THE SCOUTING NOTEBOOK: 1997

Produced by STATS, Inc.
(Sports Team Analysis and Tracking Systems, Inc.)

John Dewan, Editor
Don Zminda, Associate Editor

Statistics by STATS, Inc.

STATS
PUBLISHING

Most of the player photographs which appear in THE SCOUTING NOTE-BOOK: 1997 were furnished individually by the 28 teams that comprise Major League Baseball. Their cooperation is gratefully acknowledged: Anaheim Angels, Baltimore Orioles, Boston Red Sox, Chicago White Sox and photographer Ron Vesely, Cleveland Indians, Detroit Tigers, Kansas City Royals, Milwaukee Brewers, Minnesota Twins, New York Yankees, Oakland Athletics, Seattle Mariners, Texas Rangers, Toronto Blue Jays, Atlanta Braves, Chicago Cubs, Cincinnati Reds, Colorado Rockies, Florida Marlins, Houston Astros, Los Angeles Dodgers Inc., Montreal Expos, New York Mets, Philadelphia Phillies, Pittsburgh Pirates, St. Louis Cardinals, San Diego Padres and San Francisco Giants/Martha Jane Stanton.

Cover by Ron Freer and The Big Blue Image

Cover photos by Tony Inzerillo, *The Sporting Views*, Bensenville, IL

STATS is a trademark of Sports Team Analysis and Tracking Systems, Inc.

First Edition: January, 1997

ISBN 1-884064-35-3

Acknowledgments

The Scouting Notebook is the biggest book we do—a whopping 736 pages this year—and producing it requires the efforts of a lot of people. We'd like to thank them for helping us get it done.

This book is filled with fascinating numbers, and the Operations Department, headed by Doug Abel, works with a cast of thousands across the country to gather the data for us. The Operations staff consists of Jeff Chernow, Jason Kinsey, Jim Osborne, Matt Senter, Allan Spear and Peter Woelflein.

The Systems Department, headed by Sue Dewan, Mike Canter and Art Ashley, crunches the numbers for us. Jeff Schinski and David Pinto were the chief programmers for this book, and the rest of the Systems staff deserves a bow as well: Dave Carlson, Marty Couvillon, Mike Hammer, Stefan Kretschmann, Steve Moyer, Brent Osland, David Pinto, Pat Quinn and Kevin Thomas.

The Publications Department—the "prose boys"—produces all the editorial material you see in this book, with the help of our network of scouts. The Publications staff consists of Ethan Cooperson, Kevin Fullam, Jim Henzler, Chuck Miller, Tony Nistler and Mat Olkin. Special thanks go to Chuck, who worked many long hours making the pages of this book look first-rate. Bud Podrazik helped Chuck with the big job of cutting and pasting in the photographs and charts, and Thom Henninger helped out with numerous tasks.

The Marketing Department, headed by Jim Capuano, helps spread the STATS gospel throughout the world. Jim is assisted by Kristen Beauregard and Lori Smith, and Ron Freer works in advertising and graphic design (including the cover of this book). Thanks also go to our fantasy games department, which consists of Jim Musso and Oscar Palacios.

The Departments responsible for Publications Sales, Finances and Administration, headed by Bob Meyerhoff, handle a host of responsibilities. Bob's staff includes Marc Elman, Drew Faust, Mark Hong, Betty Moy and Mike Wenz. Stephanie Seburn manages the Administrative group's responsibilities, with assistance from Grant Blair, Ken Gilbert, Ginny Hamill, Tiffany Heingarten, Antoinette Kelly and Leena Sheth. Thanks also to John Dewan's assistant, Heather Schwarze.

— John Dewan and Don Zminda

The Scouting Staff

The Scouting Notebook writing staff consists of both baseball beat reporters and STATS reporters who cover major league games on a regular basis, and they know their stuff. We feel justifiably proud of their work, and we'd like to recognize them for their outstanding efforts.

The scouting reports in this book were written by the following people, in conjunction with our editors:

Anaheim Angels	Phil Rogers *Dallas Morning News*
Baltimore Orioles	Mike Mittleman *STATS, Inc.*
Boston Red Sox	Peter Gammons *ESPN/The Boston Globe*
Chicago White Sox	Don Zminda *STATS, Inc.*
Cleveland Indians	Paul Hoynes *Cleveland Plain Dealer*
Detroit Tigers	Peter Pascarelli *ESPN/Baseball Weekly*
Kansas City Royals	Marc Bowman *STATS, Inc.*
Milwaukee Brewers	Mat Olkin *STATS, Inc.*
Minnesota Twins	John Sickels *STATS, Inc.*
New York Yankees	John Benson *Diamond Analytics*
Oakland Athletics	Lawr Michaels *Diamond Analytics*
Seattle Mariners	Rob Neyer *Starwave/ ESPNET Sportszone*
Texas Rangers	Phil Rogers *Dallas Morning News*
Toronto Blue Jays	Mike Mittleman *STATS, Inc.*
Atlanta Braves	Mat Olkin *STATS, Inc.*
Chicago Cubs	Mat Olkin *STATS, Inc.*
Cincinnati Reds	Peter Pascarelli *ESPN/Baseball Weekly*
Colorado Rockies	Peter Pascarelli *ESPN/Baseball Weekly*
Florida Marlins	Peter Pascarelli *ESPN/Baseball Weekly*
Houston Astros	Bob Cunningham *STATS, Inc.*
Los Angeles Dodgers	Don Hartack *STATS, Inc.*
Montreal Expos	Peter Pascarelli *ESPN/Baseball Weekly*
New York Mets	John Benson *Diamond Analytics*
Philadelphia Phillies	Kevin Fullam *STATS, Inc.*
Pittsburgh Pirates	John Perrotto *Beaver County Times/ Baseball America*
St. Louis Cardinals	Bob Cunningham *STATS, Inc.*
San Diego Padres	Bob Cunningham *STATS, Inc.*
San Francisco Giants	Lawr Michaels *Diamond Analytics*

The minor league prospect reports were written by Mat Olkin. The "mini-notes" ("Other Anaheim Angels," etc.) were written by Kevin Fullam, Tony Nistler, Mat Olkin and Don Zminda.

This is STATS' third edition of *The Scouting Notebook*. Prior to that, STATS produced the 1990-94 editions of *The Scouting Report* with another publisher. We're proud to say that four of our writers have written for all *eight* editions of our "scouting books": John Benson, Marc Bowman, Paul Hoynes and John Perrotto. That's more time in the big leagues than most of the players in this book!

Special thanks to John Benson, Peter Gammons and Peter Pascarelli, three of the best baseball writers in the business, for their efforts again this year.

And my deep personal thanks to John Dewan, the scout who first noticed my work more than a decade ago. Can it really be 12 years?

— Don Zminda

Table of Contents

Foreword

by Phil Garner

Manager, Milwaukee Brewers

Competition in baseball is fierce.

In order to build a *winning* organization, you must have at least two basic ingredients: a combination of talented players who are properly trained and coached, *and* accurate information. We call this information scouting reports, and they are the lifeblood of every team.

Increasingly, the Milwaukee Brewers staff and I have turned to the *Scouting Notebook* by STATS, Inc. for information we trust on individuals throughout the major leagues. The reports on players' strengths and weaknesses have been invaluable in assessing our opposition as well as players in our own organization.

We also refer to the *Scouting Notebook* for comparisons with our own data. Effective scouting cannot be done in a vacuum, so we rely on this book to enhance our evaluations and decisions. In addition, our defensive alignments are constantly reviewed and adjusted with the help of the exclusive information found in the following pages.

I continue to find the *Scouting Notebook* by STATS, Inc. to be very accurate and very valuable in my daily preparations. I, along with my coaches and scouts, look forward to the 1997 edition!

Introduction

Welcome to the third edition of *The Scouting Notebook*. This is the eighth annual "scouting book" STATS has produced (we produced the annual *Scouting Report* from 1990 to 1994), and the underlying philosophy of these books has always remained the same: get a bunch of intelligent baseball analysts, people who collectively cover *thousands* of games every season, and have them give us their detailed scouting reports on every major league player who saw significant action last season.

The result is a veritable encyclopedia of contemporary major league baseball. Every year, we tell you about the strengths and weaknesses of hundreds of players—not just major league players, either, but also each club's top minor league prospects. We study the stats, we talk to the scouts, and we watch the games with a keen eye, recording even the smallest details. We look for the true ability that may have gotten exaggerated or obscured by the hype.

Our scouting staff includes some of the top baseball analysts around, people like Peter Gammons, Peter Pascarelli, John Benson, Paul Hoynes, Phil Rogers and John Perrotto.

New Features and Old Favorites

As was the case last year, this book contains comments on every player who performed in the majors in 1996. But we're not resting on our laurels. New features for 1997 include:

Manager Pages. A full-page essay on each team's manager, analyzing his style, strengths and weaknesses.

More Stats for Half-Page Players. Players receiving half-page essays now receive situational splits like home/road, left/right, etc.

Stats for Mini-Note Players. One of our popular new features last year were the "mini-notes," brief comments on and outlooks for the players who saw limited action the previous season (even one game). The mini-notes return for each team, but this year they include 1996 and lifetime major league stats for each player.

Along with all those lively, well-written reports,

we give you our bountiful supply of useful, easy-to-understand data. This includes hitting and pitching charts based on the 1996 season. The hitting charts show you graphically where each player hit the ball, while the pitching charts measure the effectiveness of every pitcher (in four different situations) in performing his most basic task—throwing a strike.

Then there's "Stars, Bums and Sleepers." In this section—a fantasy/rotisserie smorgasbord—you'll get a feel for what to expect from each player in 1997: whether they will improve, decline, remain consistent, or even come out of nowhere to surprise.

We'll get to the meat of the book—the full- and half-page player reports—later, but first, let's go over the other sections in which players and managers are evaluated.

The Manager's Page

This is one of our new features this year. On this page, we analyze the manager: his strengths and weaknesses; his style and strategy; and his outlook for 1997. We also provide statistical breakdowns detailing his handling of the pitching staff and his use of strategies like the sacrifice, the hit-and-run, and defensive substitutions.

Some of the terms listed in the stats column of the manager's page include:

First Batter Platoon Percentage: The percentage of times the managers' relievers had a platoon advantage over the first opposing batter (lefty-vs.-lefty, righty-vs.-righty).

High-Pitch Outings: The number of times that the manager allowed his starting pitchers to throw more than 120 pitches in a ballgame.

Hit & Run Success %: The percentage of hit and runs that result in baserunner advancement with no double play.

Mid-Inning Changes: The number of times the manager changed pitchers in the middle of an inning.

One-Batter Pitcher Appearances: The number of times the manager brought in a pitcher to face only one opposing batter.

Pitchouts with a Runner Moving: The number of times the opposition was running when the manager called a pitchout.

Platoon Percentage: Frequency that the manager gets his hitters the platoon advantage. Switch-hitters always have the advantage.

Quick/Slow Hooks: A Quick Hook is the removal of a pitcher who has pitched less than six innings and given up three runs or less. A Slow Hook occurs when a pitcher pitches more than nine innings, or allows seven or more runs, or whose combined innings pitched and runs allowed totals 13 or more.

Sacrifice Bunt Percentage: Bunts resulting in sacrifices or hits with runners on, divided by the number of attempts.

Saves with Over 1 Inning Pitched: The number of times the manager's relief pitchers worked more than one inning to earn a save.

Starting Lineups Used: Based on batting order, 1-8 for National Leaguers, 1-9 for American Leaguers.

2+ Pitching Changes in Low-Scoring Games: The manager's team gave up two runs or less in the game, but used at least three pitchers.

To qualify for the rankings, the manager needed to manage his team in at least 100 games in 1996.

The "Other" Pages ("Mini-Notes")

Some players didn't play enough last year to merit a full- or half-page essay, and aren't young enough or good enough to deserve a prospect report (see below). But they did play in the majors last year, so they require a brief evaluation. Following the half-page reports for each team, you'll find a page devoted to these part-timers, with each getting a three- or four-line summary. At the conclusion of each "mini-note" you'll find a letter grade from A to D, with the grades as follows:

A — should be an important contributor
B — should spend at least part of the season on the roster and contribute
C — unlikely to spend much time on a major league roster or contribute much if he does
D — unlikely to play in the majors at all

The grades aren't gospel, of course, and you'll need to watch spring training reports to get the best reading on where these guys will end up.

The Prospect Pages

If major leaguers aren't enough for you, *The Scouting Notebook* presents two "prospects pages" for each team. For each club, we've chosen eight promising minor league players. We try to include most of the top prospects, but our main aim is to identify the most *advanced* minor leaguers—the ones with the best chance of making an impact in 1997.

As a useful guide, we include "major league equivalencies" for the position players who played Double- or Triple-A in 1996. The MLE is a tool, adjusted for league and ballpark, devised by Bill James to indicate how a minor league hitter would have done last year at the major league level, based on his minor league stats. The system is invaluable because it irons out so many of the misleading illusions in minor league statistics.

Along with the top prospects for each team, we also include an organization overview. Some clubs are simply better at developing talent than others; it's not hard to figure out why the Braves have remained a superpower while the Phillies—who ambushed the Braves in the NLCS only four years ago—have plunged to the bottom of the heap.

In addition, just to provide the broadest possible minor league coverage, there is a paragraph titled "Others to Watch." These are other notable prospects, with their skills outlined in a sentence or two.

The Players

For each major league team, we give extensive reports on 24 major league players. Sixteen of them include a full page of scouting information, and eight players from each club receive half-page reports. Because we like to get this book into your hands as soon as possible, players are listed with their 1996 clubs, but we keep abreast of post-season moves, and all player moves which took place before December 10, 1996 are noted and discussed in the texts. If you can't find a particular player, just check the index.

The Scouting Notebook Page

The Scouting Notebook page for primary players has two columns.

The left column provides an in-depth report by an expert scout or analyst who follows the team on a daily basis. The right column contains statistical information. Starting at the top of the column, it lists:

Position: The first position shown is the player's most common position in 1996. If a position player played 10 or more games at any other positions, those positions are also shown. For pitchers, SP stands for starting pitcher and RP for relief pitcher. A second pitching position is shown if a starting pitcher relieved at least four times or if a relief pitcher started at least twice.

Bats and Throws: L=left-handed, R=right-handed, B=both (switch-hitter).

Opening Day Age: This is the player's age on March 30, the Sunday night on which the 1997 season is expected to begin.

Born: Birth date and place.

ML Seasons: This number indicates the number of different major league seasons in which this player has actually appeared. For example, if a player was called up to play in September in each of the last three seasons, the number shown would be three (3). Note that this is different from the term "Major League Service," which counts only the actual number of days a player appears on a major league roster.

Overall Statistics: These are traditional statistics for the player's 1996 season and his career through 1996.

Pitcher Strike Charts

The pitcher strike charts answer the question "How Often Does He Throw Strikes?" The charts are constructed based on pitchers' normal range of success at throwing strikes. Our data shows that pitchers generally will toss a strike between 40 and 80 percent of the time. Therefore we've constructed the chart to represent the 40-80 percent range of throwing strikes. The strike count includes swinging strikes, taken strikes, foul balls *and* balls hit in play. Even though not all balls hit into play are strikes, the theory is that most of them are, and the ones that aren't would be difficult to judge. Our charts reflect these assumptions.

The charts are broken into four categories. **All Pitches** is straightforward, as is **First Pitch**. We define **Ahead** as being any time there are more strikes than balls in the count (0-1, 0-2, 1-2). **Behind** includes counts with more balls than strikes. League averages are shown in each chart. Here are the 1996 league averages:

Strike Percentage by League — 1996		
	American	National
All Pitches	61.1%	62.5%
First Pitch	56.0%	58.0%
Ahead in the Count	58.6%	60.4%
Behind in the Count	66.3%	67.2%

You'll notice the National League throws a slightly higher percentage of strikes, as they have in all eight years we've kept track of this.

Hitting Diagrams

The hitting diagrams shown in these reports are state-of-the-art. For every major league game last year, STATS-trained reporters entered into our computers *every* ball hit into play (both hits and outs). They kept track of the *type* of batted balls—ground balls, fly balls, pop-ups, line drives and bunts—as well as the *distance* each ball traveled. *Direction* was tracked by dividing the field into 26 "wedges" projecting out from home plate. Distance is measured in 10-foot increments outward from home plate.

Below are left-handed-hitting Barry Bonds' hitting diagrams. The chart on the left shows where Bonds hit the ball against lefthanders, while the chart on the right shows what he did against righthanders.

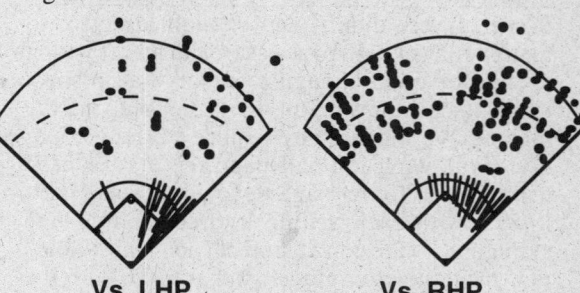

Vs. LHP   **Vs. RHP**

In the diagrams, ground balls and short line drives are shown by the lines of various lengths in the infield; the longer the line, the more ground balls and liners were hit in that direction. As you can see from the charts above, Bonds rarely hits a ground ball to the left side of the infield. When he steps up to the plate, it makes a lot of sense for the infielders to shade him to pull, no matter who's pitching.

In the outfield, batted balls are shown by dots. The dotted line in the outfield is 300 feet away from home plate, indicating a rough approximation of typical outfield defensive positions. Taking another look at Bonds, it's obvious that he has no trouble pulling the ball in the air, even against southpaws. Surprisingly, he's more likely to hit the ball to the opposite field when a *righthander* is on the mound. So even though an infield shift would make sense, if a righthander is pitching, the outfielders ought to play Bonds straight-away.

Technical Information on the Diagrams

A lot of experimentation went into producing these charts. When we first started, we tried to show every single batted ball that was put into play by each player. We found that the charts became very cluttered for everyday players. We began experimenting with trying to show only the most meaningful information. When all was said and done, here's what we ended up with:

a. Pop-ups and bunts are excluded. We excluded pop-ups because 95% of these are caught regardless of how fielders are positioned. We excluded bunts because defensing a bunt is a whole different strategy that is primarily used on a select number of players and situations.

b. Ground balls under 50 feet are excluded. These are mostly swinging bunts and are somewhat rare. We exclude them because they don't provide a true indication of the direction of a batted ball reaching an infielder or going through the infield.

c. For everyday players, we excluded what we call "isolated points" in the outfield. If a player hit only one ball in a given area of the field with no other batted balls in the vicinity all season, we exclude it from the chart. We felt that one ball does not give a true indication of a tendency. This rule did not apply to balls hit farther than 380 feet; all batted balls over 380 feet are shown. See Mark McGwire for many examples.

d. Similarly, for players who played infrequently, we expanded the data sample to create a more complete pattern of dots in the outfield. For example, Kevin Mitchell doesn't play enough to create a lot of dots on his outfield chart. If we left the chart alone, it would lead you to believe that he had no power. That wouldn't be fair.

e. For ground balls over 50 feet, we excluded only the rare isolated ground ball. For most players, almost all of their ground balls are shown.

Other notes of interest:

The field itself is drawn to precise scale, with the outfield fence reaching 400 feet in center field and 330 feet down the lines. Keep in mind that parks are configured differently so that a dot that is shown inside of the diagram might actually have been a home run. Similarly, a dot outside the fence in the diagram might actually have been in play.

Liners under 170 feet are part of the infield. We give responsibility for short line drives to the infielders.

No distinction is made between hits and outs.

1996 Situational Stats

There are eight situational breakdowns for every primary player. **Home** and **Road** show performance while playing in his home park and on the road. **First Half** and **Scnd Half** show performance before and after last year's All-Star break. For hitters, **LHP** and **RHP** show the player's performance versus left-handed pitchers and right-handed pitchers, respectively. For pitchers, **LHB** and **RHB** show how the opposition batters hit against that pitcher based on the side of the plate from which they hit. **Sc Pos** stands for Scoring Position. It shows batting performance when hitting with runners in scoring position. For pitchers, **Sc Pos** shows the opposition's batting statistics when there are men in scoring position against that pitcher.

The definition we use for **Clutch** here can be simply defined as the late innings of a close game. For those of you interested in the exact definition, clutch is when it is the seventh inning or later and the batting team is up by one run, tied, or has the tying run on base, at bat, or on deck. Our definition of Clutch is consistent with a very well-known statistic, the save.

1996 Rankings

This section shows how the player ranked against the league, against his teammates, and by position in significant categories. Thanks to the power of the STATS computer, we not only include traditional categories, but also the less traditional categories as shown in the Major League Leaders section of this book. The Definitions and Qualifications section below provides some details on these lesser-known categories. Due to space considerations, when a player ranked high in numerous categories, we omitted some of the less interesting rankings.

Major League Leaders

The chapter immediately following this introduction is a complete listing of Major League Leaders. The top three players in each category are shown for each league separately. You'll notice a STATS flavor to these leaders. Not only do we show the leaders for the common categories like batting average, home runs and ERA, but you'll also find less traditional categories like steals of third and pitches thrown.

Definitions and Qualifications

The following are definitions and qualifications for the Major League Leaders and Rankings.

Definitions:

Times on Base — Hits plus walks plus hit-by-pitch.

Ground/Fly Ratio — The ratio of all ground balls hit to fly balls and pop-ups hit. Bunts and line drives are excluded completely.

Runs/Times on Base — This is calculated by dividing Runs Scored by Times on Base.

Clutch — This category shows a player's batting average in the late innings of close games: the seventh inning or later with the batting team ahead by one, tied, or has the tying run on base, at bat, or on deck.

Bases Loaded — This category shows a player's batting average in bases loaded situations.

GDP per GDP situation — A GDP situation exists any time there is a man on first with less than two outs. This statistic measures how often a player grounds into a double play in that situation.

Percentage of Pitches Taken — This tells you how often a player lets a pitch go by without swinging.

Percentage Swings Put In Play — This tells you how often a player hits the ball into fair territory, or is retired on a foul-ball out, when he swings.

Run Support per Nine Innings — This indicates how many runs are scored for a pitcher by his team while he was pitching translated into a per-nine-inning figure.

Baserunners per Nine Innings — These are the hits, walks and hit batsmen allowed per nine innings.

Strikeout/Walk Ratio — This is simply a pitcher's strikeouts divided by his walks allowed.

Stolen Base Percentage Allowed — This figure indicates how successful opposing baserunners are when attempting a stolen base. It's stolen bases divided by stolen-base attempts.

Save Percentage — This is saves divided by save opportunities. Save opportunities include saves plus blown saves.

Blown Saves — A blown save is charged any time a pitcher comes into a game where a save situation is in place and he loses the lead.

Holds — A hold is given to a pitcher when he comes into the game in a save situation, but is removed before the end of the game while maintaining his team's lead. The pitcher must retire at least one batter to get a hold.

Percentage of Inherited Runners Scored — When a pitcher comes into a game with men already on base, these runners are called inherited runners. This statistic measures the percentage of these inherited runners that the relief pitcher allows to score.

First Batter Efficiency — This statistic tells you the batting average allowed by a relief pitcher to the first batter he faces.

Qualifications:

In order to be ranked, a player had to qualify with a minimum number of opportunities, as follows:

Batters

Batting average, slugging percentage, on-base average, home run frequency, ground/fly ratio, runs scored per time reached base and pitches seen per plate appearance — (3.1 plate appearances) times (team games)

Percentage of pitches taken, lowest percentage of swings that missed and percentage of swings put into play — (9.26 pitches seen) times (team games)

Percentage of extra bases taken as a runner — (.09 opportunities to advance) times (team games)

Stolen base percentage — (.12 stolen-base attempts) times (team games)

Runners in scoring position — (.62 plate appearances with runners in scoring position) times (team games)

Clutch — (.31 plate appearances in the clutch) times (team games)

Bases loaded — (.06 plate appearances with the bases loaded) times (team games)

GDP per GDP situation — (.31 plate appearances with a man on first and less than two outs) times (team games)

Vs LHP — (.77 plate appearances against left-handed pitchers) times (team games)

Vs RHP — (2.33 plate appearances against right-handed pitchers) times (team games)

BA at home — (1.55 plate appearances at home) times (team games)

BA on the road — (1.55 plate appearances on the road) times (team games)

Leadoff on-base average — (.93 plate appearances in the number-one spot in the batting order) times (team games)

Cleanup slugging percentage — (.93 plate appearances in the number-four spot in the batting order) times (team games)

BA on 3-1 count — (.06 plate appearances putting the ball into play or walking on a 3-1 count) times (team games)

BA with 2 strikes — (.62 plate appearances with two strikes) times (team games)

BA on 0-2 count — (.12 plate appearances putting the ball into play or striking out on a 0-2 count) times (team games)

BA on 3-2 count — (.12 plate appearances with a 3-2 count) times (team games)

Pitchers

Earned run average, run support per nine innings, baserunners per nine innings, batting average allowed, on-base average allowed, slugging percentage allowed, home runs per nine innings, strikeouts per nine innings, strikeout/walk ratio, stolen base percentage allowed, GDPs per nine innings, pitches thrown per batter and groundball/flyball ratio off — one inning pitched per team game

Winning percentage — .09 decisions per team game

GDPs induced per GDP situation — pitchers facing .19 batters in GDP situations per team game

Save Percentage — .12 save opportunities per team game

Percentage of inherited runners scoring — .19 inherited runners per team game

First batter efficiency — .25 games in relief per team game

BA allowed, runners in scoring position — pitchers facing .93 batters with men in scoring position per team game

ERA at home — .5 innings pitched at home per team game

ERA on the road — .5 innings pitched on the road per team game

Vs LHB — .77 left-handed batters faced per team game

Vs RHB — 2.33 right-handed batters faced per team game

Relief Pitchers

ERA, batting average allowed, baserunners per nine innings, strikeouts per 9 innings — .33 relief innings per team game

Fielders

Percentage caught stealing by catchers — catchers with .46 stolen-base attempts against them per team game

Fielding percentage — .62 games at a position per team game; .19 chances per team game for pitchers

1996 American League Leaders

Batters

Batting Average
Alex Rodriguez	.358
Frank Thomas	.349
Paul Molitor	.341

Home Runs
Mark McGwire	52
Brady Anderson	50
Ken Griffey Jr	49

Runs Batted In
Albert Belle	148
Juan Gonzalez	144
Mo Vaughn	143

Games Played
Cal Ripken	163
Rafael Palmeiro	162
Paul Molitor	161
Mo Vaughn	161

At Bats
Kenny Lofton	662
Paul Molitor	660
Cal Ripken	640

Runs Scored
Alex Rodriguez	141
Chuck Knoblauch	140
Roberto Alomar	132
Kenny Lofton	132

Hits
Paul Molitor	225
Alex Rodriguez	215
Kenny Lofton	210

Singles
Paul Molitor	167
Kenny Lofton	157
Darryl Hamilton	145

Doubles
Alex Rodriguez	54
Edgar Martinez	52
Ivan Rodriguez	47

Triples
Chuck Knoblauch	14
Fernando Vina	10
4 players tied with	8

Stolen Bases
Kenny Lofton	75
Tom Goodwin	66
Otis Nixon	54

Caught Stealing
Tom Goodwin	22
Kenny Lofton	17
Chuck Knoblauch	14

Walks
Tony Phillips	125
Jim Thome	123
Edgar Martinez	123

Intentional Walks
Frank Thomas	26
Mo Vaughn	19
Mark McGwire	16

Hit by Pitch
Brady Anderson	22
Chuck Knoblauch	19
Charlie O'Brien	17

Strikeouts
Jay Buhner	159
Melvin Nieves	158
Mo Vaughn	154

Ground into DP
Cal Ripken	28
Frank Thomas	25
2 players tied with	21

Sacrifice Bunts
Tom Goodwin	21
Dave Howard	17
2 players tied with	16

Sacrifice Flies
Bobby Bonilla	17
Roberto Alomar	12
Kevin Elster	11

Plate Appearances
Mo Vaughn	752
Kenny Lofton	736
Rafael Palmeiro	732

Times on Base
Mo Vaughn	316
Chuck Knoblauch	314
Frank Thomas	298

Total Bases
Alex Rodriguez	379
Albert Belle	375
Mo Vaughn	370

Slugging Percentage
Mark McGwire	.730
Juan Gonzalez	.643
Brady Anderson	.637

Slugging off LHP
Juan Gonzalez	.887
Frank Thomas	.798
Mark McGwire	.784

Slugging off RHP
Mark McGwire	.713
Jim Thome	.696
Brady Anderson	.686

Cleanup Slugging
Mark McGwire	.726
Juan Gonzalez	.647
Albert Belle	.630

On-Base Average
Mark McGwire	.467
Edgar Martinez	.464
Frank Thomas	.459

OBA off LHP
Frank Thomas	.544
Mark McGwire	.511
John Jaha	.487

OBA off RHP
Jim Thome	.489
Edgar Martinez	.461
Mark McGwire	.453

Leadoff OBA
Bob Higginson	.500
Chuck Knoblauch	.448
Roberto Alomar	.405

AB/HR Frequency
Mark McGwire	8.1
Ken Griffey Jr	11.1
Juan Gonzalez	11.5

Ground/Fly Ratio
Otis Nixon	3.0
Tom Goodwin	2.4
Derek Jeter	2.1

% Extra Bases Taken
Roberto Alomar	72.3%
Tom Goodwin	70.5
Tim Salmon	69.8

Runs/Time On Base
Alex Rodriguez	50.7%
Ken Griffey Jr	50.0
Ivan Rodriguez	49.6

SB Success %
Ray Durham	88.2%
Pat Listach	83.3
Johnny Damon	83.3

Steals of third
Kenny Lofton	24
Otis Nixon	12
Tom Goodwin	11

BA Scoring Position
Scott Brosius	.365
Chuck Knoblauch	.364
Frank Thomas	.363

BA Late & Close
Dave Nilsson	.379
Pat Meares	.356
Wade Boggs	.354

BA Bases Loaded
Bob Higginson	.667
Wil Cordero	.615
Omar Vizquel	.615

GDP/GDP Situation
Jose Valentin	3.0%
Tom Goodwin	3.1
Dave Nilsson	3.4

BA vs LH Pitchers
Roberto Kelly	.406
Frank Thomas	.403
Chuck Knoblauch	.388

BA vs RH Pitchers
Dave Nilsson	.359
Alex Rodriguez	.354
Paul Molitor	.340

BA at Home
Mo Vaughn	.380
Julio Franco	.364
Alex Rodriguez	.364

BA on the Road
Frank Thomas	.362
Kevin Seitzer	.356
Alex Rodriguez	.352

BA on 3-1 Count
Lyle Mouton	1.000
Mark Whiten	.750
Kimera Bartee	.750

BA With 2 Strikes
Chuck Knoblauch	.311
Alex Rodriguez	.290
Roberto Alomar	.284

BA on 0-2 Count
George Arias	.348
Alex Rodriguez	.333
Mo Vaughn	.323

BA on 3-2 Count
Greg Myers	.440
Fernando Vina	.421
Charlie O'Brien	.393

Pitches Seen
Tony Phillips	3051
Roberto Alomar	2953
Chuck Knoblauch	2953

Pitches Seen per PA
Jim Thome	4.46
Mickey Tettleton	4.33
Edgar Martinez	4.27

% Pitches Taken
Edgar Martinez	67.3%
Wade Boggs	65.6
Jeff Frye	64.9

% of Missed Swings

Wade Boggs	4.7%
Joey Cora	6.7
Fernando Vina	7.4

% Swings Put In Play

Gary DiSarcina	61.7%
Wade Boggs	60.1
Fernando Vina	59.8

Bunts in Play

Tom Goodwin	52
Otis Nixon	44
Kenny Lofton	38

Pitchers

Earned Run Average

Juan Guzman	2.93
Pat Hentgen	3.22
Charles Nagy	3.41

Wins

Andy Pettitte	21
Pat Hentgen	20
Mike Mussina	19

Losses

Jim Abbott	18
Erik Hanson	17
Rich Robertson	17

Win-Loss Percentage

Jamie Moyer	.813
Charles Nagy	.773
Andy Pettitte	.724

Games Pitched

Eddie Guardado	83
Mike Myers	83
Mike Stanton	81

Games Started

Mike Mussina	36
11 players tied with	35

Complete Games

Pat Hentgen	10
Roger Pavlik	7
Ken Hill	7

Shutouts

Rich Robertson	3
Pat Hentgen	3
Ken Hill	3

Games Finished

Roberto Hernandez	61
Heathcliff Slocumb	60
Jose Mesa	60

Innings Pitched

Pat Hentgen	265.2
Alex Fernandez	258.0
Ken Hill	250.2

Hits Allowed

Chris Haney	267
Mike Mussina	264
2 players tied with	262

Batters Faced

Pat Hentgen	1100
Alex Fernandez	1071
Ken Hill	1061

Runs Allowed

Tim Wakefield	151
Tom Gordon	143
Erik Hanson	143

Earned Runs Allowed

Tom Gordon	134
Mike Mussina	130
Erik Hanson	129

Home Runs Allowed

Shawn Boskie	40
Brad Radke	40
Tim Wakefield	38

Walks Allowed

Rich Robertson	116
Roger Clemens	106
Tom Gordon	105

Hit Batters

Shawn Boskie	13
Jason Grimsley	13
Orel Hershiser	12
Tim Wakefield	12

Strikeouts

Roger Clemens	257
Chuck Finley	215
Kevin Appier	207

Wild Pitches

Chuck Finley	17
Richie Lewis	14
Erik Hanson	13
Kevin Tapani	13
Jim Abbott	13

Balks

Ken Hill	4
8 players tied with	2

Run Support per 9 IP

Tom Gordon	7.3
Mike Mussina	6.8
Bobby Witt	6.8

Baserunners per 9 IP

Juan Guzman	10.5
Brad Radke	11.3
Charles Nagy	11.4

BA Allowed

Juan Guzman	.228
Roger Clemens	.237
Pat Hentgen	.241

BA Allowed Scor Pos

Richie Lewis	.184
Juan Guzman	.199
Roger Clemens	.199

Slugging Pct Allowed

Pat Hentgen	.355
Roger Clemens	.358
Juan Guzman	.363

On-Base Pct Allowed

Juan Guzman	.289
Brad Radke	.302
Charles Nagy	.306

Home Runs per 9 IP

Pat Hentgen	.678
Ken Hill	.682
Roger Clemens	.705

Strikeouts per 9 IP

Roger Clemens	9.5
Kevin Appier	8.8
Chuck Finley	8.1

Walks per 9 IP

Chris Haney	2.0
David Wells	2.0
Brad Radke	2.2

Strikeout/Walk Ratio

Juan Guzman	3.1
Mike Mussina	3.0
Alex Fernandez	2.8

Stolen Bases Allowed

Scott Erickson	32
Tim Wakefield	30
Roger Clemens	30

Caught Stealing Off

Sterling Hitchcock	14
Ken Hill	14
Roger Clemens	13

SB% Allowed

Jimmy Key	25.0%
Chris Haney	35.7
Erik Hanson	40.0

GDPs induced

Scott Erickson	36
Tim Belcher	31
Erik Hanson	28

GDPs induced per 9 IP

Scott Erickson	1.5
Erik Hanson	1.2
Tim Belcher	1.2

GDPs/GDP Situation

Paul Menhart	21.1%
Jim Corsi	20.6
Scott Erickson	19.9

Grd/Fly Ratio Off

Scott Erickson	2.8
Orel Hershiser	2.3
Charles Nagy	2.0

Pitches Thrown

Roger Clemens	4260
Alex Fernandez	4098
Pat Hentgen	4058

Pitches per Batter

Orel Hershiser	3.36
Scott Erickson	3.50
Chris Haney	3.51

Pickoff Throws

Pat Hentgen	205
Kenny Rogers	194
Chuck Finley	176

ERA at Home

Pat Hentgen	3.19
Andy Pettitte	3.22
Chuck Finley	3.29

ERA on the Road

Juan Guzman	2.24
Ken Hill	2.85
Alex Fernandez	3.16

BA Off by LH Batters

Mariano Rivera	.215
Juan Guzman	.224
David Wells	.225

BA Off by RH Batters

Kevin Appier	.228
Pat Hentgen	.233
Juan Guzman	.233

Relief ERA

Roberto Hernandez	1.91
Mariano Rivera	2.09
Troy Percival	2.31

Relief Wins

Mariano Rivera	8
Rafael Carmona	8
Arthur Rhodes	8

Relief Losses

Bill Simas	8
Norm Charlton	7
Mike Henneman	7
Jose Mesa	7

Saves

John Wetteland	43
Jose Mesa	39
Roberto Hernandez	38

Blown Saves

Jeff Montgomery	10
Heathcliff Slocumb	8
Roberto Hernandez	8
Matt Karchner	8

Save Opportunities

John Wetteland	47
Roberto Hernandez	46
Jose Mesa	44

Save Percentage		Relief Strikeouts/9 IP		Errors by Catcher		Errors by Left Field	
Troy Percival	92.3%	Troy Percival	12.2	Mike Stanley	10	Albert Belle	10
John Wetteland	91.5	Randy Myers	11.4	Ivan Rodriguez	10	Tony Phillips	7
Billy Taylor	89.5	Jeff Nelson	11.0	Sandy Alomar Jr	9	Joe Carter	7
						Garret Anderson	7

Holds		% Inher Rnnrs Scored		Errors by First Base		Errors by Center Field	
Mariano Rivera	27	Billy Taylor	14.7%	Mo Vaughn	15	Kenny Lofton	10
Mike Stanton	22	Dennis Cook	19.8	Paul Sorrento	11	Chad Curtis	7
Jeff Russell	20	Norm Charlton	20.5	Mark McGwire	10	Bernie Williams	5
				J.T. Snow	10		

Relief Innings		First Batter Efficiency		Errors by Second Base		Errors by Right Field	
Mariano Rivera	107.2	Dennis Cook	.065	Fernando Vina	16	Manny Ramirez	9
Bob Wickman	95.2	Mariano Rivera	.089	Carlos Baerga	15	Melvin Nieves	9
Tony Castillo	95.0	Troy Percival	.107	Joey Cora	13	Tim Salmon	8

Relief BA Allowed				Errors by Third Base		% CS off Catchers	
Troy Percival	.149	**Fielding**		Jeff Cirillo	18	Ivan Rodriguez	51.1%
Mariano Rivera	.189	Errors by Pitcher		Jim Thome	17	Ron Karkovice	40.7
Eric Plunk	.203	Ben McDonald	6	Dave Hollins	17	Dan Wilson	39.0

Runners/9 IP - Relief					
Troy Percival	8.6	Bob Scanlan	4	Errors by Shortstop	
Mariano Rivera	9.1	11 players tied with	3	Jose Valentin	37
John Wetteland	10.6			Derek Jeter	22
				Pat Meares	22

1996 National League Leaders

Batters

Batting Average
Tony Gwynn	.353
Ellis Burks	.344
Mike Piazza	.336

Home Runs
Andres Galarraga	47
Gary Sheffield	42
Barry Bonds	42

Runs Batted In
Andres Galarraga	150
Dante Bichette	141
Ken Caminiti	130

Games Played
Craig Biggio	162
Jeff Bagwell	162
Gary Sheffield	161
Steve Finley	161

At Bats
Lance Johnson	682
Marquis Grissom	671
Mark Grudzielanek	657

Runs Scored
Ellis Burks	142
Steve Finley	126
Barry Bonds	122

Hits
Lance Johnson	227
Ellis Burks	211
Marquis Grissom	207

Singles
Lance Johnson	166
Mark Grudzielanek	157
Eric Young	149

Doubles
Jeff Bagwell	48
Steve Finley	45
Ellis Burks	45

Triples
Lance Johnson	21
Thomas Howard	10
Marquis Grissom	10

Stolen Bases
Eric Young	53
Lance Johnson	50
Delino DeShields	48

Caught Stealing
Eric Young	19
Rickey Henderson	15
Royce Clayton	15

Walks
Barry Bonds	151
Gary Sheffield	142
Jeff Bagwell	135

Intentional Walks
Barry Bonds	30
Mike Piazza	21
Jeff Bagwell	20

Hit by Pitch
Craig Biggio	27
Eric Young	21
Andres Galarraga	17

Strikeouts
Henry Rodriguez	160
Andres Galarraga	157
Todd Hundley	146

Ground into DP
Eric Karros	27
Greg Colbrunn	22
Mike Piazza	21
John Mabry	21

Sacrifice Bunts
Denny Neagle	16
Pedro Martinez	16
Tom Glavine	15
John Smoltz	15

Sacrifice Flies
Dante Bichette	10
Rick Wilkins	10
Ken Caminiti	10

Plate Appearances
Lance Johnson	724
Craig Biggio	723
Marquis Grissom	723

Times on Base
Jeff Bagwell	324
Gary Sheffield	315
Barry Bonds	311

Total Bases
Ellis Burks	392
Andres Galarraga	376
Steve Finley	348

Slugging Percentage
Ellis Burks	.639
Gary Sheffield	.624
Ken Caminiti	.621

Slugging off LHP
Ellis Burks	.741
Ken Caminiti	.721
Andres Galarraga	.660

Slugging off RHP
Barry Bonds	.624
Gary Sheffield	.621
Todd Hundley	.620

Cleanup Slugging
Barry Bonds	.669
Larry Walker	.656
Andres Galarraga	.638

On-Base Average
Gary Sheffield	.465
Barry Bonds	.461
Jeff Bagwell	.451

OBA off LHP
Jeff Bagwell	.517
Ellis Burks	.488
Gary Sheffield	.460

OBA off RHP	
Barry Bonds	**.483**
Gary Sheffield	.466
Jeff Bagwell	.434

Leadoff OBA	
Rickey Henderson	**.409**
John Cangelosi	.401
Eric Young	.392

AB/HR Frequency	
Barry Bonds	**12.3**
Gary Sheffield	12.4
Sammy Sosa	12.4

Ground/Fly Ratio	
Rey Ordonez	**2.9**
Javy Lopez	2.1
Lance Johnson	2.0

% Extra Bases Taken	
Bernard Gilkey	**74.5%**
T. Hollandsworth	72.1
Todd Hundley	70.5

Runs/Time On Base	
Ellis Burks	**51.1%**
Steve Finley	49.4
Marvin Benard	48.4

SB Success %	
Derek Bell	**90.6%**
Larry Walker	90.0
Barry Bonds	85.1

Steals of third	
Derek Bell	**11**
3 players tied with	10

BA Scoring Position	
Brian Jordan	**.422**
Andres Galarraga	.413
Bernard Gilkey	.406

BA Late & Close	
Tony Gwynn	**.471**
Hal Morris	.369
Lance Johnson	.368

BA Bases Loaded	
Luis Gonzalez	**.800**
Brian Jordan	.684
David Segui	.600

GDP/GDP Situation	
Rich Aurilia	**1.7%**
Todd Hollandsworth	2.2
Shane Andrews	2.9

BA vs LH Pitchers	
Ellis Burks	**.427**
Jeff Conine	.393
Jeff Bagwell	.364

BA vs RH Pitchers	
Mark Grace	**.343**
Eric Young	.336
Lance Johnson	.334

BA at Home	
Eric Young	**.412**
Ellis Burks	.390
Dante Bichette	.366

BA on the Road	
Lance Johnson	**.369**
Mike Piazza	.353
John Mabry	.331

BA on 3-1 Count	
Carl Everett	**1.000**
Pete Incaviglia	.800
Benito Santiago	.778

BA With 2 Strikes	
Jim Eisenreich	**.309**
Lance Johnson	.301
Tony Gwynn	.296

BA on 0-2 Count	
Gregg Jefferies	**.375**
Rondell White	.367
J. Allensworth	.364

BA on 3-2 Count	
Bill Spiers	**.450**
Gregg Jefferies	.433
Wayne Kirby	.421

Pitches Seen	
Jeff Bagwell	**2894**
Ellis Burks	2735
Gary Sheffield	2699

Pitches Seen per PA	
Rickey Henderson	**4.48**
Barry Larkin	4.12
Todd Zeile	4.11

% Pitches Taken	
R. Henderson	**69.4%**
Todd Zeile	65.1
Walt Weiss	63.5

% of Missed Swings	
Tony Gwynn	**6.7%**
Ricky Otero	6.9
Gregg Jefferies	8.4

% Swings Put In Play	
Tony Gwynn	**60.4%**
Lance Johnson	58.9
Eric Young	58.7

Bunts in Play	
Brian McRae	**29**
Jeff Fassero	25
Walt Weiss	24
Tom Glavine	24

Pitchers

Earned Run Average	
Kevin Brown	**1.89**
Greg Maddux	2.72
Al Leiter	2.93

Wins	
John Smoltz	**24**
Andy Benes	18
Kevin Brown	17
Kevin Ritz	17

Losses	
Pat Rapp	**16**
Frank Castillo	**16**
4 players tied with	14

Win-Loss Percentage	
John Smoltz	**.750**
Ramon Martinez	.714
Ismael Valdes	.682

Games Pitched	
Brad Clontz	**81**
Bob Patterson	79
Mark Dewey	78
Jeff Shaw	78

Games Started	
Tom Glavine	**36**
5 players tied with	35

Complete Games	
Curt Schilling	**8**
John Smoltz	6
4 players tied with	5

Shutouts	
Kevin Brown	**3**
7 players tied with	2

Games Finished	
Todd Worrell	**67**
Robb Nen	66
Mel Rojas	64
Mark Wohlers	64

Innings Pitched	
John Smoltz	**253.2**
Greg Maddux	245.0
Shane Reynolds	239.0

Hits Allowed	
Jaime Navarro	**244**
Kevin Ritz	236
Darryl Kile	233

Batters Faced	
Jaime Navarro	**1007**
John Smoltz	995
Tom Glavine	994

Runs Allowed	
Kevin Ritz	**135**
Mark Leiter	128
W. VanLandingham	123

Earned Runs Allowed	
Kevin Ritz	**125**
Mark Leiter	112
W. VanLandingham	109

Home Runs Allowed	
Mark Leiter	**37**
Pete Harnisch	30
Steve Trachsel	30
Todd Stottlemyre	30

Walks Allowed	
Al Leiter	**119**
Kevin Ritz	105
Dave Burba	97
Darryl Kile	97

Hit Batters	
Darryl Kile	**16**
Kevin Brown	**16**
Mark Leiter	**16**

Strikeouts	
John Smoltz	**276**
Hideo Nomo	234
Pedro Martinez	222
Jeff Fassero	222

Wild Pitches	
Mike Williams	**16**
Jason Isringhausen	14
Joey Hamilton	14

Balks	
Ismael Valdes	**5**
Mark Leiter	4
11 players tied with	3

Run Support per 9 IP	
Kevin Ritz	**7.2**
Mark Gardner	6.8
Ramon Martinez	6.0

Baserunners per 9 IP	
John Smoltz	**9.1**
Kevin Brown	9.1
Greg Maddux	9.4

BA Allowed	
Al Leiter	**.202**
John Smoltz	.216
Hideo Nomo	.218

Slugging Pct Allowed	
Kevin Brown	**.289**
Al Leiter	.316
John Smoltz	.331

On-Base Pct Allowed	
John Smoltz	**.260**
Kevin Brown	.262
Greg Maddux	.264

Home Runs per 9 IP	
Kevin Brown	**.309**
Greg Maddux	.404
Tom Glavine	.535

Strikeouts per 9 IP	
John Smoltz	**9.8**
Hideo Nomo	9.2
Pedro Martinez	9.2

Walks per 9 IP

Greg Maddux	**1.0**
Kevin Brown	1.3
Danny Darwin	1.5

Strikeout/Walk Ratio

Greg Maddux	**6.1**
John Smoltz	5.0
Kevin Brown	4.8

Stolen Bases Allowed

Hideo Nomo	**52**
Todd Stottlemyre	30
Pedro Martinez	29

Caught Stealing Off

W. VanLandingham	**14**
Alan Benes	13
Kevin Ritz	13
Jeff Fassero	13

SB% Allowed

D. Osborne	**28.6%**
Curt Schilling	33.3
Alan Benes	38.1

GDPs induced

Pedro Astacio	**28**
Kevin Brown	26
4 players tied with	24

GDPs induced per 9 IP

Pat Rapp	**1.3**
Pedro Astacio	1.2
Mark Thompson	1.1

GDPs/GDP Situation

Jamey Wright	**22.4%**
Robb Nen	20.8
Mark Petkovsek	20.3

Grd/Fly Ratio Off

Kevin Brown	**3.4**
Greg Maddux	3.0
Joey Hamilton	2.4

BA Allowed Scor Pos

Steve Trachsel	**.137**
Kevin Brown	.188
Dave Burba	.193

Pitches Thrown

Tom Glavine	**3835**
John Smoltz	3801
Jaime Navarro	3682

Pitches per Batter

Greg Maddux	**3.10**
Bob Tewksbury	3.26
Danny Darwin	3.38

Pickoff Throws

Armando Reynoso	**237**
Mark Leiter	231
Ismael Valdes	208

ERA at Home

Kevin Brown	**1.69**
Al Leiter	2.08
Greg Maddux	2.44

ERA on the Road

Kevin Brown	**2.19**
Terry Mulholland	2.53
John Smoltz	2.95

BA Off by LH Batters

Shane Reynolds	**.209**
Curt Schilling	.215
Hideo Nomo	.216

BA Off by RH Batters

Al Leiter	**.194**
Todd Stottlemyre	.198
Danny Darwin	.199

Relief ERA

Tim Worrell	**1.54**
John Franco	1.83
Robb Nen	1.95

Relief Wins

Antonio Osuna	**9**
Trevor Hoffman	**9**
Jeff Shaw	8
Mark Petkovsek	8

Relief Losses

Rod Beck	**9**
Doug Henry	8
Francisco Cordova	7
Tim Scott	7

Saves

Jeff Brantley	**44**
Todd Worrell	**44**
Trevor Hoffman	42

Blown Saves

Todd Worrell	**9**
John Franco	8
5 players tied with	7

Save Opportunities

Todd Worrell	**53**
Jeff Brantley	49
Trevor Hoffman	49

Save Percentage

Mel Rojas	**90.0%**
Jeff Brantley	89.8
Ricky Bottalico	89.5

Holds

Jeff Shaw	**22**
Steve Reed	**22**
Doug Bochtler	20

Relief Innings

Jeff Shaw	**104.2**
Terry Adams	101.0
Toby Borland	90.2

Relief BA Allowed

Tim Worrell	**.137**
Trevor Hoffman	.161
Mel Rojas	.193

Runners/9 IP - Relief

Tim Worrell	**8.0**
Trevor Hoffman	8.5
Mel Rojas	9.6

Relief Strikeouts/9 IP

Mark Wohlers	**11.6**
Trevor Hoffman	11.4
Chan Ho Park	10.7

% Inher Rnnrs Scored

Mark Wohlers	**16.7%**
T.J. Mathews	**16.7%**
Trevor Hoffman	17.1

First Batter Efficiency

Ricky Bottalico	**.123**
Hector Carrasco	.130
Doug Bochtler	.143

Fielding

Errors by Pitcher

Mark Thompson	**5**
Jason Isringhausen	**5**
Jaime Navarro	**5**

Errors by Catcher

Jason Kendall	**18**
3 players tied with	11

Errors by First Base

Jeff Bagwell	**16**
Eric Karros	15
Andres Galarraga	14

Errors by Second Base

Luis Alicea	**24**
Delino DeShields	17
Mark Lemke	15

Errors by Third Base

Sean Berry	**22**
Jeff Kent	21
Ken Caminiti	20
Vinny Castilla	20

Errors by Shortstop

Walt Weiss	**30**
Mark Grudzielanek	27
Rey Ordonez	27

Errors by Left Field

Al Martin	**7**
Barry Bonds	6
Bernard Gilkey	6
Henry Rodriguez	6

Errors by Center Field

Lance Johnson	**12**
Brian L. Hunter	**12**
Steve Finley	7

Errors by Right Field

Raul Mondesi	**12**
Sammy Sosa	10
Dante Bichette	9

% CS off Catchers

Charles Johnson	**47.6%**
Kirt Manwaring	44.6
Tom Pagnozzi	34.3

Stars, Bums and Sleepers — Who's Who in 1997

Who will be the next Alex Rodriguez? No one has the answer, but everyone has an opinion. Here at STATS, we have our own ideas about next year's sleepers and, as we do every year, we will present them—and much more—in the following section: "Stars, Bums and Sleepers."

Last year, we listed three sleepers at the shortstop position: Alex Rodriguez, Derek Jeter and Mark Grudzielanek. Whenever a prediction works out that well, there has to be more than a little bit of luck involved. Still, there were good reasons to expect those three youngsters to perform beyond expectations. There are several similar players on the horizon for '97, and we'll tip you off on all of them.

In addition to the ever-in-demand sleeper picks, we also list the players that are most likely to improve, decline, or remain consistent. Hey, we'll admit that certain players don't present much of a challenge. For example, we're quite confident that long after Major League Baseball approves expansion to 100 teams and interleague play with the Canadian Football League, Mickey Tettleton will still be chugging right along, hitting .240-something, with power and walks. It's the Juan Guzmans that are hard; the Ben McDonalds and the Darryl Kiles. But we're proud to say that each of those pitchers were listed among our sleeper picks last year.

How do we do it? Well, we don't want give away *all* of the secrets, but we will assure you that the office dartboard plays absolutely no part in the process. Those of you familiar with the work of Bill James, particularly *The Bill James Baseball Abstract*, may recall that Bill designed a system to predict a player's future performance. The heart of the system is the simple truth that a player's past history is the best indicator of his future production. Over the past few years, Bill and John Dewan have further refined the system. Its results, combined with the subjective advice of our scouts and staff experts, help us form the lists that follow.

Of course, the system is far more complex than that. If we apply it to a .300 hitter, it won't just tell us that the guy will hit .300 next year and leave it at that. The system also takes into account certain general rules about how players' production changes over time. What are some of the rules? Well, most are pretty obvious. For example, younger players tend to get better, while older players tend to decline, with age 27 typically being the peak offensive season for a position player. Age 27 is also the most common year for a player to have a season "over his head," which we also take into account. It's likely that a player who has an unexpectedly good year will have trouble repeating it. A player who improves the previous season will tend to decline the next, and vice versa. In short, everybody gravitates toward the center. As you probably could guess, over the years we've developed several other reliable indicators.

We learn as we go along, too. Sometimes the greatest improvements in the system result from failed predictions. Last year, we advised you to "Expect A Better Year" from John Olerud, Delino DeShields and Travis Fryman. As you know, it didn't happen. Should we tweak the system to make it more wary of players whose growth stagnates in their mid-20s? Perhaps. This never will be an exact science, but as long as there's room for improvement, we'll keep tinkering.

How To Use This Section

Every position is broken into four groups: Expect A Better Year in '97, Look for Consistency, Production Will Drop, and 1997 Sleepers. Here's a key point to remember when looking at the first three of these categories: **A player is put into one of these three groups based on his 1996 performance only.** For example, Bob Higginson is shown in the category Production Will Drop. That means that you probably shouldn't expect him to hit .320 with a .577 slugging percentage again. However, this doesn't mean that we think Higginson is the next

Larry Sheets. Higgy's a good young hitter, and he should put up some pretty good numbers in 1997. His level of production might drop, but it certainly won't disappear.

We do things a little differently in the section entitled 1997 Sleepers, but we continue to do them well. We aren't trying to suggest that we expect to hit the jackpot again like we did on A-Rod, but you can bet (not literally, of course) that many of this year's crop of sleepers will wake up the baseball world. The numbers we show in this section are each player's combined minor and major league performance for 1996. The idea here is to show what this player is *capable* of doing. We've tried to factor projected playing time into the equation as this book went to press in late 1996, but you'll get a better idea as the season starts as to who's playing and who's not.

Finally, within each grouping (for example, shortstops listed under Expect a Better Year) we've ranked the players based on our own expectations of performance from best performance to worst.

How We Developed This Section

We broke down all the regular major league players from this book into their most common position played in 1996. We then looked at every player in two basic ways: statistical analysis and subjective rating. For our statistical model, we looked at historical patterns of performance to help us project performance for each player. Here are some of the factors that we plugged into our computer.

Career Trends—A player should not be judged simply on his most recent year of performance, although the tendency for most fans (and many "experts") is to do just that. While it is possible that a player who had a good year in relation to the rest of his career has suddenly become a better ballplayer, it's much more likely that it was simply a good year. Brady Anderson hit around 15 homers a year for five years, and then broke out with 50 last season. He *might* make another run at Maris, but more likely, his long-ball total will settle in somewhere between last year's and his previously established levels. In short, it's a lot easier to have a fluke year than a fluke *career*. The same is true about a player who suffered through an off year last year. If his slump does not result in a severe reduction in his

playing time, the player will usually rebound, at least to some extent.

Player Age—The "primest" year for a position player in baseball is age 27. Based on historical studies, this is the most likely age for a hitter to have his best year. So, the rule of thumb is that if a batter is less than 27, you can expect some improvement over **the level of play he's established so far in his career.** If a batter is over 27, you can expect some decrease in his playing performance from his established levels. The age when a pitcher reaches his peak is somewhat more difficult to pin down. While it isn't possible to define a specific peak age as we do for hitters, we are able to identify many factors that give us an accurate indication of whether a pitcher's potential is rising or falling.

Minor League Performance—In his book *The Bill James Baseball Abstract*, Bill found that minor league performance, when properly adjusted, is just as reliable in predicting major league performance as is prior major league performance. Therefore, we've looked at minor league performance here to help us project 1997, especially for the players we call "Sleepers."

We then added our own subjective considerations:

Playing Time—When considering how productive a player will be in a given year, you first have to estimate how often he'll play. We've done this by evaluating players compared to their teammates. As this book goes to press, Brian Giles hasn't been guaranteed a regular spot by the Indians—not yet, anyway. But he's plenty good enough to play, and we think he'll get his at-bats. Do your own research this spring to find out more about a team's plans for a player if you're not sure—and don't forget to take into account a player's injury history. Jose Canseco surely will be someone's regular DH, but the chances are that your check from Ed McMahon will arrive in the mail before Canseco ever holds up for 500 at-bats in a season.

Pitchers' Inconsistency—For every five hitters you can name as being reasonably consistent from year to year, there is probably only one pitcher who can compare in consistency. Pitchers are full of surprises; it's the nature of the beast. We used many subjective considerations in devising our pitcher evaluations.

Catcher

Expect A Better Year in '97

| | 1996 Statistics | | | |
	Avg.	HR	RBI	SB
Chris Hoiles	.258	25	73	0
Charles Johnson	.218	13	37	1
Darrin Fletcher	.266	12	57	0
Jim Leyritz	.264	7	40	2
Brad Ausmus	.221	5	35	4
Jesse Levis	.236	1	21	0
Jorge Fabregas	.287	2	26	0
Sandy Martinez	.227	3	18	0

Look for Consistency

| | 1996 Statistics | | | |
	Avg.	HR	RBI	SB
Mike Piazza	.336	36	105	0
Javy Lopez	.282	23	69	1
Joe Girardi	.294	2	45	13
Mike Macfarlane	.274	19	54	3
Sandy Alomar Jr	.263	11	50	1
Eddie Taubensee	.291	12	48	3
Ron Karkovice	.220	10	38	0
Bill Haselman	.274	8	34	4
Mike Matheny	.204	8	46	3
Jason Kendall	.300	3	42	5
Brian Johnson	.272	8	35	0
Pat Borders	.277	5	18	0
Tony Eusebio	.307	1	33	0

Production Will Drop

| | 1996 Statistics | | | |
	Avg.	HR	RBI	SB
Ivan Rodriguez	.300	19	86	5
Todd Hundley	.259	41	112	1
Mike Stanley	.270	24	69	2
Terry Steinbach	.272	35	100	0
Dan Wilson	.285	18	83	1
Rick Wilkins	.243	14	59	0
Benito Santiago	.264	30	85	2
Scott Servais	.265	11	63	0
John Flaherty	.284	13	64	3
Tom Pagnozzi	.270	13	55	4
Jeff Reed	.284	8	37	2
Greg Myers	.286	6	47	0
Joe Oliver	.242	11	46	2
Charlie O'Brien	.238	13	44	0

1997 Sleepers

| | 1996 Statistics (includes minor leagues) | | | |
	Avg.	HR	RBI	SB
Mike Sweeney	.293	21	91	4
Todd Greene	.275	7	42	2
Jayhawk Owens	.238	4	23	4
George Williams	.228	8	28	0
Kirt Manwaring	.227	1	19	0
Matt Walbeck	.228	2	33	3

First Base

Expect A Better Year in '97

| | 1996 Statistics | | | |
	Avg.	HR	RBI	SB
John Olerud	.274	18	61	1
Greg Colbrunn	.286	16	69	4
Mark Johnson	.274	13	47	6
Ron Coomer	.296	12	41	3
Rico Brogna	.255	7	30	0
Will Clark	.283	13	72	2

Look for Consistency

| | 1996 Statistics | | | |
	Avg.	HR	RBI	SB
Frank Thomas	.349	40	134	1
Jeff Bagwell	.315	31	120	21
Fred McGriff	.295	28	107	7
Tino Martinez	.292	25	117	2
Jason Giambi	.291	20	79	0
Eric Karros	.260	34	111	8
Mark Grace	.331	9	75	2
J.T. Snow	.257	17	67	1
Wally Joyner	.277	8	65	5
Scott Stahoviak	.284	13	61	3
David Segui	.286	11	58	4
Butch Huskey	.278	15	60	1
John Mabry	.297	13	74	3

Production Will Drop

| | 1996 Statistics | | | |
	Avg.	HR	RBI	SB
Mo Vaughn	.326	44	143	2
Rafael Palmeiro	.289	39	142	8
Andres Galarraga	.304	47	150	18
John Jaha	.300	34	118	3
Cecil Fielder	.252	39	117	2
Mark McGwire	.312	52	113	0
Hal Morris	.313	16	80	7
Jeff King	.271	30	111	15
Julio Franco	.322	14	76	8
Paul Sorrento	.289	23	93	0
Jose Offerman	.303	5	47	24
Mark Carreon	.281	11	65	3

1997 Sleepers

| | 1996 Statistics (includes minor leagues) | | | |
	Avg.	HR	RBI	SB
Tony Clark	.267	41	108	1
Gregg Jefferies	.285	7	51	20
Dmitri Young	.328	15	66	16
Gene Schall	.286	19	77	1
Brian Hunter	.293	14	52	1

Second Base

Expect A Better Year in '97

	1996 Statistics			
	Avg.	HR	RBI	SB
Bret Boone	.233	12	69	3
Carlos Baerga	.254	12	66	1
Delino DeShields	.224	5	41	48
Brent Gates	.263	2	30	1
Edgardo Alfonzo	.261	4	40	2
Jason Bates	.206	1	9	2
Nelson Liriano	.267	3	30	2
Ray Durham	.275	10	65	30

Look for Consistency

	1996 Statistics			
	Avg.	HR	RBI	SB
Eric Young	.324	8	74	53
Craig Biggio	.288	15	75	25
Mark Lewis	.270	11	55	6
Jose Vizcaino	.297	1	45	15
Mickey Morandini	.250	3	32	26
Jeff Frye	.286	4	41	18
Carlos Garcia	.285	6	44	16
Jody Reed	.244	2	49	2
Luis Alicea	.258	5	42	11
Mark Lemke	.255	5	37	5
Bip Roberts	.283	0	52	12
Steve Scarsone	.219	5	23	2

Production Will Drop

	1996 Statistics			
	Avg.	HR	RBI	SB
Roberto Alomar	.328	22	94	17
Chuck Knoblauch	.341	13	72	45
Ryne Sandberg	.244	25	92	12
Mike Lansing	.285	11	53	23
Fernando Vina	.283	7	46	16
Mark McLemore	.290	5	46	27
Joey Cora	.291	6	45	5
Randy Velarde	.285	14	54	7
Mariano Duncan	.340	8	56	4
Keith Lockhart	.273	7	55	11
Domingo Cedeno	.272	2	20	6

1997 Sleepers

	1996 Statistics (includes minor leagues)			
	Avg.	HR	RBI	SB
Luis Castillo	.301	2	43	68
Tony Batista	.309	14	65	9
Wil Cordero	.289	5	42	2
Tomas Perez	.258	2	32	9
Felipe Crespo	.274	10	68	12
Mark Loretta	.271	1	24	3

Third Base

Expect A Better Year in '97

	1996 Statistics			
	Avg.	HR	RBI	SB
Russ Davis	.234	5	18	2
Willie Greene	.244	19	63	0
Jeff Kent	.284	12	55	6
Mike Blowers	.265	6	38	0
Jeff Branson	.244	9	37	2

Look for Consistency

	1996 Statistics			
	Avg.	HR	RBI	SB
Travis Fryman	.268	22	100	4
Matt Williams	.302	22	85	1
Tim Naehring	.288	17	65	2
Leo Gomez	.238	17	56	1
Shane Andrews	.227	19	64	3
Joe Randa	.303	6	47	13
Wade Boggs	.311	2	41	1

Production Will Drop

	1996 Statistics			
	Avg.	HR	RBI	SB
Jim Thome	.311	38	116	2
Chipper Jones	.309	30	110	14
Vinny Castilla	.304	40	113	7
Dean Palmer	.280	38	107	2
Robin Ventura	.287	34	105	1
Jeff Cirillo	.325	15	83	4
Ken Caminiti	.326	40	130	11
Ed Sprague	.247	36	101	0
Todd Zeile	.263	25	99	1
Scott Brosius	.304	22	71	7
Sean Berry	.281	17	95	12
Gary Gaetti	.274	23	80	2
Dave Hollins	.262	16	78	6
Charlie Hayes	.253	12	75	6
B.J. Surhoff	.292	21	82	0
Terry Pendleton	.238	11	75	2

1997 Sleepers

	1996 Statistics (includes minor leagues)			
	Avg.	HR	RBI	SB
Todd Walker	.329	28	117	15
George Arias	.287	15	83	4
Scott Rolen	.307	15	79	12
Bill Mueller	.311	4	55	2
Phil Nevin	.293	32	88	7
Chris Snopek	.253	8	30	2
Dave Magadan	.258	3	21	0

Shortstop

Expect A Better Year in '97

	Avg.	HR	RBI	SB
	1996 Statistics			
John Valentin	.296	13	59	9
Alex Gonzalez	.235	14	64	16
Edgar Renteria	.309	5	31	16
Gary DiSarcina	.256	5	48	2
Jeff Blauser	.245	10	35	6
Shawon Dunston	.300	5	25	8
Ricky Gutierrez	.284	1	15	6
Norberto Martin	.350	1	14	10

Production Will Drop

	Avg.	HR	RBI	SB
	1996 Statistics			
Alex Rodriguez	.358	36	123	15
Barry Larkin	.298	33	89	36
Cal Ripken	.278	26	102	1
Jose Valentin	.259	24	95	17
Omar Vizquel	.297	9	64	35
Kevin Elster	.252	24	99	4
Walt Weiss	.282	8	48	10
Ozzie Guillen	.263	4	45	6
Dave Howard	.219	4	48	5

Look for Consistency

	Avg.	HR	RBI	SB
	1996 Statistics			
Derek Jeter	.314	10	78	14
Mark Grudzielanek	.306	6	49	33
Jay Bell	.250	13	71	6
Pat Meares	.267	8	67	9
Chris Gomez	.257	4	45	3
Royce Clayton	.277	6	35	33
Mike Bordick	.240	5	54	5
Kevin Stocker	.254	5	41	6
Greg Gagne	.255	10	55	4
Orlando Miller	.256	15	58	3
Rey Ordonez	.257	1	30	1
Jose Hernandez	.242	10	41	4

1997 Sleepers

	Avg.	HR	RBI	SB
	1996 Statistics (includes minor leagues)			
Nomar Garciaparra	.308	20	67	8
Neifi Perez	.304	7	75	18
Kurt Abbott	.275	13	44	5
Rich Aurilia	.256	3	30	5
Damion Easley	.293	6	27	8
Rey Sanchez	.209	1	13	9

Left Field

Expect A Better Year in '97

	Avg.	HR	RBI	SB
	1996 Statistics			
Bob Higginson	.320	26	81	6
Luis Gonzalez	.271	15	79	9
Marc Newfield	.278	12	57	1
Curtis Pride	.300	10	31	11
Gerald Williams	.252	5	34	10
Derrick May	.251	5	33	2
James Mouton	.263	3	34	21
Mark Sweeney	.265	3	22	3
Robert Perez	.327	2	21	3

Production Will Drop

	Avg.	HR	RBI	SB
	1996 Statistics			
Barry Bonds	.308	42	129	40
Ellis Burks	.344	40	128	32
Al Martin	.300	18	72	38
Bernard Gilkey	.317	30	117	17
Rusty Greer	.332	18	100	9
Tony Phillips	.277	12	63	13
Joe Carter	.253	30	107	7
Greg Vaughn	.260	41	117	9
Henry Rodriguez	.276	36	103	2
Rickey Henderson	.241	9	29	37
Craig Paquette	.259	22	67	5
Rich Amaral	.292	1	29	25
Pete Incaviglia	.242	18	50	2
Thomas Howard	.272	6	42	6
Dave Clark	.270	8	36	2

Look for Consistency

	Avg.	HR	RBI	SB
	1996 Statistics			
Albert Belle	.311	48	148	11
Marty Cordova	.309	16	111	11
Ryan Klesko	.282	34	93	6
Jeff Conine	.293	26	95	1
Ron Gant	.246	30	82	13
Garret Anderson	.285	12	72	7
Todd Hollandsworth	.291	12	59	21
Darryl Strawberry	.262	11	36	6
Kevin Mitchell	.316	8	39	0

1997 Sleepers

	Avg.	HR	RBI	SB
	1996 Statistics (includes minor leagues)			
Brooks Kieschnick	.264	19	70	0
Tim Raines	.288	12	48	13
Mike Greenwell	.294	9	46	4
Jeffrey Hammonds	.241	12	46	6
Bob Abreu	.283	13	69	24
Cliff Floyd	.257	7	34	9
Billy Ashley	.226	10	34	2
Billy Mcmillon	.334	17	74	5

Center Field

Expect A Better Year in '97

	1996 Statistics			
	Avg.	HR	RBI	SB
Johnny Damon	.271	6	50	25
Chad Curtis	.252	12	46	18
Brian L. Hunter	.276	5	35	35
Quinton Mccracken	.290	3	40	17
Brett Butler	.267	0	8	8
Mike Kingery	.246	3	27	2

Look for Consistency

	1996 Statistics			
	Avg.	HR	RBI	SB
Ken Griffey Jr	.303	49	140	16
Kenny Lofton	.317	14	67	75
Ray Lankford	.275	21	86	35
Jim Edmonds	.304	27	66	4
Darren Bragg	.261	10	47	14
Tom Goodwin	.282	1	35	66
Darren Lewis	.228	4	53	21
Pat Listach	.240	1	33	25
Bernie Williams	.305	29	102	17
Rich Becker	.291	12	71	19

Production Will Drop

	1996 Statistics			
	Avg.	HR	RBI	SB
Brady Anderson	.297	50	110	21
Marquis Grissom	.308	23	74	28
Brian McRae	.276	17	66	37
Steve Finley	.298	30	95	22
Lance Johnson	.333	9	69	50
Devon White	.274	17	84	22
Darryl Hamilton	.293	6	51	15
Dave Martinez	.318	10	53	15
Ernie Young	.242	19	64	7
Otis Nixon	.286	1	29	54
Eric Davis	.287	26	83	23
Jacob Brumfield	.255	14	60	15
Marvin Benard	.248	5	27	25
Ricky Otero	.273	2	32	16
F.P. Santangelo	.277	7	56	5
Lenny Dykstra	.261	3	13	3

1997 Sleepers

	1996 Statistics (includes minor leagues)			
	Avg.	HR	RBI	SB
Larry Walker	.285	21	67	18
Rondell White	.293	11	53	16
Darin Erstad	.297	10	61	14
Stan Javier	.272	2	23	14
Jermaine Allensworth	.303	12	74	36
Shannon Stewart	.293	6	44	36
Ruben Rivera	.244	12	62	21
Lee Tinsley	.226	3	19	10

Right Field

Expect A Better Year in '97

	1996 Statistics			
	Avg.	HR	RBI	SB
Tim Salmon	.286	30	98	4
Jeromy Bumitz	.265	9	40	4
Melvin Nieves	.246	24	60	1
Lyle Mouton	.294	7	39	3
Shawn Green	.280	11	45	5
Michael Tucker	.260	12	53	10
Dave Justice	.321	6	25	1
Carl Everett	.240	1	16	6
Damon Buford	.283	6	20	8
Sherman Obando	.247	8	22	2
Reggie Sanders	.258	14	34	24

Look for Consistency

	1996 Statistics			
	Avg.	HR	RBI	SB
Manny Ramirez	.309	33	112	8
Raul Mondesi	.297	24	88	14
Sammy Sosa	.273	40	100	18
Moises Alou	.281	21	96	9
Derek Bell	.263	17	113	29
Dave Nilsson	.331	17	84	2
Orlando Merced	.287	17	80	8
Troy O'Leary	.260	15	81	3
Glenallen Hill	.280	19	67	6
Matt Mieske	.278	14	64	1
Mike Devereaux	.229	8	34	8
Tony Gwynn	.353	3	50	11

Production Will Drop

	1996 Statistics			
	Avg.	HR	RBI	SB
Gary Sheffield	.314	42	120	16
Dante Bichette	.313	31	141	31
Juan Gonzalez	.314	47	144	2
Jay Buhner	.271	44	138	0
Paul O'Neill	.302	19	91	0
Bobby Bonilla	.287	28	116	1
Brian Jordan	.310	17	104	22
Danny Tartabull	.254	27	101	1
Mark Whiten	.262	22	71	17
Jim Eisenreich	.361	3	41	11
Jose Herrera	.269	6	30	8
Roberto Kelly	.323	6	47	10
Warren Newson	.255	10	31	3

1997 Sleepers

	1996 Statistics (includes minor leagues)			
	Avg.	HR	RBI	SB
Andruw Jones	.316	39	105	33
Rudy Pemberton	.331	30	113	20
Vladimir Guerrero	.351	25	97	19
Alex Ochoa	.315	12	72	9
Matt Lawton	.276	13	75	6
Jon Nunnally	.267	30	94	10
Jermaine Dye	.265	18	56	4
Angel Echevarria	.335	16	80	4
Todd Dunn	.339	19	79	13
Ozzie Timmons	.229	24	56	2
Jose Malave	.257	12	46	2
Brent Brede	.346	11	88	14

Designated Hitter

Expect A Better Year in '97

| | 1996 Statistics | | | |
	Avg.	HR	RBI	SB
Bob Hamelin	.255	9	40	5
Joe Vitiello	.241	8	40	2

Look for Consistency

| | 1996 Statistics | | | |
	Avg.	HR	RBI	SB
Carlos Delgado	.270	25	92	0
Ruben Sierra	.247	12	72	4
Jose Canseco	.289	28	82	3
Edgar Martinez	.327	26	103	3

Production Will Drop

| | 1996 Statistics | | | |
	Avg.	HR	RBI	SB
Geronimo Berroa	.290	36	106	0
Chili Davis	.292	28	95	5
Paul Molitor	.341	9	113	18
Mickey Tettleton	.246	24	83	2
Kevin Seitzer	.326	13	78	6
Harold Baines	.311	22	95	3
Eddie Murray	.260	22	79	4
Reggie Jefferson	.347	19	74	0

1997 Sleepers

| | 1996 Statistics (includes minor leagues) | | | |
	Avg.	HR	RBI	SB
Brian S. Giles	.326	25	91	4

Starting Pitchers

Expect A Better Year in '97

| | 1996 Statistics | | | | |
	W	L	ERA	Sv	BR/9
Mark Gubicza	4	12	5.13	0	1.45
Mark Langston	6	5	4.82	0	1.32
Doug Drabek	7	9	4.57	0	1.57
David Cone	7	2	2.88	0	1.19
Greg Maddux	15	11	2.72	0	1.04
David West	2	2	4.76	0	1.48
Randy Johnson	5	0	3.67	1	1.22
Kent Mercker	4	6	6.98	0	1.78
Pete Schourek	4	5	6.01	0	1.57
Ricky Bones	7	14	6.22	0	1.72
Jim Bullinger	6	10	6.54	1	1.70
Pat Rapp	8	16	5.10	0	1.71
Paul Wagner	4	8	5.40	0	1.57
Kevin Foster	7	6	6.21	0	1.55
Michael Mimbs	3	9	5.53	0	1.60
Marty Janzen	4	6	7.33	0	1.83
Amaury Telemaco	5	7	5.46	0	1.46
Rocky Coppinger	10	6	5.18	0	1.50
Dan Serafini	0	1	10.38	0	2.31
Trever Miller	0	4	9.18	0	2.34
Brian Moehler	0	1	4.35	0	1.84
Roger Clemens	10	13	3.63	0	1.34
Jack McDowell	13	9	5.11	0	1.48
Steve Avery	7	10	4.47	0	1.45
Cal Eldred	4	4	4.46	0	1.46
Rick Helling	3	3	4.31	0	1.10

Look for Consistency

| | 1996 Statistics | | | | |
	W	L	ERA	Sv	BR/9
Tom Candiotti	9	11	4.49	0	1.43
Sid Fernandez	3	6	3.43	0	1.22
Kevin Gross	11	8	5.22	0	1.59
Orel Hershiser	15	9	4.24	0	1.50
Dwight Gooden	11	7	5.01	0	1.56
Jimmy Key	12	11	4.68	0	1.36
Mark Portugal	8	9	3.98	0	1.22
Rick Aguilera	8	6	5.42	0	1.38
Bob Tewksbury	10	10	4.31	0	1.31
Bobby Witt	16	12	5.41	0	1.67
Chuck Finley	15	16	4.16	0	1.45
Kenny Rogers	12	8	4.68	0	1.51
John Smiley	13	14	3.64	0	1.22
David Wells	11	14	5.14	0	1.36
John Burkett	11	12	4.24	0	1.31
Tom Glavine	15	10	2.98	0	1.30
Ramon Martinez	15	6	3.42	0	1.46
Ken Hill	16	10	3.63	0	1.40
Todd Stottlemyre	14	11	3.87	0	1.29
Erik Hanson	13	17	5.41	0	1.62
Tom Gordon	12	9	5.59	0	1.66
Pete Harnisch	8	12	4.21	0	1.35
Kevin Appier	14	11	3.62	0	1.29
Jaime Navarro	15	12	3.92	0	1.38
Kevin Tapani	13	10	4.59	0	1.40
Kevin Ritz	17	11	5.28	0	1.66
Wilson Alvarez	15	10	4.22	0	1.46
Ben McDonald	12	10	3.90	0	1.36
Jason Grimsley	5	7	6.84	0	1.82
Shawn Boskie	12	11	5.32	0	1.62
Scott Erickson	13	12	5.02	0	1.52
Charles Nagy	17	5	3.41	0	1.27
Mark Leiter	8	12	4.92	0	1.48
Alex Fernandez	16	10	3.45	0	1.27
Scott Aldred	6	9	6.21	0	1.62

Look For Consistency (continued)

	W	L	ERA	Sv	BR/9
Dave Burba	11	13	3.83	0	1.43
Darryl Kile	12	11	4.19	0	1.58
Jeff Fassero	15	11	3.30	0	1.19
Andy Ashby	9	5	3.23	0	1.22
Frank Castillo	7	16	5.28	0	1.44
Denny Neagle	16	9	3.50	0	1.25
Mike Mussina	19	11	4.81	0	1.38
Armando Reynoso	8	9	4.96	0	1.50
Rheal Cormier	7	10	4.17	0	1.35
Mark Clark	14	11	3.43	0	1.26
Donovan Osborne	13	9	3.53	0	1.25
Roger Pavlik	15	8	5.19	0	1.50
Mike Williams	6	14	5.44	0	1.56
Pedro Astacio	9	8	3.44	0	1.34
Pedro Martinez	13	10	3.70	0	1.21
Shane Reynolds	16	10	3.65	0	1.17
Paul Quantrill	5	14	5.43	0	1.67
Tim Wakefield	14	13	5.14	0	1.61
Sterling Hitchcock	13	9	5.35	0	1.65
Mike Hampton	10	10	3.59	0	1.42
Woody Williams	4	5	4.73	0	1.46
Aaron Sele	7	11	5.32	0	1.70
Allen Watson	8	12	4.61	0	1.42
Kirk Rueter	6	8	3.97	0	1.35
Albie Lopez	5	4	6.39	0	1.68
Bobby Jones	12	8	4.42	0	1.37
Chad Ogea	10	6	4.79	0	1.35
W. VanLandingham	9	14	5.40	0	1.56
Joey Hamilton	15	9	4.17	0	1.41
Ismael Valdes	15	7	3.32	0	1.23
Felipe Lira	6	14	5.22	0	1.44
Scott Karl	13	9	4.86	0	1.46
Andy Pettitte	21	8	3.87	0	1.38
Brad Radke	11	16	4.46	0	1.26
Jason Schmidt	5	6	5.70	0	1.69
Don Wengert	7	11	5.58	0	1.65
Hideo Nomo	16	11	3.19	0	1.17
C.J. Nitkowski	2	3	8.08	0	2.34
Ariel Prieto	6	7	4.15	0	1.52
Rick Krivda	3	5	4.96	0	1.58
Jason Isringhausen	6	14	4.77	0	1.58
Bob Wolcott	7	10	5.73	0	1.61
John Wasdin	8	7	5.96	0	1.52
Mike Grace	7	2	3.49	0	1.11
Donne Wall	9	8	4.56	0	1.40
Dennis Springer	5	6	5.51	0	1.48
Osvaldo Fernandez	7	13	4.61	0	1.51
Paul Wilson	5	12	5.38	0	1.60
Calvin Maduro	0	1	3.52	0	1.17
Dennis Martinez	9	6	4.50	0	1.44
Frank Rodriguez	13	14	5.05	2	1.46
Chan Ho Park	5	5	3.64	0	1.44

Production Will Drop

1996 Statistics

	W	L	ERA	Sv	BR/9
Fernando Valenzuela	13	8	3.62	0	1.42
Danny Darwin	10	11	3.77	0	1.21
Jamie Moyer	13	3	3.98	0	1.40
Terry Mulholland	13	11	4.66	0	1.41
Kevin Brown	17	11	1.89	0	1.01
Tim Belcher	15	11	3.92	0	1.41
Al Leiter	16	12	2.93	0	1.31
John Smoltz	24	8	2.94	0	1.01
Curt Schilling	9	10	3.19	0	1.10
Mark Gardner	12	7	4.42	0	1.48
Andy Benes	18	10	3.83	1	1.29
Omar Olivares	7	11	4.89	0	1.58
Juan Guzman	11	8	2.93	0	1.16
Chris Haney	10	14	4.70	0	1.42
Pat Hentgen	20	10	3.22	0	1.27
Doug Linton	7	9	5.02	0	1.39
Greg Gohr	5	9	7.24	1	1.82
Rich Robertson	7	17	5.12	0	1.73
Dave Telgheder	4	7	4.65	0	1.50
Salomon Torres	3	3	4.59	0	1.43
Darren Oliver	14	6	4.66	0	1.59
Roger Salkeld	8	5	5.20	0	1.50
Steve Trachsel	13	9	3.03	0	1.22
Kevin Jarvis	8	9	5.98	0	1.64
Tim Vanegmond	3	5	5.27	0	1.50
Mark Thompson	9	11	5.30	0	1.63
James Baldwin	11	6	4.42	0	1.36
Ugueth Urbina	10	5	3.71	0	1.29
Doug Johns	6	12	5.98	1	1.66
Marc Valdes	1	3	4.81	0	1.79
Shawn Estes	3	5	3.60	0	1.49
Alan Benes	13	10	4.90	0	1.50

1997 Sleepers

1996 Statistics
(includes minor leagues)

	W	L	ERA	Sv	BR/9
Jim Abbott	2	20	6.79	0	1.69
Huck Flener	10	5	3.32	0	1.28
Esteban Loaiza	5	7	4.43	0	1.43
Rich Hunter	9	14	5.23	0	1.52
Jose Paniagua	14	9	2.92	0	1.26
Ramiro Mendoza	10	7	4.02	0	1.43
Justin Thompson	7	9	3.80	0	1.35
Matt Wagner	12	7	4.47	0	1.46
Willie Adams	13	8	3.87	0	1.30
Jose Rosado	18	9	3.00	0	1.21
Jeff D'Amico	11	10	4.25	0	1.23
Jamey Wright	13	7	3.31	0	1.39
Chris Peters	10	8	3.43	0	1.26
Matt Beech	14	10	3.94	0	1.14
Jason Dickson	13	17	3.89	0	1.38
Curt Lyons	15	4	2.63	0	1.27

Relief Pitchers

Expect A Better Year in '97

	W	L	ERA	Sv	BR/9
	1996 Statistics				
Roger McDowell	1	1	4.25	4	1.58
Eric Plunk	3	2	2.43	2	1.20
Mike Jackson	1	1	3.63	6	1.26
Ed Vosberg	1	1	3.27	8	1.64
Tony Castillo	5	4	3.60	2	1.28
Willie Blair	2	6	4.60	1	1.32
Gil Heredia	2	5	5.89	1	1.45
Chris Hammond	5	8	6.56	0	1.67
Darren Holmes	5	4	3.97	1	1.39
Rich DeLucia	3	6	5.84	0	1.56
Hipolito Pichardo	3	5	5.43	3	1.50
Greg McMichael	5	3	3.22	2	1.29
Julian Tavarez	4	7	5.36	0	1.54
Johnny Ruffin	1	3	5.49	0	1.76
Mark Acre	1	3	6.12	2	1.96
Brad Clontz	6	3	5.69	1	1.40
Roger Bailey	2	3	6.24	1	1.76
Joel Adamson	0	0	7.36	0	2.36
Alex Pacheco	0	0	11.12	0	1.59
Marc Wilkins	4	3	3.84	1	1.56
Jay Witasick	1	1	6.23	0	1.31
Nerio Rodriguez	0	1	4.32	0	1.56
Eric Ludwick	0	1	9.00	0	1.50
Chris Holt	0	1	5.79	0	1.71
Kurt Miller	1	3	6.80	0	1.99
Jimmy Haynes	3	6	8.29	1	2.04
Jeff Suppan	1	1	7.54	0	1.90
Billy Wagner	2	2	2.44	9	1.18

Look for Consistency

	W	L	ERA	Sv	BR/9
	1996 Statistics				
Jesse Orosco	3	1	3.40	0	1.29
Dennis Eckersley	0	6	3.30	30	1.25
John Franco	4	3	1.83	28	1.39
Todd Worrell	4	6	3.03	44	1.33
Paul Assenmacher	4	2	3.09	1	1.37
Mike Maddux	3	2	4.48	0	1.68
Norm Charlton	4	7	4.04	20	1.41
Mike Henneman	0	7	5.79	31	1.38
Jeff Montgomery	4	6	4.26	24	1.28
John Wetteland	2	3	2.83	43	1.18
Jim Corsi	6	0	4.03	3	1.47
Xavier Hernandez	5	5	4.62	6	1.37
Mike Dyer	5	5	4.40	2	1.56
Mike Stanton	4	4	3.66	1	1.33
Chuck McElroy	7	1	3.86	0	1.43
Mike Munoz	2	2	6.65	0	1.61
Rich Garces	3	2	4.91	0	1.70
Mike Timlin	1	6	3.65	31	1.18
Heathcliff Slocumb	5	5	3.02	31	1.51
Mike Magnante	2	2	5.67	0	1.59
Rod Beck	0	9	3.34	35	1.08
Mark Petkovsek	11	2	3.55	0	1.39
Doug Henry	2	8	4.68	9	1.59
Barry Manuel	4	1	3.24	0	1.20
Yorkis Perez	3	4	5.29	0	1.74
Todd Van Poppel	3	9	9.06	1	2.05
Brian Williams	3	10	6.77	2	1.95
Jeff Nelson	4	4	4.36	2	1.52
Kent Bottenfield	3	5	2.63	1	1.31
Bill Risley	0	1	3.89	0	1.39
Bob Wickman	7	1	4.42	0	1.62
Steve Reed	4	3	3.96	0	1.21
Dave Mlicki	6	7	3.30	1	1.49
Graeme Lloyd	2	6	4.29	0	1.48
John Cummings	3	4	5.35	0	1.95
Lance Painter	4	2	5.86	0	1.66
Curt Leskanic	7	5	6.23	6	1.66
Sean Bergman	6	8	4.37	0	1.36
Todd Jones	6	3	4.40	17	1.71
Hector Carrasco	4	3	3.75	0	1.40
Carlos Reyes	7	10	4.78	0	1.61
Dave Veres	6	3	4.17	4	1.58
Dave Stevens	3	3	4.66	11	1.43
Bryce Florie	2	3	4.74	0	1.62
Brad Woodall	2	2	7.32	0	1.63
Mike James	5	5	2.67	1	1.41
Troy Percival	0	2	2.31	36	0.96
Ron Villone	1	1	3.14	2	1.42
Jason Christiansen	3	3	6.70	0	1.71
Doug Bochtler	2	4	3.02	3	1.29
John Ericks	4	5	5.79	8	1.61
Matt Karchner	7	4	5.76	1	1.75
T.J. Mathews	2	6	3.01	6	1.15
Larry Thomas	2	3	3.23	0	1.60
Robert Person	4	5	4.52	0	1.37
Francisco Cordova	4	7	4.09	12	1.26
Alvin Morman	4	1	4.93	0	1.60
Dan Naulty	3	2	3.79	4	1.37
Rodney Myers	2	1	4.68	0	1.51
Mike Holtz	3	3	2.45	0	1.47

Look For Consistency (continued)

Larry Mitchell	0	0	4.50	0	1.58
Mark Wohlers	2	4	3.03	39	1.22
Jose Mesa	2	7	3.73	39	1.38
Jeff Brantley	1	2	2.41	44	1.15
Mel Rojas	7	4	3.22	36	1.06
Lee Smith	3	4	3.83	2	1.53
Jeff Russell	4	3	2.72	5	1.29
Doug Jones	7	5	4.09	9	1.48
Darren Dreifort	1	4	4.94	0	1.48
Paul Shuey	5	2	2.85	4	1.32

Production Will Drop

	1996 Statistics				
	W	L	ERA	Sv	BR/9
Rick Honeycutt	2	1	2.85	4	1.04
Mike Bielecki	4	3	2.63	2	1.27
Randy Myers	4	4	3.53	31	1.53
Dan Plesac	6	5	4.09	11	1.29
Bruce Ruffin	7	5	4.00	24	1.21
Bob Patterson	3	3	3.13	8	1.26
Jose Bautista	3	4	3.36	0	1.19
Tony Fossas	0	4	2.68	2	1.36
Dennis Cook	5	2	4.09	0	1.35
Mark Guthrie	2	3	2.22	1	1.21
Mike Fetters	3	3	3.38	32	1.50
Scott Radinsky	5	1	2.41	1	1.32
Alan Mills	3	2	4.28	3	1.39
Jeff Shaw	8	6	2.49	4	1.24
Jim Poole	6	1	2.86	0	1.43
Mark Dewey	6	3	4.21	0	1.50
Roberto Hernandez	6	5	1.91	38	1.22
Arthur Rhodes	9	1	4.08	1	1.34
Jeff Juden	5	0	3.27	0	1.35
Buddy Groom	5	0	3.84	2	1.58
Richie Lewis	4	6	4.18	2	1.63
Mike Trombley	5	1	3.01	6	1.33
Ken Ryan	3	5	2.43	8	1.31
Robb Nen	5	1	1.95	35	1.07
Trevor Hoffman	9	5	2.25	42	0.94
Mike Mohler	6	3	3.67	7	1.49
Omar Daal	4	5	4.02	0	1.28
Jerry DiPoto	7	2	4.19	0	1.80
Angel Miranda	7	6	4.94	1	1.71
Eddie Guardado	6	5	5.25	4	1.32
Turk Wendell	4	5	2.84	18	1.32

Tim Worrell	9	7	3.05	1	1.27
Mark Hutton	5	3	4.15	0	1.37
Scott Sanders	9	5	3.38	0	1.16
Cory Bailey	5	2	3.00	0	1.54
Paul Spoljaric	2	2	3.08	1	1.34
A.J. Sager	4	5	5.01	0	1.54
Billy Taylor	6	3	4.33	17	1.34
Jose Lima	5	6	5.70	3	1.57
Jon Lieber	9	5	3.99	1	1.32
Bob Wells	12	7	5.30	0	1.48
Toby Borland	7	3	4.07	0	1.42
Joey Eischen	1	2	4.21	0	1.65
Jason Jacome	0	4	4.72	1	1.91
Armando Benitez	1	0	3.77	4	0.91
Ricky Bottalico	4	5	3.19	34	1.06
Antonio Osuna	9	6	3.00	4	1.18
Greg Hansell	3	0	5.69	3	1.56
Mike Myers	1	5	5.01	6	1.67
Jose Parra	5	5	6.04	0	1.69
Rafael Carmona	8	3	4.28	1	1.69
Mariano Rivera	8	3	2.09	5	1.01
Tim Crabtree	5	3	2.54	1	1.25
Ricardo Jordan	2	2	1.80	0	1.20
Mark Brandenburg	5	5	3.43	0	1.47
Terry Adams	3	6	2.94	4	1.33
Bill Simas	2	8	4.58	2	1.61
Terrell Wade	5	0	2.97	1	1.51
Jay Powell	4	3	4.54	2	1.56

1997 Sleepers

	1996 Statistics (includes minor leagues)				
	W	L	ERA	Sv	BR/9
Bill Swift	1	1	5.18	2	1.56
Danny Jackson	1	1	3.88	0	1.35
Bobby Ayala	6	3	5.66	3	1.34
Doug Brocail	1	6	4.62	0	1.54
Dan Miceli	3	10	5.32	2	1.61
John Hudek	3	0	2.75	6	1.19
Matt Ruebel	6	4	4.60	1	1.59
Ron Blazier	7	1	4.15	12	1.28
Danny Graves	6	3	2.32	19	1.12
Dario Veras	12	4	2.65	2	1.16
Felix Heredia	9	2	2.11	5	1.24
Jaime Bluma	1	2	3.24	30	1.31
Derek Wallace	7	5	2.40	29	1.19

American League Players

Terry Collins

1996 Season

For the third time in his three seasons as manager, Terry Collins led the Houston Astros to a winning record in 1996. But Houston once again finished out of the playoffs, and owner Drayton McLane pink-slipped Collins. It was a difficult year all around for the fiery Collins, who felt himself targeted both by some of his players—most notably All-Star second baseman Craig Biggio—and some of his coaches. He was criticized for a lack of communication with his players, who felt he grew too removed from them.

Offense

Collins preaches aggressiveness, but he didn't have enough speed on his Houston teams to make much happen offensively. The longer he managed the Astros, the more he relied on the big-bat thunder of Jeff Bagwell. Collins was criticized for not finding a better way to protect Bagwell, but the fault lay in the personnel, not the lineups he filled out. Collins is expected to try some hit-and-runs and steal attempts as the new manager of the Angels, but once again his biggest challenge will be to find a way to best utilize his most productive bat, Tim Salmon.

Pitching & Defense

Like Tony La Russa, Bobby Valentine and other new-school skippers, Collins will get a reliever up at the first sign of trouble. The danger is burning out his relievers over the course of the season. Collins' Houston teams suffered fundamental lapses, in part because he often seemed to sacrifice defense in search of a little more run production.

1997 Outlook

Collins finds himself in a highly unusual situation. His pitching coach is the manager who was fired midway through last season, Marcel Lachemann. Fortunately for Collins, Lachemann is about as loyal of a company man as you can find in baseball. Still, Collins doesn't figure to have it easy in his new job.

Born: 5/27/49 in Midland, MI

Playing Experience: No major league experience

Managerial Experience: 3 seasons

Manager Statistics

Year	Team, Lg	W	L	Pct	GB	Finish
1996	Houston, NL	82	80	.506	6.0	2nd Central
3 Seasons		224	197	.532	—	—

1996 Starting Pitchers by Days Rest

	≤3	4	5	6+
Astros Starts	9	88	34	24
Astros ERA	3.82	4.52	3.09	4.90
NL Avg Starts	4	86	41	21
NL ERA	4.06	4.28	4.23	4.58

1996 Situational Stats

	Terry Collins	NL Average
Hit & Run Success %	40.0	39.0
Stolen Base Success %	74.1	71.6
Platoon Pct.	39.2	51.9
Defensive Subs	38	20
High-Pitch Outings	9	13
Quick/Slow Hooks	13/12	19/12
Sacrifice Attempts	94	92

1996 Rankings (National League)

→ 1st in steals of third base (38), least caught steals of home plate (0), double steals (20) and defensive substitutions (38)

→ 2nd in stolen base attempts (243), steals of second base (142), hit-and-run attempts (135), hit-and-run percentage (40.0%) and starts on three days rest (9)

→ 3rd in stolen base percentage (74.1%)

Jim Abbott

1996 Season

Wow. Where to start? With the three-year contract that California gave him before the season or the 2-18 return on that investment? Either way, the Angels wound up with pie on their face for bringing back the remarkable Jim Abbott, who became a folk hero in his initial stay with California in 1989-92. Abbott got so out of whack that he was not only banished to the bullpen for the first time after 226 career starts, but the Angels actually sent him to Triple-A for four starts in August. He went 0-2 there, which means he managed to lose 20 games overall.

Pitching

Scouts marveled as Abbott put together an 11-8 performance in 1995, which gave him the leverage to get a multi-year deal. He was able to win despite an apparent lack of stuff. He struggles to hit 85 MPH with his fastball and he never has had a reliable curveball. This proved to be a fatal combination last year, when he allowed one homer every 6.2 innings, a ratio that worsened to one homer every 4.0 innings at Anaheim Stadium. His strikeout total dropped for the fifth year in a row, as he actually walked 20 more than he whiffed. And the left-handed Abbott continued to be pounded by lefty swingers, who had a slugging average of close to .700 against him.

Defense

Abbott, who was born without a right hand, has always been a marvel at fielding his position. That's the one thing that has not changed. His reactions on the mound are quick and he has worked hard to hold runners.

1997 Outlook

Angels' Assistant G.M. Tim Mead is Abbott's biggest backer, which means he should get an opportunity to bounce back. But if he continues to get battered at last year's pace, the Angels will eventually have to eat what's left of his $6 million contract.

Position: SP
Bats: L **Throws:** L
Ht: 6' 3" **Wt:** 210

Opening Day Age: 29
Born: 9/19/67 in Flint, MI
ML Seasons: 8

Overall Statistics

	W	L	Pct.	ERA	G	GS	Sv	IP	H	BB	SO	HR	BR/IP
1996	2	18	.100	7.48	27	23	0	142.0	171	78	58	23	1.75
Career	80	100	.444	4.11	238	234	0	1560.1	1634	566	837	138	1.41

How Often He Throws Strikes

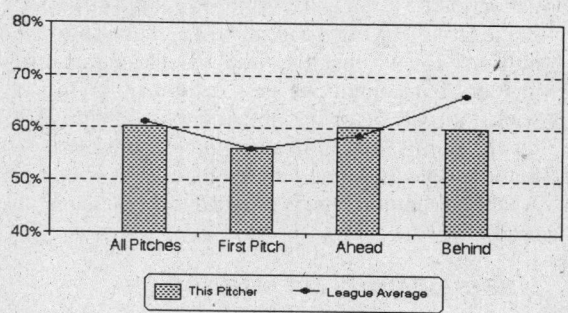

1996 Situational Stats

	W	L	ERA	Sv	IP		AB	H	HR	RBI	Avg
Home	0	8	8.52	0	56.0	LHB	119	40	10	32	.336
Road	2	10	6.80	0	86.0	RHB	439	131	13	79	.298
First Half	1	11	7.60	0	90.0	Sc Pos	163	57	8	85	.350
Scnd Half	1	7	7.27	0	52.0	Clutch	28	11	3	9	.393

1996 Rankings (American League)

→ 1st in losses and lowest winning percentage
→ 3rd in wild pitches (13), highest ERA on the road (6.80) and highest batting average allowed with runners in scoring position (.350)
→ 10th in balks (1) and highest batting average allowed vs. right-handed batters (.298)
→ Led the Angels in losses and runners caught stealing (8)

Garret Anderson

1996 Season

Garret Anderson didn't exactly suffer from the dreaded sophomore jinx, but he could not repeat the production he provided in 1995, when he finished second in the A.L. Rookie of the Year balloting. In his first full season in the major leagues, he was third on the team in RBI, but contributed to the Angels' offensive woes by refusing to take a walk. He batted everywhere except cleanup and ninth over the course of the season, and seemed exhausted by the effort, tiring at the end.

Hitting

Anderson's blessing is also his curse. He is an unusually good high-ball hitter for a left-handed batter, but he often chases pitches up and out of the strike zone, trying to tomahawk them into the outfield. He will use the whole field against left-handers but sometimes gets caught up trying to yank the ball against righthanders. Perhaps as a result, he hits lefthanders as well—if not better—than he does righthanders. He had little power at Anaheim Stadium last year and slightly less on the road.

Baserunning & Defense

Trying to awaken the Angels' disappointing offense, Marcel Lachemann and John McNamara tried to be aggressive with Anderson on base. Oops. He stole seven bases, the most of his professional career, but was caught stealing nine times. He covers ground in the outfield but is nevertheless a defensive liability. His arm is weak, even for a left fielder, and teams run on him.

1997 Outlook

Something had to give in the crowded California outfield, and eventually the Angels opted to trade DH Chili Davis to the Royals, opening up the DH spot for Anderson. But while he's assured of playing regularly for now, he needs to raise his game to make sure he's in the long-range plans. He now has run out of steam in September two years in a row, so perhaps he would benefit from a little bit more rest during the season.

Position: LF
Bats: L **Throws:** L
Ht: 6' 3" **Wt:** 190

Opening Day Age: 24
Born: 6/30/72 in Los Angeles, CA
ML Seasons: 3

Overall Statistics

	G	AB	R	H	D	T	HR	RBI	SB	BB	SO	Avg	OBP	Slg
1996	150	607	79	173	33	2	12	72	7	27	84	.285	.314	.405
Career	261	994	129	298	52	3	28	142	13	46	151	.300	.329	.443

Where He Hits the Ball

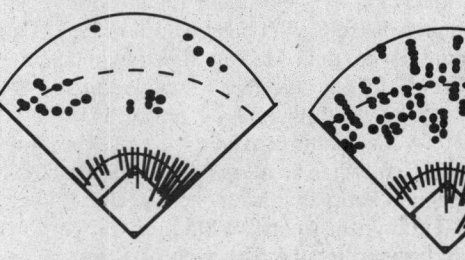

Vs. LHP   **Vs. RHP**

1996 Situational Stats

	AB	H	HR	RBI	Avg		AB	H	HR	RBI	Avg
Home	306	87	7	34	.284	LHP	212	62	3	21	.292
Road	301	86	5	38	.286	RHP	395	111	9	51	.281
First Half	355	103	9	37	.290	Sc Pos	150	36	2	51	.240
Scnd Half	252	70	3	35	.278	Clutch	98	33	2	14	.337

1996 Rankings (American League)

- → 2nd in errors in left field (7)
- → 3rd in GDPs (21) and lowest fielding percentage in left field (.977)
- → 4th in least pitches seen per plate appearance (3.38)
- → 8th in lowest on-base percentage and lowest on-base percentage vs. left-handed pitchers (.296)
- → 9th in singles
- → 10th in at-bats and caught stealing
- → Led the Angels in at-bats, hits, singles, doubles, caught stealing, GDPs (21) and batting average in the clutch (.337)

George Arias

1996 Season

Some think George Arias is the long-term answer at third base, where the Angels have been going from one stop-gap player to another since Doug DeCinces retired. Arias started the season as California's regular third baseman, skipping Triple-A entirely, but was sent to the minors after hitting .184 in his first 26 games. He earned his way back to the big leagues by hitting .337 with 55 RBI in 59 games at Triple-A, and seemed an improved product after rejoining the Angels after the All-Star break.

Hitting

Arias has plenty of power but sometimes struggles to make contact. He often appeared overanxious, putting himself in the hole by swinging at pitches out of the strike zone. It often looked like he was guess-hitting. In the minors, he drew slightly more than one walk for every two strikeouts, but with the Angels, he got only one walk for every 3.1 whiffs. Arias needs to develop more patience, especially with runners in scoring position. He really struggled on the road in his first trip through the American League. He didn't fare very well in clutch situations, either.

Baserunning & Defense

Arias, a seventh-round draft choice in 1993, was billed as a strong defensive third baseman in the minors. He made some spectacular plays in his rookie season, but was generally erratic. He runs like your basic third baseman: not very quickly.

1997 Outlook

Arias returns as the incumbent third sacker. He needs to do a better job hitting against righthanders to stay out of a platoon situation, however. He should benefit from the reduced expectations of the Angels, who will be more patient developing their young players now that they have stable ownership and a better grasp on the team's potential.

Position: 3B
Bats: R **Throws:** R
Ht: 5'11" **Wt:** 190

Opening Day Age: 25
Born: 3/12/72 in Tucson, AZ
ML Seasons: 1

Overall Statistics

	G	AB	R	H	D	T	HR	RBI	SB	BB	SO	Avg	OBP	Slg
1996	84	252	19	60	8	1	6	28	2	16	50	.238	.284	.349
Career	84	252	19	60	8	1	6	28	2	16	50	.238	.284	.349

Where He Hits the Ball

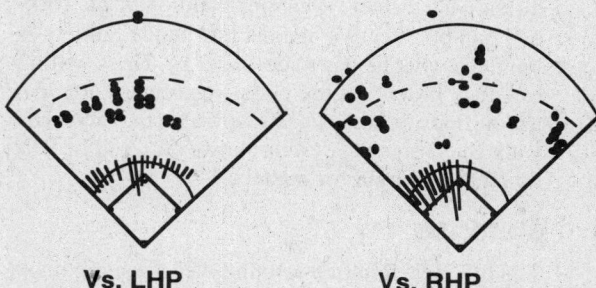

Vs. LHP   **Vs. RHP**

1996 Situational Stats

	AB	H	HR	RBI	Avg		AB	H	HR	RBI	Avg
Home	125	38	5	22	.304	LHP	82	24	3	12	.293
Road	127	22	1	6	.173	RHP	170	36	3	16	.212
First Half	76	14	1	5	.184	Sc Pos	83	17	2	22	.205
Scnd Half	176	46	5	23	.261	Clutch	25	6	0	2	.240

1996 Rankings (American League)

- → 1st in batting average on an 0-2 count (.348)
- → 9th in errors at third base (10)
- → Led the Angels in batting average on an 0-2 count (.348)

Shawn Boskie

1996 Season

There's nothing that catches the eye about Sean Boskie, but the veteran righthander has a big heart and just enough stuff to get by as a fourth or fifth starter. He was second on California's staff in both wins and innings pitched—proof of the unfulfilled expectations of others. In the Year of the Home Run, no one served up more than Boskie. He joined Minnesota's Brad Radke in allowing 40. Despite that, he won a dozen games, five more than he'd ever totaled in a season.

Pitching

Boskie is a prototype sinkerballer who gets hurt when he gets pitches up in the strike zone. He doesn't have many weapons—although his forkball can be effective against left-handed hitters—but does what he has to do to get by. He is willing to knock hitters off the plate—he hit 13 batters—and he doesn't hurt himself with a lot of walks. His walk rate was up last year, however. And he seldom has a margin for mistakes.

Defense

The 6-3 Boskie moves around well for a big man, and obviously takes fielding drills seriously. Runners don't try to steal on him all that often, but when they do go, they usually make it.

1997 Outlook

Boskie, a free agent, is entering the Scott Sanderson stage of his career. He will probably never get a long-term contract but could be a pleasant surprise for any team who signs him to a one-year deal. He would love to stay in Anaheim, where he seems to be a short-term fit, but must be willing to move from team to team if he is going to stay in the big leagues for many more years.

Position: SP/RP
Bats: R **Throws:** R
Ht: 6' 3" **Wt:** 200

Opening Day Age: 30
Born: 3/28/67 in Hawthorne, NV
ML Seasons: 7
Pronunciation: BAHSS-kee

Overall Statistics

	W	L	Pct.	ERA	G	GS	Sv	IP	H	BB	SO	HR	BR/IP
1996	12	11	.522	5.32	37	28	0	189.1	226	67	133	40	1.55
Career	42	54	.438	4.92	184	118	0	775.2	853	262	434	114	1.44

How Often He Throws Strikes

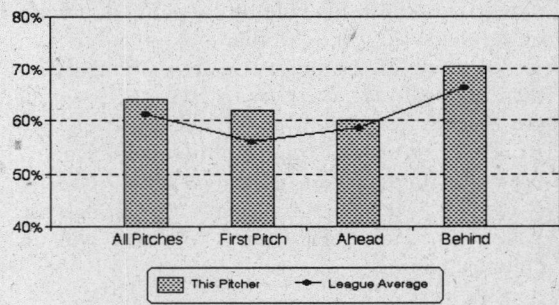

This Pitcher — League Average

1996 Situational Stats

	W	L	ERA	Sv	IP		AB	H	HR	RBI	Avg
Home	5	6	6.38	0	91.2	LHB	390	98	20	49	.251
Road	7	5	4.33	0	97.2	RHB	379	128	20	61	.338
First Half	9	3	4.27	0	111.2	Sc Pos	167	47	8	69	.281
Scnd Half	3	8	6.84	0	77.2	Clutch	59	23	2	7	.390

1996 Rankings (American League)

→ 1st in home runs allowed, hit batsmen (13), highest slugging percentage allowed (.508), most home runs allowed per 9 innings (1.90), highest ERA at home (6.38) and highest batting average allowed vs. right-handed batters (.338)

→ 2nd in highest stolen base percentage allowed (89.5%)

→ 4th in lowest groundball/flyball ratio allowed (0.9)

→ 5th in highest batting average allowed (.294)

→ 6th in highest ERA

→ 7th in highest on-base percentage allowed (.359) and most baserunners allowed per 9 innings (13.9)

Chili Davis

Position: DH
Bats: B **Throws:** R
Ht: 6' 3" **Wt:** 217

Opening Day Age: 37
Born: 1/17/60 in
Kingston, Jamaica
ML Seasons: 16

1996 Season

Someday Chili Davis is going to wear out, but it didn't happen last year. The veteran switch-hitter put together another remarkable season, and remained one of the game's most consistent run producers. Davis led the Angels in on-base percentage and was second to Tim Salmon in home runs and RBI. His 28 home runs were a California club record for a switch-hitter. His production was wasted on a second-division club, as it has been for too much of his career.

Hitting

Davis has become the consummate pro. He passed the 2,000-hit plateau last year and needs only two more home runs to reach 300 for his career. He is a proven clutch hitter who consistently delivers with runners in scoring position. Davis is equally effective from either side of the plate and is willing to work the count. He likes the ball up whether he's batting right-handed or left-handed.

Baserunning & Defense

Davis has lost the speed he had earlier in his career. He has only 15 stolen bases since he joined California in 1993, but remains a competent baserunner. Davis is a full-time designated hitter who plays the outfield only under emergency circumstances—eight times in the last six years. As you might expect, he's well below-average when asked to play in the field, and his arm is weak.

1997 Outlook

The Angels needed to do something about their glut of outfield and DH candidates, and they traded Davis to the Royals after the season. He could have a 100-RBI season if the men batting in front of him raise their production from 1996. Last season, 16 of his 28 home runs were solo shots, so he could have driven in many more runs if he'd had the opportunity. He may not hit another 28 homers, but he's a virtual lock for at least 20.

Overall Statistics

	G	AB	R	H	D	T	HR	RBI	SB	BB	SO	Avg	OBP	Slg
1996	145	530	73	155	24	0	28	95	5	86	99	.292	.387	.496
Career	2115	7617	1099	2089	372	29	298	1195	132	1022	1484	.274	.357	.448

Where He Hits the Ball

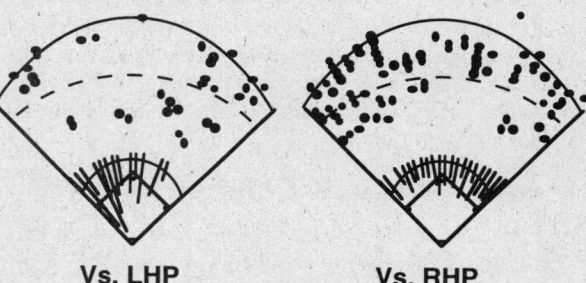

Vs. LHP **Vs. RHP**

1996 Situational Stats

	AB	H	HR	RBI	Avg		AB	H	HR	RBI	Avg
Home	267	79	15	44	.296	LHP	176	51	9	33	.290
Road	263	76	13	51	.289	RHP	354	104	19	62	.294
First Half	281	84	16	52	.299	Sc Pos	136	43	5	63	.316
Scnd Half	249	71	12	43	.285	Clutch	84	20	5	12	.238

1996 Rankings (American League)

➡ 8th in lowest cleanup slugging percentage (.489)
➡ Led the Angels in sacrifice flies (6), intentional walks (11), on-base percentage, HR frequency (18.9 ABs per HR), batting average vs. right-handed pitchers, slugging percentage vs. right-handed pitchers (.503), on-base percentage vs. right-handed pitchers (.396) and batting average

Gary DiSarcina

1996 Season

It's almost too easy to say that Gary DiSarcina simply hasn't been the same since he tore ligaments in his left thumb late in the 1995 season, but it is the truth. He couldn't duplicate the career year he was having before the thumb injury. DiSarcina's batting average fell 51 points, returning to pre-1995 levels. He has never walked much, nor had much power, so his low on-base average made him an offensive liability.

Hitting

Scouts talked about DiSarcina's bat speed increasing in mid-career, but it didn't seem quite the same last year as it had been before the thumb injury. He has always been able to cover the whole plate with a compact swing, but he did less with the balls he got his bat on last year. He's never learned to work a walk, and still hacks at too many borderline pitches. He's an easy out for right-handed pitchers, but a skilled bunter.

Baserunning & Defense

Fans who are used to seeing DiSarcina as a human vacuum cleaner were shocked by his play in 1996. He botched more routine plays in one year than he had in the two previous seasons combined. He has soft hands and quick feet, but lost his confidence. He has average speed but did not get as many chances to run in the John McNamara era as he had before the managerial change.

1997 Outlook

Don't be surprised if the Angels' top shortstop drops back permanently to number nine in the batting order, where he was when the California lineup was its most effective in 1995. He will probably never be an All-Star in a league that has been invaded by guys like Alex Rodriguez, Derek Jeter and Alex Gonzalez, but there's no reason he shouldn't regain some of the prestige he lost last season.

Position: SS
Bats: R **Throws:** R
Ht: 6' 2" **Wt:** 190

Opening Day Age: 29
Born: 11/19/67 in Malden, MA
ML Seasons: 8
Pronunciation: dee-sar-SEE-na

Overall Statistics

	G	AB	R	H	D	T	HR	RBI	SB	BB	SO	Avg	OBP	Slg
1996	150	536	62	137	26	4	5	48	2	21	36	.256	.286	.347
Career	682	2335	281	596	110	14	19	212	27	100	191	.255	.291	.339

Where He Hits the Ball

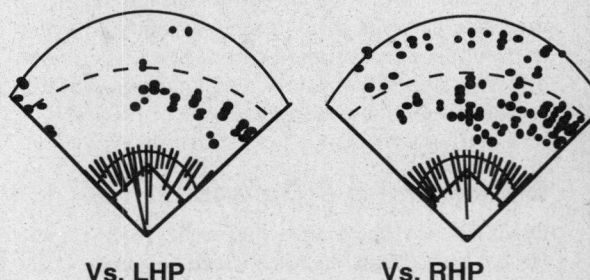

Vs. LHP   Vs. RHP

1996 Situational Stats

	AB	H	HR	RBI	Avg		AB	H	HR	RBI	Avg
Home	286	66	2	22	.231	LHP	164	48	2	14	.293
Road	250	71	3	26	.284	RHP	372	89	3	34	.239
First Half	282	69	1	29	.245	Sc Pos	124	26	3	41	.210
Scnd Half	254	68	4	19	.268	Clutch	76	15	1	9	.197

1996 Rankings (American League)

- → 1st in lowest on-base percentage vs. right-handed pitchers (.278) and highest percentage of swings put into play (61.7%)
- → 2nd in lowest on-base percentage, least pitches seen per plate appearance (3.00) and lowest batting average with runners in scoring position (.210)
- → 3rd in sacrifice bunts (16) and lowest slugging percentage vs. right-handed pitchers (.320)
- → 4th in lowest slugging percentage and lowest fielding percentage at shortstop (.971)
- → 5th in highest groundball/flyball ratio (1.9), lowest batting average at home (.231) and errors at shortstop (20)

Jim Edmonds

1996 Season

Two stays on the disabled list kept Jim Edmonds from putting up the kind of headline-grabbing numbers he had after California turned him loose in 1995. He was fairly productive when he played, but the Angels missed him when he was out with a strained left shoulder and sprained ligament in his right thumb. Pitchers made some adjustments to him, with lefthanders especially finding holes in his swing.

Hitting

In his breakthrough 1995 season, the left-handed hitting Edmonds used his sweet swing as effectively against lefthanders as righthanders. But that wasn't the case last year. Lefthanders ate his lunch by busting him in, then going away. He is developing a reputation as a guy you can get out with men in scoring position. He loses his discipline at the plate with men on base, which leads to more frequent strikeouts.

Baserunning & Defense

Edmonds is a prototype center fielder. He covers ground, catches what he gets to and shows no fear of the wall or the turf. On top of that, he's got a good arm. He has made only one error in each of the last two seasons. As a baserunner, he's surprisingly poor. He doesn't get good jumps on base hits, which makes it a struggle to score from second on sharp singles.

1997 Outlook

Edmonds should be back in center field for Anaheim, but the development of prospect Darin Erstad could make Edmonds trade bait eventually. For now Erstad figures to be in left, with Garret Anderson taking over for Chili Davis as the DH. Wherever he plays, look for Edmonds to get back to the 100-RBI level, provided he doesn't put himself on the DL running into a wall.

Position: CF
Bats: L **Throws:** L
Ht: 6' 1" **Wt:** 190

Opening Day Age: 26
Born: 6/27/70 in Fullerton, CA
ML Seasons: 4

Overall Statistics

	G	AB	R	H	D	T	HR	RBI	SB	BB	SO	Avg	OBP	Slg
1996	114	431	73	131	28	3	27	66	4	46	101	.304	.375	.571
Career	367	1339	233	387	75	9	65	214	9	129	319	.289	.354	.504

Where He Hits the Ball

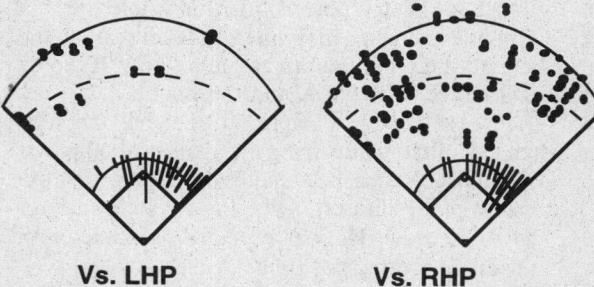

Vs. LHP   **Vs. RHP**

1996 Situational Stats

	AB	H	HR	RBI	Avg		AB	H	HR	RBI	Avg
Home	230	73	17	43	.317	LHP	122	23	2	9	.189
Road	201	58	10	23	.289	RHP	309	108	25	57	.350
First Half	187	57	13	34	.305	Sc Pos	111	27	4	36	.243
Scnd Half	244	74	14	32	.303	Clutch	67	14	2	8	.209

1996 Rankings (American League)

→ 2nd in lowest batting average vs. left-handed pitchers (.189)

→ 3rd in fielding percentage in center field (.997)

→ 7th in lowest slugging percentage vs. left-handed pitchers (.311) and lowest on-base percentage vs. left-handed pitchers (.293)

Darin Erstad

1996 Season

It's no surprise that the former University of Nebraska All-American reached the big leagues quickly. That was what California was counting on when it took him with the first pick of the 1995 draft. He vindicated that pick with a quick climb through the minors, hitting .305 in 85 games at Triple-A last year. He got the call-up when Jim Edmonds went on the disabled list in June and didn't return to the minors until August. He did a creditable job in his time in Anaheim, but showed that there are still areas of the game that need improvement.

Hitting

Erstad has been a power hitter his whole life, but is having to change his game a little bit without the benefit of an aluminum bat. He hit only 10 home runs between Triple-A and the majors last year. The Angels were pleased to see that the left-handed hitter could hang in against southpaws. Like most rookies, he sometimes seemed too anxious to prove himself, swinging at pitches out of the strike zone. He was especially anxious with runners in scoring position.

Baserunning & Defense

Erstad has good speed, which should yield 25-30 stolen bases. He plays a solid center field but paled when compared to Edmonds. So far, his arm has been unimpressive. He could be a superior left fielder, which will very likely end up being his position in the major leagues.

1997 Outlook

Erstad's arrival gave California a surplus in the outfield. For a time the club considered trading Edmonds or left fielder Garret Anderson to open up a spot for Erstad, but the club ultimately decided to trade designated hitter Chili Davis instead. Erstad is likely to open the season as Anaheim's left fielder, with Anderson the DH.

Position: CF/LF
Bats: L **Throws:** L
Ht: 6' 2" **Wt:** 210

Opening Day Age: 22
Born: 6/4/74 in Jamestown, North Dakota
ML Seasons: 1

Overall Statistics

	G	AB	R	H	D	T	HR	RBI	SB	BB	SO	Avg	OBP	Slg
1996	57	208	34	59	5	1	4	20	3	17	29	.284	.333	.375
Career	57	208	34	59	5	1	4	20	3	17	29	.284	.333	.375

Where He Hits the Ball

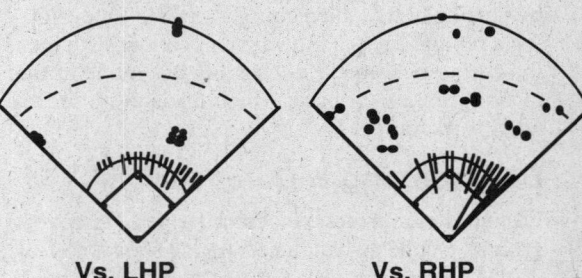

Vs. LHP   Vs. RHP

1996 Situational Stats

	AB	H	HR	RBI	Avg		AB	H	HR	RBI	Avg
Home	95	25	1	8	.263	LHP	65	20	1	9	.308
Road	113	34	3	12	.301	RHP	143	39	3	11	.273
First Half	96	30	3	13	.313	Sc Pos	49	11	0	14	.224
Scnd Half	112	29	1	7	.259	Clutch	35	11	0	4	.314

1996 Rankings (American League)

→ 1st in lowest batting average on a 3-1 count (.000)
→ 5th in lowest on-base percentage for a leadoff hitter (.338)
→ 10th in errors in center field (2)

Jorge Fabregas

1996 Season

Jorge Fabregas was supposed to establish himself as a regular last season but could not hold onto his position with California. He started the year with the Angels but was sent to the minors in June, which may have been the wake-up call his career needed. He spent three weeks there, then returned to California, where he hit much better. He batted .309 after the break, albeit with little power.

Hitting

Fabregas created expectations with a strong showing in 1994 but has struggled to match his production since then. He was a power hitter in college, but has become a contact hitter as he's progressed up the ladder. He loves the fastball and is at his best when a pitcher feeds him a first-pitch heater. And impatient as he is, he'll seldom draw a walk. He has developed an inside-out swing that seems to keep him from driving balls. He had one extra-base hit every 32 at-bats last year, which is nothing short of pitiful. He still does a good job putting the ball in play with runners in scoring position, and for a left-handed hitter, he isn't overmatched by lefties. Nevertheless, the Angels expected more.

Baserunning & Defense

The 6-foot-3 Fabregas moves slowly behind the plate and sometimes has trouble catching hard throwers like Troy Percival. He's an awkward thrower who fires too many balls into center field. On the basepaths, he stole two fewer last year than Cecil Fielder.

1997 Outlook

Fabregas may already have missed his chance to become a regular. His best hope in Anaheim may be to hang around caddying for Todd Greene. But as a left-handed-hitting catcher, he could stay in the big leagues for a long time—Jamie Quirk did.

Position: C
Bats: L **Throws:** R
Ht: 6' 3" **Wt:** 214

Opening Day Age: 27
Born: 3/13/70 in Miami, FL
ML Seasons: 3
Pronunciation: FA-ber-gas

Overall Statistics

	G	AB	R	H	D	T	HR	RBI	SB	BB	SO	Avg	OBP	Slg
1996	90	254	18	73	6	0	2	26	0	17	27	.287	.326	.335
Career	206	608	54	165	19	0	3	64	2	41	73	.271	.315	.317

Where He Hits the Ball

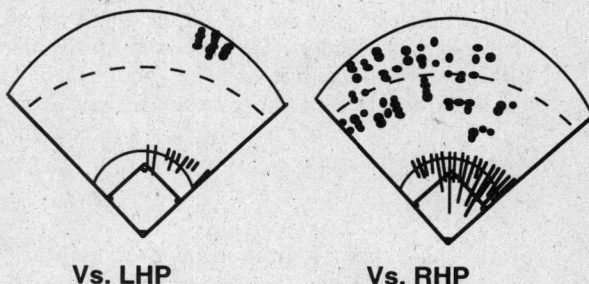

Vs. LHP   **Vs. RHP**

1996 Situational Stats

	AB	H	HR	RBI	Avg		AB	H	HR	RBI	Avg
Home	130	31	1	11	.238	LHP	30	12	1	4	.400
Road	124	42	1	15	.339	RHP	224	61	1	22	.272
First Half	115	30	2	7	.261	Sc Pos	56	17	0	23	.304
Scnd Half	139	43	0	19	.309	Clutch	32	8	1	3	.250

1996 Rankings (American League)

➡ 6th in lowest batting average on a 3-2 count (.091)
➡ 8th in errors at catcher (6)

Chuck Finley

1996 Season

While not as successful as in the early years of his career, Chuck Finley has turned into Mr. Reliable for the Angels. He led the team in victories and innings last year, which marked the seventh time in eight years he has won at least 10 games. He lowered his ERA for the second consecutive year. No wonder California went to the wall to keep him from flying the coop as a free agent before last season.

Pitching

Finley still has a good fastball, which he complements with a forkball. He does a great job throwing both from the same motion, which gives hitters no tip that the forkball is coming until it dives down to their ankles. As a result, he gets a lot of double-play grounders. He throws a slurve for strikes, which makes him extremely tough on left-handed hitters. He not only struck out a career-high 215 last year, but had the best strikeout-to-walk ratio of his career.

Defense

Finley has spent a long time around Mark Langston, but still hasn't picked up a single one of his fielding secrets. He has always been clumsy fielding his position, especially on bunts. He is among the easiest lefthanders for baserunners to run on, both because he is slow getting the ball to the plate and he doesn't expend too much energy holding men on.

1997 Outlook

Pencil Finley in for another 15 wins. There were some who thought he might be complacent in the first year of his new contract, but he proved those skeptics wrong. There's no reason to expect less in his second year. In fact, with more run support he could win 18 games, which he hasn't done since 1991. In any event, he remains the ace of the staff and one of the best lefties in the league.

Position: SP
Bats: L **Throws:** L
Ht: 6' 6" **Wt:** 214

Opening Day Age: 34
Born: 11/26/62 in Monroe, LA
ML Seasons: 11

Overall Statistics

	W	L	Pct.	ERA	G	GS	Sv	IP	H	BB	SO	HR	BR/IP
1996	15	16	.484	4.16	35	35	0	238.0	241	94	215	27	1.41
Career	129	114	.531	3.65	344	287	0	2074.1	1985	850	1584	191	1.37

How Often He Throws Strikes

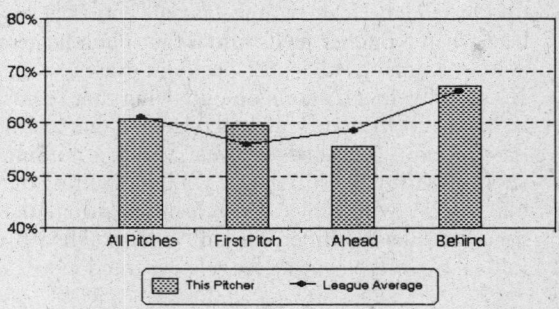

1996 Situational Stats

	W	L	ERA	Sv	IP		AB	H	HR	RBI	Avg
Home	12	6	3.29	0	139.2	LHB	124	29	5	17	.234
Road	3	10	5.40	0	98.1	RHB	792	212	22	81	.268
First Half	9	7	4.95	0	123.2	Sc Pos	215	55	5	72	.256
Scnd Half	6	9	3.31	0	114.1	Clutch	68	24	1	9	.353

1996 Rankings (American League)

- → 1st in wild pitches (17)
- → 2nd in games started, strikeouts, balks (2) and least run support per 9 innings (4.2)
- → 3rd in pickoff throws (176), most strikeouts per 9 innings (8.1), ERA at home (3.29) and errors at pitcher (3)
- → 4th in losses and pitches thrown (3,997)
- → 5th in batters faced (1,037), hit batsmen (11) and stolen bases allowed (24)
- → 6th in shutouts (1) and lowest fielding percentage at pitcher (.925)
- → 7th in innings pitched
- → 8th in wins, walks allowed, highest ground-ball/flyball ratio allowed (1.5) and most pitches thrown per batter (3.85)

Mike James

Position: RP
Bats: R **Throws:** R
Ht: 6' 3" **Wt:** 185

Opening Day Age: 29
Born: 8/15/67 in Fort Walton, FL
ML Seasons: 2

Anaheim Angels

1996 Season

Having taken a long time to reach the big leagues, Mike James did not waste any time establishing himself as one of the more reliable middle relievers in the American League. In his first full season in the big leagues, he was solid from wire to wire. He led California's staff in appearances and the bullpen in innings. As one scout said about James' teammate Troy Percival a year ago, the hitters weren't batting out of turn to hit against him.

Pitching

James has a great mound presence for a reliever. He has both a mean streak and perhaps a little bit of loose wiring. He has good stuff and isn't afraid to pitch inside, hitting one batter every eight innings last year. His delivery makes it hard for batters to see the ball coming at them. His best pitch is a fastball that runs inside on right-handed hitters, jamming them or breaking their bats. But his tricky delivery and his willingness to work inside helps him remain effective against lefties as well.

Defense

James is an average fielder. Although he has a slow delivery, basestealers have difficulty timing him. As a result, teams don't start runners against him as often as you would think they would. He is not the kind of pitcher managers are comfortable using the hit-and-run against.

1997 Outlook

James and Percival give Anaheim a terrific one-two combination in the bullpen. But while there's every reason to think Percival will sustain his success, hitters may begin to figure out James. He needs to make sure success doesn't go to his head. He doesn't want to lose the pitching pattern that has made him successful, but it wouldn't hurt to learn a new trick or two for his third season.

Overall Statistics

	W	L	Pct.	ERA	G	GS	Sv	IP	H	BB	SO	HR	BR/IP
1996	5	5	.500	2.67	69	0	1	81.0	62	42	65	7	1.28
Career	8	5	.615	3.16	115	0	2	136.2	111	68	101	13	1.31

How Often He Throws Strikes

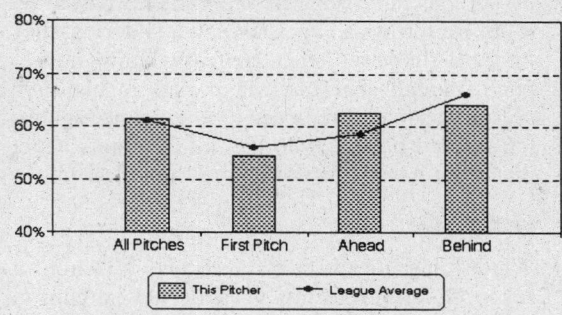

1996 Situational Stats

	W	L	ERA	Sv	IP		AB	H	HR	RBI	Avg
Home	5	1	1.16	1	46.2	LHB	131	31	3	16	.237
Road	0	4	4.72	0	34.1	RHB	159	31	4	20	.195
First Half	5	4	2.34	1	50.0	Sc Pos	70	14	3	28	.200
Scnd Half	0	1	3.19	0	31.0	Clutch	176	38	5	25	.216

1996 Rankings (American League)
- → 5th in holds (18)
- → 6th in relief ERA (2.67)
- → 8th in hit batsmen (10), relief innings (81.0) and lowest batting average allowed in relief (.214)
- → Led the Angels in games pitched, holds (18), blown saves (5) and relief innings (81.0)

Mark Langston

Position: SP
Bats: R **Throws:** L
Ht: 6' 2" **Wt:** 184

Opening Day Age: 36
Born: 8/20/60 in San Diego, CA
ML Seasons: 13

1996 Season

For the second time in three years, Mark Langston was bothered by injuries. His season ended early due to surgery to repair torn knee cartilage. He hasn't been the same since having bone chips removed from his elbow early in the 1994 season, turning in ERAs above 4.60 three years in a row. His total of six wins last year was the lowest of his career, and the three-time American League strikeout champ failed to strike out 100 for the first time since 1985.

Pitching

Langston hasn't had the same zip on his fastball since the surgery in 1994. He relies on his changeup but gets hurt trying to throw the fastball to set it up. He throws a curveball and a slider but they look a lot like each other. He really knows how to pitch, though. The one major plus to his 1996 season was that he regained his dominance against left-handed batters, who had hit 22 points better than right-handed batters against him in 1995.

Defense

While Langston did not add to his collection of seven Gold Gloves last year, he did nothing to dispel the notion that he is the Jim Kaat of his era. His mechanics are technically perfect and he could give a clinic in how to hold runners close to first base. He gobbles up comebackers. Every young pitcher should pay attention when Langston is on the mound.

1997 Outlook

Langston was averaging almost seven innings per start before going on the disabled list. There's no reason to believe he cannot have a full recovery and do a good job as a six- or seven-inning pitcher. But he's reached the point in his career where his elbow will be a constant concern. It's the price he pays for having averaged 247 innings a year between 1986 and '93.

Overall Statistics

	W	L	Pct.	ERA	G	GS	Sv	IP	H	BB	SO	HR	BR/IP
1996	6	5	.545	4.82	18	18	0	123.1	116	45	83	18	1.31
Career	172	146	.541	3.85	401	398	0	2772.0	2486	1190	2335	283	1.33

How Often He Throws Strikes

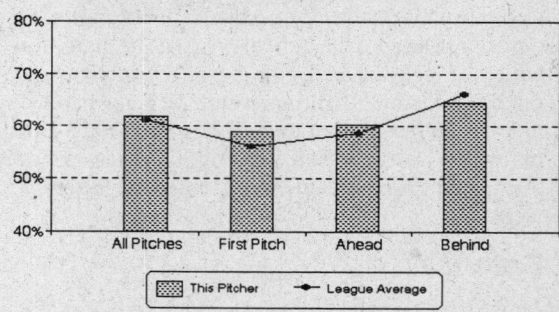

1996 Situational Stats

	W	L	ERA	Sv	IP		AB	H	HR	RBI	Avg
Home	3	2	4.17	0	49.2	LHB	48	9	0	3	.188
Road	3	3	5.25	0	73.2	RHB	421	107	18	58	.254
First Half	5	4	4.86	0	96.1	Sc Pos	99	31	3	37	.313
Scnd Half	1	1	4.67	0	27.0	Clutch	40	8	2	3	.200

1996 Rankings (American League)
- ➡ 5th in pickoff throws (165)
- ➡ Led the Angels in lowest batting average allowed vs. right-handed batters (.254)

1996 Season

No one who had ever seen him throw a fastball doubted that Troy Percival could become one of the top stoppers in the American League. The converted catcher did exactly that in his second major league season, converting 36 of 39 save opportunities, including 11 in a row early in the season. He has little first-hand knowledge of California's disappointing season. The Angels were 46-16 when he pitched and 24-75 when he did not. Cleveland was the only team that beat him.

Pitching

Goose Gossage was never nastier than this guy. He throws a fastball in the upper 90s, and it runs in on right-handed hitters. Once ahead in the count, he can put away hitters with either another fastball or a sharp-breaking curveball. He has struck out 11.8 batters per nine innings in his major league career, actually raising that average a little after his remarkable rookie performance in 1995. He sometimes supplies power for hitters. Eight of the 38 hits he allowed left the park.

Defense

Percival, who didn't make the transition to pitching until 1991, still must work to become an average fielder. He has trouble holding runners on, and made no progress in that regard last year. He never will be a plus fielder, but neither was Gossage, come to think about it.

1997 Outlook

Percival should have as much success as the Angels will allow him to have. If they improve from last year's 70-91 record, he could save 40-plus games. He is perhaps the most dominant, overpowering relief pitcher in baseball today. Percival also gives Anaheim an interesting bargaining chip as the club re-tools. If the Angels are willing to deal him, they could get a nice package of talent in return.

Position: RP
Bats: R **Throws:** R
Ht: 6' 3" **Wt:** 200

Opening Day Age: 27
Born: 8/9/69 in Fontana, CA
ML Seasons: 2

Anaheim Angels

Overall Statistics

	W	L	Pct.	ERA	G	GS	Sv	IP	H	BB	SO	HR	BR/IP
1996	0	2	.000	2.31	62	0	36	74.0	38	31	100	8	0.93
Career	3	4	.429	2.13	124	0	39	148.0	75	57	194	14	0.89

How Often He Throws Strikes

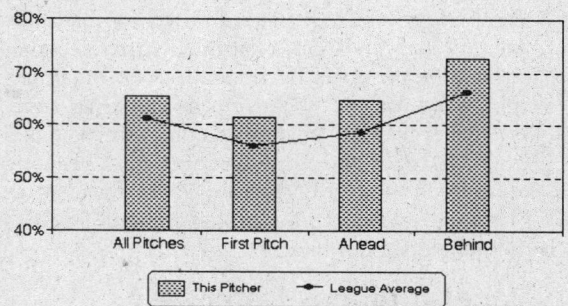

1996 Situational Stats

	W	L	ERA	Sv	IP		AB	H	HR	RBI	Avg
Home	0	1	2.41	18	37.1	LHB	133	17	2	9	.128
Road	0	1	2.21	18	36.2	RHB	122	21	6	15	.172
First Half	0	1	1.76	22	41.0	Sc Pos	67	10	3	18	.149
Scnd Half	0	1	3.00	14	33.0	Clutch	185	26	6	17	.141

1996 Rankings (American League)

→ 1st in save percentage (92.3%), lowest batting average allowed in relief with runners on base (.140), lowest batting average allowed in relief (.149), least baserunners allowed per 9 innings in relief (8.6) and most strikeouts per 9 innings in relief (12.2)

→ 3rd in first batter efficiency (.107) and relief ERA (2.31)

→ 4th in saves, save opportunities (39) and lowest batting average allowed in relief with runners in scoring position (.149)

→ 7th in games finished (52)

→ Led the Angels in saves, games finished (52), save opportunities (39), save percentage (92.3%) and first batter efficiency (.107)

Tim Salmon

1996 Season

If Tim Salmon was any other California player, he would have been adjudged to have had a great season. But by the standards he set during the two strike-shortened seasons, it was a somewhat disappointing year for the Angels' right fielder. Despite a second-half power drought, he reached 30 homers for the third time in four years. But he still failed to duplicate his 100-RBI performance from 1995. Salmon's problems were partly due to the disintegrating lineup around him, but he brought some of it on himself by pressing with men in scoring position.

Hitting

Salmon may have the strongest wrists in baseball. They allow him to generate power to all fields from a relatively short, controlled stroke that can cover all of the plate. He generally waits out pitchers, laying off any pitches up in the strike zone. When he gets the pitcher to come down, that's where he does the most damage. Last year, he occasionally tried to force the action for a struggling offense. He is just as good against righthanders as lefthanders.

Baserunning & Defense

Salmon regressed in the outfield last year, committing eight errors. His inconsistency was surprising for scouts, who had previously judged him as one of the league's best right fielders. He covers a lot of ground and has a strong arm. He is not a fast baserunner but runs aggressively, taking the extra base at every possible opportunity.

1997 Outlook

Salmon has established an enviable track record in his first four seasons, averaging close to 30 homers and 100 RBI per season. He should repeat that performance and could exceed it. He has the potential for a monster year worthy of MVP mention, although he doesn't seem to mind the lack of attention he has received thus far.

Position: RF
Bats: R **Throws:** R
Ht: 6' 3" **Wt:** 220

Opening Day Age: 28
Born: 8/24/68 in Long Beach, CA
ML Seasons: 5
Pronunciation: SA-men

Overall Statistics

	G	AB	R	H	D	T	HR	RBI	SB	BB	SO	Avg	OBP	Slg
1996	156	581	90	166	27	4	30	98	4	93	125	.286	.386	.501
Career	564	2085	369	610	115	10	120	374	16	331	496	.293	.392	.530

Where He Hits the Ball

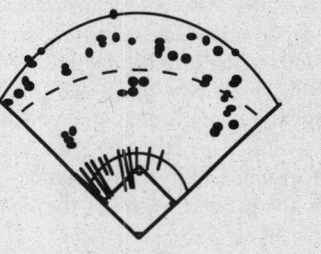
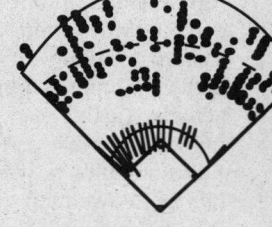

Vs. LHP   **Vs. RHP**

1996 Situational Stats

	AB	H	HR	RBI	Avg		AB	H	HR	RBI	Avg
Home	293	78	18	52	.266	LHP	164	44	10	27	.268
Road	288	88	12	46	.306	RHP	417	122	20	71	.293
First Half	321	94	22	58	.293	Sc Pos	148	38	7	66	.257
Scnd Half	260	72	8	40	.277	Clutch	87	28	3	10	.322

1996 Rankings (American League)

➡ 3rd in errors in right field (8) and highest percentage of extra bases taken as a runner (69.8%)
➡ 5th in lowest fielding percentage in right field (.975)
➡ 6th in batting average with the bases loaded (.545)
➡ 7th in lowest groundball/flyball ratio (0.7)
➡ 8th in cleanup slugging percentage (.585)
➡ 9th in pitches seen (2,792)
➡ Led the Angels in home runs, runs scored, triples, total bases (291), RBI, walks, times on base (263), strikeouts, pitches seen (2,792), plate appearances (681), games played (156) and slugging percentage

J.T. Snow

Traded To
GIANTS

Position: 1B
Bats: B **Throws:** L
Ht: 6' 2" **Wt:** 202

Opening Day Age: 29
Born: 2/26/68 in Long Beach, CA
ML Seasons: 5

Anaheim Angels

1996 Season

"Thud." That was the noise of J.T. Snow falling from the pedestal he had put himself on with a career season in 1995. Last season, few players were more disappointing than the enigmatic Snow. Not everyone expected Snow to repeat his numbers from '95 (.289-24-102) but the Angels certainly didn't expect drops of 32 points in average and 35 RBI. That decline seemed even worse in the Year of the Hitter. Simply put: he was the biggest flop this side of John Olerud.

Hitting

The switch-hitting Snow never got into a groove last year, perhaps because pitchers stopped feeding him the fastballs he'd feasted on in the first half of 1995. His longest hitting streak of the season was eight games. He has always been a little better left-handed than right-handed, but he struggled mightily from the right side last year, and his power was down from both sides. He doesn't run well, which contributed to him hitting into lots of double plays. He has never developed the confidence to take marginal pitches when behind in the count.

Baserunning & Defense

Snow is nice to watch in the field. He has good range and does a better-than-average job scooping throws. He won his second consecutive Gold Glove, but even his error total more than doubled during an all-around rotten season. He is a liability on the bases, getting thrown out on six of seven steal attempts, many of which were botched hit-and-runs.

1997 Outlook

Who knows what to expect from J.T. Snow anymore? The Angels obviously didn't, and they traded Snow to the Giants after the season. With San Francisco, he'll be expected to re-establish himself offensively. He should forget about trying to hit home runs and return to being a gap hitter who hits an occasional homer. Unless he's able to do that, his current level of production won't cut it at a hitter's position.

Overall Statistics

	G	AB	R	H	D	T	HR	RBI	SB	BB	SO	Avg	OBP	Slg
1996	155	575	69	148	20	1	17	67	1	56	96	.257	.327	.384
Career	495	1775	232	457	65	4	65	258	6	187	328	.257	.331	.408

Where He Hits the Ball

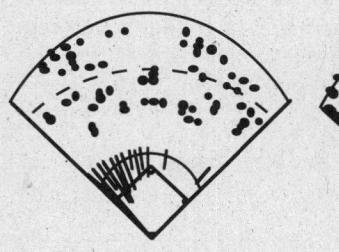 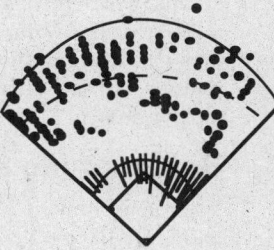

Vs. LHP   **Vs. RHP**

1996 Situational Stats

	AB	H	HR	RBI	Avg		AB	H	HR	RBI	Avg
Home	290	77	8	35	.266	LHP	186	37	3	17	.199
Road	285	71	9	32	.249	RHP	389	111	14	50	.285
First Half	318	83	11	39	.261	Sc Pos	143	37	4	49	.259
Scnd Half	257	65	6	28	.253	Clutch	84	28	1	9	.333

1996 Rankings (American League)

- → 1st in lowest on-base percentage vs. left-handed pitchers (.249)
- → 3rd in lowest batting average vs. left-handed pitchers (.199), lowest slugging percentage vs. left-handed pitchers (.274) and errors at first base (10)
- → 5th in lowest fielding percentage at first base (.993)
- → 9th in GDPs (19), lowest batting average on a 3-1 count (.111) and lowest batting average on the road (.249)
- → 10th in lowest slugging percentage
- → Led the Angels in hit by pitch (5)

Randy Velarde

1996 Season

Few heads turned when the Angels signed free agent Randy Velarde to be their regular second baseman, but it proved to be a sound move. Velarde responded well to the chance to play every day, turning in a solid all-around performance. He sustained a 21-game hitting streak in midseason and was one of the few Angels to live up to expectations.

Hitting

Velarde has some value even when he doesn't get on base, as he makes pitchers work to get him out. He is patient, taking a lot of pitches and fouling off others. He seems to always be in 2-2 and 3-2 counts, which results in both a lot of strikeouts and a lot of walks. Velarde does a good job with runners in scoring position, shortening his stroke and putting the ball in play consistently. He's also a terrific bunter.

Baserunning & Defense

Velarde is limited both in the field and on the bases. He has an adequate arm at second base but his range is average at best. His best asset is a knowledge of what it takes to play all over the field, which is under-utilized with him anchored to second base. Marcel Lachemann tried to run with him on the bases but got burned. He lacks both speed and the instincts necessary to steal bases against all but the slowest of deliveries.

1997 Outlook

Velarde returns to Anaheim, where he is expected to be back as the starting second baseman, although he may be dropped to the bottom of the order. His production has been climbing a little bit at a time. It's not out of the question to think he could hit .300, which he has never done in a full-time role. He could also attract trade interest from teams seeking a veteran utility player for the stretch run.

Position: 2B/3B
Bats: R **Throws:** R
Ht: 6' 0" **Wt:** 192

Opening Day Age: 34
Born: 11/24/62 in Midland, TX
ML Seasons: 10
Pronunciation: vuh-LARR-dee

Overall Statistics

	G	AB	R	H	D	T	HR	RBI	SB	BB	SO	Avg	OBP	Slg
1996	136	530	82	151	27	3	14	54	7	70	118	.285	.372	.426
Career	794	2465	345	662	126	13	57	262	29	256	500	.269	.342	.400

Where He Hits the Ball

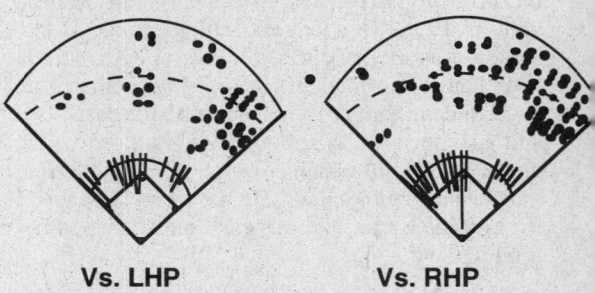

Vs. LHP   **Vs. RHP**

1996 Situational Stats

	AB	H	HR	RBI	Avg		AB	H	HR	RBI	Avg
Home	275	89	8	27	.324	LHP	152	43	3	18	.283
Road	255	62	6	27	.243	RHP	378	108	11	36	.286
First Half	284	85	6	30	.299	Sc Pos	99	33	1	40	.333
Scnd Half	246	66	8	24	.268	Clutch	80	25	2	11	.313

1996 Rankings (American League)

→ 5th in lowest fielding percentage at second base (.982)
→ 6th in lowest percentage of swings on the first pitch (15.8%)
→ 7th in most pitches seen per plate appearance (4.18), lowest batting average on the road (.243) and highest percentage of extra bases taken as a runner (63.6%)
→ 9th in lowest batting average with the bases loaded (.111)
→ 10th in errors at second base (9)
→ Led the Angels in hit by pitch (5), most pitches seen per plate appearance (4.18) and batting average with runners in scoring position (.333)

Greg Gohr

Position: SP/RP
Bats: R **Throws:** R
Ht: 6' 3" **Wt:** 205

Opening Day Age: 29
Born: 10/29/67 in Santa Clara, CA
ML Seasons: 4
Pronunciation: GOAR

Overall Statistics

	W	L	Pct.	ERA	G	GS	Sv	IP	H	BB	SO	HR	BR/IP
1996	5	9	.357	7.24	32	16	1	115.2	163	44	75	31	1.79
Career	8	11	.421	6.21	66	22	1	182.2	234	82	131	35	1.73

1996 Situational Stats

	W	L	ERA	Sv	IP		AB	H	HR	RBI	Avg
Home	1	5	5.03	0	53.2	LHB	261	82	13	46	.314
Road	4	4	9.15	1	62.0	RHB	233	81	18	41	.348
First Half	4	8	6.75	0	86.2	Sc Pos	123	37	6	55	.301
Scnd Half	1	1	8.69	1	29.0	Clutch	15	1	0	0	.067

1996 Season

As it turns out, it wasn't the depressing Tiger Stadium scenery that had been holding back the Tigers' first pick in the 1989 draft. After being acquired from Detroit in a July 31 trade for infielder Damion Easley, Greg Gohr failed to provide much return for the Angels. He had spent the first half of the season in Detroit's starting rotation, going 4-8 with a 7.17 ERA. The Angels tried him as a middle reliever and he went 1-1 with a 7.50 ERA. He was consistent, anyway.

Pitching & Defense

Gohr's high leg kick reminds some of Nolan Ryan's, but the resemblance ends there. Gohr's fastball is straight and his curveball often seems flat, which explains his .330 opposing batting average last year. He has never been considered a good fielder and was hampered further after a midseason battle with tendinitis in his left knee.

1997 Outlook

Gohr has a good enough arm to earn him a longer look than he got in 1996. He may benefit from the Angels' new regime, but this guy is not a kid anymore. At 29, it's time for results.

Todd Greene

Position: C
Bats: R **Throws:** R
Ht: 5'10" **Wt:** 200

Opening Day Age: 25
Born: 5/8/71 in Augusta, GA
ML Seasons: 1

Overall Statistics

	G	AB	R	H	D	T	HR	RBI	SB	BB	SO	Avg	OBP	Slg
1996	29	79	9	15	1	0	2	9	2	4	11	.190	.238	.278
Career	29	79	9	15	1	0	2	9	2	4	11	.190	.238	.278

1996 Situational Stats

	AB	H	HR	RBI	Avg		AB	H	HR	RBI	Avg
Home	35	6	1	2	.171	LHP	47	5	1	2	.106
Road	44	9	1	7	.205	RHP	32	10	1	7	.313
First Half	0	0	0	0	-	Sc Pos	18	5	0	6	.278
Scnd Half	79	15	2	9	.190	Clutch	10	2	1	1	.200

1996 Season

A converted outfielder, Todd Greene is expected to become Anaheim's regular catcher into the next century. He split last year between Triple-A and Anaheim, raising questions at both stops. He combined to hit 40 homers between Double-A and Triple-A in 1995 but didn't hit for power or average in a brief trial with the big club last year.

Hitting, Baserunning & Defense

Greene is an all-or-nothing hitter and a former mediocre outfielder who wasn't drafted until the 12th round. The Angels gambled by converting him to catcher. He has picked up the basics behind the plate but will play there only as a way to get his bat into an otherwise crowded lineup. He has improved a lot behind the plate since being charged with 44 passed balls in 1994 but still has a long way to go. He runs well for a catcher.

1997 Outlook

Common sense says Greene needs a full year at Triple-A before returning to the big leagues. A bust-out spring training could convince Anaheim to trust him with the catcher's chores, however.

Jason Grimsley

Position: SP/RP
Bats: R **Throws:** R
Ht: 6' 3" **Wt:** 180

Opening Day Age: 29
Born: 8/7/67 in Cleveland, TX
ML Seasons: 7

Overall Statistics

	W	L	Pct.	ERA	G	GS	Sv	IP	H	BB	SO	HR	BR/IP
1996	5	7	.417	6.84	35	20	0	130.1	150	74	82	14	1.72
Career	18	25	.419	5.39	101	68	1	426.0	450	263	283	35	1.67

1996 Situational Stats

	W	L	ERA	Sv	IP		AB	H	HR	RBI	Avg
Home	5	1	5.08	0	79.2	LHB	278	79	5	49	.284
Road	0	6	9.59	0	50.2	RHB	246	71	9	50	.289
First Half	4	5	5.05	0	87.1	Sc Pos	165	53	7	87	.321
Scnd Half	1	2	10.47	0	43.0	Clutch	28	8	1	2	.286

1996 Season

For one glorious game in May, Jason Grimsley showed a glimpse of the stuff that's made him a perennial success in the minors. He threw a complete-game shutout to beat the Yankees, allowing only five hits and three walks. But it was an otherwise wasted season, as he shuttled between the Angels' rotation and bullpen without distinguishing himself in either role.

Pitching & Defense

Grimsley's fastball has just enough velocity and movement to retire mediocre hitters. But he hasn't found a pitch that works consistently against the more patient major-leaguers, who take the trash he throws outside the strike zone and wait for something over the plate, which they generally kill. Control was also a problem as he walked 5.1 per nine innings. He is a below-average fielder and has a lot of problems holding runners.

1997 Outlook

Expansion can't get here fast enough for Grimsley. He will have to pitch well in spring training to earn a job on a big-league staff. He has teased teams like Philadelphia and Cleveland with his potential, but there's a reason he knows the American Association better than the American League.

Mike Holtz

Position: RP
Bats: L **Throws:** L
Ht: 5' 9" **Wt:** 175

Opening Day Age: 24
Born: 10/10/72 in Arlington, VA
ML Seasons: 1

Overall Statistics

	W	L	Pct.	ERA	G	GS	Sv	IP	H	BB	SO	HR	BR/IP
1996	3	3	.500	2.45	30	0	0	29.1	21	19	31	1	1.36
Career	3	3	.500	2.45	30	0	0	29.1	21	19	31	1	1.36

1996 Situational Stats

	W	L	ERA	Sv	IP		AB	H	HR	RBI	Avg
Home	2	1	2.70	0	13.1	LHB	47	12	0	6	.255
Road	1	2	2.25	0	16.0	RHB	56	9	1	4	.161
First Half	0	0	-	0	0.0	Sc Pos	32	8	0	9	.250
Scnd Half	3	3	2.45	0	29.1	Clutch	35	10	0	2	.286

1996 Season

There was no bigger surprise in the California Angels organization last year than lefthander Mike Holtz. He got off to a decent start at Double-A but shocked the major-league staff after being promoted to California in July. He pitched better in the big leagues than he had at Midland. Go figure.

Pitching & Defense

Holtz retired the first 12 hitters he faced with California and ended his rookie season with the second-lowest ERA among Angels pitchers who worked at least 30 games. He had a sneaky-quick fastball, a decent curveball, and change-up that stymied right-handed hitters. Overall, hitters hit only .204 against him, with one home run in almost 30 innings. He's got quick reactions on the mound and does a good job keeping runners close.

1997 Outlook

For a surprise like Holtz, the trick will be to do it two years in a row. He may have trouble picking up where he left off, because he was on a three-month-long roll. He showed the tools to be a valuable set-up man, but first looks can be deceiving.

Jack Howell

Position: 3B
Bats: L **Throws:** R
Ht: 6' 0" **Wt:** 190

Opening Day Age: 35
Born: 8/18/61 in Tucson, AZ
ML Seasons: 8

Rex Hudler

Position: 2B/CF
Bats: R **Throws:** R
Ht: 6' 0" **Wt:** 195

Opening Day Age: 36
Born: 9/2/60 in Tempe, AZ
ML Seasons: 11
Nickname: The Wonder Dog

Jack Howell

Overall Statistics

	G	AB	R	H	D	T	HR	RBI	SB	BB	SO	Avg	OBP	Slg
1996	66	126	20	34	4	1	8	21	0	10	30	.270	.324	.508
Career	803	2394	314	569	115	16	92	295	13	275	569	.238	.318	.414

1996 Situational Stats

	AB	H	HR	RBI	Avg		AB	H	HR	RBI	Avg
Home	67	16	4	10	.239	LHP	9	2	0	0	.222
Road	59	18	4	11	.305	RHP	117	32	8	21	.274
First Half	72	19	5	12	.264	Sc Pos	32	7	2	13	.219
Scnd Half	54	15	3	9	.278	Clutch	30	8	1	3	.267

1996 Season

Back from Japan, Jack Howell enjoyed a solid 1996 season in a limited role. He did a good job off the bench, setting a California club record with four pinch-hit home runs, and played well enough at third base to allow the Angels to take their time breaking in young George Arias.

Hitting, Baserunning & Defense

The left-handed-hitting Howell is almost entirely a platoon player, almost never facing lefties. He hit for a decent average with good power numbers against righthanders. He sometimes gets over-anxious with runners in scoring position. Howell is a defensive liability at third base. He has limited range and a below-average arm, which causes him to sometimes rush his throws. He has below-average speed but doesn't take reckless chances on the bases.

1997 Outlook

There's always a spot on the bench for a left-handed-hitting infielder with a track record as a pinch hitter. A free agent, Howell may return to Anaheim to back up third base and pinch hit. Wherever he ends up, he may get a few more at-bats next year but is unlikely to get more than 200.

Rex Hudler

Overall Statistics

	G	AB	R	H	D	T	HR	RBI	SB	BB	SO	Avg	OBP	Slg
1996	92	302	60	94	20	3	16	40	14	9	54	.311	.337	.556
Career	699	1604	242	429	91	10	51	157	106	67	285	.267	.300	.432

1996 Situational Stats

	AB	H	HR	RBI	Avg		AB	H	HR	RBI	Avg
Home	142	42	6	19	.296	LHP	139	48	9	21	.345
Road	160	52	10	21	.325	RHP	163	46	7	19	.282
First Half	182	58	11	28	.319	Sc Pos	46	12	2	20	.261
Scnd Half	120	36	5	12	.300	Clutch	40	8	2	5	.200

1996 Season

Rex "The Wonder Dog" Hudler had more than his day in 1996—he had the best season of his career, a remarkable feat considering he turned 36 in September. He provided one of the few sparks for California's underachieving offense, batting .314 with 11 homers and 22 RBIs in 35 games as the leadoff man. Three words sum up his approach to baseball: No whining allowed.

Hitting, Baserunning & Defense

Hudler has become a genuine power threat against lefthanders. He's a fastball hitter who likes pitches up in the strike zone, and has learned to lay off the low breaking ball. He is a decent hit-and-run man and accomplished bunter. He has tremendous value for a team, as he can play almost anywhere. He doesn't have sprinter's speed but he has stolen 27 bases in 32 tries over the last two seasons.

1997 Outlook

Hudler spent 10 seasons building toward the opportunity he got last season, and it paid off when he signed a free-agent contract with the Phillies. The Phils figure to use him in the same super-sub role he handled so effectively in 1996.

Chuck McElroy

Position: RP
Bats: L **Throws:** L
Ht: 6' 0" **Wt:** 195

Opening Day Age: 29
Born: 10/1/67 in Port Arthur, TX
ML Seasons: 8
Pronunciation: MACK-ill-roy

Overall Statistics

	W	L	Pct.	ERA	G	GS	Sv	IP	H	BB	SO	HR	BR/IP
1996	7	1	.875	3.86	52	0	0	49.0	45	23	45	4	1.39
Career	23	19	.548	3.48	367	0	14	403.2	376	200	340	29	1.43

1996 Situational Stats

	W	L	ERA	Sv	IP		AB	H	HR	RBI	Avg
Home	3	0	3.65	0	24.2	LHB	65	15	1	12	.231
Road	4	1	4.07	0	24.1	RHB	118	30	3	18	.254
First Half	6	0	4.55	0	31.2	Sc Pos	63	17	2	24	.270
Scnd Half	1	1	2.60	0	17.1	Clutch	52	8	0	5	.154

1996 Season

After being acquired by the Angels in May in exchange for Lee Smith, lefthander Chuck McElroy pitched well while making the transition from the National League. The set-up man won seven games against only one loss, and in a June series at Kansas City, he got wins in three consecutive games (something only seven other relievers have ever done). It was a nifty recovery from a horrible performance with Cincinnati in 1995, when he was buried by manager Davey Johnson.

Pitching & Defense

McElroy relies on a fastball and curve to set up his on-again, off-again forkball. He can generally throw strikes under pressure. It has been a few years since his fastball was good enough to make left-handed hitters uncomfortable. They hit him about as well as right-handed hitters do. McElroy is a decent fielder with a good pickoff move.

1997 Outlook

California was McElroy's third team in four years. He is likely to continue moving around the majors on one-year contracts. There's no reason he shouldn't be able to make 40-50 appearances this year.

Dennis Springer

Knuckleballer

Position: SP/RP
Bats: R **Throws:** R
Ht: 5'10" **Wt:** 185

Opening Day Age: 32
Born: 2/12/65 in Fresno, CA
ML Seasons: 2

Overall Statistics

	W	L	Pct.	ERA	G	GS	Sv	IP	H	BB	SO	HR	BR/IP
1996	5	6	.455	5.51	20	15	0	94.2	91	43	64	24	1.42
Career	5	9	.357	5.38	24	19	0	117.0	112	52	79	27	1.40

1996 Situational Stats

	W	L	ERA	Sv	IP		AB	H	HR	RBI	Avg
Home	3	4	6.49	0	52.2	LHB	194	48	12	26	.247
Road	2	2	4.29	0	42.0	RHB	169	43	12	21	.254
First Half	0	0	14.21	0	6.1	Sc Pos	62	15	3	22	.242
Scnd Half	5	6	4.89	0	88.1	Clutch	19	3	2	2	.158

1996 Season

Journeyman righthander Dennis Springer spent three stints with California, appearing in 20 games (15 starts) to fill a void left by injuries to the pitching staff. He earned the opportunity by going 10-3 with a 2.72 ERA at Triple-A. He finished the season on a roll, notching all five of his wins after the All-Star break.

Pitching & Defense

Springer's bread-and-butter is a knuckleball. He has a below-average fastball which often gets ripped, resulting in one homer every 3.9 innings. He's got to work ahead in the count to keep hitters from sitting on his fastball. He can't afford to hurt himself with walks, and his control wasn't as sharp as it had been in the minors. He is an average fielder, but holding runners is a problem.

1997 Outlook

Springer adds depth to the Anaheim staff. He could stick on the Opening Day roster as the number-five starter or return to Triple-A, where he would continue to provide good insurance for the Angels in case any more of their pitchers get hurt.

Other Anaheim Angels

Kyle Abbott (Pos: LHP, Age: 29)

	W	L	Pct.	ERA	G	GS	Sv	IP	H	BB	SO	HR	BR/IP
1996	0	1	.000	20.25	3	0	0	4.0	10	5	3	1	3.75
Career	4	17	.190	5.20	57	22	0	185.1	207	79	124	26	1.54

After pitching for the Phillies and in Japan, Abbott returned briefly to his original club last year. The results weren't pretty, and Abbott will probably try to catch on elsewhere this year. 1997 Outlook: D

Vince Coleman (Pos: LF, Age: 35, Bats: B)

	G	AB	R	H	D	T	HR	RBI	SB	BB	SO	Avg	OBP	Slg
1996	33	84	10	13	1	1	1	4	12	9	31	.155	.237	.226
Career	1365	5392	849	1424	176	89	28	346	752	476	957	.264	.324	.345

"Have Legs, Will Travel" is now the story for Coleman, who signed a minor league contract with the Angels after the Reds waived him last year. May get one last chance, but it's a long shot. 1997 Outlook: D

Ken Edenfield (Pos: RHP, Age: 30)

	W	L	Pct.	ERA	G	GS	Sv	IP	H	BB	SO	HR	BR/IP
1996	0	0	-	10.38	2	0	0	4.1	10	2	4	2	2.77
Career	0	0	-	5.82	9	0	0	17.0	25	7	10	3	1.88

After pitching in the Angel system for several years, Edenfield was dealt to the Yankees last year and pitched very well for Triple-A Columbus. He's a fine reliever; he just needs a chance. 1997 Outlook: C

Robert Eenhoorn (Pos: 2B, Age: 29, Bats: R)

	G	AB	R	H	D	T	HR	RBI	SB	BB	SO	Avg	OBP	Slg
1996	18	29	3	5	0	0	0	2	0	2	5	.172	.212	.172
Career	26	47	5	9	2	0	0	4	0	3	8	.191	.231	.234

Eenhorn was a shortstop in the Yankee system for a number of years, but never got a chance to play. He was dealt to the Angels last year, and has a chance to stick as a utility infielder. 1997 Outlook: C

Mark Eichhorn (Pos: RHP, Age: 36)

	W	L	Pct.	ERA	G	GS	Sv	IP	H	BB	SO	HR	BR/IP
1996	1	2	.333	5.04	24	0	0	30.1	36	11	24	3	1.55
Career	48	43	.527	3.00	563	7	32	885.2	825	270	640	49	1.24

Long a fine middle reliever, Eichhorn has missed most of the last two seasons with rotator cuff problems. A free agent, he will hope to show someone he's healthy this spring. 1997 Outlook: C

Robert Ellis (Pos: RHP, Age: 26)

	W	L	Pct.	ERA	G	GS	Sv	IP	H	BB	SO	HR	BR/IP
1996	0	0	-	0.00	3	0	0	5.0	4	4	5	0	0.80
Career	0	0	-	0.00	3	0	0	5.0	4	4	5	0	0.80

After several years in the White Sox system, Ellis joined the Angels in a minor league deal last year. Only 26; he throws hard and has a chance to make the club this year. 1997 Outlook: B

Ryan Hancock (Pos: RHP, Age: 25)

	W	L	Pct.	ERA	G	GS	Sv	IP	H	BB	SO	HR	BR/IP
1996	4	1	.800	7.48	11	4	0	27.2	34	17	19	2	1.84
Career	4	1	.800	7.48	11	4	0	27.2	34	17	19	2	1.84

The Angels' second-round draft pick in 1993, Hancock got into 11 games with the big club last year. The results were mixed, and he'll probably need more Triple-A experience. 1997 Outlook: C

Pep Harris (Pos: RHP, Age: 24)

	W	L	Pct.	ERA	G	GS	Sv	IP	H	BB	SO	HR	BR/IP
1996	2	0	1.000	3.90	11	3	0	32.1	31	17	20	4	1.48
Career	2	0	1.000	3.90	11	3	0	32.1	31	17	20	4	1.48

A former Indian farmhand, Harris came to the Angels for Brian Anderson last spring. Still only 24, he has plenty of minor league experience and could make the club as a swingman this year. 1997 Outlook: B

Mark Holzemer (Pos: LHP, Age: 27)

	W	L	Pct.	ERA	G	GS	Sv	IP	H	BB	SO	HR	BR/IP
1996	1	0	1.000	8.76	25	0	0	24.2	35	8	20	7	1.74
Career	1	4	.200	8.31	42	4	0	56.1	80	28	35	10	1.92

Holzemer has had three trials with the Angels, getting battered around each time. He's also had shoulder problems, and the club released him late last year. Another team might give him a chance. 1997 Outlook: D

Phil Leftwich (Pos: RHP, Age: 27)

	W	L	Pct.	ERA	G	GS	Sv	IP	H	BB	SO	HR	BR/IP
1996	0	1	.000	7.36	2	2	0	7.1	12	3	4	1	2.05
Career	9	17	.346	4.99	34	34	0	202.0	220	72	102	22	1.45

Once considered one the Angels' brightest pitching prospects, Leftwich pitched for the club in 1993-94, then came down with serious arm trouble. He seemed recovered last year and might make it back. 1997 Outlook: C

Darrell May (Pos: LHP, Age: 24)

	W	L	Pct.	ERA	G	GS	Sv	IP	H	BB	SO	HR	BR/IP
1996	0	1	.000	9.53	10	2	0	11.1	18	6	6	6	2.12
Career	0	1	.000	9.98	12	2	0	15.1	28	6	7	6	2.22

After brief trials with the Braves and Pirates, May came to the Angels in a waiver deal late last year. Hasn't shown much in the majors, but his minor league record is pretty good. 1997 Outlook: C

Rich Monteleone (Pos: RHP, Age: 34)

	W	L	Pct.	ERA	G	GS	Sv	IP	H	BB	SO	HR	BR/IP
1996	0	3	.000	5.87	12	0	0	15.1	23	2	5	5	1.63
Career	24	17	.585	3.87	210	0	0	353.1	344	119	212	43	1.31

Monteleone was once a fine reliever, but he's had two years of injuries, and the Angels released him last September. If healthy, he could make it back, but he'll need a great spring training. 1997 Outlook: C

Brad Pennington (**Pos**: LHP, **Age**: 27)

	W	L	Pct.	ERA	G	GS	Sv	IP	H	BB	SO	HR	BR/IP
1996	0	2	.000	6.20	22	0	0	20.1	11	31	20	2	2.07
Career	3	6	.333	6.90	78	0	4	75.2	66	86	83	12	2.01

Pennington has a 90+ fastball, but he can't find home plate with it. The Angels were the latest team to try and then give up on him. With his arm, he's bound to get at least one more chance. 1997 Outlook: C

Chris Pritchett (**Pos**: 1B, **Age**: 27, **Bats**: L)

	G	AB	R	H	D	T	HR	RBI	SB	BB	SO	Avg	OBP	Slg
1996	5	13	1	2	0	0	0	1	0	0	3	.154	.154	.154
Career	5	13	1	2	0	0	0	1	0	0	3	.154	.154	.154

A lefty first baseman with a good batting eye and a little bit of power, Pritchett joined the Angels last September after a solid year at Triple-A Vancouver. Might stick as a reserve/pinch hitter. 1997 Outlook: C

Scott Sanderson (**Pos**: RHP, **Age**: 40)

	W	L	Pct.	ERA	G	GS	Sv	IP	H	BB	SO	HR	BR/IP
1996	0	2	.000	7.50	5	4	0	18.0	39	4	7	5	2.39
Career	163	143	.533	3.84	472	407	5	2561.0	2590	625	1611	297	1.26

Sanderson's 19th major league season was destroyed by injuries, and the Angels finally let him go. Barring a miracle, his fine career is over. 1997 Outlook: D

Jeff Schmidt (**Pos**: RHP, **Age**: 26)

	W	L	Pct.	ERA	G	GS	Sv	IP	H	BB	SO	HR	BR/IP
1996	2	0	1.000	7.88	9	0	0	8.0	13	8	2	2	2.63
Career	2	0	1.000	7.88	9	0	0	8.0	13	8	2	2	2.63

A first-round draft pick in 1992, Schmidt had a brief trial with the Angels last year, but couldn't find home plate.

He'll probably get a longer look this year. 1997 Outlook: C

Dick Schofield (**Pos**: SS, **Age**: 34, **Bats**: R)

	G	AB	R	H	D	T	HR	RBI	SB	BB	SO	Avg	OBP	Slg
1996	13	16	3	4	0	0	0	0	1	1	1	.250	.294	.250
Career	1368	4299	505	989	137	32	56	353	120	446	684	.230	.308	.316

Schofield missed most of last year for "personal reasons," then became a free agent. Even if his problems are solved, he's 34 and a long shot to make a major league roster this year. 1997 Outlook: D

Chris Turner (**Pos**: C, **Age**: 28, **Bats**: R)

	G	AB	R	H	D	T	HR	RBI	SB	BB	SO	Avg	OBP	Slg
1996	4	3	1	1	0	0	0	1	0	1	0	.333	.400	.333
Career	92	237	33	59	12	1	2	27	4	20	48	.249	.308	.333

A backup catcher for the Angels for a couple of years, Turner spent most of 1996 at Triple-A Vancouver. He'll never be a number-one receiver, but could still make it back as a reserve. 1997 Outlook: C

Shad Williams (**Pos**: RHP, **Age**: 26)

	W	L	Pct.	ERA	G	GS	Sv	IP	H	BB	SO	HR	BR/IP
1996	0	2	.000	8.89	13	2	0	28.1	42	21	26	7	2.22
Career	0	2	.000	8.89	13	2	0	28.1	42	21	26	7	2.22

Williams has had two and a half years of Triple-A experience, but didn't show much in a 13-game trial with the Angels last year. They need pitching, so he should get another chance in '97. 1997 Outlook: C

Anaheim Angels Minor League Prospects

Organization Overview:

Although the Angels' farm system remains reasonably productive, there's an alarming lack of depth beyond the front-line prospects. Equally disturbing were the underwhelming debuts of many of their top youngsters last year. After giving looks to several of their top prospects, the Angels were somewhat disappointed by the debuts of George Arias and Todd Greene, and, to a lesser extent, Darin Erstad. It was a troubling departure from recent years, when players like Garret Anderson, Jim Edmonds and Troy Percival had been worked right in without a hitch. If the current crop of youngsters doesn't pan out, there's hardly anyone at the lower levels to pick up the baton. Unless the new ownership instills a renewed emphasis on scouting, the system soon may be running on empty.

Larry Barnes

Position: 1B
Bats: L **Throws:** L
Ht: 6' 1" **Wt:** 195

Opening Day Age: 22
Born: 7/23/74 in Bakersfield, CA

Recent Statistics

	G	AB	R	H	D	T	HR	RBI	SB	BB	SO	AVG
95 R Angels	55	194	41	61	8	3	3	37	11	26	40	.314
96 A Cedar Rapds	131	489	84	155	36	5	27	112	9	58	101	.317

Left-handed first baseman Larry Barnes bulked up over the winter, and the results showed all summer. In the Class-A Midwest League, where only two other players topped the 20-homer mark and one other player drove in 100 runs, Barnes paced the circuit with 27 homers and 112 RBI. He didn't win the Triple Crown, but his .317 average placed sixth, and he did capture the league MVP award. He's got a short swing that generates power to all fields, and he's a sharp fielder at first base. Only 22 years old next year, he may begin the year in Double-A.

Jason Dickson

Position: P
Bats: L **Throws:** R
Ht: 6' 0" **Wt:** 190

Opening Day Age: 24
Born: 3/30/73 in London, Ontario, Canada

Recent Statistics

	W	L	ERA	G	GS	Sv	IP	H	R	BB	SO	HR
96 AA Midland	5	2	3.58	8	8	0	55.1	55	27	10	40	3
96 AAA Vancouver	7	11	3.80	18	18	0	130.1	134	73	40	70	9
96 AL California	1	4	4.57	7	7	0	43.1	52	22	18	20	6

The Angels moved 23-year-old Jason Dickson into their starting rotation late in the year, and even though he didn't blow the league away, they're counting on him to nail down a rotation spot as early as next year. Dickson is a workhorse who completed 10 of his 28 minor league starts last year. His fastball doesn't quite reach the 90s, but he's got good command of three solid pitches. He began the year in Double-A, moved up to Triple-A, and made seven starts for the Angels late in the year. His totals for the three stops: 33 games started, 229 innings, and a 13-17 record.

Aaron Guiel

Position: 3B
Bats: L **Throws:** R
Ht: 5' 10" **Wt:** 190

Opening Day Age: 24
Born: 10/5/72 in Vancouver, BC, Canada

Recent Statistics

	G	AB	R	H	D	T	HR	RBI	SB	BB	SO	AVG
93 A Boise	35	104	24	31	6	4	2	12	3	26	21	.298
94 A Cedar Rapds	127	454	84	122	30	1	18	82	21	64	93	.269
95 A Lk Elsinore	113	409	73	110	25	7	7	58	7	69	96	.269
96 AA Midland	129	439	72	118	29	7	10	48	11	56	71	.269
96 MLE	129	422	57	101	24	3	8	38	7	37	77	.239

Aaron Guiel will go as far as his bat takes him. A former second baseman, severe defensive problems forced him to move to third this year, where he showed decent range but a highly erratic arm. But the left-handed hitter shows a respectable amount of power at the plate, and at age 24, he may develop a bit further. He won't hit for a great average, and his speed is not an asset, but he's got the skills to make it if he continues to progress.

Keith Luuloa

Position: 2B
Bats: R **Throws:** R
Ht: 6' 1" **Wt:** 185

Opening Day Age: 22
Born: 12/24/74 in Honolulu, HI

Recent Statistics

	G	AB	R	H	D	T	HR	RBI	SB	BB	SO	AVG
94 R Angels	28	97	14	29	4	1	1	10	3	8	14	.299
95 A Lk Elsinore	102	380	50	100	22	7	5	53	1	24	47	.263
96 AA Midland	134	531	80	138	24	2	7	44	4	47	54	.260
96 MLE	134	512	64	119	20	1	6	35	2	31	58	.232

At age 21, Keith Luuloa held his own at Double-A Midland, and showed the potential to be a useful second baseman. As a hitter, he doesn't have much power, patience or speed, but he may learn to hit for a good enough average to break into a major league lineup. He made some strides in curbing his overaggressiveness at the plate last year. A converted shortstop, Luuloa played remarkable defense in his first full year at second base. He showed very good range, and hung in well on the double play. A couple more years of seasoning may be all he needs.

Orlando Palmeiro

Position: OF
Bats: L **Throws:** R
Ht: 5' 11" **Wt:** 155
Opening Day Age: 28
Born: 1/19/69 in Hobeken, NJ

Recent Statistics

	G	AB	R	H	D	T	HR	RBI	SB	BB	SO	AVG
96 AAA Vancouver	62	245	40	75	13	4	0	33	7	30	19	.306
96 AL California	50	87	6	25	6	1	0	6	0	8	13	.287
96 MLE	62	238	36	68	11	2	0	29	5	26	20	.286

Orlando Palmeiro had little luck finding playing time in the Angels' crowded outfield last year. However, the trade of Chili Davis may relieve the logjam and enable him to get his foot in the door. He doesn't have the skills of a starting outfielder, and at age 28, he's not likely to develop them, but could make a very good fourth outfielder. He hits for a good average from the left side of the plate, and lefties don't seem to bother him. Power isn't a part of his game, but he can play all three outfield positions and steal an occasional base.

Matt Perisho

Position: P
Bats: L **Throws:** L
Ht: 6' 0" **Wt:** 190
Opening Day Age: 21
Born: 6/8/75 in Burlington, IA

Recent Statistics

	W	L	ERA	G	GS	Sv	IP	H	R	BB	SO	HR
93 R Angels	7	3	3.66	11	11	0	64.0	58	32	23	65	1
94 A Cedar Rapds	12	9	4.33	27	27	0	147.2	165	90	88	107	11
95 A Lk Elsinore	8	9	6.32	24	22	0	115.1	137	91	60	68	10
96 A Lk Elsinore	7	5	4.20	21	18	0	128.2	131	72	58	97	9
96 AA Midland	3	2	3.21	8	8	0	53.1	48	22	20	50	4

The young lefty suffered through a disastrous '95 season after undergoing arm surgery the year before. Last year, he finally recovered, and the results were astonishing. He went 7-5 in the first half at Class A, earning a promotion to Double-A Midland—one of the most hitter-friendly parks in the minors. With his back to the outfield fences and the wind in his face, Perisho posted a 3.21 ERA and fanned almost a batter per inning for Midland. For the season, he whiffed 147 batters in 182 innings. Although he's only 22 this year, he may come up quickly.

Jarrod Washburn

Position: P
Bats: L **Throws:** L
Ht: 6' 1" **Wt:** 185
Opening Day Age: 22
Born: 8/13/74 in La Crosse, WI

Recent Statistics

	W	L	ERA	G	GS	Sv	IP	H	R	BB	SO	HR
95 A Cedar Rapds	0	1	3.44	3	3	0	18.1	17	7	7	20	1
95 A Boise	3	2	3.33	8	8	0	46.0	35	17	14	54	1
96 A Lk Elsinore	6	3	3.30	14	14	0	92.2	79	38	33	93	5
96 AAA Vancouver	0	2	10.80	2	2	0	8.1	12	16	12	5	1
96 AA Midland	5	6	4.40	13	13	0	88.0	77	44	25	58	11

The Angels' second-round pick in '95, Jarrod Washburn is a young, durable lefty with a 93-MPH moving fast-

ball. He's tough to pick up, and throws a curveball and change-up with good command. With stuff like that, he had no problem reaching Triple-A last year after beginning the year in A-ball. He struck out a man per inning at Class-A Lake Elsinore, and survived a 13-start trial at Double-A Midland's bandbox. He finished with two poor starts at Triple-A, but that may have been the result of fatigue. In his first professional season last year, he threw 189 innings, a very high total for a 21 year old. If his arm survives the workload, he has a very bright future.

Mike Wolff

Position: OF
Bats: R **Throws:** R
Ht: 6' 1" **Wt:** 195
Opening Day Age: 26
Born: 12/19/70 in Wilmington, NC

Recent Statistics

	G	AB	R	H	D	T	HR	RBI	SB	BB	SO	AVG
93 A Cedar Rapds	120	407	63	100	18	5	17	72	8	74	104	.246
94 AA Midland	113	397	64	115	30	1	13	58	10	54	91	.290
95 AA Midland	127	445	76	135	28	3	14	70	10	65	83	.303
96 A Lk Elsinore	12	42	12	12	3	0	2	7	3	9	10	.286
96 AAA Vancouver	71	256	46	64	15	3	10	38	6	34	69	.250
96 MLE	71	250	41	58	13	1	9	34	4	30	73	.232

Mike Wolff spent '94 and '95 putting up solid numbers at Double-A, but no one noticed him, so last year, he decided to try to hit for more power. The effort was successful, as he boosted his home run power slightly as he moved into a much tougher home run park at Triple-A Vancouver. However, he missed half of the season with an injury, so once again, his numbers escaped notice. Wolff can play center or right field fairly well, and packs a good throwing arm. At age 26, he's a bit long in the tooth, but he isn't far away.

Others to Watch

Righthander **Brian Cooper** had a decent year at Class A Lake Elsinore. His 7-9 record and 4.21 ERA were unimpressive, but the Angels like his 155 strikeouts and 39 walks in 162.1 innings. In a system devoid of pitching prospects at the lower levels, he'll be the focus of attention... Righthander **Geoff Edsell** is a marginal prospect. He reached Triple-A last year at age 24, but needs to refine his command before he'll be able to make the jump to the majors... Catcher **Bret Hemphill** finally developed a decent bat to go with his outstanding defense. He's behind schedule at age 25, but the switch-hitter showed good power last year in A-ball. He'll likely hit well enough at Double-A Midland to keep moving up... Although he'll be only 22 years old next year, catcher **Ben Molina** is already a step ahead of Hemphill. After a .274 season at Double-A that included only 25 strikeouts, Molina will move to Triple-A to provide insurance for the Angels, who are still uncertain whether Todd Greene has the receiving skills to remain behind the plate.

Davey Johnson

1996 Season

Davey Johnson's mandate as the Orioles' new manager last year was to turn around what had been considered an underachieving, unmotivated team under former manager Phil Regan. While it took him some time to get things together, Johnson's no-nonsense style and ability to handle players paid off in a playoff spot for the O's—the first for the club in 13 years.

Offense

Former N.L. manager Johnson was expected to make the Orioles a more aggressive baserunning team, but he quickly discovered that his team's talent was better suited for slugging. Tactics such as the hit-and-run, sacrificing, and basestealing became non-existent in a lineup which set a major league record by hitting 257 home runs. Johnson did, however, platoon and use his bench more than the average American League team.

Pitching & Defense

Johnson is considered a master of handling a pitching staff, but the struggling O's staff proved a trial for him all season. His boldest move was to switch to a four-man rotation in August, and the change helped fuel the Orioles' surge to a playoff spot. He believes in using his bullpen to secure platoon advantages—even when the strategy produces questionable results—and he did a superb job in working with an injury-riddled relief corps. Johnson is keen on late-inning defensive substitutions, frequently replacing Bobby Bonilla in right field late in the season.

1997 Outlook

Johnson had some difficulties in dealing with personalities in his new managerial position. He made judgment mistakes in trying to force Bobby Bonilla into the DH spot and also in temporarily moving Cal Ripken to third base. To his credit, Johnson has always acknowledged his mistakes and put his difficulties behind him. With the team now more accustomed to his managerial style, he hopes to get the O's out of the gate a little faster this year.

Born: 1/30/43 in Orlando, FL

Playing Experience: 1965-1978, Bal, Atl, Phi, ChN

Managerial Experience: 11 seasons

Manager Statistics

Year Team, Lg	W	L	Pct	GB	Finish
1996 Baltimore, AL	88	74	.540	4.0	2nd East
11 Seasons	887	663	.572	—	—

1996 Starting Pitchers by Days Rest

	≤3	4	5	6+
Orioles Starts	23	88	13	30
Orioles ERA	5.49	5.39	5.70	6.27
AL Avg Starts	4	96	30	21
AL ERA	5.57	4.90	5.33	5.81

1996 Situational Stats

	Davey Johnson	AL Average
Hit & Run Success %	33.9	39.1
Stolen Base Success %	65.5	69.6
Platoon Pct.	69.2	61.9
Defensive Subs	38	29
High-Pitch Outings	13	23
Quick/Slow Hooks	15/28	17/20
Sacrifice Attempts	46	58

1996 Rankings (American League)

➙ 1st in least caught steals of home plate (0), slow hooks (28) and starts on three days rest (23)

Roberto Alomar

1996 Season

The Orioles' void at second base prompted them to sign Roberto Alomar as a free agent after the 1995 season. Alomar lived up to his billing as the best second baseman in the game, batting close to .400 for the first two months of the season and never hitting a slump until late in the year. But a lot of luster was lost from Alomar's season when he spit in umpire John Hirschbeck's face during the last weekend of the regular season, resulting in a controversy that still hasn't died down.

Hitting

Alomar is a switch-hitter who has historically been substantially weaker from the right side of the plate. However, he's worked hard to correct the problem, hitting over .300 from both sides during the 1996 season. Alomar has also become a more patient hitter, frequently waiting on pitches to drive them to the opposite field. Surprisingly enough, he was able to accomplish this without sacrificing any power. While he has difficulty with pitches thrown low and inside, Alomar is tough to fan, as evidenced by his .284 average when batting with two strikes.

Baserunning & Defense

Alomar has excellent quickness and was a 50-base stealer for several years. However, because of his surrounding lineup and the different roles he plays as a hitter, his stolen base attempts have dropped significantly. He's one of the best at motoring around the bases. Defensively, there is no better second baseman in the majors than the perennial Gold Glover. Alomar has incredible range and is a magician at turning the double play.

1997 Outlook

Alomar will be suspended for the first five games of 1997, but it will take more than that to put the spitting incident behind him. The Orioles can only hope the controversy will help mature a player who has been criticized in the past for being self-centered and childish. As a ballplayer, he is among the best in the game and is a vital part of the Orioles future.

Position: 2B
Bats: B **Throws:** R
Ht: 6' 0" **Wt:** 185

Opening Day Age: 29
Born: 2/5/68 in Ponce, PR
ML Seasons: 9
Pronunciation: AL-a-mar
Nickname: Robby

Overall Statistics

	G	AB	R	H	D	T	HR	RBI	SB	BB	SO	Avg	OBP	Slg
1996	153	588	132	193	43	4	22	94	17	90	65	.328	.411	.527
Career	1304	5048	829	1522	273	52	99	593	313	560	587	.302	.371	.435

Where He Hits the Ball

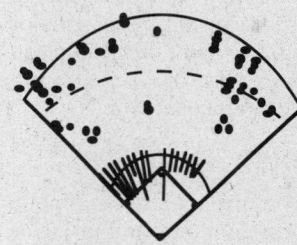

Vs. LHP   **Vs. RHP**

1996 Situational Stats

	AB	H	HR	RBI	Avg			AB	H	HR	RBI	Avg
Home	283	101	14	52	.357		LHP	192	60	9	37	.313
Road	305	92	8	42	.302		RHP	396	133	13	57	.336
First Half	327	115	11	53	.352		Sc Pos	129	41	8	75	.318
Scnd Half	261	78	11	41	.299		Clutch	86	30	3	14	.349

1996 Rankings (American League)

→ 1st in highest percentage of extra bases taken as a runner (72.3%)
→ 2nd in sacrifice flies (12) and pitches seen (2,953)
→ 3rd in runs scored, on-base percentage for a leadoff hitter (.405), batting average with two strikes (.284) and fielding percentage at second base (.985)
→ 5th in most pitches seen per plate appearance (4.22), batting average in the clutch (.349), errors at second base (11) and lowest percentage of swings on the first pitch (15.7%)

Brady Anderson

1996 Season

Without question, the Orioles' biggest surprise of 1996 was Brady Anderson, who slammed an incredible 50 home runs. Anderson, whose previous career high was only 21 homers, rewrote the record books as he led off 12 games with a home run, passed the legendary Frank Robinson as the Orioles' all-time single-season home run leader and became just the 14th player in history to reach the magic 50. Even more remarkable is the fact that Anderson accomplished these feats while suffering from appendicitis, for which he had surgery when the year ended!

Hitting

Anderson made significant modifications to his hitting approach last season. He moved closer to the plate, which—in addition to helping him lead the league in getting hit by pitches—helped him cut down markedly on his swing. Always an excellent low fastball hitter, he is susceptible to inside pitches around the belt. With Roberto Alomar on deck behind him, Anderson saw more fastballs and consequently became a dead pull hitter.

Baserunning & Defense

Anderson is a legitimate threat to steal, as evidenced by the 21 bases he swiped last year. Hustling on the basepaths, Anderson is a smart runner who frequently takes advantage of enemy outfielders' defensive liabilities. After patrolling left field during the 1995 season, Anderson looked comfortable in his return to center last year, displaying adequate range and a solid throwing arm. Still, the Orioles are more comfortable with him in left and would like to return him there this season.

1997 Outlook

It would seem unlikely that Anderson will be able to duplicate last year's heroics at the plate. He will be pitched to much more carefully and will probably start to see more junk than heat, which by itself should reduce his home run production. Luckily for them, the Orioles didn't have to negotiate with Anderson coming off his monster season last year, since they had a renewable option on his existing contract.

Position: CF
Bats: L **Throws:** L
Ht: 6' 1" **Wt:** 195

Opening Day Age: 33
Born: 1/18/64 in Silver Spring, MD
ML Seasons: 9

Overall Statistics

	G	AB	R	H	D	T	HR	RBI	SB	BB	SO	Avg	OBP	Slg
1996	149	579	117	172	37	5	50	110	21	76	106	.297	.396	.637
Career	1094	3850	629	989	201	49	122	456	208	535	699	.257	.356	.430

Where He Hits the Ball

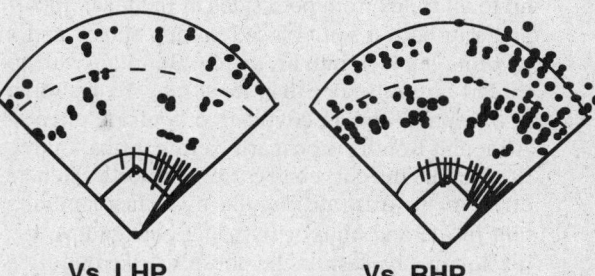

Vs. LHP   **Vs. RHP**

1996 Situational Stats

	AB	H	HR	RBI	Avg		AB	H	HR	RBI	Avg
Home	300	84	19	46	.280	LHP	187	47	13	36	.251
Road	279	88	31	64	.315	RHP	392	125	37	74	.319
First Half	307	91	30	62	.296	Sc Pos	111	23	4	47	.207
Scnd Half	272	81	20	48	.298	Clutch	79	20	3	11	.253

1996 Rankings (American League)

→ 1st in hit by pitch (22) and lowest batting average with runners in scoring position (.207)
→ 2nd in home runs
→ 3rd in slugging percentage and slugging percentage vs. right-handed pitchers (.686)
→ 4th in total bases (369) and HR frequency (11.6 ABs per HR)
→ 5th in on-base percentage for a leadoff hitter (.402), errors in center field (3) and lowest fielding percentage in center field (.992)
→ 8th in highest percentage of extra bases taken as a runner (62.2%)

Bobby Bonilla

1996 Season

In his first full season with Baltimore, Bobby Bonilla fought through myriad distractions to post strong offensive numbers. Bonilla, who spent the summer squabbling with manager Davey Johnson over his defensive role on the club, was nearly traded by GM Pat Gillick midway through the season—only to be saved at the last minute by owner Peter Angelos. Bonilla eventually won his battle to play the field and finished strongly. His powerful presence in the lineup was a key ingredient in the Orioles' success.

Hitting

Bonilla is a highly skilled switch-hitter who can hit to all fields from both sides of the plate. Incorporating both a semi-closed batting stance and a pivoting leg kick into his swing, Bonilla is able to extend himself more than most players, resulting in exceptional plate coverage on outside pitches. Although Bonilla is primarily a low fastball hitter, he also hits the curveball extremely well. Pitchers often try to frustrate Bonilla by either jamming him inside and high or by using change-ups, but it's not an easy task, as he doesn't strike out often for a power hitter.

Baserunning & Defense

While not often called upon to steal, Bonilla is a decent runner who is aggressive on the basepaths. Bonilla fought with management about his ability (or lack of it) as an outfielder, and his poor flyball judgment can make him look bad on some plays. Although he has limited range, he does have an excellent arm and was second on the team in outfield assists.

1997 Outlook

A free agent, Bonilla signed with the Florida Marlins after the season was over. The Marlins will be looking for him to give them the same kind of production he gave to the Orioles last year. He'll be reunited with Jim Leyland, his manager during his great seasons with the Pirates, and that might help spur him to a big year.

Position: RF/DH
Bats: B **Throws:** R
Ht: 6' 4" **Wt:** 240

Opening Day Age: 34
Born: 2/23/63 in New York, NY
ML Seasons: 11
Pronunciation: buh-NEE-yuh
Nickname: Bobby Bo

Overall Statistics

	G	AB	R	H	D	T	HR	RBI	SB	BB	SO	Avg	OBP	Slg
1996	159	595	107	171	27	5	28	116	1	75	85	.287	.363	.491
Career	1593	5786	916	1643	333	54	245	965	37	719	931	.284	.361	.487

Where He Hits the Ball

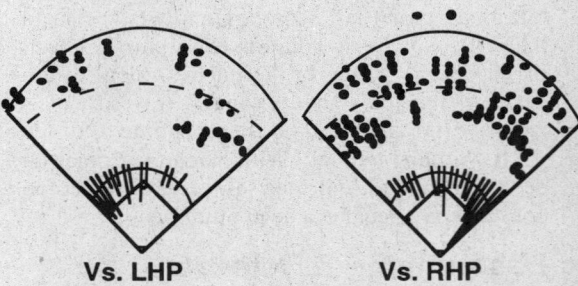

Vs. LHP   **Vs. RHP**

1996 Situational Stats

	AB	H	HR	RBI	Avg		AB	H	HR	RBI	Avg
Home	293	81	9	55	.276	LHP	195	59	10	37	.303
Road	302	90	19	61	.298	RHP	400	112	18	79	.280
First Half	308	87	10	52	.282	Sc Pos	164	47	10	92	.287
Scnd Half	287	84	18	64	.293	Clutch	83	24	7	25	.289

1996 Rankings (American League)

- → 1st in sacrifice flies (17)
- → 3rd in lowest cleanup slugging percentage (.443)
- → 4th in lowest fielding percentage in right field (.975)
- → 5th in errors in right field (5)
- → 6th in games played (159) and lowest batting average on an 0-2 count (.042)
- → Led the Orioles in sacrifice flies (17)

Rocky Coppinger

1996 Season

After a meteoric rise from Class-A to Triple-A during the 1995 season, Rocky Coppinger was regarded as the best pitching prospect in the Orioles farm system. When the Baltimore rotation had problems early last season, Coppinger was called up from Triple-A Rochester in early June and thrust into the majors ahead of schedule. Remaining in the rotation for the rest of the year, he showed his inexperience but still won 10 games, the most by an Orioles rookie since Bob Milacki won 14 in 1989.

Pitching

At 6'5" and 250 pounds, Coppinger is a big man who throws hard. He features mid-90s fastballs of both the two- and four-seam variety, and he complements these weapons with a hard-biting slider and a good circle change. As is the case with most young, inexperienced pitchers, Coppinger has a tendency to overthrow, leading to control problems. When he's laboring, his four-seam riser will start to sail and his sliders will start bouncing up to the plate. He rarely gets ahead of hitters, which led him to surrender 25 homers in just 125 innings.

Defense

Coppinger's defensive skills can best be described as adequate. He is not very quick at covering first base, nor is he agile charging in for bunts. Coppinger also has a slow delivery which hurts his ability to control the opposition's running game. To combat this, he'll usually throw a higher percentage of fastballs with men on base.

1997 Outlook

Coppinger entered the league at a young age, and his quick adjustment to the majors bodes well for his future. His winning record was somewhat deceiving given his high ERA, but once he learns how to throw more strikes, he'll be able to unleash his full potential. Coppinger will be in the Orioles rotation again this year as the fourth or fifth starter.

Position: SP
Bats: R **Throws:** R
Ht: 6' 5" **Wt:** 250

Opening Day Age: 23
Born: 3/19/74 in El Paso, TX
ML Seasons: 1

Baltimore Orioles

Overall Statistics

	W	L	Pct.	ERA	G	GS	Sv	IP	H	BB	SO	HR	BR/IP
1996	10	6	.625	5.18	23	22	0	125.0	126	60	104	25	1.49
Career	10	6	.625	5.18	23	22	0	125.0	126	60	104	25	1.49

How Often He Throws Strikes

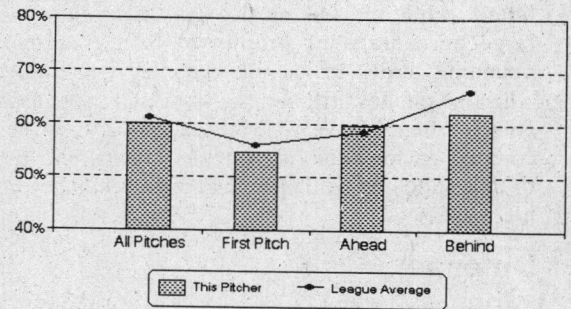

1996 Situational Stats

	W	L	ERA	Sv	IP		AB	H	HR	RBI	Avg
Home	3	2	6.75	0	49.1	LHB	220	71	14	40	.323
Road	7	4	4.16	0	75.2	RHB	259	55	11	29	.212
First Half	4	0	4.65	0	31.0	Sc Pos	102	33	6	46	.324
Scnd Half	6	6	5.36	0	94.0	Clutch	9	2	0	0	.222

1996 Rankings (American League)

→ 5th in highest batting average allowed vs. left-handed batters (.323)
→ 8th in stolen bases allowed (21)

Scott Erickson

1996 Season

Scott Erickson's first full season in Baltimore provided mixed results. Picking up where he left off in 1995 as the club's number-three starter, Erickson struggled early in the year, and he was unable to put together consistently strong outings until the latter part of the summer. Finally hitting stride in August, Erickson played a key role in the Orioles playoff drive by winning eight of his last 12 starts.

Pitching

A power pitcher who delivers his heater up to 93 MPH, Erickson rarely strays from his fastball/slider combination. He'll toss curves or change-ups only to keep hitters guessing. His conventional fastball runs away from left-handed hitters, while his sinking two-seamer produces a large percentage of ground balls. He enjoys pounding lefties inside but becomes vulnerable when his pitches drift belt high—which happened all too often last year. Erickson can usually be counted on for about six innings a start, but his troubles pitching with men on base have hampered his success.

Defense

Erickson has a decent glove and good mobility, enabling him to smoothly cover first base on grounders hit to the right side. Because his delivery leaves him heading towards the plate, he is effective charging bunts. Using an unusual sidearm pickoff throw, Erickson did not hold baserunners particularly well last season. In addition, they often disrupted his concentration, affecting his pitching performances.

1997 Outlook

Erickson is signed through the 1997 season at a salary of $2.8 million. While manager Davey Johnson would love to see the erratic Erickson pitch more consistently, he's always been a pitcher who bursts out of the gate slowly, gaining strength as the year progresses. Even with the signing of Jimmy Key, Erickson should remain in the rotation as the third starter—and for Baltimore to challenge for the pennant next year, that is precisely the slot where he needs to be.

Position: SP
Bats: R **Throws:** R
Ht: 6' 4" **Wt:** 230

Opening Day Age: 29
Born: 2/2/68 in Long Beach, CA
ML Seasons: 7

Overall Statistics

	W	L	Pct.	ERA	G	GS	Sv	IP	H	BB	SO	HR	BR/IP
1996	13	12	.520	5.02	34	34	0	222.1	262	66	100	21	1.48
Career	83	76	.522	4.33	206	203	0	1310.1	1408	468	688	111	1.43

How Often He Throws Strikes

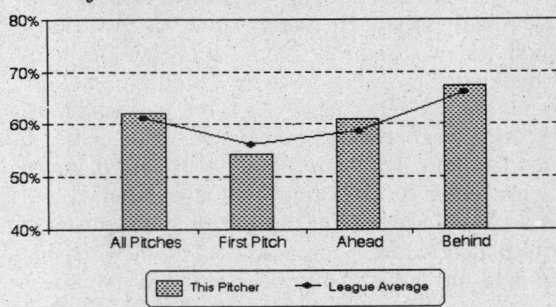

1996 Situational Stats

	W	L	ERA	Sv	IP		AB	H	HR	RBI	Avg
Home	6	5	4.76	0	107.2	LHB	475	153	10	65	.322
Road	7	7	5.26	0	114.2	RHB	406	109	11	52	.268
First Half	5	6	4.71	0	112.2	Sc Pos	229	75	5	95	.328
Scnd Half	8	6	5.33	0	109.2	Clutch	43	9	0	3	.209

1996 Rankings (American League)

- ➡ 1st in stolen bases allowed (32), GDPs induced (36), highest groundball/flyball ratio allowed (2.8), most GDPs induced per 9 innings (1.5) and least strikeouts per 9 innings (4.0)
- ➡ 2nd in highest batting average allowed (.297) and least pitches thrown per batter (3.50)
- ➡ 3rd in hits allowed, highest stolen base percentage allowed (88.9%) and most GDPs induced per GDP situation (19.9%)
- ➡ 4th in complete games (6)

Jeffrey Hammonds

1996 Season

Every year, the Orioles' front office expects Jeffrey Hammonds to finally start fulfilling his "untapped potential." Last year was no exception, either in regard to the O's expectations or Hammonds' dismal performance. Hammonds started poorly, was demoted to Triple-A in June, and was on the trading block by July. To cap it off, he suffered a knee injury and was on the disabled list from mid-August until the end of the season.

Hitting

The pressure to produce has adversely warped Hammonds' strike zone judgment, turning him into a wild swinger who lunges at anything he thinks he can reach. Although he has some pop in his bat, his inability to make contact prevents him from becoming a productive major-league hitter. Hammonds needs to learn more patience and cut down on his swing in order to stay in the big leagues. He did draw a few more walks than usual last year, and his quick bat continued to produce an occasional home run.

Baserunning & Defense

Hammonds has the speed to be an effective basestealer, but not the on-base percentage to utilize those skills. He also injured his left knee last season, further curtailing his running potential. A good defensive outfielder who has excellent range but a weak arm, Hammonds' throwing problems have relegated him to patrolling left field.

1997 Outlook

The best way to describe Hammonds' future in Baltimore is to say he is definitely on the bubble. While still young at 26, he hasn't been able to stay healthy or show any productivity since 1994. His name continually comes up in trade rumors, and with the Orioles spending so much on free agents, it is hard to see where and when Hammonds will break into their lineup.

Position: LF/RF
Bats: R **Throws:** R
Ht: 6' 0" **Wt:** 195

Opening Day Age: 26
Born: 3/5/71 in Plainfield, NJ
ML Seasons: 4

Overall Statistics

	G	AB	R	H	D	T	HR	RBI	SB	BB	SO	Avg	OBP	Slg
1996	71	248	38	56	10	1	9	27	3	23	53	.226	.301	.383
Career	229	781	111	205	45	4	24	100	16	51	138	.262	.310	.423

Where He Hits the Ball

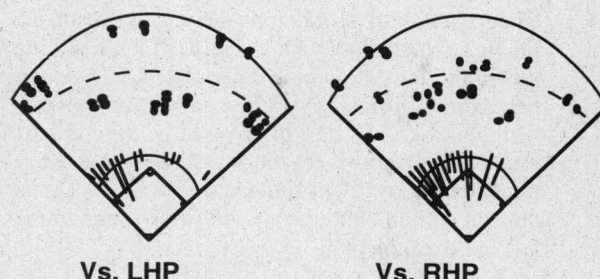

Vs. LHP   **Vs. RHP**

1996 Situational Stats

	AB	H	HR	RBI	Avg		AB	H	HR	RBI	Avg
Home	110	29	3	10	.264	LHP	81	20	2	7	.247
Road	138	27	6	17	.196	RHP	167	36	7	20	.216
First Half	194	46	6	19	.237	Sc Pos	60	12	4	21	.200
Scnd Half	54	10	3	8	.185	Clutch	46	11	2	7	.239

1996 Rankings (American League)

→ 8th in lowest batting average on a 3-2 count (.100)
→ Led the Orioles in batting average on an 0-2 count (.273)

Chris Hoiles

1996 Season

Chris Hoiles' 1996 campaign can be described as a "Tale of Two Seasons"—and oddly similar to the one he experienced in 1995. As the season started, Hoiles was once again hampered by a sore shoulder which affected him behind the plate as well as in the batter's box. In addition, it didn't exactly boost his confidence to learn that finding a new catcher would be management's top priority from day one. Batting just .222 at the end of June, Hoiles finally regained his hitting stroke after the All-Star break, and wound up posting excellent power numbers for the year.

Hitting

A power hitter with a compact swing, Hoiles is smart enough to go the opposite way with outside pitches, which is why he is successful at handling down-and-away breaking balls. Because he sometimes drops his inside shoulder and has an upward-tilting stroke, Hoiles is frequently stymied by pitches at or above the belt. Consequently, he is pitched high and away quite often. Hoiles is a good "mistake pitch" hitter who will jump on anything left out over the plate.

Baserunning & Defense

Like most catchers, Hoiles is a slow runner who is very conservative on the basepaths, with no intention of ever stealing. His shoulder ailments have hampered his ability to throw out baserunners, as he has been successful only 23 percent of the time. Hoiles doesn't have much maneuverability behind the plate, either, but he is respected for his handling of pitchers.

1997 Outlook

Hoiles has a long-term contract extending through the 1999 season at a considerably high salary level. That makes it difficult for the Orioles to trade him. But they'll probably try, since they feel they need better defense behind the plate. Hoiles might well be back with the O's this year, but it's doubtful he'll be their full-time catcher.

Position: C
Bats: R **Throws:** R
Ht: 6' 0" **Wt:** 215

Opening Day Age: 32
Born: 3/20/65 in Bowling Green, OH
ML Seasons: 8

Overall Statistics

	G	AB	R	H	D	T	HR	RBI	SB	BB	SO	Avg	OBP	Slg
1996	127	407	64	105	13	0	25	73	0	57	97	.258	.356	.474
Career	698	2233	334	586	95	2	124	344	4	346	480	.262	.366	.473

Where He Hits the Ball

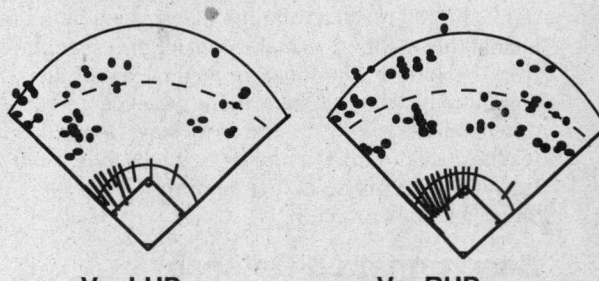

Vs. LHP   **Vs. RHP**

1996 Situational Stats

	AB	H	HR	RBI	Avg		AB	H	HR	RBI	Avg
Home	214	51	13	37	.238	LHP	125	38	9	24	.304
Road	193	54	12	36	.280	RHP	282	67	16	49	.238
First Half	210	47	12	30	.224	Sc Pos	101	24	6	47	.238
Scnd Half	197	58	13	43	.294	Clutch	54	16	4	12	.296

1996 Rankings (American League)

- ➡ 3rd in lowest percentage of runners caught stealing as a catcher (17.9%)
- ➡ 6th in errors at catcher (7)
- ➡ 9th in lowest batting average at home (.238)
- ➡ 10th in hit by pitch (9)

Eddie Murray

1996 Season

Although not the fearsome slugger he was during the 1980s, Eddie Murray still finds ways to contribute. Traded back to the Orioles by the Cleveland Indians in midseason, Murray took over as Baltimore's designated hitter, enabling the Orioles to relieve Bobby Bonilla from a role he didn't want. Along with stabilizing what had been a sinking Baltimore ship, Murray also became just the third member of the major league's 500 homer/3,000 hit club, locking up his spot in the Hall of Fame.

Hitting

Murray owes his continued productivity to his strong wrists and quick bat, attributes similar to those possessed by the great Hank Aaron, another player who enjoyed a long career. A switch-hitter who comes out swinging from the heels, Murray still uses a big piece of lumber and an open, crouched, batting stance. He is fooled often by a good change-up and does not handle the high fastball well, but he is a master at capitalizing on pitchers' mistakes—crushing pitches thrown over the middle of the plate.

Baserunning & Defense

Until last season, Murray was still getting playing time at first base, but that is no longer the case. He is the epitome of the designated hitter, in that he is no longer a good defensive player nor does he run particularly well.

1997 Outlook

Murray, a restricted free agent, will be 41 at the start of next season and will likely be offered another one-year contract. He made $2 million last year and it's hard to see him commanding that type of paycheck again, but the Orioles' management likes Murray's leadership abilities and values the role he plays on the team. Although he is capable of having another 20-home run season, decline in production due to age is inevitable.

Position: DH
Bats: B **Throws:** R
Ht: 6' 2" **Wt:** 220

Opening Day Age: 41
Born: 2/24/56 in Los Angeles, CA
ML Seasons: 20

Overall Statistics

	G	AB	R	H	D	T	HR	RBI	SB	BB	SO	Avg	OBP	Slg
1996	152	566	69	147	21	1	22	79	4	61	87	.260	.327	.417
Career	2971	11169	1614	3218	553	35	501	1899	109	1318	1490	.288	.361	.478

Where He Hits the Ball

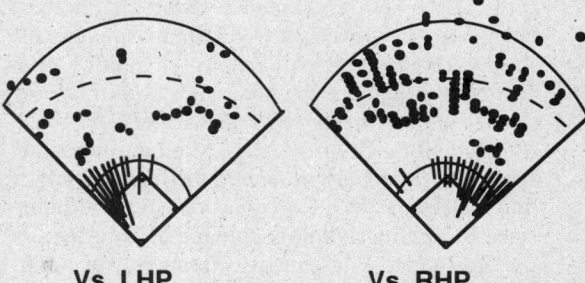

Vs. LHP   **Vs. RHP**

1996 Situational Stats

	AB	H	HR	RBI	Avg		AB	H	HR	RBI	Avg
Home	262	60	13	37	.229	LHP	156	42	6	21	.269
Road	304	87	9	42	.286	RHP	410	105	16	58	.256
First Half	323	84	11	39	.260	Sc Pos	140	32	2	51	.229
Scnd Half	243	63	11	40	.259	Clutch	88	21	5	13	.239

1996 Rankings (American League)

→ 3rd in highest percentage of swings on the first pitch (41.2%)

→ 4th in sacrifice flies (10) and lowest batting average at home (.229)

→ 7th in lowest batting average with runners in scoring position (.229)

→ 9th in GDPs (19) and lowest percentage of pitches taken (48.8%)

Mike Mussina

Position: SP
Bats: R **Throws:** R
Ht: 6' 1" **Wt:** 180

Opening Day Age: 28
Born: 12/8/68 in
Williamsport, PA
ML Seasons: 6
Pronunciation:
myoo-SEE-nuh

1996 Season

Despite winning 19 games for the second straight year Mike Mussina had a disappointing 1996. Not fully recovered from an abdominal strain suffered during spring training, Mussina struggled for much of the season, breaking out of his slump only after manager Davey Johnson decided to switch to a four-man rotation in August. Even after winning six starts in a row down the stretch, Mussina finished the year with an unusually high 4.81 ERA. His postseason work was also spotty.

Pitching

No American League starter has the array of pitches that Mussina possesses. Not satisfied with just a sharp-breaking knuckle-curve and the best change-up in the league, Mussina complements those pitches with two fastballs—a sinking two-seam cutter and a four-seam riser, both routinely thrown in the low 90s. When he is able to establish the fastball early in the game, he can dominate. However, his inability to keep the ball down hurt him in 1996, as he allowed a career-high 31 home runs. Struggling with his command more than in previous years, Mussina also frequently accumulated high pitch counts which sapped his stamina.

Defense

Mussina has good footwork coming off the mound and uses his quickness to cover first base well. With solid fielding instincts, he rarely makes mental errors on slow rollers and sacrifice bunts. Mussina is extremely adept at holding runners, using his unique windup to discourage basestealing. Only six runners stole successfully against him all year out of a meager 14 attempts.

1997 Outlook

Mussina will return as the Orioles' ace next season, determined to lower this year's unusually high ERA. To regain his success, Mussina will need to use more fastballs in the early innings of his outings, reserving his breaking pitches for crucial game situations. Although he hasn't yet had a breakthrough season, Mussina is now entering his prime and should be knocking on stardom's door for several years to come.

Overall Statistics

	W	L	Pct.	ERA	G	GS	Sv	IP	H	BB	SO	HR	BR/IP
1996	19	11	.633	4.81	36	36	0	243.1	264	69	204	31	1.37
Career	90	41	.687	3.56	161	161	0	1137.2	1066	274	760	117	1.18

How Often He Throws Strikes

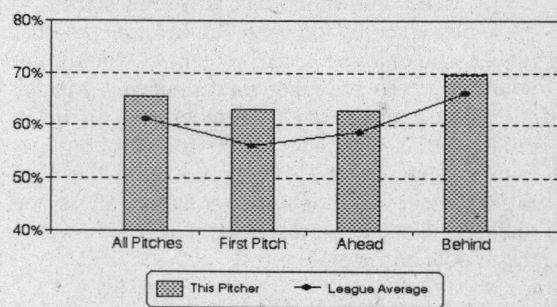

This Pitcher — League Average

1996 Situational Stats

	W	L	ERA	Sv	IP		AB	H	HR	RBI	Avg
Home	9	8	5.39	0	132.0	LHB	495	124	8	46	.251
Road	10	3	4.12	0	111.1	RHB	464	140	23	80	.302
First Half	11	5	4.87	0	129.1	Sc Pos	222	69	9	96	.311
Scnd Half	8	6	4.74	0	114.0	Clutch	75	14	3	8	.187

1996 Rankings (American League)

→ 1st in games started and fielding percentage at pitcher (1.000)
→ 2nd in hits allowed, highest strikeout/walk ratio (3.0) and most run support per 9 innings (6.8)
→ 3rd in wins
→ 4th in innings pitched, batters faced (1,039) and strikeouts
→ 5th in lowest stolen base percentage allowed (42.9%) and most strikeouts per 9 innings (7.5)
→ 6th in shutouts (1) and highest ERA at home (5.39)

Randy Myers

1996 Season

Signed by new Baltimore GM Pat Gillick to fill the closer's role that Doug Jones couldn't handle in 1995, Randy Myers had a disappointing '96 season. Myers had early success and pitched flawlessly in April, but as the summer wore on his difficulty with right-handed hitters cost him the confidence of manager Davey Johnson. Despite recovering to post good numbers in September, Myers had enough difficulties to jeopardize his place in the ranks of baseball's elite stoppers.

Pitching

Myers is a three-pitch closer, featuring a low-90s fastball, a tight slider, and a straight change-up. He rarely challenges right-handed hitters inside, preferring to shoot for the outside edge of the plate with his fastball and change. He uses his slider more often against left-handed hitters, since its sharp, late-breaking movement makes it very difficult to hit from that side of the plate. Myers' difficulties occur when he tries to finesse the strike zone, which not only saps his stamina but also forces him to use his predictable fastball—a pitch which is often very hittable when he has to work from behind in the count.

Defense

Not known for having a great pickoff move, Myers does a fair job of keeping runners honest. He's helped by the fact that he usually comes into games in situations that aren't conducive to running. He has a clean, efficient set delivery and is a decent fielder.

1997 Outlook

Myers is costing the O's $2.6 million a year, and his up-and-down '96 season didn't win him a lot of friends in Baltimore. Johnson and GM Pat Gillick won't hesitate to go to another closer if Myers continues to struggle, and a trade is also a possibility. He'll get another chance to close for somebody this year, but at 34 he'll have to prove he isn't slipping.

Position: RP
Bats: L **Throws:** L
Ht: 6' 1" **Wt:** 225

Opening Day Age: 34
Born: 9/19/62 in Vancouver, WA
ML Seasons: 12

Overall Statistics

	W	L	Pct.	ERA	G	GS	Sv	IP	H	BB	SO	HR	BR/IP
1996	4	4	.500	3.53	62	0	31	58.2	60	29	74	7	1.52
Career	38	53	.418	3.20	605	12	274	768.1	652	348	787	61	1.30

How Often He Throws Strikes

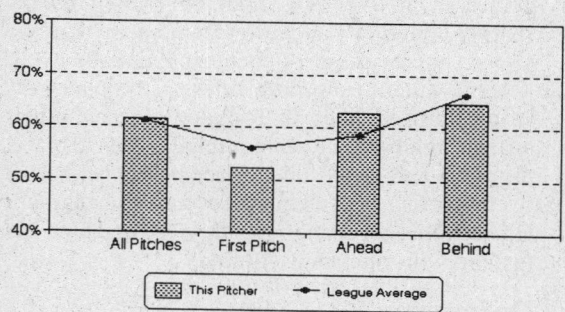

1996 Situational Stats

	W	L	ERA	Sv	IP		AB	H	HR	RBI	Avg
Home	1	1	1.61	16	28.0	LHB	48	10	3	10	.208
Road	3	3	5.28	15	30.2	RHB	178	50	4	20	.281
First Half	0	2	3.26	18	30.1	Sc Pos	62	17	2	24	.274
Scnd Half	4	2	3.81	13	28.1	Clutch	179	43	6	24	.240

1996 Rankings (American League)

→ 2nd in most strikeouts per 9 innings in relief (11.4)
→ 4th in lowest save percentage (81.6%)
→ 5th in blown saves (7)
→ 6th in saves and save opportunities (38)
→ 8th in games finished (50)
→ Led the Orioles in saves, games finished (50), save opportunities (38), save percentage (81.6%), blown saves (7) and most strikeouts per 9 innings in relief (11.4)

Jesse Orosco

1996 Season

Still effective as he nears his 40th birthday, Jesse Orosco has had two straight good seasons as the southpaw set-up man in the Orioles bullpen. Orosco had two disastrous outings in mid-April, allowing a whopping 12 earned runs, but then recovered to give up just six more earned runs in his next 50 appearances. He was outstanding during the Orioles' drive to a playoff spot, posting a 1.23 ERA after the All-Star break.

Pitching

Orosco uses three basic pitches to get the job done. In addition to a high-80s sinking fastball and a sweeping curveball, he utilizes a slider that rarely comes in at over 80 MPH, but which breaks sharply both down and away from enemy batters. Orosco mixes these pitches exceptionally well, keeping hitters from both sides of the plate off-stride. Orosco likes to backdoor his curveball against righthanders while forcing lefties to chase his down-and-away slider. Since he has neither an overpowering fastball nor a deceptive change-up, Orosco relies on changing both speed and location to disrupt his opponents' timing.

Defense

Orosco did not see many fielding chances last season, but handled them adequately just the same. He has a sure glove when fielding grounders and can be counted on to make smart decisions on sacrifice bunts. Orosco does not hold runners well: in fact, no runner was thrown out stealing on Orosco last year as he allowed six stolen bases.

1997 Outlook

Orosco was a restricted free agent eligible for arbitration, but because of his relatively inexpensive salary, the Orioles signed him for another season. Despite his age, his experience and savvy should continue to make him a valuable asset to the Baltimore bullpen.

Position: RP
Bats: R **Throws:** L
Ht: 6' 2" **Wt:** 205

Opening Day Age: 39
Born: 4/21/57 in Santa Barbara, CA
ML Seasons: 17

Overall Statistics

	W	L	Pct.	ERA	G	GS	Sv	IP	H	BB	SO	HR	BR/IP
1996	3	1	.750	3.40	66	0	0	55.2	42	28	52	5	1.26
Career	74	69	.517	2.98	885	4	133	1076.2	867	460	972	84	1.23

How Often He Throws Strikes

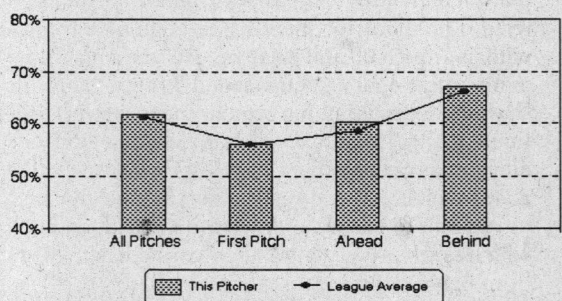

```
80%

70%

60%

50%

40%
     All Pitches   First Pitch   Ahead   Behind
```

▨ This Pitcher —●— League Average

1996 Situational Stats

	W	L	ERA	Sv	IP		AB	H	HR	RBI	Avg
Home	1	0	2.27	0	31.2	LHB	74	16	2	10	.216
Road	2	1	4.88	0	24.0	RHB	129	26	3	13	.202
First Half	2	1	5.81	0	26.1	Sc Pos	45	11	3	19	.244
Scnd Half	1	0	1.23	0	29.1	Clutch	80	12	1	9	.150

1996 Rankings (American League)

- → 4th in holds (19)
- → 5th in lowest percentage of inherited runners scored (21.7%) and lowest batting average allowed in relief (.207)
- → 7th in first batter efficiency (.186)
- → Led the Orioles in games pitched, holds (19), first batter efficiency (.186), lowest percentage of inherited runners scored (21.7%), relief ERA (3.40), lowest batting average allowed in relief (.207) and least baserunners allowed per 9 innings in relief (11.6)

Rafael Palmeiro

1996 Season

In a lineup full of All-Star hitters, Rafael Palmeiro is the man whom the Orioles most want to see at the plate in a critical situation. Palmeiro set a new club record last season with 142 RBI and matched his career high in home runs with 39, completing his metamorphosis from a solid number-three hitter to one of the best cleanup men in the league. One of the hallmarks of Palmeiro's season was his consistency, as his production levels were never affected by slumps.

Hitting

Palmeiro has one of the quickest bats in the game, allowing him to wait a bit longer on pitches than most hitters. With great hand control guiding his swing, Palmeiro has developed into an above-average two-strike hitter. He has excellent power and likes to pull lefthanders by bringing in his hands to get the barrel of his bat through the strike zone more quickly. Palmeiro's only weakness is his penchant for swinging at low-and-away breaking balls, resulting in harmless pop-ups.

Baserunning & Defense

Palmeiro is neither a serious threat to steal nor an accomplished baserunner. Defensively, he has improved immensely as a first baseman, committing just eight errors last season while becoming one of the league's best at digging low throws out of the dirt. Palmeiro is not especially quick to the hole when holding runners on base, but he does have a reliable glove.

1997 Outlook

Rafael Palmeiro will be entering the fourth year of his five-year deal with the Orioles and has become an indispensable part of the team. He is still in his prime and should continue to be the Orioles' main run producer. Although his average dipped slightly to .289 last year, it is understandable since Palmeiro has placed more emphasis on power upon recently moving to the cleanup slot.

Position: 1B
Bats: L **Throws:** L
Ht: 6' 0" **Wt:** 190

Opening Day Age: 32
Born: 9/24/64 in Havana, Cuba
ML Seasons: 11

Overall Statistics

	G	AB	R	H	D	T	HR	RBI	SB	BB	SO	Avg	OBP	Slg
1996	162	626	110	181	40	2	39	142	8	95	96	.289	.381	.546
Career	1462	5483	868	1636	336	29	233	848	68	589	637	.298	.367	.498

Where He Hits the Ball

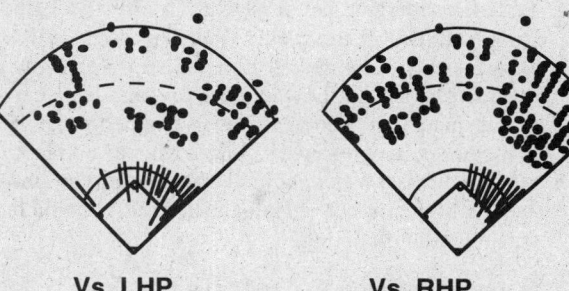

Vs. LHP   **Vs. RHP**

1996 Situational Stats

	AB	H	HR	RBI	Avg		AB	H	HR	RBI	Avg
Home	299	85	21	67	.284	LHP	244	72	14	56	.295
Road	327	96	18	75	.294	RHP	382	109	25	86	.285
First Half	332	98	22	77	.295	Sc Pos	173	56	12	101	.324
Scnd Half	294	83	17	65	.282	Clutch	82	28	5	20	.341

1996 Rankings (American League)

→ 2nd in games played (162)
→ 3rd in plate appearances (732) and lowest groundball/flyball ratio (0.6)
→ 4th in RBI and fielding percentage at first base (.995)
→ 6th in total bases (342), intentional walks (12), pitches seen (2,823) and cleanup slugging percentage (.594)
→ 7th in at-bats and errors at first base (8)
→ 9th in home runs and walks
→ 10th in doubles, times on base (279) and batting average in the clutch (.341)

Cal Ripken Jr.

1996 Season

It might surprise some to know that Cal Ripken Jr. surpassed his career averages in virtually every major statistical category in 1996. Not bad for a 36 year old who hasn't had a day's rest in 14 years. Ripken was supposed to be able to relax after dealing with "The Streak" in 1995, but instead faced new challenges that included a brief shift from shortstop to third base. In the end, though, Ripken quieted the naysayers with another outstanding season.

Hitting

Known for constantly changing his batting stance and making repeated adjustments, Ripken cast aside those habits last season in an effort to gain some stability at the plate. While his long, stiff-armed swing still makes him vulnerable to low outside pitches, he showed more restraint last year in chasing them. Though he was dropped to sixth in the order, the presence of Eddie Murray and B.J. Surhoff behind him enabled Ripken to see an unusually high number of fastballs last season, which was much to his liking.

Baserunning & Defense

While his fielding numbers don't indicate it, many people feel that Ripken has lost so much range that he's no longer a top-level shortstop. He remains as sure-handed as ever, and while he doesn't have a cannon for an arm, it's certainly strong enough for either short or third. Ripken is a slow but intelligent baserunner who is not shy when it comes to taking out infielders on the double play.

1997 Outlook

Cal Ripken Jr. is an Orioles icon who played every game again in 1996, and there's no reason to think things will change next year. Speculation continues that if the Orioles can land a top-caliber shortstop, Ripken might be moved to third base for good. Ripken wouldn't be crazy about that, but the shift might help prolong his career.

Position: SS
Bats: R **Throws:** R
Ht: 6' 4" **Wt:** 220

Opening Day Age: 36
Born: 8/24/60 in Havre de Grace, MD
ML Seasons: 16

Overall Statistics

	G	AB	R	H	D	T	HR	RBI	SB	BB	SO	Avg	OBP	Slg
1996	163	640	94	178	40	1	26	102	1	59	78	.278	.341	.466
Career	2381	9217	1366	2549	487	43	353	1369	35	960	1033	.277	.345	.454

Where He Hits the Ball

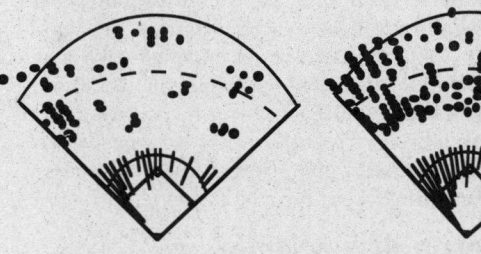

Vs. LHP   Vs. RHP

1996 Situational Stats

	AB	H	HR	RBI	Avg		AB	H	HR	RBI	Avg
Home	311	71	10	42	.228	LHP	191	55	7	23	.288
Road	329	107	16	60	.325	RHP	449	123	19	79	.274
First Half	334	96	17	65	.287	Sc Pos	161	50	6	70	.311
Scnd Half	306	82	9	37	.268	Clutch	98	33	3	18	.337

1996 Rankings (American League)

- → 1st in GDPs (28) and games played (163)
- → 3rd in at-bats and lowest batting average at home (.228)
- → 4th in fielding percentage at shortstop (.980)
- → 5th in most GDPs per GDP situation (17.2%)
- → 7th in plate appearances (707)
- → 10th in doubles and errors at shortstop (14)
- → Led the Orioles in at-bats, GDPs (28), games played (163), batting average on the road (.325) and highest percentage of swings put into play (48.5%)

B.J. Surhoff

1996 Season

One of several highly-touted free-agent signees by the Orioles, B.J. Surhoff proved to be an outstanding acquisition because of his versatility both in the field and at the plate. Surhoff posted career highs in home runs and RBI while bolstering the bottom of the Orioles batting order. In addition, he filled the void at third base for most of the year until the acquisition of Todd Zeile moved him to the outfield.

Hitting

Surhoff is one of those rare high fastball hitters who can roll his wrists on anything upstairs and still stay on top of the ball. He is an extremely good situational hitter because he is very patient and has the bat speed to catch up with virtually any type of pitch. While most of his power is to the right-center field gap, he will hit the opposite way when pitched outside. Surhoff can be tamed somewhat by breaking sliders thrown inside or split-fingered fastballs. He is a free swinger—but also a tough strikeout.

Baserunning & Defense

Considering the fact that Surhoff had not played regularly at third base since 1993, he did an admirable job filling in for Baltimore last season. Although his glove is erratic while moving to his left and he is slow to charge the bunt, Surhoff covers the line well and has a solid arm. After being placed in left field upon Zeile's arrival late in the season, he seemed quite comfortable. Surhoff does not steal, nor is he known for any great baserunning maneuvers.

1997 Outlook

Since Surhoff produced offensively even while being shifted around in the field, it is reasonable to think he might provide even more productivity with a more stable role this year. Right field is his most likely position, but there is a slight chance he could be back at third.

Position: 3B/LF
Bats: L **Throws:** R
Ht: 6' 1" **Wt:** 200

Opening Day Age: 32
Born: 8/4/64 in Bronx, NY
ML Seasons: 10

Overall Statistics

	G	AB	R	H	D	T	HR	RBI	SB	BB	SO	Avg	OBP	Slg
1996	143	537	74	157	27	6	21	82	0	47	79	.292	.352	.482
Career	1245	4421	546	1221	221	30	78	606	102	341	402	.276	.326	.393

Where He Hits the Ball

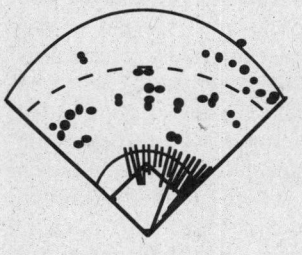

Vs. LHP   **Vs. RHP**

1996 Situational Stats

	AB	H	HR	RBI	Avg		AB	H	HR	RBI	Avg
Home	257	74	12	41	.288	LHP	162	47	3	21	.290
Road	280	83	9	41	.296	RHP	375	110	18	61	.293
First Half	275	78	13	49	.284	Sc Pos	138	43	3	61	.312
Scnd Half	262	79	8	33	.302	Clutch	87	20	4	17	.230

1996 Rankings (American League)

→ 1st in lowest fielding percentage at third base (.948)

→ 4th in batting average with the bases loaded (.615)

→ 6th in errors at third base (14)

→ 7th in batting average on a 3-1 count (.636)

→ Led the Orioles in triples, least GDPs per GDP situation (6.3%), batting average with the bases loaded (.615) and batting average on a 3-1 count (.636)

David Wells

1996 Season

Acquired in a trade prior to the 1996 season, left-hander David Wells was expected to back up Mike Mussina as the number-two starter. While pitching effectively at Camden Yards, Wells had severe problems on the road, compiling a 7.35 ERA outside of Baltimore's friendly confines. Wells also struggled against the bottom echelon of the league while saving some of his best efforts for contending clubs. But that characteristic was an asset in the postseason, where he was one of Baltimore's most reliable starters.

Pitching

While usually looking to get ahead of batters with his 90 MPH fastball, Wells has a wide arsenal of pitches to attack his opponents. He has a big-breaking curveball that he can usually place below the knees, a well controlled slider, and a change-up that he uses exclusively against right-handed hitters. Wells likes to come inside to batters on both sides of the plate, despite the fact that even the weakest hitters are able to get the bat around on him. Considered one of the best control pitchers in baseball, Wells hides the ball well, making it tough for hitters to pick up his pitches.

Defense

Wells isn't nicknamed "Boomer" for nothing—he's a large man who's out of shape and does not have good mobility in the field. Although Wells is a southpaw, he has trouble controlling opposing baserunners, mainly because he employs a high leg kick in his windup.

1997 Outlook

Wells' contract was only for one season, and he is again a free agent. It's unlikely that he'll be re-signed by the Orioles, who came close to dealing him away last July. Regardless of where he winds up, Wells must improve his concentration and consistency—particularly when facing the lower-ranked teams in the league. There will always be a demand for a left-handed veteran, so he should have little trouble finding employment.

Position: SP
Bats: L **Throws:** L
Ht: 6' 4" **Wt:** 225

Opening Day Age: 33
Born: 5/20/63 in Torrance, CA
ML Seasons: 10

Overall Statistics

	W	L	Pct.	ERA	G	GS	Sv	IP	H	BB	SO	HR	BR/IP
1996	11	14	.440	5.14	34	34	0	224.1	247	51	130	32	1.33
Career	90	75	.545	3.99	348	178	13	1413.0	1396	371	922	165	1.25

How Often He Throws Strikes

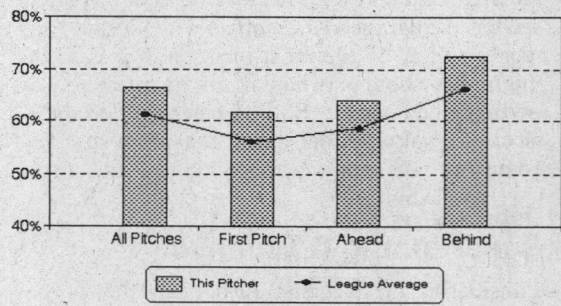

1996 Situational Stats

	W	L	ERA	Sv	IP		AB	H	HR	RBI	Avg
Home	7	6	3.53	0	130.0	LHB	191	43	4	19	.225
Road	4	8	7.35	0	94.1	RHB	675	204	28	99	.302
First Half	5	8	5.28	0	117.2	Sc Pos	189	51	8	85	.270
Scnd Half	6	6	4.98	0	106.2	Clutch	92	25	2	9	.272

1996 Rankings (American League)

→ 1st in highest ERA on the road (7.35)
→ 2nd in balks (2)
→ 3rd in lowest batting average allowed vs. left-handed batters (.225)
→ 4th in stolen bases allowed (26) and highest stolen base percentage allowed (86.7%)
→ 6th in losses, home runs allowed, least pitches thrown per batter (3.66) and least strikeouts per 9 innings (5.2)
→ 7th in GDPs induced (24), highest strikeout/walk ratio (2.5), highest slugging percentge allowed (.458), most home runs allowed per 9 innings (1.28) and ERA at home (3.53)

Todd Zeile

Signed By
DODGERS

1996 Season

Acquired in an August 29 trade from the Phillies along with outfielder Pete Incaviglia, Todd Zeile was expected to provide power for the stretch run. Zeile's presence also enabled Baltimore to move B.J. Surhoff into left field and finally obtain the everyday third baseman they were looking for. As it turned out, Zeile didn't do much for the O's in September, but he made up for it with a solid postseason.

Hitting

Zeile is a flat-swinging, line-drive hitter with decent gap power. Because of his level compact stroke, he occasionally swings over the ball, producing a lot of ground balls. Zeile has worked on generating home run power by pulling more fastballs, and his 25 homers last year were a career high. But his primary value is as a situational hitter with men on base and in scoring position. In those scenarios, Zeile is smart enough to cut down on his swing and become more of a contact hitter.

Baserunning & Defense

Though he'll never be mistaken for Brooks Robinson, Zeile has steadily improved as a third baseman since being converted from a catcher a few years ago. Of course, this means that he has merely brought his defense to an adequate level, not an outstanding one. Zeile's baserunning is of no concern to pitchers, since he rarely attempts to steal.

1997 Outlook

The Orioles were satisfied with Zeile's play last year, but with the club apparently serious about shifting Cal Ripken to third on a permanent basis, they did not make a serious bid to keep him. The Dodgers scooped him up in early December, inking the California native and former UCLA Bruin to a three-year pact. He should anchor the hot corner for LA, playing across the diamond from former UCLA teammate Eric Karros. Having played for four clubs in the last two years, he'll be happy to settle down somewhere.

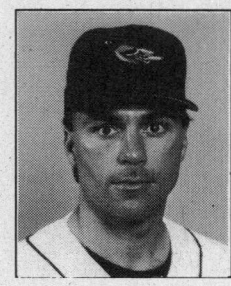

Position: 3B/1B
Bats: R **Throws:** R
Ht: 6' 1" **Wt:** 200

Opening Day Age: 31
Born: 9/9/65 in Van Nuys, CA
ML Seasons: 8
Pronunciation: ZEAL

Baltimore Orioles

Overall Statistics

	G	AB	R	H	D	T	HR	RBI	SB	BB	SO	Avg	OBP	Slg
1996	163	617	78	162	32	0	25	99	1	82	104	.263	.348	.436
Career	999	3610	468	949	197	13	109	523	34	444	567	.263	.342	.415

Where He Hits the Ball

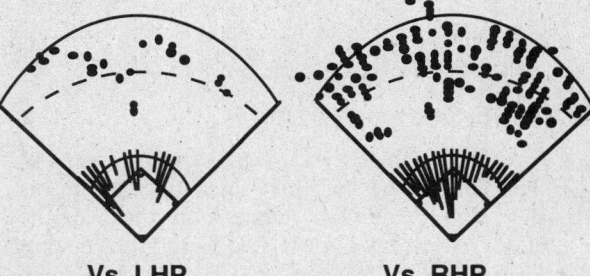

Vs. LHP   **Vs. RHP**

1996 Situational Stats

	AB	H	HR	RBI	Avg		AB	H	HR	RBI	Avg
Home	280	73	10	46	.261	LHP	118	33	6	20	.280
Road	337	89	15	53	.264	RHP	499	129	19	79	.259
First Half	328	86	13	49	.262	Sc Pos	168	50	4	68	.298
Scnd Half	289	76	12	50	.263	Clutch	100	22	4	11	.220

1996 Rankings (American League)

➡ Did not rank near the top or bottom in any category

Armando Benitez

Position: RP
Bats: R **Throws:** R
Ht: 6' 4" **Wt:** 220

Opening Day Age: 24
Born: 11/3/72 in
Ramon Santana, DR
ML Seasons: 3
Pronunciation:
buh-NEE-tez

Overall Statistics

	W	L	Pct.	ERA	G	GS	Sv	IP	H	BB	SO	HR	BR/IP
1996	1	0	1.000	3.77	18	0	4	14.1	7	6	20	2	0.91
Career	2	5	.286	4.63	65	0	6	72.0	52	47	90	10	1.38

1996 Situational Stats

	W	L	ERA	Sv	IP		AB	H	HR	RBI	Avg
Home	1	0	1.13	1	8.0	LHB	15	2	0	0	.133
Road	0	0	7.11	3	6.1	RHB	34	5	2	4	.147
First Half	1	0	6.75	0	4.0	Sc Pos	17	0	0	1	.000
Scnd Half	0	0	2.61	4	10.1	Clutch	24	3	1	2	.125

1996 Season

Hard-throwing Armando Benitez missed most of the 1996 season with a strained ligament in his right elbow. Returning in late August to share the closer role with Randy Myers, Benitez helped turn a struggling bullpen into a formidable one down the stretch.

Pitching & Defense

Armed with a mid-90s fastball, Benitez can be overpowering. However, he has had trouble settling on a complementary pitch, since control problems with both his slider and splitter have sapped his confidence in them. Because of this, Benitez has a tendency to keep throwing the fastball until he gets well ahead in the count, which can make him a little predictable. Although he doesn't have a great pickoff move, his pitches get to the plate so quickly that he keeps potential basestealers honest. Benitez is solid with the glove.

1997 Outlook

If Benitez can develop command of a second pitch, he has the arm to become one of the league's top closers. He showed coolness under fire in key games late last season, and he could be ready to take over as the Orioles' sole stopper this season.

Mike Devereaux

Position: RF/LF/CF
Bats: R **Throws:** R
Ht: 6' 0" **Wt:** 195

Opening Day Age: 33
Born: 4/10/63 in
Casper, WY
ML Seasons: 10
Pronunciation:
DEH-ver-oh

Overall Statistics

	G	AB	R	H	D	T	HR	RBI	SB	BB	SO	Avg	OBP	Slg
1996	127	323	49	74	11	2	8	34	8	34	53	.229	.305	.350
Career	1048	3655	483	930	166	33	105	472	84	286	623	.254	.308	.404

1996 Situational Stats

	AB	H	HR	RBI	Avg		AB	H	HR	RBI	Avg
Home	145	31	5	18	.214	LHP	135	33	5	19	.244
Road	178	43	3	16	.242	RHP	188	41	3	15	.218
First Half	217	54	4	22	.249	Sc Pos	75	17	1	23	.227
Scnd Half	106	20	4	12	.189	Clutch	66	15	1	1	.227

1996 Season

Signed as a free agent prior to the 1996 season, Mike Devereaux returned to the team for which he had played six seasons before leaving in 1995. Obtained as outfield insurance, Devereaux was playing regularly until the O's obtained Eddie Murray and made Bobby Bonilla the everyday right fielder.

Hitting, Baserunning & Defense

Devereaux is a high fastball hitter who has decent power, but he swings over the ball so much that he grounds out a large percentage of the time. He does generally make contact and can clear the fences occasionally as well. Used primarily in a defensive role late in the season, Devereaux is a good fielder who covers lots of outfield turf but does not own a particularly accurate or strong throwing arm. While still blessed with above-average speed, he doesn't have the necessary "first-step quickness" to be a stolen base artist.

1997 Outlook

Devereaux has become a journeyman, signing one-year deals and bouncing from team to team. Once again a free agent, he's likely to be applying his trade elsewhere in 1997.

Jimmy Haynes

Position: RP/SP
Bats: R **Throws:** R
Ht: 6' 3" **Wt:** 180

Opening Day Age: 24
Born: 9/5/72 in
LaGrange, GA
ML Seasons: 2

Overall Statistics

	W	L	Pct.	ERA	G	GS	Sv	IP	H	BB	SO	HR	BR/IP
1996	3	6	.333	8.29	26	11	1	89.0	122	58	65	14	2.02
Career	5	7	.417	7.01	30	14	1	113.0	133	70	87	16	1.80

1996 Situational Stats

	W	L	ERA	Sv	IP		AB	H	HR	RBI	Avg
Home	3	3	6.84	0	51.1	LHB	159	48	5	24	.302
Road	0	3	10.27	1	37.2	RHB	207	74	9	54	.357
First Half	2	5	6.72	1	71.0	Sc Pos	101	43	4	62	.426
Scnd Half	1	1	14.50	0	18.0	Clutch	27	5	1	4	.185

1996 Season

Rookie righthander Jimmy Haynes spent most of 1996 shuffling in and out of the number-five slot in the Baltimore rotation. He started 11 games with little distinction before manager Davey Johnson opted to go with a four-man rotation. Haynes moved to the bullpen and was eventually sent to the minors.

Pitching & Defense

Haynes possesses a live low-90s fastball which has good movement and is an effective strikeout pitch. He also mixes in a big, looping curve and an occasional change-up and slider. Haynes had extensive control problems last season and his inability to get ahead of hitters eventually forced him out of the rotation. He is still trying to develop a slide-step from the set position to keep runners honest, but he has good mobility off the mound and is a solid fielder.

1997 Outlook

Haynes was supposed to be ready for the majors last year but obviously needed more seasoning. He attended the Arizona Fall League in the offseason to sharpen his skills and control, and will be given another opportunity to break into the rotation this spring.

Pete Incaviglia

Position: LF
Bats: R **Throws:** R
Ht: 6' 1" **Wt:** 225

Opening Day Age: 32
Born: 4/2/64 in Pebble Beach, CA
ML Seasons: 10
Pronunciation: in-ca-VEEL-ee-uh
Nickname: Inky

Overall Statistics

	G	AB	R	H	D	T	HR	RBI	SB	BB	SO	Avg	OBP	Slg
1996	111	302	37	73	9	2	18	50	2	30	89	.242	.318	.464
Career	1211	4049	527	1002	189	21	201	641	33	347	1221	.247	.311	.453

1996 Situational Stats

	AB	H	HR	RBI	Avg		AB	H	HR	RBI	Avg
Home	122	31	6	19	.254	LHP	74	26	8	19	.351
Road	180	42	12	31	.233	RHP	228	47	10	31	.206
First Half	216	55	14	37	.255	Sc Pos	91	20	8	38	.220
Scnd Half	86	18	4	13	.209	Clutch	56	10	0	3	.179

1996 Season

Joining the Orioles in a late-season trade with the Phillies, Pete Incaviglia provided a little help to an already stacked Baltimore lineup. After spending the 1995 season in Japan, Incaviglia had re-entered the majors with Philadelphia and, true to form, he was dynamic against left-handed pitching.

Hitting, Baserunning & Defense

Incaviglia is a straight inside fastball hitter. His problem is that most opponents will not pitch him there, making him a frequent strikeout victim. He hurts most southpaws who are forced to pitch inside to him, but struggles mightily against righthanders, frequently chasing the down-and-away slider. Incaviglia has limited mobility both in the field and on the basepaths. Although he does have a decent arm, it's not very accurate.

1997 Outlook

The Orioles have excellent depth in the outfield and more than likely will not be interested in signing the one-dimensional Incaviglia. Look for Inky to end up on a team that is looking for some inexpensive right-handed power. He is still capable of parking 20 home runs next season no matter where he winds up playing.

Rick Krivda

Position: SP/RP
Bats: R **Throws:** L
Ht: 6' 1" **Wt:** 180

Opening Day Age: 27
Born: 1/19/70 in
McKeesport, PA
ML Seasons: 2

Overall Statistics

	W	L	Pct.	ERA	G	GS	Sv	IP	H	BB	SO	HR	BR/IP
1996	3	5	.375	4.96	22	11	0	81.2	89	39	54	14	1.57
Career	5	12	.294	4.76	35	24	0	157.0	165	64	107	23	1.46

1996 Situational Stats

	W	L	ERA	Sv	IP		AB	H	HR	RBI	Avg
Home	1	3	5.49	0	41.0	LHB	52	15	0	3	.288
Road	2	2	4.43	0	40.2	RHB	263	74	14	37	.281
First Half	2	4	4.67	0	44.1	Sc Pos	68	22	3	27	.324
Scnd Half	1	1	5.30	0	37.1	Clutch	12	2	0	1	.167

1996 Season

Lefthander Rick Krivda has been trying for a couple of years to find a permanent spot in the Orioles' starting rotation. Krivda spent most of 1996 battling with Jimmy Haynes for the number-five starter's job, but he did his most effective work as a middle reliever.

Pitching & Defense

Krivda is a finesse pitcher whose main weapon is a big curveball which can be an excellent pitch when he's on target. He tries to establish his mid-80s fastball at the outset of each appearance, and he also throws a change-up to keep hitters honest. He tends to have problems with his control, and he also has a slow delivery which hurts his ability to control enemy basestealers. Krivda is a good fielding pitcher.

1997 Outlook

Krivda turns 27 years old this year, and he has yet to prove he has enough command to be successful in the majors. With his lack of both velocity and precision control, a finesse pitcher like Krivda may be destined for a career in the high minors. This spring will be crucial for him if he expects to establish a big league career.

Roger McDowell

Position: RP
Bats: B **Throws:** R
Ht: 6' 1" **Wt:** 195

Opening Day Age: 36
Born: 12/21/60 in
Cincinnati, OH
ML Seasons: 12

Overall Statistics

	W	L	Pct.	ERA	G	GS	Sv	IP	H	BB	SO	HR	BR/IP
1996	1	1	.500	4.25	41	0	4	59.1	69	23	20	7	1.55
Career	70	70	.500	3.30	723	2	159	1050.0	1045	410	524	50	1.39

1996 Situational Stats

	W	L	ERA	Sv	IP		AB	H	HR	RBI	Avg
Home	1	1	3.48	2	31.0	LHB	92	28	1	15	.304
Road	0	0	5.08	2	28.1	RHB	141	41	6	25	.291
First Half	1	1	3.66	3	51.2	Sc Pos	82	26	2	34	.317
Scnd Half	0	0	8.22	1	7.2	Clutch	93	26	4	17	.280

1996 Season

After a promising start to his season, arm problems caught up to Roger McDowell in 1996. He was on the disabled list twice and finally went out for good with a torn rotator cuff in mid August. The usually reliable McDowell allowed 15 of his last 27 inherited runners to score, evidence of how much his arm was bothering him.

Pitching & Defense

McDowell's effectiveness depends heavily on a high-80s fastball which runs in on the hands of right-handed hitters. He'll also throw a tight slider down and in to lefthanders. Although McDowell doesn't strike out a lot of batters, thanks to his sinker he keeps the ball down in the strike zone, resulting in a high amount of ground balls. McDowell does not have a particularly good pickoff move but fields his position adequately.

1997 Outlook

McDowell will be 36 and coming off arthroscopic surgery this spring, which raises questions about his future. But he has one thing in his favor: he works cheap. Whether or not he'll be re-signed in Baltimore, McDowell is an experienced reliever who should be available for a reasonable price—meaning he will be pitching somewhere in 1997.

Alan Mills

Position: RP
Bats: B **Throws:** R
Ht: 6' 1" **Wt:** 195

Opening Day Age: 30
Born: 10/18/66 in
Lakeland, FL
ML Seasons: 7

Overall Statistics

	W	L	Pct.	ERA	G	GS	Sv	IP	H	BB	SO	HR	BR/IP
1996	3	2	.600	4.28	49	0	3	54.2	40	35	50	10	1.37
Career	26	19	.578	3.84	239	5	11	384.2	335	223	273	45	1.45

1996 Situational Stats

	W	L	ERA	Sv	IP		AB	H	HR	RBI	Avg
Home	3	0	3.34	0	29.2	LHB	70	16	2	10	.229
Road	0	2	5.40	3	25.0	RHB	122	24	8	24	.197
First Half	1	0	4.66	1	19.1	Sc Pos	58	11	3	24	.190
Scnd Half	2	2	4.08	2	35.1	Clutch	76	20	6	25	.263

1996 Season

Alan Mills entered the 1996 season still trying to recover from the arthroscopic shoulder surgery he underwent late in 1995. It took him until May to get into his first game, and he was brought along slowly until late June, when he finally started to throw effectively. Mills proved to be an important reliever for the O's down the stretch, even serving as a closer on occasion.

Pitching & Defense

Mills' main weapon is what is known as "easy gas"—a mid-90s fastball that is thrown with a deceptively slow arm motion, but which explodes when it reaches the plate. He uses a hard slider as his second pitch, generating a fairly high percentage of strikeouts off it. Mills' main weakness is his control, since his failure to define the strike zone has resulted in a disturbing number of home runs. Mills does not hold runners especially well and is an average fielder.

1997 Outlook

Mills has shown he has made a full recovery from his 1995 surgery by regaining his arm speed and pitch velocity. He is likely to move into a more prominent set-up role next season if he can improve his control.

Arthur Rhodes

Position: RP
Bats: L **Throws:** L
Ht: 6' 2" **Wt:** 205

Opening Day Age: 27
Born: 10/24/69 in
Waco, TX
ML Seasons: 6

Overall Statistics

	W	L	Pct.	ERA	G	GS	Sv	IP	H	BB	SO	HR	BR/IP
1996	9	1	.900	4.08	28	2	1	53.0	48	23	62	6	1.34
Career	26	25	.510	5.49	97	61	1	397.0	392	211	335	53	1.52

1996 Situational Stats

	W	L	ERA	Sv	IP		AB	H	HR	RBI	Avg
Home	4	1	5.23	1	31.0	LHB	65	16	6	15	.246
Road	5	0	2.45	0	22.0	RHB	134	32	0	11	.239
First Half	9	0	3.47	1	49.1	Sc Pos	46	9	1	17	.196
Scnd Half	0	1	12.27	0	3.2	Clutch	60	5	0	0	.083

1996 Season

For the most part, Arthur Rhodes had a great year in 1996. He won his first nine decisions, eight of them coming out of the bullpen. Unfortunately for Rhodes, he missed most of the last two months of the season with inflammation in his left shoulder. He was able to return to the squad just prior to the playoffs, but was not a major contributor.

Pitching & Defense

Rhodes is a flame-throwing southpaw who can hit 95 MPH on the radar gun. As a reliever, he will limit his arsenal to fastballs and curves, but he can throw an occasional slider or change-up when called upon to start. He has alternated between the bullpen and the rotation for the last couple of years, but his repertoire makes him more valuable as a set-up man from the left side. Rhodes does not have a good pickoff move but is a decent fielding pitcher.

1997 Outlook

Dependable for quality middle-relief innings, Rhodes needs to stay healthy to build on what he established last season. He has found his niche in relief and will probably not be entering the rotation any time soon.

Other Baltimore Orioles

Manny Alexander (Pos: SS, Age: 26, Bats: R)

	G	AB	R	H	D	T	HR	RBI	SB	BB	SO	Avg	OBP	Slg
1996	53	68	6	7	0	0	0	4	3	3	27	.103	.141	.103
Career	154	315	43	65	9	1	3	27	14	23	60	.206	.265	.270

It took Alexander about two weeks as their starting shortstop to finally convince the Orioles that he'd been over-hyped. Baltimore seems to have come to its senses, and no one else is after him. 1997 Outlook: C

Archie Corbin (Pos: RHP, Age: 29)

	W	L	Pct.	ERA	G	GS	Sv	IP	H	BB	SO	HR	BR/IP
1996	2	0	1.000	2.30	18	0	0	27.1	22	22	20	2	1.61
Career	2	0	1.000	2.43	20	0	0	29.2	25	24	21	2	1.65

The 29-year-old rookie pitched decently in middle relief, but experienced his usual control lapses. He's too wild to hold a rotation spot or any significant role in the bullpen. 1997 Outlook: C

Cesar Devarez (Pos: C, Age: 27, Bats: R)

	G	AB	R	H	D	T	HR	RBI	SB	BB	SO	Avg	OBP	Slg
1996	10	18	3	2	0	1	0	0	0	1	3	.111	.158	.222
Career	16	22	3	2	0	1	0	0	0	1	3	.091	.130	.182

Devarez' one decent tool—his strong throwing arm—got him into 10 games last year, but he'll be lucky if he adds anything more to his career totals. 1997 Outlook: D

Todd Frohwirth (Pos: RHP, Age: 34)

	W	L	Pct.	ERA	G	GS	Sv	IP	H	BB	SO	HR	BR/IP
1996	0	0	-	11.12	4	0	0	5.2	10	4	1	1	2.47
Career	20	19	.513	3.60	284	0	11	417.2	389	172	259	23	1.34

The 34-year-old submariner made his first appearance in two years, and quickly showed why no one missed him. His delivery remains intriguing, but his effectiveness may be a thing of the past. 1997 Outlook: C

Jeff Huson (Pos: 2B, Age: 32, Bats: L)

	G	AB	R	H	D	T	HR	RBI	SB	BB	SO	Avg	OBP	Slg
1996	17	28	5	9	1	0	0	2	0	1	3	.321	.333	.357
Career	545	1332	182	315	47	11	7	106	48	152	171	.236	.314	.304

Huson's a left-handed-hitting utility infielder who's looking for his next bench gig. He'll probably find one, at least for a little while, but he'll never play regularly again. 1997 Outlook: C

Gene Kingsale (Pos: CF, Age: 20, Bats: B)

	G	AB	R	H	D	T	HR	RBI	SB	BB	SO	Avg	OBP	Slg
1996	3	0	0	0	0	0	0	0	0	0	0	-	-	-
Career	3	0	0	0	0	0	0	0	0	0	0	-	-	-

Kingsale came up directly from Class A at age 19 and got into three games without an at-bat. He has blinding speed but remains years away from playing center field in the majors. 1997 Outlook: C

Terry Mathews (Pos: RHP, Age: 32)

	W	L	Pct.	ERA	G	GS	Sv	IP	H	BB	SO	HR	BR/IP
1996	4	6	.400	4.52	71	0	4	73.2	79	34	62	10	1.53
Career	16	15	.516	4.06	226	4	8	299.0	296	119	232	32	1.39

The chinless middle reliever came over from the Marlins and became an important set-up man for the Orioles late in the year. He'll continue in that role for them—or somebody else. 1997 Outlook: A

Mike Milchin (Pos: LHP, Age: 29)

	W	L	Pct.	ERA	G	GS	Sv	IP	H	BB	SO	HR	BR/IP
1996	3	1	.750	7.44	39	0	0	32.2	44	17	29	6	1.87
Career	3	1	.750	7.44	39	0	0	32.2	44	17	29	6	1.87

The oft-injured minor league veteran finally surfaced, with awful results. He's a classic example of a pitcher who would be selling insurance if he were right-handed. 1997 Outlook: C

Jimmy Myers (Pos: RHP, Age: 27)

	W	L	Pct.	ERA	G	GS	Sv	IP	H	BB	SO	HR	BR/IP
1996	0	0	-	7.07	11	0	0	14.0	18	3	6	4	1.50
Career	0	0	-	7.07	11	0	0	14.0	18	3	6	4	1.50

Four years ago, Myers was demoted from closer to middle reliever—while pitching in Double-A. The fact that the Orioles used the 27-year-old right-hander 11 times last year shows their desperation. 1997 Outlook: D

Mark Parent (Pos: C, Age: 35, Bats: R)

	G	AB	R	H	D	T	HR	RBI	SB	BB	SO	Avg	OBP	Slg
1996	56	137	17	31	7	0	9	23	0	5	37	.226	.252	.474
Career	401	1077	101	237	43	0	52	147	2	81	250	.220	.274	.405

Parent means power: powerful bat; powerful arm. But Parent also means slow—slow enough to be your grandparent, and almost old enough, too (35). He's probably done enough to remain a backup, for now. 1997 Outlook: B

Billy Ripken (Pos: 2B/3B, Age: 32, Bats: R)

	G	AB	R	H	D	T	HR	RBI	SB	BB	SO	Avg	OBP	Slg
1996	57	135	19	31	8	0	2	12	0	9	18	.230	.281	.333
Career	814	2452	261	598	109	5	17	200	22	160	290	.244	.293	.313

By now, everyone knows that Billy is all leather and no wood. The presence of Roberto Alomar limits his usefulness, but he may find a role if they move his brother to third base as planned. 1997 Outlook: B

Brian Sackinsky (Pos: RHP, Age: 25)

	W	L	Pct.	ERA	G	GS	Sv	IP	H	BB	SO	HR	BR/IP
1996	0	0	-	3.86	3	0	0	4.2	6	3	2	1	1.93
Career	0	0	-	3.86	3	0	0	4.2	6	3	2	1	1.93

Recovering from arm woes, the 26-year-old sinker/slider pitcher got a short look in September. He's not overpowering, and his weight is a concern. Success in Triple-A may get him a look. 1997 Outlook: B

Keith Shepherd (Pos: RHP, Age: 29)

	W	L	Pct.	ERA	G	GS	Sv	IP	H	BB	SO	HR	BR/IP
1996	0	1	.000	8.71	13	0	0	20.2	31	18	17	6	2.37
Career	2	5	.286	6.71	41	1	3	63.0	80	30	34	10	1.75

The Red Sox liked him, but shoulder problems ruined his chance there. Now 29, working on his fourth team. He gets strikeouts but needs to find a role. 1997 Outlook: C

Mark Smith (Pos: LF, Age: 26, Bats: R)

	G	AB	R	H	D	T	HR	RBI	SB	BB	SO	Avg	OBP	Slg
1996	27	78	9	19	2	0	4	10	0	3	20	.244	.298	.423
Career	67	189	20	44	7	0	7	27	3	15	44	.233	.301	.381

Smith began to tap his latent power last year, and likely earned a shot with the O's. He's a corner outfielder or DH, but hits enough to be useful. Baltimore seems to have plans for him. 1997 Outlook: B

Tony Tarasco (Pos: RF, Age: 26, Bats: L)

	G	AB	R	H	D	T	HR	RBI	SB	BB	SO	Avg	OBP	Slg
1996	31	84	14	20	3	0	1	9	5	7	15	.238	.297	.310
Career	268	689	100	173	29	4	20	70	34	67	115	.251	.318	.392

It was a long fall from starting left fielder in Baltimore, to Triple-A, to the disabled list for most of the second half. Tarasco has good tools and may turn out to be a good acquisition. 1997 Outlook: A

Esteban Yan (Pos: RHP, Age: 22)

	W	L	Pct.	ERA	G	GS	Sv	IP	H	BB	SO	HR	BR/IP
1996	0	0	-	5.79	4	0	0	9.1	13	3	7	3	1.71
Career	0	0	-	5.79	4	0	0	9.1	13	3	7	3	1.71

The young righthander has good control and gets strikeouts but still needs to find a role. A full year of Triple-A is probably in order. Yan has good upside potential if the O's can decide what to do with him. 1997 Outlook: C

Baltimore Orioles

Baltimore Orioles Minor League Prospects

Organization Overview:

The Orioles' lack of emphasis on scouting has left them with one of the most talent-poor farm systems in the majors. That talent void left them in the lurch during their pennant push when they attempted to make late-season deals for veteran help. Ultimately, they had to settle for Todd Zeile and Terry Mathews, but surrendered three of their best farmhands in the process, further eroding their meager corps of prospects. In recent years, graduates of the Baltimore system have been disappointing, due to injuries, immaturity and misjudgment of their skills. Meanwhile, the front office has emphasized building through free agency, cutting off opportunities for its youngsters. Their talent in the higher levels of the system is confined to the corner positions, where the major league club is already well-stocked. Further down, there are some promising arms, but it may be a while before anyone makes a major impact at the major league level.

Brent Bowers

Position: OF
Bats: L **Throws:** R
Ht: 6' 3" **Wt:** 200

Opening Day Age: 25
Born: 5/2/71 in Oak Lawn, IL

Recent Statistics

	G	AB	R	H	D	T	HR	RBI	SB	BB	SO	AVG
96 AA Bowie	58	228	37	71	11	1	9	25	10	17	40	.311
96 AAA Rochester	49	206	40	67	8	4	4	19	9	14	41	.325
96 AL Baltimore	21	39	6	12	2	0	0	3	0	0	7	.308
96 MLE	107	425	68	129	17	2	11	39	14	25	86	.304

After wearing out his welcome in the Toronto system, Bowers really put it together in '96. A hot start at Double-A Bowie brought a mid-season promotion to Triple-A, and the Orioles brought him up for a look in August. He can cover all three outfield spots, and he showed good range in center field in the minors. His strong arm is an asset, and he has the speed to cover more than enough ground. At the plate, he's impatient but makes good contact. He's a left-handed hitter, so if his sudden emergence isn't a fluke, he'll be able to help the Orioles as a fourth outfielder or platoon player.

Danny Clyburn

Position: OF-DH
Bats: R **Throws:** R
Ht: 6' 3" **Wt:** 217

Opening Day Age: 22
Born: 4/6/74 in Lancaster, SC

Recent Statistics

	G	AB	R	H	D	T	HR	RBI	SB	BB	SO	AVG
93 A Augusta	127	457	55	121	21	4	9	66	5	37	97	.265
94 A Salem	118	461	57	126	19	0	22	90	4	20	96	.273
95 A Winston-Sal	59	227	27	59	10	2	11	41	2	13	59	.260
95 A Frederick	15	45	4	9	4	0	0	4	1	4	18	.200
95 A High Desert	45	160	20	45	3	1	12	37	2	17	41	.281
96 AA Bowie	95	365	51	92	14	5	18	55	4	17	88	.252
96 MLE	95	358	45	85	12	3	17	49	3	13	95	.237

With impressive strengths but obvious flaws, it's not hard to see why Clyburn is currently in his third organization. His power is his one big tool, and it will have to carry him. Despite his other shortcomings, it may: he's big and strong, and when he connects, the ball jumps. The downside is that he hasn't learned to control his impulse to swing at everything. He's an awful outfielder as well, so improving his selectivity at the plate will be the key to his advancement.

Tommy Davis

Position: 1B
Bats: R **Throws:** R
Ht: 6' 1" **Wt:** 195

Opening Day Age: 23
Born: 5/21/73 in Mobile, AL

Recent Statistics

	G	AB	R	H	D	T	HR	RBI	SB	BB	SO	AVG
94 A Albany	61	216	35	59	10	1	5	35	2	18	52	.273
95 A Frederick	130	496	62	133	26	3	15	57	7	41	105	.268
95 AA Bowie	9	32	5	10	3	0	3	10	0	1	9	.313
96 AA Bowie	137	524	75	137	32	2	14	54	5	41	113	.261
96 MLE	137	513	67	126	29	1	13	48	3	31	122	.246

The Orioles' top pick in the 1994 draft (second round) hasn't quite developed into the power hitter they envisioned. Still, he remains a good gap hitter and one of the best power prospects in the system. He handled first base adequately after defensive shortcomings at third base forced a move across the diamond. He has little speed, so to make it, he'll have to turn some of those doubles into home runs.

Chris Fussell

Position: P
Bats: R **Throws:** R
Ht: 6' 2" **Wt:** 185

Opening Day Age: 20
Born: 5/19/76 in Oregon, OH

Recent Statistics

	W	L	ERA	G	GS	Sv	IP	H	R	BB	SO	HR
94 R Orioles	2	3	4.15	14	8	0	56.1	53	30	24	65	2
95 R Bluefield	9	1	2.19	12	12	0	65.2	37	18	32	98	4
96 A Frederick	5	2	2.81	15	14	0	86.1	71	36	44	94	4

Fussell is a young flamethrower with excellent stuff. Not only does he have a good moving fastball and a good breaking ball, but he possesses uncommon command for someone so young. He missed time with injuries last year, but was still able to make the jump from Rookie League to A-Ball. Against the more advanced competition, he still kept his strikeout rate over one per inning. He's still very young, but he may come quickly.

Scott McClain

Position: 3B
Bats: R **Throws:** R
Ht: 6' 3" **Wt:** 209

Opening Day Age: 24
Born: 5/19/72 in Simi Valley, CA

Recent Statistics

	G	AB	R	H	D	T	HR	RBI	SB	BB	SO	AVG
93 A Frederick	133	427	65	111	22	2	9	54	10	70	88	.260
94 AA Bowie	133	427	71	103	29	1	11	58	6	72	89	.241
95 AAA Rochester	61	199	32	50	9	1	8	22	0	23	34	.251
95 AA Bowie	70	259	41	72	14	1	13	61	2	25	44	.278
96 AAA Rochester	131	463	76	130	23	4	17	69	8	61	109	.281
96 MLE	131	453	68	120	21	2	16	62	6	54	115	.265

McClain is only 25, but he's been waiting for several years for a shot at the Orioles' third base job. Unfortunately, he's in danger of being passed by Otanez. Despite his slowness afoot, McClain has excellent range in the field and plays good overall defense. He's a big, strong hitter who just might hit for enough power to hold a major league job. To become a stronger candidate for a position, he must bump up his production at the plate another notch.

Willis Otanez

Position: 3B
Bats: R **Throws:** R
Ht: 5' 11" **Wt:** 150

Opening Day Age: 23
Born: 4/19/73 in Las Matas De Cotui, DR

Recent Statistics

	G	AB	R	H	D	T	HR	RBI	SB	BB	SO	AVG
93 A Bakersfield	95	325	34	85	11	2	10	39	1	29	63	.262
94 A Vero Beach	131	476	77	132	27	1	19	72	4	53	98	.277
95 A Vero Beach	92	354	39	92	24	0	10	53	1	28	59	.260
95 AA San Antonio	27	100	8	24	4	1	1	7	0	6	25	.240
96 AA Bowie	138	506	60	134	27	2	24	75	3	45	97	.265
96 MLE	138	496	53	124	24	1	23	67	2	34	104	.250

Otanez, a wiry, young third baseman, filled out a little more in '96. As a result, his power numbers progressed to the point where he has to be taken seriously as a prospect. He can put a charge into the ball, but has to work on cutting his strikeouts and making better contact. He can handle the leather at third, showing decent range and above-average tools. Of all the power prospects in the system, he's the one who could make the biggest immediate impact.

Nerio Rodriguez

Position: P
Bats: R **Throws:** R
Ht: 6' 1" **Wt:** 195

Opening Day Age: 24
Born: 3/22/73 in Bani, DR

Recent Statistics

	W	L	ERA	G	GS	Sv	IP	H	R	BB	SO	HR
96 A Frederick	8	7	2.26	24	17	2	111.1	83	42	40	114	10
96 AAA Rochester	1	0	1.80	2	2	0	15.0	10	3	2	6	0
96 AL Baltimore	0	1	4.32	8	1	0	16.2	18	11	7	12	2

Rodriguez took the short route to the majors last year. He dominated the Carolina League for most of the season, and when Baltimore GM Pat Gillick was looking for an extra pitcher in August, he called up Rodriguez directly to the majors. In eight games with Baltimore, Rodriguez used his good fastball and command to fan 12 batters in 16.2 innings. At age 23, he was a little advanced for A-ball, and his handling and performance indicate that he'll be on the fast track to the majors.

B.J. Waszgis

Position: C
Bats: R **Throws:** R
Ht: 6' 2" **Wt:** 210

Opening Day Age: 26
Born: 8/24/70 in Omaha, NE

Recent Statistics

	G	AB	R	H	D	T	HR	RBI	SB	BB	SO	AVG
93 A Frederick	31	109	12	27	4	0	3	9	1	9	30	.248
93 A Albany	86	300	45	92	25	3	8	52	4	27	55	.307
94 A Frederick	122	426	76	120	16	3	21	100	6	65	94	.282
95 AA Bowie	130	438	53	111	22	0	10	50	2	70	91	.253
96 AAA Rochester	96	304	37	81	16	0	11	48	2	41	87	.266
96 MLE	96	298	33	75	14	0	10	43	1	36	92	.252

Waszgis is too old to be considered a top prospect, but his skills would make him a capable backup catcher. He's got decent power for a backstop, and he's patient enough to work a walk. The combination makes him a fairly productive hitter, despite an unimpressive batting average. His defense is nothing special, but it won't keep him from getting an opportunity in the majors.

Others to Watch

The presence of **Melvin Rosario** enabled the Orioles to deal Greg Zaun late in the year. Rosario is playing for his third organization, but he came into his own last year. The switch-hitting receiver batted .310 in the California League to earn a midseason promotion to Double-A. His hitting dropped off after the promotion, but he still got a quick look at Triple-A at season's end. . . Righthander **Sidney Ponson** has emerged as one of the top prospects in the system. Ponson throws in the low-90s with good control, and could be up by the end of the year. . . **Calvin Pickering** is a big first baseman who put up even bigger numbers in Rookie ball last year. The left-handed hitter showed devastating power and led the Appalachian League with a .325 average. . . A couple of rungs ahead of Pickering was another lefty-swinging first sacker, **Chris Kirgan**. Kirgan led the California League with 35 home runs and 131 RBI, and batted .297 for the season. . . Center fielder **David Dellucci** batted .324 at Class A Frederick in the first half, and hit .291 in Double-A after a midseason promotion. The left-handed hitter will be only 23 this season, and could develop into a top-of-the-order hitter.

Jimy Williams

1996 Season

A longtime protege of Braves manager Bobby Cox, Jimy Williams has spent the last seven seasons as Cox' third-base coach. Prior to that he had succeeded Cox as the Blue Jays' manager in 1986. Williams was in a difficult situation, replacing a franchise giant, and when his authority—and that of general manager Pat Gillick—was challenged by veterans like Damaso Garcia and George Bell, the Toronto top brass stabbed him in the back. Williams never got another chance.

Offense

Williams enjoys being thought of as unpredictable when it comes to offensive strategy, whether it be in sending runners or in calling for the hit-and-run. He tries to outwit his opponent often by doing the unexpected. This measure of creativity can also cause some embarrassing plays, which got him into trouble in Toronto. One has to excel to become an everyday player for Williams because he likes to tinker with his lineup, and that means a lot of platooning for those who are not producing on a regular basis.

Pitching & Defense

One of Williams' problems in Toronto was that he was overanxious and got pitchers up and down too much in the bullpen. He learned from that experience and his new pitching coach, Joe Kerrigan, should be able to help him. He is as unconventional in his defensive strategy as he is on offense. He will move defenses around from pitch to pitch, daring to employ the unusual. He even created spring training drills to help outfielders like Otis Nixon learn to climb walls.

1997 Outlook

Williams has dealt with impossible expectations before, and a decade after his stint in Toronto, his reputation in the baseball community is more firmly established. Managing the Red Sox is never easy, but Williams is under little pressure from G.M. Dan Duquette, who feels Williams is the best man to simultaneously contend and develop.

Born: 10/04/43 in Santa Maria, CA

Playing Experience: 1966-1967, StL

Managerial Experience: 4 seasons

Manager Statistics

Year Team, Lg	W	L	Pct	GB	Finish
— —	—	—	—	—	—
4 Seasons	281	241	.538	—	—

1996 Starting Pitchers by Days Rest

	≤3	4	5	6+
Red Sox Starts	—	—	—	—
Red Sox ERA	—	—	—	—
AL Avg Starts	4	96	30	21
AL ERA	5.57	4.90	5.33	5.81

1996 Situational Stats

	Jimy Williams	AL Average
Hit & Run Success %	—	39.1
Stolen Base Success %	—	69.6
Platoon Pct.	—	61.9
Defensive Subs	—	29
High-Pitch Outings	—	23
Quick/Slow Hooks	—	17/20
Sacrifice Attempts	—	58

1996 Rankings (National League)

➡ Did not manage in the majors last year

Darren Bragg

1996 Season

The Red Sox acquired Darren Bragg from the Mariners July 30 for Jamie Moyer. While Moyer helped Seattle greatly, Bragg quickly became a sort of B-version Lenny Dykstra in Boston. The stocky, aggressive outfielder—a baseball and football foe of Mo Vaughn when Bragg was at the Taft School and Vaughn at Trinity Pawling—injected life into the slumbering Red Sox with his diving catches and fearlessness.

Hitting

Braggs is a tough out, a line-drive hitter similar to Jim Eisenreich. He is strong and has surprising power. He quickly learned to use Fenway, banging balls away from him to left field and pulling breaking balls into the open spaces in right and right-center. Bragg is a dead fastball hitter, and though he played every day, he struggled against left-handed pitching.

Baserunning & Defense

Because the Red Sox had run out of patience with the Hoseys, Coles and Cuylers, Bragg stepped in and played primarily in center for Boston. While he plays hard, catches the ball, positions himself well and has an average arm, he lacks the raw speed to play there regularly. He played well in right field, and may well end up being used as a platoon utility man who plays all three positions. Bragg has good baserunning speed and will use his body to break up the double play. He is a stolen base threat as well.

1997 Outlook

The Red Sox, who started the season with middle-of-the-lineup hitters like Will Cordero and Mike Greenwell at the front of the order, badly needed what Bragg brought to them. Though he struggled against lefties, he pounded righthanders. That should ensure that he will get at least a chance to platoon for Boston in 1997.

Position: LF/CF/RF
Bats: L **Throws:** R
Ht: 5' 9" **Wt:** 180

Opening Day Age: 27
Born: 9/7/69 in Waterbury, CT
ML Seasons: 3

Boston Red Sox

Overall Statistics

	G	AB	R	H	D	T	HR	RBI	SB	BB	SO	Avg	OBP	Slg
1996	127	417	74	109	26	2	10	47	14	69	74	.261	.366	.405
Career	187	581	98	146	32	3	13	61	23	89	116	.251	.354	.384

Where He Hits the Ball

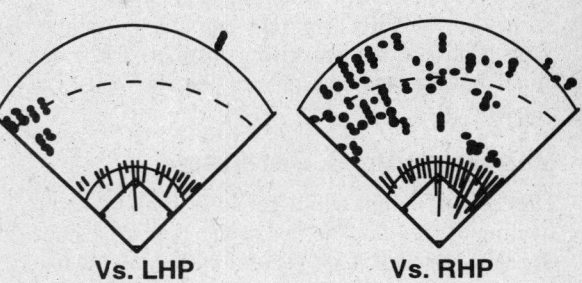

Vs. LHP   **Vs. RHP**

1996 Situational Stats

	AB	H	HR	RBI	Avg		AB	H	HR	RBI	Avg
Home	231	62	7	29	.268	LHP	84	16	1	7	.190
Road	186	47	3	18	.253	RHP	333	93	9	40	.279
First Half	157	42	7	19	.268	Sc Pos	87	24	3	37	.276
Scnd Half	260	67	3	28	.258	Clutch	51	15	0	6	.294

1996 Rankings (American League)

➡ 4th in lowest stolen base percentage (60.9%)
➡ 9th in highest percentage of pitches taken (61.1%)
➡ 10th in caught stealing (9)
➡ Led the Red Sox in on-base percentage for a leadoff hitter (.370)

Jose Canseco

1996 Season

There is a buzz that comes over the park when Jose Canseco steps to the plate, and he still has the extraordinary bat speed that makes him so terribly dangerous. The problem is that he keeps breaking down with injuries. Last April, Canseco was disabled with a hip flexor muscle strain. Then in late July, the back that had bothered him on and off for years blew out and required surgery. As a result he was limited to 96 games and only 360 at-bats.

Hitting

Canseco is still a dead-red hitter who looks fastball and can catch up to most of them. Some pitchers jam him, go up the ladder or try to get him out with breaking balls away when he gets down in the count, but he kills anything less than a quality pitch. Canseco has surprising instincts for situational hitting, and has proven that he will give himself up.

Baserunning & Defense

The loss of weight could get Jose thinking about stealing bases again, but it's been a long time since Canseco ran well. Last year he broke down when he played the outfield, but if his neck doesn't bother him, he could play left field in Fenway Park. Canseco can catch the balls he gets to, and while his arm is a shell of what it was when he broke in, he still can throw decently.

1997 Outlook

To his credit, when most of his teammates and the media doubted they would see him again, Canseco returned when the Red Sox snuck back into contention in September. He began his winter training assuring the Red Sox that his back was in its best shape since high school. We'll see; Canseco has missed more than 200 games over the last five years, and hasn't played 120 games since Fay Vincent was commissioner.

Position: DH
Bats: R **Throws:** R
Ht: 6' 4" **Wt:** 240

Opening Day Age: 32
Born: 7/2/64 in Havana, Cuba
ML Seasons: 12
Pronunciation: can-SAY-co

Overall Statistics

	G	AB	R	H	D	T	HR	RBI	SB	BB	SO	Avg	OBP	Slg
1996	96	360	68	104	22	1	28	82	3	63	82	.289	.400	.589
Career	1341	5071	864	1379	251	13	328	1033	156	623	1349	.272	.355	.521

Where He Hits the Ball

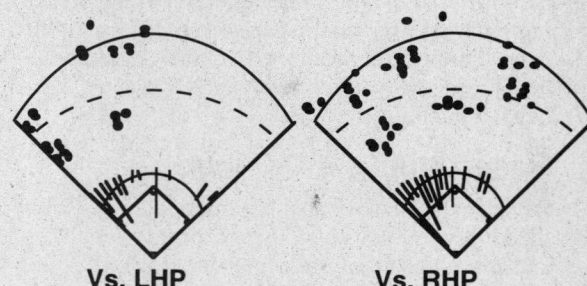

Vs. LHP   Vs. RHP

1996 Situational Stats

	AB	H	HR	RBI	Avg		AB	H	HR	RBI	Avg
Home	170	53	17	41	.312	LHP	95	31	6	23	.326
Road	190	51	11	41	.268	RHP	265	73	22	59	.275
First Half	275	84	26	63	.305	Sc Pos	117	31	8	56	.265
Scnd Half	85	20	2	19	.235	Clutch	68	18	5	14	.265

1996 Rankings (American League)

➞ 5th in cleanup slugging percentage (.599)
➞ 10th in batting average on an 0-2 count (.280)
➞ Led the Red Sox in least GDPs per GDP situation (6.2%)

Roger Clemens

1996 Season

Forget the 10-13 record, or the fact that Roger Clemens is 40-39 the last four years. In the second half of the 1996 season, it was clear that Clemens was as dominant as he was at the turn of the decade. He was 6-2, 2.09 in his last 10 starts, and after the All-Star break struck out 123 men in 111.1 innings. With better run support and a better bullpen, he could have won 16-18 games.

Pitching

Several factors converged to return Clemens to dominance. He slowed his mechanics back down. He was healthy. Catcher Bill Haselman helped make his forkball far more effective by setting up either inside or way outside, getting Roger to stay away from the middle of the plate. Often, when Haselman set up inside, hitters would guess fastball and end up swinging at split-fingered fastballs. Clemens still throws 94-95 MPH, and while many consider him to be a high fastball pitcher, what is remarkable about him is that despite all the strikeouts, he is really a sinkerball pitcher. His 1.68 groundball/flyball ratio was one of the best in the league.

Defense

Clemens works very hard at his fielding, and after a key error in September, was out working on fundamentals between starts. He holds the ball and uses a slide-step, and his high opponent steal totals are more a reflection of two factors—catchers with throwing problems and his concern with finishing hitters.

1997 Outlook

The longtime ace of the Red Sox went into the market seeking a four-year deal coming off that 40-39 four-year record. He might get it, because the way he threw at the end of the season indicated that he was back to being one of the game's few dominant power pitchers. The Red Sox were hoping to keep him, but they knew they'd be in a bidding war.

Position: SP
Bats: R **Throws:** R
Ht: 6' 4" **Wt:** 230

Opening Day Age: 34
Born: 8/4/62 in Dayton, OH
ML Seasons: 13
Nickname: Rocket

Overall Statistics

	W	L	Pct.	ERA	G	GS	Sv	IP	H	BB	SO	HR	BR/IP
1996	10	13	.435	3.63	34	34	0	242.2	216	106	257	19	1.33
Career	192	111	.634	3.06	383	382	0	2776.0	2359	856	2590	194	1.16

How Often He Throws Strikes

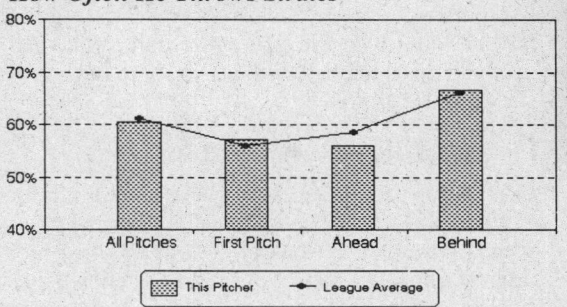

This Pitcher / League Average

1996 Situational Stats

	W	L	ERA	Sv	IP		AB	H	HR	RBI	Avg
Home	5	4	3.45	0	107.0	LHB	513	121	10	59	.236
Road	5	9	3.78	0	135.2	RHB	398	95	9	35	.239
First Half	3	8	4.04	0	131.1	Sc Pos	221	44	1	64	.199
Scnd Half	7	5	3.15	0	111.1	Clutch	94	27	4	16	.287

1996 Rankings (American League)

→ 1st in strikeouts, pitches thrown (4,260), most pitches thrown per batter (4.13) and most strikeouts per 9 innings (9.5)

→ 2nd in walks allowed, stolen bases allowed (30), lowest batting average allowed (.237) and lowest slugging percentage allowed (.358)

→ 3rd in runners caught stealing (13), least run support per 9 innings (4.3), least home runs allowed per 9 innings (.70) and lowest batting average allowed with runners in scoring position

→ 4th in complete games (6), shutouts (2) and lowest batting average allowed vs. left-handed batters

Wil Cordero

Position: 2B/DH
Bats: R **Throws:** R
Ht: 6' 2" **Wt:** 195

Opening Day Age: 25
Born: 10/3/71 in
Mayaguez, PR
ML Seasons: 5
Pronunciation:
cor-DAIR-oh

1996 Season

The trade for Montreal's Wil Cordero turned out to be one of the undoings of the 1996 Red Sox and manager Kevin Kennedy. Kennedy, coach Tim Johnson and Dan Duquette—all of whom knew Cordero from Montreal—thought he could be made into a second baseman. He couldn't. At the plate, Cordero started the season slowly but had raised his average to .287 when he fractured his right tibia on May 20. By the time he returned on August 12, Jeff Frye had taken his second base job.

Hitting

The Red Sox feel that healthy, Cordero will hit and produce. At 25, he is a .279 lifetime hitter who will likely grow stronger and stronger. He is a good fastball hitter who uses the entire field, so he can wait and drive the ball with authority to the opposite field.

Baserunning & Defense

During his first couple of years in Montreal, Cordero was a stolen base threat and he had good speed. However, he has all but abandoned any such notions the last two seasons. Felipe Alou always felt that first base or left field were Cordero's natural positions, as he has slow feet, poor range and a bad shoulder which has needed surgery. The Red Sox coaching staff felt that he lacked two of the most important requirements for playing second: quick feet and a strong arm with multiple release points. They may have to put him either at third base, where he can use his soft hands, in left field or at DH.

1997 Outlook

The Red Sox feel that Cordero can hit 20 homers and knock in 100 runs this season if he is healthy. The fact that his contract will be up has something to do with that, of course. He is at the age when many hitters begin to develop power, and a big season is possible if they can find a place for him to play.

Overall Statistics

	G	AB	R	H	D	T	HR	RBI	SB	BB	SO	Avg	OBP	Slg
1996	59	198	29	57	14	0	3	37	2	11	31	.288	.330	.404
Career	483	1728	231	482	115	8	40	215	39	131	272	.279	.337	.424

Where He Hits the Ball

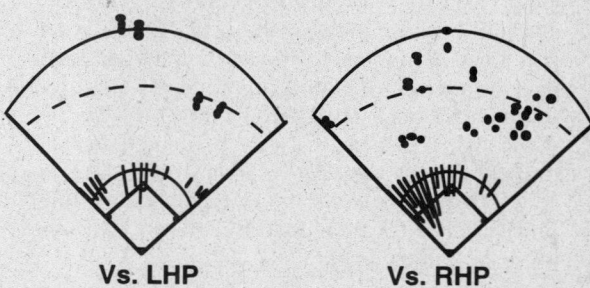

Vs. LHP   **Vs. RHP**

1996 Situational Stats

	AB	H	HR	RBI	Avg		AB	H	HR	RBI	Avg
Home	101	31	2	19	.307	LHP	59	14	0	10	.237
Road	97	26	1	18	.268	RHP	139	43	3	27	.309
First Half	157	45	2	28	.287	Sc Pos	60	22	0	32	.367
Scnd Half	41	12	1	9	.293	Clutch	38	16	1	15	.421

1996 Rankings (American League)

➡ 2nd in batting average with the bases loaded (.615)
➡ 9th in errors at second base (10)
➡ Led the Red Sox in batting average with the bases loaded (.615)

Jeff Frye

1996 Season

With Wil Cordero injured, Luis Alicea released and Jeff Manto hurt, the Red Sox took Kevin Kennedy's advice and rescued Jeff Frye from the Rangers' Triple-A Oklahoma City farm team last June. Given a new life, Frye played very well in Boston and gave them some juice up at the front of the order. When Darren Bragg came over and moved into the leadoff spot, Frye did an excellent job as a patient number-two hitter. After months of wild swingers up at the top of the order in front of Mo Vaughn, Frye and Bragg worked in tandem to reach base and work pitchers.

Hitting

Even though he takes a lot of pitches, the 5-9, 165-pound Frye is a dangerous high fastball hitter. He will push balls to right field and fight off inside fastballs, handling righthanders nearly as well as he handles lefties. He used the room in Fenway's right field to his advantage, often going the opposite way against righties. He is also a good bunter.

Baserunning & Defense

Frye does not have Roberto Alomar's skills at second base, but he has good hands and—more important on a groundball staff such as Boston's—can turn the tough double play. He also is a good athlete who can fill in a shortstop and play very well in the outfield, where he started five games split between left, center and right. A fine baserunner with good speed, he had the best year of his career on the basepaths with 18 steals in 22 attempts.

1997 Outlook

Projected over 150 games, Frye would have scored 106 runs last year. It is expected that he will fit right in with Jimy Williams, a believer in defensive positioning and studying opposing teams' tendencies, which Frye likes to do.

Position: 2B
Bats: R **Throws:** R
Ht: 5' 9" **Wt:** 165

Opening Day Age: 30
Born: 8/31/66 in Oakland, CA
ML Seasons: 4

Overall Statistics

	G	AB	R	H	D	T	HR	RBI	SB	BB	SO	Avg	OBP	Slg
1996	105	419	74	120	27	2	4	41	18	54	57	.286	.372	.389
Career	319	1136	173	325	71	8	9	100	28	123	152	.286	.360	.386

Where He Hits the Ball

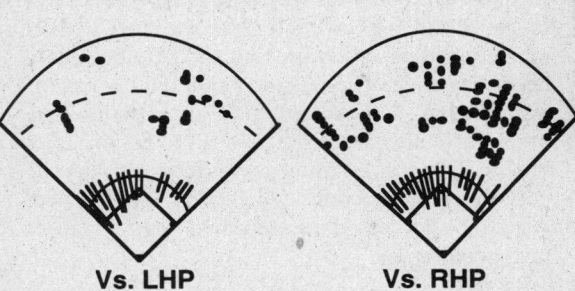

Vs. LHP   **Vs. RHP**

1996 Situational Stats

	AB	H	HR	RBI	Avg		AB	H	HR	RBI	Avg
Home	217	60	3	17	.276	LHP	121	33	0	11	.273
Road	202	60	1	24	.297	RHP	298	87	4	30	.292
First Half	116	26	0	8	.224	Sc Pos	87	23	1	33	.264
Scnd Half	303	94	4	33	.310	Clutch	51	11	0	9	.216

1996 Rankings (American League)

➡ 3rd in highest percentage of pitches taken (64.9%)
➡ 4th in stolen base percentage (81.8%)
➡ 6th in fielding percentage at second base (.983) and lowest percentage of swings that missed (9.2%)
➡ 8th in steals of third (4)
➡ 9th in lowest on-base percentage for a leadoff hitter (.354)
➡ 10th in batting average with two strikes (.262) and errors at second base (9)
➡ Led the Red Sox in stolen bases, stolen base percentage (81.8%), batting average with two strikes (.262), highest percentage of pitches taken (64.9%) and steals of third (4)

Tom Gordon

1996 Season

Few pitchers more frustrate managers than Tom Gordon. He can look like an All-Star one start, then walk the bases loaded in the first inning the next time out, or another night go six hitless innings and unravel. Going 12-9 in his first season with the Red Sox is misleading, because the Red Sox scored an astounding 7.34 runs per start for the 28-year-old veteran. It got so frustrating at one point that Kevin Kennedy considered using Gordon as a closer to try to get him to focus on his one power pitch.

Pitching

The great curveball is there, and Gordon has a nice second curveball with which he can throw strikes to get ahead. His fastball is in the 86-87 MPH range, but it has good life and sink. He definitely needs a change of some kind to get lefthanders off his curveball: lefties whacked Gordon to the tune of .301. He also needs better ways to get ahead of hitters. There is an immense difference when he gets ahead in the count: .212 ahead, .308 behind. Also to be addressed are Gordon's frequent lapses in concentration.

Defense

Gordon is small and an excellent athlete, and is, at worst, an average fielder. Because of his curveball and the leg swing in his delivery, he can be run on (17 steals, 5 caught stealing). But he does a decent job holding the ball and quickening his delivery to the plate, so those 17 steals are about average.

1997 Outlook

The man is strong. Gordon averaged 110 pitches per start and was tough in the 76-90 pitch area. But he makes too many mistakes for anyone with his stuff to be the top-of-the-rotation starter his arm says he should be. Now there is a new manager and new pitching coach in Boston, and they, too, will concentrate on trying to unlock the mystery of this million-dollar arm.

Position: SP
Bats: R **Throws:** R
Ht: 5' 9" **Wt:** 180

Opening Day Age: 29
Born: 11/18/67 in Sebring, FL
ML Seasons: 9

Overall Statistics

	W	L	Pct.	ERA	G	GS	Sv	IP	H	BB	SO	HR	BR/IP
1996	12	9	.571	5.59	34	34	0	215.2	249	105	171	28	1.64
Career	91	80	.532	4.27	308	178	3	1365.1	1289	692	1170	119	1.45

How Often He Throws Strikes

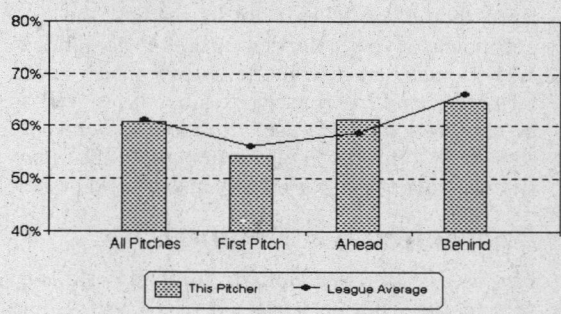

1996 Situational Stats

	W	L	ERA	Sv	IP		AB	H	HR	RBI	Avg
Home	6	4	5.36	0	131.0	LHB	478	144	15	62	.301
Road	6	5	5.95	0	84.2	RHB	398	105	13	59	.264
First Half	6	4	6.20	0	106.0	Sc Pos	238	58	8	88	.244
Scnd Half	6	5	5.01	0	109.2	Clutch	41	14	1	8	.341

1996 Rankings (American League)

→ 1st in most run support per 9 innings (7.3)
→ 2nd in highest ERA and least GDPs induced per 9 innings (0.5)
→ 3rd in walks allowed, most baserunners allowed per 9 innings (14.9) and errors at pitcher (3)
→ 5th in highest ERA on the road
→ 6th in shutouts (1), hits allowed and highest on-base percentage allowed (.359)
→ 7th in highest groundball/flyball ratio allowed (1.5), most strikeouts per 9 innings (7.1) and highest ERA at home
→ 8th in batters faced (998), strikeouts, pitches thrown (3,785) and highest slugging percentage allowed (.455)

Mike Greenwell

1996 Season

Back in the late 1980s, it looked as if Mike Greenwell was going to be a contender to what was then Don Mattingly's throne. Greenwell hit over .300, he belted over 20 homers, he knocked in 119 runs in 1988. But when 1996 ended, the hard-nosed 33-year-old Greenwell was at a stage when he was saying good-bye to Boston and knowing that he had to resurrect his career.

Hitting

Greenwell doesn't have the lightning-quick bat he possessed in his best years, but he is still a good fastball hitter who, because he always used the whole field, can drive the ball with authority to the alleys. He hasn't hit for much power the last few seasons, but if he is sitting on a fastball or gets the head out early on a breaking ball up, he can still pull the ball with power. He hangs in against lefties, carving the ball to the opposite field. However, he is prone to swinging at first pitches out of the strike zone because he is so aggressive.

Baserunning & Defense

The subtle parts of the game are not Greenwell's strong suits. While he tries hard in the outfield, he is a below-average left fielder, with injuries limiting his range and arm as well as problems with both judgment and his hands. Because he plays everything as hard as he can, he is also an oft-reckless baserunner who overestimates his speed and runs into outs.

1997 Outlook

The main reason for Greenwell's fast decline was poor health—a bad ankle, foot, shoulder, elbow and back. In the last five seasons, he averaged only 98 games, and while he batted .291 in that time, he also averaged less than 10 homers, and 51 RBI. . . second baseman numbers. He'll try to better those numbers in his new locale. One thing about Greenwell—he will never fail for wont of trying.

Position: LF
Bats: L **Throws:** R
Ht: 6' 0" **Wt:** 205

Opening Day Age: 33
Born: 7/18/63 in Louisville, KY
ML Seasons: 12

Overall Statistics

	G	AB	R	H	D	T	HR	RBI	SB	BB	SO	Avg	OBP	Slg
1996,	77	295	35	87	20	1	7	44	4	18	27	.295	.336	.441
Career	1269	4623	657	1400	275	38	130	726	80	460	364	.303	.368	.463

Where He Hits the Ball

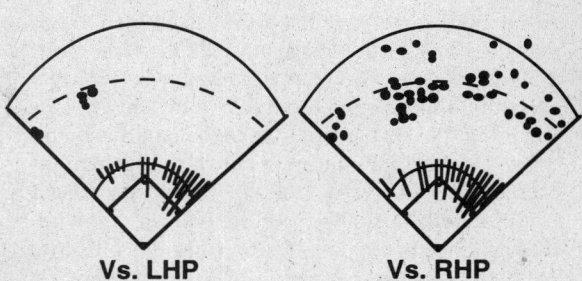

Vs. LHP   **Vs. RHP**

1996 Situational Stats

	AB	H	HR	RBI	Avg		AB	H	HR	RBI	Avg
Home	143	41	4	22	.287	LHP	81	28	0	9	.346
Road	152	46	3	22	.303	RHP	214	59	7	35	.276
First Half	90	20	1	8	.222	Sc Pos	75	25	2	35	.333
Scnd Half	205	67	6	36	.327	Clutch	49	14	1	9	.286

1996 Rankings (American League)

→ 6th in lowest batting average with the bases loaded (.100) and errors in left field (4)

Reggie Jefferson

1996 Season

Reggie Jefferson was 27 when the 1996 season began, having bounced around from Cincinnati to Cleveland to Seattle to Boston but never coming to the right place at the right time. Then Jose Canseco and Mike Greenwell got hurt, and he found himself in the same place Fred Lynn batted .350 and Wade Boggs batted .369—Fenway Park. A former switch-hitter who now hits left-handed exclusively, Jefferson did what those former Red Sox did so well—stay back, hit fastballs where they are pitched (which in Fenway often means over the wall), and drive the breaking ball. The result was a huge season.

Hitting

Jefferson did well against lefties in limited exposure, but he's struggled against them in the past. He will likely continue as a platoon hitter. He hits the ball on the ground too much to be a big home-run hitter, but he learned to take the ball down and away and get it into the air in Fenway, which might increase his power potential. Pitchers try to get him out with fastballs from the belt up, knowing that patience is not one of his virtues. He kills low balls, hangers and can fight off inside pitches.

Baserunning & Defense

Jefferson's best position is designated hitter. He can play first base, but he does not have much mobility and has struggled turning the 3-6-3 double play. Because of injuries and the logjam at DH, the Red Sox were forced to play him in left field for 45 games. He lacks range and can't throw but did a respectable job, with only two errors in left.

1997 Outlook

Jefferson has had 507 at-bats in two years with the Red Sox and produced these statistics: a .333 batting average, 38 doubles, four triples, 24 homers and 100 RBI. He probably won't be an everyday player, but he figures to be in the lineup whenever the Red Sox face a righty.

Position: DH/1B/LF
Bats: L **Throws:** L
Ht: 6' 4" **Wt:** 215

Opening Day Age: 28
Born: 9/25/68 in Tallahassee, FL
ML Seasons: 6

Overall Statistics

	G	AB	R	H	D	T	HR	RBI	SB	BB	SO	Avg	OBP	Slg
1996	122	386	67	134	30	4	19	74	0	25	89	.347	.388	.593
Career	399	1232	166	364	69	8	46	185	1	84	264	.295	.343	.476

Where He Hits the Ball

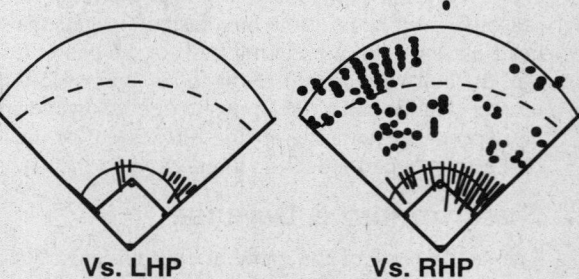

Vs. LHP   Vs. RHP

1996 Situational Stats

	AB	H	HR	RBI	Avg		AB	H	HR	RBI	Avg
Home	214	81	12	47	.379	LHP	50	16	1	9	.320
Road	172	53	7	27	.308	RHP	336	118	18	65	.351
First Half	173	65	9	33	.376	Sc Pos	99	33	2	48	.333
Scnd Half	213	69	10	41	.324	Clutch	58	19	3	13	.328

1996 Rankings (American League)
➡ Led the Red Sox in doubles

Tim Naehring

Position: 3B
Bats: R **Throws:** R
Ht: 6' 2" **Wt:** 203

Opening Day Age: 30
Born: 2/1/67 in Cincinnati, OH
ML Seasons: 7
Pronunciation: NAIR-ring

1996 Season

Tim Naehring is the player's player, one who goes at his job as hard and as professionally as anyone in the game. He is one of those rare players that every opposing manager wants to manage, and who off the field is as sincere and community-minded as they come. There's only one problem—injuries. Last year he hurt his neck diving into a dugout, pulled a hamstring and missed the last 19 games with a sore knee. Earlier in his career, he had back and shoulder operations.

Hitting

Naehring is a solid, professional hitter. He is basically a line-drive hitter who tries to use the entire field, fighting off breaking balls. He has learned to look for pitches and drive the ball for power. He had 12 homers and was slugging .502 at the All-Star break last year, only to see his numbers diminish because of injuries. He is extremely competitive and he hangs in well against righthanders, hitting .300 with 13 homers off them last year.

Baserunning & Defense

One of the reasons Naehring comes down with so many injuries is that he plays so hard—diving on the turf or into dugouts for instance. He has become a premier third baseman who has a good first step, outstanding hands and a strong, accurate arm. The back problems have slowed him down, but he has terrific baseball instincts and is a very accomplished baserunner.

1997 Outlook

Made a free agent as a result of the labor agreement which restored service time to striking players, Naehring found his services very much in demand. Over the winter, he began a different type of training to focus less on weights and bulk and more on flexibility, so maybe he will finally stay healthy. That's all he really needs to succeed. Simply put, the man is a winner.

Overall Statistics

	G	AB	R	H	D	T	HR	RBI	SB	BB	SO	Avg	OBP	Slg
1996	116	430	77	124	16	0	17	65	2	49	63	.288	.363	.444
Career	477	1613	216	453	86	3	40	210	4	198	272	.281	.363	.412

Where He Hits the Ball

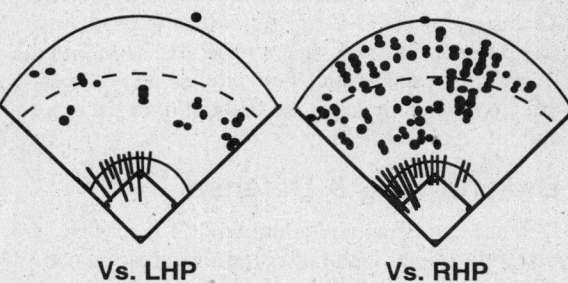

Vs. LHP   **Vs. RHP**

1996 Situational Stats

	AB	H	HR	RBI	Avg		AB	H	HR	RBI	Avg
Home	208	66	9	44	.317	LHP	107	27	4	14	.252
Road	222	58	8	21	.261	RHP	323	97	13	51	.300
First Half	241	78	12	42	.324	Sc Pos	121	36	4	49	.298
Scnd Half	189	46	5	23	.243	Clutch	59	15	5	11	.254

1996 Rankings (American League)

- ➡ 5th in fielding percentage at third base (.963)
- ➡ 7th in errors at third base (11)
- ➡ 8th in highest percentage of pitches taken (61.8%)
- ➡ 10th in highest percentage of swings put into play (53.0%) and highest percentage of extra bases taken as a runner (61.2%)
- ➡ Led the Red Sox in highest percentage of swings put into play (53.0%) and highest percentage of extra bases taken as a runner (61.2%)

Troy O'Leary

1996 Season

Troy O'Leary is yet another left-handed batter who found happiness in Fenway Park. Actually, O'Leary had always hit very well while in the Milwaukee farm system; he just never got an opportunity to play full-time. But after being acquired for one dollar from the Brewers, O'Leary has batted .322 with 15 homers in 472 at-bats at Fenway.

Hitting

O'Leary is a slasher, an aggressive, free-swinging hitter who lines the ball all over the park. He has big problems with lefties and has essentially become a platoon player. He's also an impatient hitter who likes to hack at the first baseball he sees. Teams try to get O'Leary out with offspeed stuff and pitches out of the strike zone, but he makes a living on mistakes and first pitches. He is most effective when he takes the ball out over the plate and hits it to left field.

Baserunning & Defense

Defense can be an adventure with O'Leary. He is best in left field, with fair range and a below-average arm. However, he has had his problems with angles and throwing in Fenway's spacious and treacherous right field; he has a habit of overthrowing cutoff men any time there is a runner headed for the plate, giving other baserunners free bases. O'Leary has good speed but doesn't have baserunning instincts, with only nine steals in 15 tries for his career.

1997 Outlook

O'Leary's sometimes laid-back personality got him out of favor in the middle of the '96 season, when he found himself benched for long periods of time and was sought in a trade by the Atlanta Braves. He got back into the lineup in August and his hot hitting helped spark the Red Sox back into the playoff chase. He probably won't get 497 at-bats again this year, but he figures to remain a useful platoon outfielder.

Position: RF/LF/CF
Bats: L **Throws:** L
Ht: 6' 0" **Wt:** 198

Opening Day Age: 27
Born: 8/4/69 in Compton, CA
ML Seasons: 4

Overall Statistics

	G	AB	R	H	D	T	HR	RBI	SB	BB	SO	Avg	OBP	Slg
1996	149	497	68	129	28	5	15	81	3	47	80	.260	.327	.427
Career	307	1003	140	282	63	12	27	140	9	86	165	.281	.340	.449

Where He Hits the Ball

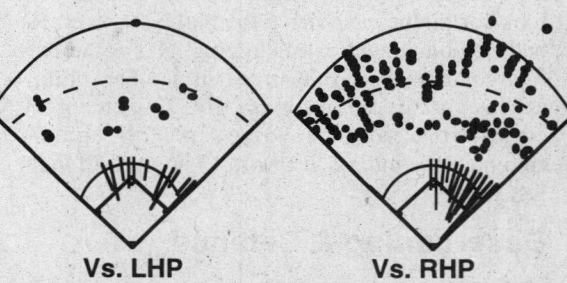

Vs. LHP   **Vs. RHP**

1996 Situational Stats

	AB	H	HR	RBI	Avg		AB	H	HR	RBI	Avg
Home	263	79	10	55	.300	LHP	106	21	0	15	.198
Road	234	50	5	26	.214	RHP	391	108	15	66	.276
First Half	283	71	8	42	.251	Sc Pos	130	44	6	70	.338
Scnd Half	214	58	7	39	.271	Clutch	72	16	3	14	.222

1996 Rankings (American League)

- ➡ 1st in lowest batting average on the road
- ➡ 3rd in lowest fielding percentage in right field (.974)
- ➡ 4th in lowest batting average on an 0-2 count (.032)
- ➡ 8th in errors in right field (4)
- ➡ 10th in errors in left field (3)
- ➡ Led the Red Sox in triples, highest ground-ball/flyball ratio (1.3) and batting average with runners in scoring position

Aaron Sele

1996 Season

The 1995 season was frustrating for Aaron Sele because of a May shoulder injury that essentially sidelined him the rest of the season. It was even more frustrating because he had to live with whispers questioning his willingness to pitch through pain. In 1996, it only got worse. After a winter in which he underwent intensive physical training, Sele suffered through an erratic season. When it was over his manager, Kevin Kennedy said, "It's time for Aaron to re-establish his priorities."

Pitching

When Sele came to the majors, he was a power pitcher with an average fastball, a big-time 12-to-6 power curveball and a Bob Welch get-me-over curveball to match. After the arm injury, he sometimes seemed reluctant to let go of his best curveball; as evidence, lefthanders batted .322 off him. He also seemed prone to nibbling and had problems getting counts in which he could use his curveball as an out pitch. Sele's fastball isn't much above the 85 MPH range, but it has a good sink, and this year he'll try to go back to his fastball and change-up more to set up his curveballs.

Defense

Overly concerned about basestealers, Sele has been using a slide-step which holds runners but detracts from his velocity. He is also less inclined to throw his best pitch, his curve, with men on base. With the new regime, it is likely that he'll be told to concentrate more on the hitters. He is an average fielder.

1997 Outlook

This will be an intense spring for Sele as he tries to turn the corner in what was once a promising career. He's probably not broken-hearted that Kennedy got fired. While Sele said nothing, it undoubtedly helps to know he'll be getting a fresh start under new manager Jimy Williams.

Position: SP
Bats: R **Throws:** R
Ht: 6' 5" **Wt:** 215

Opening Day Age: 26
Born: 6/25/70 in
Golden Valley, MN
ML Seasons: 4
Pronunciation:
SEE-lee

Boston Red Sox

Overall Statistics

	W	L	Pct.	ERA	G	GS	Sv	IP	H	BB	SO	HR	BR/IP
1996	7	11	.389	5.32	29	29	0	157.1	192	67	137	14	1.65
Career	25	21	.543	4.03	75	75	0	444.2	464	189	356	35	1.47

How Often He Throws Strikes

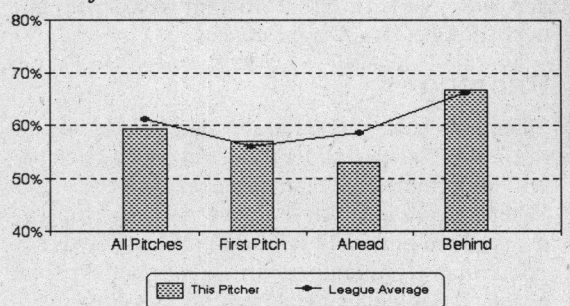

1996 Situational Stats

	W	L	ERA	Sv	IP		AB	H	HR	RBI	Avg
Home	3	5	6.37	0	65.0	LHB	339	109	9	57	.322
Road	4	6	4.58	0	92.1	RHB	295	83	5	41	.281
First Half	3	5	5.99	0	88.2	Sc Pos	174	55	3	77	.316
Scnd Half	4	6	4.46	0	68.2	Clutch	23	7	0	1	.304

1996 Rankings (American League)

→ 7th in highest batting average allowed vs. left-handed batters
→ 8th in lowest winning percentage
→ 10th in highest batting average allowed with runners in scoring position

Heathcliff Slocumb

1996 Season

Last January, the Red Sox traded Ken Ryan, Lee Tinsley and Glenn Murray for hard-throwing reliever Heathcliff Slocumb. After Slocumb's first blown save opportunity, Sox manager Kevin Kennedy told the media that he was looking for a new closer. While Slocumb was the type of inconsistent closer who will drive a manager bonkers at times, Kennedy could not ride through the difficulties, and until August the relationship was one of the Red Sox's worst problems. Slocumb has one of the most overpowering, running sinkers in the game, but he is often lacking in self-confidence, and for much of the year Kennedy's lack of faith in him showed. But Slocumb finally got it together and was 15-for-16 in save opportunities with an 0.94 ERA his last 22 appearances.

Pitching

Slocumb's basic pitches are a sinker he throws in the mid-90s, a hard slider and a forkball, a pitch he will use effectively when he's ahead in the count. When he got ahead in the count last year, opponents batted only .207 against him. His slider is so good that righthanders are virtually helpless against it. Unlike many closers, he was often used in the eighth or summoned in the middle of an inning, but that sort of usage never bothered him.

Defense

Slocumb is not exactly a detail-master. He doesn't hold runners very well (14 out of 15), and sometimes will have lapses when he seems to forget about them. He also has some adventures fielding ground balls and throwing to bases.

1997 Outlook

Slocumb is a closer, and the closer's job is to overpower people, which he can do. After a great first half in 1995 with the Phillies and a spectacular finish in 1996 with the Red Sox, this may be the season when we find out once and for all just how good Heathcliff Slocumb really is.

Position: RP
Bats: R **Throws:** R
Ht: 6' 3" **Wt:** 220

Opening Day Age: 30
Born: 6/7/66 in Jamaica, NY
ML Seasons: 6

Overall Statistics

	W	L	Pct.	ERA	G	GS	Sv	IP	H	BB	SO	HR	BR/IP
1996	5	5	.500	3.02	75	0	31	83.1	68	55	88	2	1.48
Career	21	17	.553	3.50	300	0	65	357.2	347	189	292	13	1.50

How Often He Throws Strikes

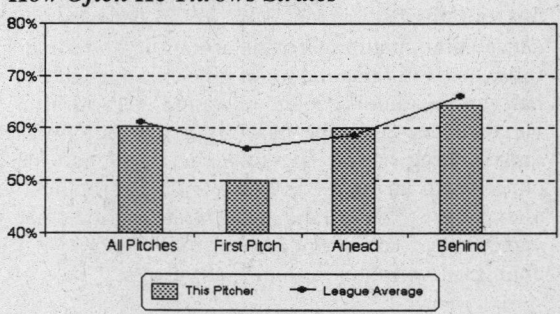

1996 Situational Stats

	W	L	ERA	Sv	IP		AB	H	HR	RBI	Avg
Home	2	3	4.78	15	37.2	LHB	165	47	1	18	.285
Road	3	2	1.58	16	45.2	RHB	141	21	1	13	.149
First Half	2	5	3.35	11	43.0	Sc Pos	101	22	1	30	.218
Scnd Half	3	0	2.68	20	40.1	Clutch	216	51	2	28	.236

1996 Rankings (American League)

- ➡ 2nd in games finished (60) and blown saves (8)
- ➡ 3rd in lowest save percentage (79.5%)
- ➡ 4th in games pitched and save opportunities (39)
- ➡ 6th in saves
- ➡ 7th in relief innings (83.1)
- ➡ 9th in wild pitches (10), lowest batting average allowed in relief with runners on base (.211) and most strikeouts per 9 innings in relief (9.5)
- ➡ 10th in relief ERA (3.02) and lowest batting average allowed in relief (.222)
- ➡ Led the Red Sox in games pitched, saves, games finished (60) and wild pitches (10)

Mike Stanley

1996 Season

It took Mike Stanley many years to overcome shoulder problems and finally get a chance to be an everyday catcher. Now, just when Stanley has established himself as one of the best-hitting catchers in the game, a new injury has raised questions about his future. After hitting 24 homers in 121 games for the Red Sox last year, the 33-year-old Stanley missed the last three weeks with a herniated disk in his lower back.

Hitting

The entire 1996 season was filled with injuries for the veteran catcher. Stanley hurt his leg in spring training and was later bothered by arm problems, but those injuries didn't affect his hitting. He is a smart veteran hitter who sticks to hitting fastballs through the middle and looks for breaking balls he can handle. He has good power to center field, and will take the breaking ball or fastball away and drive it. Stanley has long been a solid producer in clutch situations (.325 in close and late situations over the last five years), both because he understands situational hitting and because he knows his own limitations.

Baserunning & Defense

Defense has been a problem for Stanley since he had his right shoulder operated on more than a decade ago. He does not have a strong arm—and partially as a result of his injuries—opponents ran wild against him last year. Red Sox pitchers also had a 5.34 ERA with Stanley catching, 4.57 with Bill Haselman, which raised some eyebrows. In addition, he did not have the mobility behind the plate that he did when he was healthy.

1997 Outlook

Stanley exercised the renewal option on his $2.1 million contract for 1997, but there is considerable question about his future as the Red Sox catcher. On a team already loaded with DH types like Jose Canseco, Wilfredo Cordero and Reggie Jefferson, that doesn't bode well for him.

Position: C
Bats: R **Throws:** R
Ht: 6' 0" **Wt:** 190

Opening Day Age: 33
Born: 6/25/63 in Ft. Lauderdale, FL
ML Seasons: 11

Boston Red Sox

Overall Statistics

	G	AB	R	H	D	T	HR	RBI	SB	BB	SO	Avg	OBP	Slg
1996	121	397	73	107	20	1	24	69	2	69	62	.270	.383	.506
Career	971	2669	398	721	136	7	109	440	10	402	569	.270	.367	.449

Where He Hits the Ball

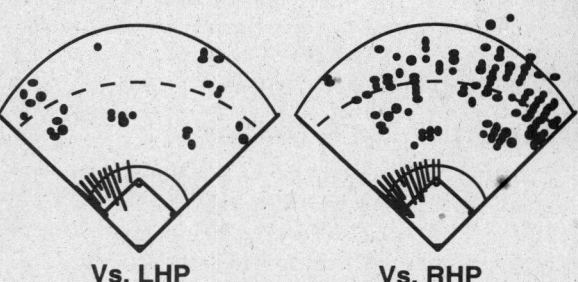

Vs. LHP   **Vs. RHP**

1996 Situational Stats

	AB	H	HR	RBI	Avg		AB	H	HR	RBI	Avg
Home	195	56	10	39	.287	LHP	106	32	10	26	.302
Road	202	51	14	30	.252	RHP	291	75	14	43	.258
First Half	242	66	12	42	.273	Sc Pos	114	30	6	47	.263
Scnd Half	155	41	12	27	.265	Clutch	56	17	2	11	.304

1996 Rankings (American League)

→ 1st in errors at catcher (10) and lowest percentage of runners caught stealing as a catcher (9.6%)

→ Led the Red Sox in slugging percentage vs. left-handed pitchers (.632)

John Valentin

1996 Season

The 1996 season ended in controversy for John Valentin. Toward the end of a solid campaign, Valentin was asked to move to third base so that the Red Sox could give rookie Nomar Garciaparra a chance to play shortstop. At the time, the Sox were still in the pennant race, and Valentin balked. At the end of the season he asked to be traded.

Hitting

Valentin is a hitter who has figured out Fenway. He gets right up on top of the plate and takes outside fastballs into the park's vast territory in right-center. Yet he can also pull the inside fastball or breaking ball and hook it up into the screen or off the fence. Nine of his 13 homers were in Fenway, where he slugged .500, compared to .381 on the road. He can handle righties, but he's a much more dangerous hitter against lefthanders.

Baserunning & Defense

The Red Sox wanted to move Valentin not so much because they were disgusted with his defensive play, but because they felt their defense would be much improved with Garciaparra and Valentin on the same side of the infield. Valentin has good street instincts, and while he doesn't have quick, natural range, he does play the ball off the bat well. The biggest knock on him has been that he'll occasionally one-hand ground balls, leading to careless errors. Valentin is a little big and heavy-legged, but he runs the bases well and should be able to improve last season's poor basestealing performance (9-for-19).

1997 Outlook

The Red Sox are expected to honor Valentin's request and trade him to a club willing to keep him at shortstop. Away from Fenway, his numbers probably won't approach his brilliant 1995 season, but he should come close to his figures from '96, when he was troubled by an injury to his left shoulder.

Position: SS/3B
Bats: R **Throws:** R
Ht: 6' 0" **Wt:** 180

Opening Day Age: 30
Born: 2/18/67 in Mineola, NY
ML Seasons: 5
Nickname: Val

Overall Statistics

	G	AB	R	H	D	T	HR	RBI	SB	BB	SO	Avg	OBP	Slg
1996	131	527	84	156	29	3	13	59	9	63	59	.296	.374	.436
Career	552	2001	316	587	145	10	65	301	36	255	258	.293	.376	.473

Where He Hits the Ball

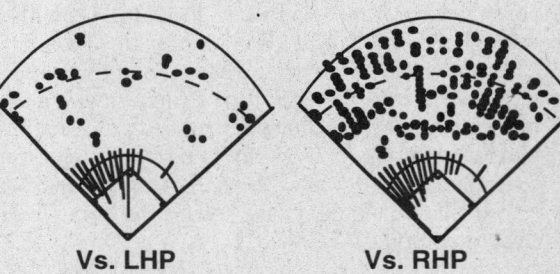

Vs. LHP   **Vs. RHP**

1996 Situational Stats

	AB	H	HR	RBI	Avg		AB	H	HR	RBI	Avg
Home	246	77	9	34	.313	LHP	129	49	1	14	.380
Road	281	79	4	25	.281	RHP	398	107	12	45	.269
First Half	346	101	10	39	.292	Sc Pos	115	32	1	41	.278
Scnd Half	181	55	3	20	.304	Clutch	80	27	4	9	.338

1996 Rankings (American League)

→ 1st in lowest stolen base percentage (47.4%)
→ 4th in batting average vs. left-handed pitchers and on-base percentage vs. left-handed pitchers (.481)
→ 5th in caught stealing (10)
→ 6th in lowest fielding percentage at shortstop (.971)
→ 7th in errors at shortstop (16)
→ Led the Red Sox in caught stealing (10), most pitches seen per plate appearance (3.86), batting average vs. left-handed pitchers, on-base percentage vs. left-handed pitchers (.481), batting average on the road and lowest percentage of swings on the first pitch (21.9%)

Mo Vaughn

1996 Season

Mo Vaughn got to start the All-Star game because of a foot injury to Frank Thomas, and to many, there was some justice that had nothing to do with Thomas. It's just that Vaughn has become one of the game's greatest sluggers, yet is stuck in the All-Star war with Thomas. Two nights earlier, Mo hit a dramatic, game-winning homer in Baltimore that won a game the Red Sox had to win, and defined Vaughn's presence on that team.

Hitting

There's no question that Vaughn is another left-handed hitter who figured out how to use Fenway. He waits on fastballs he can drive off or over the Green Monster, while laying back to pound breaking balls to deep right field. Pitchers try to jam him or go up the ladder with fastballs, and he'll sometimes chase bad breaking balls down and in and off the plate. But Mo has worked very hard at being patient and looking for pitches he knows he can handle.

Baserunning & Defense

Vaughn is a quick-footed athlete with surprising range, but his hands sometimes betray him. He has trouble scooping balls in the dirt and sometimes lets hard hit ground balls ricochet off him. But he works at it, and could be an average defensive infielder in time. His athleticism shows up on the bases, where he can steal an occasional base and can score from first on balls down the right field line in Fenway because of his surprising speed and his knowledge of the park.

1997 Outlook

Hurt, sick or attacked, Vaughn plays; he's missed five games in two years, two when he was attacked in a night spot, and last season played more than half the season with a broken middle finger. He still put up dramatic numbers, and you can expect more of the same in 1997.

Position: 1B/DH
Bats: L **Throws:** R
Ht: 6' 1" **Wt:** 240

Opening Day Age: 29
Born: 12/15/67 in Norwalk, CT
ML Seasons: 6
Nickname: The Hit Dog

Overall Statistics

	G	AB	R	H	D	T	HR	RBI	SB	BB	SO	Avg	OBP	Slg
1996	161	635	118	207	29	1	44	143	2	95	154	.326	.420	.583
Career	751	2692	430	794	144	8	155	541	26	372	656	.295	.387	.527

Where He Hits the Ball

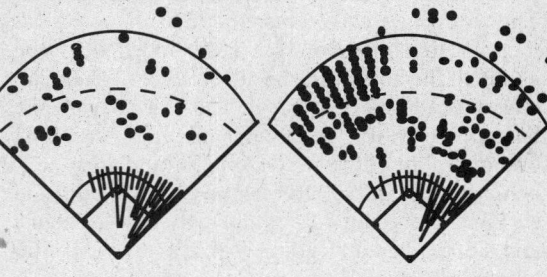

Vs. LHP   **Vs. RHP**

1996 Situational Stats

	AB	H	HR	RBI	Avg		AB	H	HR	RBI	Avg
Home	318	121	27	81	.381	LHP	200	63	10	45	.315
Road	317	86	17	62	.271	RHP	435	144	34	98	.331
First Half	341	118	26	78	.346	Sc Pos	169	55	17	102	.325
Scnd Half	294	89	18	65	.303	Clutch	92	32	5	19	.348

1996 Rankings (American League)

➡ 1st in times on base (316), plate appearances (752), batting average at home, errors at first base (15) and lowest fielding percentage at first base (.988)
➡ 2nd in intentional walks (19)
➡ 3rd in total bases (370), RBI, strikeouts, games played (161) and batting average on an 0-2 count (.323)
➡ 4th in hits, hit by pitch (14), pitches seen (2,872) and cleanup slugging percentage (.627)
➡ 5th in at-bats
➡ 6th in home runs, on-base percentage , batting average in the clutch and slugging percentage vs. right-handed pitchers (.616)

Tim Wakefield

1996 Season

Many felt that 1996 was the real breakthrough year for Tim Wakefield. Sure, he had a 14-1 run in 1995, but when he finished 2-7 that year and went 5-9, 6.24 in the first half of '96, people began recalling his experience in Pittsburgh: unhittable at first, then so bad he had to go back to the minors. Instead of backing down, Wakefield battled through his problems, and by the end of the season seemed to understand precisely what he is—a Charlie Hough who made 32 starts, threw 211.2 innings and was right around .500.

Pitching

In the second half of the season, Wakefield became more aggressive, responded to all the adjustments batters made on him and stopped worrying about all the home runs he allowed (38). There are days when Wakefield has it. There are days when he gets killed, for the knuckler is either wobbling or darting out of the strike zone so much that he is behind every hitter. He learned to hang in and survive, averaging 7.2 innings per start in August and September and going 9-4 after the All-Star break.

Defense

A converted first baseman, Wakefield is an exceptional fielder and who holds runners as well as a knuckleballer can. Before last season, basestealers were only 25 out of 47 off him, so his horrible 1996 numbers (30 of 31) may be a partial reflection of his catchers and the way the Red Sox prepared. The Sox were the only team in baseball not to throw out an opposing runner on a pitchout.

1997 Outlook

What the Red Sox hope they have in Wakefield is a reliable 200-plus inning starter who, like Hough, Wilbur Wood, Phil Niekro and most other knuckleballers, is just coming into his own at 30. They—and he—are beginning to develop the patience necessary to survive a knuckleballer's foibles, like the home runs, the five-run first innings and the numerous stolen bases.

Position: SP
Bats: R **Throws:** R
Ht: 6' 2" **Wt:** 206

Opening Day Age: 30
Born: 8/2/66 in Melbourne, FL
ML Seasons: 4

Overall Statistics

	W	L	Pct.	ERA	G	GS	Sv	IP	H	BB	SO	HR	BR/IP
1996	14	13	.519	5.14	32	32	0	211.2	238	90	140	38	1.55
Career	44	33	.571	4.12	96	92	0	627.1	622	268	369	77	1.42

How Often He Throws Strikes

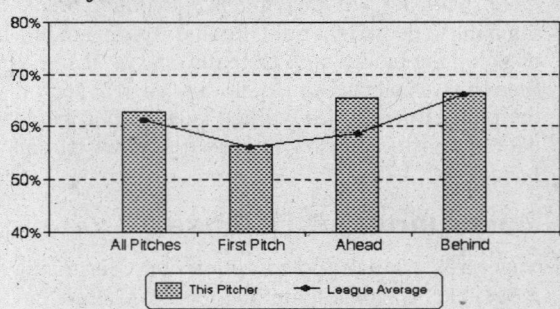

1996 Situational Stats

	W	L	ERA	Sv	IP		AB	H	HR	RBI	Avg
Home	7	6	5.42	0	108.0	LHB	454	131	14	63	.289
Road	7	7	4.86	0	103.2	RHB	397	107	24	68	.270
First Half	5	9	6.24	0	101.0	Sc Pos	226	58	11	91	.257
Scnd Half	9	4	4.15	0	110.2	Clutch	77	18	3	7	.234

1996 Rankings (American League)

→ 1st in highest stolen base percentage allowed (96.8%)
→ 2nd in stolen bases allowed (30) and most home runs allowed per 9 innings (1.62)
→ 3rd in home runs allowed and hit batsmen (12)
→ 4th in complete games (6)
→ 5th in highest slugging percentage allowed (.469), lowest groundball/flyball ratio allowed (0.9) and highest ERA at home
→ 7th in least pitches thrown per batter (3.67)
→ 8th in lowest strikeout/walk ratio (1.6) and most baserunners allowed per 9 innings (14.5)
→ 9th in highest ERA and highest on-base percentage allowed (.353)
→ 10th in walks allowed and balks (1)

Mark Brandenburg

Position: RP
Bats: R **Throws:** R
Ht: 6' 0" **Wt:** 180

Opening Day Age: 26
Born: 7/14/70 in Houston, TX
ML Seasons: 2

Overall Statistics

	W	L	Pct.	ERA	G	GS	Sv	IP	H	BB	SO	HR	BR/IP
1996	5	5	.500	3.43	55	0	0	76.0	76	33	66	8	1.43
Career	5	6	.455	4.09	66	0	0	103.1	112	40	87	13	1.47

1996 Situational Stats

	W	L	ERA	Sv	IP		AB	H	HR	RBI	Avg
Home	2	5	3.77	0	43.0	LHB	126	36	3	21	.286
Road	3	0	3.00	0	33.0	RHB	169	40	5	28	.237
First Half	1	0	2.14	0	42.0	Sc Pos	87	23	2	40	.264
Scnd Half	4	5	5.03	0	34.0	Clutch	75	24	3	15	.320

1996 Season

The Red Sox acquired sidearming middle man Mark Brandenburg from the Rangers with Kerry Lacy for Mike Stanton on July 31. He immediately became a workhorse, appearing in 29 games the last two months.

Pitching & Defense

A side-wheeler who sweeps in from third base, Brandenburg is very effective against right-handed batters, not so great against lefties. When he has his sinker and command of his slider, he can be tough if hitters don't get too many looks at him. But there were times in both Texas and Boston when he had to be overexposed—hence the eight home runs and occasional rocky outings. Despite his side-wheeling delivery, he's a decent fielder. He isn't quick to the plate, but varies his delivery and allowed only two steals last year.

1997 Outlook

The Sox believe that with his ability to get hitters to put the ball in the middle of the field, Brandenburg can be the sort of pitcher who thrives at Fenway. If the Red Sox have Heathcliff Slocumb as a consistent closer and can find some complimentary set-up men, there is a role for Brandenburg on their team.

Rich Garces

Position: RP
Bats: R **Throws:** R
Ht: 6' 0" **Wt:** 215

Opening Day Age: 25
Born: 5/18/71 in Maracay, VZ
ML Seasons: 4

Overall Statistics

	W	L	Pct.	ERA	G	GS	Sv	IP	H	BB	SO	HR	BR/IP
1996	3	2	.600	4.91	37	0	0	44.0	42	33	55	5	1.70
Career	3	4	.429	4.27	63	0	2	78.0	75	50	81	6	1.60

1996 Situational Stats

	W	L	ERA	Sv	IP		AB	H	HR	RBI	Avg
Home	3	1	3.12	0	34.2	LHB	64	20	0	11	.313
Road	0	1	11.57	0	9.1	RHB	103	22	5	21	.214
First Half	2	2	5.00	0	36.0	Sc Pos	58	16	2	27	.276
Scnd Half	1	0	4.50	0	8.0	Clutch	65	17	3	16	.262

1996 Season

Signed by the Red Sox as a minor league free agent over the winter, Rich Garces was a significant contributor to the Boston bullpen until his elbow gave out. Recalled by the Red Sox from Triple-A on April 24, he got off to a solid start, went on the DL in late July, then went out for good with a strained right rib cage in late August.

Pitching & Defense

Stuff isn't a problem for Garces. He has an above-average fastball and an outstanding curveball, his power and strikeout pitch. He is especially tough on righthanders. With his John Candy body, Garces is not a good fielder. He also has problems holding runners, who were 4-for-4 stealing off him.

1997 Outlook

Garces can pitch. His problems are: 1) health, as his constant weight problem may be a contributing factor to the forearm strain and rib cage pulls that sidelined him; 2) lack of concentration, as evidenced by the fact that as dominant as he can be against right-handed batters, he still surrendered five gopher balls to them; and 3) the lack of an offspeed pitch for lefties. With maturity and better conditioning, he can be an effective reliever.

Nomar Garciaparra (Top Prospect)

Position: SS
Bats: R **Throws:** R
Ht: 6' 0" **Wt:** 167

Opening Day Age: 23
Born: 7/23/73 in Whittier, CA
ML Seasons: 1
Pronunciation: NO-mar Gar-see-up-PARE-uh

Overall Statistics

	G	AB	R	H	D	T	HR	RBI	SB	BB	SO	Avg	OBP	Slg
1996	24	87	11	21	2	3	4	16	5	4	14	.241	.272	.471
Career	24	87	11	21	2	3	4	16	5	4	14	.241	.272	.471

1996 Situational Stats

	AB	H	HR	RBI	Avg		AB	H	HR	RBI	Avg
Home	.43	9	3	7	.209	LHP	31	5	1	5	.161
Road	44	12	1	9	.273	RHP	56	16	3	11	.286
First Half	0	0	0	0	-	Sc Pos	28	7	0	11	.250
Scnd Half	87	21	4	16	.241	Clutch	15	4	0	3	.267

1996 Season

Considered the Red Sox shortstop of the future, Nomar Garciaparra was limited to just 43 games at Triple-A Pawtucket in 1996 because of a torn tendon in his knee. He succeeded in making quite an impact in his shortened season by hitting .343 with 16 homers and 46 RBI in those 43 games. Called up to Boston in late August, he lived up to everyone's high expectations.

Hitting, Baserunning & Defense

The Red Sox' first-round draft pick in 1994, Garciaparra first gained recognition for his fielding skill and great range at shortstop. But adding muscle has turned him into an excellent hitting prospect. He showed great bat speed and keen strike zone judgment while coming up through the ranks in Class-A and Double-A. He has exceptional quickness moving both ways at shortstop as well as fine speed and basestealing ability.

1997 Outlook

Garciaparra could be Boston's starting shortstop for years to come. By adding home run distance to his swing, he has rounded his game to the point where he could become an impact player in his first full season in the majors.

Bill Haselman

Position: C
Bats: R **Throws:** R
Ht: 6' 3" **Wt:** 223

Opening Day Age: 30
Born: 5/25/66 in Long Branch, NJ
ML Seasons: 6
Pronunciation: HASS-ul-mun

Overall Statistics

	G	AB	R	H	D	T	HR	RBI	SB	BB	SO	Avg	OBP	Slg
1996	77	237	33	65	13	1	8	34	4	19	52	.274	.331	.439
Career	252	641	88	160	34	3	19	84	7	52	124	.250	.309	.401

1996 Situational Stats

	AB	H	HR	RBI	Avg		AB	H	HR	RBI	Avg
Home	104	32	5	17	.308	LHP	81	29	3	14	.358
Road	133	33	3	17	.248	RHP	156	36	5	20	.231
First Half	106	26	3	10	.245	Sc Pos	60	22	2	27	.367
Scnd Half	131	39	5	24	.298	Clutch	40	11	2	8	.275

1996 Season

At the age of 30, Bill Haselman—who was once Troy Aikman's backup at UCLA—finally got a chance to catch on a semi-regular basis due to Mike Stanley's back problems. He seemed to be learning to hit as the season ended, particularly in areas like taking opposing righthanders to right center. He also held his own defensively.

Hitting, Baserunning & Defense

Haselman is a fiercely competitive athlete who seems to hit best in difficult situations. At this point, he still has trouble with tough righthanders and breaking balls, but his lack of consistent playing time might be one reason for that. He runs well for a catcher, swiping four bases last year. Given the opportunity to catch, Haselman became a staff favorite. He was especially popular with Roger Clemens. His arm is about average.

1997 Outlook

Haselman earned the right to go into 1997 with no worse than a split of Boston's catching duties. He has improved as he's played, and he has those quarterback leadership skills that seem to translate so well to catching, which is why pitchers like to work with him.

Mike Maddux

Position: RP/SP
Bats: L **Throws:** R
Ht: 6' 2" **Wt:** 185

Opening Day Age: 35
Born: 8/27/61 in Dayton, OH
ML Seasons: 11

Overall Statistics

	W	L	Pct.	ERA	G	GS	Sv	IP	H	BB	SO	HR	BR/IP
1996	3	2	.600	4.48	23	7	0	64.1	76	27	32	12	1.60
Career	32	30	.516	3.93	341	48	19	708.1	709	227	462	51	1.32

1996 Situational Stats

	W	L	ERA	Sv	IP		AB	H	HR	RBI	Avg
Home	3	0	3.63	0	39.2	LHB	122	35	7	19	.287
Road	0	2	5.84	0	24.2	RHB	136	41	5	18	.301
First Half	0	1	4.66	0	19.1	Sc Pos	65	16	3	25	.246
Scnd Half	3	1	4.40	0	45.0	Clutch	18	7	1	3	.389

1996 Season

One of the injuries that most hurt the Red Sox early in the 1996 season came when swingman Mike Maddux went down with an elbow problem. The slightly-built Maddux was used for 40 pitches on an April Sunday, worked in an 11 a.m. game the next day and came in again on Tuesday. *Apres la, le breakdown.* Maddux eventually went on the DL and wasn't really healthy again until August.

Pitching & Defense

What makes Maddux so valuable is that his knowledge of pitching can be used in a number of roles. An ideal long man who can come into games in the early innings, he is also a useful part-time starter. Maddux has four pitches which he can get over the plate, his fastball has good sink, and he's always had excellent control. The veteran has always been consistent holding runners and he's a good fielder.

1997 Outlook

Maddux has been a very effective pitcher in Fenway Park the last two years. He is not a physical horse and has to be utilized carefully, but the Red Sox wanted the veteran free agent back and re-signed him for 1997.

Jose Malave

Position: RF
Bats: R **Throws:** R
Ht: 6' 2" **Wt:** 212

Opening Day Age: 25
Born: 5/31/71 in Cumana, Venezuela
ML Seasons: 1
Pronunciation: MAH-la-vay

Overall Statistics

	G	AB	R	H	D	T	HR	RBI	SB	BB	SO	Avg	OBP	Slg
1996	41	102	12	24	3	0	4	17	0	2	25	.235	.257	.382
Career	41	102	12	24	3	0	4	17	0	2	25	.235	.257	.382

1996 Situational Stats

	AB	H	HR	RBI	Avg		AB	H	HR	RBI	Avg
Home	40	8	1	2	.200	LHP	55	14	3	13	.255
Road	62	16	3	15	.258	RHP	47	10	1	4	.213
First Half	87	21	4	13	.241	Sc Pos	28	8	2	14	.286
Scnd Half	15	3	0	4	.200	Clutch	14	1	0	0	.071

1996 Season

Rookie outfielder Jose Malave was called up from Triple-A Pawtucket in late May to help relieve an injury-laden Red Sox outfield. Malave had hit well at Pawtucket and was able to show glimpses of power after joining the Red Sox. Unfortunately, a strained knee knocked him out of the lineup.

Hitting, Baserunning & Defense

Malave is a well-built athlete with a powerful stroke who led the Eastern League with 92 RBI in 1994 while hitting 24 homers. He continued to get stronger and increased his home-run rate when he reached Triple-A. His problem is that he tends to overswing and has trouble laying off bad pitches. Malave is not likely to hit for a good average because of his lack of discipline. He does not run particularly well and is not known for his defensive exploits.

1997 Outlook

With all the uncertainty in the Red Sox outfield, Malave could find himself being given a long look come spring. He needs to show he can get on base and hit for better average, or he'll end up back in Triple-A Pawtucket despite his power.

Jeff Suppan

Position: SP
Bats: R **Throws:** R
Ht: 6' 2" **Wt:** 210

Opening Day Age: 22
Born: 1/2/75 in
Oklahoma City, OK
ML Seasons: 2
Pronunciation:
sup-PAN

Overall Statistics

	W	L	Pct.	ERA	G	GS	Sv	IP	H	BB	SO	HR	BR/IP
1996	1	1	.500	7.54	8	4	0	22.2	29	13	13	3	1.85
Career	2	3	.400	6.75	16	7	0	45.1	58	18	32	7	1.68

1996 Situational Stats

	W	L	ERA	Sv	IP		AB	H	HR	RBI	Avg
Home	0	1	9.72	0	8.1	LHB	46	10	1	7	.217
Road	1	0	6.28	0	14.1	RHB	42	19	2	11	.452
First Half	0	0	0.00	0	1.2	Sc Pos	26	9	2	15	.346
Scnd Half	1	1	8.14	0	21.0	Clutch	5	4	0	2	.800

1996 Season

After moving steadily through the Red Sox system, Jeff Suppan opened last season in the Boston bullpen. Sent to Triple-A Pawtucket to get more work, he was leading the International League in strikeouts when Boston brought him back on August 2. However, Suppan didn't pitch with the aggressiveness that made him successful in the minors. He nibbled, walking 12 men in 20.2 innings in his four starts. He finished the season on the injured list with back and elbow problems.

Pitching & Defense

Suppan has only average velocity, but his delivery makes the ball difficult for hitters to pick up. His best pitch is his curveball, and he also throws a fosh change-up which he began learning at Double-A Trenton in 1995 from pitching coach Al Nipper. Suppan needs to work on holding runners, but that should come in time since he has a smooth, fluid delivery. He is a good athlete who fields his position well.

1997 Outlook

The Red Sox hope that Suppan is fully recovered from the injuries which cut short his 1996 season. If healthy, he should be ready to move into the starting rotation this year.

Lee Tinsley

Position: CF/LF
Bats: B **Throws:** R
Ht: 5'10" **Wt:** 195

Opening Day Age: 28
Born: 3/4/69 in
Shelbyville, KY
ML Seasons: 4

Overall Statistics

	G	AB	R	H	D	T	HR	RBI	SB	BB	SO	Avg	OBP	Slg
1996	123	244	29	54	6	1	3	16	8	17	78	.221	.277	.291
Career	312	748	119	186	28	2	13	73	39	77	197	.249	.321	.344

1996 Situational Stats

	AB	H	HR	RBI	Avg		AB	H	HR	RBI	Avg
Home	109	31	1	12	.284	LHP	63	11	0	4	.175
Road	135	23	2	4	.170	RHP	181	43	3	12	.238
First Half	137	31	1	10	.226	Sc Pos	63	10	0	13	.159
Scnd Half	107	23	2	6	.215	Clutch	41	11	0	2	.268

1996 Season

Traded to the Phillies in the Heathcliff Slocumb deal last January, Lee Tinsley was quickly reacquired when Boston needed help in center field early last season. He batted only .245 in 92 games and then was dealt in November to Mariners, who had traded Tinsley to the Red Sox in the first place back in 1994.

Hitting, Baserunning & Defense

Tinsley is a dangerous first-ball, high-ball, fastball hitter. He has alley power and can occasionally hit a ball a long way, especially batting left-handed. He also has tremendous speed, and though his throwing is subpar, he is a defensive plus in center and left fields. The problem has been that he has never put those tools together. He swings at too many balls out of the strike zone, never has been able to adjust to breaking pitches of any kind and has yet to demonstrate that he has the instincts to use his speed to steal bases.

1997 Outlook

Seattle is counting on Tinsley as a fourth outfielder and a role player this year. His tools say he could be better than that, but at 28 he has yet to harness them.

Other Boston Red Sox

Stan Belinda (Pos: RHP, Age: 30)

	W	L	Pct.	ERA	G	GS	Sv	IP	H	BB	SO	HR	BR/IP
1996	2	1	.667	6.59	31	0	2	28.2	31	20	18	3	1.78
Career	32	20	.615	3.89	376	0	74	435.1	363	184	360	42	1.26

The right-handed sidearmer suffered through an injury-plagued season and was released at the end of the year. He's come back from arm problems before, and should find another home this year. 1997 Outlook: B

Esteban Beltre (Pos: 3B, Age: 29, Bats: R)

	G	AB	R	H	D	T	HR	RBI	SB	BB	SO	Avg	OBP	Slg
1996	27	62	6	16	2	0	0	6	1	4	14	.258	.299	.290
Career	186	401	46	95	17	0	1	35	5	28	73	.237	.285	.287

Diminutive infielder Esteban Beltre rode the Boston bench for three months before they released him in June. He tried his hand in two other systems, but couldn't make it back. It may be bye-bye Beltre. 1997 Outlook: D

Phil Clark (Pos: 1B, Age: 28, Bats: R)

	G	AB	R	H	D	T	HR	RBI	SB	BB	SO	Avg	OBP	Slg
1996	3	3	0	0	0	0	0	0	0	0	1	.000	.000	.000
Career	264	543	62	150	30	0	17	65	4	27	76	.276	.317	.425

Jerald's brother went down to Pawtucket, played a whole bunch of positions, and hit fairly well. All it got him, though, was a contract to play in Japan this year. Sayonara. 1997 Outlook: D

Alex Cole (Pos: CF, Age: 31, Bats: L)

	G	AB	R	H	D	T	HR	RBI	SB	BB	SO	Avg	OBP	Slg
1996	24	72	13	16	5	1	0	7	5	8	11	.222	.296	.319
Career	573	1760	286	493	58	26	5	117	148	217	296	.280	.360	.351

Cole took a brief ride on the Red Sox' center field merry-go-round, but ended up at Pawtucket when the music stopped. The Red Sox don't need him, but he always seems to pop up somewhere. 1997 Outlook: C

Milt Cuyler (Pos: CF/RF, Age: 28, Bats: B)

	G	AB	R	H	D	T	HR	RBI	SB	BB	SO	Avg	OBP	Slg
1996	50	110	19	22	1	2	1	7	13	19	.200	.299	.300
Career	483	1380	224	326	45	23	9	116	77	120	273	.236	.303	.322

Over the first half of the season, Cuyler was used to fulfill the Red Sox' quota of speed and defense. A back injury wiped out his second half. Now a free agent, his future is grim. 1997 Outlook: D

Alex Delgado (Pos: C, Age: 26, Bats: R)

	G	AB	R	H	D	T	HR	RBI	SB	BB	SO	Avg	OBP	Slg
1996	26	20	5	5	0	0	0	1	0	3	3	.250	.348	.250
Career	26	20	5	5	0	0	0	1	0	3	3	.250	.348	.250

Delgado spent four different stints with the Red Sox last year, and played six different positions for them, including catcher. He can't hit, but his versatility makes him a great insurance policy. 1997 Outlook: C

John Doherty (Pos: RHP, Age: 29)

	W	L	Pct.	ERA	G	GS	Sv	IP	H	BB	SO	HR	BR/IP
1996	0	0	-	5.68	3	0	0	6.1	8	4	3	1	1.89
Career	32	31	.508	4.87	148	61	9	521.1	613	140	177	47	1.44

In 1997, sinkerballer John Doherty experienced the mother of all career crises: within the span of two months, both the Tigers and the Red Sox decided that they had no use for him. 'Nuff said? 1997 Outlook: D

Vaughn Eshelman (Pos: LHP, Age: 27)

	W	L	Pct.	ERA	G	GS	Sv	IP	H	BB	SO	HR	BR/IP
1996	6	3	.667	7.08	39	10	0	87.2	112	58	59	13	1.94
Career	12	6	.667	6.01	62	24	0	169.1	198	94	100	16	1.72

Lefthander Vaughn Eshelman cut his hand in the spring, and even after he returned a month later, things hardly got better. He was pummeled relentlessly, and a return to the minors may be coming. 1997 Outlook: C

Ken Grundt (Pos: LHP, Age: 27)

	W	L	Pct.	ERA	G	GS	Sv	IP	H	BB	SO	HR	BR/IP
1996	0	0	-	27.00	1	0	0	0.1	1	0	0	0	3.00
Career	0	0	-	27.00	1	0	0	0.1	1	0	0	0	3.00

Nomad southpaw Ken Grundt was called up for one week in August. He appeared in one game, got one out, and will probably retire with his 27.00 ERA intact. 1997 Outlook: D

Eric Gunderson (Pos: LHP, Age: 31)

	W	L	Pct.	ERA	G	GS	Sv	IP	H	BB	SO	HR	BR/IP
1996	0	1	.000	8.31	28	0	0	17.1	21	8	7	5	1.67
Career	6	6	.500	5.29	109	4	1	95.1	106	46	57	10	1.59

Eric Gunderson was another lefty reliever the Red Sox tried last year. He didn't do the job, but pitched well enough at Triple-A to get another shot or two this year. 1997 Outlook: C

Reggie Harris (Pos: RHP, Age: 28)

	W	L	Pct.	ERA	G	GS	Sv	IP	H	BB	SO	HR	BR/IP
1996	0	0	-	12.46	4	0	0	4.1	7	5	4	2	2.77
Career	1	0	1.000	4.81	22	1	0	48.2	37	39	37	7	1.36

Long-ago prospect Reggie Harris returned from baseball's dead to enjoy a dominant season as a closer at Double-A. His arm finally seemed healthy, but the Sox didn't use him much in September. Dead again? 1997 Outlook: C

Scott Hatteberg (Pos: C, Age: 27, Bats: L)

	G	AB	R	H	D	T	HR	RBI	SB	BB	SO	Avg	OBP	Slg
1996	10	11	3	2	1	0	0	0	0	3	2	.182	.357	.273
Career	12	13	4	3	1	0	0	0	0	3	2	.231	.375	.308

Scott Hatteberg is a left-handed-hitting catcher, so the Red Sox have kept him hanging around at Triple-A just in case they needed him. He's a decent hitter, but they probably won't give him a shot. 1997 Outlook: C

Dwayne Hosey (Pos: CF, Age: 30, Bats: B)

	G	AB	R	H	D	T	HR	RBI	SB	BB	SO	Avg	OBP	Slg
1996	28	78	13	17	2	2	1	3	6	7	17	.218	.282	.333
Career	52	146	33	40	10	3	4	10	12	15	33	.274	.342	.466

Hosey began the year as Boston's center fielder, but got demoted when the manager made him the scapegoat for the team's poor start. He can play. Being dealt to Texas may be just what he needs. 1997 Outlook: B

Joe Hudson (Pos: RHP, Age: 26)

	W	L	Pct.	ERA	G	GS	Sv	IP	H	BB	SO	HR	BR/IP
1996	3	5	.375	5.40	36	0	1	45.0	57	32	19	4	1.98
Career	3	6	.333	4.75	75	0	2	91.0	110	55	48	6	1.81

Joe Hudson spent four separate stints with the Red Sox last year, and couldn't find the plate during any of them. He's only 26, so he may yet turn it around. 1997 Outlook: C

Brent Knackert (Pos: RHP, Age: 27)

	W	L	Pct.	ERA	G	GS	Sv	IP	H	BB	SO	HR	BR/IP
1996	0	1	.000	9.00	8	0	0	10.0	16	7	5	1	2.30
Career	1	2	.333	7.04	32	2	0	47.1	66	28	33	6	1.99

Knackert saved 10 games in 11 appearances at Double-A last year, but didn't do anything at Triple-A or in the majors. For him to get back to the big show will take some doing. 1997 Outlook: D

Kerry Lacy (Pos: RHP, Age: 24)

	W	L	Pct.	ERA	G	GS	Sv	IP	H	BB	SO	HR	BR/IP
1996	2	0	1.000	3.38	11	0	0	10.2	15	8	9	2	2.16
Career	2	0	1.000	3.38	11	0	0	10.2	15	8	9	2	2.16

Lacy came over from the Rangers in the Mike Stanton deal, and pitched decently for the Red Sox in December. He's never been considered much of a prospect, but Boston must have liked something about him. 1997 Outlook: C

Pat Mahomes (Pos: RHP, Age: 26)

	W	L	Pct.	ERA	G	GS	Sv	IP	H	BB	SO	HR	BR/IP
1996	3	4	.429	6.91	31	5	2	57.1	72	33	36	13	1.83
Career	20	28	.417	5.82	125	51	5	379.0	413	195	223	70	1.60

Mahomes always posted good numbers in the minors, but flunked a zillion trials with the Twins. The Red Sox picked him up late in the year, and it seemed like they wanted to give him a look. 1997 Outlook: C

Jeff Manto (Pos: 3B, Age: 32, Bats: R)

	G	AB	R	H	D	T	HR	RBI	SB	BB	SO	Avg	OBP	Slg
1996	43	102	15	20	6	1	3	10	0	17	24	.196	.317	.363
Career	217	578	73	130	27	2	24	75	2	76	136	.225	.323	.403

From Japan, to the Boston minor league system, to Seattle, and then back to Boston, utilityman Jeff Manto truly played everywhere last year. Where he stops, nobody knows. 1997 Outlook: C

Nate Minchey (Pos: RHP, Age: 27)

	W	L	Pct.	ERA	G	GS	Sv	IP	H	BB	SO	HR	BR/IP
1996	0	2	.000	15.00	2	2	0	6.0	16	5	4	1	3.50
Career	3	7	.300	6.53	13	12	0	62.0	95	27	37	7	1.97

Minchey got bombed in both his starts with Boston, and then missed the second half with an arm injury. He's pitched well in the minors over the past few years, but his status is very much in limbo. 1997 Outlook: C

Greg Pirkl (Pos: DH, Age: 26, Bats: R)

	G	AB	R	H	D	T	HR	RBI	SB	BB	SO	Avg	OBP	Slg
1996	9	23	2	4	1	0	1	1	0	0	4	.174	.174	.348
Career	45	116	12	26	4	0	8	16	0	2	27	.224	.242	.466

Greg Pirkl has major league power but can't play anywhere besides first base. The Red Sox picked him up on waivers, and have kicked around the idea of making a pitcher out of him. Hmm. . . 1997 Outlook: D

Arquimedez Pozo (Pos: 2B, Age: 23, Bats: R)

	G	AB	R	H	D	T	HR	RBI	SB	BB	SO	Avg	OBP	Slg
1996	21	58	4	10	3	1	1	11	1	2	10	.172	.210	.310
Career	22	59	4	10	3	1	1	11	1	2	10	.169	.206	.305

Finally liberated from the Seattle chain, Pozo got a quick look at third base and second base with Boston. He's young, he can hit, and his glove isn't a huge liability. He could surprise. 1997 Outlook: B

Tony Rodriguez (Pos: SS, Age: 26, Bats: R)

	G	AB	R	H	D	T	HR	RBI	SB	BB	SO	Avg	OBP	Slg
1996	27	67	7	16	1	0	1	9	0	4	8	.239	.292	.299
Career	27	67	7	16	1	0	1	9	0	4	8	.239	.292	.299

Rodriguez is a decent backup infielder, but that's about it. He probably won't play unless there's a ton of injuries or some sort of emergency. 1997 Outlook: C

Bill Selby (Pos: 2B/3B, Age: 26, Bats: L)

	G	AB	R	H	D	T	HR	RBI	SB	BB	SO	Avg	OBP	Slg
1996	40	95	12	26	4	0	3	6	1	9	11	.274	.337	.411
Career	40	95	12	26	4	0	3	6	1	9	11	.274	.337	.411

Selby's a squat, left-handed hitter who can hit enough to fill in but not enough to start at third base. He's barely adequate at second base. We'll see him next whenever he comes back from Japan. 1997 Outlook: D

Boston Red Sox Minor League Prospects

Organization Overview:

The Red Sox' system used to be a coaching wasteland where prospects were left to take a do-it-yourself approach to their own development. All of that has changed since G.M. Dan Duquette took over in 1994. Under the command of Director of Field Operations Bob Schaefer and Scouting Director Wayne Britton, the Boston system has become a model organization, brimming with great young players that are finally beginning to reach the majors. Over the past two years, Duquette has gone outside of the organization for more advanced young players in order to buy some development time for the real prospects. His efforts have netted the Sox a number of useful young players who had been overlooked in other organizations, but now the team's philosophy may be changing. Scrounging for spare parts will need to take a back seat to the business of development. The challenge of the next couple of years will be to integrate a bumper crop of youngsters into the major league lineup.

Todd Carey

Position: 3B   **Opening Day Age:** 25
Bats: L **Throws:** R   **Born:** 8/14/71 in Lynn,
Ht: 6' 1" **Wt:** 180   MA

Recent Statistics

	G	AB	R	H	D	T	HR	RBI	SB	BB	SO	AVG
93 A Ft. Laud	118	444	41	109	14	5	3	31	2	24	44	.245
94 A Lynchburg	105	363	42	85	14	2	13	42	1	49	77	.234
95 A Sarasota	25	85	15	26	6	0	4	19	2	9	17	.306
95 AA Trenton	76	228	30	62	11	1	8	36	3	28	44	.272
96 AA Trenton	125	440	78	110	34	3	20	78	4	48	123	.250
96 MLE	125	441	73	111	37	2	18	73	2	38	131	.252

Carey is a former shortstop who plays a great third base. He can also cover both middle infield spots, so his powerful left-handed bat may earn him a bench role, at the very least. He's not tremendously fast, and his struggles at the plate in his first few seasons got him tagged as a non-prospect. But he's shown significant development in the past two years, and he doesn't need to go much further to project as a valuable backup infielder.

Walt McKeel

Position: C   **Opening Day Age:** 25
Bats: R **Throws:** R   **Born:** 1/17/72 in
Ht: 6' 2" **Wt:** 200   Wilson, NC

Recent Statistics

	G	AB	R	H	D	T	HR	RBI	SB	BB	SO	AVG
96 AA Trenton	128	464	86	140	19	1	16	78	2	60	52	.302
96 AL Boston	1	0	0	0	0	0	0	0	0	0	0	-
96 MLE	128	463	80	139	21	0	14	73	1	47	55	.300

For someone who never gets mentioned as a prospect, McKeel has proven to be a very good hitter for a catcher.

He struggled at the plate for several years, but turned it around in '95. Last year, his development continued, as he went to Double-A and put up great numbers in a difficult park. There's pop in his bat, and he rarely strikes out. He can catch as well as play first base, and he's adequate at both spots. At worst, he should be able to help as a backup. If the Red Sox give him a shot at the regular catching job, they may be pleasantly surprised.

Roberto Mejia

Position: 2B   **Opening Day Age:** 24
Bats: R **Throws:** R   **Born:** 4/14/72 in Hato
Ht: 5' 11" **Wt:** 160   Mayor, DR

Recent Statistics

	G	AB	R	H	D	T	HR	RBI	SB	BB	SO	AVG
93 AAA Col. Spmg	77	291	51	87	15	2	14	48	12	18	56	.299
94 AAA Col. Spmg	73	283	54	80	24	2	6	37	7	21	49	.283
95 AAA Col. Spmg	38	143	18	42	10	2	2	14	0	7	29	.294
96 AAA Indianapols	101	374	55	109	24	9	13	58	13	29	79	.291
96 AAA Pawtucket	21	74	9	19	4	0	0	4	4	5	18	.257
96 MLE	122	448	59	128	30	7	12	58	11	31	100	.286

Mejia blew all of his chances with the Rockies, and the Reds dealt him to the Red Sox for Kevin Mitchell late in the year. He put up good numbers at Triple-A for Cincinnati, and he's still young enough to turn it around. At the plate, he hasn't made any progress in curbing his overaggressiveness, but he still has good power for a second baseman. In the field, he has good range and a good arm, but his pivot still needs work. For someone with good speed, he doesn't steal very often.

Trot Nixon

Position: OF   **Opening Day Age:** 22
Bats: L **Throws:** L   **Born:** 4/11/74 in
Ht: 6' 1" **Wt:** 195   Durham, NC

Recent Statistics

	G	AB	R	H	D	T	HR	RBI	SB	BB	SO	AVG
96 AA Trenton	123	438	55	110	11	4	11	63	7	50	65	.251
96 AL Boston	2	4	2	2	1	0	0	0	1	0	1	.500
96 MLE	123	437	51	109	12	3	9	59	5	39	69	.249

You have to wonder if the back injury he suffered in '95 is still bothering him. He's young, and he played in a tough park last year, but any way you cut it, his numbers were underwhelming. He remains reasonably selective, but his power has regressed. Scouts have always raved about his tools, so he may yet pan out. In the field, he's moved over from center to become a terrific right fielder, with a powerful arm and good range. He's intense and wants to excel, so physical problems are the only thing that might hold him back. He's still at least a year away.

Carl Pavano

Position: P
Bats: R **Throws:** R
Ht: 6' 5" **Wt:** 225

Opening Day Age: 21
Born: 1/8/76 in New Britain, CT

Recent Statistics

	W	L	ERA	G	GS	Sv	IP	H	R	BB	SO	HR
94 R Red Sox	4	3	1.84	9	7	0	44.0	31	14	7	47	1
95 A Michigan	6	6	3.44	22	22	0	141.1	118	63	52	138	7
96 AA Trenton	16	5	2.63	27	26	0	185.0	154	66	47	146	16

After getting himself into much better shape over the offseason, Pavano became one of the game's best pitching prospects last year. He throws a 90-MPH sinking fastball and a good offspeed pitch. His control is remarkable, as is his durability. He's looked upon as one of the jewels of the Boston system, and he'll be called up as soon as he shows he's capable of handling the jump.

Rudy Pemberton

Position: OF
Bats: R **Throws:** R
Ht: 6' 1" **Wt:** 185

Opening Day Age: 27
Born: 12/17/69 in San Pedro De Macoris, DR

Recent Statistics

	G	AB	R	H	D	T	HR	RBI	SB	BB	SO	AVG
96 AAA Okla. City	17	71	6	18	3	0	2	11	1	1	10	.254
96 AAA Pawtucket	102	396	77	129	28	3	27	92	16	18	63	.326
96 AL Boston	13	41	11	21	8	0	1	10	3	2	4	.512
96 MLE	119	461	72	141	32	2	23	90	11	16	76	.306

Pemberton is a very good hitter, and someday he'll get a chance to prove it. Until now, his poor defense and questions about his attitude have held him back. Despite all of that, he went 21-for-41 in his trial with Boston last year, and now carries a major league average of .423 in 71 at-bats. He's impatient at the plate, but he has decent speed, and has always made excellent contact. He's capable of putting together a big year if given the shot.

Brian Rose

Position: P
Bats: R **Throws:** R
Ht: 6' 2" **Wt:** 190

Opening Day Age: 21
Born: 2/13/76 in ?

Recent Statistics

	W	L	ERA	G	GS	Sv	IP	H	R	BB	SO	HR
95 A Michigan	8	5	3.44	21	20	0	136.0	127	63	31	105	5
96 AA Trenton	12	7	4.01	27	27	0	163.2	157	82	45	115	21

Rose and Pavano have been compared throughout their minor league careers, but Rose's second half-slump last year left him lagging behind. He's still a premier prospect, with a moving fastball that hits 90. He's drawn raves for his poise on the mound, but he's been held back by his below-average curveball. He may be a bit farther away than Pavano, and a full year of Triple-A may be the plan for him. Still, he's a good bet to crack the Boston rotation within the next two years, unless injuries intervene.

Donnie Sadler

Position: SS
Bats: R **Throws:** R
Ht: 5' 7" **Wt:** 160

Opening Day Age: 21
Born: 6/17/75 in Clifton, TX

Recent Statistics

	G	AB	R	H	D	T	HR	RBI	SB	BB	SO	AVG
94 R Red Sox	53	206	52	56	8	6	1	16	32	23	27	.272
95 A Michigan	118	438	103	124	25	8	9	55	41	79	85	.283
96 AA Trenton	115	454	68	121	20	8	6	46	34	38	75	.267
96 MLE	115	454	63	121	22	6	5	43	24	30	80	.267

When the top prospects in baseball are listed, his name often appears. Sadler is a small shortstop whose speed is already becoming legendary. He uses it to cover a tremendous amount of ground in the field, and he's dangerous on the basepaths, too. A tremendous athlete, he has a great arm and will be a top shortstop once he smooths out his footwork. The Red Sox tried to convert him to center field (due to the presence of Nomar Garciaparra), and Sadler was uncomfortable out there despite showing great range. To be a top leadoff prospect, he only needs to address last year's decrease in walks.

Others to Watch

Fireballing righthander **Bobby Rodgers** returned from arm problems to completely dominate the NY-Penn League last year. No one could touch his 95-MPH fastball and good curveball, and he ended up fanning 108 batters in only 90 innings, to go with a sparkling 1.90 ERA. At age 22, he may be the next power arm in the Red Sox' pipeline. . . He may get some competition from **Juan Pena**, though. At the tender age of 19, Pena went 12-10 with a 2.97 ERA in the Midwest League. He showed a phenomenal combination of power and control, striking out 156 batters while walking only 34. . . Also in the mix is righthander **James Farrell**, who posted a combined record of 15-9 at two levels of Class A last year. He'll be 23 this season, and could move up quickly. . . Comparisons to Carlton Fisk are premature, but catcher **Damian Sapp** opened some eyes by batting .322 with good power at Class A last year. He figures to be about two years away. . . Former Giants' and Reds' farmhand **Adam Hyzdu** tore up the Eastern League last year. The Red Sox will try to convert him from the outfield to catcher over the winter. If he can make the adjustment, his bat will be more than good enough to get him to the majors.

Terry Bevington

1996 Season

The 1996 season was Terry Bevington's first full campaign as a major league manager, and it was a season full of controversy. Bevington was accused of overmanaging—particularly in the way he used his pitching staff—when the Sox faded down the stretch in their bid to win a wild-card berth. Bevington's communication skills also came under fire, both in the way he dealt with the media and in his relationships with his own players.

Offense

Bevington uses his whole roster, substituting frequently and giving everybody a chance to contribute. He doesn't platoon much, although he did sit down Ozzie Guillen against some lefthanders last year. His 1996 team was power-laden by White Sox standards, but he wasn't afraid to utilize the bunt or hit-and-run. He uses the stolen base intelligently, giving the green light to high-percentage stealers but shutting down the ones more likely to be thrown out.

Pitching & Defense

Given a choice between a guy who can field and a player who can hit, Bevington tends to go with the better bat. He'll save his light-hitting glove men for the late innings. When it comes to using pitchers, Bevington's the sort who will bring in a lefty pitcher to pitch to one lefty hitter in the fifth inning. His bullpen is warming up constantly, and many felt that his relievers were worn out by the All-Star break last year.

1997 Outlook

After failing in a well-publicized bid to sign Jim Leyland, the Sox surprised many when they re-signed Bevington to a two-year contract. Despite getting a two-year pact, he'll probably be gone if the team doesn't get off to a strong start.

Born: 7/27/56 in Akron, OH

Playing Experience: No major league experience

Managerial Experience: 2 seasons

Manager Statistics

Year	Team, Lg	W	L	Pct	GB	Finish
1996	Chicago, AL	85	77	.525	14.5	2nd Central
2 Seasons		142	133	.516	—	—

1996 Starting Pitchers by Days Rest

	≤3	4	5	6+
White Sox Starts	3	104	24	20
White Sox ERA	6.06	4.50	3.97	5.60
AL Avg Starts	4	96	30	21
AL ERA	5.57	4.90	5.33	5.81

1996 Situational Stats

	Terry Bevington	AL Average
Hit & Run Success %	44.0	39.1
Stolen Base Success %	71.9	69.6
Platoon Pct.	69.5	61.9
Defensive Subs	52	29
High-Pitch Outings	42	23
Quick/Slow Hooks	24/15	17/20
Sacrifice Attempts	75	58

1996 Rankings (American League)

→ 1st in least caught steals of third base (3), squeeze plays (10), pitchouts (60), pitchouts with a runner moving (16) and one-batter pitcher appearances (48)

→ 2nd in sacrifice bunt attempts (75), intentional walks (43), defensive substitutions (52), starts with over 120 pitches (42) and starts with over 140 pitches (2)

→ 3rd in hit-and-run attempts (91) and quick hooks (24)

Wilson Alvarez

1996 Season

Determined to show that his 8-11 season in 1995 was a fluke, Wilson Alvarez reported to camp in better condition last spring and reached the All-Star break with a 10-4 record. By the end of August, Alvarez had matched his career high of 15 victories, and seemed a good bet to win 18 or more. But Alvarez slumped badly down the stretch and failed to win in five September starts.

Pitching

Alvarez' best pitch is a 90-plus fastball with excellent movement, and his sharp-breaking curve is another formidable weapon. His slider and change aren't as good, but both can be effective if spotted properly. Alvarez can dominate hitters when he has command of his pitches, but control has been a career-long problem for him. He misses the strike zone so frequently that he often reaches the 100-pitch level by the sixth inning, making it difficult for him to last into the late innings. Alvarez also is guilty of poor pitch selection at times. He'll have a hitter overmatched with his fastball, then suddenly serve up a nothing change and get creamed.

Defense

Alvarez is a poor fielder, reacting slowly to balls hit up the middle and often failing to cover first quickly enough. His pickoff move is probably the best on the Sox staff, but his delivery home is pretty slow, and runners can take advantage of him.

1997 Outlook

While he's had two 15-win seasons, Alvarez hasn't reached the level of success once expected of him. Control problems have held him back, and so has his tendency to put on weight. But he's still one of the better lefthanders in the American League, and a solid number-two or three starter. A lot of teams would love a pitcher like that, and if the Sox sour on him, there'll be plenty of clubs interested in him.

Position: SP
Bats: L **Throws:** L
Ht: 6' 1" **Wt:** 235

Opening Day Age: 27
Born: 3/24/70 in Maracaibo, VZ
ML Seasons: 7

Overall Statistics

	W	L	Pct.	ERA	G	GS	Sv	IP	H	BB	SO	HR	BR/IP
1996	15	10	.600	4.22	35	35	0	217.1	216	97	181	21	1.44
Career	58	43	.574	3.91	164	138	1	918.1	855	470	660	95	1.44

How Often He Throws Strikes

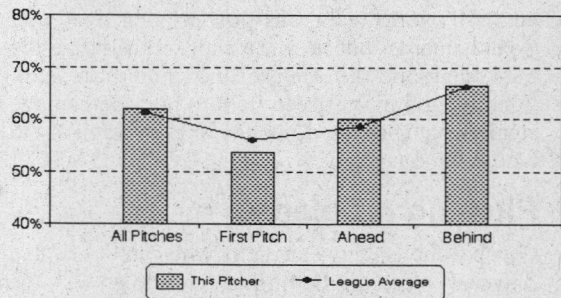

1996 Situational Stats

	W	L	ERA	Sv	IP		AB	H	HR	RBI	Avg
Home	7	6	3.79	0	92.2	LHB	145	44	1	9	.303
Road	8	4	4.55	0	124.2	RHB	693	172	20	86	.248
First Half	10	4	3.69	0	117.0	Sc Pos	216	55	6	71	.255
Scnd Half	5	6	4.84	0	100.1	Clutch	63	18	0	6	.286

1996 Rankings (American League)

→ 1st in fielding percentage at pitcher (1.000)
→ 2nd in games started and most pitches thrown per batter (4.08)
→ 5th in walks allowed and runners caught stealing (11)
→ 6th in strikeouts, pitches thrown (3,863) and most strikeouts per 9 innings (7.5)
→ 8th in wins, stolen bases allowed (21) and least home runs allowed per 9 innings (.87)
→ 9th in lowest batting average allowed (.258), most run support per 9 innings (6.3) and lowest batting average allowed vs. right-handed batters (.248)

Harold Baines

1996 Season

The White Sox retired Harold Baines' uniform number when they traded him to the Rangers back in 1989, but in his return to the Sox last season, Baines looked like he wouldn't be ready for retirement for several more years. Installed as the everyday DH, Baines wound up playing 143 games, his most since '89, and his 95 RBI were his highest total since way back in 1985. Baines gave the club a weapon it sorely needed, a power hitter to bat behind Frank Thomas in the lineup.

Hitting

Baines stands well off the plate and takes a long, smooth stroke, finishing with the top hand off the ball. He tends to pull anything hit on the ground, but he'll use the whole field when he gets the ball in the air. He's a great lowball hitter, and pitchers work him upstairs consistently. The big surprise in his return to the Sox last year was the way he handled lefthanders. Considered a platoon player by the Orioles, Baines hit southpaws so well that he seldom had to be taken out of the lineup.

Baserunning & Defense

You could tell Baines was feeling revitalized last year from the fact that he swiped three bases—this after swiping only one base in the previous nine years. It probably won't happen again, since Baines is very slow and needs to protect his extremely tender knees. The knee problems long ago turned him into a full-time designated hitter, and he hasn't played in the field in years.

1997 Outlook

Baines' return to Chicago was a success in every way, and other things being equal, the club would love to have him finish his career there. But the Albert Belle signing means the Sox will probably be a little more budget-minded with some of their other players. There's still a good chance Baines will return to the White Sox. . . but only if they feel his salary demands are reasonable.

Position: DH
Bats: L **Throws:** L
Ht: 6' 2" **Wt:** 195

Opening Day Age: 38
Born: 3/15/59 in St. Michaels, MD
ML Seasons: 17

Overall Statistics

	G	AB	R	H	D	T	HR	RBI	SB	BB	SO	Avg	OBP	Slg
1996	143	495	80	154	29	0	22	95	3	73	62	.311	.399	.503
Career	2326	8366	1113	2425	416	48	323	1356	33	877	1225	.290	.355	.467

Where He Hits the Ball

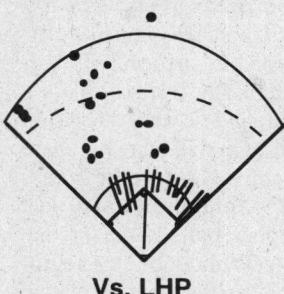

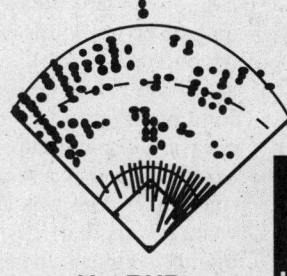

Vs. LHP   **Vs. RHP**

1996 Situational Stats

	AB	H	HR	RBI	Avg		AB	H	HR	RBI	Avg
Home	237	67	9	39	.283	LHP	105	35	4	27	.333
Road	258	87	13	56	.337	RHP	390	119	18	68	.305
First Half	264	83	15	62	.314	Sc Pos	155	41	7	69	.265
Scnd Half	231	71	7	33	.307	Clutch	96	33	6	26	.344

1996 Rankings (American League)

→ 3rd in lowest percentage of extra bases taken as a runner (28.3%)
→ 5th in GDPs (20)
→ 7th in batting average on the road (.337)
→ 8th in batting average in the clutch (.344)
→ 10th in most GDPs per GDP situation (15.5%)and
→ Led the White Sox in highest groundball/flyball ratio (1.6), batting average in the clutch (.344), cleanup slugging percentage (.516), batting average on a 3-2 count (.349)and highest percentage of swings put into play (50.4%)

Chicago White Sox

James Baldwin

1996 Season

Considered one of White Sox' top pitching prospects for the last several years, rookie righthander James Baldwin began the 1996 season at Triple-A Nashville. Recalled late in April, Baldwin won his first two starts and soon established himself as the best rookie pitcher in the American League. He won nine of his first 10 decisions, and even a late-season slump couldn't spoil a very impressive debut season.

Pitching

Baldwin came to the majors with a reputation for having one of the best curveballs in the game. The reputation is well deserved. The pitch has a sharp, late, downward break, and Baldwin proved early on that he could throw it for strikes consistently, which is all he really needed to succeed. He balances the curve with a high 80s fastball that's a solid pitch in its own right, and he also throws an occasional change-up. Baldwin will hang his share of curves, and as a result can be hurt by the home-run ball. But he was able to limit the damage last year. Nearly half his gopher balls came in one month, August, when he was undoubtedly beginning to feel the effects of the long major league season.

Defense

Baldwin has a slow delivery and only a fair move to first, so runners can take advantage of him. He's also had some problems fielding his position, committing three errors last year.

1997 Outlook

After getting lit up in a four-start trial early in 1995, Baldwin proved last year that he has both the stuff and the control to succeed at the major league level. He'll need to show that he can handle the grind of a 162-game schedule, but a 15-win season is well within his capabilities this year.

Position: SP
Bats: R **Throws:** R
Ht: 6' 3" **Wt:** 210

Opening Day Age: 25
Born: 7/15/71 in Southern Pines, NC
ML Seasons: 2

Overall Statistics

	W	L	Pct.	ERA	G	GS	Sv	IP	H	BB	SO	HR	BR/IP
1996	11	6	.647	4.42	28	28	0	169.0	168	57	127	24	1.33
Career	11	7	.611	5.10	34	32	0	183.2	200	66	137	30	1.45

How Often He Throws Strikes

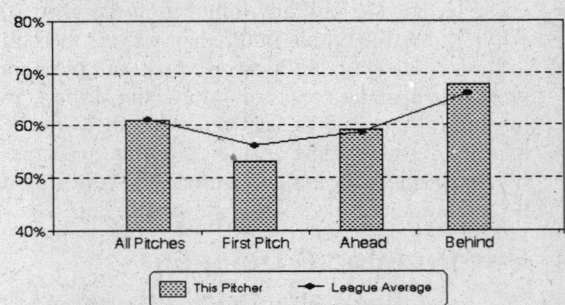

This Pitcher ▨   League Average ●—

1996 Situational Stats

	W	L	ERA	Sv	IP		AB	H	HR	RBI	Avg
Home	6	3	3.75	0	98.1	LHB	353	94	11	33	.266
Road	5	3	5.35	0	70.2	RHB	301	74	13	43	.246
First Half	7	1	3.75	0	72.0	Sc Pos	127	31	5	47	.244
Scnd Half	4	5	4.92	0	97.0	Clutch	54	12	6	8	.222

1996 Rankings (American League)

→ 1st in least GDPs induced per 9 innings (0.5)
→ 2nd in lowest groundball/flyball ratio allowed (0.7) and lowest fielding percentage at pitcher (.903)
→ 3rd in errors at pitcher (3)
→ 6th in wild pitches (12)
→ 7th in winning percentage and lowest batting average allowed vs. right-handed batters (.246)
→ 8th in lowest batting average allowed (.257), least baserunners allowed per 9 innings and most home runs allowed per 9 innings (1.28)
→ 9th in lowest on-base percentage allowed (.319)
→ 10th in balks (1)

Ray Durham

1996 Season

After breaking in with a solid rookie season in 1995, Ray Durham improved in virtually every category last season. Along with posting better hitting numbers across the board, Durham was far more sure of himself in the field, and he's developing into one of the best baserunners in baseball.

Hitting

The switch-hitting Durham greatly improved his plate work from the left side last year, and wound up hitting for a better average as a lefty. He continues to show more power as a righty, however. From either side he's a line-drive hitter with gap power and a nice, short stroke. While not a wild swinger, Durham doesn't draw an exceptional number of walks, and he's looked more comfortable hitting in the bottom half of the order. He's shown a tendency to lose bat speed late in the year, resulting in September slumps.

Baserunning & Defense

The fastest player on the White Sox team, Durham is both a superb baserunner and basestealer. He has great baserunning instincts and seldom gets thrown out trying to take an extra base, even though he's an extremely aggressive runner. Durham's athleticism helps him on defense, where he shows fine range—particularly on pop flies and plays to his left. Though he still has a few rough edges, he cut down on his errors last year, committing only 11 miscues.

1997 Outlook

Still only 25, Durham has the tools to develop into an All-Star caliber second baseman. Whether he reaches that level or not in 1997, he figures to continue to improve. A season with 15 home runs, 90 runs scored and 35 stolen bases—plus improved defense—is well within his capabilities. It'll help if he can avoid the late-season slumps that plagued him in 1995 and 1996.

Position: 2B
Bats: B **Throws:** R
Ht: 5' 8" **Wt:** 170

Opening Day Age: 25
Born: 11/30/71 in Charlotte, NC
ML Seasons: 2

Overall Statistics

	G	AB	R	H	D	T	HR	RBI	SB	BB	SO	Avg	OBP	Slg
1996	156	557	79	153	33	5	10	65	30	58	95	.275	.350	.406
Career	281	1028	147	274	60	11	17	116	48	89	178	.267	.331	.396

Where He Hits the Ball

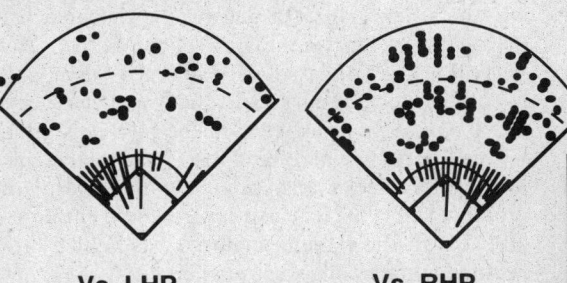

Vs. LHP   Vs. RHP

1996 Situational Stats

	AB	H	HR	RBI	Avg		AB	H	HR	RBI	Avg
Home	275	71	3	31	.258	LHP	168	44	3	21	.262
Road	282	82	7	34	.291	RHP	389	109	7	44	.280
First Half	284	75	5	31	.264	Sc Pos	126	33	2	52	.262
Scnd Half	273	78	5	34	.286	Clutch	98	25	1	8	.255

1996 Rankings (American League)

- ➡ 1st in stolen base percentage (88.2%)
- ➡ 5th in errors at second base (11) and fielding percentage at second base (.984)
- ➡ 6th in stolen bases
- ➡ 8th in hit by pitch (10)
- ➡ 10th in least GDPs per GDP situation (5.2%) and bunts in play (26)
- ➡ Led the White Sox in doubles, stolen bases, hit by pitch (10) and stolen base percentage

Alex Fernandez

1996 Season

It took him a while to get comfortable in the role, but Alex Fernandez has finally settled into the number-one starter's role that the White Sox have hoped he'd assume since they traded Jack Mc-Dowell to the Yankees after the 1994 season. Working a career-high 258 innings and striking out 200 batters for the first time in his career, Fernandez was a true staff anchor for the Sox in 1996. He was at his best down the stretch, going 4-1 in the heat of the September playoff battle.

Pitching

Throwing from a smooth, compact motion, Fernandez has beautiful mechanics. . . a big reason why he's never spent a day on the disabled list during his seven-year major league career. His fastball has excellent velocity and movement, and his other pitches—curveball, slider and change—are above-average as well. In the past he's gone through periods where he'd lose command of his pitches for weeks at a time, but that wasn't a problem in 1996. He's also settled down emotionally, and his new-found maturity has helped him become a more consistent pitcher.

Defense

Fernandez works hard at all aspects of his game, and he's developed a quick, tricky move to first that helps him control the running game better than most power pitchers. His good mechanics leave him in excellent position for fielding balls hit up the middle, and his overall defensive work is close to Gold Glove caliber.

1997 Outlook

Fernandez was one of the players who became a free agent when service time lost in 1994 was restored by the new labor agreement. The Sox made a bid to keep him, but the Miami native was lured away by the prospects of pitching for his hometown Florida Marlins. The Marlins signed Fernandez to a $36 million, five-year contract in early December. He figures to remain one of the best young starters in the game.

Position: SP
Bats: R **Throws:** R
Ht: 6' 1" **Wt:** 215

Opening Day Age: 27
Born: 8/13/69 in Miami Beach, FL
ML Seasons: 7

Overall Statistics

	W	L	Pct.	ERA	G	GS	Sv	IP	H	BB	SO	HR	BR/IP
1996	16	10	.615	3.45	35	35	0	258.0	248	72	200	34	1.24
Career	79	63	.556	3.78	199	197	0	1346.1	1306	426	951	148	1.29

How Often He Throws Strikes

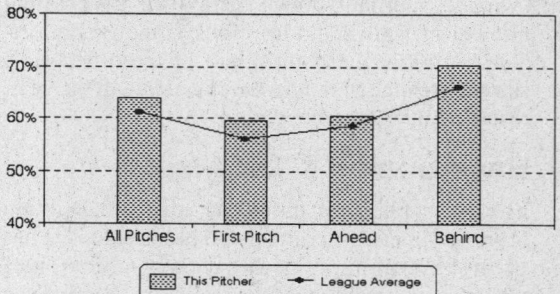

1996 Situational Stats

	W	L	ERA	Sv	IP		AB	H	HR	RBI	Avg
Home	7	7	3.74	0	130.0	LHB	535	138	18	46	.258
Road	9	3	3.16	0	128.0	RHB	445	110	16	54	.247
First Half	8	5	4.10	0	129.2	Sc Pos	172	42	4	61	.244
Scnd Half	8	5	2.81	0	128.1	Clutch	105	21	1	4	.200

1996 Rankings (American League)

→ 2nd in games started, innings pitched, batters faced (1,071) and pitches thrown (4,098)
→ 3rd in highest strikeout/walk ratio (2.8) and lowest ERA on the road (3.16)
→ 4th in ERA, complete games (6) , home runs allowed, lowest on-base percentage allowed (.307) and least baserunners allowed per 9 innings
→ 5th in wins, strikeouts and lowest batting average allowed (.253)
→ 6th in shutouts (1)
→ 7th in hits allowed and pickoff throws (159)
→ 8th in lowest slugging percentage allowed (.397) and lowest batting average allowed vs. right-handed batters (.247)

Ozzie Guillen

Position: SS
Bats: L **Throws:** R
Ht: 5'11" **Wt:** 164

Opening Day Age: 33
Born: 1/20/64 in Ocumare del Tuy, VZ
ML Seasons: 12
Pronunciation: GHEY-un

1996 Season

After batting only .248 in 1995—his worst average ever for a full season—Ozzie Guillen bounced back with a better year in 1996. Guillen raised his average 15 points to .263 and matched his career high with four home runs. But as usual his main contributions came on defense, where he continued to perform with distinction in his 12th year as the White Sox shortstop.

Hitting

If every hitter was like Guillen, there'd be a lot more two-hour games. He comes up hacking, looking for a fastball and usually jumping on the first pitch. He seldom walks, seldom strikes out and seldom hits with power, but he knows how to handle the bat. One of his favorite techniques is to chop down on a high pitch and attempt to pound it through the infield. He's also an outstanding bunter. Guillen's had major problems with left-handers in recent years, and increasingly finds himself on the bench when a southpaw is starting.

Baserunning & Defense

Guillen no longer possesses the range he had prior to tearing knee ligaments in 1992, but he remains a steady and dependable shortstop. He plays the hitters very well, and he's one of the best in the business on the double play. Guillen's speed is now only average at best, and he isn't much of a basestealer. He'll also commit an occasional baserunning gaffe, usually due to overaggressiveness.

1997 Outlook

Guillen has had a long run as the White Sox shortstop, and though he's 33 and no longer quite the player he once was, he figures to be back out there in 1997. Along with his steady play in the field, the White Sox value his spirit and leadership skills, and he continues to be a favorite with the fans. But Guillen will probably find himself sitting out more games this year than in the past.

Overall Statistics

	G	AB	R	H	D	T	HR	RBI	SB	BB	SO	Avg	OBP	Slg
1996	150	499	62	131	24	8	4	45	6	10	27	.263	.273	.367
Career	1601	5577	634	1488	219	62	20	513	158	171	436	.267	.287	.339

Where He Hits the Ball

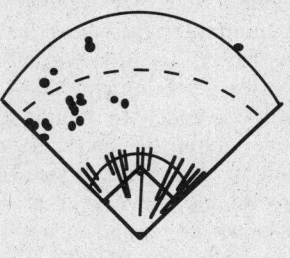
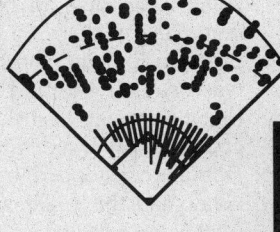

Vs. LHP   **Vs. RHP**

1996 Situational Stats

	AB	H	HR	RBI	Avg		AB	H	HR	RBI	Avg
Home	239	60	0	19	.251	LHP	117	28	1	5	.239
Road	260	71	4	26	.273	RHP	382	103	3	40	.270
First Half	294	81	2	26	.276	Sc Pos	122	32	3	39	.262
Scnd Half	205	50	2	19	.244	Clutch	104	30	1	9	.288

1996 Rankings (American League)

- → 1st in lowest on-base percentage and least pitches seen per plate appearance (2.80)
- → 2nd in lowest on-base percentage vs. right-handed pitchers (.281) and highest percentage of swings on the first pitch (48.6%)
- → 3rd in triples and fielding percentage at shortstop (.981)
- → 4th in lowest HR frequency (124.8 ABs per HR)
- → 5th in lowest slugging percentage
- → 7th in sacrifice bunts (12)
- → 9th in lowest slugging percentage vs. right-handed pitchers (.385)
- → Led the White Sox in triples

Roberto Hernandez

1996 Season

After posting 38 saves in 1993, his first full year as the White Sox closer, Roberto Hernandez went through a two-year stretch in which he was often too inconsistent to be considered a top-level finisher. Hernandez was on trial when the 1996 season began, but he quickly silenced the doubters with his brilliant relief work. He didn't allow his second earned run until June, and he entered September with 34 saves and an ERA of 1.01. He gave in to fatigue down the stretch, but still matched his career high with 38 saves.

Pitching

Hernandez possesses three excellent pitches—a 90-plus fastball, a nasty splitter and a serviceable slider—and he's all but unhittable when he has command of them. In '94 and '95 location was a problem for him, and he often got lit up when he was struggling to find the strike zone. He seemed intent on trying to strike every hitter out, and if he couldn't, he found himself in trouble. Last year Hernandez stopped trying to blow every hitter away, and the result was better command of his pitches. His strikeout rate declined a little from 1995, but he was a much better pitcher overall.

Defense

A power pitcher with a long, slow delivery, Hernandez is fairly easy to steal on, but as a closer he's usually in the game when runners are reluctant to take off. He's fairly mobile around the mound and handles his fielding responsibilities well.

1997 Outlook

Hernandez had a pretty rough September, but that was undoubtedly the result of being worked very hard because of the club's thin bullpen. More effective set-up work would help lighten his load a little, and if he can maintain the command he had in '96, he should continue to be one of the best closers in the game.

Position: RP
Bats: R **Throws:** R
Ht: 6' 4" **Wt:** 235

Opening Day Age: 32
Born: 11/11/64 in Santurce, PR
ML Seasons: 6

Overall Statistics

	W	L	Pct.	ERA	G	GS	Sv	IP	H	BB	SO	HR	BR/IP
1996	6	5	.545	1.91	72	0	38	84.2	65	38	85	2	1.22
Career	24	23	.511	2.93	299	3	134	356.2	301	132	364	27	1.21

How Often He Throws Strikes

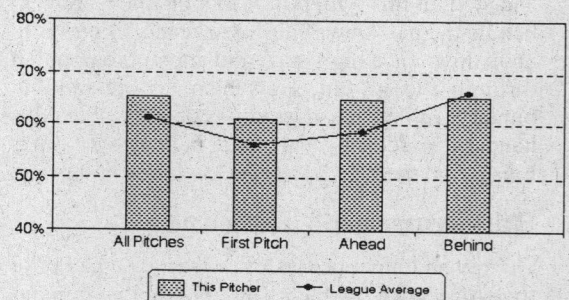

This Pitcher   League Average

1996 Situational Stats

	W	L	ERA	Sv	IP		AB	H	HR	RBI	Avg
Home	2	2	1.66	20	43.1	LHB	162	31	1	13	.191
Road	4	3	2.18	18	41.1	RHB	151	34	1	15	.225
First Half	1	0	1.20	26	45.0	Sc Pos	89	17	1	24	.191
Scnd Half	5	5	2.72	12	39.2	Clutch	247	54	2	26	.219

1996 Rankings (American League)

- → 1st in games finished (61) and relief ERA (1.91)
- → 2nd in save opportunities (46) and blown saves (8)
- → 3rd in saves
- → 5th in least GDPs induced per GDP situation (2.9%)
- → 6th in lowest save percentage (82.6%), relief wins (6) , relief innings (84.2), lowest batting average allowed in relief (.208) and least baserunners allowed per 9 innings in relief (10.9)
- → 7th in games pitched and lowest batting average allowed in relief with runners on base (.208)

Ron Karkovice

Position: C
Bats: R **Throws:** R
Ht: 6' 1" **Wt:** 219

Opening Day Age: 33
Born: 8/8/63 in Union, NJ
ML Seasons: 11
Nickname: Officer Karkovice

1996 Season

Ron Karkovice has been the White Sox' primary catcher for five seasons, and his 1995 campaign was a lot like the other four: he hit for a low average, provided an occasional longball, and played great defense. His season was cut short by knee problems, however, and he logged only seven at-bats in September.

Hitting

Karkovice isn't in the lineup for his offense. He hasn't hit over .220 since 1993, and his lifetime average is an anemic .223. He's always been a wild swinger, and pitchers usually don't have much difficulty getting him to chase high pitches out of the strike zone. He'd shown some signs of development in 1994 and '95, laying off some of the bad pitches and drawing a fair number of walks. But last year he returned to his old undisciplined ways. Karkovice does have some power, and if a pitcher makes a mistake he can jump on it and knock the ball out of the yard. He's also a fine bunter.

Baserunning & Defense

Karkovice earns his keep with his work behind the plate. His strong, accurate throwing arm is one of the best in the business, he gets rid of the ball as quickly as anyone, and he's a fine handler of pitchers. He's also excellent at blocking low pitches despite his knee problems. Once fairly fast for a catcher, he's now strictly a station-to-station runner.

1997 Outlook

Unless the Sox trade for a catcher or sign a free agent, Karkovice figures to be the club's primary receiver again in 1997. They know they can't expect much offense from him, but his package of defensive skills is enough to make up for it. He'll turn 34 in August, however, and he's begun to show some signs of wear. Figure him for 110-120 games behind the plate while the club attempts to start breaking in a younger receiver.

Overall Statistics

	G	AB	R	H	D	T	HR	RBI	SB	BB	SO	Avg	OBP	Slg
1996	111	355	44	78	22	0	10	38	0	24	93	.220	.270	.366
Career	888	2459	326	549	117	6	90	317	24	222	717	.223	.291	.386

Where He Hits the Ball

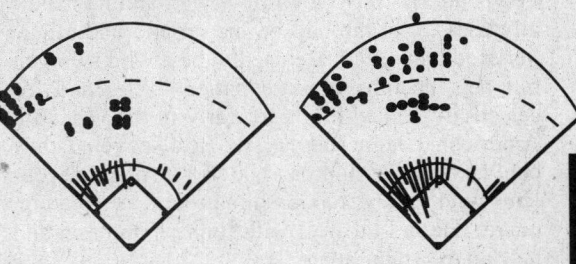

Vs. LHP   **Vs. RHP**

1996 Situational Stats

	AB	H	HR	RBI	Avg		AB	H	HR	RBI	Avg
Home	176	40	5	17	.227	LHP	85	23	2	10	.271
Road	179	38	5	21	.212	RHP	270	55	8	28	.204
First Half	230	49	7	24	.213	Sc Pos	81	14	1	22	.173
Scnd Half	125	29	3	14	.232	Clutch	51	7	1	1	.137

1996 Rankings (American League)

→ 2nd in lowest batting average in the clutch (.137) and highest percentage of runners caught stealing as a catcher (37.7%)

→ 4th in lowest batting average with the bases loaded (.083)

→ 8th in lowest batting average on an 0-2 count (.053)

→ 9th in errors at catcher (5)

Chicago White Sox

Darren Lewis

1996 Season

When the White Sox decided that Lance Johnson's salary demands were excessive last winter, they let Johnson depart via free agency and signed Darren Lewis to replace him. Lewis wasn't expected to hit like Johnson, but the Sox thought he could hit around .250 while providing Gold Glove-caliber defense. Lewis got off to a surprisingly good start at bat, and was hitting .271 at the end of May. But then he slumped badly and even his solid glove work wasn't enough to keep him in the lineup. He hit only .200 after the break and finished the year as a defensive substitute.

Hitting

Lewis doesn't have a lot of power, and he generally tries to hit the ball on the ground and utilize his excellent speed. He used to be a wild swinger, but he's become a more patient hitter and his selectivity helped him a lot early in the year. But American League pitchers soon discovered they could overpower him, and he had surprising problems with lefties, making him useless as a platoon player. He did hit well with runners on base, and he's an excellent bunter.

Baserunning & Defense

The White Sox have had a long history of great defensive center fielders, and Lewis helped continue the tradition. He has excellent speed and instincts for the ball, and he hardly ever makes a mistake. His throwing arm was a little disappointing, however. Lewis' speed helps him on the bases, and he's capable of stealing 30 or more bases in a season.

1997 Outlook

Lewis is signed for 1997, so he figures to get another chance this spring. With his speed, defensive ability and new-found patience at the plate, he doesn't need to hit a lot to be a useful player. But the Sox have plenty of outfield candidates, and Lewis will probably begin the year as a bench player.

Position: CF
Bats: R **Throws:** R
Ht: 6' 0" **Wt:** 189

Opening Day Age: 29
Born: 8/28/67 in Berkeley, CA
ML Seasons: 7

Overall Statistics

	G	AB	R	H	D	T	HR	RBI	SB	BB	SO	Avg	OBP	Slg
1996	141	337	55	77	12	2	4	53	21	45	40	.228	.321	.312
Career	720	2359	358	580	70	25	13	188	172	234	267	.246	.320	.313

Where He Hits the Ball

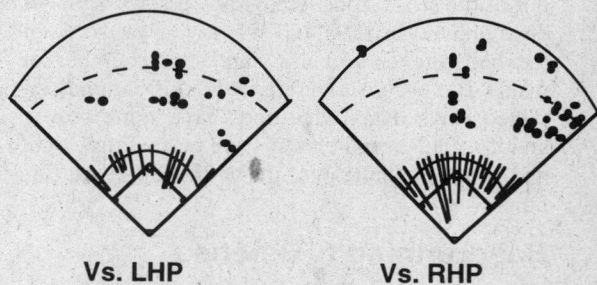

Vs. LHP   Vs. RHP

1996 Situational Stats

	AB	H	HR	RBI	Avg		AB	H	HR	RBI	Avg
Home	172	36	0	24	.209	LHP	112	21	1	14	.188
Road	165	41	4	29	.248	RHP	225	56	3	39	.249
First Half	207	51	3	35	.246	Sc Pos	87	28	2	51	.322
Scnd Half	130	26	1	18	.200	Clutch	56	9	0	6	.161

1996 Rankings (American League)

- ➡ 1st in lowest batting average vs. left-handed pitchers (.188) and lowest slugging percentage vs. left-handed pitchers (.241)
- ➡ 2nd in lowest on-base percentage vs. left-handed pitchers (.268)
- ➡ 3rd in lowest fielding percentage in center field (.990)
- ➡ 5th in sacrifice bunts (15), lowest batting average in the clutch (.161) and errors in center field (3)
- ➡ 7th in bunts in play (29)
- ➡ 8th in stolen base percentage (80.8%)
- ➡ Led the White Sox in sacrifice bunts (15), batting average with the bases loaded (.500) and bunts in play (29)

Dave Martinez

1996 Season

A lot of people thought it was a fluke when Dave Martinez hit .307 after joining the White Sox in 1995. After all, Martinez had never batted .300 in nine previous seasons, and his lifetime average was only .269. But Martinez proved the skeptics wrong by lifting his average to a career-high .318. As in '95, his versatility was a plus, and he performed capably at several different positions.

Hitting

Martinez has improved noticeably as a hitter since coming over to the American League. He's developed a quick, short, line-drive stroke, and he's learned to hang in against lefthanders, always a problem for him in the past. He's not a big home-run threat, but he has fine power to the gaps, and he can turn on a low fastball. Pitchers work him away and try to tease him with fastballs up and out of the strike zone, but he's learned to lay off stuff he can't handle. He's a fairly patient hitter, and he draws a respectable number of walks.

Baserunning & Defense

Martinez has always had fine speed, and he's a smart baserunner and effective basestealer. He's also a fine defensive player, capable of handling all three outfield positions and first base as well. His best position is probably right field, since he has a good arm and lacks the range of a classic center fielder. But wherever they put him, he does a fine job.

1997 Outlook

Martinez has been a one-man rescue squad in his two seasons with the White Sox, taking over positions where the club was short-handed and performing capably. He's signed for 1997, but this time they might be tempted to leave him in center, the position at which they have the greatest need. His defense can't match Darren Lewis', but his superior offense should be able to compensate for that.

Position: CF/1B/RF
Bats: L **Throws:** L
Ht: 5'10" **Wt:** 175

Opening Day Age: 32
Born: 9/26/64 in Brooklyn, NY
ML Seasons: 11

Overall Statistics

	G	AB	R	H	D	T	HR	RBI	SB	BB	SO	Avg	OBP	Slg
1996	146	440	85	140	20	8	10	53	15	52	52	.318	.393	.468
Career	1288	3774	514	1037	156	53	63	372	139	346	579	.275	.336	.394

Where He Hits the Ball

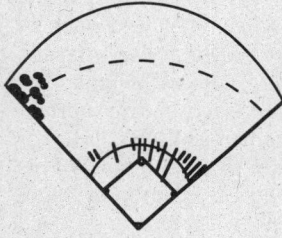

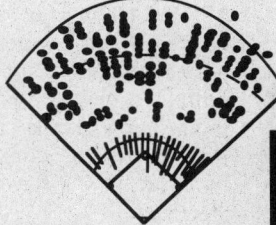

Vs. LHP   **Vs. RHP**

1996 Situational Stats

	AB	H	HR	RBI	Avg		AB	H	HR	RBI	Avg
Home	206	58	3	20	.282	LHP	74	23	1	10	.311
Road	234	82	7	33	.350	RHP	366	117	9	43	.320
First Half	206	64	5	31	.311	Sc Pos	92	31	3	42	.337
Scnd Half	234	76	5	22	.325	Clutch	85	29	1	7	.341

1996 Rankings (American League)

- ➡ 3rd in triples
- ➡ 4th in batting average on the road (.350)
- ➡ 5th in batting average with two strikes (.272)
- ➡ 6th in least GDPs per GDP situation (3.8%)
- ➡ 8th in steals of third (4)
- ➡ 9th in lowest stolen base percentage (68.2%)
- ➡ 10th in lowest batting average on a 3-1 count (.133) and lowest percentage of swings that missed (10.1%)
- ➡ Led the White Sox in triples, least GDPs per GDP situation (3.8%), batting average with two strikes (.272), lowest percentage of swings that missed (10.1%) and steals of third (4)

Lyle Mouton

1996 Season

After an impressive 58-game debut in 1995, Lyle Mouton spent the 1996 season as a reserve outfielder, getting an occasional start and coming off the bench frequently. That's a difficult role for any player, particularly a young one, but Mouton handled it very well. He displayed impressive power at times and wound up hitting .294, just a shade under his rookie average of .302. He was solid against both righties and lefties, and hit very well in pressure situations.

Hitting

Mouton is Frank Thomas-sized at 6'4" and 240 pounds, but he's yet to develop into a consistent home run threat. While the raw power is there, Mouton tends to be a wild swinger, and pitchers have had success getting him to chase offspeed pitches and low breaking stuff in the dirt. Sox hitting coach Bill Buckner has worked on shortening Mouton's stroke, and when he keeps his hands back and swings compactly, the ball jumps off his bat. But he's still working on developing more consistency.

Baserunning & Defense

Mouton has pretty good speed for a man his size and reached double figures in steals several times during his minor league career. He hasn't stolen much during his brief career with the White Sox, but he can't be taken for granted. He's a pretty good outfielder, but his throwing arm isn't really strong enough for right field, where he's spent most of his time.

1997 Outlook

Mouton has remained a bench player because the Sox have been bringing in veteran outfielders, like Tony Phillips and Danny Tartabull last year. With Tartabull already departed via free agency, Mouton might get his chance at a full-time role this year. He figures to duel with rookie Mike Cameron and several others for the regular right-field job.

Position: RF/LF/DH
Bats: R **Throws:** R
Ht: 6' 4" **Wt:** 240

Opening Day Age: 27
Born: 5/13/69 in Lafayette, LA
ML Seasons: 2
Pronunciation: Moo-TAHN

Overall Statistics

	G	AB	R	H	D	T	HR	RBI	SB	BB	SO	Avg	OBP	Slg
1996	87	214	25	63	8	1	7	39	3	22	50	.294	.361	.439
Career	145	393	48	117	24	1	12	66	4	41	96	.298	.367	.455

Where He Hits the Ball

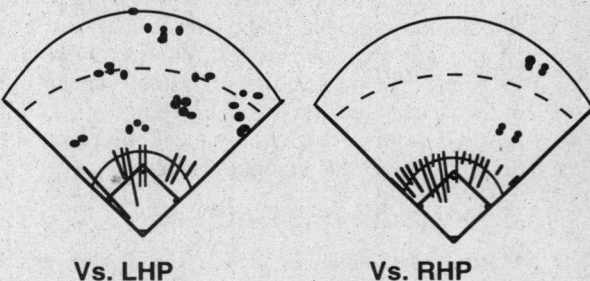

Vs. LHP   **Vs. RHP**

1996 Situational Stats

	AB	H	HR	RBI	Avg		AB	H	HR	RBI	Avg
Home	106	31	4	21	.292	LHP	125	37	3	23	.296
Road	108	32	3	18	.296	RHP	89	26	4	16	.292
First Half	108	32	4	18	.296	Sc Pos	69	21	2	32	.304
Scnd Half	106	31	3	21	.292	Clutch	35	13	3	9	.371

1996 Rankings (American League)

→ 1st in batting average on a 3-1 count (1.000)
→ Led the White Sox in batting average on a 3-1 count (1.000)

Tony Phillips

1996 Season

Signed to a two-year free-agent contract in January, Tony Phillips shocked the White Sox in spring training when he left camp and announced he was retiring. Phillips quickly returned, but that set the tone for his season, as he remained volatile and embroiled in controversy all year. The White Sox didn't mind; they loved Phillips' spirit, and loved the way he performed on the field. Drawing 125 walks and matching his career high with 119 runs scored, Phillips was outstanding as a leadoff hitter. He was also a big surprise in left field, where he played brilliantly.

Hitting

Phillips' ability to get on base makes him one of the top leadoff men in the game. Batting from a deep crouch to reduce his strike zone, he consistently draws well over 100 walks a year. A switch-hitter, he hits for a higher average from the right side but he has excellent power either way. Phillips takes a good, hard cut and strikes out as often as he walks. But as long as he reaches base nearly 300 times a year, no one is going to complain.

Baserunning & Defense

Considered a mediocre defensive player who could play a lot of positions but none particularly well, Phillips surprised the Sox with the way he performed in left field. He covered a lot of ground, made a number of highlight-film catches and displayed a solid throwing arm. An aggressive runner with decent but not great speed, Phillips is usually good for 10 to 15 steals a year.

1997 Outlook

After a torrid first half, Phillips cooled off after the break, hitting only .248 with 18 RBI. He'll turn 38 in April, so age has to be a concern, but he should have at least one more solid season in him. Albert Belle will be taking over left field from Phillips, and if he returns to the club, he'll have to play some other position. . . maybe several positions. There was also talk of trading Phillips.

Position: LF
Bats: B **Throws:** R
Ht: 5'10" **Wt:** 175

Opening Day Age: 37
Born: 4/25/59 in Atlanta, GA
ML Seasons: 15

Overall Statistics

	G	AB	R	H	D	T	HR	RBI	SB	BB	SO	Avg	OBP	Slg
1996	153	581	119	161	29	3	12	63	13	125	132	.277	.404	.399
Career	1849	6441	1094	1718	286	44	133	692	152	1099	1237	.267	.374	.387

Where He Hits the Ball

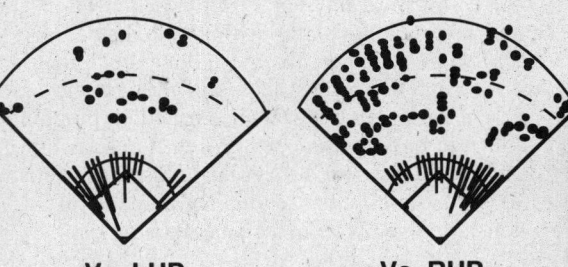

Vs. LHP　　　　**Vs. RHP**

1996 Situational Stats

	AB	H	HR	RBI	Avg		AB	H	HR	RBI	Avg
Home	284	83	6	29	.292	LHP	149	45	3	17	.302
Road	297	78	6	34	.263	RHP	432	116	9	46	.269
First Half	331	99	7	45	.299	Sc Pos	108	36	5	52	.333
Scnd Half	250	62	5	18	.248	Clutch	95	24	2	11	.253

1996 Rankings (American League)

- → 1st in walks and pitches seen (3,051)
- → 2nd in errors in left field (7)
- → 3rd in fielding percentage in left field (.981)
- → 4th in most pitches seen per plate appearance (4.24) and on-base percentage for a leadoff hitter (.403)
- → 5th in plate appearances (719)
- → 6th in times on base (290) and lowest stolen base percentage (61.9%)
- → 8th in on-base percentage vs. left-handed pitchers (.456)
- → 9th in runs scored
- → Led the White Sox in runs scored, sacrifice flies (8), caught stealing, walks, strikeouts and pitches seen (3,051)

Kevin Tapani

Position: SP
Bats: R **Throws:** R
Ht: 6' 0" **Wt:** 189

Opening Day Age: 33
Born: 2/18/64 in Des Moines, IA
ML Seasons: 8
Pronunciation: TAP-uh-nee
Nickname: Tap

1996 Season

Looking to add a veteran to their starting rotation, the White Sox signed righthander Kevin Tapani to a one-year contract just prior to spring training last year. While not a big-name star, Tapani had won in double figures during every season of the 1990s, and the Sox expected him to win a dozen games or so while pitching around 200 innings. It looked like he would far surpass those expectations when he reached the All-Star break with an 8-5 record. But Tapani had a rough last two months and wound up right around where he figured to be, posting 13 victories in 225 innings of work.

Pitching

Tapani throws a number of pitches, but his best pitch is probably his split-fingered fastball. He also features a slider, change and a fastball that is mid-to-high 80s at best. None of those pitches is overpowering, and he's always relied on pinpoint control in order to succeed. When it deserts him, as it did late last year, he's going to have problems. But he generally has enough command of his pitches to give his team a chance to win.

Defense

Tapani does the little things well. His delivery leaves him in excellent fielding position, and he's also very quick off the mound. He also does a fine job of controlling the running game. After some problems holding runners in 1995, he worked on his move last year and permitted only 10 steals in 18 attempts.

1997 Outlook

Tapani was a free agent when the '96 season ended, and while he's hardly a big star, there aren't many pitchers around who can win consistently year after year. The White Sox would love to have him back, but the price won't be as cheap as it was a year ago. Wherever he ends up, he figures to remain a dependable third or fourth starter.

Overall Statistics

	W	L	Pct.	ERA	G	GS	Sv	IP	H	BB	SO	HR	BR/IP
1996	13	10	.565	4.59	34	34	0	225.1	236	76	150	34	1.38
Career	92	75	.551	4.18	231	225	0	1461.0	1541	349	919	152	1.29

How Often He Throws Strikes

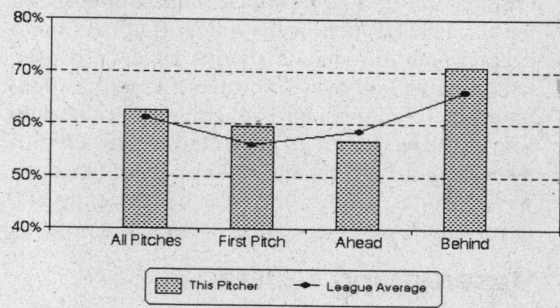

1996 Situational Stats

	W	L	ERA	Sv	IP		AB	H	HR	RBI	Avg
Home	9	3	3.91	0	119.2	LHB	441	121	21	68	.274
Road	4	7	5.37	0	105.2	RHB	439	115	13	40	.262
First Half	8	5	3.53	0	125.0	Sc Pos	196	53	5	66	.270
Scnd Half	5	5	5.92	0	100.1	Clutch	57	16	5	11	.281

1996 Rankings (American League)

→ 3rd in wild pitches (13)
→ 4th in home runs allowed
→ 6th in most home runs allowed per 9 innings (1.36)
→ 10th in innings pitched and pitches thrown (3,704)
→ Led the White Sox in losses, home runs allowed, wild pitches (13), highest ground-ball/flyball ratio allowed (1.3), lowest stolen base percentage allowed (55.6%), least pitches thrown per batter (3.81) and most GDPs induced per 9 innings (0.8)

Danny Tartabull

1996 Season

The White Sox have played "rent-a-right-fielder" for the last several years—obtaining a veteran fly-chaser, usually at a bargain-basement price, to fill the position for a year. Danny Tartabull, the latest member of the club, was even more of a gamble than Ellis Burks, Darrin Jackson and Mike Devereaux had been. But Tartabull belied his reputation as a sulking, oft-injured underachiever by belting 27 homers and reaching the 100-RBI mark for the first time since 1993. He was at his best down the stretch, hitting eight homers and driving in 24 runs in 24 September games.

Hitting

Tartabull is a hard swinger who strikes out a lot and seldom hits for much of an average. But he compensates with his home run power and his ability to draw some walks. He's a great fastball hitter who loves the high heater, and pitchers will usually try to work him downstairs, hoping he'll get impatient or fall behind in the count. But when he's on his game he'll lay off those pitches, extending the at-bat until he gets an offering he can handle.

Baserunning & Defense

Considered a poor outfielder, Tartabull showed better range than expected, and his arm was strong enough for right field. But he doesn't position himself very well, and he makes too many careless mistakes and poor throws to ever be considered a good outfielder. He's a slow runner and no threat to steal.

1997 Outlook

Like the rent-a-right-fielders who preceded him, Tartabull was a free agent at season's end and it seemed pretty likely that he too would move on. With younger and cheaper players like Lyle Mouton and Mike Cameron ready to assert themselves, the club was making little effort to bring back Tartabull.

Position: RF
Bats: R **Throws:** R
Ht: 6' 1" **Wt:** 204

Opening Day Age: 34
Born: 10/30/62 in Miami, FL
ML Seasons: 13

Overall Statistics

	G	AB	R	H	D	T	HR	RBI	SB	BB	SO	Avg	OBP	Slg
1996	132	472	58	120	23	3	27	101	1	64	128	.254	.340	.487
Career	1403	5004	754	1366	289	22	262	925	37	764	1358	.273	.368	.497

Where He Hits the Ball

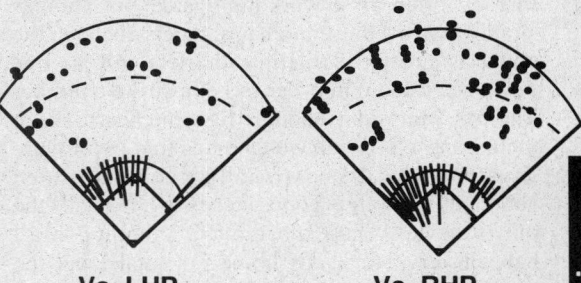

Vs. LHP　　　　**Vs. RHP**

1996 Situational Stats

	AB	H	HR	RBI	Avg		AB	H	HR	RBI	Avg
Home	225	55	11	43	.244	LHP	133	36	4	27	.271
Road	247	65	16	58	.263	RHP	339	84	23	74	.248
First Half	258	63	11	45	.244	Sc Pos	141	35	6	68	.248
Scnd Half	214	57	16	56	.266	Clutch	76	9	3	8	.118

1996 Rankings (American League)

→ 1st in lowest batting average in the clutch (.118)
→ 2nd in lowest fielding percentage in right field (.973)
→ 4th in errors in right field (7) and highest percentage of swings that missed (32.2%)
→ 7th in batting average on an 0-2 count (.300)
→ 10th in lowest batting average
→ Led the White Sox in batting average on an 0-2 count (.300)

Frank Thomas

1996 Season

On track to be be ranked among the greatest hitters of all time by the time he's through, Frank Thomas had another awesome season in 1996. Despite missing 19 games with a broken foot, Thomas hit 40 homers while reaching the 100 mark in runs scored, RBI and walks for the sixth time in six full seasons. His .349 average was the second highest of his career. He finished the year on a tear, blasting 11 home runs during the September playoff chase.

Hitting

Thomas' lethal combination of power and discipline makes him almost impossible to pitch to. Pitchers often try to work him inside, but Thomas simply lays off those pitches and gets ahead in the count as a result. Sometimes hurlers will lay one down the middle in order to get a strike over, but Thomas jumps on enough first pitches to keep them honest. His one weakness is that in pressure situations, he'll occasionally get exasperated about getting so few good pitches to hit. That's the only time he'll chase a bad pitch. . . but it doesn't happen very often. His home-run total is all the more impressive given that he plays in Comiskey Park, one of the toughest hitters' yards in baseball.

Baserunning & Defense

A huge man, Thomas has slowed down on the bases and only stole one sack in 1996. He also grounded into a career-high 25 double plays. He's a cautious baserunner and doesn't make too many mistakes. Thomas' defense at first base was greatly improved last year. Though he remains a below-average fielder, he showed improved range and made a number of outstanding plays.

1997 Outlook

Still only 28, Thomas is already the White Sox career home-run leader (he dueled Harold Baines early in the season and eventually took the lead), and there's no limit to the kind of numbers he's capable of compiling before he's through. The prospect of Thomas and Albert Belle hitting back-to-back the next few years should create nightmares for opposing pitchers.

Position: 1B
Bats: R **Throws:** R
Ht: 6' 5" **Wt:** 257

Opening Day Age: 28
Born: 5/27/68 in Columbus, GA
ML Seasons: 7
Nickname: Big Hurt

Overall Statistics

	G	AB	R	H	D	T	HR	RBI	SB	BB	SO	Avg	OBP	Slg
1996	141	527	110	184	26	0	40	134	1	109	70	.349	.459	.626
Career	930	3291	675	1077	211	8	222	729	17	770	513	.327	.452	.599

Where He Hits the Ball

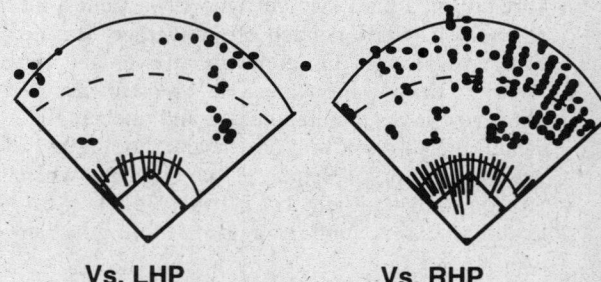

Vs. LHP   Vs. RHP

1996 Situational Stats

	AB	H	HR	RBI	Avg		AB	H	HR	RBI	Avg
Home	251	84	16	52	.335	LHP	119	48	13	37	.403
Road	276	100	24	82	.362	RHP	408	136	27	97	.333
First Half	332	116	23	85	.349	Sc Pos	146	53	10	91	.363
Scnd Half	195	68	17	49	.349	Clutch	91	28	4	19	.308

1996 Rankings (American League)

➡ 1st in intentional walks (26), on-base percentage vs. left-handed pitchers (.544) and batting average on the road (.362)
➡ 2nd in GDPs (25), batting average vs. left-handed pitchers (.403) , slugging percentage vs. left-handed pitchers (.798) and batting average
➡ 3rd in times on base (298), on-base percentage and batting average with runners in scoring position (.363)
➡ 4th in lowest fielding percentage at first base (.992)
➡ 5th in walks and errors at first base (9)
➡ 6th in slugging percentage

Robin Ventura

Position: 3B/1B
Bats: L **Throws:** R
Ht: 6' 1" **Wt:** 198

Opening Day Age: 29
Born: 7/14/67 in Santa Maria, CA
ML Seasons: 8

1996 Season

While Frank Thomas and Tony Phillips got most of the attention, Robin Ventura quietly put together the best season of his career in 1996. Ventura established career highs with 34 homers and 105 RBI, and his 96 runs scored were another personal best. Ventura also had an outstanding year on defense, winning the fourth Gold Glove of his career.

Hitting

Long a disciple of the Charlie Lau-Walt Hriniak school of hitting, Ventura changed his approach a little last year under new Sox hitting coach Bill Buckner. He began uppercutting the ball a little more, and the result was more fly balls, leading to the 34 homers—eight more than he had ever hit before. Still primarily a line-drive hitter, he has power to all fields, and he hangs in against a left-handed pitcher about as well as any lefty swinger around. He also possesses excellent discipline at the plate and doesn't strike out much for a power hitter. Pitchers tend to work inside on him, hoping to jam him.

Baserunning & Defense

After winning three straight Gold Gloves from 1991 to 1993, Ventura missed out in 1994-95 due to a few too many careless errors. He was back on track in '96, committing only 10 miscues as he nailed down another award. He's outstanding on bunts and slow rollers, and few third sackers are better at starting the 5-4-3 double play. He's a slow baserunner who's swiped only 14 sacks in eight seasons, while being caught 25 times.

1997 Outlook

One of the most consistent players in the game, Ventura has driven in 90 or more runs in five of the last six seasons while ranking among the top defensive players at his position. Despite that, he remains the subject of trade rumors. If the White Sox do trade him, they figure to get plenty in return, because he's one of the best third basemen in the business.

Overall Statistics

	G	AB	R	H	D	T	HR	RBI	SB	BB	SO	Avg	OBP	Slg
1996	158	586	96	168	31	2	34	105	1	78	81	.287	.368	.520
Career	1039	3769	547	1041	178	7	144	624	14	555	527	.276	.367	.442

Where He Hits the Ball

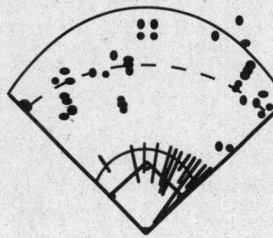

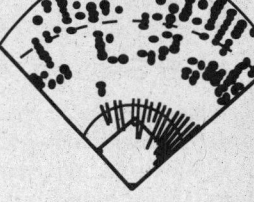

Vs. LHP   **Vs. RHP**

1996 Situational Stats

	AB	H	HR	RBI	Avg		AB	H	HR	RBI	Avg
Home	285	95	13	49	.333	LHP	185	49	14	39	.265
Road	301	73	21	56	.243	RHP	401	119	20	66	.297
First Half	312	88	19	55	.282	Sc Pos	170	46	10	74	.271
Scnd Half	274	80	15	50	.292	Clutch	115	27	2	7	.235

1996 Rankings (American League)

➡ 3rd in fielding percentage at third base (.974)
➡ 6th in lowest batting average on the road (.243)
➡ 8th in games played (158)
➡ 9th in errors at third base (10)
➡ Led the White Sox in at-bats, sacrifice flies (8) and games played (158)

Chicago White Sox

Pat Borders

Position: C
Bats: R **Throws:** R
Ht: 6' 2" **Wt:** 195

Opening Day Age: 33
Born: 5/14/63 in Columbus, OH
ML Seasons: 9

Overall Statistics

	G	AB	R	H	D	T	HR	RBI	SB	BB	SO	Avg	OBP	Slg
1996	76	220	15	61	7	0	5	18	0	9	43	.277	.306	.377
Career	880	2693	234	685	142	10	62	300	6	129	434	.254	.288	.384

1996 Situational Stats

	AB	H	HR	RBI	Avg		AB	H	HR	RBI	Avg
Home	107	38	3	12	.355	LHP	71	24	3	7	.338
Road	113	23	2	6	.204	RHP	149	37	2	11	.248
First Half	101	29	2	10	.287	Sc Pos	61	13	1	12	.213
Scnd Half	119	32	3	8	.269	Clutch	39	8	0	1	.205

1996 Season

When backup catcher Chad Kreuter was lost for the year with a fractured shoulder in mid-July, the White Sox obtained veteran receiver Pat Borders to replace him. Borders wound up playing much more than expected when number-one receiver Ron Karkovice suffered a knee injury, batting .277 in 31 games with the Sox.

Hitting, Baserunning & Defense

Borders is a line-drive hitter who's capable of hitting for a respectable average, but he doesn't have much home run power or selectivity at the plate. He struggled against righties last year, but hit lefthanders quite well and can make some contributions as a platoon player. His defensive skills are considered below average, with a weak throwing arm his biggest liability.

1997 Outlook

The MVP of the 1992 World Series, Borders is now strictly a journeyman who's played for five teams in the last two years. A lot of clubs can use a backup catcher with a good bat, so he should have no trouble finding an employer this year. He played fairly well for the White Sox after his acquisition last summer, and a return to Chicago is possible.

Tony Castillo

Position: RP
Bats: L **Throws:** L
Ht: 5'10" **Wt:** 190

Opening Day Age: 34
Born: 3/1/63 in Lara, VZ
ML Seasons: 8
Pronunciation: cas-TEE-oh

Overall Statistics

	W	L	Pct.	ERA	G	GS	Sv	IP	H	BB	SO	HR	BR/IP
1996	5	4	.556	3.60	55	0	2	95.0	95	24	57	10	1.25
Career	23	17	.575	3.54	314	6	18	437.1	443	145	277	39	1.34

1996 Situational Stats

	W	L	ERA	Sv	IP		AB	H	HR	RBI	Avg
Home	3	3	4.37	1	55.2	LHB	114	35	1	17	.307
Road	2	1	2.52	1	39.1	RHB	249	60	9	35	.241
First Half	2	1	3.71	0	53.1	Sc Pos	98	27	3	40	.276
Scnd Half	3	3	3.46	2	41.2	Clutch	125	35	5	18	.280

1996 Season

Lefty reliever Tony Castillo came to the White Sox from Toronto late last August, just in time for the stretch run. Castillo was a godsend for a club desperate for middle-relief help, posting a 1.59 ERA in 15 Chicago appearances.

Pitching & Defense

Castillo throws a high-80s fastball, a slider and a curve, and while he's usually been used as a specialist against lefties, he held right-handed batters to a lower average in both 1995 and '96. His control is usually sharp but he's vulnerable to the home-run ball, particularly against righties. He's a durable pitcher, capable of working effectively for two or more innings. Castillo fields his position smartly and has an effective pickoff move.

1997 Outlook

Good lefty relievers remain a valuable commodity, and Castillo has been one of the best in baseball over the last several years. With the Sox bullpen one of the club's weakest links last year, they figured to make an effort to keep Castillo around. If he can't come to terms with Chicago, he'll have little trouble finding another employer.

Matt Karchner

Position: RP
Bats: R **Throws:** R
Ht: 6' 4" **Wt:** 210

Opening Day Age: 29
Born: 6/28/67 in Berwick, PA
ML Seasons: 2

Overall Statistics

	W	L	Pct.	ERA	G	GS	Sv	IP	H	BB	SO	HR	BR/IP
1996	7	4	.636	5.76	50	0	1	59.1	61	41	46	10	1.72
Career	11	6	.647	4.34	81	0	1	91.1	94	53	70	12	1.61

1996 Situational Stats

	W	L	ERA	Sv	IP		AB	H	HR	RBI	Avg
Home	1	3	9.75	0	24.0	LHB	98	27	4	18	.276
Road	6	1	3.06	1	35.1	RHB	130	34	6	25	.262
First Half	7	2	4.59	1	49.0	Sc Pos	72	18	2	33	.250
Scnd Half	0	2	11.32	0	10.1	Clutch	136	36	7	25	.265

1996 Season

Righthander Matt Karchner was outstanding in a half-season of relief work as a White Sox rookie in 1995, and he began the '96 season as the primary set-up man for Roberto Hernandez. Karchner got off to a great start, but his season soon turned sour. He began to lose effectiveness after coming down with a stiff shoulder in June, and he was hammered repeatedly from then on. Finally, in August, he went out for the season with torn cartilage in his right knee. He underwent arthroscopic surgery on September 3.

Pitching & Defense

Karchner is a fastball/slider pitcher, and though he doesn't have overpowering stuff, he goes right after the hitters. That approach served him well in 1995, but in '96 his location was spotty and he was burned repeatedly by walks and gopher balls. His defensive work was also shaky, but he did a fairly good job of holding runners.

1997 Outlook

The Sox love Karchner's aggressiveness, but his 1996 season was a disaster after May. He'll have to prove he's both healthy and effective this spring before being entrusted with the major bullpen role he was given last year.

Chad Kreuter

Position: C
Bats: B **Throws:** R
Ht: 6' 2" **Wt:** 200

Opening Day Age: 32
Born: 8/26/64 in Greenbrae, CA
ML Seasons: 9
Pronunciation: CREW-ter

Overall Statistics

	G	AB	R	H	D	T	HR	RBI	SB	BB	SO	Avg	OBP	Slg
1996	46	114	14	25	8	0	3	18	0	13	29	.219	.308	.368
Career	451	1158	145	274	59	4	28	128	2	157	280	.237	.328	.367

1996 Situational Stats

	AB	H	HR	RBI	Avg		AB	H	HR	RBI	Avg
Home	43	12	2	12	.279	LHP	37	10	1	6	.270
Road	71	13	1	6	.183	RHP	77	15	2	12	.195
First Half	105	23	3	17	.219	Sc Pos	32	9	0	14	.281
Scnd Half	9	2	0	1	.222	Clutch	34	4	1	4	.118

1996 Season

Journeyman catcher Chad Kreuter signed a free-agent contract with the White Sox prior to the 1996 season, and wound up winning the job as Ron Karkovice's backup. Kreuter didn't hit much, but his leadership skills, good defense and ability to handle pitchers helped make him an important member of the team. Unfortunately Kreuter's season ended in mid-July when he suffered multiple fractures to his left shoulder in a violent home-plate collision with Kansas City's Johnny Damon.

Hitting, Baserunning & Defense

Kreuter had a big year at bat for the 1993 Tigers, but that was a fluke: during the rest of his career he's been a low-average hitter with some patience at the plate and the ability to hit an occasional longball. His forte is defense. He has a fine throwing arm, excellent mobility behind the plate and a great rapport with pitchers.

1997 Outlook

Kreuter's teammates thought so highly of him that most of them wrote his uniform number 12 on their caps to honor him after his season-ending, possibly career-ending injury. He was released by the team following the season and will be looking for a job over the winter.

Norberto Martin

Position: SS/DH
Bats: R **Throws:** R
Ht: 5'10" **Wt:** 164

Opening Day Age: 30
Born: 12/10/66 in
Santo Domingo, DR
ML Seasons: 4
Pronunciation:
mar-TEEN
Nickname: Paco

Overall Statistics

	G	AB	R	H	D	T	HR	RBI	SB	BB	SO	Avg	OBP	Slg
1996	70	140	30	49	7	0	1	14	10	6	17	.350	.374	.421
Career	195	445	69	133	21	5	4	49	19	19	59	.299	.325	.396

1996 Situational Stats

	AB	H	HR	RBI	Avg		AB	H	HR	RBI	Avg
Home	64	22	0	7	.344	LHP	66	26	1	7	.394
Road	76	27	1	7	.355	RHP	74	23	0	7	.311
First Half	49	20	0	2	.408	Sc Pos	28	9	0	12	.321
Scnd Half	91	29	1	12	.319	Clutch	24	6	0	2	.250

1996 Season

Norberto Martin's season got off to a scary start when a ball jumped off his bat on a bunt attempt, shattering several bones in his face. Martin didn't return until June, but he showed no effects from the layoff. He tore the cover off the ball for the rest of the season, hitting .350 while filling in at several positions.

Hitting, Baserunning & Defense

Martin comes out of the dugout swinging, ready to jump on the first fastball he sees. He doesn't have much power and he hardly ever draws a walk, but he belts enough line drives to make himself valuable. He can play second, short, third or the outfield, but he's below average everywhere except second base, and his arm is on the weak side. Martin can motor around the bases and is a threat to steal any time.

1997 Outlook

Martin's speed, versatility and ability to hit off the bench make him a perfect fill-in. Look for him to continue to be one of the best bench players in the game this year while logging 200 at-bats or so.

Bill Simas

Position: RP
Bats: R **Throws:** R
Ht: 6'3" **Wt:** 220

Opening Day Age: 25
Born: 11/28/71 in
Hanford, CA
ML Seasons: 2
Pronunciation:
SEE-muss

Overall Statistics

	W	L	Pct.	ERA	G	GS	Sv	IP	H	BB	SO	HR	BR/IP
1996	2	8	.200	4.58	64	0	2	72.2	75	39	65	5	1.57
Career	3	9	.250	4.26	78	0	2	86.2	90	49	81	6	1.60

1996 Situational Stats

	W	L	ERA	Sv	IP		AB	H	HR	RBI	Avg
Home	1	3	5.03	0	39.1	LHB	118	32	1	12	.271
Road	1	5	4.05	2	33.1	RHB	165	43	4	34	.261
First Half	0	4	4.09	1	44.0	Sc Pos	92	27	2	39	.293
Scnd Half	2	4	5.34	1	28.2	Clutch	148	44	2	26	.297

1996 Season

Like most of the members of the beleaguered White Sox middle-relief corps, righthander Bill Simas had an up-and-down year in 1996. Simas' brightest moment came in a big midseason series against the Indians, when he entered the game with the bases loaded and none out and escaped the jam without allowing a run. But Simas also had six blown saves, eight relief losses and plenty of other rough moments.

Pitching & Defense

One of the hardest throwers on the Sox staff, Simas has a 90-plus fastball that makes him a closer candidate in many peoples' minds. He also throws a slider and change, and when he has good location, he can dominate hitters. Unfortunately, that didn't happen often enough in 1996. Simas is a good fielder and has a decent move to first.

1997 Outlook

The Sox are desperate for effective middle men, and the hard-throwing Simas will get every chance to succeed in 1996. Only 25, he could develop into a fine set-up man if he can develop better command of his pitches.

Chris Snopek

Position: 3B/SS
Bats: R **Throws:** R
Ht: 6' 1" **Wt:** 185

Opening Day Age: 26
Born: 9/20/70 in Cynthiana, KY
ML Seasons: 2

Overall Statistics

	G	AB	R	H	D	T	HR	RBI	SB	BB	SO	Avg	OBP	Slg
1996	46	104	18	27	6	1	6	18	0	6	16	.260	.304	.510
Career	68	172	30	49	10	1	7	25	1	15	28	.285	.344	.477

1996 Situational Stats

	AB	H	HR	RBI	Avg		AB	H	HR	RBI	Avg
Home	49	12	3	7	.245	LHP	80	25	6	18	.313
Road	55	15	3	11	.273	RHP	24	2	0	0	.083
First Half	60	12	3	7	.200	Sc Pos	32	8	2	13	.250
Scnd Half	44	15	3	11	.341	Clutch	11	1	0	0	.091

1996 Season

Highly-regarded rookie infielder Chris Snopek began the 1996 season on the White Sox roster, but had trouble getting playing time behind Robin Ventura and Ozzie Guillen. Snopek wound up spending part of the year at Triple-A Nashville, but performed impressively in his 46 games with the Sox.

Hitting, Baserunning & Defense

Considered a line-drive hitter with gap power, Snopek surprised people by blasting six home runs in limited action. In addition, nearly half his hits went for extra bases. He struggled against righties, but he really didn't get many chances to face them. He also had problems in the field—especially at third, which is considered his best position. He has good speed, but he's not much of a threat to steal.

1997 Outlook

Snopek's name often comes up in trade talks, but the Sox think so highly of him that there's talk they might deal Ventura instead. It's also possible that they might try Snopek in the outfield. Snopek's too good a prospect to keep on the bench, and one way or another he figures to get considerable playing time this year. . . either with the Sox or someone else.

Larry Thomas

Position: RP
Bats: R **Throws:** L
Ht: 6' 1" **Wt:** 195

Opening Day Age: 27
Born: 10/25/69 in Miami, FL
ML Seasons: 2

Overall Statistics

	W	L	Pct.	ERA	G	GS	Sv	IP	H	BB	SO	HR	BR/IP
1996	2	3	.400	3.23	57	0	0	30.2	32	14	20	1	1.50
Career	2	3	.400	2.64	74	0	0	44.1	40	20	32	2	1.35

1996 Situational Stats

	W	L	ERA	Sv	IP		AB	H	HR	RBI	Avg
Home	2	2	2.30	0	15.2	LHB	63	18	1	11	.286
Road	0	1	4.20	0	15.0	RHB	51	14	0	2	.275
First Half	2	3	3.32	0	21.2	Sc Pos	34	10	0	10	.294
Scnd Half	0	0	3.00	0	9.0	Clutch	66	21	1	11	.318

1996 Season

After an impressive late-season debut in 1995, Larry Thomas took over as the primary lefty specialist in the White Sox bullpen last year. Thomas had a few problems, but he was one of the more effective workmen in the shaky Sox middle relief corps before missing most of the last two months with a strained left elbow.

Pitching & Defense

Thomas doesn't have a blazing fastball, but the pitch has good movement, and when he's on his game he mixes it effectively with his slider and change-up. The slider was inconsistent in 1996, however, and he had problems against the left-handed hitters he's paid to retire. He also had some trouble with opposing baserunners, but he fielded his position smartly.

1997 Outlook

Thomas will need to sharpen his slider, but if his elbow is sound he figures to be an important member of the Sox bullpen this year. Like some of the other members of the pen, he suffered the effects of a heavy workload, and he'll need to be used more carefully this year.

Other Chicago White Sox

Jason Bere (Pos: RHP, Age: 25)

	W	L	Pct.	ERA	G	GS	Sv	IP	H	BB	SO	HR	BR/IP
1996	0	1	.000	10.26	5	5	0	16.2	26	18	19	3	2.64
Career	32	23	.582	5.01	80	80	0	438.2	405	285	385	53	1.57

After going 7-15 with a 7.19 ERA in 1995, Bere missed virtually the entire '96 campaign with elbow problems that required surgery. He's not being counted on much for 1997. 1997 Outlook: D

Mike Bertotti (Pos: LHP, Age: 27)

	W	L	Pct.	ERA	G	GS	Sv	IP	H	BB	SO	HR	BR/IP
1996	2	0	1.000	5.14	15	2	0	28.0	28	20	19	5	1.71
Career	3	1	.750	7.65	19	6	0	42.1	51	31	34	11	1.94

Bertotti's had some success at the minor league level, but he's had major problems finding home plate during two trials with the White Sox. The Sox could use another lefty, but he's a long shot to contribute much this year. 1997 Outlook: C

Domingo Cedeno (Pos: 2B, Age: 28, Bats: B)

	G	AB	R	H	D	T	HR	RBI	SB	BB	SO	Avg	OBP	Slg
1996	89	301	46	82	12	2	2	20	6	15	64	.272	.308	.346
Career	202	605	83	147	20	6	6	51	8	36	140	.243	.286	.326

Cedeno came to the White Sox in a late-season deal and played very little, but he'd done a good job in 77 games with Toronto. A good defensive player who can handle second, short, or third, he should be on some team's bench this year. 1997 Outlook: B

Jeff Darwin (Pos: RHP, Age: 27)

	W	L	Pct.	ERA	G	GS	Sv	IP	H	BB	SO	HR	BR/IP
1996	0	1	.000	2.93	22	0	0	30.2	26	9	15	5	1.14
Career	0	1	.000	4.15	24	0	0	34.2	33	12	16	6	1.30

A longtime Seattle farmhand, Darwin joined the White Sox last year and was one of the more effective members of the club's beleaguered bullpen. He's not a fireballer, but he knows how to pitch. 1997 Outlook: B

Marvin Freeman (Pos: RHP, Age: 33)

	W	L	Pct.	ERA	G	GS	Sv	IP	H	BB	SO	HR	BR/IP
1996	7	9	.438	6.15	27	24	0	131.2	155	58	72	21	1.62
Career	35	28	.556	4.64	221	78	5	593.2	616	249	383	63	1.46

After getting lit up in 23 starts for the Rockies, Freeman made one late-season start for the Sox and lasted two innings. A free agent, he'll get a shot somewhere this year. 1997 Outlook: C

Stacy Jones (Pos: RHP, Age: 29)

	W	L	Pct.	ERA	G	GS	Sv	IP	H	BB	SO	HR	BR/IP
1996	0	0	-	0.00	2	0	0	2.0	0	1	1	0	0.50
Career	0	0	-	3.46	6	1	0	13.0	11	6	11	1	1.31

A veteran minor league righty, Jones began the year in the Brewer system, moved to the Sox system in May, and proceeded to record 26 saves in Double and Triple-A. Has an outside chance. 1997 Outlook: C

Brian Keyser (Pos: RHP, Age: 30)

	W	L	Pct.	ERA	G	GS	Sv	IP	H	BB	SO	HR	BR/IP
1996	1	2	.333	4.98	28	0	1	59.2	78	28	19	3	1.78
Career	6	8	.429	4.97	51	10	1	152.0	192	55	67	13	1.63

Keyser has done some fine work in the Sox minor league system, but hasn't shown much in two extended trials with the big club. He might get one last chance this year. 1997 Outlook: C

Al Levine (Pos: RHP, Age: 28)

	W	L	Pct.	ERA	G	GS	Sv	IP	H	BB	SO	HR	BR/IP
1996	0	1	.000	5.40	16	0	0	18.1	22	7	12	1	1.58
Career	0	1	.000	5.40	16	0	0	18.1	22	7	12	1	1.58

A starter for most of his minor league career, Levine was shifted to the bullpen last year and saved 12 games at Triple-A Nashville. He didn't impress much in 16 games with the Sox. 1997 Outlook: D

Robert Machado (Pos: C, Age: 23, Bats: R)

	G	AB	R	H	D	T	HR	RBI	SB	BB	SO	Avg	OBP	Slg
1996	4	6	1	4	1	0	0	2	0	0	0	.667	.667	.833
Career	4	6	1	4	1	0	0	2	0	0	0	.667	.667	.833

A catcher with fine defensive skills and an outstanding arm, Machado got a cup of coffee with the Sox when Ron Karkovice got hurt last year. Still only 23, he'll probably be in Triple-A this year. 1997 Outlook: C

Joe Magrane (Pos: LHP, Age: 32)

	W	L	Pct.	ERA	G	GS	Sv	IP	H	BB	SO	HR	BR/IP
1996	1	5	.167	6.88	19	8	0	53.2	70	25	21	10	1.77
Career	57	67	.460	3.81	190	166	0	1096.2	1081	391	564	79	1.34

After years of arm problems and ineffectiveness, Magrane pitched his way into the Sox rotation last spring. He pitched miserably and drew his release. His career is probably over. 1997 Outlook: D

Kirk McCaskill (Pos: RHP, Age: 35)

	W	L	Pct.	ERA	G	GS	Sv	IP	H	BB	SO	HR	BR/IP
1996	5	5	.500	6.97	29	4	0	51.2	72	31	28	6	1.99
Career	106	108	.495	4.12	380	242	7	1729.0	1748	665	1003	154	1.40

"Captain Kirk" had a fine, long career, but he stopped getting hitters out in the middle of 1995. When it didn't get better for him in '96, he gave up and announced his retirement. 1997 Outlook: D

Jose Munoz (Pos: 2B, Age: 29, Bats: B)

	G	AB	R	H	D	T	HR	RBI	SB	BB	SO	Avg	OBP	Slg
1996	17	27	7	7	0	0	0	1	0	4	1	.259	.355	.259
Career	17	27	7	7	0	0	0	1	0	4	1	.259	.355	.259

After spending five seasons in Triple-A while working in three different systems, Munoz finally got his first major league shot last year. He didn't do much, but his versatility gives him a chance. 1997 Outlook: C

Mike Robertson (Pos: 1B, Age: 26, Bats: L)

	G	AB	R	H	D	T	HR	RBI	SB	BB	SO	Avg	OBP	Slg
1996	6	7	0	1	1	0	0	0	0	0	1	.143	.143	.286
Career	6	7	0	1	1	0	0	0	0	0	1	.143	.143	.286

The Sox' third-round draft pick in 1991, Robertson has some power and is considered a fine defensive first baseman. Frank Thomas prevents him from getting a chance with the Sox, so he's looking for another club. 1997 Outlook: C

Scott Ruffcorn (Pos: RHP, Age: 27)

	W	L	Pct.	ERA	G	GS	Sv	IP	H	BB	SO	HR	BR/IP
1996	0	1	.000	11.37	3	1	0	6.1	10	6	3	1	2.53
Career	0	5	.000	9.68	12	5	0	30.2	44	34	13	4	2.54

A hard thrower who was the Sox' number-one draft pick in 1991, Ruffcorn has had great success in the minors, but has pitched like he's scared to death in four trials with the big club. He needs a new team, and maybe a good therapist. 1997 Outlook: B

Rich Sauveur (Pos: LHP, Age: 33)

	W	L	Pct.	ERA	G	GS	Sv	IP	H	BB	SO	HR	BR/IP
1996	0	0	-	15.00	3	0	0	3.0	3	5	1	1	2.67
Career	0	1	.000	6.56	24	3	0	35.2	45	23	21	7	1.91

One of those lefty relievers who sticks around forever, Sauveur has pitched for five major league teams, but worked only 24 games. He can get lefties out, and it's still not too late for him. 1997 Outlook: C

Mike Sirotka (Pos: LHP, Age: 25)

	W	L	Pct.	ERA	G	GS	Sv	IP	H	BB	SO	HR	BR/IP
1996	1	2	.333	7.18	15	4	0	26.1	34	12	11	3	1.75
Career	2	4	.333	5.49	21	10	0	60.2	73	29	30	5	1.68

Sirotka has been impressive in the Sox minor league system, but was ineffective in a 15-game shot with the big club last year. His best chance might be a switch to the bullpen. 1997 Outlook: C

Don Slaught (Pos: C, Age: 38, Bats: R)

	G	AB	R	H	D	T	HR	RBI	SB	BB	SO	Avg	OBP	Slg
1996	76	243	25	76	10	0	6	36	0	15	22	.313	.355	.428
Career	1307	4043	413	1151	235	28	77	476	18	306	555	.285	.338	.414

Slaught might forget what uniform he's wearing sometimes, but he never seems to forget how to hit line drives. Even at 38, he could still help a club as a backup receiver this year. 1997 Outlook: A

Chicago White Sox Minor League Prospects

Organization Overview:

The White Sox received wide acclaim several years ago when they developed a formidable starting rotation consisting of Jack McDowell, Alex Fernandez, Wilson Alvarez and Jason Bere. Since that time, however, McDowell has left and Bere has fallen injured, and the farm system has been largely unable to replace them. James Baldwin finally broke through last year, and his fine season placed him second in the A.L. Rookie of the Year voting, but after that, there was nothing. The Sox desperately needed a fifth starter, but youngsters like Scott Ruffcorn, Luis Andujar, Brian Keyser, Mike Bertotti and Mike Sirotka all came up short. It was a critical failure by the farm system, one that probably cost the Sox a postseason berth. Chris Snopek was a nice addition on the infield, but no youngster except Baldwin played a major role on the team. Fortunately, there are a number of prospects at the higher levels who appear ready to graduate to the majors soon. The front-line prospects are respectable, but there's little depth.

Jeff Abbott

Position: OF   **Opening Day Age:** 24
Bats: R **Throws:** L   **Born:** 8/17/72 in
Ht: 6' 2" **Wt:** 190   Decatur, GA

Recent Statistics

	G	AB	R	H	D	T	HR	RBI	SB	BB	SO	AVG
94 R White Sox	4	15	4	7	1	0	1	3	2	4	0	.467
94 A Hickory	63	224	47	88	16	6	6	48	2	38	33	.393
95 A Pr. William	70	264	41	92	16	0	4	47	7	26	25	.348
95 AA Birmingham	55	197	25	63	11	1	3	28	1	19	20	.320
96 AAA Nashville	113	440	64	143	27	1	14	60	12	32	50	.325
96 MLE	113	435	63	138	25	0	13	59	10	31	51	.317

Jeff Abbott is quite possibly the best pure hitter in the minors right now. Even if he never progresses another inch, he's capable of hitting well over .300 with decent power. Then where is he, you ask? The problem is that his glove confines him to left field, and his bat lacks true left field power. He's a right-handed hitter, his tools have never impressed the scouts, and he'll be 24 years old next year, so the White Sox don't regard him as a star in the making. However, Wade Boggs was given similarly lukewarm reviews during his minor league days. If Abbott plays, he'll hit.

Mike Cameron

Position: OF   **Opening Day Age:** 24
Bats: R **Throws:** R   **Born:** 1/8/73 in
Ht: 6' 1" **Wt:** 170   Lagrange, GA

Recent Statistics

	G	AB	R	H	D	T	HR	RBI	SB	BB	SO	AVG
96 AA Birmingham	123	473	120	142	34	12	28	77	39	71	117	.300
96 AL Chicago	11	11	1	1	0	0	0	0	0	1	3	.091
96 MLE	123	464	111	133	31	9	25	71	29	55	122	.287

It all clicked for Mike Cameron last year. He'd always possessed the raw tools, but he made some adjustments that helped his bat speed, and suddenly tapped into his latent power. The new-found pop enabled him to approach the 30-30 mark, and signaled his emergence as a legitimate five-tool prospect. He's got terrific speed, and possesses the best range and outfield arm in the system. The White Sox are thinking very seriously about giving him the center field or right field job next year, and he could be one the season's top rookies.

Nelson Cruz

Position: P   **Opening Day Age:** 24
Bats: R **Throws:** R   **Born:** 9/13/72 in
Ht: 6' 1" **Wt:** 160   Puerta Plaza, DR

Recent Statistics

	W	L	ERA	G	GS	Sv	IP	H	R	BB	SO	HR
95 R Bristol	0	0	9.00	1	0	0	1.0	2	1	0	0	0
95 A Pr. William	2	1	0.47	9	0	1	19.1	12	1	6	18	1
95 A Hickory	2	7	2.70	44	0	9	66.2	65	31	15	68	6
96 AA Birmingham	6	6	3.20	37	18	1	149.0	150	65	41	142	10

Righthander Nelson Cruz may have the best power arm in the White Sox' system. During his three-year minor league career, the Sox have used him as both a starter and a reliever. Last year, he worked in both roles, and performed capably in each. At Double-A Birmingham, he fanned almost a batter per inning, while posting a strikeout-to-walk ratio of better than 3-to-1. It's still unclear whether he'll end up in the rotation or the bullpen, but he's got the stuff to advance quickly.

Tom Fordham

Position: P   **Opening Day Age:** 23
Bats: L **Throws:** L   **Born:** 2/20/74 in San
Ht: 6' 2" **Wt:** 210   Diego, CA

Recent Statistics

	W	L	ERA	G	GS	Sv	IP	H	R	BB	SO	HR
93 R White Sox	1	1	1.80	3	0	0	10.0	9	2	3	12	0
93 A Sarasota	0	0	0.00	2	0	0	5.0	3	1	3	5	0
93 A Hickory	4	3	3.88	8	8	0	48.2	36	21	21	27	3
94 A Hickory	10	5	3.14	17	17	0	109.0	101	47	30	121	10
94 A South Bend	4	4	4.34	11	11	0	74.2	82	46	14	48	4
95 A Pr. William	9	0	2.04	13	13	0	84.0	66	20	35	78	7
95 AA Birmingham	6	3	3.38	14	14	0	82.2	79	35	28	51	9
96 AA Birmingham	2	1	2.65	6	6	0	37.1	26	13	14	37	4
96 AAA Nashville	10	8	3.45	22	22	0	140.2	117	60	69	118	15

Lefthander Tom Fordham started capturing attention when he went a combined 15-3 at two levels in '95. Last year, he kept up the pace as he moved up the ladder, spending most of the year in Triple-A and posting a solid 12-9 mark overall, with good supporting numbers. He's a prototypical finesse-type lefty, with a fastball that tops out in the high-80s. He succeeds by changing speeds and hitting the corners with his above-average curveball and change-up. He's still young—just 23 next year— and the White Sox don't want to rush him. They desperately needed a fifth starter last year, but chose to let Fordham remain in Triple-A. If he keeps it up, they won't be able to resist much longer.

Jimmy Hurst

Position: OF
Opening Day Age: 25
Bats: R **Throws:** R
Born: 3/1/72 in
Ht: 6' 6" **Wt:** 225
Tuscaloosa, AL

Recent Statistics

	G	AB	R	H	D	T	HR	RBI	SB	BB	SO	AVG
93 A South Bend	123	464	79	113	26	0	20	79	15	37	141	.244
94 A Pr. William	127	455	90	126	31	6	25	91	15	72	128	.277
95 AA Birmingham	91	301	47	57	11	0	12	34	12	33	95	.189
96 AA Birmingham	126	472	62	125	23	1	18	88	19	53	128	.265
96 AAA Nashville	3	6	2	2	1	0	1	2	0	1	3	.333
96 MLE	129	469	58	118	21	0	16	82	14	41	137	.252

If Mike Cameron is the "after" picture, Jimmy Hurst is the "before." His tools are tremendous, and he's got a high ceiling if he ever learns how to use them. In addition to his considerable power potential, he's got a very strong arm and good speed. Still, he remains awfully raw at the plate, and continues to work on making better contact. The White Sox would like to see some results soon, because at age 25, time may be running out.

Greg Norton

Position: SS
Opening Day Age: 24
Bats: B **Throws:** R
Born: 7/6/72 in San
Ht: 6' 1" **Wt:** 182
Leandro, CA

Recent Statistics

	G	AB	R	H	D	T	HR	RBI	SB	BB	SO	AVG
96 AA Birmingham	76	287	40	81	14	3	8	44	5	33	55	.282
96 AAA Nashville	43	164	28	47	14	2	7	26	2	17	42	.287
96 AL Chicago	11	23	4	5	0	0	2	3	0	4	6	.217
96 MLE	119	442	64	119	24	3	12	65	4	41	98	.269

Greg Norton is a switch-hitting third baseman who got himself noticed with a surprising '95 season. He's got good hands and the strongest throwing arm in the system, so the Sox have been testing his versatility by playing him at shortstop. He isn't good enough to play the position full time, but he's more than good enough for third base. He's got good speed and an excellent eye, and he hit for better power and average last year. Unfortunately, he seems to be stuck behind both Robin Ventura and Chris Snopek.

Magglio Ordonez

Position: OF
Opening Day Age: 23
Bats: R **Throws:** R
Born: 1/28/74 in
Ht: 5' 11" **Wt:** 155
Caracas, Venez

Recent Statistics

	G	AB	R	H	D	T	HR	RBI	SB	BB	SO	AVG
93 A Hickory	84	273	32	59	14	4	3	20	5	26	66	.216
94 A Hickory	132	490	86	144	24	5	11	69	16	45	57	.294
95 A Pr. William	131	487	61	116	24	2	12	65	11	41	71	.238
96 AA Birmingham	130	479	66	126	41	0	18	67	9	39	74	.263
96 MLE	130	470	61	117	37	0	16	62	7	30	77	.249

Magglio Ordonez took a big step forward in '95. There always had been worries about how much power he would be able to generate from his thin frame, but in a very tough home run park, he socked 18 round-trippers and added 41 doubles. He's got a good arm and decent range in the outfield, and can play all three positions. Only 23 years old next year, his power may continue to grow as he matures. He doesn't need to go much further before he'll be ready.

Olmedo Saenz

Position: 3B
Opening Day Age: 26
Bats: R **Throws:** R
Born: 10/8/70 in Chitre
Ht: 6' 2" **Wt:** 185
Herrera, Panama

Recent Statistics

	G	AB	R	H	D	T	HR	RBI	SB	BB	SO	AVG
93 A South Bend	13	50	3	18	4	1	0	7	1	7	7	.360
93 A Sarasota	33	121	13	31	9	4	0	27	3	9	18	.256
93 AA Birmingham	49	173	30	60	17	2	6	29	2	20	21	.347
94 AAA Nashville	107	383	48	100	27	2	12	59	3	30	57	.261
95 AAA Nashville	111	415	60	126	26	1	13	74	0	45	60	.304
96 AAA Nashville	134	476	86	124	29	1	18	63	4	53	80	.261
96 MLE	134	471	84	119	27	0	17	62	3	51	82	.253

After his third straight year at Triple-A, it's clear that Olmedo Saenz is going nowhere in the White Sox organization. He's already been passed by Chris Snopek, and the White don't exactly need to replace Robin Ventura, anyway. Now, the emergence of Greg Norton crowds him out even further. It's unfortunate, because Saenz is a decent hitter with respectable power, as well as the best defensive third baseman in the American Association. At age 26, it's time for him to find a new employer.

Others to Watch

The White Sox have some good young arms in the lower reaches of their farm system. Righthander **Carlos Castillo** struck out 158 batters and walked only 33 in two levels of A-ball. Only 22 next year, he may get a shot to open the season at Double-A. . . Converted shortstop **Jason Olsen** spent his first season on the mound last year, and went 12-6 with a 2.72 ERA at three different stops in A-ball. He showed a surprising knowledge of the art of pitching, with a strikeout-to-walk ratio of almost 3-to-1. . . Second baseman **Frankie Menechino** was already 25 years old when he reached Double-A last year, but he made the most of his opportunity. He hit .292 with decent power, and got absolutely no help from his home park. . . The White Sox may need a catcher soon, and the most likely candidate is **Julio Vinas**. He hit for a low average at Triple-A, but showed acceptable power, especially for a 23 year old.

Mike Hargrove

1996 Season

What kind of manager is Mike Hargrove? He's spent almost six seasons with tempestuous Albert Belle and both men are still alive. He communicates well with players and rarely loses his temper. When the Indians became a contender, he may have been intimidated by the stars that were added to the roster, but he adjusted. Last year's loss in the first round of the playoffs was unexpected after 99 wins during the season, but Hargrove kept a volatile clubhouse under control.

Offense

Hargrove isn't daring. He likes to call for the double steal early in the game, but that's about it. He's been content to let the best-hitting lineup in the American League swing away. He uses the hit-and-run on occasion, never squeezes, and sacrifice bunts only in obvious situations. Until last season, his bench players gathered dust. After his stale bench was exposed in the 1995 World Series, he started using backup players more often.

Pitching & Defense

Hargrove is careful with pitchers. His starters have a pitch count, and he keeps six relievers so he can create match-ups late in the game. When he has an established closer such as Jose Mesa, the ninth inning is a given. He has not shown patience with young pitchers, but the same can be said for the front office.

1997 Outlook

Hargrove will be under pressure in 1997. His contract was not extended because the front office expected a return trip to the World Series last year. The front office wants him to be tougher. Uproar caused by Belle's shenanigans and the trades of Eddie Murray and Carlos Baerga last year gave the impression that Hargrove had lost control of the club. The Indians will be contenders again, but to be more than that, Hargrove will have to keep the team focused, especially given the loss of Belle.

Born: 10/26/49 in Perryton, TX

Playing Experience: 1974-1985, Tex, Cle, SD

Managerial Experience: 6 seasons

Manager Statistics

Year	Team, Lg	W	L	Pct	GB	Finish
1996	Cleveland, AL	99	62	.615	—	1st Central
6 Seasons		449	378	.543	—	—

1996 Starting Pitchers by Days Rest

	≤3	4	5	6+
Indians Starts	1	82	48	22
Indians ERA	3.60	4.67	4.41	4.47
AL Avg Starts	4	96	30	21
AL ERA	5.57	4.90	5.33	5.81

1996 Situational Stats

	Mike Hargrove	AL Average
Hit & Run Success %	38.6	39.1
Stolen Base Success %	76.2	69.6
Platoon Pct.	62.5	61.9
Defensive Subs	25	29
High-Pitch Outings	14	23
Quick/Slow Hooks	14/17	17/20
Sacrifice Attempts	58	58

1996 Rankings (American League)

→ 1st in stolen base percentage (76.2%), steals of third base (36), least caught steals of third base (3) and double steals (10)

→ 2nd in stolen base attempts (210)

→ 3rd in steals of second base (122), steals of home plate (2), sacrifice bunt percentage (87.9%), pitchouts (41), pitchouts with a runner moving (13) and one-batter pitcher appearances (43)

Sandy Alomar

1996 Season

Finally, Sandy Alomar stayed clear of the disabled list and played 127 games in 1996—the most since his rookie year of 1990. It was the first season since 1990 that he didn't go on the DL. He hit in 21 of his first 22 games, including a career-high 17-game hitting streak. He went into the All-Star break hitting .286, but managed just a .232 average in the second half.

Hitting

Alomar is an aggressive hitter who swings early in the count. Last year he felt pressure to hit homers and consequently pulled the ball too much. As a result, he grounded into more than his share of double plays. Alomar is a much better hitter when he's patient and when he uses the whole field. His power is to left and left-center field and he's strong enough to drive the ball out of any park. He has trouble with inside fastballs, but can hit the breaking ball to right field.

Baserunning & Defense

Alomar doesn't clog the bases, but several knee operations have robbed him of his zip and daring. He throws well, but didn't get much help from his pitchers in holding runners, cutting down 32 percent of the basestealers he faced. Alomar still needs to improve his game-calling abilities, and his honest and caustic postgame evaluations of pitchers may have hurt his relationship with the Indian staff. He flashes good range and movement behind the plate for a big man and is excellent at blocking balls in the dirt.

1997 Outlook

Alomar's second-half slump worried the Indians. They went into the offseason looking for catching help, which could mean less playing time for Alomar regardless of his health. He is his own worst critic and needs to ease up on himself and enjoy the game.

Position: C
Bats: R **Throws:** R
Ht: 6' 5" **Wt:** 215

Opening Day Age: 30
Born: 6/18/66 in Salinas, PR
ML Seasons: 9
Pronunciation: AL-a-mar

Overall Statistics

	G	AB	R	H	D	T	HR	RBI	SB	BB	SO	Avg	OBP	Slg
1996	127	418	53	110	23	0	11	50	1	19	42	.263	.299	.397
Career	617	2076	246	561	103	4	53	265	22	111	233	.270	.313	.400

Where He Hits the Ball

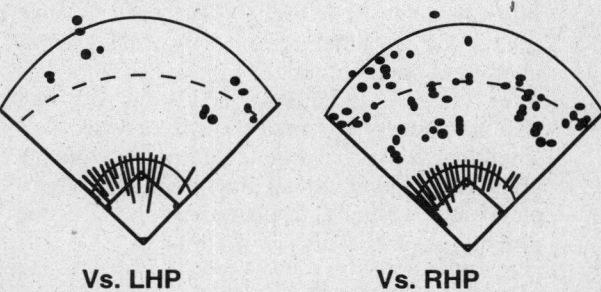

Vs. LHP   **Vs. RHP**

1996 Situational Stats

	AB	H	HR	RBI	Avg		AB	H	HR	RBI	Avg
Home	193	50	3	20	.259	LHP	115	29	4	15	.252
Road	225	60	8	30	.267	RHP	303	81	7	35	.267
First Half	241	69	6	29	.286	Sc Pos	112	31	3	41	.277
Scnd Half	177	41	5	21	.232	Clutch	65	19	3	7	.292

1996 Rankings (American League)

→ 3rd in most GDPs per GDP situation (20.8%), errors at catcher (9) and lowest fielding percentage at catcher (.988)
→ 5th in GDPs (20)
→ 6th in batting average on an 0-2 count (.300)
→ Led the Indians in GDPs (20) and batting average in the clutch (.292)

Albert Belle

1996 Season

Albert Belle hit 48 homers, led the American League with 148 RBI, served a two-game suspension and was fined a total of $75,000. In other words, it was a typical season for Hurricane Albert. Belle was fined $50,000 in spring training for cursing at a network TV reporter during Game 3 of the 1995 World Series. Later he was suspended for two games and fined $25,000 for turning Milwaukee second baseman Fernando Vina into roadkill while breaking up a double play. He also became Cleveland's franchise leader in homers with 242. Whew!

Hitting

When he's hot, Belle probably has the best plate coverage of any hitter in the league. He has power to all fields, and he's hit .311 or higher in the last three seasons. Impatience is his biggest foe. Against pitchers he doesn't know, or when he's struggling, Belle hits into a lot of first-pitch double plays. He's a good fastball hitter who pounds crippled breaking balls. Pitchers with good inside fastballs or junkballers can get him out.

Baserunning & Defense

Belle still doesn't hustle to first base, but he's better than he used to be. He'll slide hard to break up a double play, and is very effective in going from first to third. His speed is deceptive, and he was perfect as a thief last year (11-for-11). An average left fielder, Belle charges fly balls well, but will loaf after balls hit into the corner if he's playing in the gap. His arm strength and accuracy are average to below average.

1997 Outlook

A free agent, Belle signed with the Tribe's chief Central Division rival, the White Sox, after the season. One of the stormiest and most productive careers in Tribe history has come to an end. Despite the top-to-bottom strength of the Indians lineup, Belle's departure leaves them with a hole in the middle of the lineup that they can't possibly fill.

Position: LF
Bats: R **Throws:** R
Ht: 6' 2" **Wt:** 210

Opening Day Age: 30
Born: 8/25/66 in Shreveport, LA
ML Seasons: 8

Overall Statistics

	G	AB	R	H	D	T	HR	RBI	SB	BB	SO	Avg	OBP	Slg
1996	158	602	124	187	38	3	48	148	11	99	87	.311	.410	.623
Career	913	3441	592	1014	223	16	242	751	61	396	622	.295	.369	.580

Where He Hits the Ball

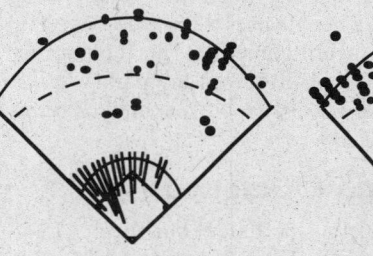

Vs. LHP   **Vs. RHP**

1996 Situational Stats

	AB	H	HR	RBI	Avg		AB	H	HR	RBI	Avg
Home	299	87	22	69	.291	LHP	151	48	15	35	.318
Road	303	100	26	79	.330	RHP	451	139	33	113	.308
First Half	321	94	27	74	.293	Sc Pos	154	54	19	110	.351
Scnd Half	281	93	21	74	.331	Clutch	91	23	6	21	.253

1996 Rankings (American League)

- → 1st in RBI and errors in left field (10)
- → 2nd in total bases (375) and lowest fielding percentage in left field (.970)
- → 3rd in cleanup slugging percentage (.630)
- → 4th in home runs and intentional walks (15)
- → 5th in times on base (293), GDPs (20) and HR frequency (12.5 ABs per HR)
- → 6th in runs scored, plate appearances (715), batting average with runners in scoring position (.351) and slugging percentage vs. left-handed pitchers (.675)
- → 7th in walks, slugging percentage, batting average with the bases loaded (.538) and slugging percentage vs. right-handed pitchers (.605)

Julio Franco

1996 Season

After seven seasons in Texas, Chicago and Japan, Julio Franco returned to Cleveland, the city where he established himself as a big leaguer. For the most part the return was a success as Franco hit .322, the second-highest average of his career, and made the postseason for the first time. Franco also received extensive playing time at first base, where he did a fair job. However, he missed two months with a strained right hamstring and played only 33 games in the season's second half. He finished the year by batting just .133 (2 for 15) in the postseason.

Hitting

Franco is an intelligent, patient hitter. He has an inside-out swing which allows him to hit inside fastballs to right field with power. He works deep into the count on almost every at-bat and possesses great strength in his upper body and hands. He uses a big (35 ounce) bat and can drive the ball through most infield shifts and into the gaps. High fastballs and sweeping breaking balls give him trouble, however.

Baserunning & Defense

Before the hamstring injury, Franco, who is 35, ran like he was 25. After the injury, he ran like he was 55. He was an adventure at first base and had trouble scooping balls out of the dirt on low throws. His defense slipped even further when he returned from his hamstring injury. He has the quick hands and the arm of a middle infielder—he came up as a shortstop—and starts the 3-6-3 double play well.

1997 Outlook

With the acquisition of Matt Williams, it appears as though the Indians will hand the first base duties over to Jim Thome and make Franco their regular DH. He hasn't lost a thing as a hitter and fits anywhere from second to seventh in the lineup. What the Indians have to do is find a way to keep him healthy.

Position: 1B/DH
Bats: R **Throws:** R
Ht: 6' 1" **Wt:** 190

Opening Day Age: 35
Born: 8/23/61 in San Pedro de Macoris, DR
ML Seasons: 14

Overall Statistics

	G	AB	R	H	D	T	HR	RBI	SB	BB	SO	Avg	OBP	Slg
1996	112	432	72	139	20	1	14	76	8	61	82	.322	.407	.470
Career	1770	6813	1036	2061	319	46	134	937	245	684	889	.303	.366	.422

Where He Hits the Ball

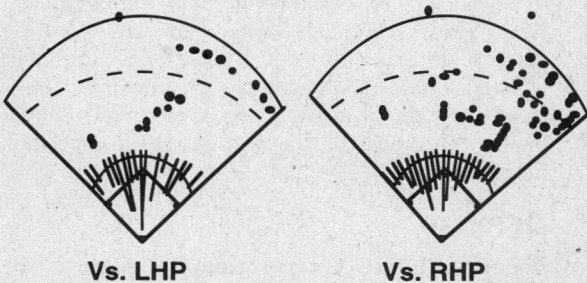

Vs. LHP   **Vs. RHP**

1996 Situational Stats

	AB	H	HR	RBI	Avg		AB	H	HR	RBI	Avg
Home	217	79	7	42	.364	LHP	128	43	2	16	.336
Road	215	60	7	34	.279	RHP	304	96	12	60	.316
First Half	304	99	10	55	.326	Sc Pos	120	42	4	64	.350
Scnd Half	128	40	4	21	.313	Clutch	63	14	2	7	.222

1996 Rankings (American League)

- → 2nd in batting average at home (.364)
- → 3rd in lowest percentage of swings on the first pitch (11.0%)
- → 4th in batting average on an 0-2 count (.313)
- → 5th in errors at first base (9)
- → 6th in batting average on a 3-1 count (.643)
- → 7th in batting average with runners in scoring position (.350)
- → 10th in highest percentage of pitches taken (61.0%)
- → Led the Indians in batting average vs. left-handed pitchers (.336), batting average on a 3-1 count (.643), batting average on an 0-2 count (.313), batting average at home (.364) and batting average with two strikes (.250)

Orel Hershiser

Position: SP
Bats: R **Throws:** R
Ht: 6' 3" **Wt:** 195

Opening Day Age: 38
Born: 9/16/58 in Buffalo, NY
ML Seasons: 14
Nickname: Bulldog

1996 Season

Orel Hershiser rode a rollercoaster last season. He was 4-4 with a 6.64 ERA in his first 12 starts before correcting a flaw in his delivery and going 11-5 with a 3.19 ERA in his final 21 starts. He won only one game in September, however, and he struggled in the postseason.

Pitching

Hershiser has five pitches: a sinking fastball, slider, curveball, change-up and splitter. When he's pitching well, he needs only his sinker and slider to get batters out. His sinker drops so hard and so fast that some hitters think he throws a spitter. He can reach 87-90 MPH with good control and hates to walk people, allowing only 2.5 walks per nine innings last season. His intense distaste for bases on balls actually gets him into trouble at times, as he sometimes allows hits instead of yielding walks. He's a six- to seven-inning pitcher who must be watched closely in the late innings.

Defense

Though he turned 38 last September, Hershiser is well conditioned and agile coming off the mound. He led the rotation with 69 total chances last year, committing only two errors and starting three double plays. He also controls the running game well: only seven runners attempted to steal against him, and three were thrown out.

1997 Outlook

Hershiser is 35-16, including the postseason, in his two seasons with the Indians. The team would like to see that production continue in this, the third and final year of his contract. He became a club leader last year after the trades of Eddie Murray and Carlos Baerga, and he'll probably enter next season as the third or fourth starter. However, Hershiser doesn't figure to last much longer, and his late-season fade has to be a concern.

Overall Statistics

	W	L	Pct.	ERA	G	GS	Sv	IP	H	BB	SO	HR	BR/IP
1996	15	9	.625	4.24	33	33	0	206.0	238	58	125	21	1.44
Career	165	117	.585	3.16	402	362	5	2529.1	2323	762	1679	168	1.22

How Often He Throws Strikes

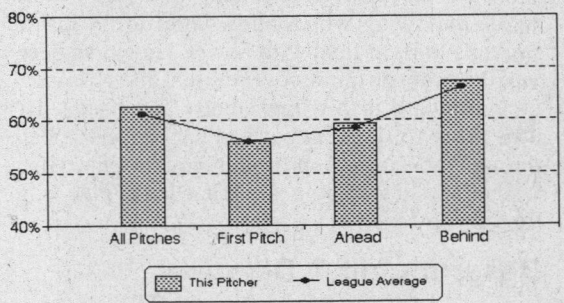

1996 Situational Stats

	W	L	ERA	Sv	IP		AB	H	HR	RBI	Avg
Home	6	2	4.04	0	84.2	LHB	459	144	7	50	.314
Road	9	7	4.38	0	121.1	RHB	369	94	14	46	.255
First Half	9	5	4.23	0	104.1	Sc Pos	210	54	3	72	.257
Scnd Half	6	4	4.25	0	101.2	Clutch	42	10	0	4	.238

1996 Rankings (American League)

→ 1st in least pitches thrown per batter (3.36)
→ 2nd in highest groundball/flyball ratio allowed (2.3)
→ 3rd in hit batsmen (12)
→ 7th in wild pitches (11) and most GDPs induced per 9 innings (1.0)
→ 8th in wins and highest batting average allowed (.287)
→ 9th in least home runs allowed per 9 innings (.92), least strikeouts per 9 innings (5.5) and highest batting average allowed vs. left-handed batters (.314)
→ 10th in balks (1), GDPs induced (23) and winning percentage

Kenny Lofton

1996 Season

Kenny Lofton set career highs in at-bats, hits, runs, doubles, homers, RBI and stolen bases in 1996. His 210 hits and 132 runs were the most by an Indian since Earl Averill had 232 hits and scored 136 runs in 1936. Lofton also added his fifth straight A.L. stolen base title, and he won his fourth straight Gold Glove.

Hitting

Lofton is a contact hitter who can slap the ball to all fields. He's at his best when he bunts or hits the ball anywhere from center field to the left field line. He'll often back away from the inside fastball because he doesn't think it's a strike, but he'll adjust and drive that pitch out of the park. Lofton has improved against the breaking ball, but still goes through phases when he thinks he's a home run hitter instead of a leadoff hitter.

Baserunning & Defense

Momentum guides Lofton on the bases. He'll steal bases in bunches, and then stop for a week or so. He posted an imposing 89-percent success rate (24-of-27) when stealing third. Despite a career-high 10 errors, he won another Gold Glove for his acrobatics in center field. Lofton has great speed and leaping ability and goes from gap-to-gap better than anyone in the league. His arm strength and accuracy are above average, but most of his errors came on bad throws.

1997 Outlook

Lofton is the key to the Tribe offense. That won't stop this year no matter how many changes take place in the lineup. This could be Lofton's final year in Cleveland depending on what happens with the labor negotiations. He could make it memorable if he walks and bunts more. . . and stays focused. The clubhouse turmoil of 1996 and his constant bickering with umpires over balls and strikes seemed to distract this talented and motivated player.

Position: CF
Bats: L **Throws:** L
Ht: 6' 0" **Wt:** 180

Opening Day Age: 29
Born: 5/31/67 in East Chicago, IN
ML Seasons: 6

Overall Statistics

	G	AB	R	H	D	T	HR	RBI	SB	BB	SO	Avg	OBP	Slg
1996	154	662	132	210	35	4	14	67	75	61	82	.317	.372	.446
Career	700	2821	551	883	133	42	39	261	327	307	343	.313	.379	.431

Where He Hits the Ball

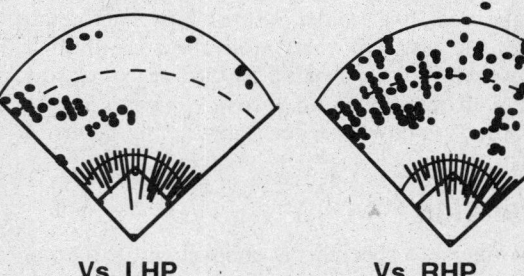

Vs. LHP **Vs. RHP**

1996 Situational Stats

	AB	H	HR	RBI	Avg			AB	H	HR	RBI	Avg
Home	321	110	7	35	.343		LHP	235	71	2	17	.302
Road	341	100	7	32	.293		RHP	427	139	12	50	.326
First Half	363	114	6	40	.314		Sc Pos	144	46	3	52	.319
Scnd Half	299	96	8	27	.321		Clutch	92	24	0	8	.261

1996 Rankings (American League)

- ➡ 1st in at-bats, stolen bases, errors in center field (10), lowest fielding percentage in center field (.975) and steals of third (24)
- ➡ 2nd in singles, caught stealing and plate appearances (736)
- ➡ 3rd in runs scored, hits and bunts in play (38)
- ➡ 4th in highest percentage of extra bases taken as a runner (69.6%)
- ➡ 5th in stolen base percentage (81.5%)
- ➡ 8th in pitches seen (2,802) and lowest percentage of swings that missed (10.1%)
- ➡ 9th in batting average at home (.343)
- ➡ Led the Indians in at-bats, runs scored, hits, singles, stolen bases, caught stealing and plate appearances (736)

Dennis Martinez

1996 Season

Last year was Dennis Martinez's final season with the Indians, and perhaps the final season of his career. He was on the disabled list three times with a strained flexor tendon in his right elbow; the injury limited him to three starts after the All-Star break. After an 8-2 start, he walked off the mound in Chicago on June 28 in the fourth inning because of pain in his elbow. He was never the same.

Pitching

When healthy, Martinez is a control pitcher who throws a fastball, curveball and change-up. He throws between 85-88 MPH, but he's deceptive and can throw any pitch at any time for a strike. His best offering is his curveball, which he can make break like a slider. A sore elbow and forearm over the last two years stole the snap from it, however. When he needs a big out late in the game, he'll drop down and throw sidearm. At 41, Martinez is now a six- or seven-inning pitcher at best.

Defense

Martinez is a specialist at controlling the running game. As soon as a runner reaches base, the game comes to a halt. He'll step off the rubber and throw to first at will in an effort to stop the other team's momentum. He can still field his position, especially on shots back up the middle. He's never been accused of having great reflexes, but he can still get off the mound and cover first.

1997 Outlook

Injury or no injury, it's unlikely Martinez will be back with the Indians because of his confrontational relationship with the front office. He still thinks he can pitch, and needs just four more wins to pass Juan Marichal as the winningest Latin American pitcher in big league history. Martinez has always been in good baseball shape, but he may have to take better care of his arm and body through strength training if he wants to extend his career any further.

Position: SP
Bats: R **Throws:** R
Ht: 6' 1" **Wt:** 180

Opening Day Age: 41
Born: 5/14/55 in Granada, Nicaragua
ML Seasons: 21

Overall Statistics

	W	L	Pct.	ERA	G	GS	Sv	IP	H	BB	SO	HR	BR/IP
1996	9	6	.600	4.50	20	20	0	112.0	122	37	48	12	1.42
Career	240	182	.569	3.63	630	548	6	3860.0	3723	1117	2070	356	1.25

How Often He Throws Strikes

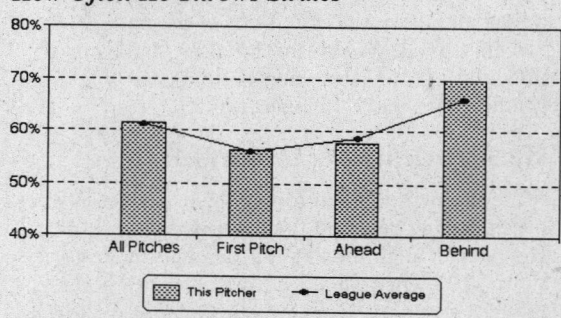

1996 Situational Stats

	W	L	ERA	Sv	IP		AB	H	HR	RBI	Avg
Home	4	4	4.68	0	65.1	LHB	221	61	4	30	.276
Road	5	2	4.24	0	46.2	RHB	218	61	8	28	.280
First Half	8	5	4.62	0	101.1	Sc Pos	95	28	4	44	.295
Scnd Half	1	1	3.38	0	10.2	Clutch	25	9	0	3	.360

1996 Rankings (American League)

➡ 6th in shutouts (1)
➡ Led the Indians in shutouts (1)

Jack McDowell

1996 Season

Jack McDowell came to the Indians last season as a free-agent starter in the prime of his career. McDowell, plagued by inconsistency and injury, had what he called "the worst season in my career." He went 5-1 in his first nine starts, and 1-5 in his next nine. On July 26, he went on the disabled list for the first time in his career with a right forearm injury. He was hit hard at first when he returned from the DL, but he recovered to go 3-0 in September.

Pitching

McDowell mixes his fastball with a forkball and a curve. The forkball is his best pitch. It's extremely effective and Black Jack's favorite pitch whenever he gets ahead of the hitter with two strikes. He throws two different varieties, one that breaks right and one that breaks left with velocity ranging from 89-91 MPH. When his forkball and curve are working, it allows him to throw high fastballs past hitters. He was reluctant to throw his curve after coming off the DL in August, though, and his other pitches got hit hard. McDowell has always pitched a lot of innings, but last year he was no longer a lock to go deep into a game.

Defense

The opposition stole an overwhelming 22 bases in 28 attempts with McDowell on the mound last year, taking full advantage of his slow delivery to the plate. At 6-5, McDowell looks awkward, but he gets off the mound well and does a decent job fielding his position, though he can be slow to cover first.

1997 Outlook

The Indians need a big season from McDowell. He put a lot of pressure on himself last year, wanting to help the club get back to the World Series. He must now show manager Mike Hargrove that he can be trusted with a lead late in the game. He also needs to be more consistent in finding the strike zone.

Position: SP
Bats: R **Throws:** R
Ht: 6' 5" **Wt:** 188

Opening Day Age: 31
Born: 1/16/66 in Van Nuys, CA
ML Seasons: 9
Nickname: Black Jack

Overall Statistics

	W	L	Pct.	ERA	G	GS	Sv	IP	H	BB	SO	HR	BR/IP
1996	13	9	.591	5.11	30	30	0	192.0	214	67	141	22	1.46
Career	119	77	.607	3.73	251	251	0	1753.1	1683	564	1216	152	1.28

How Often He Throws Strikes

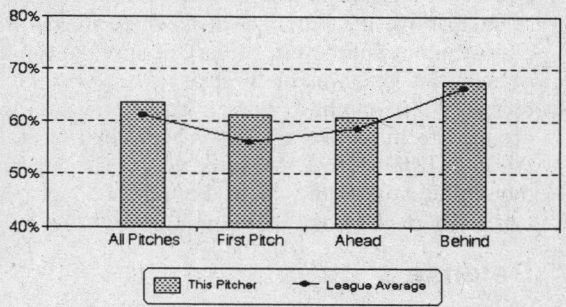

1996 Situational Stats

	W	L	ERA	Sv	IP		AB	H	HR	RBI	Avg
Home	7	5	6.28	0	90.1	LHB	424	120	12	53	.283
Road	6	4	4.07	0	101.2	RHB	336	94	10	44	.280
First Half	6	6	4.39	0	123.0	Sc Pos	195	46	1	66	.236
Scnd Half	7	3	6.39	0	69.0	Clutch	68	26	1	11	.382

1996 Rankings (American League)

→ 2nd in highest ERA at home (6.28)
→ 5th in least GDPs induced per 9 innings (0.6)
→ 6th in shutouts (1)
→ 7th in stolen bases allowed (22)
→ 8th in complete games (5)
→ 9th in highest stolen base percentage allowed (78.6%)
→ 10th in ERA on the road (4.07), lowest batting average allowed with runners in scoring position (.236) and fielding percentage at pitcher (.979)
→ Led the Indians in losses, complete games (5), shutouts (1), home runs allowed, walks allowed, pickoff throws (128) and stolen bases allowed (22)

Jose Mesa

1996 Season

Jose Mesa followed a perfect 1995 season with a flawed 1996 campaign and was criticized because of it. Two years ago, he was 46-for-48 in save opportunities with a 1.13 ERA. Last year he went 2-7 with 39 saves in 44 chances and a 3.73 ERA. He started last season by converting his first 20 save opportunities, but then he slumped. At one point Paul Shuey temporarily replaced him as the closer while pitching coach Mark Wiley worked on his mechanics.

Pitching

Mesa throws a fastball and slider. The fastball is his best pitch and he can bring a four-seam and two-seam variation. He tries to put the four-seamer above the hitter's waist, which makes it almost impossible to hit. Mesa will sink the two-seamer, and that was his best pitch last year. He threw it too much, however, and his velocity dropped from an average of 97 MPH in 1995 to 94-95 MPH in 1996. Mesa is very strong, and though he worked mostly in the ninth inning, he can easily pitch two or three innings.

Defense

Mesa does a good job containing the running game. He's quick to the plate and gives his catchers a chance to throw runners out. He's not a great fielder, but he gets off the mound well and you won't find a harder worker on the Cleveland team.

1997 Outlook

Mesa went from a dominant closer in 1995 and a good part of the first half of 1996, to a shaky one in the second half of last season. He converted 15-of-16 save opportunities after the break, but most of them were more dramatic than the team would have liked. Right-handed hitters adjusted to him, posting a .287 average when he was on the hill last year. Now it's Mesa's turn to make an adjustment. During his slump, he went into seclusion, stopped talking to reporters, and stopped having fun. Closers can't close like that.

Position: RP
Bats: R **Throws:** R
Ht: 6' 3" **Wt:** 225

Opening Day Age: 30
Born: 5/22/66 in Azua, DR
ML Seasons: 8
Pronunciation: MAY-sa

Overall Statistics

	W	L	Pct.	ERA	G	GS	Sv	IP	H	BB	SO	HR	BR/IP
1996	2	7	.222	3.73	69	0	39	72.1	69	28	64	6	1.34
Career	39	52	.429	4.48	280	95	87	780.1	816	307	470	67	1.44

How Often He Throws Strikes

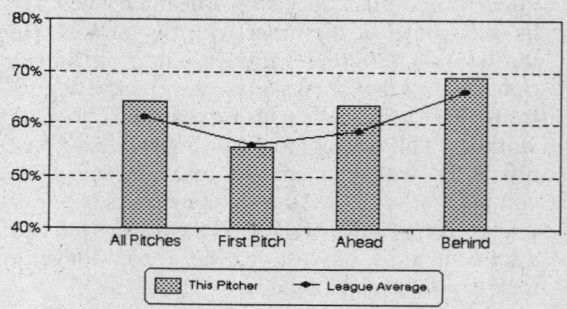

1996 Situational Stats

	W	L	ERA	Sv	IP		AB	H	HR	RBI	Avg
Home	0	6	3.66	19	39.1	LHB	133	30	2	12	.226
Road	2	1	3.82	20	33.0	RHB	136	39	4	13	.287
First Half	0	3	4.91	24	36.2	Sc Pos	52	18	0	19	.346
Scnd Half	2	4	2.52	15	35.2	Clutch	189	54	2	21	.286

1996 Rankings (American League)

→ 2nd in saves, games finished (60) and relief losses (7)
→ 3rd in save opportunities (44)
→ 4th in save percentage (88.6%)
→ Led the Indians in games pitched, saves, games finished (60), save opportunities (44), save percentage (88.6%), blown saves (5) and relief losses (7)

Charles Nagy

1996 Season

Charles Nagy should have easily won 20 games last year. He started hot and finished hot, but in between he went 1-3 in a 12-start stretch from June 21 to August 21. Eight of those 12 starts ended in no decisions, and in three of the no decisions Nagy left with a lead. Still, he had a satisfying season. Nagy went 11-1 in his first 14 starts and was the American League's starting pitcher in the All-Star game. He also pitched over 200 innings for the first time since 1992.

Pitching

Nagy has four pitches: a sinking fastball, curve, splitter, and change-up. He relies mostly on his sinker, but his breaking ball—a blend between a curve and a slider—is a deadly out pitch. What made Nagy successful last season was his great control of his two offspeed pitches. He brings his fastball in somewhere between 87-90 MPH. He is very unorthodox in his pitch selection, and hitters find it hard to sit on a certain offering because he'll throw any pitch, regardless of the count. He hates to come out of a game.

Defense

Nagy doesn't pay much attention to the running game. Only five of 24 basestealers were thrown out with him on the mound. He's a sound fielder who gets off the mound quickly, always covers first, and has good range.

1997 Outlook

If the Indians don't sign a top-shelf free agent pitcher during the offseason, Nagy should go to spring training as the number-one starter. Dennis Martinez is gone, Orel Hershiser is 38 and Jack McDowell has a long way to go to recapture his Cy Young form. Nagy is on the verge of becoming a dominant starter—since August of 1994, he's 35-11. He has always pitched behind established starters such as Greg Swindell, Tom Candiotti, Bud Black, Jack Morris, Martinez and Hershiser. He seems ready to lead now.

Position: SP
Bats: L **Throws:** R
Ht: 6' 3" **Wt:** 200

Opening Day Age: 29
Born: 5/5/67 in Fairfield, CT
ML Seasons: 7
Pronunciation: NAG-ee

Overall Statistics

	W	L	Pct.	ERA	G	GS	Sv	IP	H	BB	SO	HR	BR/IP
1996	17	5	.773	3.41	32	32	0	222.0	217	61	167	21	1.25
Career	74	54	.578	3.86	168	167	0	1127.0	1183	327	748	95	1.34

How Often He Throws Strikes

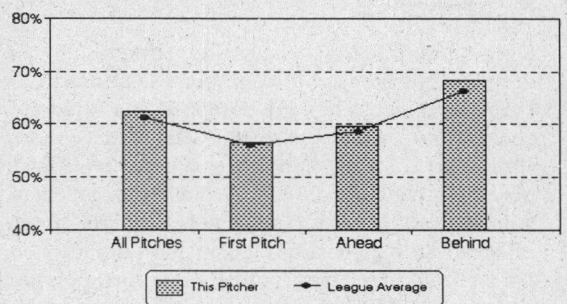

Legend: This Pitcher — League Average

1996 Situational Stats

	W	L	ERA	Sv	IP		AB	H	HR	RBI	Avg
Home	8	3	3.37	0	125.2	LHB	434	113	10	42	.260
Road	9	2	3.46	0	96.1	RHB	417	104	11	39	.249
First Half	11	2	3.53	0	122.1	Sc Pos	196	42	4	61	.214
Scnd Half	6	3	3.25	0	99.2	Clutch	87	21	4	9	.241

1996 Rankings (American League)

- ➡ 1st in fielding percentage at pitcher (1.000)
- ➡ 2nd in winning percentage
- ➡ 3rd in ERA, lowest on-base percentage allowed (.306), highest groundball/flyball ratio allowed (2.0) and least baserunners allowed per 9 innings (11.4)
- ➡ 4th in wins, ERA at home (3.37) and lowest batting average allowed with runners in scoring position (.214)
- ➡ 5th in GDPs induced (26), highest strikeout/walk ratio (2.7), most GDPs induced per 9 innings (1.1) and ERA on the road (3.46)
- ➡ 6th in lowest batting average allowed (.255)
- ➡ 7th in lowest slugging percentage allowed (.388)

Cleveland Indians

Chad Ogea

Position: SP/RP
Bats: R **Throws:** R
Ht: 6' 2" **Wt:** 200

Opening Day Age: 26
Born: 11/9/70 in Lake Charles, LA
ML Seasons: 3
Pronunciation: OH-jay

1996 Season

Chad Ogea may have finally convinced the Indians that he's a starting pitcher. Ever since they drafted him in 1991, they've viewed him as a fifth starter/long reliever with below-average stuff. But last season, especially in the second half when Dennis Martinez and Jack McDowell were injured, he became the team's most consistent starter outside of Charles Nagy. Ogea opened the year as the fifth starter, but went on the disabled list with tendinitis in his right shoulder. After a trip to Triple-A Buffalo, he returned to the Tribe on June 8 and moved into the rotation full time on July 2. He finished strong, going 5-3 with a 3.27 ERA in his last 11 starts.

Pitching

Ogea's best pitch is a change-up. Hitters sat on it in 1995, but he used his curveball last season to keep them guessing. He scrapped his slider to concentrate on the curve. He uses a deceptive, short-arm motion, and throws between 87-91 MPH. His fastball breaks late, and he can get away with some occasional high heat because of his offspeed stuff. Questions about his durability in the late innings persist, but he's intelligent on the mound.

Defense

Baserunners like to challenge Ogea, but he's getting better at stopping them. He has bad knees, so his range and quickness aren't the best. He still shows some spring off the mound, however, and can cover first base when needed.

1997 Outlook

For several seasons the Indians have been bragging about their young pitchers. Ogea, to date, has been one of the few to show he can win regularly in the big leagues. Depending on what moves the Indians make over the winter, look for Ogea to be on the staff either as a fourth or fifth starter or long reliever. He's best suited for starting, a fact he proved last year.

Overall Statistics

	W	L	Pct.	ERA	G	GS	Sv	IP	H	BB	SO	HR	BR/IP
1996	10	6	.625	4.79	29	21	0	146.2	151	42	101	22	1.32
Career	18	10	.643	4.18	53	36	0	269.1	267	81	169	35	1.29

How Often He Throws Strikes

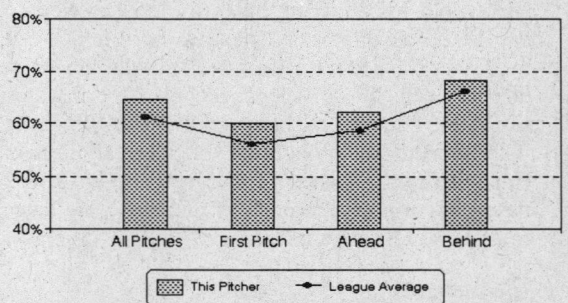

1996 Situational Stats

	W	L	ERA	Sv	IP		AB	H	HR	RBI	Avg
Home	7	1	4.54	0	77.1	LHB	306	81	11	40	.265
Road	3	5	5.06	0	69.1	RHB	261	70	11	37	.268
First Half	4	1	5.98	0	46.2	Sc Pos	126	31	3	48	.246
Scnd Half	6	5	4.23	0	100.0	Clutch	33	8	1	1	.242

1996 Rankings (American League)

- → 6th in shutouts (1)
- → 8th in runners caught stealing (9)
- → Led the Indians in shutouts (1), home runs allowed and runners caught stealing (9)

Manny Ramirez

1996 Season

In 1995, Manny Ramirez tired in September and the postseason. He finished strong in 1996, however, hitting .341 after the All-Star break and .375 (6-for-16) in the postseason against Baltimore. He came to spring training overweight and had to ride a bike around the training complex after practice to burn it off. But he worked hard the rest of the season and began to emerge as a complete player.

Hitting

Ramirez generates good bat speed with a smooth, tension-free swing. He has a slight lift to his swing, and has good power to center and right field. Ramirez hits the ball where it's pitched, he's patient and looks for certain pitches. If he's looking for a breaking ball, he'll let two hittable fastballs go until he gets the breaking ball. Split-fingers and breaking balls away give him trouble.

Baserunning & Defense

Ramirez has gone from being one of the worst baserunners in the league to a state of tentative mediocrity. He has decent speed and is looking more and more confident going from first to third. He still has trouble with the basics, such as leaving early from third base on sacrifice flies. Ramirez made great strides in right field, leading the majors with 19 outfield assists. He showed an accurate arm and consistently hit the cutoff man. His loping stride and basket catches give him a casual air, but he charges the ball and is no longer intimidated by the fence.

1997 Outlook

Ramirez jumped from the bottom of the lineup to the fifth spot last year following the trades of Eddie Murray and Carlos Baerga. He may be asked to move to cleanup since Albert Belle's departure. It will be interesting to see how he responds to the move. It's certainly his time to step up and be a consistent contributor.

Position: RF
Bats: R **Throws:** R
Ht: 6' 0" **Wt:** 190

Opening Day Age: 24
Born: 5/30/72 in Santo Domingo, DR
ML Seasons: 4

Overall Statistics

	G	AB	R	H	D	T	HR	RBI	SB	BB	SO	Avg	OBP	Slg
1996	152	550	94	170	45	3	33	112	8	85	104	.309	.399	.582
Career	402	1377	235	406	94	4	83	284	18	204	296	.295	.385	.550

Where He Hits the Ball

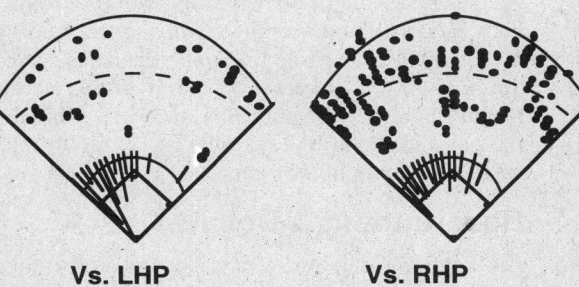

Vs. LHP   **Vs. RHP**

1996 Situational Stats

	AB	H	HR	RBI	Avg		AB	H	HR	RBI	Avg
Home	275	87	19	64	.316	LHP	149	48	7	24	.322
Road	275	83	14	48	.302	RHP	401	122	26	88	.304
First Half	292	82	20	64	.281	Sc Pos	154	47	8	81	.305
Scnd Half	258	88	13	48	.341	Clutch	81	19	7	16	.235

1996 Rankings (American League)

- ➡ 1st in errors in right field (9) and lowest fielding percentage in right field (.970)
- ➡ 6th in doubles
- ➡ 8th in sacrifice flies (9)
- ➡ 9th in total bases (320) and slugging percentage vs. right-handed pitchers (.584)
- ➡ Led the Indians in doubles and sacrifice flies (9)

Cleveland Indians

Kevin Seitzer

1996 Season

When the Indians acquired Kevin Seitzer on August 31 from Milwaukee, it was like a jolt of electricity hit the "me-first" Indians. They went 19-7 in September and played their best fundamental ball of the season. Seitzer hit .386 in 22 games with the Tribe and helped clinch the A.L. Central title with a grand slam against Chicago on September 17. He underwent arthroscopic surgery on his left knee after the season.

Hitting

Seitzer fit perfectly into the Tribe's lineup as a number-two hitter behind Kenny Lofton. It looked like Seitzer and Lofton had been teammates for years when it came to working the hit-and-run. He's a good line-drive hitter who's not afraid to work a pitcher deep into the count, thanks to a late, quick swing. Sinkers away and good inside fastballs will get him out. He's an excellent breaking-ball hitter and will take the ball to right field when he's down in the count.

Baserunning & Defense

Bad knees and all, Seitzer always runs hard to first base, making him an oddity on the Indians. He was a prime candidate to be replaced by a pinch runner late in a tight game. His range at first base was limited by a sore left knee, but he did an adequate job defensively and has a decent arm. Seitzer played some third base for the Brewers, but at this stage of his career he'll see more time at DH and first.

1997 Outlook

Cleveland wanted Seitzer back not only for his bat and his knowledge, but also for his enthusiasm and attitude, and they signed him to a new contract after the season. The Indians like what he brings to the club, and though they have plenty of other options at first, third and DH, he'll get his playing time.

Position: DH/1B/3B
Bats: R **Throws:** R
Ht: 5'11" **Wt:** 193

Opening Day Age: 35
Born: 3/26/62 in Springfield, IL
ML Seasons: 11
Pronunciation: SITE-zer

Overall Statistics

	G	AB	R	H	D	T	HR	RBI	SB	BB	SO	Avg	OBP	Slg
1996	154	573	85	187	35	3	13	78	6	87	79	.326	.416	.466
Career	1375	5080	712	1504	271	35	72	589	80	651	592	.296	.377	.406

Where He Hits the Ball

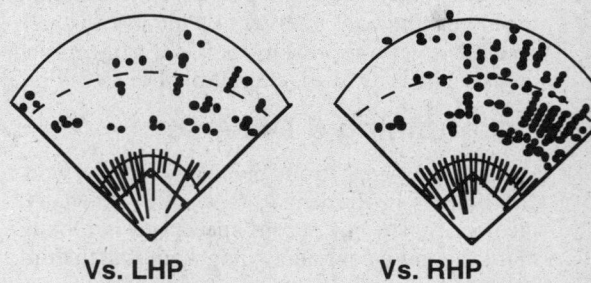

Vs. LHP   **Vs. RHP**

1996 Situational Stats

	AB	H	HR	RBI	Avg		AB	H	HR	RBI	Avg
Home	289	86	5	40	.298	LHP	174	64	3	21	.368
Road	284	101	8	38	.356	RHP	399	123	10	57	.308
First Half	312	110	10	44	.353	Sc Pos	137	41	4	60	.299
Scnd Half	261	77	3	34	.295	Clutch	70	22	2	5	.314

1996 Rankings (American League)

- → 2nd in batting average on the road (.356)
- → 4th in lowest percentage of extra bases taken as a runner (28.4%)
- → 5th in singles (136) and batting average on a 3-2 count (.388)
- → 7th in on-base percentage (.416)
- → 8th in hits (187) and lowest percentage of swings on the first pitch (17.5%)
- → 9th in batting average (.326)
- → 10th in times on base (279), highest ground-ball/flyball ratio (1.7) and batting average vs. left-handed pitchers (.368)

Paul Shuey

Position: RP
Bats: R **Throws:** R
Ht: 6' 3" **Wt:** 215

Opening Day Age: 26
Born: 9/16/70 in Lima, OH
ML Seasons: 3

1996 Season

Paul Shuey started last season upside down under a freeway after his car slipped off an icy road. Shuey, who was with Triple-A Buffalo at the time, was promoted to Cleveland soon afterward, but he was still traumatized by the accident and was sent back down. He returned June 10 and had a break-through season as a set-up man and closer.

Pitching

Shuey has always thrown hard, but before last season no one knew where the ball was going. After years of fighting the front office about his high leg kick—he wanted it, they wanted him to shorten it—he cut it down and lost 25 pounds playing winter ball in Puerto Rico. He lost veloc-ity, but found control and command. He throws a fastball in the range of 93-97 MPH, along with a curveball and splitter. His fastball is straight and can be hit. He has a big breaking curve and a nasty slider he throws at 89-90 MPH. Shuey seems to be 3-2 on every batter, but he issued only 26 walks last year.

Defense

Shuey has worked hard at stopping basestealers. He shortens his leg kick, uses a slide-step, and quickens his delivery to the plate when a runner gets on. The trimmed-down Shuey was quicker off the mound last season and stayed away from the hamstring injuries that bothered him in years past. Still, he's not a great fielder.

1997 Outlook

Many people in the Indians' front office believed Shuey, the second overall pick in 1992, was a bust when he flopped year after year. But last season he showed the ability to adjust and adapt and became an important part of the bullpen as a set-up man/closer. He figures to play a bigger role this year with the possible loss of Eric Plunk to free agency and the trade of Julian Tavarez.

Overall Statistics

	W	L	Pct.	ERA	G	GS	Sv	IP	H	BB	SO	HR	BR/IP
1996	5	2	.714	2.85	42	0	4	53.2	45	26	44	6	1.32
Career	5	5	.500	3.89	63	0	9	71.2	64	43	65	7	1.49

How Often He Throws Strikes

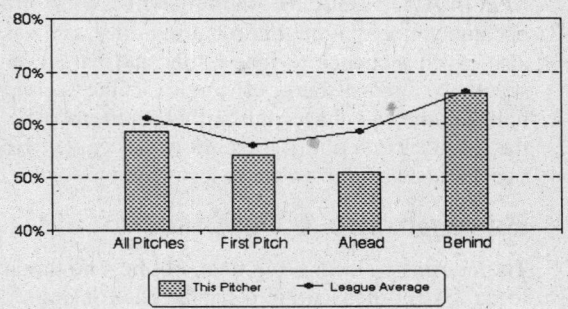

1996 Situational Stats

	W	L	ERA	Sv	IP		AB	H	HR	RBI	Avg
Home	4	1	2.20	2	28.2	LHB	93	22	1	8	.237
Road	1	1	3.60	2	25.0	RHB	102	23	5	15	.225
First Half	2	2	4.43	2	20.1	Sc Pos	49	9	1	17	.184
Scnd Half	3	0	1.89	2	33.1	Clutch	94	23	4	10	.245

1996 Rankings (American League)

→ 4th in lowest batting average allowed in relief with runners on base (.185)
→ 8th in relief ERA (2.85)
→ 9th in first batter efficiency (.189)
→ 10th in balks (1)
→ Led the Indians in balks (1), first batter effi-ciency (.189), lowest batting average allowed in relief with runners on base (.185) and low-est batting average allowed in relief with run-ners in scoring position (.184)

Jim Thome

1996 Season

After starting the season in a 1-for-20 slump, Jim Thome rebounded to have one of the best power years by a left-handed hitter in Tribe history. Thome's 38 homers were the most by a Cleveland lefty since Hal Trosky hit 42 in 1936. He also set a franchise record with 123 walks. Along with Manny Ramirez, Thome was forced to move up in the lineup after the trades of Carlos Baerga and Eddie Murray. He responded by showing everyone he was ready to be a meat-of-the-order hitter.

Hitting

One key for Thome last year was moving into the number-three spot behind Kenny Lofton and in front of Albert Belle. He shortened his swing and became a more patient hitter batting third. He was also given a chance to face lefties and batted respectably against them, especially in the second half. Thome will chase high fastballs, but can drive the outside pitch out of the park to left-center. He possesses awesome power to right field.

Baserunning & Defense

Thome runs well for a big man, but he's no threat to steal. He slides hard into second base on double plays and has a good fadeaway slide at the plate. He's worked hard at third base, but his glove and his arm are still unpredictable. His main problem is making the throw to first. If he throws from a crouch, he's fine. It's when he has time to straighten up and throw that the ball dies in the dirt.

1997 Outlook

Thome will most definitely be up for a position change. The addition of Matt Williams from the Giants most likely puts Thome at first base. He showed last season that he could move into the middle of lineup and produce. . . but this year he will have to do that without Belle hitting behind him.

Position: 3B
Bats: L **Throws:** R
Ht: 6' 4" **Wt:** 220

Opening Day Age: 26
Born: 8/27/70 in Peoria, IL
ML Seasons: 6
Pronunciation: TOE-mee

Overall Statistics

	G	AB	R	H	D	T	HR	RBI	SB	BB	SO	Avg	OBP	Slg
1996	151	505	122	157	28	5	38	116	2	123	141	.311	.450	.612
Career	500	1647	315	475	95	12	93	284	14	310	424	.288	.404	.530

Where He Hits the Ball

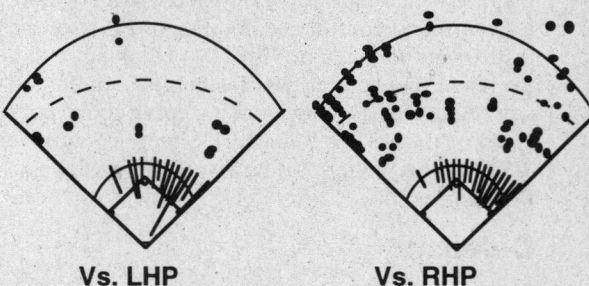

Vs. LHP   **Vs. RHP**

1996 Situational Stats

	AB	H	HR	RBI	Avg		AB	H	HR	RBI	Avg
Home	246	72	18	60	.293	LHP	160	40	7	30	.250
Road	259	85	20	56	.328	RHP	345	117	31	86	.339
First Half	258	80	16	51	.310	Sc Pos	147	45	10	76	.306
Scnd Half	247	77	22	65	.312	Clutch	85	24	5	21	.282

1996 Rankings (American League)

→ 1st in most pitches seen per plate appearance (4.46) and on-base percentage vs. right-handed pitchers (.489)
→ 2nd in walks, slugging percentage vs. right-handed pitchers (.696) and errors at third base (17)
→ 4th in on-base percentage, batting average vs. right-handed pitchers (.339) and lowest fielding percentage at third base (.953)
→ 5th in pitches seen (2,837)
→ 6th in highest percentage of pitches taken (63.7%)
→ 7th in runs scored, times on base (286) and strikeouts

Jose Vizcaino

1996 Season

Jose Vizcaino came to Cleveland from the New York Mets on July 29 with the hope that he would stabilize the Tribe's defense at second base. He handled the pressure of replacing the popular Carlos Baerga, and in 48 games with the Indians the switch-hitter posted a .285 batting average. He also played well in his first trip to the postseason, hitting .333 (4-for-12) in the Divisional Playoffs against Baltimore.

Hitting

Vizcaino is an arm-and-hands hitter. He doesn't get his legs or hips into his swing, which kills his ability to drive the ball. He is a better hitter from the left side of the plate. He handles fastballs effectively, but struggles against the breaking ball. Vizcaino needs to level out his swing and stop hitting underneath the ball. Because of his good bat control and his ability to bunt and work the hit-and-run, he can fill the number-two spot in the lineup or hit at the bottom of the order. He was dangerous with runners in scoring position for the Tribe.

Baserunning & Defense

Vizcaino runs hard to first base, and he swiped 15 bases last year despite a lack of aggressiveness on the basepaths. He's a solid middle infielder with good range and an above-average arm. He looks more comfortable at shortstop than second base, but he turned the double play well for the Tribe and showed exceptional range to his left. He was criticized for not diving for grounders in New York, but he dove for them in Cleveland.

1997 Outlook

The Indians liked what they saw in Vizcaino, but they went into the offseason looking for bigger offensive numbers from their second baseman. Consequently, Vizcaino and his $2.7 million salary were traded, along with Jeff Kent and Julian Taverez, to San Francisco in the Matt Williams deal. The Giants will get what they paid for: a defensive-oriented singles hitter.

Position: 2B
Bats: B **Throws:** R
Ht: 6' 1" **Wt:** 180

Opening Day Age: 29
Born: 3/26/68 in Palenque de San Cristobal, DR
ML Seasons: 8
Pronunciation: vis-KAH-ee-no

Overall Statistics

	G	AB	R	H	D	T	HR	RBI	SB	BB	SO	Avg	OBP	Slg
1996	144	542	70	161	17	8	1	45	15	35	82	.297	.341	.363
Career	756	2503	294	688	86	25	12	217	42	172	353	.275	.321	.344

Where He Hits the Ball

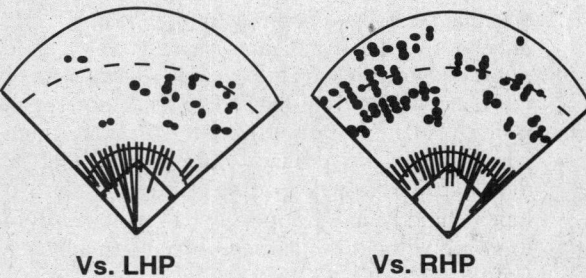

Vs. LHP   **Vs. RHP**

1996 Situational Stats

	AB	H	HR	RBI	Avg		AB	H	HR	RBI	Avg
Home	271	76	1	26	.280	LHP	153	45	0	11	.294
Road	271	85	0	19	.314	RHP	389	116	1	34	.298
First Half	293	90	1	24	.307	Sc Pos	137	42	0	39	.307
Scnd Half	249	71	0	21	.285	Clutch	87	24	0	12	.276

1996 Rankings (American League)

➡ Did not rank near the top or bottom in any category.

Omar Vizquel

Position: SS
Bats: B **Throws:** R
Ht: 5' 9" **Wt:** 165

Opening Day Age: 29
Born: 4/24/67 in Caracas, VZ
ML Seasons: 8
Pronunciation: viz-KELL

1996 Season

Omar Vizquel committed a career-high 20 errors at shortstop in 1996, but still won his fourth Gold Glove. That's an indication of the kind of respect he has gained throughout the league, and also showed that most people knew he played with a frayed labrum in his right shoulder the whole season. Vizquel made up for his defensive miscues with his best season at the plate. He set career highs in average, runs, doubles, homers, RBI and stolen bases. He also led the Tribe with a .429 batting average in the postseason.

Hitting

What Vizquel did last season was the product of three years of hard work. One key to his success was that he stopped popping up high fastballs. He either didn't swing at them or he made a concerted effort to chop down on the ball. He's a better hitter left-handed than right-handed, and can turn on an inside fastball while hitting lefty. Another thing which helped his progress was the fact that he didn't spend the whole season hitting in the two hole behind Kenny Lofton. He had more freedom to swing without the burden of trying to advance Lofton.

Baserunning & Defense

Vizquel and Lofton are the only Indians with the green light to steal. He's blossomed into a basestealer the last two years even though he's not that fast. He'll get picked off occasionally, but his instincts are very good. His range didn't suffer, but because of his shoulder injury, Vizquel tried to hurry throws. He may have the softest hands in baseball and rarely makes a bad decision when he has the ball.

1997 Outlook

Vizquel underwent surgery on his right shoulder after the season and no damage was found to the rotator cuff. He'll be back at short this year, and for many years to come after signing through 2001.

Overall Statistics

	G	AB	R	H	D	T	HR	RBI	SB	BB	SO	Avg	OBP	Slg
1996	151	542	98	161	36	1	9	64	35	56	42	.297	.362	.417
Career	1016	3481	447	914	134	17	22	284	116	311	332	.263	.322	.330

Where He Hits the Ball

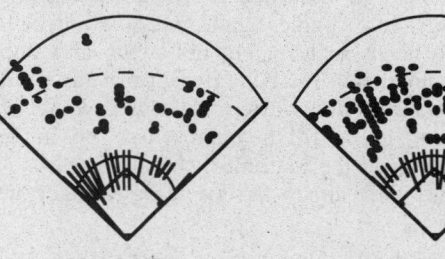

Vs. LHP **Vs. RHP**

1996 Situational Stats

	AB	H	HR	RBI	Avg		AB	H	HR	RBI	Avg
Home	281	86	2	39	.306	LHP	168	46	4	22	.274
Road	261	75	7	25	.287	RHP	374	115	5	42	.307
First Half	306	91	4	38	.297	Sc Pos	141	37	3	55	.262
Scnd Half	236	70	5	26	.297	Clutch	86	25	1	12	.291

1996 Rankings (American League)

→ 2nd in batting average with the bases loaded (.615)
→ 4th in lowest percentage of swings that missed (7.5%)
→ 5th in stolen bases, errors at shortstop (20), lowest fielding percentage at shortstop (.971), bunts in play (30) and steals of third (6)
→ 6th in highest percentage of swings put into play (55.0%)
→ 7th in sacrifice bunts (12)
→ 8th in sacrifice flies (9)
→ 10th in caught stealing (9)
→ Led the Indians in sacrifice bunts (12), sacrifice flies (9) and batting average with the bases loaded (.615)

Paul Assenmacher

Position: RP
Bats: L **Throws:** L
Ht: 6' 3" **Wt:** 210

Opening Day Age: 36
Born: 12/10/60 in Allen Park, MI
ML Seasons: 11

Overall Statistics

	W	L	Pct.	ERA	G	GS	Sv	IP	H	BB	SO	HR	BR/IP
1996	4	2	.667	3.09	63	0	1	46.2	46	14	44	1	1.29
Career	52	38	.578	3.38	685	1	49	726.2	670	264	682	57	1.29

1996 Situational Stats

	W	L	ERA	Sv	IP		AB	H	HR	RBI	Avg
Home	3	1	2.28	1	27.2	LHB	86	22	0	10	.256
Road	1	1	4.26	0	19.0	RHB	91	24	1	10	.264
First Half	0	1	2.10	1	25.2	Sc Pos	71	18	0	19	.254
Scnd Half	4	1	4.29	0	21.0	Clutch	57	16	0	9	.281

1996 Season

Paul Assenmacher had his second straight solid season in the Tribe's pen. The late-inning specialist would have ended the season with an ERA below 3.00, but he allowed five earned runs in his last two outings. Lefties hit .256 against him, which is not up to his usual standards, but the figure shrinks to .212 over the last six seasons.

Pitching & Defense

Assenmacher excels at throwing his sharp-breaking curve for strikes. It's his best pitch along with an 88 MPH fastball and change-up. He is excellent at getting ahead of hitters, and when he gets a batter 1-2 or 0-2, no one is better at putting a hitter away. Assenmacher doesn't have great range, but he's committed only two errors in 11 seasons. He has a good pickoff move, but runners can take advantage of his slow delivery.

1997 Outlook

Assenmacher turned 36 in December, but the Indians haven't abused him, so he should remain effective for another year or more. Cleveland needs him to do what he's done in the past: retire lefties, erase the first batter he faces and pitch well with runners in scoring position.

Mark Carreon

Position: 1B
Bats: R **Throws:** L
Ht: 6' 0" **Wt:** 195

Opening Day Age: 33
Born: 7/9/63 in Chicago, IL
ML Seasons: 10
Pronunciation: CARRY-on

Overall Statistics

	G	AB	R	H	D	T	HR	RBI	SB	BB	SO	Avg	OBP	Slg
1996	119	434	56	122	34	3	11	65	3	33	42	.281	.339	.449
Career	738	2012	246	557	108	5	69	289	12	140	246	.277	.327	.438

1996 Situational Stats

	AB	H	HR	RBI	Avg		AB	H	HR	RBI	Avg
Home	196	56	5	36	.286	LHP	108	31	2	13	.287
Road	238	66	6	29	.277	RHP	326	91	9	52	.279
First Half	292	76	9	51	.260	Sc Pos	120	38	4	52	.317
Scnd Half	142	46	2	14	.324	Clutch	68	17	1	13	.250

1996 Season

Mark Carreon was acquired from San Francisco at the All-Star break because the Indians needed a good hitter who could play first base when Julio Franco was injured. Carreon did an excellent job, batting .324 in 38 games. His season ended prematurely when he fouled a ball off his left shin on August 23.

Hitting, Baserunning & Defense

Carreon has loose, quick hands and stands close to the plate. He's not a pretty hitter, but he's effective, especially against fastballs. He also has some pop, though he prefers to punch line drives and hit the ball where it's pitched. He's a quality pinch hitter because he usually makes contact. At one time Carreon ran well, but knee operations have slowed him. He's a decent, if awkward, first baseman. When Kenny Lofton had sore feet, Carreon even played center field.

1997 Outlook

Carreon filed for free agency at the end of the season, and the Indians weren't that interested in bringing him back even though he played well. He's probably best suited for a National League team because of his abilities as a pinch hitter.

Brian Giles

Position: DH/LF
Bats: L **Throws:** L
Ht: 5'11" **Wt:** 195

Opening Day Age: 26
Born: 1/21/71 in El
Cajon, CA
ML Seasons: 2

Overall Statistics

	G	AB	R	H	D	T	HR	RBI	SB	BB	SO	Avg	OBP	Slg
1996	51	121	26	43	14	1	5	27	3	19	13	.355	.434	.612
Career	57	130	32	48	14	1	6	30	3	19	14	.369	.441	.631

1996 Situational Stats

	AB	H	HR	RBI	Avg		AB	H	HR	RBI	Avg
Home	54	17	2	12	.315	LHP	22	8	0	7	.364
Road	67	26	3	15	.388	RHP	99	35	5	20	.354
First Half	0	0	0	0	-	Sc Pos	41	14	2	20	.341
Scnd Half	121	43	5	27	.355	Clutch	31	11	1	3	.355

1996 Season

Brian Giles joined Cleveland from Triple-A Buffalo on July 12 and hit a game-tying, pinch hit homer in the ninth inning of a 7-5 victory. He'd already hit 20 homers in Buffalo before the All-Star break. Giles stayed hot, hitting .463 in his first 23 games with the big club. When Julio Franco came off the disabled list and Kevin Seitzer was acquired from Milwaukee, Giles became a bench player.

Hitting, Baserunning & Defense

Giles is small but powerful. He has a short, compact swing that generates a lot of power. He's good lowball hitter who can handle breaking balls and change-ups. He'll struggle against breaking balls and inside fastballs from lefties. Giles runs well, but isn't a threat to steal. The Indians think he's a solid outfielder with above-average range and arm strength. His best position is left field.

1997 Outlook

The Indians need to find out if Giles can play every day or if he's a platoon player. Given the loss of Albert Belle, he should get his chance to start.

Jeff Kent

Traded To
GIANTS

Position: 3B/1B
Bats: R **Throws:** R
Ht: 6' 1" **Wt:** 185

Opening Day Age: 29
Born: 3/7/68 in
Bellflower, CA
ML Seasons: 5

Overall Statistics

	G	AB	R	H	D	T	HR	RBI	SB	BB	SO	Avg	OBP	Slg
1996	128	437	61	124	27	1	12	55	6	31	78	.284	.330	.432
Career	602	2125	296	583	118	11	78	318	16	140	415	.274	.327	.450

1996 Situational Stats

	AB	H	HR	RBI	Avg		AB	H	HR	RBI	Avg
Home	208	57	4	26	.274	LHP	123	40	0	14	.325
Road	229	67	8	29	.293	RHP	314	84	12	41	.268
First Half	310	91	9	37	.294	Sc Pos	117	28	1	38	.239
Scnd Half	127	33	3	18	.260	Clutch	69	22	2	8	.319

1996 Season

Jeff Kent came to the Indians from the New York Mets in the Carlos Baerga trade on July 29. He went from starting at third base with the Mets to being a bench player, and his confidence suffered. He got off to a 6-for-38 start with the Indians, but finished strong. Playing first, second and third base, he hit .328 in his final 23 games.

Hitting, Baserunning & Defense

Kent studies pitchers, and the fact that he didn't know A.L. pitchers hurt him. He's a fastball hitter, but didn't see many after the trade because he had such trouble with the breaking ball in Cleveland. He has a short, quick swing and can hit for power. Kent is an average runner and played solid infield defense last year. The Mets said he was an inconsistent defender, but he didn't show many flaws in limited playing time with the Tribe.

1997 Outlook

Kent didn't appear to fit into the Tribe's plans at the end of last year, and will be in his third uniform in two seasons following his trade to the Giants. He offers a lot of pop in his bat from the second base position.

Kent Mercker

Position: SP/RP
Bats: L **Throws:** L
Ht: 6' 2" **Wt:** 195

Opening Day Age: 29
Born: 2/1/68 in Dublin, OH
ML Seasons: 8

Overall Statistics

	W	L	Pct.	ERA	G	GS	Sv	IP	H	BB	SO	HR	BR/IP
1996	4	6	.400	6.98	24	12	0	69.2	83	38	29	13	1.74
Career	35	31	.530	3.91	257	66	19	585.1	523	280	455	62	1.37

1996 Situational Stats

	W	L	ERA	Sv	IP		AB	H	HR	RBI	Avg
Home	1	4	7.41	0	37.2	LHB	56	16	1	5	.286
Road	3	2	6.47	0	32.0	RHB	223	67	12	46	.300
First Half	3	6	7.43	0	53.1	Sc Pos	63	17	4	36	.270
Scnd Half	1	0	5.51	0	16.1	Clutch	13	5	0	0	.385

1996 Season

Kent Mercker would like to forget last season. He began the season in Baltimore after a big trade with Atlanta, but proved to be a flop. The Indians acquired him in a July 21 trade for Eddie Murray, and he made 10 forgettable appearances in the Tribe bullpen. Troubled with a dead arm in Baltimore, Mercker's strength appeared to return with the Indians, but they weren't interested in paying him $3 million for 1997.

Pitching & Defense

Mercker's fastball, clocked at 83 MPH with the Orioles, improved to 88-90 MPH with the Tribe. He throws a slider, curve and change-up, but the fastball is his best pitch when it's working. He said his left arm went bad when he tried to get ready too quickly in spring training. He's a good athlete who fields his position well, though he doesn't have a great deal of range. Controlling the running game has never been his top priority.

1997 Outlook

The Tribe wasn't interested in bringing back Mercker, and he signed a one-year deal with the Reds after the season. The Reds hope the return to the National League will help him rebuild his confidence.

Tony Pena

Position: C
Bats: R **Throws:** R
Ht: 6' 0" **Wt:** 185

Opening Day Age: 39
Born: 6/4/57 in Monte Cristi, DR
ML Seasons: 17
Pronunciation: PAIN-yuh

Overall Statistics

	G	AB	R	H	D	T	HR	RBI	SB	BB	SO	Avg	OBP	Slg
1996	67	174	14	34	4	0	1	27	0	15	25	.195	.255	.236
Career	1948	6403	661	1672	294	27	107	698	80	445	830	.261	.310	.366

1996 Situational Stats

	AB	H	HR	RBI	Avg		AB	H	HR	RBI	Avg
Home	82	13	0	8	.159	LHP	62	14	1	8	.226
Road	92	21	1	19	.228	RHP	112	20	0	19	.179
First Half	83	22	1	13	.265	Sc Pos	63	19	1	27	.302
Scnd Half	91	12	0	14	.132	Clutch	18	3	0	1	.167

1996 Season

Tony Pena—the ageless catcher—may have finally aged. At 39, he hit .195 in 67 games. From June 21 to the end of the season, Pena posted a .119 (13-for-109) mark which included 0-for-24 and 0-for-20 slumps. He was still a good influence in the clubhouse, but it was clear his considerable skills were slipping.

Hitting, Baserunning & Defense

Pena has an all-or-nothing swing. He can hit a fastball if it's in his wheelhouse, but if it is not, he won't come close. Breaking balls mystified him all season long. He still has a great head on his shoulders and his ability to get inside a pitcher's head continues to be a strength. And despite his advanced age, his arm remains strong. Pena was never much of a threat to steal, but he always ran hard.

1997 Outlook

The Indians went into the offseason looking to upgrade the catching position. That meant Pena, a free agent, would not be back. The fun he brought to the clubhouse will be missed. So, too, will his guidance of young players.

Cleveland Indians

Eric Plunk

Position: RP
Bats: R **Throws:** R
Ht: 6' 6" **Wt:** 220

Opening Day Age: 33
Born: 9/3/63 in Wilmington, CA
ML Seasons: 11

Overall Statistics

	W	L	Pct.	ERA	G	GS	Sv	IP	H	BB	SO	HR	BR/IP
1996	3	2	.600	2.43	56	0	2	77.2	56	34	85	6	1.16
Career	60	46	.566	3.62	528	41	34	937.1	799	538	878	86	1.43

1996 Situational Stats

	W	L	ERA	Sv	IP		AB	H	HR	RBI	Avg
Home	2	1	2.92	1	37.0	LHB	135	32	3	13	.237
Road	1	1	1.99	1	40.2	RHB	141	24	3	13	.170
First Half	2	0	2.47	1	43.2	Sc Pos	79	16	0	18	.203
Scnd Half	1	2	2.38	1	34.0	Clutch	118	22	2	9	.186

1996 Season

Eric Plunk has given middle relievers a good name over the past few years. Last season was his fifth in the Tribe's bullpen, and every one of them has been exceptional.

Pitching & Defense

Plunk throws hard and strikes people out. He has a 92-94 MPH fastball, though it can be straight and hittable, and also adds in a sharp-breaking curve, a slow curve and dabbles with a slider. He tends to walk the first man he faces, so he's more effective when he starts an inning. He's 6' 6", wears thick glasses and is wild enough to scare right-handed hitters. Nine of 10 baserunners were successful stealing against Plunk in 1996, but he hasn't made an error in three seasons.

1997 Outlook

Plunk has been the backbone of the Tribe's bullpen for five years, but he filed for free agency. He's only 33 and hardly looks over the hill. If he *doesn't* return, the Indians will have to replace him with a hard thrower who can strike people out when the game is on the line. They're not easy to find.

Julian Tavarez

Traded To GIANTS

Position: RP/SP
Bats: R **Throws:** R
Ht: 6' 2" **Wt:** 165

Opening Day Age: 23
Born: 5/22/73 in Santiago, DR
ML Seasons: 4

Overall Statistics

	W	L	Pct.	ERA	G	GS	Sv	IP	H	BB	SO	HR	BR/IP
1996	4	7	.364	5.36	51	4	0	80.2	101	22	46	9	1.52
Career	16	12	.571	4.49	117	12	0	204.1	236	57	133	24	1.43

1996 Situational Stats

	W	L	ERA	Sv	IP		AB	H	HR	RBI	Avg
Home	2	3	5.36	0	40.1	LHB	151	56	4	27	.371
Road	2	4	5.36	0	40.1	RHB	170	45	5	30	.265
First Half	3	5	4.91	0	51.1	Sc Pos	99	30	2	47	.303
Scnd Half	1	2	6.14	0	29.1	Clutch	85	24	4	7	.282

1996 Season

In 1995, Julian Tavarez became a middle-relief sensation similar to the 1996 Mariano Rivera. He was the bridge between the American League's best rotation and closer. In 1996, the bridge collapsed. He pitched well in relief in April, then fell into a prolonged slump to close out the season.

Pitching & Defense

Tavarez has a great arm. His best pitch is a sinking 92-95 MPH fastball. A slider and splitter are his next best pitches, but the late breaking action on those weapons disappeared last season. Lefties wore him out, hitting .371 compared to .268 in 1995. When he was put in the rotation following Dennis Martinez's injury, he looked lost. Tavarez has a quick delivery to the plate to stop baserunners, and he's a decent fielder.

1997 Outlook

Several teams were interested in acquiring Tavarez after the season, and the Giants won the sweepstakes. Cleveland felt he suffered from a big head last year because of his rookie success. San Francisco hopes he's matured enough to get past that. He'll probably start this season in the bullpen, with a chance to be a starter when that maturation process has moved forward.

Other Cleveland Indians

Brian Anderson (Pos: LHP, Age: 24)

	W	L	Pct.	ERA	G	GS	Sv	IP	H	BB	SO	HR	BR/IP
1996	3	1	.750	4.91	10	9	0	51.1	58	14	21	9	1.40
Career	16	14	.533	5.35	50	45	0	264.0	299	73	117	47	1.41

The Indians traded for Anderson after the Angels committed a procedural error that left them in danger of losing him. He's young and highly regarded, but flunked out of the rotation twice last year. 1997 Outlook: B

Casey Candaele (Pos: 2B, Age: 36, Bats: B)

	G	AB	R	H	D	T	HR	RBI	SB	BB	SO	Avg	OBP	Slg
1996	24	44	8	11	2	0	1	4	0	1	9	.250	.267	.364
Career	740	1908	201	475	85	20	11	135	36	160	210	.249	.307	.332

The 36-year-old utilityman is still around because he switch-hits and plays a bunch of different positions. There's no telling how much longer he'll be able to hang on. 1997 Outlook: C

Einar Diaz (Pos: C, Age: 24, Bats: R)

	G	AB	R	H	D	T	HR	RBI	SB	BB	SO	Avg	OBP	Slg
1996	4	1	0	0	0	0	0	0	0	0	0	.000	.000	.000
Career	4	1	0	0	0	0	0	0	0	0	0	.000	.000	.000

The young catcher has a good defensive reputation and decent offensive potential. He played at Double-A last year and is probably a year away from challenging for a major league job. 1997 Outlook: C

Alan Embree (Pos: LHP, Age: 27)

	W	L	Pct.	ERA	G	GS	Sv	IP	H	BB	SO	HR	BR/IP
1996	1	1	.500	6.39	24	0	0	31.0	30	21	33	10	1.65
Career	4	5	.444	6.11	51	4	1	73.2	72	45	68	15	1.59

Embree is one of the hardest-throwing lefties around, but control problems last year left him with no role in the Indians' bullpen. Many teams covet his arm, and he could make a big breakthrough at any time. 1997 Outlook: B

Scott Leius (Pos: 3B, Age: 31, Bats: R)

	G	AB	R	H	D	T	HR	RBI	SB	BB	SO	Avg	OBP	Slg
1996	27	43	3	6	4	0	1	3	0	2	8	.140	.178	.302
Career	503	1416	204	352	62	10	27	158	15	156	222	.249	.323	.364

Leius hit .140 as a backup infielder for Cleveland in the first half. They sent him to the minors late in the year, where he didn't hit well enough to have much hope for 1997. 1997 Outlook: C

Geronimo Pena (Pos: 3B, Age: 30, Bats: B)

	G	AB	R	H	D	T	HR	RBI	SB	BB	SO	Avg	OBP	Slg
1996	5	9	1	1	0	0	1	2	0	1	4	.111	.200	.444
Career	378	1010	162	265	60	8	30	124	54	112	255	.262	.345	.427

Pena continued to be a lightning rod for injuries. He played at Triple-A for both the Cardinals and Indians, and became a free agent at the end of the year. He can play if he's healthy. *IF.* 1997 Outlook: B

Herbert Perry (Pos: 1B, Age: 27, Bats: R)

	G	AB	R	H	D	T	HR	RBI	SB	BB	SO	Avg	OBP	Slg
1996	7	12	1	1	0	0	0	0	1	1	2	.083	.154	.167
Career	63	183	25	53	14	1	3	24	2	17	31	.290	.361	.426

Perry is a good contact hitter and a fine first baseman, but the Indians sent him down to work on his power stroke. The power didn't come, but he hit well before he hurt his knee. 1997 Outlook: B

Joe Roa (Pos: RHP, Age: 25)

	W	L	Pct.	ERA	G	GS	Sv	IP	H	BB	SO	HR	BR/IP
1996	0	0	-	10.80	1	0	0	1.2	4	3	0	0	4.20
Career	0	1	.000	7.04	2	1	0	7.2	13	5	0	1	2.35

Joe Roa is only 25 years old and one of the finest control pitchers in the high minors, but no one has any confidence at all in his stuff. He probably can pitch, but we may never get the chance to find out. 1997 Outlook: C

Greg Swindell (Pos: LHP, Age: 32)

	W	L	Pct.	ERA	G	GS	Sv	IP	H	BB	SO	HR	BR/IP
1996	1	4	.200	7.14	21	6	0	51.2	66	19	36	13	1.65
Career	103	98	.512	3.90	293	268	0	1800.0	1905	391	1224	201	1.28

Fat, injury-prone, ineffective, and twice-released last year, Greg Swindell is a great bet to be one of the best pitchers of 1997—in Taiwan. 1997 Outlook: D

Ryan Thompson (Pos: CF, Age: 29, Bats: R)

	G	AB	R	H	D	T	HR	RBI	SB	BB	SO	Avg	OBP	Slg
1996	8	22	2	7	0	0	1	5	0	1	6	.318	.348	.455
Career	291	1019	129	245	53	4	40	131	8	75	282	.240	.301	.418

Thompson spent the entire year at Triple-A and displayed the same shortcomings that the Mets had always refused to acknowledge. At age 29, someday is now, and he's not good enough. 1997 Outlook: C

Nigel Wilson (Pos: DH, Age: 27, Bats: L)

	G	AB	R	H	D	T	HR	RBI	SB	BB	SO	Avg	OBP	Slg
1996	10	12	2	3	0	0	2	5	0	1	6	.250	.308	.750
Career	22	35	2	3	0	0	2	5	0	1	21	.086	.111	.257

Four years after being taken second in the 1993 expansion draft, Nigel Wilson was still at Triple-A last season. He socked 30 homers for Buffalo, then signed to play in Japan. 1997 Outlook: D

Cleveland Indians Minor League Prospects

Organization Overview:

The Cleveland organization is simply packed with talent from top to bottom. Jim Thome and Manny Ramirez were developed in-house, and last year, the farm system contributed Brian Giles and Paul Shuey to a major league roster that was already loaded. Not only do they have a long line of pitchers preparing to bolster Cleveland's staff, but they also have an advanced prospect at just about every other position. Such depth gives them great leverage and flexibility in trade talks and free-agent negotiations. The Indians have stockpiled prospects not only by drafting wisely, but by going after young players who have reached dead ends in other organizations. Most of their impact players are still a year or two away, but for the time being, they have plenty of solid players who will be able to step into the lineup and produce immediately. There's every reason to think that the Indians will remain a dynasty into the next century.

Bruce Aven

Position: OF   **Opening Day Age:** 25
Bats: R **Throws:** R   **Born:** 3/4/72 in
Ht: 5' 9" **Wt:** 180   Orange, TX

Recent Statistics

	G	AB	R	H	D	T	HR	RBI	SB	BB	SO	AVG
94 A Watertown	61	220	49	73	14	5	5	33	12	20	45	.332
95 A Kinston	130	479	70	125	23	5	23	69	15	41	109	.261
96 AA Canton-Akrn	131	481	91	143	31	4	23	79	22	43	101	.297
96 AAA Buffalo	3	9	5	6	0	0	1	2	0	1	1	.667
96 MLE	134	478	85	137	30	2	20	71	16	32	108	.287

He was too old, his speed was nothing special, and his defense was lacking—or so they said. But Bruce Aven proved them all wrong with a standout year at Double-A. Playing in a tough home run park, he remained a power threat, and stepped up his game in all other areas. He came within three points of batting .300, stole 22 bases in 28 tries, and most surprisingly, shifted to center field and didn't embarrass himself. It's true that at age 25, he's still a little old, and that he'll be limited to a corner spot in the majors, but he's shown he can hit enough to be useful at the major league level.

Bartolo Colon

Position: P   **Opening Day Age:** 21
Bats: R **Throws:** R   **Born:** 5/24/75 in
Ht: 6' 0" **Wt:** 185   Altamira, DR

Recent Statistics

	W	L	ERA	G	GS	Sv	IP	H	R	BB	SO	HR
94 R Burlington	7	4	3.14	12	12	0	66.0	46	32	44	84	3
95 A Kinston	13	3	1.96	21	21	0	128.2	91	31	39	152	8
96 AA C'nton-Akrn	2	2	1.74	13	12	0	62.0	44	17	25	56	2
96 AAA Buffalo	0	0	6.00	8	0	0	15.0	16	10	8	19	2

In each of the past two seasons, Bartolo Colon has done the same thing: he's generated tremendous fanfare with his 95-MPH fastball and excellent control, and he's missed a large part of the season with an elbow injury. The tendinitis that sidelined him in '96 was unrelated to the bone bruise he suffered in '95, but his durability remains a concern. When he returned to action in the second half of '96, he was promoted to Triple-A, where he was moved to the bullpen to save wear and tear on his arm. For the first time in his career, he was hit hard, although that may have been the lingering effects of the injury. Only 22 this year, he's been dominant wherever he's pitched, and could be an impact pitcher if his arm holds up.

Danny Graves

Position: P   **Opening Day Age:** 23
Bats: R **Throws:** R   **Born:** 8/7/73 in
Ht: 5' 11" **Wt:** 200   Saigon, Vietnam

Recent Statistics

	W	L	ERA	G	GS	Sv	IP	H	R	BB	SO	HR
96 AAA Buffalo	4	3	1.48	43	0	19	79.0	57	14	24	46	1
96 AL Cleveland	2	0	4.55	15	0	0	29.2	29	18	10	22	2

For the past two seasons, Danny Graves has been one of the most unhittable pitchers in the minors, posting an almost-surreal 1.08 ERA over 149 innings. The Indians called him up for two separate stints with the big club last year, and they apparently saw enough to reserve a middle relief spot for him for next year. Graves gets ground balls with a sinking fastball in the low 90s and a sharp slider. He's got excellent control and a closer mentality. The only concern is that he worked well over 100 innings last year. If he's at full strength, he's capable of playing a major role in their bullpen.

Damian Jackson

Position: SS   **Opening Day Age:** 23
Bats: R **Throws:** R   **Born:** 8/16/73 in Los
Ht: 5' 10" **Wt:** 160   Angeles, CA

Recent Statistics

	G	AB	R	H	D	T	HR	RBI	SB	BB	SO	AVG
96 AAA Buffalo	133	452	77	116	15	1	12	49	24	48	78	.257
96 AL Cleveland	5	10	2	3	2	0	0	1	0	1	4	.300
96 MLE	133	444	70	108	14	0	10	45	19	44	81	.243

Damian Jackson's ability is so impressive that some people have been disappointed with his progress. He's got good speed and some power, hits for a decent average, and has the range, hands and arm to be a standout shortstop. On the other hand, he tries to pull the ball too much, strikes out a lot, and makes a lot of errors on routine plays. However, he's still very young—only 23—and he's still improving. His strikeouts have dropped significantly in each of the past two years, and there's still time for him to reclaim his title as the Indians' shortstop of the future.

Albie Lopez

Position: P | **Opening Day Age:** 25
Bats: R **Throws:** R | **Born:** 8/18/71 in Mesa, AZ
Ht: 6' 2" **Wt:** 205 |

Recent Statistics

	W	L	ERA	G	GS	Sv	IP	H	R	BB	SO	HR
96 AAA Buffalo	10	2	3.87	17	17	0	104.2	90	54	40	89	13
96 AL Cleveland	5	4	6.39	13	10	0	62.0	80	47	22	45	14

Last year, Albie Lopez pitched himself out of the Cleveland rotation early in the year. They returned him to Triple-A, where he reportedly improved both his attitude and his curveball. The Tribe called him back up in August, but the improvements were not evident in his performance. Lopez has been one of the most successful pitchers in the minors over the last four years, and at age 25, the Indians know it's time to fish or cut bait. Next year may hold his most extended opportunity yet. So far, his 90-MPH fastball and good command of four pitches hasn't been enough, but he'll be given a chance to find the missing ingredient.

Alex Ramirez

Position: OF | **Opening Day Age:** 22
Bats: R **Throws:** R | **Born:** 10/3/74 in
Ht: 5' 11" **Wt:** 176 | Caracas, Venez

Recent Statistics

	G	AB	R	H	D	T	HR	RBI	SB	BB	SO	AVG
93 R Burlington	64	252	44	68	14	4	13	58	12	13	52	.270
93 A Kinston	3	12	0	2	0	0	0	1	0	0	5	.167
94 A Columbus	125	458	64	115	23	3	18	57	7	26	100	.251
95 A Bakersfield	98	406	56	131	25	2	10	52	13	18	76	.323
95 AA Canton-Akrn	33	133	15	33	3	4	1	11	3	5	24	.248
96 AA Canton-Akrn	131	513	79	169	28	12	14	85	18	16	74	.329
96 MLE	131	500	70	156	27	8	12	76	14	12	78	.312

No relation to Manny. This Ramirez has the speed to get by at all three outfield positions, but lacks the power of a corner outfielder. At the plate, he's as impatient as they come, but he knows how to put the bat on the ball. Unless he can play center, he'll have to develop into a true high-average hitter to make it. But after handling Double-A so well at age 21, that's not out of the question.

Richie Sexson

Position: 1B | **Opening Day Age:** 22
Bats: R **Throws:** R | **Born:** 12/29/74 in
Ht: 6' 6" **Wt:** 206 | Portland, OR

Recent Statistics

	G	AB	R	H	D	T	HR	RBI	SB	BB	SO	AVG
93 R Burlington	40	97	11	18	3	0	1	5	1	18	21	.186
94 A Columbus	130	488	88	133	25	2	14	77	7	37	87	.273
95 A Kinston	131	494	80	151	34	0	22	85	4	43	115	.306
96 AA Canton-Akrn	133	518	85	143	33	3	16	76	2	39	118	.276
96 MLE	133	508	76	133	32	2	14	68	1	29	125	.262

The Indians regard six-foot, six-inch Richie Sexson as their first baseman of the future. Only 22 years old this year, the big, strong right-handed hitter had a good season last in year in Double-A. He's been lauded for his work ethic and athleticism, and the Indians expect him to flower into a high-average power hitter over the next couple of years. If everything goes according to schedule, a year at Triple-A may be all that he needs.

Enrique Wilson

Position: SS | **Opening Day Age:** 21
Bats: B **Throws:** R | **Born:** 7/27/75 in Santo
Ht: 5' 11" **Wt:** 160 | Domingo, DR

Recent Statistics

	G	AB	R	H	D	T	HR	RBI	SB	BB	SO	AVG
93 R Elizabethtn	58	197	42	57	8	4	13	50	5	14	18	.289
94 A Columbus	133	512	82	143	28	12	10	72	21	44	34	.279
95 A Kinston	117	464	55	124	24	7	6	52	18	25	38	.267
96 AA Canton-Akrn	117	484	70	147	17	5	5	50	23	31	46	.304
96 AAA Buffalo	3	8	1	4	1	0	0	0		0	1	.500
96 MLE	120	479	62	138	18	3	4	44	18	23	49	.288

Budding phenom Enrique Wilson passed Damian Jackson on the Indians' depth chart at shortstop, and now the Indians have taken another step to move him onto the fast track to the majors: they've converted him to second base. Despite the fact that he's only 21 years old this year, he's considered a contender for the Indians' vacant second base spot. This is the result of his outstanding season last year in Double-A. Not only was he voted the best defensive shortstop and the player with the best infield arm in the Eastern League, but he also batted over .300. He still needs to be more selective and to better utilize his speed, but he's capable of holding a major league job right now. In a few years, he could be a standout middle infielder.

Others to Watch

Third baseman **Russell Branyan** set the South Atlantic League record with 40 homers last year. The left-handed hitter is several years away, and needs to curb his strikeouts, but his power is among the best in the system. . . **Sean Casey** won the Carolina League batting title last year. A tremendous pure hitter, the lefty-swinging first baseman will likely jump to Double-A this year at age 22. . . Former closer **Travis Driskill** was converted into a starter, with excellent results. His average fastball, good curve and slider, and tight command are better suited to starting. He went 13-7 at Double-A, and will be only 25 this year. . . Lefthander **Casey Whitten** got off to a blazing start at Double-A, but hit the wall after a promotion to Triple-A. When he's on, his superb change-up can be devastating. . Righthander **Jaret Wright** remains one of the Indians' best prospects. He used his mid-90s fastball to dominate the Carolina League last year, and he'll likely reach Double-A this year at age 21.

Buddy Bell

1996 Season

Few people could have survived Detroit's horrendous 1996 season with as much class as Buddy Bell. He and the Tigers' management knew that it would be a long year, but nothing could have prepared them for the 5-39 stretch from mid-April to early June, followed by a 4-23 finish. By the end of the year, Detroit had used 53 different players. Bell earned the respect of both veterans and young players with his refusal to rip the club publicly, and he showed the patience to remain outwardly positive throughout the long campaign.

Offense

During the course of the season, Bell transformed a Tiger offense that for years had played a plodding, high-strikeout, "wait for a home run" style. When situations and personnel allowed, he pressed the action with movement on the bases. He experimented with platoons at a number of positions. He also stressed the need for the entire lineup to cut down on its strikeouts. As it was, the Tigers whiffed 1,268 times—a new major league record.

Pitching & Defense

The staff ERA was a stupefying 6.38, the highest mark in American League history. Detroit hurlers allowed a record 241 home runs, of which a record 14 were grand slams. It's obvious that Bell did not have much with which to work. He was quick to experiment with the bullpen, which was much improved over the season's final two months. As the season wore on, he also tried tilting his lineup more toward defense in hopes of helping out his shaky pitching.

1997 Outlook

It will be another year of auditions for the Tigers. The key to everything is putting together a pitching rotation that at least keeps Detroit in games. Bell is so secure with club management that he would likely survive another season like 1996. If they win 70 games, it would be viewed as a major step forward.

Born: 8/27/51 in Pittsburgh, PA

Playing Experience: 1972-1989, Cle, Tex, Cin, Hou

Managerial Experience: 1 season

Manager Statistics

Year	Team, Lg	W	L	Pct	GB	Finish
1996	Detroit, AL	53	109	.327	39.0	5th East
1 Season		53	109	.327	—	—

1996 Starting Pitchers by Days Rest

	≤3	4	5	6+
Tigers Starts	1	80	46	21
Tigers ERA	9.00	5.45	8.08	9.41
AL Avg Starts	4	96	30	21
AL ERA	5.57	4.90	5.33	5.81

1996 Situational Stats

	Buddy Bell	AL Average
Hit & Run Success %	36.7	39.1
Stolen Base Success %	63.5	69.6
Platoon Pct.	51.1	61.9
Defensive Subs	17	29
High-Pitch Outings	26	23
Quick/Slow Hooks	17/27	17/20
Sacrifice Attempts	63	58

1996 Rankings (American League)

➡ 1st in relief appearances (426) and mid-inning pitching changes (250)

➡ 3rd in intentional walks (40), starting lineups used (128), slow hooks (27) and first batter platoon percentage (63.6%)

Brad Ausmus

1996 Season

Catcher Brad Ausmus came to Detroit in the deal which sent Chris Gomez and John Flaherty to the Padres last June. After batting below .200 in 50 games with San Diego, Ausmus went on to start 69 games behind the plate for the Tigers and was the club's primary starting catcher during the Tigers' surge toward respectability in July and August. Combining his numbers with San Diego and Detroit, he posted a career high in RBI and two of his four Tiger homers were game-winners.

Hitting

Ausmus can handle fastballs but had some difficulty adjusting to a diet of offspeed and breaking stuff. He has not yet displayed consistent power, but he could be a late-bloomer and develop into someone who can produce a dozen or so home runs in a season. He experienced trouble against left-handed pitching last year, much of that difficulty coming early in the season when, during one huge slump, he had only 21 hits in a 125 at-bat stretch.

Baserunning & Defense

The struggling Detroit pitching staff did its best work with Ausmus catching. The Tigers' ERA was nearly a run and a half lower when he was behind the plate. He has excellent catching mechanics and though his arm is average at best, he has an outstandingly quick release and good footwork. A better-than-average runner for a catcher, Ausmus is a threat to steal, though he tried to do too much on the bases last year and was thrown out eight times in 12 attempts.

1997 Outlook

Ausmus' intelligence and catching skills make him a vital part of the Tigers' rebuilding effort. He worked well with the parade of different Detroit pitchers and will be counted on to provide some needed stability behind the plate. He should also improve his offensive production now that he is more familiar with the American League.

Position: C
Bats: R **Throws:** R
Ht: 5'11" **Wt:** 190

Opening Day Age: 27
Born: 4/14/69 in New Haven, CT
ML Seasons: 4
Pronunciation: AHS-muss

Overall Statistics

	G	AB	R	H	D	T	HR	RBI	SB	BB	SO	Avg	OBP	Slg
1996	125	375	46	83	16	0	5	35	4	39	72	.221	.302	.304
Career	378	1190	153	302	52	6	22	105	27	106	219	.254	.317	.363

Where He Hits the Ball

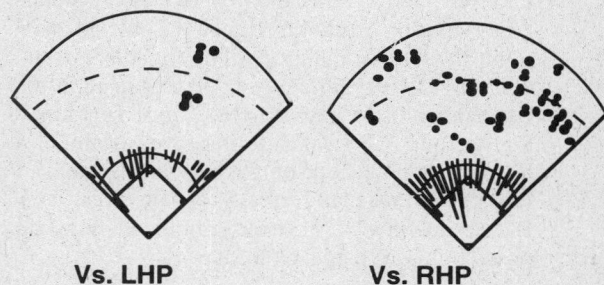

Vs. LHP   **Vs. RHP**

1996 Situational Stats

	AB	H	HR	RBI	Avg		AB	H	HR	RBI	Avg
Home	193	41	2	20	.212	LHP	90	13	2	10	.144
Road	182	42	3	15	.231	RHP	285	70	3	25	.246
First Half	189	37	1	14	.196	Sc Pos	91	19	2	31	.209
Scnd Half	186	46	4	21	.247	Clutch	69	16	2	12	.232

1996 Rankings (American League)

➡ Did not rank near the top or bottom in any category

Kimera Bartee

Position: CF
Bats: R **Throws:** R
Ht: 6' 0" **Wt:** 175

Opening Day Age: 24
Born: 7/21/72 in Omaha, NE
ML Seasons: 1

1996 Season

Kimera Bartee must have felt like a yo-yo over the winter of 1995-96. He was traded from Baltimore to Minnesota, but then was taken in the Rule 5 draft by the Orioles. When Baltimore tried to sneak him through waivers and return him to Minnesota, the Tigers grabbed him. He proved to be a pleasant surprise. After some early struggles, he established himself as the Tigers' everyday center fielder, batting .271 over his final 79 games and leading the team in stolen bases and sacrifice bunts.

Hitting

In the early going, Bartee was getting the bat knocked out of his hands by average fastballs. After working on choking up on the bat and trying to hit the ball on the ground, he found some success. He has very little power, mixing in 18 infield hits among his 55 base knocks. Detroit sent him to the Arizona Fall League to improve his ability to hit righties in the hope of making him a switch-hitter, a skill that could greatly enhance his value. Bartee hit only .178 versus righthanders as opposed to his .378 against lefties.

Baserunning & Defense

With exceptional speed but little knowledge of basestealing, Bartee still managed 20 steals in 30 attempts, and the Tigers think he is capable of eventually developing into a 40-steal player. He has excellent range in center, though he needs to work on getting a better jump on balls. He was occasionally guilty of playing too shallow in Tiger Stadium's spacious center field, but he has all the tools to be a top outfielder, including a better-than-average arm.

1997 Outlook

A raw talent who needs to refine his skills, Bartee showed Detroit more than enough to enter this season as the club's center fielder. The jury is still out on the switch-hitting experiment, but if Bartee continues to improve in making contact, he can give the Tigers some needed speed either at the top of the order or in the nine hole.

Overall Statistics

	G	AB	R	H	D	T	HR	RBI	SB	BB	SO	Avg	OBP	Slg
1996	110	217	32	55	6	1	1	14	20	17	77	.253	.308	.304
Career	110	217	32	55	6	1	1	14	20	17	77	.253	.308	.304

Where He Hits the Ball

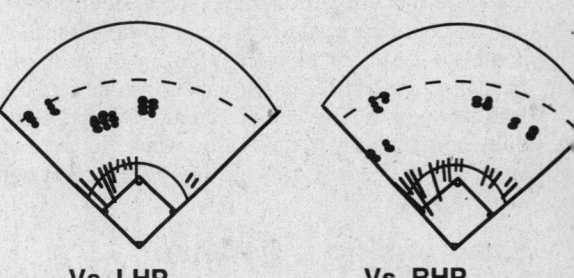

Vs. LHP   **Vs. RHP**

1996 Situational Stats

	AB	H	HR	RBI	Avg		AB	H	HR	RBI	Avg
Home	129	35	0	8	.271	LHP	82	31	1	5	.378
Road	88	20	1	6	.227	RHP	135	24	0	9	.178
First Half	61	18	0	5	.295	Sc Pos	52	10	0	13	.192
Scnd Half	156	37	1	9	.237	Clutch	21	7	0	3	.333

1996 Rankings (American League)

- → 3rd in batting average on a 3-1 count (.750)
- → 5th in caught stealing (10)
- → 6th in sacrifice bunts (13)
- → 7th in lowest stolen base percentage (66.7%) and bunts in play (29)
- → 10th in errors in center field (2)
- → Led the Tigers in sacrifice bunts (13), stolen bases, caught stealing, stolen base percentage (66.7%), batting average on a 3-1 count (.750) and bunts in play (29)

Tony Clark

Position: 1B/DH
Bats: B **Throws:** R
Ht: 6' 7" **Wt:** 245

Opening Day Age: 24
Born: 6/15/72 in El Cajon, CA
ML Seasons: 2

1996 Season

Long considered to be one of the most promising power-hitting prospects in baseball, Tony Clark established himself as a rising star in 1996. Recalled from Triple-A Toledo on June 7, Clark took over the everyday duties at first base following the July 31 trade of Cecil Fielder to the Yankees. He ended up leading the Tigers with 27 homers in only 100 games. He improved as the season progressed—smashing nine homers and driving in 25 runs in September—and was chosen A.L. Player of the Week for the season's final week.

Hitting

The question with Clark is whether he will make enough contact to put together a productive career. Strikeouts have been his problem since the 6'7" switch-hitter gave up on his pro basketball dreams and devoted all his attention to baseball. He is a free swinger with little knowledge of the strike zone and can be tied up inside with average hard stuff, especially when he bats right-handed. Clark has awesome power when he gets his arms extended, and when he learns how to cut down on his swing when behind in the count, he has the potential to be a .280-type hitter without sacrificing the long ball.

Baserunning & Defense

Clark has decent speed when he gets a head of steam, but he is a slow starter who will never be a basestealer. For a big man, he has surprisingly good range and footwork around first. He also turns the double play well for such an inexperienced first baseman.

1997 Outlook

Detroit's rebuilding effort got a huge shot in the arm from Clark's impressive second-half performance. If he cuts down on his strikeouts, he has a chance to emerge a big-time slugger, helping the Tigers forget about the loss of Cecil Fielder.

Overall Statistics

	G	AB	R	H	D	T	HR	RBI	SB	BB	SO	Avg	OBP	Slg
1996	100	376	56	94	14	0	27	72	0	29	127	.250	.299	.503
Career	127	477	66	118	19	1	30	83	0	37	157	.247	.298	.480

Where He Hits the Ball

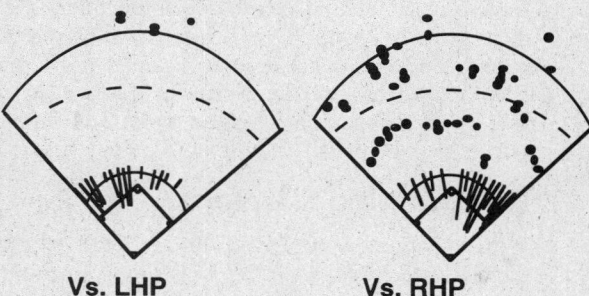

Vs. LHP   **Vs. RHP**

1996 Situational Stats

	AB	H	HR	RBI	Avg		AB	H	HR	RBI	Avg
Home	201	53	17	48	.264	LHP	93	20	5	17	.215
Road	175	41	10	24	.234	RHP	283	74	22	55	.261
First Half	99	25	6	18	.253	Sc Pos	91	22	7	50	.242
Scnd Half	277	69	21	54	.249	Clutch	57	11	1	5	.193

1996 Rankings (American League)

→ 1st in highest percentage of swings that missed (36.0%)
→ 2nd in lowest percentage of swings put into play (32.7%)
→ 6th in lowest batting average with two strikes (.126)
→ 9th in errors at first base (6)
→ Led the Tigers in home runs

Detroit Tigers

Travis Fryman

1996 Season

It was a landmark season for Travis Fryman in 1996. He drove in 100 runs for the first time in his career, finishing strong with 60 RBI in his last 90 games. And after a three-year stay at third base, Fryman ended the year back at his original position of shortstop, where he played well.

Hitting

Fryman has historically been a strikeout-prone, streaky hitter. When he keeps his swing compact and maintains patience in working counts, he is a steady run producer with extra-base power. His Achilles' heel continues to be an inability to avoid prolonged slumps. They usually occur when he finds himself behind in the count too often and then starts chasing high fastballs or offspeed pitches out of the strike zone. Fryman has long been known around the American League as a first-pitch swinger, so when he does see a first-pitch strike it's usually a mistake.

Baserunning & Defense

With average speed at best, Fryman is rarely a threat to steal. However, he is aggressive on the bases and will go hard into second to break up a double play. Well established as one of the league's better third basemen, Fryman was nevertheless moved back to shortstop when all other possible successors to Alan Trammell fell short. Fryman showed solid range at short, and made only two errors in 29 games. His strong, accurate arm fits well with the position.

1997 Outlook

Though he has nearly 1,000 major-league games behind him, Fryman is only 28 years old and will continue to be one of the foundation players upon which Detroit will try to rebuild. Several clubs have tried to take Fryman away from the Tigers, but they'd prefer to keep him in the Motor City. Ideally Detroit would like to obtain a shortstop over the winter and move him back to third base, but they know he can handle short if needed.

Position: 3B/SS
Bats: R **Throws:** R
Ht: 6' 1" **Wt:** 195

Opening Day Age: 28
Born: 3/25/69 in Lexington, KY
ML Seasons: 7

Overall Statistics

	G	AB	R	H	D	T	HR	RBI	SB	BB	SO	Avg	OBP	Slg
1996	157	616	90	165	32	3	22	100	4	57	118	.268	.329	.437
Career	942	3702	517	1013	202	26	127	577	42	344	818	.274	.336	.445

Where He Hits the Ball

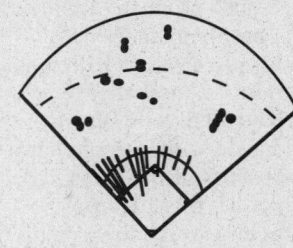
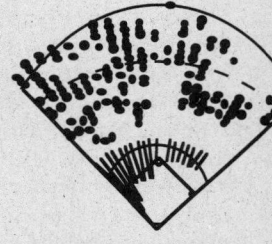

Vs. LHP   **Vs. RHP**

1996 Situational Stats

	AB	H	HR	RBI	Avg			AB	H	HR	RBI	Avg
Home	288	78	10	45	.271		LHP	125	31	3	15	.248
Road	328	87	12	55	.265		RHP	491	134	19	85	.273
First Half	328	88	13	58	.268		Sc Pos	175	48	6	74	.274
Scnd Half	288	77	9	42	.267		Clutch	84	21	5	20	.250

1996 Rankings (American League)

→ 1st in fielding percentage at third base (.979)
→ 4th in sacrifice flies (10)
→ 9th in at-bats
→ Led the Tigers in at-bats, runs scored, hits, singles, total bases (269), RBI, sacrifice flies (10), times on base (226), GDPs (18), pitches seen (2,696), plate appearances (688), games played (157) and highest percentage of extra bases taken as a runner (55.8%)

Bobby Higginson

1996 Season

In his second season in the majors, Bobby Higginson emerged as a rising star. He narrowly missed being among the top 10 hitters in the American League while belting 26 homers and compiling a .404 on-base percentage. A foot injury sidelined him for three weeks in May, but Higginson recovered and was particularly productive in the second half of the season. He hit .333 after the All-Star break and closed out the year with a .352 mark in September.

Hitting

The biggest factor in Higginson's surprising development has been his improved patience. He has learned to work counts much more consistently and has developed a strong sense of discipline at the plate. The result was a significant drop in his strikeout totals without a drop in power. Higginson now will hit the ball where it's pitched rather than try to pull everything, resulting in more opposite-field gap hits. He also has made his swing slightly more compact, allowing him to better turn around inside hard stuff. He is still uncomfortable against left-handed pitching, and only one of his 26 homers last season came against southpaws.

Baserunning & Defense

Higginson doesn't have the speed of a classic leadoff hitter, but he does run well enough and is aggressive enough to produce 10 to 15 steals a year. He has good instincts on the basepaths and looks to take the extra base when the opportunity presents itself. He can play left or right field with equal effectiveness, and though he does not have a cannon, he has a quick release and an accuracy which helped him produce nine outfield assists.

1997 Outlook

Higginson opened the Tigers eyes by batting .421 with 13 homers and 34 RBI in the leadoff spot. Those numbers, combined with his work ethic, make him a very important part of Detroit's rebuilding efforts. He should be a mainstay of the club for years to come.

Position: LF/CF/RF
Bats: L **Throws:** R
Ht: 5'11" **Wt:** 195

Opening Day Age: 26
Born: 8/18/70 in Philadelphia, PA
ML Seasons: 2

Overall Statistics

	G	AB	R	H	D	T	HR	RBI	SB	BB	SO	Avg	OBP	Slg
1996	130	440	75	141	35	0	26	81	6	65	66	.320	.404	.577
Career	261	850	136	233	52	5	40	124	12	127	173	.274	.367	.488

Where He Hits the Ball

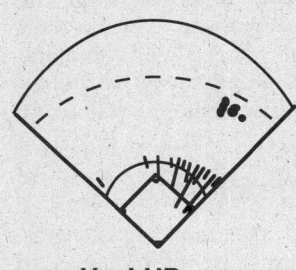

Vs. LHP **Vs. RHP**

1996 Situational Stats

	AB	H	HR	RBI	Avg		AB	H	HR	RBI	Avg
Home	232	78	15	39	.336	LHP	61	14	1	12	.230
Road	208	63	11	42	.303	RHP	379	127	25	69	.335
First Half	203	62	14	42	.305	Sc Pos	90	31	3	52	.344
Scnd Half	237	79	12	39	.333	Clutch	67	17	5	9	.254

1996 Rankings (American League)

→ 1st in batting average with the bases loaded (.667) and on-base percentage for a leadoff hitter (.500)
→ 4th in slugging percentage vs. right-handed pitchers (.623)
→ 5th in errors in right field (5)
→ 8th in batting average vs. right-handed pitchers (.335)
→ 9th in most pitches seen per plate appearance (4.11) and batting average with runners in scoring position (.344)
→ 10th in batting average at home (.336) and errors in left field (3)
→ Led the Tigers in doubles, walks, slugging percentage and on-base percentage

Mark Lewis

1996 Season

In his first full season as an everyday second baseman, Mark Lewis easily surpassed his career highs in most offensive categories. The majority of his production came in the season's first half, however. He also began breaking down physically as the season wore on, missing a week in August with a sore back and another week in September after being beaned by an Aaron Sele pitch.

Hitting

Maybe the worst thing that happened to Lewis was hitting home runs early in the season. He fell into the habit of trying to pull everything, and as a result struck out far too much for someone with so little power. He is at his best at the plate when he takes more pitches to the opposite field. Lewis is often guilty of pulling off pitches in an attempt to pull the ball, however, especially against breaking stuff. He also does not work counts very efficiently and has a low walk total as a result.

Baserunning & Defense

Prior to 1996, Lewis had spent most of his professional career either at shortstop or third base. Last year, the Tigers asked him to hold down second, and he did a decent job in making the transition, committing only one error in his last 64 games. Lewis has average range but does possess sure hands and a strong, accurate arm. He also displayed above-average aptitude for making the second-base pivot. He is an average runner who is capable of the occasional stolen base.

1997 Outlook

The Tigers had a choice to make regarding Lewis, who was eligible for arbitration after the season. They liked his performance well enough to keep him, but probably not enough to pay him what he figured to make in arbitration. As a result Lewis might be modeling his fourth uniform in four seasons in 1997.

Position: 2B
Bats: R **Throws:** R
Ht: 6' 1" **Wt:** 185

Opening Day Age: 27
Born: 11/30/69 in Hamilton, OH
ML Seasons: 6

Overall Statistics

	G	AB	R	H	D	T	HR	RBI	SB	BB	SO	Avg	OBP	Slg
1996	145	545	69	147	30	3	11	55	6	42	109	.270	.326	.396
Career	466	1568	179	425	86	5	21	158	16	105	276	.271	.317	.372

Where He Hits the Ball

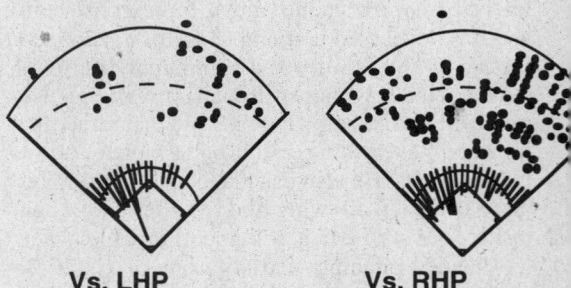

Vs. LHP   **Vs. RHP**

1996 Situational Stats

	AB	H	HR	RBI	Avg		AB	H	HR	RBI	Avg
Home	286	73	8	34	.255	LHP	131	46	3	13	.351
Road	259	74	3	21	.286	RHP	414	101	8	42	.244
First Half	325	98	8	33	.302	Sc Pos	125	36	2	43	.288
Scnd Half	220	49	3	22	.223	Clutch	77	17	1	5	.221

1996 Rankings (American League)

→ 2nd in fielding percentage at second base (.987)
→ 5th in lowest on-base percentage vs. right-handed pitchers (.299)
→ 7th in lowest slugging percentage vs. right-handed pitchers (.365)
→ 8th in lowest batting average vs. right-handed pitchers (.244)
→ 9th in lowest percentage of extra bases taken as a runner (32.6%)
→ 10th in errors at second base (9)
→ Led the Tigers in highest groundball/flyball ratio (1.4), batting average vs. left-handed pitchers (.351) and slugging percentage vs. left-handed pitchers (.496)

Richie Lewis

1996 Season

Healthy for the first time in a couple of years, Richie Lewis proved to be one of the Tigers' most reliable pitchers. Working almost exclusively as a middle reliever, he was among the league leaders in appearances while compiling the second-best ERA on the beleaguered Detroit staff. He also held up well, allowing runs in only three of his final 16 appearances.

Pitching

Lewis is basically a two-pitch pitcher, using a big, sharp-breaking over-hand curve which can be as good as any curve in the league and a decent sinking fastball. He gets in trouble when he is not throwing the curve for strikes or not breaking it off sharply, floating it into the strike zone instead. He also has bouts with wildness. He was second in the majors with 14 wild pitches in 1996. Lewis more often than not pitched off his fastball last year, using the heater to set up the curve. Throwing more fastballs early in the count helped both his control and his arm strength and was one reason opposing batters hit only .238 against him. Lewis has never had more than a mediocre change-up, which he all but junked when he became firmly established as a reliever.

Defense

With a compact delivery that is quick to the plate, Lewis keeps himself in good fielding position. He does only a fair job of holding runners, though he at times has shown a quick pickoff move.

1997 Outlook

Perceived as a throw-in when acquired from San Diego in a six-player spring training deal, Lewis became one of the few reliable pitchers for Detroit. Despite that, the Tigers released him in November rather than risk going to salary arbitration with him. He could still return to the club if they feel his demands are reasonable; if not, plenty of other teams would be willing to add him to their relief corps.

Position: RP
Bats: R **Throws:** R
Ht: 5'10" **Wt:** 175

Opening Day Age: 31
Born: 1/25/66 in Muncie, IN
ML Seasons: 5

Overall Statistics

	W	L	Pct.	ERA	G	GS	Sv	IP	H	BB	SO	HR	BR/IP
1996	4	6	.400	4.18	72	0	2	90.1	78	65	78	9	1.58
Career	12	15	.444	4.32	197	3	2	264.1	251	168	224	33	1.59

How Often He Throws Strikes

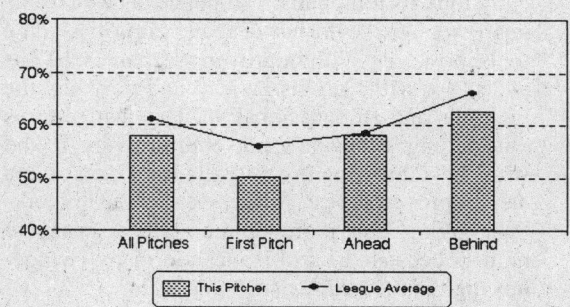

1996 Situational Stats

	W	L	ERA	Sv	IP		AB	H	HR	RBI	Avg
Home	3	3	5.40	1	48.1	LHB	131	26	1	13	.198
Road	1	3	2.79	1	42.0	RHB	197	52	8	45	.264
First Half	2	5	4.20	2	45.0	Sc Pos	125	23	1	45	.184
Scnd Half	2	1	4.17	0	45.1	Clutch	110	27	2	19	.245

1996 Rankings (American League)

→ 1st in lowest batting average allowed with runners in scoring position (.184)
→ 2nd in wild pitches (14) and balks (2)
→ 4th in relief innings (90.1)
→ 5th in relief losses (6)
→ 7th in games pitched and most baserunners allowed per 9 innings in relief (14.6)
→ Led the Tigers in wild pitches (14), balks (2), runners caught stealing (5), blown saves (4), lowest batting average allowed with runners in scoring position (.184), lowest batting average allowed in relief with runners on base (.228), lowest batting average allowed in relief with runners in scoring position (.184), relief ERA (4.18) and relief losses (6)

Jose Lima

1996 Season

After struggling for a third straight year to establish himself as a big league starting pitcher, Jose Lima took a trip to the minors and returned for the second half of the season as a reliever. The results offered some encouragement. Lima earned five wins in relief, kept his ERA under 5.00 in his last 34 appearances and was tried at times in the closer's role, earning three saves in seven opportunities.

Pitching

Lima's development has likely been retarded by the fact that he was rushed to the majors before he was ready for the competition. The resulting difficulty took its toll on his confidence, as well as his aggressiveness with his fastball. Lima has some tools, however. With improved mechanics, he has added 4-6 MPH on his fastball and now hits the high 80s and an occasional 90. His change-up is outstanding when he's not overthrowing it and when he's throwing his fastballs for strikes. Lima also improved his cut fastball as well as his forkball, giving him more options. He is prone to homers because he still leaves too many change-ups high in the strike zone.

Defense

Lima is a good athlete whose delivery keeps him in good fielding position, especially after some recent refinements. He also has improved his pickoff move and is much more aware of the need to hold runners. Only four steals were attempted against him last year.

1997 Outlook

The Tigers have too few good arms to give up on somebody with Lima's youth and ability. They liked much of what they saw from him in a relief role and likely are leaning toward keeping him in the bullpen at least to begin the season. He probably won't be a closer, but Detroit needs to get him more innings before making a decision about his future role with the organization.

Position: RP/SP
Bats: R **Throws:** R
Ht: 6' 2" **Wt:** 205

Opening Day Age: 24
Born: 9/30/72 in Santiago, DR
ML Seasons: 3
Pronunciation: LEE-muh

Overall Statistics

	W	L	Pct.	ERA	G	GS	Sv	IP	H	BB	SO	HR	BR/IP
1996	5	6	.455	5.70	39	4	3	72.2	87	22	59	13	1.50
Career	8	16	.333	6.24	57	20	3	153.0	183	43	103	25	1.48

How Often He Throws Strikes

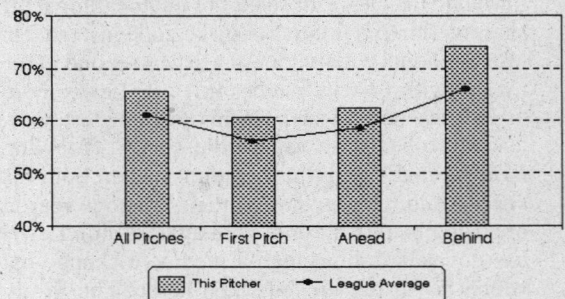

1996 Situational Stats

	W	L	ERA	Sv	IP		AB	H	HR	RBI	Avg
Home	2	2	6.35	1	34.0	LHB	147	43	7	25	.293
Road	3	4	5.12	2	38.2	RHB	147	44	6	23	.299
First Half	0	4	7.43	0	26.2	Sc Pos	83	22	3	31	.265
Scnd Half	5	2	4.70	3	46.0	Clutch	104	23	2	11	.221

1996 Rankings (American League)

➡ Led the Tigers in blown saves (4) and relief wins (5)

Felipe Lira

Position: SP
Bats: R **Throws:** R
Ht: 6' 0" **Wt:** 170

Opening Day Age: 24
Born: 4/26/72 in Miranda, VZ
ML Seasons: 2

1996 Season

Despite going winless in 13 starts after July 7 and finishing the year with a seven-game losing streak, Felipe Lira pitched better in his second year in the majors than his grim record would indicate. He led the Tigers in strikeouts and innings pitched, and the club averaged only two runs a game in his 14 losses. His best stretch came in late June when he won three straight decisions, two of those complete-game shutouts. He suffered a broken hand in late September which isn't expected to be a problem this spring.

Pitching

When Lira is battling his control, he struggles. He not only walks too many hitters but also suffers with inconsistent control in the strike zone, which largely accounts for the 30 home runs he allowed last season. He has the stuff to be a winner, though. His fastball rarely tops 90 MPH, but he has excellent movement with several pitches. He throws a cut fastball, perhaps his best pitch, a rising fastball, a slider and a change which he sinks and can move away or in to either right- or left-handed hitters.

Defense

Basestealers had a field day last year with Lira on the hill, swiping 17 bases in 21 tries. He has yet to learn a decent pickoff move and compounds the problem with a fairly slow delivery to the plate and occasional lapses in concentration. Lira otherwise fields his position well.

1997 Outlook

Detroit liked the way in which Lira did not lose his aggressiveness during his hard-luck second half of last season. He enters 1997 as one of the few givens in the Tigers' starting rotation, and he has the ability and makeup to become a dependable big league starter who is counted on for 200 innings and at least a dozen wins.

Overall Statistics

	W	L	Pct.	ERA	G	GS	Sv	IP	H	BB	SO	HR	BR/IP
1996	6	14	.300	5.22	32	32	0	194.2	204	66	113	30	1.39
Career	15	27	.357	4.83	69	54	1	341.0	355	122	202	47	1.40

How Often He Throws Strikes

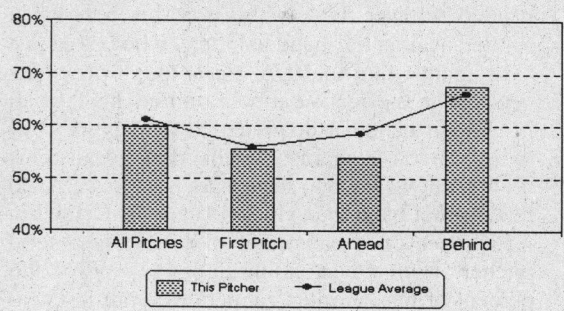

1996 Situational Stats

	W	L	ERA	Sv	IP		AB	H	HR	RBI	Avg
Home	3	9	3.85	0	112.1	LHB	409	115	18	57	.281
Road	3	5	7.11	0	82.1	RHB	348	89	12	42	.256
First Half	6	7	5.61	0	109.0	Sc Pos	153	40	6	64	.261
Scnd Half	0	7	4.73	0	85.2	Clutch	63	17	2	4	.270

1996 Rankings (American League)
- ➡ 1st in fielding percentage at pitcher (1.000)
- ➡ 2nd in highest ERA on the road (7.11)
- ➡ 4th in shutouts (2)
- ➡ 5th in lowest winning percentage, least run support per 9 innings (4.5) and most home runs allowed per 9 innings (1.39)
- ➡ 6th in losses
- ➡ 7th in highest ERA, highest stolen base percentage allowed (81.0%) and least strikeouts per 9 innings (5.2)
- ➡ 8th in hit batsmen (10)
- ➡ 9th in home runs allowed and least GDPs induced per 9 innings (0.7)
- ➡ Led the Tigers in ERA, losses, games started, shutouts (2), innings pitched and hits allowed

Mike Myers

1996 Season

No pitcher in baseball appeared in more games than lefthander Mike Myers, whose 83 appearances set a Detroit club record. He was especially busy prior to the Tigers' acquisition of lefties John Cummings and Joey Eischen, appearing in a whopping 61 of Detroit's first 107 games. Though many of his outings were rocky early in the year, he finished strong and was scored upon in only five of his last 22 games. He also notched six saves in eight opportunities.

Pitching

Detroit overused Myers last season because for much of the year he was the club's only left-handed reliever. Ideally, he is at his best when spotted against left-handed hitters, who batted just .229 against him in 1996. He is tough on lefties because he is effective at both running his fastball in on their hands or down and away. Myers' stuff is less effective against righthanders because his motion allows them to see his pitches too well, and he does not have the velocity to get his fastball in on righties on a consistent basis. He is a solid pitcher in clutch situations, allowing only 24.6 percent of his inherited runners to score last season.

Defense

Myers does not have a pickoff move that worries many baserunners, and they are easily able to read his delivery home and get consistently good jumps. Basestealers were successful on seven of nine attempts on his watch in 1996. He does a good job of fielding his position.

1997 Outlook

After bouncing around assorted organizations, Myers may have found his niche in Detroit. His reliability against left-handed hitters along with his durability are valuable assets on a staff that requires a lot of mileage from its bullpen.

Position: RP
Bats: L **Throws:** L
Ht: 6' 4" **Wt:** 197

Opening Day Age: 27
Born: 6/26/69 in Cook County, IL
ML Seasons: 2

Overall Statistics

	W	L	Pct.	ERA	G	GS	Sv	IP	H	BB	SO	HR	BR/IP
1996	1	5	.167	5.01	83	0	6	64.2	70	34	69	6	1.61
Career	2	5	.286	5.30	96	0	6	73.0	81	41	73	7	1.67

How Often He Throws Strikes

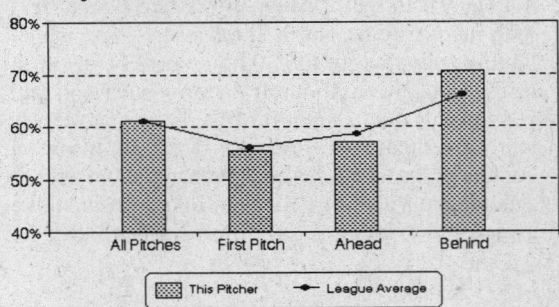

This Pitcher — League Average

1996 Situational Stats

	W	L	ERA	Sv	IP		AB	H	HR	RBI	Avg
Home	0	2	5.03	2	34.0	LHB	118	27	1	10	.229
Road	1	3	4.99	4	30.2	RHB	139	43	5	29	.309
First Half	0	4	5.90	3	39.2	Sc Pos	85	23	1	31	.271
Scnd Half	1	1	3.60	3	25.0	Clutch	114	31	1	15	.272

1996 Rankings (American League)

→ 1st in games pitched
→ 4th in first batter efficiency (.132) and most baserunners allowed per 9 innings in relief (15.0)
→ 7th in holds (17) and lowest percentage of inherited runners scored (24.6%)
→ 8th in most strikeouts per 9 innings in relief (9.6)
→ 10th in highest relief ERA (5.01)
→ Led the Tigers in games pitched, holds (17), first batter efficiency (.132), lowest percentage of inherited runners scored (24.6%) and most strikeouts per 9 innings in relief (9.6)

Phil Nevin

1996 Season

For the first time in his pro career, Phil Nevin displayed signs of the ability that made him the first player selected in the 1992 amateur draft. After spending much of the season at Double-A Jacksonville learning how to catch, Nevin ended the year back at third base. His fielding was solid and over his last 19 games, Nevin drove in 17 runs with eight homers despite playing with a sore ankle.

Hitting

The trade from Houston to Detroit served as a wake-up call for Nevin, who worked hard last winter to increase his strength. The weight work translated into his best power numbers since college. He hit 24 homers at Double-A before clubbing eight in only 120 at-bats with the Tigers. He has a smooth, short stroke and last year made progress in hitting more to the opposite field. He chases high fastballs and can be tied up inside with hard stuff, however, and has always been prone to strikeouts. He still has much to learn in terms of patience and knowledge of the strike zone. He is a decent offspeed hitter for his age and should develop more opposite-field power.

Defense & Baserunning

Nevin had made progress as a catcher, but is more comfortable at third where his good hands, above-average range and strong throwing arm serve him well. One knock on him is his tendency to be erratic and occasionally hurry his throws. Nevin also has decent outfield skills and can play left field if needed. He is an average runner and no threat to steal bases.

1997 Outlook

Nevin revived his career with his strong finish last season. With the Tigers thinking about returning Travis Fryman to third, Nevin may wind up back behind the plate or in the outfield this year. Whatever his position, he figures to get plenty of action.

Position: 3B
Bats: R **Throws:** R
Ht: 6' 2" **Wt:** 210

Opening Day Age: 26
Born: 1/19/71 in Fullerton, California
ML Seasons: 2

Overall Statistics

	G	AB	R	H	D	T	HR	RBI	SB	BB	SO	Avg	OBP	Slg
1996	38	120	15	35	5	0	8	19	1	8	39	.292	.338	.533
Career	85	276	28	63	9	1	10	32	2	26	79	.228	.305	.377

Where He Hits the Ball

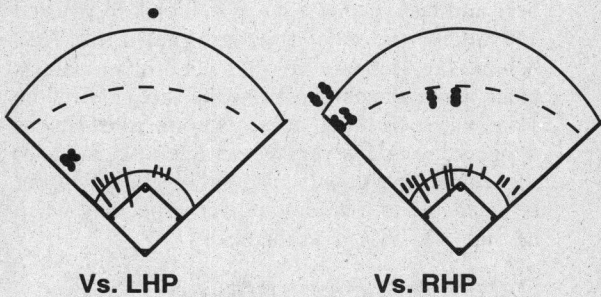

Vs. LHP　　　　**Vs. RHP**

1996 Situational Stats

	AB	H	HR	RBI	Avg		AB	H	HR	RBI	Avg
Home	70	20	3	7	.286	LHP	36	11	2	5	.306
Road	50	15	5	12	.300	RHP	84	24	6	14	.286
First Half	0	0	0	0	-	Sc Pos	24	7	3	12	.292
Scnd Half	120	35	8	19	.292	Clutch	20	5	0	1	.250

1996 Rankings (American League)

➜ Did not rank near the top or bottom in any category

Melvin Nieves

1996 Season

Tiger GM Randy Smith obtained Melvin Nieves from the Padres last year and gave him extensive playing time for the first time in the major leagues. The returns were mixed. Nieves had streaks of impressive power, including one 19-game span in which he launched 12 home runs. He also had long bouts of non-production and went the entire month of June without a single longball. Nieves also missed extensive time with two different leg injuries.

Hitting

Nieves is a classic all-or-nothing streak hitter. At every level, he has piled up huge strikeout numbers and last year was no exception. He whiffed 158 times—the second-highest total in the A.L. behind Jay Buhner. He's a switch-hitter who is much more dangerous from the left side of the plate, where he hit 20 of his 24 home runs. He has a big swing and is very vulnerable to changes of speed. Nieves will only grudgingly take walks, but he's capable of awesome power, especially when he finds a fastball over the plate.

Defense & Baserunning

To say the least, playing the outfield is an adventure for Nieves. He made 13 errors last season, more than any outfielder in the league. He is prone to misjudging too many fly balls and often appears lax in his effort to close on balls. He has a big-time arm, but he's also never met a cutoff man he didn't overthrow. Nieves is an average runner with little ability to steal bases.

1997 Outlook

Power like the kind Nieves can harness is hard to find. But with the Tigers looking to add better athletes and more hitters who make contact, Nieves could wind up with another club in 1997. He's only 25, and despite the many holes in his game, he's capable of hitting 30 or more homers this year.

Position: RF/LF/DH
Bats: B **Throws:** R
Ht: 6' 2" **Wt:** 210

Opening Day Age: 25
Born: 12/28/71 in San Juan, PR
ML Seasons: 5
Pronunciation: nee-AY-vuss

Overall Statistics

	G	AB	R	H	D	T	HR	RBI	SB	BB	SO	Avg	OBP	Slg
1996	120	431	71	106	23	4	24	60	1	44	158	.246	.322	.485
Career	259	750	109	172	31	5	41	106	3	71	284	.229	.304	.448

Where He Hits the Ball

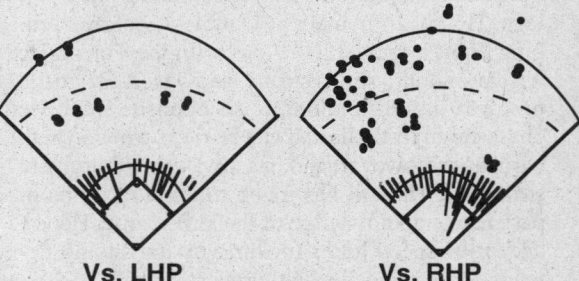

Vs. LHP   Vs. RHP

1996 Situational Stats

	AB	H	HR	RBI	Avg		AB	H	HR	RBI	Avg
Home	199	46	10	22	.231	LHP	101	22	4	18	.218
Road	232	60	14	38	.259	RHP	330	84	20	42	.255
First Half	221	53	8	25	.240	Sc Pos	89	21	5	36	.236
Scnd Half	210	53	16	35	.252	Clutch	68	22	4	8	.324

1996 Rankings (American League)

- ➡ 1st in errors in right field (9) and lowest percentage of swings put into play (31.1%)
- ➡ 2nd in strikeouts
- ➡ 3rd in highest percentage of swings that missed (33.0%)
- ➡ 4th in lowest batting average with two strikes (.123)
- ➡ 6th in errors in left field (4)
- ➡ Led the Tigers in hit by pitch (6), strikeouts and batting average in the clutch (.324)

Omar Olivares

1996 Season

It was hardly a momentous honor given the way Detroit's season went, but let it be noted that former National League hurler Omar Olivares was the Tigers' big winner with seven victories. His performance should not be entirely disparaged. After making only 30 major league appearances in his previous two years, Olivares became the most dependable innings-eater in the Tigers' beleaguered rotation. Only 18 times did a Tiger starter last eight or more innings, and Olivares accounted for eight of those outings despite making just 25 starts. His season was truncated by eight weeks due to a hamstring pull. He won three games in June and won three consecutive starts in late July and early August.

Pitching

Olivares' career had been going steadily downhill since 1993 until he showed some signs of life last year. His best pitch has always been a heavy sinking fastball, which pitching coaches have tried to make him throw at least 80 percent of the time. However, he insists on mixing in too many sliders or forkballs and that has caused inconsistent control. Olivares has now developed a decent cut fastball—which better complements his sinker—and he can be especially tough on right-handed hitters. He still walks too many hitters and is not a big strikeout man.

Defense

Olivares is a decent fielding pitcher who gets himself in good position to make plays and does not panic in the field. He also does a good job of holding runners and has come up with an effective pickoff move.

1997 Outlook

Olivares is hardly destined to be a big-time winner. But in the scheme of things for the Tigers he at least provides the potential for 150-plus innings, making him a valuable member of Detroit's rotation. . . if only for the short term.

Position: SP
Bats: R **Throws:** R
Ht: 6' 1" **Wt:** 190

Opening Day Age: 29
Born: 7/6/67 in Mayaguez, PR
ML Seasons: 7
Pronunciation: ah-liv-AIR-es

Overall Statistics

	W	L	Pct.	ERA	G	GS	Sv	IP	H	BB	SO	HR	BR/IP
1996	7	11	.389	4.89	25	25	0	160.0	169	75	81	16	1.53
Career	37	39	.487	4.35	182	112	3	807.2	824	330	427	76	1.43

How Often He Throws Strikes

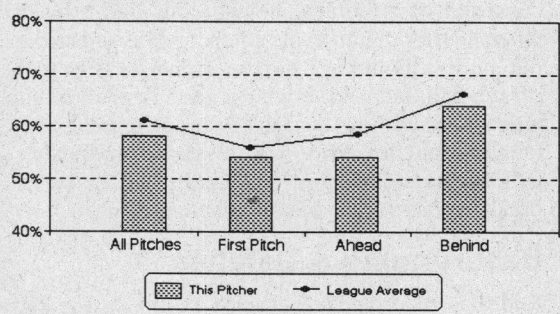

1996 Situational Stats

	W	L	ERA	Sv	IP		AB	H	HR	RBI	Avg
Home	4	4	4.35	0	70.1	LHB	309	90	8	40	.291
Road	3	7	5.32	0	89.2	RHB	306	79	8	34	.258
First Half	4	5	4.72	0	74.1	Sc Pos	167	40	4	59	.240
Scnd Half	3	6	5.04	0	85.2	Clutch	50	11	0	1	.220

1996 Rankings (American League)

→ 7th in GDPs induced (24)
→ 8th in lowest winning percentage
→ 10th in balks (1)
→ Led the Tigers in wins, complete games (4), GDPs induced (24), winning percentage, most GDPs induced per GDP situation (15.4%) and ERA on the road (5.32)

Detroit Tigers

Curtis Pride

1996 Season

One of baseball's best human interest stories, Curtis Pride showed he was more than just a good story. The hearing-impaired outfielder earned a roster spot with the Tigers during spring training and did a solid job in a platoon outfield role. After coming back from a shoulder injury that sidelined him for nearly a month, Pride finished the year strong, hitting .312 with seven dingers over the second half. He surprised the Tigers with occasional flashes of power.

Hitting

Pride has made his swing much more compact, and as a result puts the ball into play much more consistently. At times, he will fall into streaks when he tries to pull every pitch, and he will strike out against high, hard stuff when he starts to pull off the ball. He is otherwise a good fastball hitter who also is willing to go to the opposite field with breaking pitches. Pride was given little exposure to left-handed pitching and likely will make or break his career as a platoon player.

Baserunning & Defense

Pride has good speed and can be a solid basestealer who should improve his percentage as he gains more experience and exposure to big league pitchers. He is also very aggressive going into second on double plays and is always looking to take the extra base. Pride has decent range in the field with an average arm that is best suited for playing left.

1997 Outlook

Everyone in baseball is rooting for Pride, and he should stick with the Tigers as at least a utility outfielder. His ability to hit lefthanders is suspect, likely making him a platoon player. However, on a team looking for athletes, Pride should be a much-used asset considering his ability to hit for average and his speed.

Position: LF/DH
Bats: L **Throws:** R
Ht: 6' 0" **Wt:** 200

Opening Day Age: 28
Born: 12/17/68 in Washington, DC
ML Seasons: 3

Overall Statistics

	G	AB	R	H	D	T	HR	RBI	SB	BB	SO	Avg	OBP	Slg
1996	95	267	52	80	17	5	10	31	11	31	63	.300	.372	.513
Career	153	339	65	95	19	6	11	38	15	36	82	.280	.349	.469

Where He Hits the Ball

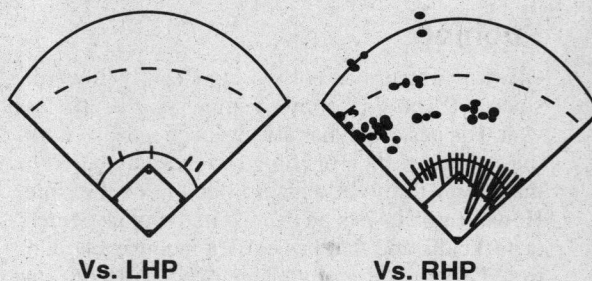

Vs. LHP   **Vs. RHP**

1996 Situational Stats

	AB	H	HR	RBI	Avg		AB	H	HR	RBI	Avg
Home	142	43	5	20	.303	LHP	12	3	0	2	.250
Road	125	37	5	11	.296	RHP	255	77	10	29	.302
First Half	126	36	3	13	.286	Sc Pos	58	16	2	20	.276
Scnd Half	141	44	7	18	.312	Clutch	44	11	1	5	.250

1996 Rankings (American League)
➡ 10th in errors in left field (3)
➡ Led the Tigers in triples

Ruben Sierra

1996 Season

Dumped on the Tigers by the New York Yankees in the Cecil Fielder trade, Ruben Sierra did little in Detroit. He hit only one home run in 46 games with the Tigers, though he did drive in enough runs with Detroit to give him 10 straight seasons with at least 70 RBI. He hit just .222 with the Tigers, and his overall average for the season was the second-lowest of his career.

Hitting

In keeping with what has become a career pattern, the switch-hitting Sierra was a much better hitter for average last season when batting from the right side of the plate but had better power when batting left-handed. Even in his glory years with Texas, the book on Sierra was to feed him breaking stuff away and out of the strike zone. . . and that hasn't changed. He has trouble driving such pitches and has resisted adjusting his hitting style to go with pitches away from him. He remains a dangerous mistake hitter and can catch up with most fastballs on the inner half of the plate.

Baserunning & Defense

At one time in his career, Sierra was a threat to steal 15-20 bases every year. However, his suspect conditioning has resulted in frequent leg problems, and last season Sierra attempted only four steals. Though he has decent overall skills and a strong arm, Sierra has recently evolved into an indifferent outfielder with bad judgment and even worse instincts. His six assists in 1996 barely offset his six errors.

1997 Outlook

The Tigers saw more than enough of Sierra in his two months in Detroit and were so anxious to move him that they agreed to pay $4.6 million of his $5.2 million contract in dealing him to Cincinnati. The Reds think they may have gotten a bargain *if* Sierra can produce 15 or so homers and his usual 70-plus RBI.

Position: DH/LF/RF
Bats: B **Throws:** R
Ht: 6' 1" **Wt:** 200

Opening Day Age: 31
Born: 10/6/65 in Rio Piedras, PR
ML Seasons: 11

Overall Statistics

	G	AB	R	H	D	T	HR	RBI	SB	BB	SO	Avg	OBP	Slg
1996	142	518	61	128	26	2	12	72	4	60	83	.247	.320	.375
Career	1596	6197	870	1675	332	52	232	1024	130	479	917	.270	.319	.453

Where He Hits the Ball

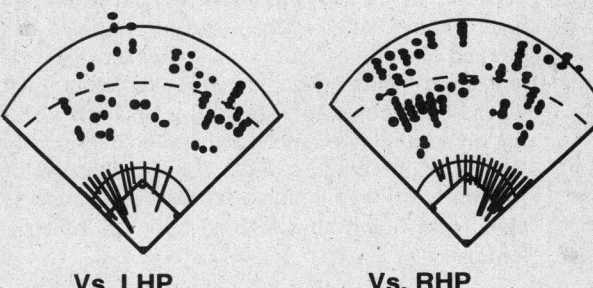

Vs. LHP   **Vs. RHP**

1996 Situational Stats

	AB	H	HR	RBI	Avg		AB	H	HR	RBI	Avg
Home	261	66	4	33	.253	LHP	158	50	2	26	.316
Road	257	62	8	39	.241	RHP	360	78	10	46	.217
First Half	301	77	9	43	.256	Sc Pos	156	37	5	62	.237
Scnd Half	217	51	3	29	.235	Clutch	69	13	1	8	.188

1996 Rankings (American League)

- → 1st in lowest batting average versus right-handed pitchers and lowest cleanup slugging percentage (.370)
- → 5th in lowest slugging percentage versus righthanded pitchers (.347) and lowest batting average on the road
- → 6th in intentional walks (12), lowest on-base percentage versus righthanded pitchers (.300) and lowest batting average
- → 7th in lowest slugging percentage
- → 8th in sacrifice flies (9) and errors in right field (4)
- → 10th in lowest on-base percentage

Detroit Tigers

Justin Thompson

1996 Season

Amid big expectations, oft-injured rookie left-hander Justin Thompson finally made his major league debut last season. Thompson, who was sidelined for the entire 1994 season with arm troubles, arrived in Detroit in late May after pitching brilliantly for Triple-A Toledo. His first two starts for Detroit were outstanding, but he had a reoccurrence of shoulder soreness and was sidelined for two months. Upon his return, he was not as effective, though he did earn his first and only major league win in late August.

Pitching

If he stays healthy, Thompson can be the total package. His fastball hits 90 MPH, he's developed hard sinking action with his heater and also has worked on adding a cut fastball. He has an excellent, sharp-breaking curve that is a strikeout pitch when he can control it. Thompson has been working on adding an offspeed pitch and occasionally shows an improving straight change. Because of the frailty of his pitching arm, there are concerns about him being able to hold his stuff past six innings.

Defense

Thompson has a decent pickoff move and does a good job of paying attention to baserunners. He is somewhat slow coming to the plate, so some basestealers will be able to burn him even if he keeps them from getting a good jump. He is somewhat awkward at the end of his delivery but otherwise appears to be a capable fielder.

1997 Outlook

Thompson had a full winter to rest and strengthen himself after his series of arm problems, so he should arrive at spring training in good condition. The Tigers believe he can develop into a major factor in their rotation. For now, the expectations should be toned down. If he's healthy enough to take the ball on a regular basis, Thompson can win 10 or so games for this year's Tigers.

Position: SP
Bats: L **Throws:** L
Ht: 6' 4" **Wt:** 215

Opening Day Age: 24
Born: 3/8/73 in San Antonio, TX
ML Seasons: 1

Overall Statistics

	W	L	Pct.	ERA	G	GS	Sv	IP	H	BB	SO	HR	BR/IP
1996	1	6	.143	4.58	11	11	0	59.0	62	31	44	7	1.58
Career	1	6	.143	4.58	11	11	0	59.0	62	31	44	7	1.58

How Often He Throws Strikes

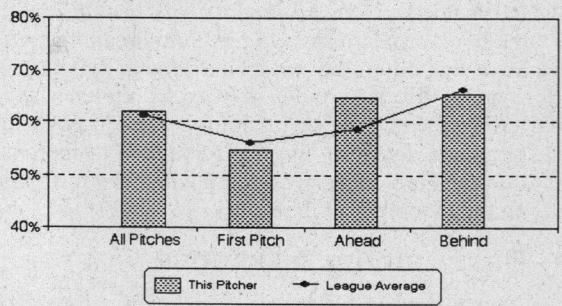

1996 Situational Stats

	W	L	ERA	Sv	IP		AB	H	HR	RBI	Avg
Home	0	3	5.40	0	30.0	LHB	47	13	2	6	.277
Road	1	3	3.72	0	29.0	RHB	185	49	5	25	.265
First Half	0	1	2.03	0	13.1	Sc Pos	61	19	2	25	.311
Scnd Half	1	5	5.32	0	45.2	Clutch	8	1	1	1	.125

1996 Rankings (American League)
➡ Led the Tigers in runners caught stealing (5)

Raul Casanova

Position: C
Bats: B **Throws:** R
Ht: 5'11" **Wt:** 200

Opening Day Age: 24
Born: 8/23/72 in Humacao, Puerto Rico
ML Seasons: 1

Overall Statistics

	G	AB	R	H	D	T	HR	RBI	SB	BB	SO	Avg	OBP	Slg
1996	25	85	6	16	1	0	4	9	0	6	18	.188	.242	.341
Career	25	85	6	16	1	0	4	9	0	6	18	.188	.242	.341

1996 Situational Stats

	AB	H	HR	RBI	Avg		AB	H	HR	RBI	Avg
Home	44	9	1	4	.205	LHP	11	3	1	1	.273
Road	41	7	3	5	.171	RHP	74	13	3	8	.176
First Half	57	8	3	5	.140	Sc Pos	21	5	1	6	.238
Scnd Half	28	8	1	4	.286	Clutch	13	2	1	2	.154

1996 Season

Recalled May 24 from Triple-A, where he'd hit eight homers in 49 games, rookie catching prospect Raul Casanova was expected to get plenty of action behind the plate. Casanova's chances of getting his feet wet in the majors ended when he suffered a broken wrist on June 18. He remained sidelined for two months and needed a minor league rehab stint before returning in September.

Hitting, Baserunning & Defense

A switch-hitter, Casanova was used primarily against right-handed pitching in his limited time last year. He has a quick bat, though he needs to be more disciplined at the plate. He has trouble with breaking stuff but showed flashes of being able to hit fastballs with power. He does not run well but has excellent potential as a receiver. Casanova possesses an above-average arm and is improving his footwork and his release.

1997 Outlook

Casanova's lost year means he must impress in spring training to win a spot on the Opening Day roster. But the Tigers regard him highly, and he has excellent potential to be at least a part-timer who could spell Brad Ausmus, especially against the tougher right-handed pitchers.

John Cummings

Position: RP
Bats: L **Throws:** L
Ht: 6'3" **Wt:** 200

Opening Day Age: 27
Born: 5/10/69 in Torrance, CA
ML Seasons: 4

Overall Statistics

	W	L	Pct.	ERA	G	GS	Sv	IP	H	BB	SO	HR	BR/IP
1996	3	4	.429	5.35	25	0	0	37.0	48	22	29	4	1.89
Career	8	15	.348	5.31	91	16	0	191.2	219	92	106	20	1.62

1996 Situational Stats

	W	L	ERA	Sv	IP		AB	H	HR	RBI	Avg
Home	1	3	7.50	0	18.0	LHB	51	15	0	15	.294
Road	2	1	3.32	0	19.0	RHB	102	33	4	19	.324
First Half	0	1	6.75	0	5.1	Sc Pos	54	19	2	31	.352
Scnd Half	3	3	5.12	0	31.2	Clutch	36	9	0	6	.250

1996 Season

Acquired last July from the Dodgers, left-handed reliever John Cummings was effective at first, winning three games and compiling a 2.13 ERA in his first 15 appearances in a Detroit uniform. However, Cummings got lit up in September, posting an ERA of nearly 8.00.

Pitching & Defense

When Cummings gets ahead in the count, he is effective because he can then bring either a decent cut fastball which approaches the high 80s or an improving change-up. He is too often pitching from behind, however, and can become a nibbler, resulting in too many walks and too many hits allowed. He is also not appreciably more effective vs. left-handed hitters, making him more of a middle man than a lefty specialist. He has an average pickoff move but does come to the plate quickly which helps against baserunners.

1997 Outlook

Cummings is one of many Tigers pitchers who will come to spring training with little job security. He can be effective in short stretches, and should be able to stick on the staff as a long man and middle reliever.

Damion Easley

Position: SS/2B
Bats: R **Throws:** R
Ht: 5'11" **Wt:** 185

Opening Day Age: 27
Born: 11/11/69 in New York, NY
ML Seasons: 5

Overall Statistics

	G	AB	R	H	D	T	HR	RBI	SB	BB	SO	Avg	OBP	Slg
1996	49	112	14	30	2	0	4	17	3	10	25	.268	.331	.393
Career	371	1166	137	286	50	5	17	116	27	107	181	.245	.315	.340

1996 Situational Stats

	AB	H	HR	RBI	Avg		AB	H	HR	RBI	Avg
Home	40	11	1	4	.275	LHP	48	16	3	10	.333
Road	72	19	3	13	.264	RHP	64	14	1	7	.219
First Half	40	7	2	7	.175	Sc Pos	28	8	2	15	.286
Scnd Half	72	23	2	10	.319	Clutch	19	5	0	4	.263

1996 Season

Once considered a top prospect by the Angels, Damion Easley saw his stock decline after weak-hitting seasons in 1994 and 1995. Easley began 1996 on the shelf with shoulder problems, and when he failed to hit after his return, the Angels dealt him to Detroit July 31. Easley continued to nurse hamstring and ankle injuries after coming to Detroit, but hit very well when he was available.

Hitting, Baserunning & Defense

A line-drive hitter with limited power, Easley had become an easy out because of his lack of selectivity and his susceptibility to getting jammed. Maybe it was an aberration, but he looked like a much smarter hitter after the trade to Detroit. Easley has above-average speed but is not a basestealing threat. He's versatile in the field, capable of playing second, short, third and the outfield. Second base is his best spot.

1997 Outlook

A change of scenery seemed to help Easley, who had become a little-used benchwarmer with the Angels. The Tigers weren't completely happy with Mark Lewis' play at second last year, and Easley could get some playing time there if he continues to hit.

Joey Eischen

Position: RP
Bats: L **Throws:** L
Ht: 6' 1" **Wt:** 190

Opening Day Age: 26
Born: 5/25/70 in West Covina, CA
ML Seasons: 3
Pronunciation: EYE-shen

Overall Statistics

	W	L	Pct.	ERA	G	GS	Sv	IP	H	BB	SO	HR	BR/IP
1996	1	2	.333	4.21	52	0	0	68.1	75	34	51	7	1.60
Career	1	2	.333	4.33	70	0	0	89.1	98	45	67	8	1.60

1996 Situational Stats

	W	L	ERA	Sv	IP		AB	H	HR	RBI	Avg
Home	1	0	3.43	0	39.1	LHB	80	23	2	11	.288
Road	0	2	5.28	0	29.0	RHB	185	52	5	34	.281
First Half	0	0	4.93	0	38.1	Sc Pos	89	28	2	37	.315
Scnd Half	1	2	3.30	0	30.0	Clutch	42	16	3	11	.381

1996 Season

Of the 27 pitchers who labored for the Tigers last season, Joey Eischen posted the lowest earned run average. He was scored upon in only six of his 24 appearances with Detroit after coming over in a trade with Los Angeles. His 3.24 ERA with the Tigers could have been even better if not for the grand slam he yielded to Albert Belle on August 27.

Pitching & Defense

Eischen throws in the low 90s and can be tough on lefthanders with his riding fastball. He also throws a decent slider but has no reliable offspeed pitch. His problem throughout his career has been control. He walks far too many hitters and becomes hittable when he is not pitching from ahead in the count. Eischen is slow to the plate, making him an easy target for basestealers. He is an average fielding pitcher.

1997 Outlook

Eischen has long been considered a solid prospect, and he gave the Tigers' staff a boost after his arrival. He enters this season as a certain part of Detroit's bullpen mix, where he likely will pitch in set-up situations.

C.J. Nitkowski

Position: SP
Bats: L **Throws:** L
Ht: 6' 3" **Wt:** 190

Opening Day Age: 24
Born: 3/3/73 in Suffren, NY
ML Seasons: 2

Overall Statistics

	W	L	Pct.	ERA	G	GS	Sv	IP	H	BB	SO	HR	BR/IP
1996	2	3	.400	8.08	11	8	0	45.2	62	38	36	7	2.19
Career	4	10	.286	7.21	31	26	0	117.1	156	73	67	18	1.95

1996 Situational Stats

	W	L	ERA	Sv	IP		AB	H	HR	RBI	Avg
Home	2	2	6.61	0	31.1	LHB	40	14	1	7	.350
Road	0	1	11.30	0	14.1	RHB	147	48	6	33	.327
First Half	1	0	1.29	0	7.0	Sc Pos	57	20	2	30	.351
Scnd Half	1	3	9.31	0	38.2	Clutch	1	0	0	0	.000

1996 Season

C.J. Nitkowski made eight starts for the Tigers last year, with distressing results. After his first outing resulted in seven innings and a victory, he lasted past the fifth inning only one other time and surrendered 48 hits in 30.2 innings.

Pitching & Defense

Nitkowski was regarded highly enough to be a number-one draft pick largely because of a heavy, sinking fastball that at times approaches 90 MPH. However, his mechanics have always been inconsistent, which too often makes the sinker flatten out in the strike zone—a big reason why opposing batters hit .332 against him last year. Nitkowski still has not come up with a second out pitch, though his change has shown some improvement. His pickoff move has improved, but he continues to have a slow delivery home. He's an adequate fielder.

1997 Outlook

Nitkowski is young, and the verdict on his long-term prospects in the major leagues is still far from being in. However, his chances could soon begin to dwindle if he doesn't step up early to claim a spot in the Detroit rotation. Otherwise, he faces another trip to Triple-A.

A.J. Sager

Position: RP/SP
Bats: R **Throws:** R
Ht: 6' 4" **Wt:** 220

Opening Day Age: 32
Born: 3/3/65 in Columbus, OH
ML Seasons: 3

Overall Statistics

	W	L	Pct.	ERA	G	GS	Sv	IP	H	BB	SO	HR	BR/IP
1996	4	5	.444	5.01	22	9	0	79.0	91	29	52	10	1.52
Career	5	9	.357	5.58	54	12	0	140.1	172	52	88	15	1.60

1996 Situational Stats

	W	L	ERA	Sv	IP		AB	H	HR	RBI	Avg
Home	1	4	5.29	0	32.1	LHB	152	45	4	10	.296
Road	3	1	4.82	0	46.2	RHB	158	46	6	31	.291
First Half	1	1	3.95	0	13.2	Sc Pos	67	16	3	29	.239
Scnd Half	3	4	5.23	0	65.1	Clutch	23	10	1	6	.435

1996 Season

Yet another of the many Tigers with former San Diego ties, A.J. Sager was recalled from Triple-A in mid-June and worked as both a starter and long reliever. He was 3-2 in his nine starts with a 5.33 ERA and added a win in relief, where he built a 4.45 ERA.

Pitching & Defense

Sager is a sinker/slider righthander whose strength has always been his good control. He has the ability to locate his fastball where he wants to, but he also works with a small margin for error since none of his pitches are overpowering. Even though he allows more hits than innings pitched, he has the ability to work out of trouble. Sager has a good pickoff move and a quick, compact delivery that is tough on baserunners, who were successful only three times in eight attempts against him last year.

1997 Outlook

While he has no star potential, Sager is a serviceable pitcher who can be a potential option for Detroit as either a spot starter or long reliever.

Todd Van Poppel

Position: RP/SP
Bats: R **Throws:** R
Ht: 6' 5" **Wt:** 210

Opening Day Age: 25
Born: 12/9/71 in Hinsdale, IL
ML Seasons: 5

Overall Statistics

	W	L	Pct.	ERA	G	GS	Sv	IP	H	BB	SO	HR	BR/IP
1996	3	9	.250	9.06	37	15	1	99.1	139	62	53	24	2.02
Career	20	33	.377	6.22	113	69	1	443.0	455	271	311	71	1.64

1996 Situational Stats

	W	L	ERA	Sv	IP		AB	H	HR	RBI	Avg
Home	1	4	8.76	0	49.1	LHB	212	80	16	62	.377
Road	2	5	9.36	1	50.0	RHB	203	59	8	36	.291
First Half	1	4	7.39	0	59.2	Sc Pos	135	48	12	82	.356
Scnd Half	2	5	11.57	1	39.2	Clutch	28	7	1	3	.250

1996 Season

Long-ballyhooed prospect Todd Van Poppel got off to a good start with Detroit after the team acquired him off waivers in early August. He won two of his first four starts and tossed his first career complete-game shutout on Aug. 30. However, he became a launching pad in his final five starts, going 0-3 with a whopping 21.89 ERA.

Pitching & Defense

Van Poppel has the raw stuff to be a winner, including a moving fastball that hits the high 80s consistently, a circle change and a curve. He has displayed only brief periods in which he maintains control of all his pitches, however. He has labored with his release point throughout his career and too often ends up pitching from behind. He then becomes tentative and his stuff suffers. Van Poppel has never held runners well, though he's a competent fielder.

1997 Outlook

The Tigers had hopes they could turn Van Poppel's career around, but changed their mind after his horrible finish. When the season ended they sold him to the Angels. He'll get another chance with California, but hopes are fading for him.

Brian Williams

Position: RP/SP
Bats: R **Throws:** R
Ht: 6' 2" **Wt:** 225

Opening Day Age: 28
Born: 2/15/69 in Lancaster, SC
ML Seasons: 6

Overall Statistics

	W	L	Pct.	ERA	G	GS	Sv	IP	H	BB	SO	HR	BR/IP
1996	3	10	.231	6.77	40	17	2	121.0	145	85	72	21	1.90
Career	23	36	.390	5.46	164	63	5	461.2	515	248	310	52	1.65

1996 Situational Stats

	W	L	ERA	Sv	IP		AB	H	HR	RBI	Avg
Home	3	3	5.42	2	79.2	LHB	260	96	12	58	.369
Road	0	7	9.36	0	41.1	RHB	217	49	9	46	.226
First Half	2	5	5.45	2	72.2	Sc Pos	143	46	6	82	.322
Scnd Half	1	5	8.75	0	48.1	Clutch	38	7	3	8	.184

1996 Season

Ex-Astro and Padre righthander Brian Williams entered the 1996 season as the Tigers' closer, but that experiment was scratched after 15 appearances. He then spent time in the Detroit rotation where he managed only three wins in 17 starts and produced a 6.65 ERA.

Pitching & Defense

Williams is one of those guys who has a "great arm" which has yet to yield the expected results. His fastball has been clocked in the mid 90s, and on occasion his curve can be unhittable. However, he has never mastered the art of consistency and his control has deteriorated to the point where he averaged 6.3 walks per nine innings last season. Williams is an excellent athlete who fields his position well and has a quick pickoff move to first.

1997 Outlook

Williams was dropped from the Tigers' 40-man roster after the season, so he has to battle non-roster odds this spring if he is to earn a spot on the staff. His stuff is good enough for him to still be a factor as either a reliever or starter, but his control has to improve if he is to stay in the majors.

Other Detroit Tigers

Mike Christopher (Pos: RHP, Age: 33)

	W	L	Pct.	ERA	G	GS	Sv	IP	H	BB	SO	HR	BR/IP
1996	1	1	.500	9.30	13	0	0	30.0	47	11	19	11	1.93
Career	5	1	.833	4.90	71	0	1	125.0	151	40	76	25	1.53

Against Christopher last season, the average AL hitter turned into Babe Ruth (.351 BA, .746 SLG). As you may have surmised, Christopher did not spend much time in the majors. Probably through at 33. 1997 Outlook: D

John Farrell (Pos: RHP, Age: 34)

	W	L	Pct.	ERA	G	GS	Sv	IP	H	BB	SO	HR	BR/IP
1996	0	2	.000	14.21	2	2	0	6.1	11	5	0	2	2.53
Career	36	46	.439	4.56	116	109	0	698.2	732	250	355	72	1.41

Farrell is a journeyman who appeared slightly out of place in a major league uniform (14.21 ERA in two starts). If you can't hack it on the *Tigers'* staff, you're out of luck. 1997 Outlook: D

Phil Hiatt (Pos: 3B, Age: 27, Bats: R)

	G	AB	R	H	D	T	HR	RBI	SB	BB	SO	Avg	OBP	Slg
1996	7	21	3	4	0	1	0	1	0	2	11	.190	.261	.286
Career	140	372	44	79	18	2	11	49	7	27	130	.212	.277	.360

Hiatt is bound for the "Land of the Rising Sun" after getting just 21 at-bats with the Tigers last season. He's definitely not a major league player, but he might surprise in Japan. 1997 Outlook: D

Tim Hyers (Pos: 1B, Age: 25, Bats: L)

	G	AB	R	H	D	T	HR	RBI	SB	BB	SO	Avg	OBP	Slg
1996	17	26	1	2	1	0	0	0	0	4	5	.077	.200	.115
Career	75	149	14	32	4	0	0	7	3	13	21	.215	.278	.242

Hyers notched just two hits in 26 major league at-bats (.077 BA) before getting shuttled down to the minors. As a first baseman who doesn't get on base or have power, his prospects are dim. 1997 Outlook: D

Greg Keagle (Pos: RHP, Age: 25)

	W	L	Pct.	ERA	G	GS	Sv	IP	H	BB	SO	HR	BR/IP
1996	3	6	.333	7.39	26	6	0	87.2	104	68	70	13	1.96
Career	3	6	.333	7.39	26	6	0	87.2	104	68	70	13	1.96

Keagle started and finshed last season strongly (3.08 ERA in April/Sep.), but was hammered during the middle of the year (10.69 ERA). Back problems that sidelined him in July could have contributed. 1997 Outlook: B

Jeff McCurry (Pos: RHP, Age: 27)

	W	L	Pct.	ERA	G	GS	Sv	IP	H	BB	SO	HR	BR/IP
1996	0	0	-	24.30	2	0	0	3.1	9	2	0	3	3.30
Career	1	4	.200	6.02	57	0	1	64.1	91	32	27	12	1.91

Another in a long line of Tigers' "prospects," McCurry was roughed up for nine earned runs during his two appearances in the majors (24.30 ERA). Now 27, he might not get another chance. 1997 Outlook: D

Shannon Penn (Pos: DH, Age: 27, Bats: B)

	G	AB	R	H	D	T	HR	RBI	SB	BB	SO	Avg	OBP	Slg
1996	6	14	0	1	0	0	0	1	0	0	3	.071	.071	.071
Career	9	23	0	4	0	0	0	1	0	1	5	.174	.208	.174

Penn was recently released by Detroit after getting just 23 major league at-bats over the last two seasons. He has speed and will take a walk (or sometimes a pitch), but he's not a prospect. 1997 Outlook: D

Duane Singleton (Pos: CF, Age: 24, Bats: L)

	G	AB	R	H	D	T	HR	RBI	SB	BB	SO	Avg	OBP	Slg
1996	18	56	5	9	1	0	0	3	0	4	15	.161	.230	.179
Career	33	87	5	11	1	0	0	3	1	5	25	.126	.183	.138

Singleton received an extensive trial in center field last spring when Bob Higginson went down with a sprained foot. After hitting .161 in the majors and .221 at Triple-A, he was waived in November. 1997 Outlook: D

Clint Sodowsky (Pos: RHP, Age: 24)

	W	L	Pct.	ERA	G	GS	Sv	IP	H	BB	SO	HR	BR/IP
1996	1	3	.250	11.84	7	7	0	24.1	40	20	9	5	2.47
Career	3	5	.375	8.50	13	13	0	47.2	64	38	23	9	2.14

After decent seasons in '95 with Detroit and Triple-A Toledo, Sodowsky began last season in the Tigers' rotation. The experiment went so well (11.84 ERA) that he was later traded to Pittsburgh. 1997 Outlook: C

Alan Trammell (Pos: SS/2B, Age: 39, Bats: R)

	G	AB	R	H	D	T	HR	RBI	SB	BB	SO	Avg	OBP	Slg
1996	66	193	16	45	2	0	1	16	6	10	27	.233	.267	.259
Career	2293	8288	1231	2365	412	55	185	1003	236	850	874	.285	.352	.415

After 20 years in the majors, Alan Trammell finally called it quits at the end of last season. A probable Hall of Famer, Trammell left soon after the departure of longtime Tigers' teammate Lou Whitaker. 1997 Outlook: D

Tom Urbani (Pos: LHP, Age: 29)

	W	L	Pct.	ERA	G	GS	Sv	IP	H	BB	SO	HR	BR/IP
1996	3	2	.600	8.15	19	4	0	35.1	46	18	21	11	1.81
Career	10	17	.370	4.98	81	36	0	260.1	316	86	149	38	1.54

After getting off to a slow start in St. Louis (7.71 ERA), Urbani was exiled to Detroit in June. There, the shell-shocked pitcher was relegated to the bullpen before finishing the year in Toledo. 1997 Outlook: C

Randy Veres (Pos: RHP, Age: 31)

	W	L	Pct.	ERA	G	GS	Sv	IP	H	BB	SO	HR	BR/IP
1996	0	4	.000	8.31	25	0	0	30.1	38	23	28	6	2.01
Career	5	13	.278	4.93	111	1	2	138.2	143	67	88	20	1.51

Obtained in a preseason deal with the Marlins, Veres lasted just over a month in the Tigers' bullpen before earning his release with a 8.31 ERA. At 31, it's doubtful that another team will rescue him. 1997 Outlook: D

Mike Walker (Pos: RHP, Age: 30)

	W	L	Pct.	ERA	G	GS	Sv	IP	H	BB	SO	HR	BR/IP
1996	0	0	-	8.46	20	0	1	27.2	40	17	13	10	2.06
Career	3	11	.214	5.09	88	12	2	161.0	181	95	76	18	1.71

Walker, like most of the Tigers' bullpen, was scorched for an 8.46 ERA in 20 early-season appearances last year. He has a history of success, so he will improve as long as the team behind him also does. 1997 Outlook: B

Eddie Williams (Pos: DH, Age: 32, Bats: R)

	G	AB	R	H	D	T	HR	RBI	SB	BB	SO	Avg	OBP	Slg
1996	77	215	22	43	5	0	6	26	0	18	50	.200	.267	.307
Career	340	1021	133	261	42	2	36	135	1	88	185	.256	.322	.406

Williams garnered occasional starts last season at the DH slot and various infield positions. Struggling mightily at the plate (.200 AVG, .307 SLG), he was forced to accept a demotion at the end of the year. 1997 Outlook: C

Detroit Tigers Minor League Prospects

Organization Overview:

Had it not been for the recent arrivals of Tony Clark and Bob Higginson, the Detroit Tigers' farm system might have been relegated to the level of the Loch Ness Monster or the second gunman in Dealey Plaza—rumored to exist, but very difficult to verify. Team President John McHale, Jr. and G.M. Randy Smith have vowed to rebuild the system from the bottom up. To this point, however, their accomplishments have been limited to collecting second-class prospects from other organizations. The farm system remains barren, and their last draft was so disappointing that they fired their farm director over it. Justin Thompson has finally arrived, and Mike Drumright and Seth Greisinger may emerge some time next year, but after that, help is a long, long ways away.

Frank Catalanotto

Position: 2B **Opening Day Age:** 22
Bats: L **Throws:** R **Born:** 4/27/74 in
Ht: 6' 0" **Wt:** 170 Smithtown, NY

Recent Statistics

	G	AB	R	H	D	T	HR	RBI	SB	BB	SO	AVG
93 R Bristol	55	199	37	61	9	5	3	22	3	15	19	.307
94 A Fayetteville	119	458	72	149	24	8	3	56	4	37	54	.325
95 AA Jacksonvlle	134	491	66	111	19	5	8	48	13	49	56	.226
96 AA Jacksonvlle	132	497	105	148	34	6	17	67	15	74	69	.298
96 MLE	132	489	100	140	31	4	17	63	11	59	74	.286

Frank Catalanotto was clearly overmatched at Double-A in 1995, but made a giant leap forward last year in his second season in the Eastern League. He raised his average 72 points to .298, and his power numbers increased across the board. Only 23 next year, the left-handed-hitting second baseman is quickly becoming a multi-talented prospect. He's got good power for a middle infielder, and knows the strike zone. He's not the most sure-handed fielder around, but he's got good range and hangs in on the double play. He's got a chance to stick with the A's after Oakland selected him in the Rule 5 draft.

Fausto Cruz

Position: SS **Opening Day Age:** 25
Bats: R **Throws:** R **Born:** 1/5/72 in Monte
Ht: 5' 11" **Wt:** 165 Christi, DR

Recent Statistics

	G	AB	R	H	D	T	HR	RBI	SB	BB	SO	AVG
96 AAA Toledo	107	384	49	96	18	2	12	59	11	33	81	.250
96 AL Detroit	14	38	5	9	2	0	0	0	0	1	11	.237
96 MLE	107	379	47	91	17	1	12	57	9	32	85	.240

Acquired from the Oakland organization in a preseason deal, Fausto Cruz knew what he had to do to impress the Tigers: hit for more power. Down at Triple-A, he managed to do that—although his average suffered and his strikeouts went up. The Tigers called him up four separate times, but never gave him an extended look at shortstop. Although he isn't fast at all, he can play the position, as well as fill in at second and third base. If the shortstop position opens back up, he could probably fill the spot about as well as Chris Gomez did.

Mike Drumright

Position: P **Opening Day Age:** 22
Bats: L **Throws:** R **Born:** 4/19/74 in
Ht: 6' 4" **Wt:** 210 Salina, KS

Recent Statistics

	W	L	ERA	G	GS	Sv	IP	H	R	BB	SO	HR
95 A Lakeland	1	1	4.29	5	5	0	21.0	19	11	9	19	2
95 AA Jacksonville	1	2	3.93	10	10	0	52.2	49	24	24	53	6
96 AA Jacksonville	6	4	3.97	18	18	0	99.2	80	51	48	109	11

The 11th overall pick in the 1995 draft, righthander Mike Drumright is looked upon as the future ace of the Detroit staff. A shoulder injury cost him two months of the '96 season, but didn't diminish his status, as he was voted the top pitching prospect in the Double-A Southern League at season's end. He's got great stuff, with a sinking fastball in the low 90s and a power curveball that was voted the best breaking pitch in the Southern League. The Tigers aren't taking any chances with his arm, but won't hesitate to call him up as soon as he's physically up to it.

Trever Miller

Position: P **Opening Day Age:** 23
Bats: R **Throws:** L **Born:** 5/29/73 in
Ht: 6' 3" **Wt:** 175 Louisville, KY

Recent Statistics

	W	L	ERA	G	GS	Sv	IP	H	R	BB	SO	HR
96 AAA Toledo	13	6	4.90	27	27	0	165.1	167	98	65	115	19
96 AL Detroit	0	4	9.18	5	4	0	16.2	28	17	9	8	3

Ah, to be young and left-handed. Trever Miller is blessed with both virtues, so no one seems to mind that he doesn't throw hard. And it doesn't hurt that he keeps the ball down and throws his curve and slider for strikes. The Tigers drafted him out of high school in the first round of the '91 draft, and it's been a long learning process for him. Last year was his best yet, with a 13-6 record at Triple-A and four September starts with Detroit. He's not the type of pitcher who'll hit the ground running, but he should be able to develop into a solid big league starter.

Detroit Tigers

Brian Moehler

Position: P
Bats: R **Throws:** R
Ht: 6' 3" **Wt:** 195
Opening Day Age: 25
Born: 12/31/71 in Rockingham, NC

Recent Statistics

	W	L	ERA	G	GS	Sv	IP	H	R	BB	SO	HR
96 AA Jacksonville	15	6	3.48	28	28	0	173.1	186	80	50	120	9
96 AL Detroit	0	1	4.35	2	2	0	10.1	11	10	8	2	1

The key to Brian Moehler's success is that he never gets hurt or misses a start. Every five days, he's out on the mound, learning how to get by with an average fastball and a sharp slider. Last year, in his second season at the Double-A level, he improved dramatically, winning 15 games and earning a late-season look from the Tigers. He's right-handed, 25 years old, and not overpowering, so he'll have to just keep pecking away until he gets his chance. With his indestructible arm, chances are that he'll be ready when the time comes—perhaps sometime in '97.

Cam Smith

Position: P
Bats: R **Throws:** R
Ht: 6' 3" **Wt:** 190
Opening Day Age: 23
Born: 9/20/73 in Brooklyn, NY

Recent Statistics

	W	L	ERA	G	GS	Sv	IP	H	R	BB	SO	HR
93 R Bristol	3	1	3.58	9	7	0	37.2	25	22	22	33	5
93 A Niagara Fal	0	0	18.00	2	2	0	5.0	12	11	6	0	0
94 A Fayetteville	5	13	6.06	26	26	0	133.2	133	100	86	128	10
95 A Fayetteville	13	8	3.81	29	29	0	149.0	110	75	87	166	6
96 A Lakeland	5	8	4.59	22	21	0	113.2	93	64	71	114	10

Hard-throwing righthander Cam Smith has spent three full seasons in Single-A, fanning a man per inning each year, with otherwise mixed results. His mid-90s fastball is one of the best in the system, but he doesn't have any other pitches to go with it, and his control is spotty. After giving him ample time to learn how to pitch, the Tigers are finally yielding to reality and making him a short reliever. He could be dominant in that role, or he could just keep spinning his wheels.

Bubba Trammell

Position: OF
Bats: R **Throws:** R
Ht: 6' 2" **Wt:** 205
Opening Day Age: 25
Born: 11/6/71 in Knoxville TN

Recent Statistics

	G	AB	R	H	D	T	HR	RBI	SB	BB	SO	AVG
94 A Jamestown	65	235	37	70	18	6	5	41	9	23	32	.298
95 A Lakeland	122	454	61	129	32	3	16	72	13	48	80	.284
96 AA Jacksonville	83	311	63	102	23	2	27	75	3	32	61	.328
96 AAA Toledo	51	180	32	53	14	1	6	24	5	22	44	.294
96 MLE	134	483	91	147	34	1	33	94	6	46	111	.304

No relation. This Trammell is a power-hitting outfielder. He got off to a monstrous start at Double-A, and didn't slow down much after his midseason promotion to Triple-A. If he gets a shot in the majors, he'll be a legitimate 30-homer threat, and probably will hit for a decent average. The only thing holding him back is. . . everything else. He's going to be 25 next year, so he's no young phenom. In left or right field, his defense has improved to the point where it's barely tolerable. It's always tough for a young DH to break in, but if he does, he'll hit.

Greg Whiteman

Position: P
Bats: L **Throws:** L
Ht: 6' 2" **Wt:** 185
Opening Day Age: 23
Born: 6/12/73 in Cumberland, MD

Recent Statistics

	W	L	ERA	G	GS	Sv	IP	H	R	BB	SO	HR
94 A Jamestown	6	5	4.04	15	15	0	75.2	72	39	35	67	2
95 A Lakeland	1	2	6.05	4	4	0	19.1	18	16	15	20	1
95 A Fayetteville	6	8	4.23	23	23	0	125.2	108	65	58	145	9
96 A Lakeland	11	10	3.71	27	27	0	150.1	134	66	89	122	5

Greg Whiteman is a 24-year-old lefthander who still hasn't gotten above A-ball. What's holding him back? Just a lack of exceptional velocity or control. His fastball has good movement but doesn't crack 90 MPH. To win, he has to be able to get his curve and change-up over the plate, and he usually does. He won't learn to throw 90, so to make it, he'll need to keep working on his command.

Others to Watch

Righthander **Willis Roberts** went 9-7 with a 2.89 ERA in A-Ball. Only 22 next year, he'll move up to Double-A to start the season. . . Converted shortstop **Brian Corey** saved 34 games in Class A last year and is regarded as Detroit's future closer. He struck out 101 batters in 82 innings, walking only 17, with a 1.21 ERA. . . Left-handed first baseman **Daryle Ward** batted .291 at Class A, and showed some power potential. Now 22 years old, he's the son of former big leaguer Gary Ward. . . Outfielder **Juan Encarnacion** took a step backward in his second full year at Class A, but remains a budding power threat. At age 21, there's still time for him to remedy his free-swinging ways. . . Big righthander **Matt Drews** was considered one of the Yankees' untouchables only a year ago, but his mechanics got so fouled up that they dealt him to Detroit. Drews' combined record at three levels last year was 1-14, but the Tigers hope that he can rediscover the form that produced a 15-7 record in A-ball the year before.

Bob Boone

1996 Season

Manager Bob Boone resembles a bargain hunter who scours garage sales. He loves recycling other organizations' castoffs. He also likes shifting established players into new roles. Recasting players gained some short-term victories, but may have stifled the growth of lesser young talents. Consider Boone's decision to move Jose Offerman to first base and replace him at shortstop with David Howard. It improved the Royals' infield defense and helped revitalize Offerman's career, but it hurt the offense and blocked opportunities for Bob Hamelin and Joe Vitiello.

Offense

Boone tailors the Royals' attack to its existing talent, so his game plan features highly aggressive, pressure baserunning. He'll use the hit-and-run regularly, but prefers straight steals, and especially the double steal of home. He'll bunt early and often, trying for a quick lead. Using platoons like he invented the concept, Boone is fanatical about inserting pinch hitters to exploit platoon situations.

Pitching & Defense

Boone eagerly turns games over to his bullpen and rapidly runs through it, using relievers in many different ways over the course of a season. As with hitters, he'll quickly change pitchers when platoon advantages occur. Boone likes versatile defensive players and won't abide by anyone who can't adjust to role changes.

1997 Outlook

Tinkering with the lineup is a Boone specialty. Everyone plays, but few play every day. So those Royals who can fill many roles will get more playing time. Royals' upper management loves Boone. His discovery of hidden talents in marginal players makes their shoestring budget work. Yet the key to a promising future in Kansas City is sticking with its core of young players, who will be prone to slumps and inconsistent play. The Royals showed faith in Boone's plans by recently extending his contract through the 1999 season.

Born: 11/19/47 in San Diego, CA

Playing Experience: 1972-1990, Phi, Cal, KC

Managerial Experience: 2 seasons

Manager Statistics

Year	Team, Lg	W	L	Pct	GB	Finish
1996	Kansas City, AL	75	86	.466	24.0	5th Central
2 Seasons		145	160	.475	—	—

1996 Starting Pitchers by Days Rest

	≤3	4	5	6+
Royals Starts	6	100	33	12
Royals ERA	7.50	4.23	3.93	4.35
AL Avg Starts	4	96	30	21
AL ERA	5.57	4.90	5.33	5.81

1996 Situational Stats

	Bob Boone	AL Average
Hit & Run Success %	37.4	39.1
Stolen Base Success %	69.6	69.6
Platoon Pct.	73.9	61.9
Defensive Subs	28	29
High-Pitch Outings	26	23
Quick/Slow Hooks	14/19	17/20
Sacrifice Attempts	93	58

1996 Rankings (American League)

→ 1st in stolen base attempts (280), steals of second base (161), steals of home plate (9), sacrifice bunt attempts (93), hit-and-run attempts (174) and starting lineups used (152)

→ 2nd in steals of third base (25), double steals (8), squeeze plays (9) and starts on three days rest (6)

→ 3rd in pinch hitters used (172)

Kevin Appier

1996 Season

In an era of rising offense, Kevin Appier turned in the third-highest ERA of his career for a full season, but still ranked fifth among league ERA leaders. He also placed third in the league with a career-best 207 strikeouts. For the third straight year, however, minor shoulder problems sidelined Appier, causing him to miss two July starts. When he returned—with a new multi-year contract in hand—Appier finished the year with a 7-4 run, fanning 61 batters over his last seven starts.

Pitching

Appier's fastball, slider and split-fingered pitch are all superior offerings that come in hard and fast to hitters. His fastball reaches the low 90s, which is good enough to blow past batters before Appier puts them away with the splitter. His overhead delivery and falling off the first-base side of the mound imparts some sideways movement to his pitches, although it can also wreak havoc for catchers assigned to block wild split-fingered fastballs in the dirt. Despite the occasionally unruly splitter, Appier has always had relatively good control for a power pitcher.

Defense

The follow-through of Appier's exaggerated delivery leaves him out of position to field grounders through the middle or chase bunts along the third base line. In addition, his throws to bases often are unpredictable. His delivery sometimes helps opposing baserunners gain an advantage, but he had reasonable success against the running game in 1996.

1997 Outlook

The unquestioned ace of the Royals' staff, Appier should remain the top dog through 1998, thanks to a big-dollar, two-year contract. One of the winningest pitchers of the 1990s (94-61), Appier is coming off his seventh consecutive winning season, despite the subpar offensive support he often receives. As long as his extreme delivery doesn't contribute to a more severe shoulder problem, Appier will remain one of baseball's best hurlers.

Position: SP
Bats: R **Throws:** R
Ht: 6' 2" **Wt:** 195

Opening Day Age: 29
Born: 12/6/67 in Lancaster, CA
ML Seasons: 8
Pronunciation: APE-e-er

Overall Statistics

	W	L	Pct.	ERA	G	GS	Sv	IP	H	BB	SO	HR	BR/IP
1996	14	11	.560	3.62	32	32	0	211.1	192	75	207	17	1.26
Career	95	65	.594	3.28	222	210	0	1429.2	1260	494	1168	89	1.23

How Often He Throws Strikes

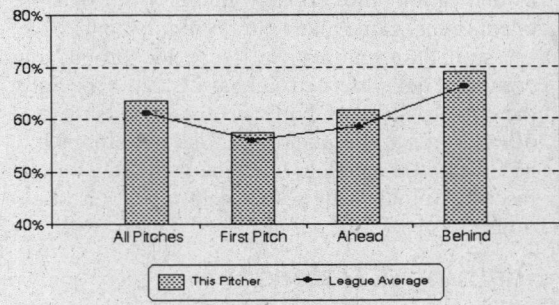

1996 Situational Stats

	W	L	ERA	Sv	IP		AB	H	HR	RBI	Avg
Home	6	5	3.43	0	97.0	LHB	427	111	11	41	.260
Road	8	6	3.78	0	114.1	RHB	356	81	6	35	.228
First Half	7	7	3.63	0	114.0	Sc Pos	185	43	1	56	.232
Scnd Half	7	4	3.61	0	97.1	Clutch	76	21	5	9	.276

1996 Rankings (American League)

→ 1st in lowest batting average allowed vs. right-handed batters (.228) and fielding percentage at pitcher (1.000)
→ 2nd in most strikeouts per 9 innings (8.8)
→ 3rd in strikeouts
→ 4th in highest strikeout/walk ratio (2.8), lowest batting average allowed (.245), lowest slugging percentage allowed (.370) and least home runs allowed per 9 innings (.72)
→ 5th in ERA, most pitches thrown per batter (3.97) and ERA at home (3.43)
→ 6th in shutouts (1), lowest on-base percentage allowed (.314) and least baserunners allowed per 9 innings
→ 7th in ERA on the road (3.78)

Tim Belcher

1996 Season

With a victory on the last day of the season, Tim Belcher tied his career high for victories in a season. He was consistent throughout the year, providing a stabilizing influence to an inexperienced staff. Except for a six-game stretch in June—brought on by a well-publicized shouting match with umpire Joe Brinkman—Belcher never went more than three starts without a victory.

Pitching

Belcher can throw four different pitches effectively, although he often needs an inning to discover what works best on any particular day. When his split-fingered fastball is working, he is in top form. He'll set hitters up with a regular fastball that reaches the upper 80s, a sharp slider, and an occasional curveball, then get them to beat grounders into the turf with the splitter. Belcher has learned to work effectively with just the fastball and slider, pitching to both sides of the plate and changing speeds. He remains prone to the gopher ball, however, allowing nearly one per start—usually on a hanging slider. No longer a power pitcher, Belcher continues to make adjustments that make him a more complete pitcher.

Defense

Belcher has always been a good fielder and 1996 was no different, as he helped himself a number of times with fine fielding plays. He moves quickly to field bunts or cover first base. Belcher also held baserunners at first with a surprisingly good pick-off move.

1997 Outlook

Belcher's fine season in 1996 led to a new two-year contract in September. His stability and stamina are especially important as the Royals expect to add at least one rookie to their rotation in 1997. A highly competitive individual, Belcher will provide experience and depth to this youthful team.

Position: SP
Bats: R **Throws:** R
Ht: 6' 3" **Wt:** 220

Opening Day Age: 35
Born: 10/19/61 in Sparta, OH
ML Seasons: 10

Overall Statistics

	W	L	Pct.	ERA	G	GS	Sv	IP	H	BB	SO	HR	BR/IP
1996	15	11	.577	3.92	35	35	0	238.2	262	68	113	28	1.38
Career	109	101	.519	3.80	295	274	5	1822.1	1721	649	1202	161	1.30

How Often He Throws Strikes

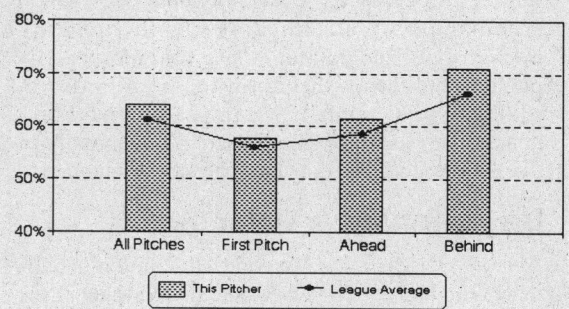

1996 Situational Stats

	W	L	ERA	Sv	IP		AB	H	HR	RBI	Avg
Home	7	4	3.97	0	118.0	LHB	510	147	12	56	.288
Road	8	7	3.88	0	120.2	RHB	421	115	16	52	.273
First Half	7	4	4.19	0	120.1	Sc Pos	198	52	5	73	.263
Scnd Half	8	7	3.65	0	118.1	Clutch	102	27	3	12	.265

1996 Rankings (American League)

- ➡ 2nd in games started, GDPs induced (31) and least strikeouts per 9 innings (4.3)
- ➡ 3rd in hits allowed and most GDPs induced per 9 innings (1.2)
- ➡ 6th in shutouts (1) and innings pitched
- ➡ 7th in batters faced (1,021)
- ➡ 8th in wins and least pitches thrown per batter (3.67)
- ➡ 9th in pitches thrown (3,751) and ERA on the road (3.88)
- ➡ 10th in ERA
- ➡ Led the Royals in wins, games started, shutouts (1), innings pitched, batters faced (1,021), pitches thrown (3,751), GDPs induced (31) and winning percentage

Johnny Damon

1996 Season

Johnny Damon's first full major league season prompted more questions than it answered. He was, at times, as good as advertised: slashing extra-base hits, stealing bases and sparking the offense. But, more often, he was just another youngster feeling his way in the big leagues. Will he be the offensive force the Royals so desperately need? Can he become a good center fielder? Will he hit for a high average and add power? Those questions remain unanswered after Damon's season of on-the-job training in 1996.

Hitting

Damon has gap power and slices hits to all fields, but he successfully pulls the ball only when righthanders make mistakes with breaking pitches. Lefthanders often make him look bad by pitching him away, then throwing heat inside, resulting in weak, tentative swings. Damon hit lefthanders in the minors and he should eventually in the majors, too. But, for now, he's overmatched.

Baserunning & Defense

Above-average speed is one of Damon's hallmarks, and he uses it very well. His 25 stolen bases were second best on the club in 1996, and as a major leaguer he has succeeded in 32 of 37 steal attempts. Damon's speed also has paid off in the outfield—and he's needed every bit of it because he rarely gets a good jump on fly balls. Damon played center field and right field in 1996, and was disappointing at both. His weak arm further compromises his defensive play.

1997 Outlook

The spotlight is on Damon as a measurement of the success of the Royals' youth movement. The success—or failure—of those youngsters, and especially Damon, will determine the club's direction and the future of its management on and off the field. While he still has a promising future, Damon must have a better year in 1997 if he is to stay on course to superstardom.

Position: CF/RF
Bats: L **Throws:** L
Ht: 6' 2" **Wt:** 190

Opening Day Age: 23
Born: 11/5/73 in Fort Riley, KS
ML Seasons: 2
Pronunciation: DAY-mun

Overall Statistics

	G	AB	R	H	D	T	HR	RBI	SB	BB	SO	Avg	OBP	Slg
1996	145	517	61	140	22	5	6	50	25	31	64	.271	.313	.368
Career	192	705	93	193	33	10	9	73	32	43	86	.274	.316	.387

Where He Hits the Ball

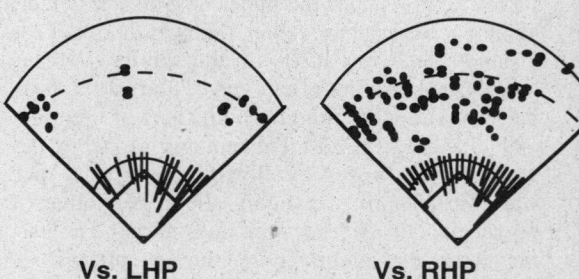

Vs. LHP   Vs. RHP

1996 Situational Stats

	AB	H	HR	RBI	Avg		AB	H	HR	RBI	Avg
Home	252	65	3	20	.258	LHP	133	30	1	15	.226
Road	265	75	3	30	.283	RHP	384	110	5	35	.286
First Half	304	86	4	28	.283	Sc Pos	113	26	2	41	.230
Scnd Half	213	54	2	22	.254	Clutch	84	13	0	4	.155

1996 Rankings (American League)

→ 2nd in stolen base percentage (83.3%)
→ 4th in lowest batting average in the clutch (.155)
→ 5th in least GDPs per GDP situation (3.7%), lowest slugging percentage vs. left-handed pitchers (.293) and errors in center field (3)
→ 6th in lowest slugging percentage and lowest batting average vs. left-handed pitchers (.226)
→ 7th in lowest on-base percentage
→ 8th in stolen bases and steals of third (4)
→ 9th in lowest batting average with runners in scoring position (.230) and bunts in play (27)
→ 10th in sacrifice bunts (10)

Tom Goodwin

1996 Season

Tom Goodwin's second full season with the Royals was a carbon copy of his first. As in 1995, Goodwin provided good hitting near the top of the order, fine center field defense and blazing speed. A sore ribcage muscle limited his play over the last two weeks of the season. Just as in 1995, this highly professional player stayed within his game and turned in another very useful year.

Hitting

A slashing hitter with little power, Goodwin is at his best against right-handed pitchers. His bunting ability and great speed force third basemen to play shallow, often allowing Goodwin to slap grounders past them. While he provides virtually no extra-base hits, he often steals the extra base when he gets on. Hard-throwing lefties frequently overpower Goodwin. His wide-open stance leaves him vulnerable to inside fastballs. Goodwin doesn't draw enough walks to emerge as a top-flight leadoff hitter, but he can succeed as a number-two hitter.

Baserunning & Defense

There's hardly a faster player in baseball. Goodwin finished second in the American League in steals to Kenny Lofton for the second straight year, accumulating 116 thefts over two seasons. He was caught stealing a league-leading 22 times in 1996, largely because he took lots of chances in the Royals' gambling offensive scheme. Great speed helps Goodwin cover acres of outfield territory. He glides effortlessly under drives to the deepest parts of the park. Only a subpar throwing arm detracts from Goodwin's defensive play.

1997 Outlook

Despite a fine track record over two big-league seasons, Goodwin still has his critics. But a team lacking power needs a player like Goodwin near the top of the batting order. Goodwin has shown that he's a major league-caliber player who can provide good defense, steady hitting and frightening speed. In the right role, Goodwin is a solid contributor.

Position: CF/LF
Bats: L **Throws:** R
Ht: 6' 1" **Wt:** 175

Opening Day Age: 28
Born: 7/27/68 in Fresno, CA
ML Seasons: 6

Overall Statistics

	G	AB	R	H	D	T	HR	RBI	SB	BB	SO	Avg	OBP	Slg
1996	143	524	80	148	14	4	1	35	66	39	79	.282	.334	.330
Career	381	1103	176	309	32	8	5	67	125	84	166	.280	.335	.337

Where He Hits the Ball

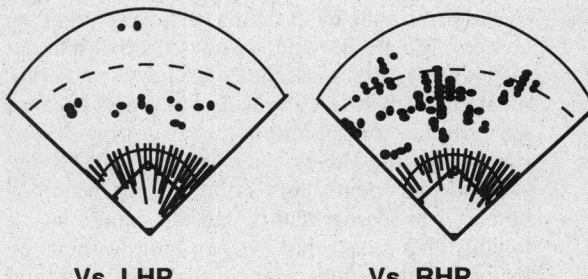

Vs. LHP   **Vs. RHP**

1996 Situational Stats

	AB	H	HR	RBI	Avg		AB	H	HR	RBI	Avg
Home	259	59	0	13	.228	LHP	162	51	0	15	.315
Road	265	89	1	22	.336	RHP	362	97	1	20	.268
First Half	317	89	1	21	.281	Sc Pos	121	35	0	34	.289
Scnd Half	207	59	0	14	.285	Clutch	71	16	0	5	.225

1996 Rankings (American League)

➡ 1st in sacrifice bunts (21), caught stealing (22), lowest HR frequency (524.0 ABs per HR), lowest slugging percentage vs. right-handed pitchers (.304) and bunts in play (52)
➡ 2nd in stolen bases, highest groundball/flyball ratio (2.4) , least GDPs per GDP situation (3.1%), lowest batting average at home (.228) and highest percentage of extra bases taken as a runner (70.5%)
➡ 3rd in lowest slugging percentage and steals of third (11)
➡ 5th in errors in center field (3)
➡ 8th in singles and batting average on the road (.336)

Chris Haney

1996 Season

Coming off a 1995 season which was shortened by back surgery, Chris Haney turned in his first full year in the majors in 1996. It was a year full of ups and downs, as Haney ran off five streaks of three or more wins or losses during the season. The lefthander's ability to throw strikes was the key to his fortune. In the nine starts in which he walked none, Haney was 8-0 with a 2.25 ERA. In 26 other starts he went 2-14 with a 5.83 ERA.

Pitching

Recently Haney has learned to trust his stuff. He's now comfortable throwing a strike with any pitch in his repertoire. In 1996 his best pitch was strike one. Once ahead in the count, Haney could open up the strike zone by throwing offspeed stuff at the corners. Mostly he works with a fastball and cut fastball that reaches the upper 80s, and he complements them with a curveball, slider and change-up. Still, his control within the strike zone has to improve before Haney can experience big-league success. Opponents bashed him for a club-high 29 homers last season, and he led the majors by allowing 267 hits. Since he can't throw heat by major league hitters, Haney must hit spots and change speeds.

Defense

For a lefthander, Haney's pickoff move is merely average. He compensates well by throwing frequently to first base to reduce leads, and opposing basestealers fared miserably against him last year. Haney's an average fielder who keeps his wits about him in tight spots.

1997 Outlook

The Royals' patience with Haney is beginning to pay off. He has become a respectable third starter and the team's top lefty. Yet Haney is at a crossroads. If he can demonstrate more consistency within the strike zone, he can become one of the league's better left-handed starters. If not, 1997 will be another season full of peaks and valleys.

Position: SP
Bats: L **Throws:** L
Ht: 6' 3" **Wt:** 195

Opening Day Age: 28
Born: 11/16/68 in Baltimore, MD
ML Seasons: 6

Overall Statistics

	W	L	Pct.	ERA	G	GS	Sv	IP	H	BB	SO	HR	BR/IP
1996	10	14	.417	4.70	35	35	0	228.0	267	51	115	29	1.39
Career	31	42	.425	4.84	112	106	0	626.1	691	217	334	68	1.45

How Often He Throws Strikes

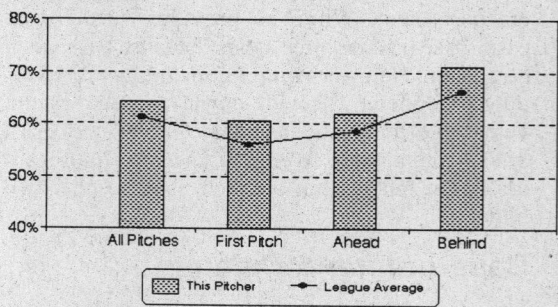

1996 Situational Stats

	W	L	ERA	Sv	IP		AB	H	HR	RBI	Avg
Home	5	7	5.01	0	116.2	LHB	181	49	4	19	.271
Road	5	7	4.37	0	111.1	RHB	737	218	25	103	.296
First Half	7	6	4.49	0	124.1	Sc Pos	211	64	7	88	.303
Scnd Half	3	8	4.95	0	103.2	Clutch	88	23	2	11	.261

1996 Rankings (American League)

→ 1st in hits allowed and in fielding percentage at pitcher (1.000)
→ 2nd in games started and lowest stolen base percentage allowed (35.7%)
→ 3rd in least pitches thrown per batter (3.51) and least strikeouts per 9 innings (4.5)
→ 6th in losses, shutouts (1) and highest batting average allowed (.291)
→ 8th in runners caught stealing (9)
→ 9th in innings pitched, batters faced (988) and highest slugging percentage allowed (.453)
→ 10th in highest strikeout/walk ratio (2.3)
→ Led the Royals in losses, games started, shutouts (1), hits allowed, home runs allowed and runners caught stealing (9)

David Howard

Position: SS
Bats: B **Throws:** R
Ht: 6' 0" **Wt:** 175

Opening Day Age: 30
Born: 2/26/67 in
Sarasota, FL
ML Seasons: 6

1996 Season

When Jose Offerman was found wanting as a shortstop and was shifted to first base, David Howard became the Royals' de facto everyday shortstop. By playing in many more games than ever before at the major league level, he reached career highs in several offensive categories while stabilizing the Royals' infield defense. However, his batting average, on-base percentage and slugging percentage actually dipped below what he'd done the previous several seasons. The Royals got what they expected from Howard in 1996: sparkling glove work and little else.

Hitting

A slap hitter with very little power, Howard may be the weakest-hitting everyday position player in the game. He can be overmatched even by mediocre pitching. Howard has trouble against fastball pitchers who throw high heat and finesse pitchers who throw breaking pitches in the dirt. He has neither a good batting eye nor the patience to wait for a good pitch. Howard can bunt—he was second on the club and in the American League with 17 sacrifice bunts—but that is the extent of his offensive expertise.

Baserunning & Defense

Capable of making difficult plays look routine and impossible plays seem possible, Howard is a marvelous defensive player. He's best used as a shortstop, but can also play second base very well. Howard has excellent range and a strong, accurate arm. Possessing average speed, Howard ran the bases tentatively and was inexplicably shy about taking an extra base on outfield hits last year.

1997 Outlook

By default, Howard is the starting shortstop going into 1997. There are no prospects in the high minors ready to step into a major league role, and no one among the infielders currently with the Royals has proven they can handle the glove work well enough. A stronger team with a better offense could more easily absorb his abysmal hitting, but barring an offseason move, Howard will be the Royals' regular shortstop in 1997.

Overall Statistics

	G	AB	R	H	D	T	HR	RBI	SB	BB	SO	Avg	OBP	Slg
1996	143	420	51	92	14	5	4	48	5	40	74	.219	.291	.305
Career	467	1237	127	281	44	12	7	117	21	108	231	.227	.290	.299

Where He Hits the Ball

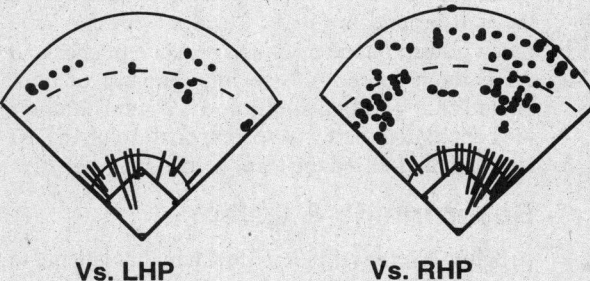

Vs. LHP   **Vs. RHP**

1996 Situational Stats

	AB	H	HR	RBI	Avg		AB	H	HR	RBI	Avg
Home	227	53	3	23	.233	LHP	146	30	3	18	.205
Road	193	39	1	25	.202	RHP	274	62	1	30	.226
First Half	269	64	2	26	.238	Sc Pos	109	27	2	45	.248
Scnd Half	151	28	2	22	.185	Clutch	77	15	0	5	.195

1996 Rankings (American League)

→ 1st in fielding percentage at shortstop (.982)
→ 2nd in sacrifice bunts (17)
→ 4th in lowest batting average vs. left-handed pitchers (.205), lowest on-base percentage vs. left-handed pitchers (.282) and bunts in play (31)
→ 6th in lowest batting average at home (.233)
→ 9th in lowest slugging percentage vs. left-handed pitchers (.322)

Keith Lockhart

1996 Season

Cruising along with a .311 batting average entering July, Keith Lockhart was the subject of All-Star speculation in Kansas City. But he wasn't selected and his second half was anything but All-Star caliber. Lockhart batted only .234 over the last three months to finish with final season totals that pale beside his 1995 performance. He went from being nearly an everyday player to platooning before finally losing his second base job to Jose Offerman.

Hitting

With his compact swing, Lockhart is a vastly better hitter against right-handed pitchers. He tries to make contact on the first hittable pitch and sprays the ball around the park. Lockhart doesn't have much power, but he can turn on inside pitches and drive them for extra-base hits. He has demonstrated clutch-hitting ability and is a good hitter off the bench: Lockhart was second on the club in RBI last year, and he led the team with eight pinch hits.

Baserunning & Defense

A below-average fielder, Lockhart has adequate range, although he occasionally has trouble on balls to his right at second base. Lockhart doesn't have the quick reflexes needed to play third base regularly, and his arm is just fair. On the basepaths, Lockhart is an integral part of the Royals' running game. He runs the bases aggressively, but without taking unnecessary risks.

1997 Outlook

Jose Offerman's rebirth as a hitter and second baseman will relegate Lockhart to a reserve role with the Royals. It's a role with which Lockhart is familiar after spending parts of 10 seasons in the minor leagues. He may never again be a regular, but Lockhart's versatility can make him a useful big-league reserve. Lockhart will be a good coach when his playing days are through. He has a deeply ingrained work ethic and a finely tuned understanding of the game.

Position: 2B/3B
Bats: L **Throws:** R
Ht: 5'10" **Wt:** 170

Opening Day Age: 32
Born: 11/10/64 in Whittier, CA
ML Seasons: 3

Overall Statistics

	G	AB	R	H	D	T	HR	RBI	SB	BB	SO	Avg	OBP	Slg
1996	138	433	49	118	33	3	7	55	11	30	40	.273	.319	.411
Career	259	750	94	215	52	6	15	94	20	48	71	.287	.330	.432

Where He Hits the Ball

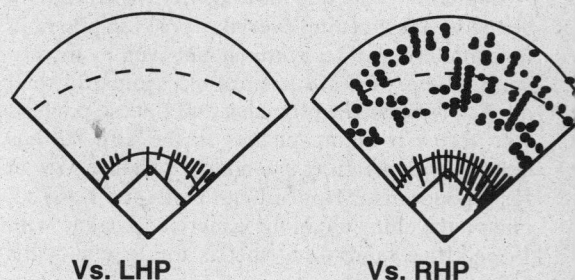

Vs. LHP   **Vs. RHP**

1996 Situational Stats

	AB	H	HR	RBI	Avg		AB	H	HR	RBI	Avg
Home	190	53	4	29	.279	LHP	62	13	0	5	.210
Road	243	65	3	26	.267	RHP	371	105	7	50	.283
First Half	243	76	3	35	.313	Sc Pos	116	30	2	43	.259
Scnd Half	190	42	4	20	.221	Clutch	61	15	1	6	.246

1996 Rankings (American League)

→ 6th in lowest percentage of pitches taken (48.0%)
→ 8th in lowest batting average on a 3-2 count (.100)
→ 9th in batting average on an 0-2 count (.286)
→ Led the Royals in doubles and batting average on an 0-2 count (.286)

Mike Macfarlane

1996 Season

After a one-year hiatus to Boston, Mike Macfarlane returned to the Royals as their primary catcher and a consistent RBI source. His 1996 campaign was a carbon copy of his last four years with the Royals (1991-94), as Macfarlane provided much-needed power, defense, and leadership. He ranked among team leaders in several power categories, and led the Royals in slugging percentage.

Hitting

One of the most extreme pull hitters in the major leagues, Macfarlane looks for high fastballs that he can drive deep to the outfield. Since his departure from Kansas City in 1994, Macfarlane has backed slightly off the plate and opened up his stance a little. The adjusted stance lets him handle inside fastballs better. Finesse pitchers give him the most trouble, often inducing Macfarlane to swing wildly at breaking pitches low and outside.

Baserunning & Defense

Unafraid to block the plate or pitches in the dirt, Macfarlane remains one of the most hard-nosed catchers in the game. His throwing has improved in recent seasons, and last year he nailed a respectable 36 percent of opposing basestealers. Macfarlane handles pitchers well, especially the mercurial Kevin Appier. As a station-to-station baserunner, Macfarlane is slow—even by catchers' standards. In the Royals' running-based offense, though, he stole a career-high three bases.

1997 Outlook

Macfarlane is in a teaching role, helping to bring the catching skills of youngsters Mike Sweeney and Sal Fasano up to big-league levels. He'll start 1997 as the regular catcher and an important slugging source for the power-starved Royals. Should Sweeney or Fasano develop as expected, Macfarlane's role with the club will substantially decrease. Even then the Royals will want Macfarlane on the roster. He's a clubhouse leader who is well regarded by pitchers.

Position: C
Bats: R **Throws:** R
Ht: 6' 1" **Wt:** 210

Opening Day Age: 32
Born: 4/12/64 in Stockton, CA
ML Seasons: 10

Overall Statistics

	G	AB	R	H	D	T	HR	RBI	SB	BB	SO	Avg	OBP	Slg
1996	112	379	58	104	24	2	19	54	3	31	57	.274	.339	.499
Career	920	2901	371	737	178	15	110	414	11	246	565	.254	.328	.440

Where He Hits the Ball

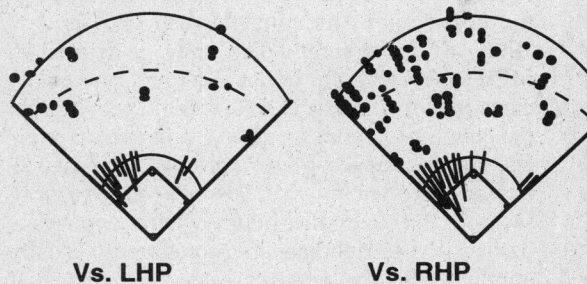

Vs. LHP   **Vs. RHP**

1996 Situational Stats

	AB	H	HR	RBI	Avg		AB	H	HR	RBI	Avg
Home	184	55	9	27	.299	LHP	116	28	8	21	.241
Road	195	49	10	27	.251	RHP	263	76	11	33	.289
First Half	189	52	9	23	.275	Sc Pos	99	24	4	35	.242
Scnd Half	190	52	10	31	.274	Clutch	60	11	1	7	.183

1996 Rankings (American League)

- ➡ 5th in fielding percentage at catcher (.993)
- ➡ 6th in batting average on a 3-2 count (.379)
- ➡ 7th in lowest batting average on a 3-1 count (.091)
- ➡ 9th in lowest on-base percentage vs. left-handed pitchers (.297)
- ➡ 10th in lowest batting average in the clutch (.183)
- ➡ Led the Royals in hit by pitch (7), slugging percentage vs. left-handed pitchers (.526) and batting average on a 3-2 count (.379)

Jeff Montgomery

1996 Season

Jeff Montgomery's 1996 campaign started out badly and only got worse. He nearly blew more saves than he had in the previous two years combined, and he developed a particularly nasty habit of serving up gopher balls shortly after entering close games. His frequency of home runs allowed more than doubled and he posted his highest single-season ERA for a full season. The dismal season finally ended for Montgomery in September, when he had season-ending surgery to repair tissue damage that caused weakness in his pitching shoulder.

Pitching

Montgomery's usual trick of trying to get ahead in the count on a first-pitch fastball backfired in 1996. His heater simply didn't have its normal 90 MPH steam, and often went back out faster than it came in to the hitters. When he could get ahead in the count, Montgomery turned to his above-average slider, change-up and curveball to put away hitters. Too often last year, however, he left a weak fastball out over the plate, where opponents bashed it. The righthanders Montgomery usually dominated hit him hard last season: more than half of their hits went for extra bases.

Defense

Because Montgomery was so often hit hard upon entering the game, few baserunners attempted to steal against him. Nevertheless, Mongtgomery has a decent move to first. He's a good fielder who is quick to cover bunts and throws well to the bases.

1997 Outlook

Shoulder surgery was deemed successful and Montgomery is expected to be ready for spring training in 1997. If he's healthy, he'll again be one of the American League's better closers. Because Montgomery has experienced shoulder problems in two of the last three years, a legitimate concern has emerged over his shelf life. Entering the second year of a lucrative two-year contract provides an added incentive to produce a better year in 1997.

Position: RP
Bats: R **Throws:** R
Ht: 5'11" **Wt:** 180

Opening Day Age: 35
Born: 1/7/62 in Wellston, OH
ML Seasons: 10

Overall Statistics

	W	L	Pct.	ERA	G	GS	Sv	IP	H	BB	SO	HR	BR/IP
1996	4	6	.400	4.26	48	0	24	63.1	59	19	45	14	1.23
Career	42	39	.519	2.86	540	1	242	702.0	602	235	604	57	1.19

How Often He Throws Strikes

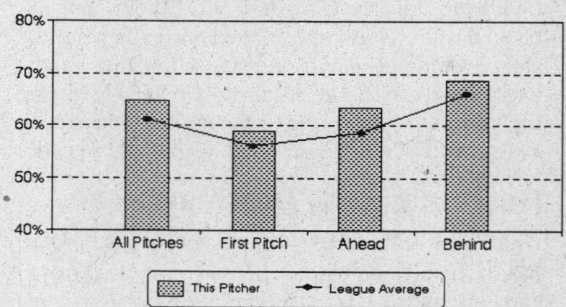

Legend: This Pitcher ▨ — League Average —●—

1996 Situational Stats

	W	L	ERA	Sv	IP		AB	H	HR	RBI	Avg
Home	3	1	2.97	9	33.1	LHB	134	32	5	18	.239
Road	1	5	5.70	15	30.0	RHB	101	27	9	18	.267
First Half	1	6	4.20	18	45.0	Sc Pos	59	16	1	19	.271
Scnd Half	3	0	4.42	6	18.1	Clutch	189	48	12	33	.254

1996 Rankings (American League)

➡ 1st in lowest save percentage (70.6%) and blown saves (10)
➡ 2nd in worst first batter efficiency (.364)
➡ 5th in relief losses (6)
➡ 9th in least baserunners allowed per 9 innings in relief (11.5)
➡ 10th in saves and save opportunities (34)
➡ Led the Royals in saves, games finished (41), save opportunities (34), save percentage (70.6%), blown saves (10), relief ERA (4.26), relief losses (6), lowest batting average allowed in relief (.251), least baserunners allowed per 9 innings in relief (11.5) and most strikeouts per 9 innings in relief (6.4)

Jose Offerman

1996 Season

No player generated more turmoil for the Royals than Jose Offerman in 1996. Yet he finished the year as one of the club's most valuable players, leading the team in batting average, on-base percentage, hits and extra-base hits while running off several late-season hitting streaks. Offerman displaced a handful of Kansas City infielders when manager Bob Boone moved him around in search of a place to play. He found new life by taking over the first base job when fan-favorite Bob Hamelin failed. Later, he replaced the injured Bip Roberts at second base and won a regular role.

Hitting

Given the controversy over where Offerman plays and his past struggles defensively, many people overlook his superior batting skills. Hitting left-handed he shows great patience, waiting for pitches away that he can slap up the middle or to left field. He's less patient batting right-handed, but he exhibits more pop. While he can be over-powered by hard throwers, he's still a highly productive hitter whose ability to get on base makes him a legitimate leadoff man.

Baserunning & Defense

As a shortstop, Offerman has the tools but makes far too many mistakes to succeed. His poor mechanics cause him to botch routine grounders and throw wildly. At first or second base, though, Offerman was quite good last year. He showed good range at both spots, and was less prone to throwing troubles. Offerman's speed and good baserunning instincts made him an essential part of the Royals' running game. Basestealing once again is a part of his game.

1997 Outlook

After becoming the Royals' starting second baseman and leadoff man in September, Offerman batted .376 and won a regular job. Finding a useful role for this Dodgers' castoff was manager Bob Boone's most impressive success. His career reborn, Offerman will bat leadoff and play second base nearly every day in 1997.

Position: 1B/2B/SS
Bats: B **Throws:** R
Ht: 6' 0" **Wt:** 190

Opening Day Age: 28
Born: 11/8/68 in San Pedro de Macoris, DR
ML Seasons: 7

Overall Statistics

	G	AB	R	H	D	T	HR	RBI	SB	BB	SO	Avg	OBP	Slg
1996	151	561	85	170	33	8	5	47	24	74	98	.303	.384	.417
Career	730	2528	342	673	98	32	13	207	85	338	422	.266	.353	.346

Where He Hits the Ball

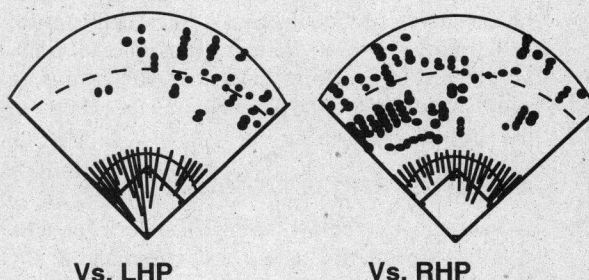

Vs. LHP   **Vs. RHP**

1996 Situational Stats

	AB	H	HR	RBI	Avg		AB	H	HR	RBI	Avg
Home	275	84	1	28	.305	LHP	193	48	4	13	.249
Road	286	86	4	19	.301	RHP	368	122	1	34	.332
First Half	274	81	1	19	.296	Sc Pos	129	36	0	38	.279
Scnd Half	287	89	4	28	.310	Clutch	78	25	0	5	.321

1996 Rankings (American League)

→ 1st in lowest batting average with the bases loaded (.000)
→ 3rd in triples
→ 5th in caught stealing and lowest HR frequency (112.2 ABs per HR)
→ 6th in highest groundball/flyball ratio (1.8)
→ 9th in on-base percentage vs. right-handed pitchers (.417)
→ 10th in batting average vs. right-handed pitchers (.332)
→ Led the Royals in at-bats, runs scored, hits, doubles, triples, total bases (234), walks, times on base (245), pitches seen (2,527), plate appearances (645), games played (151), slugging percentage and on-base percentage

Craig Paquette

1996 Season

Craig Paquette was another successful reclamation project by the budget-conscious Royals. Released by Oakland late in the spring, Paquette was signed by Kansas City and sent to Triple-A Omaha. He earned a late-April recall and was quickly inserted into the everyday lineup. Despite a September slump, he ended the year as Kansas City's leader in homers and RBI. Paquette's power was an important addition to the weak-hitting Royals.

Hitting

An extremely aggressive pull hitter, Paquette will swing from the heels when he sees a pitch that he likes—and he likes most of them. His inability to be selective is evident in his career strikeout-to-walk ratio: 311-to-49. Paquette remains especially vulnerable to breaking balls low and away; he can't make the two-strike adjustments needed to put the ball in play.

Baserunning & Defense

A versatile but below-average fielder, Paquette was used primarily as a third baseman by the Royals. He displayed a strong arm but otherwise average glove work. While he also appeared at first base, shortstop and in left field, he lacks sufficient range to play regularly at short or in the outfield. Paquette possesses decent speed and can steal a base, but he has shown questionable judgment on the basepaths.

1997 Outlook

Manager Bob Boone claims Paquette will have a job as long as he runs the Royals. What that job will be in 1997 remains to be seen, since Boone has a penchant for shifting players into new roles. The most likely scenario has Paquette as a regular corner infielder, hitting in an RBI spot. His home run bat is a critical need for the power-shy Royals' lineup. Paquette's long-range future depends on how much he can reduce his strikeout rate without losing power.

Position: 3B/1B/SS/LF
Bats: R **Throws:** R
Ht: 6' 0" **Wt:** 190

Opening Day Age: 28
Born: 3/28/69 in Long Beach, CA
ML Seasons: 4
Pronunciation: pah-KET

Overall Statistics

	G	AB	R	H	D	T	HR	RBI	SB	BB	SO	Avg	OBP	Slg
1996	118	429	61	111	15	1	22	67	5	23	101	.259	.296	.452
Career	342	1154	138	268	50	6	47	162	15	49	311	.232	.263	.408

Where He Hits the Ball

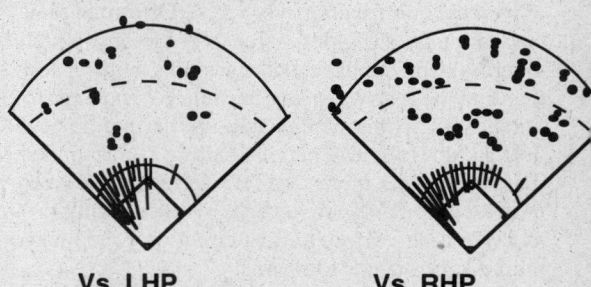

Vs. LHP   **Vs. RHP**

1996 Situational Stats

	AB	H	HR	RBI	Avg		AB	H	HR	RBI	Avg
Home	197	53	12	36	.269	LHP	141	44	7	21	.312
Road	232	58	10	31	.250	RHP	288	67	15	46	.233
First Half	181	43	10	30	.238	Sc Pos	125	29	6	49	.232
Scnd Half	248	68	12	37	.274	Clutch	68	18	2	11	.265

1996 Rankings (American League)

- ➡ 3rd in lowest batting average on an 0-2 count (.025)
- ➡ 5th in lowest percentage of pitches taken (47.8%)
- ➡ 7th in errors at third base (11)
- ➡ 10th in batting average on a 3-1 count (.600) and highest percentage of swings that missed (27.4%)
- ➡ Led the Royals in home runs, RBI, strikeouts and batting average on a 3-1 count (.600)

Joe Randa

1996 Season

Joe Randa's first full year in the big leagues was quietly impressive. Not expected to be a big contributor at the outset of the season, Randa gave the Royals productive hitting and sparkling defense. Because Randa never attracted much attention as a prospect, few Royals fans may realize he was one of just two Royals' hitters to top the .300 mark in 1996.

Hitting

The knock against Randa has always been that he won't hit enough in the majors. Yet Randa has hit at every minor league level, so his good hitting in 1996 should come as no surprise. He's not a power hitter, but he makes contact and goes with the pitch, lining base hits to all fields. He's primarily a fastball hitter with gap power, but he showed an increasing ability to adjust to offspeed stuff last year. Randa can be overmatched by hard-throwing righthanders.

Baserunning & Defense

Randa has above-average speed and the smarts to be an effective basestealer. He picks his spots well and takes advantage of anything the defense will give him. A sharp fielder, Randa combines quick reflexes at the hot corner with an accurate arm. As a second baseman his range is somewhat limited, but he has made noticeable improvement on the second-base pivot.

1997 Outlook

Randa has done everything that the Royals have asked of him. He has an intelligent, well-rounded approach that has led to success in most aspects of the game. He'll never be a star, but Randa can be a useful major league player. For 1997, expect Randa to get plenty of pinch-hitting duty and to serve as a fifth infielder who starts periodically at third or second base. With the Royals' volatile infield situation, his role could quickly expand.

Position: 3B/2B
Bats: R **Throws:** R
Ht: 5'11" **Wt:** 190

Opening Day Age: 27
Born: 12/18/69 in Milwaukee, WI
ML Seasons: 2

Overall Statistics

	G	AB	R	H	D	T	HR	RBI	SB	BB	SO	Avg	OBP	Slg
1996	110	337	36	102	24	1	6	47	13	26	47	.303	.351	.433
Career	144	407	42	114	26	1	7	52	13	32	64	.280	.331	.400

Where He Hits the Ball

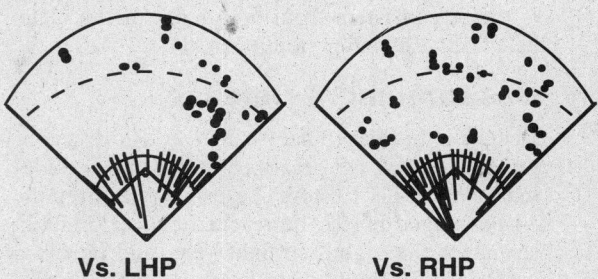

Vs. LHP   **Vs. RHP**

1996 Situational Stats

	AB	H	HR	RBI	Avg		AB	H	HR	RBI	Avg
Home	163	54	2	31	.331	LHP	147	50	1	22	.340
Road	174	48	4	16	.276	RHP	190	52	5	25	.274
First Half	157	47	2	21	.299	Sc Pos	82	29	1	37	.354
Scnd Half	180	55	4	26	.306	Clutch	51	11	0	3	.216

1996 Rankings (American League)

➡ Led the Royals in batting average vs. left-handed pitchers (.340) and on-base percentage vs. left-handed pitchers (.385)

Bip Roberts

1996 Season

Coming to Kansas City in a winter trade for popular Wally Joyner, Bip Roberts faced great expectations from Royals' fans in 1996. By most accounts he met them, fitting in well in Kansas City's speed game. But the oft-injured Roberts again lacked durability, missing nearly half the season due to various injuries.

Hitting

Using his short stroke, Roberts likes to pick on the first pitch. He'll hit the ball where it's pitched, trying to spray grounders to all fields. On those rare occasions when he muscles up for extra bases, Roberts will jump on a high fastball, slashing the pitch into an opposite field gap. Although Roberts is rather consistent from both sides of the plate, he's far too impatient to bat leadoff.

Baserunning & Defense

Despite a midseason hamstring tear, Roberts continued to show the great speed that is his trademark. While his 12 stolen bases were far from the 44 he swiped in '92, he reached double digits in steals for the eighth straight year, and he did a good job of taking extra bases on outfield hits. Despite a steady glove and arm, Roberts was merely an average second baseman for the Royals. His range to his left wasn't good and he was tentative on the double-play pivot. Roberts is not a good outfielder, displaying a weak arm and a slow jump on fly balls.

1997 Outlook

Injuries prevented Roberts from getting the 500 plate appearances necessary to invoke the second year of his lucrative contract, but the Royals moved quickly to re-sign Roberts at the end of the season. His playing time may be reduced, though, with Jose Offerman taking over at second. Still, Roberts can be an offensive sparkplug, as long as he can stay healthy.

Position: 2B/DH
Bats: B **Throws:** R
Ht: 5' 7" **Wt:** 165

Opening Day Age: 33
Born: 10/27/63 in Berkeley, CA
ML Seasons: 10

Overall Statistics

	G	AB	R	H	D	T	HR	RBI	SB	BB	SO	Avg	OBP	Slg
1996	90	339	39	96	21	2	0	52	12	25	38	.283	.331	.357
Career	987	3421	555	1011	166	29	25	284	230	337	443	.296	.360	.383

Where He Hits the Ball

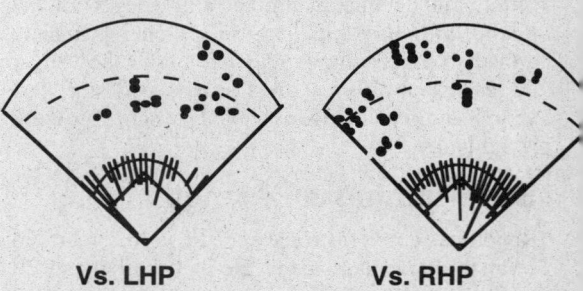

Vs. LHP   **Vs. RHP**

1996 Situational Stats

	AB	H	HR	RBI	Avg		AB	H	HR	RBI	Avg
Home	155	44	0	26	.284	LHP	112	31	0	8	.277
Road	184	52	0	26	.283	RHP	227	65	0	44	.286
First Half	222	67	0	34	.302	Sc Pos	108	36	0	52	.333
Scnd Half	117	29	0	18	.248	Clutch	57	14	0	9	.246

1996 Rankings (American League)

- → 3rd in lowest stolen base percentage (57.1%)
- → 10th in caught stealing (9)
- → Led the Royals in sacrifice flies (6), intentional walks (8) and batting average with runners in scoring position (.333)

Jose Rosado

Position: SP
Bats: L **Throws:** L
Ht: 6' 0" **Wt:** 175

Opening Day Age: 22
Born: 11/9/74 in Jersey City, NJ
ML Seasons: 1

1996 Season

From out of nowhere, rookie Jose Rosado took the Royals' rotation by storm. He didn't arrive with a lightning-quick fastball or a thunderclap curve. Rosado debuted with the kind of stuff that makes hitters wonder how he gets them out. He began the year allowing no runs in two starts at Double-A Wichita, then went 8-3 in 15 starts at Triple-A Omaha before joining the Royals rotation in July. He was an immediate success, winning team pitcher-of-the-month awards in July and August. It was a spectacular year for Rosado, who wasn't among the more highly regarded prospects when the season began. He wasn't even on the 40-man roster.

Pitching

With a veteran's poise, Rosado has learned the art of upsetting a hitter's timing. He throws fastballs at two speeds—the faster one in the upper 80s—and a superb change-up that was an effective out pitch in 1996. Rosado rarely got flustered when things didn't go his way early in the game. Instead, he kept his cool, stuck to his game plan and nearly always left the game in good shape. Rosado has yet to develop the stamina necessary to pile up a lot of innings; he's a six- or seven-inning pitcher at this point.

Defense

Rosado's glove work is nothing spectacular, but he doesn't hurt himself by trying to make the spectacular play. He also doesn't possess an especially good pickoff move. Timing is a more important element to Rosado's control of the running game.

1997 Outlook

It's easy to get excited over Rosado's bright future. However, caution is in order: he's barely been around the league once and he's just 22 years old. Still, Rosado has uncanny poise for a youngster, which bodes well for his long-term success. He'll start 1997 as the Royals' fourth starter.

Overall Statistics

	W	L	Pct.	ERA	G	GS	Sv	IP	H	BB	SO	HR	BR/IP
1996	8	6	.571	3.21	16	16	0	106.2	101	26	64	7	1.19
Career	8	6	.571	3.21	16	16	0	106.2	101	26	64	7	1.19

How Often He Throws Strikes

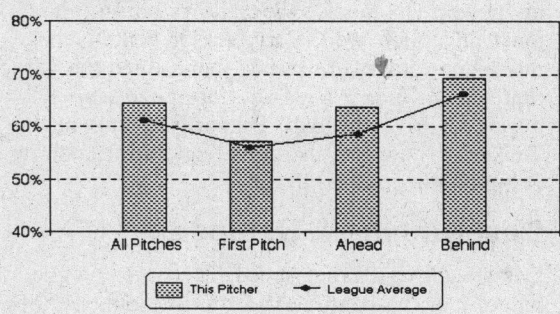

1996 Situational Stats

	W	L	ERA	Sv	IP		AB	H	HR	RBI	Avg
Home	5	3	3.03	0	62.1	LHB	76	24	2	4	.316
Road	3	3	3.45	0	44.1	RHB	330	77	5	30	.233
First Half	0	0	3.00	0	6.0	Sc Pos	91	21	2	26	.231
Scnd Half	8	6	3.22	0	100.2	Clutch	31	8	0	2	.258

1996 Rankings (American League)

- ➡ 4th in lowest batting average allowed vs. right-handed batters (.233)
- ➡ 6th in shutouts (1)
- ➡ 10th in balks (1)
- ➡ Led the Royals in shutouts (1) and balks (1)

Michael Tucker

1996 Season

Michael Tucker began his second major league season the same way he started his first—in a slump. Struggling with a .219 average entering July, Tucker suddenly found his stroke. He was a different hitter in the second half before injuring his hand on a headfirst slide in late August. He beat the tag and helped win the game, but he also finished the year on the disabled list. Tucker's season was very encouraging. He combined growing power with a penchant for late-inning heroics.

Hitting

Tucker's uppercut swing is unusually quick, and it's the quickness, not raw strength, that generates his power. His quick swing allows him to hit almost any pitch well. Early-season tentativeness made him look overmatched, but around the All-Star break, Tucker became more aggressive and began to drive the ball. Primarily a pull hitter, Tucker was the Royals' most feared hitter before going on the disabled list.

Baserunning & Defense

Despite above-average speed, Tucker isn't a good baserunner; he continues to run into outs on the basepaths. He also doesn't make use of that speed in the outfield, often getting slow jumps on fly balls. His weak arm is best suited for left field. Manager Bob Boone gave Tucker some time at first base, where his inexperience showed, but he wasn't a bad first baseman.

1997 Outlook

Tucker's talent is obvious. When he puts together a full season of hitting like he has in the second halves of the last two years, he will quickly become one of the Royals' most important hitters. The first base experiment will continue in spring training, but no matter where he ends up in the field, Tucker will be in the lineup regularly. He has potential to give what the Royals need most: a power boost in the middle of the lineup.

Position: RF/LF
Bats: L **Throws:** R
Ht: 6' 2" **Wt:** 185

Opening Day Age: 25
Born: 6/25/71 in South Boston, VA
ML Seasons: 2

Overall Statistics

	G	AB	R	H	D	T	HR	RBI	SB	BB	SO	Avg	OBP	Slg
1996	108	339	55	88	18	4	12	53	10	40	69	.260	.346	.442
Career	170	516	78	134	28	4	16	70	12	58	120	.260	.341	.422

Where He Hits the Ball

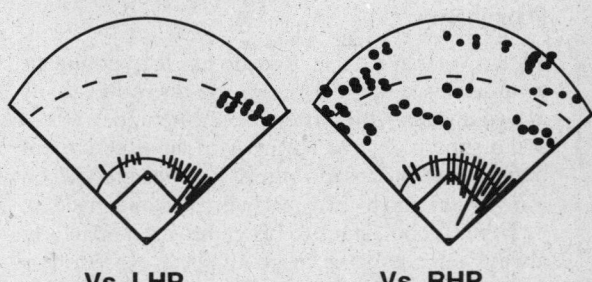

Vs. LHP   **Vs. RHP**

1996 Situational Stats

	AB	H	HR	RBI	Avg		AB	H	HR	RBI	Avg
Home	166	44	2	24	.265	LHP	72	17	5	13	.236
Road	173	44	10	29	.254	RHP	267	71	7	40	.266
First Half	211	48	8	33	.227	Sc Pos	83	23	2	41	.277
Scnd Half	128	40	4	20	.313	Clutch	48	9	2	5	.188

1996 Rankings (American League)

➡ Led the Royals in hit by pitch (7)\

Joe Vitiello

1996 Season

Joe Vitiello was expected to be a much-needed power source for the 1996 Royals. Instead he struggled to find his batting stroke, striking out about a quarter of the time. He was benched for a lengthy period, then demoted to Triple-A Omaha at midseason. When he returned in late August, Vitiello swung a more aggressive and productive bat, hitting .271 over his last 14 games.

Hitting

Vitiello is a former Triple-A batting champion, and it shows in his level, controlled stroke. Although he will periodically turn on a pitch and pull it for extra bases, he mostly tries to hit line drives back through the middle. Right-handed pitchers can get the best of Vitiello by busting fastballs in on his hands, then throwing breaking stuff low and away.

Baserunning & Defense

Knee surgery in the minor leagues several years ago has robbed Vitiello of any speed he may have once possessed. The most telling statistic about Vitiello's lack of speed was the team-leading 12 double plays he grounded into in 1996. Consequently, Vitiello is limited to first base or designated hitter duty. He's not a good first baseman; his reactions are slow and his lack of big-league experience shows.

1997 Outlook

Once regarded as an up-and-coming slugger, Vitiello's step backward in 1996 has dulled his chance for regular play in Kansas City. Manager Bob Boone prefers players who demonstrate defensive versatility, and that could keep Vitiello from ever getting a full-time shot with the Royals. The lone bright spot for Vitiello is that other first basemen from 1996 either won't be back with the Royals or will be playing other positions. He may have one more shot at gaining a regular role, but he'll have to hit for both average and power to win the job.

Position: DH
Bats: R **Throws:** R
Ht: 6' 3"   **Wt:** 230

Opening Day Age: 26
Born: 4/11/70 in Cambridge, MA
ML Seasons: 2
Pronunciation: vit-ee-ELL-o

Overall Statistics

	G	AB	R	H	D	T	HR	RBI	SB	BB	SO	Avg	OBP	Slg
1996	85	257	29	62	15	1	8	40	2	38	69	.241	.342	.401
Career	138	387	42	95	19	1	15	61	2	46	94	.245	.334	.416

Where He Hits the Ball

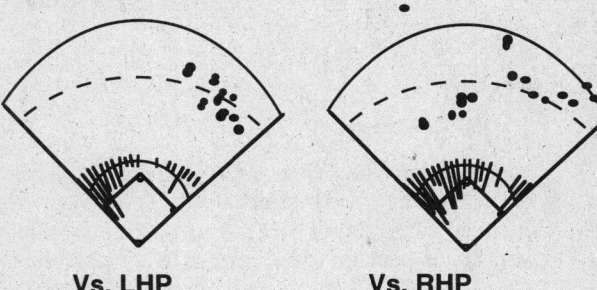

Vs. LHP   Vs. RHP

1996 Situational Stats

	AB	H	HR	RBI	Avg		AB	H	HR	RBI	Avg
Home	140	38	3	25	.271	LHP	109	28	4	21	.257
Road	117	24	5	15	.205	RHP	148	34	4	19	.230
First Half	206	49	7	32	.238	Sc Pos	66	16	2	28	.242
Scnd Half	51	13	1	8	.255	Clutch	34	11	1	5	.324

1996 Rankings (American League)

➡ 2nd in most GDPs per GDP situation (23.5%) and lowest cleanup slugging percentage (.395)

➡ Led the Royals in GDPs (12) and cleanup slugging percentage (.395)

Jaime Bluma

Position: RP
Bats: R **Throws:** R
Ht: 5'11" **Wt:** 195

Opening Day Age: 24
Born: 5/18/72 in Beaufort, SC
ML Seasons: 1

Overall Statistics

	W	L	Pct.	ERA	G	GS	Sv	IP	H	BB	SO	HR	BR/IP
1996	0	0	-	3.60	17	0	5	20.0	18	4	14	2	1.10
Career	0	0	-	3.60	17	0	5	20.0	18	4	14	2	1.10

1996 Situational Stats

	W	L	ERA	Sv	IP		AB	H	HR	RBI	Avg
Home	0	0	3.60	4	10.0	LHB	34	11	1	4	.324
Road	0	0	3.60	1	10.0	RHB	39	7	1	3	.179
First Half	0	0	-	0	0.0	Sc Pos	25	4	1	6	.160
Scnd Half	0	0	3.60	5	20.0	Clutch	38	7	0	2	.184

1996 Season

Jaime Bluma led Triple-A Omaha with 25 saves before earning a September call-up. The move was intended as a training exercise to get Bluma's feet wet, but it became a preview of Bluma's future when Jeff Montgomery underwent shoulder surgery. Bluma was thrust into the closer role and performed magnificently; 5-for-5 in save chances.

Pitching & Defense

While Bluma's high-80s fastball isn't overwhelming, it's late-breaking sink makes it effective. Bluma also throws an above-average hard slider to keep hitters off-stride. He's still learning how to set up hitters and work the corners. When he adds a change-up or cut fastball, his sinker will be all the more devastating. Bluma's inexperience was barely noticeable, as he fielded his position well and displayed a good move to first.

1997 Outlook

The Royals have been grooming Bluma for the closer's role since he was their third draft pick in 1994. The heir apparent to Jeff Montgomery has collected 48 saves as a professional, including an organization-high 30 in 1996. He figures to continue his on-the-job training in 1997 as the primary set-up man.

Mark Gubicza

Traded To ANGELS

Position: SP
Bats: R **Throws:** R
Ht: 6' 5" **Wt:** 230

Opening Day Age: 34
Born: 8/14/62 in Philadelphia, PA
ML Seasons: 13
Pronunciation: GOO-ba-zah

Overall Statistics

	W	L	Pct.	ERA	G	GS	Sv	IP	H	BB	SO	HR	BR/IP
1996	4	12	.250	5.13	19	19	0	119.1	132	34	55	22	1.39
Career	132	135	.494	3.91	382	327	2	2218.2	2226	783	1366	153	1.36

1996 Situational Stats

	W	L	ERA	Sv	IP		AB	H	HR	RBI	Avg
Home	2	8	4.50	0	72.0	LHB	265	81	9	34	.306
Road	2	4	6.06	0	47.1	RHB	199	51	13	34	.256
First Half	4	12	5.13	0	119.1	Sc Pos	97	31	5	44	.320
Scnd Half	0	0	-	0	0.0	Clutch	16	5	2	5	.313

1996 Season

One of Paul Molitor's American League-leading 225 hits was a wicked liner that fractured Mark Gubicza's left leg below the knee and ended his season in early July. It was a merciful end for Gubicza, who was well into the worst season of his lengthy career.

Pitching & Defense

Primarily a sinkerball pitcher, Gubicza will spot his below-average fastball to set-up sliders and sinkers aimed at corners. He doesn't have the velocity to pitch in the middle of the plate, so he must work both sides to fool hitters. Too often in 1996 he got pitches out over the plate, and opponents pounded him for a .476 slugging average. Gubicza, who has worked hard to become a solid fielder, also has improved his pickoff move in recent years.

1997 Outlook

The Royals traded Gubicza to the Angels after the season. However, his chances for a comeback aren't good. He owns a winning record in just one of the last seven seasons and he no longer has big-league stuff. A year after leading the majors in starts, Gubicza's career is nearly over.

Bob Hamelin

Position: DH/1B
Bats: L **Throws:** L
Ht: 6' 0" **Wt:** 235

Opening Day Age: 29
Born: 11/29/67 in
Elizabeth, NJ
ML Seasons: 4
Pronunciation:
HAM-lynn

Overall Statistics

	G	AB	R	H	D	T	HR	RBI	SB	BB	SO	Avg	OBP	Slg
1996	89	239	31	61	14	1	9	40	5	54	58	.255	.391	.435
Career	278	808	117	195	49	3	42	135	9	142	191	.241	.357	.465

1996 Situational Stats

	AB	H	HR	RBI	Avg		AB	H	HR	RBI	Avg
Home	118	26	2	15	.220	LHP	41	9	0	4	.220
Road	121	35	7	25	.289	RHP	198	52	9	36	.263
First Half	137	32	5	28	.234	Sc Pos	65	14	3	30	.215
Scnd Half	102	29	4	12	.284	Clutch	36	9	4	11	.250

1996 Season

Following a horrible 1995 season, Bob Hamelin needed to start last year swinging the bat as he did when he was the 1994 American League Rookie of the Year. He didn't, and then he got hurt. Despite hitting .284 after his July return, Hamelin was persona non grata and virtually disappeared from the lineup in September.

Hitting, Baserunning & Defense

A slightly more compact stroke let Hamelin make better contact in 1996, but it also diminished his power. He's a patient hitter—to a fault. He'll take hittable pitches when ahead in the count, then flail badly at unhittable pitches later in the same at-bat. Hamelin likes pulling low fastballs, but he struggles against high inside heat. Despite his size, he's not a bad baserunner. As a first baseman, Hamelin is average at best.

1997 Outlook

After two years of battling Royals management over his weight and hitting philosophy, Hamelin is finished in Kansas City. He wants out, and the Royals are likely to accommodate him. Hamelin can still hit, but will have to do it elsewhere, perhaps in Japan.

Jason Jacome

Position: RP
Bats: L **Throws:** L
Ht: 6' 0" **Wt:** 180

Opening Day Age: 26
Born: 11/24/70 in
Tulsa, OK
ML Seasons: 3
Pronunciation:
HOCK-a-mee

Overall Statistics

	W	L	Pct.	ERA	G	GS	Sv	IP	H	BB	SO	HR	BR/IP
1996	0	4	.000	4.72	49	2	1	47.2	67	22	32	5	1.87
Career	8	17	.320	5.01	77	29	1	206.2	255	75	112	26	1.60

1996 Situational Stats

	W	L	ERA	Sv	IP		AB	H	HR	RBI	Avg
Home	0	2	7.91	0	19.1	LHB	76	21	1	9	.276
Road	0	2	2.54	1	28.1	RHB	123	46	4	22	.374
First Half	0	2	4.34	0	37.1	Sc Pos	65	17	0	23	.262
Scnd Half	0	2	6.10	1	10.1	Clutch	36	13	2	4	.361

1996 Season

Jason Jacome began 1996 in the Royals' bullpen, but he made two terrible starts in April, resulting in a return to the pen. He enjoyed some success as Kansas City's primary left-handed set-up man, posting a 2.47 ERA in relief and earning his first career save, but he didn't really pitch as well as the low ERA would indicate.

Pitching & Defense

Jacome relies on guile instead of an overpowering fastball: his best heater registers just 83 MPH on the radar gun. Instead he tries to needle corners and induce grounders with sliders, curveballs and change-ups. He was a fairly easy puzzle for right-handed hitters, but he held his own against lefties, limiting them to just one home run. An above-average fielder, Jacome has a good pickoff move.

1997 Outlook

Jacome's inconsistency as a set-up man means he'll have to fight to keep the role. His main competition will come from Jeff Granger, a highly regarded, former number-one draft pick who recently has been converted to the bullpen. Win or lose, Jacome's days as a starter are over; for now, he's a situational lefty in the bullpen.

Doug Linton

Position: SP
Bats: R **Throws:** R
Ht: 6' 1" **Wt:** 190

Opening Day Age: 31
Born: 9/2/65 in Santa Ana, CA
ML Seasons: 5

Overall Statistics

	W	L	Pct.	ERA	G	GS	Sv	IP	H	BB	SO	HR	BR/IP
1996	7	9	.438	5.02	21	18	0	104.0	111	26	87	13	1.32
Career	16	16	.500	5.84	91	27	0	237.1	284	96	168	34	1.60

1996 Situational Stats

	W	L	ERA	Sv	IP		AB	H	HR	RBI	Avg
Home	3	5	4.34	0	58.0	LHB	213	61	5	19	.286
Road	4	4	5.87	0	46.0	RHB	197	50	8	37	.254
First Half	3	4	4.89	0	46.0	Sc Pos	102	27	2	40	.265
Scnd Half	4	5	5.12	0	58.0	Clutch	18	4	1	3	.222

1996 Season

Swingman Doug Linton had his best major league season in 1996. He achieved career highs in most pitching categories and established himself as a viable big-league starter. Linton gave the Royals several good stop-gap starts, often after lengthy stints of no work at all.

Pitching & Defense

Shoulder surgery a few years back significantly diminished Linton's fastball, but it has slowly regained its pop and now reaches the low 90s. An inability to have simultaneous command of both his fastball and sinkerball has also plagued him. When he throws both pitches for strikes, batters will beat sinkers into the ground or swing through high fastballs. Linton needs a good bullpen because he lacks the stamina to go more than six innings. He isn't a good fielder and his pickoff move is poor.

1997 Outlook

While Linton has proven himself a capable big leaguer, he lacks a role with the Royals. Considering the dearth of quality major league pitching, he'll get a chance at a regular rotation job somewhere. A more consistent Linton could even be a winner.

Mike Magnante

Position: RP
Bats: L **Throws:** L
Ht: 6' 1" **Wt:** 195

Opening Day Age: 31
Born: 6/17/65 in Glendale, CA
ML Seasons: 6
Pronunciation: mag-NAN-tee

Overall Statistics

	W	L	Pct.	ERA	G	GS	Sv	IP	H	BB	SO	HR	BR/IP
1996	2	2	.500	5.67	38	0	0	54.0	58	24	32	5	1.52
Career	10	18	.357	4.40	191	19	0	325.1	365	125	170	27	1.51

1996 Situational Stats

	W	L	ERA	Sv	IP		AB	H	HR	RBI	Avg
Home	2	0	1.15	0	31.1	LHB	72	21	3	13	.292
Road	0	2	11.91	0	22.2	RHB	134	37	2	27	.276
First Half	1	2	5.50	0	34.1	Sc Pos	59	19	2	35	.322
Scnd Half	1	0	5.95	0	19.2	Clutch	43	7	1	7	.163

1996 Season

Mike Magnante's rollercoaster season ended on a downturn, as he surrendered 10 runs over his last 7-1/3 innings. He began the year as a key left-handed reliever and ended it a forgotten man. Magnante appeared in just five of the Royals' final 29 games.

Pitching & Defense

Magnante tries to set up hitters by spotting his low-80s fastball just out of reach, then coming back with sliders and change-ups. It's an effective combination against power hitters with long swings, but most hitters merely wait him out, take what he offers, and smash a line drive. Magnante hasn't been especially effective against lefty swingers, and 1996 was no different. Magnante has a fine pickoff move and fields his position well, despite the knee braces that limit his range.

1997 Outlook

Because Magnante hasn't established a noteworthy platoon differential, Manager Bob Boone couldn't find a useful role for him in 1996. Magnante was looking forward to leaving the Royals at season's end, and the Royals obliged by handing him his release. He's a marginal major leaguer who will likely get another chance elsewhere.

Hipolito Pichardo

Position: RP
Bats: R **Throws:** R
Ht: 6' 1" **Wt:** 185

Opening Day Age: 27
Born: 8/22/69 in
Esperanza, DR
ML Seasons: 5
Pronunciation:
e-POL-ee-toe
puh-CHAR-dough

Overall Statistics

	W	L	Pct.	ERA	G	GS	Sv	IP	H	BB	SO	HR	BR/IP
1996	3	5	.375	5.43	57	0	3	68.0	74	26	43	5	1.47
Career	32	26	.552	4.36	207	49	7	508.1	553	182	251	32	1.45

1996 Situational Stats

	W	L	ERA	Sv	IP		AB	H	HR	RBI	Avg
Home	1	3	5.28	1	29.0	LHB	122	36	2	17	.295
Road	2	2	5.54	2	39.0	RHB	139	38	3	26	.273
First Half	3	3	6.21	1	37.2	Sc Pos	84	29	2	39	.345
Scnd Half	0	2	4.45	2	30.1	Clutch	141	49	2	27	.348

1996 Season

Expected to take on a primary set-up role in Kansas City's bullpen, Hipolito Pichardo wasn't up to the task and got rocked regularly. Manager Bob Boone quickly lost confidence in Pichardo, and his role was reduced to mopping up games that were already out of reach.

Pitching & Defense

Pichardo throws a 90 MPH fastball, split-fingered fastball and a slider. His control problems usually involve finding the plate, but in 1996 his difficulties with control were within the strike zone. He still threw hard enough, but his pitches were just too fat. The right-handed hitters he was expected to handle, handled him instead. He's not the smoothest glove man around, but he's quick enough and gets the job done. Pichardo's deliberate delivery gives baserunners an edge.

1997 Outlook

The emergence of Jaime Bluma will push Pichardo into a less important relief role. He'll no longer be expected to be a bridge to closer Jeff Montgomery. Pichardo's past experience as a starter may come in handy as he attempts a new long relief role.

Mike Sweeney

Top Prospect

Position: C/DH
Bats: R **Throws:** R
Ht: 6' 1" **Wt:** 195

Opening Day Age: 23
Born: 7/22/73 in
Orange, CA
ML Seasons: 2

Overall Statistics

	G	AB	R	H	D	T	HR	RBI	SB	BB	SO	Avg	OBP	Slg
1996	50	165	23	46	10	0	4	24	1	18	21	.279	.358	.412
Career	54	169	24	47	10	0	4	24	1	18	21	.278	.356	.408

1996 Situational Stats

	AB	H	HR	RBI	Avg		AB	H	HR	RBI	Avg
Home	68	18	1	9	.265	LHP	49	12	1	7	.245
Road	97	28	3	15	.289	RHP	116	34	3	17	.293
First Half	0	0	0	0	-	Sc Pos	46	13	1	21	.283
Scnd Half	165	46	4	24	.279	Clutch	17	3	0	1	.176

1996 Season

Battery mates Jose Rosado and Mike Sweeney made the same trek from Double-A Wichita through Triple-A Omaha to Kansas City in 1996. Sweeney had only slightly less success than Rosado, showing promise as a capable major league hitter whose catching skills will rank as big-league caliber with a bit of fine-tuning.

Hitting, Baserunning & Defense

Hitting from a relaxed, upright stance, Sweeney is a line-drive hitter with moderate gap power. Finesse pitchers easily fooled Sweeney when he first arrived from Omaha, but he made noticeable adjustments later in the year. He has occasionally shown a powerful arm, but he still needs to improve his footwork behind the plate. While Sweeney worked well with Rosado, learning to handle the veteran pitchers on the Royals' staff will take some time.

1997 Outlook

Sweeney will need at least one full year to get acclimated to the big leagues, and tutoring from veteran Mike Macfarlane will help him through the adjustment period in 1997. Sweeney, the Royals' catcher of the future, is projected to be a solid, everyday catcher in the majors.

Other Kansas City Royals

Brian Bevil (Pos: RHP, Age: 25)

	W	L	Pct.	ERA	G	GS	Sv	IP	H	BB	SO	HR	BR/IP
1996	1	0	1.000	5.73	3	1	0	11.0	9	5	7	2	1.27
Career	1	0	1.000	5.73	3	1	0	11.0	9	5	7	2	1.27

Bevil had a brief trial with the Royals last year, but spent most of the year in the minors, where he went 16-7 overall. He has an impressive strikeout record, and will get a long look this spring. 1997 Outlook: A

Jeff Granger (Pos: LHP, Age: 25)

	W	L	Pct.	ERA	G	GS	Sv	IP	H	BB	SO	HR	BR/IP
1996	0	0	-	6.61	15	0	0	16.1	21	10	11	3	1.90
Career	0	1	.000	7.43	18	2	0	26.2	37	18	15	5	2.06

The fifth overall pick in the 1993 draft, Granger was supposed to be starring for the Royals by now. Injuries have set him back, but he had a fine season at Triple-A Omaha last year. 1997 Outlook: B

Rick Huisman (Pos: RHP, Age: 27)

	W	L	Pct.	ERA	G	GS	Sv	IP	H	BB	SO	HR	BR/IP
1996	2	1	.667	4.60	22	0	1	29.1	25	18	23	4	1.47
Career	2	1	.667	5.31	29	0	1	39.0	39	19	35	6	1.49

A hard thrower who's had to battle back from injuries, Huisman finally got his first real major league chance last year. Results were so-so, but he has a decent chance at a bullpen job this season. 1997 Outlook: B

Mark Kiefer (Pos: RHP, Age: 28)

	W	L	Pct.	ERA	G	GS	Sv	IP	H	BB	SO	HR	BR/IP
1996	0	0	-	8.10	7	0	0	10.0	15	5	5	1	2.00
Career	5	1	.833	4.29	44	0	1	79.2	70	45	61	11	1.44

A long-time member of the Brewer system, Kiefer came to the Royals in a minor league deal last year. He got hit hard, but he pitched pretty well for Milwaukee in '95. 1997 Outlook: C

Henry Mercedes (Pos: C, Age: 27, Bats: R)

	G	AB	R	H	D	T	HR	RBI	SB	BB	SO	Avg	OBP	Slg
1996	4	4	1	1	0	0	0	0	0	0	1	.250	.250	.250
Career	56	99	14	26	4	1	0	13	1	10	30	.263	.336	.323

A backup-type catcher who's had brief chances with the A's and Royals, Mercedes was picked up by the Rangers after the 1996 season. Has a slight chance of making it as a number-two or three receiver. 1997 Outlook: C

Rod Myers (Pos: CF, Age: 24, Bats: L)

	G	AB	R	H	D	T	HR	RBI	SB	BB	SO	Avg	OBP	Slg
1996	22	63	9	18	7	0	1	11	3	7	16	.286	.357	.444
Career	22	63	9	18	7	0	1	11	3	7	16	.286	.357	.444

Myers had a solid year for the Royals' Triple-A team at Omaha last year, then looked good in 22 games with the big club. Has some power, speed and on-base ability, and could win a job. 1997 Outlook: B

Les Norman (Pos: RF/LF, Age: 28, Bats: R)

	G	AB	R	H	D	T	HR	RBI	SB	BB	SO	Avg	OBP	Slg
1996	54	49	9	6	0	0	0	0	1	6	14	.122	.232	.122
Career	78	89	15	15	0	1	0	4	1	12	20	.169	.275	.191

Norman has seen limited action with Kaycee the last couple of seasons as your basic 25th man, and shown very little. Will probably be back in the minors this year, barring some miracle. 1997 Outlook: D

Bob Scanlan (Pos: RHP, Age: 30)

	W	L	Pct.	ERA	G	GS	Sv	IP	H	BB	SO	HR	BR/IP
1996	0	1	.000	6.85	17	0	0	22.1	29	12	6	2	1.84
Career	20	33	.377	4.46	243	39	17	482.1	516	182	230	37	1.45

After getting lit up in eight games with the Tigers last year, Scanlan went down to the minors, then came back up with the Royals and pitched very well. Could stick around again this year. 1997 Outlook: B

Julio Valera (Pos: RHP, Age: 28)

	W	L	Pct.	ERA	G	GS	Sv	IP	H	BB	SO	HR	BR/IP
1996	3	2	.600	6.46	31	2	1	61.1	75	27	31	7	1.66
Career	15	20	.429	4.85	85	38	5	317.1	361	117	179	31	1.51

After a couple of years in the minors, Valera came back up to the majors wtih the Royals last season. He showed little and drew his release after the season. Has talent, might get another chance. 1997 Outlook: C

Kevin Young (Pos: 1B/RF, Age: 27, Bats: R)

	G	AB	R	H	D	T	HR	RBI	SB	BB	SO	Avg	OBP	Slg
1996	55	132	20	32	6	0	8	23	3	11	32	.242	.301	.470
Career	321	891	88	209	46	5	21	107	7	65	201	.235	.292	.368

After several disappointing seasons with the Pirates, Young was dealt to the Royals and had his best major league season last year. His versatility may keep him in the majors. 1997 Outlook: B

Kansas City Royals Minor League Prospects

Organization Overview:

Over the last four years, the Kansas City Royals' farm system has become one of the most well-respected in the game. The system produced another good rookie crop last year, as home-grown youngsters Johnny Damon, Michael Tucker, Mike Sweeney and Jose Rosado all played prominent roles on the major league club. The strength of the system is an abundance of pitching, catching and infield prospects at the higher levels, a wave of talent that is expected to make an impact over the next couple of years. The entire organization has become one of the most development-oriented in baseball, and the youngsters will be given every opportunity to advance to the majors when their time comes.

Sal Fasano

Position: C   **Opening Day Age:** 25
Bats: R **Throws:** R   **Born:** 8/10/71 in
Ht: 6' 2" **Wt:** 220   Chicago, IL

Recent Statistics

	G	AB	R	H	D	T	HR	RBI	SB	BB	SO	AVG
96 AAA Omaha	29	104	12	24	4	0	4	15	0	6	21	.231
96 AL Kansas City	51	143	20	29	2	0	6	19	1	14	25	.203

Last year was a stomach-turning roller-coaster ride for rookie catcher Sal Fasano. With no professional experience above Double-A, he nonetheless went north with the Royals in the spring. He played quite a bit in the first half, but his weight ballooned, and he was sent down after the All-Star break. Just to make sure he got the message, the Royals didn't even bother to call him up in September. Over the winter, he changed his diet, lost weight, and re-emerged as their top catching prospect. He's a great defender with a strong throwing arm, and he is got good power potential at the plate. The Royals may move Mike Sweeney to first base to make room for him.

Jed Hansen

Position: 2B   **Opening Day Age:** 24
Bats: R **Throws:** R   **Born:** 8/19/72 in
Ht: 6' 1" **Wt:** 195   Tacoma, WA

Recent Statistics

	G	AB	R	H	D	T	HR	RBI	SB	BB	SO	AVG
94 A Eugene	66	235	26	57	8	2	3	17	6	24	56	.243
95 A Springfield	122	414	86	107	27	7	9	50	44	78	73	.258
96 AA Wichita	99	405	60	116	27	4	12	50	14	29	72	.286
96 AAA Omaha	29	99	14	23	4	0	3	9	2	12	22	.232
96 MLE	128	482	55	117	26	3	10	44	10	27	94	.243

Someday very soon, Jed Hansen will be the Kansas City Royals' second baseman. He was the Royals' second-round pick in the '94 draft, and his big year at Double-A last year only accelerated his journey to the majors.

When he gets there, he'll hit for a decent average, with good power for a middle infielder. He's also a steady defender who can play all over the infield. He draws a few walks and steals some bases, and at age 24, he should keep on improving.

Mendy Lopez

Position: 3B   **Opening Day Age:** 22
Bats: R **Throws:** R   **Born:** 10/15/74 in
Ht: 6' 2" **Wt:** 165   Pimentol Provincia, DR

Recent Statistics

	G	AB	R	H	D	T	HR	RBI	SB	BB	SO	AVG
94 R Royals	59	235	56	85	19	3	5	50	19	22	27	.362
95 A Wilmington	130	428	42	116	29	3	2	36	18	28	73	.271
96 AA Wichita	93	327	47	92	20	5	6	32	14	26	67	.281
96 MLE	93	313	35	78	17	3	4	23	9	16	68	.249

Mendy Lopez is anything but your typical third base prospect; in fact, he looks a lot more like a shortstop, which he used to be. He has good speed and hits for a good average, but has very little power. He's thin as a rail, but the Royals think he'll be more of a run producer once he fills out. On defense, his range is simply astonishing, and he was voted the best defensive third baseman in the Texas League. That should add up to quite a package if he develops even a little power. Only 22 years old, he's got time yet.

Tony Medrano

Position: SS   **Opening Day Age:** 22
Bats: R **Throws:** R   **Born:** 12/8/74 in
Ht: 5' 11" **Wt:** 155   Bellflower, CA

Recent Statistics

	G	AB	R	H	D	T	HR	RBI	SB	BB	SO	AVG
93 R Blue Jays	39	158	20	42	9	0	0	9	6	10	9	.266
94 R Blue Jays	6	22	2	8	4	0	1	5	0	1	0	.364
94 A Dunedin	60	199	20	47	6	4	4	21	3	12	26	.236
95 AA Wichita	1	5	0	0	0	0	0	0	0	0	3	.000
95 A Wilmington	123	460	69	131	20	6	3	43	11	34	42	.285
96 AA Wichita	125	474	59	130	26	1	8	55	10	18	36	.274
96 MLE	125	453	44	109	22	0	5	41	6	11	36	.241

Young shortstop Tony Medrano has potential in a lot of areas. He could be a good leadoff hitter who sprays line drives to all fields, although he's still too impatient at the plate. Someday, he may be strong enough to drive the ball, but right now he's a 155-pound stick figure. He could be a standout defensive shortstop, although he's error-prone and needs to learn to position himself better. He could do a lot of things, and at age 22, he'll be given time to learn how.

Jon Nunnally

Position: OF　　**Opening Day Age:** 25
Bats: L **Throws:** R　　**Born:** 11/9/71 in
Ht: 5' 10" **Wt:** 188　　Pelham, NC

Recent Statistics

	G	AB	R	H	D	T	HR	RBI	SB	BB	SO	AVG
96 AAA Omaha	103	345	76	97	21	4	25	77	10	47	100	.281
96 AL Kansas City	35	90	16	19	5	1	5	17	0	13	25	.211
96 MLE	103	332	61	84	18	3	19	62	7	37	99	.253

After enjoying a solid rookie year in '95, Jon Nunnally was sent to Triple-A. He had a good year down there, and made strides in learning to hit lefties. Still, the Royals left him down there for most of the year, and he got only 90 at-bats with the big club. He remains a decent right fielder with a good arm and above-average speed. He's only 25, and the way the Royals have handled him has been confusing. He can help them—or someone else—either as a platoon outfielder, or as a full-timer.

Jim Pittsley

Position: P　　**Opening Day Age:** 22
Bats: R **Throws:** R　　**Born:** 4/3/74 in
Ht: 6' 7" **Wt:** 215　　Dubois, PA

Recent Statistics

	W	L	ERA	G	GS	Sv	IP	H	R	BB	SO	HR
93 A Rockford	5	5	4.26	15	15	0	80.1	76	43	32	87	3
94 A Wilmington	11	5	3.17	27	27	0	161.2	154	73	42	171	15
95 AAA Omaha	4	1	3.21	8	8	0	47.2	38	20	16	39	5
96 A Wilmington	0	1	11.00	2	2	0	9.0	13	12	5	10	4
96 AA Wichita	3	0	0.41	3	3	0	22.0	9	1	5	7	0
96 AAA Omaha	7	1	3.97	13	13	0	70.1	74	34	39	53	8

Is he really only 23 years old? It seems we've been hearing about him forever. He was on the verge of breaking through in '95 when a stiff elbow shut him down. It was feared that he'd need a full elbow reconstruction, but it turned out that all they had to do was repair the ligament. He spent last year working back up to full strength, and it took a while for his control to come around. Before the injury, he threw a 90-MPH fastball and a curve with good command, and he'll be a top prospect once again if he's able to throw like he used to. We'll find out this season.

Glendon Rusch

Position: P　　**Opening Day Age:** 22
Bats: L **Throws:** L　　**Born:** 11/7/74 in
Ht: 6' 2" **Wt:** 170　　Seattle, WA

Recent Statistics

	W	L	ERA	G	GS	Sv	IP	H	R	BB	SO	HR
93 R Royals	4	2	1.60	11	10	0	62.0	43	14	11	48	0
93 A Rockford	0	1	3.38	2	2	0	8.0	10	6	7	8	0
94 A Rockford	8	5	4.66	28	17	1	114.0	111	61	34	122	5
95 A Wilmington	14	6	1.74	26	26	0	165.2	110	41	34	147	15
96 AAA Omaha	11	9	3.98	28	28	0	169.2	177	88	40	117	15

At age 21, lefthander Glendon Rusch jumped from A-ball to Triple-A, and continued to confound hitters, without even reaching the upper-80s. In short, he's got everything you'd want except a fastball: an exceptional change-up, good breaking pitches, excellent command and uncommon poise. He was voted the best pitching prospect in the American Association, and may be less than a year away.

Chris Stynes

Position: OF-3B　　**Opening Day Age:** 24
Bats: R **Throws:** R　　**Born:** 1/19/73 in
Ht: 5' 9" **Wt:** 170　　Queens, NY

Recent Statistics

	G	AB	R	H	D	T	HR	RBI	SB	BB	SO	AVG
96 AAA Omaha	72	284	50	101	22	2	10	40	7	18	17	.356
96 AL Kansas City	36	92	8	27	6	0	0	6	5	2	5	.293
96 MLE	72	271	40	88	19	1	7	32	5	14	16	.325

Chris Stynes has the kind of tools that ensure that he'll always be underappreciated. He's a line-drive hitter with doubles power, and he's capable of hitting for a good average in the majors. His defense at second base is steady, if unspectacular, but the Royals refuse to take him seriously at that position. Instead, they've tried him at third base and left field, where his lack of home run power handicaps him. Still, in a half-season at Triple-A last year, at age 23, he hit .356 with 10 homers, and struck out only 17 times. As a second baseman, he's a prospect.

Others to Watch

Second baseman **Ramon Martinez** has little in common with his National League namesake. This Ramon hits for a decent average but is still a little raw in the field. . . Further down the ladder is another second baseman, **Carlos Febles**. He's still very young, but showed great on-base ability in A-ball last year. . . First baseman **Larry Sutton** returned from an injury last year, with a vengeance. After missing most of '95 with a broken elbow, the left-handed slugger batted .296 with 22 homers at Double-A. However, at age 27, his upside is limited. . . Left fielder **Ryan Long** developed a little more power in his second season at Double-A. He's still an impatient hitter and a defensive liability, so he's got a ways to go. . . Second baseman **Sergio Nunez** fared better in his second try at the high Class-A level. He's young and quick, and only needs to learn to get on base more.

Phil Garner

1996 Season

Phil Garner is a feisty leader who favors a National League style of play. Solid baserunning and fundamentals are important to him, as is tight defense. He doesn't mind casting his lot with young, unproven players, and he's successfully broken quite a few of them into the lineup. He always seems to get the most out of the talent he has to work with, and that continued to be the case in 1996.

Offense

Garner favors speed at the top of the lineup. Basestealing is a weapon he uses when he has the horses, but aggressive baserunning is expected of everyone at all times. He'll platoon to cover established players' weaknesses, but he'll rarely do it with a youngster. He has little patience for a player who strikes out a lot and won't make adjustments. He favors the hit-and-run, and he'll use the sacrifice and the squeeze more than most managers.

Pitching & Defense

In the middle of the diamond, Garner prefers glove men over hitters. His handling of pitchers has changed greatly in the past few seasons. When Cal Eldred blew out his elbow after years of heavy use, it made a distinct impression on Garner, who now watches his pitch counts religiously. He doesn't believe in easing a pitcher into a role—he'll take a young pitcher and immediately start using him in the role he envisions for the player.

1997 Outlook

In the past, Garner has done a good job of molding limited talent into a cohesive unit. But with a rebuilt pitching staff and an overhauled outfield, the 1997 Brewers will be a very different team. This time it will be Garner's job to meet expectations by keeping them over .500. Contention won't be demanded overnight, but there's a perception that the foundation for a winner has been laid. Garner will need to show some signs—however small—that he's actually building one.

Born: 4/30/49 in Jefferson City, TN

Playing Experience: 1973-1988, Oak, Pit, Hou, LA, SF

Managerial Experience: 5 seasons

Manager Statistics

Year	Team, Lg	W	L	Pct	GB	Finish
1996	Milwaukee, AL	80	82	.494	19.5	3rd Central
5 Seasons		359	386	.482	—	—

1996 Starting Pitchers by Days Rest

	≤3	4	5	6+
Brewers Starts	1	99	35	17
Brewers ERA	0.00	4.95	5.75	5.25
AL Avg Starts	4	96	30	21
AL ERA	5.57	4.90	5.33	5.81

1996 Situational Stats

	Phil Garner	AL Average
Hit & Run Success %	35.1	39.1
Stolen Base Success %	67.8	69.6
Platoon Pct.	59.4	61.9
Defensive Subs	46	29
High-Pitch Outings	13	23
Quick/Slow Hooks	24/24	17/20
Sacrifice Attempts	72	58

1996 Rankings (American League)

→ 1st in 2+ pitching changes in low scoring games (25)
→ 3rd in sacrifice bunt attempts (72), defensive substitutions (46) and quick hooks (24)

Jeromy Burnitz

1996 Season

At last, an opportunity! After missing his chances in New York and getting stuck behind talented outfielders in Cleveland, Jeromy Burnitz got traded to Milwaukee in August and finally got a chance to play. As their regular right fielder down the stretch, he displayed solid all-around tools, and seemed to justify the Brewers' faith that he could be their full-time right fielder.

Hitting

Burnitz is a low-ball hitter who gets good lift on the ball. He has the bat speed to put up good power numbers. He won't hit for a great average, but he is patient enough to draw his share of walks. He's never been given a full opportunity to show that he can hang in against lefthanders. If he gets a pitch he's looking for, he can hammer it, but once he falls behind in the count, he's easy prey.

Baserunning & Defense

Burnitz was a successful basestealer in the minors, and he still has good speed, but this is the first time he's played major league ball for a manager who values that aspect of his game. He has more than enough range for right field, played some left field and can even play center. His arm is strong and fairly accurate.

1997 Outlook

The Brewers have given Burnitz the right field job, and it is his to lose. He is certainly talented enough to hold the job, and after waiting in the wings for years, it isn't likely that he'll fritter away this opportunity. Although he doesn't possess any one particular skill that defines his game, he should be able to give the Brewers solid contributions across the board. If he's able to hit lefties, he projects as a productive regular.

Position: RF/CF/DH
Bats: L **Throws:** R
Ht: 6' 0" **Wt:** 190

Opening Day Age: 27
Born: 4/15/69 in Westminster, CA
ML Seasons: 4
Pronunciation: BURR-nitz

Overall Statistics

	G	AB	R	H	D	T	HR	RBI	SB	BB	SO	Avg	OBP	Slg
1996	94	200	38	53	14	0	9	40	4	33	47	.265	.377	.470
Career	234	613	117	155	29	6	25	93	8	94	158	.253	.356	.442

Where He Hits the Ball

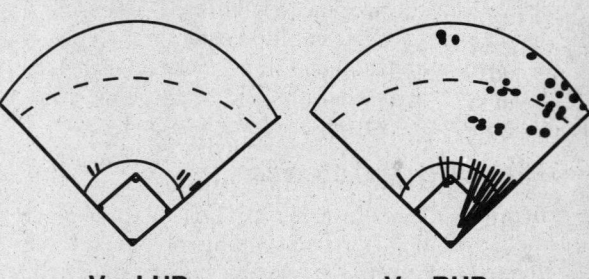

Vs. LHP   **Vs. RHP**

1996 Situational Stats

	AB	H	HR	RBI	Avg		AB	H	HR	RBI	Avg
Home	94	26	5	18	.277	LHP	26	7	1	6	.269
Road	106	27	4	22	.255	RHP	174	46	8	34	.264
First Half	50	14	3	8	.280	Sc Pos	63	16	3	32	.254
Scnd Half	150	39	6	32	.260	Clutch	38	9	3	4	.237

1996 Rankings (American League)

➡ Did not rank near the top or bottom in any category

Jeff Cirillo

Position: 3B
Bats: R **Throws:** R
Ht: 6' 2" **Wt:** 188

Opening Day Age: 27
Born: 9/23/69 in Pasadena, CA
ML Seasons: 3
Pronunciation: suh-RILL-o

1996 Season

For the second straight year, Jeff Cirillo began the season fighting Kevin Seitzer for playing time at third base. With a torrent of line drives, Cirillo once again ran Seitzer off the hot corner—this time for good. The singles and doubles came in bushels as Cirillo developed into a premier number-two hitter. By the end of the year, he had established himself as the Brewers' third baseman for many years to come.

Hitting

At the plate, Cirillo models himself after former teammate Seitzer, lining shots to all fields. He covers the whole plate by crowding it, which enables him to reach the outside pitch. If the ball is in on his hands, he has the quickness to pull his hands in and line it the other way. He knows better than to swing for the fences, but he can shoot balls into the gaps with the best of them.

Baserunning & Defense

Cirillo has decent speed and knows how to run the bases. He's never been a big basestealer, and his running game was hampered by a sore knee last year. At third base, he has all the tools to be a top-notch defender, with great reactions and one of the strongest arms in the league. His 18 errors—most coming on hurried throws—topped A.L. third basemen, but his range is very good, and he doesn't have far to go to become one of the best.

1997 Outlook

As a major building block in the Brewers' youth movement, Cirillo should be manning third base for many years to come. He's a little too old to project as a superstar, but his season shouldn't be written off as a fluke, either. Yes, the late-blooming Cirillo really *is* this good, as the rest of the league is quickly becoming aware.

Overall Statistics

	G	AB	R	H	D	T	HR	RBI	SB	BB	SO	Avg	OBP	Slg
1996	158	566	101	184	46	5	15	83	4	58	69	.325	.391	.504
Career	322	1020	175	305	74	9	27	134	11	116	127	.299	.374	.469

Where He Hits the Ball

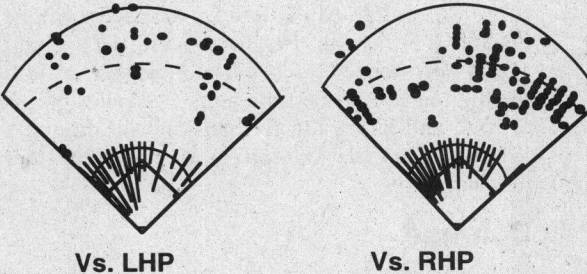

Vs. LHP   **Vs. RHP**

1996 Situational Stats

	AB	H	HR	RBI	Avg		AB	H	HR	RBI	Avg
Home	272	81	6	39	.298	LHP	161	50	6	12	.311
Road	294	103	9	44	.350	RHP	405	134	9	71	.331
First Half	277	93	6	39	.336	Sc Pos	133	44	5	63	.331
Scnd Half	289	91	9	44	.315	Clutch	72	25	2	12	.347

1996 Rankings (American League)

- ➞ 1st in errors at third base (18)
- ➞ 2nd in lowest fielding percentage at third base (.950)
- ➞ 4th in doubles
- ➞ 5th in batting average on the road (.350)
- ➞ 7th in batting average in the clutch (.347)
- ➞ 8th in games played (158) and highest groundball/flyball ratio (1.7)
- ➞ 10th in hits and caught stealing (9)
- ➞ Led the Brewers in at-bats, hits, doubles, sacrifice flies (6), caught stealing, plate appearances (643), games played (158), batting average on the road (.350) and batting average with two strikes (.256)

Jeff D'Amico

1996 Season

Boy, *that* was a quick trip up the ladder. At the start of the season, 20-year-old Jeff D'Amico was a former number-one pick who'd been bothered by injuries for most of his pro career. He was sent to Double-A to begin the year, and no one expected to see him in a big league uniform anytime soon. D'Amico, however, so completely overpowered Texas League hitters that the Brewers brought him up directly to the majors before the All-Star break. He hit some rough patches along the way, but showed enough ability to remain in the rotation for the rest of the year.

Pitching

His curveball, change-up and forkball are all useful pitches, but D'Amico's ticket to success will be his 90-MPH fastball. He still must refine his control of his offspeed pitches, which he sets up with the high heat. For the time being, he relies on his fastball and hopes the fly balls stay in the park. When he harnesses his stuff, he may put it together in a hurry.

Defense

For someone who's six-foot-seven, D'Amico is surprisingly quick off the mound. Few expected the youngster to show such polish on the finer points like fielding comebackers, covering first base and holding runners.

1997 Outlook

D'Amico made a huge leap last year, and it may take him a while to get his feet on the ground. Phil Garner has kept him under a strict pitch count, so even at his tender age, burnout shouldn't be a major concern. He has all the tools, so it's only a matter of learning how to use them. Unless an injury stops him, D'Amico should develop into one of the better pitchers in the league. Can he do it this year? It's not very *likely*, but it's certainly possible.

Position: SP
Bats: R **Throws:** R
Ht: 6' 7" **Wt:** 250

Opening Day Age: 21
Born: 12/27/75 in St. Petersburg, FL
ML Seasons: 1
Pronunciation: Da-MEE-ko

Overall Statistics

	W	L	Pct.	ERA	G	GS	Sv	IP	H	BB	SO	HR	BR/IP
1996	6	6	.500	5.44	17	17	0	86.0	88	31	53	21	1.38
Career	6	6	.500	5.44	17	17	0	86.0	88	31	53	21	1.38

How Often He Throws Strikes

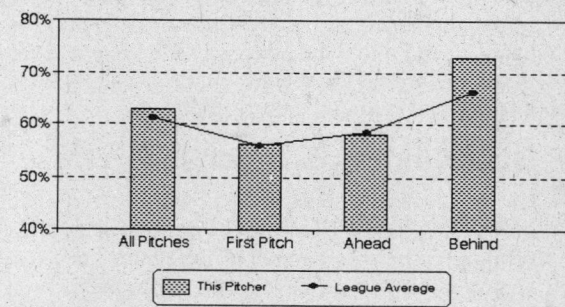

1996 Situational Stats

	W	L	ERA	Sv	IP		AB	H	HR	RBI	Avg
Home	3	4	5.65	0	43.0	LHB	185	54	12	28	.292
Road	3	2	5.23	0	43.0	RHB	145	34	9	20	.234
First Half	1	1	4.82	0	9.1	Sc Pos	59	20	4	27	.339
Scnd Half	5	5	5.52	0	76.2	Clutch	3	3	0	1	1.000

1996 Rankings (American League)

➡ 10th in balks (1)
➡ Led the Brewers in balks (1)

Cal Eldred

1996 Season

After undergoing ligament transplant surgery in June of 1995, Cal Eldred began 1996 as a major question mark. Through strenuous rehab, he brought himself back ahead of schedule and returned to the rotation at the All-Star break. It took a while for him to work his way back up to full strength. Held to a limit of 100 pitches, Eldred made impressive strides in recovering his velocity and stamina. By the end of the year, he was looking very much like the Cal Eldred of old.

Pitching

Eldred likes to work up and down in the strike zone. He comes in high with a 90-MPH fastball, and then throws an overhand curve that looks deceptively similar until it drops below the hitter's knees. He'll mix in a change-up a few times a game. When his high heat catches too much of the plate, it can often end up in the bleachers. Walks are sometimes a problem, especially when he can't get his curve over.

Defense

With a high leg kick and an unconvincing pickoff move, Eldred can be an easy target for basestealers. He doesn't give away anything with the glove, however. He's a good athlete with good reflexes, and he fields his position well.

1997 Outlook

Phil Garner seems to have learned a lesson from Eldred's injury: watch the pitch counts. Garner used to leave Eldred out there all day, but now keeps him on a strict pitch limit. With more careful handling, Eldred should continue to rebuild the stamina he lost. Although he won't be asked to throw 260 innings a year any more, he'll likely be just as effective as the Eldred of days past.

Position: SP
Bats: R **Throws:** R
Ht: 6' 4" **Wt:** 236

Opening Day Age: 29
Born: 11/24/67 in Cedar Rapids, IA
ML Seasons: 6

Milwaukee Brewers

Overall Statistics

	W	L	Pct.	ERA	G	GS	Sv	IP	H	BB	SO	HR	BR/IP
1996	4	4	.500	4.46	15	15	0	84.2	82	38	50	8	1.42
Career	45	34	.570	3.90	97	97	0	661.2	592	252	418	73	1.28

How Often He Throws Strikes

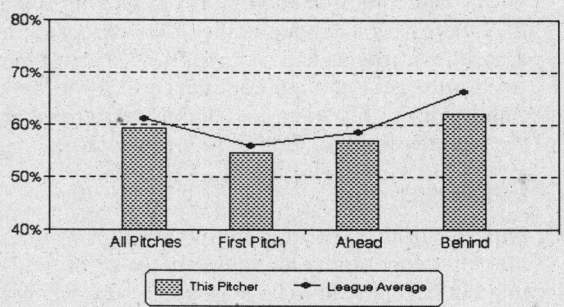

1996 Situational Stats

	W	L	ERA	Sv	IP		AB	H	HR	RBI	Avg
Home	1	3	4.96	0	45.1	LHB	164	50	5	19	.305
Road	3	1	3.89	0	39.1	RHB	153	32	3	20	.209
First Half	0	0	-	0	0.0	Sc Pos	80	24	3	31	.300
Scnd Half	4	4	4.46	0	84.2	Clutch	15	3	0	0	.200

1996 Rankings (American League)

→ Did not rank near the top or bottom in any category

Mike Fetters

1996 Season

In 1995, Mike Fetters took major steps toward solidifying his role as the Brewers' closer. Last year, he locked up the job and threw away the key. Although the Brewers' relief corps was constantly unsettled, when the ninth inning came, Phil Garner always knew whom to call. Fetters answered the bell from wire to wire, finishing fifth in the league in saves and giving the Brewers an unquestioned stopper for the first time in years.

Pitching

Fetters has become one of the best short relievers in the league by using an amazingly simple formula. When he throws his low-90s fastball at the knees, and comes back with his devastating forkball, there isn't much for a hitter to do except to hit a harmless ground ball. Although it's taken time for him to gain enough confidence to do it, he's finally junked his slider and committed to live or die with the forkball. So far, he's living large.

Defense

Fetters' turning, rolling follow-through affords him little opportunity to indulge in the art of fielding, but he's proven to be reasonably sure-handed when the occasion arises. As far as holding runners, Fetters' philosophy is to get the out at the plate. His pickoff move is a stern glare toward first base, and basestealers can get a decent jump on his stretch delivery.

1997 Outlook

For the foreseeable future, whenever the Brewers win, chances are that Fetters will be on the mound for the final out. They locked him up with a two-year deal during the season, so he isn't going anywhere. Now, on an improving club with a great defensive infield behind him, his success should continue. He has proven—to the Brewers, and to himself—that he can do the job.

Position: RP
Bats: R **Throws:** R
Ht: 6' 4"   **Wt:** 224

Opening Day Age: 32
Born: 12/19/64 in Van Nuys, CA
ML Seasons: 8

Overall Statistics

	W	L	Pct.	ERA	G	GS	Sv	IP	H	BB	SO	HR	BR/IP
1996	3	3	.500	3.38	61	0	32	61.1	65	26	53	4	1.48
Career	15	20	.429	3.37	284	6	74	379.2	378	168	246	28	1.44

How Often He Throws Strikes

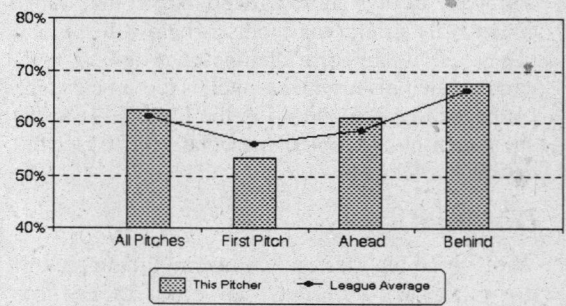

1996 Situational Stats

	W	L	ERA	Sv	IP		AB	H	HR	RBI	Avg
Home	3	2	4.60	10	31.1	LHB	136	38	3	19	.279
Road	0	1	2.10	22	30.0	RHB	101	27	1	10	.267
First Half	1	1	2.03	16	31.0	Sc Pos	76	19	1	24	.250
Scnd Half	2	2	4.75	16	30.1	Clutch	155	47	2	22	.303

1996 Rankings (American League)

→ 5th in saves and save percentage (84.2%)
→ 6th in games finished (55), save opportunities (38) and worst first batter efficiency (.327)
→ 8th in blown saves (6)
→ Led the Brewers in games pitched, saves, games finished (55), save opportunities (38), save percentage (84.2%), blown saves (6), relief ERA (3.38), lowest batting average allowed in relief (.274) and most strikeouts per 9 innings in relief (7.8)

John Jaha

Position: 1B/DH
Bats: R **Throws:** R
Ht: 6' 1" **Wt:** 222

Opening Day Age: 30
Born: 5/27/66 in Portland, OR
ML Seasons: 5

1996 Season

After John Jaha broke out with a monster partial-season in 1995, the only question was whether he could stay healthy and keep it up over a full year. By any measure, the answer was a resounding, "Yes!" Jaha was able to avoid the nagging injuries that have plagued him in the past, and kept up his blistering pace of the year before. He cracked the A.L. top 10 in RBI and provided the big bat at first base that the Brewers have been looking for since Cecil Cooper's heyday.

Hitting

Crowding the plate gives Jaha good plate coverage and enables him to hit the ball to all fields with excellent power. He likes to get an inside fastball to drive, and he'll wait patiently if he doesn't get what he's looking for. Pitchers try to negate his power by keeping the ball down, but he's still content to ground a single through the infield.

Baserunning & Defense

Jaha no longer has enough speed to even attempt to steal, but he handles himself adeptly around the first base bag. He shows good hands and decent range at first base, as well as an accurate arm.

1997 Outlook

With the trade of Greg Vaughn, the Brewers have made one thing crystal clear: they will be counting on Jaha to anchor the middle of the order from now on. His first few seasons in the majors were regarded as somewhat disappointing in light of his minor league numbers, but Jaha has finally made good on his promise. Unless the nagging injuries return, he should remain among the league's most productive hitters.

Overall Statistics

	G	AB	R	H	D	T	HR	RBI	SB	BB	SO	Avg	OBP	Slg
1996	148	543	108	163	28	1	34	118	3	85	118	.300	.398	.543
Career	520	1798	307	498	86	4	87	302	31	216	398	.277	.361	.474

Where He Hits the Ball

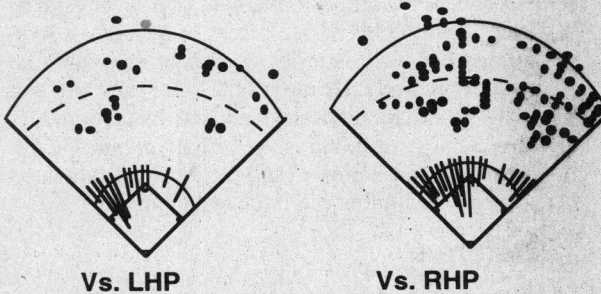

Vs. LHP   **Vs. RHP**

1996 Situational Stats

	AB	H	HR	RBI	Avg		AB	H	HR	RBI	Avg
Home	253	78	17	54	.308	LHP	124	46	7	27	.371
Road	290	85	17	64	.293	RHP	419	117	27	91	.279
First Half	289	85	16	65	.294	Sc Pos	168	51	11	87	.304
Scnd Half	254	78	18	53	.307	Clutch	69	20	3	20	.290

1996 Rankings (American League)

→ 3rd in on-base percentage vs. left-handed pitchers (.487)
→ 8th in most pitches seen per plate appearance (4.13) and batting average vs. left-handed pitchers (.371)
→ 9th in RBI and errors at first base (6)
→ 10th in batting average with the bases loaded (.500) and cleanup slugging percentage (.549)
→ Led the Brewers in home runs, runs scored, total bases (295), RBI, walks, times on base (253), GDPs (16), pitches seen (2,627), slugging percentage, HR frequency (16.0 ABs per HR), most pitches seen per plate appearance (4.13) and batting average with the bases loaded (.500)

Scott Karl

1996 Season

The 1996 season was a learning experience for the Brewers' young southpaw, Scott Karl. He started strong, finished strong, and slumped in-between, but overall, his season was a solid step forward. He showed uncommon durability, taking his turn every fifth day and pitching late into games fairly consistently. Even more importantly, he became one of the winningest lefthanders in the league, and showed the potential to solidify his spot in that rare class.

Pitching

Like many lefties, Karl gets the job done without Grade-A heat. His fastball only reaches the mid-80s, but it has good movement and he is able to keep it on the black. He mixes in a decent curve, but his out pitch is a heavy change-up, which he locates precisely. He moves the ball in and out, and isn't afraid to pitch inside. Left-handed hitters have a hard time picking up the ball on him. He did have a few problems with righties, and might need to work on another pitch to use against them.

Defense

Although he committed three errors last year, Karl is a mobile and sure-handed fielder who can handle anything hit back up the middle. His pickoff move is one of the league's best, and shuts down the running game almost completely. Baserunners are starting to take more conservative leads, but he keeps on hanging them out to dry.

1997 Outlook

Karl is young, durable, and intelligent. He knows how to pitch, and he's already experienced success in the big leagues. His lack of velocity is his only shortcoming, but many lefthanders have succeeded with less. The Brewers will continue to count on him as one of their top starters, and there's every reason to expect his maturation and development to continue in 1997.

Position: SP
Bats: L **Throws:** L
Ht: 6' 2" **Wt:** 195

Opening Day Age: 25
Born: 8/9/71 in Fontana, CA
ML Seasons: 2

Overall Statistics

	W	L	Pct.	ERA	G	GS	Sv	IP	H	BB	SO	HR	BR/IP
1996	13	9	.591	4.86	32	32	0	207.1	220	72	121	29	1.41
Career	19	16	.543	4.59	57	50	0	331.1	361	122	180	39	1.46

How Often He Throws Strikes

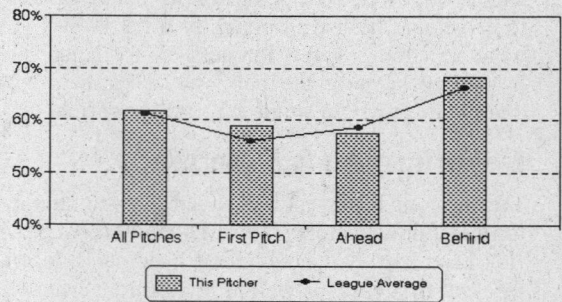

1996 Situational Stats

	W	L	ERA	Sv	IP		AB	H	HR	RBI	Avg
Home	6	6	5.64	0	99.0	LHB	156	33	5	15	.212
Road	7	3	4.15	0	108.1	RHB	657	187	24	91	.285
First Half	8	4	4.50	0	110.0	Sc Pos	179	47	6	72	.263
Scnd Half	5	5	5.27	0	97.1	Clutch	22	6	0	2	.273

1996 Rankings (American League)

- ➡ 3rd in errors at pitcher (3)
- ➡ 4th in most run support per 9 innings (6.8) and highest ERA at home (5.64)
- ➡ 5th in hit batsmen (11)
- ➡ 6th in shutouts (1)
- ➡ 7th in lowest fielding percentage at pitcher (.930)
- ➡ 8th in least strikeouts per 9 innings (5.3)
- ➡ 9th in lowest stolen base percentage allowed (46.7%)
- ➡ 10th in balks (1), highest slugging percentage allowed (.448), least pitches thrown per batter (3.68) and most home runs allowed per 9 innings (1.26)

Pat Listach

Position: CF/2B
Bats: B **Throws:** R
Ht: 5' 9" **Wt:** 180

Opening Day Age: 29
Born: 9/12/67 in
Natchitoches, LA
ML Seasons: 5

1996 Season

Pat Listach's long, strange trip continued last year. Finally healthy, he was moved to center field when Chuck Carr and David Hulse got hurt. He performed reasonably well in the outfield and in the leadoff spot (despite his .398 on-base percentage as a starter in June, his on-base percentage for the season was predictably low), and seemed to have recovered much of the speed he'd lost. But in June came a shoulder injury that landed him on the DL. When he returned, he played poorly and was traded to the Yankees, who discovered that Listach had broken his foot just before the trade. The Yanks sent him back to the Brewers, who eventually released him.

Hitting

A switch-hitter, Listach slaps the ball on the ground from either side of the plate. He's more apt to pull the ball from the right side, his strong side. Batting lefty, he's a far weaker hitter, and prefers the ball down. He has the speed to bunt but doesn't often get the ball down successfully.

Baserunning & Defense

Listach's legs were much healthier last year, and it showed. Even in part-time play, Listach was one of the league's most effective basestealers. He was rarely thrown out, and even swiped third base seven times. With little previous experience in center field, Listach showed good range but still needs to learn to read a fly ball. His average arm was adequate for the position. Second base is where he looks the most comfortable, although he can still play shortstop.

1997 Outlook

His days in Milwaukee are over. Listach found his talents in demand in Houston, and the club signed him to a one-year deal. A switch-hitting infielder/outfielder should be able to help the Astros in some capacity. He remains a solid hitter from the right side and a good defensive infielder. How much of an opportunity he'll get—and how healthy he'll be—are impossible to tell.

Overall Statistics

	G	AB	R	H	D	T	HR	RBI	SB	BB	SO	Avg	OBP	Slg
1996	87	317	51	76	16	2	1	33	25	36	51	.240	.317	.312
Career	451	1640	237	420	61	11	5	137	112	156	314	.256	.322	.316

Where He Hits the Ball

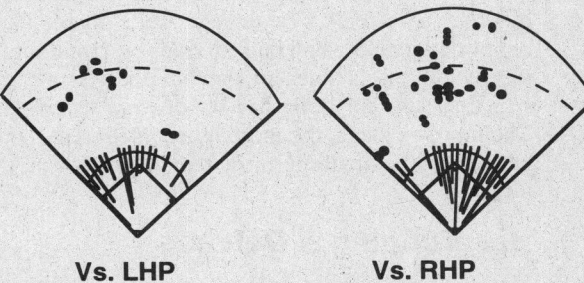

Vs. LHP   **Vs. RHP**

1996 Situational Stats

	AB	H	HR	RBI	Avg		AB	H	HR	RBI	Avg
Home	176	49	1	23	.278	LHP	121	37	1	10	.306
Road	141	27	0	10	.191	RHP	196	39	0	23	.199
First Half	192	52	1	20	.271	Sc Pos	74	22	0	31	.297
Scnd Half	125	24	0	13	.192	Clutch	43	7	0	3	.163

1996 Rankings (American League)

→ 1st in lowest batting average on a 3-2 count (.054)
→ 2nd in stolen base percentage (83.3%) and lowest on-base percentage for a leadoff hitter (.304)
→ 4th in least GDPs per GDP situation (3.6%) and steals of third (7)
→ 5th in errors in center field (3)
→ 6th in lowest batting average in the clutch (.163)
→ 8th in stolen bases
→ Led the Brewers in stolen bases, stolen base percentage (83.3%) and steals of third (7)

Mike Matheny

1996 Season

With no one else to turn to last year, the Brewers gave the catching chores to young defensive specialist Mike Matheny. At first, his bat was surprisingly potent. He drove in 30 runs over the first two months of the season, but reality soon set in. Matheny endured a horrific slump in June and July in which he not only lost his job, but even got sent back to the minors. He was recalled in September, but didn't play very often—or very well— thereafter.

Hitting

Matheny's swing is so defensive that it seems his only purpose at the plate is to avoid striking out. In spite of such efforts, pitchers have no trouble blowing a fastball by him for strike three. He chops down on the ball and survives by grounding the ball through holes in the infield. When the situation calls for it, he can lay down a sacrifice. The more he plays, the more it becomes clear that he'll never be anything more than a number-nine hitter.

Baserunning & Defense

Matheny has decent speed but rarely gets the chance to display it. His defensive skills are what's gotten him to the majors. He possesses a strong, accurate arm, and his ability to block balls in the dirt gives young pitchers the confidence to throw their breaking ball.

1997 Outlook

By the end of '96, the Brewers seemed to have given up on Matheny. Between his August demotion and September bench-riding, the handwriting was on the wall. It now seems clear that the Brewers will go outside the organization to pursue a starting catcher. However, Matheny's defense should be enough to keep him around in a backup role, to which he's well-suited.

Position: C
Bats: R **Throws:** R
Ht: 6' 3" **Wt:** 205

Opening Day Age: 26
Born: 9/22/70 in Columbus, OH
ML Seasons: 3

Overall Statistics

	G	AB	R	H	D	T	HR	RBI	SB	BB	SO	Avg	OBP	Slg
1996	106	313	31	64	15	2	8	46	3	14	80	.204	.243	.342
Career	214	532	47	117	27	3	9	69	5	29	121	.220	.267	.333

Where He Hits the Ball

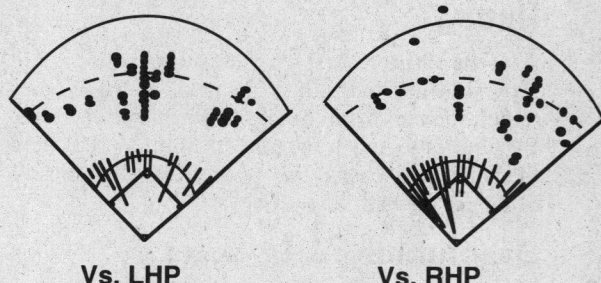

Vs. LHP　　　　**Vs. RHP**

1996 Situational Stats

	AB	H	HR	RBI	Avg		AB	H	HR	RBI	Avg
Home	147	31	5	22	.211	LHP	104	20	0	14	.192
Road	166	33	3	24	.199	RHP	209	44	8	32	.211
First Half	230	48	4	37	.209	Sc Pos	87	24	1	38	.276
Scnd Half	83	16	4	9	.193	Clutch	32	5	1	2	.156

1996 Rankings (American League)

➡ 1st in lowest batting average with two strikes (.066), lowest fielding percentage at catcher (.985) and lowest batting average on an 0-2 count (.000)
➡ 4th in errors at catcher (8)
➡ Led the Brewers in sacrifice bunts (7)

Ben McDonald

1996 Season

When the Brewers signed Ben McDonald before the season, little did they know that it would turn out to be one of the year's best free-agent signings. McDonald took his regular turn all year and showed no signs of the shoulder problems that had troubled him in 1995. What's more, he became the unquestioned ace of the staff, finishing ninth in the league in ERA. McDonald suffered through a rough stretch in August, going 0-5 with a 6.23 ERA, but recovered and finished the year strongly. The stabilizing presence of "Big Ben" was invaluable on a mound corps with few constants.

Pitching

With the shoulder completely healed, McDonald was again reaching the low 90s last year. With his hard curve and an occasional change-up, he used the same formula that had worked so well for him in Baltimore. He can get burned when he leaves his pitches up, but when he's on, he can set up the curve and make batters hit it on the ground.

Defense

McDonald can cover first when he needs to, but tends to get overanxious on comebackers—a tendency that led to six errors last year, the most in the majors by a pitcher. He has an average move to first, but his rather slow delivery puts him at a disadvantage against basestealers.

1997 Outlook

When you're looking for a staff leader, McDonald fulfills all the criteria: he takes the ball every five days and gives you a solid effort. He was handled more carefully last year, which should bode well for his future health. The Brewers will continue to build their rotation around him. At age 29, McDonald's best years still may be ahead of him. Look for his fortunes to improve as the team develops around him.

Position: SP
Bats: R **Throws:** R
Ht: 6' 7" **Wt:** 214

Opening Day Age: 29
Born: 11/24/67 in Baton Rouge, LA
ML Seasons: 8

Overall Statistics

	W	L	Pct.	ERA	G	GS	Sv	IP	H	BB	SO	HR	BR/IP
1996	12	10	.545	3.90	35	35	0	221.1	228	67	146	25	1.33
Career	70	63	.526	3.89	190	177	0	1158.1	1066	401	784	125	1.27

How Often He Throws Strikes

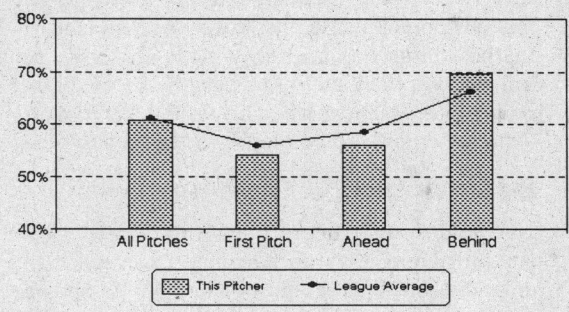

1996 Situational Stats

	W	L	ERA	Sv	IP		AB	H	HR	RBI	Avg
Home	6	7	4.16	0	119.0	LHB	496	129	16	48	.260
Road	6	3	3.61	0	102.1	RHB	367	99	9	44	.270
First Half	9	3	3.92	0	117.0	Sc Pos	205	46	2	64	.224
Scnd Half	3	7	3.88	0	104.1	Clutch	37	6	0	0	.162

1996 Rankings (American League)

→ 1st in errors at pitcher (6) and lowest fielding percentage at pitcher (.878)
→ 2nd in games started
→ 5th in lowest batting average allowed with runners in scoring position (.224)
→ 6th in least GDPs induced per 9 innings (0.6) and ERA on the road (3.61)
→ 8th in lowest on-base percentage allowed (.319)
→ 9th in ERA and highest groundball/flyball ratio allowed (1.4)
→ 10th in least baserunners allowed per 9 innings (12.2)
→ Led the Brewers in ERA, games started, innings pitched and hits allowed

Marc Newfield

1996 Season

How's that for seizing the moment? For three years, Marc Newfield couldn't find a way to break into the Seattle Mariners or San Diego Padres' lineup, but when a late-season trade to Milwaukee made him the Brewers' left fielder, he took the job and ran with it. As a Brewer, Newfield displayed the line-drive power that's always had people raving about his offensive potential. What he *didn't* show was also significant—the rumored problems about his defense and his attitude never surfaced.

Hitting

Newfield is one of those rare young hitters who can hit for power without sacrificing contact. His low strikeout rate is exceptional for someone with his RBI potential. He hits line drives and is learning how to go the other way. Although he's been impatient at the plate in the past, he seemed more relaxed late last year when he didn't have to worry about whether he'd be playing the next day.

Baserunning & Defense

Newfield simply doesn't have the speed to be anything more than an adequate baserunner and defender, but that should be enough. He showed average range in left field, to go with a throwing arm that was weak, if accurate.

1997 Outlook

Newfield was arrested for possession of marijuana in late September. As a first-time offender, he probably won't be suspended, but the arrest was a sign that he still needs to develop some maturity. He's still very young, and at 24 has plenty of time to grow into an outstanding player. All he's ever needed is for a team to have patience with him. Now, the Brewers will give him the same opportunity they gave Greg Vaughn eight years ago: they'll plant him in left field and let him grow and develop.

Position: LF/RF
Bats: R **Throws:** R
Ht: 6' 4" **Wt:** 205

Opening Day Age: 24
Born: 10/19/72 in Sacramento, CA
ML Seasons: 4

Overall Statistics

	G	AB	R	H	D	T	HR	RBI	SB	BB	SO	Avg	OBP	Slg
1996	133	370	48	103	26	0	12	57	1	27	70	.278	.332	.446
Career	212	614	69	158	38	1	18	89	1	36	106	.257	.303	.410

Where He Hits the Ball

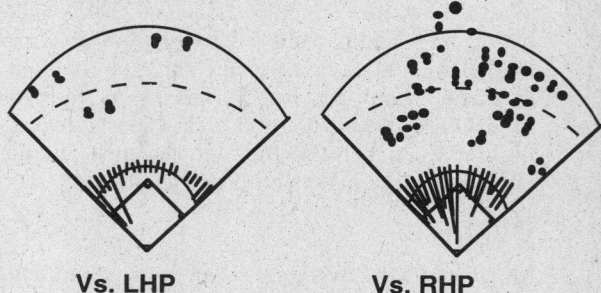

Vs. LHP   Vs. RHP

1996 Situational Stats

	AB	H	HR	RBI	Avg		AB	H	HR	RBI	Avg
Home	171	42	5	25	.246	LHP	89	26	1	11	.292
Road	199	61	7	32	.307	RHP	281	77	11	46	.274
First Half	149	43	4	22	.289	Sc Pos	114	26	4	43	.228
Scnd Half	221	60	8	35	.271	Clutch	60	16	2	8	.267

1996 Rankings (American League)
→ Did not rank near the top or bottom in any category

Dave Nilsson

1996 Season

Although he's still having trouble finding a position, Dave Nilsson is looking more and more at home in the batter's box. After missing most of April with a hairline fracture in his foot, he started hot and never cooled off, finishing with the sixth-highest average in the A.L. He played first base, right field, designated hitter—wherever they could fit him in on any given day—but one place you were always sure to find him was right in the heart of the Milwaukee batting order. Nilsson's monster season established him as one of the Brewer's most dangerous clutch hitters and most valuable run producers.

Hitting

Nilsson is a low-ball hitter who is particularly deadly against righthanders. His favorite pitch is down and in, but he can hit the outside pitch with power to left field. Long fly balls into the gaps are his trademark. Lefties still give him trouble, especially when he pulls off the breaking pitch down and away.

Baserunning & Defense

On the bases, it quickly becomes apparent that Nilsson used to be a catcher. In the outfield, he takes good angles to the ball, but his lack of speed limits his range. His arm is strong enough for right field, and his throwing accuracy has improved with experience. Still, it's apparent that his future is at first base.

1997 Outlook

With the recent infusion of young talent into the Milwaukee outfield, Nilsson may be pushed into a full-time DH role this year. That may be just what the big ex-catcher needs to finally get through a full season without an injury. He's made tremendous strides as a hitter since moving out from behind the plate. All that's left for him to do is to conquer his weakness against lefties and remain healthy for a full season.

Position: RF/1B/DH
Bats: L **Throws:** R
Ht: 6' 3" **Wt:** 231

Opening Day Age: 27
Born: 12/14/69 in Brisbane, Queensland, Australia
ML Seasons: 5
Pronunciation: NILL-son

Overall Statistics

	G	AB	R	H	D	T	HR	RBI	SB	BB	SO	Avg	OBP	Slg
1996	123	453	81	150	33	2	17	84	2	57	68	.331	.407	.525
Career	464	1573	223	446	91	8	52	271	10	169	224	.284	.351	.451

Where He Hits the Ball

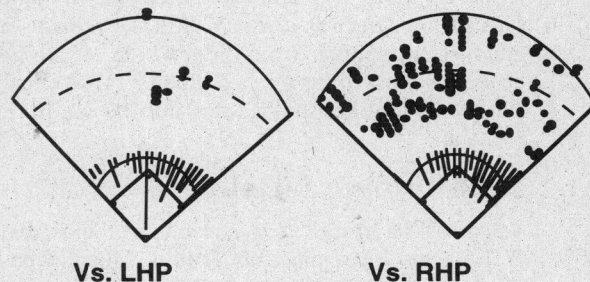

Vs. LHP   **Vs. RHP**

1996 Situational Stats

	AB	H	HR	RBI	Avg		AB	H	HR	RBI	Avg
Home	228	74	3	42	.325	LHP	105	25	1	12	.238
Road	225	76	14	42	.338	RHP	348	125	16	72	.359
First Half	181	60	9	39	.331	Sc Pos	131	44	4	63	.336
Scnd Half	272	90	8	45	.331	Clutch	58	22	2	9	.379

1996 Rankings (American League)

- → 1st in batting average in the clutch (.379) and batting average vs. right-handed pitchers (.359)
- → 3rd in least GDPs per GDP situation (3.4%)
- → 5th in on-base percentage vs. right-handed pitchers (.440)
- → 6th in batting average on the road (.338) and batting average
- → 8th in slugging percentage vs. right-handed pitchers (.595) and errors in right field (4)
- → 9th in cleanup slugging percentage (.565)
- → Led the Brewers in on-base percentage, batting average with runners in scoring position (.336) and batting average in the clutch (.379)

Jose Valentin

1996 Season

Last year, Jose Valentin exploded on the scene as a multi-dimensional talent. Combining power, speed and flashy defense, Valentin moved into the upper echelon of major league shortstops. Although he didn't make a major leap forward in any one area, he smoothed over some of the rough edges of his game and matured into a very complete player.

Hitting

After looking foolish against lefties for his entire career, the switch-hitting Valentin worked hard in the offseason to improve his swing from the right side. It worked: he raised his average over 100 points from that side and belted the first two home runs of his career as a righty. Still, he remains a much stronger hitter from the left side, where he generates most of his extra-base hits. From either side, Valentin likes the ball down so he can lift it in the air.

Baserunning & Defense

Valentin's baserunning is one of the things that Phil Garner loves most about him. Valentin has great speed—probably the best on the team—but more importantly, he runs with alertness and intelligence, and rarely gets himself thrown out. Despite his high error total, Valentin's defense is also a strength. Many of his 1996 miscues were throwing errors caused by a sore shoulder early in the year. His range is among the best in the game, and his strong arm is an asset whether he's making a play in the hole or starting a double play.

1997 Outlook

What separates Valentin from other offensive shortstops is that he can truly field his position. For next year, his assignment remains the same: improve his right-handed hitting and cut down on the errors. Considering the way he's attacked his weaknesses in the past, it's a safe bet that he'll continue to develop into one of the game's best shortstops.

Position: SS
Bats: B **Throws:** R
Ht: 5'10" **Wt:** 166

Opening Day Age: 27
Born: 10/12/69 in Manati, PR
ML Seasons: 5

Overall Statistics

	G	AB	R	H	D	T	HR	RBI	SB	BB	SO	Avg	OBP	Slg
1996	154	552	90	143	33	7	24	95	17	66	145	.259	.336	.475
Career	386	1231	210	298	76	12	47	198	46	148	319	.242	.322	.438

Where He Hits the Ball

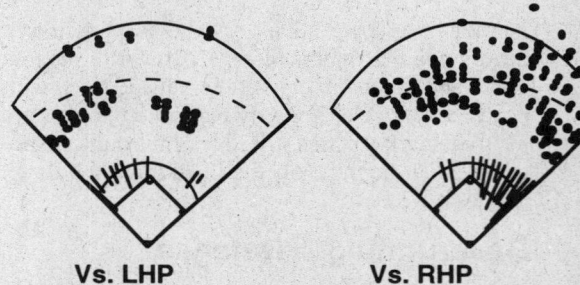

Vs. LHP   **Vs. RHP**

1996 Situational Stats

	AB	H	HR	RBI	Avg		AB	H	HR	RBI	Avg
Home	283	75	10	51	.265	LHP	121	30	2	18	.248
Road	269	68	14	44	.253	RHP	431	113	22	77	.262
First Half	307	85	12	57	.277	Sc Pos	154	45	8	73	.292
Scnd Half	245	58	12	38	.237	Clutch	76	15	4	14	.197

1996 Rankings (American League)

→ 1st in least GDPs per GDP situation (3.0%), errors at shortstop (37) and lowest fielding percentage at shortstop (.950)
→ 4th in lowest percentage of swings put into play (35.1%)
→ 5th in strikeouts
→ 6th in lowest groundball/flyball ratio (0.7) and stolen base percentage (81.0%)
→ 7th in triples
→ Led the Brewers in intentional walks (9), strikeouts and least GDPs per GDP situation (3.0%)

Fernando Vina

1996 Season

It was a breakthrough season for the Brewers' diminutive second baseman and leadoff hitter, Fernando Vina. He began the year platooning at second base, but won the job outright with a hot start at the plate. He soon worked his way into the leadoff spot, and despite cooling off in the second half, he remained the Brewers' second-sacker and leadoff man all year.

Hitting

An aggressive hitter who crowds the plate and isn't afraid of getting nicked, Vina likes to get on top of the high pitch and pull it to right field. He doesn't have any power, but he very rarely swings and misses. With two strikes he can be very tough. Lefties give him trouble, and seeing more of them last year didn't seem to help him solve them. Vina's an excellent bunter who's always a threat to lay one down.

Baserunning & Defense

Vina's not a true basestealer, but draws attention by taking big leads. He can be daring on the basepaths, as evidenced by his 10 triples, which placed second in the league. Defense is the strongest part of his game. Although he led A.L. second basemen with 16 errors, he made up for it with his tremendous range and quick hands. He teams with Jose Valentin to form one of the best double-play combos in baseball.

1997 Outlook

Although he cooled in the second half and doesn't draw as many walks as you'd like, Vina seems to have a firm hold on the Brewers leadoff job. He's the type of speed-and-defense player that fits Phil Garner's style of play, and he fits right in with the needs of this team. Still, he may have been playing a bit over his head last year, and a small dropoff wouldn't be unexpected.

Position: 2B
Bats: L **Throws:** R
Ht: 5' 9" **Wt:** 170

Opening Day Age: 27
Born: 4/16/69 in Sacramento, CA
ML Seasons: 4
Pronunciation: VEEN-yuh

Overall Statistics

	G	AB	R	H	D	T	HR	RBI	SB	BB	SO	Avg	OBP	Slg
1996	140	554	94	157	19	10	7	46	16	38	35	.283	.342	.392
Career	356	1011	165	272	34	17	10	83	31	76	77	.269	.341	.366

Where He Hits the Ball

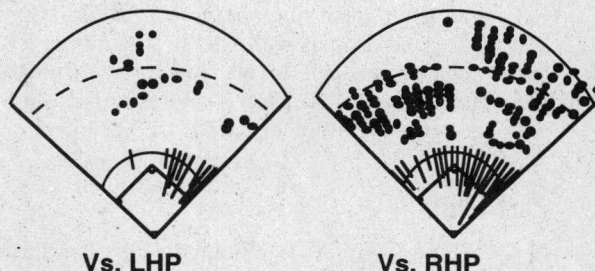

Vs. LHP   Vs. RHP

1996 Situational Stats

	AB	H	HR	RBI	Avg		AB	H	HR	RBI	Avg
Home	265	74	3	29	.279	LHP	110	24	0	8	.218
Road	289	83	4	17	.287	RHP	444	133	7	38	.300
First Half	279	87	4	24	.312	Sc Pos	115	29	2	37	.252
Scnd Half	275	70	3	22	.255	Clutch	73	17	0	3	.233

1996 Rankings (American League)

➡ 1st in errors at second base (16)
➡ 2nd in triples, lowest slugging percentage vs. left-handed pitchers (.245) and batting average on a 3-2 count (.421)
➡ 3rd in lowest fielding percentage at second base (.979), lowest percentage of swings that missed (7.4%) and highest percentage of swings put into play (59.8%)
➡ 5th in hit by pitch (13), least pitches seen per plate appearance (3.39), lowest batting average vs. left-handed pitchers (.218), lowest on-base percentage vs. left-handed pitchers (.285) and bunts in play (30)

Bob Wickman

1996 Season

Over the first half of the season, the Yankees used Bob Wickman very heavily, and he remained among the league leaders in appearances for most of the year. Just when it seemed that his needle was about to hit empty, they dealt him to Milwaukee, where he seemed to find his second wind. As has been his habit, Wickman continued to rack up victories for the Brewers, going 3-0 to improve his career record to a remarkable 34-14.

Pitching

Having lost the tip of his right index finger in a childhood accident, Wickman has truly unique movement on his pitches. His fastball barely cracks 90 MPH, but shows good sinking action. To lefties, he'll cut it and run it in on their hands. His slider has good drop as well, and he can mix in a heavy change-up. All in all, few pitchers are harder to hit a fly ball against. With runners on base, his grounders are just what the doctor ordered.

Defense

Not especially athletic, Wickman can handle comebackers but isn't terribly quick to cover first. He's never had a good pickoff move, and as baserunners continued to run on him last year, he seemed to become distracted with men on base.

1997 Outlook

The Brewers are looking for a rested and rejuvenated Bob Wickman to become a key component of their bullpen next year. He's proven to be most valuable as a set-up man, something Milwaukee sorely needs. As Phil Garner continues to go easy on his starting pitchers, Wickman should help to bridge the gap to the closers. With a less oppressive workload—only Mariano Rivera worked more relief innings among A.L. firemen last year—he should be more effective than ever.

Position: RP
Bats: R **Throws:** R
Ht: 6' 1" **Wt:** 212

Opening Day Age: 28
Born: 2/6/69 in Green Bay, WI
ML Seasons: 5

Overall Statistics

	W	L	Pct.	ERA	G	GS	Sv	IP	H	BB	SO	HR	BR/IP
1996	7	1	.875	4.42	70	0	0	95.2	106	44	75	10	1.57
Career	34	14	.708	4.17	235	28	11	436.0	444	193	273	34	1.46

How Often He Throws Strikes

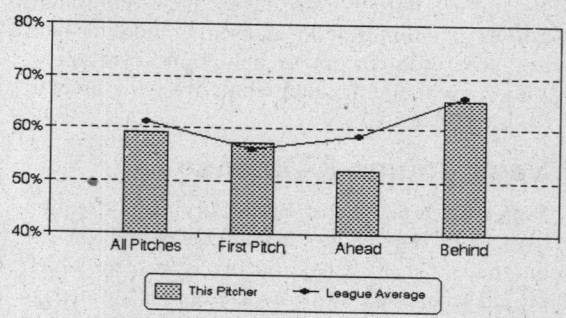

Legend: ▨ This Pitcher —●— League Average

1996 Situational Stats

	W	L	ERA	Sv	IP		AB	H	HR	RBI	Avg
Home	3	1	5.58	0	50.0	LHB	178	54	5	27	.303
Road	4	0	3.15	0	45.2	RHB	196	52	5	45	.265
First Half	3	1	3.86	0	56.0	Sc Pos	119	37	2	60	.311
Scnd Half	4	0	5.22	0	39.2	Clutch	74	18	2	11	.243

1996 Rankings (American League)

➡ 2nd in highest percentage of inherited runners scored (50.0%) and relief innings (95.2)
➡ 4th in relief wins (7)
➡ 7th in highest batting average allowed in relief (.283)
➡ 8th in most baserunners allowed per 9 innings in relief (14.6)

Gerald Williams

1996 Season

Gerald Williams began his career as a defensive replacement, worked his way up to platoon player, and last year, he finally graduated to full-time play. Admittedly, he had to get out of New York to do it. After sharing the Yankees' left field job for parts of three seasons, a late-season trade to the Brewers made him their starting center fielder. Although a strained shoulder prevented Williams from showing them his full capabilities, the Brewers were excited to get him.

Hitting

Williams has enough power to make up for the low batting average, but one question still needs to be answered: Can he hit right-handed pitching? He was never given the opportunity to do so in New York, but the Brewers are betting that he can. If they're wrong, his impatience at the plate may relegate him to part-time status again.

Baserunning & Defense

Williams is fast and daring on the basepaths—of his 10 steals, four were steals of third—but he doesn't always make his gambles pay off. Even with his tools, his stolen base percentage was among the worst in the league. In the outfield, he uses his speed to much better effect, patrolling center field with excellent range. He's always had a strong arm, and his throwing didn't suffer a bit with the move from left field to center.

1997 Outlook

Everyone has always agreed that Williams has the tools to succeed as a full-time player, but now's the time to make them translate into production. His speed and defense should give him some leeway at the plate—especially with the Brewers' prevailing philosophy—so he should get a full shot at the center field job. Unless righthanders simply over-match him, he should be able to contribute enough to keep the job.

Position: LF/CF/RF
Bats: R **Throws:** R
Ht: 6' 2" **Wt:** 190

Opening Day Age: 30
Born: 8/10/66 in New Orleans, LA
ML Seasons: 5

Overall Statistics

	G	AB	R	H	D	T	HR	RBI	SB	BB	SO	Avg	OBP	Slg
1996	125	325	43	82	19	4	5	34	10	19	57	.252	.299	.382
Career	339	687	113	170	49	9	18	87	19	46	125	.247	.298	.424

Where He Hits the Ball

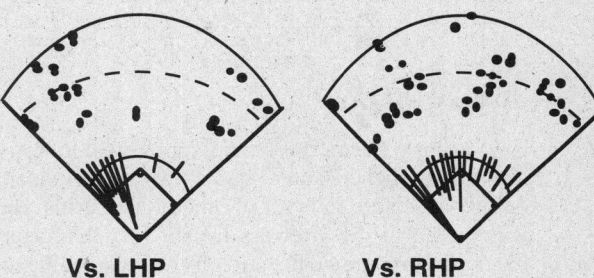

Vs. LHP   **Vs. RHP**

1996 Situational Stats

	AB	H	HR	RBI	Avg		AB	H	HR	RBI	Avg
Home	147	40	3	21	.272	LHP	124	36	4	14	.290
Road	178	42	2	13	.236	RHP	201	46	1	20	.229
First Half	183	58	5	26	.317	Sc Pos	96	22	0	25	.229
Scnd Half	142	24	0	8	.169	Clutch	38	14	0	2	.368

1996 Rankings (American League)

→ 1st in lowest batting average on a 3-1 count (.000)
→ 2nd in lowest stolen base percentage (52.6%)
→ 8th in lowest batting average with runners in scoring position (.229) and steals of third (4)
→ 9th in lowest batting average with the bases loaded (.111)
→ 10th in caught stealing (9)

Bryce Florie

Position: RP
Bats: R **Throws:** R
Ht: 5'11" **Wt:** 190

Opening Day Age: 26
Born: 5/21/70 in
Charleston, SC
ML Seasons: 3

Overall Statistics

	W	L	Pct.	ERA	G	GS	Sv	IP	H	BB	SO	HR	BR/IP
1996	2	3	.400	4.74	54	0	0	68.1	65	40	63	4	1.54
Career	4	5	.444	3.69	110	0	1	146.1	122	81	139	12	1.39

1996 Situational Stats

	W	L	ERA	Sv	IP		AB	H	HR	RBI	Avg
Home	0	2	5.21	0	38.0	LHB	118	28	3	17	.237
Road	2	1	4.15	0	30.1	RHB	144	37	1	17	.257
First Half	1	2	3.56	0	43.0	Sc Pos	83	20	1	28	.241
Scnd Half	1	1	6.75	0	25.1	Clutch	88	25	0	10	.284

1996 Season

Bryce Florie began the year pitching well in middle relief for the Padres, but soon found himself being phased out in favor of other young arms. He was traded to the Brewers in late July. Unfortunately, he tired down the stretch and wasn't able to exhibit his best form for Milwaukee.

Pitching & Defense

Florie does it with movement, not velocity. His fastball won't knock your socks off, but you could tie yourself in knots trying to follow its unpredictable route. His slider has good action as well, and the combination yields ground balls from lefthanders and righthanders alike. Florie lacks a good pickoff move, and generally ignores baserunners. He can make the plays in the field and cover first when he needs to, but he'd be more effective with the glove if he finished his delivery in a better position to field.

1997 Outlook

Strikeouts and ground balls are a dynamite combination, and Florie knows the recipe well. With a winter of rest, there's no reason why he can't pitch in Milwaukee like he did in San Diego. If he can, he'll be an important set-up man in the Brewers' bullpen.

Doug Jones

Position: RP
Bats: R **Throws:** R
Ht: 6'2" **Wt:** 205

Opening Day Age: 39
Born: 6/24/57 in
Covina, CA
ML Seasons: 12

Overall Statistics

	W	L	Pct.	ERA	G	GS	Sv	IP	H	BB	SO	HR	BR/IP
1996	7	2	.778	4.22	52	0	3	64.0	72	20	60	7	1.44
Career	50	60	.455	3.21	578	4	242	785.1	802	179	639	49	1.25

1996 Situational Stats

	W	L	ERA	Sv	IP		AB	H	HR	RBI	Avg
Home	4	0	3.57	0	35.1	LHB	111	30	5	20	.270
Road	3	2	5.02	3	28.2	RHB	145	42	2	23	.290
First Half	2	2	5.01	2	32.1	Sc Pos	84	20	2	33	.238
Scnd Half	5	0	3.41	1	31.2	Clutch	88	29	2	24	.330

1996 Season

The Cubs waived Doug Jones in June, and once more, it appeared that his career might be at an end. However, the Brewers signed him and called him up in July. Without any prior warning or justification, Jones suddenly regained his effectiveness, and pitched well for the final two months of the season.

Pitching & Defense

Jones has only one effective pitch: the change-up. All he does is change speeds and pitch to spots, continually walking the thin line between effectiveness and batting practice. It works—sometimes for up to months at a time. Jones is an average fielder for a 39 year old, which means he can handle any plays that don't include too much running. Stealing on him is not advised; his compact delivery leaves no time for a good jump.

1997 Outlook

Jones signed a minor league contract with the Brewers after last season, but it's impossible to say whether he can add yet another chapter to his improbable saga. Put it this way: when Bill James dies and goes to heaven, God will ask him, "So what do you think Doug Jones is going to do next year?"

Jesse Levis

Position: C
Bats: L **Throws:** R
Ht: 5' 9" **Wt:** 180

Opening Day Age: 28
Born: 4/14/68 in
Philadelphia, PA
ML Seasons: 5

Overall Statistics

	G	AB	R	H	D	T	HR	RBI	SB	BB	SO	Avg	OBP	Slg
1996	104	233	27	55	6	1	1	21	0	38	15	.236	.348	.283
Career	176	358	37	85	14	1	2	31	0	41	30	.237	.317	.299

1996 Situational Stats

	AB	H	HR	RBI	Avg		AB	H	HR	RBI	Avg
Home	127	31	0	13	.244	LHP	40	11	0	8	.275
Road	106	24	1	8	.226	RHP	193	44	1	13	.228
First Half	83	19	0	10	.229	Sc Pos	75	17	0	19	.227
Scnd Half	150	36	1	11	.240	Clutch	58	15	1	7	.259

1996 Season

It was an unlikely climb for Jesse Levis. He was expected to be the Indians' Triple-A catcher, but an early-season deal sent him to Milwaukee, where he became the second-stringer. When starter Mike Matheny flopped. Levis actually ended up handling the bulk of the catching chores down the stretch—rather adequately, at that.

Hitting, Baserunning & Defense

Levis is a squat left-handed hitter who tries to work a walk. If that doesn't work, he'll try to poke a single, but he rarely generates any power. His main asset is his ability to get on base. Although he'd never faced lefties much in the past, he hung in there against them last year. Despite coming to the majors with a lousy defensive reputation, he was surprisingly adequate for the Brewers. His arm isn't strong, but his release is quick enough to do the job. On the bases, he's a forceout waiting to happen.

1997 Outlook

The Brewers harbor no illusions that Levis can be their regular catcher, and he'll fight just to remain on the team as a backup.

Mark Loretta

Position: 2B/3B/SS
Bats: R **Throws:** R
Ht: 6' 0" **Wt:** 175

Opening Day Age: 25
Born: 8/14/71 in Santa
Monica, CA
ML Seasons: 2

Overall Statistics

	G	AB	R	H	D	T	HR	RBI	SB	BB	SO	Avg	OBP	Slg
1996	73	154	20	43	3	0	1	13	2	14	15	.279	.339	.318
Career	92	204	33	56	6	0	2	16	3	18	22	.275	.336	.333

1996 Situational Stats

	AB	H	HR	RBI	Avg		AB	H	HR	RBI	Avg
Home	82	23	0	6	.280	LHP	74	17	0	5	.230
Road	72	20	1	7	.278	RHP	80	26	1	8	.325
First Half	60	19	0	8	.317	Sc Pos	41	11	0	12	.268
Scnd Half	94	24	1	5	.255	Clutch	21	6	0	3	.286

1996 Season

On a limited basis, rookie infielder Mark Loretta got to show what he had to offer last year. Backing up three infield spots, Loretta hit for a decent average and played solid defense all around. A starting spot never opened up for him, but he was first in line in case one did.

Hitting, Baserunning & Defense

Loretta isn't able to generate much power from his wiry frame, but can use his strong wrists to lash the ball to all fields. He's capable of hitting for a good average, but the whole package translates into the production you'd expect from a middle infielder. At any of the infield spots, Loretta shows acceptable range with sure hands and an accurate arm. His speed is unremarkable.

1997 Outlook

Loretta showed enough last year to stick with the big club in '97. He won't start unless an injury opens up a position for him, but he's more than qualified to continue serving as a backup.

Matt Mieske

Position: RF
Bats: R **Throws:** R
Ht: 6' 0" **Wt:** 192

Opening Day Age: 29
Born: 2/13/68 in Midland, MI
ML Seasons: 4
Pronunciation:
MEE-skee

Overall Statistics

	G	AB	R	H	D	T	HR	RBI	SB	BB	SO	Avg	OBP	Slg
1996	127	374	46	104	24	3	14	64	1	26	76	.278	.324	.471
Career	351	958	136	252	50	5	39	157	6	78	197	.263	.321	.448

1996 Situational Stats

	AB	H	HR	RBI	Avg		AB	H	HR	RBI	Avg
Home	195	55	9	28	.282	LHP	145	51	7	31	.352
Road	179	49	5	36	.274	RHP	229	53	7	33	.231
First Half	220	63	9	35	.286	Sc Pos	116	31	1	44	.267
Scnd Half	154	41	5	29	.266	Clutch	53	11	1	10	.208

1996 Season

In early 1996, Matt Mieske seemed to be making real progress against right-handed pitching—his major weakness as a hitter. But by midseason, Mieske had slipped back into his old habits. By the end of the year, any hopes that he would break out of his platoon role had long since evaporated.

Hitting, Baserunning & Defense

Miekse likes to get a pitch inside and pull it in the air. He struggles against righthanders because he pulls off breaking balls on the outside corner. His inability to make more consistent contact has been frustrating. Still, he's as dangerous as anyone against a lefty. Mieske has lost the speed that made him a basestealer in the low minors. He has above-average range in right field, and his strong, accurate throwing arm is one of his biggest assets.

1997 Outlook

Mieske may have come to the end of the line in Milwaukee. The Brewers have brought in a lot of new outfield talent, so they may no longer be able to carry Mieske, who simply can't play against the majority of pitchers. He'll probably be looking for another platoon role with a different club.

Angel Miranda

Position: RP/SP
Bats: L **Throws:** L
Ht: 6' 1" **Wt:** 195

Opening Day Age: 27
Born: 11/9/69 in Arecibo, PR
ML Seasons: 4

Overall Statistics

	W	L	Pct.	ERA	G	GS	Sv	IP	H	BB	SO	HR	BR/IP
1996	7	6	.538	4.94	46	12	1	109.1	116	69	78	12	1.69
Career	17	21	.447	4.48	106	47	2	349.1	338	197	235	40	1.53

1996 Situational Stats

	W	L	ERA	Sv	IP		AB	H	HR	RBI	Avg
Home	3	2	4.69	1	55.2	LHB	120	39	3	21	.325
Road	4	4	5.20	0	53.2	RHB	299	77	9	44	.258
First Half	3	5	4.79	1	77.0	Sc Pos	112	31	3	49	.277
Scnd Half	4	1	5.29	0	32.1	Clutch	67	17	1	6	.254

1996 Season

Screwballing lefthander Angel Miranda performed well in middle relief early in the year. This earned him a promotion to the starting rotation, but he pitched his way back into the bullpen several weeks later. He spent the rest of the year performing decently in middle relief before his arm tired in September.

Pitching & Defense

Miranda throws a running, fading screwball, which he works off the outside corner to righthanders. When he can't get it over, he falls behind and has to come in with his high-80s fastball. To lefties, he throws an erratic curve, which is the major reason he's less effective against them. After a pair of knee surgeries, Miranda lacks mobility on the mound, and his follow-through makes it hard for him to get over to first base. His pickoff move has improved greatly, and as a result, he's become very tough to run on.

1997 Outlook

In the second half, Miranda seemed to find his niche as a middle reliever. He'll likely keep this role unless injuries necessitate his return to the rotation. For him to succeed as a starter, he'll need to refine his curveball.

Tim VanEgmond

Position: SP
Bats: R **Throws:** R
Ht: 6' 2" **Wt:** 180

Opening Day Age: 27
Born: 5/31/69 in
Shreveport, LA
ML Seasons: 3

Overall Statistics

	W	L	Pct.	ERA	G	GS	Sv	IP	H	BB	SO	HR	BR/IP
1996	3	5	.375	5.27	12	9	0	54.2	58	23	33	6	1.48
Career	5	9	.357	5.96	23	17	0	99.2	105	50	60	15	1.56

1996 Situational Stats

	W	L	ERA	Sv	IP		AB	H	HR	RBI	Avg
Home	2	3	5.52	0	31.0	LHB	115	29	4	15	.252
Road	1	2	4.94	0	23.2	RHB	97	29	2	10	.299
First Half	0	0	-	0	0.0	Sc Pos	56	11	2	20	.196
Scnd Half	3	5	5.27	0	54.2	Clutch	12	3	0	0	.250

1996 Season

After failing in short trials with the Red Sox in 1994 and '95, Tim VanEgmond was called up by the Brewers and inserted into the starting rotation shortly after the All-Star break. For two months, he was surprisingly successful, but he completely fell apart in September.

Pitching & Defense

VanEgmond relies almost entirely upon a two-seam fastball with a velocity in the high 80s. He cuts it and runs it in and out, counting on its movement to produce weak fly balls. When he can't find the corners with it, he's liable to get hammered. He will also mix in a slider and change-up for show. VanEgmond is quick off the mound, but an otherwise average fielder. He hasn't shown a good pickoff move, but he controls the running game reasonably well.

1997 Outlook

Which Tim VanEgmond can the Brewers expect— the one who pitched so well in July and August, or the one who looked like a minor leaguer in September? It all depends on whether he has control of his two-seamer on any particular day. He may begin the year as the fifth starter, but how long he holds the job is anyone's guess.

Ron Villone

Position: RP
Bats: L **Throws:** L
Ht: 6' 3" **Wt:** 235

Opening Day Age: 27
Born: 1/16/70 in
Englewood, NJ
ML Seasons: 2

Overall Statistics

	W	L	Pct.	ERA	G	GS	Sv	IP	H	BB	SO	HR	BR/IP
1996	1	1	.500	3.14	44	0	2	43.0	31	25	38	6	1.30
Career	3	4	.429	4.50	82	0	3	88.0	75	59	101	17	1.52

1996 Situational Stats

	W	L	ERA	Sv	IP		AB	H	HR	RBI	Avg
Home	0	0	1.90	2	23.2	LHB	53	11	1	10	.208
Road	1	1	4.66	0	19.1	RHB	97	20	5	18	.206
First Half	0	0	0.00	0	13.1	Sc Pos	46	14	4	25	.304
Scnd Half	1	1	4.55	2	29.2	Clutch	41	9	2	10	.220

1996 Season

When the Brewers traded Greg Vaughn to San Diego in late July, they made sure the Padres threw in hard-throwing lefthander Ron Villone. The story of Villone's career has been an ongoing struggle to harness his stuff, and last year marked a small step forward in the process.

Pitching & Defense

When you're left-handed and you can throw in the mid-90s, it isn't hard to figure out what you need to do to succeed: throw strikes. When Villone's doing that, he can be nearly unhittable. But when he can't get his fastball over to set up his split-fingered fastball, he can be very frustrating to watch. Simply being left-handed helps Villone control the running game, but his awkward follow-through leaves him off-balance and in poor position to field. Still, he's an excellent athlete who can get over to cover first as quickly as is needed.

1997 Outlook

Villone will go as far as his control allows him to. The Brewers will use him in a set-up role and may give him the opportunity to close out a few games if he shows he's up to it.

Other Milwaukee Brewers

Marshall Boze (Pos: RHP, Age: 25)

	W	L	Pct.	ERA	G	GS	Sv	IP	H	BB	SO	HR	BR/IP
1996	0	2	.000	7.79	25	0	1	32.1	47	25	19	5	2.23
Career	0	2	.000	7.79	25	0	1	32.1	47	25	19	5	2.23

Righthander Marshall Boze was tried as a middle reliever over the first half of the season, with disastrous results. The fiasco left little doubt that his stuff is less than major-league caliber. 1997 Outlook: D

Terry Burrows (Pos: LHP, Age: 28)

	W	L	Pct.	ERA	G	GS	Sv	IP	H	BB	SO	HR	BR/IP
1996	2	0	1.000	2.84	8	0	0	12.2	12	10	5	2	1.74
Career	4	2	.667	5.71	37	3	1	58.1	73	30	27	14	1.77

Burrows spent three unimpressive weeks with the Brewers in June, and became a free agent when he refused assignment to the minors. The Yankees' Triple-A team signed him, and he didn't do much for them. 1997 Outlook: D

Cris Carpenter (Pos: RHP, Age: 31)

	W	L	Pct.	ERA	G	GS	Sv	IP	H	BB	SO	HR	BR/IP
1996	0	0	-	7.56	8	0	0	8.1	12	2	2	1	1.68
Career	27	22	.551	3.91	291	13	7	414.1	398	131	252	38	1.28

Carpenter was a hot prospect with the Cardinals a decade or two ago, and pitched well with the Brewers' Triple-A team last year. He hasn't pitched effectively in the majors in four years. 1997 Outlook: D

Chuck Carr (Pos: CF, Age: 28, Bats: B)

	G	AB	R	H	D	T	HR	RBI	SB	BB	SO	Avg	OBP	Slg
1996	27	106	18	29	6	1	1	11	5	6	21	.274	.310	.377
Career	418	1475	217	376	67	5	9	106	132	132	225	.255	.318	.325

Carr suffered the season's grisliest injury in May when his knee buckled as he chased a fly ball. Somehow, a torn ligament was the only injury, but if he can't run, he can't play. And even if he *can* run. . . 1997 Outlook: C

Ramon Garcia (Pos: RHP, Age: 27)

	W	L	Pct.	ERA	G	GS	Sv	IP	H	BB	SO	HR	BR/IP
1996	4	4	.500	6.66	37	2	4	75.2	84	21	40	17	1.39
Career	8	8	.500	6.02	53	17	4	154.0	163	52	80	30	1.40

Garner seemed to like something about Garcia, and stuck with him—for no apparent reason—for most of the season. Houston selected him in the Rule 5 Draft in December. 1997 Outlook: C

Brian Givens (Pos: LHP, Age: 31)

	W	L	Pct.	ERA	G	GS	Sv	IP	H	BB	SO	HR	BR/IP
1996	1	3	.250	12.86	4	4	0	14.0	32	7	10	3	2.79
Career	6	10	.375	5.86	23	23	0	121.1	148	61	83	14	1.72

After pitching decently in '95, Givens began the year in the minors, was recalled for four starts in June, and got sent back down after being hit frightfully hard. He's much too old for a rebuilding team. 1997 Outlook: C

Kevin Koslofski (Pos: CF, Age: 30, Bats: L)

	G	AB	R	H	D	T	HR	RBI	SB	BB	SO	Avg	OBP	Slg
1996	25	42	5	9	3	2	0	6	0	4	12	.214	.298	.381
Career	97	205	31	50	3	4	4	21	2	22	41	.244	.325	.356

No more than an extra outfielder, Koslofski gets into a few games a year by just hanging around and waiting for someone to get hurt. Someone always does, but he may call it quits before the next time. 1997 Outlook: D

Jose Mercedes (Pos: RHP, Age: 26)

	W	L	Pct.	ERA	G	GS	Sv	IP	H	BB	SO	HR	BR/IP
1996	0	2	.000	9.18	11	0	0	16.2	20	5	6	6	1.50
Career	2	3	.400	5.40	35	0	0	55.0	54	29	23	11	1.51

Jose Mercedes pitched decently at Triple-A, but posted a major league ERA over nine for the second straight year. Streaks like that rarely make it into their third year. 1997 Outlook: D

Danny Perez (Pos: LF, Age: 26, Bats: R)

	G	AB	R	H	D	T	HR	RBI	SB	BB	SO	Avg	OBP	Slg
1996	4	4	0	0	0	0	0	0	0	0	0	.000	.000	.000
Career	4	4	0	0	0	0	0	0	0	0	0	.000	.000	.000

Danny Perez rarely hits well outside his hometown of El Paso. His attitude has been questioned, and he's never been seen as a prospect. He may mature but probably won't. 1997 Outlook: D

Mike Potts (Pos: LHP, Age: 26)

	W	L	Pct.	ERA	G	GS	Sv	IP	H	BB	SO	HR	BR/IP
1996	1	2	.333	7.15	24	0	1	45.1	58	30	21	7	1.94
Career	1	2	.333	7.15	24	0	1	45.1	58	30	21	7	1.94

Potts pitched decently in the minors for several years, so the Brewers gave him a shot. He posted an ERA over seven in the first half, and didn't fare much better after being sent down. 1997 Outlook: D

Al Reyes (Pos: RHP, Age: 25)

	W	L	Pct.	ERA	G	GS	Sv	IP	H	BB	SO	HR	BR/IP
1996	1	0	1.000	7.94	5	0	0	5.2	8	2	2	1	1.76
Career	2	1	.667	3.23	32	0	1	39.0	27	20	31	4	1.21

Reyes pitched well for the Brewers in '95 before undergoing elbow surgery. He spent most of last year recovering, but at age 26, there's still hope. 1997 Outlook: B

Steve Sparks (Pos: RHP, Age: 31)

	W	L	Pct.	ERA	G	GS	Sv	IP	H	BB	SO	HR	BR/IP
1996	4	7	.364	6.60	20	13	0	88.2	103	52	21	19	1.75
Career	13	18	.419	5.23	53	40	0	290.2	313	138	117	36	1.55

Steve Sparks completely lost command of his knuckleball last year, and as a result, the Brewers completely lost faith in him. After a brief demotion, he sat unused for most of the second half. 1997 Outlook: C

Kelly Stinnett (Pos: C, Age: 27, Bats: R)

	G	AB	R	H	D	T	HR	RBI	SB	BB	SO	Avg	OBP	Slg
1996	14	26	1	2	0	0	0	0	0	2	11	.077	.172	.077
Career	138	372	44	83	14	3	6	32	4	42	104	.223	.321	.325

The Brewers needed a catcher last year, and Stinnett was tearing it up at Triple-A, but they never gave him a real shot. He didn't play often—or well—after his August recall, and his future is elsewhere. 1997 Outlook: C

Tim Unroe (Pos: 1B, Age: 26, Bats: R)

	G	AB	R	H	D	T	HR	RBI	SB	BB	SO	Avg	OBP	Slg
1996	14	16	5	3	0	0	0	0	0	4	5	.188	.350	.188
Career	16	20	5	4	0	0	0	0	0	4	5	.200	.333	.200

Unroe accumulated 16 at-bats in four separate stints with the Brewers last year. He's an unremarkable hitter, and they don't need him at either of the corner positions. 1997 Outlook: C

Turner Ward (Pos: RF/LF, Age: 31, Bats: B)

	G	AB	R	H	D	T	HR	RBI	SB	BB	SO	Avg	OBP	Slg
1996	43	67	7	12	2	1	2	10	3	13	17	.179	.309	.328
Career	341	918	130	216	36	7	21	119	21	120	162	.235	.324	.358

Ward batted .179 before a strained shoulder put him out for the year. He may hang around as an extra outfielder, but he doesn't have all that much to offer. 1997 Outlook: C

Kevin Wickander (Pos: LHP, Age: 32)

	W	L	Pct.	ERA	G	GS	Sv	IP	H	BB	SO	HR	BR/IP
1996	2	0	1.000	4.97	21	0	0	25.1	26	17	19	2	1.70
Career	5	1	.833	4.02	150	0	2	138.2	151	85	101	12	1.70

Wickander went down with a shoulder problem in June, looked awful on rehab, and got released in August. He may be finished, but on the other hand, he's a lefty. 1997 Outlook: C

Milwaukee Brewers Minor League Prospects

Organization Overview:

Last season, Brewers' G.M. Sal Bando swung a couple of late-season deals where he gave up veterans for youngsters. The moves were necessary, not only from a payroll standpoint, but from a baseball standpoint as well. The farm system is simply devoid of talent, and Bando accepted he'd have to go outside the organization to rebuild. Dave Nilsson, Jeff Cirillo and John Jaha were all developed in-house, and last year the system produced Scott Karl, Mark Loretta and Jeff D'Amico. There is, however, very little left in the pipeline. Former first-rounders Geoff Jenkins and Antone Williamson continue to fight injuries, and after a series of fruitless drafts, the second-line talent is virtually nonexistent. It remains to be seen whether new Scouting Director Cecil Cooper will be given enough resources and support to grow anything in his empty garden.

Brian Banks

Position: OF   **Opening Day Age:** 26
Bats: B **Throws:** R   **Born:** 9/28/70 in Mesa,
Ht: 6' 3" **Wt:** 200   AZ

Recent Statistics

	G	AB	R	H	D	T	HR	RBI	SB	BB	SO	AVG
96 AAA New Orl'ns	137	487	71	132	29	7	16	64	17	66	105	.271
96 AL Milwaukee	4	7	2	4	2	0	1	2	0	1	2	.571
96 MLE	137	486	71	131	29	6	14	64	15	67	106	.270

He's not quite young enough to be a prospect, and his offense is good, but not quite good enough to make it in the outfield, so the Brewers are trying to make a catcher out of Brian Banks. It's not a completely crazy idea; Banks was a catcher in high school and his first year of college. If the experiment works, it will give them someone who can back up at catcher and all three outfield positions. He's got decent power and speed, and projects to hit for a fairly good average, so he'd be useful off the bench.

Ronnie Belliard

Position: 2B   **Opening Day Age:** 20
Bats: R **Throws:** R   **Born:** 7/4/76 in New
Ht: 5' 9" **Wt:** 176   York, NY

Recent Statistics

	G	AB	R	H	D	T	HR	RBI	SB	BB	SO	AVG
94 R Brewers	39	143	32	42	7	3	0	27	7	14	25	.294
95 A Beloit	130	461	76	137	28	5	13	56	16	36	67	.297
96 AA El Paso	109	416	73	116	20	8	3	57	26	60	51	.279
96 MLE	109	402	57	102	17	5	2	44	18	40	53	.254

Ronnie Belliard is the cousin of big league shortstop Rafael Belliard. Luckily, Ronnie also got the fielding gene—he's got great range and was voted the best defensive second baseman in the Texas League. He's equally fortunate that he *didn't* inherit Rafael's batting traits—Ronnie hit well and controlled the strike zone in Double-A at the tender age of 19. He can run, and his basestealing is improving. The Brewers regard him as their second baseman of the future, and plan to give him another year. He may take less time than that to make it.

Valerio De Los Santos

Position: P   **Opening Day Age:** 21
Bats: L **Throws:** L   **Born:** 10/6/75 in Las
Ht: 6' 4" **Wt:** 185   Matas De Farfan, DR

Recent Statistics

	W	L	ERA	G	GS	Sv	IP	H	R	BB	SO	HR
95 R Brewers	4	6	2.20	14	12	0	82.0	81	34	12	57	3
96 A Beloit	10	8	3.55	33	23	4	164.2	164	83	59	137	11

Young southpaw Valerio de los Santos tore through the Midwest League last year with only two pitches: the best fastball in the league, and a forkball. However, it was the most innings he'd ever thrown as a professional, and he slowed after an 8-0 start. A late-season move to the bullpen was intended only to preserve his arm, and he'll return to the rotation next year. Only 21 years old, he'll advance as quickly as his arm and his stuff allow him to.

Todd Dunn

Position: OF   **Opening Day Age:** 26
Bats: R **Throws:** R   **Born:** 7/29/70 in Tulsa,
Ht: 6' 5" **Wt:** 220   OK

Recent Statistics

	G	AB	R	H	D	T	HR	RBI	SB	BB	SO	AVG
96 AA El Paso	98	359	72	122	24	5	19	78	13	45	84	.340
96 AL Milwaukee	6	10	2	3	1	0	0	1	0	0	3	.300
96 MLE	98	343	56	106	21	3	14	61	9	30	88	.309

Ever since the Brewers drafted him in the first round of the '93 draft, Todd Dunn has remained an exceptional athlete who simply couldn't play baseball. He finally escaped A-ball last year at age 25—exceptionally late for someone regarded as a prospect. However, Dunn made remarkable progress last year when he finally learned to curb his free-swinging ways and lay off the breaking ball. The result was that he won the Texas League batting title, and revived the hope that he can contribute in the majors as a corner outfielder.

Geoff Jenkins

Position: DH
Bats: L **Throws:** L
Ht: 6' 1" **Wt:** 195

Opening Day Age: 22
Born: 7/21/74 in Olympia, WA

Recent Statistics

	G	AB	R	H	D	T	HR	RBI	SB	BB	SO	AVG
95 R Helena	7	28	2	9	0	1	0	9	0	3	11	.321
95 A Stockton	13	47	13	12	2	0	3	12	2	10	12	.255
95 AA El Paso	21	79	12	22	4	2	1	13	3	8	23	.278
96 AA El Paso	22	77	17	22	5	4	1	11	1	12	21	.286
96 A Stockton	37	138	27	48	8	4	3	25	3	20	32	.348

The ninth overall selection in the '95 draft, Geoff Jenkins was bothered all year by chronic looseness in his left shoulder. When he's healthy, he's got a powerful uppercut that should produce plenty of power and a good batting average. He's slow, and doesn't do much on defense, so he'll have to hope that his shoulder recovers and allows him to bat naturally. If that happens, he's a potential impact player on the strength of his bat alone. He may not need much more than one full season in the minors.

Danny Klassen

Position: SS
Bats: R **Throws:** R
Ht: 6' 0" **Wt:** 175

Opening Day Age: 21
Born: 9/22/75 in Leamington, Ontario, Canada

Recent Statistics

	G	AB	R	H	D	T	HR	RBI	SB	BB	SO	AVG
93 R Brewers	38	117	26	26	5	0	2	20	14	24	28	.222
93 R Helena	18	45	8	9	1	0	0	3	2	7	11	.200
94 A Beloit	133	458	61	119	20	3	6	54	28	58	123	.260
95 A Beloit	59	218	27	60	15	2	2	15	12	16	43	.275
96 A Stockton	118	432	58	116	22	4	2	46	14	34	77	.269

Young shortstop Danny Klassen lost half of '95 to knee surgery, but returned to have a decent year at Class A Stockton last year. He's an above-average defender with good range and a strong throwing arm, and experience should curb his errors. His speed is his best tool, and he'll need to learn to get on base more to take advantage of it. He's made significant progress on reducing his strikeouts, and he's still got plenty of time to mature as a hitter. The Brewers think he may be ready in another couple of years.

Sean Maloney

Position: P
Bats: R **Throws:** R
Ht: 6' 7" **Wt:** 210

Opening Day Age: 25
Born: 5/25/71 in South Kingstown, RI

Recent Statistics

	W	L	ERA	G	GS	Sv	IP	H	R	BB	SO	HR
93 R Helena	2	2	4.34	17	3	0	47.2	55	31	11	35	2
94 A Beloit	2	6	5.49	51	0	22	59.0	73	42	10	53	3
95 AA El Paso	7	5	4.18	43	0	15	64.2	69	41	28	54	4
96 AA El Paso	3	2	1.43	51	0	38	56.2	49	11	12	57	1

In his second year at Double-A, six foot, seven-inch righthander Sean Maloney exploded on the scene with 38 saves, the best total in the minors last year. His fastball reaches 90 MPH, but the difference this year was that he developed a good splitter to go with it. Although he's advanced in age, the Brewers added him to the 40-man roster in the belief that he can be a decent set-up man in the majors. He could be better than they think; a 1.43 ERA in the Texas League—especially at El Paso— is simply unheard-of. Maloney could be a good sleeper pick next year.

Antone Williamson

Position: 1B-DH
Bats: L **Throws:** R
Ht: 6' 1" **Wt:** 195

Opening Day Age: 23
Born: 7/18/73 in Torrance, CA

Recent Statistics

	G	AB	R	H	D	T	HR	RBI	SB	BB	SO	AVG
94 R Helena	6	26	5	11	2	1	0	4	0	2	4	.423
94 A Stockton	23	85	6	19	4	0	3	13	0	7	19	.224
94 AA El Paso	14	48	8	12	3	0	1	9	0	7	8	.250
95 AA El Paso	104	392	62	121	30	6	7	90	3	47	57	.309
96 AAA New Orlns	55	199	23	52	10	1	5	23	1	19	40	.261

Like Geoff Jenkins, Antone Williamson is a former Brewers' first-round pick ('94) who's been set back by shoulder problems. In '95, problems with his right shoulder forced him to move from third to first base, and last year, surgery for a torn labrum in his left shoulder cost him most of the season. Williamson is still young— only 23 next year—but he still hasn't shown the power that's been expected of him. He's made consistent contact, but with no other skills to speak of, he won't make it as a first baseman unless he steps up his production.

Others to Watch

Second baseman **Roberto Lopez** had a disappointing year at Triple-A, and got pushed aside by Ronnie Belliard. Lopez can turn the double play and get on base, and may surface elsewhere. . . **Mike Rennhack**, a refugee left fielder from the Houston system, batted .320 with 103 RBI for Class A Stockton. He's a switch-hitter and will be only 22 next year, so he may yet pan out. . . Despite the fact that he didn't grab a regular spot in the starting rotation until June, righthander **Travis Smith** went 13-5 between A-ball and Double-A. . . Last year, **Brad Seitzer**'s numbers in Double-A looked exactly like the ones his brother Kevin compiled in the majors. Now 27, Brad is too old to be a prospect, but he looks like a hitter.

Tom Kelly

1996 Season

Despite the catastrophic loss of Kirby Puckett to glaucoma, Tom Kelly kept the ship steady in 1996, and the Twins count the rebuilding season as a success. He may be quiet, even dour, but he demands the utmost effort from his players. He is usually patient with a struggling player, as long as that player is putting forth maximum effort. . . any sign of laziness brings swift comment. Kelly's biggest strength is his ability to keep his players motivated. The Twins are the best hustling team in the American League.

Offense

Kelly strongly emphasizes the fundamentals. The Twins are a team of excellent baserunners; they tag up aggressively on fly balls, steal bases at a very good percentage and put constant pressure on the defense. Kelly will use the hit-and-run frequently, but he calls for the bunt only half as often as the typical manager. He is not a fanatical platooner, but he uses his bench, and keeps his reserves fresh. Kelly has a cadre of players to whom he is very loyal, sometimes to a fault.

Pitching & Defense

Kelly and pitching coach Dick Such have come under fire during the rebuilding process, mostly because promising youngsters like Pat Mahomes and LaTroy Hawkins haven't developed as anticipated. But he usually pulls a starter before things get out of hand, and his pitchers stay healthy. Kelly's teams are very strong defensively. He substitutes freely, seldom issues an intentional walk, and is frugal with pitchouts.

1997 Outlook

Kelly has managed the same team for longer than any other manager or coach in the four major professional sports, and his job remains secure. In 1997, the team thinks it can contend for a wild-card spot, especially now that they have signed free agent Terry Steinbach.

Born: 8/15/50 in Graceville, MN

Playing Experience: 1975-1975, Min

Managerial Experience: 11 seasons

Manager Statistics

Year	Team, Lg	W	L	Pct	GB	Finish
1996	Minnesota, AL	78	84	.481	21.5	4th Central
11 Seasons		785	791	.498	—	—

1996 Starting Pitchers by Days Rest

	≤3	4	5	6+
Twins Starts	4	107	21	20
Twins ERA	5.57	5.12	5.54	5.62
AL Avg Starts	4	96	30	21
AL ERA	5.57	4.90	5.33	5.81

1996 Situational Stats

	Tom Kelly	AL Average
Hit & Run Success %	45.5	39.1
Stolen Base Success %	73.0	69.6
Platoon Pct.	60.2	61.9
Defensive Subs	12	29
High-Pitch Outings	14	23
Quick/Slow Hooks	11/14	17/20
Sacrifice Attempts	33	58

1996 Rankings (American League)

➡ 1st in pinch hitters used (207)

➡ 2nd in steals of second base (133), hit-and-run attempts (99) and saves with over 1 inning pitched (13)

➡ 3rd in stolen base attempts (196), steals of home plate (2) and hit-and-run percentage (45.5%)

Rick Aguilera

1996 Season

The Twins embarked upon a dangerous experiment in 1996: converting Rick Aguilera from closer back to rotation starter. Although he had not started a game since 1989, Aguilera was enthusiastic about the move. He missed most of April and all of May after hurting his wrist carrying his wife's luggage during spring training, and missed most of September after pulling his hamstring. Neither injury was because of his load as a starter, however, and his arm held up surprisingly well. He showed flashes of excellence, but was inconsistent.

Pitching

As a reliever, Aguilera relied on his sinking fastball and nasty split-finger pitch. As a starter, he rounded out his repertoire by dusting off his slider and curveball. The fastball has lost velocity since his days as a premier closer, but it still has excellent movement and his control is pinpoint. His split-finger and slider are both above-average; his curve is average, but a useful complement to his other offerings. Aggie was a consistent reliever, but as a starter he was erratic. His control was always excellent, and he had several starts where he was dominant, but on nights when his velocity was down or his command less than perfect, he could get lit up.

Defense

Aguilera is an excellent athlete and a fine fielder. He finishes his delivery in good position to field the ball, and seldom makes a mistake or throws to the wrong base. He does not have a particularly good move to first base, however, and all 11 stolen-base attempts against him last season were successful.

1997 Outlook

The 1996 experiment was neither a dramatic success nor a critical failure. The development of the Twins' young pitchers makes Aguilera's presence in the rotation less important for 1997, so Tom Kelly is considering moving him back to closer. Aguilera says he will be happy in either role, though he would probably be more consistent as a reliever.

Position: SP
Bats: R **Throws:** R
Ht: 6' 5" **Wt:** 203

Opening Day Age: 35
Born: 12/31/61 in San Gabriel, CA
ML Seasons: 12
Pronunciation: ag-yuh-LAIR-uh

Overall Statistics

	W	L	Pct.	ERA	G	GS	Sv	IP	H	BB	SO	HR	BR/IP
1996	8	6	.571	5.42	19	19	0	111.1	124	27	83	20	1.36
Career	67	62	.519	3.48	488	89	211	1033.1	992	284	822	102	1.23

How Often He Throws Strikes

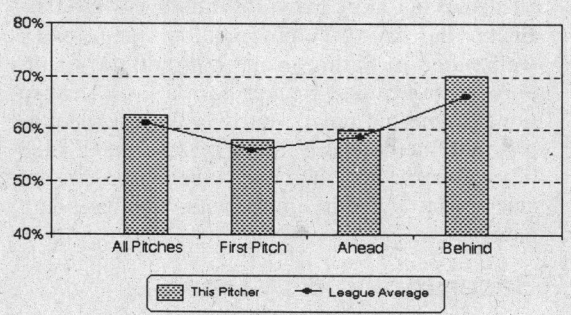

1996 Situational Stats

	W	L	ERA	Sv	IP		AB	H	HR	RBI	Avg
Home	3	4	7.13	0	53.0	LHB	243	70	10	36	.288
Road	5	2	3.86	0	58.1	RHB	207	54	10	27	.261
First Half	2	3	5.97	0	37.2	Sc Pos	106	31	7	46	.292
Scnd Half	6	3	5.13	0	73.2	Clutch	30	8	2	5	.267

1996 Rankings (American League)

➡ Did not rank near the top or bottom in any category

Rich Becker

1996 Season

Rich Becker won the Twins' center field job with a solid spring training, but got off to a horrendous start; his batting average on May 1st was .089. Manager Tom Kelly resisted the pressure to send Becker to the minors, and Rich responded to the vote of confidence. By the end of the season, Becker had fully demonstrated his broad range of offensive and defensive skills.

Hitting

Becker usually hit second in the Twins order behind Chuck Knoblauch. He is a very patient hitter, sometimes to a fault. His willingness to take pitches results in a good on-base percentage, but he strikes out more than most number-two hitters. Becker has line-drive power to both gaps, and is well suited to hitting in the Metrodome. At this point in his career, Becker hasn't shown exceptional home-run power, but the Twins expect his output to increase as he matures. A former switch-hitter, Becker now hits exclusively from the left side and struggled in limited action against southpaws.

Baserunning & Defense

Becker lost speed following a severe 1993 knee injury, but he still motors well and has excellent baserunning instincts. He is quietly emerging as one of the best defensive outfielders in the American League. He tracks balls very well, is quite reliable, and with the retirement of Kirby Puckett he has taken charge as the leader in the outfield. His arm is strong and very accurate—he led the A.L. with 19 outfield assists.

1997 Outlook

The Twins are pleased with Becker's progress, and he opens 1997 with the center field job in his hip pocket. Becker's biggest problem has been lack of self-confidence, but he has now shown everyone, including himself, that he belongs in the major leagues. With his combination of power, speed, on-base ability, and defense, he helps his team in a lot of ways. A breakout season is possible.

Position: CF/LF
Bats: L **Throws:** L
Ht: 5'10" **Wt:** 199

Opening Day Age: 25
Born: 2/1/72 in Aurora, IL
ML Seasons: 4

Overall Statistics

	G	AB	R	H	D	T	HR	RBI	SB	BB	SO	Avg	OBP	Slg
1996	148	525	92	153	31	4	12	71	19	68	118	.291	.372	.434
Career	285	1022	152	274	51	5	15	112	34	120	242	.268	.347	.372

Where He Hits the Ball

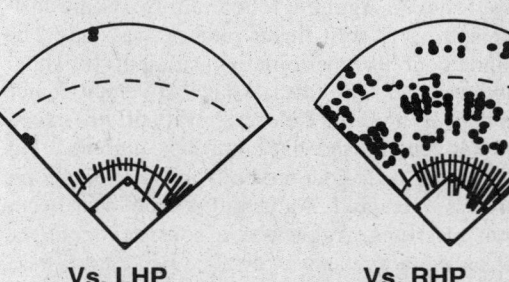

Vs. LHP	Vs. RHP

1996 Situational Stats

	AB	H	HR	RBI	Avg		AB	H	HR	RBI	Avg
Home	267	83	8	43	.311	LHP	105	18	0	9	.171
Road	258	70	4	28	.271	RHP	420	135	12	62	.321
First Half	243	62	5	20	.255	Sc Pos	144	47	2	54	.326
Scnd Half	282	91	7	51	.323	Clutch	68	17	2	12	.250

1996 Rankings (American League)

→ 4th in fielding percentage in center field (.994)
→ 8th in batting average with the bases loaded (.538)
→ 10th in errors in center field (2) and highest percentage of swings on the first pitch (35.5%)
→ Led the Twins in sacrifice bunts (5), strikeouts, stolen base percentage (79.2%) and batting average on a 3-1 count (.500)

Marty Cordova

1996 Season

What sophomore jinx? Marty Cordova, the American League's 1995 Rookie of the Year, proved that last season was no fluke with a fine all-around performance in 1996. Hitting cleanup for most of the season, Cordova hit for power and average. With his hustle and obvious offensive ability, Cordova has become a fan favorite and one of the cornerstones of the franchise.

Hitting

During his rookie year, Cordova showed major league power but struck out more than he, or the Twins, wanted, so he shortened his swing in 1996 and looked for more contact. The result was a higher batting average and more doubles, but fewer home runs and strikeouts. Despite the drop-off in the homer total, his slugging percentage was nearly the same as his 1995 mark, and his on-base percentage was better. He hits righthanders and lefthanders equally well, and doesn't scare in pressure situations. Cordova catches up to most fastballs, although he can occasionally be overpowered by hard stuff up and in.

Baserunning & Defense

Cordova surprised everybody with 20 stolen bases in 1995, but opposing batteries were more vigilant in 1996 and he managed just 11 steals. He has slightly above-average speed and is relatively aggressive, but doesn't make silly mistakes on the basepaths. An injury several years ago robbed him of arm strength, but he compensates with a quick release and usually hits the cutoff man. His range in left field is good, and he has worked hard to make himself into a solid defensive outfielder.

1997 Outlook

After his rookie campaign, the Twins gave Cordova a three-year contract, so he won't be going anywhere soon. He likes playing for the Twins and the Twins like him, so it would surprise no one if he spent the rest of his career in Minnesota. He has an excellent work ethic and should remain a quality player for many years.

Position: LF
Bats: R **Throws:** R
Ht: 6' 0" **Wt:** 193

Opening Day Age: 27
Born: 7/10/69 in Las Vegas, NV
ML Seasons: 2
Pronunciation: Core-DOE-vuh

Overall Statistics

	G	AB	R	H	D	T	HR	RBI	SB	BB	SO	Avg	OBP	Slg
1996	145	569	97	176	46	1	16	111	11	53	96	.309	.371	.478
Career	282	1081	178	318	73	5	40	195	31	105	207	.294	.362	.482

Where He Hits the Ball

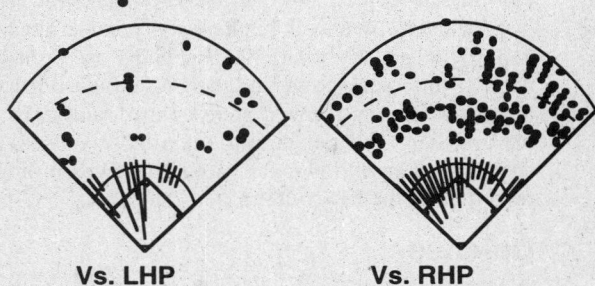

Vs. LHP   **Vs. RHP**

1996 Situational Stats

	AB	H	HR	RBI	Avg		AB	H	HR	RBI	Avg
Home	281	91	10	62	.324	LHP	129	39	4	33	.302
Road	288	85	6	49	.295	RHP	440	137	12	78	.311
First Half	291	93	7	56	.320	Sc Pos	186	58	3	90	.312
Scnd Half	278	83	9	55	.299	Clutch	76	20	2	10	.263

1996 Rankings (American League)

- ➠ 1st in fielding percentage in left field (.991) and highest percentage of swings on the first pitch (50.3%)
- ➠ 4th in doubles, lowest cleanup slugging percentage (.449) and lowest percentage of pitches taken (47.8%)
- ➠ 8th in sacrifice flies (9)
- ➠ 9th in highest percentage of extra bases taken as a runner (61.4%)
- ➠ 10th in errors in left field (3)
- ➠ Led the Twins in home runs, doubles, sacrifice flies (9) and cleanup slugging percentage (.449)

Eddie Guardado

1996 Season

ERA is normally a very good indicator of a pitcher's quality, but in Eddie Guardado's case, his 5.25 mark last season was misleading. A handful of poor games inflated his ERA; in reality, his 1996 campaign was quite successful. He tied for the major league lead with 83 appearances and emerged as a key component of the Minnesota bullpen in pressure situations.

Pitching

Guardado relies on two primary pitches: a fastball and a curve. The velocity on his heater has improved over the last two years—he now throws it in the low 90s—and the pitch is particularly difficult for left-handed hitters to pick up. His curve is good when thrown well, but he hangs it sometimes and gives up the longball, especially to right-handed hitters. A power pitcher, he struck out a batter per inning, showed good control, and gave up less than a hit per inning. Guardado is also a flyball pitcher, and is much more effective on the road than in the Metrodome.

Defense

Guardado's delivery takes him toward the third base side of the diamond, so he has trouble getting to first base in time to make putouts. Otherwise, he is a solid fielder—he catches what he gets to and doesn't make mistakes. In fact, he was not charged with an error in 1996. His move to first is decent and his delivery to the plate very quick. Guardado can also be difficult to run on; only two runners attempted to steal against him all last season.

1997 Outlook

The Twins see past his ERA mark, and now count on Guardado as an integral part of their bullpen. He was a starter in the minors, and there is occasional talk of him getting another chance at the rotation, but that seems unlikely now. Count on another season in relief.

Position: RP
Bats: R **Throws:** L
Ht: 6' 0" **Wt:** 193

Opening Day Age: 26
Born: 10/2/70 in Stockton, CA
ML Seasons: 4
Pronunciation: Gwar-DAH-doe

Overall Statistics

	W	L	Pct.	ERA	G	GS	Sv	IP	H	BB	SO	HR	BR/IP
1996	6	5	.545	5.25	83	0	4	73.2	61	33	74	12	1.28
Career	13	24	.351	5.73	157	25	6	276.2	309	118	199	41	1.54

How Often He Throws Strikes

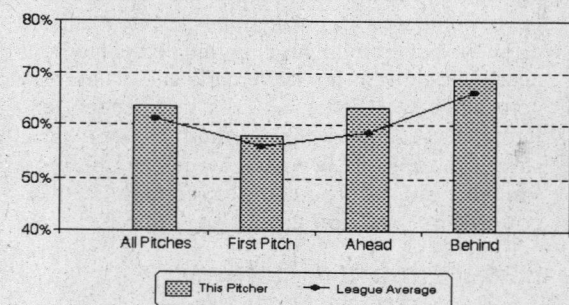

This Pitcher / League Average

1996 Situational Stats

	W	L	ERA	Sv	IP		AB	H	HR	RBI	Avg
Home	3	4	6.88	2	35.1	LHB	111	22	2	13	.198
Road	3	1	3.76	2	38.1	RHB	156	39	10	28	.250
First Half	4	3	4.84	2	44.2	Sc Pos	67	21	1	29	.313
Scnd Half	2	2	5.90	2	29.0	Clutch	132	31	8	23	.235

1996 Rankings (American League)

→ 1st in games pitched
→ 5th in holds (18) and first batter efficiency (.162)
→ 6th in relief wins (6)
→ 9th in highest relief ERA (5.25) and relief losses (5)
→ 10th in most strikeouts per 9 innings in relief (9.0)
→ Led the Twins in games pitched, holds (18), first batter efficiency (.162), lowest percentage of inherited runners scored (31.0%), relief wins (6), relief losses (5), least baserunners allowed per 9 innings in relief (11.9) and most strikeouts per 9 innings in relief (9.0)

Roberto Kelly

1996 Season

Seeking veteran leadership for their young out-fielders, the Twins signed Roberto Kelly to a one-year contract before the 1996 season. Kelly split time between center and right fields, platooning with Rich Becker and Matt Lawton, and despite missing two weeks in midseason with a hamstring pull, he responded with his best season in years.

Hitting

Kelly hits out of a slightly open stance, which gives him a good view of offerings from south-paws. In fact, he crushed them for an average in excess of .400 last season, making him very valu-able as a platoon player. Kelly has line-drive power, particularly to right-center field. He can be overpowered by fastballs up and in, and also chases sliders away. His plate discipline has never been exceptional; his walk rate is mediocre, and he strikes out quite a bit. Kelly hits the ball on the ground a lot, and grounds into a large number of double plays for a man with his speed.

Baserunning & Defense

Kelly has always had excellent speed, but his per-formance as a basestealer had declined in recent years. The Twins strongly emphasize baserunning fundamentals, and Kelly responded to the coach-ing, stealing 10 bases in 12 attempts. Kelly's de-fense had declined over the last two years as well, but he arrested the deterioration in 1996 and turned in a solid season in the field. He has above-average range, and is capable at any of the outfield spots. Though his arm isn't terrific, he seldom makes mistakes with it.

1997 Outlook

The Twins were pleased with Kelly's performance in 1996, and re-signed him for 1997. After playing for five different teams over a three-year period, Kelly thrived in the environment of the Twin Cit-ies. The Twins think they can contend in 1997, and Kelly would provide a useful option off the bench.

Position: RF/CF
Bats: R **Throws:** R
Ht: 6' 2" **Wt:** 202

Opening Day Age: 32
Born: 10/1/64 in Panama City, Panama
ML Seasons: 10
Nickname: Gray

Overall Statistics

	G	AB	R	H	D	T	HR	RBI	SB	BB	SO	Avg	OBP	Slg
1996	98	322	41	104	17	4	6	47	10	23	53	.323	.375	.457
Career	1060	3857	536	1110	190	24	87	442	220	265	686	.288	.337	.417

Where He Hits the Ball

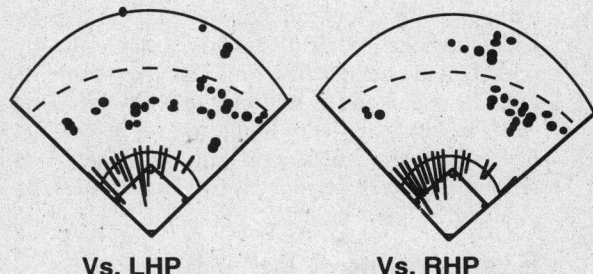

Vs. LHP   **Vs. RHP**

1996 Situational Stats

	AB	H	HR	RBI	Avg		AB	H	HR	RBI	Avg
Home	158	50	3	21	.316	LHP	128	52	4	21	.406
Road	164	54	3	26	.329	RHP	194	52	2	26	.268
First Half	173	54	1	22	.312	Sc Pos	88	28	2	41	.318
Scnd Half	149	50	5	25	.336	Clutch	42	13	0	3	.310

1996 Rankings (American League)

→ 1st in batting average vs. left-handed pitchers (.406)

→ 4th in most GDPs per GDP situation (20.0%) and batting average with two strikes (.274)

→ 7th in on-base percentage vs. left-handed pitchers (.462)

→ Led the Twins in batting average vs. left-handed pitchers (.406) and slugging percent-age vs. left-handed pitchers (.594)

Chuck Knoblauch

1996 Season

Amidst a lengthy contract negotiation, the forced retirement of Kirby Puckett, and Paul Molitor's pursuit of the 3,000-hit mark, Chuck Knoblauch continued his march of excellence. For much of the season, Knoblauch led the American League in batting average, but an August slump attributed to a nagging finger injury ruined his chances. Knoblauch still had a stellar campaign, but that's becoming normal for him.

Hitting

Knoblauch hits out of an exaggerated yet compact stance, holding his bat well back in the strike zone. His plate discipline has improved from very good to exceptional, and as he has gotten stronger, his ability to drive the ball has increased. He pulls balls down the left-field line, drives singles up the middle, and punches balls into the alleys. He hits most fastballs, and is seldom fooled by breaking stuff. Knoblauch's very high on-base percentage makes him an ideal leadoff hitter, and he's also refined the art of getting hit by pitches—he was plunked 19 times in 1996.

Baserunning & Defense

Knoblauch isn't a burner, but his speed is above-average. He gets excellent jumps, and is very good at reading pitchers and advancing on sacrifice flies. On a team of good baserunners, he's the best. Knoblauch anchors the Twins infield, and has mastered the difficult Metrodome artificial turf. His error rate is low, he has quick hands, he turns the double play, and has above-average range. Many scouts consider him to be the best defensive second baseman in the American League.

1997 Outlook

Knoblauch's on-again-off-again contract hassles with the Twins have been resolved; he has signed a long-term deal and should be manning second base in Minnesota through the year 2000. His hustle, intensity and desire have never been questioned. Chuck Knoblauch is now the centerpiece of the Minnesota franchise, and one of the game's brightest stars.

Position: 2B
Bats: R **Throws:** R
Ht: 5' 9" **Wt:** 181

Opening Day Age: 28
Born: 7/7/68 in Houston, TX
ML Seasons: 6
Pronunciation: NOB-lock

Overall Statistics

	G	AB	R	H	D	T	HR	RBI	SB	BB	SO	Avg	OBP	Slg
1996	153	578	140	197	35	14	13	72	45	98	74	.341	.448	.517
Career	857	3328	596	1019	184	41	34	333	214	429	369	.306	.391	.417

Where He Hits the Ball

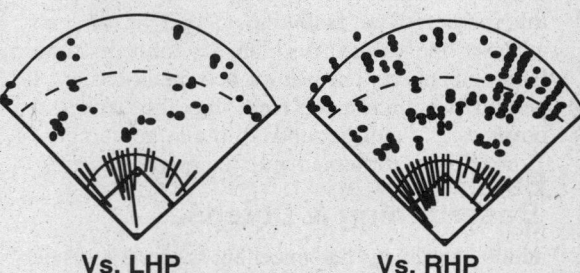

Vs. LHP   Vs. RHP

1996 Situational Stats

	AB	H	HR	RBI	Avg		AB	H	HR	RBI	Avg
Home	300	104	7	40	.347	LHP	147	57	4	19	.388
Road	278	93	6	32	.335	RHP	431	140	9	53	.325
First Half	308	114	8	45	.370	Sc Pos	110	40	2	53	.364
Scnd Half	270	83	5	27	.307	Clutch	71	12	0	9	.169

1996 Rankings (American League)

→ 1st in triples, batting average with two strikes (.311) and fielding percentage at second base (.988)

→ 2nd in runs scored, hit by pitch (19), times on base (314), pitches seen (2,953), batting average with runners in scoring position (.364) and on-base percentage for a leadoff hitter (.448)

→ 3rd in caught stealing and batting average vs. left-handed pitchers (.388)

→ 4th in stolen bases, lowest percentage of swings on the first pitch (12.6%) and batting average

Pat Meares

Position: SS
Bats: R **Throws:** R
Ht: 6' 0" **Wt:** 188

Opening Day Age: 28
Born: 9/6/68 in Salina, KS
ML Seasons: 4
Pronunciation: MEERS

1996 Season

Pat Meares entered the 1996 season hoping to build on the progress made during 1995. As usual he got off to a hot start, but fell into a deep slump which lasted most of the spring and early summer. An August rebound brought his stats back to respectable levels, but he did little to build on his 1995 progress.

Hitting

Meares hits out of a slightly closed stance. He tries desperately to keep his swing compact, and when he does he can turn on pitches for power. But then he gets power-conscious and falls into bad habits, resulting in long midseason slumps. When Meares' swing gets long, he tries to pull everything, and pitchers get him out with breaking stuff away or hard stuff up and in. His plate discipline isn't good, so his on-base percentages are low and he strikes out too much for someone with limited power.

Baserunning & Defense

Meares is reasonably fast on the bases. He's a good athlete, and although he is not particularly skilled as a basestealer, he seldom gets himself out. His defense is average across the board. He has a good backhand to his right, and generally quick reactions, but his range to his left is limited—especially on artificial turf—and his strong arm sometimes goes wild on him. Meares works well with keystone partner Chuck Knoblauch, but is not in Knoblauch's class with the glove.

1997 Outlook

Meares is a very hard worker, and no one can accuse him of lack of effort. He does what he can with average ability, and has emerged as a serviceable major league shortstop despite his deficiencies. While he is not a championship-quality shortstop, he's not terrible either. The Twins like him because of his work ethic, and the shortstop job is his until someone better comes along.

Overall Statistics

	G	AB	R	H	D	T	HR	RBI	SB	BB	SO	Avg	OBP	Slg
1996	152	517	66	138	26	7	8	67	9	17	90	.267	.298	.391
Career	459	1482	185	391	71	15	22	173	28	53	260	.264	.296	.377

Where He Hits the Ball

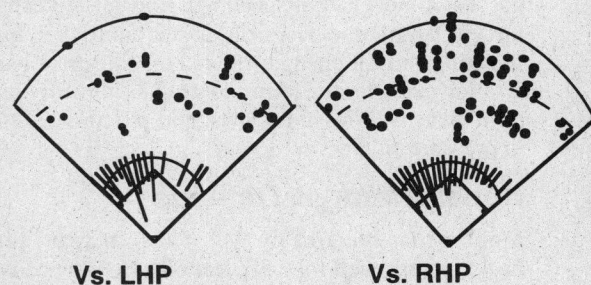

Vs. LHP   **Vs. RHP**

1996 Situational Stats

	AB	H	HR	RBI	Avg		AB	H	HR	RBI	Avg
Home	272	69	3	35	.254	LHP	138	41	4	25	.297
Road	245	69	5	32	.282	RHP	379	97	4	42	.256
First Half	275	70	5	39	.255	Sc Pos	135	37	5	57	.274
Scnd Half	242	68	3	28	.281	Clutch	59	21	0	11	.356

1996 Rankings (American League)

- → 2nd in batting average in the clutch (.356), errors at shortstop (22) and lowest fielding percentage at shortstop (.965)
- → 3rd in lowest on-base percentage and lowest on-base percentage vs. right-handed pitchers (.285)
- → 6th in lowest slugging percentage vs. right-handed pitchers (.356)
- → 7th in triples and lowest percentage of pitches taken (48.3%)
- → 8th in most GDPs per GDP situation (16.5%)
- → 9th in GDPs (19)
- → 10th in hit by pitch (9) and least pitches seen per plate appearance (3.50)

Paul Molitor

1996 Season

In 1996, Paul Molitor followed in Dave Winfield's footsteps and returned home to his native Minnesota in pursuit of his 3,000th hit. Many observers expected him to rebound from a disappointing 1995 season despite his advanced age, but not even the most optimistic expected the monster season he produced for the Twins. Molitor was durable, consistent, and amazingly productive. His 225 hits and 113 RBI were career highs.

Hitting

Molitor's swing is a thing of beauty: he keeps his head in perfect position, has great hip action and lashes line drives with his short, sharp stroke. He has lost almost no bat speed over the years, keeps up with all but the best heat, is seldom tricked by breaking stuff or change-ups and his line drive bat is tailor-made for the Metrodome. Molitor still hits righties as well as southpaws, and remains tough in pressure situations.

Baserunning & Defense

Molitor runs remarkably well for a 40 year old: heck, he runs well for a 30 year old. He is a heady baserunner who is difficult to pick off, takes the extra base at every opportunity and steals bases at a good percentage. Molitor was mainly a designated hitter in 1996, but he did play 17 games at first base and demonstrated that he can still play defense when called upon. The Twins try to keep him off the field, however, to minimize the risk of injury.

1997 Outlook

Molitor had a free-agency option in his contract, but signed a two-year contract with the Twins shortly after the season ended. He intends to remain a Twin for the remainder of his career. The Twins love his veteran presence in a young clubhouse, and couldn't be happier with his performance. At his age, a decline in his output has to be expected, but he gave no indication in 1996 that it would happen any time soon. He is a class act on and off the field.

Position: DH/1B
Bats: R **Throws:** R
Ht: 6' 0" **Wt:** 190

Opening Day Age: 40
Born: 8/22/56 in St. Paul, MN
ML Seasons: 19
Pronunciation: MOLL-uh-ter
Nickname: The Igniter

Overall Statistics

	G	AB	R	H	D	T	HR	RBI	SB	BB	SO	Avg	OBP	Slg
1996	161	660	99	225	41	8	9	113	18	56	72	.341	.390	.468
Career	2422	9795	1644	3014	544	105	220	1149	484	1004	1130	.308	.372	.452

Where He Hits the Ball

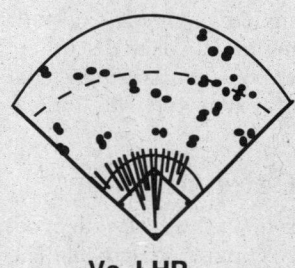

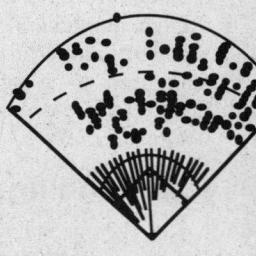

Vs. LHP   **Vs. RHP**

1996 Situational Stats

	AB	H	HR	RBI	Avg		AB	H	HR	RBI	Avg
Home	334	120	6	62	.359	LHP	148	51	2	23	.345
Road	326	105	3	51	.322	RHP	512	174	7	90	.340
First Half	354	115	6	54	.325	Sc Pos	209	70	2	98	.335
Scnd Half	306	110	3	59	.359	Clutch	96	33	3	18	.344

1996 Rankings (American League)

- → 1st in hits and singles
- → 2nd in at-bats
- → 3rd in triples, GDPs (21), games played (161), batting average vs. right-handed pitchers (.340) and batting average
- → 4th in plate appearances (729), highest groundball/flyball ratio (1.9) and batting average at home (.359)
- → 5th in highest percentage of extra bases taken as a runner (64.7%)
- → 8th in doubles, sacrifice flies (9), times on base (284) and least pitches seen per plate appearance (3.44)
- → 9th in batting average in the clutch (.344)

Greg Myers

Position: C
Bats: L **Throws:** R
Ht: 6' 2" **Wt:** 215

Opening Day Age: 30
Born: 4/14/66 in Riverside, CA
ML Seasons: 9

1996 Season

The Twins signed Greg Myers to a one-year contract prior to the 1996 season. He opened the season platooning with Matt Walbeck and quickly proved his worth, hitting for average and some power through the end of June. He slumped in July, however, and then spent two weeks in mid-summer on the disabled list with a strained abdominal muscle. Myers didn't play particularly well after his return.

Hitting

Myers is one of those guys who looks like he should produce more than he does. He is a strong man, and his left-handed pull swing seems ideally suited for the short porch in right field in the Metrodome. His power is actually somewhat limited, although he can turn a mediocre fastball around if the pitcher gets it in the wrong spot. Myers is impatient at times, and strikes out too frequently. His best role is as a platoon catcher, though he hit lefties well enough in limited action against them last year.

Baserunning & Defense

Myers is slow even for a catcher. He doesn't have good baserunning instincts, and is one of the few Minnesota runners who doesn't tag up and advance aggressively on fly balls. His defense is adequate: his arm strength, accuracy and release times are average, and his footwork is neither very good nor very bad. He caught 35 percent of runners attempting to steal on him in 1996. Myers also did an adequate job of working with a young pitching staff, although some pitchers preferred throwing to Walbeck.

1997 Outlook

Myers is a useful complementary player: a platoon catcher with a decent bat and a glove that won't hurt you. The Twins liked the job he did last year, but there were rumors that they intended to pursue free agent and Minnesota native Terry Steinbach this winter. Myers re-signed with the Twins in October, but how much he'll play depends on whether or not they bring in a veteran like Steinbach.

Overall Statistics

	G	AB	R	H	D	T	HR	RBI	SB	BB	SO	Avg	OBP	Slg
1996	97	329	37	94	22	3	6	47	0	19	52	.286	.320	.426
Career	583	1708	172	434	88	6	38	205	3	113	276	.254	.298	.379

Where He Hits the Ball

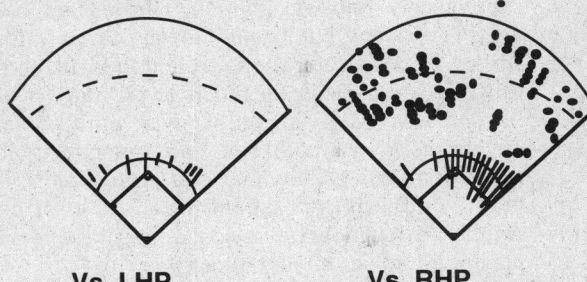

Vs. LHP   **Vs. RHP**

1996 Situational Stats

	AB	H	HR	RBI	Avg		AB	H	HR	RBI	Avg
Home	180	52	3	22	.289	LHP	31	9	0	4	.290
Road	149	42	3	25	.282	RHP	298	85	6	43	.285
First Half	219	69	6	40	.315	Sc Pos	97	26	1	40	.268
Scnd Half	110	25	0	7	.227	Clutch	52	16	1	7	.308

1996 Rankings (American League)

→ 1st in batting average on a 3-2 count (.440)
→ 4th in errors at catcher (8)
→ Led the Twins in batting average on a 3-2 count (.440)

Dan Naulty

1996 Season

A year ago, Dan Naulty was an obscure minor league pitcher with a good arm but no track record of consistent success. A stint in the Arizona Fall League went well, and then he opened eyes with a great spring training, making the team as a middle reliever. He was very effective from April to July, but just as the Twins moved him into the closer role, he came down with a numb arm. Tests revealed an arterial impingement; he had surgery to remove a rib that was blocking blood flow to his arm, and missed the last eight weeks of the season.

Pitching

Naulty generates 90-92 MPH velocity with a deceptive arms-and-legs motion. His fastball has great movement, but he can't always throw it for strikes. He also features a slider and forkball, both of which are difficult for hitters to pick up out of his delivery. Naulty's control gives him trouble, but he gets a few ground balls and isn't vulnerable to the home run. Naulty takes his profession seriously, and was a frequent sidekick of Rick Aguilera throughout the season, asking the veteran pitcher for advice about bullpen work.

Defense

Naulty's height and delivery leave him vulnerable to basestealers. He has tried to work on this problem, but there is only so much he can do about it. He is a fine athlete, and quite a good fielder.

1997 Outlook

Naulty had just been given the closer job when he hurt his arm. The injury is similar to those suffered by Mark Guthrie and Roberto Hernandez in recent years, so the long-term prospects for recovery are quite good. The Twins expect him back for 1997, but middle relief will be his role. He won't get the closer job back until he proves his arm is healthy.

Position: RP
Bats: R **Throws:** R
Ht: 6' 6" **Wt:** 211

Opening Day Age: 27
Born: 1/6/70 in Los Angeles, CA
ML Seasons: 1

Overall Statistics

	W	L	Pct.	ERA	G	GS	Sv	IP	H	BB	SO	HR	BR/IP
1996	3	2	.600	3.79	49	0	4	57.0	43	35	56	5	1.37
Career	3	2	.600	3.79	49	0	4	57.0	43	35	56	5	1.37

How Often He Throws Strikes

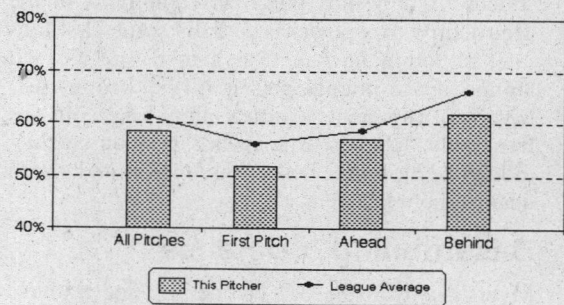

1996 Situational Stats

	W	L	ERA	Sv	IP		AB	H	HR	RBI	Avg
Home	2	1	1.47	1	30.2	LHB	88	14	4	14	.159
Road	1	1	6.49	3	26.1	RHB	120	29	1	14	.242
First Half	3	0	3.13	1	46.0	Sc Pos	49	14	1	22	.286
Scnd Half	0	2	6.55	3	11.0	Clutch	70	13	1	14	.186

1996 Rankings (American League)

➡ 4th in lowest batting average allowed in relief (.207)

➡ 8th in worst first batter efficiency (.302) and highest percentage of inherited runners scored (39.4%)

➡ Led the Twins in blown saves (5), most GDPs induced per GDP situation (13.3%), lowest batting average allowed in relief with runners on base (.223) and lowest batting average allowed in relief (.207)

Brad Radke

Position: SP
Bats: R **Throws:** R
Ht: 6' 2" **Wt:** 186

Opening Day Age: 24
Born: 10/27/72 in Eau Claire, WI
ML Seasons: 2

1996 Season

Coming into 1996, Brad Radke was the Twins' ace-by-default. Radke had been rushed to the majors in 1995 and showed flashes of potential, but at times was overwhelmed. In 1996, he was much better. He endured a slump in June and early July, but regained effectiveness and finished the season strongly. All throughout, he showed improving command and mental toughness, and emerged as the most polished of the Twins' young pitchers and the leader of the staff.

Pitching

Radke's fastball usually runs about 87 MPH. He has experimented with different grips to get more movement on the pitch, and is quite adept at throwing it on the corners of the plate. His curveball has improved from average to above-average, and his change-up is very deceptive. His slider can also be effective. Radke has outstanding control, and he never gives in to the hitter. He gives up lots of home runs, but most of them come with the bases empty. His strikeout rate doubled last year—without loss of control—which is an excellent sign for his future. He is very bright, emotionally mature and extremely durable. He has never been injured in his professional career.

Defense

Radke is a fine athlete, and is an excellent fielder. His compact motion and solid move to first base make him difficult to steal on, he fields bunts well and knows the fundamentals of infield play. He has obviously been well coached.

1997 Outlook

There is no more default about it: Radke is the Twins' ace. His 11-16 record in 1996 was due in part to poor run support. . . he could easily reverse that mark in 1997. He is maturing as a pitcher and as an individual. The Twins love Radke's mental approach to pitching, and although he doesn't have the stuff of a hard-throwing dominator, he should be a very fine pitcher for years to come.

Overall Statistics

	W	L	Pct.	ERA	G	GS	Sv	IP	H	BB	SO	HR	BR/IP
1996	11	16	.407	4.46	35	35	0	232.0	231	57	148	40	1.24
Career	22	30	.423	4.84	64	63	0	413.0	426	104	223	72	1.28

How Often He Throws Strikes

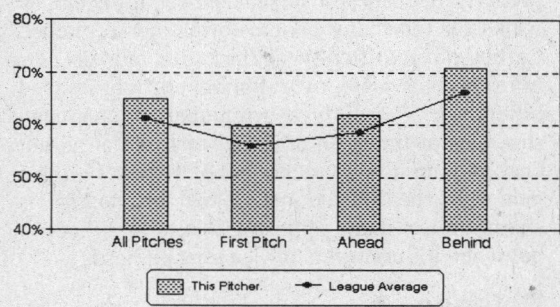

1996 Situational Stats

	W	L	ERA	Sv	IP		AB	H	HR	RBI	Avg
Home	6	7	3.63	0	124.0	LHB	518	133	24	65	.257
Road	5	9	5.42	0	108.0	RHB	383	98	16	48	.256
First Half	5	10	4.79	0	124.0	Sc Pos	168	47	10	70	.280
Scnd Half	6	6	4.08	0	108.0	Clutch	68	21	5	10	.309

1996 Rankings (American League)

- → 1st in home runs allowed, lowest ground-ball/flyball ratio allowed (0.7) and fielding percentage at pitcher (1.000)
- → 2nd in games started, lowest on-base percentage allowed (.302) and least baserunners allowed per 9 innings (11.3)
- → 4th in losses, least pitches thrown per batter (3.63), most home runs allowed per 9 innings (1.55) and least GDPs induced per 9 innings (0.6)
- → 6th in highest strikeout/walk ratio (2.6) and highest slugging percentage allowed (.464)
- → 7th in lowest batting average allowed (.256) and least run support per 9 innings (4.8)
- → 8th in innings pitched

Rich Robertson

1996 Season

The Twins were impressed with Rich Robertson's work late in 1995, and gave him a rotation spot in 1996. Robertson was erratic, but held his starting slot all season. He threw three shutouts and led the Twins staff with five complete games, but also had his share of disastrous outings and did not win back-to-back starts all season.

Pitching

Robertson is a tall, thin lefthander with adequate stuff. His fastball hits the upper 80s on a good day, while his slider and curveball are average major league pitches. Robertson says his change-up is his best pitch, and it is quite good when thrown properly. He doesn't have a power arm, but he walks far too many people for a finesse pitcher. Lefties have difficulty against him, but he gets himself in trouble by nibbling to right-handed hitters. He is mainly a groundball pitcher, and struggles at times on artificial turf, which is not encouraging for a pitcher who throws half his games in the Metrodome. When his control is sharp, he can make opposing hitters look bad. . . but when his control is off, he gets hit hard.

Defense

Robertson uses his left-handedness to good advantage against baserunners. He has a good move to first and is difficult to steal against. He is a mediocre fielder, however. He is adequate fielding bunts and is in generally good fielding position, but he has made his share of mistakes.

1997 Outlook

Robertson has little star ability, but he could still develop into a useful pitcher and will probably make the rotation again in 1997. He needs to improve his control—he finished with more walks than strikeouts in 1996—and consistency to get the most out of his average ability. His win-loss record in 1996 was hurt by poor run support, but he probably isn't better than a .500 pitcher in any event.

Position: SP/RP
Bats: L **Throws:** L
Ht: 6' 4" **Wt:** 175

Opening Day Age: 28
Born: 9/15/68 in Nacogdoches, TX
ML Seasons: 4

Overall Statistics

	W	L	Pct.	ERA	G	GS	Sv	IP	H	BB	SO	HR	BR/IP
1996	7	17	.292	5.12	36	31	0	186.1	197	116	114	22	1.68
Career	9	18	.333	5.00	78	35	0	262.2	280	161	165	28	1.68

How Often He Throws Strikes

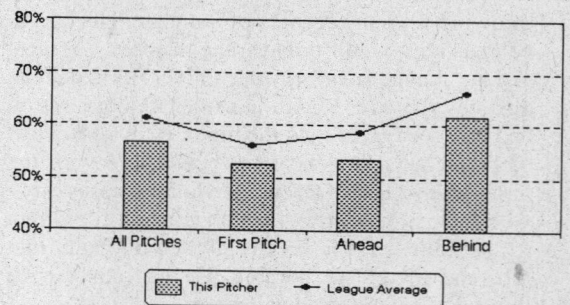

1996 Situational Stats

	W	L	ERA	Sv	IP		AB	H	HR	RBI	Avg
Home	3	11	5.06	0	105.0	LHB	146	33	3	18	.226
Road	4	6	5.20	0	81.1	RHB	576	164	19	79	.285
First Half	3	9	4.76	0	104.0	Sc Pos	183	49	8	76	.268
Scnd Half	4	8	5.57	0	82.1	Clutch	23	6	1	3	.261

1996 Rankings (American League)

- 1st in shutouts (3), walks allowed, lowest strikeout/walk ratio (1.0), highest on-base percentage allowed (.378), most baserunners allowed per 9 innings and least run support per 9 innings (3.7)
- 2nd in losses
- 4th in lowest winning percentage and most GDPs induced per 9 innings (1.1)
- 8th in complete games (5)
- 10th in GDPs induced (23), least strikeouts per 9 innings (5.5) and fielding percentage at pitcher (.979)
- Led the Twins in losses, complete games (5), shutouts (3), walks allowed, hit batsmen (9) and pickoff throws (67)

Frankie Rodriguez

1996 Season

Acquired from the Red Sox in exchange for Rick Aguilera midway through 1995, Frankie Rodriguez was counted on to be an integral part of the Minnesota rotation in 1996. He was erratic from start to start, however, showing great stuff and decent command at times, while struggling badly at others. He did make progress, impressing the Twins and others with his stuff and athletic ability.

Pitching

Rodriguez has the best arm on the team. His fastball runs 90-95 MPH, with excellent movement. His curveball and slider are also good pitches, and he has made progress developing a change-up. Control of all his offerings is a problem—his pitches have so much movement that he doesn't know where they are going to end up much of the time, although his command is better than it was a year ago. His strikeout rate is low for someone with his raw stuff, which indicates that further refinement is necessary. Lefthanders don't seem to have much of an advantage against him, and unlike many young pitchers, he isn't intimidated by the Metrodome. He shows good durability, and his arm is resilient.

Defense

Rodriguez entered pro ball as a shortstop, and he is an outstanding athlete on the mound, with terrific range and a strong and accurate arm on defense. He makes mistakes of inexperience, but that should resolve itself with time. His move to first is good and runners were thrown out 42 percent of the time on his watch.

1997 Outlook

Rodriguez spent a week as the Twins' closer in midsummer, but the organization sees him as a potential ace starter and he will be in the rotation in 1997. He is still unpolished and has a lot to learn about pitching, but he's less raw than he was a year ago. He's still very young, and continued progress could put him into the elite class. He certainly has the physical talent to dominate.

Position: SP/RP
Bats: R **Throws:** R
Ht: 6' 0" **Wt:** 195

Opening Day Age: 24
Born: 12/11/72 in Brooklyn, NY
ML Seasons: 2

Overall Statistics

	W	L	Pct.	ERA	G	GS	Sv	IP	H	BB	SO	HR	BR/IP
1996	13	14	.481	5.05	38	33	2	206.2	218	78	110	27	1.43
Career	18	22	.450	5.42	63	51	2	312.1	332	135	169	38	1.50

How Often He Throws Strikes

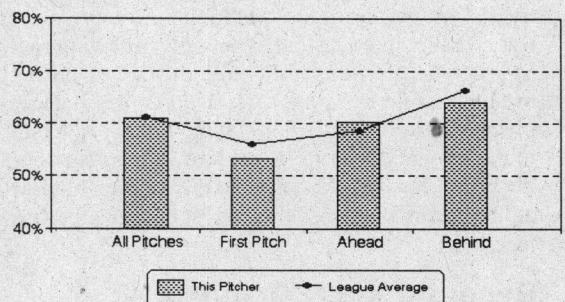

1996 Situational Stats

	W	L	ERA	Sv	IP		AB	H	HR	RBI	Avg
Home	6	5	3.90	0	101.2	LHB	441	121	12	56	.274
Road	7	9	6.17	2	105.0	RHB	361	97	15	56	.269
First Half	8	7	5.29	0	112.1	Sc Pos	201	58	8	89	.289
Scnd Half	5	7	4.77	2	94.1	Clutch	73	18	3	11	.247

1996 Rankings (American League)

→ 3rd in lowest strikeout/walk ratio (1.4)
→ 4th in highest ERA on the road (6.17)
→ 5th in least pitches thrown per batter (3.65) and least strikeouts per 9 innings (4.8)
→ 6th in losses
→ Led the Twins in wins, winning percentage, highest groundball/flyball ratio allowed (1.4) and most run support per 9 innings (5.5)

Scott Stahoviak

1996 Season

Scott Stahoviak entered the 1996 campaign in a tenuous position: the Twins were still searching for a suitable replacement for Kent Hrbek, and weren't sure Stahoviak was the guy. He opened the season in a platoon with Ron Coomer, and was productive in streaks—he was very hot in April, June, and July, but cool in May, August, and September. Overall, the platoon combo worked out great: Stahoviak and Coomer combined for 25 homers and 102 RBI.

Hitting

Stahoviak has the physique of a slugger but does not produce consistent power. He hit several long home runs last year, but also went through protracted power droughts. Stahoviak is very selective. He hits most fastballs, but gets his swing tied up when he tries too hard to pull the ball, resulting in slumps. He does best when he drives outside pitches to the opposite field. Stahoviak hits the ball in the air and doesn't ground into very many double plays. He has platooned in the majors, but has done decently against the few southpaws he has faced.

Baserunning & Defense

Stahoviak has long legs and runs well for a big guy. He can be tentative on the basepaths, but has worked hard to improve his reactions and is now a decent baserunner. Stahoviak used to be a third baseman, but an erratic arm forced his move to first base. He is an excellent defensive first baseman, with lightning-quick reactions and above-average range.

1997 Outlook

Stahoviak doesn't appear to have Hrbek-like potential, but his on-base percentage, occasional power and excellent glove make him a useful player. He is well-regarded for his work ethic and fits in well with the hustling Twins. Barring an offseason transaction, he'll continue platooning with Coomer and should remain productive. Stahoviak turns 27 in March 1997, an age when many players have their best years.

Position: 1B
Bats: L **Throws:** R
Ht: 6' 5" **Wt:** 222

Opening Day Age: 27
Born: 3/6/70 in Waukegan, IL
ML Seasons: 3

Overall Statistics

	G	AB	R	H	D	T	HR	RBI	SB	BB	SO	Avg	OBP	Slg
1996	130	405	72	115	30	3	13	61	3	59	114	.284	.376	.469
Career	244	725	101	196	53	3	16	85	8	92	197	.270	.353	.418

Where He Hits the Ball

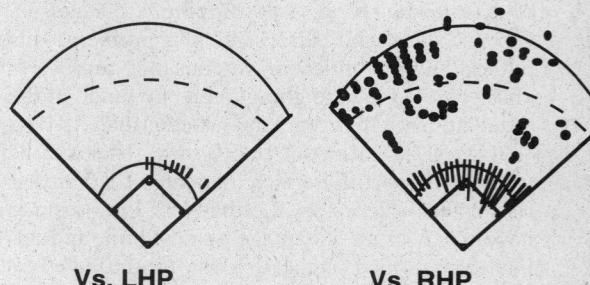

Vs. LHP   **Vs. RHP**

1996 Situational Stats

	AB	H	HR	RBI	Avg		AB	H	HR	RBI	Avg
Home	208	65	8	31	.313	LHP	29	8	1	3	.276
Road	197	50	5	30	.254	RHP	376	107	12	58	.285
First Half	199	59	7	32	.296	Sc Pos	125	35	5	51	.280
Scnd Half	206	56	6	29	.272	Clutch	50	14	1	5	.280

1996 Rankings (American League)

➔ 5th in fielding percentage at first base (.994)
➔ 6th in lowest percentage of swings put into play (35.3%)

Mike Trombley

1996 Season

Mike Trombley began 1996 in the minors, just another failed pitching prospect in a long line of failed Twins pitching prospects. He didn't sulk, however, and used his time in Triple-A exile to work on a new pitch: a split-fingered fastball. He was extremely effective at Salt Lake City, and when recalled in June, he moved into the Twins bullpen and continued to pitch well. He remained effective all season, and finished the year as the main right-handed option out of the Minnesota pen.

Pitching

Trombley has always had decent stuff. His fastball has average velocity and movement, but he has a nasty curveball that right-handed hitters bail out on. His problem in the past has been a need for a third pitch. Attempts to develop a standard change-up were unsuccessful, and it wasn't until he began using the split-fingered fastball that he had a true out pitch. Trombley remains more effective against righties than lefties. His control is usually good, and he is one of the few Twins pitchers who isn't vulnerable to the gopher ball. He has a resilient arm, and can work on consecutive days.

Defense

Trombley has worked hard to make his delivery more compact, but he will never be terrific at holding baserunners—opponents were successful on six of eight stolen base attempts against him in 1996. He's a pretty good athlete, however, and handles his position well. Like most Twins pitchers, he doesn't make fielding mistakes very often and is alert and active on the field.

1997 Outlook

By the end of the season, Trombley was the most reliable member of the Twins pen, and he will open the 1997 season as the main right-handed set-up man. He finally has lived up to the promise he showed in the minor leagues.

Position: RP
Bats: R **Throws:** R
Ht: 6' 2" **Wt:** 206

Opening Day Age: 29
Born: 4/14/67 in Springfield, MA
ML Seasons: 5
Pronunciation: TROM-blee

Overall Statistics

	W	L	Pct.	ERA	G	GS	Sv	IP	H	BB	SO	HR	BR/IP
1996	5	1	.833	3.01	43	0	6	68.2	61	25	57	2	1.25
Career	20	17	.541	4.72	141	35	8	375.1	398	143	280	50	1.44

How Often He Throws Strikes

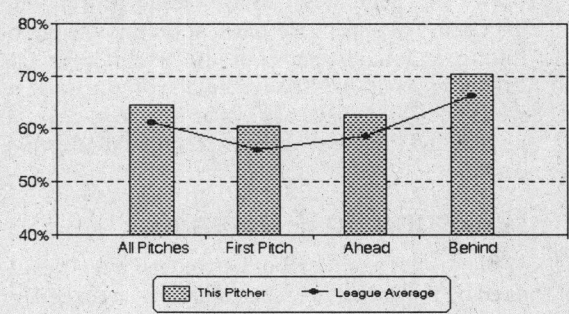

This Pitcher — League Average

1996 Situational Stats

	W	L	ERA	Sv	IP		AB	H	HR	RBI	Avg
Home	3	1	4.54	3	35.2	LHB	111	33	2	20	.297
Road	2	0	1.36	3	33.0	RHB	148	28	0	18	.189
First Half	2	0	1.93	1	23.1	Sc Pos	90	23	1	35	.256
Scnd Half	3	1	3.57	5	45.1	Clutch	112	25	0	15	.223

1996 Rankings (American League)

➡ 6th in highest percentage of inherited runners scored (43.1%)

➡ 9th in relief ERA (3.01)

➡ Led the Twins in lowest batting average allowed in relief with runners in scoring position (.256) and relief ERA (3.01)

Todd Walker

1996 Season

The Twins signed veteran Dave Hollins last December to buy time for heralded 1994 first-round draft pick Todd Walker. No one questioned Walker's offense, but the Twins felt the converted second baseman needed a year of Triple-A to settle in at his new position at third base. Walker hit for average and power in the Pacific Coast League, and worked hard on his defense. The Twins traded Hollins in August, and handed the position to Walker.

Hitting

Walker is a pure hitter. He has a compact stroke from the left side, and despite his lack of imposing brawn, he generates above-average power with excellent bat speed. He has a solid knowledge of hitting, and understands not just the fundamentals of hitting, but the fundamentals of pitching as well. The Twins have always been able to develop hitters, and they see Walker as their next offensive prodigy.

Baserunning & Defense

Walker is not a burner, but like most players developed by the Twins in recent years, he has excellent baserunning instincts, can steal bases when called upon and advances on the basepaths aggressively. He stole 13 bases at Salt Lake City, and two more in the majors. Walker is a decent defensive second baseman, but the presence of Chuck Knoblauch precludes his use at that position. He has worked hard to develop his glove skills at third base. He has good range and quick hands, but his arm is only average and he needs more experience at the hot corner.

1997 Outlook

The Twins are very confident in Walker, and barring a complete collapse or catastrophic injury, the third base job is his. His hitting ability and excellent work ethic have endeared him to the front office. Walker will play every day in 1997, and should be one of the leading candidates for American League Rookie of the Year.

Position: 3B
Bats: L **Throws:** R
Ht: 6' 0" **Wt:** 170

Opening Day Age: 23
Born: 5/25/73 in Bakersfield, CA
ML Seasons: 1

Overall Statistics

	G	AB	R	H	D	T	HR	RBI	SB	BB	SO	Avg	OBP	Slg
1996	25	82	8	21	6	0	0	6	2	4	13	.256	.281	.329
Career	25	82	8	21	6	0	0	6	2	4	13	.256	.281	.329

Where He Hits the Ball

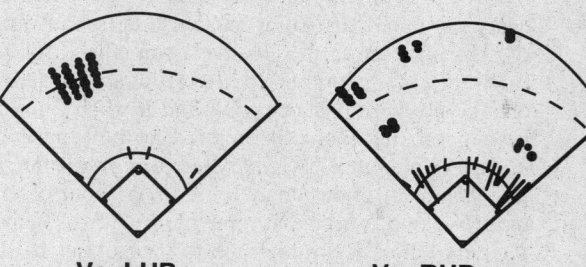

Vs. LHP   **Vs. RHP**

1996 Situational Stats

	AB	H	HR	RBI	Avg		AB	H	HR	RBI	Avg
Home	30	9	0	2	.300	LHP	16	3	0	0	.188
Road	52	12	0	4	.231	RHP	66	18	0	6	.273
First Half	0	0	0	0	-	Sc Pos	23	3	0	4	.130
Scnd Half	82	21	0	6	.256	Clutch	11	2	0	0	.182

1996 Rankings (American League)

➡ Did not rank near the top or bottom in any category

Scott Aldred

Position: SP/RP
Bats: L **Throws:** L
Ht: 6' 4" **Wt:** 215

Opening Day Age: 28
Born: 6/12/68 in Flint, MI
ML Seasons: 5

Overall Statistics

	W	L	Pct.	ERA	G	GS	Sv	IP	H	BB	SO	HR	BR/IP
1996	6	9	.400	6.21	36	25	0	165.1	194	68	111	29	1.58
Career	13	23	.361	6.13	75	52	0	314.0	364	151	196	52	1.64

1996 Situational Stats

	W	L	ERA	Sv	IP		AB	H	HR	RBI	Avg
Home	3	2	7.21	0	68.2	LHB	151	49	7	30	.325
Road	3	7	5.49	0	96.2	RHB	509	145	22	83	.285
First Half	3	7	7.78	0	83.1	Sc Pos	176	57	9	86	.324
Scnd Half	3	2	4.61	0	82.0	Clutch	34	8	1	4	.235

1996 Season

Scott Aldred opened the season with the woeful Tigers, but was so ineffective that Detroit gave up on him and placed him on waivers in late May. The Twins, looking for a left-handed pitcher, claimed him. He pitched a bit better for Minnesota, particularly in August and September.

Pitching & Defense

Aldred has a 90 MPH fastball and his curve has good movement, but he has trouble throwing strikes. . . and he doesn't have much of a change-up. The Twins thought he struggled with the Tigers because he didn't throw his curveball enough, so they encouraged him to do so and it seemed to help. He is a definite flyball pitcher. Left-handed hitters hit him better than righthanders do, so he isn't well-suited for short relief. Aldred's fielding skills are average at best, as is his ability to hold runners.

1997 Outlook

The Twins are encouraged by the progress Aldred made late in the season, but given his inconsistent track record, it's hard to get excited about him. He has a good arm, but so do a lot of others. He will be in the running for the fifth starter/long reliever job in 1997.

Ron Coomer

Position: 1B/RF
Bats: R **Throws:** R
Ht: 5'11" **Wt:** 195

Opening Day Age: 30
Born: 11/18/66 in Crest Hill, IL
ML Seasons: 2

Overall Statistics

	G	AB	R	H	D	T	HR	RBI	SB	BB	SO	Avg	OBP	Slg
1996	95	233	34	69	12	1	12	41	3	17	24	.296	.340	.511
Career	132	334	49	95	15	2	17	60	3	26	35	.284	.335	.494

1996 Situational Stats

	AB	H	HR	RBI	Avg		AB	H	HR	RBI	Avg
Home	126	36	5	20	.286	LHP	146	45	10	31	.308
Road	107	33	7	21	.308	RHP	87	24	2	10	.276
First Half	139	41	8	26	.295	Sc Pos	64	17	1	26	.266
Scnd Half	94	28	4	15	.298	Clutch	34	6	1	3	.176

1996 Season

Acquired from the Dodgers as part of the Kevin Tapani deal in 1995, Ron Coomer platooned with Scott Stahoviak at first base for the Twins in 1996. The Twins expected him to do well, but he exceeded their expectations and thrived as their primary right-handed first baseman.

Hitting, Baserunning & Defense

Coomer hits the ball where it is pitched and doesn't try to pull everything, resulting in above-average power to all fields. His swing is compact and he shows no weaknesses against left-handed pitching, crushing most fastballs. He shows much less power against righthanders, making him primarily a platoon player. He is slow and cautious on the bases. Coomer has a decent glove at first, and can fill in at third if needed. He also played right field, but his inexperience showed. He has a strong outfield arm but poor range.

1997 Outlook

Coomer combined with Scott Stahoviak to form a productive platoon combination, and there is no reason to believe things will change for 1997. As a veteran minor leaguer, he is just happy to have a major league job, and as long as he keeps hitting, the Twins will have one for him.

Greg Hansell

Position: RP
Bats: R **Throws:** R
Ht: 6' 5" **Wt:** 215

Opening Day Age: 26
Born: 3/12/71 in
Bellflower, CA
ML Seasons: 2

Overall Statistics

	W	L	Pct.	ERA	G	GS	Sv	IP	H	BB	SO	HR	BR/IP
1996	3	0	1.000	5.69	50	0	3	74.1	83	31	46	14	1.53
Career	3	1	.750	6.05	70	0	3	93.2	112	37	59	19	1.59

1996 Situational Stats

	W	L	ERA	Sv	IP		AB	H	HR	RBI	Avg
Home	2	0	5.36	2	48.2	LHB	127	30	8	20	.236
Road	1	0	6.31	1	25.2	RHB	164	53	6	37	.323
First Half	3	0	5.12	3	51.0	Sc Pos	84	25	2	40	.298
Scnd Half	0	0	6.94	0	23.1	Clutch	43	10	1	7	.233

1996 Season

Part of the payment for Kevin Tapani, Greg Hansell was out of options to begin the 1996 campaign, so the Twins had to keep him in the majors or risk losing him on waivers. He spent the season pitching long relief out of the Minnesota bullpen, but failed to distinguish himself.

Pitching & Defense

Hansell is a big guy and a hard thrower. His fastball is consistently in the low 90s and his curve has great movement. But he doesn't change speeds very well, and his control is nothing special. He is a flyball pitcher who is very vulnerable to the home run. Hansell has the arm to dominate a game, but that didn't happen very often in 1996. He is a decent athlete, but is average as a fielder. His move to first is pretty good for a righthander.

1997 Outlook

Hansell's job in 1996 was to watch and learn. He's not an old man by any means, and as long as he can throw hard, a job will be available for him. He was picked up by Boston on waivers in the offseson and will have to show improvement to get beyond the role of long reliever in 1997.

Matt Lawton

Position: RF/CF
Bats: L **Throws:** R
Ht: 5'10" **Wt:** 196

Opening Day Age: 25
Born: 11/3/71 in
Gulfport, MS
ML Seasons: 2

Overall Statistics

	G	AB	R	H	D	T	HR	RBI	SB	BB	SO	Avg	OBP	Slg
1996	79	252	34	65	7	1	6	42	4	28	28	.258	.339	.365
Career	100	312	45	84	11	2	7	54	5	35	39	.269	.354	.385

1996 Situational Stats

	AB	H	HR	RBI	Avg		AB	H	HR	RBI	Avg
Home	110	25	1	17	.227	LHP	49	12	0	6	.245
Road	142	40	5	25	.282	RHP	203	53	6	36	.261
First Half	139	32	2	21	.230	Sc Pos	74	23	3	38	.311
Scnd Half	113	33	4	21	.292	Clutch	38	9	1	9	.237

1996 Season

Matt Lawton opened 1996 as Kirby Puckett's replacement in right field. He got off to a slow start, and spent much of May and June in the minor leagues. He returned in July and played well for the remainder of the season.

Hitting, Baserunning & Defense

Lawton hits out of a crouch and reminds some people of Tony Phillips. He is patient and seldom swings at bad pitches, and though he is not a big home run threat, he has pop and can be dangerous. Lawton has well above-average speed, but was not aggressive on the bases in 1996. The converted infielder still struggles at times in the outfield, but his speed allows him to outrun most of his mistakes. His arm is not very strong.

1997 Outlook

Lawton did a decent job last year, and the Twins think he can do even better. Barring a trade or free-agent signing, he is the favorite to open in right field for 1997, at least as part of a platoon. The Twins like his attitude and offensive potential, and at the very least, he is a solid fourth outfielder.

Jose Parra

Position: RP/SP
Bats: R **Throws:** R
Ht: 5'11" **Wt:** 165

Opening Day Age: 24
Born: 11/28/72 in Jacagua, DR
ML Seasons: 2
Pronunciation: PAHR-uh

Overall Statistics

	W	L	Pct.	ERA	G	GS	Sv	IP	H	BB	SO	HR	BR/IP
1996	5	5	.500	6.04	27	5	0	70.0	88	27	50	15	1.64
Career	6	10	.375	6.59	47	17	0	142.0	181	55	86	28	1.66

1996 Situational Stats

	W	L	ERA	Sv	IP		AB	H	HR	RBI	Avg
Home	3	2	6.99	0	37.1	LHB	140	47	7	24	.336
Road	2	3	4.96	0	32.2	RHB	146	41	8	26	.281
First Half	1	3	6.83	0	27.2	Sc Pos	79	23	4	35	.291
Scnd Half	4	2	5.53	0	42.1	Clutch	14	5	2	3	.357

1996 Season

Another part of the Kevin Tapani deal with the Dodgers, Jose Parra had a sore arm in spring training and opened the season at Triple-A. He was recalled in April, sent back down, then recalled again in July and spent the rest of the season in Minnesota. He made five spot starts, but most of his appearances were in relief.

Pitching & Defense

Parra is a small guy, but with an arm that belies his stature. His fastball has above-average velocity and movement, and he usually throws it for strikes. He also shows a plus slider at times, and has worked to develop a change-up. Despite his stuff, he gives up too many hits: he throws strikes, but he leaves too many pitches up in the strike zone. He also gives up a lot of home runs. Parra is a fine athlete, with a quick delivery to the plate that can make him tough to steal against.

1997 Outlook

The Twins have remained high on Parra despite his struggles, and he is still very young. . . but he needs to show signs of progress soon. He will get big league innings in 1997, but his role is uncertain.

Jeff Reboulet

Position: SS/1B/2B/3B
Bats: R **Throws:** R
Ht: 6' 0" **Wt:** 171

Opening Day Age: 32
Born: 4/30/64 in Dayton, OH
ML Seasons: 5
Pronunciation: REB-uh-lay

Overall Statistics

	G	AB	R	H	D	T	HR	RBI	SB	BB	SO	Avg	OBP	Slg
1996	107	234	20	52	9	0	0	23	4	25	34	.222	.298	.261
Career	450	1016	135	252	46	2	9	100	13	128	154	.248	.335	.324

1996 Situational Stats

	AB	H	HR	RBI	Avg		AB	H	HR	RBI	Avg
Home	106	26	0	10	.245	LHP	86	20	0	6	.233
Road	128	26	0	13	.203	RHP	148	32	0	17	.216
First Half	129	27	0	12	.209	Sc Pos	55	16	0	22	.291
Scnd Half	105	25	0	11	.238	Clutch	40	13	0	5	.325

1996 Season

Jeff Reboulet has served as the Twins' primary utility infielder since 1992, and his role didn't change in 1996. He had a surprisingly good 1995 campaign, but he returned to earth in 1996 and did little with the bat.

Hitting, Baserunning & Defense

Reboulet is one of Tom Kelly's favorite players, but it isn't because of his bat. He works the count and usually makes contact, but he doesn't drive the ball and shows little power. He does bunt very well, however. His speed is average, but he is a solid baserunner with sound judgment. With the glove, Reboulet is a jack-of-all-trades. He has great hands, decent range and an average arm, and is capable at all four infield positions, though he is probably best at shortstop. He has played the outfield on occasion and doesn't embarrass himself, and also serves as the emergency catcher.

1997 Outlook

Tom Kelly is very loyal to his bench players, so Reboulet's hold on the utility job, while not guaranteed, is stronger than one might think given his weak hitting performance in 1996. His main competition is Denny Hocking, who is even less effective with the bat and not as polished defensively.

Dave Stevens

Position: RP
Bats: R **Throws:** R
Ht: 6' 3" **Wt:** 205

Opening Day Age: 27
Born: 3/4/70 in
Fullerton, CA
ML Seasons: 3

Overall Statistics

	W	L	Pct.	ERA	G	GS	Sv	IP	H	BB	SO	HR	BR/IP
1996	3	3	.500	4.66	49	0	11	58.0	58	25	29	12	1.43
Career	13	9	.591	5.39	129	0	21	168.2	187	80	100	32	1.58

1996 Situational Stats

	W	L	ERA	Sv	IP		AB	H	HR	RBI	Avg
Home	3	2	6.35	4	28.1	LHB	113	36	6	24	.319
Road	0	1	3.03	7	29.2	RHB	107	22	6	14	.206
First Half	1	0	3.29	11	27.1	Sc Pos	70	18	3	26	.257
Scnd Half	2	3	5.87	0	30.2	Clutch	96	27	6	22	.281

1996 Season

Dave Stevens opened the 1996 season as the Twins' closer, but erratic performances and an elbow nerve problem put his job in jeopardy. Out of frustration, he punched a locker in Cleveland July 20, ripping a gash in his pitching hand that required stitches. When he came off the disabled list in August, his closer role was gone, but he finished the season on a strong note in middle relief.

Pitching & Defense

Stevens' velocity is consistently in the low 90s. The fastball can be too straight at times, so he has worked to develop a second pitch. A marginal slider has given way to a split-fingered fastball, which shows potential to be an out pitch for him. He is vulnerable to the home run and to lefties. Stevens is a good athlete and holds runners very well for a righthander.

1997 Outlook

Stevens finished the season pitching very well, but no one is talking about him regaining the closer job. His role now seems to be middle relief. He could get another shot at being the stopper eventually, but the Twins would like to see him develop more consistency first.

Matt Walbeck

Position: C
Bats: B **Throws:** R
Ht: 5'11" **Wt:** 188

Opening Day Age: 27
Born: 10/2/69 in
Sacramento, CA
ML Seasons: 4

Overall Statistics

	G	AB	R	H	D	T	HR	RBI	SB	BB	SO	Avg	OBP	Slg
1996	63	215	25	48	10	0	2	24	3	9	34	.223	.252	.298
Career	286	976	98	224	42	1	9	109	7	52	148	.230	.269	.302

1996 Situational Stats

	AB	H	HR	RBI	Avg		AB	H	HR	RBI	Avg
Home	100	18	1	9	.180	LHP	74	21	1	10	.284
Road	115	30	1	15	.261	RHP	141	27	1	14	.191
First Half	48	11	0	3	.229	Sc Pos	62	16	1	22	.258
Scnd Half	167	37	2	21	.222	Clutch	35	3	0	0	.086

1996 Season

The Twins finally gave up on Matt Walbeck as an everyday catcher, and platooned the switch-hitter with the lefty-hitting Greg Myers. Walbeck saw some regular action during Myers' injury, and while he continued to display good glove skills, his offensive production remained disappointing.

Hitting, Baserunning & Defense

Walbeck is a switch-hitter, but hits so poorly from the left side of the plate that the Twins have toyed with the idea of making him strictly a right-handed hitter. He shows doubles power and a decent batting average from the right side, but from the left side all he produces are ground balls to second base. He is impatient from both sides. Walbeck is also slow and a station-to-station runner. He is a fine defensive catcher. His arm is average, but he has a very quick release, blocks the plate well and has a good rapport with the pitching staff.

1997 Outlook

Walbeck has blown the opportunity to start, and will likely spend the rest of his career in a reserve role. It may help him to hit only from the right side. If he does that he could become a decent option as a platoon catcher.

Other Minnesota Twins

Erik Bennett (Pos: RHP, Age: 28)

	W	L	Pct.	ERA	G	GS	Sv	IP	H	BB	SO	HR	BR/IP
1996	2	0	1.000	7.90	24	0	1	27.1	33	16	13	7	1.79
Career	2	0	1.000	7.81	25	0	1	27.2	33	16	13	7	1.77

A burly righthander who spent several years in Triple-A, Bennett got his first real major league chance last year. He had problems keeping the ball in the park, but might get another chance this year. 1997 Outlook: C

Mike Durant (Pos: C, Age: 27, Bats: R)

	G	AB	R	H	D	T	HR	RBI	SB	BB	SO	Avg	OBP	Slg
1996	40	81	15	17	3	0	0	5	3	10	15	.210	.293	.247
Career	40	81	15	17	3	0	0	5	3	10	15	.210	.293	.247

While primarily a catcher, Durant can play several positions, and he has excellent speed for a receiver. He throws pretty well, and could be a useful backup if he can improve his hitting a little. 1997 Outlook: B

Chip Hale (Pos: 2B, Age: 32, Bats: L)

	G	AB	R	H	D	T	HR	RBI	SB	BB	SO	Avg	OBP	Slg
1996	85	87	8	24	5	0	1	16	0	6	16	.276	.347	.368
Career	319	563	62	158	27	1	7	78	2	56	64	.281	.349	.369

One of baseball's best pinch hitters, Hale had another good year for the Twins in 1996, then signed a free agent contract with the Dodgers after the season. Should continue as a useful bench player. 1997 Outlook: A

LaTroy Hawkins (Pos: RHP, Age: 24)

	W	L	Pct.	ERA	G	GS	Sv	IP	H	BB	SO	HR	BR/IP
1996	1	1	.500	8.20	7	6	0	26.1	42	9	24	8	1.94
Career	3	4	.429	8.44	13	12	0	53.1	81	21	33	11	1.91

Considered a top pitching prospect, Hawkins has shown little in two chances to crack the Minnesota rotation. Tom Kelly doesn't seem to think much of him, but other teams would love to have him. 1997 Outlook: B

Denny Hocking (Pos: RF, Age: 26, Bats: B)

	G	AB	R	H	D	T	HR	RBI	SB	BB	SO	Avg	OBP	Slg
1996	49	127	16	25	6	0	1	10	3	8	24	.197	.243	.268
Career	84	219	30	45	10	2	1	15	7	16	38	.205	.258	.283

Hocking was expected to play a lot for the Twins last year, but a broken jaw and torn-up knee wrecked his season. If healthy, he could fashion a career as a utility infielder, but that's about it. 1997 Outlook: C

Scott Klingenbeck (Pos: RHP, Age: 26)

	W	L	Pct.	ERA	G	GS	Sv	IP	H	BB	SO	HR	BR/IP
1996	1	1	.500	7.85	10	3	0	28.2	42	10	15	5	1.81
Career	4	5	.444	7.10	35	13	0	115.1	149	56	62	28	1.78

Klingenbeck came to the Twins in the Scott Erickson deal in 1995, then spent most of the '96 season in Triple-A. He hasn't shown much in the majors yet, but could break through this year. 1997 Outlook: B

Travis Miller (Pos: LHP, Age: 24)

	W	L	Pct.	ERA	G	GS	Sv	IP	H	BB	SO	HR	BR/IP
1996	1	2	.333	9.23	7	7	0	26.1	45	9	15	7	2.05
Career	1	2	.333	9.23	7	7	0	26.1	45	9	15	7	2.05

A first-round pick in 1994, Miller moved quickly through the Twins system, then got eight late-season starts last year. He struggled, but will probably get another chance this spring. 1997 Outlook: C

Minnesota Twins Minor League Prospects

Organization Overview:

The Minnesota Twins' farm system has had its share of flops—Pat Mahomes and LaTroy Hawkins come to mind—but all in all, it's plugged quite a few holes for its small-market parent club. Over the past few years, it's given them a full three-man outfield and several young pitchers; if you go back even further, it produced a pretty fair double-play combination that still hasn't been broken up. Now, the system's crown jewel, Todd Walker, is set to take over at third base, and there are some good young pitchers and outfielders fine-tuning their skills in the higher levels of the system. Down deeper lies a second wave of talent, consisting mostly of pitchers and catchers. G.M. Terry Ryan has been forced to deal off a lot of high-priced talent, but in every deal, he's gotten a useful young player or two in return. All in all, it's one of the better assembly lines around, and should enable the Twins to remain competitive despite continuing free agent defections.

Brent Brede

Position: OF   **Opening Day Age:** 25
Bats: L **Throws:** L   **Born:** 9/13/71 in
Ht: 6' 4" **Wt:** 190   Belleville, IL

Recent Statistics

	G	AB	R	H	D	T	HR	RBI	SB	BB	SO	AVG
96 AAA Salt Lake	132	483	102	168	38	8	11	86	14	87	87	.348
96 AL Minnesota	10	20	2	6	0	1	0	2	0	1	5	.300
96 MLE	132	462	81	147	34	5	9	68	10	70	94	.318

Brent Brede is a left-handed hitting corner outfielder who could be a good major league leadoff man if given the chance. He doesn't have good instincts in the outfield or much home run power at the plate, but he does have one important skill: he gets on base. In the majors, Brede could hit around .300 with a good number of doubles and walks. He may not get much of a chance, however, because he's a little too old—25 this year—and his tools never have impressed the scouts. He can play, though.

Torii Hunter

Position: OF   **Opening Day Age:** 21
Bats: R **Throws:** R   **Born:** 7/18/75 in Pine
Ht: 6' 2" **Wt:** 205   Bluff, AR

Recent Statistics

	G	AB	R	H	D	T	HR	RBI	SB	BB	SO	AVG
93 R Twins	28	100	6	19	3	0	0	8	4	4	23	.190
94 A Fort Wayne	91	335	57	98	17	1	10	50	8	25	80	.293
95 A Fort Myers	113	391	64	96	15	2	7	36	7	38	77	.246
96 A Fort Myers	4	16	1	3	0	0	0	1	1	2	5	.188
96 AA New Britain	99	342	49	90	20	3	7	33	7	28	60	.263
96 MLE	99	339	47	87	20	2	7	31	5	23	66	.257

Scouts have always swooned at Torii Hunter's five-tool talent, but his production has always seemed to fall short

of expectations. Upon closer examination, however, his '96 season was remarkably productive for a 20 year old in Double-A. As one of the youngest players in the Eastern League, he played in one of the toughest hitter's parks in the minors, and still batted .263 with decent power. He played great defense in center field, with superior range and a strong arm. Once he figures out how to stay on breaking pitches, and discovers how to use his good speed to steal bases, he could be a monster.

J.J. Johnson

Position: OF   **Opening Day Age:** 23
Bats: R **Throws:** R   **Born:** 8/31/73 in
Ht: 6' 0" **Wt:** 195   Sharon, CT

Recent Statistics

	G	AB	R	H	D	T	HR	RBI	SB	BB	SO	AVG
93 A Utica	43	170	33	49	17	4	2	27	5	9	34	.288
93 A Lynchburg	25	94	10	24	3	0	4	17	1	7	20	.255
94 A Lynchburg	131	515	66	120	28	4	14	51	4	36	132	.233
95 A Sarasota	107	391	49	108	16	4	10	43	7	26	74	.276
95 AA Trenton	2	6	1	3	0	0	0	1	0	0	0	.500
96 AA New Britain	119	440	62	120	23	3	16	59	10	40	90	.273
96 AAA Salt Lake	13	56	8	19	3	1	1	13	0	1	11	.339
96 MLE	132	489	65	132	25	2	16	66	8	33	110	.270

J.J. Johnson came over to the Twins after the '95 season as "the player to be named" in the deal that sent Rick Aguilera to Boston. Last year, Johnson made that deal look better and better for the Twins. He moved from center to left field to accommodate Torii Hunter, and began to show the power the Red Sox had envisioned when they selected him in the first round of the '91 draft. Although he's not a basestealer, he's got good speed, and projects to be a multi-dimensional talent. He's not far off.

Brian Raabe

Position: 2B   **Opening Day Age:** 29
Bats: R **Throws:** R   **Born:** 11/5/67 in New
Ht: 5' 9" **Wt:** 170   Ulm, NM

Recent Statistics

	G	AB	R	H	D	T	HR	RBI	SB	BB	SO	AVG
96 AAA Salt Lake	116	482	103	169	39	4	18	69	8	47	19	.351
96 AL Minnesota	7	9	0	2	0	0	0	1	0	0	1	.222
96 MLE	116	462	82	149	35	2	15	55	6	38	20	.323

Second baseman Brian Raabe developed late and was prematurely written off as a prospect. It's a shame, because he's become one of the better second baseman in baseball—the majors included. Last year, he batted .351 to win the Pacific Coast League batting title. He's always had amazing bat control, and last year, he began to hit for more power. The result: 18 homers, with only 19 strikeouts. Is he a defensive liability? No. He's got decent range, sure hands and a strong arm. He's done developing at age 29, but he could hit over .300 in the majors and contribute in many other ways.

Ryan Radmanovich

Position: OF
Bats: L **Throws:** R
Ht: 6' 2" **Wt:** 185

Opening Day Age: 25
Born: 8/9/71 in Calgary, Alberta, Canada

Recent Statistics

	G	AB	R	H	D	T	HR	RBI	SB	BB	SO	AVG
93 A Fort Wayne	62	204	36	59	7	5	8	38	8	30	60	.289
94 A Fort Myers	26	85	11	16	4	0	2	9	3	7	19	.188
94 A Fort Wayne	101	383	64	105	20	6	19	69	19	45	98	.274
95 A Fort Myers	12	41	3	13	2	0	0	5	0	2	8	.317
96 AA New Britain	125	453	77	127	31	2	25	86	4	49	122	.280
96 MLE	125	449	74	123	31	1	25	83	3	41	134	.274

Ryan Radmanovich is a late-blooming power hitter who returned from an injury-marred '95 season to have a remarkable year last year. Playing in a notoriously tough home park, he established himself as a serious left-handed hitting power prospect. He still gets fooled by breaking pitches at times, and he's getting a bit old to be hanging around in the minors. He may break out with an even bigger year in '97 when he moves up to the hitter-friendly Pacific Coast League.

Mark Redman

Position: P
Bats: L **Throws:** L
Ht: 6' 5" **Wt:** 220

Opening Day Age: 23
Born: 1/5/74 in San Diego, CA

Recent Statistics

	W	L	ERA	G	GS	Sv	IP	H	R	BB	SO	HR
95 A Fort Myers	2	1	2.76	8	5	0	32.2	28	13	13	26	4
96 A Fort Myers	3	4	1.85	13	13	0	82.2	63	24	34	75	1
96 AA New Britain	7	7	3.81	16	16	0	106.1	101	51	50	96	5
96 AAA Salt Lake	0	0	9.00	1	1	0	4.0	7	4	2	4	1

The 13th overall pick in the '95 draft, lefthander Mark Redman climbed from A-ball to Triple-A during his first full season in the minors. He gets strikeouts with a great circle change, a good breaking ball, and a moving fastball in the high 80s. At the lower levels, he was dominant, but the more advanced competition revealed that his control still needs some refinement. If he's slow to remedy that flaw, it may take him a little longer than expected to work his way through Triple-A, which is a difficult place to pitch in the Twins' system.

Dan Serafini

Position: P
Bats: B **Throws:** L
Ht: 6' 1" **Wt:** 185

Opening Day Age: 23
Born: 1/25/74 in San Francisco, CA

Recent Statistics

	W	L	ERA	G	GS	Sv	IP	H	R	BB	SO	HR
96 AAA Salt Lake	7	7	5.58	25	23	0	130.2	164	84	58	109	20
96 AL Minnesota	0	1	10.38	1	1	0	4.1	7	5	2	1	1

As a lefty without overpowering stuff, Dan Serafini does all the things he needs to do to succeed. He shuts down the running game, throws four pitches for strikes, changes speeds and moves the ball around. His arm is durable, and he's never missed a professional start due to an arm injury. Only 23 this year, he may be given another year at Triple-A to refine his game. If he can win down there with his stuff, he can succeed in the majors.

Hector Trinidad

Position: P
Bats: R **Throws:** R
Ht: 6' 2" **Wt:** 190

Opening Day Age: 23
Born: 9/8/73 in Los Angeles, CA

Recent Statistics

	W	L	ERA	G	GS	Sv	IP	H	R	BB	SO	HR
93 A Peoria	7	6	2.47	22	22	0	153.0	142	56	29	118	6
93 AA Orlando	1	3	6.57	4	4	0	24.2	34	19	7	13	5
94 A Daytona	11	9	3.23	28	27	0	175.2	171	72	40	142	8
95 AA New Britain	4	11	4.61	23	22	0	121.0	137	67	22	92	6
96 AA New Britain	6	6	3.84	25	24	0	138.1	137	75	31	93	6

In one of the more unique trades in recent years, Hector Trinidad was traded from the Cubs in exchange for former Twins' G.M. Andy McPhail. The 23-year-old righthander possesses remarkable control, although he doesn't throw hard and tires easily. He showed some improvement in his second year at Double-A, but still needs to build up some stamina before he'll be ready for the big time. Give him at least another year.

Others to Watch

Catcher **Jose Valentin** was heralded as one of the top prospects in baseball after a big year in A-ball in '95. His hitting dropped off last year, but he moved up two more levels to finish in Double-A at age 20. The switch-hitter still figures to develop into one of the game's better receivers. . . The last thing the Twins need is another outfielder, but **Chris Latham** is worth keeping. The switch-hitting center fielder has decent power and speed, and is close to being ready. . .Righthander **Jason Bell** used excellent command to fan 177 batters between A-ball and Double-A. He tailed off after a midseason promotion, and the Twins plan to take it slow with Bell, who'll be 22 years old this year. . . There's still hope for third baseman **Chad Roper**, who improved slightly in his second season at the Double-A level. He's got a great infield arm, but needs to develop his power and smooth out his glovework. . . **A.J. Pierzynski** would be the top catching prospect in most other organizations. He's got power from the left side of the plate, a strong arm, and he's only 20 years old.

Joe Torre

1996 Season

Joe Torre is an all-business manager. Although he considers players' feelings and communicates effectively, the team always comes first—no exceptions. Torre prefers familiar veterans over newcomers. He was instrumental in bringing Joe Girardi and Mariano Duncan to New York, moves that helped the team. He also brought Gerald Perry to spring training, an idea that didn't work. When Torre likes a youngster, however, he makes a real commitment, like naming Derek Jeter his starting shortstop before spring training even began. Torre puts players into situations where they are likely to succeed, and then stands by them. The result in 1996 was a total success.

Offense

With a slow team that stole only 50 bases in 1995, Torre injected speed and upped the steal total to 96. The resurgence of Darryl Strawberry as a speed threat reflects Torre's aggressiveness, to the point of diminishing returns. Torre shifts his style toward bunting and other one-run tactics when he expects a pitching duel, not waiting until the late innings. His starting lineup reflects his scoring expectations; Tim Raines in left field means Torre expects a low-scoring game. Torre pinch hit sparingly in 1996 with poor results (.231 average).

Pitching & Defense

With Mariano Rivera and John Wetteland a well-defined duo in the pen, Torre was quick to seek relief. Starters' pitch counts were often held under 100 in 1996. Torre likes to manage specific match-ups. The acquisition of lefty Graeme Lloyd at the expense of defensive super-sub Gerald Williams reflected the desire for pitching specialists. Sticking with Lloyd through his early problems helped New York become a winner.

1997 Outlook

Torre got about all he could from his 1996 roster. Following up a co-Manager of the Year performance will be a challenge in 1997, but Torre's team will likely be there at the end.

Born: 7/18/40 in Brooklyn, NY

Playing Experience: 1960-1977, Mil, Atl, StL, NYN

Managerial Experience: 15 seasons

Manager Statistics

Year	Team, Lg	W	L	Pct	GB	Finish
1996	New York, AL	92	70	.568	—	1st East
15 Seasons		1,028	1,127	.477	—	—

1996 Starting Pitchers by Days Rest

	≤3	4	5	6+
Yankees Starts	7	96	20	29
Yankees ERA	7.09	4.43	7.06	5.36
AL Avg Starts	4	96	30	21
AL ERA	5.57	4.90	5.33	5.81

1996 Situational Stats

	Joe Torre	AL Average
Hit & Run Success %	48.8	39.1
Stolen Base Success %	67.6	69.6
Platoon Pct.	65.4	61.9
Defensive Subs	55	29
High-Pitch Outings	22	23
Quick/Slow Hooks	26/12	17/20
Sacrifice Attempts	53	58

1996 Rankings (American League)

→ 1st in hit-and-run percentage (48.8%), defensive substitutions (55), quick hooks (26) and 2+ pitching changes in low scoring games (25)

→ 2nd in steals of home plate (4), double steals (8), squeeze plays (9) and starting lineups used (131)

→ 3rd in relief appearances (411)

Wade Boggs

Hall of Famer

Position: 3B
Bats: L **Throws:** R
Ht: 6' 2" **Wt:** 197

Opening Day Age: 38
Born: 6/15/58 in Omaha, NE
ML Seasons: 15

1996 Season

For Wade Boggs, 1996 was an off year. He got through the first half well enough, but by midsummer he was slowed by a stiff back. His symptoms included increased difficulty getting around on tough left-handed pitchers, and he had the lowest RBI total of his 15-year career. General Manager Bob Watson was prompted to acquire righty-hitting Charlie Hayes, and Boggs appeared in only 14 games during September.

Hitting

Not many hitters can hit .311 in a bad year; that's how good Boggs is. His quick hands still work wonders. Boggs is especially adept at poking outside pitches into left field. His strike zone judgment is the best of his generation. One negative is that his power is fading with age, as he doesn't pull pitches like he used to.

Baserunning & Defense

A slow runner, Boggs has never stolen more than three bases in a season, but he remains alert to baserunning opportunities and can't be ignored by pitchers. His defense was sharp enough for a Gold Glove two years ago, and he still helps his team with astute positioning. At age 38 his lateral movement is not what it used to be.

1997 Outlook

Boggs enters the second year of a three-year contract in 1997. He has reacted well to a shifting role that had him looking like a platoon player at the end of last season, even if manager Joe Torre declined to use that term. Boggs' high on-base percentage makes him a viable leadoff batter on a team that doesn't steal many bases, but another change to watch for in 1997 is Boggs hitting second. He will also assume more designated hitter duty and appear lower in the batting order on occasion. Even with all these cautions, he still ranks among the top third basemen in the American League.

Overall Statistics

	G	AB	R	H	D	T	HR	RBI	SB	BB	SO	Avg	OBP	Slg
1996	132	501	80	156	29	2	2	41	1	67	32	.311	.389	.389
Career	2123	8100	1367	2697	518	55	105	905	20	1280	630	.333	.422	.449

Where He Hits the Ball

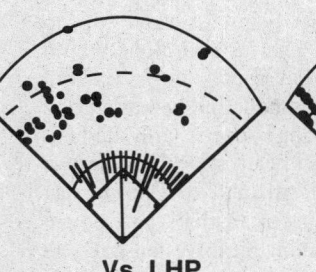
Vs. LHP

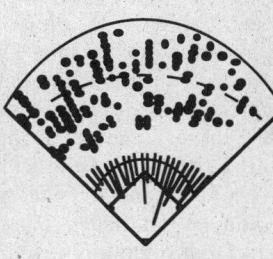
Vs. RHP

1996 Situational Stats

	AB	H	HR	RBI	Avg		AB	H	HR	RBI	Avg
Home	273	90	2	25	.330	LHP	138	37	0	12	.268
Road	228	66	0	16	.289	RHP	363	119	2	29	.328
First Half	293	97	2	26	.331	Sc Pos	104	31	0	33	.298
Scnd Half	208	59	0	15	.284	Clutch	65	23	0	6	.354

1996 Rankings (American League)

→ 1st in lowest percentage of swings that missed (4.7%) and lowest percentage of swings on the first pitch (10.4%)

→ 2nd in fielding percentage at third base (.974), highest percentage of pitches taken (65.6%) and highest percentage of swings put into play (60.1%)

→ 3rd in lowest HR frequency (250.5 ABs per HR) and highest batting average in the clutch (.354)

→ 7th in on-base percentage for a leadoff hitter (.384)

→ 8th in lowest slugging percentage vs. left-handed pitchers (.319)

New York Yankees

David Cone

1996 Season

David Cone started his 1996 season brilliantly, jumping out to a 4-1 record with a 2.03 ERA in early May. But then came the bad news: numbness in Cone's pitching hand was caused by an aneurysm, and he required surgery to graft a vein from his thigh into his pitching shoulder. There was no certainty that Cone would pitch again in 1996, but he came back September 2, helped the Yankees hold their dwindling lead in the American League East, and altered the course of the World Series with his superb start in Game 3. Cone finished the year as he began: on top of the pitching profession.

Pitching

Cone is a rare talent. He can throw his 90+ MPH heater to precise locations, using different grips to get various movements. The fastball alone would be effective, but Cone has much more. His out pitch is a split-fingered fastball, and he has a good hard curve. Cone can change speeds with the fastball or the curve. He also has a slider that he can throw overhand or sidearm, and in Florida last spring he sharpened his cut fastball and began using that pitch more often. Simply stated, Cone baffles hitters.

Defense

Cone has matured over the years, and he is more alert and steadier on defense than he used to be. His hard-throwing motion, however, leaves him out of position to field balls hit back toward the mound. Cone has never been good at holding runners. The opposition has been stealing nearly one base per game against him for years.

1997 Outlook

Given his strong comeback from surgery, Cone is again a frontrunner for a Cy Young award. He has two years remaining on a three-year contract with the Yankees. If any pitcher can look like a 20-game winner before the season starts, Cone is that man.

Position: SP
Bats: L **Throws:** R
Ht: 6' 1" **Wt:** 190

Opening Day Age: 34
Born: 1/2/63 in Kansas City, MO
ML Seasons: 11

Overall Statistics

	W	L	Pct.	ERA	G	GS	Sv	IP	H	BB	SO	HR	BR/IP
1996	7	2	.778	2.88	11	11	0	72.0	50	34	71	3	1.17
Career	136	80	.630	3.16	299	270	1	1994.0	1639	750	1812	154	1.20

How Often He Throws Strikes

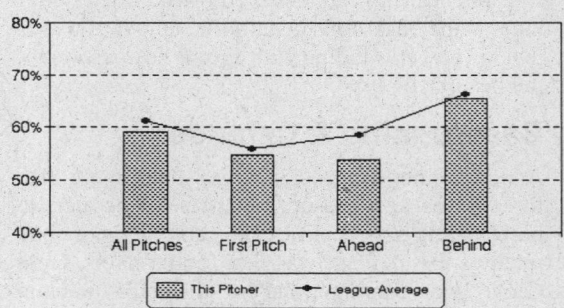

1996 Situational Stats

	W	L	ERA	Sv	IP		AB	H	HR	RBI	Avg
Home	3	1	2.91	0	34.0	LHB	147	29	1	10	.197
Road	4	1	2.84	0	38.0	RHB	106	21	2	11	.198
First Half	4	1	2.03	0	40.0	Sc Pos	49	11	1	18	.224
Scnd Half	3	1	3.94	0	32.0	Clutch	16	1	0	1	.063

1996 Rankings (American League)

➡ 10th in balks (1)
➡ Led the Yankees in balks (1)

Mariano Duncan

1996 Season

Acquired by the Yankees as a veteran utility infielder, Mariano Duncan was a major surprise last season. When starting second baseman Pat Kelly was injured in spring training, Yankee management announced, almost apologetically, that they would use a platoon of Duncan and Andy Fox. Duncan ended up with most of the playing time, although he was sidelined for 18 days in May with a strained groin. He provided an unexpected offensive spark.

Hitting

Duncan is aggressive and uses all fields. A free swinger, he almost never draws a base on balls. Duncan has not walked 20 times in a season since 1990, and he has had under 10 in each of the last two years. He readily swings at the first pitch, looking for a fastball he can drive. American League pitchers could not exploit this aggressiveness, however. Duncan makes consistent contact despite his undisciplined ways, and remains a dangerous hitter even with two strikes. His all-fields hitting style makes it difficult for defenses to plan positioning.

Baserunning & Defense

With good raw speed, Duncan needs watching on the bases. Although he was unfamiliar with American League pitchers, Duncan ran more in 1996 than he did in 1995. Still, he has lost half a step since stealing 48 bases for the Dodgers 10 years ago. Duncan is just a fair fielder. He showed good range at second base, but has always been erratic. In 1996 he was often removed in the late innings for a defensive replacement.

1997 Outlook

His offensive production made Duncan a good candidate to keep his starting role in 1997. However, don't expect him to hit .300 again, let alone .340. He offers versatility at the infield skill positions, which makes him valuable coming off the bench. That flexibility, although an asset for the team, could diminish Duncan's 1997 playing time.

Position: 2B
Bats: R **Throws:** R
Ht: 6' 0" **Wt:** 185

Opening Day Age: 34
Born: 3/13/63 in San Pedro de Macoris, DR
ML Seasons: 11

New York Yankees

Overall Statistics

	G	AB	R	H	D	T	HR	RBI	SB	BB	SO	Avg	OBP	Slg
1996	109	400	62	136	34	3	8	56	4	9	77	.340	.352	.500
Career	1190	4338	583	1167	219	37	86	466	168	189	835	.269	.303	.396

Where He Hits the Ball

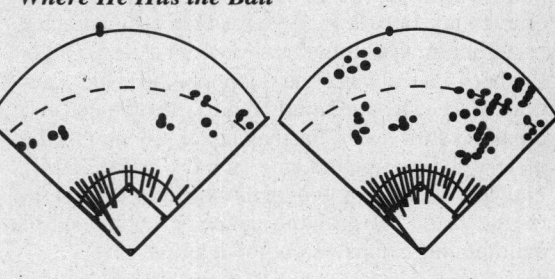

Vs. LHP   **Vs. RHP**

1996 Situational Stats

	AB	H	HR	RBI	Avg		AB	H	HR	RBI	Avg
Home	160	65	5	31	.406	LHP	123	39	2	19	.317
Road	240	71	3	25	.296	RHP	277	97	6	37	.350
First Half	201	63	4	27	.313	Sc Pos	114	37	1	48	.325
Scnd Half	199	73	4	29	.367	Clutch	51	13	0	7	.255

1996 Rankings (American League)

➡ 2nd in lowest fielding percentage at second base (.975)
➡ 5th in errors at second base (11)
➡ Led the Yankees in batting average with the bases loaded (.467)

Cecil Fielder

1996 Season

The Yankees acquired Cecil Fielder at the July 31st trading deadline, hoping his bat would help neutralize the left-handed pitching that opposing teams lined up against New York's lefty-dominant batting order. As the everyday designated hitter, Fielder did his job. He also performed well during the postseason, leading the Yankees with a .391 average in the World Series.

Hitting

Fielder is an aggressive free swinger, with extremely quick hands and wrists that can pull almost any pitch. At this point in his career he is more willing to line an outside pitch to right field, or even take a ball. In 1996 his increased patience brought him to within three walks of a career high. Pitchers have always had to approach Fielder cautiously. The standard method is to use offspeed and breaking stuff away. Fastballs over any part of the plate, or just outside, are always risky. While Fielder's batting average has been dropping in recent years, his growing patience has helped to maintain his offensive output at a high level.

Baserunning & Defense

Fielder stole his first base ever in 1996. That is not a sign of new-found speed; pitchers simply stopped watching him years ago. He rarely takes an extra base, and although he hustles, his size makes him an easy groundball double-play opportunity. At first base, Fielder is steady and has soft hands, but his range is clearly below average. Even before leaving Detroit, he was making the shift from first base to DH.

1997 Outlook

With 28 or more home runs in each of the last seven years, Fielder is major league baseball's leading home run hitter of the 1990s, with 258, and he ranks first in RBI over the same span with 791. If 1996 was not a comeback year for him, at least it showed that his decline has been exaggerated by some writers. He should continue to remain a fearsome slugger in 1997, but it might not be for the Yankees.

Position: 1B/DH
Bats: R **Throws:** R
Ht: 6' 3" **Wt:** 250

Opening Day Age: 33
Born: 9/21/63 in Los Angeles, CA
ML Seasons: 11
Nickname: Big Daddy

Overall Statistics

	G	AB	R	H	D	T	HR	RBI	SB	BB	SO	Avg	OBP	Slg
1996	160	591	85	149	20	0	39	117	2	87	139	.252	.350	.484
Career	1255	4380	655	1122	168	6	289	879	2	589	1118	.256	.346	.495

Where He Hits the Ball

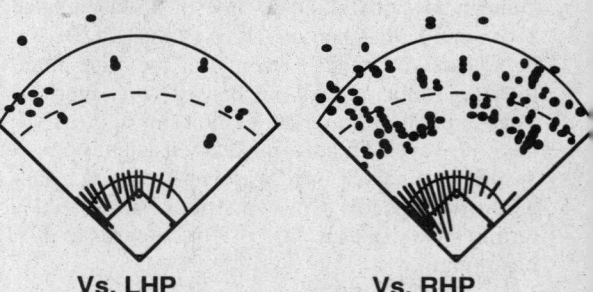

Vs. LHP   **Vs. RHP**

1996 Situational Stats

	AB	H	HR	RBI	Avg		AB	H	HR	RBI	Avg
Home	273	71	18	62	.260	LHP	138	38	11	28	.275
Road	318	78	21	55	.245	RHP	453	111	28	89	.245
First Half	318	77	19	60	.242	Sc Pos	152	42	8	75	.276
Scnd Half	273	72	20	57	.264	Clutch	80	15	4	9	.188

1996 Rankings (American League)

- ➡ 5th in games played (160)
- ➡ 6th in intentional walks (12) and pitches seen (2,823)
- ➡ 7th in lowest cleanup slugging percentage (.472), lowest percentage of extra bases taken as a runner (32.2%) and lowest batting average (.252)
- ➡ 8th in strikeouts (139), lowest batting average on the road (.245) and errors at first base (7)
- ➡ 9th in home runs (39), highest percentage of swings that missed (27.7%) and lowest percentage of swings put into play (36.1%)
- ➡ 10th in RBI (117) and lowest batting average vs. right-handed pitchers (.245)

Joe Girardi

1996 Season

When the Yankees let Mike Stanley go to Boston and brought in Joe Girardi as the starting catcher for 1996, fans and media were skeptical. By September all skepticism had turned into excitement. Girardi hit better than expected, posting a higher batting average than in any of his three seasons in Colorado. More importantly, Girardi handled a pitching staff that suffered numerous setbacks in 1996, yet came through very well in a championship season.

Hitting

Girardi is no power hitter. He didn't get an American League home run until August 18. He does make good contact, however, generally hitting the ball on the ground. Moving to the American League, where the breaking ball is more predominant than in the National League, may have helped Girardi. He can hit low-breaking junk better than he can catch up with a rising fastball. For a guy who isn't a big run producer, Girardi could be more patient at the plate.

Baserunning & Defense

Girardi's speed, surprising for a catcher, helps him beat out grounders for hits. In 1996 he took full advantage of pitchers who didn't watch him closely. His 13 stolen bases were a career high and he even stole home once. On defense, Girardi moves well around the plate and has an average throwing arm. He excels at handling pitchers and calling a game, subtle skills that were appreciated by manager and former catcher Joe Torre, but were less visible to fans and media. Girardi caught Dwight Gooden's no-hitter on May 14. By midsummer, Mike Stanley had been forgotten.

1997 Outlook

You can't argue with success, and the Yankees became big winners with Girardi behind the plate. Although his biggest strengths are not box score items, Girardi has won over the fans in New York. A free agent, he signed a two-year contract to remain with the Yankees.

Position: C
Bats: R **Throws:** R
Ht: 5'11" **Wt:** 195

Opening Day Age: 32
Born: 10/14/64 in Peoria, IL
ML Seasons: 8

Overall Statistics

	G	AB	R	H	D	T	HR	RBI	SB	BB	SO	Avg	OBP	Slg
1996	124	422	55	124	22	3	2	45	13	30	55	.294	.346	.374
Career	732	2417	273	660	101	17	20	235	35	157	340	.273	.321	.354

Where He Hits the Ball

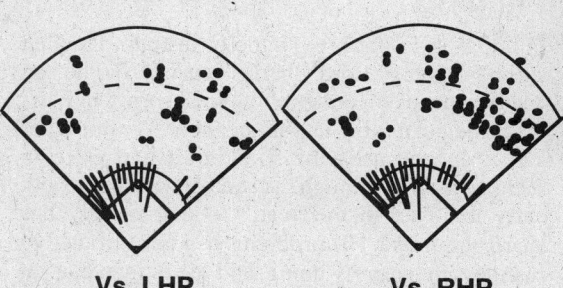

Vs. LHP   **Vs. RHP**

1996 Situational Stats

	AB	H	HR	RBI	Avg		AB	H	HR	RBI	Avg
Home	214	65	1	20	.304	LHP	136	35	0	9	.257
Road	208	59	1	25	.284	RHP	286	89	2	36	.311
First Half	225	66	0	21	.293	Sc Pos	101	30	1	43	.297
Scnd Half	197	58	2	24	.294	Clutch	57	20	0	5	.351

1996 Rankings (American League)

- → 1st in fielding percentage at catcher (.996)
- → 3rd in lowest on-base percentage vs. left-handed pitchers (.282)
- → 4th in batting average in the clutch (.351)
- → 9th in sacrifice bunts (11)
- → 10th in lowest slugging percentage vs. left-handed pitchers (.324) and lowest batting average on a 3-2 count (.105)
- → Led the Yankees in sacrifice bunts (11) and bunts in play (19)

1996 Season

After more than a year away from baseball, Dwight Gooden didn't have many believers after the 1995 season. But the Yankees saw Gooden's 94 MPH fastball in autumn instructional camp and signed the comeback candidate. Gooden struggled with his control in spring training and briefly lost his rotation spot in April, but pitching coach Mel Stottlemyre suggested some mechanical adjustments, and Gooden began a long streak of good starts on April 27. His comeback was capped with his first no-hitter on May 14. Later in the year, Gooden tired and was left off the postseason roster.

Pitching

In addition to the high-velocity fastball, Gooden still has his big "Lord Charles" curve. And he can change speeds on either pitch. Last spring in Florida he began mixing in a slider about five times per game, and he used the straight change more in 1996, as well. Although his control was shaky both early and late in the year, Gooden usually has sharp command. His problems can be attributed to rustiness in the early going, and the fatigue that set in as the year wore on. He hadn't pitched a full season since 1993.

Defense

Gooden's high leg kick has always made him easy prey for stolen bases. Nothing changed with Gooden's arrival in the American League, which is less known for the running game: 24 of 29 stolen base attempts against him were successful. Gooden fields his position well, getting off the mound quickly and making strong, accurate throws.

1997 Outlook

Gooden has shown he can still pitch effectively. Despite his late-summer swoon, the Yankees exercised their 1997 option on this comeback gem. Once again a fan favorite in New York, Gooden is very much in the Yankees' plans for their 1997 rotation.

Position: SP
Bats: R **Throws:** R
Ht: 6' 3" **Wt:** 210

Opening Day Age: 32
Born: 11/16/64 in Tampa, FL
ML Seasons: 12
Nickname: Doc, Dr. K.

Overall Statistics

	W	L	Pct.	ERA	G	GS	Sv	IP	H	BB	SO	HR	BR/IP
1996	11	7	.611	5.01	29	29	0	170.2	169	88	126	19	1.51
Career	168	92	.646	3.24	334	332	1	2340.1	2067	739	2001	142	1.20

How Often He Throws Strikes

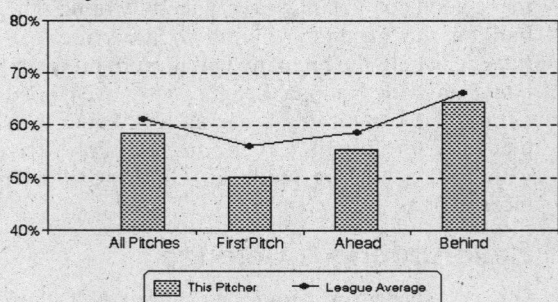

This Pitcher — League Average

1996 Situational Stats

	W	L	ERA	Sv	IP		AB	H	HR	RBI	Avg
Home	8	1	3.56	0	101.0	LHB	382	97	10	46	.254
Road	3	6	7.11	0	69.2	RHB	271	72	9	41	.266
First Half	8	4	4.20	0	94.1	Sc Pos	178	40	5	62	.225
Scnd Half	3	3	6.01	0	76.1	Clutch	44	3	0	0	.068

1996 Rankings (American League)

→ 3rd in most pitches thrown per batter (4.01) and least GDPs induced per 9 innings (0.6)
→ 4th in lowest strikeout/walk ratio (1.4)
→ 5th in stolen bases allowed (24) and highest stolen base percentage allowed (82.8%)
→ 6th in shutouts (1) and lowest batting average allowed with runners in scoring position (.225)
→ 8th in ERA at home (3.56)
→ 9th in least run support per 9 innings (5.0) and lowest batting average allowed vs. left-handed batters (.254)
→ 10th in balks (1), lowest batting average allowed (.259) and highest on-base percentage allowed (.352)

Derek Jeter

1996 Season

Derek Jeter was the Yankees' sixth Opening Day shortstop in six years. The search is now over. Jeter won the everyday shortstop job before the season began, and he just kept getting better. Jeter was an on-field team leader by the second half of the season, often sparking the team with his timely hitting in crucial games. His defense was consistently superior. He performed like a veteran in the Yankees' drive to the World Championship, hitting .361 in 15 postseason games, then capped his season by being a unanimous choice for American League Rookie of the Year.

Hitting

Jeter has a smooth swing and good strike zone judgment. His high strikeout total in 1996 reflected a little rookie over-aggressiveness. The Yankees used him as their leadoff batter in 38 games, and he rewarded them with a .328 average in that role. Jeter has good line drive power, using the whole field. He will hit more home runs as he matures.

Baserunning & Defense

Jeter has good raw speed, aggressive instincts on the bases, and an ability to read baserunning situations that is rare for a youngster. He always gets a good jump, and he troubles pitchers even when he isn't trying to steal. In the field he has excellent range, good lateral movement, and sure hands. His throwing arm might be his weakest asset, and it is above average.

1997 Outlook

With his strong second half and September flourish (.356 average, 25 runs and 18 RBI in his final 101 at-bats), Jeter offers hope that he can actually improve on his terrific rookie season. Certainly there is no evidence that he is headed for a sophomore slump. He has the tools and makeup to eventually rate among the best to ever play shortstop for the Yankees.

Position: SS
Bats: R **Throws:** R
Ht: 6' 3" **Wt:** 185

Opening Day Age: 22
Born: 6/26/74 in Pequannock, NJ
ML Seasons: 2
Pronunciation: JEE-ter

Overall Statistics

	G	AB	R	H	D	T	HR	RBI	SB	BB	SO	Avg	OBP	Slg
1996	157	582	104	183	25	6	10	78	14	48	102	.314	.370	.430
Career	172	630	109	195	29	7	10	85	14	51	113	.310	.365	.425

Where He Hits the Ball

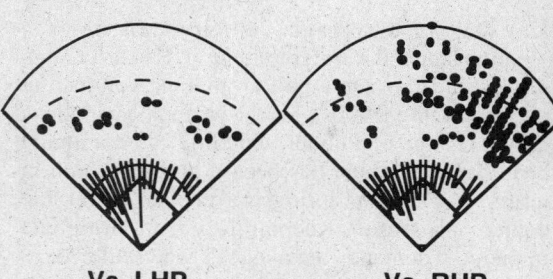

Vs. LHP   **Vs. RHP**

1996 Situational Stats

	AB	H	HR	RBI	Avg		AB	H	HR	RBI	Avg
Home	285	86	3	40	.302	LHP	162	55	2	12	.340
Road	297	97	7	38	.327	RHP	420	128	8	66	.305
First Half	285	79	4	38	.277	Sc Pos	155	42	2	67	.271
Scnd Half	297	104	6	40	.350	Clutch	80	21	3	13	.263

1996 Rankings (American League)

→ 2nd in errors at shortstop (22)
→ 3rd in highest groundball/flyball ratio (2.1) and lowest fielding percentage at shortstop (.969)
→ 4th in singles
→ 8th in sacrifice flies (9), lowest stolen base percentage (66.7%) and highest on-base percentage for a leadoff hitter (.379)
→ 10th in hit by pitch (9)
→ Led the Yankees in hits, singles, sacrifice flies (9), hit by pitch (9), strikeouts, games played (157), highest groundball/flyball ratio (2.1), batting average on the road (.327), highest percentage of extra bases taken as a runner (61.2 %) and batting average

Jimmy Key

Signed By ORIOLES

Position: SP
Bats: R **Throws:** L
Ht: 6' 1" **Wt:** 185

Opening Day Age: 35
Born: 4/22/61 in
Huntsville, AL
ML Seasons: 13

1996 Season

After rotator cuff surgery in July 1995, Jimmy Key wasn't expected to pitch again for a year. He went to spring training last February, however, expecting to be ready for Opening Day. "I never considered any other plan," said Key. He should have listened to his doctors. He pitched valiantly before going on the disabled list on May 17 with a sore shoulder and an ERA over 6.00. After resting the shoulder and missing more time in June because of a strained calf muscle, he came back in prime form and pitched 20 consecutive scoreless innings in July, winning five games that month. Fittingly, he started the World Series clincher for New York.

Pitching

Key has just average velocity, but he is a grandmaster at the craft of pitching. He can change speeds and move the ball around as well as any pitcher of the 1990s. Key's weapons include a curve, change and slider which he can command beautifully. Stamina has been a problem, both in terms of pitching during a game and over the course of a season. Keeping Key from tiring late in the year demands a manager's watchful eye.

Defense

Fielding is part of Key's total package of getting batters out. His motion leaves him well positioned, and he moves quickly and confidently around the mound, valuable skills for a pitching style that induces many grounders and slow rollers. Despite missing so much time, he led all Yankee pitchers except Andy Pettitte and Kenny Rogers in assists in 1996. Key holds runners exceptionally well, and yielded only two steals last year.

1997 Outlook

Expecting big things from Key, Baltimore signed him to a two-year, $7.5 million contract after the season. The O's must be careful not to over-work Key, but given ample rest, he could return to the form he showed in 1993 and 1994, when he won 35 games for the Yankees.

Overall Statistics

	W	L	Pct.	ERA	G	GS	Sv	IP	H	BB	SO	HR	BR/IP
1996	12	11	.522	4.68	30	30	0	169.1	171	58	116	21	1.35
Career	164	104	.612	3.49	411	344	10	2300.0	2231	563	1344	225	1.21

How Often He Throws Strikes

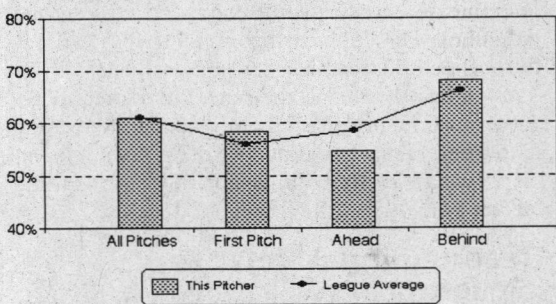

1996 Situational Stats

	W	L	ERA	Sv	IP		AB	H	HR	RBI	Avg
Home	4	5	5.05	0	76.2	LHB	95	16	1	7	.168
Road	8	6	4.37	0	92.2	RHB	548	155	20	74	.283
First Half	5	6	5.05	0	76.2	Sc Pos	136	37	5	55	.272
Scnd Half	7	5	4.37	0	92.2	Clutch	21	5	0	1	.238

1996 Rankings (American League)

- 1st in lowest stolen base percentage allowed (25.0%)
- 4th in most pitches thrown per batter (3.98)
- 6th in most GDPs induced per 9 innings (1.0)
- Led the Yankees in losses, lowest on-base percentage allowed (.326), lowest stolen base percentage allowed (25.0%), least baserunners allowed per 9 innings, most GDPs induced per 9 innings (1.0) and ERA on the road (4.37)

Tino Martinez

1996 Season

Don Mattingly is a tough act to follow, but Tino Martinez blended into the Yankee lineup just fine, helping fans forget Donnie Baseball. The main question about Martinez was whether his 1995 surge, largely built on improvement against left-handed pitching, would continue. Martinez again did well against southpaws in 1996, solidifying his status as a heart-of-the-order slugger. He produced the most RBI by a Yankee first baseman since Mattingly's big 1985 season. Martinez' 15th-inning grand slam on May 1, a season highlight, was his second game-winning home run in two days.

Hitting

Martinez is a powerful line-drive hitter who uses the whole field. He can turn on an inside pitch and pull a homer down the right field line—a necessity for a lefty hitter at Yankee Stadium—and he also can go with outside pitches against either righties or lefties. Martinez has shown better patience the last two years, with a career-high 68 walks in 1996. For a hard swinger, he is not an easy strike-out.

Baserunning & Defense

Regarded as a slow runner by most teams, Martinez can surprise a pitcher who doesn't pay attention. Alert, but lacking raw speed, Martinez is not much of a baserunning asset. Fielding is one area where Martinez will never approach Mattingly, but Tino gets the job done. His range is just average, but he has soft hands and good footwork, and his positioning has improved with experience.

1997 Outlook

Martinez has a five-year contract extending to the year 2000, and he faces no challengers for the starting first base job. He is in the prime of his career right now. Martinez may not be an All-Star in a league that contains Frank Thomas and Mo Vaughn, but he is just what New York needs for the next few years.

Position: 1B
Bats: L **Throws:** R
Ht: 6' 2" **Wt:** 210

Opening Day Age: 29
Born: 12/7/67 in Tampa, FL
ML Seasons: 7

Overall Statistics

	G	AB	R	H	D	T	HR	RBI	SB	BB	SO	Avg	OBP	Slg
1996	155	595	82	174	28	0	25	117	2	68	85	.292	.364	.466
Career	698	2491	332	676	134	6	113	429	5	266	394	.271	.342	.466

Where He Hits the Ball

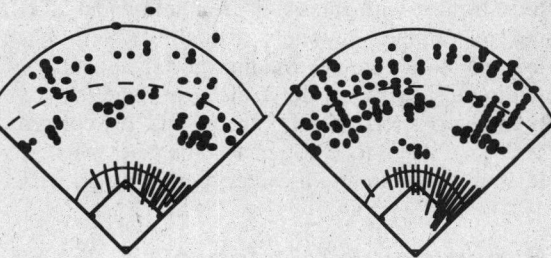

Vs. LHP   **Vs. RHP**

1996 Situational Stats

	AB	H	HR	RBI	Avg		AB	H	HR	RBI	Avg
Home	286	81	9	64	.283	LHP	219	61	6	40	.279
Road	309	93	16	53	.301	RHP	376	113	19	77	.301
First Half	330	93	14	63	.282	Sc Pos	180	61	10	98	.339
Scnd Half	265	81	11	54	.306	Clutch	82	26	6	24	.317

1996 Rankings (American League)

→ 2nd in fielding percentage at first base (.996)
→ 5th in batting average on an 0-2 count (.308) and lowest percentage of extra bases taken as a runner (31.5%)
→ 9th in batting average with two strikes (.267)
→ 10th in RBI, batting average with runners in scoring position (.339) and lowest percentage of swings on the first pitch (17.9%)
→ Led the Yankees in at-bats, RBI, pitches seen (2,588), plate appearances (671), batting average on an 0-2 count (.308), cleanup slugging percentage (.534) and batting average with two strikes (.267)

Paul O'Neill

1996 Season

Despite some mishaps, Paul O'Neill delivered a solid season that helped New York win a championship. Highlights included a career-high 14-game hitting streak and a .400 average during the month of April. Lowlights included an August 28th brawl with the Mariners (yes, again) which got O'Neill suspended for two games, and a sore hamstring that limited his mobility in September and throughout the postseason.

Hitting

The American League batting champion when he hit over .300 against lefties in 1994, O'Neill has struggled with southpaws ever since. He has the most trouble with curveballs from lefthanders, but he can clobber anyone's fastball. O'Neill has learned to use Yankee Stadium to his advantage, pulling inside pitches down the right field line and lining gap shots to left-center field on outside pitches. O'Neill took patience at the plate to a new level in 1996, setting a career high in walks with 102.

Baserunning & Defense

Although he stole 20 bases with Cincinnati in 1989, O'Neill does not offer much speed on the bases. He is, however, alert and competitive, and never shy about breaking up a double play. After some shuttling between right field and left in past years, O'Neill settled in as the Yankees' regular right fielder in 1996. He responded by continuing a 213-game errorless streak that started in July 1995. Runners respect his strong throwing arm, so he doesn't get many assists.

1997 Outlook

O'Neill's contract extends through 1998, and the Yankees are happy with him as their everyday right fielder and number-three hitter. Dropping down in the batting order when facing lefty starters—and more frequent days off against selected southpaws—will become a consideration eventually. It is unlikely that O'Neill, now 34, can return to the form he showed in 1994, but he still is a very productive hitter.

Position: RF
Bats: L **Throws:** L
Ht: 6' 4" **Wt:** 215

Opening Day Age: 34
Born: 2/25/63 in Columbus, OH
ML Seasons: 12

Overall Statistics

	G	AB	R	H	D	T	HR	RBI	SB	BB	SO	Avg	OBP	Slg
1996	150	546	89	165	35	1	19	91	0	102	76	.302	.411	.474
Career	1320	4490	631	1269	271	14	178	756	69	595	733	.283	.365	.468

Where He Hits the Ball

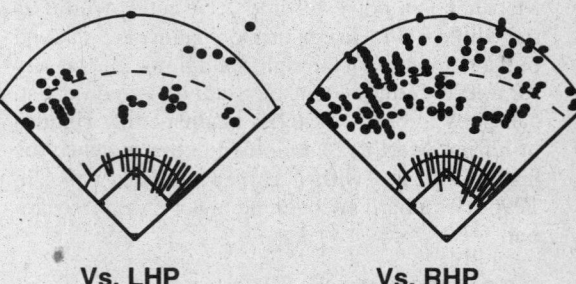

Vs. LHP **Vs. RHP**

1996 Situational Stats

	AB	H	HR	RBI	Avg		AB	H	HR	RBI	Avg
Home	252	82	7	41	.325	LHP	197	47	7	34	.239
Road	294	83	12	50	.282	RHP	349	118	12	57	.338
First Half	306	98	8	52	.320	Sc Pos	143	46	4	68	.322
Scnd Half	240	67	11	39	.279	Clutch	63	18	2	9	.286

1996 Rankings (American League)

→ 1st in fielding percentage in right field (1.000)
→ 4th in on-base percentage vs. right-handed pitchers (.445)
→ 5th in GDPs (20) and batting average vs. right-handed pitchers (.338)
→ 6th in walks
→ 10th in on-base percentage and lowest batting average vs. left-handed pitchers (.239)
→ Led the Yankees in doubles, walks, times on base (271), GDPs (20), on-base percentage, batting average vs. right-handed pitchers (.338), slugging percentage vs. right-handed pitchers (.521) and on-base percentage vs. right-handed pitchers (.445)

Andy Pettitte

1996 Season

The Yankees' most promising young southpaw in more than a decade, Andy Pettitte positively blossomed in 1996. He paced New York to a World Championship, and pitched well enough to compete for the Cy Young Award in just his second season, though Pat Hentgen edged him for the award. Pettitte also became the first Yankee to win 20 games since Ron Guidry. A true ace, Pettitte was 13-3 in games after a Yankee loss, and he was 3-0 against divisional rival Baltimore. He was outstanding in one of the Yankees' most important games of the year, a 1-0 win over the Braves in Game 5 of the World Series.

Pitching

Pettitte has all the tools. He throws a fastball in the low 90s, complemented by a sinker, a hard curve, and a cut fastball. Pettitte has good command of all four, and can change speeds off the fastball or the curve. When he's on, he is untouchable. On one of his rare bad days, Pettitte gets his breaking pitches up, where they become hittable. More often, he can keep any pitch down to get a ground ball, or use his big fastball for a strikeout or pop fly.

Defense

Adept at holding runners, Pettitte forced the opposition to lose more than half of their stolen base attempts in 1996 (10 steals, 11 caught). Even more impressive is his pickoff move, which is a difficult read for even the most astute baserunner. He also is an excellent fielder with good range, who led all Yankee pitchers in assists last year.

1997 Outlook

Predicting that any pitcher will win 20 games is a stretch, but Pettitte has the air of a big winner. His toughness at home in New York makes him a natural Opening Day starter, and he has been a bulldog in the clutch ever since he reached the majors. Look for another big year.

Position: SP
Bats: L **Throws:** L
Ht: 6' 5" **Wt:** 235

Opening Day Age: 24
Born: 6/15/72 in Baton Rouge, LA
ML Seasons: 2
Pronunciation: PET-it

New York Yankees

Overall Statistics

	W	L	Pct.	ERA	G	GS	Sv	IP	H	BB	SO	HR	BR/IP
1996	21	8	.724	3.87	35	34	0	221.0	229	72	162	23	1.36
Career	33	17	.660	4.00	66	60	0	396.0	412	135	276	38	1.38

How Often He Throws Strikes

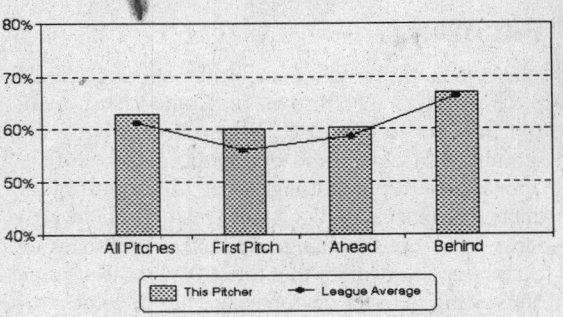

1996 Situational Stats

	W	L	ERA	Sv	IP		AB	H	HR	RBI	Avg
Home	10	4	3.22	0	120.1	LHB	152	50	1	12	.329
Road	11	4	4.65	0	100.2	RHB	692	179	22	76	.259
First Half	13	4	3.81	0	115.2	Sc Pos	193	49	6	67	.254
Scnd Half	8	4	3.93	0	105.1	Clutch	62	15	1	2	.242

1996 Rankings (American League)

- ➡ 1st in wins
- ➡ 2nd in ERA at home (3.22)
- ➡ 3rd in winning percentage and errors at pitcher (3)
- ➡ 4th in highest groundball/flyball ratio allowed (1.7)
- ➡ 5th in runners caught stealing (11)
- ➡ 6th in pickoff throws (164)
- ➡ 8th in ERA, most run support per 9 innings (6.4) and lowest fielding percentage at pitcher (.936)
- ➡ 10th in balks (1), GDPs induced (23), lowest slugging percentage allowed (.404), lowest stolen base percentage allowed (47.6%) and least home runs allowed per 9 innings (.94)

Mariano Rivera

1996 Season

The Yankees never had a better idea than converting Mariano Rivera from a starter to a reliever. There was a glimpse of what to expect when Rivera pitched 5-1/3 scoreless innings with eight strikeouts during the 1995 playoffs. In 1996 Rivera became a reliable and dominant blow-them-away set-up man, producing a 26-inning scoreless streak in April and May. Later he filled in as closer when John Wetteland went on the disabled list in August. Rivera had many impressive stats, but among his most glittering was the batting average of the first batter faced in each game: .089. Rivera's postseason dominance was critical to the Yankees' championship.

Pitching

There is nothing subtle or crafty about Rivera's pitching style. He throws high and rising heat, typically 94 to 96 MPH. When Rivera is on the mound, outfielders and corner infielders shift to opposite-field positioning, even with a pull hitter at bat. No one can pull a Rivera fastball. In the past Rivera has used a change-up, and he still uses an occasional hard slider that tops 90 MPH. But since converting to relief his repertoire has become simple. He even has mothballed a split-fingered pitch that he was experimenting with in 1995. Rivera is blessed with a resilient arm that can go day after day.

Defense

A remarkable fielder for a hard thrower, Rivera moves well around the mound and picks up bunts quickly and flawlessly. He also keeps an eye on the few runners who get on base against him. Opponents stole just three bases against Rivera in 1996.

1997 Outlook

With John Wetteland expected to return in 1997, and Rivera one of the Yankees' most untouchable players, it looks like another season of set-up work is in store for the young Panamanian. On any other team he would be promoted to closer immediately.

Position: RP
Bats: R **Throws:** R
Ht: 6' 2" **Wt:** 168

Opening Day Age: 27
Born: 11/29/69 in Panama City, Panama
ML Seasons: 2

Overall Statistics

	W	L	Pct.	ERA	G	GS	Sv	IP	H	BB	SO	HR	BR/IP
1996	8	3	.727	2.09	61	0	5	107.2	73	34	130	1	0.99
Career	13	6	.684	3.40	80	10	5	174.2	144	64	181	12	1.19

How Often He Throws Strikes

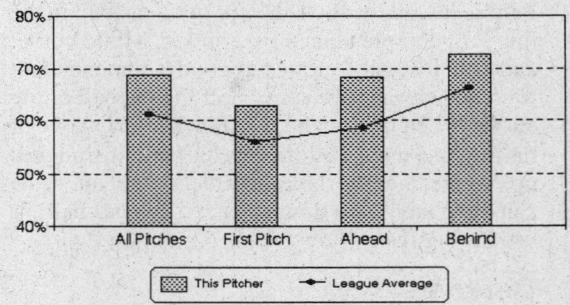

This Pitcher — League Average

1996 Situational Stats

	W	L	ERA	Sv	IP		AB	H	HR	RBI	Avg
Home	6	2	1.80	4	50.0	LHB	214	46	1	15	.215
Road	2	1	2.34	1	57.2	RHB	172	27	0	13	.157
First Half	3	1	1.80	2	60.0	Sc Pos	88	15	0	25	.170
Scnd Half	5	2	2.45	3	47.2	Clutch	239	45	1	19	.188

1996 Rankings (American League)

➡ 1st in holds (27), lowest batting average allowed vs. left-handed batters (.215), relief wins (8) and relief innings (107.2)

➡ 2nd in first batter efficiency (.089), relief ERA (2.09), lowest batting average allowed in relief (.189) and least baserunners allowed per 9 innings in relief (9.1)

➡ 4th in most strikeouts per 9 innings in relief (10.9)

➡ 8th in lowest batting average allowed in relief with runners on base (.210)

➡ 9th in lowest batting average allowed in relief with runners in scoring position (.170)

➡ Led the Yankees in holds (27)

Kenny Rogers

1996 Season

Much was expected of Kenny Rogers, who came to the Yankees with a rich four-year contract after going 17-7 with a 3.38 ERA in 1995. New York didn't get numbers like those, but they did get a solid starter. Actually, Rogers found himself in the bullpen for the first three weeks of the season, after Jimmy Key and Dwight Gooden emerged to join David Cone and Andy Pettitte in a four-man rotation when the team didn't need five starters. In his first start on April 21, Rogers took a no-hitter into the sixth inning. He then took a no-hitter into the eighth on May 28. Though he slipped in July and August, registering a 6.00 ERA for those two months, he came on strong in September (2.53) before enduring a rough postseason.

Pitching

Rogers has a good enough fastball, but his big strength is a deceptive change-up that is especially tough on lefty hitters. Rogers also has good command of his curveball and cut fastball, and he knows how to use the pitches that are working best for him in each outing. His simple game plan is to change speeds and move the ball around to keep hitters off balance. When he does that, he can beat anyone.

Defense

Extremely good at holding runners, Rogers held the opposition to four stolen bases in 10 attempts in 1996. He also has a great pickoff move. Rogers is an above-average fielder who moves well around the mound. He can be too quick sometimes, forcing a play that results in an occasional error.

1997 Outlook

Although his All-Star peak in 1995 is history, Rogers' contract ensures a prominent role in New York. He is far above average for a fourth starter, and his ability to suppress lefty hitting will make him the starter of choice in many big games.

Position: SP
Bats: L **Throws:** L
Ht: 6' 1" **Wt:** 205

Opening Day Age: 32
Born: 11/10/64 in Savannah, GA
ML Seasons: 8

Overall Statistics

	W	L	Pct.	ERA	G	GS	Sv	IP	H	BB	SO	HR	BR/IP
1996	12	8	.600	4.68	30	30	0	179.0	179	83	92	16	1.46
Career	82	59	.582	4.01	406	130	28	1122.1	1104	453	772	113	1.39

How Often He Throws Strikes

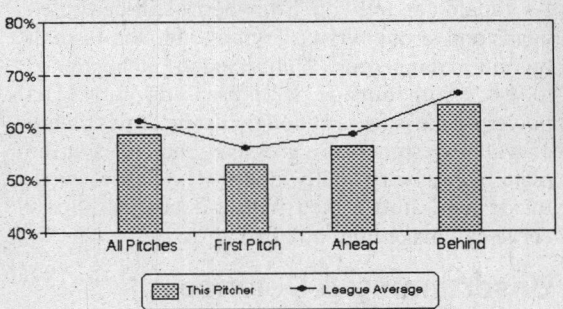

1996 Situational Stats

	W	L	ERA	Sv	IP		AB	H	HR	RBI	Avg
Home	9	5	4.27	0	109.2	LHB	110	23	3	12	.209
Road	3	3	5.32	0	69.1	RHB	576	156	13	67	.271
First Half	6	4	4.25	0	97.1	Sc Pos	145	44	3	58	.303
Scnd Half	6	4	5.18	0	81.2	Clutch	38	12	1	4	.316

1996 Rankings (American League)

- → 2nd in pickoff throws (194) and lowest strikeout/walk ratio (1.1)
- → 4th in lowest stolen base percentage allowed (40.0%) and least strikeouts per 9 innings (4.6)
- → 5th in lowest slugging percentage allowed (.378) and least home runs allowed per 9 innings (.80)
- → 6th in shutouts (1) and least run support per 9 innings (4.6)
- → 10th in highest groundball/flyball ratio allowed (1.4)
- → Led the Yankees in complete games (2), shutouts (1), pickoff throws (194) and lowest slugging percentage allowed (.378)

Darryl Strawberry

1996 Season

One of the few players ever to come back from an independent league to the majors, Darryl Strawberry revived his career by hitting .435 with 18 home runs in 108 at-bats for St. Paul of the Northern League. The Yankees gave him a minor league contract on July 4, watched him hit three homers in eight at-bats with Triple-A Columbus, and brought him to New York on July 6. His successful half-season with the Yankees included a three-homer game against Chicago's Kevin Tapani on August 6. Appearing in the World Series capped one of the best comeback stories of the 1990s.

Hitting

As Tapani can tell you, Strawberry still has quick hands and strong wrists. Trying to blow a fastball by him is dangerous. Right-handed pitchers need to work him outside with breaking stuff. His power stroke is feared enough that he draws plenty of walks, despite his aggressive tendencies at the plate. Strawberry really doesn't hit lefties well. Inside hard stuff mixed with a decent southpaw curve can make him look bad.

Baserunning & Defense

Under the aggressive style of Joe Torre, Strawberry began stealing bases again for the first time since 1993. He has good raw speed, although not what he had when he stole 36 bases for the Mets in 1987. If age has slowed him, it has also made him a bit wiser on the basepaths. In the field Strawberry still shows flashes of ability to cover his territory quickly, and his arm remains sound. He made no errors in 1996, but still must be regarded as somewhat erratic when it comes to concentration.

1997 Outlook

The Yankees exercised their 1997 option on the new, improved Strawberry, after letting him go following the 1995 season. There is still some lightning in his bat, and New York fans once again appreciate him.

Position: LF/DH
Bats: L **Throws:** L
Ht: 6' 6" **Wt:** 215

Opening Day Age: 35
Born: 3/12/62 in Los Angeles, CA
ML Seasons: 14
Nickname: Straw

Overall Statistics

	G	AB	R	H	D	T	HR	RBI	SB	BB	SO	Avg	OBP	Slg
1996	63	202	35	53	13	0	11	36	6	31	55	.262	.359	.490
Career	1447	5045	843	1309	239	36	308	935	211	750	1237	.259	.356	.504

Where He Hits the Ball

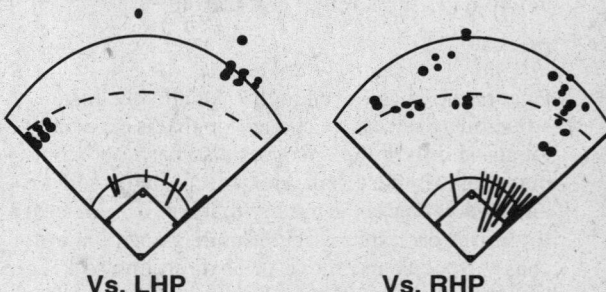

Vs. LHP   **Vs. RHP**

1996 Situational Stats

	AB	H	HR	RBI	Avg			AB	H	HR	RBI	Avg
Home	100	33	8	23	.330		LHP	53	11	4	9	.208
Road	102	20	3	13	.196		RHP	149	42	7	27	.282
First Half	4	0	0	0	.000		Sc Pos	47	13	3	23	.277
Scnd Half	198	53	11	36	.268		Clutch	38	11	1	5	.289

1996 Rankings (American League)

- ➞ 4th in batting average on a 3-2 count (.393)
- ➞ Led the Yankees in batting average on a 3-2 count (.393)

John Wetteland

1996 Season

With the same sweat-stained cap on his head all year, John Wetteland carried the weight of being the Yankees' ace reliever from their new spring home in Tampa to a World Series Championship in New York. Despite missing 24 days with a strained groin muscle, he led the league in saves and became the first Yankee to surpass 40 saves since Dave Righetti in 1986. Wetteland had saves in four consecutive games twice during the regular season, and the World Series MVP executed the feat again in the final four games of the Series.

Pitching

With a rising fastball that normally comes in at 95 MPH, Wetteland doesn't need any subtlety or tricks to get batters out. He is a classic strike-out/pop-up style closer. Having been a starter when he first came up in 1989, he does have other pitches. His second best is a big-breaking curve. He also has a slider, sinker, straight change and splitter, but rarely uses his third-best pitch. He just doesn't need it. Wetteland is a no-nonsense, come-at-you pitcher with good stamina.

Defense

Wetteland doesn't spend much time worrying about baserunners. While baserunners were rare, they succeeded on eight of 10 steal attempts against him in 1996. With his pitching style, he doesn't get many grounders back to the mound, but he is a solid fielder who made no errors last year. He moves well and knows what to do with the ball.

1997 Outlook

Second behind Randy Myers in the major leagues with 179 saves since 1992, Wetteland is arguably the single best relief pitcher in the game today. He had an option for 1997 which enabled him to file for free agency after the season, and he chose to exercise it. Wetteland was being hotly pursued by the Yankees, who have gone to the postseason in both of Wetteland's years as their closer.

Position: RP
Bats: R **Throws:** R
Ht: 6' 2" **Wt:** 215

Opening Day Age: 30
Born: 8/21/66 in San Mateo, CA
ML Seasons: 8
Pronunciation: WET-land

Overall Statistics

	W	L	Pct.	ERA	G	GS	Sv	IP	H	BB	SO	HR	BR/IP
1996	2	3	.400	2.83	62	0	43	63.2	54	21	69	9	1.18
Career	28	33	.459	2.92	370	17	180	512.0	392	174	556	43	1.11

How Often He Throws Strikes

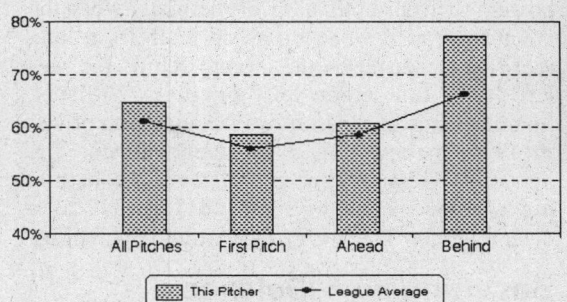

This Pitcher —— League Average

1996 Situational Stats

	W	L	ERA	Sv	IP		AB	H	HR	RBI	Avg
Home	2	0	1.86	18	29.0	LHB	144	41	7	24	.285
Road	0	3	3.63	25	34.2	RHB	97	13	2	5	.134
First Half	0	1	3.03	29	38.2	Sc Pos	67	12	2	19	.179
Scnd Half	2	2	2.52	14	25.0	Clutch	187	42	7	26	.225

1996 Rankings (American League)

➡ 1st in saves and save opportunities (47)
➡ 2nd in save percentage (91.5%)
➡ 3rd in least baserunners allowed per 9 innings in relief (10.6)
➡ 4th in games finished (58)
➡ 7th in relief ERA (2.83) and most strikeouts per 9 innings in relief (9.8)
➡ 10th in first batter efficiency (.190)
➡ Led the Yankees in saves, games finished (58), save opportunities (47), save percentage (91.5%) and blown saves (4)

Bernie Williams

1996 Season

For years the *Scouting Notebook* has been touting Bernie Williams as a budding superstar. In 1996 he put up the numbers to justify the rave previews. Williams sparked the Yankee surge to their bulging midseason lead, hitting .368 in May and .362 in June. Even more important, he hit .367 against divisional rival Baltimore. One offensive highlight was a grand slam against Minnesota on April 26, setting the trend for a host of Yankee come-from-behind victories. Williams also was a star on defense, reaching a career high in assists.

Hitting

Williams can do it all: hit for average, hit for power, hit from both sides of the plate, work the count to draw a walk, hit a bad pitch for a long sacrifice fly, or hit on the ground behind the runner. He is murder on lefty pitching. Williams' line-drive power blossomed into home run power in 1996, making him a manager's dream. The versatile Williams appeared all over the batting order, from second to sixth, and hit .372 as a cleanup hitter. There is no safe way to pitch him.

Baserunning & Defense

A tentative runner when he first came up, Williams now moves with more confidence. He gets a good jump and has excellent raw speed, explaining his career high in stolen bases in 1996. In the field he has the good range that it takes to play center in Yankee Stadium, and his throwing arm cut down 10 opportunistic baserunners last year.

1997 Outlook

The only question is whether Williams can possibly improve. He is in his prime, but the key to his emergence was his budding self-confidence, which suggests he can reach an even higher level in 1997. A quiet leader who could be the team's MVP for years, Williams would make the Yankees very happy simply by repeating what he did in 1996.

Position: CF
Bats: B **Throws:** R
Ht: 6' 2" **Wt:** 205

Opening Day Age: 28
Born: 9/13/68 in San Juan, PR
ML Seasons: 6

Overall Statistics

	G	AB	R	H	D	T	HR	RBI	SB	BB	SO	Avg	OBP	Slg
1996	143	551	108	168	26	3	29	102	17	82	72	.305	.391	.535
Career	681	2670	430	760	148	27	79	369	67	348	423	.285	.368	.449

Where He Hits the Ball

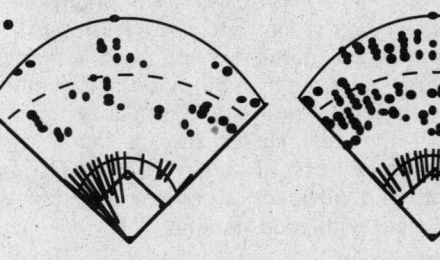

Vs. LHP   Vs. RHP

1996 Situational Stats

	AB	H	HR	RBI	Avg		AB	H	HR	RBI	Avg
Home	259	85	12	47	.328	LHP	173	65	16	39	.376
Road	292	83	17	55	.284	RHP	378	103	13	63	.272
First Half	270	88	16	56	.326	Sc Pos	146	52	6	73	.356
Scnd Half	281	80	13	46	.285	Clutch	75	22	3	13	.293

1996 Rankings (American League)

➡ 2nd in lowest fielding percentage in center field (.986)

➡ 3rd in errors in center field (5)

➡ 5th in batting average with runners in scoring position (.356) and slugging percentage vs. left-handed pitchers (.694)

➡ 6th in stolen base percentage (81.0%) and batting average vs. left-handed pitchers (.376)

➡ 7th in triples

➡ 10th in on-base percentage vs. left-handed pitchers (.447)

➡ Led the Yankees in home runs, runs scored, triples, total bases (295), stolen bases, slugging percentage, HR frequency (19.0 ABs per HR) and stolen base percentage (81.0%)

Ricky Bones

Position: SP/RP
Bats: R **Throws:** R
Ht: 6' 0" **Wt:** 193

Opening Day Age: 27
Born: 4/7/69 in Salinas, PR
ML Seasons: 6
Pronunciation: BONE-us

Overall Statistics

	W	L	Pct.	ERA	G	GS	Sv	IP	H	BB	SO	HR	BR/IP
1996	7	14	.333	6.22	36	24	0	152.0	184	68	63	30	1.66
Career	51	62	.451	4.72	166	149	0	944.0	1016	325	356	131	1.42

1996 Situational Stats

	W	L	ERA	Sv	IP		AB	H	HR	RBI	Avg
Home	4	6	5.24	0	77.1	LHB	330	109	20	47	.330
Road	3	8	7.23	0	74.2	RHB	281	75	10	46	.267
First Half	6	10	5.80	0	111.2	Sc Pos	142	40	6	64	.282
Scnd Half	1	4	7.36	0	40.1	Clutch	35	10	2	4	.286

1996 Season

When Pat Listach came to New York unable to play after an August 23 trade with Milwaukee, the Brewers amended the trade by throwing in Ricky Bones, who had been a mediocre starter for them. The Yankees got little from Bones, who appeared in just four games for them. In those four outings he gave up two hits per inning and had an ERA over 14.00. Bones has fallen a long way since being the Brewers' Opening Day starter in 1996.

Pitching & Defense

Bones has neither good velocity nor fine control. His fastball, slider, curve and change all have fair movement, and if batters put the ball in play near fielders, Bones can deliver a workmanlike outing. He is good at holding runners and usually helps himself in the field.

1997 Outlook

Bones had a poor season in 1996, and the Yankees felt he was not good enough to start for them. After the season he signed a one-year deal with the Reds, and he hopes the change in leagues will revive his career.

Andy Fox

Position: 2B/3B
Bats: L **Throws:** R
Ht: 6' 4" **Wt:** 205

Opening Day Age: 26
Born: 1/12/71 in Sacramento, CA
ML Seasons: 1

Overall Statistics

	G	AB	R	H	D	T	HR	RBI	SB	BB	SO	Avg	OBP	Slg
1996	113	189	26	37	4	0	3	13	11	20	28	.196	.276	.265
Career	113	189	26	37	4	0	3	13	11	20	28	.196	.276	.265

1996 Situational Stats

	AB	H	HR	RBI	Avg		AB	H	HR	RBI	Avg
Home	90	16	1	6	.178	LHP	29	5	1	3	.172
Road	99	21	2	7	.212	RHP	160	32	2	10	.200
First Half	117	24	2	8	.205	Sc Pos	48	8	1	9	.167
Scnd Half	72	13	1	5	.181	Clutch	18	5	0	0	.278

1996 Season

An Arizona Fall League alumnus, Andy Fox went to spring training hoping to land a backup utility role. When Pat Kelly succumbed to a sore shoulder Fox rose to the job of platoon second baseman before the season began. Mariano Duncan's superior hitting cut into Fox's playing time, but he got into 113 games, often as a defensive substitute at second, third or shortstop.

Hitting, Baserunning & Defense

Fox can do much better than his rookie stats would indicate. He hit .348 in 302 at-bats with Triple-A Columbus in 1995. He has line-drive power and very good speed and is often used as a pinch runner. His main defensive asset is versatility, as he can play all three infield positions. He has good range but is error-prone.

1997 Outlook

At 26 Fox is still young enough to project as a major league utility player, capable of producing a respectable batting average and filling in anywhere needed in the infield. The Yankees are very likely to give him another clear shot at establishing himself in 1997.

Charlie Hayes

Position: 3B
Bats: R **Throws:** R
Ht: 6' 0" **Wt:** 224

Opening Day Age: 31
Born: 5/29/65 in
Hattiesburg, MS
ML Seasons: 9

Overall Statistics

	G	AB	R	H	D	T	HR	RBI	SB	BB	SO	Avg	OBP	Slg
1996	148	526	58	133	24	2	12	75	6	37	90	.253	.300	.375
Career	1089	3896	419	1037	199	15	106	527	38	249	650	.266	.311	.407

1996 Situational Stats

	AB	H	HR	RBI	Avg		AB	H	HR	RBI	Avg
Home	234	62	5	36	.265	LHP	112	31	4	16	.277
Road	292	71	7	39	.243	RHP	414	102	8	59	.246
First Half	299	74	9	45	.247	Sc Pos	134	41	0	59	.306
Scnd Half	227	59	3	30	.260	Clutch	86	21	2	12	.244

1996 Season

Charlie Hayes came into baseball as the successor to Mike Schmidt as the Phillies' third baseman, and he's been in the shadows ever since. Hayes' acquisition on August 30th was one of Yankee GM Bob Watson's good moves during the 1996 season. Hayes filled in frequently when Wade Boggs had a stiff back in September. Hayes batted .284 as a Yankee, played a steady third base, and won a place in history by parking under the pop-fly that won the World Series.

Hitting, Baserunning & Defense

Hayes can work the count, pull a pitch, or go the opposite way. He has hit over 10 home runs every year for seven years. In the field he has adequate range and quick hands. Most of his errors come on errant throws. On the bases he has more speed than his build suggests, and he needs watching.

1997 Outlook

Hayes proves every year that he can help any major league team at third base. He exercised his right to demand to be traded after the season, but that's a contractual ploy and he could still return to New York. If he stays with the Yankees he'll lose his everyday player status, but a Boggs/Hayes platoon can obviously support a winner.

Jim Leyritz

Traded To
ANGELS

Position: C/3B/DH
Bats: R **Throws:** R
Ht: 6' 0" **Wt:** 195

Opening Day Age: 33
Born: 12/27/63 in
Lakewood, OH
ML Seasons: 7
Pronunciation:
LAY-ritz

Overall Statistics

	G	AB	R	H	D	T	HR	RBI	SB	BB	SO	Avg	OBP	Slg
1996	88	265	23	70	10	0	7	40	2	30	68	.264	.355	.381
Career	522	1561	203	416	70	1	57	243	5	193	349	.266	.361	.422

1996 Situational Stats

	AB	H	HR	RBI	Avg		AB	H	HR	RBI	Avg
Home	132	38	3	24	.288	LHP	87	21	0	5	.241
Road	133	32	4	16	.241	RHP	178	49	7	35	.275
First Half	170	41	4	24	.241	Sc Pos	79	21	1	31	.266
Scnd Half	95	29	3	16	.305	Clutch	30	7	0	2	.233

1996 Season

Andy Pettitte's favorite catcher, Jim Leyritz was a useful utility player for the 1996 Yankees. In addition to being backup catcher, Leyritz played some third base and left field and started 10 games as DH. He helped the Yankees jump out to an early lead by hitting .340 in April. And his momentum-changing three-run homer in Game 4 of the World Series was a career highlight.

Hitting, Baserunning & Defense

Leyritz still has pull-hitter power against righties or lefties, and he has learned how to use all fields later in his career. He is a mistake-punisher but can be overcome with a mid-90s fastball—leaving a mystery as to why Mark Wohlers threw him all those sliders. Leyritz has always been a good athlete and retains enough speed to steal a base. He is alert when running. His defense and throwing are just adequate.

1997 Outlook

Despite his postseason heroics, Leyritz was traded to the Angels after the season. He considers it a break, since he'll probably play more in Anaheim than he did in New York.

Graeme Lloyd

Position: RP
Bats: L **Throws:** L
Ht: 6' 7" **Wt:** 234

Opening Day Age: 29
Born: 4/9/67 in
Geelong, Victoria,
Australia
ML Seasons: 4

Overall Statistics

	W	L	Pct.	ERA	G	GS	Sv	IP	H	BB	SO	HR	BR/IP
1996	2	6	.250	4.29	65	0	0	56.2	61	22	30	4	1.46
Career	7	18	.280	4.06	196	0	7	199.1	202	58	105	17	1.30

1996 Situational Stats

	W	L	ERA	Sv	IP		AB	H	HR	RBI	Avg
Home	1	1	2.64	0	30.2	LHB	89	21	1	17	.236
Road	1	5	6.23	0	26.0	RHB	132	40	3	17	.303
First Half	2	2	2.13	0	38.0	Sc Pos	67	22	2	31	.328
Scnd Half	0	4	8.68	0	18.2	Clutch	104	30	1	12	.288

1996 Season

The Yankees obtained lefty reliever Graeme Lloyd, along with utility man Pat Listach, in an August 23 trade with the Brewers. Listach turned up lame and had to be returned to the Brewers, and when Lloyd began his Yankee tenure with a disastrous West Coast road trip, New York fans and media were up in arms. Lloyd came back and pitched well in late September, however, and he was vital to New York's postseason success.

Pitching & Defense

Lloyd is among the sharper lefty set-up relievers in the American League when his big curve, sinker and slider are in the strike zone. He is useful both for getting lefty hitters out, and for inducing groundballs to get double plays. For a large guy, he moves well around the mound, and he has always been good at holding runners.

1997 Outlook

The World Series exposure did Lloyd's career a world of good. Though bothered with arm soreness at times during 1996, he showed that he can work through that problem and come back strong. If there is any limitation for 1997, it is that he probably won't be used as frequently as he was earlier in his career.

Jeff Nelson

Position: RP
Bats: R **Throws:** R
Ht: 6' 8" **Wt:** 235

Opening Day Age: 30
Born: 11/17/66 in
Baltimore, MD
ML Seasons: 5

Overall Statistics

	W	L	Pct.	ERA	G	GS	Sv	IP	H	BB	SO	HR	BR/IP
1996	4	4	.500	4.36	73	0	2	74.1	75	36	91	6	1.49
Career	17	17	.500	3.43	300	0	11	336.1	296	161	338	25	1.36

1996 Situational Stats

	W	L	ERA	Sv	IP		AB	H	HR	RBI	Avg
Home	1	3	6.03	1	34.1	LHB	127	36	5	20	.283
Road	3	1	2.93	1	40.0	RHB	159	39	1	14	.245
First Half	3	2	4.91	2	40.1	Sc Pos	72	18	3	25	.250
Scnd Half	1	2	3.71	0	34.0	Clutch	81	26	2	12	.321

1996 Season

"It isn't New York so much as it's trying to do too much to impress a new team," said Yankee manager Joe Torre when Jeff Nelson began the 1996 season with less effectiveness than he had previously shown with Seattle. Nelson settled down, however, and became an integral part of the Yankees' highly effective bullpen. He posted a 1.46 ERA in 13 September appearances, and finished his year with three solid performances in the World Series.

Pitching & Defense

Nelson is a hard-throwing sidearmer with a good fastball and a sharp slider. His obvious specialty is retiring righty hitters with his sweeping motion. Nelson has a resilient arm, and he isn't tentative against lefty hitters when he faces them. He is only fair at holding runners, and his defense is a bit below average.

1997 Outlook

It has been an odyssey for Nelson since he became a dominant set-up man for the championship Mariners in 1995. His strong finish with New York ensures an opportunity somewhere in 1997, and Nelson's presence has meant success for two teams in two years.

Tim Raines

Position: LF
Bats: B **Throws:** R
Ht: 5' 8" **Wt:** 186

Opening Day Age: 37
Born: 9/16/59 in Sanford, FL
ML Seasons: 18
Nickname: Rock

Overall Statistics

	G	AB	R	H	D	T	HR	RBI	SB	BB	SO	Avg	OBP	Slg
1996	59	201	45	57	10	0	9	33	10	34	29	.284	.383	.468
Career	2112	7967	1419	2352	381	109	155	862	787	1168	838	.295	.385	.429

1996 Situational Stats

	AB	H	HR	RBI	Avg		AB	H	HR	RBI	Avg
Home	112	35	7	16	.313	LHP	39	10	0	5	.256
Road	89	22	2	17	.247	RHP	162	47	9	28	.290
First Half	84	24	2	10	.286	Sc Pos	52	13	2	25	.250
Scnd Half	117	33	7	23	.282	Clutch	30	9	1	4	.300

1996 Season

Although sidelined with a strained hamstring from May 22nd to August 11th, Tim Raines was a key factor in the Yankees' 1996 championship. When the team's division lead was shrinking, Raines sparked the offense with his baserunning and surprising power. Raines had a pair of two-homer games down the stretch.

Hitting, Baserunning & Defense

A former National League batting champion, Raines retains good strike zone judgment and ability to drive a pitch to any field. Though used mainly against right-handed pitching in 1996, the switch-hitting Raines can still handle himself from both sides of the plate. His speed is down considerably since he was a perennial 70-steal man ten years ago, but Raines is still aggressive and alert. Raines has good range in left, but often has problems judging fly balls. His arm is weak.

1997 Outlook

Raines has lost the everyday status that he last had with the White Sox in 1995, but that is mainly a reflection of the Yankees' surplus of outfield talent. Raines has another year on his contract with New York, and should see plenty of action this year.

Ruben Rivera

Position: RF/LF/CF
Bats: R **Throws:** R
Ht: 6' 3" **Wt:** 200

Opening Day Age: 23
Born: 11/14/73 in La Chorrera, Panama
ML Seasons: 2

Overall Statistics

	G	AB	R	H	D	T	HR	RBI	SB	BB	SO	Avg	OBP	Slg
1996	46	88	17	25	6	1	2	16	6	13	26	.284	.381	.443
Career	51	89	17	25	6	1	2	16	6	13	27	.281	.377	.438

1996 Situational Stats

	AB	H	HR	RBI	Avg		AB	H	HR	RBI	Avg
Home	24	7	0	6	.292	LHP	25	7	2	6	.280
Road	64	18	2	10	.281	RHP	63	18	0	10	.286
First Half	47	13	1	10	.277	Sc Pos	36	10	0	14	.278
Scnd Half	41	12	1	6	.293	Clutch	13	3	1	2	.231

1996 Season

Although he played little for New York in 1996, Ruben Rivera was a critical part of the team. Down the stretch he was the Yankees' best defensive outfield replacement, filling an important role after the trade of Gerald Williams to Milwaukee. Rivera actually played better for the Yankees than he did at Triple-A Columbus, where he spent most of the year.

Hitting, Baserunning & Defense

Rivera has all the offensive tools: speed, power, and ability to draw a walk. He has been a high-strikeout victim, but he's young. He has stolen over 20 bases per year (all leagues combined) three years in a row, adding increased knowledge to his fine raw speed. In right field he has very good range and an outstanding arm.

1997 Outlook

One of the most highly-praised prospects on the Yankee farm, Rivera was a disappointment in hitting .235 at Columbus in 1996. He was also disciplined for skipping a game. His attitude has been aloof at times, and coachability is a concern. Despite these cautions, Rivera looks like one of the best outfield talents for the next decade, though maybe not in New York.

Other New York Yankees

Mike Aldrete (Pos: DH, Age: 36, Bats: L)

	G	AB	R	H	D	T	HR	RBI	SB	BB	SO	Avg	OBP	Slg
1996	63	108	16	23	6	0	6	20	0	14	19	.213	.301	.435
Career	930	2147	277	565	104	9	41	271	19	314	381	.263	.356	.377

Acquired in a June trade with California, Aldrete spelled various Yankees at the DH, first base, and outfield slots. He hit well for a part-time player, but is now a free agent. 1997 Outlook: B

Brian Boehringer (Pos: RHP, Age: 27)

	W	L	Pct.	ERA	G	GS	Sv	IP	H	BB	SO	HR	BR/IP
1996	2	4	.333	5.44	15	3	0	46.1	46	21	37	6	1.45
Career	2	7	.222	7.73	22	6	0	64.0	70	43	47	11	1.77

Boehringer was hammered hard as a starter in June but returned to the majors to post effective numbers from the Yankees' bullpen (3.34 ERA). He's got good strike-out rates and a promising future. 1997 Outlook: B

Billy Brewer (Pos: LHP, Age: 28)

	W	L	Pct.	ERA	G	GS	Sv	IP	H	BB	SO	HR	BR/IP
1996	1	0	1.000	9.53	4	0	0	5.2	7	8	8	0	2.65
Career	9	7	.563	4.20	148	0	3	128.2	120	64	92	19	1.43

Joining New York after a midseason trade with the Dodgers, Brewer was decidedly unimpressive in four relief appearances. He walked eight batters in five-plus innings of work—not a positive sign. 1997 Outlook: C

Paul Gibson (Pos: LHP, Age: 37)

	W	L	Pct.	ERA	G	GS	Sv	IP	H	BB	SO	HR	BR/IP
1996	0	0	-	6.23	4	0	0	4.1	6	0	3	1	1.38
Career	22	24	.478	4.07	319	15	11	556.2	570	236	345	55	1.45

Gibson was released in May after four mediocre bullpen appearances. He didn't latch on to another team, so his career is probably over at age 37. 1997 Outlook: D

Matt Howard (Pos: 2B, Age: 29, Bats: R)

	G	AB	R	H	D	T	HR	RBI	SB	BB	SO	Avg	OBP	Slg
1996	35	54	9	11	1	0	1	9	1	2	8	.204	.228	.278
Career	35	54	9	11	1	0	1	9	1	2	8	.204	.228	.278

Howard served as infield insurance for New York last summer in three separate stints in the major leagues. He's played well at Triple-A Colombus, but is now 29 and no longer a prospect. 1997 Outlook: C

Steve Howe (Pos: LHP, Age: 39)

	W	L	Pct.	ERA	G	GS	Sv	IP	H	BB	SO	HR	BR/IP
1996	0	1	.000	6.35	25	0	1	17.0	19	6	5	1	1.47
Career	47	41	.534	3.03	497	0	91	606.1	586	139	328	32	1.20

Everyone's favorite drug felon, Howe's career *finally* came to an end in June when he was released after posting a 6.35 ERA in 25 appearances. Soon coming to a street corner near you. 1997 Outlook: D

Dion James (Pos: LF, Age: 34, Bats: L)

	G	AB	R	H	D	T	HR	RBI	SB	BB	SO	Avg	OBP	Slg
1996	6	12	1	2	0	0	0	1	0	1	2	.167	.231	.167
Career	917	2708	362	781	142	21	32	266	43	318	307	.288	.364	.392

James was released in May—less than a month after he signed with the Yankees—when it became obvious that his playing days in the majors were through. 1997 Outlook: D

Scott Kamieniecki (Pos: RHP, Age: 32)

	W	L	Pct.	ERA	G	GS	Sv	IP	H	BB	SO	HR	BR/IP
1996	1	2	.333	11.12	7	5	0	22.2	36	19	15	6	2.43
Career	36	39	.480	4.33	113	94	1	627.1	644	282	323	65	1.48

When it became apparent that Kamieniecki had no-where near regained full strength from his elbow surgery in '95 (11.12 ERA in seven outings), he spent the year in the minors. Future propects are dim. 1997 Outlook: D

Pat Kelly (Pos: 2B, Age: 29, Bats: R)

	G	AB	R	H	D	T	HR	RBI	SB	BB	SO	Avg	OBP	Slg
1996	13	21	4	3	0	0	0	2	0	2	9	.143	.217	.143
Career	524	1599	193	402	91	10	24	173	48	108	317	.251	.308	.366

After sharing the second base duties with Randy Velarde over the past few years, Kelly was plagued with an assortment of injuries last season. He's 29, and not the type of player that ages well. 1997 Outlook: B

Matt Luke (Pos: DH, Age: 26, Bats: L)

	G	AB	R	H	D	T	HR	RBI	SB	BB	SO	Avg	OBP	Slg
1996	1	0	1	0	0	0	0	0	0	0	0	-	-	-
Career	1	0	1	0	0	0	0	0	0	0	0	-	-	-

Luke had just one plate appearance in the majors last year before getting sent down to Triple-A Columbus for the entire season. He certainly has power, but he also has no concept of the strike zone. 1997 Outlook: D

Tim McIntosh (Pos: C, Age: 32, Bats: R)

	G	AB	R	H	D	T	HR	RBI	SB	BB	SO	Avg	OBP	Slg
1996	3	3	0	0	0	0	0	0	0	0	0	.000	.000	.000
Career	71	117	12	21	5	0	2	10	1	4	22	.179	.211	.274

McIntosh made his first appearance in the big leagues since '93 when he surfaced for three games last spring. His lackluster performance in the minors won't bring him back anytime soon. 1997 Outlook: D

Jim Mecir (Pos: RHP, Age: 26)

	W	L	Pct.	ERA	G	GS	Sv	IP	H	BB	SO	HR	BR/IP
1996	1	1	.500	5.13	26	0	0	40.1	42	23	38	6	1.61
Career	1	1	.500	4.60	28	0	0	45.0	47	25	41	6	1.60

Mecir has overpowering stuff, but he struggled with his control in the majors last season (23 BB's in 40-plus innings). His minor league numbers (2.27 ERA at Triple-A) indicate he has ability. 1997 Outlook: B

Dave Pavlas (Pos: RHP, Age: 34)

	W	L	Pct.	ERA	G	GS	Sv	IP	H	BB	SO	HR	BR/IP
1996	0	0	-	2.35	16	0	1	23.0	23	7	18	0	1.30
Career	2	0	1.000	2.65	34	0	1	51.0	57	13	33	3	1.37

Despite outstanding numbers at Triple-A Columbus *and* in the majors, Pavlus was released at the end of last season. He could return to the European leagues if he's not offered a job in the U.S. 1997 Outlook: C

Dale Polley (Pos: LHP, Age: 32)

	W	L	Pct.	ERA	G	GS	Sv	IP	H	BB	SO	HR	BR/IP
1996	1	3	.250	7.89	32	0	0	21.2	23	11	14	5	1.57
Career	1	3	.250	7.89	32	0	0	21.2	23	11	14	5	1.57

Polley was rudely greeted by major league hitters upon joining the Yankees in June, accumulating a 7.89 ERA through 32 appearances. Released at the end of the year, his career is in jeopardy. 1997 Outlook: D

Luis Sojo (Pos: 2B/3B/SS, Age: 31, Bats: R)

	G	AB	R	H	D	T	HR	RBI	SB	BB	SO	Avg	OBP	Slg
1996	95	287	23	63	10	1	1	21	2	11	17	.220	.250	.272
Career	531	1698	199	440	68	9	25	160	20	79	118	.259	.295	.354

Sojo filled in admirably at a host of infield positions after being claimed off waivers in August. While he's not much of a hitter, he could return as the Yanks' utility man this season. 1997 Outlook: A

Dave Weathers (Pos: RHP, Age: 27)

	W	L	Pct.	ERA	G	GS	Sv	IP	H	BB	SO	HR	BR/IP
1996	2	4	.333	5.48	42	12	0	88.2	108	42	53	8	1.69
Career	17	24	.415	5.48	125	57	0	377.2	455	185	235	34	1.69

Traded from Florida just before the deadline, Weathers struggled immensely in the AL (9.35 ERA in 11 games). But then he pitched well in the playoffs, allowing just a single run in 11 postseason innings. 1997 Outlook: B

Wally Whitehurst (Pos: RHP, Age: 32)

	W	L	Pct.	ERA	G	GS	Sv	IP	H	BB	SO	HR	BR/IP
1996	1	1	.500	6.75	2	2	0	8.0	11	2	1	1	1.63
Career	20	37	.351	4.02	163	66	3	487.2	525	130	313	43	1.34

Finally returning to the majors after having a bone spur removed in '94, Whitehurst's comeback lasted all of 10 days. Following a poor September start against the Angels, he was returned to the minors. 1997 Outlook: D

New York Yankees Minor League Prospects

Organization Overview:

The New York Yankees have always seemed to think that the purpose of their farm system was to manufacture trade bait. Last year, that philosophy seemed to change, as home-growns like Mariano Rivera, Andy Pettitte and Derek Jeter each made enormous contributions to the major league club. But now, after years of dealing away prospects, and with their best youngsters already entrenched at the major league level, there is very little left down on the farm. They've still got some highly-coveted outfielders who are almost ready to surface, and a handful of promising pitchers dot the lower levels, but beyond that, there's almost no depth at all. A number of potential contributors have stalled or been set back by injuries. Even the most successful ones know that their parent club very rarely gives an extended opportunity to any of its youngsters. After last October's purge, it's unclear whether the new player development regime will be able to live up to the accomplishments of their predecessors.

Brian Buchanan

Position: OF **Opening Day Age:** 23
Bats: R **Throws:** R **Born:** 7/21/73 in
Ht: 6' 4" **Wt:** 220 Miami, FL

Recent Statistics

	G	AB	R	H	D	T	HR	RBI	SB	BB	SO	AVG
94 A Oneonta	50	177	28	40	9	2	4	26	5	24	53	.226
95 A Greensboro	23	96	19	29	3	0	3	12	7	9	17	.302
96 A Tampa	131	526	65	137	22	4	10	58	23	37	108	.260

Brian Buchanan, the Yankees' first-round pick in the '94 draft, missed most of '95 and nearly had his foot amputated after a severe compound dislocation. Club officials were relieved to see him return to action last year, but the lost year of development was still costly for Buchanan, who has great tools but never played much baseball before college. He's got great raw power, but at age 23, it's about time he figured out how to use it. The right fielder probably will begin the year in Double-A.

Ricky Ledee

Position: OF **Opening Day Age:** 23
Bats: L **Throws:** L **Born:** 11/22/73 in
Ht: 6' 2" **Wt:** 160 Ponce, PR

Recent Statistics

	G	AB	R	H	D	T	HR	RBI	SB	BB	SO	AVG
93 A Oneonta	52	192	32	49	7	6	8	20	7	25	46	.255
94 A Greensboro	134	484	87	121	23	9	22	71	10	91	126	.250
95 A Greensboro	89	335	65	90	16	6	14	49	10	51	66	.269
96 AA Norwich	39	137	27	50	11	1	8	37	2	16	25	.365
96 AAA Columbus	96	358	79	101	22	6	21	64	6	44	95	.282
96 MLE	135	483	90	139	29	3	26	86	5	48	123	.288

Despite a nagging shoulder injury, Ricky Ledee put together such a fine year in '96 that some people in the organization now like him even better than Ruben Rivera. Ledee isn't too pretty in left field, but at the plate, he's easy to love. He hits for power and average, and a weakness against lefties is his only blemish. If the Yankees give him a chance this year, he's capable of duplicating Derek Jeter's Rookie of the Year honors.

Rafael Medina

Position: P **Opening Day Age:** 22
Bats: R **Throws:** R **Born:** 2/15/75 in
Ht: 6' 3" **Wt:** 194 Panama City, Panama

Recent Statistics

	W	L	ERA	G	GS	Sv	IP	H	R	BB	SO	HR
93 R Yankees	2	0	0.66	5	5	0	27.1	16	6	12	21	0
94 A Oneonta	3	7	4.66	14	14	0	73.1	67	54	35	59	7
95 A Tampa	2	2	2.37	6	6	0	30.1	29	12	12	25	0
95 A Greensboro	4	4	4.01	19	19	0	98.2	86	48	38	108	8
96 AA Norwich	5	8	3.06	19	19	0	103.0	78	48	55	112	7

Rafael Medina's got great stuff, and now all he needs to do is mature. With a fastball in the low 90s and a good overhand curve, he's struck out almost a batter per inning wherever he's pitched. As soon as he refines his control and builds some stamina, he may come quickly. He's only 22 this year, but probably will spend a good portion of the season in Triple-A.

Ramiro Mendoza

Position: P **Opening Day Age:** 24
Bats: R **Throws:** R **Born:** 6/15/72 in Los
Ht: 6' 2" **Wt:** 154 Santos, Panama

Recent Statistics

	W	L	ERA	G	GS	Sv	IP	H	R	BB	SO	HR
96 AAA Columbus	6	2	2.51	15	15	0	97.0	96	30	19	61	2
96 AL New York	4	5	6.79	12	11	0	53.0	80	43	10	34	5

Panamanian sinkerballer Ramiro Mendoza got 11 starts with the Yanks last year, but got hit hard, and drew criticism for his immaturity. Although he's not overpowering, he throws strikes and keeps the ball down. His sinking fastball has great life, and he may add some velocity as he fills out. He'll likely perform better in his next trial.

Jorge Posada

Position: C **Opening Day Age:** 25
Bats: B **Throws:** R **Born:** 8/17/71 in
Ht: 6' 0" **Wt:** 167 Santurce, PR

Recent Statistics

	G	AB	R	H	D	T	HR	RBI	SB	BB	SO	AVG
96 AAA Columbus	106	354	76	96	22	6	11	62	3	79	86	.271
96 AL New York	8	14	1	1	0	0	0	0	0	1	6	.071
96 MLE	106	344	65	86	19	3	10	53	2	65	87	.250

Switch-hitting catcher Jorge Posada is one of the most underappreciated prospects in the entire Yankees' organization. He's a good receiver with a strong arm, and he can hit. He's spent three years at Triple-A (although he's only 25), and he's improved each year. He's a productive hitter in an understated way: he hits for a decent average with pretty good power and a lot of walks. There are many major league catchers who are far worse.

Danny Rios

Position: P   **Opening Day Age:** 24
Bats: R **Throws:** R   **Born:** 11/11/72 in
Ht: 6' 2" **Wt:** 208   Madrid, Spain

Recent Statistics

	W	L	ERA	G	GS	Sv	IP	H	R	BB	SO	HR
93 R Yankees	2	1	3.52	24	0	6	38.1	34	18	16	29	0
94 A Greensboro	3	2	0.87	37	0	17	41.1	32	4	13	36	1
94 A Tampa	0	0	0.00	9	0	2	10.1	6	2	4	11	0
95 A Tampa	0	4	2.00	57	0	24	67.1	67	24	20	72	1
96 AA Norwich	3	1	2.09	38	0	17	43.0	34	14	21	38	0
96 AAA Columbus	4	1	1.95	24	0	0	27.2	22	7	6	22	1

If anyone in the entire organization has the potential to duplicate what Mariano Rivera has done, it's Danny Rios. The righthander with the 95 MPH fastball blew hitters away at Double-A and Triple-A last year, and has nothing left to prove down there. In his minor league career, he's struck out 208 hitters in 228 innings with a 1.97 ERA, while allowing only three home runs. The Yanks probably will play it conservatively and send him back to Triple-A, but Rios may force the issue fairly soon.

Shane Spencer

Position: OF   **Opening Day Age:** 25
Bats: R **Throws:** R   **Born:** 2/20/72 in Key
Ht: 5' 11" **Wt:** 182   West, FL

Recent Statistics

	G	AB	R	H	D	T	HR	RBI	SB	BB	SO	AVG
93 A Greensboro	122	431	89	116	35	2	12	80	14	52	62	.269
94 A Tampa	90	334	44	97	22	3	8	53	5	30	53	.290
95 A Tampa	134	500	87	150	31	3	16	88	14	61	60	.300
96 AA Norwich	126	450	70	114	19	0	29	89	4	68	99	.253
96 AAA Columbus	9	31	7	11	4	0	3	6	0	5	5	.355
96 MLE	135	467	66	111	20	0	26	82	2	53	108	.238

It took the Yankees four years to figure out that Shane Spencer was good enough to play above A-ball. Last year, at age 24, they finally gave him a shot at Double-A.

Playing in a very tough home run park, he blasted 29 round-trippers, and added three more during a nine-game stint at Triple-A—despite playing most of the year with a hip-flexor injury. In left field, he's pure first base material, but the combination of his power and good eye should be enough to get him a look.

Jay Tessmer

Position: P   **Opening Day Age:** 24
Bats: R **Throws:** R   **Born:** 12/26/72 in
Ht: 6' 3" **Wt:** 190   Meadville, PA

Recent Statistics

	W	L	ERA	G	GS	Sv	IP	H	R	BB	SO	HR
95 A Oneonta	2	0	0.95	34	0	20	38.0	27	8	12	52	0
96 A Tampa	12	4	1.48	68	0	35	97.1	68	18	19	104	2

Although at age 23, he was a bit old for the Class-A Florida State League, righthander Jay Tessmer was completely dominant there last year, in only his first season of pro ball. Despite the excellent strikeout numbers, the former college star isn't overpowering, and relies on location and savvy. It's odd the Yankees haven't moved him up faster.

Others to Watch

Ivan Cruz is old, doesn't hit for average, and can't play defense, but he's got major league power. The left-handed hitter bashed 28 homers at Triple-A, three less than he hit in '95. . . Righthander **Ray Ricken** regressed after a strong '95 season. He began the year at Double-A, but struggled so badly after a promotion to Triple-A that he was moved to the bullpen. Only 23, he may rebound. . . First baseman **Nick Delvecchio** gets hit by pitches so often that he can hardly stay in the lineup. But when he plays, the lefty-swinging first baseman has good power and knows how to get on base. . . He's a long shot, but **Dan Donato** might find a way to make it. He's a left-handed hitting third baseman, and he hits for a decent average, but his lack of power is a major handicap. . . Lefty **Matt Dunbar** got a brief look with the Marlins in '95. Last year, he went back down to the minors, compiling a sub-2.00 ERA at three stops, and fanned almost a batter an inning.

Art Howe

Born: 12/15/46 in Pittsburgh, PA

Playing Experience: 1974-1985, Pit, Hou, StL

Managerial Experience: 6 seasons

1996 Season

Laid-back Art Howe was the perfect fit for the rebuilding Oakland team. Unlike his very successful predecessor Tony La Russa, Howe showed an almost limitless ability to let his players gain experience, and the results showed. The A's were flirting with the .500 mark into August and finished well above expectations. Even stalwart veterans like Terrry Steinbach and Mark McGwire, who had gotten used to La Russa's disciplined style, not only enjoyed playing but produced their finest seasons under the new manager.

Offense

Scoring runs wasn't much of an issue for Oakland last year. Oakland hit homers in bunches, but they lacked speed on the bases. Howe was forced to play "Earl Weaver" three-run homer baseball. He didn't have too many bunters or basestealers available, so his hands were largely tied.

Pitching & Defense

Despite so many questions on the pitching staff, Howe was at his best with his pitchers. Assisted by pitching coach Bob Cluck, Howe assembled, reassembled and tinkered with his starting rotation and bullpen, cajoling an amazing 78 wins from a group of unknowns and rookies. The Athletics are a good defensive team; their biggest roadblock is experience, or the lack thereof. The skill and technique of the Bordicks and McGwires has not been lost on the Giambis and Brosiuses. That will continue.

1997 Outlook

The learning is theoretically over, and now it is time for Howe and his team to really establish themselves. The signing of a veteran starting pitcher who is capable of 200 innings, and the development (or acquisition) of a closer, are necessary for the team to take the next step. Simlarly, re-signing Mike Bordick will help the team make the jump to contender. If these needs can be met, the A's should be a .500 team in 1997 and contend for a championship somewhere down the line.

Manager Statistics

Year	Team, Lg	W	L	Pct	GB	Finish
1996	Oakland, AL	78	84	.481	12.0	3rd West
6 Seasons		470	502	.484	—	—

1996 Starting Pitchers by Days Rest

	≤3	4	5	6+
Athletics Starts	1	88	42	19
Athletics ERA	6.00	5.84	4.84	5.08
AL Avg Starts	4	96	30	21
AL ERA	5.57	4.90	5.33	5.81

1996 Situational Stats

	Art Howe	AL Average
Hit & Run Success %	43.6	39.1
Stolen Base Success %	62.4	69.6
Platoon Pct.	49.9	61.9
Defensive Subs	40	29
High-Pitch Outings	7	23
Quick/Slow Hooks	15/19	17/20
Sacrifice Attempts	49	58

1996 Rankings (American League)

➡ 1st in least caught steals of third base (3) and intentional walks (49)

➡ 2nd in relief appearances (419), saves with over 1 inning pitched (13) and first batter platoon percentage (64.1%)

➡ 3rd in least caught steals of second base (30) and mid-inning pitching changes (229)

Willie Adams

1996 Season

While it's fair to say that almost the entire A's pitching staff moved from obscurity to the majors last season, no one illustrated the trend more than rookie righthander Willie Adams. He made a single spot start for the A's in June, then returned to the club for good in late July. Inserted into the rotation in the second half, he coolly established himself as the A's preeminent control specialist.

Pitching

Relying primarily on a sinker, Adams sets up his money pitch with a fastball in the high 80s. He is always around the plate, and when he's on, he can be very tough. Adams also has good stamina, pitching into the sixth inning in all but one of his 12 starts. He gave up more than his share of home runs early on, but seemed to gain confidence as the season progressed, and gave up only one home run over his final 38 innings. As a pitcher, his role models are fellow Stanford alums Mike Mussina and Jack McDowell.

Defense

Adams is not particularly quick off the mound, but when he gets to the ball he takes care of business. He must work on holding baserunners. His slow motion allows them to get a good jump, as evidenced by the number of runners caught stealing while he was on the mound last year: none.

1997 Outlook

Adams could easily pitch 200 innings and become a mainstay of the A's rotation this year. He could use a little more velocity on his fastball, but that may come with experience and maturity—both physical and mental. The A's will be happy to give him the chance to develop in their rotation next year.

Position: SP
Bats: R **Throws:** R
Ht: 6' 7" **Wt:** 215

Opening Day Age: 24
Born: 10/8/72 in Gallup, NM
ML Seasons: 1

Overall Statistics

	W	L	Pct.	ERA	G	GS	Sv	IP	H	BB	SO	HR	BR/IP
1996	3	4	.429	4.01	12	12	0	76.1	76	23	68	11	1.30
Career	3	4	.429	4.01	12	12	0	76.1	76	23	68	11	1.30

How Often He Throws Strikes

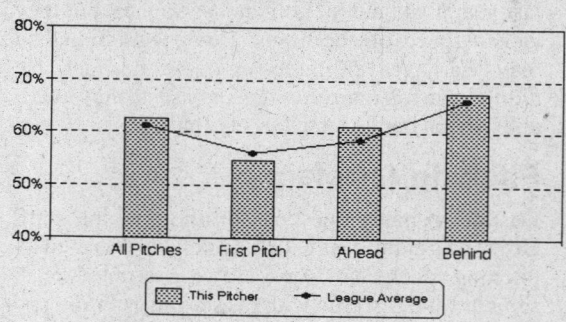

This Pitcher ▢   League Average ◆

1996 Situational Stats

	W	L	ERA	Sv	IP		AB	H	HR	RBI	Avg
Home	3	2	2.90	0	40.1	LHB	173	40	7	18	.231
Road	0	2	5.25	0	36.0	RHB	123	36	4	15	.293
First Half	0	0	6.00	0	6.0	Sc Pos	68	14	3	20	.206
Scnd Half	3	4	3.84	0	70.1	Clutch	13	4	0	0	.308

1996 Rankings (American League)

➡ 6th in shutouts (1)
➡ Led the Athletics in shutouts (1)

Tony Batista

Position: 2B/3B
Bats: R **Throws:** R
Ht: 6' 0" **Wt:** 165

Opening Day Age: 23
Born: 12/9/73 in Puerto Plata, DR
ML Seasons: 1

1996 Season

When it came to securing a starting job in the 1996 Oakland infield, Tony Batista was the ultimate darkhorse. Thought to be at least a couple of years away from the bigs, Batista arrived well ahead of schedule, thanks to Brent Gates' injury and Rafael Bournigal's weak hitting. Batista seized the opportunity, and by season's end, he'd established himself as the second baseman.

Hitting

Batista overcame an early slump and improved his average as the season progressed, showing that he was adjusting well to major league pitching. As with his minor league career, Batista showed good power with six homers in less than half a season, but he also showed very little ability to draw walks. Despite this handicap, he still performed well in the leadoff spot. However, he must work on his strike-zone judgment to ensure long-term success.

Baserunning & Defense

Using his good speed, Batista swiped seven bases during his limited tenure with the A's. A converted shortstop, Batista has better-than-average range at second and knows how to turn two. In 52 games at second base, he committed only three errors—a remarkable feat, especially for a rookie.

1997 Outlook

Batista has firmly established himself as Oakland's second baseman for now—and perhaps for good. He has all the tools you look for: speed, range, a good glove and, most surprisingly for a middle infielder, power. He must work on refining his approach at the plate, but the thought of teaming up Batista with future shortstop Miguel Tejada gives the A's a lot to be excited about. In a year or two, Batista may comprise one-half of the best young keystone combo in the league.

Overall Statistics

	G	AB	R	H	D	T	HR	RBI	SB	BB	SO	Avg	OBP	Slg
1996	74	238	38	71	10	2	6	25	7	19	49	.298	.350	.433
Career	74	238	38	71	10	2	6	25	7	19	49	.298	.350	.433

Where He Hits the Ball

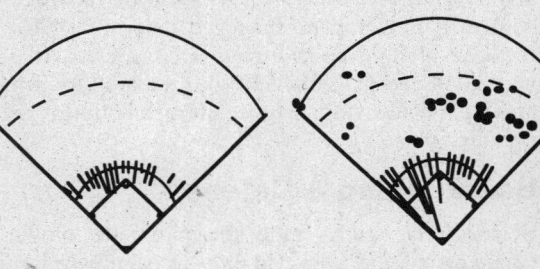

Vs. LHP   **Vs. RHP**

1996 Situational Stats

	AB	H	HR	RBI	Avg		AB	H	HR	RBI	Avg
Home	110	28	1	14	.255	LHP	65	18	2	9	.277
Road	128	43	5	11	.336	RHP	173	53	4	16	.306
First Half	40	14	1	1	.350	Sc Pos	42	16	1	17	.381
Scnd Half	198	57	5	24	.288	Clutch	32	7	2	6	.219

1996 Rankings (American League)

→ 6th in on-base percentage for a leadoff hitter (.401)
→ Led the Athletics in on-base percentage for a leadoff hitter (.401)

Oakland Athletics

273

Geronimo Berroa

1996 Season

Add Geronimo Berroa to the list of players who, at worst, moved the level of the "Peter Principle" up a notch, and at best, established themselves as baseball's new power elite. Setting career highs in just about every offensive category, Berroa topped both the 30 homer and 100 RBI totals for the first time in 1996. There was never any doubt that "The Chief" could hit; he drove that point—and quite a few baserunners—home last year.

Hitting

Berroa is the type of free swinger who drives managers—and discerning fans—looney. One day he looks incapable of holding his own in a whiffle ball league, and the next day he will hit three homers (something he managed *twice* in 1996). Because of his free-swinging ways, Berroa is a very good bad-ball hitter. He'll often look foolish making a wild swing, then tee off on an offering in the same place.

Baserunning & Defense

Berroa possesses average speed, but he knows where his strengths lie. He didn't steal a base last year, preferring to advance by bat—either his own, or those of his teammates. Berroa simply has no business playing in the field. He has poor range, gets a poor jump on the ball and doesn't have much of an arm.

1997 Outlook

Despite a prolific 1996, Berroa's time with Oakland could be running out. His marketability is at its peak, and the A's have a surplus of hitting and a shortfall of pitching. With the injury-prone Mark McGwire and young Jason Giambi ready to fill the DH and first base spots, Berroa could prove expendable. He certainly will get 500 at-bats *somewhere* in 1997.

Position: DH/LF/RF
Bats: R **Throws:** R
Ht: 6' 0" **Wt:** 195

Opening Day Age: 32
Born: 3/18/65 in Santo Domingo, DR
ML Seasons: 7
Nickname: The Chief

Overall Statistics

	G	AB	R	H	D	T	HR	RBI	SB	BB	SO	Avg	OBP	Slg
1996	153	586	101	170	32	1	36	106	0	47	122	.290	.344	.532
Career	505	1661	255	470	78	6	73	268	14	163	323	.283	.347	.469

Where He Hits the Ball

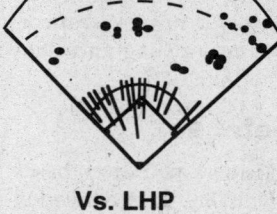

Vs. LHP   **Vs. RHP**

1996 Situational Stats

	AB	H	HR	RBI	Avg		AB	H	HR	RBI	Avg
Home	290	89	21	63	.307	LHP	135	46	8	29	.341
Road	296	81	15	43	.274	RHP	451	124	28	77	.275
First Half	319	94	19	56	.295	Sc Pos	146	44	8	64	.301
Scnd Half	267	76	17	50	.285	Clutch	84	26	5	14	.310

1996 Rankings (American League)

➡ Led the Athletics in at-bats, hits, singles, total bases (312), sacrifice flies (6), strikeouts, GDPs (16), pitches seen (2,573) and plate appearances (643)

Mike Bordick

1996 Season

Turning in a typical workmanlike season, Mike Bordick provided stability for both the middle infield and the large contingent of youngsters who called the Oakland Coliseum home last summer. Bordick doesn't hit much, but he has seamlessly eased into the role of veteran leader and shortstop.

Hitting

Bordick's never been much of an offensive performer, and his numbers dipped despite the hitting explosion of 1996. He is good at hitting the breaking pitch, and he uses his short stroke to try to punch the ball around the field. But he has very little power, and can be overpowered pretty easily by a pitcher with a good fastball. He generally makes contact, and he's a pretty good hit-and-run man.

Baserunning & Defense

An adequate baserunner, Bordick can steal an occasional base, but he isn't much of a threat any more. His main attribute is his glove. He possesses excellent range, a strong arm, quick reflexes and a smooth motion when making any kind of play. The A's defense led the majors in double plays in '96, and Bordick was a big reason why.

1997 Outlook

The new labor agreement made Bordick a free agent, and question marks abound over his possible departure from Oakland. Several clubs were looking for shortstops in the offseason, and Bordick's services were very much in demand. The A's have powerful young shortstop Miguel Tejada waiting in the wings, but Tejada is not ready just yet, so they would be plenty happy to keep Bordick and his steady play around for at least another season. If they are unable to, look for someone to pay Bordick a lot of money just to bring his glove.

Position: SS
Bats: R **Throws:** R
Ht: 5'11" **Wt:** 175

Opening Day Age: 31
Born: 7/21/65 in Marquette, MI
ML Seasons: 7

Overall Statistics

	G	AB	R	H	D	T	HR	RBI	SB	BB	SO	Avg	OBP	Slg
1996	155	525	46	126	18	4	5	54	5	52	59	.240	.307	.318
Career	823	2643	273	682	94	15	21	252	48	240	309	.258	.324	.329

Where He Hits the Ball

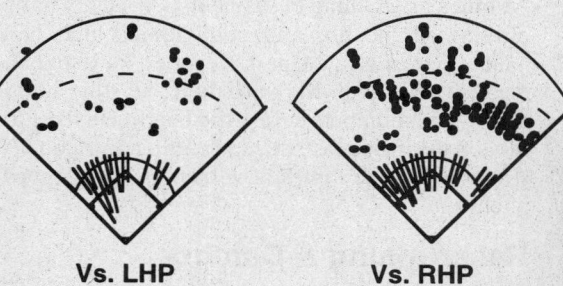

Vs. LHP   **Vs. RHP**

1996 Situational Stats

	AB	H	HR	RBI	Avg		AB	H	HR	RBI	Avg
Home	260	68	2	27	.262	LHP	137	31	1	13	.226
Road	265	58	3	27	.219	RHP	388	95	4	41	.245
First Half	278	62	2	30	.223	Sc Pos	146	36	1	48	.247
Scnd Half	247	64	3	24	.259	Clutch	81	22	1	13	.272

1996 Rankings (American League)

- → 1st in lowest slugging percentage
- → 2nd in lowest batting average on the road (.219) and lowest batting average
- → 4th in lowest slugging percentage vs. left-handed pitchers (.292) and lowest slugging percentage vs. right-handed pitchers (.327)
- → 5th in fielding percentage at shortstop (.979)
- → 6th in lowest on-base percentage and lowest on-base percentage vs. left-handed pitchers (.287)
- → 7th in lowest HR frequency (105.0 ABs per HR), lowest batting average vs. left-handed pitchers (.226), errors at shortstop (16) and highest percentage of swings put into play (53.9%)

Oakland Athletics

Scott Brosius

1996 Season

What a difference a new season—or better yet, a new manager—can make. Under Tony La Russa, the role of Scott Brosius (four positions, some platooning, some benching) was highly unclear, but he flourished last year under Oakland's new manager, Art Howe. Installed Opening Day as the starting third baseman, Brosius exceeded expectations on defense and provided both power and consistency on offense. The impact of his presence was visible, as the A's played better both before Brosius missed seven weeks with a fractured left ulna, and then again after his return.

Hitting

As much as anything else, playing on a daily basis eliminated the hot and cold streaks that had haunted Brosius in the past. Despite a long stint on the disabled list in May and June, he still put up career-high numbers across the board. He likes to turn on the inside fastball, and cutting down on his stroke has made him less vulnerable to offspeed pitches.

Baserunning & Defense

Brosius' consistency was a welcome addition on offense, but much-improved defense was an absolute revelation. Seemingly possessed by the ghost of Carney Lansford, Brosius played an aggressive and effective third base, committing only two errors over his first 350 innings at the hot corner. However, his error rate more than doubled, committing eight errors, in his final 596 innings. He is a solid baserunner, with good speed and the ability to steal a base.

1997 Outlook

Brosius is a key component of the new A's. With the rebuilding of 1996 out of the way, the A's may have the makings for a real contender. Brosius, whose confidence should continue to build, will be a main cog as he enters his peak production years. If he can stay healthy this year, he's capable of putting up some impressive numbers.

Position: 3B
Bats: R **Throws:** R
Ht: 6' 1" **Wt:** 185

Opening Day Age: 30
Born: 8/15/66 in Hillsboro, OR
ML Seasons: 6
Pronunciation: BRO-shus

Overall Statistics

	G	AB	R	H	D	T	HR	RBI	SB	BB	SO	Avg	OBP	Slg
1996	114	428	73	130	25	0	22	71	7	59	85	.304	.393	.516
Career	477	1509	221	397	75	4	65	208	25	144	270	.263	.332	.447

Where He Hits the Ball

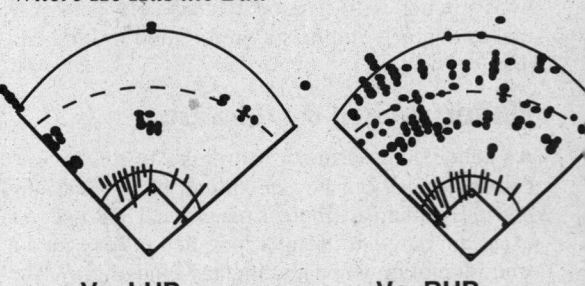

Vs. LHP   Vs. RHP

1996 Situational Stats

	AB	H	HR	RBI	Avg		AB	H	HR	RBI	Avg
Home	221	69	15	42	.312	LHP	90	32	4	17	.356
Road	207	61	7	29	.295	RHP	338	98	18	54	.290
First Half	139	46	11	34	.331	Sc Pos	115	42	5	52	.365
Scnd Half	289	84	11	37	.291	Clutch	60	19	5	14	.317

1996 Rankings (American League)

- → 1st in batting average with runners in scoring position (.365)
- → 4th in fielding percentage at third base (.969)
- → 9th in errors at third base (10)
- → Led the Athletics in batting average with runners in scoring position (.365), batting average in the clutch (.317), batting average at home (.312) and batting average with two strikes (.237)

Jason Giambi

1996 Season

During his first full season as a big leaguer, Jason Giambi fulfilled all of his promise, and then some. He hit for both average and power and established himself as an integral part of what may well be a new wave of Oakland champions. Only a series of nagging injuries—some coming as a direct result of his aggressiveness—slowed Giambi's production late in the year.

Hitting

Giambi is a solid line-drive hitter with a smooth, easy swing. He credits teammate Mark McGwire with helping him to develop his power. Mac and "Gumby" talked baseball and pumped iron together on a regular basis in 1996. It paid off as Giambi, who'd never hit more than 12 homers in a minor league season, blasted 20 out of the yard. He'll need to show he can handle lefties, and he needs to learn to pace himself better in order to maintain his effectiveness at the plate during the long, grueling season.

Baserunning & Defense

Giambi is too young to be confined to the role of designated hitter, but Oakland's having problems finding him a defensive position. He spelled McGwire at first base and Scott Brosius at third base during their respective injuries, playing adequately but not spectacularly at each spot. With those two veterans in the lineup, Giambi played enthusiastically, if unremarkably, in the outfield. He knows his limits and played an errorless left field despite never having played there before as a professional. Giambi doesn't so much run as he *rumbles;* the man is no threat to steal.

1997 Outlook

Giambi's emergence as a pure hitter, and especially as a power source, bodes well for future seasons. He undoubtedly possesses the best swing on the club, and when he gets hot, he can be next to impossible to get out. As he gains experience, his resilience and production should continue to improve.

Position: 1B/3B/LF/DH
Bats: L **Throws:** R
Ht: 6' 2" **Wt:** 200

Opening Day Age: 26
Born: 1/8/71 in West Covina, CA
ML Seasons: 2
Pronunciation: gee-AHM-bee

Overall Statistics

	G	AB	R	H	D	T	HR	RBI	SB	BB	SO	Avg	OBP	Slg
1996	140	536	84	156	40	1	20	79	0	51	95	.291	.355	.481
Career	194	712	111	201	47	1	26	104	2	79	126	.282	.357	.461

Where He Hits the Ball

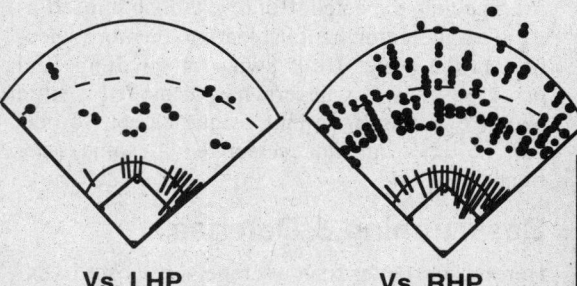

Vs. LHP   **Vs. RHP**

1996 Situational Stats

	AB	H	HR	RBI	Avg			AB	H	HR	RBI	Avg
Home	234	73	6	35	.312		LHP	126	30	2	14	.238
Road	302	83	14	44	.275		RHP	410	126	18	65	.307
First Half	316	102	16	60	.323		Sc Pos	136	41	7	60	.301
Scnd Half	220	54	4	19	.245		Clutch	82	22	1	7	.268

1996 Rankings (American League)

- ➡ 6th in lowest batting average with the bases loaded (.100)
- ➡ 9th in lowest batting average vs. left-handed pitchers (.238)
- ➡ 10th in doubles
- ➡ Led the Athletics in doubles, most pitches seen per plate appearance (4.01), batting average vs. right-handed pitchers (.307), batting average on a 3-2 count (.321) and highest percentage of extra bases taken as a runner (45.2%)

Jose Herrera

1996 Season

Slated to spend the 1996 season in the minors, rookie outfielder Jose Herrera became a beneficiary of Oakland's rebuilding process. Herrera started the year at Double-A Huntsville, but Pedro Munoz' bad hamstring and Allen Battle's bad hitting precipitated an early promotion. Herrera's performance proved somewhat ironic: his defense, which had been touted as a strength, was subpar, whereas his offense, which had been questioned, improved during the '96 campaign.

Hitting

Although Herrera didn't tear the cover off the ball, he showed signs of power and hit for a better average than expected. But to establish himself as a big league hitter, he must learn to be more selective at the plate. He'll swing at anything, and pitchers know it. Herrera has displayed a little patience during his minor league career, so perhaps he'll become more selective with some experience.

Baserunning & Defense

Herrera has better than average speed, but to exploit it, he must improve his ability to get on base. His defense—which drew raves in the minors—nearly proved to be his undoing. Several defensive gaffes, including two during a critical road trip back East, relegated Herrera to the bench and caused speculation that his days with the A's were numbered. His five errors in right field says more about his head than his glove. He disdains going all the way to the wall, among other things. Herrera does have a tremendous arm, and few challenge it. Those who do regret it.

1997 Outlook

Herrera's sometimes-lackadaisical play (on both offense and defense) put him in disfavor with both A's management and fans last year. Occasionally his skills make him look like a star, but more often, his concentration makes him look like a journeyman. He is young, though, and a full season in Triple-A would do him a lot of good.

Position: RF/CF
Bats: L **Throws:** L
Ht: 6' 0" **Wt:** 165

Opening Day Age: 24
Born: 8/30/72 in Santo Domingo, DR
ML Seasons: 2

Overall Statistics

	G	AB	R	H	D	T	HR	RBI	SB	BB	SO	Avg	OBP	Slg
1996	108	320	44	86	15	1	6	30	8	20	59	.269	.318	.378
Career	141	390	53	103	16	3	6	32	9	26	70	.264	.314	.367

Where He Hits the Ball

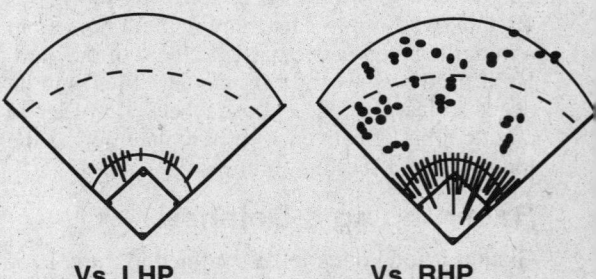

Vs. LHP   **Vs. RHP**

1996 Situational Stats

	AB	H	HR	RBI	Avg		AB	H	HR	RBI	Avg
Home	145	45	3	15	.310	LHP	27	8	0	3	.296
Road	175	41	3	15	.234	RHP	293	78	6	27	.266
First Half	176	50	4	21	.284	Sc Pos	68	18	1	23	.265
Scnd Half	144	36	2	9	.250	Clutch	44	8	1	4	.182

1996 Rankings (American League)

→ 1st in lowest on-base percentage for a leadoff hitter (.302)
→ 5th in errors in right field (5)
→ Led the Athletics in bunts in play (16)

Doug Johns

1996 Season

Doug Johns started 1996 with a flurry, giving up only two runs over his first 15 innings. As with many finesse pitchers, however, he was much less successful once the league got a better look at him. He remained in the rotation until August, when he was sent to the bullpen. He continued to struggle in that role.

Pitching

Like most of the Oakland pitchers, Johns is hardly overpowering. He spots his pitches and must rely on precise control of his sharp slider to get hitters out. His high-80s fastball is adequate, and as a good student of pitching coach Bob Cluck, he uses his change-up to set up his out pitch. Johns is prone to fits of wildness within games, and during some starts he never seems to have his control at all. Unlike a veteran, he's unable to compensate, and the results can be just plain ugly. Johns does have the mental toughness and durability to survive as a starter, but he may not have the stuff.

Defense

Johns' glove is adequate but not much more. He committed a couple of errors last year, and no one on the entire staff committed more. As a southpaw, he ought to be good at holding runners, but he isn't. He must work on it.

1997 Outlook

Because there are so many opportunities for a pitcher to grab a starting spot in the Oakland rotation, Johns could wind up with one. He did not flourish in the bullpen, so making it in the rotation is a must. Since he is now 29 years old, he must make his mark while he still has the chance. That means he has to establish himself in 1997, or else he'll probably lose his spot to a youngster.

Position: SP/RP
Bats: R **Throws:** L
Ht: 6' 2" **Wt:** 185

Opening Day Age: 29
Born: 12/19/67 in South Bend, IN
ML Seasons: 2

Overall Statistics

	W	L	Pct.	ERA	G	GS	Sv	IP	H	BB	SO	HR	BR/IP
1996	6	12	.333	5.98	40	23	1	158.0	187	69	71	21	1.62
Career	11	15	.423	5.63	51	32	1	212.2	231	95	96	26	1.53

How Often He Throws Strikes

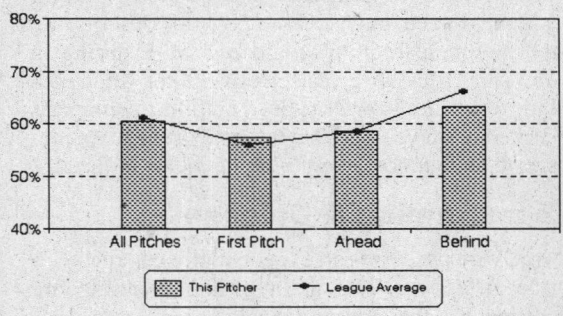

1996 Situational Stats

	W	L	ERA	Sv	IP		AB	H	HR	RBI	Avg
Home	3	7	4.83	1	87.2	LHB	138	39	4	14	.283
Road	3	5	7.42	0	70.1	RHB	492	148	17	81	.301
First Half	5	10	6.18	0	106.1	Sc Pos	172	52	3	68	.302
Scnd Half	1	2	5.57	1	51.2	Clutch	28	10	3	5	.357

1996 Rankings (American League)

- ➡ 4th in GDPs induced (27)
- ➡ 5th in most GDPs induced per GDP situation (19.1%)
- ➡ 7th in lowest winning percentage
- ➡ 9th in highest batting average allowed vs. right-handed batters (.301)
- ➡ Led the Athletics in losses, walks allowed, wild pitches (9), pickoff throws (146), GDPs induced (27), ERA at home (4.83) and lowest batting average allowed vs. right-handed batters (.301)

Oakland Athletics

Mark McGwire

1996 Season

It is hard to think of "what ifs" in a season where a guy hit 50-plus home runs. But in Mark McGwire's case, you have to wonder: "What if he hadn't missed 30 games due to injury?" "What if," indeed. Give McGwire 103 more plate appearances, and factor in a homer every 8.13 at bats, and Roger Maris becomes a mere asterisk again. But on the other hand, such speculation only serves to diminish the truly fabulous year McGwire had.

Hitting

McGwire has established himself as one of the most electrifying and powerful hitters in the game. The re-designed Coliseum may be much more of a homer haven, but McGwire's 450-foot shots into the new construction would be awe-inspiring in any park. McGwire is a selective hitter who regularly exceeds 80 walks, but compiles a slugger's strikeout total as well. He has an extreme uppercut swing, and almost everything he hits is in the air.

Baserunning & Defense

McGwire possesses an excellent glove and plays a fine first base. His main problems afield are caused by the nagging back and foot injuries which have haunted him throughout his career. As a baserunner, McGwire is sluggish. Half of his total runs scored were the result of his home runs.

1997 Outlook

McGwire is an important part of the Oakland rebuilding process. He is more than a just respected veteran: he is the core of the offense, the voice of experience, and the link to the past championship teams. By his own admission, he went into 1996 skeptical, fearful that the team had no direction. By midseason he was won over by the youth movement, saying he "had never had so much fun playing ball before." Every effort will be made to keep him happy—and injury-free—in 1997.

Position: 1B/DH
Bats: R **Throws:** R
Ht: 6' 5" **Wt:** 250

Opening Day Age: 33
Born: 10/1/63 in Pomona, CA
ML Seasons: 11

Overall Statistics

	G	AB	R	H	D	T	HR	RBI	SB	BB	SO	Avg	OBP	Slg
1996	130	423	104	132	21	0	52	113	0	116	112	.312	.467	.730
Career	1224	4082	725	1053	171	5	329	860	7	789	945	.258	.380	.544

Where He Hits the Ball

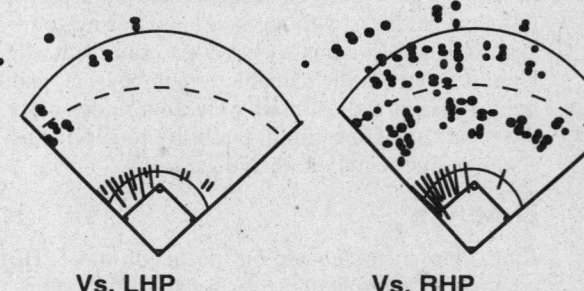

Vs. LHP   **Vs. RHP**

1996 Situational Stats

	AB	H	HR	RBI	Avg		AB	H	HR	RBI	Avg
Home	213	66	24	56	.310	LHP	102	38	12	26	.373
Road	210	66	28	57	.314	RHP	321	94	40	87	.293
First Half	211	70	28	60	.332	Sc Pos	103	37	14	61	.359
Scnd Half	212	62	24	53	.292	Clutch	51	16	3	8	.314

1996 Rankings (American League)

→ 1st in home runs, slugging percentage, on-base percentage, HR frequency (8.1 ABs per HR), lowest groundball/flyball ratio (0.4), cleanup slugging percentage (.726) and slugging percentage vs. right-handed pitchers (.713)

→ 2nd in on-base percentage vs. left-handed pitchers (.511)

→ 3rd in intentional walks (16), slugging percentage vs. left-handed pitchers (.784), on-base percentage vs. right-handed pitchers (.453), errors at first base (10) and lowest fielding percentage at first base (.990)

Mike Mohler

1996 Season

Mike Mohler began the 1996 season as a left-handed set-up man, and was reasonably effective in that role. When Jim Corsi faltered, Mohler moved into the closer spot. He didn't handle it very well, and it was back to set-up, where he toiled for the rest of the year with acceptable results. Mohler wound up pitching in a career-high 72 games, and tied Buddy Groom for the most appearances on the club.

Pitching

Not a power pitcher by any stretch, Mohler relies on a combination of forkballs, sinkers and assorted junk to get hitters out. His fastball isn't overpowering, and he simply cannot afford to rely upon it too heavily. He can survive when his defense supports him and his control is sharp enough. His location was more precise in '95. He went the entire season without surrendering a home run, but he only pitched 23.2 innings. Last year, he was not as sharp, and surrendered nine "big flies"—most of them coming in critical situations.

Defense

Mohler fields his position well and makes few mistakes. He is good at getting to balls hit his way and is able to cover first. He holds runners close, and has a surprisingly good move to first for a relief specialist.

1997 Outlook

If the 1996 season proves anything, it shows that Mike Mohler is not a closer. He lacks a power pitch, and his command of his offspeed pitches just isn't good enough for him to continually survive in pressure situations. But he is well-suited to work as a set-up man and as a situational lefty, although he is equally effective against left-handed and right-handed hitters. He should continue in a middle relief role, most likely giving the A's a number of solid innings in the '97 season.

Position: RP
Bats: R **Throws:** L
Ht: 6' 2" **Wt:** 195

Opening Day Age: 28
Born: 7/26/68 in Dayton, OH
ML Seasons: 4

Overall Statistics

	W	L	Pct.	ERA	G	GS	Sv	IP	H	BB	SO	HR	BR/IP
1996	6	3	.667	3.67	72	0	7	81.0	79	41	64	9	1.48
Career	8	11	.421	4.36	143	10	8	171.1	154	105	125	20	1.51

How Often He Throws Strikes

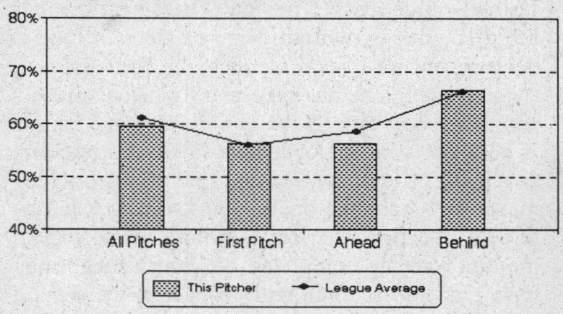

1996 Situational Stats

	W	L	ERA	Sv	IP		AB	H	HR	RBI	Avg
Home	1	1	3.93	3	36.2	LHB	99	26	4	21	.263
Road	5	2	3.45	4	44.1	RHB	201	53	5	29	.264
First Half	4	0	2.57	6	49.0	Sc Pos	88	22	4	40	.250
Scnd Half	2	3	5.34	1	32.0	Clutch	176	48	5	30	.273

1996 Rankings (American League)

- → 6th in relief wins (6)
- → 7th in games pitched and highest percentage of inherited runners scored (41.3%)
- → 8th in blown saves (6) and relief innings (81.0)
- → Led the Athletics in games pitched, games finished (30), wild pitches (9), holds (13), blown saves (6), relief wins (6) and relief innings (81.0)

Ariel Prieto

1996 Season

Cuban righthander Ariel Prieto began last season with confusion, moved on to disappointment, and then emerged from the ashes to post great numbers down the stretch. Prieto arrived at spring training overweight and out of shape, struggled through his first nine starts, then went down with a sore arm. When he was ready to return, management wisely kept him at Triple-A Edmonton, where he completed a handful of very good starts before returning to the A's. He continued to pitch effectively after his return.

Pitching

Prieto has a smooth delivery and a very good fastball which reaches the low 90s. His problem as a big leaguer is twofold: first, he doesn't have a deep repertoire to complement the fastball; and, second, though he has successfully faced "professional" Cuban hitters, the quality of those batters is nowhere near major league level. A's pitching coach Bob Cluck, who insists that all his pitchers must throw a change-up, has worked with Prieto to remedy the first problem. Leaving Prieto in Edmonton after he completed his injury rehab may have put him on track with respect to the second one. He returned a much more focused pitcher, posting an ERA a shade over three over his last 12 starts. Prieto pitched six or more innings in all of those starts save the last.

Defense

Prieto covers his position more than adequately. He gets to balls hit within his range deceptively fast and covers first very well too. He doesn't hold runners very well, however.

1997 Outlook

If Prieto can pick up where he left off, he could not only emerge as the number-one Oakland starter, but fulfill the promise that made him so sought-after when he was first signed. He could easily win 15 or more games this year.

Position: SP
Bats: R **Throws:** R
Ht: 6' 3" **Wt:** 225

Opening Day Age: 27
Born: 10/22/69 in Havana, Cuba
ML Seasons: 2
Pronunciation: pree-AY-to

Overall Statistics

	W	L	Pct.	ERA	G	GS	Sv	IP	H	BB	SO	HR	BR/IP
1996	6	7	.462	4.15	21	21	0	125.2	130	54	75	9	1.46
Career	8	13	.381	4.41	35	30	0	183.2	187	86	112	13	1.49

How Often He Throws Strikes

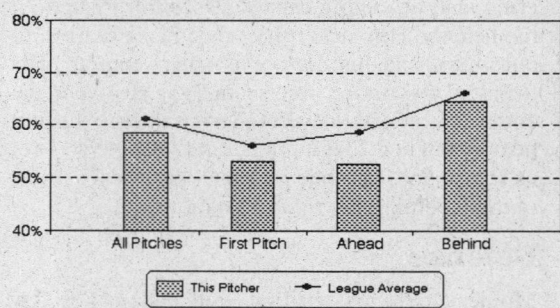

1996 Situational Stats

	W	L	ERA	Sv	IP		AB	H	HR	RBI	Avg
Home	4	3	5.06	0	58.2	LHB	280	72	6	28	.257
Road	2	4	3.36	0	67.0	RHB	196	58	3	29	.296
First Half	2	3	6.37	0	41.0	Sc Pos	117	29	2	44	.248
Scnd Half	4	4	3.08	0	84.2	Clutch	25	6	1	2	.240

1996 Rankings (American League)

- → 2nd in balks (2)
- → 10th in lowest batting average allowed vs. left-handed batters (.257)
- → Led the Athletics in complete games (2), hit batsmen (7), balks (2), runners caught stealing (6) and lowest batting average allowed vs. left-handed batters (.257)

Carlos Reyes

1996 Season

There were a lot of decisions to be made regarding the composition of the A's 1996 starting rotation, but Carlos Reyes' situation didn't need much thought. He was in, simple as that. But he lasted only until May 21 as a starter, and spent the remainder of the season doomed to middle relief and mop-up work. Reyes was considerably more effective in relief, delivering an ERA under four and earning over half of his victories in that role.

Pitching

As his sinker goes, so goes Reyes. When he can keep his bread-and-butter pitch down, he's fine, but when he gets it up, it often goes out of the park. Reyes' fastball only reaches the low 80s, but he has a good slider and he mixes his pitches well. At times, he can have complete command, and the results can be a tight, efficient complete-game performance. More often, however, he loses concentration and digs himself a hole, and that is his undoing. Since he is most successful during the first few innings, he is well suited to the middle relief role.

Defense

Reyes fields his position well, getting to more than his share of grounders, but he will hurry and bobble the ball on occasion. Reyes' pickoff move is non-existent, but his quick delivery provides a decent defense against potential basestealers.

1997 Outlook

Based on his performance in the second half of last year, Reyes figures to continue in his role as a middle reliever. He is durable and doesn't need much rest between appearances. Plus Reyes has the ability to provide a long relief appearance or an occasional spot start when needed.

Position: RP/SP
Bats: B **Throws:** R
Ht: 6' 1" **Wt:** 190

Opening Day Age: 27
Born: 4/4/69 in Miami, FL
ML Seasons: 3
Pronunciation: RAY-ess

Overall Statistics

	W	L	Pct.	ERA	G	GS	Sv	IP	H	BB	SO	HR	BR/IP
1996	7	10	.412	4.78	46	10	0	122.1	134	61	78	19	1.59
Career	11	19	.367	4.68	113	20	1	269.1	276	133	183	39	1.52

How Often He Throws Strikes

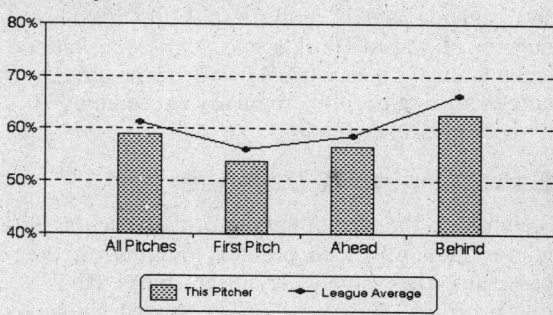

This Pitcher — League Average

1996 Situational Stats

	W	L	ERA	Sv	IP		AB	H	HR	RBI	Avg
Home	1	4	5.17	0	62.2	LHB	246	67	8	38	.272
Road	6	6	4.37	0	59.2	RHB	230	67	11	44	.291
First Half	4	10	5.51	0	85.0	Sc Pos	120	39	8	68	.325
Scnd Half	3	0	3.13	0	37.1	Clutch	43	11	0	3	.256

1996 Rankings (American League)

→ 3rd in highest percentage of inherited runners scored (50.0%)
→ 5th in most baserunners allowed per 9 innings in relief (14.9)
→ 6th in highest batting average allowed with runners in scoring position (.325)
→ 10th in balks (1)
→ Led the Athletics in strikeouts

Terry Steinbach

Signed By
TWINS

1996 Season

Still getting better at the age of 34, Terry Steinbach obliterated his career highs in homers, RBI and slugging percentage last year. He and teammate Mark McGwire provided experience and guidance to the young and powerful A's. On defense, he aided the maturation of the Oakland pitching staff—something the young hurlers hope will continue.

Hitting

Steinbach has always had a moderate amount of power, but he exploded in 1996, more than doubling his previous career high in home runs. Steinbach is deadly at hitting the fastball, and shows good plate discipline despite drawing a low number of walks. He is a good two-strike hitter and has always been extremely effective with runners in scoring position, regularly exceeding .300 in those pressure situations.

Baserunning & Defense

Steinbach is the type of middle-of-the-order hitter whose lack of speed creates logjams on the basepaths. Defensively, Steinbach shines. He is a fine backstop, allowing only six passed balls in 1140 innings behind the plate. Even more importantly, he handles pitchers very well. His presence was invaluable to the flock of young Oakland starters, many of whom had never before been in a major league rotation before. Steinbach has a strong arm, although the young pitchers held down his caught-stealing total last year.

1997 Outlook

Steinbach was an important veteran member of the A's. But he wanted to finish his career in his native Minnesota and the Twins signed the backstop to a two-year $6 million deal after the season. He is both durable and dependable, and the Twins will surely be glad to have him around.

Position: C
Bats: R **Throws:** R
Ht: 6' 1" **Wt:** 195

Opening Day Age: 35
Born: 3/2/62 in New Ulm, MN
ML Seasons: 11

Overall Statistics

	G	AB	R	H	D	T	HR	RBI	SB	BB	SO	Avg	OBP	Slg
1996	145	514	79	140	25	1	35	100	0	49	115	.272	.342	.529
Career	1199	4162	498	1144	205	14	132	595	15	307	689	.275	.328	.426

Where He Hits the Ball

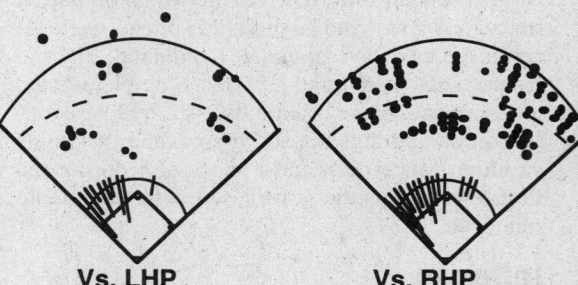

Vs. LHP   **Vs. RHP**

1996 Situational Stats

	AB	H	HR	RBI	Avg		AB	H	HR	RBI	Avg
Home	254	70	16	52	.276	LHP	120	35	9	15	.292
Road	260	70	19	48	.269	RHP	394	105	26	85	.266
First Half	280	76	18	46	.271	Sc Pos	133	41	9	65	.308
Scnd Half	234	64	17	54	.274	Clutch	80	18	4	12	.225

1996 Rankings (American League)

- → 2nd in lowest percentage of extra bases taken as a runner (27.9%)
- → 3rd in lowest percentage of pitches taken (47.3%)
- → 5th in lowest fielding percentage at catcher (.991) and highest percentage of swings on the first pitch (41.0%)
- → 6th in errors at catcher (7)
- → 9th in least pitches seen per plate appearance (3.48)
- → 10th in HR frequency (14.7 ABs per HR)
- → Led the Athletics in GDPs (16) and batting average with the bases loaded (.450)

Billy Taylor

1996 Season

Billy Taylor played a large role as a set-up man for the 1994 A's, then missed the entire 1995 season with a torn anterior cruciate ligament in his left knee. He returned in 1996 and grabbed the closer position for the majority of the season. Once established, Taylor filled the role pretty well, but a groin injury slowed him in the second half.

Pitching

Taylor is probably the closest thing Oakland has to a real closer. He has a good moving fastball in the high 80s, a slider and a change-up. His stuff isn't overpowering, but he knows how to work a hitter, and he usually won't have problems unless he starts falling behind in the count, enabling the hitter to sit on his fastball. A cool customer who served a long minor-league apprenticeship before reaching the majors as a 32-year-old rookie in 1994, Taylor seems to thrive in pressure situations. He was consistently able to stifle the opposition last year when he came in with runners on base. He has a very durable arm, and working two or three days in a row doesn't bother him at all.

Defense

Taylor is not adept at holding baserunners; in fact, basestealers are a perfect 11-for-11 against him in his major league career. On the other hand, he fields his position quite well, getting to balls quickly and covering first base when he needs to.

1997 Outlook

Taylor holds the closer's job going into the season, but he really cannot be considered a long-term solution to the problem. First, he will be 35 years old in 1997, with only two major league seasons under his belt. Second, over the past three years, he's been out with injuries half of the time. Set-up is really the ideal role for him.

Position: RP
Bats: R **Throws:** R
Ht: 6' 8"   **Wt:** 200

Opening Day Age: 35
Born: 10/16/61 in Monticello, FL
ML Seasons: 2

Overall Statistics

	W	L	Pct.	ERA	G	GS	Sv	IP	H	BB	SO	HR	BR/IP
1996	6	3	.667	4.33	55	0	17	60.1	52	25	67	5	1.28
Career	7	6	.538	3.97	96	0	18	106.2	90	43	115	9	1.25

How Often He Throws Strikes

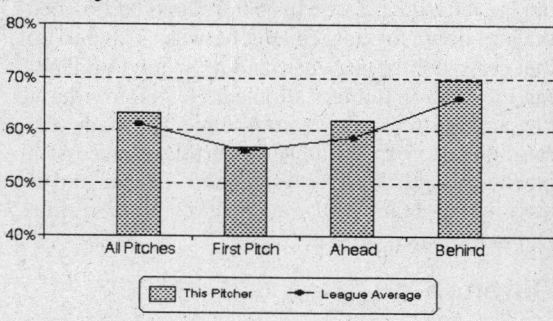

1996 Situational Stats

	W	L	ERA	Sv	IP		AB	H	HR	RBI	Avg
Home	4	2	5.87	7	30.2	LHB	87	21	2	11	.241
Road	2	1	2.73	10	29.2	RHB	138	31	3	16	.225
First Half	4	1	2.94	7	33.2	Sc Pos	68	14	2	23	.206
Scnd Half	2	2	6.08	10	26.2	Clutch	147	31	2	19	.211

1996 Rankings (American League)

→ 1st in lowest percentage of inherited runners scored (14.7%)
→ 3rd in save percentage (89.5%)
→ 5th in most strikeouts per 9 innings in relief (10.0)
→ 6th in relief wins (6)
→ 8th in first batter efficiency (.188)
→ Led the Athletics in saves, games finished (30), save opportunities (19), save percentage (89.5%), first batter efficiency (.188), lowest percentage of inherited runners scored (14.7%), relief wins (6), lowest batting average allowed in relief (.231), least baserunners allowed per 9 innings in relief (12.1) and most strikeouts per 9 innings in relief (10.0)

Oakland Athletics

Don Wengert

1996 Season

After a solid rookie debut as an A's reliever in 1996, Don Wengert began last season back in the bullpen, where he had fair success. But with the A's hurting for starters, he was shifted back to the starting role he had held through most of his minor league career. Wengert pitched well at first, but had problems remaining consistently effective. He struggled with the heat of summer, rebounded in August, then was hit frighteningly hard in September.

Pitching

Wengert is a crafty pitcher who features a serviceable fastball in the mid 80s, a sinker and a change-up. He relies heavily on his control and has to keep the ball down to succeed. But he wasn't able to do that consistently last year, and he wound up leading the team in homers allowed. He is fairly durable and didn't miss a start once he made the rotation last year. While he wasn't very successful on the mound, Wengert is a good listener and is anxious to learn and succeed, something that Oakland's management likes.

Defense

Wengert is quick off the mound and fields his position very well. He does not have much of a move to first, but holds runners reasonably well. As he works to refine his game, this should improve.

1997 Outlook

Wengert certainly took his lumps last year, but manager Art Howe and pitching coach Bob Cluck are hoping it was a learning experience for him. They like his attitude, so he figures to continue in the Oakland rotation. He will probably start the year as the fourth or fifth starter, but will need more success than he found in 1996 in order to stay there.

Position: SP/RP
Bats: R **Throws:** R
Ht: 6' 2" **Wt:** 205

Opening Day Age: 27
Born: 11/6/69 in Sioux City, IA
ML Seasons: 2

Overall Statistics

	W	L	Pct.	ERA	G	GS	Sv	IP	H	BB	SO	HR	BR/IP
1996	7	11	.389	5.58	36	25	0	161.1	200	60	75	29	1.61
Career	8	12	.400	5.23	55	25	0	191.0	230	72	91	32	1.58

How Often He Throws Strikes

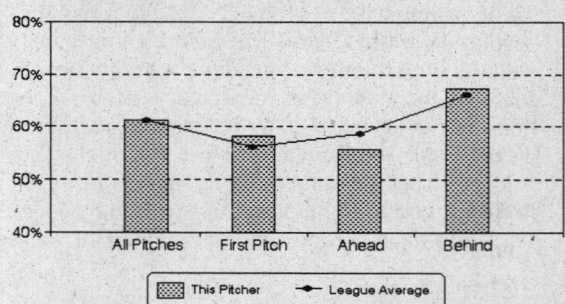

This Pitcher ▦   —●— League Average

1996 Situational Stats

	W	L	ERA	Sv	IP		AB	H	HR	RBI	Avg
Home	3	4	5.26	0	92.1	LHB	346	106	18	55	.306
Road	4	7	6.00	0	69.0	RHB	305	94	11	39	.308
First Half	3	6	4.96	0	89.0	Sc Pos	156	40	3	57	.256
Scnd Half	4	5	6.35	0	72.1	Clutch	41	10	0	1	.244

1996 Rankings (American League)

- ➡ 6th in shutouts (1) and highest batting average allowed vs. right-handed batters (.308)
- ➡ 8th in lowest winning percentage
- ➡ 9th in highest ERA at home (5.26)
- ➡ Led the Athletics in games started, shutouts (1), innings pitched, hits allowed, batters faced (725), home runs allowed, pitches thrown (2,699) and lowest batting average allowed with runners in scoring position (.256)

Ernie Young

1996 Season

Encouraged by manager Art Howe's support, Ernie Young settled comfortably into the Athletics' lineup last year. By season's end, he was firmly established as Oakland's center fielder. Young, who had nothing else to achieve in the minors, proved to be up to the task. He showed good power and played strong defense, boding well for the future.

Hitting

Young has been a slow learner at all levels of professional baseball, but, once he's gotten the hang of the next level, he's been successful. Since coming to the majors, Young has shortened his big swing somewhat. He is a good fastball hitter, and despite reports to the contrary, also hits curveballs well. He has patience at the plate along with streaky power. His performance in pressure situations has been subpar, but that should improve as his confidence grows.

Baserunning & Defense

Young has adequate speed and can steal a base now and then. Still, he has a lot to learn about baserunning, and he often appeared tentative on the sacks last year. In the field Young isn't a classic center fielder, but he has good range and a solid glove. His arm is strong and accurate, though not overwhelmingly so.

1997 Outlook

Though he claimed center field in '97, the A's really envision Young as their future left fielder. He has had a full season to get acclimated to the big leagues, so now it is time to show what he really can do. Young has always improved during his second season at a new level, so he may do the same here. He certainly possesses the best combination of bat and glove of all the outfielders on the Oakland roster.

Position: CF/RF
Bats: R **Throws:** R
Ht: 6' 1" **Wt:** 190

Opening Day Age: 27
Born: 7/8/69 in Chicago, IL
ML Seasons: 3

Overall Statistics

	G	AB	R	H	D	T	HR	RBI	SB	BB	SO	Avg	OBP	Slg
1996	141	462	72	112	19	4	19	64	7	52	118	.242	.326	.424
Career	178	542	83	124	23	4	21	72	7	61	138	.229	.313	.402

Where He Hits the Ball

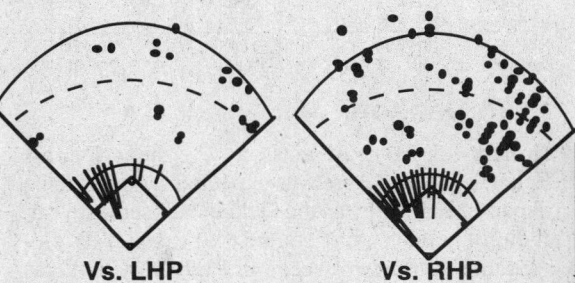

Vs. LHP   Vs. RHP

1996 Situational Stats

	AB	H	HR	RBI	Avg		AB	H	HR	RBI	Avg
Home	231	60	10	27	.260	LHP	127	35	6	16	.276
Road	231	52	9	37	.225	RHP	335	77	13	48	.230
First Half	271	65	12	41	.240	Sc Pos	116	27	3	40	.233
Scnd Half	191	47	7	23	.246	Clutch	71	13	5	12	.183

1996 Rankings (American League)

→ 2nd in fielding percentage in center field (.997)

→ 3rd in lowest batting average with the bases loaded (.071), lowest on-base percentage for a leadoff hitter (.309), lowest batting average on the road (.225) and lowest batting average

→ 4th in lowest batting average vs. right-handed pitchers (.230)

→ 5th in highest percentage of swings that missed (30.7%)

→ 6th in highest percentage of swings on the first pitch (38.7%)

→ 9th in lowest batting average in the clutch (.183)

Mark Acre

Position: RP
Bats: R **Throws:** R
Ht: 6' 8" **Wt:** 240

Opening Day Age: 28
Born: 9/16/68 in
Concord, CA
ML Seasons: 3

Overall Statistics

	W	L	Pct.	ERA	G	GS	Sv	IP	H	BB	SO	HR	BR/IP
1996	1	3	.250	6.12	22	0	2	25.0	38	9	18	4	1.88
Career	7	6	.538	5.09	99	0	2	111.1	114	60	86	15	1.56

1996 Situational Stats

	W	L	ERA	Sv	IP		AB	H	HR	RBI	Avg
Home	1	1	5.93	1	13.2	LHB	51	18	1	10	.353
Road	0	2	6.35	1	11.1	RHB	61	20	3	11	.328
First Half	0	0	6.94	0	11.2	Sc Pos	37	11	0	15	.297
Scnd Half	1	3	5.40	2	13.1	Clutch	32	13	2	8	.406

1996 Season

Hailed for several years as the next Dennis Eckersley, Mark Acre was expected to succeed the departed Eckersley as the Oakland closer last year. It didn't happen. Acre started the season in Triple-A, came up for two weeks in early May and was clobbered, and was quickly demoted again. He returned to Oakland in August and fared no better.

Pitching & Defense

The forkball is Acre's bread-and-butter. He throws it hard, and when he's got confidence in it, he can mix it with a good fastball to get batters out. With no one on base, he tries to come right in with it, but he doesn't have the stuff to get by with that approach. Acre fields well enough, gets to balls and covers the bag. He doesn't hold runners very well.

1997 Outlook

Although many closers work their way up through different roles, Acre has been groomed as a closer from the start. Oakland needs someone to take the ball in the late innings, and they would like Acre to take the bull by the horns. If he doesn't start to produce, their patience with him may run out soon.

Rafael Bournigal

Position: 2B/SS
Bats: R **Throws:** R
Ht: 5'11" **Wt:** 165

Opening Day Age: 30
Born: 5/12/66 in Azua, DR
ML Seasons: 4
Pronunciation: BORN-nuh-gal

Overall Statistics

	G	AB	R	H	D	T	HR	RBI	SB	BB	SO	Avg	OBP	Slg
1996	88	252	33	61	14	2	0	18	4	16	19	.242	.290	.313
Career	146	406	36	99	19	3	0	32	4	26	28	.244	.296	.305

1996 Situational Stats

	AB	H	HR	RBI	Avg		AB	H	HR	RBI	Avg
Home	128	26	0	8	.203	LHP	62	13	0	4	.210
Road	124	35	0	10	.282	RHP	190	48	0	14	.253
First Half	127	38	0	10	.299	Sc Pos	59	15	0	18	.254
Scnd Half	125	23	0	8	.184	Clutch	34	12	0	6	.353

1996 Season

Rafael Bournigal started the 1996 season on the bench, but assumed the Athletics' second base job in June as a result of Brent Gates' broken leg. He went on a tear after claiming the full-time job, but soon fizzled and wound up back on the bench for the final third of the season. He played well in the field, however, and proved to be valuable utility man.

Hitting, Baserunning & Defense

Bournigal is a prototypical contact-hitting utility infielder. He doesn't walk, he doesn't strike out, and he doesn't hit for power. Bournigal has better-than-average speed, and although he isn't much of a basestealer, he does run the bases aggressively. His real strength is his defense—he is equally adept at both second and short.

1997 Outlook

Although no one is madly trumpeting his attributes, Bournigal has proved himself to be a valuable fill-in last year. He will not be involved in the 1997 battle for the starting second base spot, but he probably will remain on the Athletics roster, ready to step in again in a utility role.

Jim Corsi

Position: RP
Bats: R **Throws:** R
Ht: 6' 1" **Wt:** 220

Opening Day Age: 35
Born: 9/9/61 in Newton, MA
ML Seasons: 7

Overall Statistics

	W	L	Pct.	ERA	G	GS	Sv	IP	H	BB	SO	HR	BR/IP
1996	6	0	1.000	4.03	57	0	3	73.2	71	34	43	6	1.43
Career	13	16	.448	3.23	222	1	5	320.1	296	127	179	20	1.32

1996 Situational Stats

	W	L	ERA	Sv	IP		AB	H	HR	RBI	Avg
Home	4	0	5.23	0	31.0	LHB	113	37	3	21	.327
Road	2	0	3.16	3	42.2	RHB	150	34	3	15	.227
First Half	3	0	3.55	2	38.0	Sc Pos	74	20	3	31	.270
Scnd Half	3	0	4.54	1	35.2	Clutch	109	25	6	13	.229

1996 Season

Veteran righthander Jim Corsi was one of several men who briefly filled the Oakland stopper role last season. Much better suited for set-up work, Corsi turned in a creditable number of innings and provided some veteran experience to the bullpen in 1996.

Pitching & Defense

Corsi can still bring his fastball in the high 80s, but his out pitch is his ground ball inducing palmball. He is very effective against right-handed hitters. Corsi is not capable of more than a couple of performances over a short period without a rest. He does his job well on defense, quickly grabbing the grounders he so often serves up. He also is very good at holding baserunners and has a good move to first, although hitters seem to pick up the ball better when he goes into the stretch.

1997 Outlook

Corsi is a serviceable set-up pitcher, and he turned in a decent, injury-free season. He is not expected to be back in Oakland, though, so he'll probably be setting up somewhere else.

Brent Gates

Position: 2B
Bats: B **Throws:** R
Ht: 6' 1" **Wt:** 180

Opening Day Age: 27
Born: 3/14/70 in Grand Rapids, MI
ML Seasons: 4

Overall Statistics

	G	AB	R	H	D	T	HR	RBI	SB	BB	SO	Avg	OBP	Slg
1996	64	247	26	65	19	2	2	30	1	18	35	.263	.316	.381
Career	403	1539	179	419	83	9	16	179	14	141	226	.272	.331	.369

1996 Situational Stats

	AB	H	HR	RBI	Avg		AB	H	HR	RBI	Avg
Home	123	33	1	10	.268	LHP	55	10	0	6	.182
Road	124	32	1	20	.258	RHP	192	55	2	24	.286
First Half	247	65	2	30	.263	Sc Pos	61	12	0	24	.197
Scnd Half	0	0	0	0	-	Clutch	40	7	0	3	.175

1996 Season

Brent Gates started 1996 as the A's regular second baseman, but suffered a season of disappointment. At the plate, he had a miserable April (.237), followed by a better May (.272). He was getting into a groove in June (.293) when he suffered a season-ending broken leg. He then watched Tony Batista take his position, probably on a permanent basis.

Hitting, Baserunning & Defense

Gates has regressed since 1993, when he batted .290 as a 23-year-old rookie. A switch-hitter, he hits line drives with occasional power, but he's had a lot of problems with inside pitches. Gates is a good baserunner, although he isn't much of a basestealer. He has good range and a steady glove, but tends to bail out while turning the double play. He'll sometimes boot the routine balls while handling the tough ones.

1997 Outlook

Gates' days with Oakland are probably numbered. He is certainly more than a serviceable second sacker, but with Batista claiming second base and Rafael Bournigal available as a backup, Gates becomes prime trade bait.

Oakland Athletics

Buddy Groom

Position: RP
Bats: L **Throws:** L
Ht: 6' 2" **Wt:** 200

Opening Day Age: 31
Born: 7/10/65 in
Dallas, TX
ML Seasons: 5

Overall Statistics

	W	L	Pct.	ERA	G	GS	Sv	IP	H	BB	SO	HR	BR/IP
1996	5	0	1.000	3.84	72	1	2	77.1	85	34	57	8	1.54
Career	7	13	.350	5.36	180	15	5	240.1	293	114	149	28	1.69

1996 Situational Stats

	W	L	ERA	Sv	IP		AB	H	HR	RBI	Avg
Home	0	0	5.50	0	37.2	LHB	123	33	2	16	.268
Road	5	0	2.27	2	39.2	RHB	179	52	6	31	.291
First Half	3	0	3.45	2	47.0	Sc Pos	96	29	4	42	.302
Scnd Half	2	0	4.45	0	30.1	Clutch	76	17	1	9	.224

1996 Season

Appearing in 72 games for Oakland—71 of them as a relief pitcher—veteran lefty Buddy Groom pitched well for most of the season. Groom had one bad month (August), but otherwise proved to be a very effective set-up man.

Pitching & Defense

Groom has a decent high-80s fastball, but he's learned to spot it more carefully than in the past, making the pitch even more effective. He relies more heavily these days on his slider, curve and change. Though he does well when he's in control of himself, he tends to panic under pressure, often giving up big hits with men on base. He also seemed to tire as the season progressed. Groom has only an average move to first, and runners can take advantage of him. He's not a good fielder and is slow getting to balls hit near him.

1997 Outlook

Groom wore down a bit under the strain of working a career-high 72 games last year, but overall it was the best season of his career. He figures to continue working in the same middle-relief role next year.

Dave Telgheder

Position: SP
Bats: R **Throws:** R
Ht: 6' 3" **Wt:** 212

Opening Day Age: 30
Born: 11/11/66 in
Middletown, NY
ML Seasons: 4
Pronunciation:
TAIL-gade-urr

Overall Statistics

	W	L	Pct.	ERA	G	GS	Sv	IP	H	BB	SO	HR	BR/IP
1996	4	7	.364	4.65	16	14	0	79.1	92	26	43	12	1.49
Career	11	12	.478	4.96	53	25	0	190.2	219	62	98	28	1.47

1996 Situational Stats

	W	L	ERA	Sv	IP		AB	H	HR	RBI	Avg
Home	3	5	4.43	0	44.2	LHB	173	56	6	21	.324
Road	1	2	4.93	0	34.2	RHB	142	36	6	13	.254
First Half	0	0	-	0	0.0	Sc Pos	75	14	0	19	.187
Scnd Half	4	7	4.65	0	79.1	Clutch	18	9	0	3	.500

1996 Season

Recalled to help the struggling Oakland staff after the All-Star break, Dave Telgheder put together an up-and-down series of starts that were almost as confusing as his career. Of his 14 starts, seven were excellent, four were very poor, and the other three were somewhere in-between.

Pitching & Defense

After being freed from the Mets' system, Telgheder brought his assortment of offspeed stuff to Oakland. He throws a good split-fingered fastball, saving his mid-80s fastball for when he needs it. When he hits his spots, he can be very effective. Telgheder covers his position very well, and gets to the base quickly. He is not very adept at holding runners.

1997 Outlook

It almost seems like a broken record, but there are so many unknowns about the Oakland starting staff that a fourth or fifth spot may go to Telgheder almost by default. The A's like his tenacity and experience, but his inconsistency perplexes them. He cannot endure too many more bad performances if he is to keep his job.

John Wasdin

Position: SP
Bats: R **Throws:** R
Ht: 6' 2" **Wt:** 190

Opening Day Age: 24
Born: 8/5/72 in Fort Belvoir, VA
ML Seasons: 2

Overall Statistics

	W	L	Pct.	ERA	G	GS	Sv	IP	H	BB	SO	HR	BR/IP
1996	8	7	.533	5.96	25	21	0	131.1	145	50	75	24	1.48
Career	9	8	.529	5.81	30	23	0	148.2	159	53	81	28	1.43

1996 Situational Stats

	W	L	ERA	Sv	IP		AB	H	HR	RBI	Avg
Home	6	3	4.96	0	74.1	LHB	269	84	14	53	.312
Road	2	4	7.26	0	57.0	RHB	243	61	10	35	.251
First Half	6	2	4.75	0	55.0	Sc Pos	112	38	9	64	.339
Scnd Half	2	5	6.84	0	76.1	Clutch	24	10	1	8	.417

1996 Season

After being the final player cut last spring, rookie righthander John Wasdin returned to the A's in late May and moved into the club's revolving-door rotation. Wasdin pitched fairly well at first, but by July the league was wise to him and he began to struggle. He finished the season in the bullpen.

Pitching & Defense

Wasdin features good command of his mid-80s fastball, curve and slider. He will come at hitters, rarely walking anyone, and he has the stuff to pile up some strikeouts. Lefties have given him trouble, however, and opposing managers tended to stack their lineups with them. He wields a good glove, but is terrible at holding baserunners.

1997 Outlook

Wasdin got his major league experience a little sooner than anticipated, and did about as well as could have been expected. His role as a member of the rotation is probably secure. With a year under his belt, he'll likely put up better numbers in 1997, which would make him an important cog on the Oakland staff.

George Williams

Position: C/DH
Bats: B **Throws:** R
Ht: 5'10" **Wt:** 190

Opening Day Age: 27
Born: 4/22/69 in Lacrosse, WI
ML Seasons: 2

Overall Statistics

	G	AB	R	H	D	T	HR	RBI	SB	BB	SO	Avg	OBP	Slg
1996	56	132	17	20	5	0	3	10	0	28	32	.152	.311	.258
Career	85	211	30	43	10	1	6	24	0	39	53	.204	.337	.346

1996 Situational Stats

	AB	H	HR	RBI	Avg		AB	H	HR	RBI	Avg
Home	72	11	0	3	.153	LHP	34	6	0	2	.176
Road	60	9	3	7	.150	RHP	98	14	3	8	.143
First Half	97	16	3	9	.165	Sc Pos	27	3	1	7	.111
Scnd Half	35	4	0	1	.114	Clutch	27	2	0	0	.074

1996 Season

George Williams began the season on the A's roster, backing up Terry Steinbach behind the plate. He had trouble finding his stroke and was sent down to Triple-A, where a .404 average got him a quick ticket back to Oakland. But Williams immediately went back into his slump once he returned. In the Year of the Hitter, he wound up hitting .152.

Hitting, Baserunning & Defense

A switch-hitter, Williams is capable of hitting for average and power, but he exhibited neither in '96. Though he made decent contact, he couldn't handle the breaking pitches and change-ups that American League hitters must face. Williams is slow on the bases and behind the plate, displaying an average glove and an erratic throwing arm.

1997 Outlook

Despite the tribulations of Williams' 1996 season, he has several pluses. First, he has nowhere to go but up. Second, he has handled minor league pitching effectively as both a hitter and receiver. Third, the potential departure of Steinbach could leave a gap at the position. Williams, by virtue of a familiarity with the pitching staff, would become a prime candidate for the starting job.

Oakland Athletics

Other Oakland Athletics

Allen Battle (Pos: CF/LF, Age: 28, Bats: R)

	G	AB	R	H	D	T	HR	RBI	SB	BB	SO	Avg	OBP	Slg
1996	47	130	20	25	3	0	1	5	10	17	26	.192	.293	.238
Career	108	248	33	57	8	0	1	7	13	32	52	.230	.324	.274

Acquired before the '96 season in a trade with St. Louis, Battle was a starting outfielder for two months before the A's realized he couldn't hit (.192 BA). Things went downhill from there. . . 1997 Outlook: C

John Briscoe (Pos: RHP, Age: 29)

	W	L	Pct.	ERA	G	GS	Sv	IP	H	BB	SO	HR	BR/IP
1996	0	1	.000	3.76	17	0	1	26.1	18	24	14	2	1.59
Career	5	5	.500	5.67	100	2	2	139.2	124	129	115	18	1.81

Despite averaging nearly a walk an inning over his six-year career, Briscoe has somehow managed to stay in the majors. His luck ran out last year, as he was sent down to Triple-A Edmonton in May. 1997 Outlook: C

Bobby Chouinard (Pos: RHP, Age: 24)

	W	L	Pct.	ERA	G	GS	Sv	IP	H	BB	SO	HR	BR/IP
1996	4	2	.667	6.10	13	11	0	59.0	75	32	32	10	1.81
Career	4	2	.667	6.10	13	11	0	59.0	75	32	32	10	1.81

Chouinard pitched very well at Triple-A last season and got several opportunities to establish himself in the Oakland rotation. He was hammered (6.10 ERA) but should get another shot. 1997 Outlook: B

Paul Fletcher (Pos: RHP, Age: 30)

	W	L	Pct.	ERA	G	GS	Sv	IP	H	BB	SO	HR	BR/IP
1996	0	0	-	20.25	1	0	0	1.1	6	1	0	0	5.25
Career	1	0	1.000	6.60	12	0	0	15.0	21	10	10	2	2.07

Fletcher spent a grand total of six days in the majors last season before wearing out his welcome with a horrendous outing (3 ER, 1 1/3 IP). He did pitch well in the minors, but is now 30. 1997 Outlook: C

Webster Garrison (Pos: 2B, Age: 31, Bats: R)

	G	AB	R	H	D	T	HR	RBI	SB	BB	SO	Avg	OBP	Slg
1996	5	9	0	0	0	0	0	0	0	1	0	.000	.100	.000
Career	5	9	0	0	0	0	0	0	0	1	0	.000	.100	.000

Garrison provided some infield support during his brief stint with Oakland last season. He's hit decently in the minors, but at 31, his chances of ever holding down a regular job are finished. 1997 Outlook: D

Patrick Lennon (Pos: LF, Age: 28, Bats: R)

	G	AB	R	H	D	T	HR	RBI	SB	BB	SO	Avg	OBP	Slg
1996	14	30	5	7	3	0	0	1	0	7	10	.233	.378	.333
Career	24	40	7	8	4	0	0	2	0	10	11	.200	.360	.300

After refusing a reassignment request by Kansas City, Lennon signed a minor league deal with Oakland and had a big year with the bat. He's not young (29) so he'll have to produce in a hurry. 1997 Outlook: C

Brian Lesher (Pos: LF/RF, Age: 26, Bats: R)

	G	AB	R	H	D	T	HR	RBI	SB	BB	SO	Avg	OBP	Slg
1996	26	82	11	19	3	0	5	16	0	5	17	.232	.281	.451
Career	26	82	11	19	3	0	5	16	0	5	17	.232	.281	.451

Lesher saw some September action in the outfield after posting decent numbers at Triple-A Edmonton. He slammed five homers in only 82 at-bats, but has never met a pitch he didn't like. 1997 Outlook: C

Torey Lovullo (Pos: 1B/3B, Age: 31, Bats: B)

	G	AB	R	H	D	T	HR	RBI	SB	BB	SO	Avg	OBP	Slg
1996	65	82	15	18	4	0	3	9	1	11	17	.220	.323	.378
Career	280	680	76	153	34	1	13	54	9	76	108	.225	.304	.335

Waived in June by Oakland, his fifth team in as many years, Lovullo appears to be out of options. He's versatile (five different positions) and draws walks, but he can't hit a lick. 1997 Outlook: D

Damon Mashore (Pos: LF/RF, Age: 27, Bats: R)

	G	AB	R	H	D	T	HR	RBI	SB	BB	SO	Avg	OBP	Slg
1996	50	105	20	28	7	1	3	12	4	16	31	.267	.366	.438
Career	50	105	20	28	7	1	3	12	4	16	31	.267	.366	.438

Brought to the majors in June, Mashore was having a good season at the plate before a dislocated shoulder curtailed his year. He should receive plenty of playing time in the A's outfield this season. 1997 Outlook: A

Izzy Molina (Pos: C, Age: 25, Bats: R)

	G	AB	R	H	D	T	HR	RBI	SB	BB	SO	Avg	OBP	Slg
1996	14	25	0	5	2	0	0	1	0	1	3	.200	.231	.280
Career	14	25	0	5	2	0	0	1	0	1	3	.200	.231	.280

Molina took over at backup catcher in August when the A's sent George Williams to the minors. He hit poorly, as was to be expected, but he could return this season. 1997 Outlook: C

Steve Montgomery (Pos: RHP, Age: 26)

	W	L	Pct.	ERA	G	GS	Sv	IP	H	BB	SO	HR	BR/IP
1996	1	0	1.000	9.22	8	0	0	13.2	18	13	8	5	2.27
Career	1	0	1.000	9.22	8	0	0	13.2	18	13	8	5	2.27

Montgomery made his major league debut early last season but was clearly overmatched, walking 13 batters in 13-plus innings and racking up a 9.22 ERA. He pitched well at Triple-A and is poised to return. 1997 Outlook: C

Kerwin Moore (Pos: CF, Age: 26, Bats: B)

	G	AB	R	H	D	T	HR	RBI	SB	BB	SO	Avg	OBP	Slg
1996	22	16	4	1	1	0	0	0	1	2	6	.063	.167	.125
Career	22	16	4	1	1	0	0	0	1	2	6	.063	.167	.125

Moore is a speed demon who was called up to the big leagues in September despite a mediocre season (.230 BA at Triple-A). He can walk and steal bases, but is a non-factor with the bat. 1997 Outlook: C

Pedro Munoz (Pos: DH/RF, Age: 28, Bats: R)

	G	AB	R	H	D	T	HR	RBI	SB	BB	SO	Avg	OBP	Slg
1996	34	121	17	31	5	0	6	18	0	9	31	.256	.308	.446
Career	517	1708	203	467	75	8	67	252	11	100	418	.273	.315	.444

Munoz never recovered from straining his knee in June—not that Oakland missed him terribly. He has some power, but his low on-base percentage makes him an offensive liability. 1997 Outlook: C

Phil Plantier (Pos: LF, Age: 28, Bats: L)

	G	AB	R	H	D	T	HR	RBI	SB	BB	SO	Avg	OBP	Slg
1996	73	231	29	49	8	1	7	31	2	28	56	.212	.304	.346
Career	558	1762	247	427	82	3	86	274	13	224	446	.242	.332	.439

Plantier, after starting the year as the A's regular left fielder, was waived in June—only to be re-signed in August. Now devoid of power, it's apparent that his '93 year (34 HRs) was a fluke. 1997 Outlook: C

Aaron Small (Pos: RHP, Age: 25)

	W	L	Pct.	ERA	G	GS	Sv	IP	H	BB	SO	HR	BR/IP
1996	1	3	.250	8.16	12	3	0	28.2	37	22	17	3	2.06
Career	2	3	.400	7.05	20.	3	0	37.0	49	30	22	5	2.14

Small, who's been wildly inconsistent throughout his baseball career, received chances in April and September to establish himself on the A's staff. The results (8.16 ERA) haven't been promising. 1997 Outlook: C

Matt Stairs (Pos: RF/LF, Age: 29, Bats: L)

	G	AB	R	H	D	T	HR	RBI	SB	BB	SO	Avg	OBP	Slg
1996	61	137	21	38	5	1	10	23	1	19	23	.277	.367	.547
Career	119	263	32	69	15	2	11	47	1	30	45	.262	.339	.460

Stairs, in his first consistent stretch of major league playing time, showed he had power and could get on base (.367 OBP, .547 SLG). He's seems to have found a nitch as the A's fourth outfielder. 1997 Outlook: B

Steve Wojciechowski (Pos: LHP, Age: 26)

	W	L	Pct.	ERA	G	GS	Sv	IP	H	BB	SO	HR	BR/IP
1996	5	5	.500	5.65	16	15	0	79.2	97	28	30	10	1.57
Career	7	8	.467	5.47	30	22	0	128.1	148	56	43	17	1.59

Wojciechowski spent the first half of last season providing the reasons that Oakland *shouldn't* keep him on the roster (5.65 ERA, 97 hits in 79-plus innings). Weak minor league record. 1997 Outlook: C

Oakland Athletics

Oakland Athletics Minor League Prospects

Organization Overview:

The Oakland Athletics made a lot of headlines in the early '90s by drafting pitchers with high draft picks. Not a single one of their first-round selections panned out, but the A's were undeterred. They've now completely re-stocked their minor league system with young pitchers, but this time, they've focused on quantity rather than quality. Hey, they can't *all* get hurt this time, right? A large number of them got their first extended major league trials last year. The results were underwhelming, but they all survived the process and many of them should improve in the coming years. If that doesn't happen, there's still a boatload of young hurlers down on the farm waiting to replace them. Last year, the A's broke in several new regulars, including Jason Giambi, Tony Batista and Ernie Young. Further down on the farm, the A's have a few blue-chippers like Ben Grieve and Wil Tejada. By the time they're ready, the A's may have found a few aces among their pitchers.

Steven Cox

Position: 1B   **Opening Day Age:** 22
Bats: L **Throws:** L   **Born:** 10/31/74 in
Ht: 6' 4" **Wt:** 200   Delano, CA

Recent Statistics

	G	AB	R	H	D	T	HR	RBI	SB	BB	SO	AVG
93 A Sou. Oregon	15	57	10	18	4	1	2	16	0	5	15	.316
94 A W. Michigan	99	311	37	75	19	2	6	32	2	41	95	.241
95 A Modesto	132	483	95	144	29	3	30	110	5	84	88	.298
96 AA Huntsville	104	381	59	107	21	1	12	61	2	51	65	.281
96 MLE	104	370	52	96	19	0	9	53	1	37	69	.259

Left-handed first baseman Steve Cox hopes to be Oakland's next great power hitter. He's fairly disciplined and he's got power to all fields, but his home run stroke is still developing. Only 22 years old, he'll probably get at least another year or two to work on pulling the ball. He got contact lenses during the season last year, and the benefits may become evident this year.

Ben Grieve

Position: OF   **Opening Day Age:** 20
Bats: L **Throws:** R   **Born:** 5/4/76 in
Ht: 6' 4" **Wt:** 200   Arlington, TX

Recent Statistics

	G	AB	R	H	D	T	HR	RBI	SB	BB	SO	AVG
94 A Sou. Oregon	72	252	44	83	13	0	7	50	2	51	48	.329
95 A W. Michigan	102	371	53	97	16	1	4	62	11	60	75	.261
95 A Modesto	28	107	17	28	5	0	2	14	2	15	22	.262
96 A Modesto	72	281	61	100	20	1	11	51	8	38	52	.356
96 AA Huntsville	63	232	34	55	8	1	8	32	0	35	53	.237
96 MLE	63	226	29	49	7	0	6	28	0	25	56	.217

Ben Grieve was the most highly-regarded high school player in the '94 draft, and he's had his ups and downs since the A's selected him with the second overall pick that year. Last year, he tore up the California League, but had a much tougher time after a midseason promotion to Double-A. Grieve bats lefty, and projects to hit for both power and average. He's got great patience and hits to all fields, but he's got very little speed and no range in either left or right field. Still, he's got tremendous upside, and the fact that he made it to Double-A at age 20 says a lot about how advanced his bat is.

Ramon Hernandez

Position: C   **Opening Day Age:** 20
Bats: R **Throws:** R   **Born:** 5/20/76 in
Ht: 6' 0" **Wt:** 170   Caracas, Venez

Recent Statistics

	G	AB	R	H	D	T	HR	RBI	SB	BB	SO	AVG
95 R Athletics	48	143	37	52	9	6	4	37	6	39	16	.364
96 A W. Michigan	123	447	62	114	26	2	12	68	2	69	62	.255

If things break right, Ramon Hernandez could develop into a rare two-way catcher. He plays good defense, showing solid throwing and ball-blocking skills. At the plate, he has an uncommonly good understanding of the strike zone for someone so young. He's already got a bit of power, and he's got the tools to hit for a much better average. Right now, he's at least two years away, but his timetable could move up if his development enables him to pass the Athletics' other catching prospects.

Willie Morales

Position: C   **Opening Day Age:** 24
Bats: R **Throws:** R   **Born:** 9/7/72 in
Ht: 5' 10" **Wt:** 182   Tucson, AZ

Recent Statistics

	G	AB	R	H	D	T	HR	RBI	SB	BB	SO	AVG
93 A Sou. Oregon	60	208	34	56	16	0	1	27	0	19	36	.269
94 A W. Michigan	111	380	47	101	26	0	13	51	3	36	64	.266
95 A Modesto	109	419	49	116	32	0	4	60	1	28	75	.277
96 AA Huntsville	108	377	54	110	24	0	18	73	0	38	67	.292
96 MLE	108	366	47	99	22	0	15	64	0	27	71	.270

Willie Morales is the most advanced of the Oakland catching prospects. He's still a bit impatient at the plate, but he hits for good power and average, and projects to develop into one of the better-hitting receivers in the game. And he's not just out there for his bat—he's got a strong arm, and nailed 42.6% of opposing basestealers last year, the third-best figure in the Southern League. Now that Terry Steinbach has departed, Morales will be able to step right in and do the job.

Brad Rigby

Position: P
Bats: R **Throws:** R
Ht: 6' 6" **Wt:** 194

Opening Day Age: 23
Born: 5/14/73 in
Milwaukee, WI

Recent Statistics

	W	L	ERA	G	GS	Sv	IP	H	R	BB	SO	HR
94 A Modesto	2	1	3.80	11	1	2	23.2	20	10	10	28	0
95 A Modesto	11	4	3.84	31	23	2	154.2	135	79	48	145	5
96 AA Huntsville	9	12	3.95	26	26	0	159.1	161	89	59	127	13

After being named the best pitching prospect in the California League in 1995, Brad Rigby moved up to Double-A last year and did nothing to soil his reputation. Rigby's got a very good fastball that regularly tops 90 MPH, two good breaking pitches and a change-up. The six-foot, six-inch righthander is close to being ready, and may need only a year at Triple-A or less.

Scott Spiezio

Position: 3B
Bats: B **Throws:** R
Ht: 6' 2" **Wt:** 195

Opening Day Age: 24
Born: 9/21/72 in Joliet,
IL

Recent Statistics

	G	AB	R	H	D	T	HR	RBI	SB	BB	SO	AVG
96 AAA Edmonton	140	523	87	137	30	4	20	91	6	56	66	.262
96 AL Oakland	9	29	6	9	2	0	0	4	0	4	4	.310
96 MLE	140	506	73	120	27	2	15	76	4	45	69	.237

If Scott Spiezio's name sounds familiar, it's because he's the son of former big leaguer Ed Spiezio. Like his dad, he's a third baseman, and a low-average hitter with medium-range power. He's an excellent defender, with great range and a cannon arm. Fortunately, his dad taught him to switch-hit. He's equally adept from both sides of the plate, but his power will have to improve because his other skills are unremarkable. At age 24 there's still time.

Miguel Tejada

Position: SS
Bats: R **Throws:** R
Ht: 5' 10" **Wt:** 170

Opening Day Age: 20
Born: 5/25/76 in Bani,
DR

Recent Statistics

	G	AB	R	H	D	T	HR	RBI	SB	BB	SO	AVG
95 A Sou. Oregon	74	269	45	66	15	5	8	44	19	41	54	.245
96 A Modesto	114	458	97	128	12	5	20	72	27	51	93	.279

It's no exaggeration to say that Miguel Tejada may have as high a ceiling as any prospect in the game. He's a legitimate five-tool player, and he's already got all five of them working. He's got uncommon power for someone so young, and his defense is something to behold.

With great hands and a cannon arm, he makes spectacular plays on a regular basis. Now, all he needs to do is to cut down on his errors and work on his command of the strike zone. Last year, in his first full season, he tackled high Class A at age 20. Next year's he's on to Double-A, and the sky's the limit.

Jay Witasick

Position: P
Bats: R **Throws:** R
Ht: 6' 4" **Wt:** 205

Opening Day Age: 24
Born: 8/28/72 in
Baltimore, MD

Recent Statistics

	W	L	ERA	G	GS	Sv	IP	H	R	BB	SO	HR
96 AA Huntsville	0	3	2.30	25	6	4	66.2	47	21	26	63	3
96 AAA Edmonton	0	0	4.15	6	0	2	8.2	9	4	6	9	1
96 AL Oakland	1	1	6.23	12	0	0	13.0	12	9	5	12	5

Jay Witasick was another top prospect in the St. Louis chain who came to Oakland in the Stottlemyre deal. All he's ever thrown is a 90-MPH moving fastball and a hard slider. When he joined the Oakland organization, they took one look at his two-pitch arsenal and immediately sent him to the bullpen. Now, he's seen as a potentially dominant closer. His short relief work at Double-A was so impressive that the A's called him up for a look late in the year. He still needs a little more time, but a half-year at Triple-A should do it.

Others to Watch

Lefthander **Bret Wagner** came over from the St. Louis organization in the Todd Stottlemyre deal. His control suffered as he moved up to Double-A, and he's lost both velocity and status in the past two years. Primarily a breaking-ball pitcher, he used to be considered one of the Cardinals' best prospects. . . **Steve Karsay** has a message for the world: "I'm not dead yet!" After missing most of '94 and all of '95 with arm miseries, Karsay threw 34 innings at Class A on a rehab assignment last year. He's still got great command—he fanned 31 batters and walked only one. It's hard to believe he'll be only 24 years old this year. . . One of the more intriguing players in the system is **David Newhan**. The left-handed hitter batted .301 and smacked 25 homers in A-ball last year. He can play all over the field, and the A's plan on moving him to second base next year. . . Converted shortstop **Mark Bellhorn** has intriguing power for a second baseman. He's only 22, so the A's will give him time to learn to make better contact. . . Right-handed starter **Mike Rossiter** continued his comeback from injuries last year, showing good control at Double-A at age 23.

Lou Piniella

1996 Season

Lou Piniella's Mariners didn't win a pennant, but they did contend for a playoff berth until the final weekend despite a pitching staff which claimed Sterling Hitchcock as its "ace" for most of the season. If only for that, "Uncle Lou" deserves credit.

Offense

Early in the season, Piniella showed a strange infatuation with the sacrifice bunt. On May 12, for example, Piniella asked Alex Rodriguez—then hitting .303 with power—to lay down a bunt in the fifth inning. In Rodriguez' other three at-bats that evening, he homered twice and doubled. Piniella soon realized his M's were one of the more prodigious run-scoring teams of all time, but he never did rely entirely on the long ball. As Alex Rodriguez noted, "The thing about playing for Lou is you know he'll try anything, any time. He keeps you aggressive because that's the way he manages. He's always taking the game to the other team."

Pitching & Defense

The combination of injuries and ineffectiveness forced the Mariners to try 10 starting pitchers in their first 60 games, or one more than they used in all of 1995. It's hard for a manager to look good when that happens. Piniella tried a number of young starters, but he's never been the most patient man when it comes to inexperienced players, and pitchers like Matt Wagner, Bob Wolcott and Salomon Torres didn't get many chances to succeed. On the other hand, he showed the patience of Job with his relievers, especially Bobby Ayala.

1997 Outlook

The Mariners would like to find a reliable leadoff man for left field, but they're set at every other position. For Piniella and the M's, the 1997 season boils down to one thing: the health of Randy Johnson. Blessed with the most talented lineup in the game, just a decent pitching staff should mean another West title for Seattle.

Born: 8/28/43 in Tampa, FL

Playing Experience: 1964-1984, Bal, Cle, KC, NYA

Managerial Experience: 10 seasons

Manager Statistics

Year	Team, Lg	W	L	Pct	GB	Finish
1996	Seattle, AL	85	76	.528	4.5	2nd West
10 Seasons		774	709	.522	—	—

1996 Starting Pitchers by Days Rest

	≤3	4	5	6+
Mariners Starts	7	94	22	25
Mariners ERA	4.46	5.57	5.04	6.11
AL Avg Starts	4	96	30	21
AL ERA	5.57	4.90	5.33	5.81

1996 Situational Stats

	Lou Piniella	AL Average
Hit & Run Success %	33.9	39.1
Stolen Base Success %	69.8	69.6
Platoon Pct.	56.8	61.9
Defensive Subs	14	29
High-Pitch Outings	15	23
Quick/Slow Hooks	26/9	17/20
Sacrifice Attempts	65	58

1996 Rankings (American League)

→ 1st in least caught steals of home plate (0), quick hooks (26), saves with over 1 inning pitched (14) and 2+ pitching changes in low scoring games (25)

→ 2nd in pinch hitters used (190), starts on three days rest (6) and mid-inning pitching changes (245)

→ 3rd in intentional walks (40)

Jay Buhner

1996 Season

Few hitters got off to a hotter start last spring than Jay Buhner. Through June 11, the hulking right fielder hit exactly .300, with 21 home runs and 61 RBI in only 60 games. However, that evening he sprained his thumb, missed a week, and was never quite the same. After returning to the lineup on June 19, Buhner batted .253 with 23 dingers and 77 RBI in 90 games—still good numbers, but not spectacular. Nevertheless, Buhner managed to drive in 138 runs, the second-highest total in club history.

Hitting

Like most power hitters with long swings, Buhner is vulnerable to the breaking ball away. He's generally patient, though. That patience results in plenty of strikeouts, but it also allows Buhner to frequently get ahead in the count. And once he does that, he's particularly dangerous. Much like Gary Gaetti, Buhner is a devastating "cripple hitter"; when he knows what's coming, the ball ends up in the seats as often as not. Buhner will take the pitch to all fields, hitting many of his homers from left-center around to right-center.

Baserunning & Defense

Buhner runs the bases very conservatively and hasn't stolen a sack since 1993. He doesn't have great range in the outfield, but much like Carl Furillo of the great Brooklyn Dodger squads, Buhner sports a very strong arm and has learned to play a close and tricky right-field wall/scoreboard to near perfection. In October, he was rewarded with his first Gold Glove.

1997 Outlook

Buhner's 1996 percentages—batting, slugging, on-base—were very similar to his numbers in both 1994 and '95, which suggests he's as sure a bet as anyone to maintain his current level of performance. And with the likes of Alex Rodriguez, Ken Griffey and Edgar Martinez batting ahead of him, Buhner should knock in another 130-plus runs this season. He'll have a bit of added incentive, because 1997 is the last year of his current contract.

Position: RF
Bats: R **Throws:** R
Ht: 6' 3" **Wt:** 210

Opening Day Age: 32
Born: 8/13/64 in
Louisville, KY
ML Seasons: 10
Pronunciation:
Buu-ner
Nickname: Bone

Overall Statistics

	G	AB	R	H	D	T	HR	RBI	SB	BB	SO	Avg	OBP	Slg
1996	150	564	107	153	29	0	44	138	0	84	159	.271	.369	.557
Career	1025	3554	570	922	175	16	213	686	6	499	953	.259	.353	.497

Where He Hits the Ball

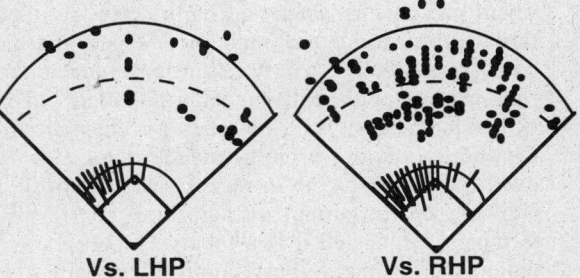

Vs. LHP   **Vs. RHP**

1996 Situational Stats

	AB	H	HR	RBI	Avg			AB	H	HR	RBI	Avg
Home	267	72	21	65	.270	LHP		125	38	11	32	.304
Road	297	81	23	73	.273	RHP		439	115	33	106	.262
First Half	291	83	23	72	.285	Sc Pos		184	58	16	101	.315
Scnd Half	273	70	21	66	.256	Clutch		83	22	5	24	.265

1996 Rankings (American League)

- → 1st in strikeouts and lowest percentage of extra bases taken as a runner (25.0%)
- → 2nd in highest percentage of swings that missed (33.0%)
- → 4th in sacrifice flies (10) and fielding percentage in right field (.989)
- → 5th in lowest cleanup slugging percentage (.458)
- → 6th in home runs, RBI and HR frequency (12.8 ABs per HR)
- → 7th in lowest percentage of swings put into play (35.9%) and highest percentage of swings on the first pitch (36.1%)
- → 10th in total bases (314) and hit by pitch (9)

Norm Charlton

1996 Season

The sight and sound were getting to be familiar. The Mariners have a late lead, and in from the bullpen strides "The Sheriff," Norm Charlton, accompanied by Garth Brooks' "Not Goin' Down." Usually, the only things goin' down were opposing hitters. Charlton saved 14 of 15 opportunities after signing with the M's in 1995, and he opened 1996 with a 12-for-13 string. Then came an awful run in late July and early August, including three straight blown saves. When he asked Lou Piniella to move him from the closer's role, Charlton was 2-6 with a 5.19 earned-run average. He did rebound with six saves in September.

Pitching

There's not much mystery to Charlton. He can still throw some serious heat, and once he gets ahead with the fastball, the hitter is often reduced to flailing away at forkballs in the dirt. It might only be two pitches, but it's a devastating combination. Charlton is murder on left-handed hitters. However, for the first time in recent years, Charlton showed an occasional vulnerability to righty swingers, which led to his relatively poor campaign. During the August slump, hitters simply weren't swinging at the forkball.

Defense

Charlton wants little to do with baserunners, so he pretty much just ignores them. The runners, in turn, take the appropriate liberties, and over the past two seasons are 13-for-14 in steal attempts. Charlton falls heavily toward third base at the conclusion of his delivery, leaving him in poor position to field comebackers.

1997 Outlook

Charlton's heart was never a question last season, and he dealt with his occasional failures with all the grace one could hope for. By reaching pre-set statistical goals last season, Charlton's Mariner contract was automatically extended through the 1997 season, so Kingdome fans will once again be treated to the strains of "Not Goin' Down" on a regular basis.

Position: RP
Bats: B **Throws:** L
Ht: 6' 3" **Wt:** 205

Opening Day Age: 34
Born: 1/6/63 in Fort Polk, LA
ML Seasons: 8
Nickname: The Sheriff

Overall Statistics

	W	L	Pct.	ERA	G	GS	Sv	IP	H	BB	SO	HR	BR/IP
1996	4	7	.364	4.04	70	0	20	75.2	68	38	73	7	1.40
Career	40	40	.500	3.12	397	37	81	680.2	565	276	612	49	1.24

How Often He Throws Strikes

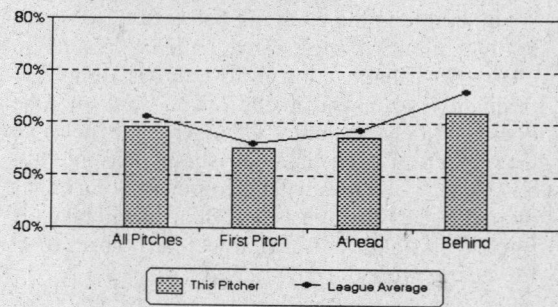

1996 Situational Stats

	W	L	ERA	Sv	IP		AB	H	HR	RBI	Avg
Home	3	2	3.98	9	43.0	LHB	75	14	0	7	.187
Road	1	5	4.13	11	32.2	RHB	204	54	7	32	.265
First Half	2	3	4.30	13	37.2	Sc Pos	97	22	3	31	.227
Scnd Half	2	4	3.79	7	38.0	Clutch	176	41	5	29	.233

1996 Rankings (American League)

- ➡ 2nd in lowest save percentage (74.1%) and relief losses (7)
- ➡ 3rd in lowest percentage of inherited runners scored (20.5%)
- ➡ 5th in blown saves (7)
- ➡ 8th in games finished (50)
- ➡ Led the Mariners in saves, games finished (50), wild pitches (9), save opportunities (27), save percentage (74.1%), blown saves (7), lowest percentage of inherited runners scored (20.5%) and relief losses (7)

Joey Cora

1996 Season

With Joey Cora, you know what you're getting. Following a hot start, he struggled. Cora then maintained a torrid midsummer pace—including a career-best 18-game hitting streak—that lifted his average from .217 on June 1 to .298 through August 3. At season's end, Cora's "percentages"—batting, slugging, on-base—were close to the same as he's posted since becoming a regular back in 1993. Starting against primarily right-handed pitchers, Cora was a constant in the Mariner lineup which led the major leagues in runs scored.

Hitting

The switch-hitting Cora has generally hit equally well from both sides of the plate, but for some reason Lou Piniella seldom lets Cora start against a left-handed pitcher. A prototypical contact hitter, Cora rarely walks or strikes out, preferring instead to slap the first good pitch he sees to either field. He does pull the ball slightly more than one would expect, and last season Cora blasted six home runs, doubling his previous career high. Most of those came on fastballs up and in, which Cora has learned to turn on. Interestingly, three of Cora's homers came in April, and the other three in September.

Baserunning & Defense

Cora and his sometime platoon partner Rich Amaral are the fastest Mariners. However, Cora ran very little last season, and his five stolen bases were his lowest figure since 1989. At second base Cora generally avoided the errors which have typically dragged down his fielding percentage. He shows decent range, but his throwing arm is, at best, weak.

1997 Outlook

With the Mariners having traded infield prospects Arquimedez Pozo and Desi Relaford, the club doesn't have many options at second base, which means Cora will be back in '97. Though more suited to hitting low in the order, Cora will continue to bat leadoff—and score runs in bunches—until Seattle finds a true leadoff man.

Position: 2B
Bats: B **Throws:** R
Ht: 5' 8" **Wt:** 162

Opening Day Age: 31
Born: 5/14/65 in Caguas, PR
ML Seasons: 9

Overall Statistics

	G	AB	R	H	D	T	HR	RBI	SB	BB	SO	Avg	OBP	Slg
1996	144	530	90	154	37	6	6	45	5	35	32	.291	.340	.417
Career	815	2558	408	697	104	31	13	208	96	254	227	.272	.343	.353

Where He Hits the Ball

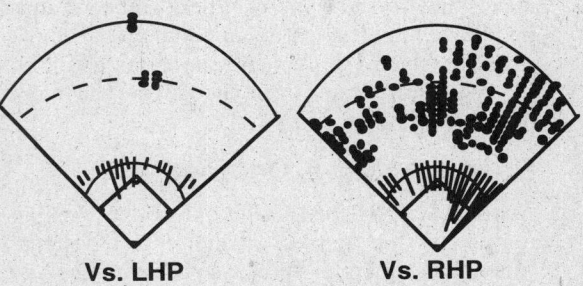

Vs. LHP   **Vs. RHP**

1996 Situational Stats

	AB	H	HR	RBI	Avg		AB	H	HR	RBI	Avg
Home	267	77	2	18	.288	LHP	55	12	0	4	.218
Road	263	77	4	27	.293	RHP	475	142	6	41	.299
First Half	288	81	3	25	.281	Sc Pos	115	32	0	37	.278
Scnd Half	242	73	3	20	.302	Clutch	80	18	0	5	.225

1996 Rankings (American League)

- → 2nd in lowest percentage of swings that missed (6.7%)
- → 3rd in errors at second base (13)
- → 4th in lowest fielding percentage at second base (.979) and highest percentage of swings put into play (59.7%)
- → 6th in least pitches seen per plate appearance (3.41)
- → 10th in lowest HR frequency (88.3 ABs per HR) and lowest batting average on an 0-2 count (.065)
- → Led the Mariners in triples, bunts in play (15), lowest percentage of swings that missed (6.7%) and highest percentage of swings put into play (59.7%)

Ken Griffey Jr.

Gold Glover

1996 Season

Ken Griffey Jr. hit 49 home runs, third in the American League, and knocked in 140 runs, fifth in the league. Both marks set new team records. Impressive? One can only wonder what Griffey might have done if not for a broken bone in his right hand that cost him 20 games in mid-summer.

Hitting

As usual, Griffey had little trouble with left-handed pitching, showing much more power against lefties than righties. Whereas many sluggers hit long, towering fly balls, Griffey's homers more often than not are line-drive laser beams to straightaway right field. In the Kingdome, that means they fly out right over the scoreboard. Lest one think Junior is just a Kingdome hitter, however, note that he was actually *more* productive on the road last season even though he had more power at home.

Baserunning & Defense

Anyone who watched Griffey score the winning run against the Yankees in the 1995 Divisional Championship Series knows the Kid can run. And last season he was an effective basestealer as well, swiping 16 bases while being caught only once. One caveat: Griffey doesn't always run all-out, especially on hits to the outfield. He plays relatively deep, resulting in numerous spectacular catches at the warning track and beyond. However, Griffey's positioning costs the Mariners innumerable singles in shallow center. Griffey and the Seattle coaching staff obviously think they come out ahead on that deal. His throwing arm is not powerful, but fairly accurate. Griffey collected another Gold Glove, his seventh straight.

1997 Outlook

Strange as it might seem, Griffey was eclipsed on his own team in 1996 by another player, Alex Rodriguez. Nevertheless, he remains one of baseball's biggest stars, and looms as a serious threat to the 60-homer mark if only he could remain healthy for an entire season.

Position: CF
Bats: L **Throws:** L
Ht: 6' 3" **Wt:** 205

Opening Day Age: 27
Born: 11/21/69 in Donora, PA
ML Seasons: 8

Overall Statistics

	G	AB	R	H	D	T	HR	RBI	SB	BB	SO	Avg	OBP	Slg
1996	140	545	125	165	26	2	49	140	16	78	104	.303	.392	.628
Career	1057	3985	695	1204	227	21	238	725	108	504	634	.302	.381	.549

Where He Hits the Ball

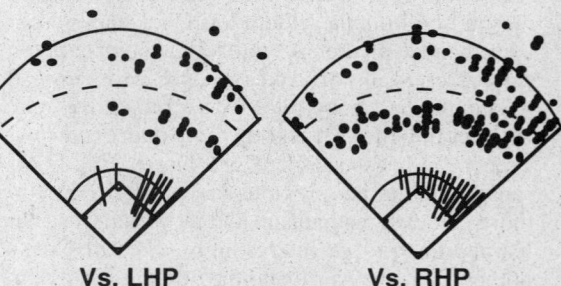

Vs. LHP   **Vs. RHP**

1996 Situational Stats

	AB	H	HR	RBI	Avg			AB	H	HR	RBI	Avg
Home	270	79	26	64	.293		LHP	158	47	21	53	.297
Road	275	86	23	76	.313		RHP	387	118	28	87	.305
First Half	261	78	23	60	.299		Sc Pos	155	47	16	94	.303
Scnd Half	284	87	26	80	.306		Clutch	76	21	5	11	.276

1996 Rankings (American League)

→ 2nd in HR frequency (11.1 ABs per HR)
→ 3rd in home runs
→ 4th in slugging percentage vs. left-handed pitchers (.741), errors in center field (4) and lowest fielding percentage in center field (.990)
→ 5th in runs scored, RBI, intentional walks (13), slugging percentage and steals of third (6)
→ 6th in total bases (342)
→ 8th in lowest groundball/flyball ratio (0.7) and least GDPs per GDP situation (4.4%)
→ Led the Mariners in home runs, RBI, intentional walks (13) and HR frequency (11.1 ABs per HR)

Sterling Hitchcock

1996 Season

Coming over from the Yankees prior to last season in a big trade, Sterling Hitchcock was slated as Seattle's number-two starter behind the incomparable Randy Johnson. Unfortunately, an injury to Johnson left Hitchcock as the club's nominal "ace," a role for which he was ill-suited. Hitchcock's All-Star break numbers, especially his 8-3 record, were acceptable, but he was simply awful down the stretch. Despite his struggles, Hitchcock was the only constant in the Mariner rotation last season, as he led the club with 13 victories and missed just one start all season (in August).

Pitching

Hitchcock's fastball tops out around 88-89 MPH, but that figure drops by two or three miles an hour when the southpaw is tired. Armed with a full repertoire of pitches, Hitchcock also throws a sinker, split-fingered fastball, a slider and a straight change-up. At times last season, it seemed that Hitchcock was telegraphing his offspeed pitches with severely slower movement in the second half of his delivery.

Defense

Thanks to his own solid pickoff move and the superior performance of catcher Dan Wilson, Hitchcock limited opposition basestealers to only 12 steals in 26 attempts last season. Hitchcock's easy motion leaves him in excellent fielding position, and he'll make all the routine plays.

1997 Outlook

Hitchcock boasts a career winning record, but that's mostly because of the healthy run support he seems to get every year. His 5.03 career ERA is certainly not eye-catching, but the Padres felt a change of scenery could lower that figure, so they acquired him in a trade for Scott Sanders. He should hold down the number-three spot in the rotation behind Andy Ashby and Joey Hamilton. If Hitchcock can find the skills he displayed as a Yankee, he could clear the 15-win plateau.

Position: SP
Bats: L **Throws:** L
Ht: 6' 1"   **Wt:** 192

Opening Day Age: 25
Born: 4/29/71 in Fayetteville, NC
ML Seasons: 5

Overall Statistics

	W	L	Pct.	ERA	G	GS	Sv	IP	H	BB	SO	HR	BR/IP
1996	13	9	.591	5.35	35	35	0	196.2	245	73	132	27	1.62
Career	29	24	.547	5.03	94	76	2	458.1	503	190	322	58	1.51

How Often He Throws Strikes

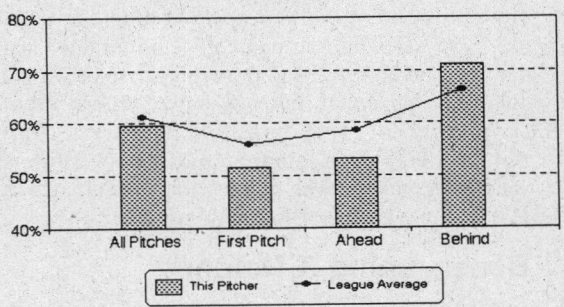

1996 Situational Stats

	W	L	ERA	Sv	IP		AB	H	HR	RBI	Avg
Home	6	5	5.19	0	102.1	LHB	166	38	3	17	.229
Road	7	4	5.53	0	94.1	RHB	628	207	24	101	.330
First Half	8	3	4.81	0	116.0	Sc Pos	182	68	8	87	.374
Scnd Half	5	6	6.14	0	80.2	Clutch	38	12	0	4	.316

1996 Rankings (American League)

→ 1st in runners caught stealing (14), highest batting average allowed (.309) and highest batting average allowed with runners in scoring position (.374)

→ 2nd in games started

→ 3rd in highest slugging percentage allowed (.476), highest on-base percentage allowed (.368), highest batting average allowed vs. right-handed batters (.330), errors at pitcher (3) and lowest fielding percentage at pitcher (.906)

→ 4th in most baserunners allowed per 9 innings (14.9) 7th in highest ERA on the road (5.53)

Seattle Mariners

Dave Hollins

Signed By
ANGELS

1996 Season

It was a strange campaign for Dave Hollins. He opened the season as the Minnesota Twins' regular third baseman, and in 25 April games he hit seven homers and racked up 22 RBI. In 25 May games, Hollins batted .185 with *zero* home runs and *four* RBI. Hollins, a diabetic, attributed some of his midseason problems to bouts of weakness brought on by low blood sugar. He battled back, and was having a solid August when the Twins traded him to Seattle on the 29th of that month. Hollins helped key the Mariners' ultimately unsuccessful playoff push, batting .353 with 25 RBI in September.

Hitting

Hollins is one of the more patient hitters around, and even when his batting average plummeted last summer, he continued to draw his share of walks. As usual, the switch-hitter was much more effective against left-handed pitchers than righthanders. Upon joining the Mariners, Hollins seemed to take fewer pitches than usual, which resulted in a lot of early-count base hits.

Baserunning & Defense

Much faster than you'd think from looking at him, Hollins is an aggressive runner but doesn't often run into outs. He used his speed to beat out 12 bunt hits last season. Hollins has always been shaky at third base, to the point where he's been tried at first base and right field in past seasons. But last year was one of his best defensive campaigns ever, some late-season throwing problems notwithstanding.

1997 Outlook

After consecutive injury-plagued seasons which saw Hollins hit .222 and .225, his 1996 campaign should be considered a major comeback. Still, feeling that Russ Davis would be fully recovered from his broken leg by next sping, the Mariners decided that Davis, not Hollins, would be the regular third baseman in 1997. Hollins signed a free-agent contract with the Angels in November and will probably be their first baseman this year.

Position: 3B
Bats: B **Throws:** R
Ht: 6' 1" **Wt:** 210

Opening Day Age: 30
Born: 5/25/66 in Orchard Park, NY
ML Seasons: 7

Overall Statistics

	G	AB	R	H	D	T	HR	RBI	SB	BB	SO	Avg	OBP	Slg
1996	149	516	88	135	29	0	16	78	6	84	117	.262	.377	.411
Career	690	2290	404	592	116	13	83	352	20	352	467	.259	.366	.429

Where He Hits the Ball

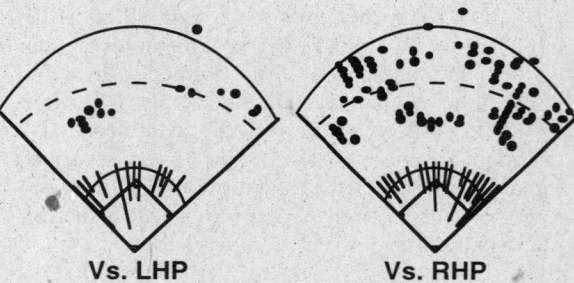

Vs. LHP   Vs. RHP

1996 Situational Stats

	AB	H	HR	RBI	Avg		AB	H	HR	RBI	Avg
Home	252	69	7	37	.274	LHP	135	44	5	24	.326
Road	264	66	9	41	.250	RHP	381	91	11	54	.239
First Half	281	65	10	37	.231	Sc Pos	158	36	3	52	.228
Scnd Half	235	70	6	41	.298	Clutch	80	22	4	13	.275

1996 Rankings (American League)

- → 2nd in errors at third base (17)
- → 5th in hit by pitch (13) and lowest fielding percentage at third base (.955)
- → 6th in lowest batting average with runners in scoring position (.228) and lowest batting average vs. right-handed pitchers (.239)
- → 8th in lowest slugging percentage vs. right-handed pitchers (.378)
- → 10th in lowest batting average on the road (.250)

Mike Jackson

1996 Season

Mike Jackson spent four seasons with the Mariners, beginning in 1988. Then came three seasons in San Francisco and one in Cincinnati, as Jackson established himself as one of baseball's top set-up men. In 1994 and '95 Jackson suffered first elbow, then shoulder tendinitis, and as a result the Mariners were able to sign him relatively cheaply before last season. Healthy all season, Jackson allowed less than a hit per inning and averaged nearly a strikeout per frame. For most of the campaign, he was Lou Piniella's surest bet out of the bullpen.

Pitching

So you like watching finesse pitchers? Turn off the TV set when Jackson enters the game, because he's pure power. Especially against right-handed hitters, Jackson likes to start off with a low-90s heater inside, get ahead in the count, and then make the hitter chase hard sliders away. He'll also throw a nice sinker. Jackson throws a change-up, too, but you'll see that about as often as Junior Griffey lays down a bunt. Jackson's slider makes him a bit more effective against right-handed hitters, but he's certainly not easy pickings for lefty swingers, either.

Defense

For a power pitcher, Jackson employs a relatively smooth delivery which leaves him in good defensive position, though he will unleash the occasional wild throw. He doesn't bother much with men on base, but given his hard deliveries and decent control, runners don't exactly go wild on Jackson.

1997 Outlook

Even though Jackson's ERA last season was his highest since 1992, Lou Piniella would love to have the free agent back in '97. Assuming he can remain healthy, Jackson will be a much-needed rock of stability in someone's bullpen.

Position: RP
Bats: R **Throws:** R
Ht: 6' 2" **Wt:** 225

Opening Day Age: 32
Born: 12/22/64 in Houston, TX
ML Seasons: 11

Overall Statistics

	W	L	Pct.	ERA	G	GS	Sv	IP	H	BB	SO	HR	BR/IP
1996	1	1	.500	3.63	73	0	6	72.0	61	24	70	11	1.18
Career	47	51	.480	3.33	623	7	44	810.0	639	346	721	83	1.22

How Often He Throws Strikes

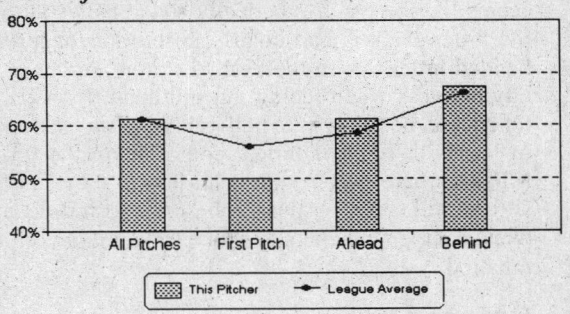

1996 Situational Stats

	W	L	ERA	Sv	IP		AB	H	HR	RBI	Avg
Home	1	0	2.65	4	37.1	LHB	97	26	4	19	.268
Road	0	1	4.67	2	34.2	RHB	174	35	7	32	.201
First Half	1	1	4.95	3	40.0	Sc Pos	80	17	1	34	.213
Scnd Half	0	0	1.97	3	32.0	Clutch	112	23	6	20	.205

1996 Rankings (American League)

- ➔ 5th in games pitched
- ➔ 8th in least baserunners allowed per 9 innings in relief (11.4)
- ➔ 10th in holds (15)
- ➔ Led the Mariners in games pitched, holds (15), lowest batting average allowed in relief with runners on base (.221), relief ERA (3.63), lowest batting average allowed in relief (.225), least baserunners allowed per 9 innings in relief (11.4) and most strikeouts per 9 innings in relief (8.8)

Seattle Mariners

Randy Johnson

1996 Season

Including postseason games, the Seattle Mariners are 38-5 in Randy Johnson's last 43 starts. Problem was, only eight of those 43 starts came in 1996, as Johnson spent most of the season on the disabled list with a herniated disk in his back. The Mariners finished 4 1/2 games behind the Rangers in the A.L. West. Does anyone doubt that a healthy Big Unit would have meant another pennant for Seattle?

Pitching

You might not have seen Johnson pitch last season, but we'll bet you remember him nevertheless. At 6'10", by the time Johnson releases the pitch it seems like he could practically shake hands with the hitter. This is particularly unsettling for left-handed hitters, even the best of whom are generally helpless when facing the southpaw Johnson. Of course, he throws the ball as hard as any starter in baseball. Even if hitters could sit on the 95-MPH fastball, they couldn't hit it. But they can't sit on the heater, because Johnson also throws a wicked slider, which makes for a truly unfair combination.

Defense

Early in his career, Johnson was somewhat erratic with the glove, but in the last few seasons he's improved his defense immensely, and is now at least adequate. And of course, as an extreme power pitcher he's forced to field fewer ground balls than most hurlers. As usual, Johnson's elongated pitching motion left him vulnerable to the stolen base, though he has worked on improving his move to first over the years.

1997 Outlook

Those fellows down in Arlington notwithstanding, the Mariners have to be considered the favorites in the West this season. . . *if* Randy Johnson is healthy all season. Unfortunately, when this book went to press Johnson's status was still in question. His September back surgery was declared a success, but it remains to be seen how the Big Unit responds.

Position: SP/RP
Bats: R **Throws:** L
Ht: 6'10" **Wt:** 230

Opening Day Age: 33
Born: 9/10/63 in Walnut Creek, CA
ML Seasons: 9
Nickname: The Big Unit

Overall Statistics

	W	L	Pct.	ERA	G	GS	Sv	IP	H	BB	SO	HR	BR/IP
1996	5	0	1.000	3.67	14	8	1	61.1	48	25	85	8	1.19
Career	104	64	.619	3.53	232	224	2	1521.0	1173	780	1709	126	1.28

How Often He Throws Strikes

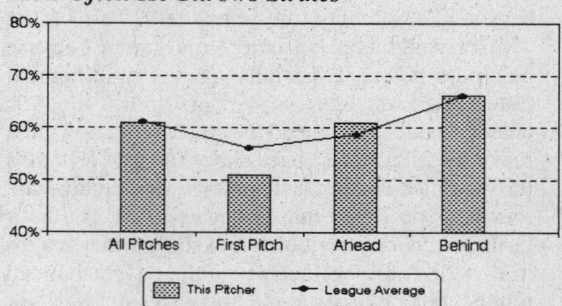

1996 Situational Stats

	W	L	ERA	Sv	IP		AB	H	HR	RBI	Avg
Home	4	0	2.43	1	40.2	LHB	39	8	1	4	.205
Road	1	0	6.10	0	20.2	RHB	189	40	7	20	.212
First Half	5	0	3.83	0	44.2	Sc Pos	57	5	2	13	.088
Scnd Half	0	0	3.24	1	16.2	Clutch	24	7	2	4	.292

1996 Rankings (American League)

➡ 10th in balks (1)
➡ Led the Mariners in balks (1)

Edgar Martinez

1996 Season

On July 20, Edgar Martinez was hitting .334, and with 44 doubles was on pace to shatter the American League record. With the Mariners getting absolutely no production from their various third basemen, Lou Piniella decided to shift Martinez from designated hitter to the hot corner. Bad idea. In his second inning in the field, Martinez and catcher John Marzano collided in pursuit of a pop-up, and Martinez suffered four fractured ribs. Martinez did hit .309 after his return in mid-August, but he suffered a serious power outage, slugging only .441 through the end of the season.

Hitting

His first at-bat of every game, Martinez takes special care to destroy any last vestige of the rear demarcation of the batter's box. Then he takes his stance as far back as the umpire will allow, and waits for a pitch he can drive. Inside, outside, high, low. . . it doesn't matter. Martinez is a fantastic hitter because he can hit anything in the strike zone to the appropriate field. All those doubles? Liners over third base, gappers to left center, drives off the right-field wall, etc. Like all great hitters, there's no set way to pitch Martinez, because he's so adept at making adjustments.

Baserunning & Defense

Martinez is one of the slower non-catchers in the game, though from time to time he will take advantage of a sleeping battery and swipe second base. Defense? Martinez played 33 innings in the field all season, three at third, and we know how that turned out.

1997 Outlook

Martinez played every Mariner game in 1995, and if not for his misadventure afield might well have done the same in 1996. Piniella has vowed to restrict Martinez to the DH slot, so he should be relatively healthy this season. Given a full campaign and fully-healed ribs, Martinez could contend for his third batting title.

Position: DH
Bats: R **Throws:** R
Ht: 5'11" **Wt:** 200

Opening Day Age: 34
Born: 1/2/63 in New York, NY
ML Seasons: 10

Overall Statistics

	G	AB	R	H	D	T	HR	RBI	SB	BB	SO	Avg	OBP	Slg
1996	139	499	121	163	52	2	26	103	3	123	84	.327	.464	.595
Career	936	3276	604	1031	256	11	117	484	30	555	465	.315	.417	.507

Where He Hits the Ball

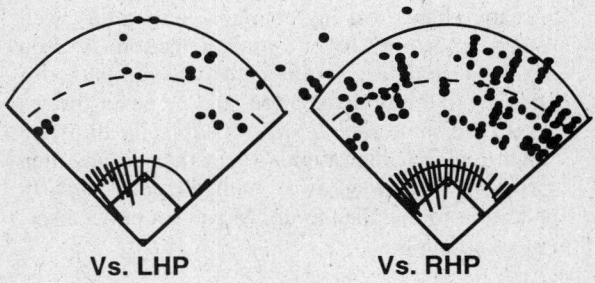

Vs. LHP **Vs. RHP**

1996 Situational Stats

	AB	H	HR	RBI	Avg		AB	H	HR	RBI	Avg
Home	238	82	14	55	.345	LHP	115	39	8	21	.339
Road	261	81	12	48	.310	RHP	384	124	18	82	.323
First Half	315	109	22	78	.346	Sc Pos	151	45	3	68	.298
Scnd Half	184	54	4	25	.293	Clutch	64	20	0	6	.313

1996 Rankings (American League)

→ 1st in highest percentage of pitches taken (67.3%)

→ 2nd in doubles, walks, on-base percentage and on-base percentage vs. right-handed pitchers (.461)

→ 3rd in most pitches seen per plate appearance (4.27)

→ 4th in times on base (294)

→ 6th in intentional walks (12), on-base percentage vs. left-handed pitchers (.473) and batting average with two strikes (.270)

→ 7th in cleanup slugging percentage (.587) and lowest percentage of swings on the first pitch (16.3%)

Jamie Moyer

1996 Season

Left-handed finesse pitchers often mature some-what late, but this is ridiculous. At the ripe old age of 33, Jamie Moyer enjoyed his finest season. Opening the campaign with Boston, Moyer was 7-1 as a starter/reliever. On July 30, he was traded to Seattle for outfielder Darren Bragg. With the Mariner rotation in desperate straits, Moyer went 4-1 with a 3.29 ERA in his first six starts. By season's end, he had set a career high in both wins and winning percentage.

Pitching

There was an old-time pitcher who once described his pitch repertoire like this: "I got my change, I got my change off my change, and I got my change off my change off my change." That pretty well sums up Jamie Moyer's pitch selection. As Lou Piniella said last summer, "He never puts two pitches in the same location, and he never throws them the same speed." Moyer typically throws a right-handed hitter a mid-80s fastball inside, then works away, away, away with offspeed stuff. In addition to the change-up, Moyer employs a ser-viceable curve.

Defense

After Moyer releases a pitch, he lands with his legs spread far apart, which somewhat limits his mobil-ity. However, when he does field the ball he knows what to do with it. For a lefthander, Moyer does a pretty poor job against prospective basestealers. Between his starts with Boston and Seattle, Moyer allowed 16 steals, while only three runners were caught.

1997 Outlook

While it's always possible he's turned the corner, Moyer has a history of pitching well one season out of three or four. Despite that, the Mariners re-signed Moyer for 1997. He probably won't go 13-3 again, but he's capable of winning in double figures.

Position: SP/RP
Bats: L **Throws:** L
Ht: 6' 0" **Wt:** 170

Opening Day Age: 34
Born: 11/18/62 in Sellersville, PA
ML Seasons: 10

Overall Statistics

	W	L	Pct.	ERA	G	GS	Sv	IP	H	BB	SO	HR	BR/IP
1996	13	3	.813	3.98	34	21	0	160.2	177	46	79	23	1.39
Career	72	79	.477	4.44	250	198	0	1277.1	1372	434	756	154	1.41

How Often He Throws Strikes

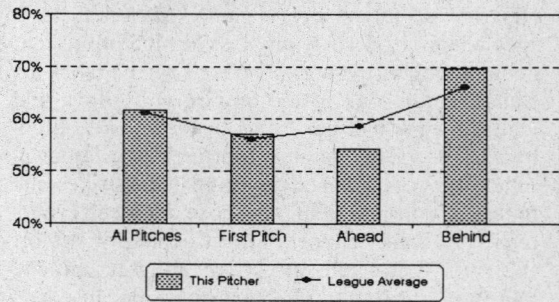

1996 Situational Stats

	W	L	ERA	Sv	IP		AB	H	HR	RBI	Avg
Home	7	2	3.87	0	86.0	LHB	152	47	7	24	.309
Road	6	1	4.10	0	74.2	RHB	490	130	16	54	.265
First Half	4	1	5.45	0	69.1	Sc Pos	143	34	4	53	.238
Scnd Half	9	2	2.86	0	91.1	Clutch	19	5	0	0	.263

1996 Rankings (American League)
- ➡ 1st in winning percentage (.813)
- ➡ 3rd in errors at pitcher (3)
- ➡ 4th in lowest fielding percentage at pitcher (.912)
- ➡ 10th in balks (1)

Terry Mulholland

Signed By
CUBS

Position: SP
Bats: R **Throws:** L
Ht: 6' 3" **Wt:** 212

Opening Day Age: 34
Born: 3/9/63 in
Uniontown, PA
ML Seasons: 10

1996 Season

After horrible 1994 and '95 campaigns, Terry Mulholland returned to Philadelphia, site of his greatest glories. He pitched reasonably well, but just a few hours before the August 1 trade deadline, the Phillies sent Mulholland to Seattle in exchange for minor league infielder Desi Relaford. As a Phillie, Mulholland was one game over .500 (8-7) with a 4.67 ERA; as a Mariner he was one game over .500 (5-4) with a 4.66 ERA.

Pitching

Mulholland is still struggling to make the transition from power pitcher to finesse pitcher. The funny thing is, he was never *really* a power pitcher. But he spotted his merely adequate fastball so well, it worked for him. Now the fastball is somewhat less than adequate, but Mulholland still relies on the pitch to set up his other pitcher: slider, change-up, and occasional splitter. Though he gives up too many hits these days, Mulholland compensates somewhat with his still-amazing control. In fact, he might be better off throwing slightly *fewer* strikes, given the hittable nature of his fastball.

Defense

As most baseball fans—and nearly every baserunner in either league—know so well, Mulholland is nearly impossible to run on. In the last five seasons, he has permitted six stolen bases. That's right. Six. On the other hand, Mulholland's career fielding percentage is .903, which means you're better off hitting a hard grounder straight to the mound than trying to steal a base.

1997 Outlook

Mulholland's 4.67 ERA with the Mariners was better than most of the other Seattle starters, and he did well enough to give Seattle some interest in bringing him back. However, he was lured away by the friendly confines of Wrigley Field, and will start for the Cubs next season.

Overall Statistics

	W	L	Pct.	ERA	G	GS	Sv	IP	H	BB	SO	HR	BR/IP
1996	13	11	.542	4.66	33	33	0	202.2	232	49	86	22	1.39
Career	81	89	.476	4.30	263	230	0	1521.0	1617	379	792	149	1.31

How Often He Throws Strikes

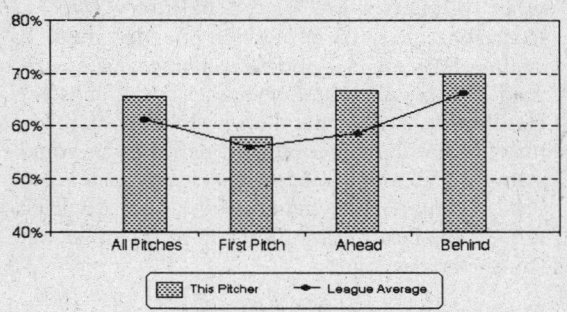

1996 Situational Stats

	W	L	ERA	Sv	IP		AB	H	HR	RBI	Avg
Home	6	7	6.33	0	86.2	LHB	147	36	2	15	.245
Road	7	4	3.41	0	116.0	RHB	651	196	20	84	.301
First Half	6	6	5.40	0	101.2	Sc Pos	168	54	2	68	.321
Scnd Half	7	5	3.92	0	101.0	Clutch	64	19	2	7	.297

1996 Rankings (American League)

➡ Did not rank near the top or bottom in any category

Seattle Mariners

Alex Rodriguez

1996 Season

Where does one start? It's easy to throw out numbers, many of which come in fives: Alex Rodriguez was the fifth-youngest player to hit 30 home runs, the fifth-youngest to clear 100 RBI, the fifth shortstop to hit 30 home runs. . . and the youngest batting champion since Al Kaline hit .340 as a 20 year old in 1955.

Hitting

How do you pitch Alex Rodriguez? If you know, there are approximately 150 American League pitchers who'd like to talk to you. After waving feebly at offspeed pitches in 1995, Rodriguez began to take those same offerings for balls. And when pitchers were forced to throw strikes, Rodriguez made them pay. He pounded the ball against lefties and righties, at home and on the road. Did clutch situations bother the youngster? Hardly. Rodriguez' numbers were consistent no matter what the situation, and he hit three grand slams in 15 bases-loaded at-bats. If he can develop just a bit more plate patience, Rodriguez will be not just the best-hitting shortstop in the game, but simply the best *hitter*.

Baserunning & Defense

Oh, you can add "very good baserunner" to the kid's resume. He runs the bases with intelligence and speed, and he runs out every ground ball (something his "mentor" Ken Griffey doesn't always do). Rodriguez was steady at shortstop last season, but he's still learning the hitters and his overall range was average at best. Like most power-hitting infielders, he does boast a strong throwing arm.

1997 Outlook

Rodriguez was so brilliant last season that we shouldn't expect a repeat performance, even if he *is* still only 21 years old. Of course, even if he loses 10 home runs and 50 points of batting average—neither decline seems likely—he'll still be a superstar. On the other hand, it's possible that we haven't seen Rodriguez' best, in which case he'll be one of the best players. . . ever.

Position: SS
Bats: R **Throws:** R
Ht: 6' 3" **Wt:** 195

Opening Day Age: 21
Born: 7/27/75 in New York, NY
ML Seasons: 3

Overall Statistics

	G	AB	R	H	D	T	HR	RBI	SB	BB	SO	Avg	OBP	Slg
1996	146	601	141	215	54	1	36	123	15	59	104	.358	.414	.631
Career	211	797	160	259	60	3	41	144	22	68	166	.325	.377	.562

Where He Hits the Ball

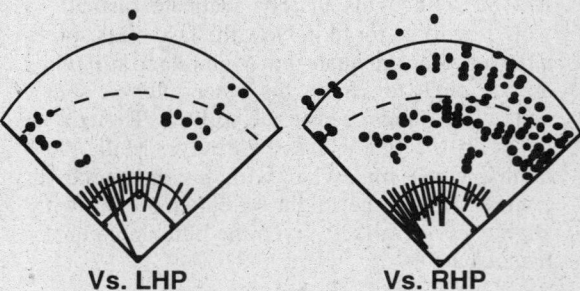

Vs. LHP   Vs. RHP

1996 Situational Stats

	AB	H	HR	RBI	Avg		AB	H	HR	RBI	Avg
Home	294	107	18	56	.364	LHP	143	53	9	35	.371
Road	307	108	18	67	.352	RHP	458	162	27	88	.354
First Half	289	97	17	65	.336	Sc Pos	149	52	11	83	.349
Scnd Half	312	118	19	58	.378	Clutch	92	30	7	21	.326

1996 Rankings (American League)

- → 1st in runs scored, doubles, total bases (379) and batting average
- → 2nd in hits, batting average vs. right-handed pitchers (.354), batting average on an 0-2 count (.333) and batting average with two strikes (.290)
- → 3rd in batting average at home (.364) and batting average on the road (.352)
- → 4th in slugging percentage
- → 5th in slugging percentage vs. right-handed pitchers (.620)
- → 6th in fielding percentage at shortstop (.977)
- → 7th in slugging percentage vs. left-handed pitchers (.664)

Paul Sorrento

1996 Season

After the 1995 season, the Mariners had a choice. They could attempt to re-sign free agent Tino Martinez for upwards of $2 million per season, or they could sign the more reasonably priced Paul Sorrento. The M's opted for Sorrento, and it turned out to be a great move. For less than half the money Martinez wound up getting from the Yankees, Sorrento produced numbers not far off what Tino had in 1995, albeit in a platoon role.

Hitting

Once a hitter who used all fields, Sorrento had become an extreme pull hitter in Cleveland, and in 1995 the result was a .235 batting average—though with plenty of power. Seattle hoped Sorrento could make some adjustments. "We wanted to open up left-center field to him," Mariners hitting coach Lee Elia said. "If he gets out on that front foot, he can still pull the ball, but he can drive the ball away from him, too." Perhaps, but Sorrento quickly learned to take advantage of the Kingdome's short porch in right field, and he hit substantially better at home than on the road. He's rarely shown any ability at all to hit lefthanders.

Baserunning & Defense

Sorrento is built a little like a linebacker, which means he's big and he's slow. But if he doesn't exactly scoot around the bases, at least he's smart enough to know his limits, and doesn't make many mistakes out there. At 220-plus pounds, Sorrento isn't the deftest of first basemen, though he does have reasonably soft hands and ably scoops low throws. Just don't expect him to range far down the line in search of foul pops.

1997 Outlook

The Mariners had an option on Sorrento's contract for 1997, and they exercised it immediately after the season ended. Given the characteristics of the Kingdome and the certainty that Sorrento will continue to face right-handed pitching almost exclusively, he should again post solid numbers.

Position: 1B
Bats: L **Throws:** R
Ht: 6' 2" **Wt:** 220

Opening Day Age: 31
Born: 11/17/65 in Somerville, MA
ML Seasons: 8

Overall Statistics

	G	AB	R	H	D	T	HR	RBI	SB	BB	SO	Avg	OBP	Slg
1996	143	471	67	136	32	1	23	93	0	57	103	.289	.370	.507
Career	711	2226	306	586	116	4	107	386	5	272	498	.263	.343	.463

Where He Hits the Ball

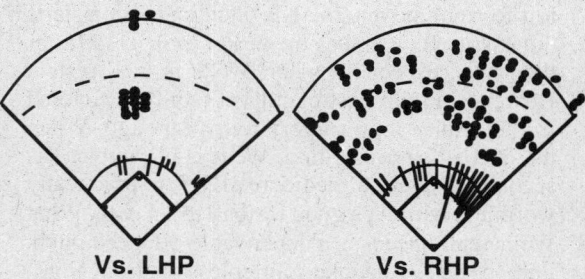

Vs. LHP   **Vs. RHP**

1996 Situational Stats

	AB	H	HR	RBI	Avg		AB	H	HR	RBI	Avg
Home	230	72	13	50	.313	LHP	60	10	2	11	.167
Road	241	64	10	43	.266	RHP	411	126	21	82	.307
First Half	253	81	15	54	.320	Sc Pos	135	42	8	73	.311
Scnd Half	218	55	8	39	.252	Clutch	72	22	4	13	.306

1996 Rankings (American League)
- ➝ 2nd in errors at first base (11) and lowest fielding percentage at first base (.989)
- ➝ Led the Mariners in batting average with the bases loaded (.435)

Bob Wells

Position: RP/SP
Bats: R **Throws:** R
Ht: 6' 0" **Wt:** 180

Opening Day Age: 30
Born: 11/1/66 in
Yakima, WA
ML Seasons: 3

1996 Season

Pitching in relief as the season began, righthander Bob Wells got off to an excellent start, posting a 4-1 record with a 1.79 ERA through the end of May. At that point, Sterling Hitchcock was the only healthy Seattle starter with an ERA below 6.00, so Lou Piniella decided to try Wells in the rotation. He did win his first five starts, but Wells' 6.70 ERA as a starter marked the experiment as a failure. Perhaps suffering from a tired arm, Wells pitched sparingly over the second half of the season.

Pitching

Wells doesn't try anything fancy on the mound. His stock in trade is a plus fastball with decent left-to-right movement. His pitching motion starts out easy, which makes the heater look a tad faster than it is, especially when Wells is well rested. However, his arm strength isn't fully recovered from Tommy John surgery four years ago. When the fastball's not working, Wells is in trouble. His secondary pitch, a mediocre slider, is practically worthless without a good fastball to set it up. What Wells really needs is a dependable offspeed pitch. Perhaps he should take splitter lessons from Norm Charlton.

Defense

Wells is momentarily off balance after completing his motion, which leaves him in poor position to field hard come-backers up the middle. His move to first is decent enough; that, and the presence of Dan Wilson behind the plate, keeps runners from taking many liberties.

1997 Outlook

Wells showed enough last spring to warrant another shot with the Mariners, but he'll likely be restricted to relief duties. Given a healthy arm, Wells could easily serve as a useful middle reliever, but don't expect anything more.

Overall Statistics

	W	L	Pct.	ERA	G	GS	Sv	IP	H	BB	SO	HR	BR/IP
1996	12	7	.632	5.30	36	16	0	130.2	141	46	94	25	1.43
Career	18	10	.643	5.33	73	20	0	216.1	237	89	138	36	1.51

How Often He Throws Strikes

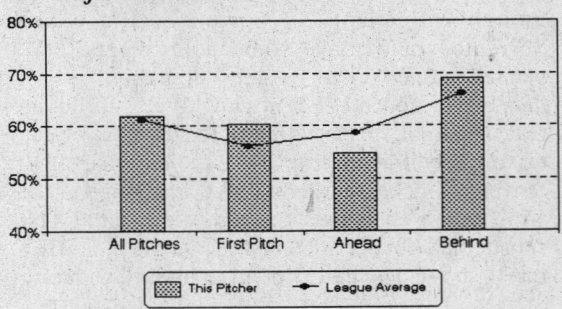

1996 Situational Stats

	W	L	ERA	Sv	IP		AB	H	HR	RBI	Avg
Home	4	3	5.25	0	61.2	LHB	257	77	13	36	.300
Road	8	4	5.35	0	69.0	RHB	258	64	12	39	.248
First Half	9	2	3.79	0	80.2	Sc Pos	102	29	7	47	.284
Scnd Half	3	5	7.74	0	50.0	Clutch	16	7	0	2	.438

1996 Rankings (American League)

- ➡ 6th in shutouts (1)
- ➡ 9th in winning percentage
- ➡ Led the Mariners in complete games (1), shutouts (1), winning percentage and lowest batting average allowed vs. left-handed batters (.300)

Mark Whiten

Position: RF/LF
Bats: B **Throws:** R
Ht: 6' 3" **Wt:** 235

Opening Day Age: 30
Born: 11/25/66 in Pensacola, FL
ML Seasons: 7
Pronunciation: WIT-en

1996 Season

Mark Whiten's 1996 campaign was an odd one. On June 17, he was released by one of the National League's worst teams, the Phillies, and shortly afterward, signed by the NL's best, the Braves. Whiten wasn't bad in Atlanta, but he was surplus talent with the emergence of rookies Jermaine Dye and Andruw Jones. So on August 14, Whiten was traded to Seattle in exchange for minor-league pitcher Roger Blanco. In 40 games as a Mariner, Whiten batted .300 and hit 12 home runs. Along with fellow newcomer Dave Hollins, Whiten helped key the M's September surge which nearly resulted in a playoff berth.

Hitting

No one can deny Whiten's strength. On September 13 in the Metrodome, he smashed a 461-foot grand slam, the longest homer all season by a Seattle hitter. Yet for a man with so much power, Whiten hits fewer home runs than you'd expect. He takes a lot of pitches, which results in lots of walks and strikeouts. It also means Whiten often ends up having to protect the strike zone, which helps explain his relative lack of power. He just might be one of those hitters who needs to be a bit *more* aggressive at the plate.

Baserunning & Defense

It was strange to see Mark Whiten in left field, but of course the Mariners weren't going to shift Jay Buhner. With Whiten in left, Buhner in right and Griffey in center, the M's undoubtedly had one of the strongest-armed outfields in history. But while few players throw *harder* than Whiten, he's not particularly accurate or intelligent with his throws.

1997 Outlook

The Mariners have a vacancy in left field, but many in the organization believe prospect Jose Cruz, Jr. might be ready for the majors as early as this spring. If not, Whiten showed enough in September to merit a long look.

Overall Statistics

	G	AB	R	H	D	T	HR	RBI	SB	BB	SO	Avg	OBP	Slg
1996	136	412	76	108	20	1	22	71	17	70	127	.262	.372	.476
Career	769	2631	396	677	102	20	93	365	72	313	599	.257	.337	.417

Where He Hits the Ball

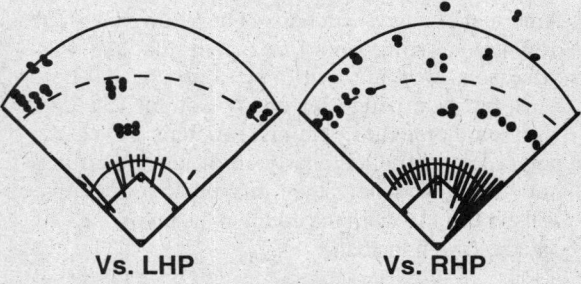

Vs. LHP   **Vs. RHP**

1996 Situational Stats

	AB	H	HR	RBI	Avg		AB	H	HR	RBI	Avg
Home	164	47	9	33	.287	LHP	94	23	6	20	.245
Road	248	61	13	38	.246	RHP	318	85	16	51	.267
First Half	211	51	7	24	.242	Sc Pos	105	33	8	53	.314
Scnd Half	201	57	15	47	.284	Clutch	76	19	5	15	.250

1996 Rankings (American League)

➥ 2nd in batting average on a 3-1 count (.750)
➥ Led the Mariners in batting average on a 3-1 count (.750)

Dan Wilson

1996 Season

Dan Wilson was one of the bigger surprises of the young season. On April 11 at Tiger Stadium, Wilson hit his first home run of the year . . . and his second, and his third. Seventeen days later Wilson hit a pair of homers in Milwaukee, and he finished April with seven dingers, just two short of his career high. He also knocked in 21 runners, which meant Wilson was on pace for approximately 45 homers and 130 RBI. He obviously fell well short of those numbers, but Wilson's season was a pleasant surprise for Lou Piniella.

Hitting

"Even my wife asked, 'What got into you?'" Wilson said in May. "It's a lot of things: I know American League pitchers better now, I've cut down my swing and I've spent the last two offseasons working with a strength coach." Perhaps, but from August 1 on, Wilson hit just .215 with four home runs, reminiscent of his 1994 campaign. Wilson pulled nearly all of his home runs, but he sprayed his other hits in all directions. Wilson likes to work the count in his favor, then sit on a belt-high fastball.

Baserunning & Defense

With most of Seattle's pitchers relying on a variety of offspeed offerings, Wilson's ability to stop pitches in the dirt was particularly valuable. In that regard, Chris Bosio described Wilson as "the best I've ever thrown to." Wilson threw out 32 percent of the runners trying to steal, one of the better figures in the American League.

1997 Outlook

Wilson faces no job competition this season, not with the season he had last year. But remember that (1) he was 27 last season, the best age for a hitter, and (2) he faded badly, perhaps worn down by his nearly-everyday catching duties. In 1997, Wilson will likely return to the .260 range, with just a modicum of power. Nevertheless, that would suit Lou Piniella just fine.

Position: C
Bats: R   **Throws:** R
Ht: 6' 3"   **Wt:** 190

Opening Day Age: 28
Born: 3/25/69 in Barrington, IL
ML Seasons: 5

Overall Statistics

	G	AB	R	H	D	T	HR	RBI	SB	BB	SO	Avg	OBP	Slg
1996	138	491	51	140	24	0	18	83	1	32	88	.285	.330	.444
Career	396	1273	123	338	64	5	30	172	4	87	232	.266	.313	.394

Where He Hits the Ball

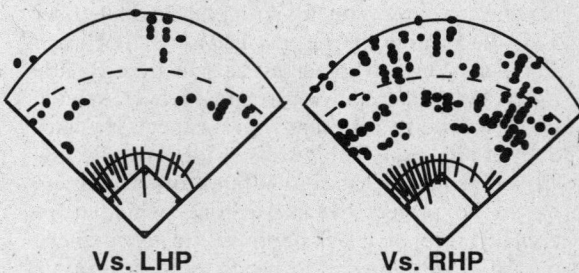

Vs. LHP   Vs. RHP

1996 Situational Stats

	AB	H	HR	RBI	Avg		AB	H	HR	RBI	Avg
Home	259	69	7	37	.266	LHP	128	33	4	25	.258
Road	232	71	11	46	.306	RHP	363	107	14	58	.295
First Half	273	84	12	52	.308	Sc Pos	141	46	5	65	.326
Scnd Half	218	56	6	31	.257	Clutch	75	24	2	22	.320

1996 Rankings (American League)

→ 2nd in fielding percentage at catcher (.996)
→ 10th in lowest on-base percentage vs. left-handed pitchers (.297)
→ Led the Mariners in sacrifice bunts (9) and GDPs (16)

Rich Amaral

Position: LF/2B/CF
Bats: R **Throws:** R
Ht: 6' 0" **Wt:** 175

Opening Day Age: 34
Born: 4/1/62 in Visalia, CA
ML Seasons: 6
Pronunciation: AM-r-all

Overall Statistics

	G	AB	R	H	D	T	HR	RBI	SB	BB	SO	Avg	OBP	Slg
1996	118	312	69	91	11	3	1	29	25	47	55	.292	.392	.356
Career	444	1267	215	351	62	8	9	117	74	131	191	.277	.348	.360

1996 Situational Stats

	AB	H	HR	RBI	Avg		AB	H	HR	RBI	Avg
Home	144	38	1	18	.264	LHP	147	43	1	16	.293
Road	168	53	0	11	.315	RHP	165	48	0	13	.291
First Half	158	45	0	17	.285	Sc Pos	70	18	0	26	.257
Scnd Half	154	46	1	12	.299	Clutch	44	9	0	3	.205

1996 Season

By season's end, Rich Amaral had done what he always does: inject a little speed into a slugging lineup, and plug just about any hole in the field. He played especially well in June and July, when filling in for the injured Ken Griffey in center field.

Hitting, Baserunning & Defense

One of the more consistent hitters around, Amaral raised his game a bit with increased patience, and those 47 walks were 14 more than his previous career best. He may be 35 years old, but you can't tell from watching Amaral run. Over the last two seasons, he's swiped 46 bases—in part-time play—while being caught only eight times. Amaral played all three outfield positions last season, plus all the infield spots except shortstop. Left field, where his speed allows him to reach many balls, is probably Amaral's best position, though he doesn't have an outfielder's arm.

1997 Outlook

Amaral may not be a good defensive player, but his versatility and his ability to reach base should keep him at the top of the lineup when the Mariners face southpaw starters. Look for him to put up close to the same numbers he did last year.

Bobby Ayala

Position: RP
Bats: R **Throws:** R
Ht: 6' 3" **Wt:** 210

Opening Day Age: 27
Born: 7/8/69 in Ventura, CA
ML Seasons: 5
Pronunciation: eye-YA-luh

Overall Statistics

	W	L	Pct.	ERA	G	GS	Sv	IP	H	BB	SO	HR	BR/IP
1996	6	3	.667	5.88	50	0	3	67.1	65	25	61	10	1.34
Career	25	22	.532	4.81	207	14	43	322.0	319	139	302	38	1.42

1996 Situational Stats

	W	L	ERA	Sv	IP		AB	H	HR	RBI	Avg
Home	4	2	6.09	1	34.0	LHB	135	41	7	27	.304
Road	2	1	5.67	2	33.1	RHB	119	24	3	18	.202
First Half	1	1	6.85	0	23.2	Sc Pos	63	21	4	34	.333
Scnd Half	5	2	5.36	3	43.2	Clutch	120	31	4	20	.258

1996 Season

Not many major leaguers have started a season worse than Bobby Ayala did last year. On April 19, Ayala allowed six runs in two innings. On April 22, he gave up four runs in three frames, bloating his ERA to 13.06. Following that game, Ayala punched out a window, resulting in nine stitches and two months on the disabled list. Ayala did pitch fairly well immediately after his return, but finished with another awful stretch in September.

Pitching & Defense

In some ways, Ayala is a mirror image of bullpen mate Norm Charlton. Like Charlton, Ayala employs a high leg kick—Ayala's is perhaps the highest in the majors—as part of an unorthodox motion. And like Charlton, Ayala's repertoire consists almost entirely of a solid fastball and a hard slider. Lou Piniella said Ayala was throwing 93-94 MPH after coming off the DL in June, though his velocity was off some late in the season. Ayala's delivery leaves him in terrible fielding position, and he pays little attention to baserunners.

1997 Outlook

There's nothing wrong with Ayala's arm, but his head is another question. At this point, a change of scenery might do wonders.

Rafael Carmona

Position: RP
Bats: L **Throws:** R
Ht: 6' 2" **Wt:** 185

Opening Day Age: 24
Born: 10/2/72 in Rio Piedras, PR
ML Seasons: 2

Overall Statistics

	W	L	Pct.	ERA	G	GS	Sv	IP	H	BB	SO	HR	BR/IP
1996	8	3	.727	4.28	53	.1	1	90.1	95	55	62	11	1.66
Career	10	7	.588	4.76	68	4	2	138.0	150	89	90	20	1.73

1996 Situational Stats

	W	L	ERA	Sv	IP		AB	H	HR	RBI	Avg
Home	4	2	1.64	1	44.0	LHB	158	53	7	22	.335
Road	4	1	6.80	0	46.1	RHB	190	42	4	26	.221
First Half	5	0	4.20	1	45.0	Sc Pos	115	30	6	42	.261
Scnd Half	3	3	4.37	0	45.1	Clutch	96	21	6	15	.219

1996 Season

With Seattle's young starters suffering growth pains all season long, Rafael Carmona—himself only 23 years old last year—saw plenty of action as the club's busiest long reliever. Amazingly, he finished third among Seattle hurlers with eight victories despite starting only one game (a loss).

Pitching & Defense

The slender Carmona pitches exclusively from the stretch, like most relievers these days. Though he started three games in 1995 and one more last season, his 0-3 record and 12-plus ERA in those starts has pretty well convinced the Mariners that Carmona's place is in the bullpen. His fastball is nothing special, so he'll throw it just about anywhere except over the plate: inside, outside, and letter-high. Carmona's only other reliable pitch is his slider, which makes up in movement what it lacks in speed. He's a solid fielder with a decent move to first.

1997 Outlook

Still only 24, Carmona should receive every chance to develop his skills. If he can just improve his control a bit, he could well become a quality set-up man.

Russ Davis

Position: 3B
Bats: R **Throws:** R
Ht: 6' 0" **Wt:** 195

Opening Day Age: 27
Born: 9/13/69 in Birmingham, AL
ML Seasons: 3

Overall Statistics

	G	AB	R	H	D	T	HR	RBI	SB	BB	SO	Avg	OBP	Slg
1996	51	167	24	39	9	0	5	18	2	17	50	.234	.312	.377
Career	95	279	38	68	14	2	7	31	2	27	80	.244	.317	.384

1996 Situational Stats

	AB	H	HR	RBI	Avg		AB	H	HR	RBI	Avg
Home	97	23	3	11	.237	LHP	49	15	2	7	.306
Road	70	16	2	7	.229	RHP	118	24	3	11	.203
First Half	167	39	5	18	.234	Sc Pos	43	9	1	12	.209
Scnd Half	0	0	0	0	-	Clutch	27	8	1	6	.296

1996 Season

No one was looking for Russ Davis to be the new Mike Schmidt. But after acquiring him from the Yankees before last season, the Mariners hoped for at least an adequate replacement for Mike Blowers. Davis was solid in April, but a dreadful May had Lou Piniella thinking about a change. Such a move became unnecessary, because on June 7 in Kansas City, Davis fractured his left fibula while chasing a foul ball, ending his season.

Hitting, Baserunning & Defense

Mariner coaches felt that Davis was concentrating too much on pulling the ball, which certainly doesn't make sense for a right-handed hitter in the Kingdome. For most of May, Davis simply looked lost at the plate, though one suspects he would have turned things around had his season not ended early. Davis' minor-league record suggests 15-20 homer power, with a fair number of walks. Once he gets on, Davis proceeds around the bases with caution. He often looked shaky at third base.

1997 Outlook

The Mariners are committed to Davis as their regular third baseman, and remain confident he'll straighten out his swing and provide solid, if unspectacular, production this season.

Brian Hunter

Position: 1B/LF
Bats: R **Throws:** L
Ht: 6' 0" **Wt:** 225

Opening Day Age: 29
Born: 3/4/68 in El Toro, CA
ML Seasons: 6

Overall Statistics

	G	AB	R	H	D	T	HR	RBI	SB	BB	SO	Avg	OBP	Slg
1996	75	198	21	53	10	0	7	28	0	15	43	.268	.327	.424
Career	436	1122	134	266	64	5	49	193	3	83	233	.237	.288	.434

1996 Situational Stats

	AB	H	HR	RBI	Avg		AB	H	HR	RBI	Avg
Home	96	27	2	15	.281	LHP	111	30	3	18	.270
Road	102	26	5	13	.255	RHP	87	23	4	10	.264
First Half	93	33	3	17	.355	Sc Pos	53	12	2	22	.226
Scnd Half	105	20	4	11	.190	Clutch	28	10	3	6	.357

1996 Season

Signed to a minor-league contract prior to last season, Brian Hunter got off to a hot start at Triple-A Tacoma and soon found himself in the Kingdome. Playing both left field and first base, Hunter was hitting .355 at the All-Star break. Then he fell off the earth, batting just .190 the remainder of the season.

Hitting, Baserunning & Defense

Hunter is a dead-pull hitter, and six of his seven homers sailed over the fence in straightaway left field. He can murder a fastball when he knows it's coming, but when Hunter gets behind in the count, he's easy pickings for a pitcher with any kind of breaking ball. Hunter is quite slow and almost never runs. Once regarded as a fine outfielder, Hunter has little range in left field and is merely an adequate first baseman.

1997 Outlook

In October, Hunter refused a minor-league assignment, thus becoming a free agent once more. Still, the Mariners need a first-base platoon partner for Paul Sorrento, which means Hunter could be a Mariner again. He'll get a chance this spring with someone, but his days as a big leaguer appear numbered.

Doug Strange

Position: 3B
Bats: B **Throws:** R
Ht: 6' 1" **Wt:** 185

Opening Day Age: 32
Born: 4/13/64 in Greenville, SC
ML Seasons: 7

Overall Statistics

	G	AB	R	H	D	T	HR	RBI	SB	BB	SO	Avg	OBP	Slg
1996	88	183	19	43	7	1	3	23	1	14	31	.235	.290	.333
Career	499	1347	145	318	63	5	19	150	13	109	215	.236	.297	.333

1996 Situational Stats

	AB	H	HR	RBI	Avg		AB	H	HR	RBI	Avg
Home	71	17	2	9	.239	LHP	14	2	0	0	.143
Road	112	26	1	14	.232	RHP	169	41	3	23	.243
First Half	83	19	1	11	.229	Sc Pos	58	12	2	22	.207
Scnd Half	100	24	2	12	.240	Clutch	53	14	1	9	.264

1996 Season

Lou Piniella likes Doug Strange, and for that, Strange must utter a prayer of thanks every night. Strange entered last season as a career .236 hitter, and that's .236 with little power and not much patience. He almost exactly matched his anemic career stats in 1996, yet he somehow never lost his spot on the Mariner roster.

Hitting, Baserunning & Defense

Nominally a switch-hitter, Strange is very rarely allowed to face a left-handed pitcher. Frequently called upon to pinch hit, Strange generally follows the pinch-hitter's prescription: take a rip at the first fastball you see. Given his performance last season, it might be time for a new strategy. Strange is no sprinter on the basepaths. . . shoot, he's barely even a jogger. Strange is a passable third baseman, and also started six games in left field, where he displayed a weak arm and a startling lack of range.

1997 Outlook

Will Doug continue his Strange career? He'll likely draw an invite to spring training somewhere, perhaps even with the Mariners, but it's about time for Strange to find another line of work.

Seattle Mariners

Salomon Torres

Position: SP
Bats: R **Throws:** R
Ht: 5'11" **Wt:** 165

Opening Day Age: 25
Born: 3/11/72 in San Pedro de Macoris, DR
ML Seasons: 4

Overall Statistics

	W	L	Pct.	ERA	G	GS	Sv	IP	H	BB	SO	HR	BR/IP
1996	3	3	.500	4.59	10	7	0	49.0	44	23	36	5	1.37
Career	11	25	.306	5.30	54	43	0	258.0	276	133	148	36	1.59

1996 Situational Stats

	W	L	ERA	Sv	IP		AB	H	HR	RBI	Avg
Home	1	1	6.16	0	19.0	LHB	97	26	3	10	.268
Road	2	2	3.60	0	30.0	RHB	85	18	2	14	.212
First Half	0	1	8.56	0	13.2	Sc Pos	36	11	1	18	.306
Scnd Half	3	2	3.06	0	35.1	Clutch	6	2	0	1	.333

1996 Season

Once one of baseball's top pitching prospects, Salomon Torres opened last season with Triple-A Tacoma. Torres was recalled to Seattle in late May, but 13.2 innings and 13 runs later he was heading back down I-5 for Tacoma. Despite just-decent numbers there, Torres was again recalled in September, and he gave the Mariners a big boost, going 3-2 with a 3.06 ERA for the month.

Pitching & Defense

With Randy Johnson on the disabled list in September, no Mariner pitcher had a better fastball than Torres. His heater routinely reaches the low 90s, and it's got nice movement as well. Torres throws a slider too, but he's still searching for a dependable offspeed pitch. He struggles with his control at times, but even then he's rarely far from the plate. Torres is quick off the mound, but hasn't developed much of a move to first.

1997 Outlook

Torres showed enough in September to earn a solid shot at the rotation this spring. His arm is still a wonderful thing, and despite his ups and downs, he's only 25. Even if he doesn't make it as a starter, Torres might well become an effective reliever one day.

Bob Wolcott

Position: SP
Bats: R **Throws:** R
Ht: 6' 0" **Wt:** 190

Opening Day Age: 23
Born: 9/8/73 in Huntington Beach, CA
ML Seasons: 2

Overall Statistics

	W	L	Pct.	ERA	G	GS	Sv	IP	H	BB	SO	HR	BR/IP
1996	7	10	.412	5.73	30	28	0	149.1	179	54	78	26	1.56
Career	10	12	.455	5.47	37	34	0	186.0	222	68	97	32	1.56

1996 Situational Stats

	W	L	ERA	Sv	IP		AB	H	HR	RBI	Avg
Home	2	7	5.77	0	78.0	LHB	308	108	15	48	.351
Road	5	3	5.68	0	71.1	RHB	294	71	11	41	.241
First Half	5	7	6.11	0	91.1	Sc Pos	133	36	7	57	.271
Scnd Half	2	3	5.12	0	58.0	Clutch	32	9	0	1	.281

1996 Season

Bob Wolcott entered last season on an up note. In his only 1995 postseason start, Wolcott escaped a bases-loaded jam in the first inning and wound up beating the powerful Cleveland Indians. That, as much as anything, ensured him a spot in the Mariner rotation last spring. He remained there through mid-August, but rarely strung together consecutive decent outings. On August 17 Wolcott and his 5.65 ERA were sent to AAA. He returned in September but struggled, especially in relief.

Pitching & Defense

Wolcott throws a solid fastball and curve, but the combination isn't quite enough in the major leagues. He needed a third pitch especially against left-handed hitters, and Wolcott struggled to find command of his change-up all season long. As a result, the Mariners have him working on a forkball, and the success of that experiment might well determine his future. In 186 major-league innings, he has yet to permit a stolen base or make an error.

1997 Outlook

If Seattle is to win another pennant, it needs a healthy Randy Johnson and solid work from two young starting pitchers. Wolcott is still a top candidate.

Other Seattle Mariners

Chris Bosio (Pos: RHP, Age: 33)

	W	L	Pct.	ERA	G	GS	Sv	IP	H	BB	SO	HR	BR/IP
1996	4	4	.500	5.93	18	9	0	60.2	72	24	39	8	1.58
Career	94	93	.503	3.96	309	246	9	1710.0	1742	481	1059	162	1.30

An 11-year major league veteran who twirled a no-hitter for the Mariners in 1993, Bosio spent all of June and most of July on the shelf with a knee injury. He'll get another chance, but probably not in Seattle. 1997 Outlook: C

Tim Davis (Pos: LHP, Age: 26)

	W	L	Pct.	ERA	G	GS	Sv	IP	H	BB	SO	HR	BR/IP
1996	2	2	.500	4.01	40	0	0	42.2	43	17	34	4	1.41
Career	6	5	.545	4.50	87	6	2	116.0	130	60	81	10	1.64

Tim Davis' 1996 campaign was shortened considerably when he went on the disabled list with a fractured leg in late May. He returned in mid-July and pitched very effectively in 20 relief appearances. 1997 Outlook: B

Scott Davison (Pos: RHP, Age: 26)

	W	L	Pct.	ERA	G	GS	Sv	IP	H	BB	SO	HR	BR/IP
1996	0	0	-	9.00	5	0	0	9.0	11	3	9	6	1.56
Career	0	0	-	8.10	8	0	0	13.1	18	4	12	7	1.65

Originally drafted as a shortstop, Davison continues his quest to become a reliever. He made five appearances for the M's in late May, but was sent back to Tacoma after posting a 9.00 ERA in nine innings. 1997 Outlook: C

Alex Diaz (Pos: LF, Age: 28, Bats: B)

	G	AB	R	H	D	T	HR	RBI	SB	BB	SO	Avg	OBP	Slg
1996	38	79	11	19	2	0	1	5	6	2	8	.241	.274	.304
Career	274	614	86	156	23	7	5	51	37	25	66	.254	.285	.339

Bone spurs in his left ankle kept Diaz out of the lineup for most of June and July, while bone chips in his elbow ruined his August. He signed a minor league contract with the Mets in November. 1997 Outlook: B

Lee Guetterman (Pos: LHP, Age: 38)

	W	L	Pct.	ERA	G	GS	Sv	IP	H	BB	SO	HR	BR/IP
1996	0	2	.000	4.09	17	0	0	11.0	11	10	6	0	1.91
Career	38	36	.514	4.33	425	23	25	658.1	717	222	287	52	1.43

Lee Guetterman finished the season the same way he began it: in the minors. In between, he pitched reasonably well in 17 games for Seattle. His 38-year-old arm must be running out of gas, however. 1997 Outlook: C

Tim Harikkala (Pos: RHP, Age: 25)

	W	L	Pct.	ERA	G	GS	Sv	IP	H	BB	SO	HR	BR/IP
1996	0	1	.000	12.46	1	1	0	4.1	4	2	1	1	1.38
Career	0	1	.000	14.09	2	1	0	7.2	11	3	2	2	1.83

Harikkala's moment in the sun was short-lived. He was called up on June 19 to make his first major league start, got shelled, and was sent back the next day. His 13-24 record at Triple-A does not bode well. 1997 Outlook: D

Edwin Hurtado (Pos: RHP, Age: 27)

	W	L	Pct.	ERA	G	GS	Sv	IP	H	BB	SO	HR	BR/IP
1996	2	5	.286	7.74	16	4	2	47.2	61	30	36	10	1.91
Career	7	7	.500	6.32	30	14	2	125.1	142	70	69	21	1.69

Hurtado began the season on the Mariners roster as a reliever and spot starter, but a 7.74 ERA had him back in Tacoma by late June. Right elbow surgery then landed him on the 60-day DL in September. 1997 Outlook: C

Ricky Jordan (Pos: 1B, Age: 31, Bats: R)

	G	AB	R	H	D	T	HR	RBI	SB	BB	SO	Avg	OBP	Slg
1996	15	28	4	7	0	0	1	4	0	1	6	.250	.290	.357
Career	677	2104	261	592	116	10	55	304	10	77	303	.281	.308	.424

Jordan began the season in a platoon role with Paul Sorrento at first base, but shoulder problems all but ended his season after just 12 games. After eight seasons in the bigs, health is a big concern. 1997 Outlook: C

Joe Klink (Pos: LHP, Age: 35)

	W	L	Pct.	ERA	G	GS	Sv	IP	H	BB	SO	HR	BR/IP
1996	0	0	-	3.86	3	0	0	2.1	3	1	2	1	1.71
Career	10	6	.625	4.26	176	0	3	164.2	171	75	94	10	1.49

After logging just over two innings with his fourth different major league club in early May, Klink was sent back to the minors and then released by the M's. The 35-year-old reliever may be out of options. 1997 Outlook: D

John Marzano (Pos: C, Age: 34, Bats: R)

	G	AB	R	H	D	T	HR	RBI	SB	BB	SO	Avg	OBP	Slg
1996	41	106	8	26	6	0	0	6	0	7	15	.245	.316	.302
Career	212	574	59	135	35	1	6	50	0	23	99	.235	.273	.331

Age may be creeping up on Marzano, but he still has fire. He was suspended for two games in September for fighting in a game against the Yankees. The backup catcher had his troubles at the plate, however. 1997 Outlook: B

Greg McCarthy (Pos: LHP, Age: 28)

	W	L	Pct.	ERA	G	GS	Sv	IP	H	BB	SO	HR	BR/IP
1996	0	0	-	1.86	10	0	0	9.2	8	4	7	0	1.24
Career	0	0	-	1.86	10	0	0	9.2	8	4	7	0	1.24

Called up from Tacoma in late August, McCarthy saw his first career action in the majors. He pitched very effectively in 10 appearances for Seattle, and everyone knows the value of a good lefty reliever. 1997 Outlook: B

Rusty Meacham (Pos: RHP, Age: 29)

	W	L	Pct.	ERA	G	GS	Sv	IP	H	BB	SO	HR	BR/IP
1996	1	1	.500	5.74	15	5	1	42.1	57	13	25	9	1.65
Career	22	14	.611	4.19	189	9	9	303.0	334	81	182	33	1.37

Meacham was traded from KC to Seattle in late June. He saw duty in the bullpen and also started five games, but the righty continued to struggle against right-handed hitters, which is not a good omen. 1997 Outlook: C

Paul Menhart (Pos: RHP, Age: 28)

	W	L	Pct.	ERA	G	GS	Sv	IP	H	BB	SO	HR	BR/IP
1996	2	2	.500	7.29	11	6	0	42.0	55	25	18	9	1.90
Career	3	6	.333	5.74	32	15	0	120.2	127	72	68	18	1.65

After spending much of the 1994 season on the DL, Menhart ended up doing the same in 1996 with a shoulder injury. His growing injury list and his growing ERA (7.29 with Seattle) are cause for concern. 1997 Outlook: C

Bob Milacki (Pos: RHP, Age: 32)

	W	L	Pct.	ERA	G	GS	Sv	IP	H	BB	SO	HR	BR/IP
1996	1	4	.200	6.86	7	4	0	21.0	30	15	13	3	2.14
Career	39	47	.453	4.38	143	125	1	795.2	817	301	387	85	1.41

For the second year in a row, eight-year vet Bob Milacki posted more walks than strikeouts and an ERA over 6.00 in his time in the majors. In November, he decided to ply his wares in Japan. 1997 Outlook: D

Blas Minor (Pos: RHP, Age: 31)

	W	L	Pct.	ERA	G	GS	Sv	IP	H	BB	SO	HR	BR/IP
1996	0	1	.000	4.24	28	0	0	51.0	50	17	34	10	1.31
Career	12	10	.545	4.39	146	0	4	213.0	218	65	178	28	1.33

Minor made 17 appearances for the Mets in 1996 before coming to Seattle in a trade in early June. He possesses average stuff that became even more average once he joined the Mariners. 1997 Outlook: C

Makoto Suzuki (Pos: RHP, Age: 21)

	W	L	Pct.	ERA	G	GS	Sv	IP	H	BB	SO	HR	BR/IP
1996	0	0	-	20.25	1	0	0	1.1	2	2	1	0	3.00
Career	0	0	-	20.25	1	0	0	1.1	2	2	1	0	3.00

Suzuki has thrown his fastball in the mid to upper 90s in the minors, but shoulder problems have hampered his development. He was hit hard at Tacoma and in his one appearance with the M's and remains a risk. 1997 Outlook: C

Seattle Mariners Minor League Prospects

Organization Overview:

During the past two years, the Seattle Mariners have looted their farm system in a series of deals intended to help the major league team over the short run. Some players like Marc Newfield, Darren Bragg and Desi Relaford, were traded for pitching. However, in other deals, the M's allowed powerful young arms like Shawn Estes and Ron Villone to get away. And finally, some players, like Greg Pirkl and Arquimedez Pozo, were basically given away. In the meantime, the farm system hasn't produced any pitchers of note for the major league club, although they can boast of producing one of the greatest young players of all time, Alex Rodriguez. Besides Alex, the Mariners haven't shown much faith in their youngsters, and when spots opened up at first base and left field, they went outside the organization to fill them—despite the fact that they had deserving minor leaguers on hand to audition. They won't have to grapple with that situation again for a while; all they've got left is Jose Cruz, Jr., and a handful of pitchers.

James Bonnici

Position: 1B **Opening Day Age:** 25
Bats: R **Throws:** R **Born:** 1/21/72 in
Ht: 6' 4" **Wt:** 230 Omaha, NE

Recent Statistics

	G	AB	R	H	D	T	HR	RBI	SB	BB	SO	AVG
93 A Riverside	104	375	69	115	21	1	9	58	0	58	72	.307
94 A Riverside	113	397	71	111	23	3	10	71	1	58	81	.280
95 AA Port City	138	508	75	144	36	3	20	91	2	76	97	.283
96 AAA Tacoma	139	497	76	145	25	0	26	74	1	59	100	.292
96 MLE	139	490	71	138	26	0	24	69	0	56	109	.282

A converted catcher and devoted weightlifter, Jim Bonnici makes himself into a better hitter every year. Last year, he was named the best power hitter in the Pacific Coast League. He's been ready for two years now, and as soon as he gets a chance, he'll prove that he's capable of hitting for both power and average. Unfortunately, the Mariners have blocked his path, and he's getting on in years. Someone who needs a first baseman would be wise to trade for this guy.

Dean Crow

Position: P **Opening Day Age:** 24
Bats: L **Throws:** R **Born:** 8/21/72 in
Ht: 6' 5" **Wt:** 212 Garland, TX

Recent Statistics

	W	L	ERA	G	GS	Sv	IP	H	R	BB	SO	HR
93 A Bellingham	5	3	1.89	25	0	4	47.2	31	14	21	38	1
94 A Appleton	2	4	7.04	16	0	2	15.1	25	15	7	11	4
95 A Riverside	3	4	2.63	51	0	22	61.2	54	21	13	46	1
96 AA Port City	2	3	3.04	60	0	26	68.0	64	35	20	43	4

Dean Crow is a short reliever in the classic mold: he relies on a moving 95-MPH fastball, and mixes in a change-up and a forkball no more than he needs to. Using sheer heat, he saved 26 games for a Double-A team that had the worst record in the entire league. He's only 24 this year, and the Mariners sure could use him in their bullpen. Suffice to say, he may not spend the entire season in Triple-A.

Jose Cruz, Jr.

Position: OF **Opening Day Age:** 22
Bats: B **Throws:** R **Born:** 4/19/74 in
Ht: 6' 0" **Wt:** 190 Arroyo, PR

Recent Statistics

	G	AB	R	H	D	T	HR	RBI	SB	BB	SO	AVG
95 A Everett	3	11	6	5	0	0	0	2	1	3	3	.455
95 A Riverside	35	144	34	37	7	1	7	29	3	24	50	.257
96 A Lancaster	53	203	38	66	17	1	6	43	7	39	33	.325
96 AA Port City	47	181	39	51	10	2	3	31	5	27	38	.282
96 AAA Tacoma	22	76	15	18	1	2	6	15	1	18	12	.237
96 MLE	69	255	53	67	12	2	9	45	4	40	56	.263

Soon, the Mariners will have two "Juniors" in the outfield. The third overall pick in the '95 draft, Jose Cruz, Jr. is a five-tool talent who's known mainly for his power potential. The switch-hitter rocketed through three levels of the Mariners' system last year, and showed great power, patience and bat control at all three stops. Many expect the 23 year old to arrive sometime next year and remain in left field for a decade or more.

Raul Ibanez

Position: OF **Opening Day Age:** 24
Bats: L **Throws:** R **Born:** 6/2/72 in
Ht: 6' 2" **Wt:** 200 Manhattan, NY

Recent Statistics

	G	AB	R	H	D	T	HR	RBI	SB	BB	SO	AVG
96 AA Port City	19	76	12	28	8	1	1	13	3	8	7	.368
96 AAA Tacoma	111	405	59	115	20	3	11	47	7	44	56	.284
96 AL Seattle	4	5	0	0	0	0	0	0	0	0	1	.000
96 MLE	130	477	67	139	28	2	12	56	7	47	68	.291

Raul Ibanez was drafted as an outfielder, converted to catcher, and finally moved back to the outfield. He's also been tried at first base. He may never find a position in the field, but he's right at home in the batter's box. Ibanez hits all pitches to all fields, and shows tremendous bat control for someone with decent power potential. He's a left-handed hitter, and he can even catch in a pinch, so there's a million ways to use him.

Alex Pacheco

Position: P
Bats: R **Throws:** R
Ht: 6' 3" **Wt:** 170
Opening Day Age: 23
Born: 7/19/73 in Caracas, Venez

Recent Statistics

	W	L	ERA	G	GS	Sv	IP	H	R	BB	SO	HR
96 AA Harrisburg	5	2	2.73	18	0	0	26.1	26	10	12	27	2
96 AAA Ottawa	2	2	6.48	33	0	6	41.2	47	32	18	34	6
96 NL Montreal	0	0	11.12	5	0	0	5.2	8	7	1	7	2

Alex Pacheco is a young, raw, hard-throwing righthander who was acquired from the Expos' organization in the Jeff Fassero deal. He was signed out of Venezuela at age 16, and has worked for seven years to get his fastball and his temper under control. Even with all those years of experience, he's still only 23 years old. Sometimes Lou Piniella takes a liking to a young reliever who throws hard, and Pacheco may find himself in the Mariners' bullpen sometime next year.

Andy Sheets

Position: SS
Bats: R **Throws:** R
Ht: 6' 2" **Wt:** 180
Opening Day Age: 25
Born: 11/19/71 in Baton Rouge, LA

Recent Statistics

	G	AB	R	H	D	T	HR	RBI	SB	BB	SO	AVG
96 AAA Tacoma	62	232	44	83	16	5	5	33	6	25	56	.358
96 AL Seattle	47	110	18	21	8	0	0	9	2	10	41	.191
96 MLE	62	227	41	78	16	3	4	30	5	23	61	.344

As a shortstop in the Seattle system, Andy Sheets has the career expectancy of an illiterate librarian. For purposes of survival, he's learned to play third base—quite well, in fact. The only problem there is that he lacks the power for the position. He could hit enough to make it at shortstop for some other team, but it looks like the best he'll be able to do with Seattle is to become a utility infielder.

Sal Urso

Position: P
Bats: R **Throws:** L
Ht: 5' 11" **Wt:** 175
Opening Day Age: 25
Born: 1/19/72 in Tampa, FL

Recent Statistics

	W	L	ERA	G	GS	Sv	IP	H	R	BB	SO	HR
93 A Appleton	4	4	3.35	36	1	2	53.2	57	24	24	50	2
94 A Riverside	1	2	5.97	30	1	0	34.2	44	27	14	26	4
95 AA Port City	2	0	2.17	51	0	1	45.2	41	13	21	44	0
96 AAA Tacoma	6	2	2.35	46	0	3	72.2	69	22	32	45	5

Sal Urso never gets mentioned as a prospect, but over the past two seasons, he's pitched as well as any left-hander in the system. Perhaps the reason is that he has an uncommon weakness for *left-handed* hitters; in any event, he's so effective against righties that he's likely to find a role somehow. He features a fastball in the low-90s, a slider, and a good change-up that he saves for righthanders. Maybe he needs to learn to throw it to lefties? Oh well; as soon as he figures them out he'll be ready.

Jason Varitek

Position: C
Bats: B **Throws:** R
Ht: 6' 2" **Wt:** 210
Opening Day Age: 24
Born: 4/11/72 in Rochester MN

Recent Statistics

	G	AB	R	H	D	T	HR	RBI	SB	BB	SO	AVG
95 AA Port City	104	352	42	79	14	2	10	44	0	61	126	.224
96 AA Port City	134	503	63	132	34	1	12	67	7	66	93	.262
96 MLE	134	503	63	132	38	0	13	67	5	58	106	.262

The 14th pick in the country in the '94 draft, Jason Varitek sat out the '94 season in a dispute over his signing bonus. The effects of the long layoff were apparent when he debuted at Double-A in '95, but he repeated at that level last year and recovered somewhat. He's an average receiver with a decent arm, but he projects to hit for decent power from both sides of the plate. His path has been cleared now that Chris Widger has been dealt away, and he'll be a viable alternative if Dan Wilson goes down.

Others to Watch

Most of the Mariners' second-line talent lies at the lower end of their system. Right-handed starter **Ken Cloude** went 15-4 in A-ball, and fanned almost a man per inning. He'll be only 21 this year. . . **Greg Wooten** is another righthander who had a good year at the Class A level. He went 15-5 with two teams, but at age 23, it's time to move up and face some real competition. . . Outfielder **Shane Monahan** drove in almost 100 runs in the California League. He's a left-handed hitter who should see Double-A this year at age 22. . . A speed-and-defense guy all the way, left-handed center fielder **Jack Sturdivant** may learn to poke enough singles to survive as a fourth outfielder. . .Righthander **Brett Iddon** moved to the bullpen and enjoyed a solid season in the Midwest League. The 20 year old fanned well over one batter per inning and posted a 2.78 ERA.

Johnny Oates

1996 Season

In his second year with the Texas Rangers, Johnny Oates did something he could not do in four seasons with the Baltimore Orioles—win a division title. It was his most enjoyable year in baseball, he said, largely because he felt better about himself as a husband and father than he did in 1995, when he wrestled with concerns about his family. Oates led Texas to 90 victories, his fifth consecutive winning record as a manager.

Offense

In two seasons with Texas, Oates has shown that he adjusts to his personnel. He used 92 different batting orders in 144 games in 1995, shuttling players around to patch holes in a team riddled by injuries. But he locked into one lineup early last year and rode it all the way to the American League West title. Five regulars played at least 140 games, which may have hurt the Rangers down the stretch. They went 8-15 after September 15, including a four-game Division Series loss to New York. Oates is not averse to playing small ball when the game dictates it, but he was not very creative in maximizing the 1996 team's run production. While Texas was fifth in the league in batting, eight other teams scored more runs.

Pitching & Defense

Oates generally uses 120 pitches as his de facto pitch limit. But he leaned on his starting pitchers more than usual last year. He countered the absence of a dominating closer by effectively using several relievers, including three lefties. All he wants out of his fielders is to make the routine plays. He will take a lack of range—even at shortstop—in exchange for reliability.

1997 Outlook

Oates and general manager Doug Melvin have succeeded in building a team that follows the Baltimore model of pitching and defense. But Oates' belief in the importance of a team-first concept could be tested as Texas comes off a division championship season.

Born: 1/21/46 in Sylva, NC

Playing Experience: 1970-1981, Bal, Atl, Phi, LA, NYA

Managerial Experience: 6 seasons

Manager Statistics

Year	Team, Lg	W	L	Pct	GB	Finish
1996	Texas, AL	90	72	.552	—	1st West
6 Seasons		455	412	.525	—	—

1996 Starting Pitchers by Days Rest

	≤3	4	5	6+
Rangers Starts	1	109	32	14
Rangers ERA	1.13	4.53	5.43	6.99
AL Avg Starts	4	96	30	21
AL ERA	5.57	4.90	5.33	5.81

1996 Situational Stats

	Johnny Oates	AL Average
Hit & Run Success %	36.0	39.1
Stolen Base Success %	76.2	69.6
Platoon Pct.	61.7	61.9
Defensive Subs	21	29
High-Pitch Outings	31	23
Quick/Slow Hooks	14/15	17/20
Sacrifice Attempts	41	58

1996 Rankings (American League)

→ 1st in least caught steals of third base (3), least caught steals of home plate (0) and first batter platoon percentage (67.3%)

→ 2nd in stolen base percentage (76.2%), least caught steals of second base (23), sacrifice bunt percentage (90.2%), starts with over 140 pitches (2) and one-batter pitcher appearances (44)

→ 3rd in starts with over 120 pitches (31)

John Burkett

Position: SP
Bats: R **Throws:** R
Ht: 6' 3" **Wt:** 215

Opening Day Age: 32
Born: 11/28/64 in New Brighton, PA
ML Seasons: 8
Pronunciation: BURR-kitt

1996 Season

The August 8 acquisition of John Burkett was a critical move by general manager Doug Melvin. Burkett was Texas' most reliable starter down the stretch, going 5-2 in his American League debut. He's a workhorse who averaged nearly seven innings per start in 1996, and almost always kept his team in the game.

Pitching

Few righthanders are as tough on left-handed hitters as Burkett. The key is a running fastball that starts on the inside half of the plate and then moves in toward the hitters' hands. It has the exact same effect as lefthander Fernando Valenzuela's screwball, except that it will move back in over the plate at the last moment when he's getting optimum movement. Burkett mixes his pitches well, throwing a slider that is nasty at times, a curveball that he uses almost exclusively against right-handed hitters, and the occasional split-fingered fastball. Burkett works down in the strike zone, coercing lots of ground balls when he is on. His durability is noteworthy: he has never been on the disabled list in his career, and he has taken every turn as a starter for the last seven years.

Defense

He's a bowler, not an athlete. So, while Burkett has worked to become a skilled pitcher, don't expect him to be graceful on the mound. He is a below-average fielder, in part because he often falls off to the left side of the mound. He has an average pickoff move that is improving.

1997 Outlook

Burkett triggered a contract option for 1997 with his 1996 workload. He joins Ken Hill and Darren Oliver to form the nucleus of what should be a solid starting rotation. With any kind of run support, he should reach the 15-win plateau for the first time since 1993, and could make a run at 20.

Overall Statistics

	W	L	Pct.	ERA	G	GS	Sv	IP	H	BB	SO	HR	BR/IP
1996	11	12	.478	4.24	34	34	0	222.2	229	58	155	19	1.29
Career	92	68	.575	3.96	227	221	1	1408.1	1462	360	872	125	1.29

How Often He Throws Strikes

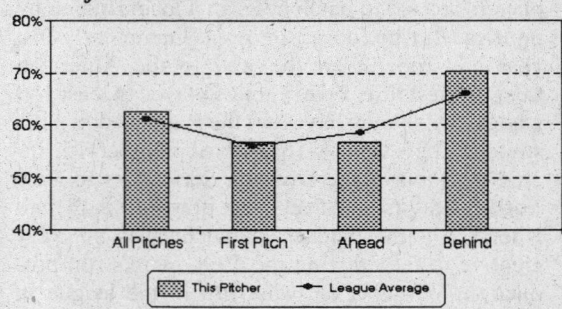

This Pitcher — League Average

1996 Situational Stats

	W	L	ERA	Sv	IP		AB	H	HR	RBI	Avg
Home	5	6	4.81	0	97.1	LHB	406	103	7	50	.254
Road	6	6	3.81	0	125.1	RHB	447	126	12	57	.282
First Half	5	8	3.73	0	120.2	Sc Pos	182	62	5	85	.341
Scnd Half	6	4	4.85	0	102.0	Clutch	83	26	2	14	.313

1996 Rankings (American League)

➜ 6th in shutouts (1)

Will Clark

1996 Season

When Rangers president Tom Schieffer committed $30 million to sign Will Clark three years ago, he was banking as much on Clark's intangibles as his production. His mandate was to help Texas win its first division title, and by that standard Clark's 1996 season was a success. Clark has set the tone in a clubhouse that has gone from fragmented to cohesive. Otherwise, it has been a long time since he has been able to carry a team offensively. In 1996 he lost 46 games to injuries while his power numbers and run production continued to decline.

Hitting

One at-bat sums up the difference between the Clark-entering-middle-age model and the younger version. In the ninth inning of Game 4 of the Division Series, Clark came to the plate with two on and one out. He ripped a pitch from John Wetteland to left-center. Clark thought the ball would at least reach the wall but it fell harmlessly into Tim Raines' glove. He no longer has the bat speed to pull good pitches, and lacks the power to do much damage to the opposite field. Last season Clark had more strikeouts than walks for the first time since 1993.

Baserunning & Defense

Clark remains a technically solid first baseman, committing just four errors in 1996. He is always into the game, especially with runners on first base and Pudge Rodriguez in the lineup. He has a weak but accurate arm. Although his speed is just average, he does a good job scoring from second base on singles.

1997 Outlook

A slower bat may cause Clark to hit lower in the Texas lineup. While his contract runs through 1998, he also may see his playing time diminish. He seldom stays healthy over a full season. Look for Johnny Oates to give him more time off against tough lefties this season. He could benefit from the rest.

Position: 1B
Bats: L **Throws:** L
Ht: 6' 1" **Wt:** 200

Opening Day Age: 33
Born: 3/13/64 in New Orleans, LA
ML Seasons: 11

Overall Statistics

	G	AB	R	H	D	T	HR	RBI	SB	BB	SO	Avg	OBP	Slg
1996	117	436	69	124	25	1	13	72	2	64	67	.284	.377	.436
Career	1510	5548	914	1667	325	43	218	953	59	709	920	.300	.379	.492

Where He Hits the Ball

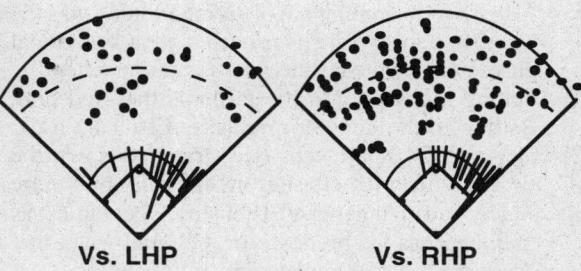

Vs. LHP   **Vs. RHP**

1996 Situational Stats

	AB	H	HR	RBI	Avg			AB	H	HR	RBI	Avg
Home	220	65	9	48	.295		LHP	134	33	4	18	.246
Road	216	59	4	24	.273		RHP	302	91	9	54	.301
First Half	241	72	6	43	.299		Sc Pos	129	35	4	57	.271
Scnd Half	195	52	7	29	.267		Clutch	59	14	4	14	.237

1996 Rankings (American League)

→ 3rd in fielding percentage at first base (.996)
→ 9th in highest percentage of swings on the first pitch (35.5%)
→ Led the Rangers in hit by pitch (5)

Kevin Elster

1996 Season

Healthy, mature, and facing one final chance, Kevin Elster was the biggest surprise in the American League last year. Rangers general manager Doug Melvin invited him to spring training as a favor to old friend Gene Michael, and was glad he did. Elster was battling for a reserve infielder's job in spring training, but got a chance to start when Benji Gil was forced to undergo surgery to repair a herniated disk. "They'll never get me out of the lineup," Elster told his brother/agent Pat, and he was right. Elster started 155 games, making major contributions to the Rangers' title season with his bat and his defense.

Hitting

Elster's forte coming out of spring training was the sacrifice bunt. While he proved a great situational player, he stunned American League pitchers by putting a charge into the fastballs they fed him. Batting in the number-nine hole, Elster hit a career-high 24 home runs. He struggled down the stretch when pitchers starting throwing him more sliders and change-ups. Elster struck out almost as frequently as his predecessor, Gil, and was especially prone to fanning against righthanders.

Baserunning & Defense

Elster has lost range since his days as a New York Mets phenom, but he compensates with intelligent positioning. Nevertheless, there were plenty of ground balls he did not get to, especially late in the season. He proved extremely reliable on routine plays, committing just 14 errors. Elster is a smart baserunner but has sub-par speed for a middle infielder.

1997 Outlook

Elster was a bargain-basement find for Texas in 1996 and deserves a hefty raise for 1997. Yet there's no way of knowing his free-agent value in these unsure times without testing the market. Elster would like to return to Texas, but with Gil still in the system and Elster's slow finish, the shortstop's future is uncertain.

Position: SS
Bats: R **Throws:** R
Ht: 6' 2" **Wt:** 200

Opening Day Age: 32
Born: 8/3/64 in San Pedro, CA
ML Seasons: 10

Overall Statistics

	G	AB	R	H	D	T	HR	RBI	SB	BB	SO	Avg	OBP	Slg
1996	157	515	79	130	32	2	24	99	4	52	138	.252	.317	.462
Career	737	2189	256	498	112	9	59	282	14	203	405	.228	.292	.368

Where He Hits the Ball

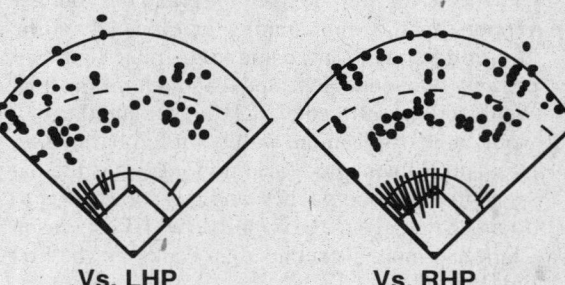

Vs. LHP   Vs. RHP

1996 Situational Stats

	AB	H	HR	RBI	Avg		AB	H	HR	RBI	Avg
Home	244	58	9	48	.238	LHP	159	45	4	32	.283
Road	271	72	15	51	.266	RHP	356	85	20	67	.239
First Half	272	71	13	58	.261	Sc Pos	156	36	4	65	.231
Scnd Half	243	59	11	41	.243	Clutch	69	10	0	10	.145

1996 Rankings (American League)

→ 2nd in fielding percentage at shortstop (.981)
→ 3rd in sacrifice bunts (16), sacrifice flies (11) and lowest batting average in the clutch (.145)
→ 4th in lowest groundball/flyball ratio (0.7)
→ 5th in lowest batting average vs. right-handed pitchers (.239)
→ 7th in lowest batting average on an 0-2 count (.053) and lowest on-base percentage vs. right-handed pitchers (.302)
→ 8th in lowest batting average at home (.238) and lowest batting average
→ 9th in lowest on-base percentage
→ 10th in strikeouts, lowest batting average with runners in scoring position (.231) and errors at shortstop (14)

Juan Gonzalez

1996 Season

Finally, some bang for the buck. In the third year of his hefty five-year contract, Juan Gonzalez broke through and won the Most Valuable Player Award, finally showing he was the stud who deserved to be the team's best-paid player. Gonzalez not only gave Texas a powerful bat in the middle of the lineup, he returned to the outfield and improved the team's defensive make-up after two years of on-again, off-again back troubles. Credit goes to general manager Doug Melvin for getting him to cut out his offseason body building.

Hitting

Gonzalez is a man to be feared when he lays off sliders in the dirt. He did that far more successfully in 1996, and set career highs in home runs and RBI while batting over .300 for the first time since 1993. Instrumental to his success was taking more pitches, as he cut down on his strikeouts and increased his walks. Hitting instructor Rudy Jaramillo also helped him with hitting inside pitches, which allowed him to hit line drives inside the foul line, rather than pulling them foul into the stands.

Baserunning & Defense

Gonzalez played right field in the minors, and he thrived when Johnny Oates gave him another chance there in 1996. He was charged with just two errors all year, playing in a park with a tricky corner. Gonzalez has average range and an average arm for a right fielder. He throws accurately. He's not a base-clogger, but often runs tentatively.

1997 Outlook

Who knows how Gonzalez will react to renewed success? The last time he had an MVP-type season he followed it with two subpar years. While he has the contractual luxury to coast, as his deal runs through 1998, the Rangers hope he will remain dedicated to the conditioning work that freed him from back trouble.

Position: RF/DH
Bats: R **Throws:** R
Ht: 6' 3" **Wt:** 220

Opening Day Age: 27
Born: 10/16/69 in Vega Baja, PR
ML Seasons: 8

Overall Statistics

	G	AB	R	H	D	T	HR	RBI	SB	BB	SO	Avg	OBP	Slg
1996	134	541	89	170	33	2	47	144	2	45	82	.314	.368	.643
Career	817	3130	480	887	172	13	214	659	16	214	609	.283	.334	.552

Where He Hits the Ball

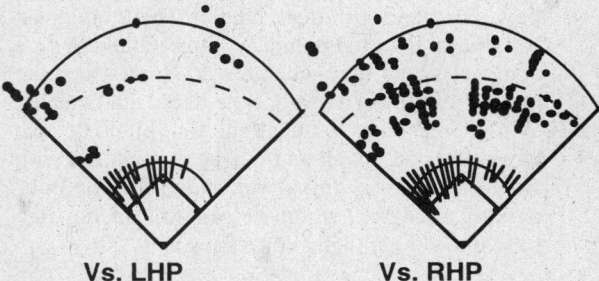

Vs. LHP   **Vs. RHP**

1996 Situational Stats

	AB	H	HR	RBI	Avg			AB	H	HR	RBI	Avg
Home	237	79	23	69	.333		LHP	141	53	20	47	.376
Road	304	91	24	75	.299		RHP	400	117	27	97	.293
First Half	244	78	22	70	.320		Sc Pos	168	54	11	93	.321
Scnd Half	297	92	25	74	.310		Clutch	67	16	3	14	.239

1996 Rankings (American League)

→ 1st in slugging percentage vs. left-handed pitchers (.887)
→ 2nd in RBI, slugging percentage and cleanup slugging percentage (.647)
→ 3rd in HR frequency (11.5 ABs per HR)
→ 5th in home runs, total bases (348), batting average vs. left-handed pitchers (.376) and fielding percentage in right field (.988)
→ 6th in intentional walks (12)
→ 7th in least pitches seen per plate appearance (3.41)
→ 8th in lowest percentage of pitches taken (48.7%)
→ Led the Rangers in home runs, total bases (348), RBI and intentional walks (12)

Texas Rangers

Rusty Greer

1996 Season

Manager Johnny Oates knows how valuable Rusty Greer is to his team. The man who delivered the most clutch hits on his 1995 club was sidelined with a rib injury for 15 games last September, and Oates watched a nine-game lead over Seattle dwindle to just two. Greer's teammates seemed to be waiting for his return. He ended the wait with a home run in his second at-bat back in the lineup, and Texas went on to win six of its last eight games. Oates acknowledged Greer's value midway through the season, moving him into the number-three spot in the order, which had belonged to Will Clark.

Hitting

Few left-handed hitters hang in better against southpaws than the mentally tough Greer. With a compact swing that generates good bat speed, he hits lefties almost as well as he does righthanders. While Greer likes to attack the first pitch, he also works the count well and can be a tough out with two strikes. His swing is well suited for The Ballpark in Arlington, where he can pull pitches into the right-field corner or into the stands.

Baserunning & Defense

Greer is perfectly suited for the broad pastures of left field at The Ballpark, where he executed dozens of running and diving catches. He also has no fear going back toward the wall. His arm is average, but accurate. He has good speed but doesn't often get to use it hitting in front of Juan Gonzalez.

1997 Outlook

Greer has learned a lot about how to handle himself by watching Will Clark for three years. That knowledge will be useful, as he figures to grow into the role of team leader. Greer signed a three-year contract before the 1996 season, but there's no chance that he will get comfortable. He knows only one way to play the game—all out.

Position: LF
Bats: L **Throws:** L
Ht: 6' 0" **Wt:** 190

Opening Day Age: 28
Born: 1/21/69 in Fort Rucker, AL
ML Seasons: 3

Overall Statistics

	G	AB	R	H	D	T	HR	RBI	SB	BB	SO	Avg	OBP	Slg
1996	139	542	96	180	41	6	18	100	9	62	86	.332	.397	.530
Career	350	1236	190	380	78	9	41	207	12	163	198	.307	.386	.485

Where He Hits the Ball

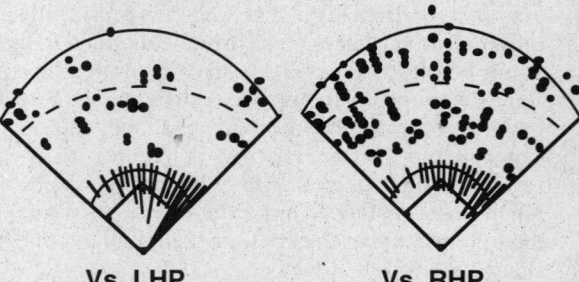

Vs. LHP   **Vs. RHP**

1996 Situational Stats

	AB	H	HR	RBI	Avg		AB	H	HR	RBI	Avg
Home	271	97	9	59	.358	LHP	174	56	6	35	.322
Road	271	83	9	41	.306	RHP	368	124	12	65	.337
First Half	299	95	8	54	.318	Sc Pos	159	51	6	78	.321
Scnd Half	243	85	10	46	.350	Clutch	65	19	1	13	.292

1996 Rankings (American League)

- ➡ 2nd in fielding percentage in left field (.984)
- ➡ 4th in sacrifice flies (10)
- ➡ 5th in batting average at home (.358), errors in left field (5) and batting average
- ➡ 6th in batting average vs. right-handed pitchers (.337)
- ➡ 8th in doubles
- ➡ 9th in batting average with the bases loaded (.500)
- ➡ Led the Rangers in triples, times on base (245), on-base percentage, batting average with the bases loaded (.500), batting average vs. right-handed pitchers (.337), batting average on a 3-1 count (.480) and on-base percentage vs. right-handed pitchers (.405)

Darryl Hamilton

1996 Season

It didn't bother Darryl Hamilton that Rangers general manager Doug Melvin courted four other center fielders before offering him a 1996 contract. He wanted to play in Texas, and he responded with a solid performance after being signed to a one-year deal. Hamilton supplanted Otis Nixon as both the center fielder and leadoff hitter. He was healthy enough to play more than 135 games for the first time in his pro career, but he wore down as the season wore on. Still, his solid play in center keyed an outfield that was surprisingly strong defensively.

Hitting

Hamilton is a contact hitter who is capable of working tough pitchers. However, he doesn't draw enough walks for a leadoff man. He's a good bunter, though, and can lay one down for a base hit. Like most left-handed hitters, he likes the ball down in the strike zone.

Baserunning & Defense

Hamilton forces outfielders to be on their toes because he's always capable of stretching a single into a double. He was not, however, the stolen-base threat Texas hoped he would be, possibly because of leg injuries that kept him in the training room long after games. He's a prototypical center fielder, taking charge and making all the plays he should make. He set a major league record last season for most chances by an outfielder without an error (390), and takes a streak of 166 consecutive errorless games into 1997. However, runners have been challenging Hamilton's arm successfully since he had Tommy John surgery in 1994.

1997 Outlook

Hamilton didn't have anything left in the final weeks of the season, perhaps because of insufficient rest given him by Johnny Oates. Concern over Hamilton's stamina may prompt Melvin to shop for a new center fielder, and Hamiton, a free agent, may well be playing elsewhere in 1997.

Position: CF
Bats: L **Throws:** R
Ht: 6' 1" **Wt:** 185

Opening Day Age: 32
Born: 12/3/64 in Baton Rouge, LA
ML Seasons: 8

Overall Statistics

	G	AB	R	H	D	T	HR	RBI	SB	BB	SO	Avg	OBP	Slg
1996	148	627	94	184	29	4	6	51	15	54	66	.293	.348	.381
Career	814	2820	417	821	123	25	29	304	124	260	281	.291	.351	.383

Where He Hits the Ball

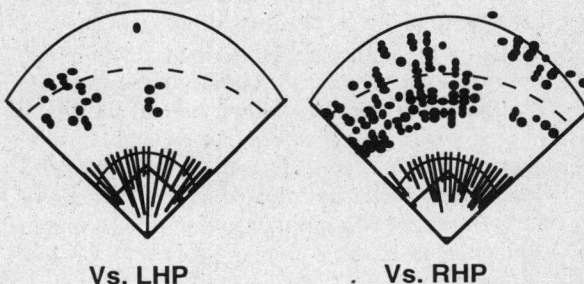

Vs. LHP   **Vs. RHP**

1996 Situational Stats

	AB	H	HR	RBI	Avg		AB	H	HR	RBI	Avg
Home	306	99	2	30	.324	LHP	182	48	1	17	.264
Road	321	85	4	21	.265	RHP	445	136	5	34	.306
First Half	341	105	2	28	.308	Sc Pos	136	34	0	41	.250
Scnd Half	286	79	4	23	.276	Clutch	81	15	1	5	.185

1996 Rankings (American League)

➡ 1st in fielding percentage in center field (1.000)
➡ 3rd in singles
➡ 5th in lowest percentage of swings that missed (8.9%)
➡ 6th in at-bats
➡ 7th in highest groundball/flyball ratio (1.8)
➡ 8th in lowest HR frequency (104.5 ABs per HR) and lowest on-base percentage for a leadoff hitter (.348)
➡ 9th in lowest slugging percentage
➡ 10th in hits and plate appearances (696)
➡ Led the Rangers in singles, pitches seen (2,678), plate appearances (696) and highest groundball/flyball ratio (1.8)

Mike Henneman

1996 Season

It's hard to knock a 10-year veteran closer coming off a career-high in saves, but here goes. Mike Henneman's disappointing performance with Texas last year could be cited as a reason to make changes to the save rule. He piled up 31 saves while throwing just 42 innings, often coming in to start the ninth inning with a two- or three-run lead. He rarely cruised through easy save opportunities, as his 5.79 ERA illustrates. Concerns about Henneman caused Johnny Oates to look elsewhere for late-inning relief down the stretch. Henneman picked up just 10 saves after the All-Star break.

Pitching

Gone, it seems, are the days when Henneman could get outs on his fastball if his split-fingered fastball wasn't working. His velocity has slipped, leaving him nibbling at the corners of the plate. He complicates matters by falling behind too many hitters. While he can still induce ground balls, he gets in trouble when the count requires him to challenge hitters. He allowed one homer every seven innings last year after giving up just one in 50 innings in 1995.

Defense

Henneman is quick to the plate, making it tough for teams to run on him. It wasn't even an option with Pudge Rodriguez behind the plate. He generally fields his position well, but is showing his age on comebackers up the middle.

1997 Outlook

Never say never with relief pitchers, but Henneman might have hit the end of the road last year. He let it be known that he wanted to end his career pitching in Texas, where he has lived for a decade. He failed to reach the level of appearances and innings that would have guaranteed a contract option for 1997, thus becoming a free agent. If he goes to spring training, it will probably be on a make-good contract.

Position: RP
Bats: R **Throws:** R
Ht: 6' 3" **Wt:** 210

Opening Day Age: 35
Born: 12/11/61 in St. Charles, MO
ML Seasons: 10
Pronunciation: HENN-uh-min

Overall Statistics

	W	L	Pct.	ERA	G	GS	Sv	IP	H	BB	SO	HR	BR/IP
1996	0	7	.000	5.79	49	0	31	42.0	41	17	34	6	1.38
Career	57	42	.576	3.21	561	0	193	732.2	686	271	533	47	1.31

How Often He Throws Strikes

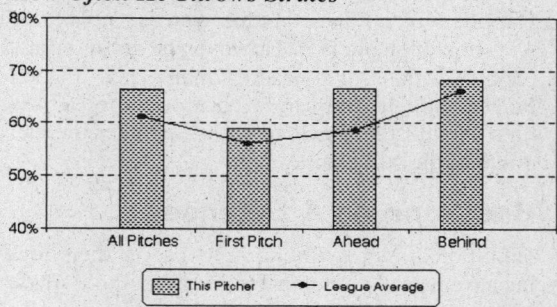

This Pitcher · League Average

1996 Situational Stats

	W	L	ERA	Sv	IP		AB	H	HR	RBI	Avg
Home	0	2	4.22	15	21.1	LHB	78	23	3	13	.295
Road	0	5	7.40	16	20.2	RHB	81	18	3	12	.222
First Half	0	7	7.90	21	27.1	Sc Pos	39	14	3	21	.359
Scnd Half	0	0	1.84	10	14.2	Clutch	120	33	4	23	.275

1996 Rankings (American League)

→ 2nd in relief losses (7)
→ 6th in saves and save percentage (83.8%)
→ 8th in blown saves (6)
→ 9th in save opportunities (37) and highest batting average allowed in relief with runners on base (.343)
→ 10th in games finished (45)
→ Led the Rangers in saves, games finished (45), save opportunities (37), save percentage (83.8%), blown saves (6) and relief losses (7)

Ken Hill

Position: SP
Bats: R **Throws:** R
Ht: 6' 2" **Wt:** 205

Opening Day Age: 31
Born: 12/14/65 in Lynn, MA
ML Seasons: 9

1996 Season

For Texas general manager Doug Melvin, Ken Hill was as good as a full house. His desire to join the Rangers allowed Melvin to call Kenny Rogers' bluff, telling him and agent Scott Boras to peddle their wares elsewhere. Hill, signed to a three-year contract, did what few free-agent pitchers (including Rogers) could do: deliver on his promise to be the staff ace. He led Texas in starts, innings and strikeouts while tying Bobby Witt for the team lead with 16 victories. His ERA was a full run lower than anyone else on the staff who made more than 10 starts.

Pitching

Cleveland pitching coach Mark Wiley restored Hill's velocity with some adjustments late in the 1995 season, and Hill has had no major problems since then. Hill is a power pitcher who hits the low 90s with his fastball, and complements it with an impressive forkball, a slider and a change-up. He is as tough on left-handed batters as right-handed batters. Hill gave up just one homer for every 13.2 innings in 1996, and he generated plenty of double-play grounders. Right-handed hitters actually put up better power numbers against Hill than lefties.

Defense

A fine athlete, Hill has terrific reactions and does a great job fielding his position. He can be slow to the plate, though, and has never developed anything beyond a pedestrian pickoff move. Baserunners will challenge him, even with Pudge Rodriguez behind the plate.

1997 Outlook

Hill is in the prime of his career. He should be Texas' Opening Day starter and an All-Star candidate in 1997. And there is no reason to believe he cannot remain effective for years to come. The Rangers might want to consider a contract extension before this guy gets back into the free-agent pool.

Overall Statistics

	W	L	Pct.	ERA	G	GS	Sv	IP	H	BB	SO	HR	BR/IP
1996	16	10	.615	3.63	35	35	0	250.2	250	95	170	19	1.38
Career	90	71	.559	3.66	233	226	0	1462.2	1375	570	890	103	1.33

How Often He Throws Strikes

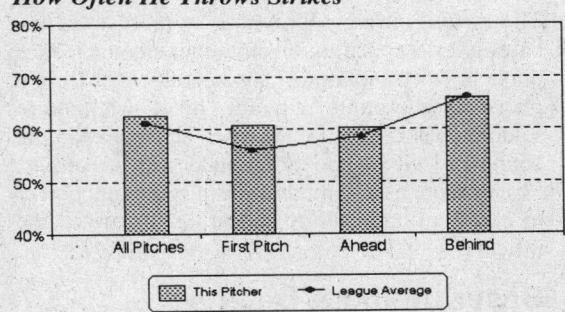

1996 Situational Stats

	W	L	ERA	Sv	IP		AB	H	HR	RBI	Avg
Home	9	7	4.45	0	121.1	LHB	501	132	5	44	.263
Road	7	3	2.85	0	129.1	RHB	448	118	14	49	.263
First Half	9	5	4.03	0	131.2	Sc Pos	222	50	3	69	.225
Scnd Half	7	5	3.18	0	119.0	Clutch	61	14	1	5	.230

1996 Rankings (American League)

- → 1st in shutouts (3), balks (4) and runners caught stealing (14)
- → 2nd in games started, complete games (7), least home runs allowed per 9 innings (.68) and ERA on the road (2.85)
- → 3rd in innings pitched and batters faced (1,061)
- → 5th in wins, hits allowed, pitches thrown (3,901) and GDPs induced (26)
- → 6th in ERA and lowest slugging percentage allowed (.378)
- → 7th in walks allowed, lowest stolen base percentage allowed (44.0%) and lowest batting average allowed with runners in scoring position (.225)

Texas Rangers

Mark McLemore

1996 Season

Mark McLemore's athleticism has long made him one of the most versatile players in the American League. But he found a home as the Rangers' regular second baseman in 1996. He also helped balance the lineup by giving Johnny Oates a switch hitter near the bottom of the order. McLemore isn't one to concern himself with where he plays or bats, embodying the unselfish spirit that worked so well in the Texas clubhouse last summer. His steady—and sometimes spectacular—fielding wasn't taken for granted by the Rangers' pitching staff.

Hitting

The switch-hitting McLemore is more effective batting left-handed, but from either side he makes pitchers work and almost always puts the ball into play on the ground. A patient hitter, McLemore seldom chases bad pitches when he's ahead in the count. In 1996 he had more walks than strikeouts. Feared more as a bunter, he has just enough power to keep outfielders from cheating in toward the infield.

Baserunning & Defense

While McLemore has a big body for a middle infielder, he moves well. He's better going to his right than his left, and makes accurate throws from his knees when he must. He is terrific chasing down pop-ups in the outfield or foul territory. He needed rotator cuff surgery after the 1995 season and no longer throws well. He compensates as best he can with a quick release on the double play. His speed seems to be diminishing, but he is still capable of 25-30 steals.

1997 Outlook

McLemore would go to Bosnia to play for Oates. He was eligible for free agency, but no one was surprised when he quickly re-signed with Texas. The Rangers have a young second baseman on the way, but aren't likely to pencil him into the lineup until 1998. McLemore helped Texas win its first division title, and now he'll try to get the Rangers into the World Series.

Position: 2B
Bats: B **Throws:** R
Ht: 5'11" **Wt:** 207

Opening Day Age: 32
Born: 10/4/64 in San Diego, CA
ML Seasons: 11

Overall Statistics

	G	AB	R	H	D	T	HR	RBI	SB	BB	SO	Avg	OBP	Slg
1996	147	517	84	150	23	4	5	46	27	87	69	.290	.389	.379
Career	930	3030	445	782	118	23	22	290	145	373	457	.258	.338	.334

Where He Hits the Ball

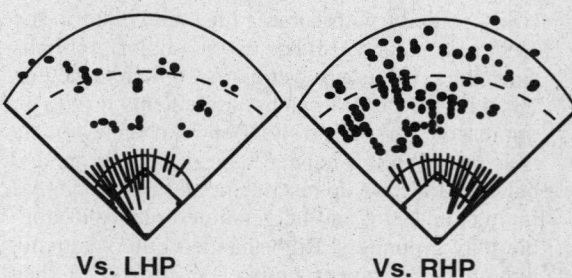

Vs. LHP   Vs. RHP

1996 Situational Stats

	AB	H	HR	RBI	Avg		AB	H	HR	RBI	Avg
Home	252	74	3	24	.294	LHP	160	40	1	10	.250
Road	265	76	2	22	.287	RHP	357	110	4	36	.308
First Half	265	81	2	29	.306	Sc Pos	116	32	1	39	.276
Scnd Half	252	69	3	17	.274	Clutch	71	23	0	5	.324

1996 Rankings (American League)

→ 4th in errors at second base (12), fielding percentage at second base (.985) and highest percentage of pitches taken (64.8%)
→ 5th in caught stealing and highest percentage of swings put into play (57.6%)
→ 6th in lowest slugging percentage vs. left-handed pitchers (.294)
→ 7th in stolen bases
→ 8th in lowest slugging percentage
→ 9th in lowest HR frequency (103.4 ABs per HR) and highest groundball/flyball ratio (1.7)
→ Led the Rangers in stolen bases, caught stealing (10), GDPs (15), on-base percentage vs. right-handed pitchers (.405) and steals of third (2)

Darren Oliver

1996 Season

Talk about a quick recovery. Darren Oliver had surgery to repair a torn rotator cuff in August 1995, but dedicated himself fully to a winter of rehabilitation. He arrived in spring training with surprising zip on his fastball and turned into the most pleasant surprise on the Texas pitching staff. Oliver experienced little fatigue and stayed free of injuries in 1996, establishing career highs as a pro in both victories and innings pitched. He capped the season with eight strong innings against New York in the Division Series.

Pitching

Oliver has a smooth delivery and above-average stuff. He has one of the best change-ups in the American League, which he sets up with a hard-breaking curve and a fastball that tops out around 85-87 MPH. Oliver is particularly tough on left-handed batters. He demonstrates a toughness on the mound that belies his mild demeanor; he doesn't hesitate to pitch inside when hitters crowd the plate. Control can be a problem. He walked 3.9 hitters per nine innings in 1996.

Defense

Oliver, the son of former major leaguer Bob Oliver, is a good athlete who fields his position well. Occasionally he will try to make the impossible play, but he has countered that tendency with more experience. Oliver has one of the best pickoff moves around.

1997 Outlook

Oliver's history makes health an annual concern. There aren't any specific ailments that suggest problems, but Oliver has had surgery for three different injuries within the last six years. Manager Johnny Oates believes Oliver gets tired when he is used too much and plans to give him occasional breaks, pushing him back a day or two whenever the schedule allows. The Rangers would love another 30-start season.

Position: SP
Bats: R **Throws:** L
Ht: 6' 2" **Wt:** 200

Opening Day Age: 26
Born: 10/6/70 in
Kansas City, MO
ML Seasons: 4

Overall Statistics

	W	L	Pct.	ERA	G	GS	Sv	IP	H	BB	SO	HR	BR/IP
1996	14	6	.700	4.66	30	30	0	173.2	190	76	112	20	1.53
Career	22	8	.733	4.34	92	37	2	276.0	279	144	205	28	1.53

How Often He Throws Strikes

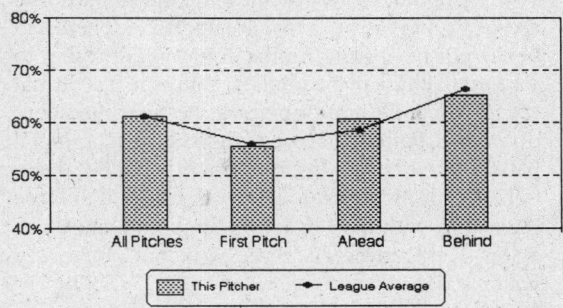

1996 Situational Stats

	W	L	ERA	Sv	IP		AB	H	HR	RBI	Avg
Home	9	2	4.27	0	103.1	LHB	106	24	2	11	.226
Road	5	4	5.25	0	70.1	RHB	576	166	18	69	.288
First Half	7	2	3.82	0	94.1	Sc Pos	169	39	3	59	.231
Scnd Half	7	4	5.67	0	79.1	Clutch	26	5	1	1	.192

1996 Rankings (American League)

- → 4th in winning percentage
- → 5th in lowest strikeout/walk ratio (1.5) and most run support per 9 innings (6.6)
- → 6th in shutouts (1)
- → 8th in hit batsmen (10), highest on-base percentage allowed (.356) and lowest batting average allowed with runners in scoring position (.231)
- → 9th in most baserunners allowed per 9 innings
- → 10th in balks (1)
- → Led the Rangers in hit batsmen (10), stolen bases allowed (11), winning percentage, highest groundball/flyball ratio allowed (1.4) and ERA at home (4.27)

Texas
Rangers

Dean Palmer

1996 Season

Dean Palmer played next to the Comeback Player of the Year in 1996. But if not for Kevin Elster, Palmer would have been a strong candidate for that award himself. He showed no signs of being bothered by the biceps tendon he tore in a grotesque at-bat early in 1995. Palmer picked up offensively where he left off, raising his batting average from its pre-1995 level while hitting with the usual power. He was an important presence for the Rangers.

Hitting

No matter how much time he spends with hitting instructor Rudy Jaramillo, Palmer has holes in his swing. He can be retired on breaking pitches that are down and fastballs that are up. But pitchers had better not fall behind in the count while trying to get him to chase those pitches. While he has the bat speed to handle tough pitches, he kills mediocre offerings. Palmer showed signs of becoming a patient hitter before his injury in '95, but he's back to being his old, overanxious self. He tried to force the action with men in scoring position, and once again averaged nearly three strikeouts for every walk.

Baserunning & Defense

Coach Bucky Dent has improved Palmer's throwing mechanics, but under pressure he still sometimes reverts to the poor footwork that leads to throws tailing up the first-base line. He has quick reactions and cuts off hits going either way, but he has trouble on plays in front of him. His 16-error season in 1996 represented progress. He runs like a power-hitting third baseman.

1997 Outlook

Texas faces a major decision with Palmer: sign him to a long-term contract or risk losing him to free agency after the 1997 season. It's not an automatic call one way or the other. For now, general manager Doug Melvin will listen to trade offers for Palmer, but there's no replacement in the organization.

Position: 3B
Bats: R **Throws:** R
Ht: 6' 1" **Wt:** 210

Opening Day Age: 28
Born: 12/27/68 in Tallahassee, FL
ML Seasons: 7

Overall Statistics

	G	AB	R	H	D	T	HR	RBI	SB	BB	SO	Avg	OBP	Slg
1996	154	582	98	163	26	2	38	107	2	59	145	.280	.348	.527
Career	680	2390	378	590	113	8	140	396	27	253	673	.247	.323	.477

Where He Hits the Ball

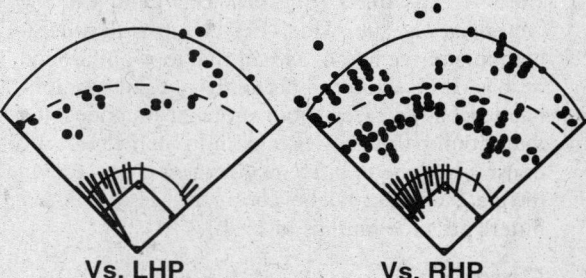

Vs. LHP   **Vs. RHP**

1996 Situational Stats

	AB	H	HR	RBI	Avg		AB	H	HR	RBI	Avg
Home	275	76	19	55	.276	LHP	152	46	12	31	.303
Road	307	87	19	52	.283	RHP	430	117	26	76	.272
First Half	310	90	20	66	.290	Sc Pos	164	35	8	61	.213
Scnd Half	272	73	18	41	.268	Clutch	74	24	6	13	.324

1996 Rankings (American League)

→ 3rd in lowest batting average with runners in scoring position (.213) and lowest fielding percentage at third base (.953)

→ 4th in errors at third base (16)

→ 5th in strikeouts and lowest groundball/flyball ratio (0.7)

→ Led the Rangers in hit by pitch (5), strikeouts, GDPs (15) and batting average in the clutch (.324)

Roger Pavlik

1996 Season

Inconsistency has marked Roger Pavlik's five-year career, and the trend continued even in his first All-Star season. Pavlik won 11 games in the first half—thanks largely to great run support—but finished the year out of the postseason rotation. He tied teammate Ken Hill for second in the American League with seven complete games, yet made his lone Division Series appearance out of the bullpen and took the loss in the decisive Game 4. It was a complete reversal from 1995, when he was awful in the first half of the season and reliable down the stretch.

Pitching

Pavlik is his own counsel, which leaves him wandering about the woods for too long when his unconventional delivery gets out of whack. He has rejected the attempts of pitching coaches Claude Osteen and Dick Bosman to refine his across-the-body motion. When everything is working, he is tough because of a decent fastball and a good sinker that acts like a split-fingered fastball. He doesn't have many options for days when he struggles, which turns him into a roller coaster ride for his manager.

Defense

Pavlik is tough to run on by getting the ball to the plate quickly. He doesn't do a very good job holding runners on, though, which causes problems on those days when Pudge Rodriguez is not behind the plate. He moves awkwardly around the infield and is a below-average fielder.

1997 Outlook

Pavlik should be coming into his own but remains a question mark. His erratic performance and the risk of injury from his across-the-body delivery make offering salary arbitration a difficult decision for the Rangers. His statistics stacked naked against the performance of other pitchers might require the slow-talking, slow-walking Houston native to experience life outside the Lone Star State.

Position: SP
Bats: R **Throws:** R
Ht: 6' 2" **Wt:** 220

Opening Day Age: 29
Born: 10/4/67 in Houston, TX
ML Seasons: 5

Overall Statistics

	W	L	Pct.	ERA	G	GS	Sv	IP	H	BB	SO	HR	BR/IP
1996	15	8	.652	5.19	34	34	0	201.0	216	81	127	28	1.48
Career	43	33	.566	4.61	115	114	0	671.1	668	315	483	76	1.46

How Often He Throws Strikes

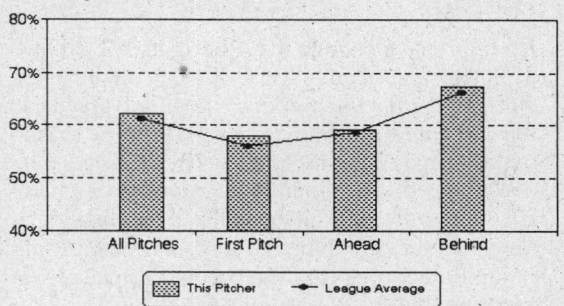

1996 Situational Stats

	W	L	ERA	Sv	IP		AB	H	HR	RBI	Avg
Home	9	3	4.82	0	106.1	LHB	411	118	13	57	.287
Road	6	5	5.61	0	94.2	RHB	373	98	15	49	.263
First Half	11	2	4.82	0	112.0	Sc Pos	191	55	4	74	.288
Scnd Half	4	6	5.66	0	89.0	Clutch	52	15	2	7	.288

1996 Rankings (American League)

- → 2nd in complete games (7)
- → 6th in winning percentage and highest ERA on the road (5.61)
- → 7th in lowest groundball/flyball ratio allowed (1.0) and most run support per 9 innings (6.4)
- → 8th in highest ERA and wins
- → 9th in lowest strikeout/walk ratio (1.6)
- → 10th in most GDPs induced per 9 innings (0.9)
- → Led the Rangers in complete games (7), home runs allowed, wild pitches (8), pickoff throws (112) and lowest batting average allowed vs. right-handed batters (.263)

Texas Rangers

Ivan Rodriguez

1996 Season

Gentlemen, start your adjectives. Ivan Rodriguez defies hyperbole. Before turning 25 this offseason, Rodriguez went to his fifth All-Star game in 1996, his fourth as a starter. The five-time Gold Glove winner improved both offensively and defensively, setting new career highs in doubles, homers and extra-base hits. While the national media pushed Juan Gonzalez as an MVP candidate, Rodriguez was equally as valuable to the Rangers. And here's one final adjective: durable. Rodriguez caught 147 games last year. He finished the season with 639 at-bats, breaking Johnny Bench's record for a catcher.

Position: C
Bats: R **Throws:** R
Ht: 5' 9"   **Wt:** 205

Opening Day Age: 25
Born: 11/30/71 in Vega Baja, PR
ML Seasons: 6
Nickname: Pudge

Overall Statistics

	G	AB	R	H	D	T	HR	RBI	SB	BB	SO	Avg	OBP	Slg
1996	153	639	116	192	47	3	19	86	5	38	55	.300	.342	.473
Career	730	2667	347	761	158	11	68	340	19	143	330	.285	.324	.429

Hitting

It's impressive enough that Rodriguez hit .300 for a second consecutive year. But he did it while working to improve his power, not his average. He fell one short of his home run goal for the season but still set a career high. He's a free swinger who doesn't need to see many pitches to hit one hard. He sprays the ball all over the field, making it tough to defense him. Hitting instructor Rudy Jaramillo believes Rodriguez could someday win a batting title.

Where He Hits the Ball

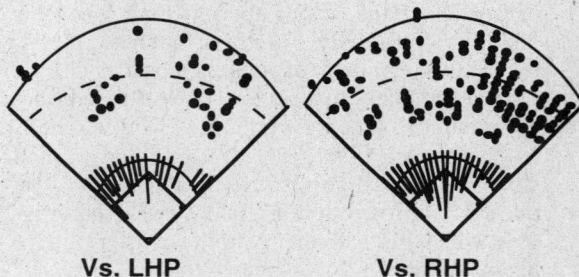

Vs. LHP   **Vs. RHP**

Baserunning & Defense

After throwing out 34 and 44 percent of potential base stealers in 1994 and 1995, Rodriguez retired runners at an amazing 49-percent rate (48-for-98) last season, another career best. He has won five consecutive Gold Gloves. Rodriguez has addressed two criticisms from his early years in the majors, doing a much better job handling the pitching staff and blocking runners off the plate. He can steal a base when he picks his spots.

1996 Situational Stats

	AB	H	HR	RBI	Avg		AB	H	HR	RBI	Avg
Home	295	96	10	51	.325	LHP	190	59	10	36	.311
Road	344	96	9	35	.279	RHP	449	133	9	50	.296
First Half	342	107	10	49	.313	Sc Pos	156	40	2	57	.256
Scnd Half	297	85	9	37	.286	Clutch	81	19	0	5	.235

1997 Outlook

Rodriguez is in an enviable position. He is eligible for free agency after the 1997 season, forcing Texas to sign him to a Juan Gonzalez-sized package or allow him to become the main course in the 1998 buffet. One imagines that expansion franchises in Phoenix and Tampa Bay could do worse than building their teams around a 26-year-old backstop already putting up Hall of Fame numbers.

1996 Rankings (American League)

→ 1st in errors at catcher (10) and highest percentage of runners caught stealing as a catcher (48.9%)
→ 2nd in lowest percentage of pitches taken (45.0%)
→ 3rd in doubles and least pitches seen per plate appearance (3.38)
→ 4th in at-bats
→ 7th in hits
→ Led the Rangers in at-bats, runs scored, hits, doubles, GDPs (15), batting average on an 0-2 count (.218) and batting average with two strikes (.248)

Mike Stanton

1996 Season

After surviving the wear and tear that comes from being in Kevin Kennedy's bullpen, Mike Stanton still had something left when Boston traded him to Texas on August 31. He was a manager's best friend: a left-handed reliever who could be brought into a game to face a left-handed hitter, then remain in the game without having to issue batting helmets to the fans in the left-field bleachers. Johnny Oates did a great job handling his bullpen, but left himself open to criticism by not handing a 2-1 lead over to Stanton to start the ninth inning of a Game 3 Division Series loss to New York.

Pitching

Stanton comes at hitters with a big body and a five-piece delivery. He makes it tough to pick up the ball early, especially for left-handed hitters. Stanton throws lots of fastballs. They usually look better coming to the plate than on the radar gun after they've hit the catcher's mitt. Rare is the time when he hits 90 MPH. His fastball has some natural movement, including good sinking action. However, it tends to straighten out when he overthrows under pressure. He has a good slider as well, but it comes and goes over the course of the season.

Defense

Stanton's unorthodox delivery makes it tough for baserunners to read his leg kick. While his motion deters a good jump, he has just an average pickoff move. He has never been an especially good fielder.

1997 Outlook

It's a mystery why Stanton has only 56 career saves. He is as durable as almost anyone, and he was equally effective against right-handed and left-handed hitters last year. He had chances to develop into a stopper with Atlanta, but could never keep it together for a full season. It might be time he gets another look, especially if he stays in Texas.

Position: RP
Bats: L **Throws:** L
Ht: 6' 1" **Wt:** 215

Opening Day Age: 29
Born: 6/2/67 in Houston, TX
ML Seasons: 8

Overall Statistics

	W	L	Pct.	ERA	G	GS	Sv	IP	H	BB	SO	HR	BR/IP
1996	4	4	.500	3.66	81	0	1	78.2	78	27	60	11	1.33
Career	23	25	.479	3.88	407	0	56	389.1	372	149	293	36	1.34

How Often He Throws Strikes

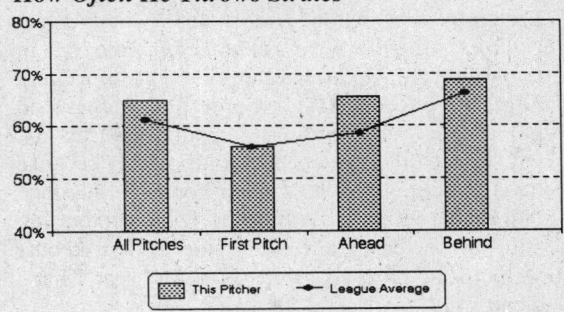

1996 Situational Stats

	W	L	ERA	Sv	IP		AB	H	HR	RBI	Avg
Home	3	2	4.01	1	33.2	LHB	114	30	1	19	.263
Road	1	2	3.40	0	45.0	RHB	180	48	10	29	.267
First Half	4	2	3.42	1	50.0	Sc Pos	92	27	3	39	.293
Scnd Half	0	2	4.08	0	28.2	Clutch	144	38	6	18	.264

1996 Rankings (American League)

- ➡ 2nd in balks (2) and holds (22)
- ➡ 3rd in games pitched (81)
- ➡ 9th in worst first batter efficiency (.301)
- ➡ 10th in relief innings (78.2)

Mickey Tettleton

1996 Season

Mickey Tettleton's second season in Texas was a difficult one. He wasn't able to produce the kind of clutch hits he delivered with regularity in 1995, most likely because he had played right field with a bad right knee for much of '95. Playing on a disabled right knee may have brought on the pain in his left knee that forced him to play much of the 1996 season in a brace. While he improved upon his batting average and RBI total as a full-time designated hitter, he didn't seem nearly as much a part of the team.

Hitting

The switch-hitting Tettleton loves hitting at The Ballpark in Arlington. Unfortunately, he has had trouble taking his success at home onto the road in two years with Texas. He can still be an infuriating hitter for pitchers, taking borderline pitches and going deep into counts. But scouts insist his bat has slowed down in recent years, possibly because he is not able to use his lower body like he once did. He has more power hitting left-handed but can still hit the seats from either side. His strikeouts were up and his walks were down last year. That's a bad sign.

Baserunning & Defense

Tettleton played only 23 games in the field last season, all at first base. He has diminishing value as a third catcher, but Johnny Oates barely uses two catchers, let alone three. Tettleton is a station-to-station runner who is often lifted for pinch runners.

1997 Outlook

Tettleton will remain the Rangers' DH, as he signed a two-year contract before the 1996 season. He is a proud professional who might fool his critics by rebounding from a season that suggested he was nearing the end. But he could find his work load reduced if he doesn't get off to a quick start.

Position: DH/1B
Bats: B **Throws:** R
Ht: 6' 2" **Wt:** 212

Opening Day Age: 36
Born: 9/16/60 in Oklahoma City, OK
ML Seasons: 13

Overall Statistics

	G	AB	R	H	D	T	HR	RBI	SB	BB	SO	Avg	OBP	Slg
1996	143	491	78	121	26	1	24	83	2	95	137	.246	.366	.450
Career	1468	4654	706	1128	209	16	242	728	23	946	1295	.242	.371	.450

Where He Hits the Ball

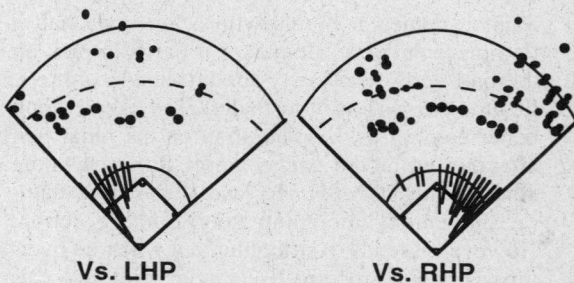

Vs. LHP   Vs. RHP

1996 Situational Stats

	AB	H	HR	RBI	Avg		AB	H	HR	RBI	Avg
Home	243	62	14	47	.255	LHP	155	38	6	21	.245
Road	248	59	10	36	.238	RHP	336	83	18	62	.247
First Half	286	73	15	47	.255	Sc Pos	136	35	5	57	.257
Scnd Half	205	48	9	36	.234	Clutch	61	18	1	12	.295

1996 Rankings (American League)

→ 2nd in most pitches seen per plate appearance (4.33) and lowest percentage of swings on the first pitch (10.7%)

→ 4th in lowest batting average on the road (.238) and lowest batting average

→ 5th in highest percentage of pitches taken (64.3%)

→ 7th in lowest batting average with two strikes (.127)

→ 8th in sacrifice flies (9)

→ 9th in walks and lowest batting average on an 0-2 count (.063)

→ Led the Rangers in walks, most pitches seen per plate appearance (4.33) and lowest percentage of swings on the first pitch (10.7%)

Bobby Witt

1996 Season

Free from the burdensome "next Nolan Ryan" label which dogged him in his early years with Texas, Bobby Witt is enjoying life as a major league pitcher. He is not going to dominate many games, but he has definite value as a fourth or fifth starter. That's the role Doug Melvin signed him to fill. He responded with an injury-free, 16-win performance—his highest victory total since 1990—and his first postseason start.

Pitching

Witt doesn't blow hitters away like he could when he arrived in the big leagues, but he still has good stuff. He can hit the low 90s with his fastball, but it never has had much movement. His out pitch has become a nasty sinker that he throws when he is ahead in the count. It produces strikeouts and ground-ball double plays. He has learned a cut fastball that acts as a change-up. Wildness was more of a problem last year: he walked 4.3 batters per nine innings, up from 3.6 per nine innings in 1995.

Defense

Witt has a big leg kick and lots of motion in his delivery, which makes him an easy target for basestealers. He benefited more than perhaps anyone from Ivan Rodriguez's cannon arm, which made baserunners think twice before trying to steal second. He is an average fielder who sometimes gets flustered under pressure.

1997 Outlook

For the third year in a row, Witt headed into free agency after the season, but he quickly re-signed with Texas, once again inking a one-year contract. He is a good fit for at least one more year, as none of the young pitchers in the Rangers' much-improved farm system are ready. Witt might not be able to duplicate his 16-win season, but he'll eat up innings at the bottom end of the rotation.

Position: SP
Bats: R **Throws:** R
Ht: 6' 2" **Wt:** 205

Opening Day Age: 32
Born: 5/11/64 in Arlington, VA
ML Seasons: 11

Overall Statistics

	W	L	Pct.	ERA	G	GS	Sv	IP	H	BB	SO	HR	BR/IP
1996	16	12	.571	5.41	33	32	0	199.2	235	96	157	28	1.66
Career	112	119	.485	4.61	312	306	0	1900.1	1821	1121	1616	165	1.55

How Often He Throws Strikes

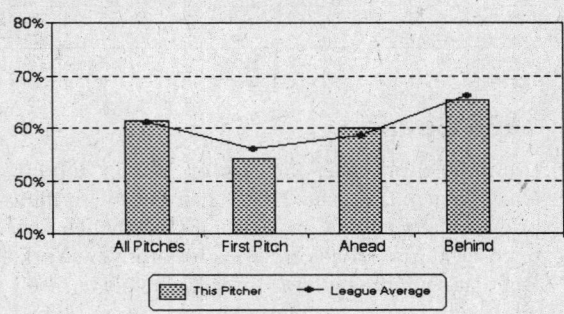

1996 Situational Stats

	W	L	ERA	Sv	IP		AB	H	HR	RBI	Avg
Home	10	4	5.87	0	104.1	LHB	436	128	14	56	.294
Road	6	8	4.91	0	95.1	RHB	360	107	14	52	.297
First Half	7	8	5.96	0	108.2	Sc Pos	174	52	7	71	.299
Scnd Half	9	4	4.75	0	91.0	Clutch	32	8	1	1	.250

1996 Rankings (American League)

- ➥ 2nd in highest on-base percentage allowed (.370) and most baserunners allowed per 9 innings
- ➥ 3rd in highest ERA, highest batting average allowed (.295), most run support per 9 innings (6.8) and highest ERA at home (5.87)
- ➥ 4th in highest slugging percentage allowed (.471)
- ➥ 5th in wins
- ➥ 6th in walks allowed
- ➥ 7th in runners caught stealing (10) and most pitches thrown per batter (3.89)
- ➥ 8th in most strikeouts per 9 innings (7.1)
- ➥ 9th in most home runs allowed per 9 innings (1.26)

Damon Buford

Position: RF/LF/CF
Bats: R **Throws:** R
Ht: 5'10" **Wt:** 170

Opening Day Age: 26
Born: 6/12/70 in
Baltimore, MD
ML Seasons: 4

Overall Statistics

	G	AB	R	H	D	T	HR	RBI	SB	BB	SO	Avg	OBP	Slg
1996	90	145	30	41	9	0	6	20	8	15	34	.283	.348	.469
Career	215	394	80	94	19	0	12	43	20	49	89	.239	.329	.378

1996 Situational Stats

	AB	H	HR	RBI	Avg		AB	H	HR	RBI	Avg
Home	81	25	3	11	.309	LHP	90	26	5	15	.289
Road	64	16	3	9	.250	RHP	55	15	1	5	.273
First Half	86	24	4	13	.279	Sc Pos	34	10	2	13	.294
Scnd Half	59	17	2	7	.288	Clutch	15	3	0	4	.200

1996 Season

Damon Buford was the top option on Johnny Oates' bench last year. That is damning with faint praise. The Rangers' lack of a quality bench was exposed in the Division Series loss to New York. But that's not the fault of Buford, who played well while not getting as much playing time as he had hoped he would.

Hitting, Baserunning & Defense

Surprisingly, Buford's bat was a plus. He had batted just .213 in 125 previous major league games with Baltimore and the Mets, but flirted with .300 for much of the year. He hits lefthanders well, but hard-throwing righthanders often overpowered him. While he has good speed, he has yet to develop into a potent basestealing threat. He has excellent range in center field and played errorless defense in 1996. His arm is a liability.

1997 Outlook

Darryl Hamilton slowed down last season, which suggests Buford may get more playing time in his second season with Texas. He is getting to the point in his career where he must establish himself as a regular, or accept an existence as a bench player.

Dennis Cook

Position: RP
Bats: L **Throws:** L
Ht: 6'3" **Wt:** 190

Opening Day Age: 34
Born: 10/4/62 in
Lamarque, TX
ML Seasons: 9

Overall Statistics

	W	L	Pct.	ERA	G	GS	Sv	IP	H	BB	SO	HR	BR/IP
1996	5	2	.714	4.09	60	0	0	70.1	53	35	64	2	1.25
Career	37	30	.552	3.93	295	71	3	689.2	649	253	425	92	1.31

1996 Situational Stats

	W	L	ERA	Sv	IP		AB	H	HR	RBI	Avg
Home	4	1	3.60	0	35.0	LHB	107	22	1	22	.206
Road	1	1	4.58	0	35.1	RHB	141	31	1	15	.220
First Half	4	1	3.00	0	45.0	Sc Pos	96	17	1	35	.177
Scnd Half	1	1	6.04	0	25.1	Clutch	58	10	2	12	.172

1996 Season

No one in Johnny Oates' 1996 bullpen was busier than Dennis Cook. He almost always was the first lefthander into the game, often working two-inning stints. Cook was on pace for 70 appearances before developing tenderness in his shoulder late in the season. He was effective as both a middle and long reliever.

Pitching & Defense

Cook's collection of offspeed pitches makes it tough for left-handed hitters to get good swings at him. He has to successfully spot his fastball, forkball and slider to keep right-handed hitters from hitting the ball hard. He will pitch around hitters he fears rather than challenge them. Such caution bloats his walk totals, but allowed him to give up just two homers in 1996. Cook has a good move to first and is quick to the plate.

1997 Outlook

Cook should pick up where he left off. But he is getting to the age where his employer has to worry about the zip on his fastball. Certainly he has learned enough throughout his career to get by with a little less stuff. A free agent, he should have little trouble finding an employer if the Rangers don't want to bring him back.

Kevin Gross

Position: SP/RP
Bats: R **Throws:** R
Ht: 6' 5" **Wt:** 227

Opening Day Age: 35
Born: 6/8/61 in
Downey, CA
ML Seasons: 14

Overall Statistics

	W	L	Pct.	ERA	G	GS	Sv	IP	H	BB	SO	HR	BR/IP
1996	11	8	.579	5.22	28	19	0	129.1	151	50	78	19	1.55
Career	140	157	.471	4.09	462	365	5	2462.1	2489	966	1707	226	1.40

1996 Situational Stats

	W	L	ERA	Sv	IP		AB	H	HR	RBI	Avg
Home	6	2	4.85	0	59.1	LHB	263	78	11	35	.297
Road	5	6	5.53	0	70.0	RHB	252	73	8	37	.290
First Half	9	6	5.59	0	96.2	Sc Pos	118	33	5	55	.280
Scnd Half	2	2	4.13	0	32.2	Clutch	35	8	0	1	.229

1996 Season

Kevin Gross came to camp in great shape last year and improved upon his dismal 1995 performance. Nevertheless, he found himself in the bullpen after the Rangers traded for John Burkett on July 31. He thrived in a middle relief role, going 2-1 with an 0.89 ERA in nine appearances before being sidelined by a herniated disk. He required surgery after the season.

Pitching & Defense

Gross has lost the fastball he had for most of his career, leaving him in trouble against lineups stacked with left-handed hitters. He had some bite on his slider and curveball, but made too many mistakes out over the plate that landed in the bleachers. He has a long, awkward delivery that makes him easy to run on. His reactions have slowed dramatically, leaving him jabbing at air after comebackers have gone past the mound.

1997 Outlook

Gross' contract expired after 1996, but he does not seem ready to call it a career. He would love to come back with Texas as a middle reliever, and might get a chance if he is realistic when it is time to talk contract.

Gil Heredia

Position: RP
Bats: R **Throws:** R
Ht: 6' 1" **Wt:** 210

Opening Day Age: 31
Born: 10/26/65 in
Nogales, AZ
ML Seasons: 6
Pronunciation:
herr-AY-dee-uh

Overall Statistics

	W	L	Pct.	ERA	G	GS	Sv	IP	H	BB	SO	HR	BR/IP
1996	2	5	.286	5.89	44	0	1	73.1	91	14	43	12	1.43
Career	19	21	.475	4.34	170	39	4	402.2	450	89	254	38	1.34

1996 Situational Stats

	W	L	ERA	Sv	IP		AB	H	HR	RBI	Avg
Home	0	2	3.89	1	44.0	LHB	116	32	2	14	.276
Road	2	3	8.90	0	29.1	RHB	186	59	10	40	.317
First Half	1	3	7.13	0	41.2	Sc Pos	85	28	3	39	.329
Scnd Half	1	2	4.26	1	31.2	Clutch	73	21	3	18	.288

1996 Season

Most of the Rangers' acquisitions worked out well last year. Then there was Gil Heredia. The Rangers thought they had stolen a quality right-handed reliever from the free-agent pool, but they ended the season with a hole in the bullpen where Heredia was supposed to be. He had compiled a 1.32 ERA as a reliever for the Expos in 1995, but it climbed to almost 6.00 in 1996 before Texas shipped him to Triple-A Oklahoma City in August.

Pitching & Defense

Heredia's calling-card is his control, but there were times last year when Johnny Oates wished he was wild. He came to spring training without his split-fingered fastball and slider, and he never got much bite on either of them. The former Expo does, however, have a good pickoff move. He holds runners close and fields his position well.

1997 Outlook

The Rangers released Heredia after the season. Despite his troubles with Texas, a National League team will have a job for Heredia, based on the credentials he established in 1995. He's going to have to prove he's ready in spring training, though, because he's done nothing recently to build a manager's confidence.

Warren Newson

Position: RF
Bats: L **Throws:** L
Ht: 5' 7" **Wt:** 202

Opening Day Age: 32
Born: 7/3/64 in
Newnan, GA
ML Seasons: 6
Nickname: The Deacon

Overall Statistics

	G	AB	R	H	D	T	HR	RBI	SB	BB	SO	Avg	OBP	Slg
1996	91	235	34	60	14	1	10	31	3	37	82	.255	.355	.451
Career	398	802	132	208	29	3	24	95	11	164	234	.259	.385	.393

1996 Situational Stats

	AB	H	HR	RBI	Avg		AB	H	HR	RBI	Avg
Home	115	27	5	19	.235	LHP	24	4	0	2	.167
Road	120	33	5	12	.275	RHP	211	56	10	29	.265
First Half	156	43	8	26	.276	Sc Pos	59	12	0	17	.203
Scnd Half	79	17	2	5	.215	Clutch	41	11	0	4	.268

1996 Season

Looking for someone who could come off the bench and provide insurance at designated hitter, the Rangers signed veteran Warren Newson. The Deacon provided some good moments when he was in the lineup, but uncharacteristally fell short as a pinch hitter (3-for-17). His defense was a problem when he filled in for Rusty Greer or Juan Gonzalez in the outfield.

Hitting, Baserunning & Defense

Newson is a patient hitter who will wait for a fastball he likes. He draws a high number of walks, but he'll also swing and miss on a lot of those heaters, resulting in numerous strikeouts. Newson's a line-drive hitter with power to all fields. He has never hit lefthanders, and did a poor job of hitting in the clutch last year. His fireplug body doesn't provide any speed on the bases or range in the outfield, but he's an intelligent player who almost always makes the smart play.

1997 Outlook

Newson won't command a large salary, but should have a job somewhere. Comfortable as a role player coming off the bench, he should be an asset to anyone's bench.

Jeff Russell

Position: RP
Bats: R **Throws:** R
Ht: 6' 3" **Wt:** 205

Opening Day Age: 35
Born: 9/2/61 in
Cincinnati, OH
ML Seasons: 14

Overall Statistics

	W	L	Pct.	ERA	G	GS	Sv	IP	H	BB	SO	HR	BR/IP
1996	3	3	.500	3.38	55	0	3	56.0	58	22	23	5	1.43
Career	56	73	.434	3.75	589	79	186	1099.2	1065	415	693	100	1.35

1996 Situational Stats

	W	L	ERA	Sv	IP		AB	H	HR	RBI	Avg
Home	1	2	3.49	2	28.1	LHB	85	28	2	12	.329
Road	2	1	3.25	1	27.2	RHB	131	30	3	19	.229
First Half	1	1	4.30	1	29.1	Sc Pos	66	16	2	27	.242
Scnd Half	2	2	2.36	2	26.2	Clutch	132	35	3	15	.265

1996 Season

You can't tell it by looking at his statistics, but it was a dream season for Jeff Russell. He not only helped Texas win its first division title, but he did it without having to undergo the weekly cortisone shots that he endured in 1995. Relinquishing the closer's job to Mike Henneman, Russell pitched adequately as a set-up man.

Pitching & Defense

Russell no longer blows hitters away with the fastball, which now tops out below 90 MPH. He also throws a slider and an occasional split-fingered fastball, but his command of those pitches last season wasn't good enough to keep left-handed hitters from sitting on his fastball and doing damage. He can still be tough on righthanders. Russell's delivery makes him tough to run on. He is a good athlete, but doesn't move around the mound as well as he once did.

1997 Outlook

Winning an American League West title was special to Russell, who is the Rangers' all-time leader in games. He probably would return for another season, but there's no guarantee of a job when general manager Doug Melvin finishes rebuilding his bullpen.

Dave Valle

Position: C
Bats: R **Throws:** R
Ht: 6' 2" **Wt:** 220

Opening Day Age: 36
Born: 10/30/60 in Bayside, NY
ML Seasons: 13
Pronunciation: VAL-ee

Overall Statistics

	G	AB	R	H	D	T	HR	RBI	SB	BB	SO	Avg	OBP	Slg
1996	42	86	14	26	6	1	3	17	0	9	17	.302	.368	.500
Career	970	2775	314	658	121	12	77	350	5	258	413	.237	.314	.373

1996 Situational Stats

	AB	H	HR	RBI	Avg		AB	H	HR	RBI	Avg
Home	44	13	0	7	.295	LHP	22	11	2	10	.500
Road	42	13	3	10	.310	RHP	64	15	1	7	.234
First Half	43	12	1	8	.279	Sc Pos	25	12	2	16	.480
Scnd Half	43	14	2	9	.326	Clutch	6	2	0	0	.333

1996 Season

Dave Valle should be thankful that there are less demanding jobs than being Ivan Rodriguez's backup. He could be Telly Savalas' barber or Dennis Rodman's publicist. Valle hit surprisingly well on the rare occasions when he was in the lineup last year. Still, Johnny Oates wasn't tempted to use him as a pinch hitter.

Hitting, Baserunning & Defense

Valle gets fed a steady diet of fastballs, and he made pitchers pay for it last year. He has a short stroke that allows him to put the ball in play. He has never had much speed, but has become even more of a base-clogger as he progresses in years. Behind the plate, he knows the pitchers almost as well as Rodriguez and does a good job handling the staff. His throwing arm is now average at best.

1997 Outlook

Valle's two-year contract expired after last season. He doesn't have many, if any, years left, though he is coming off an excellent season in a limited role. He could return for one more year as Rodriguez's backup, which would allow prospect Kevin Brown to spend a year at Triple-A Oklahoma City.

Ed Vosberg

Position: RP
Bats: L **Throws:** L
Ht: 6' 1" **Wt:** 190

Opening Day Age: 35
Born: 9/28/61 in Tucson, AZ
ML Seasons: 5

Overall Statistics

	W	L	Pct.	ERA	G	GS	Sv	IP	H	BB	SO	HR	BR/IP
1996	1	1	.500	3.27	52	0	8	44.0	51	21	32	4	1.64
Career	7	10	.412	4.03	135	3	12	131.2	137	63	100	13	1.52

1996 Situational Stats

	W	L	ERA	Sv	IP		AB	H	HR	RBI	Avg
Home	0	0	1.75	5	25.2	LHB	67	17	2	14	.254
Road	1	1	5.40	3	18.1	RHB	104	34	2	9	.327
First Half	0	0	2.86	5	22.0	Sc Pos	56	15	1	20	.268
Scnd Half	1	1	3.68	3	22.0	Clutch	75	21	1	10	.280

1996 Season

Ed Vosberg could be forgiven if he grew complacent in 1996. It marked the first time since 1987-88 that he returned to the locale where he pitched the previous year. Vosberg quietly did his part in a bullpen that depended on all its parts. He was second on the club to Mike Henneman in saves, but spent most of the year as a set-up man. It was a good year for a late bloomer.

Pitching & Defense

Vosberg's best pitch is a curveball that sharply breaks down and away from left-handed hitters. It can be almost unhittable. Vosberg's fastball is average, which leaves him nibbling around the edges of the strike zone when he is missing with the curve. He does a good job fielding his position and has a textbook pickoff move. He did not allow a steal last year.

1997 Outlook

Vosberg figures to return as an integral part of the Rangers' bullpen because Johnny Oates loves having three lefties there. He is unlikely to get as many save opportunities if Mike Stanton, who was acquired from Boston in a late-season trade, returns for another season.

Texas Rangers

Other Texas Rangers

Jose Alberro (Pos: RHP, Age: 27)

	W	L	Pct.	ERA	G	GS	Sv	IP	H	BB	SO	HR	BR/IP
1996	0	1	.000	5.79	5	1	0	9.1	14	7	2	1	2.25
Career	0	1	.000	6.90	17	1	0	30.0	40	19	12	3	1.97

Switched from relieving to a starter's role while at Triple-A Oklahoma City in 1995, Alberro had a good year for the 89ers in 1996. Has not shown much in two major league trials. 1997 Outlook: C

Rikkert Faneyte (Pos: CF, Age: 27, Bats: R)

	G	AB	R	H	D	T	HR	RBI	SB	BB	SO	Avg	OBP	Slg
1996	8	5	0	1	0	0	0	1	0	0	0	.200	.200	.200
Career	80	132	10	23	7	1	0	9	1	16	42	.174	.264	.242

Once considered a pretty good prospect by the Giants, Faneyte joined the Rangers last year and struggled at Triple-A Oklahoma City, hitting .236. He can run and field, but that isn't enough. 1997 Outlook: D

Lou Frazier (Pos: LF/DH, Age: 32, Bats: B)

	G	AB	R	H	D	T	HR	RBI	SB	BB	SO	Avg	OBP	Slg
1996	30	50	5	13	2	1	0	5	4	8	10	.260	.373	.340
Career	302	541	82	138	16	3	1	46	54	57	89	.255	.332	.301

Frazier has no power, but he can run, pinch hit and play several positions. The Rangers don't seem to think much of him, though, and he spent most of the year in the minors. 1997 Outlook: C

Benji Gil (Pos: SS, Age: 24, Bats: R)

	G	AB	R	H	D	T	HR	RBI	SB	BB	SO	Avg	OBP	Slg
1996	5	5	0	2	0	0	0	1	0	1	1	.400	.500	.400
Career	157	477	39	100	20	3	9	49	3	32	170	.210	.260	.321

Expected to be the Ranger shortstop last year, Gil came down with back problems, and by the time he was ready to return, Kevin Elster had won the position. Only 24, he could win the job back this year. 1997 Outlook: A

Rene Gonzales (Pos: 1B/3B, Age: 35, Bats: R)

	G	AB	R	H	D	T	HR	RBI	SB	BB	SO	Avg	OBP	Slg
1996	51	92	19	20	4	0	2	5	0	10	11	.217	.288	.326
Career	703	1537	185	367	59	4	19	135	23	161	230	.239	.314	.319

The versatile Gonzales got into 51 games for the Rangers last year, but could never find his batting stroke. He'll try to make the Padres roster this spring, but at 35 the clock is ticking. 1997 Outlook: C

Lee Stevens (Pos: 1B, Age: 29, Bats: L)

	G	AB	R	H	D	T	HR	RBI	SB	BB	SO	Avg	OBP	Slg
1996	27	78	6	18	2	3	3	12	0	6	22	.231	.291	.449
Career	218	696	67	157	38	3	17	90	3	63	173	.226	.289	.362

After returning from Japan, Stevens signed a minor league contract with the Rangers last year and got a chance with Texas when Will Clark got hurt. Has power, and might get a chance with someone. 1997 Outlook: C

Kurt Stillwell (Pos: 2B, Age: 31, Bats: B)

	G	AB	R	H	D	T	HR	RBI	SB	BB	SO	Avg	OBP	Slg
1996	46	77	12	21	4	0	1	4	0	10	11	.273	.364	.364
Career	998	3125	362	779	151	30	34	310	38	274	455	.249	.311	.349

Another of the Rangers' "Back from the Dead" pickups last year, Stillwell filled in at several positions and made a nice contribution. Could make a club as a utility infielder this year. 1997 Outlook: C

Jack Voigt (Pos: LF, Age: 30, Bats: R)

	G	AB	R	H	D	T	HR	RBI	SB	BB	SO	Avg	OBP	Slg
1996	5	9	1	1	0	0	0	0	0	0	2	.111	.111	.111
Career	165	365	57	91	19	1	11	51	1	53	74	.249	.344	.397

Voigt has played for Johnny Oates with both the Orioles and Rangers, but he spent most of '96 at Oklahoma City, where he had a fine year. Has fine offensive skills, and might latch on with someone. 1997 Outlook: C

Matt Whiteside (Pos: RHP, Age: 29)

	W	L	Pct.	ERA	G	GS	Sv	IP	H	BB	SO	HR	BR/IP
1996	0	1	.000	6.68	14	0	0	32.1	43	11	15	8	1.67
Career	10	9	.526	4.48	181	0	9	247.1	263	92	150	27	1.44

Once one of the Rangers' primary relievers, Whiteside came down with elbow problems, began to struggle, and wound up back in the minors. He'll get another chance this spring. 1997 Outlook: C

Craig Worthington (Pos: 3B, Age: 31, Bats: R)

	G	AB	R	H	D	T	HR	RBI	SB	BB	SO	Avg	OBP	Slg
1996	13	19	2	3	0	0	1	4	0	6	3	.158	.333	.316
Career	393	1234	126	284	50	0	33	144	3	162	264	.230	.322	.351

A one-time major league regular who's now strictly a fringe player, Worthington got one last chance with the Rangers last year but drew his release in June. Probably out of major league chances. 1997 Outlook: D

Texas Rangers Minor League Prospects

Organization Overview:

The well has run dry in Texas in recent years. The Rangers have a few good prospects who are poised to break through in the next year or two, but if they don't make it, Texas will be out of luck. Their upper levels are littered with career minor leaguers, and while the Rangers did draft well last year, the impact won't be felt for a few years. Their system was woefully short of pitching prospects, even before a couple of trades cost them several of their better young arms last year. Their top prospects divided themselves into two groups last year: one group developed more quickly than expected, and the other stalled completely. The Rangers didn't have a large number of talented youngsters to begin with, so the rash of setbacks was especially troublesome.

Mike Bell

Position: 3B
Bats: R **Throws:** R
Ht: 6' 2" **Wt:** 185

Opening Day Age: 22
Born: 12/7/74 in Cincinnati, OH

Recent Statistics

	G	AB	R	H	D	T	HR	RBI	SB	BB	SO	AVG
93 R Rangers	60	230	48	73	13	6	3	34	9	27	23	.317
94 A Charlstn-SC	120	475	58	125	22	6	6	58	16	47	76	.263
95 A Charlotte	129	470	49	122	20	1	5	52	9	48	72	.260
96 AA Tulsa	128	484	62	129	31	3	16	59	3	42	75	.267
96 MLE	128	471	54	116	27	2	12	51	2	31	80	.246

The "other" son of Buddy Bell made good progress at Double-A last year. He improved his power numbers, and cut down on his throwing errors. Bell doesn't have spectacular tools, but he's solid across the board, and fundamentally sound. He's got good range and a strong arm at third base, and his power may be enough to get him to the majors. He isn't fast and won't hit for a great average, so he'll need to keep improving his run production.

Kevin L. Brown

Position: C
Bats: R **Throws:** R
Ht: 6' 2" **Wt:** 200

Opening Day Age: 23
Born: 4/21/73 in Valparaiso, IN

Recent Statistics

	G	AB	R	H	D	T	HR	RBI	SB	BB	SO	AVG
96 AA Tulsa	128	460	77	121	27	1	26	86	0	73	150	.263
96 AL Texas	3	4	1	0	0	0	0	1	0	2	2	.000
96 MLE	128	447	67	108	24	0	20	75	0	54	160	.242

Not only does Kevin Brown have a big league name, he's got big league power. A second-round pick in '94, the big receiver has curbed his free-swinging tendencies enough to emerge as a serious longball prospect. His defense is not nearly as promising; despite a strong throwing arm, his receiving skills are adequate at best. The Rangers envision him as a part-time catcher and full-time hitter.

Edwin Diaz

Position: 2B
Bats: R **Throws:** R
Ht: 5' 11" **Wt:** 170

Opening Day Age: 22
Born: 1/15/75 in Bayamon, PR

Recent Statistics

	G	AB	R	H	D	T	HR	RBI	SB	BB	SO	AVG
93 R Rangers	43	154	27	47	10	5	1	23	12	19	21	.305
94 A Charlstn-SC	122	413	52	109	22	7	11	60	11	22	107	.264
95 A Charlotte	115	450	48	128	26	5	8	56	8	33	94	.284
96 AA Tulsa	121	499	70	132	33	6	16	65	8	25	122	.265
96 MLE	121	486	61	119	29	5	12	56	5	18	130	.245

Edwin Diaz has an intriguing mix of strengths and weaknesses. On one hand, he's got great bat speed, and possesses good power for someone so young. But on the other hand, he may not have the defensive skills to remain at second base, and he just can't lay off pitches out of the strike zone. He's got good speed, and his bat alone could easily get him to the majors. However, if he's forced to move to another position, the offensive demands will be even greater. This year will be a crucial one in his development.

Jonathan Johnson

Position: P
Bats: R **Throws:** R
Ht: 6' 0" **Wt:** 180

Opening Day Age: 22
Born: 7/16/74 in Ocala, FL

Recent Statistics

	W	L	ERA	G	GS	Sv	IP	H	R	BB	SO	HR
95 A Charlotte	1	5	2.70	8	7	0	43.1	34	14	16	25	2
96 AAA Okla. City	1	0	0.00	1	1	0	9.0	2	0	1	6	0
96 AA Tulsa	13	10	3.56	26	25	0	174.1	176	86	41	97	15

In the early 90s, the Rangers were repeatedly burned when they selected raw "tools" players high in the draft. In '95, they decided to go in the exact opposite direction, and took righthander Jonathan Johnson with their first pick. He'd been a successful pitcher in college, and seemed close to the majors, although his ceiling wasn't all that high for a first-rounder. A year later, the same estimation holds true. He's got an average fastball and a good curve, and he knows how to use them. He's ready to break through, but he probably won't ever be a number-one starter.

Mark Little

Position: OF
Bats: R **Throws:** R
Ht: 6' 0" **Wt:** 200

Opening Day Age: 24
Born: 7/11/72 in
Edwardsville, IL

Recent Statistics

	G	AB	R	H	D	T	HR	RBI	SB	BB	SO	AVG
94 A Hudson Vall	54	208	33	61	15	5	3	27	14	22	38	.293
95 A Charlotte	115	438	75	112	31	8	9	50	20	51	108	.256
96 AA Tulsa	101	409	69	119	24	2	13	50	22	48	88	.291
96 MLE	101	398	60	108	21	1	10	43	15	35	94	.271

If the Rangers' center field spot opens up this year, Mark Little could be a dark-horse candidate. He's one of the fastest players in the Rangers' system, and last year, he was named the best defensive outfielder in the Texas League. The guy can hit a little, too—he hits for a decent average with a little power. All in all, he's already advanced enough to be a solid big league center fielder. At age 24, he may have a little bit more development left in him.

Danny Patterson

Position: P
Bats: R **Throws:** R
Ht: 6' 0" **Wt:** 168

Opening Day Age: 26
Born: 2/17/71 in San
Gabriel, CA

Recent Statistics

	W	L	ERA	G	GS	Sv	IP	H	R	BB	SO	HR
96 AAA Okla. City	6	2	1.68	44	0	10	80.1	79	22	15	53	5
96 AL Texas	0	0	0.00	7	0	0	8.2	10	4	3	5	0

Righthander Danny Patterson missed most of '95 following elbow surgery, but rebounded last year to become one of their best pitching prospects. He throws a fastball, a slider, and what he calls a "vulcan splitter,"a pitch held between the middle and ring fingers. He's got good control of it, and there's been talk that the Rangers might even give him a chance to be their closer next year. At the very least, he should be able to help them in a set-up role.

Julio Santana

Position: P
Bats: R **Throws:** R
Ht: 6' 0" **Wt:** 175

Opening Day Age: 24
Born: 1/20/73 in San
Pedro De Macoris, DR

Recent Statistics

	W	L	ERA	G	GS	Sv	IP	H	R	BB	SO	HR
93 R Rangers	4	1	1.38	26	0	7	39.0	31	9	7	50	0
94 A Charlstn-SC	6	7	2.46	16	16	0	91.1	65	38	44	103	3
94 AA Tulsa	7	2	2.90	11	11	0	71.1	50	26	41	45	1
95 AAA Okla. City	0	2	39.00	2	2	0	3.0	9	14	7	6	3
95 A Charlotte	0	3	3.73	5	5	0	31.1	32	16	16	27	1

95 AA Tulsa	6	4	3.23	15	15	0	103.0	91	40	52	71	8
96 AAA Okla. City	11	12	4.02	29	29	0	185.2	171	102	66	113	12

Julio Santana was the Rangers' top pitching prospect before the '96 season, but his indifferent performance at Triple-A didn't even merit a September call-up. He showed up to camp out of shape, and during the season, he made no progress in refining his command of his 90-MPH fastball. He'll have to learn to locate his heater, because his breaking pitch and offspeed pitch are not very useful. He's got good upside potential, but it's about time we saw some signs of progress.

Theodore Silva

Position: P
Bats: R **Throws:** R
Ht: 6' 0" **Wt:** 170

Opening Day Age: 22
Born: 8/4/74 in
Inglewood, CA

Recent Statistics

	W	L	ERA	G	GS	Sv	IP	H	R	BB	SO	HR
95 A Charlstn-SC	5	4	3.38	11	11	0	66.2	59	26	12	66	4
96 A Charlotte	10	2	2.86	16	16	0	113.1	98	39	27	95	9
96 AA Tulsa	7	2	2.99	11	11	0	75.1	72	27	16	27	5

Righthander Ted Silva surprised everyone by compiling a combined 17-4 record at two levels last year. Still, there was some concern that he might hit the wall in the higher levels of the system. He continued pitching well after his promotion to Double-A, but the dropoff in his strikeout rate was alarming. He's not overpowering, and doesn't have a high ceiling. Still, he was a huge success in his first full year out of college, and he may continue to surprise.

Others to Watch

A year ago, outfielder **Andrew Vessel** was being compared to a young Dave Parker. However, after he showed up in camp looking like an *old* Parker, the Rangers shipped him back to A-ball. He played without intensity, suffered a groin pull, and his wasted season leaves his prospect status in doubt. . . Righthander **Dan Kolb** has an outstanding fastball, and probably will begin the year in Double-A at age 22. . . Right fielder **Mark Sagmoen** rebounded from a poor '95 season to hit 15 homers in Double-A and Triple-A. At age 26, he projects as a role player. . . Young shortstop **Hanley Frias** showed good range and a solid bat at Double-A. A switch-hitter, Frias may be next in line when Kevin Elster returns to earth. . . Righthander **Jeff Davis** missed half the season with an injury, but the converted reliever went 7-2 in 15 starts at Double-A.

Cito Gaston

1996 Season

Cito Gaston has long been known as the quintessential player's manager. While he is often criticized for being too laid back, he has the unequivocal support of his players, especially his star performers. This philosophy has earned him two World Series rings, but is being tested by the host of young, inexperienced players now on the Toronto roster. Under those circumstances, the Jays' performance in 1996 has to be rated as positive.

Offense

Gaston is a big believer in platooning, and with so many youngsters on this squad, it's easy to see why. Gaston is conservative in his game tactics, but uses the hit-and-run and the sacrifice in appropriate situations. He is very quick to pull hitters out of the lineup for pinch hitters, trying to play the percentages with lefty vs. righty match-ups.

Pitching & Defense

Gaston's supportive style occasionally leads to criticism that he allows his starters to stay in too long. He owns the league's most durable starter in Pat Hentgen, but several games got away from the Jays in 1996 because of big middle innings by the opposition with his starters still in the game, suggesting Gaston should have gone to his bullpen earlier. His "players-first" style also means that Gaston believes in the one-man, one-job philosophy with his closer and his set-up men. However, he is far less patient with rookies. Gaston is conventional with his defensive substitutions.

1997 Outlook

Gaston had his contract extended for another year, and he will be out to prove that he can develop his young players into major leaguers while keeping the team competitive. He will get more support from G.M. Gord Ash with free agents, which should lighten the load. He figures to be more aggressive with the running game, considering the club's power limitations.

Born: 3/17/44 in San Antonio, TX

Playing Experience: 1967-1978, Atl, SD, Pit

Managerial Experience: 8 seasons

Manager Statistics

Year	Team, Lg	W	L	Pct	GB	Finish
1996	Toronto, AL	74	88	.457	18.0	4th East
8 Seasons		611	551	.526	—	—

1996 Starting Pitchers by Days Rest

	≤3	4	5	6+
Blue Jays Starts	1	99	35	17
Blue Jays ERA	1.13	4.40	4.94	6.11
AL Avg Starts	4	96	30	21
AL ERA	5.57	4.90	5.33	5.81

1996 Situational Stats

	Cito Gaston	AL Average
Hit & Run Success %	33.3	39.1
Stolen Base Success %	75.3	69.6
Platoon Pct.	69.7	61.9
Defensive Subs	11	29
High-Pitch Outings	23	23
Quick/Slow Hooks	12/27	17/20
Sacrifice Attempts	63	58

1996 Rankings (American League)

→ 1st in least caught steals of third base (3)
→ 3rd in stolen base percentage (75.3%), steals of third base (24) and slow hooks (27)

Joe Carter

1996 Season

Joe Carter remained the key RBI man in the Blue Jays' lineup in 1996, knocking in 100-plus runs for the seventh time in the last eight years. With the Jays re-tooling their ballclub by fielding an inexperienced team, Carter's role took on added significance: the productive veteran was called upon to provide leadership. He played nearly every game, but seemed to tire during the second half of the season.

Hitting

Carter is still a dead-red low fastball hitter who has tried to hit more to the opposite field in order to cope with all of the outside pitches he receives. The results have been mixed, primarily due to his lack of plate coverage. Carter is more comfortable when he pulls the ball and can still generate good power. His bat speed has slowed somewhat, however, and in addition to struggling with outside breaking balls, he has trouble with the high heater.

Baserunning & Defense

Carter's production on the basepaths is not bad for a 37-year-old player. He doesn't have the stolen-base success ratio he once had, but he legs out the extra bases extremely well. He alternated between first base and the outfield more often last year, and while he's not a liability, he does not possess great defensive skills either. He *does* have decent arm strength but is not accurate enough with his throws, and runners will try and take advantage.

1997 Outlook

Carter is one of the few Blue Jays in recent memory to have his contract extended during a regular season. This illustrates the good faith management has in the veteran slugger. While Carter's power production is still likely to be formidable, his batting average continues to hover in the .250 range. He hopes to improve that figure by hitting the opposite way with better success.

Position: LF/1B/DH
Bats: R **Throws:** R
Ht: 6' 3" **Wt:** 215

Opening Day Age: 37
Born: 3/7/60 in Oklahoma City, OK
ML Seasons: 14

Overall Statistics

	G	AB	R	H	D	T	HR	RBI	SB	BB	SO	Avg	OBP	Slg
1996	157	625	84	158	35	7	30	107	7	44	106	.253	.306	.475
Career	1906	7422	1043	1940	380	48	357	1280	219	463	1221	.261	.308	.470

Where He Hits the Ball

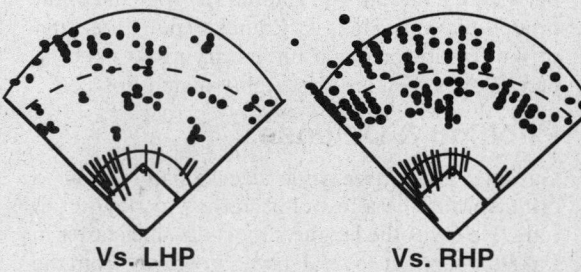

Vs. LHP   **Vs. RHP**

1996 Situational Stats

	AB	H	HR	RBI	Avg		AB	H	HR	RBI	Avg
Home	321	77	14	52	.240	LHP	166	41	6	24	.247
Road	304	81	16	55	.266	RHP	459	117	24	83	.255
First Half	342	97	20	70	.284	Sc Pos	174	48	12	76	.276
Scnd Half	283	61	10	37	.216	Clutch	91	23	3	14	.253

1996 Rankings (American League)

→ 1st in lowest fielding percentage in left field (.961) and lowest percentage of pitches taken (42.6%)

→ 2nd in lowest groundball/flyball ratio (0.6) and errors in left field (7)

→ 4th in highest percentage of swings on the first pitch (41.2%)

→ 5th in lowest on-base percentage

→ 7th in triples

→ 8th in at-bats

→ 9th in lowest cleanup slugging percentage (.490), lowest on-base percentage vs. right-handed pitchers (.307) and lowest batting average

→ 10th in lowest batting average at home (.240)

Tim Crabtree

1996 Season

Just after he had evolved into the Blue Jays' primary set-up reliever, Tim Crabtree developed bone chips in his elbow, cutting his season short. Crabtree first showed promise during the 1995 season and successfully built on that performance by posting a superb 2.54 ERA with 17 holds in 1996. He was consistent and reliable up until the time of his injury, doing much to boost the caliber of Toronto's late-inning relief corps.

Pitching

Crabtree uses a 92 MPH sinking fastball to induce a lot of ground balls. His secondary pitch is a hard slider, used with great effectiveness to right-handed hitters. When he keeps the slider low and away, it's another good groundball pitch. He is effective against left-handed hitters by using the inside part of the plate, and he always seems to keep the ball down. Though he's still working on it, he has also come up with a circle change to enhance his pitch selection and strikeout totals. He has good control, working a high percentage of favorable counts and keeping the ball in the yard.

Defense

Holding runners is not one of Crabtree's assets. He has a straight delivery to the plate using the traditional leg kick, and runners can take advantage of him. However, he is a good fielding pitcher and very mobile coming off the mound. He can cover first base effectively, as well as charge in for the bunt.

1997 Outlook

Crabtree expects to be ready for spring training after undergoing arthroscopic surgery on his pitching elbow last September. He is an integral part of the Blue Jays' bullpen and could be relied upon to take over the closer's role should Toronto lose Mike Timlin anytime soon. For now, he will remain in his key set-up role as he continues to develop more pitches.

Position: RP
Bats: R **Throws:** R
Ht: 6' 4" **Wt:** 195

Opening Day Age: 27
Born: 10/13/69 in Jackson, MI
ML Seasons: 2

Overall Statistics

	W	L	Pct.	ERA	G	GS	Sv	IP	H	BB	SO	HR	BR/IP
1996	5	3	.625	2.54	53	0	1	67.1	59	22	57	4	1.20
Career	5	5	.500	2.72	84	0	1	99.1	89	35	78	5	1.25

How Often He Throws Strikes

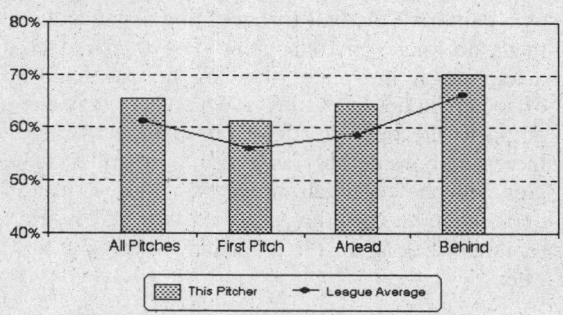

1996 Situational Stats

	W	L	ERA	Sv	IP		AB	H	HR	RBI	Avg
Home	4	2	1.36	1	33.0	LHB	119	27	1	13	.227
Road	1	1	3.67	0	34.1	RHB	136	32	3	19	.235
First Half	3	2	2.27	1	43.2	Sc Pos	82	19	0	25	.232
Scnd Half	2	1	3.04	0	23.2	Clutch	161	43	3	24	.267

1996 Rankings (American League)

- → 5th in relief ERA (2.54)
- → 7th in holds (17) and least baserunners allowed per 9 innings in relief (11.2)
- → 10th in worst first batter efficiency (.300)
- → Led the Blue Jays in holds (17) and relief ERA (2.54)

Carlos Delgado

1996 Season

Expected to become the next power source in the Toronto lineup, Carlos Delgado showed sparks of brilliance in the first half of 1996. He slugged 15 homers and drove in 60 runs by the All-Star break. Despite cooling off considerably in the latter half, Delgado played regularly for the first time in his career and became a cornerstone of the batting order, hitting in the number-three spot for much of the season.

Hitting

Delgado came into the league as a one-dimensional fastball hitter who was unable to handle the curveball. He still remains a potent fastball threat who can drive the ball for awesome distance, but that's no longer his only hope. He improved his discipline at the plate, showing he can handle offspeed pitches by cutting down on his swing and going to the opposite field. His batting average increased considerably as a result. He still struggles with the curveball, however, and is a sitting duck when he is in the hole with two strikes. He remains weak against lefthanders, striking out too often.

Baserunning & Defense

Used exclusively at first base when not a DH, Delgado has a pretty good glove, but does not have much quickness in either direction in the field. His speed is limited, and he did not attempt a single steal in 1996. He is the type of baserunner who will play it safe and hold up rather than forcing the throw.

1997 Outlook

The Blue Jays are depending on Delgado to be one of their key offensive threats. His home-run power got him to this point, and his rapid improvement in batting average—if it continues—could take him to the next level. He must improve against lefties if he is to continue his progress; otherwise he's in danger of becoming a platoon player.

Position: DH/1B
Bats: L **Throws:** R
Ht: 6' 3" **Wt:** 206

Opening Day Age: 24
Born: 6/25/72 in Aguadilla, PR
ML Seasons: 4

Overall Statistics

	G	AB	R	H	D	T	HR	RBI	SB	BB	SO	Avg	OBP	Slg
1996	138	488	68	132	28	2	25	92	0	58	139	.270	.353	.490
Career	220	710	92	175	33	2	37	127	1	90	211	.246	.337	.455

Where He Hits the Ball

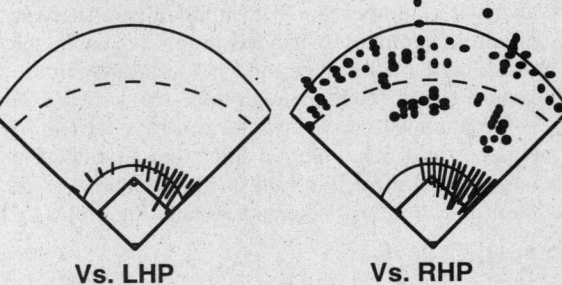

Vs. LHP   **Vs. RHP**

1996 Situational Stats

	AB	H	HR	RBI	Avg		AB	H	HR	RBI	Avg
Home	241	68	12	39	.282	LHP	92	14	2	10	.152
Road	247	64	13	53	.259	RHP	396	118	23	82	.298
First Half	285	82	15	60	.288	Sc Pos	130	38	9	71	.292
Scnd Half	203	50	10	32	.246	Clutch	76	15	3	9	.197

1996 Rankings (American League)

→ 3rd in lowest percentage of swings put into play (34.1%)
→ 8th in strikeouts and highest percentage of swings that missed (28.5%)
→ 10th in hit by pitch (9)
→ Led the Blue Jays in sacrifice flies (8), GDPs (13), most pitches seen per plate appearance (4.09), batting average with runners in scoring position (.292), batting average with the bases loaded (.455), batting average vs. right-handed pitchers (.298), slugging percentage vs. right-handed pitchers (.538), batting average at home (.282) and lowest percentage of swings on the first pitch (28.1%)

Alex Gonzalez

1996 Season

Alex Gonzalez's sophomore season was very similar to his rookie year; he hit for a very slight .235 average and continued to make a high number of errors in the field. On the plus side, Gonzalez hit for more power and played most of the season at a demanding position without wearing down. He found himself at the bottom of the order after some experimentation at the number-two spot.

Hitting

Gonzalez is a free swinger who strikes out often, but one who hits with excellent power for a middle infielder. He stands away from the plate, which results in opposing pitchers feeding him a high percentage of outside offerings. He has great difficulty with the outside slider as well as the fastball up and in. To his credit, Gonzalez knows how to go the opposite way, although with only moderate success. His primary fault is that he overswings, leading to plenty of whiffs and ground balls.

Baserunning & Defense

Gonzalez is a good basestealer, and with more opportunities he could probably achieve some significant numbers. He rarely gets caught and has excellent first-step quickness. That same quickness is his biggest asset at shortstop as well. He covers as much ground as anyone in the league and has a bazooka for an arm. It's his unsteady glove which has held him back from becoming an elite middle infielder.

1997 Outlook

Gonzalez is still viewed as part of the Blue Jays' re-tooling plans, and after two major league seasons, the jury is still out on whether or not he will break through. He will turn just 24 years old this year, but he will be under more scrutiny from the Jays' front office than ever before. He must work on his plate discipline if he ever hopes to fulfill his potential as a hitter.

Position: SS
Bats: R **Throws:** R
Ht: 6' 0" **Wt:** 182

Opening Day Age: 23
Born: 4/8/73 in Miami, FL
ML Seasons: 3

Overall Statistics

	G	AB	R	H	D	T	HR	RBI	SB	BB	SO	Avg	OBP	Slg
1996	147	527	64	124	30	5	14	64	16	45	127	.235	.300	.391
Career	273	947	122	221	52	10	24	107	23	93	258	.233	.305	.385

Where He Hits the Ball

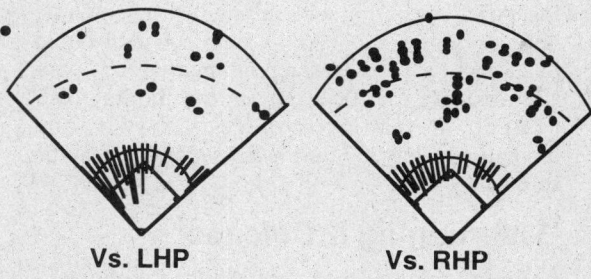

Vs. LHP   **Vs. RHP**

1996 Situational Stats

	AB	H	HR	RBI	Avg		AB	H	HR	RBI	Avg
Home	270	56	3	32	.207	LHP	163	41	3	17	.252
Road	257	68	11	32	.265	RHP	364	83	11	47	.228
First Half	297	72	6	35	.242	Sc Pos	133	32	2	43	.241
Scnd Half	230	52	8	29	.226	Clutch	90	17	3	12	.189

1996 Rankings (American League)

- ➡ 1st in lowest batting average at home (.207) and lowest batting average
- ➡ 3rd in lowest batting average vs. right-handed pitchers (.228)
- ➡ 4th in lowest on-base percentage, lowest on-base percentage vs. right-handed pitchers (.296) and errors at shortstop (21)
- ➡ 7th in fielding percentage at shortstop (.973)
- ➡ 8th in steals of third (4)
- ➡ 10th in lowest slugging percentage vs. right-handed pitchers (.387)
- ➡ Led the Blue Jays in sacrifice bunts (7)

Shawn Green

1996 Season

On the heels of a promising rookie season in 1995, Shawn Green struggled mightily until after the All-Star break. By the end of the season, he was able to lift his batting average to a respectable .280, but he had to become a different type of hitter to do so. He was another example of manager Cito Gaston's platooning strategy, seldom playing against left-handed pitchers.

Hitting

Green started his 1996 campaign determined to become more of a power hitter. The experiment took its toll on Green's average, however. He came to the plate constantly trying to pull the ball and completely lost his stride against offspeed pitching. After consulting with hitting instructor Willie Upshaw, Green changed his approach and started to sit back on pitches, slapping them to the opposite field. He sacrificed power, but the improvement in his batting average was swift and dramatic: he hit .337 during the second half of the season.

Baserunning & Defense

As Green gains more experience, the Jays hope he will continue to smooth out the rough edges that persist with his defensive game. His judgment of fly balls sometimes is lacking, causing him to get rattled and look uncomfortable in the outfield. However, he does have good range and a solid throwing arm. He is also a fast runner, but does not steal very often at this early stage in his career. As he becomes more knowledgeable of pitchers' tendencies, he will become more of a threat.

1997 Outlook

Toronto is looking for some consistency from Green before they crown him their everyday right fielder. His performance in 1996 showed that he is best when playing the role of contact hitter rather than swinging for the fences. Entering his third season in the majors, he needs to improve his mental toughness when facing lefthanders and in pressure situations.

Position: RF
Bats: L **Throws:** L
Ht: 6' 4" **Wt:** 190

Opening Day Age: 24
Born: 11/10/72 in Des Plaines, IL
ML Seasons: 4

Overall Statistics

	G	AB	R	H	D	T	HR	RBI	SB	BB	SO	Avg	OBP	Slg
1996	132	422	52	118	32	3	11	45	5	33	75	.280	.342	.448
Career	270	840	105	230	64	7	26	100	7	54	152	.274	.324	.460

Where He Hits the Ball

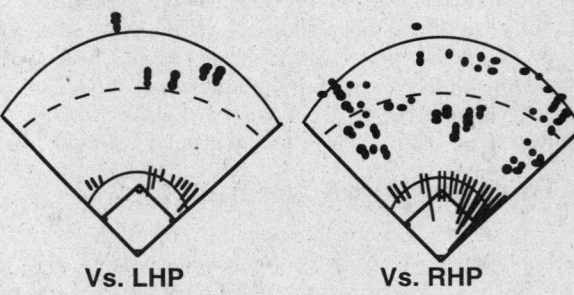

Vs. LHP　　　　**Vs. RHP**

1996 Situational Stats

	AB	H	HR	RBI	Avg		AB	H	HR	RBI	Avg
Home	202	55	7	20	.272	LHP	59	15	1	7	.254
Road	220	63	4	25	.286	RHP	363	103	10	38	.284
First Half	229	53	7	26	.231	Sc Pos	103	22	1	28	.214
Scnd Half	193	65	4	19	.337	Clutch	67	20	1	5	.299

1996 Rankings (American League)

→ 3rd in fielding percentage in right field (.992)
→ 4th in lowest batting average with runners in scoring position (.214)
→ 10th in lowest percentage of pitches taken (49.6%)
→ Led the Blue Jays in batting average in the clutch (.299)

Juan Guzman

1996 Season

After his dismal 1995 season, there was considerable doubt as to whether Juan Guzman would be re-signed by the Blue Jays for 1996. The Jays took a chance, and Guzman did not disappoint. He posted a league-best 2.93 ERA and built a winning record again. By getting back to the basics which made him one of the most dominant pitchers in the game three years ago, Guzman was able to bring back his high strikeout-to-walk ratio. He was finally derailed in September when he had to undergo an appendectomy.

Pitching

Guzman stopped being a power pitcher in 1995, losing velocity and showing a reluctance to pitch inside. In 1996, Guzman's fastball returned to 94 MPH and his slider was tougher than ever to hit, coming in at 87 MPH. Guzman still maintains a split-fingered pitch in his repertoire, using it primarily as a two-strike pitch. Catcher Charlie O'Brien deserves a lot of credit in getting Guzman to throw according to a plan instead of wandering off like he did in 1995. His pitch counts came down and his old effectiveness returned.

Defense

Guzman's biggest weakness is that he still has not worked on any type of move to first base. Runners take off almost at will because of his slow, predictable delivery to the plate. Although he is on the stocky side, he has decent fielding instincts and covers first base well.

1997 Outlook

Last winter, the Blue Jays were faced with a tough decision: offer Guzman 80 percent of his former salary as a minimum tender or lose him. It cost the Jays $2.2 million and they were rewarded. So was Guzman, who was given a new three-year, $15 million contract by the Jays after the season. Health permitting, he should continue to hold down the second spot in the rotation.

Position: SP
Bats: R **Throws:** R
Ht: 5'11" **Wt:** 195

Opening Day Age: 30
Born: 10/28/66 in Santo Domingo, DR
ML Seasons: 6
Pronunciation: GOOZ-man

Overall Statistics

	W	L	Pct.	ERA	G	GS	Sv	IP	H	BB	SO	HR	BR/IP
1996	11	8	.579	2.93	27	27	0	187.2	158	53	165	20	1.12
Career	67	44	.604	3.97	160	160	0	1010.2	918	450	865	82	1.35

How Often He Throws Strikes

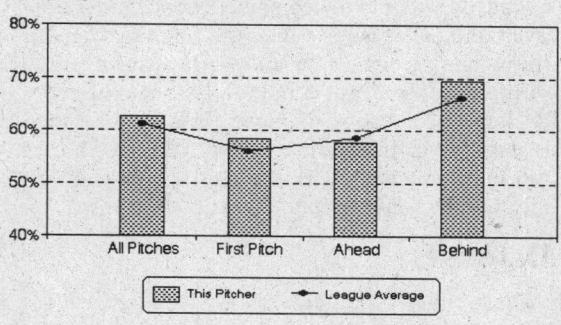

1996 Situational Stats

	W	L	ERA	Sv	IP		AB	H	HR	RBI	Avg
Home	4	3	3.71	0	87.1	LHB	353	79	8	27	.224
Road	7	5	2.24	0	100.1	RHB	339	79	12	32	.233
First Half	7	6	3.25	0	116.1	Sc Pos	136	27	4	38	.199
Scnd Half	4	2	2.40	0	71.1	Clutch	57	15	3	7	.263

1996 Rankings (American League)

→ 1st in ERA, highest strikeout/walk ratio (3.1), lowest batting average allowed (.228), lowest on-base percentage allowed (.289), least baserunners allowed per 9 innings (10.5) and ERA on the road (2.24)

→ 2nd in lowest batting average allowed vs. left-handed batters (.224) and lowest batting average allowed with runners in scoring position (.199)

→ 3rd in lowest slugging percentage allowed (.363), lowest batting average allowed vs. right-handed batters (.233) and errors at pitcher (3)

→ 4th in pickoff throws (166) and least run support per 9 innings (4.3)

Toronto Blue Jays

351

Erik Hanson

1996 Season

Erik Hanson came to the Blue Jays last season as a free agent expected to fill the void left by the departure of Al Leiter to Florida. The tall right-hander had trouble duplicating what he did for Boston in 1995. Hanson's biggest problem was allowing too many men to reach base. He had one of the worst baserunners-per-nine-innings ratios in the league until August, when he finally began throwing strikes more consistently.

Pitching

Hanson relies heavily on two breaking pitches: the backup slider and the curveball. His fastball is of moderate velocity—in the 88-89 MPH range—and he uses it only to keep hitters honest. The slow overhand curve is his punch-out pitch and he will throw it anywhere in the count. He is surprisingly vulnerable to right-handed batters when the backup slider hangs over the plate, and he then reverts to his uninspiring fastball. Hanson throws too many pitches, working high counts continually, and does not keep the ball down.

Defense

With so many baserunners to practice against, it's no wonder that Hanson has developed a good motion to first, along with a slide-step towards the plate. Basestealers were thrown out over 50 percent of the time against Hanson in 1996. However, he is an unreliable fielder who is prone to errors.

1997 Outlook

The Blue Jays prefer to look at Hanson's 1996 season as an off year and not indicative of what he can do for them. He signed a three-year deal and is locked in through 1998, but will have to show improvement if he expects to stay in Toronto beyond next season. He must work on his command of the strike zone by forcing the ball down more often in order to avoid surrendering such a high percentage of hits and walks.

Position: SP
Bats: R **Throws:** R
Ht: 6' 6" **Wt:** 215

Opening Day Age: 31
Born: 5/18/65 in Kinnelon, NJ
ML Seasons: 9

Overall Statistics

	W	L	Pct.	ERA	G	GS	Sv	IP	H	BB	SO	HR	BR/IP
1996	13	17	.433	5.41	35	35	0	214.2	243	102	156	26	1.61
Career	89	81	.524	4.04	231	228	0	1491.1	1516	469	1136	126	1.33

How Often He Throws Strikes

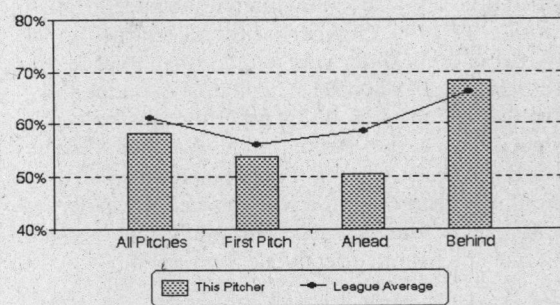

1996 Situational Stats

	W	L	ERA	Sv	IP		AB	H	HR	RBI	Avg
Home	5	7	5.31	0	96.2	LHB	425	114	13	61	.268
Road	8	10	5.49	0	118.0	RHB	417	129	13	63	.309
First Half	8	10	6.11	0	113.1	Sc Pos	215	66	6	89	.307
Scnd Half	5	7	4.62	0	101.1	Clutch	51	14	1	6	.275

1996 Rankings (American League)

→ 2nd in losses, games started and most GDPs induced per 9 innings (1.2)

→ 3rd in wild pitches (13), GDPs induced (28), lowest stolen base percentage allowed (40.0%) and errors at pitcher (3)

→ 4th in highest ERA, walks allowed, runners caught stealing (12) and highest on-base percentage allowed (.365)

→ 5th in highest batting average allowed vs. right-handed batters (.309)

→ 6th in shutouts (1), highest groundball/flyball ratio allowed (1.6) and most baserunners allowed per 9 innings (14.5)

→ 7th in lowest strikeout/walk ratio (1.5) and highest batting average allowed (.289)

Pat Hentgen

1996 Season

Many observers felt that Pat Hentgen was the best starting pitcher in the American League in 1996 and he was rewarded following the season with the Cy Young Award. Hentgen's only weakness was pitching for a mediocre team, but voters obviously discounted that in casting their ballots. The ace of the Blue Jays' staff led the league with 10 complete games, three shutouts and 265.2 innings pitched, and finished second in ERA to teammate Juan Guzman. His durability is remarkable; he topped the 200-inning mark for the third time in the past four seasons.

Pitching

Hentgen is a power pitcher who throws two of the best moving fastballs in the league. They serve as the key ingredients to his success. He has a terrific 92-93 MPH cutter which is very tough on left-handed hitters. His second fastball is a four-seamer which rises at 94 MPH and is his key out pitch when facing power hitters who are unable to lay off the letter-high heat. He employs an excellent slider and likes to throw a big overhand curve for effect. He even has an in-between pitch known as a slurve, which he will throw in a two-strike count.

Defense

Hentgen is very good at both holding runners and helping his catcher gun down would-be basestealers. He works quickly, uses a slide-step delivery from the set position and throws a lot of fastballs. He is close to being a flawless fielder, committing only one error in 1996, and covers first base in a hurry.

1997 Outlook

Hentgen turned around a lackluster 1995 campaign and again became one of the very best pitchers in the game. He improved his control of his breaking ball and will again be poised to start next season as the Blue Jays' ace starter. He is signed through the 1998 season, and with his stamina, that could mean a lot of wins.

Position: SP
Bats: R **Throws:** R
Ht: 6' 2" **Wt:** 200

Opening Day Age: 28
Born: 11/13/68 in Detroit, MI
ML Seasons: 6

Overall Statistics

	W	L	Pct.	ERA	G	GS	Sv	IP	H	BB	SO	HR	BR/IP
1996	20	10	.667	3.22	35	35	0	265.2	238	94	177	20	1.25
Career	67	43	.609	3.93	154	124	0	915.0	901	352	623	100	1.37

How Often He Throws Strikes

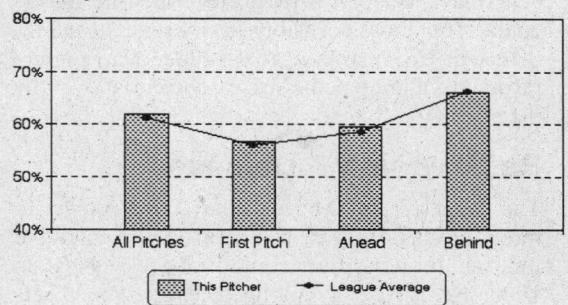

Legend: This Pitcher / League Average

1996 Situational Stats

	W	L	ERA	Sv	IP		AB	H	HR	RBI	Avg
Home	9	7	3.19	0	152.1	LHB	507	126	14	53	.249
Road	11	3	3.26	0	113.1	RHB	481	112	6	45	.233
First Half	8	6	3.86	0	133.0	Sc Pos	213	51	2	71	.239
Scnd Half	12	4	2.58	0	132.2	Clutch	99	23	1	8	.232

1996 Rankings (American League)

→ 1st in complete games (10), shutouts (3), innings pitched, batters faced (1,100), pickoff throws (205), lowest slugging percentage allowed (.355), least home runs allowed per 9 innings (.68) and ERA at home (3.19)

→ 2nd in ERA, wins, games started and lowest batting average allowed vs. right-handed batters (.233)

→ 3rd in pitches thrown (4,058) and lowest batting average allowed (.241)

→ 4th in ERA on the road (3.26)

→ 5th in winning percentage, lowest on-base percentage allowed (.308) and least baserunners allowed per 9 innings (11.4)

Toronto Blue Jays

Sandy Martinez

Position: C
Bats: L **Throws:** R
Ht: 6' 2" **Wt:** 200

Opening Day Age: 24
Born: 10/3/72 in Villa Mella, DR
ML Seasons: 2

1996 Season

When the Blue Jays made the decision to re-tool their ballclub last year and go with youth, it was reasonable to assume that Sandy Martinez would get more playing time in 1996 than he did in his rookie year. It didn't happen that way for two reasons: Martinez continued to struggle at the plate, and Charlie O'Brien proved to be too valuable to the pitching staff.

Hitting

Martinez is an undisciplined swinger who goes after a lot of pitches out of the strike zone. He seldom walks, strikes out often and hits for a low average. He is a powerfully built young man who can smack the ball a long way when he makes contact, but those occasions have been few and far between. He is strictly a pull hitter who prefers fastballs either up in the strike zone or out over the plate.

Baserunning & Defense

The biggest asset Martinez has is his powerful throwing arm. He was successful 35 percent of the time at throwing out would-be base stealers in 1996. He is also a mobile receiver who reacts quickly to balls thrown in the dirt, and does not make many fielding mistakes. Martinez runs fairly well for a catcher, but is never given the opportunity to steal.

1997 Outlook

Still part of the Blue Jays' future plans, Martinez hopes to make more progress in his third season. While many thought he was rushed up from Double-A in his rookie year due to extenuating circumstances (i.e., the Jays needed a catcher at the time), he must improve his hitting if he expects to stay around. He likely will play winter ball to give him more at-bats and to develop his timing, and with the signing of Benito Santiago, he should get plenty of time in the minors in 1997 to continue that development.

Overall Statistics

	G	AB	R	H	D	T	HR	RBI	SB	BB	SO	Avg	OBP	Slg
1996	76	229	17	52	9	3	3	18	0	16	58	.227	.288	.332
Career	138	420	29	98	21	3	5	43	0	23	103	.233	.280	.333

Where He Hits the Ball

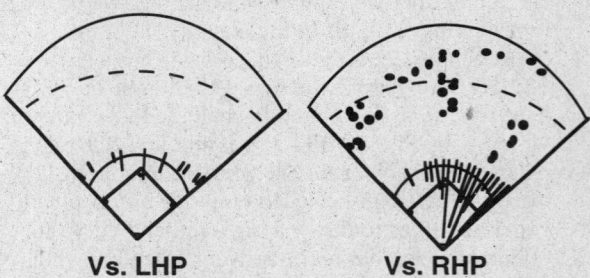

Vs. LHP   Vs. RHP

1996 Situational Stats

	AB	H	HR	RBI	Avg		AB	H	HR	RBI	Avg
Home	117	27	2	12	.231	LHP	42	10	1	4	.238
Road	112	25	1	6	.223	RHP	187	42	2	14	.225
First Half	151	36	2	14	.238	Sc Pos	54	9	0	15	.167
Scnd Half	78	16	1	4	.205	Clutch	35	6	0	1	.171

1996 Rankings (American League)

- ➡ 1st in lowest batting average on an 0-2 count (.000)
- ➡ 2nd in lowest batting average on a 3-2 count (.067)
- ➡ 5th in lowest batting average with two strikes (.124)

Otis Nixon

1996 Season

Signed as a free agent to replace the departed Devon White, Otis Nixon did a fine job of filling the Blue Jays' gap in center field and the leadoff spot. He reached base 38 percent of the time and ranked in the top five in fielding percentage for center fielders. At age 37, Nixon was the oldest Blue Jay but still remained one of the premier basestealers, ranking third in the league.

Hitting

Nixon is a switch-hitter with virtually no power who slaps the ball on the ground. . . most often to the opposite field. He uses an exaggerated open stance, somewhat crouched, choking up on the bat. He is a notorious first-pitch swinger, and because of his speed and tactics, he is always a threat to bunt. Nixon has become a more patient hitter over the years, and his 71 walks last year were a career high.

Baserunning & Defense

Nixon does not seem to be losing much speed as he gets older. He is a sure bet to steal while sitting on first, and stole third 12 times as well. As a baserunner, he usually has the green light to round third and attempt to score on any type of single. Nixon is a sure-handed outfielder who has terrific range. His only flaw is his lack of a throwing arm, which is both weak and inaccurate. He posted five assists in 1996—very near his average of 4.8 over the past seven seasons.

1997 Outlook

Nixon is signed through the 1997 season and will be patrolling center field at the Skydome as a 38-year-old outfielder. So far, Nixon has proven that the age factor has not been relevant in his case. Even though Nixon falls short of filling Devon White's shoes in terms of power and overall defense, the Jays are content to keep him as their leadoff man this year.

Position: CF
Bats: B **Throws:** R
Ht: 6' 2" **Wt:** 180

Opening Day Age: 38
Born: 1/9/59 in Evergreen, NC
ML Seasons: 14

Overall Statistics

	G	AB	R	H	D	T	HR	RBI	SB	BB	SO	Avg	OBP	Slg
1996	125	496	87	142	15	1	1	29	54	71	68	.286	.377	.327
Career	1370	3940	692	1062	116	17	8	246	498	453	545	.270	.344	.314

Where He Hits the Ball

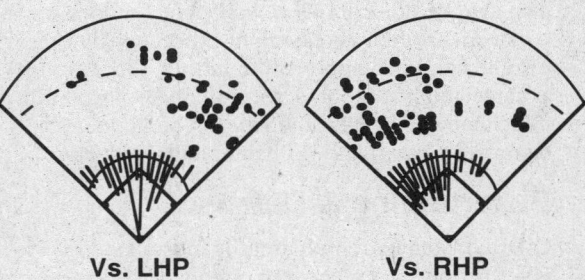

Vs. LHP   **Vs. RHP**

1996 Situational Stats

	AB	H	HR	RBI	Avg		AB	H	HR	RBI	Avg
Home	258	68	1	14	.264	LHP	151	45	0	12	.298
Road	238	74	0	15	.311	RHP	345	97	1	17	.281
First Half	243	69	1	12	.284	Sc Pos	104	29	0	28	.279
Scnd Half	253	73	0	17	.289	Clutch	62	18	0	3	.290

1996 Rankings (American League)

- ➡ 1st in highest groundball/flyball ratio (3.0)
- ➡ 2nd in lowest slugging percentage, lowest HR frequency (496.0 ABs per HR), lowest slugging percentage vs. right-handed pitchers (.319), bunts in play (44) and steals of third (12)
- ➡ 3rd in stolen bases
- ➡ 4th in caught stealing (13)
- ➡ 5th in fielding percentage in center field (.994)
- ➡ 6th in highest percentage of extra bases taken as a runner (64.6%)
- ➡ 9th in on-base percentage for a leadoff hitter (.377)
- ➡ 10th in singles (125)

Charlie O'Brien

1996 Season

The Blue Jays are fond of the tutorial method of catching, one in which they keep a veteran receiver to work with their youngsters. Charlie O'Brien was signed in the offseason to supplant the role previously held by Lance Parrish, but O'Brien provided much more than just wisdom. He ended up playing the majority of games and was credited for turning around starters Juan Guzman and Pat Hentgen with his game-calling skills.

Hitting

O'Brien is a hacker who comes to the plate looking to put wood on the ball any way he can. As a result, he is the epitome of the streak hitter; someone who looks great one month and atrocious the next. He seldom draws a walk, but he does not strike out as often as one might expect considering his undisciplined approach to hitting. O'Brien hit a career-high 13 home runs in 1996—yanking more than a few balls down the left-field line—but he remains easy pickings behind in the count.

Baserunning & Defense

O'Brien is an extremely intelligent backstop who gives his pitchers a boost of confidence whenever he's behind the plate. He threw out 38 percent of potential basestealers, which was well above the league average, and he is fearless defending the plate against oncoming runners. However, he is a bit slow chasing foul pops and jumping out of the box after bunts. O'Brien is a slow runner who rarely notches a steal himself.

1997 Outlook

Signed for 1997, O'Brien will back up free-agent acquisition Benito Santiago and continue to work on developing Sandy Martinez' skills. O'Brien's presence on this team cannot be measured in pure statistical terms. He is an experienced veteran, has caught nine Cy Young winners, played in a championship series and above all is a respected team leader.

Position: C
Bats: R **Throws:** R
Ht: 6' 2" **Wt:** 205

Opening Day Age: 35
Born: 5/1/61 in Tulsa, OK
ML Seasons: 11

Overall Statistics

	G	AB	R	H	D	T	HR	RBI	SB	BB	SO	Avg	OBP	Slg
1996	109	324	33	77	17	0	13	44	0	29	68	.238	.331	.410
Career	633	1751	177	389	94	3	46	210	1	174	257	.222	.307	.358

Where He Hits the Ball

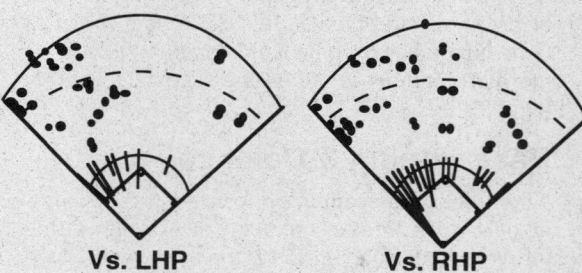

Vs. LHP   **Vs. RHP**

1996 Situational Stats

	AB	H	HR	RBI	Avg		AB	H	HR	RBI	Avg
Home	164	40	8	26	.244	LHP	123	29	4	14	.236
Road	160	37	5	18	.231	RHP	201	48	9	30	.239
First Half	157	39	6	24	.248	Sc Pos	88	19	3	26	.216
Scnd Half	167	38	7	20	.228	Clutch	63	14	3	8	.222

1996 Rankings (American League)

→ 1st in lowest batting average with the bases loaded (.000)

→ 3rd in hit by pitch (17), batting average on a 3-2 count (.393) and fielding percentage at catcher (.995)

→ 5th in lowest batting average with runners in scoring position (.216) and lowest batting average on an 0-2 count (.037)

→ 8th in lowest batting average vs. left-handed pitchers (.236)

→ Led the Blue Jays in hit by pitch (17) and batting average on a 3-2 count (.393)

John Olerud

1996 Season

John Olerud experienced another disappointing year in 1996. While no one expected him to reach the incredible .363 he posted in 1993, his batting average plummeted so rapidly that he struggled to stay in the .270s. More distressing to Olerud was the fact that he was reduced to a platoon player by manager Cito Gaston.

Hitting

Despite Olerud's declining batting average, he *did* hit for more power than in previous years (with the exception of 1993). He made a conscious effort to pull the ball more but remained a threat to hit to all fields. Olerud has an easy swing and handles inside fastballs relatively well. The outside part of the plate has been a different story, however, because he is one of those rare hitters who does not extend himself well. He prefers to use the inside-out approach to protect the outside portion of the zone.

Baserunning & Defense

Olerud is one of the most reliable fielders in the league and committed just two errors at first base. He is very good on the short-hop throws and has a big stretch with his 6'5" frame. Although his glove is excellent, he is not very quick to either side defending against the hard-hit balls. Olerud's baserunning prowess is negligible at best. He is a slow runner and is not a threat to steal, but he does use his head and rarely makes any judgment mistakes when trying for the extra base.

1997 Outlook

Olerud's huge $6.5 million salary and his inability to meet expectations have landed him on the trading block. The high salary makes him tough to deal, which means the Blue Jays will have to decide whether or not to absorb a portion of it. In a league with so many powerful first baseman, Olerud does not make the Blue Jays feel comfortable.

Position: 1B/DH
Bats: L **Throws:** L
Ht: 6' 5" **Wt:** 220

Opening Day Age: 28
Born: 8/5/68 in Seattle, WA
ML Seasons: 8
Pronunciation: OAL-uh-rude

Overall Statistics

	G	AB	R	H	D	T	HR	RBI	SB	BB	SO	Avg	OBP	Slg
1996	125	398	59	109	25	0	18	61	1	60	37	.274	.382	.472
Career	920	3103	464	910	213	6	109	471	3	514	430	.293	.395	.471

Where He Hits the Ball

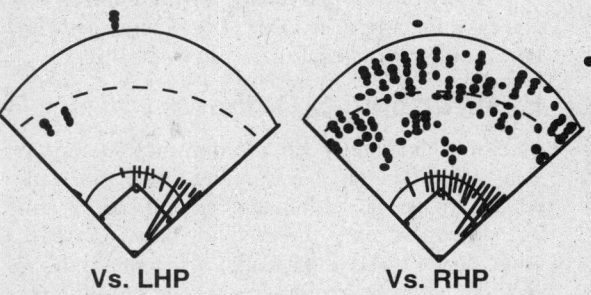

Vs. LHP   **Vs. RHP**

1996 Situational Stats

	AB	H	HR	RBI	Avg		AB	H	HR	RBI	Avg
Home	201	61	9	33	.303	LHP	64	14	1	6	.219
Road	197	48	9	28	.244	RHP	334	95	17	55	.284
First Half	235	61	14	40	.260	Sc Pos	102	25	4	45	.245
Scnd Half	163	48	4	21	.294	Clutch	62	17	3	11	.274

1996 Rankings (American League)

→ 1st in fielding percentage at first base (.998)
→ 8th in hit by pitch (10) and highest percentage of swings put into play (53.5%)
→ 9th in batting average on a 3-1 count (.600)
→ Led the Blue Jays in intentional walks (6), on-base percentage vs. right-handed pitchers (.396), highest percentage of pitches taken (61.0%), lowest percentage of swings that missed (10.9%) and highest percentage of swings put into play (53.5%)

Robert Perez

1996 Season

Playing mostly in a platoon role and as a substitute whenever Joe Carter needed a rest in left field, Robert Perez made the most of his limited at-bats last season. As a platoon player he saw plenty of left-handed pitching, but Perez impressed most observers with his consistency.

Hitting

Make no mistake: when Perez comes to bat he is swinging away. He is an impatient hitter who rarely walks, but he puts the ball in play much more often than not. He is a line-drive hitter with a little bit of power when he hits to the gaps, but he's not a big longball threat. Because he swings at so many pitches and makes regular contact, it's not easy for a pitcher to develop a strategy with Perez, either with location or pitch selection.

Baserunning & Defense

Perez has average speed and does not attempt to steal very often. His baserunning instincts are adequate, though he seldom tests an outfielder's arm and attempted only three stolen bases in 1996. Perez doesn't have a particularly strong arm himself. He covers a decent amount of territory whether playing right or left field, but he's had problems running in to make catches and lets some hits get by him.

1997 Outlook

Perez has achieved good numbers while in the minors and in his limited role in the majors. However, he is being held back from a full-time assignment in Toronto by the presence of Joe Carter. Perez is now 27 years old and is at a crossroads as far as his future with the organization is concerned. Unless the Jays move Carter to first, Perez will again be placed in a supporting role, which might not be in his best interests.

Position: LF/RF
Bats: R **Throws:** R
Ht: 6' 3" **Wt:** 205

Opening Day Age: 27
Born: 6/4/69 in Bolivar, VZ
ML Seasons: 3

Overall Statistics

	G	AB	R	H	D	T	HR	RBI	SB	BB	SO	Avg	OBP	Slg
1996	86	202	30	66	10	0	2	21	3	8	17	.327	.354	.406
Career	107	258	32	76	12	0	3	24	3	8	23	.295	.317	.376

Where He Hits the Ball

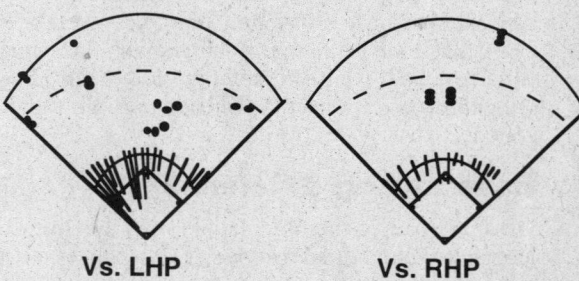

Vs. LHP   **Vs. RHP**

1996 Situational Stats

	AB	H	HR	RBI	Avg		AB	H	HR	RBI	Avg
Home	102	35	0	10	.343	LHP	143	47	2	17	.329
Road	100	31	2	11	.310	RHP	59	19	0	4	.322
First Half	105	35	0	11	.333	Sc Pos	45	18	1	19	.400
Scnd Half	97	31	2	10	.320	Clutch	32	8	0	1	.250

1996 Rankings (American League)

→ 5th in lowest batting average with the bases loaded (.091)
→ Led the Blue Jays in batting average vs. left-handed pitchers (.329)

Tomas Perez

1996 Season

One of four preseason candidates for the second base job vacated by Roberto Alomar, Tomas Perez lost out and was assigned to Triple-A Syracuse. He made it back to Toronto in late May and played regularly thereafter. Perez had a solid month of June—both at the plate and in the field—but tapered off considerably during the latter part of the year. Nonetheless, he picked up valuable experience.

Hitting

Perez is a contact hitter who swings freely from both sides of the plate and sprays the ball to all fields. Like most contact hitters, he can afford to wait a bit longer on pitches and still catch up with his fast hands. He prefers fastballs to the offspeed stuff, but he doesn't hit anything with much power. His level swing, which produces a lot of groundballs, can be an advantage because of his speed.

Baserunning & Defense

Perez has the versatility to play both middle-infield positions as well as third base if necessary. He favors second base where he shows very good range thanks to his quickness. He was under a lot of pressure last year to fill Alomar's shoes, perhaps making him somewhat of a nervous fielder; he committed 11 errors in 75 games at that position. Perez is a timid baserunner and does not often steal, but that's got more to do with his inexperience than his lack of speed.

1997 Outlook

Perez played adequately in 1996, but did not clinch the starting second-base assignment for next year. He will be considered a favorite heading into spring training, but Toronto still has a number of challengers vying for the job. It might not be settled at spring training, either. Competitor Domingo Cedeno is gone, but Miguel Cairo, Tilson Brito and Felipe Crespo will all be back trying to unseat Perez.

Position: 2B/3B
Bats: B **Throws:** R
Ht: 5'11" **Wt:** 165

Opening Day Age: 23
Born: 12/29/73 in Barquisimeto, VZ
ML Seasons: 2

Overall Statistics

	G	AB	R	H	D	T	HR	RBI	SB	BB	SO	Avg	OBP	Slg
1996	91	295	24	74	13	4	1	19	1	25	29	.251	.311	.332
Career	132	393	36	98	16	5	2	27	1	32	47	.249	.306	.331

Where He Hits the Ball

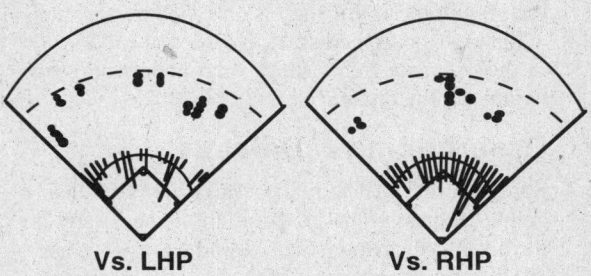

Vs. LHP   **Vs. RHP**

1996 Situational Stats

	AB	H	HR	RBI	Avg		AB	H	HR	RBI	Avg
Home	149	30	1	10	.201	LHP	94	23	1	11	.245
Road	146	44	0	9	.301	RHP	201	51	0	8	.254
First Half	105	29	1	9	.276	Sc Pos	78	15	1	18	.192
Scnd Half	190	45	0	10	.237	Clutch	39	8	0	3	.205

1996 Rankings (American League)

➡ 5th in errors at second base (11)
➡ 6th in most GDPs per GDP situation (16.9%)

Ed Sprague

1996 Season

Ed Sprague made his presence felt around the American League in 1996 by developing into one of the loop's top home run hitters. He led the Blue Jays with 36 longballs, doubling his previous career high and surpassing the 100-RBI plateau for the first time as well. He was a mainstay in the lineup, missing just three games.

Hitting

Another one of the Blue Jays' dead fastball hitters, Sprague has developed more of an uppercut swing in recent years, a key factor in his increased home-run output. Thanks to his excellent bat speed, he will murder any heat from the belt to the letters. He does not hit for high average because, coming to the plate looking for the fastball, he has problems adjusting to offspeed stuff. He does not like to go to the opposite field, which also makes him vulnerable to the outside slider.

Baserunning & Defense

Sprague continues to make strides in his defensive game. He has improved going to his backhand on the hot smashes down the line and has always been good cutting across the diamond. He has a solid arm, and because he is a gamer, he will sacrifice his body to knock down anything hit towards him. Sprague is a slow but determined runner on the basepaths who did not attempt any steals last year.

1997 Outlook

The Blue Jays and Sprague met eye-to-eye when he signed a long-term deal keeping him in Toronto all the way through the 1999 season. He has iron-man qualities, which will enable manager Cito Gaston to count on him as an automatic in the lineup every day. He would like to improve his batting average somewhat, but not at the expense of his power output.

Position: 3B
Bats: R **Throws:** R
Ht: 6' 2" **Wt:** 210

Opening Day Age: 29
Born: 7/25/67 in Castro Valley, CA
ML Seasons: 6

Overall Statistics

	G	AB	R	H	D	T	HR	RBI	SB	BB	SO	Avg	OBP	Slg
1996	159	591	88	146	35	2	36	101	0	60	146	.247	.325	.496
Career	645	2270	276	567	121	6	82	319	2	195	472	.250	.320	.417

Where He Hits the Ball

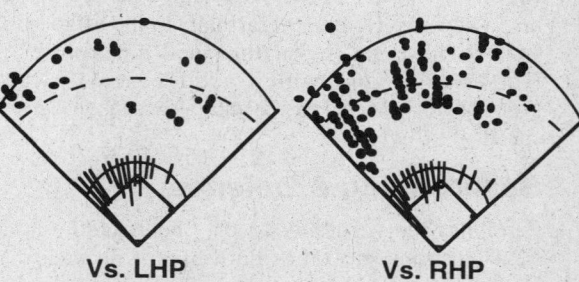

Vs. LHP   **Vs. RHP**

1996 Situational Stats

	AB	H	HR	RBI	Avg		AB	H	HR	RBI	Avg
Home	295	69	17	42	.234	LHP	155	48	14	38	.310
Road	296	77	19	59	.260	RHP	436	98	22	63	.225
First Half	308	83	23	62	.269	Sc Pos	140	36	12	66	.257
Scnd Half	283	63	13	39	.223	Clutch	88	18	6	13	.205

1996 Rankings (American League)

- → 2nd in lowest batting average vs. right-handed pitchers (.225)
- → 4th in strikeouts
- → 5th in errors at third base (15) and lowest batting average
- → 6th in games played (159) and fielding percentage at third base (.956)
- → 7th in hit by pitch (12) and lowest batting average at home (.234)
- → 8th in batting average on a 3-1 count (.615) and lowest on-base percentage vs. right-handed pitchers (.303)
- → 9th in slugging percentage vs. left-handed pitchers (.645)
- → 10th in lowest groundball/flyball ratio (0.7)

Mike Timlin

1996 Season

Awarded the Jays' closer's job right out of spring training, Mike Timlin was inconsistent until he finally found himself during the latter part of the season. He converted 82 percent of his save opportunities and finished the year on a high note, logging eight saves in September.

Pitching

Timlin has a few more pitches in his arsenal than most closers. Most often he throws a tough two-seam sinking fastball and a running heater that both come into the batter at 94 MPH. In cases where he finds himself working a long ninth inning, he offsets his power pitches with a good slider and is even capable of dealing a knee-buckling curveball from time to time. While Timlin has decent control, his lack of command within the strike zone can cause him problems. This becomes noticeable when his fastballs start to tail out over the heart of the plate.

Defense

Normally making his entrance into games in save situations, Timlin does not have to deal with many runners who are given the green light. In 56⅔ innings, only three runners attempted to steal on his watch all season. He comes to the plate with plenty of high-velocity fastballs which makes it tough for runners to gain any advantage. Timlin is an average fielder with below-average mobility.

1997 Outlook

Timlin earned his stripes in his first full year as the Jays' closer, and he signed a new contract with the club after the season. The Jays were not about to go shopping to replace someone with Timlin's potential, especially after serving his apprenticeship last year. He is poised to come into his own for the 1997 season.

Position: RP
Bats: R **Throws:** R
Ht: 6' 4" **Wt:** 210

Opening Day Age: 31
Born: 3/10/66 in Midland, TX
ML Seasons: 6

Overall Statistics

	W	L	Pct.	ERA	G	GS	Sv	IP	H	BB	SO	HR	BR/IP
1996	1	6	.143	3.65	59	0	31	56.2	47	18	52	4	1.15
Career	20	20	.500	3.72	267	3	43	346.1	328	152	295	23	1.39

How Often He Throws Strikes

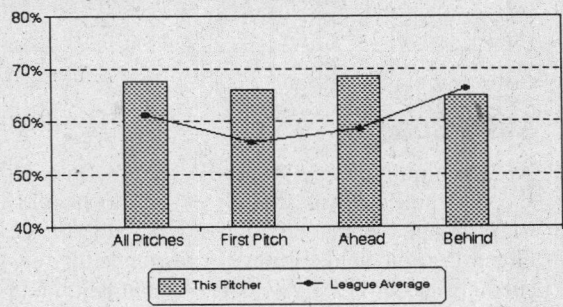

1996 Situational Stats

	W	L	ERA	Sv	IP		AB	H	HR	RBI	Avg
Home	0	0	1.66	12	21.2	LHB	116	30	1	14	.259
Road	1	6	4.89	19	35.0	RHB	89	17	3	10	.191
First Half	0	1	2.57	15	28.0	Sc Pos	46	11	1	17	.239
Scnd Half	1	5	4.71	16	28.2	Clutch	133	35	3	21	.263

1996 Rankings (American League)

→ 4th in lowest save percentage (81.6%) and least baserunners allowed per 9 innings in relief (10.6)

→ 5th in games finished (56), blown saves (7) and relief losses (6)

→ 6th in saves and save opportunities (38)

→ Led the Blue Jays in games pitched, saves, games finished (56), save opportunities (38), save percentage (81.6%), blown saves (7), first batter efficiency (.208), relief losses (6), lowest batting average allowed in relief (.229), least baserunners allowed per 9 innings in relief (10.6) and most strikeouts per 9 innings in relief (8.3)

Jacob Brumfield

Position: CF/LF/RF
Bats: R **Throws:** R
Ht: 6' 0" **Wt:** 185

Opening Day Age: 31
Born: 5/27/65 in Bogalusa, LA
ML Seasons: 5

Overall Statistics

	G	AB	R	H	D	T	HR	RBI	SB	BB	SO	Avg	OBP	Slg
1996	119	388	63	99	28	2	14	60	15	29	75	.255	.311	.446
Career	430	1214	209	323	78	9	28	122	69	104	215	.266	.327	.414

1996 Situational Stats

	AB	H	HR	RBI	Avg		AB	H	HR	RBI	Avg
Home	192	52	8	29	.271	LHP	187	53	5	28	.283
Road	196	47	6	31	.240	RHP	201	46	9	32	.229
First Half	213	53	9	28	.249	Sc Pos	94	31	6	47	.330
Scnd Half	175	46	5	32	.263	Clutch	75	11	2	8	.147

1996 Season

After beginning the 1996 season with the Pirates, Jacob Brumfield was traded to Toronto in mid-May to add depth and to platoon with Shawn Green in right field. Brumfield responded by exceeding his previous year's power numbers, and he helped spark a lagging Blue Jays offense.

Hitting, Baserunning & Defense

Brumfield spent most of his time at the top of the Blue Jays' lineup, particularly when Otis Nixon was out with injuries. He is not really suited for that role due to his low on-base percentage, but he has decent power to both gaps and is a good breaking-ball hitter. Brumfield is a free swinger who struggles against righthanders when they pitch him low and away. He is very fast and is a good percentage basestealer. He is better defensively when in either corner of the outfield rather than in center and has a decent arm.

1997 Outlook

Brumfield may have to be patient if he expects to play every day in Toronto. His best chance for an opening could be in right field if Shawn Green falters, but for now he is likely to platoon and will continue to play a supporting role.

Huck Flener

Position: SP
Bats: B **Throws:** L
Ht: 5'11" **Wt:** 175

Opening Day Age: 28
Born: 2/25/69 in Austin, TX
ML Seasons: 2

Overall Statistics

	W	L	Pct.	ERA	G	GS	Sv	IP	H	BB	SO	HR	BR/IP
1996	3	2	.600	4.58	15	11	0	70.2	68	33	44	9	1.43
Career	3	2	.600	4.54	21	11	0	77.1	75	37	46	9	1.45

1996 Situational Stats

	W	L	ERA	Sv	IP		AB	H	HR	RBI	Avg
Home	2	1	3.80	0	45.0	LHB	62	13	1	8	.210
Road	1	1	5.96	0	25.2	RHB	209	55	8	27	.263
First Half	0	0	-	0	0.0	Sc Pos	61	15	0	23	.246
Scnd Half	3	2	4.58	0	70.2	Clutch	23	8	0	3	.348

1996 Season

Lefthander Huck Flener was called up in mid-July after compiling excellent innings at Triple-A Syracuse. Flener pitched extremely well during his first five starts, but struggled thereafter.

Pitching & Defense

Flener is a finesse pitcher who relies heavily on mixing a good circle change with a low-velocity (85 MPH) fastball and working the outside corner to right-handed hitters. He replaces the change-up with a slow-breaking curveball to left-handed batters. Flener's basic pitching philosophy is based upon two goals: get the hitter to chase the outside pitch and disrupt his timing. Flener's vulnerability is exposed when batters wait him out, as his fastball is not quick enough to challenge hitters. He is an average fielder but holds runners fairly well.

1997 Outlook

The Jays would love to have a left-handed starter in their rotation to fill the gap left when Al Leiter signed with Florida. Flener has to increase his velocity over the winter and can't be afraid of coming into the hitters more often if he expects to lock up a starting role in 1997.

Marty Janzen

Position: SP
Bats: R **Throws:** R
Ht: 6' 3" **Wt:** 200

Opening Day Age: 23
Born: 5/31/73 in Homestead, FL
ML Seasons: 1

Overall Statistics

	W	L	Pct.	ERA	G	GS	Sv	IP	H	BB	SO	HR	BR/IP
1996	4	6	.400	7.33	15	11	0	73.2	95	38	47	16	1.81
Career	4	6	.400	7.33	15	11	0	73.2	95	38	47	16	1.81

1996 Situational Stats

	W	L	ERA	Sv	IP		AB	H	HR	RBI	Avg
Home	4	4	6.32	0	47.0	LHB	141	50	6	27	.355
Road	0	2	9.11	0	26.2	RHB	158	45	10	30	.285
First Half	4	4	6.33	0	48.1	Sc Pos	77	22	4	40	.286
Scnd Half	0	2	9.24	0	25.1	Clutch	26	3	0	0	.115

1996 Season

Immediately tagged as the Blue Jays' top minor league pitching prospect when he was acquired from the Yankees in the David Cone deal, Marty Janzen made his major league debut last May. He looked solid in three May appearances, only to have the bottom fall out shortly thereafter.

Pitching & Defense

Janzen is not a hard thrower. He has a running fastball that only reaches the mid- to high-80s. He also mixes in a big overhand curve and a tight slider. As a fifth starter, Janzen had stamina problems, pitching well for three or four innings only to get clobbered around the 60-pitch mark. He seemed nervous and lacked poise when pitching from behind, and as a result, the ball would start to rise in the strike zone, resulting in numerous gopher balls. Janzen is a below average fielder and average at best at holding runners.

1997 Outlook

There's little question that Janzen needs more seasoning. He has good stuff, but needs to mature and *that* process is best done at the minor league level. He did show glimpses of effective relief work, which also could be in the cards for his future.

Paul Quantrill

Position: SP/RP
Bats: L **Throws:** R
Ht: 6' 1" **Wt:** 185

Opening Day Age: 28
Born: 11/3/68 in London, Ontario, Canada
ML Seasons: 5
Pronunciation: KWON-trill

Overall Statistics

	W	L	Pct.	ERA	G	GS	Sv	IP	H	BB	SO	HR	BR/IP
1996	5	14	.263	5.43	38	20	0	134.1	172	51	86	27	1.66
Career	27	44	.380	4.47	182	64	3	554.0	654	169	307	68	1.49

1996 Situational Stats

	W	L	ERA	Sv	IP		AB	H	HR	RBI	Avg
Home	1	8	6.02	0	64.1	LHB	293	91	18	48	.311
Road	4	6	4.89	0	70.0	RHB	250	81	9	36	.324
First Half	4	9	6.13	0	86.2	Sc Pos	117	33	4	53	.282
Scnd Half	1	5	4.15	0	47.2	Clutch	63	22	3	9	.349

1996 Season

Acquired in an offseason trade with Philadelphia, Canadian-born Paul Quantrill returned to his hometown area to be the Blue Jays' fourth starter. It was not a successful homecoming, however, as Quantrill had a difficult campaign in 1996. He was shuttled back and forth between the starting rotation and the bullpen for most of the season, with most of his success coming out of the pen.

Pitching & Defense

Quantrill throws a two-seam sinking fastball, and a more conventional running fastball with good tailing action. He generates decent velocity, bringing his best fastball in at around 92 MPH. He will normally go back and forth between the fastballs and a down-and-away short slider, with the odd change-up thrown in. He likes to work quickly but tires easily, losing velocity in the process. Quantrill holds runners well and was not charged with a single error in 1996.

1997 Outlook

It's tough to see how the Blue Jays will include Quantrill in their starting rotation this season unless he improves his stamina. With his lack of stamina, he might be better off as a full-time reliever.

Bill Risley

Position: RP
Bats: R **Throws:** R
Ht: 6' 2" **Wt:** 230

Opening Day Age: 29
Born: 5/29/67 in Chicago, IL
ML Seasons: 5

Overall Statistics

	W	L	Pct.	ERA	G	GS	Sv	IP	H	BB	SO	HR	BR/IP
1996	0	1	.000	3.89	25	0	0	41.2	33	25	29	7	1.39
Career	12	8	.600	3.44	110	1	1	162.1	125	65	159	22	1.17

1996 Situational Stats

	W	L	ERA	Sv	IP		AB	H	HR	RBI	Avg
Home	0	0	5.87	0	15.1	LHB	59	11	1	8	.186
Road	0	1	2.73	0	26.1	RHB	90	22	6	18	.244
First Half	0	0	4.84	0	22.1	Sc Pos	44	10	4	23	.227
Scnd Half	0	1	2.79	0	19.1	Clutch	36	7	4	11	.194

1996 Season

Many people were surprised when the Mariners agreed to part with righty reliever Bill Risley in an offseason deal with Toronto. Coming off a solid 1995 season, Risley did not have a good chance to show all of his stuff with the Blue Jays because of two trips to the DL with shoulder problems.

Pitching & Defense

Risley is predominantly a fastball/slider pitcher. He varies speeds on his fastball anywhere from 87 to 92 MPH. He also likes to throw a backup curve to righthanders. He is more effective against left-handed hitters because of the tailing action of his fastball—it moves off the plate, making it hard for lefties to reach. Risley's poor control is his weakness. His long delivery also makes him easy to steal against, though he is an adequate fielding pitcher.

1997 Outlook

Once Risley got over his shoulder difficulties, he returned to the form that made others take notice while he was in Seattle. He needs to work on his control, but otherwise should be poised to make a solid contribution out of the bullpen this year.

Juan Samuel

Position: DH/1B/RF
Bats: R **Throws:** R
Ht: 5'11" **Wt:** 180

Opening Day Age: 36
Born: 12/9/60 in San Pedro de Macoris, DR
ML Seasons: 14
Pronunciaiton: sam-WELL

Overall Statistics

	G	AB	R	H	D	T	HR	RBI	SB	BB	SO	Avg	OBP	Slg
1996	69	188	34	48	8	3	8	26	9	15	65	.255	.319	.457
Career	1632	5936	846	1542	280	98	157	686	378	423	1401	.260	.315	.419

1996 Situational Stats

	AB	H	HR	RBI	Avg		AB	H	HR	RBI	Avg
Home	87	26	4	9	.299	LHP	137	38	7	22	.277
Road	101	22	4	17	.218	RHP	51	10	1	4	.196
First Half	97	24	4	12	.247	Sc Pos	50	15	2	17	.300
Scnd Half	91	24	4	14	.264	Clutch	36	5	0	1	.139

1996 Season

Signed to a minor league contract during the winter, veteran Juan Samuel spent most of 1996 as a bench player whom the Blue Jays used mostly against lefthanders. He split his limited playing time in the field between first base and the outfield.

Hitting, Baserunning & Defense

Despite his age, Samuel still remains one of the better fastball hitters around. He has good power, and most often tries to pull the ball. His experience makes him tougher to pitch to with men on base, but he is susceptible to the offspeed breaking stuff. Samuel has excellent baserunning instincts and knows how to steal—he was nine of 10 in that category in 1996. He is a below-average first baseman and has limitations as an outfielder as well.

1997 Outlook

Since Samuel comes so cheaply, he could well be back in a Toronto uniform. However, the Jays have to be thinking about his age and about using his place on the roster for developing some talent for the future. . . making him vulnerable to release. With his hitting skills and versatility, he should have little trouble finding a job.

Paul Spoljaric

Position: RP
Bats: R **Throws:** L
Ht: 6' 3" **Wt:** 205

Opening Day Age: 26
Born: 9/24/70 in
Kelowna, BC
ML Seasons: 2
Pronunciaiton:
spaul-JARE-ick

Overall Statistics

	W	L	Pct.	ERA	G	GS	Sv	IP	H	BB	SO	HR	BR/IP
1996	2	2	.500	3.08	28	0	1	38.0	30	19	38	6	1.29
Career	2	3	.400	5.13	30	1	1	40.1	35	28	40	9	1.56

1996 Situational Stats

	W	L	ERA	Sv	IP		AB	H	HR	RBI	Avg
Home	1	2	3.15	0	20.0	LHB	50	13	2	10	.260
Road	1	0	3.00	1	18.0	RHB	90	17	4	8	.189
First Half	0	0	3.21	0	14.0	Sc Pos	38	7	2	14	.184
Scnd Half	2	2	3.00	1	24.0	Clutch	39	6	1	1	.154

1996 Season

British Columbia native Paul Spoljaric settled into the role of left-handed middle reliever extremely well after being called up from Triple-A Syracuse in mid-May. He pitched even better after coming off a stint on the DL in late August. He was definitely one of the bright spots in the Blue Jays' bullpen in 1996.

Pitching & Defense

Spoljaric is an economical southpaw who has a blazing 93 MPH fastball which he offsets with a big, sweeping curve and a slider. Surprisingly, he is more effective against right-handers because he is relentless at coming inside and tight on the batter's hands. He is a power pitcher with less than average control whose wildness sometimes gets him in trouble. Spoljaric does not have any special talent for holding runners, but is a solid fielder.

1997 Outlook

Spoljaric will continue to work in middle relief as well as in the situational set-up role next season. He, Tim Crabtree and Bill Risley all have the potential to be future closers, and they emphasize the depth Toronto has developed in its bullpen.

Woody Williams

Position: SP
Bats: R **Throws:** R
Ht: 6' 0" **Wt:** 190

Opening Day Age: 30
Born: 8/19/66 in
Houston, TX
ML Seasons: 4

Overall Statistics

	W	L	Pct.	ERA	G	GS	Sv	IP	H	BB	SO	HR	BR/IP
1996	4	5	.444	4.73	12	10	0	59.0	64	21	43	8	1.44
Career	9	11	.450	4.09	103	13	0	209.0	192	104	164	21	1.42

1996 Situational Stats

	W	L	ERA	Sv	IP		AB	H	HR	RBI	Avg
Home	2	4	5.00	0	36.0	LHB	139	40	4	13	.288
Road	2	1	4.30	0	23.0	RHB	91	24	4	12	.264
First Half	0	0	7.71	0	2.1	Sc Pos	49	14	3	19	.286
Scnd Half	4	5	4.61	0	56.2	Clutch	17	2	0	0	.118

1996 Season

After undergoing offseason surgery on his right shoulder, Woody Williams was placed on the 60-day DL and wasn't activated until late May. He returned to the DL almost immediately, but really didn't get started again until August, finishing the season with mixed results.

Pitching & Defense

Williams expanded his pitching arsenal in 1996 by adding a split-fingered pitch to the fastball, curve and slider he already had. A large variety of pitches is Williams' method of making up for a less-than-imposing (87 MPH) fastball which overpowers no one. He tends to be a streaky performer, pitching superbly in one outing but looking mediocre the next. His performance often depends on how well he is locating the ball. He is not adept at holding runners but is a flawless fielder.

1997 Outlook

Williams has been trying to break through as a permanent starter in the Blue Jay rotation for the last two seasons, but he's been held back by injuries and a lack of consistency. Short of the Jays buying a free-agent starter, Williams will get another opportunity this season.

Other Toronto Blue Jays

Luis Andujar (Pos: RHP, Age: 24)

	W	L	Pct.	ERA	G	GS	Sv	IP	H	BB	SO	HR	BR/IP
1996	1	3	.250	6.99	8	7	0	37.1	46	16	11	8	1.66
Career	3	4	.429	5.32	13	12	0	67.2	72	30	20	12	1.51

The Chicago White Sox gave Andujar two different chances to pitch with the parent club last year before trading him to Toronto in late August. He struggled with both teams. He's young, but it looks as though he may not be fully recovered from a 1994 elbow operation. 1997 Outlook: B

Brian Bohanon (Pos: LHP, Age: 28)

	W	L	Pct.	ERA	G	GS	Sv	IP	H	BB	SO	HR	BR/IP
1996	0	1	.000	7.77	20	0	1	22.0	27	19	17	4	2.09
Career	12	15	.444	5.71	159	47	2	398.2	469	180	229	46	1.63

Bohanon began the year as a left-handed specialist in the Blue Jay bullpen. He struggled against lefties and righties, however, and was sent to Syracuse. He has shown little promise as a big leaguer. 1997 Outlook: C

Scott Brow (Pos: RHP, Age: 28)

	W	L	Pct.	ERA	G	GS	Sv	IP	H	BB	SO	HR	BR/IP
1996	1	0	1.000	5.59	18	1	0	38.2	45	25	23	5	1.81
Career	2	4	.333	5.78	42	4	2	85.2	98	54	45	11	1.77

Scott Brow closed out his third season with the Blue Jays with a 5.59 ERA in 18 appearences. It was his best campaign with Toronto, but not good enough. The Braves picked him up off waivers in October. 1997 Outlook: C

Miguel Cairo (Pos: 2B, Age: 22, Bats: R)

	G	AB	R	H	D	T	HR	RBI	SB	BB	SO	Avg	OBP	Slg
1996	9	27	5	6	2	0	0	1	0	2	9	.222	.300	.296
Career	9	27	5	6	2	0	0	1	0	2	9	.222	.300	.296

Cairo saw his first action in the majors at the end of September for the Blue Jays, but was traded to the Cubs after the season. His speed and his flashy glove should earn him a spot on the roster. 1997 Outlook: B

Dane Johnson (Pos: RHP, Age: 34)

	W	L	Pct.	ERA	G	GS	Sv	IP	H	BB	SO	HR	BR/IP
1996	0	0	-	3.00	10	0	0	9.0	5	5	7	0	1.11
Career	2	1	.667	5.06	25	0	0	21.1	21	16	14	2	1.73

Named best reliever in the American Association in 1994, Johnson has recorded 68 saves in Triple-A over the past three seasons. The Athletics acquired him off waivers to help fill out their bullpen. 1997 Outlook: B

Julio Mosquera (Pos: C, Age: 25, Bats: R)

	G	AB	R	H	D	T	HR	RBI	SB	BB	SO	Avg	OBP	Slg
1996	8	22	2	5	2	0	0	2	0	0	3	.227	.261	.318
Career	8	22	2	5	2	0	0	2	0	0	3	.227	.261	.318

If Sandy Martinez continues to struggle at the plate, Toronto may take a longer look at Mosquera behind the plate. His defense, reflexes and rocket arm are not a question. . . his punchless bat is. 1997 Outlook: C

Ken Robinson (Pos: RHP, Age: 27)

	W	L	Pct.	ERA	G	GS	Sv	IP	H	BB	SO	HR	BR/IP
1996	1	0	1.000	6.00	5	0	0	6.0	9	3	5	0	2.00
Career	2	2	.500	4.00	26	0	0	45.0	34	25	36	7	1.31

The Blue Jays re-acquired Robinson off waivers in early May and sent him to Triple-A Syracuse for the remainder of the season. He continues to compile decent strikeout totals in middle relief. 1997 Outlook: C

Jose Silva (Pos: RHP, Age: 23)

	W	L	Pct.	ERA	G	GS	Sv	IP	H	BB	SO	HR	BR/IP
1996	0	0	-	13.50	2	0	0	2.0	5	0	0	1	2.50
Career	0	0	-	13.50	2	0	0	2.0	5	0	0	1	2.50

Silva was sent to Pittsburgh as part of the deal which brought Orlando Merced and Carlos Garcia to the Jays. Obviously the Pirates hold his mid-90s fastball in high regard despite elbow troubles. 1997 Outlook: A

Frank Viola (Pos: LHP, Age: 36)

	W	L	Pct.	ERA	G	GS	Sv	IP	H	BB	SO	HR	BR/IP
1996	1	3	.250	7.71	6	6	0	30.1	43	21	18	6	2.11
Career	176	150	.540	3.73	421	420	0	2836.1	2827	864	1844	294	1.30

Attempting a second comeback from major elbow surgery in 1994, Viola posted a 1-3 record and a 7.71 ERA for the Jays before being released in early June. Don't expect another comeback attempt. 1997 Outlook: D

Jeff Ware (Pos: RHP, Age: 26)

	W	L	Pct.	ERA	G	GS	Sv	IP	H	BB	SO	HR	BR/IP
1996	1	5	.167	9.09	13	4	0	32.2	35	31	11	6	2.02
Career	3	6	.333	7.47	18	9	0	59.0	63	52	29	8	1.95

Jeff Ware has built a hefty 7.74 ERA in nine starts and nine relief appearances for Toronto over the past two seasons. Arm troubles continue to diminish his velocity and his future value. 1997 Outlook: D

Toronto Blue Jays Minor League Prospects

Organization Overview:

Although it isn't what it once was, the Toronto Blue Jays' farm system remains productive. Last year, it delivered several important new components of the Toronto ballclub, including DH Carlos Delgado, and pitchers Paul Spoljaric and Tim Crabtree. Although it's recently produced other mainstays like Alex Gonzalez and Shawn Green, the organization has had a terrible time developing young pitchers. They have many talented arms in the pipeline, but far too many of them seemed to suffer setbacks of one form or another last year. At the major league level, the system has been unable to address a severe need for pitching. However, they have maintained enough depth to be able to deal away pitchers when the need arises—as was the case when the Pittsburgh Pirates came calling. Overall, they maintain an impressive collection of position players, and a decent stock of long-range pitching prospects.

Tilson Brito

Position: SS
Bats: R **Throws:** R
Ht: 6' 0" **Wt:** 170

Opening Day Age: 24
Born: 5/28/72 in Santo Domingo, DR

Recent Statistics

	G	AB	R	H	D	T	HR	RBI	SB	BB	SO	AVG
96 AAA Syracuse	108	400	63	111	22	8	10	54	11	38	65	.278
96 AL Toronto	26	80	10	19	7	0	1	7	1	10	18	.238
96 MLE	108	388	51	99	20	5	9	44	8	30	70	.255

Error-prone shortstop Tilson Brito was given a short trial at second base by the Blue Jays last year. At Triple-A, he overcame an injury-plagued '95 season to prove that he's got decent pop for a shortstop. He's got decent speed, and if he's able to convert to second base, he may get a real shot at the position in Toronto. Now 25 years old, it's time for him to break through or be passed by.

Chris Carpenter

Position: P
Bats: R **Throws:** R
Ht: 6' 6" **Wt:** 220

Opening Day Age: 21
Born: 4/27/75 in Exeter, NH

Recent Statistics

	W	L	ERA	G	GS	Sv	IP	H	R	BB	SO	HR
94 R Medicne Hat	6	3	2.76	15	15	0	84.2	76	40	39	80	3
95 AA Knoxville	3	7	5.18	12	12	0	64.1	71	47	31	53	3
95 A Dunedin	3	5	2.17	15	15	0	99.1	83	29	50	56	3
96 AA Knoxville	7	9	3.94	28	28	0	171.1	161	94	91	150	13

Chris Carpenter's second trip around Double-A was far more successful. As a 20 year old in '95, he couldn't make it on stuff alone, but last season, he posted numbers more like those expected from a young power pitcher. The won-loss record wasn't pretty, but the big righthander finally began to use his 90 MPH heat to rack up strikeouts. If he's able to develop a good offspeed pitch to go with his power curve, he may take another big step forward.

Felipe Crespo

Position: 2B
Bats: B **Throws:** R
Ht: 5' 11" **Wt:** 190

Opening Day Age: 24
Born: 3/5/73 in Rio Piedras, PR

Recent Statistics

	G	AB	R	H	D	T	HR	RBI	SB	BB	SO	AVG
96 A Dunedin	9	34	3	11	1	0	2	6	1	2	3	.324
96 AAA Syracuse	98	355	53	100	25	0	8	58	10	56	39	.282
96 AL Toronto	22	49	6	9	4	0	0	4	1	12	13	.184
96 MLE	98	343	43	88	23	0	7	47	7	45	43	.257

Felipe Crespo is an above-average hitter for a second baseman, but his defense gives it all back. He's got an abnormally-shaped arm from a childhood injury, and it leads to throwing errors no matter where he plays. It's a shame, because he's got good power for a second baseman, runs well and hits for a good average. If he were moved to the outfield, he wouldn't be anything special. It will be hard for the Blue Jays to figure out how to use him.

Tom Evans

Position: 3B-DH
Bats: R **Throws:** R
Ht: 6' 1" **Wt:** 180

Opening Day Age: 22
Born: 7/9/74 in Kirkland, WA

Recent Statistics

	G	AB	R	H	D	T	HR	RBI	SB	BB	SO	AVG
93 A Hagerstown	119	389	47	100	25	1	7	54	9	53	61	.257
94 A Hagerstown	95	322	58	88	16	2	13	48	2	51	80	.273
95 A Dunedin	130	444	63	124	29	3	9	66	7	51	80	.279
96 AA Knoxville	120	394	87	111	27	1	17	65	4	115	113	.282
96 MLE	120	383	72	100	25	0	15	53	2	80	124	.261

Despite chronically sore knees, Tom Evans busted out with a truly impressive season in '96. Even though he was one of the youngest players in Double-A, he hit for good power with a decent average, and drew a ton of walks. He's got good range and a bazooka arm at third base, although his knees sometimes force him to DH. Once he gets another year of growth behind him, he may be seriously pushing Ed Sprague for the Blue Jays' third base job.

Mike Halperin

Position: P
Bats: L **Throws:** L
Ht: 5' 10" **Wt:** 170

Opening Day Age: 23
Born: 9/8/73 in Naples, FL

Recent Statistics

	W	L	ERA	G	GS	Sv	IP	H	R	BB	SO	HR
94 A St. Cathrns	2	1	1.13	9	1	1	24.0	11	5	5	19	0
94 A Hagerstown	2	1	1.20	6	6	0	30.0	25	4	7	27	1
95 A Dunedin	3	5	3.62	14	12	0	69.2	70	36	29	63	4
96 AA Knoxville	13	7	3.48	28	28	0	155.0	156	67	112	112	6

Mike Halperin isn't big, strong or fast, but he's left-handed, and he wins. At age 22, he went 13-7 at Double-A, and didn't miss a start all year. His stuff may not translate into huge success at the major league level, but there are plenty of teams who wouldn't mind finding out. The Blue Jays don't have a ton of pitching prospects in the higher levels of their system, so if Halperin keeps it up, they'll have to give him a chance.

Ryan Jones

Position: 1B **Opening Day Age:** 22
Bats: R **Throws:** R **Born:** 11/5/74 in
Ht: 6' 3" **Wt:** 220 Torrance, CA

Recent Statistics

	G	AB	R	H	D	T	HR	RBI	SB	BB	SO	AVG
93 R Medicne Hat	47	171	20	42	5	0	3	27	1	12	46	.246
94 A Hagerstown	115	402	60	96	29	0	18	72	1	45	124	.239
95 A Dunedin	127	478	65	119	28	0	18	78	1	41	92	.249
96 AA Knoxville	134	506	70	137	26	3	20	97	2	60	88	.271
96 MLE	134	492	57	123	24	2	18	80	1	42	97	.250

Ryan Jones has one tool: power. However, that one tool is so impressive that it may be enough to get him to the majors. After earning a reputation as a wild swinger, he made progress in controlling the strike zone last year. He can't run or field, but there aren't too many prospects who are able to hit 20 homers in Double-A at the age of 21. If Jones develops as expected, he may have more in common with Ryan Klesko than just his first name.

Jeff Patzke

Position: 2B **Opening Day Age:** 23
Bats: B **Throws:** R **Born:** 11/19/73 in
Ht: 6' 0" **Wt:** 170 Klamath Falls, OR

Recent Statistics

	G	AB	R	H	D	T	HR	RBI	SB	BB	SO	AVG
93 R Medicne Hat	71	273	45	80	11	2	1	22	5	34	31	.293
94 A Hagerstown	80	271	43	55	10	1	4	22	7	36	57	.203
95 A Dunedin	129	470	68	124	32	6	11	75	5	85	81	.264
96 AA Knoxville	124	429	70	130	31	4	4	66	6	80	103	.303
96 MLE	124	414	57	115	29	3	3	54	4	56	115	.278

Without doing anything flashy, Jeff Patzke makes a lot of small contributions. He hits for a pretty good average, knocks a few doubles, draws walks and plays reliable defense at second base. That all adds up to a very solid player. Patzke is a switch-hitter and he's only 23. It may take him longer than usual to get noticed, but if he gets a chance to play, he'll be productive.

Shannon Stewart

Position: OF **Opening Day Age:** 23
Bats: R **Throws:** R **Born:** 2/25/74 in
Ht: 6' 1" **Wt:** 185 Cincinnati, OH

Recent Statistics

	G	AB	R	H	D	T	HR	RBI	SB	BB	SO	AVG
96 AAA Syracuse	112	420	77	125	26	8	6	42	35	54	61	.298
96 AL Toronto	7	17	2	3	1	0	0	2	1	1	4	.176
96 MLE	112	406	62	111	23	5	5	34	26	44	65	.273

Speedy center fielder Shannon Stewart had a breakout year at Double-A in '95, and after a slow start last season, he was able to repeat his numbers from the year before. Stewart's speed is his ticket to the big leagues—it enables him to be a good basestealer and rangy fly-catcher in center field. It must be comforting to the Blue Jays to know that if Otis Nixon goes down, they have an equally talented player waiting in the wings.

Others to Watch

Righthander **Mark Sievert** got off to a blazing 9-2 start at Double-A, but after his promotion to Triple-A, he went 2-5 with an ERA approaching 6.00. He's got a good fastball and curve, but may need more time. . . Former first-round pick **Roy Halladay** went 15-7 in the Florida State League at age 19. He throws in the 90s, but needs to work on his knuckle-curve. . . Former football player **Anthony Sanders** is still learning the game, but his combination of power and speed is intriguing. He may be a center field prospect down the road. . . Young Venezuelan **Kelvim Escobar** blew hitters away in A-ball, but struggled in Double-A. Only 21 years old this year, he throws in the mid-90s and fanned almost a man per inning last year. . . Shortstop **Kevin Witt** was the Blue Jays' top pick in the '94 draft. His defensive problems may force a move to third base, but he's a left-handed hitter with good offensive potential.

National League Players

Bobby Cox

1996 Season

Bobby Cox has been baseball's most successful manager of the 1990s, and few skippers are more highly respected by their players and their peers. On a team with a seemingly endless supply of young talent, he's eased young players into vital roles with patience and restraint. All the while, as the youngsters have been learning how to make up for the loss of departed veterans, he's maintained a core to build around, and has just kept on winning.

Offense

Cox favors offense at the corners, but he'll find a smaller role for a player who's an obvious defensive liability. At other spots, he'll tolerate a weak hitter if the player makes up for it in the field. He sometimes will platoon a youngster in order to break him into the lineup gradually. There are usually one or two players on his bench who are kept around mainly to pinch hit.

Pitching & Defense

Cox and pitching coach Leo Mazzone have kept the Braves' pitchers more injury-free than any other staff. Cox has an excellent feel for the individual limits of each of his pitchers, and he knows exactly how many pitches they should be allowed to throw and how much rest they need between appearances. In the bullpen, he rarely rides the hot hand. His pen has well-defined roles and it takes an extended slump or hot streak before a pitcher will be moved to a different role. He stresses defense up the middle and at third base, in order to allow his pitchers to throw strikes with confidence.

1997 Outlook

It's hard to imagine a scenario which would result in the firing of Bobby Cox. Admittedly, the expectations are always high for him and the Braves, but Cox has been living up to those expectations for several years now. Another division title is the order for '97, and Cox has the talent on hand to deliver it, and more.

Born: 5/21/41 in Tulsa, OK

Playing Experience: 1968-1969, NYA

Managerial Experience: 15 seasons

Manager Statistics

Year	Team, Lg	W	L	Pct	GB	Finish
1996	Atlanta, NL	96	66	.593	—	1st East
15 Seasons		1,211	1,029	.541	—	—

1996 Starting Pitchers by Days Rest

	≤3	4	5	6+
Braves Starts	16	105	20	13
Braves ERA	3.36	3.25	3.77	4.06
NL Avg Starts	4	86	41	21
NL ERA	4.06	4.28	4.23	4.58

1996 Situational Stats

	Bobby Cox	NL Average
Hit & Run Success %	39.1	39.0
Stolen Base Success %	65.9	71.6
Platoon Pct.	62.1	51.9
Defensive Subs	27	20
High-Pitch Outings	19	13
Quick/Slow Hooks	25/13	19/12
Sacrifice Attempts	90	92

1996 Rankings (National League)

→ 1st in starts with over 140 pitches (1) and starts on three days rest (14)

→ 2nd in least caught steals of home plate (1), intentional walks (48), starts with over 120 pitches (19) and 2+ pitching changes in low scoring games (28)

→ 3rd in least caught steals of second base (38) and defensive substitutions (27)

Steve Avery

1996 Season

In 1996, Steve Avery hoped to rebound from his two-year slump and return to his former mastery. For the first two months of the season, he seemed to do just that, but his season unraveled in June, and a pulled muscle in his side knocked him out of action for most of July and August. When he returned late in the year, the injury still hindered him; he pitched inconsistently and never recovered his spot in the rotation.

Pitching

Avery comes straight over the top with a low-90s fastball, a curve and a straight change. His control has evolved to the point where he can spot all three pitches on the black fairly consistently, but his command suffers when he works out of the stretch. His arm is remarkably resilient, and he's never missed a start due to an arm injury.

Defense & Hitting

Avery's delivery limits his mobility, but he has good reactions and handles whatever he reaches. He's always had an excellent pickoff move, but he still used to be one of the easiest pitchers to run on, due to his high leg kick. But last year, he suddenly became one of the *toughest* to steal against when he learned to mix in a slide step at unpredictable times. As a hitter, he's one of the best among moundsmen, with 11 RBI and a .500 slugging average last year.

1997 Outlook

The Braves have already filled Avery's spot in the rotation, so when he entered the offseason as a free agent, Atlanta didn't put a high priority on re-signing him. His injury isn't the type that's likely to recur, and his arm is sound as always. Although it seems like he's been around forever, he's only 27 and should be just entering his peak years. Wherever he ends up, look for him to reclaim his spot among the game's elite lefthanders.

Position: SP
Bats: L **Throws:** L
Ht: 6' 4" **Wt:** 205

Opening Day Age: 26
Born: 4/14/70 in Trenton, MI
ML Seasons: 7

Overall Statistics

	W	L	Pct.	ERA	G	GS	Sv	IP	H	BB	SO	HR	BR/IP
1996	7	10	.412	4.47	24	23	0	131.0	146	40	86	10	1.42
Career	72	62	.537	3.83	203	201	0	1222.1	1180	371	815	103	1.27

How Often He Throws Strikes

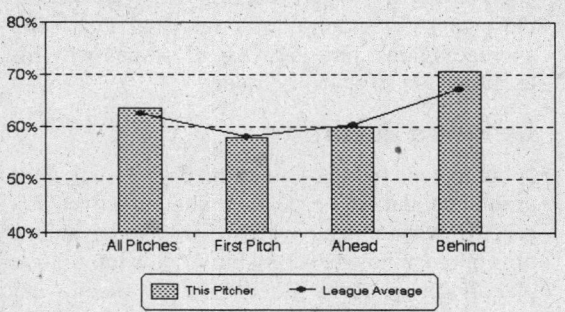

1996 Situational Stats

	W	L	ERA	Sv	IP		AB	H	HR	RBI	Avg
Home	3	4	3.95	0	73.0	LHB	90	23	0	11	.256
Road	4	6	5.12	0	58.0	RHB	423	123	10	48	.291
First Half	7	7	3.97	0	118.0	Sc Pos	107	40	1	47	.374
Scnd Half	0	3	9.00	0	13.0	Clutch	17	4	0	1	.235

1996 Rankings (National League)

→ Led the Braves in hit batsmen (4)

Brad Clontz

1996 Season

Brad Clontz's 1996 season went slowly down the drain. He spent much of the season as an important set-up man out of the Atlanta bullpen, but a league-leading 81 appearances took their toll. A terrible slump over the last two months of the season severely eroded his role, and by the time the postseason rolled around, he was rarely being summoned in important situations any more.

Pitching

Clontz's biggest asset is his unique motion, a low-sidearm, nearly submarine delivery. Right-handed hitters have a hard time connecting with his high-80s fastball and his darting slider, a pitch that has good lateral break but little drop. He's never come close to solving lefties, though, and their .363 average against him last year illustrates why his usefulness is so severely limited.

Defense & Hitting

A competent fielder, Clontz reaches his share of grounders, but isn't especially quick to cover first base. Baserunners have started to take advantage of him since he's been unable to develop a good pickoff move. As a hitter, he's completely unproven, although he did draw a couple of walks in four trips to the plate last year.

1997 Outlook

Since he's so effective against right-handed hitters, Clontz will remain useful if he can just make some progress in a couple of areas. First, he'll need to come up with a way to deal with lefties, which may require adding a new pitch. And second, he'll need to prove he can hold up better over the course of a long season. Although his role may be more limited next year, he'll get a chance to make the necessary adjustments.

Position: RP
Bats: R **Throws:** R
Ht: 6' 1" **Wt:** 180

Opening Day Age: 25
Born: 4/25/71 in Stuart, VA
ML Seasons: 2

Overall Statistics

	W	L	Pct.	ERA	G	GS	Sv	IP	H	BB	SO	HR	BR/IP
1996	6	3	.667	5.69	81	0	1	80.2	78	33	49	11	1.38
Career	14	4	.778	4.75	140	0	5	149.2	149	55	104	16	1.36

How Often He Throws Strikes

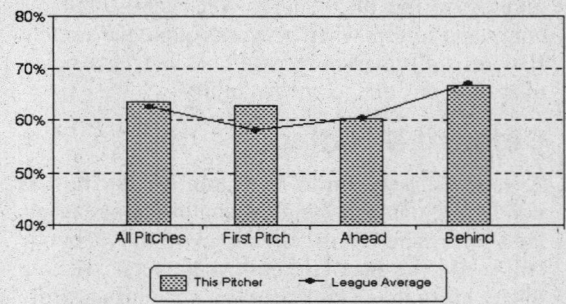

1996 Situational Stats

	W	L	ERA	Sv	IP		AB	H	HR	RBI	Avg
Home	5	2	3.38	1	42.2	LHB	80	29	6	14	.363
Road	1	1	8.29	0	38.0	RHB	226	49	5	39	.217
First Half	5	2	4.30	1	44.0	Sc Pos	86	23	3	42	.267
Scnd Half	1	1	7.36	0	36.2	Clutch	118	29	4	20	.246

1996 Rankings (National League)

➡ 1st in games pitched
➡ 3rd in highest relief ERA (5.69)
➡ 4th in least strikeouts per 9 innings in relief (5.5)
➡ 6th in holds (17)
➡ 10th in relief wins (6)
➡ Led the Braves in games pitched, balks (1) and relief wins (6)

Jermaine Dye

1996 Season

In his first trip to the plate in the major leagues, Jermaine Dye dug in and promptly hit a home run on his first swing of the bat. His tremendous tools continued to garner him attention for the rest of the year. Called up in May to replace the injured David Justice, Dye became one of the season's top rookies at the tender age of 22.

Hitting

Dye has a lightning-quick line-drive bat that can turn around anyone's fastball. He makes excellent contact. His production is even more remarkable when you consider that he still hasn't learned how to work the count. One day, he'll figure out what happens when he allows the pitcher to throw ball four, and when that happens, the pitchers will truly have a problem on their hands.

Baserunning & Defense

Dye has the tools to be an outstanding right fielder, with good speed and one of the strongest arms in the game. His throws are accurate, and he can cover all three outfield spots, but he looks raw at times in his approach to the ball. Dye still doesn't have a clue about reading pitchers' deliveries, but if he works at it, he has the speed to be a basestealer.

1997 Outlook

The Braves have been so pleased with Dye's emergence that they have begun to regard Fred McGriff as expendable. If McGriff is moved, Ryan Klesko will move to first and Dye will battle Andruw Jones and David Justice for playing time in either left or right field. Trading Justice is another option. Whatever happens, Dye figures to see plenty of action. He is certainly capable of continuing to produce at last year's level—which would be just fine—and his upside is very exciting.

Position: RF/LF
Bats: R **Throws:** R
Ht: 6' 4" **Wt:** 210

Opening Day Age: 23
Born: 1/28/74 in Oakland, CA
ML Seasons: 1

Overall Statistics

	G	AB	R	H	D	T	HR	RBI	SB	BB	SO	Avg	OBP	Slg
1996	98	292	32	82	16	0	12	37	1	8	67	.281	.304	.459
Career	98	292	32	82	16	0	12	37	1	8	67	.281	.304	.459

Where He Hits the Ball

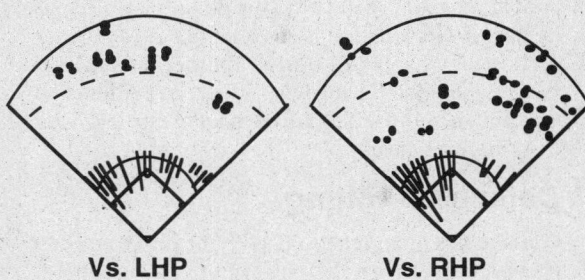

Vs. LHP   **Vs. RHP**

1996 Situational Stats

	AB	H	HR	RBI	Avg		AB	H	HR	RBI	Avg
Home	126	39	4	17	.310	LHP	93	30	5	12	.323
Road	166	43	8	20	.259	RHP	199	52	7	25	.261
First Half	84	26	5	14	.310	Sc Pos	82	21	2	24	.256
Scnd Half	208	56	7	23	.269	Clutch	60	13	1	5	.217

1996 Rankings (National League)

→ 4th in most GDPs per GDP situation (18.6%)
→ 10th in batting average on a 3-2 count (.381), errors in left field (4) and errors in right field (4)
→ Led the Braves in batting average on a 3-2 count (.381)

Tom Glavine

1996 Season

Somewhere between John Smoltz's launch into orbit and Greg Maddux's return to earth (such as it was), Tom Glavine quietly put together another stellar season. He led the league in starts, finished fifth in ERA (right behind teammate John Smoltz), and remained one of the best lefties around. The only disappointment was that unlike 1995, his chance to pitch the decisive game in the World Series never came.

Pitching

By now, everybody knows exactly where Tom Glavine makes his home. Why, it's right on the corner—the *outside* corner. He'll throw his 90 MPH fastball and wonderful change-up to that spot all day, and will come inside only as often as he has to. His location is so exact that he can work off the plate, and still throw a borderline strike if he gets behind. He throws a slider to lefties, and was much more effective against them last year than in years past.

Defense & Hitting

Glavine has great reactions with the glove and can handle anything hit back up the middle. Baserunners found him much tougher to read last year after he began to vary his stretch delivery. With the bat, Glavine is as dangerous as any pitcher in baseball. He led all pitchers with a .289 average last year, and was awarded the Silver Slugger.

1997 Outlook

Predicting another good year for Glavine is about as bold as predicting another good year for Microsoft—how can you go wrong? At the start of the season, Glavine was one of the game's top pitchers in nearly every facet of the game, except for holding runners and pitching to lefties. By the end of the year, he'd made major strides in each of his weak areas, while maintaining his superiority in everything else. The Braves picked up his option for 1997.

Position: SP
Bats: L **Throws:** L
Ht: 6' 1" **Wt:** 185

Opening Day Age: 31
Born: 3/25/66 in Concord, MA
ML Seasons: 10
Pronunciation: GLA-vin

Overall Statistics

	W	L	Pct.	ERA	G	GS	Sv	IP	H	BB	SO	HR	BR/IP
1996	15	10	.600	2.98	36	36	0	235.1	222	85	181	14	1.30
Career	139	92	.602	3.45	298	298	0	1956.1	1871	664	1212	127	1.30

How Often He Throws Strikes

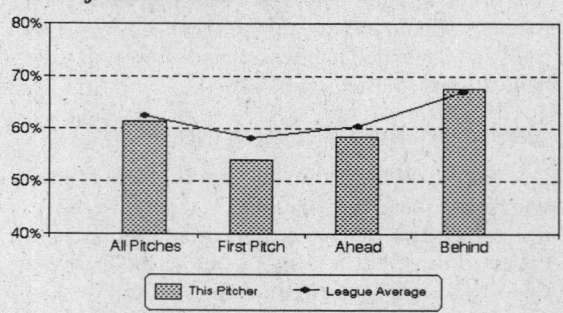

1996 Situational Stats

	W	L	ERA	Sv	IP		AB	H	HR	RBI	Avg
Home	8	3	2.45	0	114.0	LHB	152	35	1	9	.230
Road	7	7	3.49	0	121.1	RHB	740	187	13	68	.253
First Half	9	5	2.53	0	124.2	Sc Pos	205	45	3	58	.220
Scnd Half	6	5	3.50	0	110.2	Clutch	89	29	1	9	.326

1996 Rankings (National League)

- → 1st in games started and pitches thrown (3,835)
- → 3rd in sacrifice bunts (15), batters faced (994), least home runs allowed per 9 innings (.54) and bunts in play (24)
- → 4th in ERA at home (2.45)
- → 5th in ERA and innings pitched
- → 7th in lowest slugging percentage allowed (.353), lowest stolen base percentage allowed (50.0%) and most pitches thrown per batter (3.86)
- → 8th in hits allowed and ERA on the road (3.49)
- → 9th in wins and walks allowed
- → 10th in fielding percentage at pitcher (.985)

Marquis Grissom

1996 Season

After a so-so first season in Atlanta, Marquis Grissom finally delivered what the Braves had been expecting last season. He played his usual first-rate defense, but also came through with his best year yet at the plate. He batted over .300 and broke the 20-homer barrier—reaching each of those plateaus for the first time—while scoring 106 runs and finishing third in the league in hits. As an all-around center fielder, few were better last year.

Hitting

At the plate, Grissom's goal is to get a pitch he's looking for, rather than to work the count in his favor. He's a first-ball, fastball hitter, and will sometimes go after a fastball out of the zone. He hits the ball where it's pitched, showing good power to the alleys. As a leadoff man, his ability to get on base isn't all that impressive, but he makes up for that with what he does once he gets on base.

Baserunning & Defense

Grissom is one of the fastest and most aggressive baserunners in the league, although he's scaled back his running game a bit with Atlanta's powerful sluggers following him in the order. He often goes for the extra base, and very rarely gets thrown out trying. On defense, he's the complete package. His uncommon ability to go back on the ball enables him to play unusually shallow, seemingly covering everything from the infield to the warning track. His arm is strong and true. Last year, he made only one error, and was rewarded with his fourth straight Gold Glove.

1997 Outlook

Grissom has quietly become one of the most irreplaceable Braves—a crucial part of both their lineup and their defense. Luckily for the Braves, durability is another one of Grissom's strengths, so he remains an excellent bet to put up another good all-around season next year.

Position: CF
Bats: R **Throws:** R
Ht: 5'11" **Wt:** 190

Opening Day Age: 29
Born: 4/17/67 in Atlanta, GA
ML Seasons: 8

Overall Statistics

	G	AB	R	H	D	T	HR	RBI	SB	BB	SO	Avg	OBP	Slg
1996	158	671	106	207	32	10	23	74	28	41	73	.308	.349	.489
Career	995	3900	616	1096	185	36	89	392	323	296	507	.281	.332	.415

Where He Hits the Ball

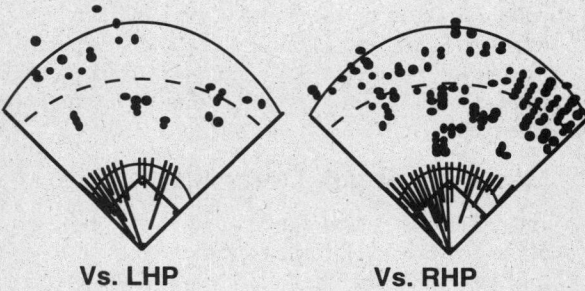

Vs. LHP   **Vs. RHP**

1996 Situational Stats

	AB	H	HR	RBI	Avg		AB	H	HR	RBI	Avg
Home	337	105	11	38	.312	LHP	168	52	9	24	.310
Road	334	102	12	36	.305	RHP	503	155	14	50	.308
First Half	367	108	13	39	.294	Sc Pos	148	43	5	56	.291
Scnd Half	304	99	10	35	.326	Clutch	99	30	1	10	.303

1996 Rankings (National League)

→ 2nd in at-bats, triples, plate appearances (723) and fielding percentage in center field (.997)
→ 3rd in hits
→ 4th in singles
→ 5th in least pitches seen per plate appearance (3.35)
→ 7th in total bases (328) and caught stealing
→ 9th in on-base percentage for a leadoff hitter (.350)
→ 10th in batting average on the road (.305)
→ Led the Braves in at-bats, hits, singles, triples, total bases (328), stolen bases, caught stealing, plate appearances (723), stolen base percentage (71.8%) and slugging percentage vs. left-handed pitchers (.565)

Chipper Jones

1996 Season

Chipper Jones has played two years in the majors, and mankind has yet to discover something that he *can't* do on a baseball field. He hit for power, he hit for average, he drew walks, he stole bases, he started the All-Star game at third base, and when the Braves needed a shortstop, he moved back to his old position and played like he'd never been away. The only thing he didn't do was take home a World Series ring, although he did bat .286 with three doubles in the Series.

Hitting

Well, it's now safe to say that Jones' 1995 power surge was no fluke. Among his other skills, Jones knows how to wait for his pitch. He can wait out a walk, but lights up the board when a pitcher tries to get ahead by just laying it in on the first pitch. He likes the ball up from either side of the plate, and laces line drives all over the field, covering the entire plate.

Baserunning & Defense

Jones has such good range at third that he can afford to play much further off the line than most third basemen. He has soft hands and a third baseman's arm, and his errors have dropped dramatically as he's grown accustomed to his new position. He played 38 games at shortstop last year, making only four errors and showing decent range. Jones has good speed, and is wise beyond his years on the basepaths, knowing exactly when to steal or to take the extra base.

1997 Outlook

Jones, who will be only 25 years old next year, has a higher ceiling than the Houston Astrodome. At this point, the only question seems to be whether he'll be one of the game's best shortstops or third basemen. In any event, he will swing the bat around which the Atlanta lineup will be built for years to come.

Position: 3B/SS
Bats: B **Throws:** R
Ht: 6' 3" **Wt:** 200

Opening Day Age: 24
Born: 4/24/72 in DeLand, FL
ML Seasons: 3

Overall Statistics

	G	AB	R	H	D	T	HR	RBI	SB	BB	SO	Avg	OBP	Slg
1996	157	598	114	185	32	5	30	110	14	87	88	.309	.393	.530
Career	305	1125	203	326	55	8	53	196	22	161	188	.290	.375	.494

Where He Hits the Ball

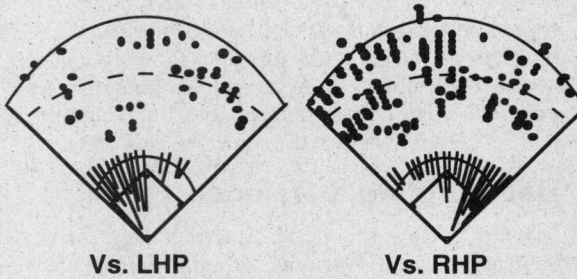

Vs. LHP   **Vs. RHP**

1996 Situational Stats

	AB	H	HR	RBI	Avg		AB	H	HR	RBI	Avg
Home	292	99	18	69	.339	LHP	173	51	6	29	.295
Road	306	86	12	41	.281	RHP	425	134	24	81	.315
First Half	327	98	17	66	.300	Sc Pos	159	51	6	75	.321
Scnd Half	271	87	13	44	.321	Clutch	91	32	7	29	.352

1996 Rankings (National League)

- → 2nd in lowest fielding percentage at third base (.947)
- → 4th in highest percentage of extra bases taken as a runner (66.7%)
- → 5th in batting average in the clutch (.352)
- → 6th in walks and times on base (272)
- → 8th in runs scored
- → 9th in batting average vs. right-handed pitchers (.315), batting average on a 3-1 count (.600), on-base percentage vs. right-handed pitchers (.404) and errors at third base (13)
- → 10th in pitches seen (2,609), lowest batting average with the bases loaded (.143) and batting average at home (.339)

David Justice

Position: RF
Bats: L **Throws:** L
Ht: 6' 3" **Wt:** 200

Opening Day Age: 30
Born: 4/14/66 in
Cincinnati, OH
ML Seasons: 8

1996 Season

Ouch. On May 15, with his World Series-winning home run still fresh in everyone's minds, David Justice took a swing at a pitch, and missed. His high, twisting, Statue-of-Liberty follow-through usually serves as little more than a personal trademark, but this time it resulted in a dislocation of his right shoulder. The resulting surgery put him out for the rest of the season, giving other young outfielders the opportunity to showcase their skills and push Justice out of the Braves' plans—which they did.

Hitting

Justice hits the ball to all fields with power, and hits lefties and righties equally well. He makes uncommonly good contact for a power hitter, and remains dangerous with two strikes. The low inside pitch is his favorite, and his slight uppercut works best against low fastballs. His biggest weakness is that he tends to be a bit streaky, although he hasn't been as prone to slumps in recent years since learning to hit the ball to left field more.

Baserunning & Defense

Although he has good speed, stealing bases isn't part of Justice's game. He will run the bases aggressively, though, and generally makes it pay off. His range, positioning and reliability in the outfield have improved markedly, although his formerly strong throwing arm has deteriorated.

1997 Outlook

With one swing of the bat, Justice went from being a central member of the World Champions to trade bait with a questionable future. Supposedly, he'll be completely recovered from the shoulder injury by next spring, but his unique swing carries the risk of a possible recurrence. It remains to be seen which team will be willing to take such a gamble when he's signed to such a hefty salary. With the glut of young talent in the Braves' outfield, Justice may have played his last game in an Atlanta uniform.

Overall Statistics

	G	AB	R	H	D	T	HR	RBI	SB	BB	SO	Avg	OBP	Slg
1996	40	140	23	45	9	0	6	25	1	21	22	.321	.409	.514
Career	817	2858	475	786	127	16	160	522	33	452	492	.275	.374	.499

Where He Hits the Ball

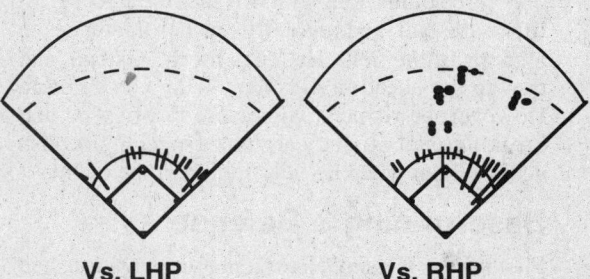

Vs. LHP   **Vs. RHP**

1996 Situational Stats

	AB	H	HR	RBI	Avg		AB	H	HR	RBI	Avg
Home	79	27	5	20	.342	LHP	53	17	3	8	.321
Road	61	18	1	5	.295	RHP	87	28	3	17	.322
First Half	140	45	6	25	.321	Sc Pos	31	10	2	21	.323
Scnd Half	0	0	0	0	-	Clutch	20	7	1	2	.350

1996 Rankings (National League)

→ 1st in lowest batting average on a 3-1 count (.000)

Ryan Klesko

1996 Season

After serving a two-year apprenticeship as a platoon player, young slugger Ryan Klesko finally got to play every day last year. The results were mixed: his overall numbers were as good as had been expected, but his efforts to solve lefthanders seemed to prevent him from making any progress in other areas of his game. He remains a work-in-progress, with his tremendous strengths sometimes overshadowed by his gaping weaknesses.

Hitting

Klesko brings power to the plate, and plenty of it. His 34 homers led the team, but he didn't fare well in his first extended trial against lefties, hitting only three of his home runs off them. He gets great lift on the ball, and regularly reaches the fences in all parts of the field. He looks for the fastball, and tries to get ahead in the count so he can sit on it. However, he remains vulnerable to offspeed and breaking pitches, and can look especially foolish against them when he falls behind in the count.

Baserunning & Defense

First base is Klesko's least unnatural position, and his conversion to left field two years ago was a bit rocky. He has improved, but not yet to the point where he can be considered average. His range and arm are poor, and he still wavers under a fly ball like Lonnie Smith staring into the sun. He went a surprising six-for-nine on stolen bases, but he doesn't have nearly enough speed to keep that up.

1997 Outlook

Klesko's goals remain the same for next year: upgrade the defense, make progress against the lefties and learn how to read offspeed pitches. That's a long laundry list, but even with those flaws, he's still become one of the league's best power hitters. How much farther he goes will depend on how well he's able to round out his game.

Position: LF
Bats: L **Throws:** L
Ht: 6' 3" **Wt:** 220

Opening Day Age: 25
Born: 6/12/71 in Westminster, CA
ML Seasons: 5

Overall Statistics

	G	AB	R	H	D	T	HR	RBI	SB	BB	SO	Avg	OBP	Slg
1996	153	528	90	149	21	4	34	93	6	68	129	.282	.364	.530
Career	387	1133	183	325	60	9	76	216	12	144	258	.287	.367	.557

Where He Hits the Ball

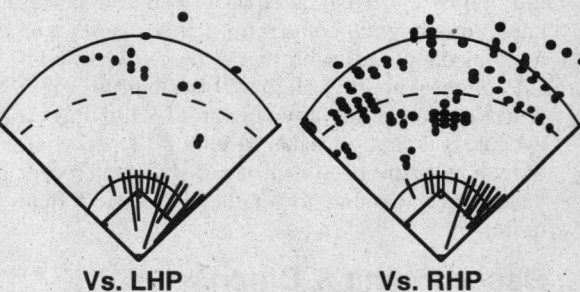

Vs. LHP   **Vs. RHP**

1996 Situational Stats

	AB	H	HR	RBI	Avg		AB	H	HR	RBI	Avg
Home	266	86	20	51	.323	LHP	139	32	3	12	.230
Road	262	63	14	42	.240	RHP	389	117	31	81	.301
First Half	299	85	22	52	.284	Sc Pos	129	34	9	59	.264
Scnd Half	229	64	12	41	.279	Clutch	84	18	0	7	.214

1996 Rankings (National League)

- ➡ 4th in lowest on-base percentage vs. left-handed pitchers (.285) and lowest fielding percentage in left field (.975)
- ➡ 5th in slugging percentage vs. right-handed pitchers (.604) and errors in left field (5)
- ➡ 6th in strikeouts and lowest slugging percentage vs. left-handed pitchers (.324)
- ➡ 7th in lowest batting average vs. left-handed pitchers (.230)
- ➡ 8th in highest percentage of swings that missed (28.0%)
- ➡ 10th in HR frequency (15.5 ABs per HR), lowest groundball/flyball ratio (1.0), lowest batting average on the road (.240) and lowest percentage of swings put into play (37.1%)

Mark Lemke

1996 Season

Last year, Mark Lemke delivered exactly what everyone has grown to expect from him: unremarkable hitting, consistent, rock-solid defense and, ultimately, postseason heroics. He missed two months in the first half with a sprained ligament in his thumb, and the injury affected his hitting upon his return. But he still provided a nightly clinic on second-base defense, and his hot hitting was a key to the Braves' comeback win in the NLCS.

Hitting

A switch-hitter, Lemke likes to chop down on the high pitch, generating little power, but spraying a decent number of hits around. He hit in the number-two hole most of last year, and his ability to make contact, hit behind the runner and lay down a bunt helps him in that role. He's usually a stronger hitter from the right side, but had trouble from that side of the plate last year—possibly due to his lingering thumb injury.

Baserunning & Defense

Lemke doesn't have exceptional speed, but his amazing quickness makes him a top-flight defender. He somehow seems to start toward the ball before it's even hit, and his small steps allow him to stay low as he glides to the ball. With quick hands and perfect footwork, he's one of the best at starting the double play or turning the pivot. His feet aren't nearly as effective on offense, and the best that can be said is that he runs the bases intelligently.

1997 Outlook

Lemke's contract was up at the end of 1996 and it's possible he won't return to Atlanta. That would be a loss for the club. He may not remain in the upper half of the batting order, but anyone who watches the Braves knows that his defense has been a critical element of Atlanta's continuing success.

Position: 2B
Bats: B **Throws:** R
Ht: 5' 9" **Wt:** 167

Opening Day Age: 31
Born: 8/13/65 in Utica, NY
ML Seasons: 9

Overall Statistics

	G	AB	R	H	D	T	HR	RBI	SB	BB	SO	Avg	OBP	Slg
1996	135	498	64	127	17	0	5	37	5	53	48	.255	.323	.319
Career	929	2788	306	692	104	14	30	237	9	309	275	.248	.321	.328

Where He Hits the Ball

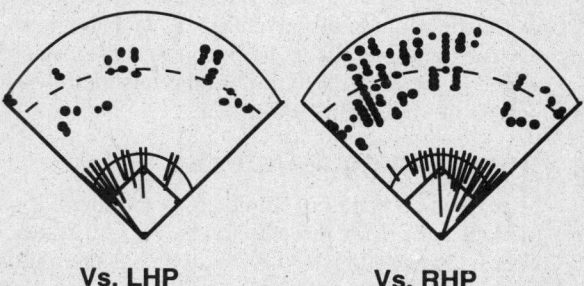

Vs. LHP   **Vs. RHP**

1996 Situational Stats

	AB	H	HR	RBI	Avg		AB	H	HR	RBI	Avg
Home	269	80	3	24	.297	LHP	128	28	3	7	.219
Road	229	47	2	13	.205	RHP	370	99	2	30	.268
First Half	253	70	4	21	.277	Sc Pos	106	28	0	31	.264
Scnd Half	245	57	1	16	.233	Clutch	74	19	0	6	.257

1996 Rankings (National League)

→ 1st in lowest batting average on the road (.205)
→ 3rd in errors at second base (15) and lowest fielding percentage at second base (.977)
→ 4th in lowest slugging percentage, lowest slugging percentage vs. right-handed pitchers (.319) and highest percentage of swings put into play (57.5%)
→ 5th in lowest slugging percentage vs. left-handed pitchers (.320)
→ 6th in lowest batting average vs. left-handed pitchers (.219)
→ 7th in lowest HR frequency (99.6 ABs per HR)

Javy Lopez

1996 Season

Javy Lopez's breakthrough season in 1995 earned him more playing time last year, and he put it to good use. In the past, Bobby Cox had been reluctant to give any one catcher too much of the load, but last year, he allowed Lopez to start almost every game that Greg Maddux and Steve Avery weren't scheduled to pitch. Lopez responded by socking 23 homers, solidifying his spot as one of the best-hitting catchers in the league.

Hitting

Lopez is an impatient hitter who has excellent power to center and right-center field. The low pitch is his favorite, and he can go down and get any pitcher's breaking ball. He's a terror when he works the count to his advantage, so he may grow by leaps and bounds as he becomes more disciplined at the plate. Still, he has the bat control to protect the plate with two strikes.

Baserunning & Defense

Lopez's main handicap on defense is an inability to block balls in the dirt effectively. This frustrates pitchers like Maddux and Avery, who must be able to throw their breaking pitches without fear in order to be effective. Lopez has a strong arm, and is unafraid to throw to any base at any time. He doesn't run well, and was successful on only one of his seven stolen-base attempts last year.

1997 Outlook

Lopez has undoubtedly broken into the upper echelon of major league catchers, but he has a lot to work on before he can be called a true star. The holes in his game—both at the plate and behind it—are not enormous, but he has considerable room for improvement. Still only 26, he'll probably take another small step closer to stardom next year.

Position: C
Bats: R **Throws:** R
Ht: 6' 3" **Wt:** 200

Opening Day Age: 26
Born: 11/5/70 in Ponce, PR
ML Seasons: 5

Overall Statistics

	G	AB	R	H	D	T	HR	RBI	SB	BB	SO	Avg	OBP	Slg
1996	138	489	56	138	19	1	23	69	1	28	84	.282	.322	.466
Career	335	1131	124	323	42	6	51	159	1	59	205	.286	.325	.469

Where He Hits the Ball

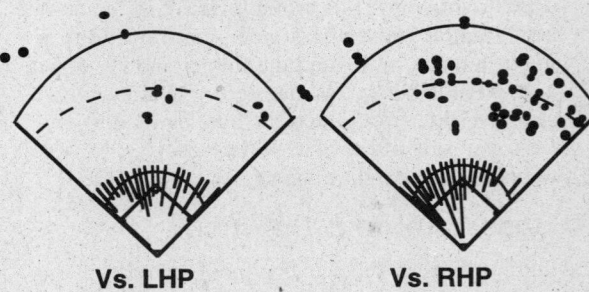

Vs. LHP   **Vs. RHP**

1996 Situational Stats

	AB	H	HR	RBI	Avg		AB	H	HR	RBI	Avg
Home	237	66	10	37	.278	LHP	113	34	4	17	.301
Road	252	72	13	32	.286	RHP	376	104	19	52	.277
First Half	269	76	12	38	.283	Sc Pos	120	31	2	41	.258
Scnd Half	220	62	11	31	.282	Clutch	102	29	3	18	.284

1996 Rankings (National League)

- ➡ 2nd in highest groundball/flyball ratio (2.1) and fielding percentage at catcher (.994)
- ➡ 3rd in lowest batting average with the bases loaded (.091)
- ➡ 6th in least pitches seen per plate appearance (3.36)
- ➡ 8th in batting average on an 0-2 count (.283) and highest percentage of swings on the first pitch (42.6%)
- ➡ Led the Braves in highest groundball/flyball ratio (2.1) and batting average on an 0-2 count (.283)

Greg Maddux

Position: SP
Bats: R **Throws:** R
Ht: 6' 0" **Wt:** 175

Opening Day Age: 30
Born: 4/14/66 in San Angelo, TX
ML Seasons: 11

Atlanta Braves

1996 Season

How good is Greg Maddux? He's so good that last year, he won 15 games for the ninth consecutive season, allowed 17 unintentional walks while fanning 172 batters, and finished second in the league in ERA, but the only thing anyone seemed to ask was, "What's wrong with Greg Maddux?" It must have been one of the most remarkable "off years" in history.

Pitching

Maddux' pitches defy classification. His hardest fastball approaches the high-80s, and he can cut it and run it in and out. He's constantly taking something off it—a little, then a lot—and when he wants to hit the brakes completely, he uses his circle change. He also throws a curve, a slider, and a million breaking balls that fall somewhere in-between. His exceptional movement and pinpoint control enable him to paint the corners and make the batter pound the ball into the ground early in the count. As a result, he's the master of efficiency, finishing second in the league in innings pitched last year without ever throwing 120 pitches in a single contest.

Hitting & Defense

Maddux, who won his seventh straight Gold Glove last year, is generally regarded as the game's best-fielding pitcher. He can hit, too, rarely striking out, and laying down a bunt when needed. Holding runners is his only weakness, since he doesn't waste time throwing to first.

1997 Outlook

Despite all the head-scratching, the answer to everyone's question is simple: there was *nothing* "wrong" with Greg Maddux last year. He threw only one less quality start than John Smoltz did, but poor run support left Maddux with a far inferior won-loss record. That likely won't keep up next year, so Maddux is an excellent bet to recapture his crown as "King of the Hill."

Overall Statistics

	W	L	Pct.	ERA	G	GS	Sv	IP	H	BB	SO	HR	BR/IP
1996	15	11	.577	2.72	35	35	0	245.0	225	28	172	11	1.03
Career	165	104	.613	2.86	336	332	0	2365.2	2102	589	1643	119	1.14

How Often He Throws Strikes

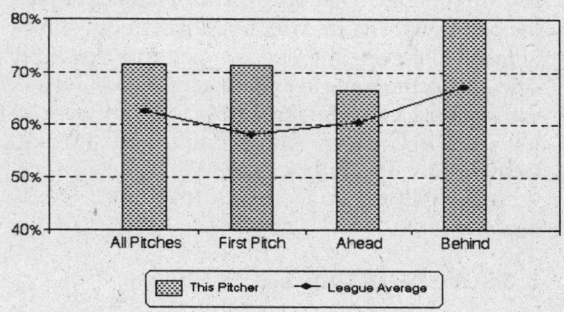

1996 Situational Stats

	W	L	ERA	Sv	IP		AB	H	HR	RBI	Avg
Home	12	3	2.44	0	140.0	LHB	423	95	4	26	.225
Road	3	8	3.09	0	105.0	RHB	511	130	7	52	.254
First Half	9	6	2.89	0	143.1	Sc Pos	199	51	5	69	.256
Scnd Half	6	5	2.48	0	101.2	Clutch	112	30	3	13	.268

1996 Rankings (National League)

- ➡ 1st in highest strikeout/walk ratio (6.1) and least pitches thrown per batter (3.10)
- ➡ 2nd in ERA, games started, innings pitched, highest groundball/flyball ratio allowed (3.0) and least home runs allowed per 9 innings (.40)
- ➡ 3rd in complete games (5), GDPs induced (24), lowest on-base percentage allowed (.264), least baserunners allowed per 9 innings and ERA at home (2.44)
- ➡ 4th in lowest slugging percentage allowed (.337) and ERA on the road (3.09)
- ➡ 5th in batters faced (978)
- ➡ 6th in hits allowed and lowest batting average allowed vs. left-handed batters (.225)

Fred McGriff

1996 Season

Was it a good year, or an off year? Fred McGriff's numbers are so consistent that it can be impossible to tell. On one hand, he batted .295, started in the All-Star game, and drove in a career-high 107 runs even without David Justice to protect him. But on the other hand, he failed to reach his customary 30-home run plateau, and suffered through a two-month slump in the middle of the season. On balance, his season was—like McGriff himself—unspectacular, but highly valuable.

Hitting

Unlike most power hitters today, McGriff stands well off the plate. He generates his power by getting full extension of his arms. He likes to pull the ball down and in, which results in quite a few homers but even more groundouts to the right side—causing some teams to employ an infield shift against him. He can also hit the ball hard to left field if you give him a pitch up and away. Lefties don't bother him, except for those who can keep the ball down and away from him consistently.

Baserunning & Defense

Although McGriff looks like he ought to run fairly well, he doesn't. He's mostly a station-to-station baserunner, and his improbable seven-for-10 basestealing performance last year equalled the best of his career. He has ordinary range around the first base bag, and nothing in particular to distinguish himself with the glove.

1997 Outlook

At age 33, McGriff may no longer be a lock for 30 homers and 100 RBI. But he's remarkably consistent, and there's no reason to think he'll fall apart any time soon. His days in Atlanta may be numbered, however. The Braves have an abundance of talented outfielders, and there was talk over the winter of dealing McGriff and moving Ryan Klesko to his natural position, first base. Wherever McGriff ends up this year, he should remain one of the top sluggers in the game.

Position: 1B
Bats: L **Throws:** L
Ht: 6' 3" **Wt:** 215

Opening Day Age: 33
Born: 10/31/63 in Tampa, FL
ML Seasons: 11
Nickname: Crime Dog

Overall Statistics

	G	AB	R	H	D	T	HR	RBI	SB	BB	SO	Avg	OBP	Slg
1996	159	617	81	182	37	1	28	107	7	68	116	.295	.365	.494
Career	1450	5129	869	1466	266	18	317	910	55	812	1135	.286	.383	.530

Where He Hits the Ball

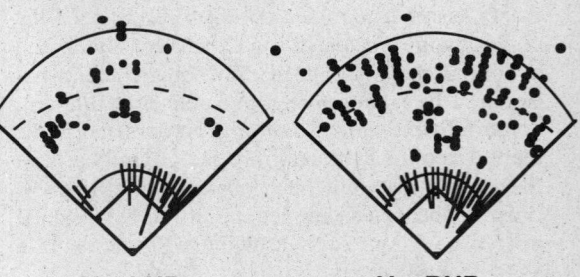

Vs. LHP   **Vs. RHP**

1996 Situational Stats

	AB	H	HR	RBI	Avg			AB	H	HR	RBI	Avg
Home	312	88	17	64	.282		LHP	200	65	11	41	.325
Road	305	94	11	43	.308		RHP	417	117	17	66	.281
First Half	341	101	20	68	.296		Sc Pos	172	46	8	72	.267
Scnd Half	276	81	8	39	.293		Clutch	92	26	3	11	.283

1996 Rankings (National League)

- → 4th in errors at first base (12) and lowest fielding percentage at first base (.992)
- → 5th in GDPs (20)
- → 6th in batting average with the bases loaded (.556)
- → 7th in games played (159)
- → 8th in intentional walks (12), lowest batting average on an 0-2 count (.038) and batting average on the road (.308)
- → 9th in lowest cleanup slugging percentage (.499)
- → Led the Braves in doubles, intentional walks (12), GDPs (20), games played (159) and batting average with the bases loaded (.556)

Greg McMichael

Position: RP
Bats: R **Throws:** R
Ht: 6' 3" **Wt:** 215

Opening Day Age: 30
Born: 12/1/66 in
Knoxville, TN
ML Seasons: 4

Atlanta Braves

1996 Season

Greg McMichael emerged as one of the league's best set-up men in 1995, and remained just as effective in '96 until elbow tendinitis slowed him during the season's final month. Before his late slump hit, he was one of the most valuable and frequently-used members of the Atlanta bullpen. His ill health was especially damaging in the postseason, where his ineffectiveness or unavailability led to several late-inning debacles.

Pitching

McMichael pitches like he prays to a statue of Doug Jones. He has no fastball to speak of, and relies almost exclusively upon his change-up. He varies its speed and location, slinging it toward the corners with his sidearm delivery. He'll mix in a slider for show, but like so many of the Braves' pitchers, he makes his living on the low outside corner. To make it all work, he needs to hit his spots, keep the ball down, and vary his velocity. When he's able to do that, he gets a surprisingly high number of strikeouts.

Hitting & Defense

McMichael is competent but unremarkable at fielding and at holding runners. He induces ground balls, and reaches a fair number of them himself. As a hitter, he's still looking for his first hit after 11 at-bats in the majors.

1997 Outlook

McMichael's poor postseason sealed his fate with the Braves, and they traded him to the New York Mets in November. He figures to handle the same middle relief role in New York that he had in Atlanta, and if he's healthy he should be able to return to effectiveness. His success will depend largely on the status of his cranky elbow.

Overall Statistics

	W	L	Pct.	ERA	G	GS	Sv	IP	H	BB	SO	HR	BR/IP
1996	5	3	.625	3.22	73	0	2	86.2	84	27	78	4	1.28
Career	18	14	.563	2.89	265	0	44	317.2	282	107	288	16	1.22

How Often He Throws Strikes

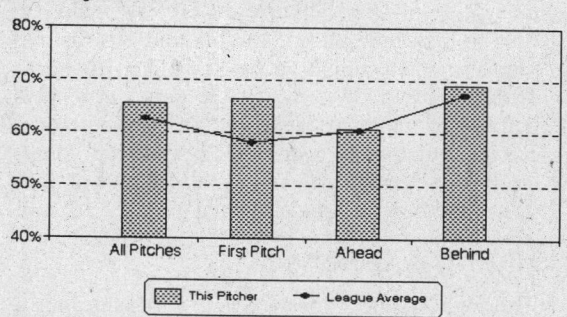

1996 Situational Stats

	W	L	ERA	Sv	IP		AB	H	HR	RBI	Avg
Home	4	0	3.42	0	50.0	LHB	176	51	3	23	.290
Road	1	3	2.95	2	36.2	RHB	156	33	1	18	.212
First Half	3	1	3.10	1	49.1	Sc Pos	95	24	1	35	.253
Scnd Half	2	2	3.38	1	37.1	Clutch	160	42	2	23	.263

1996 Rankings (National League)

→ 5th in holds (18)
→ 7th in relief innings (86.2)
→ 8th in games pitched and blown saves (6)
→ Led the Braves in balks (1), holds (18), blown saves (6) and relief innings (86.2)

Denny Neagle

1996 Season

In 1992, the Pirates acquired Denny Neagle as part of a package from the Minnesota Twins in exchange for a star lefthander (John Smiley) that the Pirates couldn't afford to keep. Last year, Neagle himself became the star lefthander that the Pirates couldn't afford to keep, and they sent him to the Braves at the trading deadline for another package of young talent. It took Neagle a while to get settled in the Braves' All-Star rotation, but he pitched well in both of his postseason starts, and finally seemed to relax under the heat of the spotlight.

Pitching

Neagle's low-three-quarters delivery makes it hard to pick the ball up, and his mid-80s fastball seems to rise as it approaches the plate. His beautiful change-up looks exactly the same until it dies halfway to the plate. He also offers a slider and a change, but changing speeds is his bread-and-butter. With a durable arm and excellent control, he's one of the best lefthanders in the game.

Hitting & Defense

Although Neagle's good move to first nabs quite a few unsuspecting baserunners, his long stretch delivery still gives them a good step or two toward second base. He's good with the glove and very quick off the mound. At the plate, he's nothing special when he swings the bat—but he's become one of the best bunters around, and uses that skill to good advantage.

1997 Outlook

After Neagle found such success in Pittsburgh, everyone was eager to see how much better he could be with the Atlanta Braves behind him. We'll soon find out, because the Braves won an intense bidding war by signing Neagle to a four-year, $17.5 million pact after the season. If his postseason performance is any indication, he seems to have made the transition from small-market ace to big-time performer.

Position: SP
Bats: L **Throws:** L
Ht: 6' 2" **Wt:** 216

Opening Day Age: 28
Born: 9/13/68 in Gambrills, MD
ML Seasons: 6
Pronunciation: NAY-gull

Overall Statistics

	W	L	Pct.	ERA	G	GS	Sv	IP	H	BB	SO	HR	BR/IP
1996	16	9	.640	3.50	33	33	0	221.1	226	48	149	26	1.24
Career	45	39	.536	4.10	200	104	3	755.2	773	229	585	86	1.33

How Often He Throws Strikes

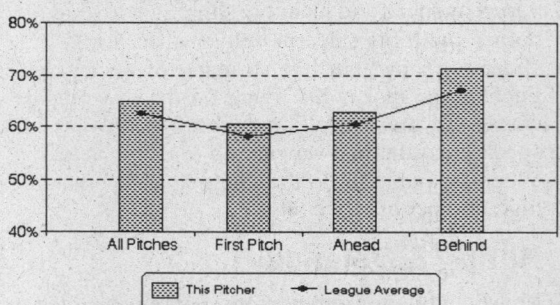

1996 Situational Stats

	W	L	ERA	Sv	IP		AB	H	HR	RBI	Avg
Home	9	2	3.11	0	107.0	LHB	110	31	2	6	.282
Road	7	7	3.86	0	114.1	RHB	735	195	24	80	.265
First Half	9	4	2.93	0	113.2	Sc Pos	167	47	4	59	.281
Scnd Half	7	5	4.10	0	107.2	Clutch	80	28	2	6	.350

1996 Rankings (National League)

→ 1st in sacrifice bunts (16)
→ 5th in wins (16), hits allowed (226) and runners caught stealing (12)
→ 6th in winning percentage (.640)
→ 9th in GDPs induced (21) and bunts in play (19)

John Smoltz

1996 Season

How did an underachieving righthander with a career record eight games over .500 suddenly break out to win 24 games and a Cy Young Award? Was it the result of finally feeling 100 percent healthy, after pitching in pain for years, and spending 1995 rebuilding arm strength after finally undergoing elbow surgery? Was it the relief and maturity that comes from finally shedding the "unfulfilled potential" label? Was it the sudden evening-out of an entire career's worth of bad luck? Indeed, it was all that and more.

Pitching

John Smoltz' stuff has always been among the best in baseball. He combines a moving, mid-90s fastball with a slider and a curveball that each rate among the best in the game. He also features a nasty split-fingered fastball, and has developed superb command of all of his pitches. His combination of power and control is virtually unrivaled in baseball. A true workhorse, he always answers the bell and throws as many pitches as it takes to get the job done. Although he's not quite as tough from the stretch, he can be virtually unhittable from the full windup.

Hitting & Defense

As if his pitching weren't enough, Smoltz also fields his position well, and makes life hard for enemy basestealers. He hits, too: he led all pitchers with 12 RBI last year, and is adept at laying down bunts.

1997 Outlook

Until last year, John Smoltz had been regarded as a disappointment for his entire career. Now he may be in danger of falling short of some people's expectations again. However, he won't allow this to eat away at him as it has in the past. His new outlook should enable him to remain one of the best righthanders in the game, which should satisfy just about everyone, including—most importantly—John Smoltz. He tested the free-agent waters during the offseason and got a huge nibble from the Indians, but he ultimately signed a four-year, $31 million deal to remain with the Braves.

Position: SP
Bats: R **Throws:** R
Ht: 6' 3" **Wt:** 185

Opening Day Age: 29
Born: 5/15/67 in Warren, MI
ML Seasons: 9

Atlanta Braves

Overall Statistics

	W	L	Pct.	ERA	G	GS	Sv	IP	H	BB	SO	HR	BR/IP
1996	24	8	.750	2.94	35	35	0	253.2	199	55	276	19	1.00
Career	114	90	.559	3.45	266	266	0	1804.1	1545	627	1528	150	1.20

How Often He Throws Strikes

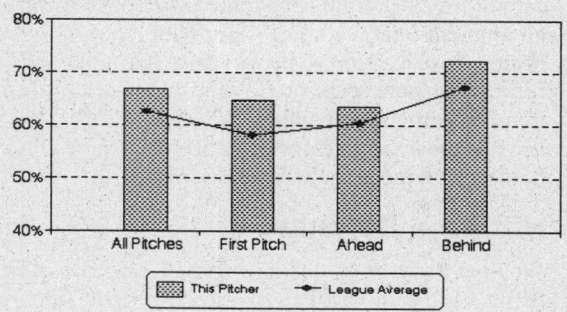

1996 Situational Stats

	W	L	ERA	Sv	IP		AB	H	HR	RBI	Avg
Home	13	3	2.94	0	131.2	LHB	394	87	5	28	.221
Road	11	5	2.95	0	122.0	RHB	528	112	14	61	.212
First Half	14	4	3.16	0	134.0	Sc Pos	174	46	5	65	.264
Scnd Half	10	4	2.71	0	119.2	Clutch	98	20	2	9	.204

1996 Rankings (National League)

➡ 1st in wins, innings pitched, strikeouts, winning percentage, lowest on-base percentage allowed (.260), least baserunners allowed per 9 innings and most strikeouts per 9 innings (9.8)

➡ 2nd in games started, complete games (6), shutouts (2), batters faced (995), pitches thrown (3,801), highest strikeout/walk ratio (5.0) and lowest batting average allowed (.216)

➡ 3rd in sacrifice bunts (15), lowest slugging percentage allowed (.331), least GDPs induced per 9 innings (0.5) and ERA on the road (2.95)

Mark Wohlers

1996 Season

What do you get when you add precise control to the game's best fastball? Why, you get Mark Wohlers, that's what. Last year, he used that unique combination to save 39 games for the Atlanta Braves, emerging as one of the most dominant—and, finally, most *effective*—short relievers in the game.

Pitching

Wohlers' fastball is the only one in the game that consistently flirts with triple-digits, and observers have long wondered what he could do if he ever fully harnessed it. Well, we can stop wondering now: not only has he gotten control of the pitch, he even went 29 straight appearances without issuing an unintentional walk last year. With that kind of heater, he can afford to use his mid-80s slider and forkball as mere scenery. He'll probably be a little more careful about using the slider after Jim Leyritz creamed one for a game-tying three-run homer in Game 4 of the World Series.

Hitting & Defense

Wohlers' fastball is such a weapon that he doesn't really have to hold runners—so he doesn't (they stole 12 bases in 13 attempts on him last year). Since he's so hard to hit, he doesn't have to field well—so he doesn't (three errors in 10 chances). And as a short reliever, he doesn't have to hit much—so he doesn't (three at-bats, three strikeouts). But no one really complains.

1997 Outlook

Can Wohlers keep rolling? Why not? There were concerns that his workload was wearing him down at season's end, but his fastball remained in the high-90s all the way through the World Series. Unless his World Series catastrophe seriously affects his psyche—which doesn't seem likely, given his makeup—Mark Wohlers should remain one of the most imposing mound presences in the game.

Position: RP
Bats: R **Throws:** R
Ht: 6' 4" **Wt:** 207

Opening Day Age: 27
Born: 1/23/70 in Holyoke, MA
ML Seasons: 6
Pronunciation: WOHL-ers

Overall Statistics

	W	L	Pct.	ERA	G	GS	Sv	IP	H	BB	SO	HR	BR/IP
1996	2	4	.333	3.03	77	0	39	77.1	71	21	100	8	1.19
Career	26	14	.650	3.28	288	0	71	296.0	255	127	323	14	1.29

How Often He Throws Strikes

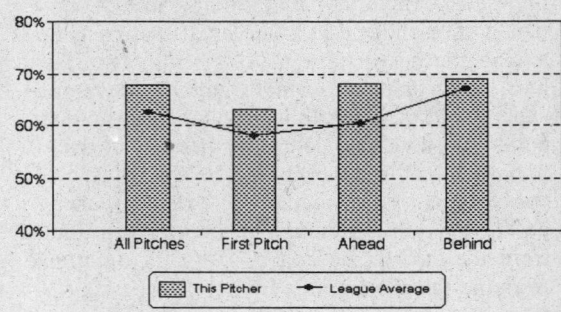

1996 Situational Stats

	W	L	ERA	Sv	IP		AB	H	HR	RBI	Avg
Home	2	4	4.75	21	41.2	LHB	137	27	3	12	.197
Road	0	0	1.01	18	35.2	RHB	159	44	5	19	.277
First Half	0	1	2.81	18	41.2	Sc Pos	99	19	0	21	.192
Scnd Half	2	3	3.28	21	35.2	Clutch	201	46	4	22	.229

1996 Rankings (National League)

- → 1st in lowest percentage of inherited runners scored (16.7%) and most strikeouts per 9 innings in relief (11.6)
- → 3rd in games finished (64)
- → 4th in saves, save opportunities (44) and save percentage (88.6%)
- → 5th in games pitched
- → 6th in errors at pitcher (3)
- → 8th in wild pitches (10)
- → Led the Braves in saves, games finished (64), wild pitches (10), save opportunities (44), save percentage (88.6%), lowest batting average allowed in relief with runners in scoring position (.192), lowest percentage of inherited runners scored (16.7%) and relief ERA (3.03)

Mike Bielecki

Position: RP/SP
Bats: R **Throws:** R
Ht: 6' 3" **Wt:** 200

Opening Day Age: 37
Born: 7/31/59 in Baltimore, MD
ML Seasons: 13
Pronunciation: bye-LECK-ee

Overall Statistics

	W	L	Pct.	ERA	G	GS	Sv	IP	H	BB	SO	HR	BR/IP
1996	4	3	.571	2.63	40	5	2	75.1	63	33	71	8	1.27
Career	67	66	.504	4.19	297	178	3	1173.2	1180	475	723	107	1.41

1996 Situational Stats

	W	L	ERA	Sv	IP		AB	H	HR	RBI	Avg
Home	3	1	1.41	1	38.1	LHB	124	31	3	10	.250
Road	1	2	3.89	1	37.0	RHB	157	32	5	15	.204
First Half	1	2	3.10	1	29.0	Sc Pos	53	12	1	17	.226
Scnd Half	3	1	2.33	1	46.1	Clutch	43	6	0	3	.140

1996 Season

Mike Bielecki's odyssey of 1996 went something like this: in the spring, he was a 36-year-old free agent pondering retirement. Then he became a non-roster invitee to the Braves' camp. Then he became a little-used middle reliever for Atlanta. Then he became an effective set-up man and spot starter. Finally, in the World Series, he became an important set-up man in the Atlanta bullpen.

Pitching, Defense & Hitting

Under the tutelage of pitching coach Leo Mazzone, Bielecki got his fastball back into the low-90s, throwing harder than he had since 1989. He uses his heater, a decent forkball and an occasional slider to work the corners and stay away from hitters' strengths. He's a decent fielder, but can't hold a runner to save his life. He's also one of the most harmless hitters in the majors.

1997 Outlook

One might almost think that if the '96 season had continued for another month, Bielecki would have become the ace of the staff. He's a free agent, however, and all he's likely earned is another invitation to pitch middle relief for the Braves or for someone else. His resurgence is noteworthy, but probably won't be long-lived.

Jeff Blauser

Position: SS
Bats: R **Throws:** R
Ht: 6' 1" **Wt:** 180

Opening Day Age: 31
Born: 11/8/65 in Los Gatos, CA
ML Seasons: 10
Pronunciation: BLAU-zer

Overall Statistics

	G	AB	R	H	D	T	HR	RBI	SB	BB	SO	Avg	OBP	Slg
1996	83	265	48	65	14	1	10	35	6	40	54	.245	.356	.419
Career	1033	3442	511	900	170	24	92	391	56	413	691	.261	.347	.405

1996 Situational Stats

	AB	H	HR	RBI	Avg		AB	H	HR	RBI	Avg
Home	152	33	4	16	.217	LHP	67	14	3	12	.209
Road	113	32	6	19	.283	RHP	198	51	7	23	.258
First Half	235	58	10	31	.247	Sc Pos	58	16	3	25	.276
Scnd Half	30	7	0	4	.233	Clutch	33	7	3	8	.212

1996 Season

Jeff Blauser remained an injury magnet for the third straight season last year. He was hampered by a bad right knee all season long, and he missed most of the second half after a pitch broke his hand on July 15. He returned in time for the postseason, but his play never returned to its first-half level.

Hitting, Baserunning & Defense

Blauser's lost power and strike-zone judgment seemed to have returned before the hand injury. On defense, however, the knee seemed to impair his footwork and mobility, leading to 23 errors and the lowest fielding percentage for any shortstop in the league. He seemed to have scaled back his aggressiveness on the basepaths as well, although he did steal six bases without being caught.

1997 Outlook

Going into the final year of a fat contract, Blauser's job is in obvious jeopardy. The Braves need someone to stay healthy and stabilize the shortstop position, but if Blauser can't do it, they'll explore other options. Blauser needs to step up and prove that injuries haven't eroded his skills too severely.

Andruw Jones (Top Prospect)

Position: RF/CF
Bats: R **Throws:** R
Ht: 6' 1" **Wt:** 185

Opening Day Age: 19
Born: 4/23/77 in
Wellemstad, Curacao
ML Seasons: 1

Overall Statistics

	G	AB	R	H	D	T	HR	RBI	SB	BB	SO	Avg	OBP	Slg
1996	31	106	11	23	7	1	5	13	3	7	29	.217	.265	.443
Career	31	106	11	23	7	1	5	13	3	7	29	.217	.265	.443

1996 Situational Stats

	AB	H	HR	RBI	Avg		AB	H	HR	RBI	Avg
Home	52	14	3	6	.269	LHP	29	11	5	11	.379
Road	54	9	2	7	.167	RHP	77	12	0	2	.156
First Half	0	0	0	0	-	Sc Pos	30	7	1	8	.233
Scnd Half	106	23	5	13	.217	Clutch	18	3	0	1	.167

1996 Season

Last year, at age 19, Andruw Jones traveled from A-ball, to Double-A, to Triple-A, to the majors, and finally, to the World Series. At each stop, he left souvenirs testifying that "Andruw Jones homered here." His incredible journey earned him his second-straight Minor League Player of the Year award from *Baseball America* magazine. It's safe to say he won't get the chance to win a third one.

Hitting, Baserunning & Defense

Yes, yes and yes. Jones is a five-tool player who seems to be able to do anything he puts his young mind to. He can play all three outfield spots, run, throw and hit with power. He's understandably raw at the plate and in the field, but has shown signs of maturity, like hitting outside breaking balls the other way.

1997 Outlook

Jones is the best prospect in baseball, and the Braves regard him as their left fielder, or right fielder, of the very near future. His youthfulness won't prevent him from putting up decent power numbers right off the bat, and his long-term future is virtually limitless.

Mike Mordecai

Position: 2B
Bats: R **Throws:** R
Ht: 5'11" **Wt:** 175

Opening Day Age: 29
Born: 12/13/67 in
Birmingham, AL
ML Seasons: 3

Overall Statistics

	G	AB	R	H	D	T	HR	RBI	SB	BB	SO	Avg	OBP	Slg
1996	66	108	12	26	5	0	2	8	1	9	24	.241	.297	.343
Career	139	187	23	48	11	0	6	22	1	19	40	.257	.322	.412

1996 Situational Stats

	AB	H	HR	RBI	Avg		AB	H	HR	RBI	Avg
Home	47	9	0	3	.191	LHP	31	6	0	2	.194
Road	61	17	2	5	.279	RHP	77	20	2	6	.260
First Half	47	12	0	3	.255	Sc Pos	24	4	0	6	.167
Scnd Half	61	14	2	5	.230	Clutch	29	7	1	4	.241

1996 Season

Last year, Mike Mordecai solidified his spot as a backup infielder, but the Braves made it clear that they'll ask him to go no further than that. He performed capably as a pinch hitter and a backup infielder, but when shortstop Jeff Blauser went down with an injury, the Braves never considered using Mordecai to fill the spot.

Hitting, Baserunning & Defense

Mordecai hits the ball in the air and has decent power for a middle infielder, but he's not dangerous enough to be a truly effective pinch hitter. He can handle the glove at any of the infield spots, showing good range and a strong arm. His speed is unremarkable, although he had decent success as a basestealer in the minors.

1997 Outlook

When the Braves tried Ed Giovanola and Chipper Jones at shortstop without giving a look to Mordecai, it seemed to define his role pretty clearly. The Braves consider him a decent backup, and nothing more. He can fill that role adequately until they come up with something better.

Terry Pendleton

Position: 3B
Bats: B **Throws:** R
Ht: 5' 9" **Wt:** 195

Opening Day Age: 36
Born: 7/16/60 in Los
Angeles, CA
ML Seasons: 13

Overall Statistics

	G	AB	R	H	D	T	HR	RBI	SB	BB	SO	Avg	OBP	Slg
1996	153	568	51	135	26	1	11	75	2	41	111	.238	.290	.345
Career	1764	6682	823	1808	337	39	136	900	124	459	916	.271	.316	.394

1996 Situational Stats

	AB	H	HR	RBI	Avg		AB	H	HR	RBI	Avg
Home	281	69	6	42	.246	LHP	112	20	1	13	.179
Road	287	66	5	33	.230	RHP	456	115	10	62	.252
First Half	305	76	5	40	.249	Sc Pos	159	47	2	62	.296
Scnd Half	263	59	6	35	.224	Clutch	98	27	3	8	.276

1996 Season

Terry Pendleton returned to Atlanta for the stretch run, but found that at age 35, you can't go home again. He didn't hit at all when they entrusted him with the third base job, and when he was relegated to pinch hitting and DH-ing in the postseason, he didn't produce in that role, either.

Hitting, Baserunning & Defense

A switch-hitter, Pendleton used to be stronger from the right side, but he produced only one extra-base hit from that side last year. As a left-handed hitter, he likes the ball down, but doesn't generate enough bat speed to hit with much home run power any more. His speed is gone, and his glove is about the only thing he has left. The range isn't what it used to be, but he still has the softest hands around.

1997 Outlook

Pendleton is a free agent, and his tenure in Atlanta proved that he'll have to find a role with someone else. He'll provide solid defense and veteran leadership, but that may no longer outweigh his wilting bat.

Eddie Perez

Position: C
Bats: R **Throws:** R
Ht: 6' 1" **Wt:** 175

Opening Day Age: 28
Born: 5/4/68 in Cuidad
Ojeda, VZ
ML Seasons: 2

Overall Statistics

	G	AB	R	H	D	T	HR	RBI	SB	BB	SO	Avg	OBP	Slg
1996	68	156	19	40	9	1	4	17	0	8	19	.256	.293	.404
Career	75	169	20	44	10	1	5	21	0	8	21	.260	.294	.420

1996 Situational Stats

	AB	H	HR	RBI	Avg		AB	H	HR	RBI	Avg
Home	74	23	2	13	.311	LHP	50	11	1	4	.220
Road	82	17	2	4	.207	RHP	106	29	3	13	.274
First Half	81	25	3	11	.309	Sc Pos	38	11	1	13	.289
Scnd Half	75	15	1	6	.200	Clutch	22	5	1	3	.227

1996 Season

Eddie Perez is one-half of the best battery in baseball—that's because he happens to be Greg Maddux' personal catcher. He works primarily with Maddux and Steve Avery, and each pitcher enjoyed much greater success last year when Perez was calling the pitches.

Hitting, Baserunning & Defense

Perez hits like your average backup catcher. He's an impatient hitter, and probably doesn't have as much power as he appeared to last year. He's no threat to steal, but his defense is an asset. He's very good at blocking balls in the dirt, he throws well and his pitch-calling is highly respected.

1997 Outlook

Perez' ability to work so well with Greg Maddux should be more than enough to keep him around. He'll never displace the offense-minded Javy Lopez, but he may end up carrying a larger share of the catching load. If any of the other Braves' pitchers begin to have problems working with Lopez, Perez may have a chance to try his hand with another battery mate or two.

Dwight Smith

Position: RF
Bats: L **Throws:** R
Ht: 5'11" **Wt:** 195

Opening Day Age: 33
Born: 11/8/63 in
Tallahassee, FL
ML Seasons: 8

Overall Statistics

	G	AB	R	H	D	T	HR	RBI	SB	BB	SO	Avg	OBP	Slg
1996	101	153	16	31	5	0	3	16	1	17	42	.203	.285	.294
Career	813	1807	244	497	88	20	46	226	42	150	334	.275	.333	.422

1996 Situational Stats

	AB	H	HR	RBI	Avg		AB	H	HR	RBI	Avg
Home	68	11	2	7	.162	LHP	7	0	0	0	.000
Road	85	20	1	9	.235	RHP	146	31	3	16	.212
First Half	103	23	3	11	.223	Sc Pos	46	7	0	12	.152
Scnd Half	50	8	0	5	.160	Clutch	42	7	0	5	.167

1996 Season

All Dwight Smith can do is hit, but last year he didn't even do that. A first-half slump ruined Bobby Cox's confidence in him, and by the end of the year, he'd been largely relieved of his pinch-hitting duties. After serving as the Braves' top pinch hitter for two years, Smith appears to be on his way out of Atlanta.

Hitting, Baserunning & Defense

Smith doesn't hit lefties, but he's always been effective against righties, especially on breaking balls down and in. He has pretty good speed, but he's never been able to put it to good use in the outfield or on the basepaths. He was given a short trial in right field last year, and wasn't quite as awful as he'd been reputed to be.

1997 Outlook

Question: what do you call a pinch hitter who doesn't hit? Answer: unemployed. Smith probably will get another shot on the basis of his past record, but it doesn't look like it will come with the Braves.

Terrell Wade

Position: RP/SP
Bats: L **Throws:** L
Ht: 6'3" **Wt:** 205

Opening Day Age: 24
Born: 1/25/73 in
Rembert, SC
ML Seasons: 2

Overall Statistics

	W	L	Pct.	ERA	G	GS	Sv	IP	H	BB	SO	HR	BR/IP
1996	5	0	1.000	2.97	44	8	1	69.2	57	47	79	9	1.49
Career	5	1	.833	3.05	47	8	1	73.2	60	51	82	10	1.51

1996 Situational Stats

	W	L	ERA	Sv	IP		AB	H	HR	RBI	Avg
Home	1	0	2.73	0	33.0	LHB	56	16	2	7	.286
Road	4	0	3.19	1	36.2	RHB	195	41	7	17	.210
First Half	2	0	1.32	1	27.1	Sc Pos	69	13	2	16	.188
Scnd Half	3	0	4.04	0	42.1	Clutch	40	9	1	4	.225

1996 Season

Rookie lefthander Terrell Wade pitched surprisingly well in middle relief early on, and showed good stuff—if not stamina—when moved into the rotation later in the year. He was shifted back to the pen in September, where he crashed and burned. Despite his inconsistency, he showed exciting promise at times.

Pitching, Baserunning & Defense

What excites people about Wade is his low-90s fastball. But what frustrates them is his inability to throw an offspeed or breaking pitch for strikes. For now, he can get by on stuff alone, but only for a few innings at a time. He's an adequate fielder, but he's got a lot of work to do on holding runners. He hit well in the minors and his bat may prove to be above average.

1997 Outlook

The Braves will bring Wade along slowly, as they do with all of their pitchers. He's not cut out to be a one-out specialist, so he'll probably begin next year as a long reliever and set-up man. If he builds up his stamina, he could get another shot at starting.

Other Atlanta Braves

Joe Ayrault (Pos: C, Age: 25, Bats: R)

	G	AB	R	H	D	T	HR	RBI	SB	BB	SO	Avg	OBP	Slg
1996	7	5	0	1	0	0	0	0	0	0	1	.200	.333	.200
Career	7	5	0	1	0	0	0	0	0	0	1	.200	.333	.200

Ayrault is a defensive specialist who'll have a tough time making it on his glove alone. The Braves already have Eddie Perez, so Ayrault won't get much of a chance in Atlanta unless an injury hits. 1997 Outlook: D

Danny Bautista (Pos: RF/LF, Age: 24, Bats: R)

	G	AB	R	H	D	T	HR	RBI	SB	BB	SO	Avg	OBP	Slg
1996	42	84	13	19	2	0	2	9	1	11	20	.226	.323	.321
Career	179	515	59	116	18	1	14	60	9	27	116	.225	.265	.346

A frightful beaning ended Bautista's season in June. He's still young enough to get a few more chances, but it's about time he figured out how to use his tools on the ballfield. 1997 Outlook: C

Rafael Belliard (Pos: SS/2B, Age: 35, Bats: R)

	G	AB	R	H	D	T	HR	RBI	SB	BB	SO	Avg	OBP	Slg
1996	87	142	9	24	7	0	0	3	3	2	22	.169	.179	.218
Career	1076	2210	207	488	52	14	1	138	43	135	366	.221	.272	.258

Belliard is still one of the best defensive shortstops around, but he's also the most impotent hitter in the majors. The Braves value his glove and re-signed him for 1997. 1997 Outlook:B

Pedro Borbon (Pos: LHP, Age: 29)

	W	L	Pct.	ERA	G	GS	Sv	IP	H	BB	SO	HR	BR/IP
1996	3	0	1.000	2.75	43	0	1	36.0	26	7	31	1	0.92
Career	5	3	.625	3.42	89	0	3	71.0	60	28	67	3	1.24

Borbon came into his own as a lefty bullpen specialist last year, but reconstructive surgery on his elbow makes him a question mark for next season. The Braves need him back, but it may take time. 1997 Outlook: B

Joe Borowski (Pos: RHP, Age: 25)

	W	L	Pct.	ERA	G	GS	Sv	IP	H	BB	SO	HR	BR/IP
1996	2	4	.333	4.85	22	0	0	26.0	33	13	15	4	1.77
Career	2	4	.333	4.05	28	0	0	33.1	38	17	18	4	1.65

Borowski was hit hard in his first extended trial in the majors, but made the Braves' postseason roster anyway. His mediocre stuff probably won't translate into major league success. 1997 Outlook: B

Ed Giovanola (Pos: SS, Age: 28, Bats: L)

	G	AB	R	H	D	T	HR	RBI	SB	BB	SO	Avg	OBP	Slg
1996	43	82	10	19	2	0	0	7	1	8	13	.232	.304	.256
Career	56	96	12	20	2	0	0	7	1	11	18	.208	.294	.229

The Braves gave Giovanola a short trial at shortstop, but quickly concluded that he's better suited to a utility role. He bats left, knows how to get on base, and can play all over the infield. 1997 Outlook: B

Dean Hartgraves (Pos: LHP, Age: 30)

	W	L	Pct.	ERA	G	GS	Sv	IP	H	BB	SO	HR	BR/IP
1996	1	0	1.000	4.78	39	0	0	37.2	34	23	30	4	1.51
Career	3	0	1.000	4.01	79	0	0	74.0	64	39	54	6	1.39

When Pedro Borbon went down, the Braves got Hartgraves to replace him, but he wasn't quite effective enough against the lefties. His sidearm motion will surface somewhere else if he doesn't stick in Atlanta. 1997 Outlook: B

Kevin Lomon (Pos: RHP, Age: 25)

	W	L	Pct.	ERA	G	GS	Sv	IP	H	BB	SO	HR	BR/IP
1996	0	0	-	4.91	6	0	0	7.1	7	3	1	0	1.36
Career	0	1	.000	5.94	12	0	0	16.2	24	8	7	0	1.92

Lomon has spent three years in Triple-A, working as a starter, a reliever, and then as a starter again. He's never been regarded as a serious prospect, and probably won't get much of a look in Atlanta. 1997 Outlook: C

Pablo Martinez (Pos: SS, Age: 27, Bats: B)

	G	AB	R	H	D	T	HR	RBI	SB	BB	SO	Avg	OBP	Slg
1996	4	2	1	1	0	0	0	0	0	0	0	.500	.500	.500
Career	4	2	1	1	0	0	0	0	0	0	0	.500	.500	.500

A minor league lifer with a forgettable name and unremarkable skills. He got into four games with the Braves last year, something he'll certainly tell his grandkids about. 1997 Outlook: D

Luis Polonia (Pos: LF/DH, Age: 32, Bats: L)

	G	AB	R	H	D	T	HR	RBI	SB	BB	SO	Avg	OBP	Slg
1996	80	206	28	55	4	1	2	16	9	11	23	.267	.306	.325
Career	1175	4163	634	1214	154	57	19	343	292	324	479	.292	.342	.370

After being traded to Atlanta, Polonia got red-hot and took over Dwight Smith's role as the top pinch hitter off the bench. Smith held that role for years, and Polonia may inherit the spot. 1997 Outlook: B

Carl Schutz (Pos: LHP, Age: 25)

	W	L	Pct.	ERA	G	GS	Sv	IP	H	BB	SO	HR	BR/IP
1996	0	0	-	2.70	3	0	0	3.1	3	2	5	0	1.50
Career	0	0	-	2.70	3	0	0	3.1	3	2	5	0	1.50

He's a hard-throwing lefty, but he's still too wild to allow us to say that he comes in and "Schutz" the door. He probably needs another year but may eventually develop into a power set-up man. 1997 Outlook: C

Tom Thobe (Pos: LHP, Age: 27)

	W	L	Pct.	ERA	G	GS	Sv	IP	H	BB	SO	HR	BR/IP
1996	0	1	.000	1.50	4	0	0	6.0	5	0	1	1	0.83
Career	0	1	.000	4.82	7	0	0	9.1	12	0	3	1	1.29

Another lucky beneficiary of the Braves' all-consuming search for lefty relievers, Thobe was promoted despite the fact that he completely fell apart at Triple-A. He may get it back together. 1997 Outlook: C

Jerome Walton (Pos: LF, **Age**: 31, **Bats**: R)

	G	AB	R	H	D	T	HR	RBI	SB	BB	SO	Avg	OBP	Slg
1996	37	47	9	16	5	0	1	4	0	5	10	.340	.389	.511
Career	560	1471	229	392	73	8	22	120	58	132	264	.266	.332	.372

Walton did well in the early going as Ryan Klesko's "relief fielder," but went down for the season with a strained hip in May. The Braves released him after the season, but he'll find work. 1997 Outlook: B

Atlanta Braves Minor League Prospects

Organization Overview:

It was another banner year for the Braves' farm system. When David Justice went down with an injury, Jermaine Dye stepped in and filled the void. Andruw Jones won his second straight Minor League Player of the Year award, and showed that he could hit in the majors as well. Rookies Terrell Wade and Eddie Perez played notable roles on the major league team, and joined a core that already included recent grads like Javy Lopez, Ryan Klesko and Chipper Jones. For all their accomplishments, the Braves' system was named Organization of the Year by Baseball America. However, it may be difficult for the Braves to take that award again next year. The talent in the upper levels of their system is thinner than it's been in years, which may impair their ability to continue packaging prospects for big-name players. Most of their impact players are at least a year or two away. Although the talent level isn't what it used to be, it remains impressive by the standards of a normal team.

Tony Graffanino

Position: 2B
Bats: R **Throws:** R
Ht: 6' 1" **Wt:** 200

Opening Day Age: 24
Born: 6/6/72 in Amityville, NY

Recent Statistics

	G	AB	R	H	D	T	HR	RBI	SB	BB	SO	AVG
96 AAA Richmond	96	353	57	100	29	2	7	33	11	34	72	.283
96 NL Atlanta	22	46	7	8	1	1	0	2	0	4	13	.174
96 MLE	96	342	48	89	26	1	6	27	7	28	74	.260

A serious back injury in '95 set back Tony Graffanino's progress, but he recovered most of his skills last year. He's lost a little speed, but he still hits for a good average with decent power for a second baseman. He was voted the best defensive second baseman in the International League last year, so he's a good all-around package if he's healthy. The Braves regard him as good insurance in case they aren't able to re-sign Mark Lemke.

Wesley Helms

Position: 3B
Bats: R **Throws:** R
Ht: 6' 4" **Wt:** 210

Opening Day Age: 20
Born: 5/12/76 in Gastonia, NC

Recent Statistics

	G	AB	R	H	D	T	HR	RBI	SB	BB	SO	AVG
94 R Braves	56	184	22	49	15	1	4	29	6	22	36	.266
95 A Macon	136	539	89	149	32	1	11	85	2	50	107	.276
96 A Durham	67	258	40	83	19	2	13	54	1	12	51	.322
96 AA Greenville	64	231	24	59	13	2	4	22	1	13	48	.255
96 MLE	64	219	16	47	10	1	2	15	1	7	50	.215

With all of the Braves best prospects having been promoted or traded away, the banner of "top prospect in the system" falls to third baseman Wes Helms. He got off to a great start in A-ball last year, but couldn't keep up with the advanced competition in Double-A. Still, at age 21, he remains a powerful, if impatient, hitter, and a tremendous defensive third baseman. As he matures and learns the strike zone over the next couple of years, he should become another powerful young Brave.

Wonder Monds

Position: OF
Bats: R **Throws:** R
Ht: 6' 3" **Wt:** 190

Opening Day Age: 24
Born: 1/11/73 in Fort Pierce, FL

Recent Statistics

	G	AB	R	H	D	T	HR	RBI	SB	BB	SO	AVG
93 R Idaho Falls	60	214	47	64	13	8	4	35	16	25	43	.299
94 A Durham	18	53	7	11	2	0	2	10	5	2	11	.208
94 A Macon	104	365	70	106	23	12	10	41	42	22	82	.290
95 R Braves	4	15	1	2	0	0	0	1	2	1	8	.133
95 A Durham	81	297	44	83	17	0	6	33	28	17	63	.279
96 R Braves	3	5	3	2	0	0	2	3	0	2	1	.400
96 AA Greenville	32	110	17	33	9	1	2	14	7	9	17	.300

Wonderful Terrific Monds was enjoying a good (but not wonderful or terrific) year when a broken hand ended his season in May. He may not have right-field power, but he's got good speed, hits for a pretty good average, and steals bases. He probably doesn't have the necessary skills to play regularly in the majors, but he's close to being ready to help as a bench player.

Damian Moss

Position: P
Bats: R **Throws:** L
Ht: 6' 0" **Wt:** 187

Opening Day Age: 20
Born: 11/24/76 in Darlinghurst, NSW Australia

Recent Statistics

	W	L	ERA	G	GS	Sv	IP	H	R	BB	SO	HR
94 R Danville	2	5	3.58	12	12	0	60.1	30	28	55	77	1
95 A Macon	9	10	3.56	27	27	0	149.1	134	73	70	177	13
96 A Durham	9	1	2.25	14	14	0	84.0	52	25	40	89	9
96 AA Greenville	2	5	4.97	11	10	0	58.0	57	41	35	48	5

Australian lefty Damian Moss used his 90-MPH fastball and sharp curve to dazzle A-ball hitters last year. His 9-1 mark earned him a promotion to Double-A, where he struggled with his control and wasn't nearly as effective. However, the mere fact that he reached Double-A at age 19 was impressive enough by itself. Moss is still maturing and filling out, and it's scary to think what he can do once he learns a change-up and masters the art of pitching.

Randall Simon

Position: 1B
Bats: L **Throws:** L
Ht: 6' 0" **Wt:** 180

Opening Day Age: 21
Born: 5/26/75 in
Willemstad, Curacao,
Netherlands

Recent Statistics

	G	AB	R	H	D	T	HR	RBI	SB	BB	SO	AVG
93 R Danville	61	232	28	59	17	1	3	31	1	10	34	.254
94 A Macon	106	358	45	105	23	1	10	54	7	6	56	.293
95 A Durham	122	420	56	111	18	1	18	79	6	36	63	.264
96 AA Greenville	134	498	74	139	26	2	18	77	4	37	61	.279
96 MLE	134	473	50	114	21	1	13	52	2	21	64	.241

Part of the reason the Braves were willing to part with Ron Wright was the presence of left-handed first baseman Randall Simon. At age 21, he held his own in the Double-A Southern League, improved his knowledge of the strike zone, and continued to flash excellent power potential. He's got a good defensive reputation at first base, and is capable of playing left field in a pinch. He makes excellent contact for a young power hitter, and a full year at Triple-A in '97 may be all he needs.

Bobby Smith

Position: 3B
Bats: R **Throws:** R
Ht: 6' 3" **Wt:** 190

Opening Day Age: 22
Born: 4/10/74 in
Oakland, CA

Recent Statistics

	G	AB	R	H	D	T	HR	RBI	SB	BB	SO	AVG
93 A Macon	108	384	53	94	16	7	4	38	12	23	81	.245
94 A Durham	127	478	49	127	27	2	12	71	18	41	112	.266
95 AA Greenville	127	444	75	116	27	3	14	58	12	40	109	.261
96 AAA Richmond	124	445	49	114	27	0	8	58	15	32	114	.256
96 MLE	124	433	41	102	24	0	6	49	10	26	117	.236

Playing third base in the Braves' system is a dead-end job, but Bobby Smith may have found a way out. He was such a tremendous defender that the Atlanta organization decided to convert him to shortstop last year. The transition was predictably rough at first, but he seems to have the tools to play the position. At the plate, he's very rough and overaggressive, and his power receded last year as he concentrated on his glovework. But he's only 23 this year, and may develop into a decent two-way shortstop.

Juan Williams

Position: OF
Bats: L **Throws:** R
Ht: 6' 0" **Wt:** 180

Opening Day Age: 24
Born: 10/9/72 in Los
Angeles, CA

Recent Statistics

	G	AB	R	H	D	T	HR	RBI	SB	BB	SO	AVG
93 A Durham	124	403	49	93	16	2	11	44	11	36	120	.231
94 A Durham	122	394	55	86	14	0	19	57	7	54	131	.218
95 AA Greenville	62	192	40	60	14	2	15	39	4	19	44	.313
95 AAA Richmond	45	129	18	34	5	0	5	11	1	17	38	.264
96 AAA Richmond	119	357	55	97	22	2	15	52	5	51	127	.272
96 MLE	119	349	46	89	19	1	14	43	3	42	130	.255

Juan Williams isn't considered a future regular, but he has what it takes to be a valuable fourth outfielder. He can play all three outfield positions, he bats lefty, and he's got some power. The Braves will have to make a decision on him before the '97 season. If they decide to keep him around, he may pay dividends.

Brad Woodall

Position: P
Bats: B **Throws:** L
Ht: 6' 0" **Wt:** 175

Opening Day Age: 27
Born: 6/25/69 in
Atlanta, GA

Recent Statistics

	W	L	ERA	G	GS	Sv	IP	H	R	BB	SO	HR
96 AAA Richmond	9	7	3.38	21	21	0	133.1	124	59	36	74	10
96 NL Atlanta	2	2	7.32	8	3	0	19.2	28	19	4	20	4

Lefthander Brad Woodall imitates Tom Glavine's approach to pitching, but he doesn't seem to have the stuff to get by with it at the major league level. It takes pinpoint control to consistently throw breaking balls off the corner of the plate. Sometimes Woodall is able to do that, and sometimes he isn't. He's topped out at age 28, so if he doesn't come up with something else quick, he may be out of luck.

Others to Watch

Center fielder **Damon Hollins** was highly touted after a big season at Double-A in '95, and expectations rose even further after he played well in spring camp. He got off to a terrible start at Triple-A, however, and suffered a season-ending arm injury in May. He's still young, and his raw power and speed are exciting. . . Down in A-ball, left-handed-hitting outfielder **George Lombard** has similar skills. He hasn't hit for much of an average, but the organization likes his combination of power and speed. Now 21 years old, he'll likely begin the year in Double-A. . . Young righthander **John Leroy** made great strides last year, going 7-4 in A-ball and performing well in eight starts at Double-A. He's only 22 this year, but based on his showing last year, the Braves may start him at Triple-A. . . Left-handed closer **Adam Butler** saved 30 games at three levels, although he struggled with his control after a midseason promotion to Double-A. Butler is not overpowering, but he's young and has a closer's mentality. . . Second baseman **Marty Malloy** sounds like a Mark Lemke clone. He doesn't project to hit much, but carries a super glove.

Jim Riggleman

1996 Season

Jim Riggleman is a regular guy who takes the "El" to the park like everyone else. When a player wants to talk, he shuts the door and listens. Instead of barking out orders at his troops, he goes out of his way to treat them like professionals. But Riggleman is no pushover. He has very strong ideas about the way a team ought to be run, and he's willing to stick by them in the face of strong criticism—from the press, or even from his own players.

Offense

Riggleman is unwilling to sacrifice speed and defense just to get some extra muscle in the lineup. He prefers to field players who are skilled defenders and situational hitters. The hit-and-run is a favorite weapon, and he demands that his players try to advance runners even with their outs. He'll platoon when he's convinced it's best for the team, even if the players involved are uncomfortable.

Pitching & Defense

Riggleman absolutely refuses to allow his starters to run up high pitch counts, and won't cave in to their demands to be left in the game longer. As a result, he uses his entire bullpen, giving four or five relievers plenty of work and expecting each of them to be ready at any point in the game. He's also a strong believer that young pitchers need seasoning in the majors before they're ready to close out games. Defense is very important to him, and sometimes he'll keep a player in the lineup even if defense is the player's only notable skill.

1997 Outlook

The Cubs are taking a patient, farsighted approach to developing a winner, and they've got the perfect manager to implement that plan. Riggleman will be expected to continue to develop the foundation of a contender, but he certainly won't be fired if the team fails to make the playoffs.

Born: 11/09/52 in Fort Dix, NJ

Playing Experience: No major league experience

Managerial Experience: 5 seasons

Manager Statistics

Year	Team, Lg	W	L	Pct	GB	Finish
1996	Chicago, NL	76	86	.469	12.0	4th Central
5 Seasons		261	336	.437	—	—

1996 Starting Pitchers by Days Rest

	≤3	4	5	6+
Cubs Starts	6	86	45	17
Cubs ERA	5.90	5.23	3.98	5.66
NL Avg Starts	4	86	41	21
NL ERA	4.06	4.28	4.23	4.58

1996 Situational Stats

	Jim Riggleman	NL Average
Hit & Run Success %	46.1	39.0
Stolen Base Success %	68.4	71.6
Platoon Pct.	50.7	51.9
Defensive Subs	21	20
High-Pitch Outings	7	13
Quick/Slow Hooks	17/11	19/12
Sacrifice Attempts	79	92

1996 Rankings (National League)

→ 1st in least caught steals of third base (2), hit-and-run percentage (46.1%) and pinch hitters used (326)

→ 2nd in relief appearances (439) and mid-inning pitching changes (178)

→ 3rd in sacrifice bunt percentage (86.1%), pitchouts (65), first batter platoon percentage (62.6%) and one-batter pitcher appearances (34)

Terry Adams

Position: RP
Bats: R **Throws:** R
Ht: 6' 3" **Wt:** 205

Opening Day Age: 24
Born: 3/6/73 in Mobile, AL
ML Seasons: 2

1996 Season

Someday, everyone agrees, Terry Adams will save a lot of games for the Chicago Cubs. But it was not to be in '96; manager Jim Riggleman brought him along slowly and confined him to mostly middle relief. Still, Adams proved to be both effective and resilient, and his performance only solidified his position as the future closer. Unlike most of his teammates, he finished the season strongly, posting a 1.32 ERA in 11 September appearances.

Pitching

Adams has the classic repertoire for a short reliever: an overpowering mid-90s fastball and a hard slider. He also has a curveball, but he's rarely used it since moving to the bullpen three years ago. Location can still be a problem at times—such as when he walked pitcher Chan Ho Park to force in the winning run on June 19—but his control improved as the year progressed. Another good sign is his ability to keep the ball down, a necessity at Wrigley Field.

Defense & Hitting

Last year, Adams got his first six professional at-bats, but he's still looking for his first hit. He wasn't terribly effective at holding runners, and his pickoff move needs work. As a fielder, he's only adequate, but sure-handed.

1997 Outlook

This year, Adams will go as far as his arm and his manager will allow him to. Jim Riggleman believes that short relievers need seasoning at the major league level, and has resisted the urge to rush Adams into the role of closer. Now, Mel Rojas has been signed, so Adams will continue his apprenticeship for another year, at least.

Overall Statistics

	W	L	Pct.	ERA	G	GS	Sv	IP	H	BB	SO	HR	BR/IP
1996	3	6	.333	2.94	69	0	4	101.0	84	49	78	6	1.32
Career	4	7	.364	3.48	87	0	5	119.0	106	59	93	6	1.39

How Often He Throws Strikes

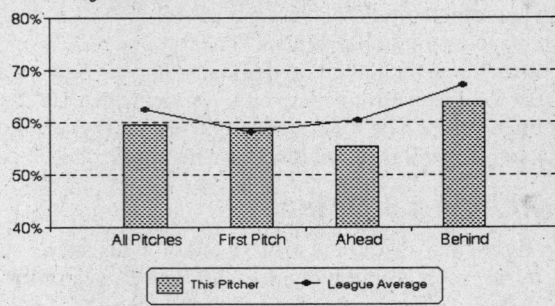

This Pitcher ▧   League Average ●—

1996 Situational Stats

	W	L	ERA	Sv	IP			AB	H	HR	RBI	Avg
Home	2	4	3.57	2	53.0		LHB	145	34	3	12	.234
Road	1	2	2.25	2	48.0		RHB	218	50	3	24	.229
First Half	2	2	2.43	1	55.2		Sc Pos	93	19	0	27	.204
Scnd Half	1	4	3.57	3	45.1		Clutch	165	35	4	18	.212

1996 Rankings (National League)

➡ 2nd in relief innings (101.0)
➡ 5th in relief losses (6)
➡ Led the Cubs in most GDPs induced per GDP situation (17.1%), relief losses (6) and relief innings (101.0)

Frank Castillo

Position: SP
Bats: R **Throws:** R
Ht: 6' 1" **Wt:** 200

Opening Day Age: 27
Born: 4/1/69 in El Paso, TX
ML Seasons: 6
Pronunciation: cas-TEE-yoh

1996 Season

Coming off the best season of his career (11-10, 3.21), Frank Castillo saw it all fall apart in the first half of 1996. His curveball suddenly deserted him, and hitters began crushing his fastball whenever he left it upstairs. He barely hung on to his spot in the rotation, until a second-half hot streak put him on firmer footing. Still, a September slump left Castillo confused about his future in the organization. He wound up tying for the league lead with 16 losses, and his 5.28 ERA was the highest of his career.

Pitching

Castillo throws strikes, works fast and changes speeds. He has an excellent change-up, but he can't get by on that and his 85-MPH fastball alone. He can cut the fastball, but it's the curveball that allows him to stay one step ahead of the hitter. When he can't get his offspeed pitches over consistently, he simply doesn't have the velocity to get by.

Defense & Hitting

Castillo is quick in the field, but is known to throw the ball away on occasion. While he was tougher to run on last year—opposing runners were successful 14 times in 24 attempts—much of the credit should go to catcher Scott Servais. At the plate, Castillo's an easy out.

1997 Outlook

Can Castillo return to his 1995 form? Certainly. He's overcome off-years before and, all in all, his record wasn't as bad as it would first appear to be. Castillo seemed to be jinxed all year, suffering bad breaks at every turn. There were many games where he pitched well only to have it all unravel in one horrible inning. On a team short of starters, he'll be given the opportunity to rebound and put '96 behind him, and that may be all he needs.

Overall Statistics

	W	L	Pct.	ERA	G	GS	Sv	IP	H	BB	SO	HR	BR/IP
1996	7	16	.304	5.28	33	33	0	182.1	209	46	139	28	1.40
Career	41	53	.436	4.16	146	142	0	851.2	861	238	585	97	1.29

How Often He Throws Strikes

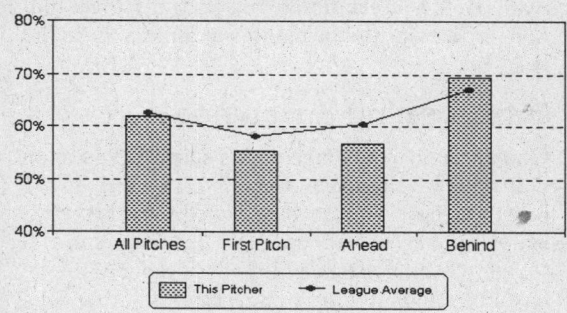

1996 Situational Stats

	W	L	ERA	Sv	IP		AB	H	HR	RBI	Avg
Home	5	7	4.92	0	89.2	LHB	291	77	8	29	.265
Road	2	9	5.63	0	92.2	RHB	435	132	20	70	.303
First Half	2	11	6.26	0	96.1	Sc Pos	135	48	7	68	.356
Scnd Half	5	5	4.19	0	86.0	Clutch	31	9	0	2	.290

1996 Rankings (National League)

- ➡ 1st in losses and highest batting average allowed with runners in scoring position (.356)
- ➡ 2nd in lowest winning percentage
- ➡ 3rd in most pitches thrown per batter (3.88) and highest ERA on the road (5.63)
- ➡ 5th in highest ERA, home runs allowed, highest slugging percentage allowed (.471), most home runs allowed per 9 innings (1.38) and highest ERA at home (4.92)
- ➡ 6th in highest batting average allowed (.288), highest batting average allowed vs. right-handed batters (.303) and errors at pitcher (3)
- ➡ 7th in lowest fielding percentage at pitcher (.932)

Leo Gomez

1996 Season

Signed prior to the season to platoon with Dave Magadan, Leo Gomez found himself holding the full-time job when his platoon partner went down with an injury early on. Gomez had a good first half, and remained a regular until Magadan returned in late May. From that point on, Gomez didn't hit much, and soon found himself back in a platoon role.

Hitting

A pull hitter with an uppercut, Gomez keeps opposing left fielders on their toes. He hits the ball hard, and they often can't reach his drives. He pays the price in strikeouts, but knows how to work a walk. He's a streak hitter, and he'll often get red-hot—or ice-cold—for months at a time, as he did last year.

Baserunning & Defense

Gomez came to Chicago with a suspect reputation with the glove, but he ultimately gave the Cubs the best third-base defense they'd had in several years. A lot of that had to do with the long grass at Wrigley, which masked his lack of range. Still, he has soft hands and a strong, accurate arm. As a baserunner, he lumbers off to the next base only when he has no other choice. For some reason, Gomez attempted five steals last year, and he actually slid in safely on one occasion.

1997 Outlook

The Cubs saw both sides of Leo Gomez last year, and came away with a much better understanding of why the Orioles ultimately became so frustrated with him. After six years of trying, it seems clear that he's simply unable to remain hot at the plate—and healthy enough to show it—for a full season. The Cubs, however, will take what they can get. If Gomez can be part of a workable platoon and provide insurance off the bench, that should be enough to keep him around.

Position: 3B
Bats: R **Throws:** R
Ht: 6' 0" **Wt:** 208

Opening Day Age: 30
Born: 3/2/67 in Canovanas, PR
ML Seasons: 7

Overall Statistics

	G	AB	R	H	D	T	HR	RBI	SB	BB	SO	Avg	OBP	Slg
1996	136	362	44	86	19	0	17	56	1	53	94	.238	.344	.431
Career	611	1916	241	466	92	2	79	259	4	255	399	.243	.336	.417

Where He Hits the Ball

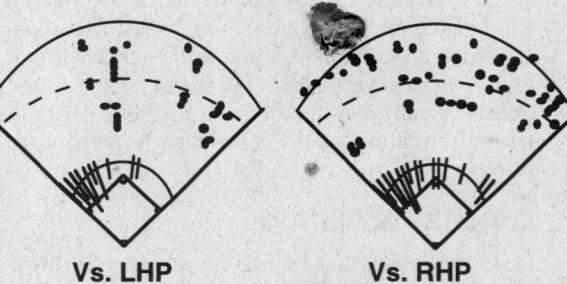

Vs. LHP   **Vs. RHP**

1996 Situational Stats

	AB	H	HR	RBI	Avg		AB	H	HR	RBI	Avg
Home	193	45	10	33	.233	LHP	113	32	3	18	.283
Road	169	41	7	23	.243	RHP	249	54	14	38	.217
First Half	226	59	13	36	.261	Sc Pos	92	20	3	36	.217
Scnd Half	136	27	4	20	.199	Clutch	65	14	2	8	.215

1996 Rankings (National League)

→ 1st in fielding percentage at third base (.972)
→ 6th in lowest batting average with runners in scoring position (.217)
→ 7th in lowest batting average on an 0-2 count (.036)
→ Led the Cubs in on-base percentage vs. left-handed pitchers (.388)

Luis Gonzalez

1996 Season

As the Cubs' platoon left fielder last year, Luis Gonzalez did the little things well. As expected, he took his walks, made good contact and played solid defense. Unfortunately, the Cubs needed him to do more of the *big* things, like hit homers and drive in runs. By the end of the year, he had grown dissatisfied with the platoon arrangement, and the Cubs were openly shopping for a more powerful left fielder.

Hitting

A classic left-handed low-ball hitter, Gonzalez makes good contact with his smooth swing, and rarely fails to make contact. He added 10 pounds in the offseason by lifting weights, but the extra muscle didn't translate into additional power. When the Cubs were forced to bat him fifth—and then fourth, after Sammy Sosa's injury—it was clear that Gonzalez was not ideally suited for the role. The Cubs chose to platoon him, although he'd never had trouble with lefties in the past. The less he saw of them, however, the tougher they became for him to hit.

Baserunning & Defense

With his long, tall frame, Gonzalez uses his above-average speed to cover a lot of ground in left field. His throws are accurate, so his weak arm isn't that much of a handicap. Although he's never mastered the finer points of basestealing, he remains an aggressive baserunner who isn't afraid to take the extra base.

1997 Outlook

Gonzalez's '96 season wasn't a disappointment; it just turned out that the Cubs needed him to do things that weren't a part of his game. Although he probably won't be back next year, he shouldn't have any problem finding a new home. The move away from Wrigley may take a small bite out of his batting average, but wherever he goes, he will remain a productive and well-rounded hitter.

Position: LF
Bats: L **Throws:** R
Ht: 6' 2" **Wt:** 185

Opening Day Age: 29
Born: 9/3/67 in Tampa, FL
ML Seasons: 7

Chicago Cubs

Overall Statistics

	G	AB	R	H	D	T	HR	RBI	SB	BB	SO	Avg	OBP	Slg
1996	146	483	70	131	30	4	15	79	9	61	49	.271	.354	.443
Career	816	2767	370	748	171	31	74	411	67	280	410	.270	.341	.435

Where He Hits the Ball

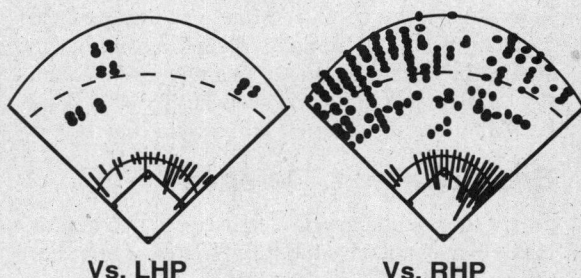

Vs. LHP   **Vs. RHP**

1996 Situational Stats

	AB	H	HR	RBI	Avg		AB	H	HR	RBI	Avg
Home	229	71	6	48	.310	LHP	80	15	2	8	.188
Road	254	60	9	31	.236	RHP	403	116	13	71	.288
First Half	260	70	6	44	.269	Sc Pos	114	40	4	63	.351
Scnd Half	223	61	9	35	.274	Clutch	74	19	0	9	.257

1996 Rankings (National League)

→ 1st in batting average with the bases loaded (.800) and fielding percentage in left field (.988)

→ 7th in batting average on a 3-1 count (.667)

→ 9th in batting average with runners in scoring position (.351) and lowest batting average on the road (.236)

→ 10th in lowest percentage of swings that missed (11.6%) and highest percentage of extra bases taken as a runner (62.2%)

→ Led the Cubs in intentional walks (8), batting average with runners in scoring position (.351), batting average with the bases loaded (.800) and batting average on a 3-1 count (.667)

399

Mark Grace

1996 Season

By now, when you say that Mark Grace had an-other "Mark Grace year," everybody knows what you mean. Aside from a two-week stretch in June when he was sidelined with back pain, Grace was pretty durable and was in the lineup every day, making major contributions with his line-drive bat and soft glove. He gave another season-long clinic on how to use the whole field, and finished the year with the fifth-best batting average in the league.

Hitting

If there's a way to consistently get him out, it has yet to be discovered. Grace covers the entire plate by hitting the ball where it's pitched—on a line. He knows the strike zone, and rarely swings through a pitch. While he remains dangerous with two strikes, he doesn't often *get* to a two-strike count. On the first good pitch he sees, he'll swing—and he'll almost always turn it into a solid line drive.

Baserunning & Defense

To get to second base, Grace uses his bat, not his legs. He may not have the speed to steal, but he has the smarts to run the bases effectively. He still has great first-step quickness, which gives him great range afield. In the field his soft hands are a major asset, and his accurate arm isn't a hindrance, ei-ther. Overall, his defense at first base sets the standard. He has won Gold Gloves in four of the last five seasons, including 1996.

1997 Outlook

Grace has committed to return to Wrigley next year, something the Cubs and their fans were quite happy to hear. He isn't quite approaching the age where you'd expect him to start slowing down, so he should continue lining hits all over the field. By the end of '97, we'll probably be standing back and admiring another typical "Mark Grace sea-son."

Position: 1B
Bats: L **Throws:** L
Ht: 6' 2" **Wt:** 190

Opening Day Age: 32
Born: 6/28/64 in Winston-Salem, NC
ML Seasons: 9

Overall Statistics

	G	AB	R	H	D	T	HR	RBI	SB	BB	SO	Avg	OBP	Slg
1996	142	547	88	181	39	1	9	75	2	62	41	.331	.396	.455
Career	1297	4903	696	1514	300	29	91	664	57	587	388	.309	.381	.437

Where He Hits the Ball

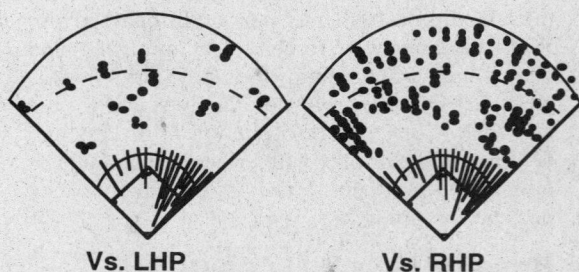

Vs. LHP   Vs. RHP

1996 Situational Stats

	AB	H	HR	RBI	Avg		AB	H	HR	RBI	Avg
Home	290	99	4	42	.341	LHP	153	46	1	15	.301
Road	257	82	5	33	.319	RHP	394	135	8	60	.343
First Half	275	92	3	34	.335	Sc Pos	129	45	2	65	.349
Scnd Half	272	89	6	41	.327	Clutch	86	21	0	5	.244

1996 Rankings (National League)

- → 1st in batting average vs. right-handed pitch-ers (.343)
- → 2nd in fielding percentage at first base (.997)
- → 4th in batting average with the bases loaded (.600), on-base percentage vs. right-handed pitchers (.412) and batting average on the road (.319)
- → 5th in singles and batting average
- → 7th in batting average at home (.341)
- → 8th in lowest percentage of swings that missed (10.2%) and highest percentage of swings put into play (55.2%)
- → 9th in on-base percentage and batting average with two strikes (.257)
- → 10th in doubles

Jose Hernandez

1996 Season

It was a frustrating year for Jose Hernandez—and for the Cubs as well. He became the starting short-stop when Rey Sanchez got hurt in June, but soon exasperated the Cubs with his frequent strikeouts and poor situational hitting. He suffered through a perplexing fielding slump later in the year, before being benched in favor of Sanchez in September.

Hitting

Hernandez has proven to be a decent hitter, and he hit well for the three months he played as a starter. He didn't fare as well when he had to come off the bench, though. At the plate, he shows surprising power—he proved last year that it wasn't a fluke when he hit 13 homers in 245 at-bats in 1995—but he hits the ball mostly on the ground. He's also an adept bunter. He often has trouble making contact, and he had a hard time making adjustments and going to right field last year.

Baserunning & Defense

Usually an above-average shortstop, Hernandez cost the Cubs several games late in the year with his glove. His range leaves something to be desired, but his arm is strong enough for third base, which he has played adequately on occasion. He has average speed and he's nothing special on the bases, although he did make good on all four of his steal attempts last year.

1997 Outlook

Despite ample opportunities, Hernandez failed to convince the Cubs that he deserves to be their starting shortstop. The Cubs preferred to play Rey Sanchez whenever he was available, so Hernandez will probably back up the left side of the infield unless another injury opens up a spot. A change of scenery might help, but the holes in his game will probably always remain.

Position: SS/3B
Bats: R **Throws:** R
Ht: 6' 1" **Wt:** 180

Opening Day Age: 27
Born: 7/14/69 in Vega Alta, PR
ML Seasons: 5

Overall Statistics

	G	AB	R	H	D	T	HR	RBI	SB	BB	SO	Avg	OBP	Slg
1996	131	331	52	80	14	1	10	41	4	24	97	.242	.293	.381
Career	328	810	115	190	29	9	24	94	7	48	228	.235	.278	.381

Where He Hits the Ball

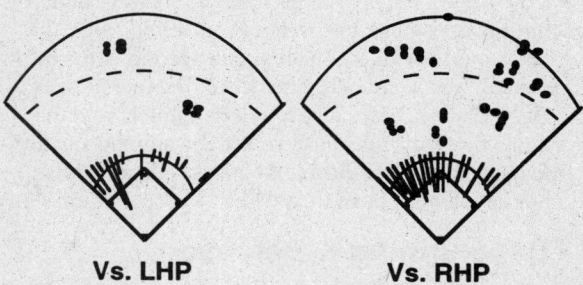

Vs. LHP   **Vs. RHP**

1996 Situational Stats

	AB	H	HR	RBI	Avg		AB	H	HR	RBI	Avg
Home	163	41	4	20	.252	LHP	81	14	1	5	.173
Road	168	39	6	21	.232	RHP	250	66	9	36	.264
First Half	185	41	3	18	.222	Sc Pos	74	18	0	25	.243
Scnd Half	146	39	7	23	.267	Clutch	68	19	3	8	.279

1996 Rankings (National League)

→ 1st in lowest batting average on a 3-1 count (.000)
→ 6th in errors at shortstop (19)

Brian McRae

1996 Season

Serious, intense, and intolerant of losing, Brian McRae does whatever it takes to make the Cubs a better team. In the field, he caught everything that came his way. At the plate, he had a good year from the leadoff spot, even though he would have preferred to hit lower in the order. When Sammy Sosa went down with an injury, he urged the front office to deal for a run-producer. From McRae, you get constructive criticism when it's warranted, but never complaints. And you always get production.

Hitting

A switch-hitter, McRae has always been stronger from the right side, but he brought his left-handed hitting up to par last year. From either side, he takes a powerful, controlled cut. He looks for the fastball away, and will attack the first one he sees. He's always been an excellent bunter, and put more bunts in play last year than anyone in the league. His 14 second-half homers were a surprise, but he may not have the power to keep that up.

Baserunning & Defense

McRae is an aggressive baserunner who's never afraid to swipe second, or even third. He's got great speed, so he rarely gets thrown out. In center field, his defense is among the best in the game. He gets a great jump on the ball, and has the instincts to take his eye off the ball and still beat it to its destination. A weak throwing arm hasn't been a major hindrance.

1997 Outlook

The Cubs locked up McRae with a three-year deal after the season. The power surge may prove illusory, but his contributions in other areas make him a top-flight center fielder. The Cubs will continue to benefit from his presence at the top of the order, in center field, and in the clubhouse.

Position: CF
Bats: B **Throws:** R
Ht: 6' 0" **Wt:** 196

Opening Day Age: 29
Born: 8/27/67 in Bradenton, FL
ML Seasons: 7

Overall Statistics

	G	AB	R	H	D	T	HR	RBI	SB	BB	SO	Avg	OBP	Slg
1996	157	624	111	172	32	5	17	66	37	73	84	.276	.360	.425
Career	908	3597	522	966	179	44	59	362	157	286	564	.269	.327	.392

Where He Hits the Ball

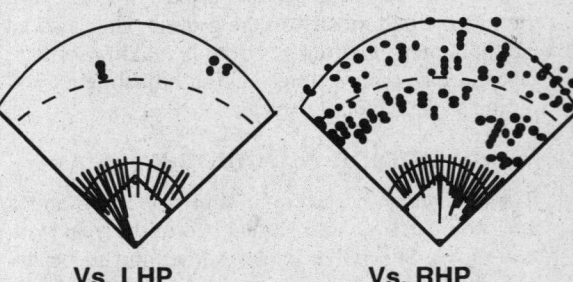

Vs. LHP   **Vs. RHP**

1996 Situational Stats

	AB	H	HR	RBI	Avg		AB	H	HR	RBI	Avg
Home	304	88	9	33	.289	LHP	142	42	2	21	.296
Road	320	84	8	33	.263	RHP	482	130	15	45	.270
First Half	354	93	3	27	.263	Sc Pos	121	33	2	47	.273
Scnd Half	270	79	14	39	.293	Clutch	104	27	2	16	.260

1996 Rankings (National League)

- ➡ 1st in bunts in play (29)
- ➡ 4th in errors in center field (5)
- ➡ 5th in pitches seen (2,678) and lowest fielding percentage in center field (.986)
- ➡ 6th in stolen bases and plate appearances (716)
- ➡ 7th in hit by pitch (12)
- ➡ 8th in on-base percentage for a leadoff hitter (.361) and steals of third (7)
- ➡ Led the Cubs in at-bats, runs scored, triples, stolen bases, caught stealing, walks, times on base (257), pitches seen (2,678), plate appearances (716), games played (157), highest groundball/flyball ratio (1.8) and stolen base percentage (80.4%)

Jaime Navarro

1996 Season

In the first half of '96, Jaime Navarro was unable to build upon the success he'd had the year before. Frustrated by a lack of run support, he blamed his teammates for not scoring for him, and once exploded at manager Jim Riggleman—right in the dugout—over what Navarro felt was a quick hook. But Navarro got his slider working better in the second half, and went on to win eight straight decisions at one point. Although he never got comfortable with Riggleman's early hooks, by the end of the year, he had re-asserted himself as the ace of the staff.

Pitching

Navarro's 90-MPH fastball and hard slider are his bread and butter, and when control of his slider deserted him early in the year, he was unable to compensate by going to his forkball and straight change. He's never been afraid to pitch inside, as evidenced by his 10 hit batsmen last year. His ability to keep the ball down has been a major asset at Wrigley Field. Despite his good stuff and excellent command, he can beat himself when things don't go his way.

Defense & Hitting

Navarro isn't particularly mobile on defense, and sometimes throws the ball away when he rushes himself. His total of five errors last year was topped by only one other major league pitcher. His pickoff move needs work, and baserunners don't find him particularly challenging. At the plate, he's a pure hacker, but somehow, he manages to drop in his share of hits.

1997 Outlook

Navarro was a free agent this winter, and the Cubs were one of many teams bidding for his services. If he ever has a year where he remains in a good frame of mind all season, there's no reason why he can't win 20 games. But to do so, he needs to grow up and learn to deal with failure—both his own, and that of his teammates. He's gone quite a long way on physical ability, and with a better mindset, he can go even further.

Position: SP
Bats: R **Throws:** R
Ht: 6' 4" **Wt:** 230

Opening Day Age: 29
Born: 3/27/68 in Bayamon, PR
ML Seasons: 8
Pronunciation: JAY-mee Nuh-VARR-oh

Overall Statistics

	W	L	Pct.	ERA	G	GS	Sv	IP	H	BB	SO	HR	BR/IP
1996	15	12	.556	3.92	35	35	0	236.2	244	72	158	25	1.34
Career	91	77	.542	4.10	247	215	1	1480.0	1563	446	810	124	1.36

How Often He Throws Strikes

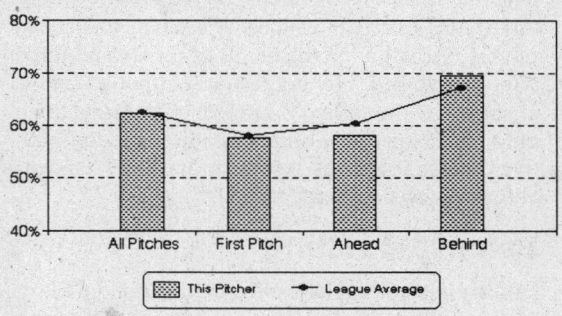

1996 Situational Stats

	W	L	ERA	Sv	IP		AB	H	HR	RBI	Avg
Home	5	7	4.24	0	114.2	LHB	374	101	10	38	.270
Road	10	5	3.61	0	122.0	RHB	532	143	15	64	.269
First Half	6	8	3.73	0	137.2	Sc Pos	202	49	7	73	.243
Scnd Half	9	4	4.18	0	99.0	Clutch	76	19	5	9	.250

1996 Rankings (National League)

→ 1st in hits allowed, batters faced (1,007), errors at pitcher (5) and lowest fielding percentage at pitcher (.868)
→ 2nd in games started
→ 3rd in pitches thrown (3,682) and GDPs induced (24)
→ 4th in innings pitched
→ 5th in stolen bases allowed (24) and runners caught stealing (12)
→ 7th in complete games (4) and highest ERA at home (4.24)
→ 8th in hit batsmen (10), wild pitches (10) and highest groundball/flyball ratio allowed (1.8)
→ 9th in wins, losses and shutouts (1)
→ 10th in ERA on the road (3.61)

Bob Patterson

1996 Season

No one expected all that much from the 37-year-old lefthander, but over the first half of the season, Bob Patterson surprised everyone by working every other day and posting a sub-2.00 ERA. Although he faded after the All-Star break, he remained the Cubs' main lefty out of the pen, and even converted eight of 10 save opportunities. By the end of the year, he was more than just a situational lefty—he was one of the Cubs' three co-closers. He wound up working in 79 games, the highest total of his 11-year career.

Pitching

Patterson can still crack 90 MPH on a good day, but what makes him effective is his excellent control of his fastball and slider. When he's on, he can run his fastball in on the hands of lefties and force a lot of pop-ups. His biggest asset, though, is his uncommon durability. Manager Jim Riggleman used Patterson a few hitters at a time on consecutive days many times last year, and the lefty was almost always up to the task.

Defense & Hitting

Patterson keeps runners close with a good pickoff move, and makes all the plays in the field. He's an average hitter for a pitcher, but as a short reliever, he rarely gets to bat anyway.

1997 Outlook

Patterson re-signed with the Cubs when the 1996 season was over. Given his age and his history, it's highly unlikely that he will save many more games for the Cubs. He's much better suited to work as a lefty specialist, and it's only a matter of time before younger arms ascend to the closer role. As a rubber-armed southpaw who throws strikes, Patterson should remain a valued member of the bullpen, albeit in a set-up role.

Position: RP
Bats: R **Throws:** L
Ht: 6' 2" **Wt:** 195

Opening Day Age: 37
Born: 5/16/59 in Jacksonville, FL
ML Seasons: 11

Overall Statistics

	W	L	Pct.	ERA	G	GS	Sv	IP	H	BB	SO	HR	BR/IP
1996	3	3	.500	3.13	79	0	8	54.2	46	22	53	6	1.24
Career	37	33	.529	4.03	450	21	27	537.2	536	158	408	59	1.29

How Often He Throws Strikes

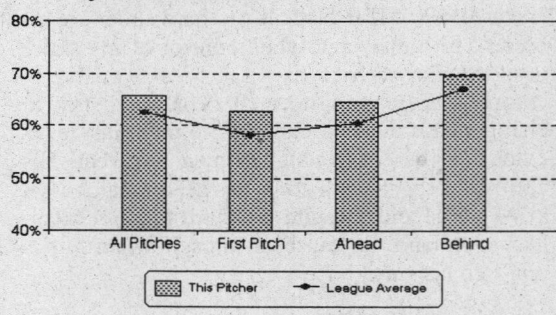

This Pitcher   League Average

1996 Situational Stats

	W	L	ERA	Sv	IP		AB	H	HR	RBI	Avg
Home	3	1	2.76	3	29.1	LHB	78	15	1	9	.192
Road	0	2	3.55	5	25.1	RHB	123	31	5	22	.252
First Half	3	2	1.78	1	30.1	Sc Pos	63	15	2	26	.238
Scnd Half	0	1	4.81	7	24.1	Clutch	114	23	1	14	.202

1996 Rankings (National League)

- ➝ 2nd in games pitched
- ➝ 5th in lowest percentage of inherited runners scored (23.3%)
- ➝ 8th in holds (15)
- ➝ 10th in lowest batting average allowed in relief with runners on base (.200)
- ➝ Led the Cubs in games pitched, holds (15), least baserunners allowed per 9 innings in relief (11.4) and most strikeouts per 9 innings in relief (8.7)

Rey Sanchez

1996 Season

It was a difficult season for Rey Sanchez. With Shawon Dunston departing via free agency, Sanchez got the opportunity to take over as the Cubs' full-time shortstop, but he was held back by continuing pain in his left hand. A fractured hamate bone in his left hand bothered him and affected his hitting until he went on the disabled list in early June. He returned in late July and eventually reclaimed his job as shortstop, but the hand was never 100 percent, and it affected his hitting all year.

Hitting

Sanchez has never been a big run producer or on-base threat at the plate, and with a painful hand injury, he was even more ineffective than ever. It's a good thing he doesn't own a dog, because he truly hates to take a walk. All he does is punch the ball on the ground toward the left side, which generates very few extra-base hits.

Baserunning & Defense

It is Sanchez' defense that sets him apart. Returning to shortstop after two years at second base, Sanchez proved to be one of the game's top defensive shortstops, making spectacular plays almost regularly. He's got it all: quick feet, great range and a great arm. Few are better at going into the hole, and he's also skilled at starting the double play. When the Cubs played him over Jose Hernandez—a far superior power hitter—no one had to ask why. His speed is nothing special, but he was sneaky enough to bag seven bases on eight attempts last year.

1997 Outlook

The health of his left hand will determine what 1997 holds for Rey Sanchez. His average may come back up as his hand recovers, but he won't have to worry about being benched for not hitting. As long as he's able to play, the Cubs will be willing to put up with his meager offense just to get his stellar glovework.

Position: SS
Bats: R **Throws:** R
Ht: 5' 9" **Wt:** 175

Opening Day Age: 29
Born: 10/5/67 in Rio Piedras, PR
ML Seasons: 6

Overall Statistics

	G	AB	R	H	D	T	HR	RBI	SB	BB	SO	Avg	OBP	Slg
1996	95	289	28	61	9	0	1	12	7	22	42	.211	.272	.253
Career	497	1630	171	430	69	8	5	112	18	85	161	.264	.306	.325

Where He Hits the Ball

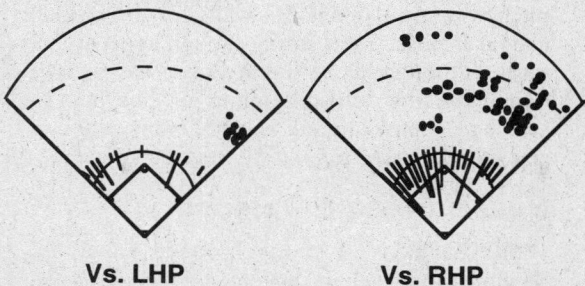

Vs. LHP   **Vs. RHP**

1996 Situational Stats

	AB	H	HR	RBI	Avg		AB	H	HR	RBI	Avg
Home	136	24	1	6	.176	LHP	51	10	0	2	.196
Road	153	37	0	6	.242	RHP	238	51	1	10	.214
First Half	161	34	1	7	.211	Sc Pos	60	8	0	10	.133
Scnd Half	128	27	0	5	.211	Clutch	38	14	0	1	.368

1996 Rankings (National League)

➡ 1st in lowest batting average on a 3-1 count (.000)
➡ Led the Cubs in sacrifice bunts (8)

Ryne Sandberg

1996 Season

After being out of the game for nearly two seasons, Ryne Sandberg returned to baseball with a renewed desire to play the game. At first, the rust showed as he suffered through his customary slow start, but his power returned quickly. Even when he wasn't hitting for a great average, he continued to do the little things on offense as well as drive in runs. By the end of the year, he'd finally found his groove, enjoying a hot September while flashing his old Gold Glove defense.

Hitting

In an effort to pull out of his slump last season, Sandberg tried a number of different approaches at the plate. His preference for looking over the first pitch was still evident. He waits for the fastball, and his hands are still strong enough to get around on it. Although his batting average was a disappointment, the ball still jumps off his bat. He seemed to come alive in key situations, and consistently delivered big hits all season.

Baserunning & Defense

While he hasn't lost much speed since '94, Sandberg's stolen base percentage—which used to be one of his strengths—was the worst in the league. In the field, he was truly the Sandberg of old, covering a lot of ground and making all the plays. He's still catching up on his positioning, but his hands are still the surest around, and his overall game is still top-notch.

1997 Outlook

Sandberg was a free agent this winter, but he re-signed with the Cubs in Novermber. It's not often that you'd expect a 37-year-old player to *improve* his numbers, but Sandberg may be the exception to the rule. His career-low batting average for a full season seemed more the result of rustiness than from a deterioration of his skills, and his power numbers were still the best of any N.L. second baseman. Sandberg badly wants to regain what he's lost, and there's no doubt that he'll work hard to improve.

Position: 2B
Bats: R **Throws:** R
Ht: 6' 2" **Wt:** 190

Opening Day Age: 37
Born: 9/18/59 in Spokane, WA
ML Seasons: 15
Nickname: Ryno

Overall Statistics

	G	AB	R	H	D	T	HR	RBI	SB	BB	SO	Avg	OBP	Slg
1996	150	554	85	135	28	4	25	92	12	54	116	.244	.316	.444
Career	2029	7938	1264	2268	377	76	270	997	337	733	1166	.286	.346	.454

Where He Hits the Ball

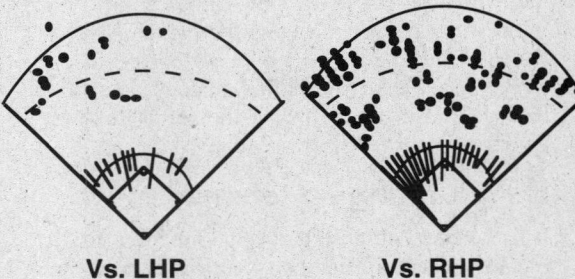

Vs. LHP　　　　**Vs. RHP**

1996 Situational Stats

	AB	H	HR	RBI	Avg		AB	H	HR	RBI	Avg
Home	287	69	12	47	.240	LHP	117	28	12	27	.239
Road	267	66	13	45	.247	RHP	437	107	13	65	.245
First Half	296	73	14	49	.247	Sc Pos	135	40	7	64	.296
Scnd Half	258	62	11	43	.240	Clutch	92	22	4	18	.239

1996 Rankings (National League)

- → 1st in lowest stolen base percentage (60.0%) and lowest percentage of swings on the first pitch (5.5%)
- → 2nd in fielding percentage at second base (.991)
- → 5th in lowest batting average vs. right-handed pitchers (.245) and lowest batting average
- → 6th in most pitches seen per plate appearance (4.04), batting average with the bases loaded (.556), slugging percentage vs. left-handed pitchers (.615) and lowest batting average at home (.240)
- → 7th in lowest on-base percentage
- → 9th in lowest batting average vs. left-handed pitchers (.239)

Scott Servais

1996 Season

It was a productive but painful year for the Cubs' cerebral receiver, Scott Servais. In his first full season as a major league regular, he got off to a hot start, only to be worn down by a variety of assaults upon his person. On May 11, Mets' pitcher Pete Harnisch sucker-punched him, inciting an ugly brawl; he bruised his knee in June; and over the course of the season, he set a team record by being hit with a pitch 14 times. Of course, Servais was also involved in a goodly number of home plate collisions. While he remained a quality catcher all year, the constant beating took its toll on the offensive side of his game.

Hitting

Servais likes the ball up, but he didn't see many waist-high pitches after his April home run spree. He's an impatient hitter who likes to hit the fastball, and when he gets one, he can hit it in the air with occasional power. He hasn't yet learned to shorten up and protect the plate with two strikes.

Baserunning & Defense

On the bases, Servais is constantly in danger of being overgrown by Wrigley's ivy. Defense, however, is his strong suit. Servais calls a good game and has a well-deserved reputation for working closely with the pitchers, who—almost to a man—love to throw to him. His arm isn't tremendously strong, but his release is quick, and he throws out his share of basestealers.

1997 Outlook

A free agent, Servais re-signed with the Cubs after the season. If he is able to avoid much of the physical abuse he suffered through last year, the difference will probably manifest itself in his offensive totals. But even if it doesn't, he'll remain an important member of the Cubs' lineup. Servais fits right in with Jim Riggleman's emphasis on pitching and defense, and he may yet learn to take better advantage of Wrigley Field.

Position: C
Bats: R **Throws:** R
Ht: 6' 2" **Wt:** 205

Opening Day Age: 29
Born: 6/4/67 in LaCrosse, WI
ML Seasons: 6
Pronunciation: SURR-viss

Overall Statistics

	G	AB	R	H	D	T	HR	RBI	SB	BB	SO	Avg	OBP	Slg
1996	129	445	42	118	20	0	11	63	0	30	75	.265	.327	.384
Career	465	1460	143	355	80	1	44	204	2	109	249	.243	.306	.390

Where He Hits the Ball

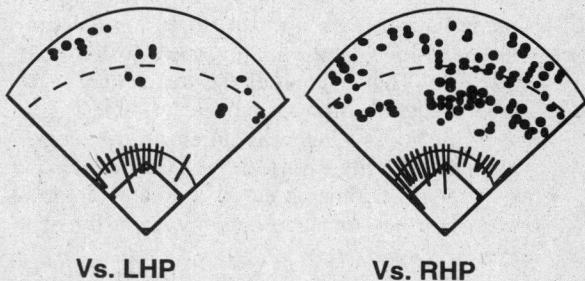

Vs. LHP   **Vs. RHP**

1996 Situational Stats

	AB	H	HR	RBI	Avg		AB	H	HR	RBI	Avg
Home	231	64	6	32	.277	LHP	101	23	3	20	.228
Road	214	54	5	31	.252	RHP	344	95	8	43	.276
First Half	252	67	9	37	.266	Sc Pos	112	30	1	44	.268
Scnd Half	193	51	2	26	.264	Clutch	86	29	4	15	.337

1996 Rankings (National League)

- ➡ 2nd in errors at catcher (11)
- ➡ 3rd in most GDPs per GDP situation (19.1%)
- ➡ 5th in hit by pitch (14) and lowest fielding percentage at catcher (.987)
- ➡ 6th in lowest batting average with two strikes (.128)
- ➡ Led the Cubs in sacrifice flies (7), hit by pitch (14), GDPs (18) and batting average in the clutch (.337)

Sammy Sosa

1996 Season

For his entire career, Sammy Sosa's name has been synonymous with the word "potential," but for five months last year, he showed that he finally was ready to fulfill everyone's lofty expectations. By the end of July—when he was named N.L. Player of the Month—he was close to a pace to break the N.L. record for home runs. Then came an inside pitch that broke a bone in his wrist, bringing a premature end to what might have been a landmark season.

Hitting

For years, the book on Sosa was well known: get ahead in the count, then give him a breaking ball away. He still tries to pull that pitch from time to time, but he stays on it much better now—letting it go by at times, and sometimes even taking it to right field. That makes all the difference in the world, because without that one weakness, he's one of the most dangerous hitters in the league. Although he's still as impatient as they come, and his swings still come up empty a great deal of the time, when he connects, he's always a threat to leave the yard.

Baserunning & Defense

Sosa's defense improved last year, too. His fearsome arm is much more effective now that he's come to understand exactly why the cutoff man tries so hard to get his attention. His positioning has also improved, while his errors and bonehead plays have become more infrequent. On the bases, he doesn't run as often as he used to, but he's running more effectively than ever.

1997 Outlook

When you project out Sosa's numbers from last year, you get a sense of what he's capable of. There aren't many players around with Sosa's combination of power, speed and defense—and we're not talking about *tools* here anymore, we're talking about *production*.

Position: RF
Bats: R **Throws:** R
Ht: 6' 0" **Wt:** 190

Opening Day Age: 28
Born: 11/12/68 in San Pedro de Macoris, DR
ML Seasons: 8

Overall Statistics

	G	AB	R	H	D	T	HR	RBI	SB	BB	SO	Avg	OBP	Slg
1996	124	498	84	136	21	2	40	100	18	34	134	.273	.323	.564
Career	926	3379	503	874	131	29	171	523	177	232	853	.259	.310	.466

Where He Hits the Ball

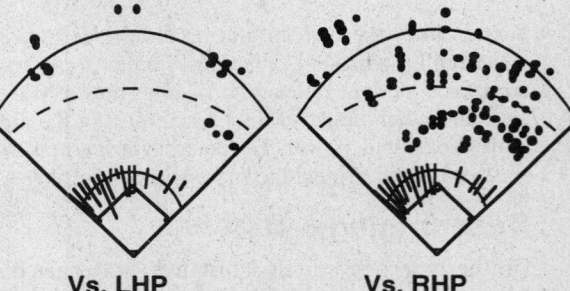

Vs. LHP   **Vs. RHP**

1996 Situational Stats

	AB	H	HR	RBI	Avg		AB	H	HR	RBI	Avg
Home	266	75	26	61	.282	LHP	113	28	8	19	.248
Road	232	61	14	39	.263	RHP	385	108	32	81	.281
First Half	353	91	27	63	.258	Sc Pos	142	35	13	60	.246
Scnd Half	145	45	13	37	.310	Clutch	92	28	7	24	.304

1996 Rankings (National League)

- ➡ 1st in highest percentage of swings that missed (33.6%)
- ➡ 2nd in errors in right field (10), lowest fielding percentage in right field (.964), lowest percentage of pitches taken (43.7%) and lowest percentage of swings put into play (32.4%)
- ➡ 3rd in HR frequency (12.4 ABs per HR)
- ➡ 4th in strikeouts
- ➡ 5th in home runs and lowest groundball/flyball ratio (0.8)
- ➡ 6th in cleanup slugging percentage (.577) and highest percentage of swings on the first pitch (43.9%)
- ➡ 7th in lowest batting average with the bases loaded (.111)

Amaury Telemaco

Position: SP/RP
Bats: R **Throws:** R
Ht: 6' 3" **Wt:** 210

Opening Day Age: 23
Born: 1/19/74 in Higuey, DR
ML Seasons: 1

1996 Season

It was a perplexing rookie season for Amaury Telemaco. At first he was brilliant, throwing 5.2 innings of no-hit ball in his major league debut before finishing with one hit allowed over seven shutout innings. After a few more good starts, he lapsed into inconsistency, and often showed his frustration on the mound. Finally, he got hurt, going on the disabled list with a strained right shoulder on August 20. He returned in September but only worked out of the bullpen for the rest of the season.

Pitching

Telemaco has excellent control of an average fastball and a sharp slider, but his change-up remains a work in progress. Despite his good command, he misses upstairs far too often—a weakness that a Cub pitcher can't afford. His may need to develop an offspeed pitch to throw to left-handed hitters. He wears his heart on his sleeve and can be fun to watch when he's pitching well, but there's a downside to that. The Cubs would like him to work on his concentration and maturity, and to stop reacting so visibly when things don't go his way.

Defense & Hitting

Telemaco's delivery is quick enough to deter basestealers, and he pays a lot of attention to runners, although he lacks a good move to first. So far, he's shown an ability to make all the plays in the field. His hitting only amounts to a strong argument for the DH.

1997 Outlook

At the tender age of 23, Telemaco may encounter a few more bumps on the road to success, but he's got a good chance to reach his destination. Such good control of a breaking pitch is uncommon for someone so young, and it shouldn't be all that difficult for him to make the necessary adjustments to deal with lefties. The Cubs only hope that he doesn't have to continue learning the hard way.

Overall Statistics

	W	L	Pct.	ERA	G	GS	Sv	IP	H	BB	SO	HR	BR/IP
1996	5	7	.417	5.46	25	17	0	97.1	108	31	64	20	1.43
Career	5	7	.417	5.46	25	17	0	97.1	108	31	64	20	1.43

How Often He Throws Strikes

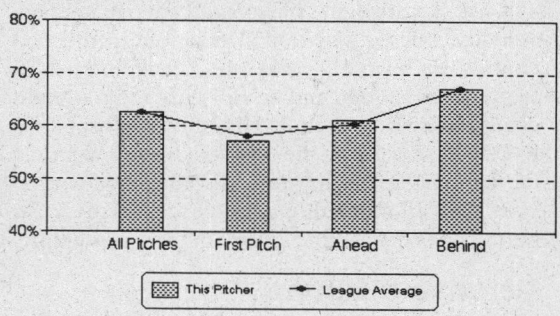

1996 Situational Stats

	W	L	ERA	Sv	IP		AB	H	HR	RBI	Avg
Home	2	4	5.98	0	46.2	LHB	158	55	9	32	.348
Road	3	3	4.97	0	50.2	RHB	227	53	11	28	.233
First Half	4	4	4.98	0	56.0	Sc Pos	84	28	6	42	.333
Scnd Half	1	3	6.10	0	41.1	Clutch	14	4	1	2	.286

1996 Rankings (National League)

→ Did not rank near the top or bottom in any category

Steve Trachsel

Position: SP
Bats: R **Throws:** R
Ht: 6' 4" **Wt:** 205

Opening Day Age: 26
Born: 10/31/70 in Oxnard, CA
ML Seasons: 4
Pronunciation: TRACK-sil

1996 Season

Coming off an awful 1995 season, Steve Trachsel worked on his split-fingered fastball, made some mechanical adjustments in the spring, and boom! He became an All-Star. He showed that things would be different in his first start of the year, when he threw six shutout innings in Wrigley Field—a place where he'd previously had a 3-16 career mark. Although he faded somewhat in the second half, he had a great year overall, finishing sixth in the league in ERA and very nearly becoming the first Cub to post a sub-3.00 ERA since Greg Maddux and Mike Morgan in 1992.

Pitching

Trachsel's fastball has only slightly above-average velocity, but he can run it in or out with good control. He's largely junked his breaking pitch in favor of his splitter, and he still mixes in a straight change from time to time. His entire philosophy is to get ahead early in the count so he can work off the corners, and with the bases empty he simply goes right after the hitter. As a result, 26 of the 30 home runs he gave up came with the bases empty.

Defense & Hitting

Trachsel is a mobile fielder with good reactions. He can handle himself at the plate, although he had a poor year with the stick in '96. He hasn't learned to cut off the running game, and his pickoff move remains average at best.

1997 Outlook

Trachsel may not make the All-Star team again in '96, but his sharp control and groundball proficiency should enable him to continue to succeed in the Cubs' rotation. By now, it's clear that he isn't the second coming of Greg Maddux, but if Jaime Navarro is around, there will be no pressure on him to be the staff ace. All he has to do is live up to the standards he set last year. He certainly has the tools and the intelligence to do it.

Overall Statistics

	W	L	Pct.	ERA	G	GS	Sv	IP	H	BB	SO	HR	BR/IP
1996	13	9	.591	3.03	31	31	0	205.0	181	62	132	30	1.19
Career	29	31	.483	3.78	86	85	0	531.1	504	195	371	78	1.32

How Often He Throws Strikes

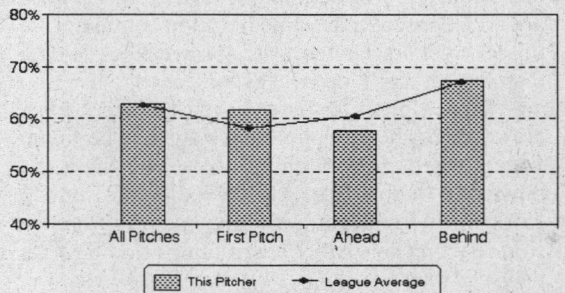

1996 Situational Stats

	W	L	ERA	Sv	IP		AB	H	HR	RBI	Avg
Home	9	5	2.58	0	118.2	LHB	282	68	13	28	.241
Road	4	4	3.65	0	86.1	RHB	487	113	17	45	.232
First Half	7	5	2.14	0	109.1	Sc Pos	182	25	2	39	.137
Scnd Half	6	4	4.05	0	95.2	Clutch	65	19	4	9	.292

1996 Rankings (National League)

→ 1st in lowest batting average allowed with runners in scoring position (.137)
→ 2nd in shutouts (2) and home runs allowed
→ 5th in ERA at home (2.58)
→ 6th in ERA and highest groundball/flyball ratio allowed (1.9)
→ 8th in lowest batting average allowed (.235)
→ 9th in most home runs allowed per 9 innings (1.32) and lowest batting average allowed vs. left-handed batters (.241)
→ Led the Cubs in ERA, shutouts (2), home runs allowed, balks (2), pickoff throws (128), winning percentage, lowest batting average allowed (.235) and lowest slugging percentage allowed (.411)

Turk Wendell

1996 Season

There comes a time in life when everyone has to grow up, even Turk Wendell. At the request of Cub manager Jim Riggleman, Wendell gave up his compulsive licorice-chewing and tooth-brushing, and concentrated on being a pitcher instead of a character. The result was a surprising season in which he pitched well enough to be the Cubs closer, and even seemed to settle into that role for weeks at a time. Riggleman, however, was reluctant to give him too much of the load. Riggleman varied Wendell's usage, pitching him anywhere from the seventh to the ninth inning. Wherever he was used, he was effective, compiling the 10th-best relief ERA in the league.

Pitching

Wendell's fastball is nothing special, but a sharp slider helped him to convert 18 of 21 save opportunities. There were very few times he couldn't get it over, so an offspeed pitch was never really needed. He snapped off the slider to lefties and righties alike, inducing them to pound it into the dirt. His arm bounced back nicely from the frequent work, and he had no trouble working every other day.

Defense & Hitting

Wendell holds runners with an effective pickoff move, and he's a capable fielder as well. He hasn't shown much in his limited opportunities as a hitter, but as a short reliever, he doesn't need to hit very often.

1997 Outlook

The signing of Mel Rojas finally clarifies Wendell's role: he's going to be a set-up man. He's well-qualified for the job, based on last year's showing. With his new-found maturity, he should continue to pitch effectively, even without the licorice.

Position: RP
Bats: L **Throws:** R
Ht: 6' 2" **Wt:** 195

Opening Day Age: 29
Born: 5/19/67 in Pittsfield, MA
ML Seasons: 4
Pronunciation: WENN-dull

Overall Statistics

	W	L	Pct.	ERA	G	GS	Sv	IP	H	BB	SO	HR	BR/IP
1996	4	5	.444	2.84	70	0	18	79.1	58	44	75	8	1.29
Career	8	9	.471	4.48	126	6	18	176.2	175	86	149	22	1.48

How Often He Throws Strikes

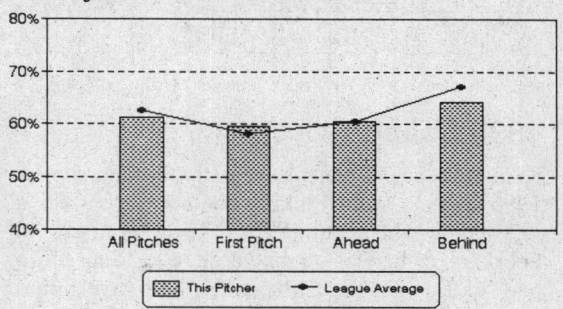

This Pitcher — League Average

1996 Situational Stats

	W	L	ERA	Sv	IP		AB	H	HR	RBI	Avg
Home	3	3	2.00	8	45.0	LHB	113	25	2	9	.221
Road	1	2	3.93	10	34.1	RHB	175	33	6	18	.189
First Half	4	2	2.30	7	43.0	Sc Pos	73	13	2	16	.178
Scnd Half	0	3	3.47	11	36.1	Clutch	169	32	5	17	.189

1996 Rankings (National League)

→ 3rd in least GDPs induced per GDP situation (1.9%)

→ 6th in lowest batting average allowed in relief with runners on base (.178), lowest percentage of inherited runners scored (25.8%) and lowest batting average allowed in relief (.201)

→ 7th in save percentage (85.7%)

→ 8th in first batter efficiency (.172)

→ 10th in relief ERA (2.84)

→ Led the Cubs in saves, games finished (49), balks (2), save opportunities (21), save percentage (85.7%), first batter efficiency (.172) and lowest batting average allowed in relief (.201)

Kent Bottenfield

Position: RP
Bats: R **Throws:** R
Ht: 6' 3" **Wt:** 237

Opening Day Age: 28
Born: 11/14/68 in Portland, OR
ML Seasons: 4

Overall Statistics

	W	L	Pct.	ERA	G	GS	Sv	IP	H	BB	SO	HR	BR/IP
1996	3	5	.375	2.63	48	0	1	61.2	59	19	33	3	1.26
Career	12	18	.400	4.31	111	30	3	280.0	297	111	125	30	1.46

1996 Situational Stats

	W	L	ERA	Sv	IP		AB	H	HR	RBI	Avg
Home	1	1	2.06	0	35.0	LHB	89	26	0	4	.292
Road	2	4	3.38	1	26.2	RHB	142	33	3	17	.232
First Half	0	0	1.13	0	16.0	Sc Pos	63	11	0	15	.175
Scnd Half	3	5	3.15	1	45.2	Clutch	77	20	0	4	.260

1996 Season

Kent Bottenfield wasn't even supposed to *have* a 1996 season. After flunking major league trials in '93 and '94, he spent 1995 in Triple-A. Then, in February, as he was on the verge of heading off to play in Taiwan, the Cubs called and gave him a tryout. He showed enough to get a Triple-A contract, and after they called him up in June, he pitched surprisingly well in middle relief.

Pitching, Defense & Hitting

Bottenfield can survive for an inning at a time on his 92-MPH fastball, although he doesn't have much of a breaking pitch to go with it. He simply moves the ball around and tries to keep it off the fat part of the bat. He has no pickoff move, and runners can take off on him whenever they please. His fielding is indifferent. At the plate, he's been inexplicably successful, compiling a .246 career batting average.

1997 Outlook

Man cannot live on a fastball alone—a lesson Bottenfield has learned the hard way, several times. His success may continue for a time, but chances are that his luck will run out sooner rather than later.

Scott Bullett

Position: LF/CF/RF
Bats: L **Throws:** L
Ht: 6' 2" **Wt:** 220

Opening Day Age: 28
Born: 12/25/68 in Martinsburg, WV
ML Seasons: 4

Overall Statistics

	G	AB	R	H	D	T	HR	RBI	SB	BB	SO	Avg	OBP	Slg
1996	109	165	26	35	5	0	3	16	7	10	54	.212	.256	.297
Career	247	374	49	87	10	9	6	42	19	25	102	.233	.283	.356

1996 Situational Stats

	AB	H	HR	RBI	Avg		AB	H	HR	RBI	Avg
Home	80	19	2	10	.238	LHP	12	2	0	1	.167
Road	85	16	1	6	.188	RHP	153	33	3	15	.216
First Half	56	16	2	6	.286	Sc Pos	49	11	1	14	.224
Scnd Half	109	19	1	10	.174	Clutch	53	8	0	4	.151

1996 Season

When the Cubs needed speed, defense, or a pinch hitter last year, they turned to Scott Bullett. Given short trials in the outfield, he failed to break out of his bench role.

Hitting, Baserunning & Defense

A left-handed hitter, Bullett mostly slaps the ball the other way and tries to leg it out. He sometimes tries to pull, but he doesn't have the power to succeed with that approach. He's impatient and rarely waits to watch ball four. His speed is among the best on the team, which enables him to cover all three outfield positions. His arm is adequate for all three, and he makes for a serviceable defensive replacement. He can steal a base also, but his reputation as a speed-and-defense guy brings him too much attention when he's on base.

1997 Outlook

The versatile Bullett was released by the Cubs after the season, but he stands a reasonable chance of catching on somewhere. He's a valuable guy to have on the bench because of the various ways he can be used.

Jim Bullinger

Position: SP/RP
Bats: R **Throws:** R
Ht: 6' 2" **Wt:** 190

Opening Day Age: 31
Born: 8/21/65 in New Orleans, LA
ML Seasons: 5

Overall Statistics

	W	L	Pct.	ERA	G	GS	Sv	IP	H	BB	SO	HR	BR/IP
1996	6	10	.375	6.54	37	20	1	129.1	144	68	90	15	1.64
Career	27	28	.491	4.77	148	63	11	481.0	473	230	301	45	1.46

1996 Situational Stats

	W	L	ERA	Sv	IP		AB	H	HR	RBI	Avg
Home	2	5	5.40	1	63.1	LHB	222	60	6	35	.270
Road	4	5	7.64	0	66.0	RHB	287	84	9	46	.293
First Half	3	7	5.96	1	80.0	Sc Pos	137	39	5	62	.285
Scnd Half	3	3	7.48	0	49.1	Clutch	39	9	0	1	.231

1996 Season

Jim Bullinger began 1996 as the Cubs' fourth starter, but got knocked around his first time through the order in so many games that he was dropped from the rotation by the middle of June. Although he pitched better out of the pen, he didn't like it there, and said so. Given more chances to return to the rotation, he flopped.

Pitching, Defense & Hitting

Bullinger relies heavily on a moving, sinking fastball. His problems last year were easy to trace: his fastball lost its sink, and he had trouble locating it. When he fell behind with it, he had to shoot for the center of the plate, and everyone in the park knew what was coming. As a former minor league shortstop, Bullinger is one of the best-hitting and best-fielding pitchers in the majors. He doesn't have much of a move to first, though, and baserunners frequently have their way.

1997 Outlook

It's safe to say that the Cubs don't want Bullinger back, and the feeling is mutual. Look for him to catch on somewhere, and perhaps even pitch well if his control returns and his infield defense supports him.

Kevin Foster

Position: SP
Bats: R **Throws:** R
Ht: 6' 1" **Wt:** 170

Opening Day Age: 28
Born: 1/13/69 in Evanston, IL
ML Seasons: 4

Overall Statistics

	W	L	Pct.	ERA	G	GS	Sv	IP	H	BB	SO	HR	BR/IP
1996	7	6	.538	6.21	17	16	0	87.0	98	35	53	16	1.53
Career	22	22	.500	4.76	62	58	0	342.1	330	142	280	58	1.38

1996 Situational Stats

	W	L	ERA	Sv	IP		AB	H	HR	RBI	Avg
Home	5	1	4.47	0	46.1	LHB	167	45	6	20	.269
Road	2	5	8.19	0	40.2	RHB	173	53	10	39	.306
First Half	3	2	7.65	0	40.0	Sc Pos	86	30	3	43	.349
Scnd Half	4	4	4.98	0	47.0	Clutch	26	8	0	2	.308

1996 Season

Kevin Foster seemed to be making good progress up until 1996, but he developed a tired arm out of spring training and lost confidence in his fastball. An extended trip to the minors seemed to rejuvenate him, however. He pitched very well upon his return in August before running out of gas in September.

Pitching, Defense & Hitting

Foster gets by with a good fastball and a decent change-up. It's obvious that he needs to add a breaking pitch, but so far he's been unable to master one. The lack of one may be his undoing, because right now he gives up too many fly balls and home runs to survive. Foster may be the best-hitting pitcher in the majors—last year he batted .296, with surprising power and walks. He's a good fielder, but can't control the running game, mostly because of his high leg kick.

1997 Outlook

Foster has the raw skills to be a reliable starter, but needs to make major adjustments to get there. The Cubs still like his potential, and he'll probably get a few more chances to succeed with them.

Tyler Houston

Position: C/1B
Bats: L **Throws:** R
Ht: 6' 2" **Wt:** 210

Opening Day Age: 26
Born: 1/17/71 in Las Vegas, NV
ML Seasons: 1

Overall Statistics

	G	AB	R	H	D	T	HR	RBI	SB	BB	SO	Avg	OBP	Slg
1996	79	142	21	45	9	1	3	27	3	9	27	.317	.358	.458
Career	79	142	21	45	9	1	3	27	3	9	27	.317	.358	.458

1996 Situational Stats

	AB	H	HR	RBI	Avg		AB	H	HR	RBI	Avg
Home	57	17	1	12	.298	LHP	5	1	0	0	.200
Road	85	28	2	15	.329	RHP	137	44	3	27	.321
First Half	37	13	1	12	.351	Sc Pos	41	17	2	23	.415
Scnd Half	105	32	2	15	.305	Clutch	32	5	0	4	.156

1996 Season

A former number-one pick of the Braves, Tyler Houston flopped in the Atlanta system and got branded with a "bad attitude" label. In Chicago, however, he exploded upon the scene with a sizzling month of July. A bulging disc slowed him somewhat in August and September, but the Cubs remained excited about finding a left-handed-hitting catcher with such offensive promise.

Hitting, Baserunning & Defense

Houston never displayed this type of hitting ability in the minors, and may have been over his head last year. He has a moderate amount of power, but he's terribly impatient, and another .300 average would be a major upset. Houston is a tolerable receiver with below-average throwing skills. What makes him valuable is his versatility, as he can play both first and third base. As a lefty swinger, he gives the roster tremendous late-inning flexibility. His speed is better than that of most catchers.

1997 Outlook

The Cubs saw enough of Houston last year to know that they want to see more. He may not look as special next time around, but if he can remain half as productive, his versatility will be a major asset off the bench.

Dave Magadan

Position: 3B
Bats: L **Throws:** R
Ht: 6' 3" **Wt:** 210

Opening Day Age: 34
Born: 9/30/62 in Tampa, FL
ML Seasons: 11

Overall Statistics

	G	AB	R	H	D	T	HR	RBI	SB	BB	SO	Avg	OBP	Slg
1996	78	169	23	43	10	0	3	17	0	29	23	.254	.360	.367
Career	1117	3271	421	944	174	11	32	389	9	566	415	.289	.391	.378

1996 Situational Stats

	AB	H	HR	RBI	Avg		AB	H	HR	RBI	Avg
Home	72	18	2	7	.250	LHP	8	3	0	0	.375
Road	97	25	1	10	.258	RHP	161	40	3	17	.248
First Half	42	7	0	2	.167	Sc Pos	48	9	0	14	.188
Scnd Half	127	36	3	15	.283	Clutch	31	7	0	2	.226

1996 Season

Signed over the winter to be the platoon third baseman, Dave Magadan missed most of the first half with a painful bone spur in his left hand. When he finally got healthy in the second half, he worked his way back into a platoon arrangement at third, and contributed his usual good number of singles and walks.

Hitting, Baserunning & Defense

Magadan doesn't have a broad range of skills, but he is able to do the one most important thing you can do on a baseball field: get on base. He's extremely selective and makes good contact, which leads to a great on-base percentage year after year. He has no power against lefties and little against righties, but at this point, no one expects him to have much. Magadan is an adequate third baseman, and Wrigley's long grass no doubt helped. His hands and arm are tolerable at best. He has no speed, and plays it conservatively on the bases.

1997 Outlook

Until something better comes along, the Cubs seem content to allow Magadan to play third whenever a right-handed pitcher takes the mound. Magadan contributes whenever he's in the lineup, so the Cubs could do a lot worse.

Rodney Myers

Position: RP
Bats: R **Throws:** R
Ht: 6' 1" **Wt:** 200

Opening Day Age: 27
Born: 6/26/69 in Rockford, IL
ML Seasons: 1

Overall Statistics

	W	L	Pct.	ERA	G	GS	Sv	IP	H	BB	SO	HR	BR/IP
1996	2	1	.667	4.68	45	0	0	67.1	61	38	50	6	1.47
Career	2	1	.667	4.68	45	0	0	67.1	61	38	50	6	1.47

1996 Situational Stats

	W	L	ERA	Sv	IP		AB	H	HR	RBI	Avg
Home	0	0	5.34	0	28.2	LHB	92	22	1	19	.239
Road	2	1	4.19	0	38.2	RHB	159	39	5	28	.245
First Half	1	1	3.89	0	37.0	Sc Pos	82	23	4	41	.280
Scnd Half	1	0	5.64	0	30.1	Clutch	21	4	0	1	.190

1996 Season

The Chicago Cubs selected righthander Rodney Myers from the Royals organization in the Rule V Draft prior to the 1996 season. Despite showing some rough edges, he stuck with the team and vindicated the Cubs' belief that his arm was good enough to take a chance on.

Pitching, Defense & Hitting

It's not hard to see Myers' flaws. His control is spotty; his slider is nothing special; his change-up is virtually nonexistent; and he has problems from the stretch position. But there's one thing that may allow him to overcome all of that: his fastball consistently reaches the low 90s. Baserunners drive him to distraction, and his delivery is too long to deter them. He hasn't distinguished himself in the field. In his first five professional at-bats last year, he went hitless and stuck out four times.

1997 Outlook

Myers got the Cubs' attention last year, and they'll give him at least a few more chances. He may continue as a middle reliever, or could even be tried in the rotation. In any event, he's a longshot to go much beyond where he is now.

Ozzie Timmons

Position: LF/RF
Bats: R **Throws:** R
Ht: 6' 2" **Wt:** 220

Opening Day Age: 26
Born: 9/18/70 in Tampa, FL
ML Seasons: 2

Overall Statistics

	G	AB	R	H	D	T	HR	RBI	SB	BB	SO	Avg	OBP	Slg
1996	65	140	18	28	4	0	7	16	1	15	30	.200	.282	.379
Career	142	311	48	73	14	1	15	44	4	28	62	.235	.299	.431

1996 Situational Stats

	AB	H	HR	RBI	Avg		AB	H	HR	RBI	Avg
Home	74	14	6	11	.189	LHP	76	16	3	8	.211
Road	66	14	1	5	.212	RHP	64	12	4	8	.188
First Half	58	7	1	1	.121	Sc Pos	29	5	1	8	.172
Scnd Half	82	21	6	15	.256	Clutch	32	3	2	3	.094

1996 Season

After a good showing as a rookie in 1995, Ozzie Timmons got squeezed out of the picture last year. He was unable to nail down part of the Cubs' left field job, and was returned to Triple-A for a substantial chunk of the season. When he finally made it back to Chicago, his game hadn't progressed much.

Hitting, Baserunning & Defense

Timmons likes to get a fastball to pull, and has become more patient at the plate. He has good power and could hit 20 homers in a full season, but he doesn't bring much else to the table offensively. In the field Timmons doesn't have great range, speed, or a strong arm, but he gives a good effort and doesn't make rookie mistakes. He steals a base or two a year by using his head, not his legs.

1997 Outlook

Unless Timmons shows something soon, he's in acute danger of being overrun by the Cubs' younger, more glamorous outfield prospects. The Cubs are looking for a power-hitting left fielder, but his name hasn't come up. Unless he's traded, he may spend next year in another frustrating holding pattern.

Other Chicago Cubs

Bret Barberie (**Pos**: 2B, **Age**: 29, **Bats**: B)

	G	AB	R	H	D	T	HR	RBI	SB	BB	SO	Avg	OBP	Slg
1996	15	29	4	1	0	0	1	2	0	5	11	.034	.176	.138
Career	479	1434	163	388	73	6	16	133	16	164	268	.271	.356	.363

In 29 at-bats with the Cubs, Barberie hit one home run and made 28 outs. Since he can switch hit and get by at a few positions on the infield, he should be able to find a bench role somewhere. 1997 Outlook: B

Mike Campbell (**Pos**: RHP, **Age**: 33)

	W	L	Pct.	ERA	G	GS	Sv	IP	H	BB	SO	HR	BR/IP
1996	3	1	.750	4.46	13	5	0	36.1	29	10	19	7	1.07
Career	12	19	.387	5.86	51	41	0	233.1	242	95	135	44	1.44

Triple-A founding father Mike Campbell had a few good starts for the Cubs before his elbow flared up. After the season, the Red Sox claimed him, dropped him, and he went to Japan. Next stop: Mars. 1997 Outlook: D

Larry Casian (**Pos**: LHP, **Age**: 31)

	W	L	Pct.	ERA	G	GS	Sv	IP	H	BB	SO	HR	BR/IP
1996	1	1	.500	1.88	35	0	0	24.0	14	11	15	2	1.04
Career	11	10	.524	4.22	197	3	2	200.1	230	68	96	22	1.49

Casian pitched well for the Cubs in the second half as their number-two lefty specialist out of the pen. He's got a good shot at remaining in that role, but he'll never be anything more. 1997 Outlook: B

Brian Dorsett (**Pos**: C, **Age**: 35, **Bats**: R)

	G	AB	R	H	D	T	HR	RBI	SB	BB	SO	Avg	OBP	Slg
1996	17	41	3	5	0	0	1	3	0	4	8	.122	.196	.195
Career	163	411	38	92	15	0	9	51	0	32	73	.224	.281	.326

Archeologists believe Dorsett caught Mike Campbell in his youth. The 35-year-old catcher sat on the Cubs' bench for two months, then got sent down and missed most of the year with an ankle injury. 1997 Outlook: D

Felix Fermin (**Pos**: 2B, **Age**: 33, **Bats**: R)

	G	AB	R	H	D	T	HR	RBI	SB	BB	SO	Avg	OBP	Slg
1996	11	16	4	2	1	0	0	1	0	2	0	.125	.222	.188
Career	903	2767	294	718	86	11	4	207	27	166	147	.259	.305	.303

Fermin was signed in desperation when injuries left the Cubs thin at shortstop. He played in 11 games, hit .125 and was released. It's unlikely that any team would ever be that desperate again. 1997 Outlook: D

Todd Haney (**Pos**: 2B, **Age**: 31, **Bats**: R)

	G	AB	R	H	D	T	HR	RBI	SB	BB	SO	Avg	OBP	Slg
1996	49	82	11	11	1	0	0	3	1	7	15	.134	.200	.146
Career	98	202	28	50	10	0	3	12	3	17	29	.248	.306	.342

Haney pinch hit and backed up Ryne Sandberg for part of the year. He's a fair defensive player who can hit for a decent average, but it's hard to stay around when your batting average drops 277 points. 1997 Outlook: C

Mike Hubbard (**Pos**: C, **Age**: 26, **Bats**: R)

	G	AB	R	H	D	T	HR	RBI	SB	BB	SO	Avg	OBP	Slg
1996	21	38	1	4	0	0	1	4	0	0	15	.105	.103	.184
Career	36	61	3	8	0	0	1	5	0	2	17	.131	.156	.180

Hubbard's got a little speed and versatility, but seems to have missed out on his chance to become the Cubs' backup catcher. He's a fair hitter, and he's still young enough to make it, in time. 1997 Outlook: C

Mike Perez (**Pos**: RHP, **Age**: 32)

	W	L	Pct.	ERA	G	GS	Sv	IP	H	BB	SO	HR	BR/IP
1996	1	0	1.000	4.67	24	0	0	27.0	29	13	22	2	1.56
Career	22	16	.579	3.56	297	0	22	325.2	319	112	207	24	1.32

Perez was ineffective in middle relief for the Cubs. They sent him down in June, and he pitched horrendously in Triple-A. He's survived worse crises, but no one's banking on another comeback. 1997 Outlook: C

Terry Shumpert (**Pos**: 3B, **Age**: 30, **Bats**: R)

	G	AB	R	H	D	T	HR	RBI	SB	BB	SO	Avg	OBP	Slg
1996	27	31	5	7	1	0	2	6	0	2	11	.226	.286	.452
Career	332	825	97	182	37	8	16	86	44	56	174	.221	.274	.343

Shumpert pinch hit and played some third base for the Cubs, and even got a couple of big hits. He doesn't hit enough to play anywhere except for second base. The Cubs released him, so he'll keep looking. 1997 Outlook: C

Tanyon Sturtze (**Pos**: RHP, **Age**: 26)

	W	L	Pct.	ERA	G	GS	Sv	IP	H	BB	SO	HR	BR/IP
1996	1	0	1.000	9.00	6	0	0	11.0	16	5	7	3	1.91
Career	1	0	1.000	9.00	8	0	0	13.0	18	6	7	4	1.85

Sturtze pitched 11 innings for the Cubs in July, and that was enough for them to confirm that he didn't belong there. He was outrighted to Triple-A in October, and may spend the rest of his career there. 1997 Outlook: D

Dave Swartzbaugh (**Pos**: RHP, **Age**: 29)

	W	L	Pct.	ERA	G	GS	Sv	IP	H	BB	SO	HR	BR/IP
1996	0	2	.000	6.38	6	5	0	24.0	26	14	13	3	1.67
Career	0	2	.000	4.88	13	5	0	31.1	31	17	18	3	1.53

Originally a starter in the minors, Swartzbaugh revived his career by moving to the bullpen. He pitched well in Triple-A after returning to the rotation. The Cubs gave him five starts in September. 1997 Outlook: C

Chicago Cubs Minor League Prospects

Organization Overview:

The Cubs are trying to develop from within, but they've gotten little help from their farm system so far. Terry Adams was a major find last year, but most of their other young pitchers have remained maddeningly inconsistent. Meanwhile, the farms have produced hardly any talented hitters over the past few years. There is hope, though; the Cubs have some exciting young arms down at the lower levels. They have a good number of position players on the way, but most of them are outfielders, a commodity that's hardly in demand at Wrigley. For some reason, the Cubs' top draft picks have had an extraordinarily difficult time advancing and developing within the system. Still, if the Cubs remain true to their professed philosophy, 1997 will be a year of opportunity for long-awaited farmhands like Brooks Kieschnick, Kevin Orie and Robin Jennings.

Brant Brown

Position: 1B
Bats: L **Throws:** L
Ht: 6' 3" **Wt:** 220
Opening Day Age: 25
Born: 6/22/71 in Porterville, CA

Recent Statistics

	G	AB	R	H	D	T	HR	RBI	SB	BB	SO	AVG
96 AAA Iowa	94	342	48	104	25	3	10	43	6	19	65	.304
96 NL Chicago	29	69	11	21	1	0	5	9	3	2	17	.304
96 MLE	94	336	43	98	23	2	9	39	4	17	68	.292

Labeled a singles-hitter in the minors, first baseman Brant Brown went a long way toward dispelling that image when he launched three homers in a doubleheader in his first week with the Cubs. Despite his impressive debut, no one really believes that he's anything but a poor man's Mark Grace. Brown shines in the field and hits for a decent average, but the power just isn't there, and at age 26, he doesn't project to be much more than a pinch hitter.

Doug Glanville

Position: OF
Bats: R **Throws:** R
Ht: 6' 2" **Wt:** 170
Opening Day Age: 26
Born: 8/25/70 in Hackensack, NJ

Recent Statistics

	G	AB	R	H	D	T	HR	RBI	SB	BB	SO	AVG
96 AAA Iowa	90	373	53	115	23	3	3	34	15	12	35	.308
96 NL Chicago	49	83	10	20	5	1	1	10	2	3	11	.241
96 MLE	90	364	48	106	21	2	2	31	12	10	36	.291

Outstanding speed may get you drafted in the first round, and it may enable you to play a great center field, but it won't make you into a baseball player. For all his speed, Doug Glanville has no power, doesn't know how to steal a base, and refuses to take a walk. Considering the fact that he's 26 and bats right-handed, there's little hope that he'll ever be anything more than a defensive replacement.

Geremis Gonzalez

Position: P
Bats: R **Throws:** R
Ht: 6' 1" **Wt:** 180
Opening Day Age: 22
Born: 1/8/75 in Maracaibo, Zulia, Venez

Recent Statistics

	W	L	ERA	G	GS	Sv	IP	H	R	BB	SO	HR
93 R Huntington	3	9	6.25	12	12	0	67.2	82	59	38	42	6
94 A Peoria	1	7	5.55	13	13	0	71.1	86	53	32	39	4
94 A Williamsprt	4	6	4.24	16	12	1	80.2	83	46	29	64	6
95 A Rockford	4	4	5.10	12	12	0	65.1	63	43	28	36	4
95 A Daytona	5	1	1.22	19	2	4	44.1	34	15	13	30	0
96 AA Orlando	6	3	3.34	17	14	0	97.0	95	39	28	85	6

Twenty-two year-old righthander Geremis Gonzalez finally found his command, and got off to a blazing start at Double-A. Unfortunately, a tender elbow slowed him in June and put him out of action for most of the second half. He's got a good arm, but with his youth and inexperience, the Cubs probably will have him start the year back in Double-A. From what he showed when he was healthy, he could come quickly.

Robin Jennings

Position: OF
Bats: L **Throws:** L
Ht: 6' 2" **Wt:** 200
Opening Day Age: 24
Born: 4/11/72 in Singapore

Recent Statistics

	G	AB	R	H	D	T	HR	RBI	SB	BB	SO	AVG
96 AAA Iowa	86	331	53	94	15	6	18	56	2	32	53	.284
96 NL Chicago	31	58	7	13	5	0	0	4	1	3	9	.224
96 MLE	86	325	48	88	14	4	16	51	1	29	55	.271

Last year, Robin Jennings proved that his power surge in '95 was no fluke. At Triple-A, he stepped up his production even more, although he couldn't get the bat going in a short trial with the Cubs. A left-handed hitter, Jennings hangs in against all types of pitchers, and only needs a chance to prove it. He's a decent right fielder, and could help the Cubs in left if they let him.

Brooks Kieschnick

Position: 1B-OF
Bats: L **Throws:** R
Ht: 6' 4" **Wt:** 228
Opening Day Age: 24
Born: 6/6/72 in Robstown, TX

Recent Statistics

	G	AB	R	H	D	T	HR	RBI	SB	BB	SO	AVG
96 AAA Iowa	117	441	47	114	20	1	18	64	0	37	108	.259
96 NL Chicago	25	29	6	10	2	0	1	6	0	3	8	.345
96 MLE	117	434	42	107	18	0	16	58	0	33	113	.247

With no place to put him, the Cubs were forced to send Brooks Kieschnick to Triple-A for the second straight year. With nothing left to prove down there, his hitting fell off a bit. Although his defense in left field is a bit shaky, he's got more than enough power to hold his own in the majors. Time is growing short for the former number-one pick, and the Cubs may not be able to keep him down much longer.

Kevin Orie

Position: 3B | **Opening Day Age:** 24
Bats: R **Throws:** R | **Born:** 9/1/72 in
Ht: 6' 4" **Wt:** 215 | Westchester, PA

Recent Statistics

	G	AB	R	H	D	T	HR	RBI	SB	BB	SO	AVG
93 A Peoria	65	238	28	64	17	1	7	45	3	21	51	.269
94 A Daytona	6	17	4	7	3	1	1	5	0	8	4	.412
95 A Daytona	119	409	54	100	17	4	9	51	5	42	71	.244
96 AA Orlando	82	296	42	93	25	0	8	58	2	48	52	.314
96 AAA Iowa	14	48	5	10	1	0	2	6	0	6	10	.208
96 MLE	96	334	40	93	22	0	8	54	1	40	65	.278

A good showing in the Arizona Fall League was the best thing that could have happened to Kevin Orie. He was hampered by wrist problems for two years, and when he finally got going last year, he separated his shoulder and missed the second half. He's got good offensive potential and plays a great third base, and the Cubs will give him a long look next spring—*if* he can prove that he's finally healthy. He now appears to be sound, and he could be one of this year's best rookies.

Steve Rain

Position: P | **Opening Day Age:** 21
Bats: R **Throws:** R | **Born:** 6/2/75 in Los
Ht: 6' 6" **Wt:** 225 | Angeles, CA

Recent Statistics

	W	L	ERA	G	GS	Sv	IP	H	R	BB	SO	HR
93 R Cubs	1	3	3.89	10	6	0	37.0	37	20	17	29	0
94 R Huntington	3	3	2.65	14	10	0	68.0	55	26	19	55	2
95 A Rockford	5	2	1.21	53	0	23	59.1	38	12	23	66	0
96 AA Orlando	1	0	2.56	35	0	10	38.2	32	15	12	48	4
96 AAA Iowa	2	1	3.12	26	0	10	26.0	17	9	8	23	3

Steve Rain has fought an uphill battle to establish himself as a serious prospect in short relief, but the numbers don't lie. He dominated A-ball in '95, but what really began to convince people was his uninterrupted march through Double-A and Triple-A last year. His velocity isn't exceptional—which may be the root of people's skepticism—but his fastball has good movement and his slider is a reliable out pitch. Rain should be able to find a role somewhere in the Cubs' bullpen this year.

Pedro Valdes

Position: OF | **Opening Day Age:** 23
Bats: L **Throws:** L | **Born:** 6/29/73 in
Ht: 6' 1" **Wt:** 160 | Fajardo, PR

Recent Statistics

	G	AB	R	H	D	T	HR	RBI	SB	BB	SO	AVG
96 AAA Iowa	103	397	61	117	23	0	15	60	2	31	57	.295
96 NL Chicago	9	8	2	1	1	0	0	1	0	1	5	.125
96 MLE	103	390	55	110	21	0	13	54	1	28	59	.282

The Cubs have three good outfield prospects waiting in line at Triple-A, and, unfortunately, Valdes is third in line. He's a good contact hitter who sprays the ball around, and he began to show a little bit of power last year. He bats lefty and plays all three outfield spots decently, so there may be a future for him as a fourth outfielder. It would be hard, though, to envision him leapfrogging over the rest of the Cubs' young outfielders.

Others to Watch

The Cubs selected **Kerry Wood** with the fourth overall pick in the '95 amateur draft, and his first full professional season last year was anything but a disappointment. The 19-year old absolutely dominated A-ball, going 10-2 and fanning well over a batter per inning. He throws a mid-90s fastball and a good curve, and the Cubs think it may take him only two more years to arrive in Wrigley. . . Righthander **Justin Speier**, the son of former big-leaguer Chris Speier, saved 19 games between A-ball and Double-A last year. He's held his own as he's moved up the ladder, and may surface as a middle reliever before long. . . Catcher **Pat Cline** is the best position prospect in the lower end of the system. He's a good receiver with great power potential, and may turn out to be the complete package in a year or two. . . Switch-hitting second baseman **Shane Livsey** has good speed and makes good contact. After only a half-season above A-ball, he'll need more time.

Ray Knight

1996 Season

Prior to last year, Ray Knight had never managed anywhere, and his inexperience often showed. An emotional skipper, he often got too enthusiastic when he won and took losing too hard when he didn't. However, he did an excellent job of keeping the Reds afloat during a season in which they were riddled by injuries and distracted by the circumstances surrounding owner Marge Schott. Knight had a habit of making up his mind quickly about players, often losing patience with veterans and kids alike.

Offense

Knight preaches aggressive baseball. He tries to press the action with stealing and movement on the bases. He may have been guilty of overmanaging his offense last year, as the Reds frequently ran into outs on the bases. But he showed the ability to use all of his available talent with an assortment of platoons, pinch hitters and in-game substitutions. His goal was to try and achieve the best match-ups with a roster often depleted by injuries.

Pitching & Defense

Like many inexperienced skippers, Knight was often guilty of warming up his bullpen at every first sign of trouble. However, he did a good job of protecting closer Jeff Brantley, who almost never warmed up without appearing in the game. Knight had a quick hook with his starters, which was the best route for a rotation that was injured all season and didn't have a true ace. When given the choice, he usually opted for his best potential offensive mix instead of substituting for defense.

1997 Outlook

Knight's hyper personality rubbed some Reds and many opponents the wrong way. However, he is an upbeat person and popular with Cincinnati fans. He did about as well as could be expected with the situation he had last year. If he has a healthy roster, Knight should have the Reds in contention.

Born: 12/28/52 in Albany, GE

Playing Experience: 1974-1988, Cin, Hou, NYN, Bal, Det

Managerial Experience: 1 season

Manager Statistics

Year	Team, Lg	W	L	Pct	GB	Finish
1996	Cincinnati, NL	81	81	.500	7.0	3rd Central
1 Season		81	81	.500	—	—

1996 Starting Pitchers by Days Rest

	≤3	4	5	6+
Reds Starts	4	80	38	30
Reds ERA	6.52	4.59	4.44	4.27
NL Avg Starts	4	86	41	21
NL ERA	4.06	4.28	4.23	4.58

1996 Situational Stats

	Ray Knight	NL Average
Hit & Run Success %	37.7	39.0
Stolen Base Success %	73.1	71.6
Platoon Pct.	56.7	51.9
Defensive Subs	27	20
High-Pitch Outings	9	13
Quick/Slow Hooks	29/8	19/12
Sacrifice Attempts	96	92

1996 Rankings (National League)

→ 1st in intentional walks (50), starting lineups used (147) and starts with over 140 pitches (1)

→ 2nd in steals of third base (36), double steals (8), pinch hitters used (313) and quick hooks (29)

→ 3rd in stolen base attempts (234), steals of second base (133), squeeze plays (9) and defensive substitutions (27)

Bret Boone

1996 Season

Sometimes toughness and competitiveness can have a negative effect on a season. Such was the case with Bret Boone in 1996. Boone insisted on playing through several nagging injuries and in the process got himself off to a slow start that he was never able to turn around. Boone did manage to exceed his RBI total from the previous year, but his overall production dropped in every area except defense.

Hitting

Hitting coaches have waged a constant battle to get Boone to cut down on his swing. However, he remains a big swinger who would love to hit more home runs. As a result, his strikeout totals have always remained high. A thumb injury last year caused him to be even more gun-shy than normal on inside pitches. In addition, a back problem hurt his ability to drive the ball to the opposite field— one reason why his doubles total plummeted. When he's healthy, Boone can turn around heat and is very aggressive early in the count.

Baserunning & Defense

Boone is hardly a burner, but he runs intelligently and can steal a base on occasion. He has developed into perhaps the best defensive second baseman in the National League. His range is about average, but he more than makes up for that with smart positioning based on his excellent knowledge of opposing hitters. He turns the double play as well as anyone and his league-leading fielding percentage among second basemen last year underscores the sureness of his hands.

1997 Outlook

Because his salary is rising, Boone was shopped over the winter by Cincinnati. Whoever has him in their lineup this year will have one of the game's better second basemen. He should bounce back from his tough season and approach .280 with 20 homers.

Position: 2B
Bats: R **Throws:** R
Ht: 5'10" **Wt:** 180

Opening Day Age: 27
Born: 4/6/69 in El Cajon, CA
ML Seasons: 5

Overall Statistics

	G	AB	R	H	D	T	HR	RBI	SB	BB	SO	Avg	OBP	Slg
1996	142	520	56	121	21	3	12	69	3	31	100	.233	.275	.354
Career	497	1814	224	473	96	9	55	258	14	117	344	.261	.310	.415

Where He Hits the Ball

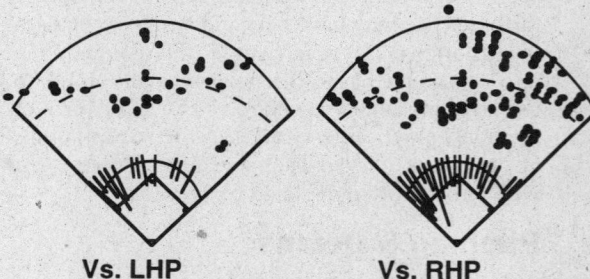

Vs. LHP   **Vs. RHP**

1996 Situational Stats

	AB	H	HR	RBI	Avg		AB	H	HR	RBI	Avg
Home	242	59	7	44	.244	LHP	117	27	6	20	.231
Road	278	62	5	25	.223	RHP	403	94	6	49	.233
First Half	237	57	8	36	.241	Sc Pos	125	32	1	54	.256
Scnd Half	283	64	4	33	.226	Clutch	79	23	0	11	.291

1996 Rankings (National League)

→ 1st in lowest on-base percentage, lowest on-base percentage vs. right-handed pitchers (.267) and fielding percentage at second base (.991)

→ 2nd in lowest batting average vs. right-handed pitchers (.233) and lowest batting average

→ 4th in sacrifice flies (9) and lowest batting average on the road (.223)

→ 6th in lowest slugging percentage vs. right-handed pitchers (.328)

→ 8th in lowest batting average vs. left-handed pitchers (.231), lowest on-base percentage vs. left-handed pitchers (.303), lowest batting average at home (.244) and lowest percentage of swings on the first pitch (21.7%)

Jeff Branson

1996 Season

Until Willie Greene started to show his power late last year, Jeff Branson was the Reds' main left-handed platoon player at third base. Branson wound up playing 64 games at third, but his greatest worth was as a versatile utility player who could fill in at second and short while also serving as a frequent left-handed pinch hitter. He managed 29 extra-base hits among his 76 hits.

Hitting

Branson has worked hard over the last three years to add more strength, and the work has paid off in improved power numbers. He is strictly a fastball hitter who does most of his damage off the heater. Branson has also moved up on the plate to allow him to pull more easily; while that has helped with more extra-base hits, he is still prone to striking out. He has difficulty with offspeed pitches, and he is strictly a platoon weapon who has never proven he can hit lefthanders.

Baserunning & Defense

When he was younger, Branson was an outstanding athlete who had excellent range both as a shortstop and third baseman. Knee problems have robbed him of much of his range as well as his speed. He is not a basestealing threat. Branson is now something of a liability at short, especially on the Cinergy Field artificial turf. He is a decent third baseman, though he does not have great hands and can occasionally be erratic with his throws.

1997 Outlook

It is a fact of life that the Reds are a better club if Branson is a reserve rather than someone getting everyday playing time. He will continue to be a utility player who offers occasional punch and a solid work ethic to the Cincinnati bench.

Position: 3B/2B/SS
Bats: L **Throws:** R
Ht: 6' 0" **Wt:** 180

Opening Day Age: 30
Born: 1/26/67 in Waynesboro, MS
ML Seasons: 5

Overall Statistics

	G	AB	R	H	D	T	HR	RBI	SB	BB	SO	Avg	OBP	Slg
1996	129	311	34	76	16	4	9	37	2	31	67	.244	.312	.408
Career	506	1247	147	319	60	9	30	135	8	104	241	.256	.311	.391

Where He Hits the Ball

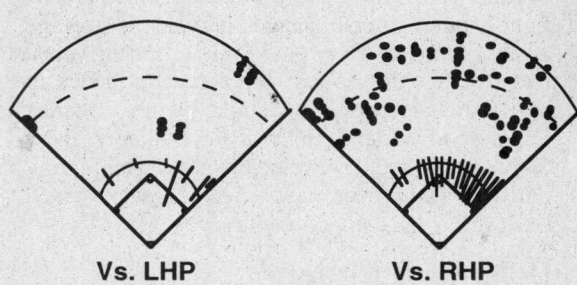

Vs. LHP   **Vs. RHP**

1996 Situational Stats

	AB	H	HR	RBI	Avg		AB	H	HR	RBI	Avg
Home	124	35	5	17	.282	LHP	55	11	2	9	.200
Road	187	41	4	20	.219	RHP	256	65	7	28	.254
First Half	189	44	5	22	.233	Sc Pos	65	12	1	24	.185
Scnd Half	122	32	4	15	.262	Clutch	64	13	4	12	.203

1996 Rankings (National League)

→ 8th in lowest batting average with the bases loaded (.125)
→ 10th in most GDPs per GDP situation (17.3%) and lowest batting average on an 0-2 count (.043)

Jeff Brantley

1996 Season

In his ninth major league season, Jeff Brantley broke through with the best year of his career—and one of the best years for any recent reliever. He led the majors with 44 saves while blowing only five save opportunities and holding opposing batters to a .215 average. He accomplished all this despite starting the season on the disabled list with a stress fracture in his right foot and despite allowing home runs in two of his first eight appearances.

Pitching

It's no secret around the National League that Brantley's money pitch, especially against right-handed hitters, is his split-fingered fastball. The splitter, along with a sharp-breaking slider, is why right-handed hitters managed only a .185 average against him last year. However, in recent years, Brantley has developed increased confidence in his fastball, especially a cutter he uses against left-handed batters. He will occasionally show hitters a curve and a circle change as well, giving him rare variety for a closer. His greatest asset, however, is his competitiveness.

Defense & Hitting

Brantley's compact delivery usually leaves him in good fielding position. He can be susceptible to stolen bases because he does not have any real pickoff move, but in the situations he normally appears in, stolen bases are rarely attempted. He isn't much of a hitter, but he rarely bats, so it's not a problem.

1997 Outlook

Brantley may not match his career year, but he remains a top-echelon closer who can be relied upon for at least 30 saves a year. He showed his affection for Cincinnati, where he is a team leader, and for manager Ray Knight by signing a new contract late last season. After his big season, he could have commanded a bidding war, but he elected to stay with the Reds at what was likely a below-market price.

Position: RP
Bats: R **Throws:** R
Ht: 5'10" **Wt:** 190

Opening Day Age: 33
Born: 9/5/63 in Florence, AL
ML Seasons: 9

Overall Statistics

	W	L	Pct.	ERA	G	GS	Sv	IP	H	BB	SO	HR	BR/IP
1996	1	2	.333	2.41	66	0	44	71.0	54	28	76	7	1.15
Career	39	30	.565	3.05	471	18	129	712.0	610	295	585	74	1.27

How Often He Throws Strikes

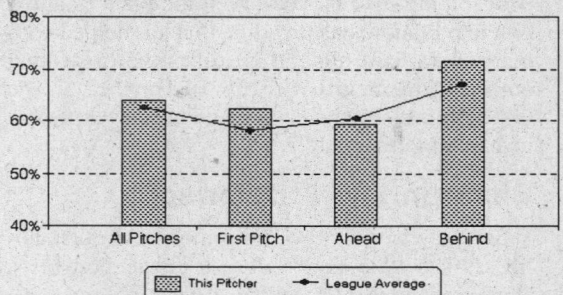

1996 Situational Stats

	W	L	ERA	Sv	IP		AB	H	HR	RBI	Avg
Home	0	0	2.45	21	33.0	LHB	121	30	2	5	.248
Road	1	2	2.37	23	38.0	RHB	130	24	5	18	.185
First Half	1	1	3.07	22	41.0	Sc Pos	45	7	2	17	.156
Scnd Half	0	1	1.50	22	30.0	Clutch	172	35	6	18	.203

1996 Rankings (National League)

- ➡ 1st in saves
- ➡ 2nd in save opportunities (49) and save percentage (89.8%)
- ➡ 4th in lowest batting average allowed in relief with runners on base (.165)
- ➡ 6th in games finished (61) and relief ERA (2.41)
- ➡ 8th in least baserunners allowed per 9 innings in relief (10.4)
- ➡ 10th in lowest batting average allowed in relief with runners in scoring position (.156) and most strikeouts per 9 innings in relief (9.6)
- ➡ Led the Reds in saves, games finished (61) and save opportunities (49)

Dave Burba

1996 Season

While injuries were weakening the rest of the Reds' rotation, Dave Burba took the ball every time he was asked and gave Cincinnati a solid workhorse season. Burba ended up with a career-best 11 wins, holding opposing hitters to a .244 average in the process. He finished off his year with wins in his last two starts.

Pitching

Burba has explosive movement on his fastball, but sometimes it moves too much for his own good. His heater can run six inches and at times he will have major control troubles because of his fastball's unpredictability. He will have streaks of wildness, which account for his high walk totals. He often does his best by simply aiming for the center of the plate and letting his 90-plus fastball move to either side of the plate. Burba also has a hard, late-breaking slider. Since becoming a full-time starting pitcher, Burba has needed to come up with something offspeed and worked last year on a straight change.

Defense & Hitting

With a high, slow leg kick and no pickoff move of any quality, Burba is easy pickings for opposing basestealers, who last year were successful 22 times in 30 attempts. He is not very agile and his delivery throws him toward first base, which makes him a mediocre fielder at best. Burba can be dangerous with the bat when he's able to make contact. Last year he hit the only two home runs produced by Reds pitchers.

1997 Outlook

Throughout his career, Burba has been shuttled between the bullpen and the starting rotation. He is now a starter to stay and certain to be part of the Reds' rotation which opens the season. He can be counted on to win at least a dozen games and pitch around 200 innings.

Position: SP
Bats: R **Throws:** R
Ht: 6' 4" **Wt:** 240

Opening Day Age: 30
Born: 7/7/66 in Dayton, OH
ML Seasons: 7

Cincinnati Reds

Overall Statistics

	W	L	Pct.	ERA	G	GS	Sv	IP	H	BB	SO	HR	BR/IP
1996	11	13	.458	3.83	34	33	0	195.0	179	97	148	18	1.42
Career	38	35	.521	4.13	248	60	1	586.1	545	277	483	56	1.40

How Often He Throws Strikes

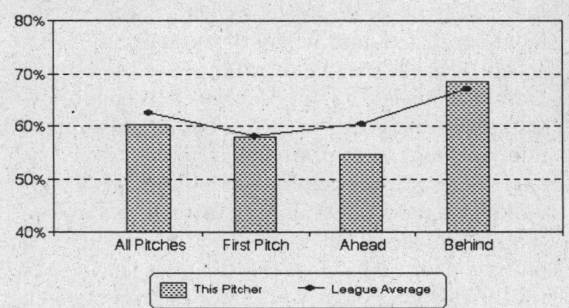

1996 Situational Stats

	W	L	ERA	Sv	IP		AB	H	HR	RBI	Avg
Home	6	9	3.75	0	117.2	LHB	314	80	8	32	.255
Road	5	4	3.96	0	77.1	RHB	419	99	10	49	.236
First Half	3	9	4.05	0	104.1	Sc Pos	192	37	1	53	.193
Scnd Half	8	4	3.57	0	90.2	Clutch	42	10	2	3	.238

1996 Rankings (National League)

→ 3rd in walks allowed and lowest batting average allowed with runners in scoring position (.193)
→ 7th in losses and lowest strikeout/walk ratio (1.5)
→ 8th in lowest fielding percentage at pitcher (.935)
→ 9th in most pitches thrown per batter (3.82)
→ 10th in lowest batting average allowed (.244)
→ Led the Reds in walks allowed, wild pitches (9), pitches thrown (3,247), stolen bases allowed (22), lowest batting average allowed (.244), lowest slugging percentage allowed (.381) and most run support per 9 innings (4.7)

Eric Davis

Position: CF/LF
Bats: R **Throws:** R
Ht: 6' 3" **Wt:** 190

Opening Day Age: 34
Born: 5/29/62 in Los Angeles, CA
ML Seasons: 12

1996 Season

No comeback story last year was more unlikely than that of Eric Davis. Out of baseball for a year after hitting .183 for the 1994 Tigers, Davis realized how much he missed the game. He got his battered body healthy, and after being given a courtesy spring-training tryout by the Reds, went on to become one of Cincinnati's most consistent players. He carried the team through the early weeks of the season and ended up with 26 homers—his best power year since 1989.

Hitting

In his prime, Davis would start his hands low and toward the front of his body, then bring them back into hitting position. He got by with all that movement because of his quick wrists and excellent bat speed. The bat speed isn't what it used to be, but Davis has made some adjustments. His hands now start slightly higher and farther back in his stance, allowing him to turn around fastballs as well as ever. He also waits better on breaking balls. Davis will chase an occasional high fastball, but he has the knowledge of the strike zone to maintain an on-base percentage close to .400. Davis has power to all fields, particularly to center and right-center.

Baserunning & Defense

The year off gave Davis time to heal his nagging back, hamstrings and knees. As a result, he has regained his aggressiveness on the bases, stealing 23 bases in 32 attempts last year. Davis remains a solid center fielder. He may have lost a step or two of range, but he can still track down a fly ball. He has always had a strong and accurate arm.

1997 Outlook

Davis has revived his career, and as a free agent in the offseason, he attracted considerable interest. If healthy, he has the skills to remain a 20-homer, 80-RBI player for a few years to come.

Overall Statistics

	G	AB	R	H	D	T	HR	RBI	SB	BB	SO	Avg	OBP	Slg
1996	129	415	81	119	20	0	26	83	23	70	121	.287	.394	.523
Career	1229	4110	746	1076	169	20	231	728	329	603	1096	.262	.357	.481

Where He Hits the Ball

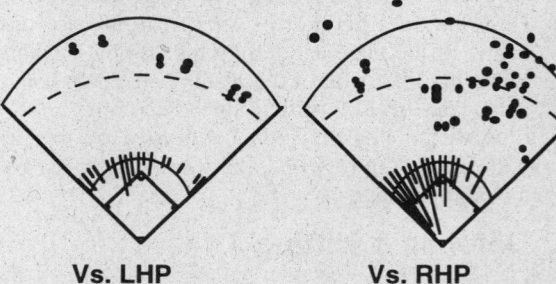

Vs. LHP   **Vs. RHP**

1996 Situational Stats

	AB	H	HR	RBI	Avg		AB	H	HR	RBI	Avg
Home	186	53	8	35	.285	LHP	93	23	4	14	.247
Road	229	66	18	48	.288	RHP	322	96	22	69	.298
First Half	203	57	14	50	.281	Sc Pos	107	35	8	57	.327
Scnd Half	212	62	12	33	.292	Clutch	64	13	4	12	.203

1996 Rankings (National League)

→ 1st in lowest cleanup slugging percentage (.394)

→ 4th in fielding percentage in center field (.988)

→ 5th in highest percentage of swings that missed (29.0%)

→ 6th in on-base percentage vs. right-handed pitchers (.409) and highest percentage of pitches taken (62.2%)

→ 9th in errors in center field (3)

→ Led the Reds in strikeouts, batting average with runners in scoring position (.327), cleanup slugging percentage (.394) and slugging percentage vs. right-handed pitchers (.556)

Willie Greene

1996 Season

After years of slow development, Willie Greene has finally started realizing his considerable promise. Greene was the Reds' third baseman for most of the last two months, and he used that time to demonstrate the power which has made him such a hot prospect. Playing almost exclusively against right-handed pitching, Greene blasted eight homers in September, six of them coming in the season's last week. For the year he had 19 dingers and 63 RBI in only 287 at-bats.

Hitting

Scouts think Greene's bat speed rivals anyone's in the game. He is a powerful pull hitter who looks to drive anything he gets on the inner half of the plate. He is primarily a low-ball hitter and has problems handling hard stuff high in the strike zone. Greene also remains vulnerable to breaking stuff off the plate. He hit only one home run off a left-handed pitcher last year and has not shown the ability yet to play against all kinds of pitching.

Baserunning & Defense

It might be difficult to find a position for Greene in order to keep his bat in the lineup. He is a liability at third, as he has poor hands and negligible range. His arm, though strong, is very erratic. The Reds gave him a brief look in left field last year, but he did not look comfortable there. The next option could be first base, though his hands of stone could be a problem there as well. Greene is a below-average runner and no threat to steal.

1997 Outlook

The Reds need to be convinced that Greene's big second half was legitimate. There is no questioning his power and bat speed, but his helplessness against lefthanders and his defensive liabilities mean that Cincinnati can't yet count on him as an everyday player. That said, Greene also has the ability to emerge as a 30-homer hitter.

Position: 3B
Bats: L **Throws:** R
Ht: 5'11" **Wt:** 192

Opening Day Age: 25
Born: 9/23/71 in Milledgeville, GA
ML Seasons: 5

Cincinnati Reds

Overall Statistics

	G	AB	R	H	D	T	HR	RBI	SB	BB	SO	Avg	OBP	Slg
1996	115	287	48	70	5	5	19	63	0	36	88	.244	.327	.495
Career	183	486	71	113	13	8	23	84	0	57	151	.233	.311	.434

Where He Hits the Ball

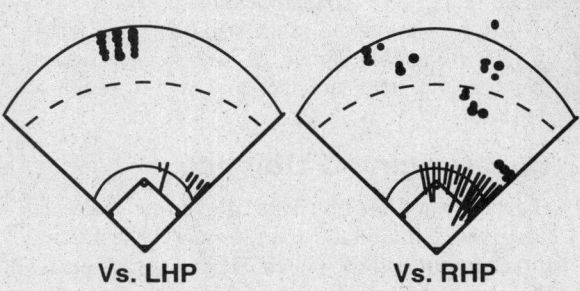

Vs. LHP   **Vs. RHP**

1996 Situational Stats

	AB	H	HR	RBI	Avg		AB	H	HR	RBI	Avg
Home	133	34	11	34	.256	LHP	44	7	1	6	.159
Road	154	36	8	29	.234	RHP	243	63	18	57	.259
First Half	122	31	8	30	.254	Sc Pos	95	22	8	43	.232
Scnd Half	165	39	11	33	.236	Clutch	46	7	2	5	.152

1996 Rankings (National League)

➡ 1st in lowest batting average on an 0-2 count (.000)
➡ 3rd in lowest batting average in the clutch (.152)
➡ 7th in errors at third base (15)
➡ 10th in lowest batting average with runners in scoring position (.232) and lowest batting average on a 3-2 count (.091)
➡ Led the Reds in intentional walks (6)

Lenny Harris

1996 Season

With injuries a constant problem for the Reds last year, the versatility of Lenny Harris was never more valuable. Harris played six different positions while also serving as Cincinnati's busiest pinch hitter. Harris was also among the Reds' best hitters in the clutch, batting .353 with runners in scoring position.

Hitting

What makes Harris such a good role player is that he can hit both left- and right-handed pitching while usually making contact. He keeps his strikeouts to a minimum and occasionally surprises people with his power. Harris is an excellent fastball hitter, but he also hangs in against breaking balls. He can be jammed up in the strike zone where he is most vulnerable. However, he has gap power to the opposite field and that makes him tough to defense.

Baserunning & Defense

Harris has not lost much speed over the years and he gives Cincinnati a legitimate basestealing threat coming off the bench. He has always been a high-percentage basestealer and last year was successful on 14 of 20 attempts. Harris' best defensive position these days might be left field, where he has decent range and an accurate arm of moderate strength. Harris also does a decent job at third, though his range is only average. In addition, he plays an adequate first base and can fill in on a short-term basis at second, though he does have some trouble turning the double play.

1997 Outlook

Cincinnati can hardly do much better for a bench player than Harris. In addition to his veteran experience at a number of positions, Harris is a very positive influence in the Reds' clubhouse. Re-signed to a two-year contract, he should again be a key piece of the puzzle in manager Ray Knight's plans.

Position: 3B/1B/LF/RF
Bats: L **Throws:** R
Ht: 5'10" **Wt:** 210

Opening Day Age: 32
Born: 10/28/64 in Miami, FL
ML Seasons: 9

Overall Statistics

	G	AB	R	H	D	T	HR	RBI	SB	BB	SO	Avg	OBP	Slg
1996	125	302	33	86	17	2	5	32	14	21	31	.285	.330	.404
Career	947	2344	289	639	88	13	17	204	98	170	203	.273	.323	.343

Where He Hits the Ball

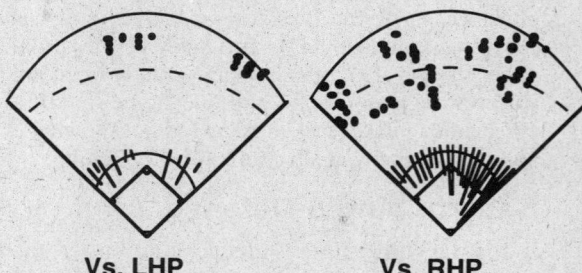

Vs. LHP   Vs. RHP

1996 Situational Stats

	AB	H	HR	RBI	Avg		AB	H	HR	RBI	Avg
Home	137	36	2	15	.263	LHP	45	14	1	7	.311
Road	165	50	3	17	.303	RHP	257	72	4	25	.280
First Half	107	30	2	13	.280	Sc Pos	68	24	1	25	.353
Scnd Half	195	56	3	19	.287	Clutch	53	14	0	5	.264

1996 Rankings (National League)

➡ Did not rank near the top or bottom in any category

Thomas Howard

1996 Season

Thomas Howard missed spring training and opened the season on the disabled list with a broken wrist, the result of an offseason accident. However, he ended up playing more games in the injury-plagued Reds' outfield than any other Cincinnati player. The added playing time helped Howard produce career highs in several categories, including RBI, doubles and triples.

Hitting

Howard has always been much more effective batting against right-handed pitching and last year was no exception. He is a low fastball hitter who can hit the ball to all fields and is at his best when he tries to slap or line the ball instead of trying to lift fly balls. Howard struggles with breaking pitches and can be busted with hard stuff upstairs. He wastes his speed by being unable to work bases on balls. However, Howard had success last year in the clutch and had the second-best average among all Cincinnati players when hitting with runners in scoring position (.329).

Baserunning & Defense

Howard has good speed and is aggressive on the bases, as shown by his 10 triples last year—a total that was tied for third in the majors. However, he is a poor percentage basestealer who last year was successful only six times in 11 attempts. He can play any of the three outfield positions, though his best position is probably left. He does not have a right fielder's arm, and while his range is above average, he occasionally misjudges the ball when playing center.

1997 Outlook

Howard is a decent extra outfielder who can help with his speed and extra-base potential. However, he probably won't be on Ray Knight's bench after being given his release by Cincinnati. The team did not want to offer him arbitration and risk spending too much on a spare player.

Position: LF/CF/RF
Bats: L **Throws:** R
Ht: 6' 2" **Wt:** 205

Opening Day Age: 32
Born: 12/11/64 in Middletown, OH
ML Seasons: 7

Overall Statistics

	G	AB	R	H	D	T	HR	RBI	SB	BB	SO	Avg	OBP	Slg
1996	121	360	50	98	19	10	6	42	6	17	51	.272	.307	.431
Career	677	1824	235	493	89	20	27	182	62	112	309	.270	.312	.385

Where He Hits the Ball

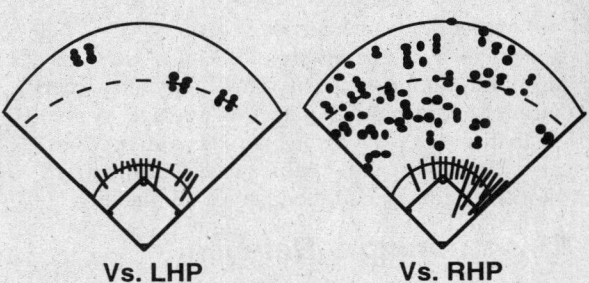

Vs. LHP   **Vs. RHP**

1996 Situational Stats

	AB	H	HR	RBI	Avg		AB	H	HR	RBI	Avg
Home	188	49	1	15	.261	LHP	67	15	0	10	.224
Road	172	49	5	27	.285	RHP	293	83	6	32	.283
First Half	133	33	3	17	.248	Sc Pos	70	23	1	34	.329
Scnd Half	227	65	3	25	.286	Clutch	63	22	2	19	.349

1996 Rankings (National League)

- 2nd in triples and lowest on-base percentage for a leadoff hitter (.292)
- 3rd in lowest batting average on a 3-2 count (.059)
- 6th in batting average in the clutch (.349)
- Led the Reds in triples and on-base percentage for a leadoff hitter (.292)

Barry Larkin

1996 Season

Barry Larkin did not repeat as National League Most Valuable Player, but he had a better season statistically than he had in his 1995 MVP year. Larkin's 33 homers and 89 RBI were career highs, easily outdistancing his '95 power numbers. He had his big year while playing his way through a slow start and several persistent injuries, including a neck problem that bothered him throughout the second half of the season.

Hitting

It's hard to believe that someone as good as Larkin can keep getting better. But with Cincinnati hurting for home runs last year, Larkin made himself a legitimate power hitter by looking for pitches to pull rather than concentrating on spraying the ball as had always been his style. Because he's such a disciplined hitter, his focus on hitting more homers did not appreciably damage his average. A great fastball hitter whose only weakness is occasionally chasing breaking balls away, Larkin is a remarkably consistent hitter against all pitching.

Baserunning & Defense

Hitting more often in the middle of the lineup caused Larkin to run less last year. However, he remains one of baseball's best basestealers. He rarely makes a mistake in trying to take an extra base and he aggressively breaks up double play attempts. Larkin has few equals in the field. His range at shortstop remains as good as anyone's and his arm is one of the best. He is a true Gold Glover.

1997 Outlook

Still getting better as he nears his 33rd birthday, Larkin remains the standard by which all National League shortstops must be judged. He should be the league's premier player at his position for years to come. And just as importantly, he is the unquestioned leader of the Reds' franchise, someone who keeps the club focused on the field despite the frequent sideshows created by owner Marge Schott.

Position: SS
Bats: R **Throws:** R
Ht: 6' 0" **Wt:** 195

Opening Day Age: 32
Born: 4/28/64 in Cincinnati, OH
ML Seasons: 11

Overall Statistics

	G	AB	R	H	D	T	HR	RBI	SB	BB	SO	Avg	OBP	Slg
1996	152	517	117	154	32	4	33	89	36	96	52	.298	.410	.567
Career	1328	4946	828	1476	254	48	135	626	275	545	483	.298	.369	.451

Where He Hits the Ball

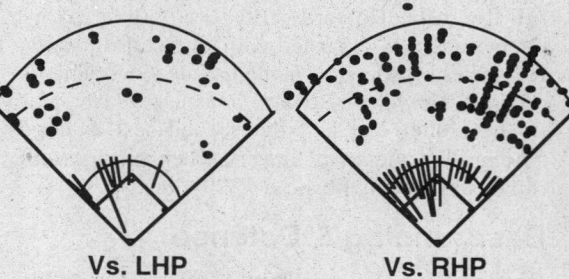

Vs. LHP   **Vs. RHP**

1996 Situational Stats

	AB	H	HR	RBI	Avg		AB	H	HR	RBI	Avg
Home	269	80	14	45	.297	LHP	121	36	9	24	.298
Road	248	74	19	44	.298	RHP	396	118	24	65	.298
First Half	266	76	12	34	.286	Sc Pos	120	37	6	53	.308
Scnd Half	251	78	21	55	.311	Clutch	69	19	7	11	.275

1996 Rankings (National League)

- → 2nd in most pitches seen per plate appearance (4.12) and steals of third (10)
- → 3rd in lowest percentage of swings on the first pitch (10.1%)
- → 4th in fielding percentage at shortstop (.975) and highest percentage of pitches taken (62.9%)
- → 5th in walks, GDPs (20) and on-base percentage vs. left-handed pitchers (.435)
- → 6th in runs scored, on-base percentage, batting average on an 0-2 count (.296) and batting average with two strikes (.275)
- → 7th in slugging percentage
- → 8th in stolen bases and errors at shortstop (17)

Kevin Mitchell

1996 Season

A bust in Boston and rarely in playing shape, Kevin Mitchell ended up back with the Reds last summer. When he was able get his overweight, injury-prone body onto the field, Mitchell showed he is still one of the game's great hitters. But just when he was heating up for the stretch run, a blown hamstring ended his season with two weeks left.

Hitting

Few teams have ever figured out how to pitch to Mitchell. He crowds the plate and is difficult to knock off the inside corner because it is so tough to get a fastball in past his quick hands. He is powerful enough to hit the ball out of any part of the ballpark, and he won't chase offspeed stuff off the outside corner. Primarily a low-ball hitter, he has learned to lay off the high pitches he cannot handle. Mitchell also has an uncanny knack of adjusting his stance from game to game and pitcher to pitcher. Because of his weight, he is not as quick with his bat as he once was, and he can sometimes be tied up inside. However, Mitchell will kill anything left over the plate.

Baserunning & Defense

Despite his lack of conditioning, Mitchell is a smart baserunner who is as aggressive as anyone when trying to break up a double play or take an extra base. However, he is no threat to steal. He catches what he reaches in left, but that isn't very much. Mitchell also will misjudge balls occasionally. His arm is only fair.

1997 Outlook

A free agent once again, Mitchell represents a huge waste of talent. With just a modest commitment to routine conditioning, he would still be among the game's most fearsome hitters. However, he cannot be trusted to be in playing shape, and he represents a huge gamble for anyone enticed by his tremendous hitting ability.

Position: LF/RF
Bats: R **Throws:** R
Ht: 5'11" **Wt:** 244

Opening Day Age: 35
Born: 1/13/62 in San Diego, CA
ML Seasons: 11

Overall Statistics

	G	AB	R	H	D	T	HR	RBI	SB	BB	SO	Avg	OBP	Slg
1996	64	206	27	65	15	0	8	39	0	37	30	.316	.420	.505
Career	1152	3948	609	1135	216	24	228	728	29	473	682	.287	.364	.528

Where He Hits the Ball

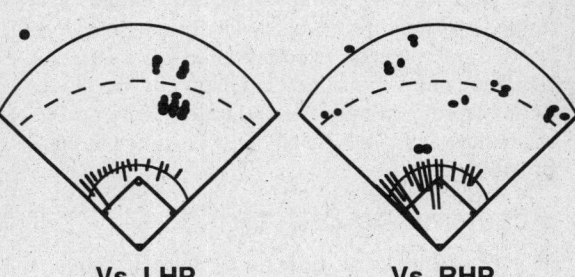

Vs. LHP   **Vs. RHP**

1996 Situational Stats

	AB	H	HR	RBI	Avg		AB	H	HR	RBI	Avg
Home	110	39	6	31	.355	LHP	50	20	3	13	.400
Road	96	26	2	8	.271	RHP	156	45	5	26	.288
First Half	58	17	1	7	.293	Sc Pos	60	18	3	31	.300
Scnd Half	148	48	7	32	.324	Clutch	38	10	0	1	.263

1996 Rankings (National League)

→ Did not rank near the top or bottom in any category

Hal Morris

1996 Season

Despite missing 20 games with various ailments, Hal Morris had the best overall season of his career. He reached career bests in home runs (16) and RBI (80) and hit .372 over his last month to finish with a .313 average. It was the fifth time Morris has batted .310 or better in his seven years with the Reds.

Hitting

Working with then-Reds hitting coach Hal McRae, Morris eliminated some of the movement in his stance which was costing him power and making him prone to being overpowered by inside hard stuff. As a result, he was able to pull more balls and hit more home runs. The changes also helped Morris improve his production against left-handed pitching; he even homered off a lefty for the first time in four years. That said, Morris remains largely an opposite-field hitter who prefers the ball away from him. He will also take his share of walks.

Baserunning & Defense

Morris can steal an occasional base if pitchers forget about him. However, he has only average speed, though he did have four triples last year along with 32 doubles. Morris' range at first base is limited but he has sure hands and a fairly accurate arm. He does a good job of digging low throws out of the dirt.

1997 Outlook

The Reds annually seem to weigh moving Morris because of his lack of consistent power at what should be a power position. So it's not surprising to hear talk that Cincinnati might move powerful young Willie Greene to first. However, Morris made strides in the run-production area last year while remaining a career .300 hitter. Considering that he turns 32 in April, he has a chance to produce several more solid seasons.

Position: 1B
Bats: L **Throws:** L
Ht: 6' 4" **Wt:** 210

Opening Day Age: 31
Born: 4/9/65 in Fort Rucker, AL
ML Seasons: 9

Overall Statistics

	G	AB	R	H	D	T	HR	RBI	SB	BB	SO	Avg	OBP	Slg
1996	142	528	82	165	32	4	16	80	7	50	76	.313	.374	.479
Career	844	2922	409	902	181	17	71	410	41	260	406	.309	.365	.455

Where He Hits the Ball

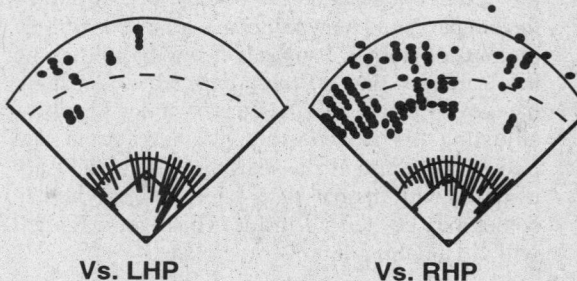

Vs. LHP   **Vs. RHP**

1996 Situational Stats

	AB	H	HR	RBI	Avg		AB	H	HR	RBI	Avg
Home	250	85	7	46	.340	LHP	132	36	1	16	.273
Road	278	80	9	34	.288	RHP	396	129	15	64	.326
First Half	274	80	7	31	.292	Sc Pos	127	39	1	58	.307
Scnd Half	254	85	9	49	.335	Clutch	84	31	2	13	.369

1996 Rankings (National League)
- 2nd in batting average in the clutch (.369)
- 5th in batting average vs. right-handed pitchers (.326)
- 6th in errors at first base (8) and fielding percentage at first base (.993)
- 8th in lowest slugging percentage vs. left-handed pitchers (.341)
- 9th in batting average at home (.340)
- Led the Reds in at-bats, hits, singles, doubles, highest groundball/flyball ratio (1.7), batting average in the clutch (.369), batting average vs. right-handed pitchers (.326), batting average at home (.340), bunts in play (14) and batting average

Mark Portugal

1996 Season

Plagued by a hamstring injury and a sore elbow, Mark Portugal struggled in his first full year with the Reds. He managed 26 starts and a decent 3.98 earned run average, but did not have a decision in the season's last three weeks. He finished with less than 10 victories for only the second time since 1990.

Pitching

Portugal is a craftsman who mixes speeds well. He throws a good curveball and slider along with a fastball he either tries to sink or cut away from left-handed hitters. His margin for error is not very great, and when he falls behind and gets himself into a fastball count, he's in trouble. Portugal is prone to streaks where he'll give up a lot of home runs. However, he's the sort of battler who will throw a change-up at any time. Unfortunately, he has never kept himself in good condition, and he has trouble holding his stuff much past six innings.

Defense & Hitting

Despite his rumpled appearance, Portugal is a fairly good athlete with decent agility on the mound. He is a poised fielder who keeps himself in good fielding position. However, he does not have a great pickoff move and his slow pitching motion, coupled with his penchant for change-ups and breaking balls, combine to make him vulnerable to the stolen base. Portugal is capable of occasionally helping himself at bat. He led the Reds in sacrifice bunts last year.

1997 Outlook

The Reds elected to allow Portugal to enter free agency after the season. They wouldn't mind retaining his services, but only if they can lower his salary. He should still have a few seasons left of delivering around 10 wins a year.

Position: SP
Bats: R **Throws:** R
Ht: 6' 0" **Wt:** 190

Opening Day Age: 34
Born: 10/30/62 in Los Angeles, CA
ML Seasons: 12

Overall Statistics

	W	L	Pct.	ERA	G	GS	Sv	IP	H	BB	SO	HR	BR/IP
1996	8	9	.471	3.98	27	26	0	156.0	146	42	93	20	1.21
Career	92	76	.548	3.83	286	227	5	1496.0	1431	529	949	155	1.31

How Often He Throws Strikes

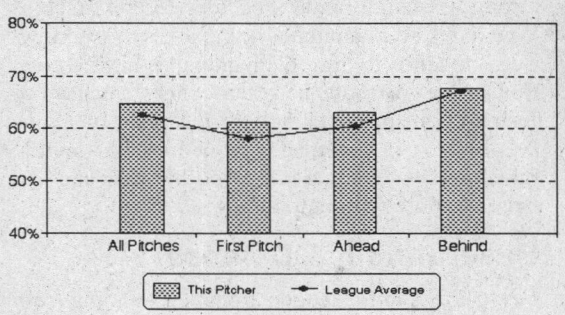

1996 Situational Stats

	W	L	ERA	Sv	IP		AB	H	HR	RBI	Avg
Home	5	6	3.48	0	88.0	LHB	234	56	7	20	.239
Road	3	3	4.63	0	68.0	RHB	355	90	13	51	.254
First Half	5	5	3.97	0	99.2	Sc Pos	122	33	5	46	.270
Scnd Half	3	4	3.99	0	56.1	Clutch	38	9	2	3	.237

1996 Rankings (National League)

→ 8th in lowest batting average allowed vs. left-handed batters (.239)
→ 9th in shutouts (1)
→ Led the Reds in home runs allowed, ERA at home (3.48) and lowest batting average allowed vs. left-handed batters (.239)

Reggie Sanders

1996 Season

There were few bigger disappointments for the Reds last year than Reggie Sanders, who was unable to play through a series of injuries—most of them related to back problems. In a year when the Reds thought he would blossom into stardom, Sanders appeared in only 81 games, managing just 33 RBI in 287 at-bats.

Hitting

Sanders was rarely healthy last year. However, using his miserable 1995 League Championship Series performance as a guide, opposing pitchers constantly challenged him with high stuff, and he has yet to prove he can handle it. Sanders has very strong wrists but his bat speed is deceptive. He is very quick on low pitches or mistakes away. However, he tends to drag his hands into hitting position and as a result, he often cannot catch up to fastballs on the inner half of the plate or above belt-high. As a result, he is prone to striking out in bunches. Sanders has improved his patience and become more willing to take walks.

Baserunning & Defense

Few players in the league are better at going from first to third than Sanders. He is a good basestealer who nevertheless needs a good jump because it takes him a few strides to get his speed into gear. An excellent right fielder, Sanders has great range, is quick to the ball, gets a good jump and has one of the better arms in the game.

1997 Outlook

There were whispers around the Reds last year that Sanders was a little too willing to nurse his aches and pains rather than trying to play hurt. This may be a crossroads season for him as he tries to quiet his critics and re-establish himself as an emerging star. For Cincinnati to return to the playoffs, they need Sanders to again be one of the league's best all-around players.

Position: RF
Bats: R **Throws:** R
Ht: 6' 1" **Wt:** 185

Opening Day Age: 29
Born: 12/1/67 in Florence, SC
ML Seasons: 6

Overall Statistics

	G	AB	R	H	D	T	HR	RBI	SB	BB	SO	Avg	OBP	Slg
1996	81	287	49	72	17	1	14	33	24	44	86	.251	.353	.463
Career	584	2092	364	573	115	25	92	316	125	253	547	.274	.355	.485

Where He Hits the Ball

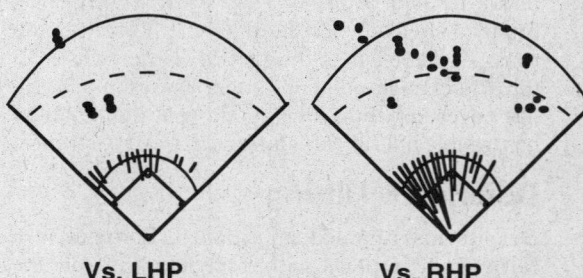

Vs. LHP   Vs. RHP

1996 Situational Stats

	AB	H	HR	RBI	Avg		AB	H	HR	RBI	Avg
Home	128	31	7	19	.242	LHP	62	16	2	2	.258
Road	159	41	7	14	.258	RHP	225	56	12	31	.249
First Half	141	40	7	17	.284	Sc Pos	79	14	2	19	.177
Scnd Half	146	32	7	16	.219	Clutch	44	10	3	6	.227

1996 Rankings (National League)

→ 2nd in lowest batting average with runners in scoring position (.177)

Pete Schourek

1996 Season

Nothing damaged the Reds' chances of repeating as N.L. Central champions last year more than the loss of ace lefty Pete Schourek. For two months, Schourek tried pitching through a sore shoulder and elbow, but the Reds finally had to shut him down after 12 starts, and he was lost for the season with elbow surgery. They had no one to replace Schourek, who went 18-7 in 1995.

Pitching

When he is healthy, Schourek is one of the league's toughest lefthanders. By making his delivery more compact and more reliant on leg drive, Schourek has added velocity to the point where he can throw consistently in the low-to-mid 90s while cutting the ball away from right-handed hitters. He has developed an outstanding straight change that is very tough to read and uses two different curves: a big slow-breaking curve and a harder one with a sharper break. Schourek's shortened delivery not only added velocity, but improved his control. He now pitches ahead in the count more consistently than in the past.

Defense & Hitting

Schourek has a decent move to first but last year had lapses in concentration with runners on—a reflection, the Reds believe, of the constant distraction from his shoulder discomfort. He does a good job of fielding his position for such a tall pitcher. Schourek is one of the league's better hitting pitchers. Last year he had five hits, five sacrifices and two RBI in his 25 plate appearances.

1997 Outlook

One of the keys to the Reds' season will be the status of Schourek. They probably won't know until late in spring training how much of a contribution he will be capable of making this season. If he does bounce back from the elbow surgery, the Reds will again have one of the best lefthanders in the league.

Position: SP
Bats: L **Throws:** L
Ht: 6' 5" **Wt:** 205

Opening Day Age: 27
Born: 5/10/69 in Austin, TX
ML Seasons: 6
Pronunciation: SHUR-ek

Overall Statistics

	W	L	Pct.	ERA	G	GS	Sv	IP	H	BB	SO	HR	BR/IP
1996	4	5	.444	6.01	12	12	0	67.1	79	24	54	7	1.53
Career	45	38	.542	4.32	161	98	2	689.2	714	230	482	64	1.37

How Often He Throws Strikes

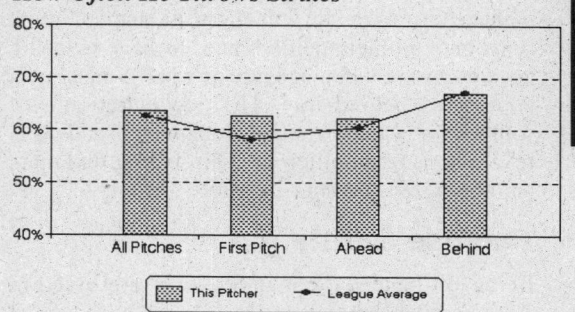

1996 Situational Stats

	W	L	ERA	Sv	IP		AB	H	HR	RBI	Avg
Home	4	2	4.03	0	38.0	LHB	47	14	2	11	.298
Road	0	3	8.59	0	29.1	RHB	223	65	5	33	.291
First Half	4	5	6.01	0	67.1	Sc Pos	79	26	2	35	.329
Scnd Half	0	0	-	0	0.0	Clutch	11	5	1	5	.455

1996 Rankings (National League)

➡ Did not rank near the top or bottom in any category

John Smiley

1996 Season

Though often plagued by a lack of run support, John Smiley was the ace of the Reds' staff last season. He was among the league leaders in games started and despite some hamstring and groin problems, he led the Reds in innings pitched. He pitched two shutouts along the way.

Pitching

Smiley throws a 90+ MPH fastball that he can sink or tail. He is excellent at hitting his spots with the fastball, and he's also able to get consistent location with both his outstanding change-up and slider. Smiley, who posts solid strikeout-to-walk ratios year after year, is almost always around the plate, a reason why he will allow his share of home runs. One problem he continues to have is losing his composure when in a jam or when a misplay is committed behind him. His concentration will sometimes waver when that happens, and as a result, he is often bitten by a big inning that mars an otherwise solid starting effort.

Defense & Hitting

Being left-handed is one of Smiley's only assets in coping with basestealers. He does not have a good pickoff move and his high leg kick makes him fairly easy for basestealers to read. His delivery sends him flopping toward third, which takes him out of fielding position. Smiley can occasionally help himself at the plate. . . if he makes contact. He also strikes out in at least a third of his plate appearances.

1997 Outlook

The Reds knew that Smiley's so-so numbers last year were deceptive. Smiley also was very content to stay in Cincinnati, which is why he signed a contract extension late last season. He remains a quality lefty who should be good for at least 12 to 15 wins for the next few seasons.

Position: SP
Bats: L **Throws:** L
Ht: 6' 4" **Wt:** 210

Opening Day Age: 32
Born: 3/17/65 in Phoenixville, PA
ML Seasons: 11

Overall Statistics

	W	L	Pct.	ERA	G	GS	Sv	IP	H	BB	SO	HR	BR/IP
1996	13	14	.481	3.64	35	34	0	217.1	207	54	171	20	1.20
Career	115	89	.564	3.67	335	254	4	1753.1	1658	455	1164	159	1.21

How Often He Throws Strikes

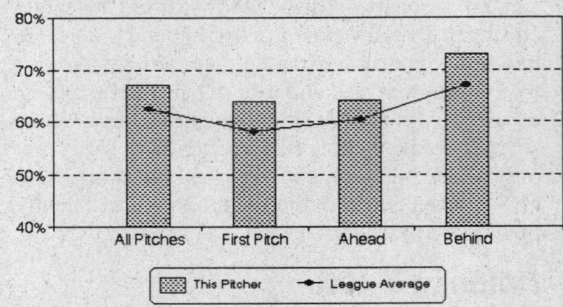

1996 Situational Stats

	W	L	ERA	Sv	IP		AB	H	HR	RBI	Avg
Home	7	7	3.87	0	107.0	LHB	127	35	4	16	.276
Road	6	7	3.43	0	110.1	RHB	681	172	16	72	.253
First Half	8	7	4.34	0	105.2	Sc Pos	175	45	3	62	.257
Scnd Half	5	7	2.98	0	111.2	Clutch	54	12	0	3	.222

1996 Rankings (National League)

- → 2nd in shutouts (2)
- → 3rd in losses
- → 7th in games started and ERA on the road (3.43)
- → 8th in least pitches thrown per batter (3.54)
- → 10th in highest strikeout/walk ratio (3.2), least baserunners allowed per 9 innings (11.0) and least run support per 9 innings (4.3)
- → Led the Reds in ERA, wins, losses, games started, complete games (2), shutouts (2), innings pitched, hits allowed, batters faced (889), home runs allowed, strikeouts, runners caught stealing (9), GDPs induced (18), winning percentage, highest strikeout/walk ratio (3.2)

Eddie Taubensee

1996 Season

Eddie Taubensee continues to give Cincinnati excellent production as a platoon catcher. Indeed, the combination of Taubensee and Joe Oliver combined for the best offensive production at catcher of any National League club except the Mets with Todd Hundley, the Dodgers with Mike Piazza and the Phillies with Benito Santiago. Taubensee and Oliver combined for 23 homers and 94 RBI, with Taubensee personally achieving career highs in homers and RBI.

Hitting

Like most left-handed hitters, Taubensee is a low-ball hitter. However, he has shown good power to the opposite field and can take a fastball up and away and drive it to left-center. He has trouble with fastballs up in the strike zone and strikes out frequently when he chases breaking balls away from the plate. Taubensee hit .333 versus lefthanders last year with two home runs. However, he has never shown the ability to hit lefties consistently enough to justify getting everyday playing duty.

Baserunning & Defense

Taubensee is a better-than-average runner for a catcher who can occasionally surprise with a stolen base. He also is a hustler out of the batter's box and is smart about trying to take an extra base. On defense, Taubensee has worked hard to improve his footwork and quicken his release. He managed to throw out 23 percent of opposing basestealers last year, an improvement over recent years. He has also improved himself as a receiver and handler of pitchers.

1997 Outlook

It remains unclear whether the Reds will keep their catching platoon intact. However, Taubensee has made himself into a very solid catcher, even if he is kept in part-time duty. Left-handed hitting catchers are hard to find, and with Taubensee's improving power, he has to be considered one of the league's most underrated players.

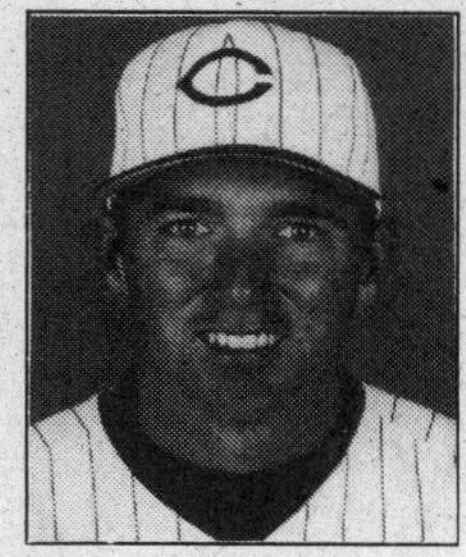

Position: C
Bats: L **Throws:** R
Ht: 6' 4" **Wt:** 205

Opening Day Age: 28
Born: 10/31/68 in Beeville, TX
ML Seasons: 6
Pronunciation: TAW-ben-see

Overall Statistics

	G	AB	R	H	D	T	HR	RBI	SB	BB	SO	Avg	OBP	Slg
1996	108	327	46	95	20	0	12	48	3	26	64	.291	.338	.462
Career	478	1383	161	364	70	6	43	191	10	120	285	.263	.321	.416

Where He Hits the Ball

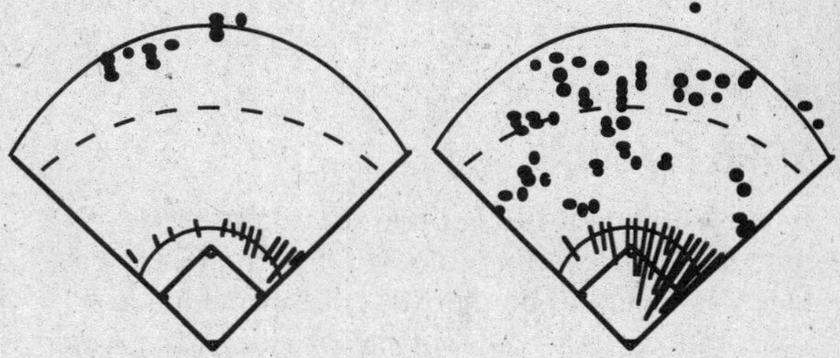

Vs. LHP Vs. RHP

1996 Situational Stats

	AB	H	HR	RBI	Avg		AB	H	HR	RBI	Avg
Home	139	44	6	27	.317	LHP	48	16	2	10	.333
Road	188	51	6	21	.271	RHP	279	79	10	38	.283
First Half	184	52	5	27	.283	Sc Pos	83	23	4	35	.277
Scnd Half	143	43	7	21	.301	Clutch	63	17	2	13	.270

1996 Rankings (National League)

- ➡ 2nd in errors at catcher (11) and lowest fielding percentage at catcher (.981)
- ➡ Led the Reds in least GDPs per GDP situation (7.4%)

Cincinnati Reds

Hector Carrasco

Position: RP
Bats: R **Throws:** R
Ht: 6' 2" **Wt:** 180

Opening Day Age: 27
Born: 10/22/69 in San Pedro de Macoris, DR
ML Seasons: 3
Pronunciation: kuh-RASS-koh

Overall Statistics

	W	L	Pct.	ERA	G	GS	Sv	IP	H	BB	SO	HR	BR/IP
1996	4	3	.571	3.75	56	0	0	74.1	58	45	59	6	1.39
Career	11	16	.407	3.51	165	0	11	218.0	186	121	164	10	1.41

1996 Situational Stats

	W	L	ERA	Sv	IP		AB	H	HR	RBI	Avg
Home	0	1	3.76	0	40.2	LHB	113	29	5	22	.257
Road	4	2	3.74	0	33.2	RHB	158	29	1	13	.184
First Half	2	2	3.71	0	34.0	Sc Pos	75	22	2	31	.293
Scnd Half	2	1	3.79	0	40.1	Clutch	107	24	2	11	.224

1996 Season

Inconsistent control continues to retard the development of fireballing reliever Hector Carrasco. Once expected to be the Reds closer, he made 56 appearances last year, but only twice was given save opportunities. . . both of which he blew. Carrasco did do a pretty good job as a specialist against right-handed hitters, however. Righties managed only a .184 average against him.

Pitching, Defense & Hitting

There are few better arms than Carrasco's. He routinely gets radar clockings in the mid to high 90s. However, he labors to harness all that heat and too often pitches from behind in the count. He also lacks command of any second pitch. Carrasco's wild delivery usually puts him out of fielding position. He also pays little attention to baserunners, who were 8-for-9 in steal attempts against him last year. He is a brutal hitter.

1997 Outlook

You don't give up on stuff like Carrasco's, but he nevertheless has not developed as the Reds had hoped. They have the luxury of keeping him in set-up roles with the presence of Jeff Brantley. However, they would like Carrasco to start making more progress as a pitcher.

Kevin Jarvis

Position: SP
Bats: L **Throws:** R
Ht: 6' 2" **Wt:** 200

Opening Day Age: 27
Born: 8/1/69 in Lexington, Kentucky
ML Seasons: 3

Overall Statistics

	W	L	Pct.	ERA	G	GS	Sv	IP	H	BB	SO	HR	BR/IP
1996	8	9	.471	5.98	24	20	0	120.1	152	43	63	17	1.62
Career	12	14	.462	5.97	49	34	0	217.0	265	80	106	34	1.59

1996 Situational Stats

	W	L	ERA	Sv	IP		AB	H	HR	RBI	Avg
Home	6	2	4.07	0	48.2	LHB	220	69	11	34	.314
Road	2	7	7.28	0	71.2	RHB	278	83	6	42	.299
First Half	2	1	3.73	0	41.0	Sc Pos	137	42	4	56	.307
Scnd Half	6	8	7.15	0	79.1	Clutch	11	0	0	0	.000

1996 Season

After unimpressive trials in 1994 and 1995, Kevin Jarvis got another chance to make the Reds' injury-riddled rotation last year. Jarvis ended up making a career-high 20 starts, and he had two of the Reds' six complete games and one shutout. But his overall work wasn't very good, particularly during the second half of the year.

Pitching, Defense & Hitting

With velocity in the mid-80s at best, Jarvis doesn't make many hitters miss. He relies on control and command of his sinking fastball, slider and change. But when he doesn't hit his spots, he is going to get hit, which is evident from the .305 opponents' batting average last year. Jarvis is a good athlete who does an adequate job of fielding but does not hold runners very well. He can occasionally help himself with the bat.

1997 Outlook

At best, Jarvis is no better than a fifth starter. However, he can be a useful member of the staff because he can pitch out of the bullpen and still be available to spot start if needed.

Joe Oliver

Position: C
Bats: R **Throws:** R
Ht: 6' 3" **Wt:** 220

Opening Day Age: 31
Born: 7/24/65 in Memphis, TN
ML Seasons: 8

Overall Statistics

	G	AB	R	H	D	T	HR	RBI	SB	BB	SO	Avg	OBP	Slg
1996	106	289	31	70	12	1	11	46	2	28	54	.242	.311	.405
Career	755	2396	225	595	127	2	70	350	7	180	445	.248	.301	.391

1996 Situational Stats

	AB	H	HR	RBI	Avg		AB	H	HR	RBI	Avg
Home	147	33	6	24	.224	LHP	110	26	4	15	.236
Road	142	37	5	22	.261	RHP	179	44	7	31	.246
First Half	137	32	4	19	.234	Sc Pos	80	19	2	33	.238
Scnd Half	152	38	7	27	.250	Clutch	37	6	0	2	.162

1996 Season

Joe Oliver returned to his Cincinnati roots and gave the Reds a solid season in a platoon situation with Eddie Taubensee. Oliver showed his power is back with 11 home runs, his second straight double-figure homer season, and fifth in the last six years, while adding 46 RBI in 289 at-bats.

Hitting, Baserunning & Defense

Oliver pulls off too many pitches to ever be a high-average hitter. Plus, he has never had the discipline to lay off outside breaking pitches. However, he can be very dangerous when he gets high fastballs over the plate. Though basically a pull hitter, he has the strength to drive balls to the opposite field. He has a quick throwing release which helped him gun down nearly 30 percent of enemy basestealers last year. He also is an excellent handler of pitchers. Oliver is a below-average runner, though he will occasionally steal a base.

1997 Outlook

Oliver was a free agent after the season, but the Reds hope to re-sign him. Cincinnati is not likely to be able to improve on their Oliver/Taubensee catching combination. In Oliver, they have a link to former championship teams and a solid veteran who knows how to work with his pitchers.

Jose Rijo

Position: SP
Bats: R **Throws:** R
Ht: 6' 3" **Wt:** 215

Opening Day Age: 31
Born: 5/13/65 in San Cristobal, DR
ML Seasons: 12
Pronunciation: REE-ho

Overall Statistics

	W	L	Pct.	ERA	G	GS	Sv	IP	H	BB	SO	HR	BR/IP
1996					Did Not Play								
Career	111	87	.561	3.16	332	260	3	1786.0	1602	634	1556	132	1.25

1996 Situational Stats

	W	L	ERA	Sv	IP		AB	H	HR	RBI	Avg
Home	—	—	—	—	—	LHB	—	—	—	—	—
Road	—	—	—	—	—	RHB	—	—	—	—	—
First Half	—	—	—	—	—	Sc Pos	—	—	—	—	—
Scnd Half	—	—	—	—	—	Clutch	—	—	—	—	—

1996 Season

After undergoing reconstructive elbow surgery in August of 1995, Jose Rijo tried to come back last season. But after reaching the point where he seemed close to being able to do a rehab stint in the minors, Rijo's elbow acted up again and he did not pitch all season.

Pitching, Defense & Hitting

A healthy Rijo is one of the best pitchers in baseball. At his best, he would combine a fastball in the low 90s with a great change-up, a late-breaking slider and one of the league's best forkballs. He had great command of all his pitches and was a great competitor who would hold his stuff into the late innings. He is also an excellent fielding pitcher who does a good job of holding runners. Rijo has never been a threat as a hitter.

1997 Outlook

Rijo required a second elbow operation shortly after the end of the season and the Reds are not counting on him to pitch at all this season. The only good news is that this is the last year of his $5 million per year contract.

Johnny Ruffin

Position: RP
Bats: R **Throws:** R
Ht: 6' 3" **Wt:** 170

Opening Day Age: 25
Born: 7/29/71 in Butler, AL
ML Seasons: 4

Overall Statistics

	W	L	Pct.	ERA	G	GS	Sv	IP	H	BB	SO	HR	BR/IP
1996	1	3	.250	5.49	49	0	0	62.1	71	37	69	10	1.73
Career	10	6	.625	3.88	131	0	3	183.1	168	86	154	21	1.39

1996 Situational Stats

	W	L	ERA	Sv	IP		AB	H	HR	RBI	Avg
Home	0	0	4.88	0	31.1	LHB	91	27	2	18	.297
Road	1	3	6.10	0	31.0	RHB	152	44	8	22	.289
First Half	1	3	6.02	0	40.1	Sc Pos	78	19	2	29	.244
Scnd Half	0	0	4.50	0	22.0	Clutch	50	16	1	8	.320

1996 Season

Righty reliever Johnny Ruffin was shut down the last three weeks of the season with shoulder stiffness. While his overall numbers weren't great, he did a decent job as a set-up man when he was healthy. Ruffin was particularly effective with inherited runners, allowing only four of 20 to score.

Pitching, Defense & Hitting

Ruffin has a fluid delivery and can get his fastball up in the 90s with good movement. He also has a hard slider and developing change. He got hit more than normal when he started losing velocity late in the season. Ruffin is just a mediocre fielder who often is out of position. He also does not hold runners very well and basestealers last year were successful in 11 of 13 attempts. He was a .500 hitter (two for four) last year.

1997 Outlook

If he can stay healthy, Ruffin is young enough and talented enough to emerge as a major factor for the Reds. There has been some thought given to making him a starting pitcher, but he can also be valuable as a bullpen set-up man.

Roger Salkeld

Position: SP/RP
Bats: R **Throws:** R
Ht: 6' 5" **Wt:** 215

Opening Day Age: 26
Born: 3/6/71 in Burbank, CA
ML Seasons: 3

Overall Statistics

	W	L	Pct.	ERA	G	GS	Sv	IP	H	BB	SO	HR	BR/IP
1996	8	5	.615	5.20	29	19	0	116.0	114	54	82	18	1.45
Career	10	10	.500	5.61	45	34	0	189.1	203	103	141	25	1.62

1996 Situational Stats

	W	L	ERA	Sv	IP		AB	H	HR	RBI	Avg
Home	5	3	3.99	0	65.1	LHB	189	47	7	25	.249
Road	3	2	6.75	0	50.2	RHB	247	67	11	38	.271
First Half	4	2	3.63	0	67.0	Sc Pos	110	33	5	42	.300
Scnd Half	4	3	7.35	0	49.0	Clutch	8	2	0	1	.250

1996 Season

Roger Salkeld was one of several Reds pitchers given a chance in their injury-riddled starting rotation last year. Salkeld made 19 starts and pitched pretty well during the first half of the season, but then he started getting shelled. He wound up in the bullpen, where some of his effectiveness returned.

Pitching, Defense & Hitting

Once one of baseball's most promising pitching prospects, Salkeld has never been able to fully come back from shoulder problems that plagued him during his days as a Seattle farmhand. He throws a hard, running fastball, a big-breaking curveball and a decent change. His problem is location. He pitches too often from behind in the count and he then starts aiming the ball, which costs him velocity. Salkeld fields his position well, but his high leg kick makes him vulnerable to stolen bases. He is a terrible hitter.

1997 Outlook

Depending on what moves the Reds make, Salkeld may get another chance to compete for a spot in the rotation. His stuff is also good enough for him to pitch in relief.

Jeff Shaw

Position: RP
Bats: R **Throws:** R
Ht: 6' 2" **Wt:** 200

Opening Day Age: 30
Born: 7/7/66 in
Washington
Courthouse, OH
ML Seasons: 7

Overall Statistics

	W	L	Pct.	ERA	G	GS	Sv	IP	H	BB	SO	HR	BR/IP
1996	8	6	.571	2.49	78	0	4	104.2	99	29	69	8	1.22
Career	19	31	.380	4.05	281	19	9	468.1	479	154	276	53	1.35

1996 Situational Stats

	W	L	ERA	Sv	IP		AB	H	HR	RBI	Avg
Home	6	2	2.08	3	47.2	LHB	160	31	2	13	.194
Road	2	4	2.84	1	57.0	RHB	233	68	6	36	.292
First Half	2	3	3.08	2	49.2	Sc Pos	129	26	1	40	.202
Scnd Half	6	3	1.96	2	55.0	Clutch	189	50	5	27	.265

1996 Season

One of the Reds' best bargain pickups was reliever Jeff Shaw, who was their busiest reliever. Pitching mostly as a set-up man, Shaw led the Reds with 78 appearances. He also won eight games in relief and added four saves, though he blew seven other opportunities during a period when he was the closer during Jeff Brantley's absence.

Pitching, Defense & Hitting

Shaw's best pitch is his split-fingered fastball, which he uses to particularily tie up left-handed hitters who managed only a .194 average against him last year. Shaw has problems when his splitter isn't biting because his stuff is otherwise average. When he has to throw fastballs, he can get hit for the long ball. Shaw is usually around the plate. He is a good fielder but has trouble holding on runners. He is no factor as a hitter.

1997 Outlook

Serviceable veterans like Shaw can be very valuable, and the Reds will gladly take the same year from Shaw which he produced in 1996.

Lee Smith

Position: RP
Bats: R **Throws:** R
Ht: 6' 6" **Wt:** 269

Opening Day Age: 39
Born: 12/4/57 in
Jamestown, LA
ML Seasons: 17

Overall Statistics

	W	L	Pct.	ERA	G	GS	Sv	IP	H	BB	SO	HR	BR/IP
1996	3	4	.429	3.74	54	0	2	55.1	57	26	41	4	1.50
Career	71	91	.438	2.98	997	6	473	1268.1	1105	478	1236	87	1.25

1996 Situational Stats

	W	L	ERA	Sv	IP		AB	H	HR	RBI	Avg
Home	1	0	3.52	2	30.2	LHB	99	22	1	11	.222
Road	2	4	4.01	0	24.2	RHB	117	35	3	14	.299
First Half	1	2	3.71	2	26.2	Sc Pos	71	15	0	21	.211
Scnd Half	2	2	3.77	0	28.2	Clutch	87	28	2	14	.322

1996 Season

Unhappy with Lee Smith's resistance to being a set-up man for Troy Percival, California traded baseball's all-time save leader to the Reds early last season. Things didn't improve for Smith in Cincinnati. He blew four of his six save chances with the Reds and wound up a marginally effective middle reliever.

Pitching, Defense & Hitting

Once one of the most feared power pitchers in baseball, Smith now has only average velocity. He's become a breaking-ball pitcher who will throw more sliders and forkballs than he will fastballs. Smith has always had good control but now that his stuff isn't what it used to be, being around the plate can be costly. Smith has always been a poor fielder who can't hold runners. His lack of hitting ability is the least of his concerns.

1997 Outlook

The Reds don't have much interest in bringing Smith back and it is uncertain where he might surface this year. He can no longer be trusted as a closer, and his Hall of Fame career is clearly about over.

Other Cincinnati Reds

Giovanni Carrara (Pos: RHP, Age: 29)

	W	L	Pct.	ERA	G	GS	Sv	IP	H	BB	SO	HR	BR/IP
1996	1	1	.500	8.05	19	5	0	38.0	54	25	23	11	2.08
Career	3	5	.375	7.58	31	12	0	86.2	118	50	50	21	1.94

Carrara is a veteran minor leaguer who was acquired off waivers in early July. He was hit fairly hard during the several starts he made in September. 1997 Outlook: C

Brook Fordyce (Pos: C, Age: 26, Bats: R)

	G	AB	R	H	D	T	HR	RBI	SB	BB	SO	Avg	OBP	Slg
1996	4	7	0	2	1	0	0	1	0	3	1	.286	.500	.429
Career	8	9	1	3	2	0	0	1	0	4	1	.333	.538	.556

Fordyce spent most of the year in Triple-A Indianapolis after being waived by the Mets last season. Unimpressive in the minors, Fordyce saw action in four September games with the Reds. 1997 Outlook: C

Curtis Goodwin (Pos: CF, Age: 24, Bats: L)

	G	AB	R	H	D	T	HR	RBI	SB	BB	SO	Avg	OBP	Slg
1996	49	136	20	31	3	0	0	5	15	19	34	.228	.323	.250
Career	136	425	60	107	14	3	1	29	37	34	87	.252	.308	.306

Bouncing up and down from the minors and majors all season, Goodwin got significant playing time in the Reds' outfield in September and June. He struggled, but is still young (24) and will take a walk. 1997 Outlook: B

Mike Kelly (Pos: CF, Age: 26, Bats: R)

	G	AB	R	H	D	T	HR	RBI	SB	BB	SO	Avg	OBP	Slg
1996	19	49	5	9	4	0	1	7	4	9	11	.184	.333	.327
Career	146	263	45	56	20	2	6	33	11	22	77	.213	.285	.373

Traded from the Braves before the '96 season, Kelly started the year with the Reds but was sent down to the minors after a miserable April performance. He won't receive too many more chances. 1997 Outlook: C

Derek Lilliquist (Pos: LHP, Age: 31)

	W	L	Pct.	ERA	G	GS	Sv	IP	H	BB	SO	HR	BR/IP
1996	0	0	-	7.36	5	0	0	3.2	5	0	1	1	1.36
Career	25	34	.424	4.13	262	52	17	483.2	532	134	261	59	1.38

At age 31, Lilliquist might have run out of shots in the majors. He was released by his second team in two years after pitching in just five games with the Reds. 1997 Outlook: D

Pedro A. Martinez (Pos: LHP, Age: 28)

	W	L	Pct.	ERA	G	GS	Sv	IP	H	BB	SO	HR	BR/IP
1996	0	0	-	6.30	9	0	0	10.0	13	8	9	2	2.10
Career	6	3	.667	3.71	114	1	3	136.0	117	86	110	13	1.49

Obtained in a September trade with the Mets, Martinez saw action in four games before he was shipped down to the minors. Cincinnati is his fourth team in the last three years. 1997 Outlook: C

Keith Mitchell (Pos: LF, Age: 27, Bats: R)

	G	AB	R	H	D	T	HR	RBI	SB	BB	SO	Avg	OBP	Slg
1996	11	15	2	4	1	0	1	3	0	1	3	.267	.313	.533
Career	105	209	34	54	3	0	8	23	3	27	37	.258	.345	.388

Mitchell had a stellar year at Triple-A Indianapolis last season and saw some playing time in the majors in September. He could surprise if he makes the team. 1997 Outlook: B

Marcus Moore (Pos: RHP, Age: 26)

	W	L	Pct.	ERA	G	GS	Sv	IP	H	BB	SO	HR	BR/IP
1996	3	3	.500	5.81	23	0	2	26.1	26	22	27	3	1.82
Career	7	5	.583	6.25	79	0	2	86.1	89	63	73	11	1.76

After starting the season in the Reds' bullpen, Moore was shelled in May and June before being sent down to the minors. He pitched well for the remainder of the year, so he should get another look. 1997 Outlook: B

Mike Morgan (Pos: RHP, Age: 37)

	W	L	Pct.	ERA	G	GS	Sv	IP	H	BB	SO	HR	BR/IP
1996	6	11	.353	4.63	23	23	0	130.1	146	47	74	16	1.48
Career	108	155	.411	4.02	389	329	3	2175.1	2247	736	1086	192	1.37

His career apparently over at 37, Morgan surprised everybody when he pitched well for Cincinnati in five September starts. Due to his age and injury history, the Reds shouldn't count on him. 1997 Outlook: B

Chad Mottola (Pos: RF, Age: 25, Bats: R)

	G	AB	R	H	D	T	HR	RBI	SB	BB	SO	Avg	OBP	Slg
1996	35	79	10	17	3	0	3	6	2	6	16	.215	.271	.367
Career	35	79	10	17	3	0	3	6	2	6	16	.215	.271	.367

Rated the best power-hitting Reds prospect by *Baseball America*, Mottola struggled during various stints in right field. He should get a longer look this season. 1997 Outlook: B

Eric Owens (Pos: LF, Age: 26, Bats: R)

	G	AB	R	H	D	T	HR	RBI	SB	BB	SO	Avg	OBP	Slg
1996	88	205	26	41	6	0	0	9	16	23	38	.200	.281	.229
Career	90	207	26	43	6	0	0	10	16	23	38	.208	.288	.237

Originally projected as a third baseman, Owens spent most of his rookie season spot-starting in left field. He has speed, but he struggled to hit his weight and has absolutely no power whatsoever. 1997 Outlook: C

Eduardo Perez (Pos: 1B, Age: 27, Bats: R)

	G	AB	R	H	D	T	HR	RBI	SB	BB	SO	Avg	OBP	Slg
1996	18	36	8	8	0	0	3	5	0	5	9	.222	.317	.472
Career	137	416	43	92	17	3	13	58	8	38	86	.221	.291	.370

Perez showed considerable power and good plate discipline during his brief July and September stints with the Reds. He should get a shot as a backup first baseman/pinch hitter this year. 1997 Outlook: B

Tim Pugh (Pos: RHP, Age: 30)

	W	L	Pct.	ERA	G	GS	Sv	IP	H	BB	SO	HR	BR/IP
1996	1	2	.333	7.27	29	1	0	52.0	66	23	36	12	1.71
Career	24	27	.471	4.97	105	56	0	407.2	473	153	210	.51	1.54

Pugh bounced back and forth between Cincinnati and Kansas City all season long before ending the year with the Reds. He refused a minor league assignment in October, and is now a free agent. 1997 Outlook: C

Mike Remlinger (Pos: LHP, Age: 31)

	W	L	Pct.	ERA	G	GS	Sv	IP	H	BB	SO	HR	BR/IP
1996	0	1	.000	5.60	19	4	0	27.1	24	19	19	4	1.57
Career	3	8	.273	4.88	44	19	0	123.2	124	79	78	19	1.64

Joining the big-league club for good in late August, Remlinger was extremely wild and largely ineffective. At age 31, his future is in doubt. 1997 Outlook: C

Chris Sabo (Pos: 3B, Age: 35, Bats: R)

	G	AB	R	H	D	T	HR	RBI	SB	BB	SO	Avg	OBP	Slg
1996	54	125	15	32	7	1	3	16	2	18	27	.256	.354	.400
Career	911	3354	494	898	214	17	116	426	120	274	460	.268	.326	.445

Returning to Cincinnati, Sabo was mediocre at third base for the Reds before being sidelined for the season with a torn right knee. He is a free agent, and at 35, chances are that his career is over. 1997 Outlook: D

Scott Service (Pos: RHP, Age: 30)

	W	L	Pct.	ERA	G	GS	Sv	IP	H	BB	SO	HR	BR/IP
1996	1	0	1.000	3.94	34	1	0	48.0	51	18	46	7	1.44
Career	7	5	.583	4.48	107	1	2	144.2	143	63	141	20	1.42

In his second stint with the Reds, Service spent the second half of the year in the majors and was decent, posting good strikeout/walk numbers. 1997 Outlook: A

Jerry Spradlin (Pos: RHP, Age: 29)

	W	L	Pct.	ERA	G	GS	Sv	IP	H	BB	SO	HR	BR/IP
1996	0	0	-	0.00	1	0	0	0.1	0	0	0	0	0.00
Career	2	1	.667	4.40	44	0	2	57.1	56	11	28	6	1.17

Spradlin faced just one batter at Cincinnati before getting released at the end of the season. He pitched well at Triple-A Indianapolis last year. 1997 Outlook: C

Scott Sullivan (Pos: RHP, Age: 26)

	W	L	Pct.	ERA	G	GS	Sv	IP	H	BB	SO	HR	BR/IP
1996	0	0	-	2.25	7	0	0	8.0	7	5	3	0	1.50
Career	0	0	-	3.09	10	0	0	11.2	11	7	5	0	1.54

After an excellent season in the minors, Sullivan saw significant action after getting called up in September. He should contend for a bullpen spot this season. 1997 Outlook: A

Cincinnati Reds

Cincinnati Reds Minor League Prospects

Organization Overview:

The Cincinnati Reds have long disdained scouting and player development, and the current state of their minor league system is a testament to that philosophy. The lower end of the system is barren, and in the upper levels, the remaining prospects —almost without exception—have failed to develop. Many players who looked promising at the lower levels have stalled before reaching the majors, and of the ones who have made it, almost every one who's been given a major league trial in the past two years has fallen flat on his face. A small group of legitimate prospects remains, but it's hard to be optimistic about their future development. If they don't make it, the Reds will have nothing left to counteract the erosion of their major league talent.

Paul Bako

Position: C | **Opening Day Age:** 24
Bats: L **Throws:** R | **Born:** 6/20/72 in
Ht: 6' 2" **Wt:** 205 | Lafayette, LA

Recent Statistics

	G	AB	R	H	D	T	HR	RBI	SB	BB	SO	AVG
93 R Billings	57	194	34	61	11	0	4	30	5	22	37	.314
94 A Winston-Sal	90	289	29	59	9	1	3	26	2	35	81	.204
95 A Winston-Sal	82	249	29	71	11	2	7	27	3	42	66	.285
96 AA Chattanooga	110	360	53	106	27	0	8	48	1	48	93	.294
96 MLE	110	349	43	95	25	0	6	39	0	34	96	.272

Over the past two seasons, so-called "defensive specialist" Paul Bako has learned how to swing the bat. He's always been an adequate thrower and a quality receiver, and now his left-handed swing is an asset as well. He's ready to handle a major league job, and could hit for a good average if given the chance. He's a good bet to surface sometime within the next year or two.

Tim Belk

Position: 1B | **Opening Day Age:** 26
Bats: R **Throws:** R | **Born:** 4/6/70 in
Ht: 6' 3" **Wt:** 200 | Cincinnati, OH

Recent Statistics

	G	AB	R	H	D	T	HR	RBI	SB	BB	SO	AVG
96 AAA Indianapolis	120	436	63	125	27	3	15	63	5	27	72	.287
96 NL Cincinnati	7	15	2	3	0	0	0	0	0	1	2	.200
96 MLE	120	422	52	111	25	2	12	52	3	23	73	.263

Tim Belk is a major league hitter, but still isn't much of a prospect. As a low-power right-handed first baseman, he isn't very useful, despite the fact that he can hit for average and really pick it around the bag. He tried to hit for more power last year, but his average went down, his strikeouts went up, and the power numbers hardly changed. Now 27 years old, his chance may have passed him by.

Aaron Boone

Position: 3B | **Opening Day Age:** 24
Bats: R **Throws:** R | **Born:** 3/9/73 in La
Ht: 6' 2" **Wt:** 190 | Mesa, CA

Recent Statistics

	G	AB	R	H	D	T	HR	RBI	SB	BB	SO	AVG
94 R Billings	67	256	48	70	15	5	7	55	6	36	35	.273
95 AA Chattanooga	23	66	6	15	3	0	0	3	2	5	12	.227
95 A Winston-Sal	108	395	61	103	19	1	14	50	11	43	77	.261
96 AA Chattanooga	136	548	86	158	44	7	17	95	21	38	77	.288
96 MLE	136	529	70	139	41	4	13	77	15	27	79	.263

It all came together for Aaron Boone last year. Always noted for his major league-caliber defense at third base, he broke out with a Southern League-record 44 doubles, and put to rest any concerns that he wouldn't hit enough to make it in the majors. Boone now projects as a similar hitter to his brother Bret, and the two Boones probably will find themselves on the same infield at some point this season.

Ray Brown

Position: 1B | **Opening Day Age:** 24
Bats: L **Throws:** R | **Born:** 7/30/72 in Simi
Ht: 6' 2" **Wt:** 205 | Valley, CA

Recent Statistics

	G	AB	R	H	D	T	HR	RBI	SB	BB	SO	AVG
94 R Billings	60	218	50	80	19	3	9	49	3	27	32	.367
95 A Winston-Sal	122	445	63	118	26	0	19	77	3	52	85	.265
95 A Charlstn-WV	6	17	3	2	1	0	0	0	0	4	3	.118
96 AA Chattanooga	115	364	68	119	26	5	13	52	2	52	62	.327
96 MLE	115	351	55	106	24	3	11	42	1	37	64	.302

Around the bag, Ray Brown has some work to do, but at the plate, he's almost all the way there. A tremendous pure hitter, the lefty-swinging Brown makes excellent contact, and his power is coming along. He's capable of hitting for a good average in the majors after only one season of Double-A, and at age 24, he's still on the way up. If his defense improves, he could become a Hal Morris-type of player.

Steve Gibralter

Position: OF | **Opening Day Age:** 24
Bats: R **Throws:** R | **Born:** 10/9/72 in
Ht: 6' 0" **Wt:** 170 | Dallas, TX

Recent Statistics

	G	AB	R	H	D	T	HR	RBI	SB	BB	SO	AVG
96 AAA Indianapolis	126	447	58	114	29	2	11	54	2	26	114	.255
96 NL Cincinnati	2	2	0	0	0	0	0	0	0	0	2	.000
96 MLE	126	434	48	101	27	1	9	45	1	22	116	.233

In 1995, Steve Gibralter came out of nowhere to emerge as a potential five-tool player. Last year, he went back to nowhere. He failed to grab the Reds' wide-open center field spot in the spring, and he floundered at Triple-A as the Reds gave major league trials to just about every other outfielder in the system. The reason for his decline may have been a bad shoulder, and if he's able to overcome it, he will remain a great defensive center fielder with exciting offensive potential.

Curt Lyons

Position: P **Opening Day Age:** 22
Bats: R **Throws:** R **Born:** 10/17/74 in
Ht: 6' 5" **Wt:** 228 Greencastle, IN

Recent Statistics

	W	L	ERA	G	GS	Sv	IP	H	R	BB	SO	HR
96 AA Chatt'nooga	13	4	2.41	24	24	0	141.2	113	48	52	176	8
96 NL Cincinnati	2	0	4.50	3	3	0	16.0	17	8	7	14	1

Young righthander Curt Lyons led all of Double-A and Triple-A with 176 strikeouts last year, and even fanned 14 batters in 16 innings with the Reds. Regardless of what you might assume, however, he is not a flamethrower. He gets his K's with an outstanding change-up and a good breaking pitch. He's got good command, and the combination has worked for him wherever he's pitched. He won't steal the strikeout crown from John Smoltz, but he's a good bet to pitch well for the Reds this year.

Pokey Reese

Position: SS **Opening Day Age:** 23
Bats: R **Throws:** R **Born:** 6/10/73 in
Ht: 6' 0" **Wt:** 160 Columbia, SC

Recent Statistics

	G	AB	R	H	D	T	HR	RBI	SB	BB	SO	AVG
93 AA Chattanooga	102	345	35	73	17	4	3	37		8	23	77	.212
94 AA Chattanooga	134	484	77	130	23	4	12	49	21	43	75	.269
95 AAA Indianapols	89	343	51	82	21	1	10	46	8	36	81	.239
96 AAA Indianapols	79	280	26	65	16	0	1	23	5	21	46	.232
96 MLE	79	272	21	57	15	0	0	19	3	18	46	.210

We're *still* waiting. Trumpeted for years as the next great Reds shortstop, Pokey Reese has stagnated at Triple-A for two years. It's become increasingly clear that the Reds won't need his services anytime soon, which leaves him in limbo. He's a tremendous athlete, and many feel that his range and arm make him one of the best defensive shortstops in the entire game. Set back by repeated injuries, his bat hasn't developed at all, and has even begun to regress. Something needs to happen for him, soon.

Brett Tomko

Position: P **Opening Day Age:** 23
Bats: R **Throws:** R **Born:** 4/7/73 in
Ht: 6' 4" **Wt:** 205 Cleveland, OH

Recent Statistics

	W	L	ERA	G	GS	Sv	IP	H	R	BB	SO	HR
95 A Charlstn-WV	4	2	1.84	9	7	0	49.0	41	12	9	46	1
96 AA Chatt'nooga	11	7	3.88	27	27	0	157.2	131	73	54	164	20

After Curt Lyons, the next-highest strikeout total in the high minors belonged to Brett Tomko. Like Lyons, Tomko throws strikes, but unlike Lyons, this guy throws hard. He was the Reds' top pick (second round) in the '95 draft, and he might have been promoted to Triple-A last summer if it hadn't been his first full year as a professional. This year may include a promotion to Cincinnati.

Others to Watch

Clint Koppe continued to win as he climbed through the system. He went 12-4 between A-ball and Double-A, but doesn't have a high ceiling as a right-handed finesse pitcher. . . Southpaw **Gabe White** was once a highly-regarded prospect in the Montreal chain. He's only 25, and went 6-3 in 11 starts at Triple-A last year. . . Young shortstop **Ricky Magdaleno** is a raw defender and wild swinger, but he's got some pop in his bat. He's got a long way to go, but may develop into a powerful middle infielder. . . **Chris Reed** lacks good command, but he's uncommonly durable and won 13 games at Double-A Chattanooga last year. Now only 23 years old, he's worth keeping an eye on. . . Righthander **Jim Nix** isn't a coming star at age 26, but he could give the Reds some solid middle relief after two straight solid seasons at Double-A. Nix isn't a big guy, but his heater cracks 90 MPH.

Don Baylor

Born: 6/28/49 in Austin, TX

Playing Experience: 1970-1988, Bal, Oak, Cal, NYA, Bos, Min

Managerial Experience: 4 seasons

1996 Season

Don Baylor has firmly established himself as "The Boss" in Colorado. Baylor has proved popular in the clubhouse with his ability to relate to both veterans and younger players. However, his short temper and criticism of other teams' styles often get his club involved in brushback battles. Baylor has managed conservatively on the road, something which critics say contributes to the Rockies' road woes.

Offense

Though he has a lineup loaded with power, Baylor tries to keep the pressure on enemy pitchers with aggressive baserunning. The Rockies stole more bases than any club in baseball and—more importantly—were second in the National League in stolen base success rates. Because of the many high-scoring games his club is involved in, Baylor uses more pinch hitters than any other club in the league.

Pitching & Defense

By necessity, Baylor has worked his bullpen extensively because he has never had any consistent starting pitching. However, he has also been guilty of overusing many of his relievers, not only in actual games but in continually calling on pitchers to warm up in the bullpen. Steve Reed, Bruce Ruffin, and Darren Holmes have gone through stretches in which they threw several times a night for several nights in a row. As a result, Colorado relievers have had their share of physical problems.

1997 Outlook

For the first time in his managerial career, Baylor has a chance to command a consistent starting rotation, which should take the pressure off his harried bullpen. His job is secure with a recent contract extension, but expectations have changed in Colorado: the Rockies are now expected to contend every year. Baylor's club will be perceived as a failure with anything less than a playoff berth this season.

Manager Statistics

Year	Team, Lg	W	L	Pct	GB	Finish
1996	Colorado, NL	83	79	.512	8.0	3rd West
4 Seasons		280	305	.479	—	—

1996 Starting Pitchers by Days Rest

	≤3	4	5	6+
Rockies Starts	0	90	31	30
Rockies ERA	0.00	5.83	6.10	4.96
NL Avg Starts	4	86	41	21
NL ERA	4.06	4.28	4.23	4.58

1996 Situational Stats

	Don Baylor	NL Average
Hit & Run Success %	40.0	39.0
Stolen Base Success %	75.3	71.6
Platoon Pct.	50.8	51.9
Defensive Subs	16	20
High-Pitch Outings	12	13
Quick/Slow Hooks	13/23	19/12
Sacrifice Attempts	115	92

1996 Rankings (National League)

→ 1st in stolen base attempts (267), steals of second base (173), steals of home plate (3), pitchouts with a runner moving (24), slow hooks (23) and relief appearances (447)

→ 2nd in stolen base percentage (75.3%), sacrifice bunt attempts (115), hit-and-run percentage (40.0%) and pitchouts (91)

→ 3rd in steals of third base (25) and hit-and-run attempts (130)

Dante Bichette

1996 Season

Despite being hampered all season by a knee ailment which required offseason surgery, Dante Bichette put together his second consecutive monster season. He placed second in the league in RBI to teammate Andres Galarraga, and he joined the elite 30/30 club (home runs and stolen bases) for the first time in his career. Most impressively, however, Bichette proved to be a true gamer by playing through last season's injuries and appearing in 159 games.

Hitting

Like all Rockies hitters, Bichette is a demonstrably better hitter at home than on the road. However, he has power to hit home runs in any ballpark. An early-count, fastball hitter, Bichette can be busted inside and will chase low and away sliders and curves. In keeping with his free-swinging teammates, who drew fewer bases on balls than all but six clubs last season, Bichette lacks plate discipline and is always reluctant to take a walk.

Baserunning & Defense

For a big man with both knee and weight problems, Bichette is a remarkably good basestealer. He does not have outstanding speed, but he is adept at getting good jumps. With teammate Larry Walker injured for much of the year, Bichette played in right field, his natural position, for most of the season. His arm is above average but he will occasionally make judgment mistakes with his throws. Bichette does not often get good jumps on fly balls and has trouble running down line drives hit over his head.

1997 Outlook

Bichette's season will hinge on whether his recovery from his knee operation this past winter is successful. The Rockies are especially concerned that he will add even more unwanted weight during his rehabilitation. If he is physically fit, Bichette will continue to be one of the National League's premier run producers—as long as he remains in Colorado.

Position: RF/LF
Bats: R **Throws:** R
Ht: 6' 3" **Wt:** 235

Opening Day Age: 33
Born: 11/18/63 in West Palm Beach, FL
ML Seasons: 9
Pronunciation: DON-tay bah-SHET

Overall Statistics

	G	AB	R	H	D	T	HR	RBI	SB	BB	SO	Avg	OBP	Slg
1996	159	633	114	198	39	3	31	141	31	45	105	.313	.359	.531
Career	979	3599	527	1056	222	18	157	629	119	174	661	.293	.327	.496

Where He Hits the Ball

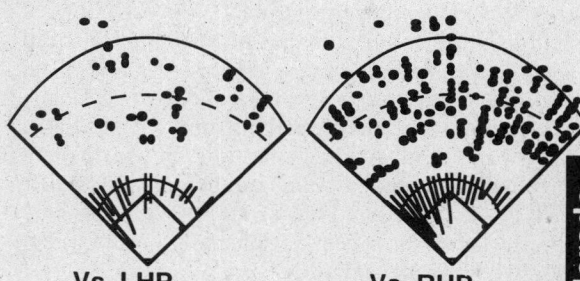

Vs. LHP　　　　**Vs. RHP**

1996 Situational Stats

	AB	H	HR	RBI	Avg		AB	H	HR	RBI	Avg
Home	336	123	22	99	.366	LHP	139	49	8	35	.353
Road	297	75	9	42	.253	RHP	494	149	23	106	.302
First Half	358	120	17	80	.335	Sc Pos	193	67	13	108	.347
Scnd Half	275	78	14	61	.284	Clutch	95	32	6	29	.337

1996 Rankings (National League)

→ 1st in sacrifice flies (10) and lowest fielding percentage in right field (.963)
→ 2nd in RBI
→ 3rd in batting average at home (.366) and errors in right field (9)
→ 4th in caught stealing (12)
→ 5th in hits and highest percentage of swings on the first pitch (44.6%)
→ 6th in total bases (336), batting average vs. left-handed pitchers (.353) and lowest cleanup slugging percentage (.464)
→ 7th in at-bats, games played (159), slugging percentage vs. left-handed pitchers (.612) and lowest percentage of pitches taken (45.8%)
→ 8th in runs scored

Ellis Burks

Position: LF/CF
Bats: R **Throws:** R
Ht: 6' 2" **Wt:** 198

Opening Day Age: 32
Born: 9/11/64 in Vicksburg, MS
ML Seasons: 10

1996 Season

Ellis Burks washed away years of injuries and underachievements with one of the league's best all-around offensive seasons. Burks joined Hank Aaron in becoming only the second player ever to accumulate 40 homers, 200 hits, and 30 steals in the same season. (Of course, Hammerin' Hank never played in Coors Field. . . .) Despite developing chronic back problems in August and September, Burks was outstanding to the bitter end, finishing his remarkable season by batting .469 over his last 20 games.

Hitting

There are few better fastball hitters than Burks. After finally recovering from a two-year-old wrist injury, he capitalized on his outstanding bat speed by becoming much more aggressive at the plate. Burks also developed into a quality two-strike and breaking-ball hitter by driving more pitches to the opposite field. At the same time, he was patient enough to draw a solid number of walks. His improved all-around hitting ability was especially reflected in his success against all types of pitching, both home and away.

Baserunning & Defense

Though he no longer runs as well as he did when he first entered the majors, Burks is still a high-percentage basestealer who has both above-average speed and outstanding judgment. Burks prefers playing left field rather than center since his back problems have hampered his range and throwing arm.

1997 Outlook

Burks, who recently signed a new contract to remain with the Rockies, cannot be expected to duplicate last year's monster numbers. Turning 32 next season, Burks will no longer be in his prime, but with his back healed and his business address in Colorado, he should continue to produce incredible offensive statistics for the next year or two.

Overall Statistics

	G	AB	R	H	D	T	HR	RBI	SB	BB	SO	Avg	OBP	Slg
1996	156	613	142	211	45	8	40	128	32	61	114	.344	.408	.639
Career	1169	4333	731	1255	247	48	177	662	141	427	772	.290	.355	.491

Where He Hits the Ball

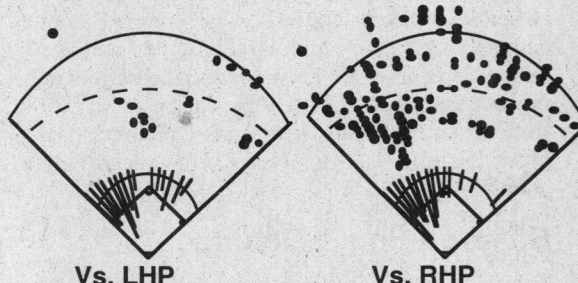

Vs. LHP   **Vs. RHP**

1996 Situational Stats

	AB	H	HR	RBI	Avg		AB	H	HR	RBI	Avg
Home	331	129	23	79	.390	LHP	143	61	8	26	.427
Road	282	82	17	49	.291	RHP	470	150	32	102	.319
First Half	334	114	22	72	.341	Sc Pos	174	63	8	83	.362
Scnd Half	279	97	18	56	.348	Clutch	83	24	2	14	.289

1996 Rankings (National League)

→ 1st in runs scored, total bases (392), slugging percentage, batting average vs. left-handed pitchers (.427) and slugging percentage vs. left-handed pitchers (.741)

→ 2nd in hits, doubles, pitches seen (2,735), on-base percentage vs. left-handed pitchers (.488), batting average at home (.390) and batting average

→ 4th in times on base (278), stolen base percentage (84.2%) and slugging percentage vs. right-handed pitchers (.609)

→ 5th in home runs, triples, RBI, errors in left field (5) and fielding percentage in left field (.978)

Vinny Castilla

1996 Season

Over the first two months of last season, Vinny Castilla struggled to produce the power he demonstrated in 1995 and was labeled as a one-year wonder. Castilla emphatically answered such criticism, hitting .314 over his last 100 games with 33 homers and 77 RBI. He added two grand slams along the way as he shattered all of his previous year's career highs. Like the other Rockies sluggers, however, Castilla was given a big boost by Coors Field, where he had 27 of his 40 homers and nearly two-thirds of his RBI.

Hitting

Castilla is known around the league as a notorious first-ball, fastball hitter—and he is dangerous when he gets ahead in the count. However, he has improved his handling of offspeed pitches and has also shown an ability to lay off breaking balls he knows he cannot handle. Though he is not a patient hitter, Castilla tries to limit his strikeouts.

Baserunning & Defense

Though his range is quite limited and his arm at times is erratic, Castilla is a solid third baseman who consistently makes the routine plays. He has good hands, with the majority of his errors coming on throwing mistakes. Castilla has below-average speed but he has learned to pick spots for occasional stolen base attempts. On the basepaths, he's aggressive in breaking up double plays.

1997 Outlook

As much as any of the Blake Street Bombers, Castilla's production has been viewed skeptically, and rightfully so. On the road he hits with some power, but his lack of selectivity and low on-base percentage make him, on balance, a barely average performer for his position. So while he should continue to post big numbers in 1997, he really can't be considered one of baseball's elite sluggers.

Position: 3B
Bats: R **Throws:** R
Ht: 6' 1" **Wt:** 200

Opening Day Age: 29
Born: 7/4/67 in Oaxaca, MX
ML Seasons: 6
Pronunciation: kas-TEE-yah

Overall Statistics

	G	AB	R	H	D	T	HR	RBI	SB	BB	SO	Avg	OBP	Slg
1996	160	629	97	191	34	0	40	113	7	35	88	.304	.343	.548
Career	477	1644	233	488	89	10	84	252	13	86	249	.297	.333	.516

Where He Hits the Ball

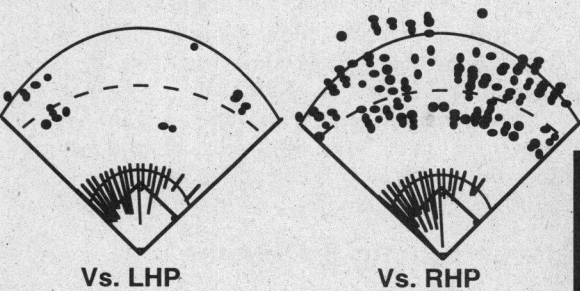

Vs. LHP   **Vs. RHP**

1996 Situational Stats

	AB	H	HR	RBI	Avg		AB	H	HR	RBI	Avg
Home	328	113	27	74	.345	LHP	137	35	5	22	.255
Road	301	78	13	39	.259	RHP	492	156	35	91	.317
First Half	338	103	17	56	.305	Sc Pos	142	47	10	71	.331
Scnd Half	291	88	23	57	.302	Clutch	88	30	6	21	.341

1996 Rankings (National League)

→ 1st in lowest percentage of pitches taken (43.0%) and highest percentage of swings on the first pitch (50.5%)
→ 3rd in least pitches seen per plate appearance (3.09) and errors at third base (20)
→ 4th in total bases (345) and fielding percentage at third base (.960)
→ 5th in home runs, GDPs (20) and games played (160)
→ 6th in batting average at home (.345)
→ 7th in hits and slugging percentage vs. right-handed pitchers (.583)
→ 8th in batting average in the clutch (.341) and batting average vs. right-handed pitchers (.317)

Andres Galarraga

1995 Season

In the Year of the Hitter, few sluggers posted better numbers than Andres Galarraga. The Big Cat led the National League with a career-high 47 homers, and his 150 RBI not only led both leagues, but marked him as the first player to reach the 150-RBI mark in 34 years. Like most Rockies, however, Galarraga's numbers were given a huge boost by Coors field, where he had 32 homers and an amazing 103 RBI. He was far less dangerous on the road, but his numbers were certainly respectable.

Hitting

Only three players struck out more times last year than Galarraga. However, his lack of plate discipline was easier to swallow because of his huge offensive production. Galarraga has always chased pitches outside of the strike zone—in particular, sliders and changes up and away from him. His open stance gives him great plate coverage and any pitch that he's able to reach is liable to be crushed.

Baserunning & Defense

Some observers have placed Galarraga among the ranks of baseball's all-time greatest defensive first baseman. He has outstanding range, agility, and hands, and is surpassed by few at snaring low throws in the dirt. Galarraga's recent conditioning efforts have made him much more mobile on the bases. He set a career mark for thefts last year with 18, and he's been a high-percentage stealer despite his advanced age, going 38-for-51 (74.5 percent) over the last three years.

1997 Outlook

His career fueled by both his excellent relationship with manager Don Baylor and the advantage of playing at Coors, Galarraga figures to post big numbers again in 1997. While the park makes him look a whole lot better than he really is, he's a quality player and a big asset to the Rockies.

Position: 1B
Bats: R **Throws:** R
Ht: 6' 3" **Wt:** 235

Opening Day Age: 35
Born: 6/18/61 in Caracas, VZ
ML Seasons: 12
Pronunciation: gah-lah-RAH-guh
Nickname: Big Cat

Overall Statistics

	G	AB	R	H	D	T	HR	RBI	SB	BB	SO	Avg	OBP	Slg
1996	159	626	119	190	39	3	47	150	18	40	157	.304	.357	.601
Career	1467	5474	788	1561	306	26	247	911	99	350	1328	.285	.336	.486

Where He Hits the Ball

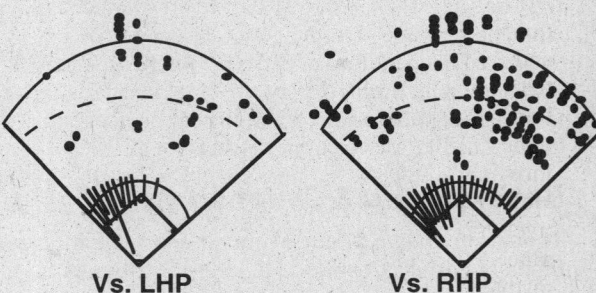

Vs. LHP   Vs. RHP

1996 Situational Stats

	AB	H	HR	RBI	Avg		AB	H	HR	RBI	Avg
Home	320	115	32	103	.359	LHP	141	46	12	42	.326
Road	306	75	15	47	.245	RHP	485	144	35	108	.297
First Half	321	88	22	75	.274	Sc Pos	189	78	18	115	.413
Scnd Half	305	102	25	75	.334	Clutch	89	26	5	15	.292

1996 Rankings (National League)

➡ 1st in home runs and RBI

➡ 2nd in total bases (376), strikeouts and batting average with runners in scoring position (.413)

➡ 3rd in hit by pitch (17), cleanup slugging percentage (.638), slugging percentage vs. left-handed pitchers (.660), errors at first base (14) and lowest fielding percentage at first base (.992)

➡ 4th in runs scored, batting average at home (.359) and highest percentage of swings that missed (29.7%)

➡ 5th in slugging percentage and HR frequency (13.3 ABs per HR)

Darren Holmes

1996 Season

Unable to handle the closer role at the beginning of the season, Darren Holmes settled in as the Rockies' set-up man and had a solid season in the busy Colorado bullpen. Holmes forfeited his chance to be the team's stopper by blowing all but one of his eight save opportunities. Once out of the high-pressure position, Holmes pitched well: he was scored upon in only four of his last 20 outings. He retired 22 straight batters down the stretch, a streak that he kept until his last appearance of the season.

Pitching

Always known for his big-breaking curveball, Holmes found out that his curve does not break quite as consistently in Denver's high altitude—and that hanging pitches leave Coors Field more than anywhere else in the majors. Holmes was burned with eight homers on the season, three of them coming in save situations. When asked to throw more than one inning in a set-up role, Holmes started to mix his offerings more effectively. The Rockies have always wanted him to place more trust in both his sinking and cut fastballs.

Defense & Hitting

Holmes' odd delivery puts him in awkward fielding positions and he often misplays balls hit around the mound. He is also very slow in delivering to the plate, but he's developed a good pickoff move that makes it more difficult for opponents to steal with him on the mound. Holmes rarely bats and doesn't help himself at the plate.

1997 Outlook

Though Colorado had hoped for years that Holmes would develop into their bullpen ace, management isn't likely to trust him with that job in the near future. However, with high-scoring games as frequent as the sunrise in Denver, Rockies' starters rarely come close to finishing what they start, making a durable and consistent middle reliever like Holmes an important part of their staff.

Position: RP
Bats: R **Throws:** R
Ht: 6' 0" **Wt:** 202

Opening Day Age: 30
Born: 4/25/66 in Asheville, NC
ML Seasons: 7

Overall Statistics

	W	L	Pct.	ERA	G	GS	Sv	IP	H	BB	SO	HR	BR/IP
1996	5	4	.556	3.97	62	0	1	77.0	78	28	73	8	1.38
Career	19	20	.487	4.08	316	0	52	374.2	368	149	336	30	1.38

How Often He Throws Strikes

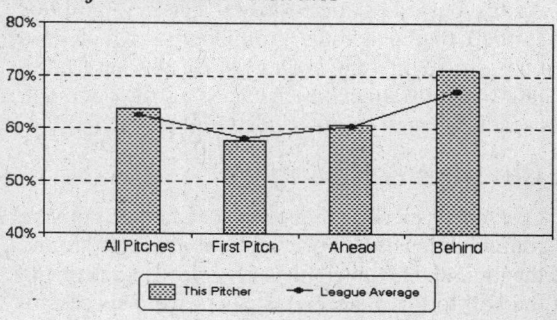

1996 Situational Stats

	W	L	ERA	Sv	IP		AB	H	HR	RBI	Avg
Home	5	1	4.28	0	40.0	LHB	117	29	2	18	.248
Road	0	3	3.65	1	37.0	RHB	183	49	6	33	.268
First Half	2	3	5.73	1	37.2	Sc Pos	91	27	2	43	.297
Scnd Half	3	1	2.29	0	39.1	Clutch	114	37	5	21	.325

1996 Rankings (National League)

➡ 3rd in blown saves (7)
➡ 6th in errors at pitcher (3) and highest percentage of inherited runners scored (41.2%)
➡ Led the Rockies in blown saves (7) and relief innings (77.0)

Curtis Leskanic

Position: RP
Bats: R **Throws:** R
Ht: 6' 0"   **Wt:** 180

Opening Day Age: 28
Born: 4/2/68 in
Homestead, PA
ML Seasons: 4

1996 Season

Curtis Leskanic started last season as the Rockies' closer and recorded six saves, along with two victories, in his first dozen appearances. Soon afterwards, Leskanic developed elbow and shoulder problems and was replaced as Colorado's bullpen ace. Leskanic had sporadic success in other relief roles, but he would not save another game, finishing the year with an unsightly 6.23 ERA.

Pitching

Leskanic's arm problems cost him most of his velocity and aggressiveness. He became prone to aiming the ball and got too many pitches up in the strike zone, resulting in numerous home run balls. At his best, Leskanic throws a heavy, mid-90s fastball that generates groundballs—which is a necessity to pitching in Denver. He also has a hard, late-breaking slider which can be a strikeout pitch, especially against left-handed hitters.

Defense & Hitting

Leskanic is a good athlete who can handle both the routine defensive plays and bunt attempts around the mound. However, he is very slow in delivering the ball to the plate: basestealers were successful in seven of 11 attempts last season. Leskanic can handle the bat very well for a reliever, and recorded a double in three at-bats last year.

1997 Outlook

By the end of last season, the Rockies didn't know what to expect of Leskanic. After undergoing post-season arthroscopic surgery on his elbow and shoulder, Leskanic will enter spring training as one of Colorado's major question marks. If he regains his confidence and stays healthy, he has the stuff to be Colorado's closer, but he could also quickly sink into a mop-up role—or the unemployment lines—if he does not regain the aggressiveness that made him such a promising pitcher.

Overall Statistics

	W	L	Pct.	ERA	G	GS	Sv	IP	H	BB	SO	HR	BR/IP
1996	7	5	.583	6.23	70	0	6	73.2	82	38	76	12	1.63
Career	15	14	.517	4.88	172	11	16	251.0	251	108	230	28	1.43

How Often He Throws Strikes

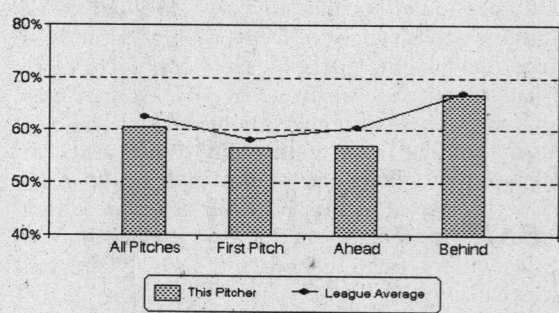

1996 Situational Stats

	W	L	ERA	Sv	IP		AB	H	HR	RBI	Avg
Home	4	0	5.87	2	38.1	LHB	129	30	7	26	.233
Road	3	5	6.62	4	35.1	RHB	159	52	5	28	.327
First Half	5	3	6.15	6	33.2	Sc Pos	82	23	4	38	.280
Scnd Half	2	2	6.30	0	40.0	Clutch	135	36	6	26	.267

1996 Rankings (National League)

- ➡ 1st in highest relief ERA (6.23)
- ➡ 3rd in worst first batter efficiency (.359) and highest batting average allowed in relief (.285)
- ➡ 4th in most baserunners allowed per 9 innings in relief (14.9)
- ➡ 5th in relief wins (7)
- ➡ Led the Rockies in relief wins (7)

Quinton McCracken

1996 Season

One of the Rockies' most pleasant surprises in 1996, Quinton McCracken made the most of his first opportunity at extensive major league playing time. McCracken stepped up during Larry Walker's long absence and filled the club's hole at center field. Batting much of the time in the second spot in the order, he had a solid on-base percentage and provided quality RBI production. . . at least when he was playing in Coors Field. On the road he was a singles hitter with a low on-base average.

Hitting

Unlike many switch-hitters, McCracken handles himself equally from both sides of the plate. Getting the majority of his playing time against righthanders, he generated most of his power from the left side. Like most Rockies, McCracken is an aggressive first-ball hitter, but he has some trouble handling pitches up in the strike zone and is prone to chasing breaking balls—which have resulted in a high number of strikeouts.

Baserunning & Defense

With above-average speed and good instincts, McCracken is a solid basestealing threat and aggressive in trying to take the extra base. He has good range in the outfield, though he occasionally will get a poor break on balls hit over his head. McCracken has a decent throwing arm and releases the ball quickly.

1997 Outlook

If Colorado's top three outfielders—Bichette, Burks and Walker—are all healthy, McCracken will serve as both the fourth outfielder and as one of the Rockies' primary pinch hitters. Since all three of the aforementioned players have had histories of injury problems, McCracken is certain to get more than his share of playing time. Like most of his teammates, he'll be working to prove he isn't just a "Coors Field hitter."

Position: CF
Bats: B **Throws:** R
Ht: 5' 7" **Wt:** 173

Opening Day Age: 27
Born: 3/16/70 in Wilmington, NC
ML Seasons: 2
Nickname: Q

Overall Statistics

	G	AB	R	H	D	T	HR	RBI	SB	BB	SO	Avg	OBP	Slg
1996	124	283	50	82	13	6	3	40	17	32	62	.290	.363	.410
Career	127	284	50	82	13	6	3	40	17	32	63	.289	.362	.408

Where He Hits the Ball

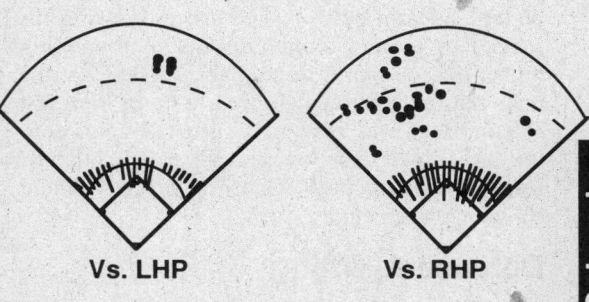

Vs. LHP   **Vs. RHP**

1996 Situational Stats

	AB	H	HR	RBI	Avg		AB	H	HR	RBI	Avg
Home	139	46	2	28	.331	LHP	68	19	0	6	.279
Road	144	36	1	12	.250	RHP	215	63	3	34	.293
First Half	94	24	0	10	.255	Sc Pos	88	30	2	37	.341
Scnd Half	189	58	3	30	.307	Clutch	53	15	0	8	.283

1996 Rankings (National League)

➡ 4th in errors in center field (5)
➡ 7th in bunts in play (21)
➡ 9th in sacrifice bunts (12)

Steve Reed

Position: RP
Bats: R **Throws:** R
Ht: 6' 2" **Wt:** 212

Opening Day Age: 31
Born: 3/11/66 in Los Angeles, CA
ML Seasons: 5

1996 Season

One of the mainstays of the Colorado bullpen for the last four years, Steve Reed again was a workhorse in 1996. He was one of three Rockies relievers who made at least 70 appearances, and he continued to neutralize right-handed hitters with his tricky sidearm delivery. Reed struggled at times during the season, surrendering five home runs in August alone. But he recovered and finished the season strongly.

Pitching

When Reed keeps his fastball low, he is a very effective pitcher. He especially dominates right-handed hitters because of his peculiar style. Reed gets in trouble when he strays from his "bread and butter" sidearm delivery and starts throwing his fastball overhand, which results in it moving higher over the strike zone. This problem was the main reason why Reed allowed 11 home runs last season. Reed was very inconsistent with his control and velocity last year and struggled with lefties, against whom the Rockies had hoped he would show improvement.

Defense & Hitting

Though he rarely gets a chance to hit, Reed can handle the bat fairly well and is usually able to make contact. His mechanics prevent him from establishing good fielding position, but he makes the routine plays and has solid defensive instincts. Reed has a slow delivery to the plate and runners can take advantage of it. However, he helps neutralize them with a decent pickoff move.

1997 Outlook

Reed was a disappointment at times last year, especially when the Rockies briefly used him as their closer. He blew all six of his save opportunities. However, he remains a durable specialty reliever who will continue to fill a key role in the Rockies' bullpen this season.

Overall Statistics

	W	L	Pct.	ERA	G	GS	Sv	IP	H	BB	SO	HR	BR/IP
1996	4	3	.571	3.96	70	0	0	75.0	66	19	51	11	1.13
Career	22	12	.647	3.54	284	0	9	323.0	299	99	243	43	1.23

How Often He Throws Strikes

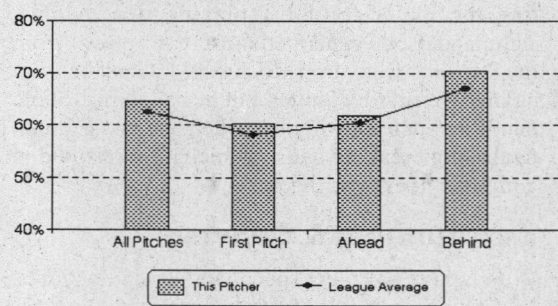

1996 Situational Stats

	W	L	ERA	Sv	IP		AB	H	HR	RBI	Avg
Home	1	1	3.02	0	41.2	LHB	102	29	5	16	.284
Road	3	2	5.13	0	33.1	RHB	174	37	6	26	.213
First Half	1	2	4.40	0	45.0	Sc Pos	73	21	1	26	.288
Scnd Half	3	1	3.30	0	30.0	Clutch	132	32	6	27	.242

1996 Rankings (National League)

- 1st in holds (22)
- 8th in blown saves (6)
- 9th in least strikeouts per 9 innings in relief (6.1)
- Led the Rockies in holds (22), lowest batting average allowed in relief with runners on base (.269), lowest percentage of inherited runners scored (31.3%) and relief ERA (3.96)

Armando Reynoso

Position: SP
Bats: R **Throws:** R
Ht: 6' 0" **Wt:** 204

Opening Day Age: 30
Born: 5/1/66 in San Luis Potosi, MX
ML Seasons: 6
Pronunciation: ray-NOH-so

1996 Season

Armando Reynoso seemed to be on his way to finishing his season strongly after winning three straight decisions in August. However, he did not win a game after August 21 and ended the year with a string of no decisions. On a more positive note, Reynoso proved he had recovered from the major elbow surgery he had undergone prior to the 1995 season. He stayed healthy while making 30 starts and placed third on his team in innings pitched.

Pitching

There is nothing overpowering about Reynoso's stuff, which is why he has always allowed more than a hit per inning. He throws a cut fastball that is clocked at no better than the mid-80s but can have good movement. In addition, he mixes in a forkball or an occasional screwball or curve, changing speeds on any or all of them. Reynoso also likes to vary his delivery to come at hitters from a variety of different angles. To be effective, Reynoso needs pinpoint control; when he pitches from behind in the count, he gets hammered.

Defense & Hitting

Few pitchers help themselves more in the field than Reynoso. He is very agile coming off the mound and makes all the plays that are required of a pitcher. Reynoso also may have the best right-handed pickoff move in baseball. While nine of 11 steals were successful against him, he also picked off eight runners. Reynoso strikes out in about half of his at-bats, but did manage nine hits and seven sacrifices last season.

1997 Outlook

With his marginal ability, Reynoso will probably never be a big winner. Since Colorado is hoping to develop its own pitching prospects, he was living on borrowed time there, and it was no surprise when the Rockies traded him to the Mets after the season. Reynoso's professionalism and competitiveness may help earn him a spot as a fourth or fifth starter on the Mets' injury-plagued staff.

Overall Statistics

	W	L	Pct.	ERA	G	GS	Sv	IP	H	BB	SO	HR	BR/IP
1996	8	9	.471	4.96	30	30	0	168.2	195	49	88	27	1.45
Career	33	32	.508	4.72	98	93	1	534.0	608	182	282	72	1.48

How Often He Throws Strikes

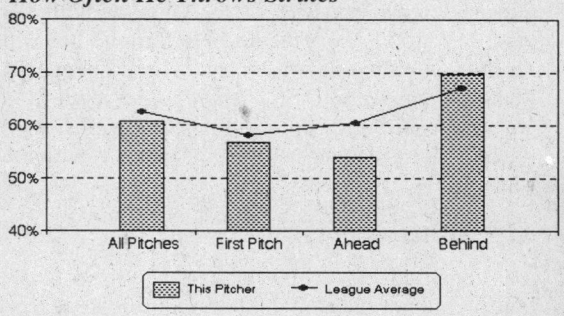

This Pitcher — League Average

1996 Situational Stats

	W	L	ERA	Sv	IP		AB	H	HR	RBI	Avg
Home	6	4	4.81	0	88.0	LHB	281	88	9	41	.313
Road	2	5	5.13	0	80.2	RHB	388	107	18	49	.276
First Half	4	6	4.68	0	98.0	Sc Pos	154	45	6	60	.292
Scnd Half	4	3	5.35	0	70.2	Clutch	16	4	1	3	.250

1996 Rankings (National League)

→ 1st in pickoff throws (237) and highest slugging percentage allowed (.483)
→ 2nd in most home runs allowed per 9 innings (1.44) and least strikeouts per 9 innings (4.7)
→ 3rd in balks (3) and highest batting average allowed (.291)
→ 4th in most run support per 9 innings (5.9)
→ 6th in highest ERA at home (4.81) and errors at pitcher (3)
→ 7th in highest ERA and highest batting average allowed vs. left-handed batters (.313)
→ 8th in highest stolen base percentage allowed (81.8%)
→ 9th in home runs allowed

Kevin Ritz

1996 Season

Last year was a breakthrough season for Kevin Ritz, who proved that you *can* pitch in Denver and still be effective. Ritz was Colorado's Opening Day starter and became the staff workhorse in the Rockies' rotation. He achieved career highs in starts, innings, and victories. Included in the stand-out campaign was a six-game winning streak from late May to late June, and wins in four of his final six starts of the season.

Pitching

Ritz had very poor walk/strikeout data last season, an indication that, although durable, he also doesn't overpower anybody. However, he is by no means defenseless. Ritz' fastball hits the high 80s and has good movement. In addition, he also throws a quality slider and mixes in a change-up that he turns over to help it sink. Ritz' control is erratic, resulting in high numbers of walks, wild pitches, long counts, and a fair amount of home runs.

Defense & Hitting

By the middle of last year, there was no better hitting pitcher than Ritz. After opening the season 1-for-18, he went on to hit .298 the rest of the way, including a home run and five RBI. Ritz gets himself in good fielding position and handles most defensive plays capably. However, he does not have any pickoff move to speak of and is one of the worst pitchers in the league at holding baserunners.

1997 Outlook

The way the Rockies score and allow runs, they vitally need starting pitchers who can give them innings and not be intimidated by Coors Field. That's what Ritz can do. He will be counted on again to be the staff's ace next season, and with Colorado's firepower behind him, there's no reason why he shouldn't win between 15 and 20 games again.

Position: SP
Bats: R **Throws:** R
Ht: 6' 4" **Wt:** 222

Opening Day Age: 31
Born: 6/8/65 in Eatonstown, NJ
ML Seasons: 7

Overall Statistics

	W	L	Pct.	ERA	G	GS	Sv	IP	H	BB	SO	HR	BR/IP
1996	17	11	.607	5.28	35	35	0	213.0	236	105	105	24	1.60
Career	39	46	.459	5.19	131	110	2	637.0	689	329	403	52	1.60

How Often He Throws Strikes

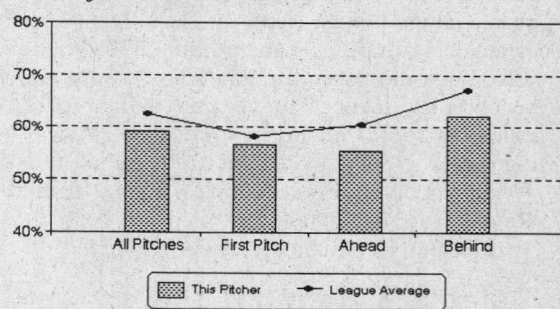

1996 Situational Stats

	W	L	ERA	Sv	IP		AB	H	HR	RBI	Avg
Home	8	4	5.93	0	104.2	LHB	337	99	10	50	.294
Road	9	7	4.65	0	108.1	RHB	500	137	14	66	.274
First Half	10	5	4.53	0	117.1	Sc Pos	237	60	9	91	.253
Scnd Half	7	6	6.21	0	95.2	Clutch	36	11	3	9	.306

1996 Rankings (National League)

→ 1st in most run support per 9 innings (7.2), least strikeouts per 9 innings (4.4), highest ERA at home (5.93) and fielding percentage at pitcher (1.000)

→ 2nd in games started, hits allowed, walks allowed, runners caught stealing (13), lowest strikeout/walk ratio (1.0), highest on-base percentage allowed (.368) and most baserunners allowed per 9 innings

→ 3rd in wins

→ 4th in highest ERA and stolen bases allowed (27)

→ 5th in hit batsmen (12), pickoff throws (198) and highest groundball/flyball ratio allowed (2.0)

Bruce Ruffin

1996 Season

When all other Rockies' relievers failed, it was left to Bruce Ruffin to serve as the club's closer from May until the end of year. Ruffin came through with a strong season in which he blew only five of 29 save opportunities on the way to setting a career high for saves and earning his best win total in nine years. Ruffin finished the season at the top of his game, converting 11 of his last 12 save chances.

Pitching

Ruffin's slider has always been his best pitch—especially against right-handed batters, whom he limited last year to a .192 average. However, Ruffin has also added three to five miles per hour on his hard sinking fastball, which can be effective on those days when his slider is not biting. Ruffin, who has displayed excellent durability throughout his career, has always been prone to wild streaks, especially when he starts to overthrow his breaking ball.

Defense & Hitting

Ruffin has decent fielding instincts, though his delivery often causes him to fall towards first base. He has improved in holding runners, but his slow delivery home doesn't give his catchers much of a shot at throwing out basestealers. Ruffin has always been one of the weakest hitting pitchers in the league, but he rarely gets a chance to bat these days—no great loss for the Rockies' offense.

1997 Outlook

Ruffin is capable of filling any number of roles in the Colorado bullpen this season. However, despite his occasional shortcomings with control and mechanics, Ruffin will likely be manager Don Baylor's first option as closer. He is not a potential 40-save star, but, if used correctly, he can be counted on to close 25 to 30 games. His proven ability to fill the pressure-packed role gives him an advantage over the Rockies' other relief candidates.

Position: RP
Bats: B **Throws:** L
Ht: 6' 2" **Wt:** 215

Opening Day Age: 33
Born: 10/4/63 in Lubbock, TX
ML Seasons: 11

Overall Statistics

	W	L	Pct.	ERA	G	GS	Sv	IP	H	BB	SO	HR	BR/IP
1996	7	5	.583	4.00	71	0	24	69.2	55	29	74	5	1.21
Career	60	80	.429	4.17	446	152	56	1246.0	1327	547	812	89	1.50

How Often He Throws Strikes

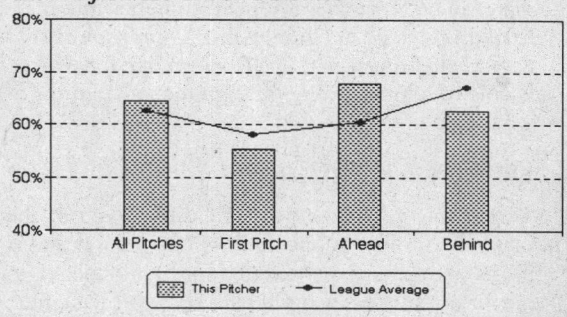

1996 Situational Stats

	W	L	ERA	Sv	IP		AB	H	HR	RBI	Avg
Home	6	2	3.96	12	36.1	LHB	62	17	0	5	.274
Road	1	3	4.05	12	33.1	RHB	198	38	5	28	.192
First Half	3	3	5.00	13	36.0	Sc Pos	73	17	2	28	.233
Scnd Half	4	2	2.94	11	33.2	Clutch	168	36	3	25	.214

1996 Rankings (National League)

- ➥ 3rd in lowest save percentage (82.8%)
- ➥ 5th in relief wins (7)
- ➥ 6th in first batter efficiency (.152)
- ➥ 8th in games finished (56), wild pitches (10) and lowest batting average allowed in relief (.212)
- ➥ Led the Rockies in games pitched, saves, games finished (56), save opportunities (29), save percentage (82.8%), first batter efficiency (.152), lowest batting average allowed in relief with runners in scoring position (.233), relief wins (7), lowest batting average allowed in relief (.212), least baserunners allowed per 9 innings in relief (10.9) and most strikeouts per 9 innings in relief (9.6)

Colorado Rockies

Mark Thompson

1996 Season

In his first full year in the Rockies' rotation, Mark Thompson held his own and developed into a solid addition to the Colorado staff. Thompson had quality starts in 54 percent of his outings and made a bit of history along the way on August 6, when he became the only Rockies pitcher to throw a complete-game shutout at Coors Field.

Pitching

Thompson has gained a solid foothold in the majors after developing a more consistent change-up; he now has an offspeed alternative to his sinking fastball and hard late-breaking slider. Thompson is not a strikeout pitcher, but he's usually around the plate, so batters generally put his pitches into play. Like all pitchers at Coors Field, Thompson is susceptible to home runs. The Rockies like the way he is able to remain strong through the late innings of a ballgame.

Defense & Hitting

Thompson gets into good fielding position the majority of time, but he tends to hurry plays and is prone to mistakes: he was tied for first in the NL in errors committed by a pitcher. Thompson is quick to the plate, which helps him against basestealers, though he does not have a good pickoff move to first. He can help himself with the bat, managing eight hits last year, including three doubles and two RBI.

1997 Outlook

Since their creation, the Rockies have generally used their top amateur picks to select pitchers, and Thompson is the first of the home-grown arms to establish himself in the Colorado rotation. He is tough enough mentally to cope with pitching in Coors Field, and he has the kind of talent and durability to contribute as a much-needed "innings eater" for the Rockies. Thompson will enter the spring in firm control of a spot in the rotation and should develop into a consistent 12- to 15-game winner.

Position: SP/RP
Bats: R **Throws:** R
Ht: 6' 2" **Wt:** 205

Opening Day Age: 25
Born: 4/7/71 in
Russellville, KY
ML Seasons: 3

Overall Statistics

	W	L	Pct.	ERA	G	GS	Sv	IP	H	BB	SO	HR	BR/IP
1996	9	11	.450	5.30	34	28	0	169.2	189	74	99	25	1.55
Career	12	15	.444	5.72	57	35	0	229.2	278	104	134	34	1.66

How Often He Throws Strikes

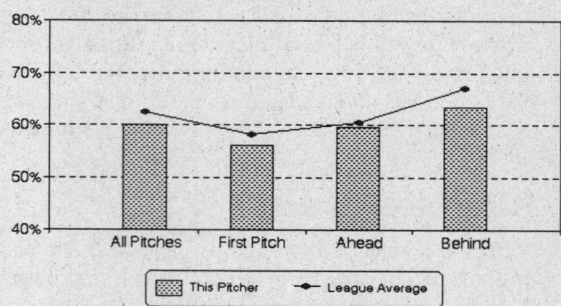

1996 Situational Stats

	W	L	ERA	Sv	IP		AB	H	HR	RBI	Avg
Home	5	4	6.41	0	80.0	LHB	299	87	12	41	.291
Road	4	7	4.32	0	89.2	RHB	364	102	13	52	.280
First Half	3	7	6.26	0	87.2	Sc Pos	185	48	5	65	.259
Scnd Half	6	4	4.28	0	82.0	Clutch	14	5	0	2	.357

1996 Rankings (National League)

- → 1st in errors at pitcher (5)
- → 2nd in lowest fielding percentage at pitcher (.875)
- → 3rd in highest ERA, highest on-base percentage allowed (.367), most baserunners allowed per 9 innings (14.6) and most GDPs induced per 9 innings (1.1)
- → 4th in hit batsmen (13), lowest strikeout/walk ratio (1.3) and highest slugging percentage allowed (.475)
- → 5th in most run support per 9 innings (5.7)
- → 7th in least strikeouts per 9 innings (5.3)
- → 8th in highest batting average allowed (.285) and most home runs allowed per 9 innings (1.33)

Larry Walker

1996 Season

The 1996 season was largely lost for Larry Walker after he suffered a broken collarbone in early June. He returned to action in late August but was mediocre at best, experiencing soreness that limited his playing time. Walker had gotten off to a solid start, hitting 14 homers in 53 games prior to his injury.

Hitting

It's not unusual for a Rockies hitter to have better numbers at home than on the road, but Walker's disparity last year was almost unbelievable: he hit under .150 on the road last year—over 250 points lower than at Coors Field. One reason for the huge difference is that he fell into the habit of taking uppercut swings in search of more home runs. Thus he pulled off too many pitches and became more prone to chasing breaking balls out of the strike zone.

Baserunning & Defense

Colorado opened the season with a controversial shift of Walker into center field. Walker had problems adjusting to his new position after establishing himself as one of the game's best right fielders. By year's end, he was back in right, where he has few equals. Walker has one of the best arms in baseball, and while he's occasionally guilty of lapses in concentration, he is a defensive stalwart. He is also an excellent runner with outstanding basestealing judgment.

1997 Outlook

Walker enters this season under a cloud of uncertainty about his physical condition. Though his collarbone is likely to be fully healed, he suffered a setback this winter when he separated his shoulder in a fishing accident. The Rockies hope that he will be at full strength by spring, and if he is, he will again take his place as one of the league's better outfielders. However, Walker needs to produce more on the road to rejoin the ranks of the major league elite.

Position: CF/RF
Bats: L   **Throws:** R
Ht: 6' 3"   **Wt:** 225

Opening Day Age: 30
Born: 12/1/66 in Maple Ridge, BC, Canada
ML Seasons: 8

Overall Statistics

	G	AB	R	H	D	T	HR	RBI	SB	BB	SO	Avg	OBP	Slg
1996	83	272	58	75	18	4	18	58	18	20	58	.276	.342	.570
Career	888	3132	522	892	196	25	153	543	132	333	604	.285	.359	.510

Where He Hits the Ball

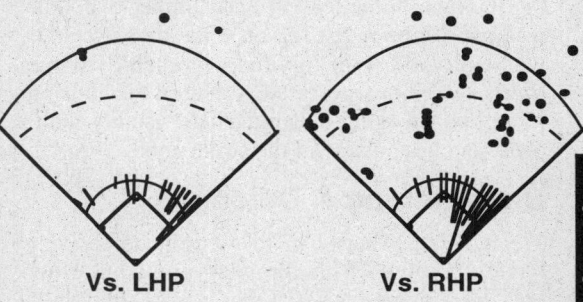

Vs. LHP   **Vs. RHP**

1996 Situational Stats

	AB	H	HR	RBI	Avg		AB	H	HR	RBI	Avg
Home	145	57	12	45	.393	LHP	75	21	5	15	.280
Road	127	18	6	13	.142	RHP	197	54	13	43	.274
First Half	198	56	14	43	.283	Sc Pos	95	25	4	38	.263
Scnd Half	74	19	4	15	.257	Clutch	35	7	0	3	.200

1996 Rankings (National League)

➡ 2nd in stolen base percentage (90.0%) and cleanup slugging percentage (.656)
➡ Led the Rockies in stolen base percentage (90.0%), cleanup slugging percentage (.656) and steals of third (5)

Walt Weiss

1996 Season

Amid all the Blake Street Bombers, there was no more valuable Rockies player than shortstop Walt Weiss. Colorado's field general, Weiss posted the best offensive season of his career, setting personal highs in virtually every offensive category. Like most Rockies, he struggled miserably on the road, but his defensive contributions continued to make him an important member of the team.

Hitting

The switch-hitting Weiss is equally effective against both right- and left-handed pitching. Previously used almost exclusively in the eighth spot of the order, Weiss proved his versatility by holding his own in the leadoff and number-two slots, walking 80 times last season. Like most Rockies, whatever power he produces comes at home. Weiss can be overpowered with hard fastballs but is a good breaking-ball hitter and usually won't chase pitches outside of the strike zone.

Baserunning & Defense

Weiss slumped early in the season defensively, largely because of his throwing problems. However, he remains one of baseball's most solid shortstops. Weiss annually handles as many chances as any player in the game because of his above-average range and intelligent positioning, and he's also fearless in turning the double play. Weiss has just average speed but uses it wisely and is a high-percentage basestealer.

1997 Outlook

There has been talk that the Rockies will deal Weiss to save some money and make room for top prospect Neifi Perez. However, many in the Colorado organization believe Weiss is far too valuable as a team leader to let him go. In addition, the Rockies believe he can be an excellent mentor for the talented Perez. Unless offered an incredible deal, the Rockies are likely to start the season with this poised and proven commodity manning the infield once again.

Position: SS
Bats: B **Throws:** R
Ht: 6' 0" **Wt:** 175

Opening Day Age: 33
Born: 11/28/63 in Tuxedo, NY
ML Seasons: 10

Overall Statistics

	G	AB	R	H	D	T	HR	RBI	SB	BB	SO	Avg	OBP	Slg
1996	155	517	89	146	20	2	8	48	10	80	78	.282	.381	.375
Career	1088	3475	440	891	122	18	19	274	76	472	469	.256	.347	.318

Where He Hits the Ball

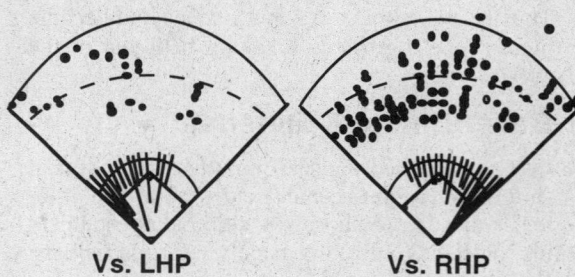

Vs. LHP   **Vs. RHP**

1996 Situational Stats

	AB	H	HR	RBI	Avg		AB	H	HR	RBI	Avg
Home	261	88	5	32	.337	LHP	141	39	0	10	.277
Road	256	58	3	16	.227	RHP	376	107	8	38	.285
First Half	290	88	2	25	.303	Sc Pos	117	26	1	36	.222
Scnd Half	227	58	6	23	.256	Clutch	71	24	1	7	.338

1996 Rankings (National League)

→ 1st in errors at shortstop (30) and lowest fielding percentage at shortstop (.957)
→ 3rd in bunts in play (24) and highest percentage of pitches taken (63.5%)
→ 4th in lowest slugging percentage vs. left-handed pitchers (.319)
→ 5th in sacrifice bunts (14)
→ 6th in lowest batting average on the road (.227)
→ 7th in highest groundball/flyball ratio (1.9)
→ 8th in walks and lowest batting average with runners in scoring position (.222)
→ 9th in batting average in the clutch (.338) and highest percentage of swings put into play (55.1%)

Jamey Wright

Position: SP
Bats: R **Throws:** R
Ht: 6' 5" **Wt:** 203

Opening Day Age: 22
Born: 12/24/74 in
Oklahoma City, OK
ML Seasons: 1

1996 Season

Colorado's number-one draft pick in 1993, Jamey Wright swept through the Rockies' farm system and snared a spot in their rotation by midseason. Wright quickly showed he belonged in the majors, winning three of his first four major league decisions and averaging six innings an outing before missing the final two weeks of the year with a minor knee injury.

Pitching

Wright has an excellent pitching foundation on which to build. His fastball moves all over the plate and is routinely clocked in the low to mid-90s. While Wright also throws a hard slider, he needs to establish a consistent offspeed pitch to take the pressure off his heater, which at times moves too much for his own good, causing him control problems. Despite his faults, Wright has loads of poise for a young pitcher and his pitches usually stays low in the strike zone, which is critically important when pitching in Colorado.

Defense & Hitting

With a deliberate delivery to the plate, Wright can be easy pickings for basestealers. However, he does have the makings of a solid pickoff move. Wright is an outstanding athlete who gets himself in good fielding position and is very agile coming off the mound. He struck out in half of his at-bats, but he did manage two hits in his rookie year and could develop into a passable hitter.

1997 Outlook

In less than three full minor league seasons, Wright has vaulted ahead of all of the other Rockies' pitching prospects. With a bright future ahead of him, he'll enter spring training secure in knowing that he has a spot in the Colorado rotation. He has the ability to develop into the kind of consistent winner the Rockies desperately need on their staff.

Overall Statistics

	W	L	Pct.	ERA	G	GS	Sv	IP	H	BB	SO	HR	BR/IP
1996	4	4	.500	4.93	16	15	0	91.1	105	41	45	8	1.60
Career	4	4	.500	4.93	16	15	0	91.1	105	41	45	8	1.60

How Often He Throws Strikes

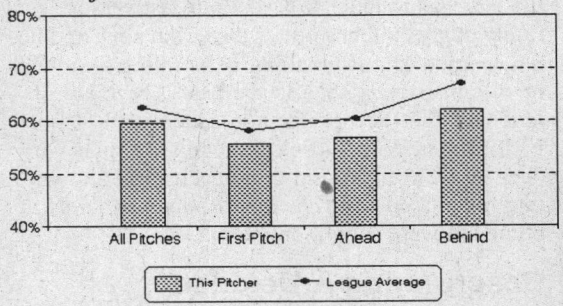

This Pitcher — League Average

1996 Situational Stats

	W	L	ERA	Sv	IP		AB	H	HR	RBI	Avg
Home	2	1	6.38	0	42.1	LHB	165	52	3	24	.315
Road	2	3	3.67	0	49.0	RHB	187	53	5	28	.283
First Half	0	0	2.84	0	6.1	Sc Pos	107	35	1	44	.327
Scnd Half	4	4	5.08	0	85.0	Clutch	18	6	0	4	.333

1996 Rankings (National League)

→ 1st in most GDPs induced per GDP situation (22.4%)
→ 8th in lowest fielding percentage at pitcher (.935)
→ Led the Rockies in most GDPs induced per GDP situation (22.4%)

Colorado Rockies

459

Eric Young

1996 Season

After missing much of the first month with a broken hand, Eric Young was chosen to the All-Star team and flirted with the batting title for much of the season. More importantly to the Rockies, Young improved significantly as a defensive second baseman and strengthened the Colorado infield. But while 1996 was a breakthrough year for Young, his total ineptitude away from Coors Field raises questions about his true effectiveness at the plate.

Hitting

A good fastball hitter, Young has become one of the most disciplined hitters in the league: no one in the NL was tougher to strike out last season. He rarely chases pitches out of the strike zone and he has learned to put breaking balls into play much more consistently than in the past. The big problem was that he became too much of a "Coors Field" hitter. With outfielders required to play very deep in Denver, Young grew accustomed to getting his hits on soft flies that dropped in safely at home but were caught on the road.

Baserunning & Defense

With excellent speed and very quick acceleration, Young is a threat to steal no matter who's behind the plate or on the mound. Defensively, he has worked hard to make himself a solid second baseman and opposing scouts say few players have come further with the glove than he has. His arm is only adequate, but he has improved his range and double-play pivot considerably.

1997 Outlook

Despite his huge season, many feel that Young's road problems are a major factor in the Rockies' inability to win away from home. That's why there is talk about dealing him now when his value is at its peak so that they can work prospect Neifi Perez into the lineup at second.

Position: 2B
Bats: R **Throws:** R
Ht: 5' 9" **Wt:** 170

Opening Day Age: 29
Born: 5/18/67 in New Brunswick, NJ
ML Seasons: 5
Nickname: E.Y.

Overall Statistics

	G	AB	R	H	D	T	HR	RBI	SB	BB	SO	Avg	OBP	Slg
1996	141	568	113	184	23	4	8	74	53	47	31	.324	.393	.421
Career	544	1784	309	528	74	22	25	193	154	205	127	.296	.376	.404

Where He Hits the Ball

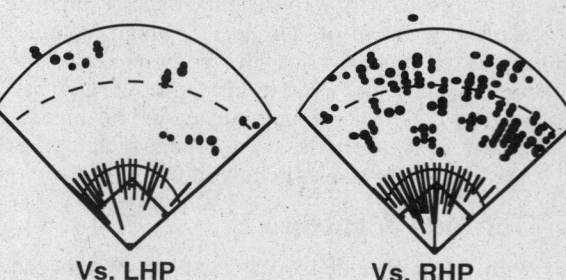

Vs. LHP   Vs. RHP

1996 Situational Stats

	AB	H	HR	RBI	Avg		AB	H	HR	RBI	Avg
Home	308	127	7	55	.412	LHP	140	40	3	13	.286
Road	260	57	1	19	.219	RHP	428	144	5	61	.336
First Half	275	95	4	38	.345	Sc Pos	144	48	0	64	.333
Scnd Half	293	89	4	36	.304	Clutch	67	19	0	15	.284

1996 Rankings (National League)

- ➡ 1st in stolen bases, caught stealing (19) and batting average at home (.412)
- ➡ 2nd in hit by pitch (21) and batting average vs. right-handed pitchers (.336)
- ➡ 3rd in singles, on-base percentage for a lead-off hitter (.392), lowest batting average on the road (.219) and highest percentage of swings put into play (58.7%)
- ➡ 4th in errors at second base (12)
- ➡ 5th in lowest fielding percentage at second base (.985)
- ➡ 6th in lowest percentage of swings that missed (9.6%)
- ➡ 7th in highest percentage of extra bases taken as a runner (64.1%) and batting average

Roger Bailey

Position: RP/SP
Bats: R **Throws:** R
Ht: 6' 1" **Wt:** 180

Opening Day Age: 26
Born: 10/3/70 in
Chattahoochee, FL
ML Seasons: 2

Overall Statistics

	W	L	Pct.	ERA	G	GS	Sv	IP	H	BB	SO	HR	BR/IP
1996	2	3	.400	6.24	24	11	1	83.2	94	52	45	7	1.75
Career	9	9	.500	5.62	63	17	1	165.0	182	91	78	16	1.65

1996 Situational Stats

	W	L	ERA	Sv	IP		AB	H	HR	RBI	Avg
Home	2	0	7.12	1	36.2	LHB	143	45	4	29	.315
Road	0	3	5.55	0	47.0	RHB	183	49	3	24	.268
First Half	0	1	8.00	0	18.0	Sc Pos	92	27	2	44	.293
Scnd Half	2	2	5.76	1	65.2	Clutch	16	2	0	0	.125

1996 Season

Roger Bailey settled in as a swing man and spot starter on the Rockies' staff in his second major league season. After getting hammered consistently in both roles, Bailey finished the year as a middle reliever, where he earned his two wins.

Pitching, Defense & Hitting

Bailey is not overpowering with his sinker-slider repertoire but he has recently come up with a decent change-up. His strikeout/walk ratio has been very disturbing, though, and his only shot at effectiveness is to keep his fastball low in the strike zone so he can generate ground balls. Bailey is an adequate fielder, but had problems holding runners last year. He has developed into a good hitter, slamming a home run and a triple in his 19 at-bats last season.

1997 Outlook

The Rockies will give Bailey a chance in spring training to earn a spot in the rotation, but his marginal talent will probably end up relegating him to a long-relief slot where he is probably best suited to pitch.

Jason Bates

Position: 2B/3B/SS
Bats: B **Throws:** R
Ht: 5'11" **Wt:** 185

Opening Day Age: 26
Born: 1/5/71 in
Downey, CA
ML Seasons: 2

Overall Statistics

	G	AB	R	H	D	T	HR	RBI	SB	BB	SO	Avg	OBP	Slg
1996	88	160	19	33	8	1	1	9	2	23	34	.206	.312	.288
Career	204	482	61	119	25	5	9	55	5	65	104	.247	.341	.376

1996 Situational Stats

	AB	H	HR	RBI	Avg		AB	H	HR	RBI	Avg
Home	73	20	1	7	.274	LHP	42	10	0	4	.238
Road	87	13	0	2	.149	RHP	118	23	1	5	.195
First Half	96	21	1	5	.219	Sc Pos	39	9	0	8	.231
Scnd Half	64	12	0	4	.188	Clutch	29	4	0	2	.138

1996 Season

With the emergence of Eric Young at second base, Jason Bates became a utility infielder and pinch hitter for the Rockies. He struggled to make a significant contribution in the part-time role, managing only six hits in 33 pinch-hit at-bats.

Hitting, Baserunning & Defense

A switch-hitter, Bates has hit much better from the left side for most of his career, but last year his lefty stroke deserted him almost completely. Reasonably patient, Bates can be overmatched against pitchers with above-average fastballs or those who use rapidly varying speeds. A fast runner, Bates is still a bit raw at stealing and is not a real threat on the bases. Defensively, second base is his best position, since he turns the double play well. He can also handle third and short, though his range and arm at those positions are just average.

1997 Outlook

The Rockies like Bates' aggressive makeup, but unless he significantly improves his hitting, he won't be able to compete with more talented players like Eric Young or Neifi Perez. He will likely remain in a bench role this season.

Mike Munoz

Position: RP
Bats: L **Throws:** L
Ht: 6' 2" **Wt:** 192

Opening Day Age: 31
Born: 7/12/65 in
Baldwin Park, CA
ML Seasons: 8
Pronunciation:
MOON-yohz

Overall Statistics

	W	L	Pct.	ERA	G	GS	Sv	IP	H	BB	SO	HR	BR/IP
1996	2	2	.500	6.65	54	0	0	44.2	55	16	45	4	1.59
Career	11	13	.458	5.38	286	0	5	220.2	240	124	162	22	1.65

1996 Situational Stats

	W	L	ERA	Sv	IP		AB	H	HR	RBI	Avg
Home	2	0	6.95	0	22.0	LHB	60	12	2	3	.200
Road	0	2	6.35	0	22.2	RHB	122	43	3	25	.352
First Half	0	1	7.13	0	24.0	Sc Pos	49	15	1	21	.306
Scnd Half	2	1	6.10	0	20.2	Clutch	53	21	2	10	.396

1996 Season

When he was spotted against left-handed hitters last year, veteran lefty reliever Mike Munoz was very effective, holding lefties to a .200 average. However, he struggled mightily at home and on the road, as right-handed bats continually teed off on him.

Pitching, Defense & Hitting

Munoz has a good sinking fastball which he uses to complement his change-up. However, he is prone to getting his balls up in the strike zone, and he does not have the talent to survive when that starts to happen. Munoz is tough to steal against because he delivers the ball to the plate very quickly. An adequate fielder, Munoz rarely gets an opportunity to use the bat.

1997 Outlook

Without any southpaw alternative at middle relief, the Rockies have given Munoz more than his fair share of chances. However, two straight poor seasons could make him expendable this spring should they find a suitable replacement. His ability to handle left-handed hitters should be enough to get him another chance someplace, but he won't succeed unless he can find some way to neutralize righties.

Jayhawk Owens

Position: C
Bats: R **Throws:** R
Ht: 6' 1" **Wt:** 213

Opening Day Age: 28
Born: 2/10/69 in
Cincinnati, OH
ML Seasons: 4

Overall Statistics

	G	AB	R	H	D	T	HR	RBI	SB	BB	SO	Avg	OBP	Slg
1996	73	180	31	43	9	1	4	17	4	27	56	.239	.338	.367
Career	130	323	54	75	16	2	11	36	5	38	104	.232	.318	.396

1996 Situational Stats

	AB	H	HR	RBI	Avg		AB	H	HR	RBI	Avg
Home	104	32	3	11	.308	LHP	93	23	2	13	.247
Road	76	11	1	6	.145	RHP	87	20	2	4	.230
First Half	102	23	3	11	.225	Sc Pos	48	9	0	11	.188
Scnd Half	78	20	1	6	.256	Clutch	17	2	0	3	.118

1996 Season

Hampered by thumb injuries all season, Jayhawk Owens was not able to take charge of the full-time catching job which was his to lose early in the year. He spent most of the campaign as a backup and played very little over the final six weeks of the season.

Hitting, Baserunning & Defense

Owens has occasional pop at the plate but he can be overpowered with good fastballs. He strikes out far too much for someone of his limited power. He has above-average speed for a catcher and can steal an occasional base. Owens greatest strength is his defensive ability: he handles the Colorado staff well, blocks pitches effectively, and has a strong arm and quick release to send enemy baserunners to the dugout.

1997 Outlook

Though there are mixed opinions about him within the Rockies' organization, Owens is a favorite of GM Bob Gebhard, who made him a second-round draft pick when he was with Minnesota and selected him in the expansion draft. With such friends in high places, Owens will likely get another crack at being the Rockies' number-one catcher this spring.

Lance Painter

Position: RP
Bats: L **Throws:** L
Ht: 6' 1" **Wt:** 197

Opening Day Age: 29
Born: 7/21/67 in
Bedford, England
ML Seasons: 4

Overall Statistics

	W	L	Pct.	ERA	G	GS	Sv	IP	H	BB	SO	HR	BR/IP
1996	4	2	.667	5.86	34	1	0	50.2	56	25	48	12	1.60
Career	13	10	.565	5.65	92	22	1	208.2	254	70	141	35	1.55

1996 Situational Stats

	W	L	ERA	Sv	IP		AB	H	HR	RBI	Avg
Home	3	0	5.81	0	31.0	LHB	52	13	1	7	.250
Road	1	2	5.95	0	19.2	RHB	148	43	11	34	.291
First Half	4	2	6.44	0	43.1	Sc Pos	60	18	4	29	.300
Scnd Half	0	0	2.45	0	7.1	Clutch	31	10	0	2	.323

1996 Season

The Rockies had hoped Lance Painter could be a southpaw stopper in their bullpen. However, he was a bust as a closer, and last year he worked almost exclusively in middle relief. Plagued by shoulder problems which eventually required surgery, he had a disappointing season.

Pitching, Defense & Hitting

Painter can be tough when he is hitting his spots with both of his strikeout pitches, his tailing fastball and late-breaking slider. However, he gets in trouble when he challenges hitters by tossing his offerings over the heart of the plate. As a result, he allowed an incredible number of 12 home runs in only 50-plus innings of work. Painter has a decent move to first, reacts smoothly in the field and handles the bat very well for a pitcher.

1997 Outlook

Painter was claimed on waivers by the Cardinals after the season. He is still a fairly hard thrower. However, he is now 29 years old and coming off a serious operation; if he's fully recovered from shoulder surgery, he will compete for a middle-relief role, but one shouldn't rely on sore-armed hurlers too heavily.

Jeff Reed

Position: C
Bats: L **Throws:** R
Ht: 6' 2" **Wt:** 190

Opening Day Age: 34
Born: 11/12/62 in
Joliet, IL
ML Seasons: 13

Overall Statistics

	G	AB	R	H	D	T	HR	RBI	SB	BB	SO	Avg	OBP	Slg
1996	116	341	34	97	20	1	8	37	2	43	65	.284	.365	.419
Career	838	2101	170	508	91	7	28	184	4	230	328	.242	.316	.332

1996 Situational Stats

	AB	H	HR	RBI	Avg		AB	H	HR	RBI	Avg
Home	179	55	7	25	.307	LHP	30	7	2	4	.233
Road	162	42	1	12	.259	RHP	311	90	6	33	.289
First Half	189	53	7	27	.280	Sc Pos	80	22	2	29	.275
Scnd Half	152	44	1	10	.289	Clutch	49	10	0	2	.204

1996 Season

A career backup, Jeff Reed was the Rockies' starting catcher for much of last season. Reed set career highs in numerous categories, including at-bats, hits, homers and RBI. He batted over .300 in his last 55 starts of the year.

Hitting, Baserunning & Defense

Reed is an opposite-field hitter with a little power who took advantage of Coors Field, slamming seven of his career-high eight homers at home. He is a reasonably patient hitter who can be handled with hard inside fastballs or sliders. Reed is a below-average runner who, last season, stole his first two bases in eight years. He is an excellent handler of pitchers and does a good job of blocking errant balls. Reed's arm is occasionally erratic, but he has a quick release.

1997 Outlook

Reed is one of those players who must fight every spring for a roster spot. However, left-handed hitting catchers are always a valuable commodity, so his job is not in very much jeopardy. Reed is a solid defender behind the plate who more than likely will continue to play in a backup capacity.

Colorado Rockies

Bill Swift

Position: RP/SP
Bats: R **Throws:** R
Ht: 6' 0" **Wt:** 197

Opening Day Age: 35
Born: 10/27/61 in
South Portland, ME
ML Seasons: 11

Overall Statistics

	W	L	Pct.	ERA	G	GS	Sv	IP	H	BB	SO	HR	BR/IP
1996	1	1	.500	5.40	7	3	2	18.1	23	5	5	1	1.53
Career	79	63	.556	3.64	360	181	27	1389.2	1420	430	661	84	1.33

1996 Situational Stats

	W	L	ERA	Sv	IP			AB	H	HR	RBI	Avg
Home	1	1	6.23	1	13.0	LHB		33	10	1	4	.303
Road	0	0	3.38	1	5.1	RHB		42	13	0	6	.310
First Half	0	0	5.40	0	3.1	Sc Pos		22	8	0	8	.364
Scnd Half	1	1	5.40	2	15.0	Clutch		10	2	0	0	.200

1996 Season

Sidelined with shoulder troubles for virtually the entire 1996 season, Bill Swift returned for the final five weeks and ended up offering a glimmer of hope for his future. Returned to his former role as a reliever, Swift converted his only two save opportunities.

Pitching, Defense & Hitting

The only question with Swift is health. He has one of baseball's best sinkers and mixes in an excellent slider and change-up. If he's back to full strength, his pitching style is perfectly suited for Coors Field. However, Swift has not been healthy in three years. One of the best fielding pitchers in the league, he handles the bat well and is not an automatic out at the plate.

1997 Outlook

Swift is a proven winner who unfortunately has never been healthy enough to give the Rockies a return on their investment. However, he threw well at the end of last season, and with a full winter to strengthen his shoulder, Colorado thinks he can finally pay dividends in their rotation this year.

John Vander Wal

Position: LF
Bats: L **Throws:** L
Ht: 6' 2" **Wt:** 198

Opening Day Age: 30
Born: 4/29/66 in Grand
Rapids, MI
ML Seasons: 6

Overall Statistics

	G	AB	R	H	D	T	HR	RBI	SB	BB	SO	Avg	OBP	Slg
1996	104	151	20	38	6	2	5	31	2	19	38	.252	.335	.417
Career	532	851	106	214	36	11	25	125	14	103	176	.251	.332	.408

1996 Situational Stats

	AB	H	HR	RBI	Avg			AB	H	HR	RBI	Avg
Home	72	22	5	24	.306	LHP		10	2	0	2	.200
Road	79	16	0	7	.203	RHP		141	36	5	29	.255
First Half	102	26	4	23	.255	Sc Pos		46	17	3	27	.370
Scnd Half	49	12	1	8	.245	Clutch		35	10	2	6	.286

1996 Season

John Vander Wal, one of baseball's premier pinch hitters, turned in another solid year in 1996. He had 16 pinch hits—three of which were home runs—and got sporadic playing time both at first base and in left field. Do we really need to mention that all of his home runs were hit in Colorado?

Hitting, Baserunning & Defense

Vander Wal sometimes is hesitant to pull the trigger at the plate, but he's a good fastball hitter who can capitalize on hanging breaking balls with occasional power. Due to his problems with southpaws, he almost never is asked to face left-handed pitching. Though he has a weak arm and just average speed, Vander Wal catches everything he reaches in left field. First base, however, is his best position.

1997 Outlook

On a team that churns through pitchers by the dozen, good pinch hitting is a must—which is why Vander Wal will continue to be a valued part of the Rockies' bench. He's also extra insurance at first base in the unlikely event of Andres Galarraga's demise.

Other Colorado Rockies

Garvin Alston (Pos: RHP, Age: 25)

	W	L	Pct.	ERA	G	GS	Sv	IP	H	BB	SO	HR	BR/IP
1996	1	0	1.000	9.00	6	0	0	6.0	9	3	5	1	2.00
Career	1	0	1.000	9.00	6	0	0	6.0	9	3	5	1	2.00

Alston spent most of the year at Triple-A Colorado Springs, but joined the Rockies for the month of June to alleviate their bullpen troubles. He didn't pitch well, but should be back in the future. 1997 Outlook: C

Eric Anthony (Pos: RF/LF, Age: 29, Bats: L)

	G	AB	R	H	D	T	HR	RBI	SB	BB	SO	Avg	OBP	Slg
1996	79	185	32	45	8	0	12	22	0	32	56	.243	.353	.481
Career	635	1925	241	444	78	6	76	264	22	205	473	.231	.304	.396

Plagued by injury problems over the past few years, Anthony was sold to the Rockies at the end of July. He can still get on base, but his .233 average at Coors Field was disturbing. 1997 Outlook: C

Robbie Beckett (Pos: LHP, Age: 24)

	W	L	Pct.	ERA	G	GS	Sv	IP	H	BB	SO	HR	BR/IP
1996	0	0	-	13.50	5	0	0	5.1	6	9	6	3	2.81
Career	0	0	-	13.50	5	0	0	5.1	6	9	6	3	2.81

Beckett is a 24-year-old pitching prospect who walked nine batters in his five innings of September work. He hasn't shown consistent success at any minor league level. 1997 Outlook: C

Jorge Brito (Pos: C, Age: 30, Bats: R)

	G	AB	R	H	D	T	HR	RBI	SB	BB	SO	Avg	OBP	Slg
1996	8	14	1	1	0	0	0	0	0	1	8	.071	.235	.071
Career	26	65	6	12	3	0	0	7	1	3	25	.185	.254	.231

Brito split the catching duties with Jeff Reed until Jayhawk Owens arrived on the scene. He had a good season at Triple-A, but managed just one hit out of 14 April at-bats with the Rockies. 1997 Outlook: C

John Burke (Pos: RHP, Age: 27)

	W	L	Pct.	ERA	G	GS	Sv	IP	H	BB	SO	HR	BR/IP
1996	2	1	.667	7.47	11	0	0	15.2	21	7	19	3	1.79
Career	2	1	.667	7.47	11	0	0	15.2	21	7	19	3	1.79

Brought up to help the Colorado bullpen finish out the year, Burke notched 11 September appearances. He was hit pretty hard, but his strikeout/walk numbers were excellent. 1997 Outlook: B

Pedro Castellano (Pos: 2B, Age: 27, Bats: R)

	G	AB	R	H	D	T	HR	RBI	SB	BB	SO	Avg	OBP	Slg
1996	13	17	1	2	0	0	0	2	0	3	6	.118	.286	.118
Career	51	93	13	15	2	0	3	9	1	13	25	.161	.271	.280

Castellano's lackluster appearance in May overshadowed what was a fine season in the minors. Currently a free agent, he was not offered a contract by Colorado. Maybe they know something we don't. 1997 Outlook: D

Alan Cockrell (Pos: RF, Age: 34, Bats: R)

	G	AB	R	H	D	T	HR	RBI	SB	BB	SO	Avg	OBP	Slg
1996	9	8	0	2	1	0	0	2	0	0	4	.250	.222	.375
Career	9	8	0	2	1	0	0	2	0	0	4	.250	.222	.375

Cockrell accumulated a few pinch hit at-bats after being called up in September. He had a decent year at Triple-A, but at 34, his days are numbered. 1997 Outlook: D

Steve Decker (Pos: C, Age: 31, Bats: R)

	G	AB	R	H	D	T	HR	RBI	SB	BB	SO	Avg	OBP	Slg
1996	67	147	24	36	3	0	2	20	1	18	29	.245	.323	.306
Career	235	625	55	137	15	2	13	67	2	63	115	.219	.291	.312

Decker was bought from San Francisco in August and started occasionally at catcher near the end of the season. He'll have competition, but he could snare a backup role this season. 1997 Outlook: B

Mike Farmer (Pos: LHP, Age: 28)

	W	L	Pct.	ERA	G	GS	Sv	IP	H	BB	SO	HR	BR/IP
1996	0	1	.000	7.71	7	4	0	28.0	32	13	16	8	1.61
Career	0	1	.000	7.71	7	4	0	28.0	32	13	16	8	1.61

Another pitcher who was overwhelmed by the looming presence of Coors Field, Farmer was terrible in his May stint with the Rockies. He should get another shot, but he's getting older (28). 1997 Outlook: C

Ryan Hawblitzel (Pos: RHP, Age: 25)

	W	L	Pct.	ERA	G	GS	Sv	IP	H	BB	SO	HR	BR/IP
1996	0	1	.000	6.00	8	0	0	15.0	18	6	7	2	1.60
Career	0	1	.000	6.00	8	0	0	15.0	18	6	7	2	1.60

Hawblitzel made eight appearances from the bullpen over the summer. Amazingly enough, he pitched better at home than on the road, but still poorly nonetheless. 1997 Outlook: C

Terry Jones (Pos: CF, Age: 26, Bats: B)

	G	AB	R	H	D	T	HR	RBI	SB	BB	SO	Avg	OBP	Slg
1996	12	10	6	3	0	0	0	1	0	0	3	.300	.273	.300
Career	12	10	6	3	0	0	0	1	0	0	3	.300	.273	.300

Jones saw limited action in September as a pinch hitter and as a defensive replacement in center field. His minor league numbers aren't that great, and it'll be tough to crack the strong Colorado outfield. 1997 Outlook: C

Dave Nied (Pos: RHP, Age: 28)

	W	L	Pct.	ERA	G	GS	Sv	IP	H	BB	SO	HR	BR/IP
1996	0	2	.000	13.50	6	1	0	5.1	5	8	4	1	2.44
Career	17	18	.486	5.06	52	41	0	241.2	262	105	146	26	1.52

Nied has been shuffled back and forth from the minors ever since he sustained elbow ligament damage a year ago. He has yet to come close to his outstanding 1994 season. Nied will get a new start this year with the Reds, who signed him to a minor league contract. 1997 Outlook: C

Harvey Pulliam (Pos: LF, Age: 29, Bats: R)

	G	AB	R	H	D	T	HR	RBI	SB	BB	SO	Avg	OBP	Slg
1996	10	15	2	2	0	0	0	0	0	2	6	.133	.235	.133
Career	64	120	16	30	8	0	5	13	0	8	34	.250	.302	.442

After injuring his right knee in April, Pulliam got a few starts with the Rockies in June before he was sent down to Triple-A Colorado Springs for the rest of the season. He's not a prospect. 1997 Outlook: D

Bryan Rekar (Pos: RHP, Age: 24)

	W	L	Pct.	ERA	G	GS	Sv	IP	H	BB	SO	HR	BR/IP
1996	2	4	.333	8.95	14	11	0	58.1	87	26	25	11	1.94
Career	6	10	.375	6.59	29	25	0	143.1	182	50	85	22	1.62

Rekar pitched well in '95, but was hammered hard and often by enemy hitters last season. He was still shaky after spending time in the minors, but he'll be effective if he regains his confidence. 1997 Outlook: B

Milt Thompson (Pos: LF, Age: 38, Bats: L)

	G	AB	R	H	D	T	HR	RBI	SB	BB	SO	Avg	OBP	Slg
1996	62	66	3	7	2	0	0	3	1	7	13	.106	.192	.136
Career	1359	3761	491	1029	156	37	47	357	214	336	635	.274	.335	.372

Acquired off waivers in June, Thompson saw some pinch-hitting action before being designated for reassignment a month later. At 38 with a .106 average last year, his career is undoubtedly over. 1997 Outlook: D

Colorado Rockies Minor League Prospects

Organization Overview:

It's too soon to evaluate the Rockies' farm system on the basis of the major league talent it's produced. Colorado has built its major league team through trades and free agency, and very few young players have had a chance to break through. A few young pitchers have been brought along, but their progress has been understandably slow. Jamey Wright's progress was encouraging last year, but Bryan Rekar—who had been equally impressive the year before—cracked under the pressure. In the draft, the Rockies have gone after pitchers almost exclusively, and a wave of talented arms is percolating up from the depths of the system. There are three potential impact players among their position prospects, but beyond that, the offensive talent is thin. The biggest challenge will be to ease their pitchers into Coors Field when the time comes.

Mark Brownson

Position: P
Bats: R **Throws:** R
Ht: 6' 2" **Wt:** 175

Opening Day Age: 21
Born: 6/17/75 in West Palm Beach, FL

Recent Statistics

	W	L	ERA	G	GS	Sv	IP	H	R	BB	SO	HR
94 R Rockies	4	1	1.66	19	4	3	54.1	48	18	6	72	2
95 AA New Haven	0	0	1.50	1	1	0	6.0	4	2	1	4	1
95 A Salem	2	1	4.02	9	1	1	15.2	16	8	10	9	0
95 A Asheville	6	7	4.01	23	12	1	98.2	106	52	29	94	12
96 AA New Haven	8	13	3.50	37	19	3	144.0	141	73	43	155	10

The Rockies still can't decide whether Mark Brownson should be a starter or a reliever. His stuff seems to be better-suited to starting: he's not overpowering, but throws several breaking and offspeed pitches for strikes. So far, he's been able to get a lot of strikeouts with his limited stuff, but that may change as he moves up the ladder. His future will depend on how well he's able to adjust to Triple-A this year.

Angel Echevarria

Position: OF
Bats: R **Throws:** R
Ht: 6' 4" **Wt:** 215

Opening Day Age: 25
Born: 5/25/71 in Bridgeport, CT

Recent Statistics

	G	AB	R	H	D	T	HR	RBI	SB	BB	SO	AVG
96 AAA Col. Sprng	110	415	67	140	19	2	16	74	4	38	81	.337
96 NL Colorado	26	21	2	6	0	0	0	6	0	2	5	.286
96 MLE	110	424	56	149	19	1	19	62	3	32	81	.351

Although he's too old to get really excited about, Angel Echevarria could put up good numbers in the majors—especially in Colorado. He's not much of an outfielder,

and it looks like the best he'll be able to do there is pinch hit and fill in. Still, he's got the bat to excel in that role, and may earn himself a larger opportunity if things break right.

Derrick Gibson

Position: OF
Bats: R **Throws:** R
Ht: 6' 2" **Wt:** 227

Opening Day Age: 22
Born: 2/5/75 in Winter Haven, FL

Recent Statistics

	G	AB	R	H	D	T	HR	RBI	SB	BB	SO	AVG
93 R Rockies	34	119	13	18	2	2	0	10	3	5	55	.151
94 A Bend	73	284	47	75	19	5	12	57	14	29	102	.264
95 A Asheville	135	506	91	148	16	10	32	115	31	29	136	.292
96 AA New Haven	122	449	58	115	21	4	15	62	3	31	125	.256
96 MLE	122	474	62	140	24	4	23	67	2	28	128	.295

Derrick Gibson is built like a football player, and he plays like one, too. He's big and strong, and runs well, but there a lot of things about the game of baseball that he just hasn't learned yet. When the Rockies jumped him to Double-A last year, the pitchers were able to exploit his flaws, and his production fell off dramatically. His defense and basestealing were unacceptable. The tremendous raw power was apparent, but so was his equally tremendous inability to read pitches. On balance, his run production is fairly advanced for someone his age, and his upside is among the best in baseball, but his development will hinge upon his ability to close the gaping holes in his game.

Todd Helton

Position: 1B
Bats: L **Throws:** L
Ht: 6' 2" **Wt:** 195

Opening Day Age: 23
Born: 8/20/73 in Knoxville, TN

Recent Statistics

	G	AB	R	H	D	T	HR	RBI	SB	BB	SO	AVG
95 A Asheville	54	201	24	51	11	1	1	15	1	25	32	.254
96 AA New Haven	93	319	46	106	24	2	7	51	2	51	37	.332
96 AAA Col. Sprng	21	71	13	25	4	1	2	13	0	11	12	.352
96 MLE	114	404	60	145	32	3	11	66	1	56	50	.359

In the entire history of the Colorado franchise, they've used all of their high draft picks on pitchers, except one. In 1995, they took Todd Helton with the eighth pick in the country, and it's paid off. Helton has become perhaps the best raw hitter in the minors, a high-average hitter with doubles power and tremendous ability to make contact. He's capable of hitting .300 in the majors right now; in Coors Field, he could contend for the batting title.

Doug Million

Position: P
Bats: L **Throws:** L
Ht: 6' 4" **Wt:** 175

Opening Day Age: 21
Born: 10/13/75 in Fort Thomas, KY

Recent Statistics

	W	L	ERA	G	GS	Sv	IP	H	R	BB	SO	HR
94 R Rockies	1	0	1.50	3	3	0	12.0	8	3	3	19	0
94 A Bend	5	3	2.34	10	10	0	57.2	50	23	21	75	4
95 A Salem	5	7	4.62	24	23	0	111.0	111	71	79	85	6
96 A Salem	7	5	2.53	17	16	0	106.2	84	37	60	99	1
96 AA New Haven	3	3	3.15	10	10	0	54.1	54	23	40	40	2

Doug Million was the Rockies' top pick in the '94 draft, and last year he began to show why. He showed up to camp in much better shape, and when the Rockies returned him to the Carolina League, where he'd struggled in '95, he found the groove. His command suffered after a promotion to Double-A, but Million remained well-advanced for his age. His hard-breaking curveball has been called one of the best breaking pitches in the minors, and he'll make great strides as he refines his command.

Neifi Perez

Position: SS
Bats: B **Throws:** R
Ht: 6' 0" **Wt:** 164

Opening Day Age: 22
Born: 2/2/75 in Villa Mella, DR

Recent Statistics

	G	AB	R	H	D	T	HR	RBI	SB	BB	SO	AVG
96 AAA Col. Spmg	133	570	77	180	28	12	7	72	16	21	48	.316
96 NL Colorado	17	45	4	7	2	0	0	3	2	0	8	.156
96 MLE	133	577	65	187	31	14	9	61	12	17	47	.324

No one expected shortstop Neifi Perez to have a standout season in the Pacific Coast League at age 21, but he did, and now his timetable has been vastly accelerated. In fact, the Rockies would like to get him into the lineup immediately, either at shortstop or second base. He's ready for it, too. His defense is major league caliber—he was voted the best defensive shortstop in the PCL—and he's capable of hitting for a good average already. In time, he may develop some home run power; for now, he hits lots of doubles and triples. If the Rockies can find a way to slot him in, he could be one the top rookies of '97.

John Thomson

Position: P
Bats: R **Throws:** R
Ht: 6' 3" **Wt:** 170

Opening Day Age: 23
Born: 10/1/73 in Vicksburg, MS

Recent Statistics

	W	L	ERA	G	GS	Sv	IP	H	R	BB	SO	HR
93 R Rockies	3	5	4.62	11	11	0	50.2	43	40	31	36	0
94 A Asheville	6	6	2.85	19	15	0	88.1	70	34	33	79	3
94 A Central Val	3	1	3.28	9	8	0	49.1	43	20	18	41	0
95 AA New Haven	7	8	4.18	26	24	0	131.1	132	69	56	82	8
96 AA New Haven	9	4	2.86	16	16	0	97.2	82	35	27	86	8
96 AAA Col. Spmg	4	7	5.04	11	11	0	69.2	76	45	26	62	6

Righthander John Thomson has good stuff, but can't get by on velocity. He mixes his pitches, and can be very effective when he hits his spots. He was able to do that in the first half in Double-A, but got hit hard in the second half at Triple-A. His overall numbers were still impressive, and he'll probably fare better in the PCL during his second time around. He's only 23, so the Rockies may give him a while to prepare himself for the even-bigger jump to Colorado.

Andy Velazquez

Position: OF
Bats: R **Throws:** R
Ht: 6' 0" **Wt:** 170

Opening Day Age: 21
Born: 12/15/75 in Santurce, PR

Recent Statistics

	G	AB	R	H	D	T	HR	RBI	SB	BB	SO	AVG
93 R Rockies	39	147	20	36	4	2	2	20	7	16	35	.245
94 A Asheville	119	447	50	106	22	3	11	39	9	23	120	.237
95 A Salem	131	497	74	149	25	6	13	69	7	40	102	.300
96 AA New Haven	132	486	72	141	29	4	19	62	5	53	114	.290
96 MLE	132	516	78	171	33	4	30	67	5	48	117	.331

Andy Velazquez's strong throwing arm isn't the only resemblance he bears to his uncle, Roberto Clemente. Velazquez is also a powerful hitter, with a tremendous ability to drive the ball for someone so young. He's still filling out, and his power should continue to grow. Next year, he'll move up to Colorado Springs, where his production could really take off. He's also got good speed, and enough range to cover center field. He's a blue-chipper in every phase of his game.

Others to Watch

A deceptive short-arm delivery helped righthander **Chris Macca** to ring up 30 saves with an incredible 1.20 ERA between A-ball and Double-A. Macca can hit 90 on the gun, and is only 22 years old this year. Look for him to begin the year in Double-A. . . Lefthander **Mike Kusiewicz** posted good numbers in Double-A at age 19. He has great control, but must prove that his arm can handle the rigors of starting for a full season. . . Righthander **Mike Saipe** will move up to Triple-A after posting good results in the Eastern League. He has excellent control, but pitching in the Pacific Coast League will test his limits in a hurry. . . Short reliever **Jake Viano** was completely unable to make the jump from Double-A to Triple-A. All he's got is a curveball, so he must have his confidence in order to succeed. He may fare better in his second try. . . Catcher **Blake Barthol** hit for good power and average in his first full season of pro ball. He'll likely see Double-A this year at age 24.

Jim Leyland

1996 Season

Jim Leyland is regarded as one of baseball's best managers for several reasons. He has an excellent rapport with his players, but he is also a no-nonsense leader who makes it clear who's the boss. He has won with young teams and veteran teams, and has learned to be patient during his various lean years with the undermanned Pirates. One adjustment he will need to make this year is managing a Marlin team with much higher expectations than those in Pittsburgh the last few years.

Offense

Like all successful managers, Leyland can adapt his style to the talents of his roster. He has always liked aggressive baseball and will steal and hit and run when given the opportunity. He also has looked for places to use platoon players as a way to keep his bench fresh. He will often gamble with mid-inning pinch-hit moves, especially if he has confidence in his bullpen.

Pitching & Defense

Pitchers who have played for Leyland rave about his feel for keeping them fresh. He will not overwork his key relievers, even if it means sacrificing a game along the way to ensure they don't blow out. He has always used a bullpen by committee. With the Marlins he might have some adjustments to make since he has a big-time closer for the first time, namely Robb Nen. Leyland calls more than his share of pitchouts and looks for ways to substitute for defense in the late innings.

1997 Outlook

Leyland already knows the Marlins' personnel and has pushed to add at least one more big hitter and another established starter. He knows the mountain he must climb in trying to catch the Braves in the N.L. East, but Leyland and the Marlins fully expect to be in the wild-card hunt at the very least this year.

Born: 12/15/44 in Pittsburgh, PA

Playing Experience: No major league experience

Managerial Experience: 11 seasons

Manager Statistics

Year	Team, Lg	W	L	Pct	GB	Finish
1996	Pittsburgh, NL	73	89	.451	15.0	5th Central
11 Seasons		851	863	.496	—	—

1996 Starting Pitchers by Days Rest

	≤3	4	5	6+
Pirates Starts	0	87	41	17
Pirates ERA	0.00	4.89	3.62	6.33
NL Avg Starts	4	86	41	21
NL ERA	4.06	4.28	4.23	4.58

1996 Situational Stats

	Jim Leyland	NL Average
Hit & Run Success %	40.0	39.0
Stolen Base Success %	72.0	71.6
Platoon Pct.	50.8	51.9
Defensive Subs	14	20
High-Pitch Outings	10	13
Quick/Slow Hooks	27/8	19/12
Sacrifice Attempts	101	92

1996 Rankings (National League)

➡ 1st in steals of home plate (3), squeeze plays (11) and starts with over 140 pitches (1)

➡ 2nd in least caught steals of home plate (1), double steals (8) and hit-and-run percentage (40.0%)

➡ 3rd in least caught steals of second base (38), pinch hitters used (299) and quick hooks (27)

Kurt Abbott

1996 Season

Kurt Abbott entered 1996 as one of the Marlins' more promising young players, but his career took a turn for the worse last year. Shoulder and hamstring troubles sidelined him early in the year. Then he was sent to Triple-A Charlotte on a rehab assignment after he had problems with dizziness, and he remained in the minors until June 13. When he returned, Abbott was moved off shortstop by rookie Edgar Renteria. He saw some duty at second and then finally settled at third base, where he made 27 starts.

Hitting

Abbott has the strength and bat speed to be a 20-homer man. However, he remains a frequent strikeout victim because of his inability to adjust to breaking balls and his overall lack of plate discipline. He has never learned how to lay off sliders or offspeed stuff. A first-ball, fastball hitter, Abbott becomes very defensive when he falls behind in the count and is easy prey for pitchers who can keep the ball off the plate.

Baserunning & Defense

A good athlete, Abbott aggressively goes after the extra base. However, he has only average speed and is a low-percentage basestealer in his few attempts. Abbott's range at shortstop is adequate, so a move to third base suits his skills. His strong arm is helped by the extra time he has to throw from third. He has only fair hands. Abbott had difficulty adjusting to turning the double play in his brief stint at second.

1997 Outlook

Abbott has been replaced as the Marlins' shortstop by Renteria, so third base is his next option. The Marlins have made no secret about wanting to obtain an established third baseman, so Abbott's role will likely be reduced to utility duty if he sticks around. His power-hitting potential makes him potential trade bait.

Position: SS/2B/3B
Bats: R **Throws:** R
Ht: 6' 0" **Wt:** 185

Opening Day Age: 27
Born: 6/2/69 in Zanesville, OH
ML Seasons: 4

Overall Statistics

	G	AB	R	H	D	T	HR	RBI	SB	BB	SO	Avg	OBP	Slg
1996	109	320	37	81	18	7	8	33	3	22	99	.253	.307	.428
Career	350	1146	149	289	54	17	37	135	12	77	327	.252	.305	.426

Where He Hits the Ball

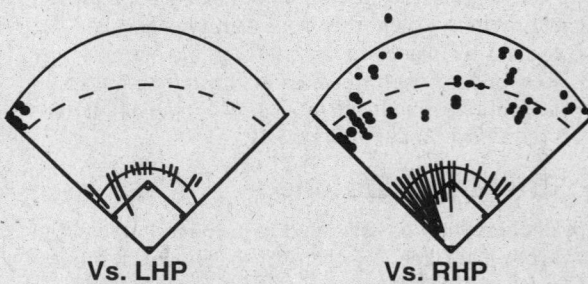

Vs. LHP   **Vs. RHP**

1996 Situational Stats

	AB	H	HR	RBI	Avg		AB	H	HR	RBI	Avg
Home	135	41	6	22	.304	LHP	67	23	2	9	.343
Road	185	40	2	11	.216	RHP	253	58	6	24	.229
First Half	165	41	3	8	.248	Sc Pos	63	15	2	25	.238
Scnd Half	155	40	5	25	.258	Clutch	53	12	1	4	.226

1996 Rankings (National League)

➡ 8th in triples
➡ Led the Marlins in triples

Alex Arias

1996 Season

In his fourth season with the Marlins, Alex Arias continued his career-long role as one of baseball's best utility men. While he played more often at third base than anywhere else, Arias saw action at all four infield positions, including his first career game at first base. His most important job was as a pinch hitter, going 10 for 28 with eight RBI in that role.

Hitting

With little power, Arias is a spray hitter who neither strikes out nor walks with much frequency. He is a decent fastball hitter who is content to take outside pitches to the opposite field. He occasionally can turn on a pitch for an infrequent extra-base hit, but is usually unable to pull anything but offspeed stuff. He handles the bat fairly well and can be used in hit-and-run situations.

Baserunning & Defense

Though Arias can fill in at any infield position, the reality is that he plays none of them very well. He probably is most comfortable at second base, where he has average range and arm strength. Arias is also a serviceable third baseman, though his arm is somewhat short to play that position regularly. He is a liability at shortstop, where is range is adequate. He also can be erratic with his throws. Arias' speed is good enough to steal an occasional base or stretch a long hit into a triple. However, he has never been a burner on the basepaths.

1997 Outlook

With his weak defense and lack of power, Arias will never be an everyday player. However, he has made himself into a productive pinch hitter and he fills a niche on Jim Leyland's bench. Look for him to get his usual 200 at-bats this year while getting into about 100 contests.

Position: 3B/SS
Bats: R **Throws:** R
Ht: 6' 3" **Wt:** 185

Opening Day Age: 29
Born: 11/20/67 in New York, NY
ML Seasons: 5

Overall Statistics

	G	AB	R	H	D	T	HR	RBI	SB	BB	SO	Avg	OBP	Slg
1996	100	224	27	62	11	2	3	26	2	17	28	.277	.335	.384
Career	381	901	94	243	36	5	8	94	4	86	98	.270	.338	.347

Where He Hits the Ball

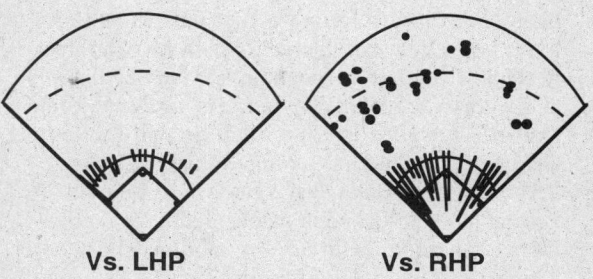

Vs. LHP **Vs. RHP**

1996 Situational Stats

	AB	H	HR	RBI	Avg		AB	H	HR	RBI	Avg
Home	109	35	1	15	.321	LHP	55	15	0	4	.273
Road	115	27	2	11	.235	RHP	169	47	3	22	.278
First Half	108	31	2	11	.287	Sc Pos	68	18	1	24	.265
Scnd Half	116	31	1	15	.267	Clutch	45	11	0	7	.244

1996 Rankings (National League)
➡ Did not rank near the top or bottom in any category

Florida Marlins

Kevin Brown

1996 Season

Though he finished second in the Cy Young voting to John Smoltz, no starting pitcher was better last season than Kevin Brown. His earned run average was lower, by nearly a full run, than any other starter in the majors and he was among league leaders in virtually every pitching category. Only the worst run-support of any regular starter in the league prevented him from winning 20 games.

Pitching

Few pitchers have a better combination of nasty stuff and outstanding control than Brown. He has what most scouts consider the best sinker in baseball, a heavy fastball that produces groundballs and so many broken bats that batting against it has been compared to hitting a shot put. Brown also has an excellent cut fastball, which he can throw in the low 90s and is tough on left-handed hitters, and a top-rate slider. He can also throw a rising fastball, though it is not a pitch he will use very frequently, and he has an above-average change-up. Brown's success last year was a product of getting himself locked in mechanically, in particular staying on top with his arm motion. The result was both a remarkable strikeout-to-walk ratio and an improved ability to carry his best stuff into the late innings.

Defense & Hitting

Brown fields his position well while also doing a good job of holding runners with an above-average pickoff move. His only pre-1996 major league at-bat came in 1990 and it showed.

1997 Outlook

Brown has always been tough to hit, so no one should have been surprised at how dominating he was last season. He has gained maturity and consistency which means that with Florida likely to have a better offense, Brown has a great chance to break through and become a 20-game winner again this year.

Position: SP
Bats: R **Throws:** R
Ht: 6' 4" **Wt:** 195

Opening Day Age: 32
Born: 3/14/65 in McIntyre, GA
ML Seasons: 10

Overall Statistics

	W	L	Pct.	ERA	G	GS	Sv	IP	H	BB	SO	HR	BR/IP
1996	17	11	.607	1.89	32	32	0	233.0	187	33	159	8	0.94
Career	105	84	.556	3.52	245	244	0	1684.0	1664	509	1018	103	1.29

How Often He Throws Strikes

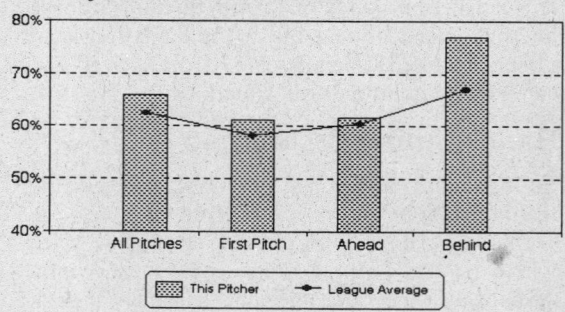

1996 Situational Stats

	W	L	ERA	Sv	IP		AB	H	HR	RBI	Avg
Home	12	4	1.69	0	138.1	LHB	411	91	3	20	.221
Road	5	7	2.19	0	94.2	RHB	438	96	5	30	.219
First Half	7	7	1.89	0	119.0	Sc Pos	149	28	1	39	.188
Scnd Half	10	4	1.89	0	114.0	Clutch	107	28	1	10	.262

1996 Rankings (National League)

→ 1st in ERA, shutouts (3), hit batsmen (16), lowest slugging percentage allowed (.289), highest groundball/flyball ratio allowed (3.4), least run support per 9 innings (3.5), least home runs allowed per 9 innings (.31), ERA at home (1.69) and ERA on the road (2.19)

→ 2nd in GDPs induced (26), lowest on-base percentage allowed (.262), least baserunners allowed per 9 innings (9.1) and lowest batting average allowed with runners in scoring position (.188)

→ 3rd in wins, complete games (5) and highest strikeout/walk ratio (4.8)

→ 4th in lowest batting average allowed (.220)

Gregg Colbrunn

Position: 1B
Bats: R **Throws:** R
Ht: 6' 0" **Wt:** 200

Opening Day Age: 27
Born: 7/26/69 in
Fontana, CA
ML Seasons: 5

1996 Season

Gregg Colbrunn followed what the Marlins had hoped was a breakthrough 1995 season with a disappointing '96 campaign. He had flashes of brilliance, including a 21-game hitting streak that ended in June, but he suffered a wrist injury in late July—another in what has been a series of hand and wrist injuries for Colbrunn. He came back to make August his best month of the year, but he finished with a weak September, and overall the Marlins were disappointed with his lack of RBI production.

Hitting

Colbrunn has a compact swing and the power to hit home runs as far as anyone. However, he remains inconsistent in his pitch selection. Though he does not run up big strikeout totals, Colbrunn does not work deep counts and is often content just to put balls into play instead of waiting for a pitch he can cream. He also crowds the plate, which makes him vulnerable to hard stuff inside and prone to getting hit in the hands and wrists.

Baserunning & Defense

A former catcher, Colbrunn has only fair speed, though he will occasionally surprise with a stolen base. He has decent hands at first, but his range is just so-so. He has improved over the last two years in his ability to dig low throws out of the dirt.

1997 Outlook

Florida officials believe Colbrunn's mediocre production at a power position was a major factor in their lack of run-scoring ability last year. So the Marlins have openly looked to add punch at the position, either by acquiring a new first baseman or by moving Jeff Conine in from left field. Colbrunn would seem to be prime trade bait; if he sticks with the Marlins, he'll probably be relegated to part-time duty.

Overall Statistics

	G	AB	R	H	D	T	HR	RBI	SB	BB	SO	Avg	OBP	Slg
1996	141	511	60	146	26	2	16	69	4	25	76	.286	.333	.438
Career	448	1515	174	423	75	3	51	230	23	68	239	.279	.317	.434

Where He Hits the Ball

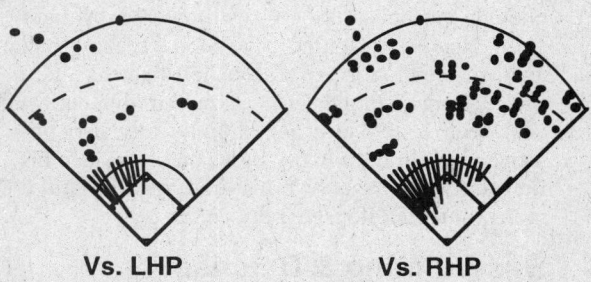

Vs. LHP   **Vs. RHP**

1996 Situational Stats

	AB	H	HR	RBI	Avg		AB	H	HR	RBI	Avg
Home	242	72	7	34	.298	LHP	113	37	6	17	.327
Road	269	74	9	35	.275	RHP	398	109	10	52	.274
First Half	321	95	8	36	.296	Sc Pos	146	39	2	52	.267
Scnd Half	190	51	8	33	.268	Clutch	90	25	0	10	.278

1996 Rankings (National League)

- ➡ 2nd in GDPs (22) and most GDPs per GDP situation (20.2%)
- ➡ 3rd in fielding percentage at first base (.995)
- ➡ 4th in lowest percentage of pitches taken (45.1%)
- ➡ 5th in hit by pitch (14)
- ➡ 7th in batting average with two strikes (.270)
- ➡ 10th in errors at first base (6)
- ➡ Led the Marlins in hit by pitch (14), GDPs (22), highest groundball/flyball ratio (1.4) and batting average with two strikes (.270)

Jeff Conine

1996 Season

A career high in home runs and another solid RBI season further established Jeff Conine's reputation as one of the league's most consistent performers. Last year Conine was often used at his original position, first base, and he seemed to welcome the shift from left field, where he was never completely comfortable. Conine finished the year on a tear, hitting .312 with a .516 slugging average in September.

Hitting

Conine has a short, powerful stroke but he takes some time getting his hands into hitting position, which makes him susceptible to high fastballs. As a result, he is prone to long spells when he loses enough bat speed to get overpowered by hard stuff. However, Conine is a good breaking-ball and offspeed hitter. He crushes left-handed pitching, ranking among the best against southpaws last year with a .393 average. Conine has also improved his ability to work bases on balls since his first few seasons as he's matured, making him a more valuable offensive performer.

Baserunning & Defense

Conine has below-average speed and only rarely attempts to steal. However, he is an aggressive runner who is very tough when trying to break up double plays. He is only a fair outfielder with poor range and just an average arm. However, he's a good first baseman with excellent hands and polished skills. A world-class racquetball player, he has quick reactions around the bag.

1997 Outlook

It was likely a sign of things to come when Conine was moved to first last year. Florida is a better club if it obtains an established left fielder and puts Conine at first where he has always preferred to play. The result should be better defense for the Marlins, and more .300-25-100 seasons from the dependable Conine.

Position: LF/1B
Bats: R **Throws:** R
Ht: 6' 1" **Wt:** 220

Opening Day Age: 30
Born: 6/27/66 in Tacoma, WA
ML Seasons: 6
Pronunciation: COH-nine

Overall Statistics

	G	AB	R	H	D	T	HR	RBI	SB	BB	SO	Avg	OBP	Slg
1996	157	597	84	175	32	2	26	95	1	62	121	.293	.360	.484
Career	604	2237	304	667	116	15	81	372	6	230	470	.298	.362	.472

Where He Hits the Ball

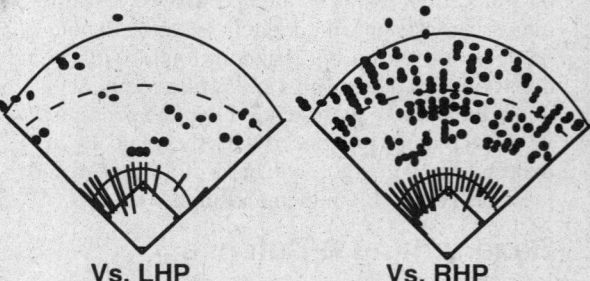

Vs. LHP   Vs. RHP

1996 Situational Stats

	AB	H	HR	RBI	Avg		AB	H	HR	RBI	Avg
Home	292	91	15	61	.312	LHP	122	48	9	31	.393
Road	305	84	11	34	.275	RHP	475	127	17	64	.267
First Half	321	96	15	49	.299	Sc Pos	171	46	5	65	.269
Scnd Half	276	79	11	46	.286	Clutch	100	29	4	14	.290

1996 Rankings (National League)

- ➡ 2nd in batting average vs. left-handed pitchers (.393) and lowest cleanup slugging percentage (.417)
- ➡ 3rd in lowest fielding percentage in left field (.975)
- ➡ 4th in slugging percentage vs. left-handed pitchers (.656) and on-base percentage vs. left-handed pitchers (.449)
- ➡ 5th in errors in left field (5)
- ➡ 7th in highest percentage of swings on the first pitch (43.8%)
- ➡ 8th in lowest groundball/flyball ratio (0.9)
- ➡ 10th in batting average on a 3-1 count (.600)
- ➡ Led the Marlins in at-bats, hits, singles and strikeouts

Chris Hammond

1996 Season

After a 9-6 season as a member of the Marlins rotation in 1995, Chris Hammond wound up being bounced from the Marlins' starting rotation early last year. Hammond was sent to the bullpen after going 1-5 with a 10.88 ERA in his first six starts. He fared better in relief, posting a 3.38 ERA in 29 outings. However, Hammond was not trusted with many important assignments.

Pitching

Throughout his career, Hammond has had difficulty maintaining his aggressiveness. He becomes tentative when he gets into trouble and gets reluctant to throw his fastball, instead falling in love with his change-up and slider. More than one pitching coach and manager have told him that he can't win unless he establishes his fastball, but the advice never seems to sink in for very long. Hammond only throws in the mid-80s but when he loses his will to throw the fastball, it makes his excellent change-up too easy to time. That's what happened last year. As a result, opposing hitters batted .315 with 14 homers in only 81 innings against him.

Defense & Hitting

Hammond has one of the best pickoff moves in baseball. Only four runners attempted to steal off him last year, and only three players have stolen successfully against him since 1994. Hammond is also a fair fielding pitcher and can help himself with the bat, though he struggled at the plate last season.

1997 Outlook

It's always difficult to give up on lefthanders, but Hammond is not likely to remain in the Marlins' future plans. He has only marginal value in the bullpen and Florida does not intend to put him back into the rotation, which means he will likely be pitching elsewhere in 1997.

Position: RP/SP
Bats: L **Throws:** L
Ht: 6' 1" **Wt:** 195

Opening Day Age: 31
Born: 1/21/66 in Atlanta, GA
ML Seasons: 7

Overall Statistics

	W	L	Pct.	ERA	G	GS	Sv	IP	H	BB	SO	HR	BR/IP
1996	5	8	.385	6.56	38	9	0	81.0	104	27	50	14	1.62
Career	43	49	.467	4.39	159	125	0	764.2	801	278	457	73	1.41

How Often He Throws Strikes

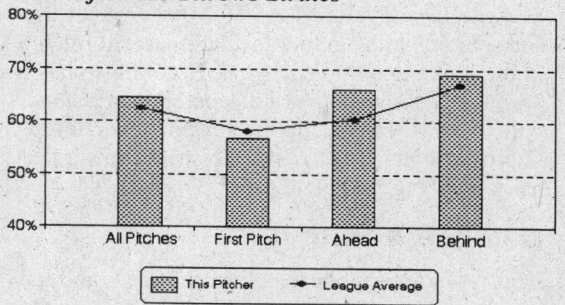

1996 Situational Stats

	W	L	ERA	Sv	IP		AB	H	HR	RBI	Avg
Home	2	2	4.32	0	33.1	LHB	88	27	3	21	.307
Road	3	6	8.12	0	47.2	RHB	242	77	11	46	.318
First Half	2	5	7.22	0	38.2	Sc Pos	94	33	4	51	.351
Scnd Half	3	3	5.95	0	42.1	Clutch	48	11	1	5	.229

1996 Rankings (National League)

➡ Did not rank near the top or bottom in any category

Mark Hutton

1996 Season

Acquired in the late-season deal that sent David Weathers to the Yankees, Mark Hutton opened the Marlins' eyes with a series of solid starting efforts. Hutton made nine starts for Florida, winning four of them and pitching impressively. He worked eight shutout innings in his final start of the year.

Pitching

Hutton had long been a top prospect in the New York organization, but injuries—first a serious groin problem, then shoulder trouble—retarded his progress. He was seldom used in the Yanks' bullpen before the trade. The 6'6" righthander has been slow to master his pitching mechanics. However, he has developed a 90+ MPH fastball that sinks, along with another fastball that will ride up in the strike zone on occasion. Hutton also has a decent slider and has started developing a change-up, but he is first of all a power pitcher. With his improved control, he has made strides toward finally realizing his potential.

Defense & Hitting

It takes Hutton a while to deliver the ball home and he doesn't have a great pickoff move. As a result, he had problems with opposing baserunners last year. He does not always get himself into good fielding position and sometimes makes judgment mistakes on defense. Hutton enjoyed his first chance to bat as a professional last year, managing six hits in his first 19 major-league at bats, including a home run.

1997 Outlook

It is common for tall pitchers to develop later, and the Australian-born Hutton, who did not face great competition early in his career, is even more likely to be a late bloomer. He did well last year in his first chance to start regularly and could end up being a steal for Florida. He is capable of winning 10 to 12 games this season as the Marlins' fourth or fifth starter.

Position: RP/SP
Bats: R **Throws:** R
Ht: 6' 6" **Wt:** 240

Opening Day Age: 27
Born: 2/6/70 in Adelaide, Australia
ML Seasons: 3

Overall Statistics

	W	L	Pct.	ERA	G	GS	Sv	IP	H	BB	SO	HR	BR/IP
1996	5	3	.625	4.15	25	11	0	86.2	79	36	56	9	1.33
Career	6	4	.600	4.49	34	15	0	112.1	107	53	69	11	1.42

How Often He Throws Strikes

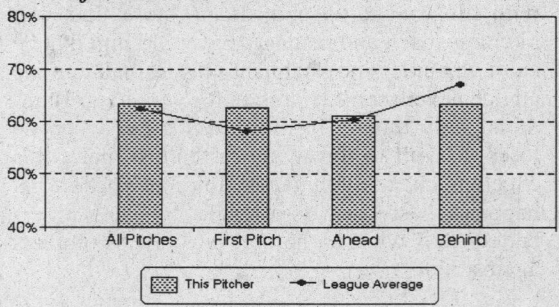

1996 Situational Stats

	W	L	ERA	Sv	IP		AB	H	HR	RBI	Avg
Home	1	1	5.40	0	28.1	LHB	152	39	5	17	.257
Road	4	2	3.55	0	58.1	RHB	179	40	4	15	.223
First Half	0	0	5.40	0	16.2	Sc Pos	68	14	2	23	.206
Scnd Half	5	3	3.86	0	70.0	Clutch	23	1	0	0	.043

1996 Rankings (National League)

➡ Did not rank near the top or bottom in any category

Charles Johnson

1996 Season

Second-year catcher Charles Johnson struggled for much of 1996 to keep his average above .200. His rough year was further complicated when he missed more than a month with a sprained finger ligament. However, Johnson held his own during the second half, when he batted .241. And he continued to be one of the game's great defensive catchers, winning his second consecutive Gold Glove.

Hitting

Johnson remains overmatched against high fastballs and changes of speed and there were times last year when he had difficulty just making contact. However, he shows flashes of potential to be a useful hitter. For one thing, he has good power which he can use the opposite field. He is a decent breaking-ball hitter and when he remains reasonably patient, he can put together solid streaks of consistent production. Johnson presses too much at times, particularly with men on base. He hit only .155 last year with runners in scoring position.

Baserunning & Defense

Only Texas' Ivan Rodriguez is comparable defensively to Johnson, whose catching skills begin with his great arm and quick release. Johnson threw out 46 percent of opposition basestealers last year, the best ratio in the league. He is skillful at blocking balls in the dirt and for a young player, he is also an excellent handler of pitchers. Johnson is a below-average runner and little threat on the bases.

1997 Outlook

What's impressive about Johnson is that he has not taken his batting difficulties behind the plate. He has the strength to be a 20-homer threat and with the Marlins' lineup likely to be improved, he should feel less pressure to produce. Johnson is not far from becoming one of the league's elite all-around catchers and he is talented enough to blossom quickly as a hitter.

Position: C
Bats: R **Throws:** R
Ht: 6' 2" **Wt:** 215

Opening Day Age: 25
Born: 7/20/71 in Fort Pierce, Florida
ML Seasons: 3

Overall Statistics

	G	AB	R	H	D	T	HR	RBI	SB	BB	SO	Avg	OBP	Slg
1996	120	386	34	84	13	1	13	37	1	40	91	.218	.292	.358
Career	221	712	79	168	29	2	25	80	1	87	166	.236	.321	.388

Where He Hits the Ball

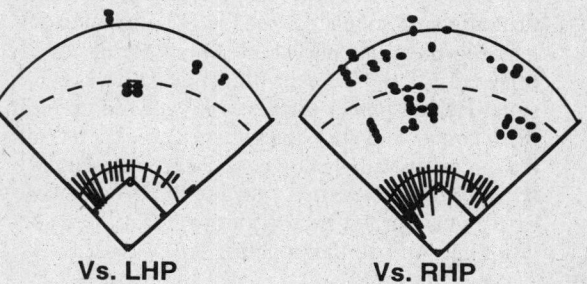

Vs. LHP   **Vs. RHP**

1996 Situational Stats

	AB	H	HR	RBI	Avg		AB	H	HR	RBI	Avg
Home	208	46	9	22	.221	LHP	87	18	1	6	.207
Road	178	38	4	15	.213	RHP	299	66	12	31	.221
First Half	274	57	9	26	.208	Sc Pos	97	15	3	23	.155
Scnd Half	112	27	4	11	.241	Clutch	57	18	2	9	.316

1996 Rankings (National League)

→ 1st in most GDPs per GDP situation (22.5%), lowest batting average with runners in scoring position (.155) and fielding percentage at catcher (.995)
→ 5th in GDPs (20)

Al Leiter

1996 Season

Some people thought the Marlins had made a mistake when they signed lefthander Al Leiter to a big free-agent contract prior to last season. But Leiter proved to be a wise investment with the best year of his career. Leiter's 16 victories were a career high and his 2.93 earned run average was topped in the N.L. only by Kevin Brown and Greg Maddux. For good measure, he pitched the first no-hitter in Florida history when he blanked the Colorado Rockies on May 11.

Pitching

Few lefthanders this side of Randy Johnson have better stuff than Leiter's. He throws a heavy sinking fastball in the low 90s, a hard slider, a cut fastball that also reaches the low 90s and an excellent big-breaking curveball which serves as an offspeed pitch. There is little finesse to Leiter's style. He is a power pitcher who will run up high pitch counts and walk many batters. Leiter has led the majors in walks allowed in each of the last two seasons. However, he is so tough to hit and so rarely gets burned by the longball that the walks don't hurt him all that much.

Defense & Hitting

Leiter is poised and agile on the mound, allowing him to make all the plays expected of a pitcher. He also keeps baserunners guessing with a good pick-off move and quick delivery home. Leiter's years in the American League were evident in how he hit. He struck out 45 times in 70 at-bats.

1997 Outlook

Scouts have been raving about Leiter's stuff ever since he was a 20-year-old prospect in the Yankees' organization. Now healthy and mature, he has become a top-echelon starting pitcher with plenty of good years ahead of him. There's no reason why he can't approach 16 to 20 wins again this season.

Position: SP
Bats: L **Throws:** L
Ht: 6' 3" **Wt:** 215

Opening Day Age: 31
Born: 10/12/65 in Toms River, NJ
ML Seasons: 10
Pronunciation: LITE-er

Overall Statistics

	W	L	Pct.	ERA	G	GS	Sv	IP	H	BB	SO	HR	BR/IP
1996	16	12	.571	2.93	33	33	0	215.1	153	119	200	14	1.26
Career	49	44	.527	3.94	146	116	2	737.1	643	428	639	54	1.45

How Often He Throws Strikes

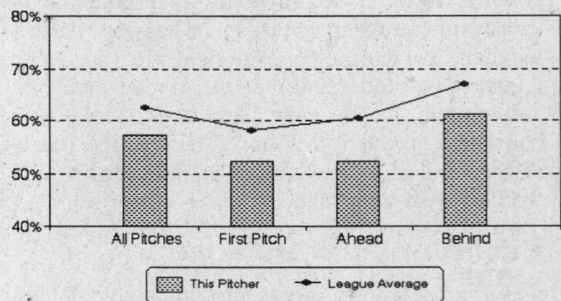

1996 Situational Stats

	W	L	ERA	Sv	IP		AB	H	HR	RBI	Avg
Home	11	3	2.08	0	116.2	LHB	127	31	1	9	.244
Road	5	9	3.92	0	98.2	RHB	629	122	13	53	.194
First Half	9	7	2.43	0	118.2	Sc Pos	150	29	3	43	.193
Scnd Half	7	5	3.54	0	96.2	Clutch	38	9	1	3	.237

1996 Rankings (National League)

→ 1st in walks allowed, lowest batting average allowed (.202), most pitches thrown per batter (4.09) and lowest batting average allowed vs. right-handed batters (.194)

→ 2nd in lowest slugging percentage allowed (.316) and ERA at home (2.08)

→ 3rd in ERA

→ 4th in pitches thrown (3,669), lowest stolen base percentage allowed (43.8%), least home runs allowed per 9 innings (.59) and lowest batting average allowed with runners in scoring position (.193)

→ 5th in wins

→ 7th in hit batsmen (11), strikeouts and GDPs induced (23)

Robb Nen

Position: RP
Bats: R **Throws:** R
Ht: 6' 4" **Wt:** 190

Opening Day Age: 27
Born: 11/28/69 in San Pedro, CA
ML Seasons: 4

1996 Season

There is no longer any question about who the Marlins' closer is: Robb Nen has emphatically established himself as one of the league's best. In 1996 Nen was among league leaders in most relief pitching categories, including saves (35) and appearances (75), while averaging 10 strikeouts per nine innings pitched. Nen finished the season by converting 20 of his last 21 save opportunities, giving him an outstanding career save percentage of 85 percent.

Pitching

Nen, who is known for his gas, can throw his fastball in the mid to upper 90s. However, Nen has broken through as a big-time closer largely because he has developed confidence in his other pitches. Along with the fastball, he features an outstanding curveball that at times is his best strikeout pitch. He also throws a hard, late-breaking slider that is especially tough on left-handed hitters. As he's become more and more sound mechanically, Nen has developed outstanding control over all his pitches.

Defense & Hitting

A tall pitcher with a somewhat slow delivery, Nen has done a poor job of holding runners in the past, but he worked on his move last year and was greatly improved. He fields his position fairly well but does not have great agility. He is still hitless in his major-league career.

1997 Outlook

The hard-throwing Nen is one of the emerging pitching stars in the National League. All he needs to get the recognition he deserves is to be a successful closer in the heat of a pennant race. That's something over which he does not have control, but in the meantime Nen should continue to be one of the best relievers in baseball.

Overall Statistics

	W	L	Pct.	ERA	G	GS	Sv	IP	H	BB	SO	HR	BR/IP
1996	5	1	.833	1.95	75	0	35	83.0	67	21	92	2	1.06
Career	12	14	.462	3.53	205	4	73	262.2	238	107	259	20	1.31

How Often He Throws Strikes

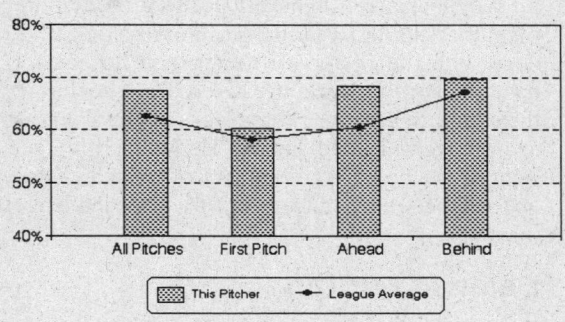

1996 Situational Stats

	W	L	ERA	Sv	IP		AB	H	HR	RBI	Avg
Home	4	0	0.82	19	44.0	LHB	141	34	0	15	.241
Road	1	1	3.23	16	39.0	RHB	157	33	2	11	.210
First Half	3	1	2.35	17	46.0	Sc Pos	78	19	1	23	.244
Scnd Half	2	0	1.46	18	37.0	Clutch	210	46	2	22	.219

1996 Rankings (National League)

- ➡ 2nd in games finished (66) and most GDPs induced per GDP situation (20.8%)
- ➡ 3rd in blown saves (7) and relief ERA (1.95)
- ➡ 5th in save opportunities (42), lowest save percentage (83.3%) and least baserunners allowed per 9 innings in relief (9.7)
- ➡ 6th in games pitched, saves and most strikeouts per 9 innings in relief (10.0)
- ➡ Led the Marlins in games pitched, saves, games finished (66), save opportunities (42), save percentage (83.3%), blown saves (7), most GDPs induced per GDP situation (20.8%), lowest batting average allowed in relief with runners on base (.213), relief ERA (1.95), relief wins (5) and relief innings (83.0)

Yorkis Perez

1996 Season

After kicking around various organizations and pitching briefly in Japan, Yorkis Perez appeared to have settled into a role as a lefty specialist in the Florida bullpen. But in 1996, Perez struggled at his specialty—retiring left-handed hitters. Perez did have problems over the last two months, but he struck out 36 batters in his final 38 innings of the season.

Pitching

Perez does not have any one outstanding pitch, and he hurt himself last year by becoming too predictable. Perez likes to start hitters off with a fastball in hopes of getting ahead in the count, then keep them off-balance with his offspeed stuff. But more often than not last year, he was missing the strike zone with the first-pitch heater, and he doesn't have the stuff to work effectively from behind in the count. In addition, Perez lacks aggressiveness against right-handed hitters. He will try to get righties to chase his assortment of breaking stuff and offspeed slop and rarely tries to challenge them.

Defense & Hitting

Perez has only a fair move to first and can be run on with pretty good success. He also is a mediocre fielder who at times is too casual with his defensive work. He remains hitless as a major leaguer, something that is not very worrisome since in his specialty role, he rarely hits.

1997 Outlook

If Perez can't retire left-handed hitters with any frequency, his value to the Marlins is pretty negligible. He'll get the chance in spring training because lefties are at such a premium, but with the way Jim Leyland uses a bullpen, he won't be around long if he does not regain some consistency.

Position: RP
Bats: L **Throws:** L
Ht: 6' 0" **Wt:** 180

Opening Day Age: 29
Born: 9/30/67 in Bajos de Haina, DR
ML Seasons: 4

Overall Statistics

	W	L	Pct.	ERA	G	GS	Sv	IP	H	BB	SO	HR	BR/IP
1996	3	4	.429	5.29	64	0	0	47.2	51	31	47	2	1.72
Career	9	10	.474	4.65	180	0	1	139.1	121	75	138	12	1.41

How Often He Throws Strikes

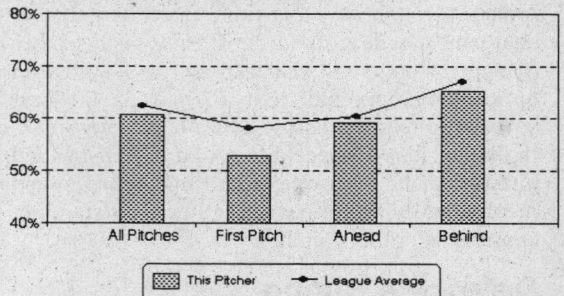

1996 Situational Stats

	W	L	ERA	Sv	IP		AB	H	HR	RBI	Avg
Home	2	1	4.50	0	22.0	LHB	88	26	1	16	.295
Road	1	3	5.96	0	25.2	RHB	98	25	1	19	.255
First Half	2	2	3.66	0	32.0	Sc Pos	61	19	0	32	.311
Scnd Half	1	2	8.62	0	15.2	Clutch	73	16	1	6	.219

1996 Rankings (National League)
➡ Did not rank near the top or bottom in any category

Jay Powell

Position: RP
Bats: R **Throws:** R
Ht: 6' 4" **Wt:** 225

Opening Day Age: 25
Born: 1/19/72 in
Meridian, MS
ML Seasons: 2

1996 Season

In his first full year in the majors, Jay Powell settled in to be a solid set-up man for Robb Nen. After missing nearly a month early in the season with a ribcage muscle pull, Powell ended up making 67 appearances, with 16 of them coming in a busy August. Along with setting up Nen, he earned his first two major league saves.

Pitching

Powell was a reliever at Mississippi State but when he was a Baltimore farmhand, he was given a trial as a starter. The switch didn't work and he seems much better suited to a relief role. His fastball is of closer's quality. He throws consistently in the low 90s and when he has his good sinking action, Powell can be overpowering. He will struggle at times with his location, and he also lacks a quality offspeed pitch or breaking-ball to lean on when he's not hitting his spots with his fastball. However, he has developed an improved cut fastball and he has the kind of makeup that allows the Marlins to use him occasionally as a closer when Nen needs a night off.

Defense & Hitting

Powell is easy pickings for basestealers, who were successful on six of seven attempts last year. He is tall with a slow delivery home that lands him in awkward fielding position. He put the ball into play twice in six plate appearances last year and is obviously no threat with the bat.

1997 Outlook

When they acquired Powell from Baltimore, Florida felt he had a chance to develop into a closer. If that happens, it won't be for a while because Nen is too good and Powell still too raw. However, Powell has the arm and the ability to continue to be an excellent set-up man for Nen again this year.

Overall Statistics

	W	L	Pct.	ERA	G	GS	Sv	IP	H	BB	SO	HR	BR/IP
1996	4	3	.571	4.54	67	0	2	71.1	71	36	52	5	1.50
Career	4	3	.571	4.18	76	0	2	79.2	78	42	56	5	1.51

How Often He Throws Strikes

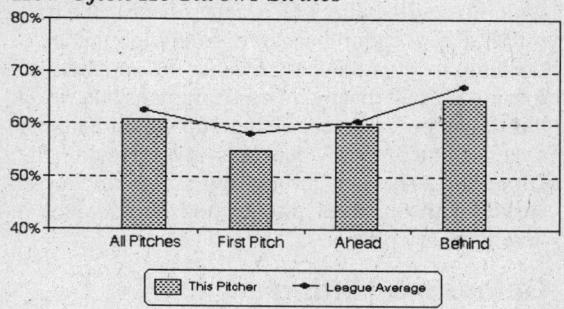

1996 Situational Stats

	W	L	ERA	Sv	IP		AB	H	HR	RBI	Avg
Home	3	0	2.97	2	33.1	LHB	112	28	3	18	.250
Road	1	3	5.92	0	38.0	RHB	166	43	2	25	.259
First Half	2	0	3.58	1	27.2	Sc Pos	96	23	2	33	.240
Scnd Half	2	3	5.15	1	43.2	Clutch	124	29	2	13	.234

1996 Rankings (National League)

→ 10th in highest batting average allowed in relief with runners on base (.308)
→ Led the Marlins in lowest percentage of inherited runners scored (30.4%)

Pat Rapp

1996 Season

Pat Rapp fell to earth last season after a strong 1995 campaign in which he developed into Florida's ace. Rapp pitched respectably during the first half of the season, but poor run support doomed him to a 4-11 record. After the break he simply fell apart. He ended up losing a league-leading 16 games while having more walks than strikeouts, more hits than innings pitched and one of the league's highest wild-pitch totals. By the end of the year, he was trade bait.

Pitching

Throughout his career, Rapp has struggled to maintain a consistent release point—particularity with his curveball, which is probably his best pitch. Rapp cannot survive solely on his two fastballs, a cutter that only reaches the mid 80s and a rising fastball that too often straightens out. Rapp has developed a decent change-up which he turns over at times. But when he's not throwing his curve for strikes, it affects his ability to throw strikes with his other pitches and he becomes a very ordinary pitcher.

Defense & Hitting

Rapp combines a good move to first with a quick delivery home to make it tough for basestealers. Only half of the 20 who tried stealing against him were successful last year. Rapp is an adequate fielder who gets himself in fundamentally sound fielding position. He is capable of occasionally helping himself with the bat.

1997 Outlook

After Florida traded John Burkett to Texas last August, the rumors about Rapp's departure faded—but only for the time being. The Marlins signed Alex Fernandez in the offseason, and intend to give some of their young arms a chance to stick in their rotation. That means Rapp is likely on borrowed time unless he makes a dramatic reversal back to his 1995 form.

Position: SP
Bats: R **Throws:** R
Ht: 6' 3"   **Wt:** 215

Opening Day Age: 29
Born: 7/13/67 in Jennings, LA
ML Seasons: 5

Overall Statistics

	W	L	Pct.	ERA	G	GS	Sv	IP	H	BB	SO	HR	BR/IP
1996	8	16	.333	5.10	30	29	0	162.1	184	91	86	12	1.69
Career	33	39	.458	4.17	101	98	0	567.0	583	281	323	42	1.52

How Often He Throws Strikes

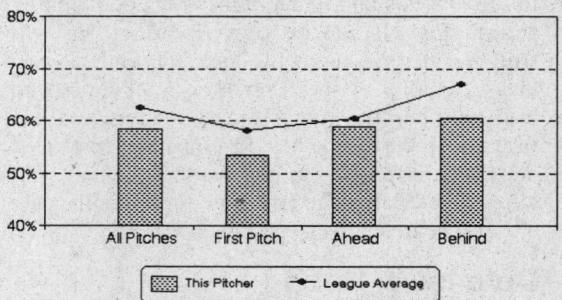

This Pitcher   League Average

1996 Situational Stats

	W	L	ERA	Sv	IP		AB	H	HR	RBI	Avg
Home	6	7	3.82	0	94.1	LHB	292	90	5	35	.308
Road	2	9	6.88	0	68.0	RHB	319	94	7	48	.295
First Half	4	11	4.09	0	101.1	Sc Pos	162	49	1	61	.302
Scnd Half	4	5	6.79	0	61.0	Clutch	33	10	1	4	.303

1996 Rankings (National League)

→ 1st in losses, lowest strikeout/walk ratio (0.9), highest batting average allowed (.301), highest on-base percentage allowed (.390), most baserunners allowed per 9 innings (15.4) and most GDPs induced per 9 innings (1.3)

→ 3rd in least strikeouts per 9 innings (4.8)

→ 4th in wild pitches (13)

→ 5th in lowest winning percentage

→ 6th in highest ERA and walks allowed

→ 7th in GDPs induced (23), least home runs allowed per 9 innings (.67) and highest batting average allowed with runners in scoring position (.302)

→ 8th in highest batting average allowed vs. left-handed batters (.310)

Edgar Renteria

1996 Season

One of the most highly regarded prospects in baseball, Edgar Renteria lived up to his billing with an outstanding debut season. Recalled from Triple-A on May 9, Renteria quickly proved he belonged in the majors, especially in the second half when he was as good as any shortstop in the league. Renteria hit .334 after the All-Star break, including a club-record 22-game hitting streak.

Hitting

The Marlins think Renteria has only scratched the surface of his offensive potential. He has made remarkable strides thus far even though not yet fully matured physically. His power has begun to surface and he already shows a very quick bat that can turn around above-average fastballs. He's cutting down his strikeouts as he gains experience and a better knowledge of the strike zone. He also shows the potential to become a good RBI man.

Baserunning & Defense

Renteria has outstanding speed and he already has a good idea of how to exploit it, stealing 16 bases in 18 attempts last season. He is a very teachable youngster who will become a big-time stolen-base threat as he learns pitchers' moves and the art of getting a jump. As a defensive shortstop, he already is among the elite in all of baseball. His range can be breathtaking, he has soft hands and is acrobatic in turning the double play. Renteria will make his share of errors because he reaches so many balls. In addition, he is sometimes a little too willing to show off his big-time arm.

1997 Outlook

It's hard to believe Renteria is only 21 years old. His arrival in the majors is at least a year ahead of schedule, but he obviously belongs. Renteria seems destined to be a big-time star and perhaps the heir to Barry Larkin as the N.L.'s best shortstop.

Position: SS
Bats: R **Throws:** R
Ht: 6' 1" **Wt:** 172

Opening Day Age: 21
Born: 8/7/75 in Barranquilla, Colombia
ML Seasons: 1
Pronunciation: ren-ter-EEE-uh

Overall Statistics

	G	AB	R	H	D	T	HR	RBI	SB	BB	SO	Avg	OBP	Slg
1996	106	431	68	133	18	3	5	31	16	33	68	.309	.358	.399
Career	106	431	68	133	18	3	5	31	16	33	68	.309	.358	.399

Where He Hits the Ball

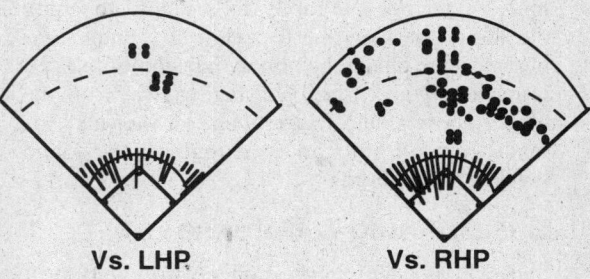

Vs. LHP   **Vs. RHP**

1996 Situational Stats

	AB	H	HR	RBI	Avg		AB	H	HR	RBI	Avg
Home	188	58	2	17	.309	LHP	90	22	2	9	.244
Road	243	75	3	14	.309	RHP	341	111	3	22	.326
First Half	129	32	1	7	.248	Sc Pos	85	25	0	23	.294
Scnd Half	302	101	4	24	.334	Clutch	63	21	1	7	.333

1996 Rankings (National League)

→ 2nd in fielding percentage at shortstop (.979)
→ 4th in batting average on a 3-1 count (.750)
→ 7th in batting average on the road (.309)
→ Led the Marlins in batting average in the clutch (.333), batting average on a 3-1 count (.750), batting average on the road (.309), bunts in play (10), lowest percentage of swings that missed (16.5%) and highest percentage of swings put into play (45.7%)

Florida Marlins

Gary Sheffield

1996 Season

Completely healthy for the first time in several years, Gary Sheffield had a monster year that reaffirmed his status as one of the game's greatest hitters. He reached career highs in virtually every category, including homers (42), RBI (120) and walks (142). Sheffield started fast with a record-tying 11 homers in April and never stopped hitting the rest of the way. More importantly, he proved he could hold up over an entire season, appearing in all but one game last year.

Hitting

Opponents and teammates alike still marvel at Sheffield's incredible bat speed, which many consider the best in baseball. Because he can wait so long on pitches, he rarely falls victim to going outside the strike zone to swing at a pitch. Few pitchers dare challenge him with fastballs unless it is absolutely necessary. But staying away from the heater doesn't help them much, as Sheffield has made himself into an excellent offspeed and breaking-ball hitter.

Baserunning & Defense

Sheffield is a good baserunner who could steal more bases if so inclined. However, he prefers to pick his spots and attempted only 25 steals last year. He is also one of the league's toughest runners at going into second to break up a double play. Sheffield has worked hard to become a solid right fielder. His range has improved and he has a strong, accurate arm with improved mechanics.

1997 Outlook

Sheffield said that getting shot in an offseason incident prior to last season made him take stock of his career. Whatever the reason, he was a great player last year. Sheffield had his spats with the front office but those are likely behind him now that Jim Leyland has arrived in the manager's office. Sheffield should be a happy player for Leyland and continue to produce awesome numbers for years to come.

Position: RF
Bats: R **Throws:** R
Ht: 5'11" **Wt:** 190

Opening Day Age: 28
Born: 11/18/68 in Tampa, FL
ML Seasons: 9

Overall Statistics

	G	AB	R	H	D	T	HR	RBI	SB	BB	SO	Avg	OBP	Slg
1996	161	519	118	163	33	1	42	120	16	142	66	.314	.465	.624
Career	891	3215	517	937	172	13	159	550	112	440	361	.291	.380	.501

Where He Hits the Ball

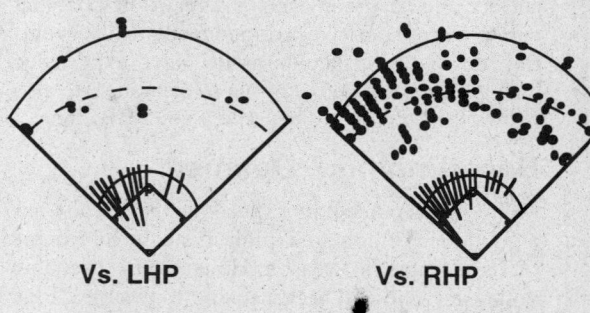

Vs. LHP   Vs. RHP

1996 Situational Stats

	AB	H	HR	RBI	Avg		AB	H	HR	RBI	Avg
Home	233	76	19	60	.326	LHP	99	31	9	26	.313
Road	286	87	23	60	.304	RHP	420	132	33	94	.314
First Half	290	86	25	62	.297	Sc Pos	132	44	14	77	.333
Scnd Half	229	77	17	58	.336	Clutch	77	22	4	18	.286

1996 Rankings (National League)

→ 1st in on-base percentage
→ 2nd in home runs, walks, times on base (315), slugging percentage, HR frequency (12.4 ABs per HR), slugging percentage vs. right-handed pitchers (.621) and on-base percentage vs. right-handed pitchers (.466)
→ 3rd in pitches seen (2,699), games played (161), lowest stolen base percentage (64.0%) and on-base percentage vs. left-handed pitchers (.460)
→ 4th in intentional walks (19) and lowest fielding percentage in right field (.976)
→ 5th in runs scored, cleanup slugging percentage (.579) and slugging percentage vs. left-handed pitchers (.636)

Devon White

1996 Season

Expectations were high when Gold Glove outfielder Devon White signed a three-year contract with the Marlins prior to the 1996 season. Plagued by a sore hamstring during the season's first six weeks, White got off to a slow start with his new club. But he recovered and ended up having a solid first season in the National League. He had his second-highest totals ever in home runs (17) and RBI (84) while setting a Marlins club record for doubles in a season with 37.

Hitting

The switch-hitting White has never been a prototypical leadoff hitter, since he hits with power and doesn't draw many walks. When he struggled in the leadoff spot early last year, the Marlins moved him to the fifth spot in the order, and his season turned around. Hitting fifth, he was able to concentrate more on pulling balls for extra-base power than simply trying to make contact. He has always been a lowball hitter from either side of the plate but usually has hit better from the left side. However, last year White hit nearly 100 points better as a righty.

Baserunning & Defense

Once he was over his hamstring woes, White returned to being the excellent baserunner he's always been. He continued to run aggressively despite being moved down in the batting order and ended up with 22 steals in 28 attempts. Defensively, there are few better outfielders. White's range is outstanding, as are his timing and leaping ability. He pulled back three certain home runs last year alone with leaping catches. White has above-average arm strength and his accuracy is outstanding.

1997 Outlook

White has had his share of minor injuries over the last couple of years but as he's grown older, his power and RBI production have improved. He should give the Marlins at least another two or three years of outstanding center-field play.

Position: CF
Bats: B **Throws:** R
Ht: 6' 2" **Wt:** 190

Opening Day Age: 34
Born: 12/29/62 in Kingston, Jamaica
ML Seasons: 12
Nickname: Devo

Overall Statistics

	G	AB	R	H	D	T	HR	RBI	SB	BB	SO	Avg	OBP	Slg
1996	146	552	77	151	37	6	17	84	22	38	99	.274	.325	.455
Career	1414	5494	866	1435	283	64	148	599	271	391	1146	.261	.314	.417

Where He Hits the Ball

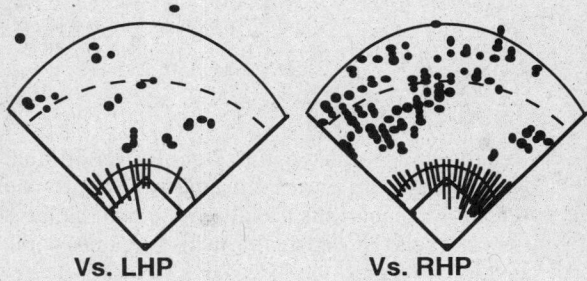

Vs. LHP   **Vs. RHP**

1996 Situational Stats

	AB	H	HR	RBI	Avg		AB	H	HR	RBI	Avg
Home	282	72	5	34	.255	LHP	119	41	6	33	.345
Road	270	79	12	50	.293	RHP	433	110	11	51	.254
First Half	303	83	7	33	.274	Sc Pos	128	44	5	69	.344
Scnd Half	249	68	10	51	.273	Clutch	93	24	3	16	.258

1996 Rankings (National League)

- → 3rd in lowest on-base percentage for a leadoff hitter (.307)
- → 4th in sacrifice flies (9)
- → 5th in fielding percentage in center field (.987)
- → 6th in errors in center field (4)
- → 7th in batting average vs. left-handed pitchers (.345)
- → 8th in lowest on-base percentage vs. right-handed pitchers (.307)
- → 10th in slugging percentage vs. left-handed pitchers (.597)
- → Led the Marlins in doubles, sacrifice flies (9), stolen bases and least GDPs per GDP situation (7.3%)

Luis Castillo

Great Speed

Position: 2B
Bats: B **Throws:** R
Ht: 5'11" **Wt:** 155

Opening Day Age: 21
Born: 9/12/75 in San Pedro de Macoris, DR
ML Seasons: 1
Pronunciation: cas-TEE-oh

Overall Statistics

	G	AB	R	H	D	T	HR	RBI	SB	BB	SO	Avg	OBP	Slg
1996	41	164	26	43	2	1	1	8	17	14	46	.262	.320	.305
Career	41	164	26	43	2	1	1	8	17	14	46	.262	.320	.305

1996 Situational Stats

	AB	H	HR	RBI	Avg		AB	H	HR	RBI	Avg
Home	93	23	0	3	.247	LHP	38	11	1	3	.289
Road	71	20	1	5	.282	RHP	126	32	0	5	.254
First Half	0	0	0	0	-	Sc Pos	31	5	0	7	.161
Scnd Half	164	43	1	8	.262	Clutch	17	5	0	2	.294

1996 Season

Recalled in August from Double-A Portland, where he was an Eastern League All-Star, rookie second baseman Luis Castillo more than held his own last year. He had 43 hits in his 41 games while stealing 17 bases. He also did a solid job defensively at second base.

Hitting, Baserunning & Defense

The 21-year old Castillo is slightly built and at times he had the bat knocked out of his hands by good hard stuff. He also has difficulty holding off on breaking stuff. Castillo is unlikely ever to have any power, and he needs to learn to shorten his swing and make more consistent contact. He has the kind of speed that could translate into 50 stolen bases someday if he gets on base enough. He also has outstanding range and quickness at second base.

1997 Outlook

The jury is out on whether Castillo is mature enough physically to play every day in the majors. And there are questions about whether he'll hit enough to stay in the lineup on a regular basis. However, his speed, defensive talent and potential make him a strong contender to be the Marlins' Opening Day second baseman.

Rick Helling

Position: SP/RP
Bats: R **Throws:** R
Ht: 6'3" **Wt:** 215

Opening Day Age: 26
Born: 12/15/70 in Devils Lake, ND
ML Seasons: 3

Overall Statistics

	W	L	Pct.	ERA	G	GS	Sv	IP	H	BB	SO	HR	BR/IP
1996	3	3	.500	4.31	11	6	0	48.0	37	16	42	9	1.10
Career	6	7	.462	5.29	23	18	0	112.1	116	42	72	25	1.41

1996 Situational Stats

	W	L	ERA	Sv	IP		AB	H	HR	RBI	Avg
Home	2	1	5.61	0	25.2	LHB	81	19	5	14	.235
Road	1	2	2.82	0	22.1	RHB	99	18	4	9	.182
First Half	1	1	4.96	0	16.1	Sc Pos	37	8	2	15	.216
Scnd Half	2	2	3.98	0	31.2	Clutch	21	3	1	2	.143

1996 Season

Acquired from Texas in the John Burkett deal last September, Rick Helling made four late-season starts for the Marlins and pitched extremely well. He earned two victories, had an excellent 1.69 ERA and averaged nearly a strikeout per inning.

Pitching, Defense & Hitting

Helling is a former number-one pick with considerable ability and good velocity. He has a good sinking fastball, but control problems and the lack of a consistent offspeed pitch have retarded his progress. He's developed an improving circle change to go along with his sinker and cutter. Helling is an excellent athlete who fields his position well. He has much to learn about holding runners and he has never had to hit prior to joining the Marlins.

1997 Outlook

A highly-regarded prospect who seems ready to make a major-league impact, Helling is among the early favorites to win a spot as a fourth or fifth starter with the Marlins this year. He is also capable of filling a role as long reliever.

Felix Heredia

Position: RP
Bats: L **Throws:** L
Ht: 6' 0" **Wt:** 165

Opening Day Age: 20
Born: 6/18/76 in Barahona, DR
ML Seasons: 1
Pronunciation: her-EEE-dee-uh

Overall Statistics

	W	L	Pct.	ERA	G	GS	Sv	IP	H	BB	SO	HR	BR/IP
1996	1	1	.500	4.32	21	0	0	16.2	21	10	10	1	1.86
Career	1	1	.500	4.32	21	0	0	16.2	21	10	10	1	1.86

1996 Situational Stats

	W	L	ERA	Sv	IP		AB	H	HR	RBI	Avg
Home	1	0	3.18	0	5.2	LHB	26	4	0	1	.154
Road	0	1	4.91	0	11.0	RHB	41	17	1	10	.415
First Half	0	0	-	0	0.0	Sc Pos	22	5	0	9	.227
Scnd Half	1	1	4.32	0	16.2	Clutch	15	4	1	2	.267

1996 Season

After an outstanding year at Double-A Portland, lefthander Felix Heredia was recalled by the Marlins on August 8. Making 21 appearances out of the Florida bullpen, he proved effective against left-handed hitters, who batted only .154 against him. However, he needs to find some weapons to handle righties, who creamed him at a .415 clip.

Pitching, Defense & Hitting

Heredia turned 20 only last June, so he obviously is an unfinished product. Last season was his first full year as a reliever, but he has the makeup to be a factor out of the bullpen. He throws in the high 80s and his velocity is expected to increase as he matures physically. He does not yet have a reliable offspeed pitch, though he does have the makings of an effective slider. He is quick off the mound but has nothing yet resembling a refined move to first. He has never batted.

1997 Outlook

With a season of winter ball under his belt, the raw Heredia will be given a long look this spring. The Marlins have a big need for lefthanders in the bullpen, and Heredia will get a shot at one of the jobs.

Kurt Miller

Position: RP/SP
Bats: R **Throws:** R
Ht: 6' 5" **Wt:** 205

Opening Day Age: 24
Born: 8/24/72 in Bakersfield, CA
ML Seasons: 2

Overall Statistics

	W	L	Pct.	ERA	G	GS	Sv	IP	H	BB	SO	HR	BR/IP
1996	1	3	.250	6.80	26	5	0	46.1	57	33	30	5	1.94
Career	2	6	.250	7.19	30	9	0	66.1	83	40	-41	8	1.85

1996 Situational Stats

	W	L	ERA	Sv	IP		AB	H	HR	RBI	Avg
Home	1	0	4.09	0	22.0	LHB	91	32	3	23	.352
Road	0	3	9.25	0	24.1	RHB	91	25	2	16	.275
First Half	1	1	5.35	0	35.1	Sc Pos	65	22	3	33	.338
Scnd Half	0	2	11.45	0	11.0	Clutch	38	14	0	8	.368

1996 Season

Long considered a top prospect, Kurt Miller has seen his career drift to the point where Florida is now trying him as a reliever. He had two tours of duty last year with Florida, starting five games and posting a 7.36 ERA and making 21 relief appearances with a 6.29 ERA.

Pitching, Defense & Hitting

Miller was the fifth overall pick, taken by Pittsburgh, in the 1990 draft. He moved on to Texas and then to Florida with Robb Nen in a deal for pitcher Cris Carpenter. Miller has a good arm but has never developed consistent mechanics. He labors with his control and has nothing to lean on consistently except his better-than-average fastball. He is somewhat awkward coming off the mound, taking him out of good fielding position, and he is only fair at holding runners. He can handle the bat, getting three hits in his eight at-bats last year.

1997 Outlook

Until he comes up with more variety in his pitches and more consistency in his location, Miller will continue to be a fringe pitcher. He'll have trouble making a major league roster this spring.

Ralph Milliard

Position: 2B
Bats: R **Throws:** R
Ht: 5'11" **Wt:** 170

Opening Day Age: 23
Born: 12/30/73 in Willemstad, Curacao
ML Seasons: 1

Overall Statistics

	G	AB	R	H	D	T	HR	RBI	SB	BB	SO	Avg	OBP	Slg
1996	24	62	7	10	2	0	0	1	2	14	16	.161	.312	.194
Career	24	62	7	10	2	0	0	1	2	14	16	.161	.312	.194

1996 Situational Stats

	AB	H	HR	RBI	Avg		AB	H	HR	RBI	Avg
Home	13	2	0	1	.154	LHP	21	5	0	0	.238
Road	49	8	0	0	.163	RHP	41	5	0	1	.122
First Half	41	7	0	1	.171	Sc Pos	10	0	0	1	.000
Scnd Half	21	3	0	0	.143	Clutch	10	1	0	0	.100

1996 Season

Ralph Milliard had several tours of duty with the Marlins last year. A defensive whiz, Milliard seemed unable to cope with major league pitching. He managed only 10 hits, two of them bunt singles.

Hitting, Baserunning & Defense

Milliard has shown improving power during his minor-league career, but he looked overmatched in his brief time with the Marlins. He has decent patience at the plate but could not catch up with average fastballs and had difficulty hitting the breaking ball. He has very good speed and could be a solid basestealer. . . if he can get on base. Milliard shines on defense. He has great range and hands at second, where he can play with anyone in the majors right now.

1997 Outlook

A native of Curacao like the storied Andruw Jones, Milliard does not have Jones' superstar future. However, the Marlins think he can become a useful major league player, perhaps this season in a utility role.

Bob Natal

Position: C
Bats: R **Throws:** R
Ht: 5'11" **Wt:** 190

Opening Day Age: 31
Born: 11/13/65 in Long Beach, CA
ML Seasons: 5
Pronunciation: NAY-tul

Overall Statistics

	G	AB	R	H	D	T	HR	RBI	SB	BB	SO	Avg	OBP	Slg
1996	44	90	4	12	1	1	0	2	0	15	31	.133	.257	.167
Career	116	285	11	55	9	3	3	16	2	28	68	.193	.273	.277

1996 Situational Stats

	AB	H	HR	RBI	Avg		AB	H	HR	RBI	Avg
Home	48	6	0	1	.125	LHP	19	2	0	0	.105
Road	42	6	0	1	.143	RHP	71	10	0	2	.141
First Half	29	4	0	0	.138	Sc Pos	22	4	0	2	.182
Scnd Half	61	8	0	2	.131	Clutch	11	0	0	0	.000

1996 Season

Bob Natal was the main backup catcher to Charles Johnson last year, meaning he didn't play very much. Natal made only 29 starts and produced only 15 total bases and two RBI. He hit safely in consecutive games only twice all season.

Hitting, Baserunning & Defense

Natal simply cannot get around on good fastballs. He also gets easily fooled with offspeed stuff, which means he has trouble simply making contact. He does get his share of walks for a weak hitter but otherwise has never shown any hint of developing into a useful hitter. He has poor speed but is a good receiver with a strong, though sometimes erratic, throwing arm.

1997 Outlook

Florida would like to add a better backup catching option. However, Natal is one of those "good guys to have around" who would probably be willing to hang around helping out at Triple-A and occasionally filling in at the big-league level if the Marlins can't find a regular backup job for him.

Joe Orsulak

Position: LF/CF/RF
Bats: L **Throws:** L
Ht: 6' 1" **Wt:** 205

Opening Day Age: 34
Born: 5/31/62 in Glen Ridge, NJ
ML Seasons: 13
Pronunciation: ORR-suh-lack

Overall Statistics

	G	AB	R	H	D	T	HR	RBI	SB	BB	SO	Avg	OBP	Slg
1996	120	217	23	48	6	1	2	19	1	16	38	.221	.274	.286
Career	1388	4143	546	1139	174	36	56	398	93	300	385	.275	.325	.375

1996 Situational Stats

	AB	H	HR	RBI	Avg		AB	H	HR	RBI	Avg
Home	115	30	2	18	.261	LHP	22	6	0	3	.273
Road	102	18	0	1	.176	RHP	195	42	2	16	.215
First Half	83	16	1	6	.193	Sc Pos	57	13	1	17	.228
Scnd Half	134	32	1	13	.239	Clutch	52	12	1	7	.231

1996 Season

After three seasons with the Mets, veteran outfielder Joe Orsulak signed a two-year deal with the Marlins last year. A real pro in every sense, Orsulak led the Marlins with 10 pinch hits while also serving as an occasional backup outfielder. However, his .221 average was a career low and he recorded only nine extra-base hits.

Hitting, Baserunning & Defense

Though strictly a part-time player these days, Orsulak is a seasoned hitter who knows the strike zone and can surprise with the occasional gap power. He usually puts the ball in play, which is why he is such a valuable pinch hitter. Orsulak can play all three outfield positions and not hurt a team defensively. His arm is above average. He is not a threat to steal any bases.

1997 Outlook

Role players like Orsulak are not easy to find and with the way Jim Leyland manages, such players are of considerable value. So Orsulak will probably keep his position on a Florida bench that needs veterans. But he'll be in danger of losing his job if he doesn't hit better than he did in 1996.

Marc Valdes

Position: SP
Bats: R **Throws:** R
Ht: 6' 0" **Wt:** 187

Opening Day Age: 25
Born: 12/20/71 in Dayton, OH
ML Seasons: 2

Overall Statistics

	W	L	Pct.	ERA	G	GS	Sv	IP	H	BB	SO	HR	BR/IP
1996	1	3	.250	4.81	11	8	0	48.2	63	23	13	5	1.77
Career	1	3	.250	5.98	14	11	0	55.2	80	32	15	6	2.01

1996 Situational Stats

	W	L	ERA	Sv	IP		AB	H	HR	RBI	Avg
Home	1	3	4.03	0	22.1	LHB	83	31	4	12	.373
Road	0	0	5.47	0	26.1	RHB	117	32	1	14	.274
First Half	0	0	-	0	0.0	Sc Pos	59	17	1	18	.288
Scnd Half	1	3	4.81	0	48.2	Clutch	15	6	0	1	.400

1996 Season

Recalled from the minors on July 29, Marc Valdes made eight starts with the Marlins last year. The former number-one draft pick also made the first relief appearances of his professional career. He won his only game in a starting role, working 6.2 innings against Chicago. But for the most part he struggled.

Pitching, Defense & Hitting

Valdes throws a good sinking fastball in the high 80s and has always had an above-average slider. He worked last year on adding a more reliable offspeed pitch which he will need if he is to stick as a major leaguer. He has good reactions on the mound but does not hold runners well and allowed seven steals in as many attempts last year. He rarely makes contact for base hits as a hitter, but he did strike out only twice in 16 at-bats.

1997 Outlook

Valdes is part of a group that includes Kurt Miller, Mark Hutton, Rick Helling and Livian Hernandez. All will be candidates for perhaps one open spot in the rotation. However, the Marlins are likely to also look at Valdes as a long reliever.

Florida Marlins

Other Florida Marlins

Miguel Batista (Pos: RHP, Age: 26)

	W	L	Pct.	ERA	G	GS	Sv	IP	H	BB	SO	HR	BR/IP
1996	0	0	-	5.56	9	0	0	11.1	9	7	6	0	1.41
Career	0	0	-	6.08	10	0	0	13.1	13	10	7	1	1.73

It took four years to get back to the majors, but Batista surfaced with the Marlins in August and appeared in nine games. With the way he pitched, we may not see him again for another four. 1997 Outlook: D

Josh Booty (Pos: 3B, Age: 21, Bats: R)

	G	AB	R	H	D	T	HR	RBI	SB	BB	SO	Avg	OBP	Slg
1996	2	2	1	1	0	0	0	0	0	0	0	.500	.500	.500
Career	2	2	1	1	0	0	0	0	0	0	0	.500	.500	.500

A hot two-sport prospect when he signed with the Marlins as the fifth overall pick in 1994, Booty has power, but has struggled to hit .200 in the low minors. There are rumors he's about to ditch the Marlins and return to his first love, football. 1997 Outlook: D

Jerry Brooks (Pos: RF, Age: 30, Bats: R)

	G	AB	R	H	D	T	HR	RBI	SB	BB	SO	Avg	OBP	Slg
1996	8	5	2	2	0	1	0	3	0	1	1	.400	.571	.800
Career	17	14	4	4	1	1	1	4	0	1	3	.286	.375	.714

Brooks is a career minor leaguer who was rewarded for his stellar season at Triple-A Charlotte with a September promotion to the majors. At 30, his future with the Marlins is dim. 1997 Outlook: C

Andre Dawson (Pos: LF, Age: 42, Bats: R)

	G	AB	R	H	D	T	HR	RBI	SB	BB	SO	Avg	OBP	Slg
1996	42	58	6	16	2	0	2	14	0	2	13	.276	.311	.414
Career	2627	9927	1373	2774	503	98	438	1591	314	589	1509	.279	.323	.482

"The Hawk" finally retired this past season after 21 years in the majors. While he was always somewhat overrated as a hitter, Dawson has certainly racked up a long list of impressive achievements. 1997 Outlook: D

Craig Grebeck (Pos: 2B, Age: 32, Bats: R)

	G	AB	R	H	D	T	HR	RBI	SB	BB	SO	Avg	OBP	Slg
1996	50	95	8	20	1	0	1	9	0	4	14	.211	.245	.253
Career	464	1166	137	293	63	6	13	119	2	139	166	.251	.334	.349

The club's utility infielder last season, Grebeck struggled at the plate in 95 at-bats. A free agent, he signed with the Angels for 1997. 1997 Outlook: A

Bill Hurst (Pos: RHP, Age: 26)

	W	L	Pct.	ERA	G	GS	Sv	IP	H	BB	SO	HR	BR/IP
1996	0	0	-	0.00	2	0	0	2.0	3	1	1	0	2.00
Career	0	0	-	0.00	2	0	0	2.0	3	1	1	0	2.00

Hurst was effective at Double-A Portland before making two September appearances with the Marlins. He's extremely wild, but also overpowering. 1997 Outlook: B

Andy Larkin (Pos: RHP, Age: 22)

	W	L	Pct.	ERA	G	GS	Sv	IP	H	BB	SO	HR	BR/IP
1996	0	0	-	1.80	1	1	0	5.0	3	4	2	0	1.40
Career	0	0	-	1.80	1	1	0	5.0	3	4	2	0	1.40

Larkin is a 23-year-old pitcher who rang up impressive stats at Double-A Portland and pitched well in one start at the end of the season. He's a bonafide prospect for the future if he stays healthy. 1997 Outlook: B

Matt Mantei (Pos: RHP, Age: 23)

	W	L	Pct.	ERA	G	GS	Sv	IP	H	BB	SO	HR	BR/IP
1996	1	0	1.000	6.38	14	0	0	18.1	13	21	25	2	1.85
Career	1	1	.500	5.68	26	0	0	31.2	25	34	40	3	1.86

A hard thrower who started the season well, Mantei was hammered in May and June before going down for the year with a rotator cuff injury. He's young, but he may not be back for a while. 1997 Outlook: D

Russ Morman (Pos: 1B, Age: 34, Bats: R)

	G	AB	R	H	D	T	HR	RBI	SB	BB	SO	Avg	OBP	Slg
1996	6	6	0	1	1	0	0	0	0	1	2	.167	.286	.333
Career	203	463	48	115	16	4	9	41	2	35	100	.248	.304	.359

Morman got six at-bats with the Marlins early in the season, but spent most of the year compiling huge offensive numbers at Triple-A Charlotte. He's now 35, so his prospects aren't great. 1997 Outlook: C

Donn Pall (Pos: RHP, Age: 35)

	W	L	Pct.	ERA	G	GS	Sv	IP	H	BB	SO	HR	BR/IP
1996	1	1	.500	5.79	12	0	0	18.2	16	9	9	3	1.34
Career	24	22	.522	3.53	303	0	10	469.2	474	131	252	46	1.29

Making it back to the big leagues after spending all of '95 in the minors, Pall appeared in 12 games with the Marlins last summer. Ineffective (5.79 ERA) and 35 years old, his career looks to be through. 1997 Outlook: D

Alejandro Pena (Pos: RHP, Age: 37)

	W	L	Pct.	ERA	G	GS	Sv	IP	H	BB	SO	HR	BR/IP
1996	0	1	.000	4.50	4	0	0	4.0	4	1	5	2	1.25
Career	56	52	.519	3.11	503	72	74	1057.1	959	331	839	75	1.22

Pena pitched in four games before missing the rest of the season with a strained rotator cuff. He hasn't been injury-free in many years, and at age 38, he won't probably start now. 1997 Outlook: D

Joe Siddall (Pos: C, Age: 29, Bats: L)

	G	AB	R	H	D	T	HR	RBI	SB	BB	SO	Avg	OBP	Slg
1996	18	47	0	7	1	0	0	3	0	2	8	.149	.184	.170
Career	44	77	4	12	2	0	0	5	0	6	16	.156	.226	.182

Siddall filled in at catcher for Charles Johnson in August when Johnson went down with a bruised finger. His performance (.149 average) was far from impressive—but then again, neither was Johnson's. 1997 Outlook: C

Jesus Tavarez (Pos: CF/LF/RF, Age: 26, Bats: B)

	G	AB	R	H	D	T	HR	RBI	SB	BB	SO	Avg	OBP	Slg
1996	98	114	14	25	3	0	0	6	5	7	18	.219	.264	.246
Career	178	343	49	87	9	2	2	23	13	24	50	.254	.304	.309

Tavarez was Florida's main outfield defensive replacement, getting into 98 games and spending time at all three positions. He wasn't great at the plate, but should keep his role this year. 1997 Outlook: B

Quilvio Veras (Pos: 2B, Age: 25, Bats: B)

	G	AB	R	H	D	T	HR	RBI	SB	BB	SO	Avg	OBP	Slg
1996	73	253	40	64	8	1	4	14	8	51	42	.253	.381	.340
Career	197	693	126	179	28	8	9	46	64	131	110	.258	.383	.361

Although an effective hitter, Veras' reluctance to abuse his ailing hamstring by stealing bases got him sent down to the minors in August in favor of prospect Luis Castillo. He was traded to the Padres after the season, and will probably be their second baseman this year. 1997 Outlook: A

Greg Zaun (Pos: C, Age: 25, Bats: B)

	G	AB	R	H	D	T	HR	RBI	SB	BB	SO	Avg	OBP	Slg
1996	60	139	20	34	9	1	2	15	1	14	20	.245	.318	.367
Career	100	243	38	61	14	1	5	29	2	30	34	.251	.336	.379

Traded from Baltimore in August, Zaun took over the backup catching duties from Bob Natal. Zaun is young and a good hitter, which bodes well for his future prospects. 1997 Outlook: B

Florida Marlins

Florida Marlins Minor League Prospects

Organization Overview:

Not only did the Marlins come up with a great young shortstop last year, but they also delivered a double-play partner for him as well. The impressive debuts of Luis Castillo and Edgar Renteria were a testament to the Marlins' strong scouting and development staff. Along with home-grown catcher Charles Johnson, the Marlins figure to be strong up the middle for years to come. A few more hitters are on the way to fill out the rest of the lineup, but the true strength of the system is its cache of pitching prospects. Several of them saw their first major league action last year, and an increasing number of them will make their presence felt over the next couple of years. The Marlins have a strong commitment to player development, but they have also put together the elements of a contender at the major league level. When the kids arrive, they should be able to relax and adjust to the majors in a winning environment.

Joel Adamson

Position: P **Opening Day Age:** 25
Bats: L **Throws:** L **Born:** 7/2/71 in
Ht: 6' 4" **Wt:** 180 Lakewood, CA

Recent Statistics

	W	L	ERA	G	GS	Sv	IP	H	R	BB	SO	HR
96 AAA Charlotte	6	6	3.78	44	8	3	97.2	108	48	28	84	15
96 NL Florida	0	0	7.36	9	0	0	11.0	18	9	7	7	1

For most of his minor league career, Joel Adamson has struggled with the inevitable injuries that befall current and ex-members of the Phillies' system. Now with Florida, Adamson seems to have found his niche as a long reliever. He's especially tough on lefties, so it won't be hard to find a role for him. His control is as good as always, and he's probably one good spring away from a major league job. The Brewers picked him up in an offseason minor league deal.

Will Cunnane

Position: P **Opening Day Age:** 22
Bats: R **Throws:** R **Born:** 4/24/74 in
Ht: 6' 2" **Wt:** 165 Suffern, NY

Recent Statistics

	W	L	ERA	G	GS	Sv	IP	H	R	BB	SO	HR
93 R Marlins	3	3	2.70	16	9	2	66.2	75	32	8	64	1
94 A Kane County	11	3	1.43	32	16	1	138.2	110	27	23	106	2
95 AA Portland	9	2	3.67	21	21	0	117.2	120	48	34	83	10
96 AA Portland	10	12	3.74	25	25	0	151.2	156	73	30	101	15

Lacking an overpowering fastball or outstanding breaking pitches, Will Cunnane gets by on control alone. The Marlins keep hoping that he'll add velocity as he fills out, but his second season at Double-A last year wasn't any better than the first. The suspicion is growing that he'll never be able to duplicate the success he enjoyed at the lower levels. Still, he's intelligent, and may figure out how to get quite a bit further with the stuff he's got. The Marlins left him off their 40-man roster, and the Padres grabbed him in the Rule 5 draft.

Todd Dunwoody

Position: OF **Opening Day Age:** 21
Bats: L **Throws:** L **Born:** 4/11/75 in W.
Ht: 6' 2" **Wt:** 185 Lafayette, IN

Recent Statistics

	G	AB	R	H	D	T	HR	RBI	SB	BB	SO	AVG
93 R Marlins	31	109	13	21	2	2	0	7	5	7	28	.193
94 A Kane County	15	45	7	5	0	0	1	1	1	5	17	.111
94 R Marlins	46	169	32	44	6	6	1	25	11	21	28	.260
95 A Kane County	132	494	80	140	20	8	14	89	39	52	105	.283
96 AA Portland	138	552	88	153	30	8	24	93	24	45	149	.277
96 MLE	138	529	68	130	25	4	16	72	16	29	159	.246

Todd Dunwoody doesn't have any one tool that defines his game, but almost all of his tools are well-above average. He projects to hit for a decent average with pretty good power, and his speed and defense in center field are strengths. He's got to work on making better contact, but a young left-handed hitter with skills like that is hard to find. In another year, Dunwoody may form the final piece in Florida's core of youngsters up the middle.

Livan Hernandez

Position: P **Opening Day Age:** 22
Bats: R **Throws:** R **Born:** 2/20/75 in Villa
Ht: 6' 2" **Wt:** 220 Clara, Cuba

Recent Statistics

	W	L	ERA	G	GS	Sv	IP	H	R	BB	SO	HR
96 AAA Charlotte	2	4	5.14	10	10	0	49.0	61	32	34	45	3
96 AA Portland	9	2	4.34	15	15	0	93.1	81	48	34	95	14
96 NL Florida	0	0	0.00	1	0	0	3.0	3	0	2	2	0

Cuban defector Livan Hernandez was given a $2.5 million bonus to sign with the Marlins, but when he showed up for camp, he looked like he'd spent about half of his bonus money on junk food. After 10 disastrous Triple-A starts, he was demoted to Double-A. Once he worked his way back into shape, his mid-90s fastball returned, and the turnaround was dramatic. The plan now is to give him a shot at making the major league rotation next year—as long as he can keep from raiding the fridge too often over the winter.

Billy McMillon

Position: OF   **Opening Day Age:** 25
Bats: L **Throws:** L   **Born:** 11/17/71 in
Ht: 5' 11" **Wt:** 172   Otero, NM

Recent Statistics

	G	AB	R	H	D	T	HR	RBI	SB	BB	SO	AVG
96 AAA Charlotte	97	347	72	122	32	2	17	70	5	36	76	.352
96 NL Florida	28	51	4	11	0	0	0	4	0	5	14	.216
96 MLE	97	324	51	99	26	1	10	50	3	25	79	.306

Billy McMillon is one of the most advanced hitters in the minors, but the Marlins are having trouble finding room for him. As an outfielder, he's limited to left field, which presents a problem because he doesn't have left field power. Instead, he shoots line drives to all fields with enough skill to bat .300 in the majors. He's getting on a bit in years—he'll be 25 this year—so the Marlins aren't worried that they're stifling a potential superstar. He'll be lucky to stick as a fourth outfielder, but he certainly can hit enough to help.

Kevin Millar

Position: 1B   **Opening Day Age:** 25
Bats: R **Throws:** R   **Born:** 9/24/71 in Los
Ht: 6' 1" **Wt:** 195   Angeles, CA

Recent Statistics

	G	AB	R	H	D	T	HR	RBI	SB	BB	SO	AVG
94 A Kane County	135	477	75	144	35	2	19	93	3	74	88	.302
95 A Brevard Cty	129	459	53	132	32	2	13	68	4	70	66	.288
96 AA Portland	130	472	69	150	32	0	18	86	6	37	53	.318
96 MLE	130	451	53	129	27	0	13	67	4	24	56	.286

This guy just keeps defying the odds. He wasn't drafted, so he went to play in the Independent Northern League. He got lucky when the Marlins signed him, and hit surprisingly well in his first two years in the organization. Last year, he got stuck behind John Roskos at first base, so they tried him at third, and he didn't embarrass himself. All the while, he kept on hitting. Power's all he's got, and it may not be enough to land him on a major league bench, but you never know with this guy.

Johnny Roskos

Position: 1B   **Opening Day Age:** 22
Bats: R **Throws:** R   **Born:** 11/19/74 in
Ht: 5' 11" **Wt:** 198   Victorville, CA

Recent Statistics

	G	AB	R	H	D	T	HR	RBI	SB	BB	SO	AVG
93 R Marlins	11	40	6	7	1	0	1	3	1	5	11	.175
94 A Elmira	39	136	11	38	7	0	4	23	0	27	37	.279
95 A Kane County	114	418	74	124	36	3	12	88	2	42	86	.297
96 AA Portland	121	396	53	109	26	3	9	58	3	67	102	.275

| 96 MLE | 121 | 381 | 41 | 94 | 22 | 2 | 6 | 45 | 1 | 44 | 109 | .247 |

Regarded as one of the best pure hitters in the Florida system, John Roskos was shifted from catcher to first base this year to enhance his development as a hitter. Unfortunately, his bat didn't cooperate. His power fell off with the move to Double-A, and he's got a long way to go before he'll be productive enough to make it as a first baseman. His raw power still excites the scouts, and he may rebound his second time around the league. He's still young, and may yet pan out.

Tony Saunders

Position: P   **Opening Day Age:** 22
Bats: L **Throws:** L   **Born:** 4/29/74 in
Ht: 6' 1" **Wt:** 189   Baltimore, MD

Recent Statistics

	W	L	ERA	G	GS	Sv	IP	H	R	BB	SO	HR
93 A Kane County	6	1	2.27	23	10	1	83.1	72	23	32	87	3
94 A Brevard Cty	5	5	3.15	10	10	0	60.0	54	24	9	46	4
95 A Brevard Cty	6	5	3.04	13	13	0	71.0	60	29	15	54	6
96 AA Portland	13	4	2.63	26	26	0	167.2	121	51	62	156	10

Lefthander Tony Saunders compiled a dazzling record during the first two years of his minor league career, but torn elbow ligaments cut short his '94 season, and he spent most of '95 building his arm back up. Last year, it all came together for him: he dominated the Eastern League with a 13-4 record and 156 strikeouts, and no lefthander in the high minors topped his K total. Although his heater doesn't crack 90, he throws a great curve and change-up, and knows how to use them. The Marlins will probably give him a long look at Triple-A before calling him up.

Others to Watch

Lefthander **Vic Darensbourg** made a nice recovery from elbow surgery that had kept him out for all of '95. The former starter shifted to the bullpen and fanned over a man per inning at Triple-A. . . The Marlins received hard-throwing righthander **Ryan Dempster** from the Rangers as partial payment for John Burkett. Dempster fanned 157 hitters at Class A last year. . . Southpaw **Bryan Ward** regressed slightly in his second season of Double-A ball, but he's still only 25 and features excellent control. . . Another lefty, **Travis Burgus**, posted a 1.78 ERA and fanned well over one batter per inning at the A level. He's 24 years old this year, so it's time for him to move up. . . Teenager **Victor Hurtado** went 15-7 in the Midwest League last year. Check on him in a couple of years.

Larry Dierker

1996 Season

Houston's selection of broadcaster Larry Dierker to replace Terry Collins as manager was a shock to those who followed the team, but few can question Dierker's knowledge of the Astros or his loyalty to the organization. It is the first managerial position at any level for Dierker, the former Houston righthander who had been the color commentator for the Astros' radio broadcasts since 1979.

Offense

Dierker's challenge will be in figuring out how to best utilize his team's strengths. Collins was unusual in this area, since he suppressed an inherently strong running attack to give big guns such as Jeff Bagwell and Derek Bell a chance to flex their offensive might. Dierker figures to loosen his club's reins, running aggressively on the basepaths and phasing out station-to-station baseball.

Pitching & Defense

Pitching is where Dierker is likely to have the largest impact. Collins got decent results out of his hurlers, but was criticized for coddling his starters at the expense of the bullpen. Dierker figures to enter his rookie season as skipper by implementing a "show me" attitude: the pitchers that show him success are the ones who will enter heavily in his plans. Dierker is not likely to be excessively loyal to veterans such as Doug Drabek and Danny Darwin, since he knows that Collins was ousted in an effort to rid the team of its dead wood.

1997 Outlook

It will take more than a managerial change for Houston to overcome its collapses of the past two years. Collins was respected by the players and posted a winning record at the helm, but that wasn't enough to keep his job. Dierker will clearly have his work cut out for him this year. If he falls flat on his face, the organization will be set even farther back.

Born: 9/22/46 in Hollywood, CA

Playing Experience: 1964-1977, Hou, StL

Managerial Experience: No major league managing experience

Manager Statistics

Year Team, Lg	W	L	Pct	GB	Finish
— —	—	—	—	—	—
— —	—	—	—	—	—

1996 Starting Pitchers by Days Rest

	≤3	4	5	6+
Astros Starts	—	—	—	—
Astros ERA	—	—	—	—
NL Avg Starts	4	86	41	21
NL ERA	4.06	4.28	4.23	4.58

1996 Situational Stats

	Larry Dierker	NL Average
Hit & Run Success %	—	39.0
Stolen Base Success %	—	71.6
Platoon Pct.	—	51.9
Defensive Subs	—	20
High-Pitch Outings	—	13
Quick/Slow Hooks	—	19/12
Sacrifice Attempts	—	92

1996 Rankings (National League)

→ Did not manage in the majors last year

Jeff Bagwell

1996 Season

Last season, Jeff Bagwell was able to show what is he is capable of when he remains healthy for an entire summer. After missing parts of three of the last four years with wrist injuries, Bagwell played in all 162 games and made a run at his second National League MVP Award in three years. His chances of winning the award were damaged by the Astros' fade down the stretch, but he nevertheless eclipsed the .300-30-100 barrier for the second time in his career.

Hitting

Bagwell's open stance and unorthodox crouching style continue to pay dividends for him. Unfortunately, the unique stance is the main reason why he's missed so much time in the past after getting hit on the hands and wrists. Like most power hitters, he likes to get his arms extended, but unlike the typical slugger, Bagwell doesn't feel the need to pull everything in sight. Despite his big swing, Bagwell has evolved into a superstar because of his ability to get the head of his bat through the strike zone with alarming quickness.

Baserunning & Defense

Although not a constant threat to run, Bagwell has good speed and is capable of taking the occasional base: in fact, his 21 steals last season were a career high. He is aggressive on the bases, especially when it comes to breaking up potential double plays. Defensively, Bagwell is one of the NL's top first basemen, both in terms of range and in digging errant throws from his teammates.

1997 Outlook

Still only 28, Bagwell is capable of surpassing the lofty feats he has achieved to date. As long as he can stay healthy, he figures to be one of the top players in the National League again this year.

Position: 1B
Bats: R **Throws:** R
Ht: 6' 0" **Wt:** 195

Opening Day Age: 28
Born: 5/27/68 in Boston, MA
ML Seasons: 6

Overall Statistics

	G	AB	R	H	D	T	HR	RBI	SB	BB	SO	Avg	OBP	Slg
1996	162	568	111	179	48	2	31	120	21	135	114	.315	.451	.570
Career	846	3091	545	950	206	18	144	589	78	500	567	.307	.406	.525

Where He Hits the Ball

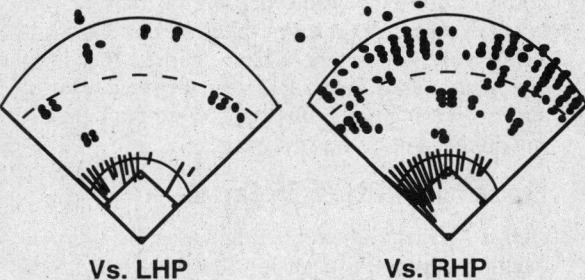

Vs. LHP   **Vs. RHP**

1996 Situational Stats

	AB	H	HR	RBI	Avg		AB	H	HR	RBI	Avg
Home	278	92	16	62	.331	LHP	110	40	3	21	.364
Road	290	87	15	58	.300	RHP	458	139	28	99	.303
First Half	317	99	22	74	.312	Sc Pos	160	50	6	81	.313
Scnd Half	251	80	9	46	.319	Clutch	86	31	9	23	.360

1996 Rankings (National League)

→ 1st in doubles, times on base (324), pitches seen (2,894), games played (162), on-base percentage vs. left-handed pitchers (.517), errors at first base (16) and lowest fielding percentage at first base (.989)

→ 3rd in walks, intentional walks (20), on-base percentage, lowest groundball/flyball ratio (0.8), batting average vs. left-handed pitchers (.364) and on-base percentage vs. right-handed pitchers (.434)

→ 4th in batting average in the clutch (.360)

→ 5th in plate appearances (719)

→ 6th in RBI and slugging percentage

→ 7th in most pitches seen per plate appearance (4.03)

Derek Bell

1996 Season

Derek Bell's second season with the Astros was both satisfying and frustrating. On the one hand, Bell drove in 113 runs, belted 60 extra-base hits and stole 29 bases—all career highs for the talented outfielder. On the other hand, his average dropped from .334 in 1995 to .263 in '96, and he batted just .233 with runners in scoring position. Bell also finished the year in a deep slump, and his poor September performance was cited as a major reason why the Astros didn't make the playoffs.

Hitting

Bell has tremendous bat speed and a big swing, and he takes a huge cut whether he's ahead in the count or not. He can murder any fastball, and he loves to take a rip at a first-pitch heater. Unfortunately for Bell, pitchers have learned that he'll swing at anything, and last year they had a lot of success teasing him with offspeed stuff and breaking pitches out of the strike zone.

Baserunning & Defense

Bell is a superb athlete. On the bases, he still gets caught napping on occasion, but his great speed enables him to leg out numerous extra-base hits, and he's developed into a superb basestealer. With excellent speed, good instincts, and a powerful throwing arm, Bell has also developed into one of the league's top defensive right fielders. Bell also does a good job when he's called upon to fill in at center field, even though he's more comfortable in right.

1997 Outlook

Despite his impressive numbers last year, Bell is still looked upon by many as a player who hasn't quite fulfilled his tremendous potential. A lot of his critics seem to reside in the Houston front office, and the word was that the Astros were shopping him this winter. Plenty of other teams would love to have him.

Position: RF
Bats: R **Throws:** R
Ht: 6' 2" **Wt:** 215

Opening Day Age: 28
Born: 12/11/68 in Tampa, FL
ML Seasons: 6

Overall Statistics

	G	AB	R	H	D	T	HR	RBI	SB	BB	SO	Avg	OBP	Slg
1996	158	627	84	165	40	3	17	113	29	40	123	.263	.311	.418
Career	607	2244	302	636	106	9	62	341	116	146	443	.283	.333	.422

Where He Hits the Ball

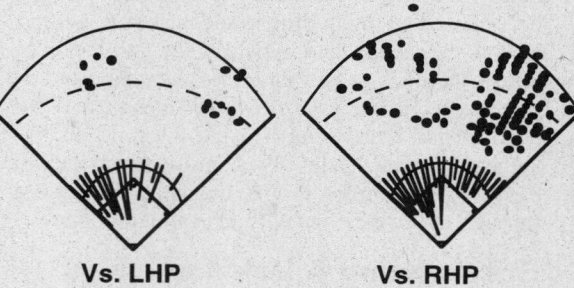

Vs. LHP   **Vs. RHP**

1996 Situational Stats

	AB	H	HR	RBI	Avg		AB	H	HR	RBI	Avg
Home	311	81	8	65	.260	LHP	134	38	4	19	.284
Road	316	84	9	48	.266	RHP	493	127	13	94	.258
First Half	361	104	9	66	.288	Sc Pos	219	51	3	91	.233
Scnd Half	266	61	8	47	.229	Clutch	102	29	2	27	.284

1996 Rankings (National League)

- → 1st in stolen base percentage (90.6%) and steals of third (11)
- → 3rd in lowest cleanup slugging percentage (.428)
- → 4th in sacrifice flies (9)
- → 5th in highest groundball/flyball ratio (2.0), errors in right field (7) and fielding percentage in right field (.977)
- → 6th in doubles and lowest on-base percentage
- → 9th in RBI, strikeouts and lowest on-base percentage vs. left-handed pitchers (.312)
- → 10th in at-bats and highest percentage of swings on the first pitch (41.9%)
- → Led the Astros in at-bats, sacrifice flies (9), strikeouts and GDPs (18)

Sean Berry

1996 Season

Acquired in a preseason trade from the Montreal Expos, Sean Berry was an unqualified success as the Astros' primary third baseman. Despite not playing every day, Berry placed third on the club in RBI and established personal bests in virtually every offensive category. Although his error total was cause for concern, he generally played solid defense at the hot corner.

Hitting

Berry is teammate Jeff Bagwell's polar opposite—his bat speed is suspect, but his swing is natural and fundamentally sound. His stroke produces surprising power, and he would have topped 25 homers if he wasn't playing in the spacious Astrodome. He was one of the team's top hitters in the clutch, batting well over .300 with runners in scoring position. It was the second year in a row that Berry had surpassed the .300 mark in clutch situations, an indication of his progress in both managing the strike zone and approaching situational hitting.

Baserunning & Defense

Although Berry isn't a fast runner, he does get sneaky occasionally, as evidenced by last season's 12 stolen bases. Knowing his speed is suspect, he usually makes sound decisions on the basepaths. Viewed as a defensive liability coming into the season, Berry may have been the NL's most improved third baseman. He improved significantly in fielding the hot shots as well as the bunts and slow rollers. His arm is as strong as any in the N.L., but it's also erratic, accounting for most his errors.

1997 Outlook

It's time for Berry to take the next step in his career and develop into the 25 home run/100 RBI man Houston believes he can become. With his first real chance to become a full-time player, Berry has settled in quite nicely with the Astros. He'll need to keep working on his defense, but he seems primed to have the best season of his career.

Position: 3B
Bats: R **Throws:** R
Ht: 5'11" **Wt:** 200

Opening Day Age: 31
Born: 3/22/66 in Santa Monica, CA
ML Seasons: 7

Overall Statistics

	G	AB	R	H	D	T	HR	RBI	SB	BB	SO	Avg	OBP	Slg
1996	132	431	55	121	38	1	17	95	12	23	58	.281	.328	.492
Career	523	1504	198	420	99	7	57	249	43	129	270	.279	.340	.468

Where He Hits the Ball

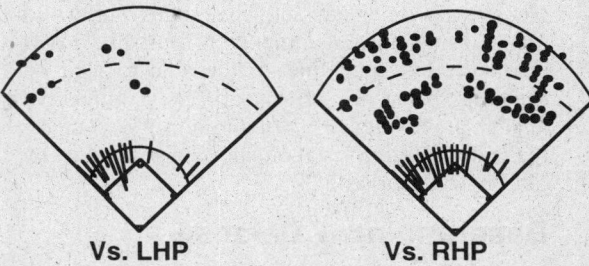

Vs. LHP   Vs. RHP

1996 Situational Stats

	AB	H	HR	RBI	Avg		AB	H	HR	RBI	Avg
Home	183	48	4	31	.262	LHP	106	28	3	21	.264
Road	248	73	13	64	.294	RHP	325	93	14	74	.286
First Half	269	77	11	55	.286	Sc Pos	156	49	7	79	.314
Scnd Half	162	44	6	40	.272	Clutch	63	19	3	20	.302

1996 Rankings (National League)

→ 1st in errors at third base (22) and lowest fielding percentage at third base (.922)
→ 6th in lowest batting average on an 0-2 count (.030)

Craig Biggio

1996 Season

Since becoming a full-time second baseman five years ago, Craig Biggio has ranked among the game's best and most consistent performers. Although not quite as spectacular last year as he was in 1995, he was again voted to the NL All-Star team. Biggio was frequently shifted around the batting order by former manager Terry Collins several years ago, but settled into the second spot the past two years. The only down note on his season was a September slump that badly hurt the Astros' attempt to win a playoff spot.

Hitting

Despite his relative lack of size, Biggio has developed into a gap hitter with solid home run power. He crowds the plate and challenges hurlers to come inside, turning quickly to pull his drives down the left field line. While able to wait on breaking balls, Biggio also offers a quick bat against power pitchers. Not afraid to "take one for the team," Biggio led the majors in getting hit by pitches last year with 27.

Baserunning & Defense

In addition to his excellent running speed, Biggio is also smart on the basepaths. Though never hesitant to be aggressive when the situation demands it, he rarely runs his team out of an inning. Despite being right-handed, he is quick out of the batter's box and grounds into very few double plays. Biggio has become one of the NL's top defensive second basemen, winning his third straight Gold Glove in '96.

1997 Outlook

Biggio's 1996 season ended on a down note, but he's still one of the top second basemen in the game. If Brian Hunter develops into an everyday leadoff hitter, Biggio will return to the second slot in the lineup, a role for which he is well-suited. The Astros will probably try to give him an occasional day off this year to avoid another late slump.

Position: 2B
Bats: R **Throws:** R
Ht: 5'11" **Wt:** 180

Opening Day Age: 31
Born: 12/14/65 in Smithtown, NY
ML Seasons: 9
Pronunciation: BIDG-jee-oh

Overall Statistics

	G	AB	R	H	D	T	HR	RBI	SB	BB	SO	Avg	OBP	Slg
1996	162	605	113	174	24	4	15	75	25	75	72	.288	.386	.415
Career	1217	4485	728	1279	245	28	94	464	221	550	646	.285	.371	.415

Where He Hits the Ball

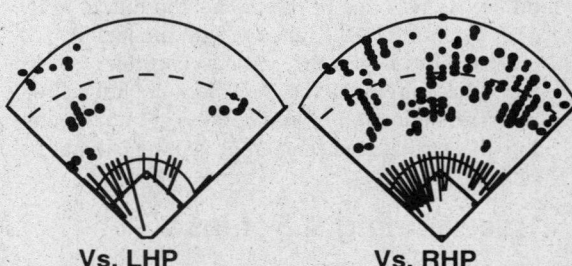

Vs. LHP   Vs. RHP

1996 Situational Stats

	AB	H	HR	RBI	Avg		AB	H	HR	RBI	Avg
Home	289	80	7	40	.277	LHP	125	41	5	20	.328
Road	316	94	8	35	.297	RHP	480	133	10	55	.277
First Half	333	100	10	47	.300	Sc Pos	143	45	4	57	.315
Scnd Half	272	74	5	28	.272	Clutch	97	25	3	13	.258

1996 Rankings (National League)

→ 1st in hit by pitch (27) and games played (162)
→ 2nd in plate appearances (723)
→ 3rd in fielding percentage at second base (.988)
→ 4th in lowest batting average with the bases loaded (.091)
→ 5th in times on base (276), pitches seen (2,678) and steals of third (8)
→ 7th in singles, on-base percentage vs. left-handed pitchers (.423) and errors at second base (10)
→ 8th in sacrifice flies (8)
→ 10th in runs scored
→ Led the Astros in runs scored, singles, triples, hit by pitch (27) and plate appearances (723)

Danny Darwin

1996 Season

One of baseball's ageless wonders, Danny Darwin joined the Astros in a mid-July trade after posting seven wins for the last-place Pittsburgh Pirates. Houston wanted the 19-year veteran to lend depth and experience to its rotation as a spot starter, but Darwin struggled with the Astros, posting an ERA of nearly 6.00 in 15 appearances.

Pitching

As is the case with most 40 year olds, Darwin has survived in the majors by pitching intelligently and avoiding mistakes. While his fastball is merely average at best these days, his slider and forkball still carry a decent bite, and his unorthodox delivery baffles younger hitters. Darwin's control remains first-rate, as evidenced by his excellent three-to-one strikeout/walk ratio. Despite his rapidly-cooling heater, Darwin is not a nibbler: he's not afraid to challenge hitters and is willing to come inside to just about anyone, refusing to allow age to become a factor in his makeup as a pitcher.

Defense & Hitting

Although he doesn't snare shots back through the box as he did in his prime, Darwin fields his position respectably. His pickoff move is above average, but runners who are able to read his move can take advantage of his slow delivery. Darwin is a poor hitter even by pitchers' standards, striking out in more than half of his appearances and recording just one hit in 10 at-bats as an Astro.

1997 Outlook

A free agent this winter, Darwin isn't ready to throw in the towel just yet. Ideally, the Texas native would prefer to finish his career in his home state, but his first priority is to land a job with a contender. Houston may end up accommodating the veteran, but the Astros would prefer to take their chances on a younger starter.

Position: SP/RP
Bats: R **Throws:** R
Ht: 6' 3" **Wt:** 202

Opening Day Age: 41
Born: 10/25/55 in Bonham, TX
ML Seasons: 19

Overall Statistics

	W	L	Pct.	ERA	G	GS	Sv	IP	H	BB	SO	HR	BR/IP
1996	10	11	.476	3.77	34	25	0	164.2	160	27	96	16	1.14
Career	158	161	.495	3.71	652	322	32	2711.1	2594	780	1769	272	1.24

How Often He Throws Strikes

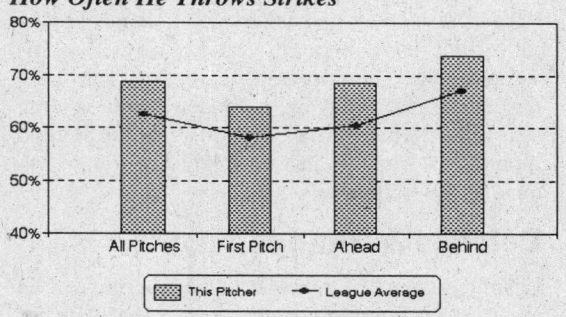

1996 Situational Stats

	W	L	ERA	Sv	IP		AB	H	HR	RBI	Avg
Home	5	5	3.86	0	91.0	LHB	276	91	9	34	.330
Road	5	6	3.67	0	73.2	RHB	347	69	7	37	.199
First Half	7	8	2.89	0	115.1	Sc Pos	146	32	3	56	.219
Scnd Half	3	3	5.84	0	49.1	Clutch	76	23	0	9	.303

1996 Rankings (National League)

→ 1st in highest batting average allowed vs. left-handed batters (.330)
→ 3rd in balks (3), least pitches thrown per batter (3.38) and lowest batting average allowed vs. right-handed batters (.199)
→ 5th in hit batsmen (12)
→ 6th in least strikeouts per 9 innings (5.2)
→ 7th in highest strikeout/walk ratio (3.6) and least GDPs induced per 9 innings (0.5)
→ 8th in least baserunners allowed per 9 innings (10.9)
→ 10th in lowest on-base percentage allowed (.297) and lowest batting average allowed with runners in scoring position (.219)

Houston Astros

Doug Drabek

1996 Season

Former Cy Young Award winner Doug Drabek saw his role on the Astros' pitching staff substantially reduced last season. No longer the ace of the staff, Drabek won just seven of his 30 starts and was outshone by younger hurlers such as Shane Reynolds and Mike Hampton. It was another disappointing season for Drabek, the former Pirate star whose four years with the Astros have produced only 38 wins.

Pitching

When he was in his prime, Drabek had the ability to position his fastballs and breakers as well as anyone not named Greg Maddux. Now in the twilight of his career, he has developed control problems that have become critical now that his weapons have deteriorated. Drabek offsets some of his shortcomings with tenacity and veteran savvy, but when he is constantly falling behind hitters—as was the case in 1996—he's going to have trouble winning.

Defense & Hitting

In some respects, Drabek has become more of an asset for his complementary skills rather than for his pitching. He fields his position extremely well, is quick off the mound to handle bunts, and does a solid job of holding baserunners. One of the best-hitting pitchers in the league, Drabek comes up with the occasional gapper and puts the ball in play more often than not.

1997 Outlook

At 34, Drabek's best days are behind him. Houston's normally abundant farm system is somewhat thin at starting pitcher, which could mean that the free agent could re-sign and serve as the fourth starter this season. Drabek would prefer to finish his career with the Astros, but he might be more valuable to a team with a staff of youngsters in need of veteran tutelage.

Position: SP
Bats: R **Throws:** R
Ht: 6' 1" **Wt:** 185

Opening Day Age: 34
Born: 7/25/62 in Victoria, TX
ML Seasons: 11
Pronunciation: DRAY-bek

Overall Statistics

	W	L	Pct.	ERA	G	GS	Sv	IP	H	BB	SO	HR	BR/IP
1996	7	9	.438	4.57	30	30	0	175.1	208	60	137	21	1.53
Career	137	112	.550	3.41	344	335	0	2257.0	2140	606	1454	196	1.22

How Often He Throws Strikes

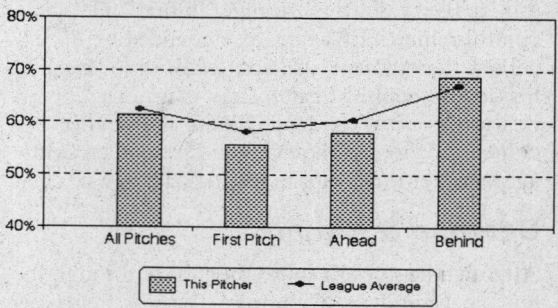

1996 Situational Stats

	W	L	ERA	Sv	IP		AB	H	HR	RBI	Avg
Home	5	4	3.64	0	94.0	LHB	314	87	10	40	.277
Road	2	5	5.64	0	81.1	RHB	385	121	11	50	.314
First Half	4	6	4.82	0	97.0	Sc Pos	184	43	5	67	.234
Scnd Half	3	3	4.25	0	78.1	Clutch	29	6	1	2	.207

1996 Rankings (National League)

- → 1st in highest batting average allowed vs. right-handed batters (.314)
- → 2nd in highest batting average allowed (.298) and highest ERA on the road (5.64)
- → 5th in lowest fielding percentage at pitcher (.930)
- → 6th in most baserunners allowed per 9 innings (14.1) and errors at pitcher (3)
- → 7th in highest on-base percentage allowed (.355)
- → 8th in highest slugging percentage allowed (.455)
- → Led the Astros in home runs allowed, stolen bases allowed (19) and most run support per 9 innings (5.0)

Mike Hampton

1996 Season

Mike Hampton emerged as one of the NL's top left-handed starting pitchers last season, winning 10 games. Hampton might have done even better, but he came down with shoulder tendinitis late in the year and was able to make only one start in September.

Pitching

Hampton depends primarily on four pitches, mixing a cut fastball, slider, curve, and change-up into his arsenal. The cutter, a pitch which produces numerous ground balls, is probably his best pitch. While he possesses excellent control for a young southpaw, Hampton isn't a power pitcher, instead relying on changing speeds and precision placement to confuse his foes. He prefers running the ball in on righties with his cutter while baffling lefties with his assortment of breaking pitches. Hampton knows when to challenge hitters and when to paint the corners, getting batters to chase pitches that aren't ideally located.

Defense & Hitting

Although Hampton has a decent pickoff move, he also has a slow delivery to the plate, and runners can take advantage of him at times. He's worked on this area of his game, however, and did a much better job of stopping opposing runners last year. Hampton is an above-average fielder who's regarded as the best athlete on the Astros staff, and he knows how to help himself with his bat.

1997 Outlook

This could be the breakout season for Hampton, who has all the earmarks of becoming a 15-to-17-game winner. He'll need to show he's recovered from last season's injury, but if his shoulder is at full strength this spring, he'll begin the year as Houston's number-three starter. . . with a chance to move up.

Position: SP
Bats: R **Throws:** L
Ht: 5'10" **Wt:** 180

Opening Day Age: 24
Born: 9/9/72 in Brooksville, FL
ML Seasons: 4

Overall Statistics

	W	L	Pct.	ERA	G	GS	Sv	IP	H	BB	SO	HR	BR/IP
1996	10	10	.500	3.59	27	27	0	160.1	175	49	101	12	1.40
Career	22	22	.500	3.78	108	54	1	369.1	390	131	248	32	1.41

How Often He Throws Strikes

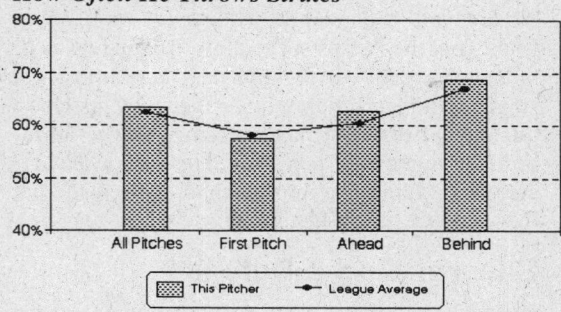

1996 Situational Stats

	W	L	ERA	Sv	IP		AB	H	HR	RBI	Avg
Home	6	4	3.45	0	86.0	LHB	127	35	2	12	.276
Road	4	6	3.75	0	74.1	RHB	498	140	10	62	.281
First Half	6	5	3.20	0	98.1	Sc Pos	173	43	3	56	.249
Scnd Half	4	5	4.21	0	62.0	Clutch	37	5	0	5	.135

1996 Rankings (National League)

→ 9th in shutouts (1)
→ Led the Astros in shutouts (1) and GDPs induced (18)

Brian L. Hunter

1996 Season

After hitting .302 in 78 games for the Astros as a rookie in 1995, Brian Hunter was expected to take over as Houston's leadoff hitter for the next decade. After 1996, however, the Astros might be thinking about changing their plans. Hunter's average tumbled 26 points to .276 last year, and his undisciplined style at the plate made him a less-than-ideal number-one hitter. His failure to draw walks forced manager Terry Collins to bury him at the bottom of the order midway through the summer. To top it all off, Hunter also missed a month of the season with a broken thumb.

Hitting

At 6-4 and 180 pounds, Hunter sports a slight frame, but the Astros still believe he can hit 15-20 homers a year. Up to now he's been mostly a singles-doubles hitter with a tendency to chase pitches out of the strike zone, resulting in an inordinate number of pop flies. The Astros desperately want him to be more patient at the plate, but thus far they haven't had much success.

Baserunning & Defense

Hunter has all the skills to develop into one of the NL's premier defensive center fielders. With lightning fast reactions, tremendous footspeed, and a fearless demeanor, Houston fans are already projecting future Gold Gloves for the young Astro. His throwing arm tends to be erratic, however. While he still needs to brush up on the finer points of baserunning fundamentals, Hunter's speed is a nightmare for enemy pitchers and catchers.

1997 Outlook

The Astros are hoping this is the season Hunter firmly establishes himself as a quality player. While Houston's projections for Hunter are probably a bit out of reach due to his problems controlling the strike zone, he remains a potential star. He could break the .300 average/40 stolen base plateau this year.

Position: CF
Bats: R **Throws:** R
Ht: 6' 4" **Wt:** 180

Opening Day Age: 26
Born: 3/5/71 in Portland, OR
ML Seasons: 3

Overall Statistics

	G	AB	R	H	D	T	HR	RBI	SB	BB	SO	Avg	OBP	Slg
1996	132	526	74	145	27	2	5	35	35	17	92	.276	.297	.363
Career	216	871	128	248	42	7	7	63	61	39	150	.285	.315	.373

Where He Hits the Ball

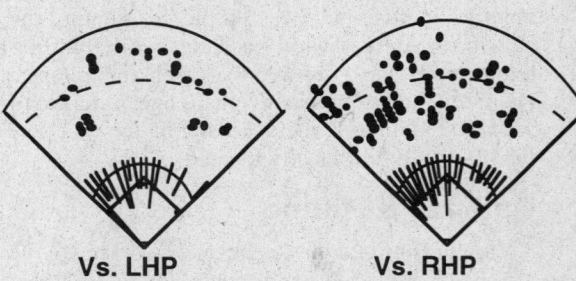

Vs. LHP   **Vs. RHP**

1996 Situational Stats

	AB	H	HR	RBI	Avg		AB	H	HR	RBI	Avg
Home	252	76	1	10	.302	LHP	131	34	0	7	.260
Road	274	69	4	25	.252	RHP	395	111	5	28	.281
First Half	314	85	2	22	.271	Sc Pos	124	23	0	29	.185
Scnd Half	212	60	3	13	.283	Clutch	83	27	1	9	.325

1996 Rankings (National League)

→ 1st in errors in center field (12) and lowest fielding percentage in center field (.960)
→ 2nd in lowest on-base percentage vs. left-handed pitchers (.267) and steals of third (10)
→ 4th in lowest batting average with runners in scoring position (.185) and lowest on-base percentage for a leadoff hitter (.313)
→ 5th in lowest on-base percentage
→ 6th in lowest HR frequency (105.2 ABs per HR) and highest percentage of extra bases taken as a runner (65.1%)
→ 9th in stolen bases, lowest batting average with the bases loaded (.125) and lowest slugging percentage vs. left-handed pitchers (.344)

Todd Jones

1996 Season

Todd Jones began last season trying to prove that his successful 1995 stint replacing closer John Hudek was no fluke. Jones had a few problems, but he was on his way to a 30-save season when his shoulder began to bother him last July. Jones wound up on the disabled list, and while he was out, rookie phenom Billy Wagner seized the closer's role. Wagner later came up lame himself, but Jones wasn't healthy enough to take back his old job.

Pitching

Jones relies on a 90+ MPH fastball, a curve and a change-up to do battle with opposing hitters. The fastball is his best pitch; it has a little bit of a sink to it, resulting in a good percentage of groundball outs. When he keeps the ball down in the strike zone, Jones can be overpowering—but when it starts to rise, if often finds a seat in the bleachers. While he attacks righthanders with his entire arsenal, he tends to nibble against lefties, who rocked him for a .316 average last season.

Defense & Hitting

Jones is considered a liability with the glove because of his poor reaction time and his difficulties in charging bunts. He also has trouble controlling runners, since he doesn't modify his delivery with runners on base. Jones rarely sees the batter's box and is not an offensive threat.

1997 Outlook

Jones had some problems last year, but he did a good job as long as he was healthy. He'll need to show he's recovered from his shoulder problems this spring, but even if he is, he might not be able to reclaim the Astros' closer's job. With both Hudek and Wagner around, Jones might return to his old set-up role, a job he has proven he can handle in the past.

Position: RP
Bats: L **Throws:** R
Ht: 6' 3" **Wt:** 200

Opening Day Age: 28
Born: 4/24/68 in Marietta, GA
ML Seasons: 4

Overall Statistics

	W	L	Pct.	ERA	G	GS	Sv	IP	H	BB	SO	HR	BR/IP
1996	6	3	.667	4.40	51	0	17	57.1	61	32	44	5	1.62
Career	18	12	.600	3.27	194	0	39	267.0	230	125	228	20	1.33

How Often He Throws Strikes

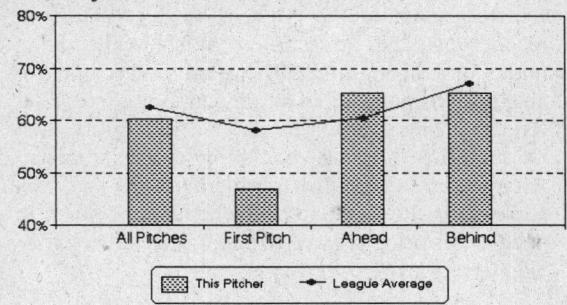

1996 Situational Stats

	W	L	ERA	Sv	IP		AB	H	HR	RBI	Avg
Home	4	2	4.24	7	23.1	LHB	95	30	3	17	.316
Road	2	1	4.50	10	34.0	RHB	128	31	2	19	.242
First Half	6	1	3.43	16	42.0	Sc Pos	73	21	1	30	.288
Scnd Half	0	2	7.04	1	15.1	Clutch	144	45	4	29	.313

1996 Rankings (National League)

→ 1st in lowest save percentage (73.9%)
→ 3rd in most baserunners allowed per 9 innings in relief (15.4)
→ 6th in highest batting average allowed in relief (.274)
→ 8th in blown saves (6) and highest percentage of inherited runners scored (37.8%)
→ 10th in relief wins (6)
→ Led the Astros in saves, games finished (37), save opportunities (23), save percentage (73.9%), blown saves (6), most GDPs induced per GDP situation (13.8%), first batter efficiency (.250) and relief wins (6)

Darryl Kile

1996 Season

A candidate for the NL's Comeback Player of the Year Award last season, Darryl Kile put together a solid campaign that quieted the naysayers in Houston. Sporting one of the finest curveballs in the game, Kile won 12 games and fanned more than 200 batters while averaging a strikeout per inning. While he still had some control problems, he didn't let his struggles disrupt his game, as he sometimes did in 1995.

Pitching

Kile's curveball was once rated the best in the NL by a poll of managers. Although it's a curve, the pitch behaves more like a forkball, since the bottom drops out of the pitch a few feet before it reaches the plate. To complement his breaker, Kile mixes in a strong mid-90s fastball and a straight change. The pressure of a tight game used to rattle Kile, but he's learned to rely on his ability and maintain his focus on controlling the strike zone. Along with his control problems, Kile has had some difficulties with left-handed hitters, and he'll need to develop a way to neutralize lefties this year.

Defense & Hitting

Kile works hard at holding runners, but his big leg kick and wildness have hurt his efforts. Tall and lanky, Kile covers a lot of ground around the mound and is a solid defender. At the plate, he strikes out nearly half the time but is able to lay down the sacrifice bunt.

1997 Outlook

After disappointing performances in 1994 and 1995, Kile seems to have returned to the form he displayed in 1993, when he won 15 games and threw a no-hitter. Entering spring training as the Astros' number-two starter, Kile could win 15 or more games if he can maintain his control and develop an effective pitch to use against left-handed hitters.

Position: SP
Bats: R **Throws:** R
Ht: 6' 5" **Wt:** 185

Opening Day Age: 28
Born: 12/2/68 in Garden Grove, CA
ML Seasons: 6

Overall Statistics

	W	L	Pct.	ERA	G	GS	Sv	IP	H	BB	SO	HR	BR/IP
1996	12	11	.522	4.19	35	33	0	219.0	233	97	219	16	1.51
Career	52	58	.473	4.12	175	148	0	944.1	920	468	768	70	1.47

How Often He Throws Strikes

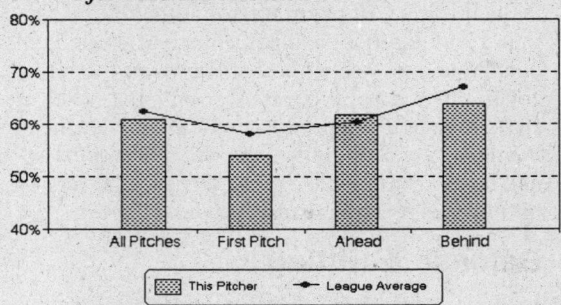

1996 Situational Stats

	W	L	ERA	Sv	IP		AB	H	HR	RBI	Avg
Home	4	6	3.79	0	109.1	LHB	405	128	9	48	.316
Road	8	5	4.60	0	109.2	RHB	438	105	7	51	.240
First Half	8	5	3.66	0	123.0	Sc Pos	213	52	2	72	.244
Scnd Half	4	6	4.88	0	96.0	Clutch	85	19	1	4	.224

1996 Rankings (National League)

→ 1st in hit batsmen (16)

→ 3rd in hits allowed, walks allowed, balks (3) and highest batting average allowed vs. left-handed batters (.316)

→ 4th in wild pitches (13), most baserunners allowed per 9 innings (14.2) and most strikeouts per 9 innings (9.0)

→ 5th in strikeouts, highest on-base percentage allowed (.359) and lowest fielding percentage at pitcher (.930)

→ 6th in batters faced (975), least home runs allowed per 9 innings (.66) and errors at pitcher (3)

→ 7th in complete games (4) and pitches thrown (3,513)

Kirt Manwaring

Signed By
ROCKIES

Position: C
Bats: R **Throws:** R
Ht: 5'11" **Wt:** 203

Opening Day Age: 31
Born: 7/15/65 in
Elmira, NY
ML Seasons: 10
Pronunciation:
man-WAIR-ing

1996 Season

After a lengthy career in San Francisco, Kirt Manwaring joined Houston in midseason in a trade for fellow catcher Rick Wilkins. Although he struggled at the plate for the Astros, Manwaring did an admirable job handling the pitching staff and helping shore up what had been a weak defensive position.

Hitting

Manwaring has never been regarded as much of a hitter, but he's usually been able to keep his average in the .240-.250 range. He's no power threat, and he's content to simply try to hit the ball where it's pitched. Pitchers usually come inside on him since his power doesn't instill fear in them. His main weakness lies in the fact that he lacks the bat speed to be a consistently productive hitter.

Baserunning & Defense

Manwaring runs like, well. . . a catcher. He is a station-to-station baserunner, rarely attempting to score from second on a single, even when there are two outs. Defensively, Manwaring is an excellent all-around player who not only does a great job blocking the plate, but who is also widely regarded as among the league's best at handling pitchers and calling ball games. In addition, he has a strong, accurate throwing arm—making potential basestealers think twice about running on him. Manwaring knows that the day his defense slips is the day his big-league career comes to an end.

1997 Outlook

Although it seems like he's been around the league forever, Manwaring will be only 31 at the start of this season. A free agent, he signed a two-year deal with the Rockies after the season. He figures to be Colorado's number-one receiver, and the shift to Coors Field ought to give a big boost to his hitting numbers.

Overall Statistics

	G	AB	R	H	D	T	HR	RBI	SB	BB	SO	Avg	OBP	Slg
1996	86	227	14	52	9	0	1	18	0	19	40	.229	.300	.282
Career	746	2217	179	544	86	12	16	211	8	163	355	.245	.307	.317

Where He Hits the Ball

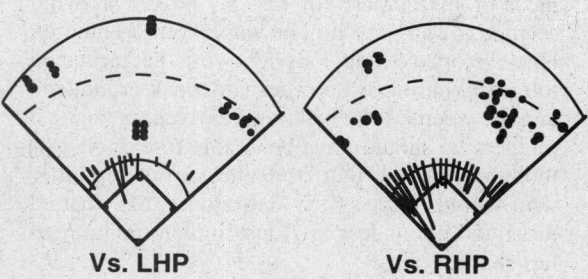

Vs. LHP   **Vs. RHP**

1996 Situational Stats

	AB	H	HR	RBI	Avg		AB	H	HR	RBI	Avg
Home	116	30	1	11	.259	LHP	60	12	1	3	.200
Road	111	22	0	7	.198	RHP	167	40	0	15	.240
First Half	119	29	1	13	.244	Sc Pos	46	9	0	16	.196
Scnd Half	108	23	0	5	.213	Clutch	37	12	0	1	.324

1996 Rankings (National League)

➡ 2nd in highest percentage of runners caught stealing as a catcher (41.8%)

Derrick May

1996 Season

The Astros obtained Derrick May from Milwaukee in midseason 1995, and May impressed his new club by hitting for both average and power throughout the rest of the year. Houston hoped May would be able to provide the same kind of production in '96, but his performance was extremely disappointing. Injuries to teammates Brian Hunter and James Mouton gave May a chance to be an everyday player last year, but he failed to capitalize on the opportunity. He finished the year as a part-time starter and left-handed pinch hitter.

Hitting

May has been a consistent line-drive hitter through most of his career, but his '95 power showing seemed to convince him he was a home-run hitter. He developed a long, looping swing that produced too many harmless pop flies and weak grounders, and he seemed to lack aggressiveness against pitchers he should have been able to exploit. Although he would figure to be the sort of gap hitter who would thrive at the Astrodome, May batted nearly 50 points less in Houston than on the road last season.

Baserunning & Defense

Although not blessed with exceptional speed, May covers the outfield turf fairly well with his long strides. However, he doesn't get a great jump on the ball, and his throwing arm is only average. May is an intelligent baserunner, but not overly aggressive, taking the extra base only when he's expected to do so. He's not much of a threat to steal.

1997 Outlook

Though he should be in the prime of his career, May is now considered nothing more than a part-time outfielder and platoon player by the Astros. With other, younger players available, they don't figure to have much interest in bringing him back. He's been a useful player in the past and will probably look to revive his career with another club.

Position: LF
Bats: L **Throws:** R
Ht: 6' 4" **Wt:** 225

Opening Day Age: 28
Born: 7/14/68 in Rochester, NY
ML Seasons: 7

Overall Statistics

	G	AB	R	H	D	T	HR	RBI	SB	BB	SO	Avg	OBP	Slg
1996	109	259	24	65	12	3	5	33	2	30	33	.251	.330	.378
Career	603	1822	218	506	90	9	42	270	26	133	198	.278	.327	.406

Where He Hits the Ball

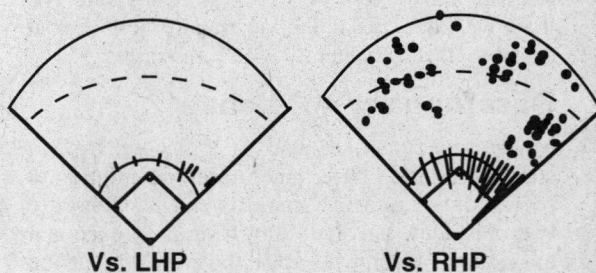

Vs. LHP   Vs. RHP

1996 Situational Stats

	AB	H	HR	RBI	Avg		AB	H	HR	RBI	Avg
Home	102	23	2	11	.225	LHP	13	2	0	1	.154
Road	157	42	3	22	.268	RHP	246	63	5	32	.256
First Half	138	37	3	23	.268	Sc Pos	81	18	1	25	.222
Scnd Half	121	28	2	10	.231	Clutch	39	9	2	5	.231

1996 Rankings (National League)

→ 9th in lowest batting average with runners in scoring position (.222)
→ 10th in least GDPs per GDP situation (5.9%) and errors in left field (4)
→ Led the Astros in least GDPs per GDP situation (5.9%)

Orlando Miller

1996 Season

As a power-hitting shortstop, Orlando Miller has developed into a valuable commodity. Miller reached double figures in home runs for the first time in his career and served as a decent middle-infield complement to second baseman Craig Biggio. Due to knee problems, the Astros juggled Miller at third base for 30 games last season, but for the most part he was an everyday fixture in the Houston lineup.

Hitting

Miller has supposedly worked hard to improve his discipline at the plate. . . but you can't tell it by looking at his numbers. The free-swinging Miller, who sported an abysmal 8:1 strikeout/walk ratio last year, will chase virtually anything when behind in the count. When he makes contact, however, the ball travels, as evidenced by his considerable extra-base power. Miller has struggled with the bat at home, and he must learn that the key to success in the Astrodome is to drive the ball into the gaps.

Baserunning & Defense

Miller's poor baserunning sabotaged many a Houston rally last season. His frame suggests that he should possess above-average speed, but he was horrendous when trying to steal, getting thrown out more than two-thirds of the time. On defense, Miller has decent range at shortstop, but at times it seems that he should be able to cover more ground. Blessed with an outstanding arm and excellent intuition, Miller certainly has proven to be a fine all-around fielder.

1997 Outlook

The Astros weren't completely happy with Miller's play last year, feeling that he lacks the consistency to be a top shortstop. With their top shortstop prospect, Russ Johnson, at least a full season away from being ready for major-league action, they were considering bringing in someone new to handle the position. If they fail to do so they can always go back to Miller.

Position: SS/3B
Bats: R **Throws:** R
Ht: 6' 1" **Wt:** 180

Opening Day Age: 28
Born: 1/13/69 in Changuinola, Panama
ML Seasons: 3

Overall Statistics

	G	AB	R	H	D	T	HR	RBI	SB	BB	SO	Avg	OBP	Slg
1996	139	468	43	120	26	2	15	58	3	14	116	.256	.291	.417
Career	247	832	82	218	46	4	22	103	7	38	199	.262	.307	.406

Where He Hits the Ball

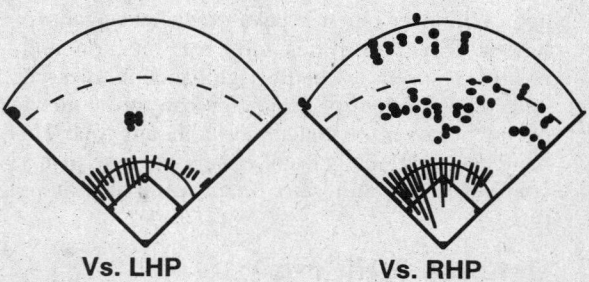

Vs. LHP   Vs. RHP

1996 Situational Stats

	AB	H	HR	RBI	Avg		AB	H	HR	RBI	Avg
Home	230	55	7	29	.239	LHP	91	17	2	5	.187
Road	238	65	8	29	.273	RHP	377	103	13	53	.273
First Half	249	67	7	36	.269	Sc Pos	127	31	2	43	.244
Scnd Half	219	53	8	22	.242	Clutch	77	25	5	10	.325

1996 Rankings (National League)

- ➡ 2nd in lowest fielding percentage at shortstop (.958)
- ➡ 5th in lowest batting average with the bases loaded (.100)
- ➡ 6th in errors at shortstop (19)
- ➡ 7th in lowest on-base percentage vs. right-handed pitchers (.306)
- ➡ 8th in lowest percentage of pitches taken (45.8%)
- ➡ 9th in hit by pitch (10) and lowest percentage of swings put into play (36.5%)
- ➡ 10th in highest percentage of swings that missed (27.6%)

Shane Reynolds

1996 Season

Firmly establishing himself as one of the National League's top pitchers, Shane Reynolds led the Astros starting staff in virtually every category last year. Not only did he produce wins, but he was often so dominating that he sparked the entire team for days at a time. If the bullpen was in need of rest, Reynolds would lend a hand by tossing a complete game to give them a day off. If his run support was lacking, he would step up his level of performance. Only a late-season slump prevented Reynolds from winning 20 games.

Pitching

Reynolds has finally mastered the split-fingered fastball that he began to tinker with several years ago. While the pitch breaks down and away to lefties, Reynolds relies more on location and changing speeds to battle righthanders. Blessed with pinpoint control, Reynolds can throw all of his pitches over the plate at virtually any time. He hates to intentionally walk batters because of his confidence in getting any hitter out in any situation.

Defense & Hitting

Reynolds' deliberate delivery sometimes hurts his ability to hold runners, but he did an effective job of shutting down the running game last year. Although Reynolds is limited at the plate, he cracked a pair of home runs last year and is a solid bunter. He is a decent fielder on the mound.

1997 Outlook

If there was a flaw to Reynolds' 1996 performance, it was that he sputtered to the finish line, failing to win a game in September. No doubt he was feeling the effects of the heaviest workload of his career, but he still had an outstanding season. He should remain one of the best starting pitchers in the league again this year.

Position: SP
Bats: R **Throws:** R
Ht: 6' 3" **Wt:** 210

Opening Day Age: 29
Born: 3/26/68 in Bastrop, LA
ML Seasons: 5

Overall Statistics

	W	L	Pct.	ERA	G	GS	Sv	IP	.H	BB	SO	HR	BR/IP
1996	16	10	.615	3.65	35	35	0	239.0	227	44	204	20	1.13
Career	35	29	.547	3.56	111	85	0	588.2	604	114	509	47	1.22

How Often He Throws Strikes

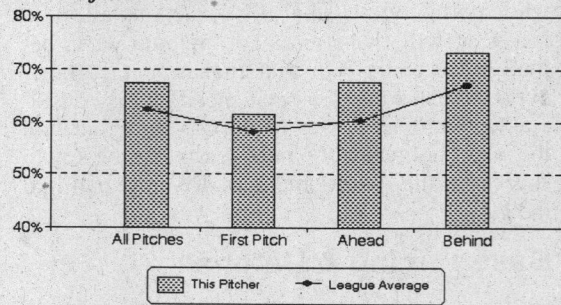

1996 Situational Stats

	W	L	ERA	Sv	IP		AB	H	HR	RBI	Avg
Home	8	4	3.34	0	126.2	LHB	412	86	7	31	.209
Road	8	6	4.01	0	112.1	RHB	499	141	13	58	.283
First Half	10	5	3.76	0	129.1	Sc Pos	198	45	3	65	.227
Scnd Half	6	5	3.53	0	109.2	Clutch	72	19	0	8	.264

1996 Rankings (National League)

→ 1st in least GDPs induced per 9 innings (0.4) and lowest batting average allowed vs. left-handed batters (.209) and fielding percentage at pitcher (1.000)
→ 2nd in games started
→ 3rd in innings pitched
→ 4th in hits allowed, batters faced (981) and highest strikeout/walk ratio (4.6)
→ 5th in sacrifice bunts (14), wins, lowest on-base percentage allowed (.288) and least baserunners allowed per 9 innings (10.5)
→ 6th in strikeouts
→ 7th in complete games (4)
→ 8th in pitches thrown (3,496)
→ 9th in shutouts (1) and winning percentage

Billy Wagner

1996 Season

With John Hudek hurt and Todd Jones struggling, the Astros decided to make rookie lefthander Billy Wagner their closer last summer—and the results were impressive. The hard-throwing lefty excelled in his new role, intimidating hitters with his dominating fastball. Unfortunately Wagner suffered a groin injury in late August and needed to be placed on the disabled list. He came back and pitched very well in September, though he failed to record another save.

Pitching

Flame-throwing lefthanders are a rare commodity, which was why *Baseball America* named Wagner one of its top 10 prospects for the 1996 season. His fastball is routinely clocked in the mid-90s, and it's complemented with well-timed breaking balls that are extremely effective when delivered right after one of his heaters. Wagner still has much to learn in terms of handling hitters in certain situations, but his raw talent alone is enough for him to excel in the majors.

Defense & Hitting

Wagner is a decent fielder who pays close attention to baserunners—occasionally *too* much attention—and is effective in holding them close. Despite that, his high leg kick makes him vulnerable to the stolen base. He's still looking for his first major league hit, which will only be a concern if he's shifted out of the bullpen.

1997 Outlook

Despite his effectiveness in the closer role last year, there's no guarantee that Wagner will remain in the bullpen. He enjoyed an outstanding minor league career as a starter, and the Astros, with other viable closer candidates, might move Wagner into their rotation if it starts to falter. One thing is a virtual certainty—Wagner will be an impact player no matter what task he is assigned.

Position: RP
Bats: L **Throws:** L
Ht: 5'11" **Wt:** 180

Opening Day Age: 25
Born: 6/25/71 in Tannersville, VA
ML Seasons: 2

Overall Statistics

	W	L	Pct.	ERA	G	GS	Sv	IP	H	BB	SO	HR	BR/IP
1996	2	2	.500	2.44	37	0	9	51.2	28	30	67	6	1.12
Career	2	2	.500	2.42	38	0	9	52.0	28	30	67	6	1.12

How Often He Throws Strikes

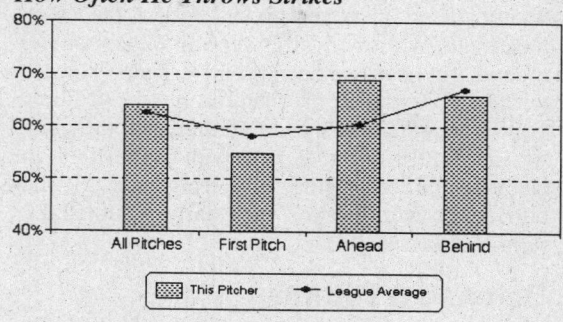

1996 Situational Stats

	W	L	ERA	Sv	IP		AB	H	HR	RBI	Avg
Home	2	1	2.40	4	30.0	LHB	23	2	0	1	.087
Road	0	1	2.49	5	21.2	RHB	147	26	6	17	.177
First Half	1	0	2.11	2	21.1	Sc Pos	52	6	1	11	.115
Scnd Half	1	2	2.67	7	30.1	Clutch	99	19	5	15	.192

1996 Rankings (National League)

→ 3rd in lowest batting average allowed in relief with runners on base (.135) and lowest batting average allowed in relief with runners in scoring position (.115)

→ Led the Astros in lowest batting average allowed in relief with runners on base (.135) and lowest batting average allowed in relief with runners in scoring position (.115)

Houston Astros

Donne Wall

1996 Season

Rookie righthander Donne Wall began last season at Triple-A Tucson, but was promoted to the big club on May 14. Installed in the starting rotation, Wall got off to an impressive start, winning his first six decisions. He began to slump after the All-Star break, recovered with a solid month of August, and then suffered through a disastrous September in which he went 0-4 with an 8.74 ERA.

Pitching

Wall isn't a dominating pitcher, but he sports good control and does an excellent job at mixing both his pitch and speed selections. He likes to keep hitters guessing, never giving batters the same look twice in a row. Wall is very intelligent on the mound, but he's also been prone to making costly mistakes. At times, his stamina has been questioned, and it has been asserted that his future may lie in middle relief. Since Wall is hesitant to challenge hitters inside, preferring to work the outside corner, he was especially troubled by right-handed batters.

Defense & Hitting

Wall is a solid, if unspectacular, fielder on the mound. His pickoff move is respectable, helping him shut down enemy basestealing threats. Wall enjoyed his occasional opportunities at the plate, but he produced just one extra-base hit and drove in only one run.

1997 Outlook

Wall would love to show the Astros that he's regained last season's early form, but questions over his stamina could relegate him to bullpen duties in a middle relief or set-up role. While competition for Houston's last two starting rotation spots figures to be feverish, Wall's chances will be dramatically enhanced if the ballclub chooses not to retain veterans Doug Drabek and Danny Darwin.

Position: SP
Bats: R **Throws:** R
Ht: 5'11" **Wt:** 180

Opening Day Age: 29
Born: 7/11/67 in Potosi, MO
ML Seasons: 2
Pronuciation: DONN-ee Wall

Overall Statistics

	W	L	Pct.	ERA	G	GS	Sv	IP	H	BB	SO	HR	BR/IP
1996	9	8	.529	4.56	26	23	0	150.0	170	34	99	17	1.36
Career	12	9	.571	4.70	32	28	0	174.1	203	39	115	22	1.39

How Often He Throws Strikes

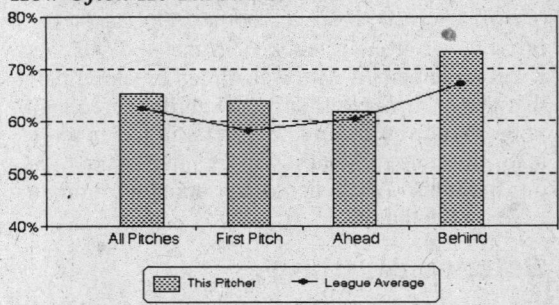

1996 Situational Stats

	W	L	ERA	Sv	IP		AB	H	HR	RBI	Avg
Home	3	3	3.84	0	75.0	LHB	244	62	6	26	.254
Road	6	5	5.28	0	75.0	RHB	350	108	11	48	.309
First Half	6	1	3.75	0	69.2	Sc Pos	156	43	4	54	.276
Scnd Half	3	7	5.27	0	80.1	Clutch	42	12	1	8	.286

1996 Rankings (National League)

→ 2nd in highest batting average allowed vs. right-handed batters (.309)
→ 9th in shutouts (1)
→ Led the Astros in shutouts (1)

Doug Brocail

Position: RP/SP
Bats: L **Throws:** R
Ht: 6' 5" **Wt:** 235

Opening Day Age: 29
Born: 5/16/67 in
Clearfield, PA
ML Seasons: 5

Overall Statistics

	W	L	Pct.	ERA	G	GS	Sv	IP	H	BB	SO	HR	BR/IP
1996	1	5	.167	4.58	23	4	0	53.0	58	23	34	7	1.53
Career	11	22	.333	4.63	98	38	1	289.2	326	97	169	36	1.46

1996 Situational Stats

	W	L	ERA	Sv	IP		AB	H	HR	RBI	Avg
Home	1	1	3.54	0	28.0	LHB	79	28	4	12	.354
Road	0	4	5.76	0	25.0	RHB	122	30	3	18	.246
First Half	1	3	4.10	0	37.1	Sc Pos	49	18	1	21	.367
Scnd Half	0	2	5.74	0	15.2	Clutch	33	9	1	4	.273

1996 Season

Righthander Doug Brocail missed much of the 1996 season with a shoulder problem that put him on the disabled list for nearly three months. Finally activated in mid-August, he showed the effects of the layoff and did little to help the Astros' unsuccessful bid to win a playoff berth.

Pitching, Defense & Hitting

Brocail throws a fastball, slider and change-up, but none of his pitches are overpowering, and he needs good location to be effective. He's never been able to develop a pitch that can neutralize left-handed hitters, and lefties continued to pound him last year. Brocail is a solid fielder, but does a very poor job of holding baserunners. He's not much of a threat at the plate, but he can help himself with a bunt.

1997 Outlook

Brocail was still recovering from his injury late last year, so the Astros will probably be patient with him. He will probably start the year as a long reliever in the bullpen, hoping he can pitch well enough to earn a more substantial role.

John Cangelosi

Position: LF/CF
Bats: B **Throws:** L
Ht: 5' 8" **Wt:** 160

Opening Day Age: 34
Born: 3/10/63 in
Brooklyn, NY
ML Seasons: 10

Overall Statistics

	G	AB	R	H	D	T	HR	RBI	SB	BB	SO	Avg	OBP	Slg
1996	108	262	49	69	11	4	1	16	17	44	41	.263	.378	.347
Career	824	1635	281	410	56	15	10	112	147	309	262	.251	.377	.322

1996 Situational Stats

	AB	H	HR	RBI	Avg		AB	H	HR	RBI	Avg
Home	155	44	1	11	.284	LHP	32	5	1	4	.156
Road	107	25	0	5	.234	RHP	230	64	0	12	.278
First Half	145	43	1	13	.297	Sc Pos	57	12	1	16	.211
Scnd Half	117	26	0	3	.222	Clutch	53	10	0	4	.189

1996 Season

For the second straight year, John Cangelosi was a sparkplug off the bench for the Astros. Getting into over 100 games as a spot starter and a late-inning defensive replacement, Cangelosi was a vital contributor to a team that lacked depth. As in '95, he gave the Astros speed, on-base ability and late-inning defense.

Hitting, Baserunning & Defense

A pesky hitter who drives enemy pitchers crazy with his unrelenting batting style, Cangelosi is extremely effective at battling for walks, bunting for hits, and wreaking havoc on the basepaths. Despite his age (34), he continues to run extremely well and is capable of stealing bases in critical situations. On defense, Cangelosi has outstanding range in center field and is capable of snaring high flies at the fence despite his diminutive stature. His arm is weak, however.

1997 Outlook

A free agent, Cangelosi signed a two-year, $1,075,000 deal with the Florida Marlins after the season. He figures to see plenty of action a fourth outfielder and pinch hitter under his old Pirate manager, Jim Leyland.

Houston Astros

Tony Eusebio

Position: C
Bats: R **Throws:** R
Ht: 6' 2" **Wt:** 210

Opening Day Age: 29
Born: 4/27/67 in San Jose De Los Llamos, DR
ML Seasons: 4
Pronunciation: you-SAY-bee-oh

Overall Statistics

	G	AB	R	H	D	T	HR	RBI	SB	BB	SO	Avg	OBP	Slg
1996	58	152	15	41	7	2	1	19	0	18	20	.270	.343	.362
Career	236	698	83	200	38	4	12	107	0	63	120	.287	.343	.404

1996 Situational Stats

	AB	H	HR	RBI	Avg		AB	H	HR	RBI	Avg
Home	86	22	1	12	.256	LHP	44	10	1	6	.227
Road	66	19	0	7	.288	RHP	108	31	0	13	.287
First Half	49	11	1	5	.224	Sc Pos	43	11	1	17	.256
Scnd Half	103	30	0	14	.291	Clutch	32	10	1	7	.313

1996 Season

Although he's established himself as a major league hitter, Tony Eusebio's difficulties behind the plate prevented him from receiving consistent playing time last season. As a result, Eusebio rode the bench after the Astros traded for former Gold Glove receiver Kirt Manwaring in midseason.

Hitting, Baserunning & Defense

Eusebio doesn't have a lot of power, but he has a nice line drive stroke that's enabled him to hit for a respectable average. He won't beat out too many infield hits, but he runs reasonably well for a catcher. Defense is where Eusebio comes up short. He's worked on his receiving and his catching skills have improved, but he still has a considerable amount of work to do in this area. His arm is strong, but his throwing has been inconsistent.

1997 Outlook

Eusebio's playing time will be closely linked to his defensive development. While he could rebound and post a good year with the bat, he'll still probably lose playing time to Manwaring, the better receiver. But with his good bat skills, Eusebio would figure to be a very useful backup receiver.

Ricky Gutierrez

Position: SS
Bats: R **Throws:** R
Ht: 6' 1" **Wt:** 175

Opening Day Age: 26
Born: 5/23/70 in Miami, FL
ML Seasons: 4
Pronunciation: goo-TIER-uhz

Overall Statistics

	G	AB	R	H	D	T	HR	RBI	SB	BB	SO	Avg	OBP	Slg
1996	89	218	28	62	8	1	1	15	6	23	42	.284	.359	.344
Career	364	1087	153	281	35	8	7	81	17	115	226	.259	.334	.325

1996 Situational Stats

	AB	H	HR	RBI	Avg		AB	H	HR	RBI	Avg
Home	112	39	1	8	.348	LHP	68	22	0	2	.324
Road	106	23	0	7	.217	RHP	150	40	1	13	.267
First Half	139	43	0	11	.309	Sc Pos	51	9	0	13	.176
Scnd Half	79	19	1	4	.241	Clutch	36	13	1	4	.361

1996 Season

Ricky Gutierrez was expected to be a light-hitting glove wizard at shortstop when Houston acquired him in the 11-player megadeal with San Diego prior to the 1995 season. But while Gutierrez has hit better than .275 in both his seasons with the Astros, he hasn't been the defensive upgrade to Orlando Miller they thought he would be. As a result, he's remained a part-time player.

Hitting, Baserunning & Defense

Gutierrez is a spray hitter who slaps the ball where it's pitched. Although he strikes out more than he should and has virtually no power, Gutierrez has some patience at the plate and gets on base often enough to be a useful offensive player. He's also a fine baserunner who possesses excellent speed. His defensive inadequacies have baffled the Astros management, since he had developed a reputation as a standout shortstop while playing in the San Diego farm system.

1997 Outlook

A useful bench player, Gutierrez is slated to remain the backup at shortstop, since the Astros have more invested in Miller's development. He also figures to fill in at second and third.

Xavier Hernandez

Position: RP
Bats: L **Throws:** R
Ht: 6' 2" **Wt:** 195

Opening Day Age: 31
Born: 8/16/65 in Port
Arthur, TX
ML Seasons: 8

Overall Statistics

	W	L	Pct.	ERA	G	GS	Sv	IP	H	BB	SO	HR	BR/IP
1996	5	5	.500	4.62	61	0	6	78.0	77	28	81	13	1.35
Career	34	25	.576	3.88	373	7	34	563.2	527	214	485	55	1.31

1996 Situational Stats

	W	L	ERA	Sv	IP		AB	H	HR	RBI	Avg
Home	3	2	5.11	5	37.0	LHB	100	30	4	18	.300
Road	2	3	4.17	1	41.0	RHB	199	47	9	29	.236
First Half	0	4	6.00	1	36.0	Sc Pos	83	22	2	33	.265
Scnd Half	5	1	3.43	5	42.0	Clutch	137	31	7	21	.226

1996 Season

Former Astros' middle man Xavier Hernandez returned to Houston after being released by the Reds early last season. Following a sluggish first half, Hernandez posted solid numbers down the stretch as the Astros' right-handed set-up man. Overall it was his best stint of pitching since his first tour of duty with the Astros ended in 1993.

Pitching, Defense & Hitting

There's nothing complicated about Hernandez. He goes right after the hitters, hammering away at them with his 90 MPH fastball, split-fingered fastball and slider. The splitter is his best pitch, and when he has command of it as he did late last year, he can be extremely effective. Very poor at holding baserunners, Hernandez is a solid glove man who fields sacrifice bunts very aggressively. He doesn't get to bat much, which is just as well since he's 1-for-37 in his career.

1997 Outlook

Hernandez revived his career after returning to Houston, and the free agent figured to draw some interest over the winter. The Astros would like to have him back if his demands are reasonable. If he can maintain command of his splitter, he should remain a useful set-up man.

John Hudek

Position: RP
Bats: B **Throws:** R
Ht: 6' 1" **Wt:** 200

Opening Day Age: 30
Born: 8/8/66 in Tampa,
FL
ML Seasons: 3
Pronunciation:
HOO-dek

Overall Statistics

	W	L	Pct.	ERA	G	GS	Sv	IP	H	BB	SO	HR	BR/IP
1996	2	0	1.000	2.81	15	0	2	16.0	12	5	14	2	1.06
Career	4	4	.500	3.58	76	0	25	75.1	55	28	82	10	1.10

1996 Situational Stats

	W	L	ERA	Sv	IP		AB	H	HR	RBI	Avg
Home	2	0	0.00	1	9.1	LHB	19	6	0	2	.316
Road	0	0	6.75	1	6.2	RHB	39	6	2	5	.154
First Half	0	0	-	0	0.0	Sc Pos	20	3	1	5	.150
Scnd Half	2	0	2.81	2	16.0	Clutch	30	3	1	2	.100

1996 Season

John Hudek didn't get much playing time last season, as complications resulting from elbow surgery forced him onto the disabled list in June. Hudek finally returned to the active roster in time to fan 14 batters in 16 innings while showing flashes of his 1993-94 form.

Pitching, Defense & Hitting

Hudek's recovery from injury problems—he also suffered a torn scalene muscle in his neck last spring—has been arduous, but he may finally have turned the corner. Before the injuries, he relied on combining a darting, mid-90s fastball with a sharp slider. Adept defensively, he has a quick delivery that freezes would-be base stealers, and he does a reasonably good job of holding runners. Hudek has only handled the bat once in his career.

1997 Outlook

Time will tell whether Hudek can make a full recovery. Though they would be foolish to count on his return, the Astros would enjoy being presented with the "problem" of whether to use Hudek or young phenom Billy Wagner as their closer. If Hudek's healthy, he could well win the job.

Alvin Morman

Position: RP
Bats: L **Throws:** L
Ht: 6' 3" **Wt:** 210

Opening Day Age: 28
Born: 1/6/69 in Rockingham, NC
ML Seasons: 1

Overall Statistics

	W	L	Pct.	ERA	G	GS	Sv	IP	H	BB	SO	HR	BR/IP
1996	4	1	.800	4.93	53	0	0	42.0	43	24	31	8	1.60
Career	4	1	.800	4.93	53	0	0	42.0	43	24	31	8	1.60

1996 Situational Stats

	W	L	ERA	Sv	IP		AB	H	HR	RBI	Avg
Home	3	0	5.94	0	16.2	LHB	71	17	1	8	.239
Road	1	1	4.26	0	25.1	RHB	94	26	7	27	.277
First Half	1	1	5.55	0	24.1	Sc Pos	61	16	4	30	.262
Scnd Half	3	0	4.08	0	17.2	Clutch	47	16	1	11	.340

1996 Season

Although still a relative unknown, rookie left-hander Alvin Morman placed second on the Astros in appearances with 53 while working in middle relief. His numbers weren't overly impressive, but he won four of five decisions and recorded seven holds. He was ex-manager Terry Collins' first option against tough left-handed batters.

Pitching, Defense & Hitting

Morman uses a herky-jerky delivery, disorienting hitters with his wildly flailing limbs. He throws a decent fastball as well as a variety of offspeed pitches. The lefty specialist proved tough against left-handed hitters, but he had major problems with righties, who slugged him at a .564 clip. Morman is average defensively, but he manages to hold baserunners close to the bag because they find it difficult deciphering his unusual motion. He failed to record a plate appearance last season.

1997 Outlook

Morman should return this year as the Astros' primary left-handed set-up/middle man, unless Houston decides to add another southpaw to their bullpen. Success won't be guaranteed, however, unless he finds some way to neutralize right-handed hitters.

James Mouton

Position: LF/CF
Bats: R **Throws:** R
Ht: 5' 9" **Wt:** 175

Opening Day Age: 28
Born: 12/29/68 in Denver, Colorado
ML Seasons: 3
Pronunciation: MOO-tawn

Overall Statistics

	G	AB	R	H	D	T	HR	RBI	SB	BB	SO	Avg	OBP	Slg
1996	122	300	40	79	15	1	3	34	21	38	55	.263	.343	.350
Career	325	908	125	233	44	3	9	77	70	90	183	.257	.328	.341

1996 Situational Stats

	AB	H	HR	RBI	Avg		AB	H	HR	RBI	Avg
Home	151	42	2	17	.278	LHP	115	39	1	15	.339
Road	149	37	1	17	.248	RHP	185	40	2	19	.216
First Half	147	37	1	24	.252	Sc Pos	78	22	0	26	.282
Scnd Half	153	42	2	10	.275	Clutch	55	15	0	3	.273

1996 Season

Despite possessing considerable potential, James Mouton has never been successful in shedding his "part-time player" label. Mouton's 1996 performance was respectable, particularly against lefties, but he continued to struggle against righthanders. Overall, he never played well enough to put in a strong claim for a full-time job.

Hitting, Baserunning & Defense

Mouton can torment lefthanders, but against righties he often chases bad pitches and he's prone to overswinging as well. He's not a big home run threat, but he does have some power to the gaps. Mouton possesses excellent speed, stealing 21 bases last season in a part-time role. In the outfield, he is able to track down everything, but is hampered by a below-average throwing arm.

1997 Outlook

The Astros view their outfield vacancies as a problem to be solved during spring training. That means Mouton will probably be given another chance to win a full-time job, but at 28 he's nearly out of chances. It's likely he'll wind up as a part-time player again, and he has the skills to contribute in that role.

Other Houston Astros

Andujar Cedeno (**Pos**: SS, **Age**: 27, **Bats**: R)

	G	AB	R	H	D	T	HR	RBI	SB	BB	SO	Avg	OBP	Slg
1996	104	335	30	71	6	3	10	38	5	15	70	.212	.247	.337
Career	616	2051	221	485	98	13	47	223	26	143	488	.236	.292	.366

Cedeno was a one-man traveling show—and offensive nightmare—in '96, getting traded twice before landing in Houston, where he started his career. Given the competition, he won't be around too long. 1997 Outlook: C

Terry Clark (**Pos**: RHP, **Age**: 36)

	W	L	Pct.	ERA	G	GS	Sv	IP	H	BB	SO	HR	BR/IP
1996	1	3	.250	8.75	17	0	0	23.2	44	9	17	4	2.24
Career	9	16	.360	5.39	78	18	1	175.1	229	66	85	15	1.68

Clark was picked up by Houston in July after being released by the Royals. With an 11.37 ERA through five relief appearances, his career is pretty much through. 1997 Outlook: D

Jim Dougherty (**Pos**: RHP, **Age**: 29)

	W	L	Pct.	ERA	G	GS	Sv	IP	H	BB	SO	HR	BR/IP
1996	0	2	.000	9.00	12	0	0	13.0	14	11	6	2	1.92
Career	8	6	.571	5.58	68	0	0	80.2	90	36	55	9	1.56

Plagued by a bout of early-season wildness, Dougherty was hammered in May and June, earning a one-way ticket to the minors. He should get a shot to make this year's team, but his future is shaky. 1997 Outlook: C

Jerry Goff (**Pos**: C, **Age**: 32, **Bats**: L)

	G	AB	R	H	D	T	HR	RBI	SB	BB	SO	Avg	OBP	Slg
1996	1	4	1	2	0	0	1	2	0	0	1	.500	.500	1.250
Career	90	214	22	46	5	0	7	19	0	33	73	.215	.320	.336

Goff caught one game with Houston in May after starter Tony Eusebio went under the knife to have a cyst removed. He draws an obscene amount of walks, but will not get significant major league playing time. 1997 Outlook: C

Dave Hajek (**Pos**: 3B, **Age**: 29, **Bats**: R)

	G	AB	R	H	D	T	HR	RBI	SB	BB	SO	Avg	OBP	Slg
1996	8	10	3	3	1	0	0	0	0	2	0	.300	.417	.400
Career	13	12	3	3	1	0	0	0	1	3	1	.250	.400	.333

Hajek's been compiling superstar numbers at Triple-A Tuscon over the past few years, but he's never gotten a decent shot in the majors. Detroit claimed him off waivers, so that could change. 1997 Outlook: B

John Johnstone (**Pos**: RHP, **Age**: 28)

	W	L	Pct.	ERA	G	GS	Sv	IP	H	BB	SO	HR	BR/IP
1996	1	0	1.000	5.54	9	0	0	13.0	17	5	5	2	1.69
Career	2	4	.333	5.62	37	0	0	49.2	63	30	36	8	1.87

Johnstone spent a month in the Astros' bullpen last season and was largely ineffective. Consistently posting yearly ERA's in the upper fives, his future would appear to be questionable at best. 1997 Outlook: C

Randy Knorr (**Pos**: C, **Age**: 28, **Bats**: R)

	G	AB	R	H	D	T	HR	RBI	SB	BB	SO	Avg	OBP	Slg
1996	37	87	7	17	5	0	1	7	0	5	18	.195	.245	.287
Career	172	464	57	105	18	2	16	64	0	37	116	.226	.285	.377

Bought from Toronto in May, Knorr served as the Astros' backup catcher for the remainder of the season. His hitting performance (.187 average) might inspire the team to search for possible alternatives. 1997 Outlook: B

Ray Montgomery (**Pos**: LF, **Age**: 27, **Bats**: R)

	G	AB	R	H	D	T	HR	RBI	SB	BB	SO	Avg	OBP	Slg
1996	12	14	4	3	1	0	1	4	0	1	5	.214	.267	.500
Career	12	14	4	3	1	0	1	4	0	1	5	.214	.267	.500

Montgomery joined the Astros for brief stints in July and September as a break from terrorizing Pacific Coast League pitchers. He might get a shot to make the club this year as a utility outfielder. 1997 Outlook: C

Gregg Olson (**Pos**: RHP, **Age**: 30)

	W	L	Pct.	ERA	G	GS	Sv	IP	H	BB	SO	HR	BR/IP
1996	4	0	1.000	4.99	52	0	8	52.1	55	35	37	7	1.72
Career	24	26	.480	2.94	411	0	172	450.1	383	225	415	22	1.35

It's been a rapid free-fall for Olson: the one-time Orioles' closer spent last season with *four* different teams. Ever since he started to have arm problems several years ago, he's never been the same. 1997 Outlook: C

Mike Simms (**Pos**: LF, **Age**: 30, **Bats**: R)

	G	AB	R	H	D	T	HR	RBI	SB	BB	SO	Avg	OBP	Slg
1996	49	68	6	12	2	1	1	8	1	4	16	.176	.233	.279
Career	181	361	43	79	14	1	15	53	4	37	100	.219	.298	.388

Despite his abysmal offensive performance last season, Simms managed to stay in the majors for most of the year. Now that he's 30, there's doubt if he'll last too much longer. 1997 Outlook: C

Mark Small (**Pos**: RHP, **Age**: 29)

	W	L	Pct.	ERA	G	GS	Sv	IP	H	BB	SO	HR	BR/IP
1996	0	1	.000	5.92	16	0	0	24.1	33	13	16	1	1.89
Career	0	1	.000	5.92	16	0	0	24.1	33	13	16	1	1.89

Small is a streaky reliever who got three shots in the Astros' bullpen last season but failed to stick around. He pitched well in the minors last year, but is now 29 and might not get another opportunity. 1997 Outlook: C

Bill Spiers (**Pos**: 3B, **Age**: 30, **Bats**: L)

	G	AB	R	H	D	T	HR	RBI	SB	BB	SO	Avg	OBP	Slg
1996	122	218	27	55	10	1	6	26	7	20	34	.252	.320	.390
Career	742	1982	263	503	69	19	22	215	59	152	309	.254	.308	.341

Spiers was *the* utility man for Houston last year, manning six different positions as well as getting 41 pinch hit at-bats. His versatility and offensive success ensure that he'll be back. 1997 Outlook: A

Houston Astros

Jeff Tabaka (Pos: LHP, Age: 33)

	W	L	Pct.	ERA	G	GS	Sv	IP	H	BB	SO	HR	BR/IP
1996	0	2	.000	6.64	18	0	1	20.1	28	14	18	5	2.07
Career	4	3	.571	4.89	91	0	2	92.0	87	58	75	8	1.58

Tabaka pitched well in '95 upon joining the Astros in a trade, but was sent down to Triple-A Tuscon for most of last season after getting shelled in the majors. It's unlikely that he'll see much action. 1997 Outlook: C

Anthony Young (Pos: RHP, Age: 31)

	W	L	Pct.	ERA	G	GS	Sv	IP	H	BB	SO	HR	BR/IP
1996	3	3	.500	4.59	28	0	0	33.1	36	22	19	4	1.74
Career	15	48	.238	3.89	181	51	20	460.0	471	167	245	41	1.39

Young began the year in Houston's bullpen but was exiled to the minors in June after giving up eight earned runs in six appearances. He was quickly sidelined with elbow problems (again) and is now a free agent. 1997 Outlook: D

Houston Astros Minor League Prospects

Organization Overview:

In the past few years, the Houston Astros have had a lot more luck developing pitchers than hitters. Last year, Billy Wagner showed that he was everything he was advertised to be, and Donne Wall proved to be a solid starter in the Shane Reynolds mold. However, the progress of Brian Hunter, Orlando Miller and James Mouton remained disappointing. Besides highly-touted outfielders Richard Hidalgo and Bob Abreu, there aren't many position players left to look forward to. A handful of pitchers are on the way up, but most of them are a year or more away. The Venezuelan pipeline that netted them Hidalgo and Abreu hasn't quite made up for their weak drafts and limited bonus budget. At least one of their outfielders should be able to make an impact this year, but other than that, they may not receive much help from the farm for a while.

Bob Abreu

Position: OF   **Opening Day Age:** 23
Bats: L **Throws:** R   **Born:** 3/11/74 in
Ht: 6' 0" **Wt:** 160   Maracay, Venez

Recent Statistics

	G	AB	R	H	D	T	HR	RBI	SB	BB	SO	AVG
96 AAA Tucson	132	484	86	138	14	16	13	68	24	83	111	.285
96 NL Houston	15	22	1	5	1	0	0	1	0	2	3	.227
96 MLE	132	461	66	115	12	9	8	52	16	62	123	.249

We've been hearing about this multi-talented Venezuelan for a while, and hopefully, he'll be ready to make the jump to the majors this year. He didn't show much progress in his second season in Triple-A, although he did lead the minors in triples for the second straight year. That illustrates two things about his game: he hits the ball hard into the gaps, and he's got the speed and aggressiveness to take the extra base. In the outfield, he's got the range and arm to play a good right field. He's still young, and has great upside potential, particularly in the power department.

Kary Bridges

Position: 2B   **Opening Day Age:** 25
Bats: L **Throws:** R   **Born:** 10/27/71 in
Ht: 5' 10" **Wt:** 165   Columbus, MS

Recent Statistics

	G	AB	R	H	D	T	HR	RBI	SB	BB	SO	AVG
93 A Quad City	65	263	37	74	9	0	3	24	15	31	18	.281
94 A Quad City	117	447	66	135	20	4	1	53	14	38	29	.302
95 AA Jackson	118	418	56	126	22	4	3	43	10	48	18	.301
96 AA Jackson	87	338	51	110	12	2	4	33	4	32	14	.325
96 AAA Tucson	42	140	24	44	9	1	1	21	1	9	8	.314
96 MLE	129	461	63	137	18	1	3	45	3	29	23	.297

Kary Bridges is just a little guy who signed late, and his defense at second base doesn't impress anyone. What makes him intriguing is the fact that he bats lefty, hits for a good average, and almost never strikes out. When you consider that he's also capable of playing the outfield, you have to conclude that he could help a major league team in a bench role. It's not very likely that he'll get the chance, but if he does, he may surprise.

Scott Elarton

Position: P   **Opening Day Age:** 21
Bats: R **Throws:** R   **Born:** 2/23/76 in
Ht: 6' 8" **Wt:** 225   Lamar, CO

Recent Statistics

	W	L	ERA	G	GS	Sv	IP	H	R	BB	SO	HR
94 R Astros	4	0	0.00	5	5	0	28.0	9	0	5	28	0
94 A Quad City	4	1	3.29	9	9	0	54.2	42	23	18	42	4
95 A Quad City	13	7	4.45	26	26	0	149.2	149	86	71	112	12
96 A Kissimmee	12	7	2.92	27	27	0	172.1	154	67	54	130	13

Lefthander Scott Elarton was selected 24th overall in the '94 draft, and his style seems to have changed since then. His fastball, which reportedly used to reach the mid-90s, now tops out at only 90, and his curveball has become his out pitch. It's odd to see someone so young making that type of adjustment, but he's continued to pitch well in spite of it. He excelled in the Florida State League last year, and he may be tried at Double-A this year at age 21. The Astros see him as one of their best young arms.

Richard Hidalgo

Position: OF   **Opening Day Age:** 21
Bats: R **Throws:** R   **Born:** 7/2/75 in
Ht: 6' 2" **Wt:** 175   Caracas, Venez

Recent Statistics

	G	AB	R	H	D	T	HR	RBI	SB	BB	SO	AVG
93 A Asheville	111	403	49	109	23	3	10	55	21	30	76	.270
94 A Quad City	124	476	68	139	47	6	12	76	12	23	80	.292
95 AA Jackson	133	489	59	130	28	6	14	59	8	32	76	.266
96 AA Jackson	130	513	66	151	34	2	14	78	11	29	55	.294
96 MLE	130	497	58	135	31	1	11	69	8	21	62	.272

When Billy Wagner was called up to the big club, it left Richard Hidalgo as the best prospect left in the system. That's no knock; Hidalgo's a potential five-tool talent with seemingly unlimited possibilities. The organization would like him to drive the ball more, but he's still got a very advanced bat for someone his age. His strikeouts dropped last year, and he projects to hit for both power and average. In center field, he covers a lot of ground, and intimidates baserunners with one of the best arms in the game. He's a year or two away, and the Astros are probably counting the days.

Houston Astros

Chris Holt

Position: P | **Opening Day Age:** 25
Bats: R **Throws:** R | **Born:** 9/18/71 in
Ht: 6' 4" **Wt:** 205 | Dallas, TX

Recent Statistics

	W	L	ERA	G	GS	Sv	IP	H	R	BB	SO	HR
96 AAA Tucson	9	6	3.62	28	27	0	186.1	208	87	38	137	11
96 NL Houston	0	1	5.79	4	0	0	4.2	5	3	3	0	0

Control artist Chris Holt encountered much more success in his second stint at Triple-A. This time around, he regained the fine command of his 90-MPH sinking fastball, and was able to duplicate the success he had in the low minors. His raw stuff won't excite the scouts, but his record was very impressive for a pitcher in the run-crazed Pacific Coast League. Like Shane Reynolds was, Holt may be surprisingly effective once he receives an extended trial in the majors.

Russ Johnson

Position: SS | **Opening Day Age:** 24
Bats: R **Throws:** R | **Born:** 2/22/73 in Baton
Ht: 5' 10" **Wt:** 185 | Rouge, LA

Recent Statistics

	G	AB	R	H	D	T	HR	RBI	SB	BB	SO	AVG
95 AA Jackson	132	476	65	118	16	2	9	53	10	50	61	.248
96 AA Jackson	132	496	86	154	24	5	15	74	9	56	50	.310
96 MLE	132	479	76	137	22	3	12	65	6	41	56	.286

Last year, Russ Johnson displayed the power the Astros envisioned when they took him with the 30th overall pick in the '94 draft. Johnson's a solid shortstop—nothing flashy, but he makes all the plays. Based on what he did last year, he should be able to hit enough to hold the Astros' shortstop job. It should make for an interesting competition with Orlando Miller in the spring; Johnson may not be nearly as exciting to watch, but he can be a more productive player than Miller.

Mitch Meluskey

Position: C | **Opening Day Age:** 23
Bats: B **Throws:** R | **Born:** 9/18/73 in
Ht: 5' 11" **Wt:** 185 | Yakima, WA

Recent Statistics

	G	AB	R	H	D	T	HR	RBI	SB	BB	SO	AVG
93 A Columbus	101	342	36	84	18	3	3	47	1	35	69	.246
94 A Kinston	100	319	36	77	16	1	3	41	3	49	62	.241
95 A Kinston	8	29	5	7	5	0	0	2	0	2	9	.241
95 A Kissimmee	78	261	23	56	18	1	3	31	3	27	33	.215
96 A Kissimmee	74	231	29	77	19	0	1	31	1	29	26	.333
96 AA Jackson	38	134	18	42	11	0	0	21	0	18	24	.313

Mitch Meluskey came over from the Cleveland organization in a minor deal early in the '95 season. He didn't hit at all that year, but last year, the switch-hitting receiver suddenly found something that worked for him at the plate. After never having hit above .246 in pro ball, he batted .333 at Kissimmee, and was leading the Florida State League in batting when he was promoted to Double-A. Not even the tougher competition was able to slow his bat. He's a little rough behind the plate, and he's got no power or speed, but at age 23, he's forcing the Astros to pay attention to him.

Edgar Ramos

Position: P | **Opening Day Age:** 22
Bats: R **Throws:** R | **Born:** 3/6/75 in
Ht: 6' 4" **Wt:** 170 | Cuinana Edo Sucre, Venez

Recent Statistics

	W	L	ERA	G	GS	Sv	IP	H	R	BB	SO	HR
93 R Astros	5	2	2.16	14	12	0	75.0	59	23	13	70	0
94 A Quad City	2	8	4.47	22	16	1	98.2	110	59	30	92	3
95 A Quad City	0	1	15.43	2	2	0	4.2	5	9	7	5	0
95 A Kissimmee	4	0	0.41	4	4	0	22.0	11	4	1	16	1
95 R Astros	0	1	1.84	5	5	0	14.2	14	6	5	16	0
96 A Kissimmee	9	0	1.51	11	11	0	77.2	51	17	15	81	0
96 AA Jackson	4	5	4.88	12	12	0	66.1	63	41	29	52	2

Another product of the Astros' vast scouting network in Venezuela, righthander Edgar Ramos pitched his way right out of A-ball by starting the season 9-0. His success didn't continue at Double-A, but it still was a breakthrough season for the young righthander. His fastball is nothing special, but he throws a beautiful change-up with excellent command. He'll have a chance to make the Phillies' staff after they selected him with the first pick in the Rule 5 draft.

Others to Watch

Lefthander **Tony Mounce** doesn't throw hard, but he's got one of the nastiest curveballs in the system. After putting up a 2.25 ERA at Class A, the 22-year-old hurler figures to get his first taste of Double-A this season. . . Third baseman **Tim Forkner** has good range afield and a line-drive bat. He doesn't have a corner man's power, but his sweet left-handed stroke should land him in Triple-A this year. . . Keep an eye on righthander **Mike Grzanich**. The 24-year old middle reliever fanned over a man per inning at Double-A. . . Don't try to run on lefthander **John Halama**—he's got one of the most deceptive pickoff moves in the game. He posted solid numbers at Double-A last year, and will try his hand in the Pacific Coast League this season. . . Left-handed relievers are always in demand, and 25-year-old southpaw **Jamie Walker** had a breakthrough season in the bullpen at Double-A. The Braves will give him a look after taking him in the Rule 5 draft.

Bill Russell

1996 Season

On the surface, Bill Russell could not be less like his mentor, Tommy Lasorda. For one thing, the new Dodger manager is stoic and calm. He does not overreact, and the Dodgers love his no-nonsense approach. Though he is known by some as "Mr. Agitator," Russell is actually quite positive. He doesn't even have a doghouse: when he benched Raul Mondesi for missing the team bus, it blew over by the following day.

Offense

Strategically, Russell is not terribly different from Lasorda. While both are fairly aggressive, Russell seems a bit less predictable than his predecessor. Russell is more likely to call a squeeze, and will often send a runner just to avoid the double play. Once he decides on platoons, he sticks with them, and he seldom allows a pinch hitter to bat against a pitcher tossing from the same side.

Pitching & Defense

By the time Russell took over, his pitchers' roles were well-defined and he did little to alter them. However, he did manipulate his staff down the stretch, juggling the rotation to ensure that Ramon Martinez would pitch the first playoff game and that Tom Candiotti would be relegated to the bullpen. He showed a slightly quicker hook than Lasorda, but the half-year sample of data is not large enough to be statistically significant. Defensively, Russell's hands were tied: the Dodgers were not a team of many interchangeable parts.

1997 Outlook

It will be very interesting to see if Russell and general manager Fred Claire can agree on the Dodgers' future. This team was supposed to win, but its dismal showing in the last two playoffs has exposed its weaknesses. Russell has been given a two-year deal, so he now has the chance to help create an exciting, aggressive contender in his own image.

Born: 10/21/48 in Pittsburg, KS

Playing Experience: 1969-1986, LA

Managerial Experience: 1 season

Manager Statistics

Year	Team, Lg	W	L	Pct	GB	Finish
1996	Los Angeles, NL	49	37	.570	1.0	2nd West
1 Season		49	37	.570	—	—

1996 Starting Pitchers by Days Rest

	≤3	4	5	6+
Dodgers Starts	0	47	27	12
Dodgers ERA	0.00	3.32	3.84	4.34
NL Avg Starts	4	86	41	21
NL ERA	4.06	4.28	4.23	4.58

1996 Situational Stats

	Bill Russell*	NL Average
Hit & Run Success %	45.9	39.0
Stolen Base Success %	77.4	71.6
Platoon Pct.	44.2	51.9
Defensive Subs	12	20
High-Pitch Outings	12	13
Quick/Slow Hooks	6/7	19/12
Sacrifice Attempts	44	92

* Russell managed the Dodgers for 86 games

1996 Rankings (National League)

➡ Did not rank near the top in any category

Pedro Astacio

1996 Season

Before the start of last season, pitching coach Dave Wallace convinced Pedro Astacio to ease up on his antics on the mound. The young Dominican mellowed and responded with his first winning year since 1993. Astacio was quite consistent except for a bad stretch in June, and as always, he finished very strongly. Over his career, he is now 22-12 with a 3.03 ERA after the All-Star break.

Pitching

Astacio throws an above-average sinking fastball, a decent change-up, and a variety of breaking balls. His most effective weapon is a circle curveball, and he'll also occasionally drop in a slider and another curve delivered with a semi-sidearm motion. Astacio's command tends to waver, and his stuff is only effective when he is ahead in the count. When the hitters know that the heater is coming, or when he gets his pitches up in the strike zone, Astacio runs into trouble. He runs out of stamina very quickly, so the Dodger bullpen always tends to rustle around the seventh inning in his starts.

Defense & Hitting

Astacio has an awkward delivery and does not release his pitches in very good fielding position. He will also toss the ball away when rushed. However, Astacio is quite fast and gets off the mound in a hurry. He is horrendous at the plate, rarely making contact, but is an average bunter who had eight successful sacrifices last season.

1997 Outlook

The Dodgers have a slew of hard-throwing young pitchers and it is just a matter of time before Chan Ho Park joins their starting rotation, making Astacio expendable. It would not shock anyone to see Astacio wearing a different uniform this year. *Caveat emptor*: let the buyer beware. Away from pitcher-friendly Dodger Stadium, Astacio's career ERA is 4.34.

Position: SP
Bats: R **Throws:** R
Ht: 6' 2" **Wt:** 195

Opening Day Age: 27
Born: 11/28/69 in Hato Mayor, DR
ML Seasons: 5
Pronunciation: uh-STAH-see-oh

Overall Statistics

	W	L	Pct.	ERA	G	GS	Sv	IP	H	BB	SO	HR	BR/IP
1996	9	8	.529	3.44	35	32	0	211.2	207	67	130	18	1.29
Career	41	38	.519	3.60	148	108	0	733.0	697	231	483	63	1.27

How Often He Throws Strikes

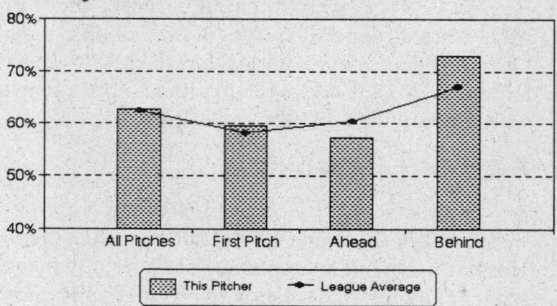

1996 Situational Stats

	W	L	ERA	Sv	IP		AB	H	HR	RBI	Avg
Home	5	4	2.86	0	110.0	LHB	336	92	8	30	.274
Road	4	4	4.07	0	101.2	RHB	457	115	10	42	.252
First Half	4	7	3.81	0	106.1	Sc Pos	176	36	6	55	.205
Scnd Half	5	1	3.08	0	105.1	Clutch	70	21	2	7	.300

1996 Rankings (National League)

- → 1st in GDPs induced (28)
- → 2nd in most GDPs induced per 9 innings (1.2)
- → 4th in least pitches thrown per batter (3.43)
- → 6th in least run support per 9 innings (4.0) and errors at pitcher (3)
- → 7th in lowest batting average allowed with runners in scoring position (.205)
- → 9th in highest groundball/flyball ratio allowed (1.7) and ERA at home (2.86)
- → Led the Dodgers in hit batsmen (9), GDPs induced (28), highest groundball/flyball ratio allowed (1.7), lowest stolen base percentage allowed (70.0%), least pitches thrown per batter (3.43) and most GDPs induced per 9 innings (1.2)

Mike Blowers

1996 Season

Mike Blowers, a lifetime .203 hitter in April, staggered out to his usual abysmal start in 1996. When the calendar turned over, however, Blowers began to hit. He batted .288 from May 1st until late July, when he blew out his knee in a baserunning mishap. The third baseman had become a crucial weapon in the Dodgers' attack and their offense suffered after his untimely departure.

Hitting

Blowers exhibits an excellent knowledge of the strike zone, but takes his cuts when he sees a pitch he likes, regardless of where it's located. Both his strikeout and walk totals are fairly high; he forces pitchers to work deep counts against him. Blowers has a bit of a hitch in his swing, but when he makes contact, he generally hits hard line drives and ground balls. He has gap power to all fields with surprising pop to right and right-center.

Baserunning & Defense

Like many of his teammates, Blowers' lack of speed strictly limits him to station-to-station baserunning. At third base, Blowers proved to be unspectacular defensively, finishing close to the bottom in zone ratings and range factor among starting third basemen. Blowers showed good range to his right, and was excellent at barehanding slow rollers. Though his arm is no howitzer, it's certainly strong enough to get the job done.

1997 Outlook

Though Dodger Stadium cut into his power numbers, Blowers was putting together a solid season when it abruptly came to a halt. He was greatly valued for both his RBI production and his solid protection of teammate Raul Mondesi, who bats ahead of him in the lineup. Nonetheless, the Dodgers released him after the season. Assuming that he can recover completely from the serious knee injury, he should be able to help some other club this year.

Position: 3B
Bats: R **Throws:** R
Ht: 6' 2"   **Wt:** 210

Opening Day Age: 31
Born: 4/24/65 in Wurzburg, Germany
ML Seasons: 8
Pronunciation: BLAU-ers

Overall Statistics

	G	AB	R	H	D	T	HR	RBI	SB	BB	SO	Avg	OBP	Slg
1996	92	317	31	84	19	2	6	38	0	37	77	.265	.341	.394
Career	545	1695	210	439	86	6	60	267	6	184	449	.259	.332	.423

Where He Hits the Ball

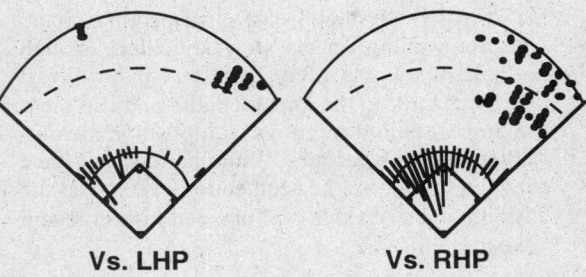

Vs. LHP   **Vs. RHP**

1996 Situational Stats

	AB	H	HR	RBI	Avg		AB	H	HR	RBI	Avg
Home	168	44	4	20	.262	LHP	68	17	2	9	.250
Road	149	40	2	18	.268	RHP	249	67	4	29	.269
First Half	296	78	6	36	.264	Sc Pos	77	15	1	29	.195
Scnd Half	21	6	0	2	.286	Clutch	54	14	3	10	.259

1996 Rankings (National League)

→ 5th in most GDPs per GDP situation (18.3%)

Tom Candiotti

Position: SP
Bats: R **Throws:** R
Ht: 6' 2" **Wt:** 221

Opening Day Age: 39
Born: 8/31/57 in
Walnut Creek, CA
ML Seasons: 13
Pronunciation:
kan-dee-AH-tee

1996 Season

The end would appear to be near for Tom Candiotti. His 152 innings pitched last season was the lowest total of his long major league career, even including the strike-shortened seasons. There is nothing physically wrong with Candiotti's arm; though he spent a stint on the disabled list after getting struck with a line drive, the reduced workload was purely due to the club's lack of confidence in the veteran's ability to get hitters out.

Pitching

Though he will argue that he is a pitcher first and a knuckleballer second, Candiotti floats his trademark pitch up there about 75 percent of the time. When he needs a strike, Candiotti will try to slip his 78 MPH "fastball" past unsuspecting hitters who are waiting on his slow knuckler. Though he'll also showcase a flat slider once in a while, it all comes back to the knuckleball—and if it's not moving, Candiotti might as well position his outfielders in the bleachers. While he may not have seen much success, he seemed to have solved the early inning woes that had plagued him in recent years.

Defense & Hitting

Candiotti has a decent move to first, but enemy basestealers still run wild on his hard-to-handle knuckleball. An average fielder, Candiotti is methodical and solid, rather than flashy, on the mound. At the plate, he is not an automatic out: he usually makes contact and is able to solidly execute sacrifice bunts. On the bases, however, he is a plodder.

1997 Outlook

The Dodgers inexplicably signed Candiotti to a two-year deal before last season. Now they are so desperate to unload him that they are reportedly willing to pay part of his $3 million salary if another team will take him off their hands. Knuckleballers often pitch well into their 40s, so someone may want to take a chance on him.

Overall Statistics

	W	L	Pct.	ERA	G	GS	Sv	IP	H	BB	SO	HR	BR/IP
1996	9	11	.450	4.49	28	27	0	152.1	172	43	79	18	1.41
Career	126	135	.483	3.53	359	346	0	2317.2	2226	750	1507	185	1.28

How Often He Throws Strikes

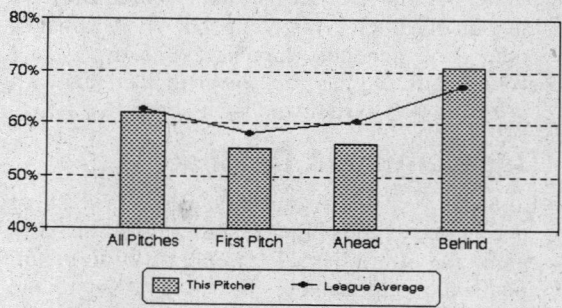

This Pitcher   League Average

1996 Situational Stats

	W	L	ERA	Sv	IP		AB	H	HR	RBI	Avg
Home	5	5	5.58	0	71.0	LHB	272	73	10	37	.268
Road	4	6	3.54	0	81.1	RHB	326	99	8	44	.304
First Half	6	7	4.06	0	99.2	Sc Pos	144	43	2	56	.299
Scnd Half	3	4	5.30	0	52.2	Clutch	17	7	1	4	.412

1996 Rankings (National League)

➡ 5th in highest batting average allowed vs. right-handed batters (.304)
➡ 9th in ERA on the road (3.54)
➡ Led the Dodgers in losses and ERA on the road (3.54)

Delino DeShields

Signed By
CARDINALS

1996 Season

Where has the real Delino DeShields gone? After disappointing seasons with the Dodgers in 1994 and 1995, DeShields was a complete disaster last year. Stumbling from the gates, DeShields went completely into the tank in the second half of the year. Despite his problems, the Dodgers kept playing him, hoping to no avail that DeShields might rediscover his batting stroke. The moody second baseman looked like a whipped puppy by season's end, his every move greeted by a chorus of hometown boos.

Hitting

DeShields has always had a big swing for a small player. He is a selective hitter with a fair understanding of the strike zone, but it hasn't helped him much now that he can't catch up to an above-average fastball. At his best, DeShields is a sharp groundball hitter who uses the whole field. These days, however, he seldom hits the ball hard anywhere, regardless of the pitch or the count.

Baserunning & Defense

DeShields can still run extremely well. After all, it's no easy task to steal 48 bases with a .288 on-base percentage. Though he closes quickly on balls hit to his left, DeShields is just an average fielder, and his weak arm makes double plays difficult for him. In addition, he tends to take his lack of hitting success onto the field, which has led to a lot of sulking on the edge of the outfield grass.

1997 Outlook

There was no love lost between DeShields and ex-manager Tommy Lasorda, so Bill Russell's hiring offered a ray of hope for him. When his performance plummeted even further under Russell, DeShields signed his death warrant with the Dodgers. DeShields occasionally has mentioned recurring pain in his upper leg and hip, so there may be a physical reason for his offensive woes. He signed with the Cardinals as a free agent during the offseason, and hopes to make a big comeback with the Redbirds.

Position: 2B
Bats: L **Throws:** R
Ht: 6' 1" **Wt:** 175

Opening Day Age: 28
Born: 1/15/69 in Seaford, DE
ML Seasons: 7

Overall Statistics

	G	AB	R	H	D	T	HR	RBI	SB	BB	SO	Avg	OBP	Slg
1996	154	581	75	130	12	8	5	41	48	53	124	.224	.288	.298
Career	908	3399	501	894	120	39	38	292	301	457	679	.263	.351	.355

Where He Hits the Ball

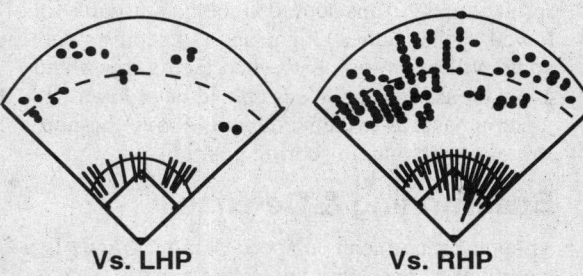

Vs. LHP   **Vs. RHP**

1996 Situational Stats

	AB	H	HR	RBI	Avg		AB	H	HR	RBI	Avg
Home	261	58	3	20	.222	LHP	133	28	1	13	.211
Road	320	72	2	21	.225	RHP	448	102	4	28	.228
First Half	342	86	5	29	.251	Sc Pos	125	25	1	32	.200
Scnd Half	239	44	0	12	.184	Clutch	97	26	0	5	.268

1996 Rankings (National League)

→ 1st in lowest batting average vs. right-handed pitchers (.228), lowest on-base percentage for a leadoff hitter (.273), lowest slugging percentage vs. right-handed pitchers (.292), lowest on-base percentage vs. left-handed pitchers (.257) and lowest batting average

→ 2nd in lowest slugging percentage, lowest on-base percentage, lowest slugging percentage vs. left-handed pitchers (.316), lowest batting average at home (.222), errors at second base (17) and lowest fielding percentage at second base (.975)

→ 3rd in stolen bases and lowest batting average vs. left-handed pitchers (.211)

Greg Gagne

Position: SS
Bats: R **Throws:** R
Ht: 5'11" **Wt:** 180

Opening Day Age: 35
Born: 11/12/61 in Fall River, MA
ML Seasons: 14
Pronunciation: GAG-nee

1996 Season

The Dodgers got exactly what they wanted out of free-agent signee Greg Gagne last season: solid defense and solid offensive production. Gagne, who nearly matched his career numbers, bounced around in the lineup at the start of the year before settling into the eighth spot in the order. After missing a month with a severely sprained ankle in mid-May, the veteran came back strong throughout the summer. However, he faded a bit down the stretch, hitting just .213 in September.

Hitting

Gagne is aggressive at the plate, looking to drive fastballs into the outfield gaps. Once he settles into the batter's box, he will take walks, which doesn't result in many runs scored since he's usually followed by the pitcher. Gagne has a sweeping swing, so he will often look bad when facing down-and-away breaking balls. He is able to bear down with men on base, as evidenced by his above-the-norm average with men in scoring position.

Baserunning & Defense

Though by no means a speed demon, Gagne is a smart baserunner who will take the extra base on hits to the outfield. He is a smart shortstop, with exceptional range complementing a strong and accurate throwing arm. Gagne has no weaknesses in the field and is one of the league's best in turning the double play.

1997 Outlook

Gagne's defensive superiority over ex-Dodger shortstop Jose Offerman masks the fact that he was not as productive at the plate or on the basepaths as his predecessor. The lifelong American Leaguer cautiously chose to sign a one-year deal with Los Angeles last winter, but then re-signed with the club after the season. The Dodgers were quite happy with Gagne's play and look forward to another year of his quiet leadership and solid glove.

Overall Statistics

	G	AB	R	H	D	T	HR	RBI	SB	BB	SO	Avg	OBP	Slg
1996	128	428	48	109	13	2	10	55	4	50	93	.255	.333	.364
Career	1654	5159	663	1311	276	47	102	547	106	336	1001	.254	.302	.385

Where He Hits the Ball

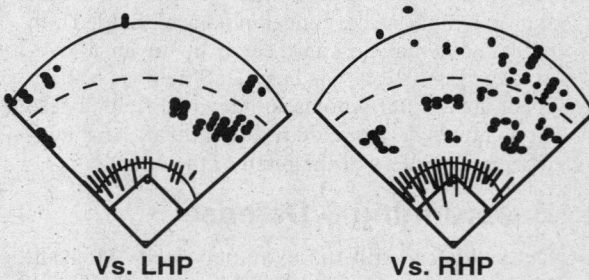

Vs. LHP   **Vs. RHP**

1996 Situational Stats

	AB	H	HR	RBI	Avg		AB	H	HR	RBI	Avg
Home	198	42	3	24	.212	LHP	93	23	3	17	.247
Road	230	67	7	31	.291	RHP	335	86	7	38	.257
First Half	180	49	5	22	.272	Sc Pos	105	30	2	43	.286
Scnd Half	248	60	5	33	.242	Clutch	81	17	1	7	.210

1996 Rankings (National League)

- ➡ 5th in errors at shortstop (21) and lowest fielding percentage at shortstop (.966)
- ➡ 9th in batting average with the bases loaded (.500)
- ➡ 10th in lowest slugging percentage vs. right-handed pitchers (.355)
- ➡ Led the Dodgers in batting average with the bases loaded (.500)

Mark Guthrie

1996 Season

Mark Guthrie was an unsung hero for the Dodgers last season. As a set-up man, the veteran lefty was virtually unhittable in the first half of the year. Though he started to slip a bit after the All-Star break, he kept his team in many games by holding the opposition at bay for an inning or two. He suffered from neck spasms late in the season, limiting his availability and effectiveness, but rebounded to pitch well down the stretch.

Pitching

Guthrie is a finesse pitcher who mixes an average fastball with a curve and change-up to retire opposing left-handed hitters. His bread-and-butter weapon, however, is an excellent splitter, which helps the southpaw remain surprisingly effective versus righties, who hit just .232 against him. Guthrie has good command of all of his pitches, and although he may walk a few batters, he has been through many battles and seldom gets rattled.

Defense & Hitting

For a lefthander, Guthrie is not very adept at holding runners. His big leg kick and mediocre pickoff move are an inviting combination for opposing basestealers. On the mound, Guthrie is an average fielder who seldom makes mistakes. Although he doesn't get to the plate very often, the longtime American Leaguer shows promise, making contact in his only three at-bats of the season.

1997 Outlook

The Dodgers have made it very clear that they would like to have Guthrie back for this season and re-signed him in early November. Guthrie should make himself comfortable in the Los Angeles bullpen. He's probably going to stay there for at least a couple more years.

Position: RP
Bats: R **Throws:** L
Ht: 6' 4" **Wt:** 207

Opening Day Age: 31
Born: 9/22/65 in Buffalo, NY
ML Seasons: 8

Overall Statistics

	W	L	Pct.	ERA	G	GS	Sv	IP	H	BB	SO	HR	BR/IP
1996	2	3	.400	2.22	66	0	1	73.0	65	22	56	3	1.19
Career	31	32	.492	3.93	330	43	9	582.1	611	205	463	52	1.40

How Often He Throws Strikes

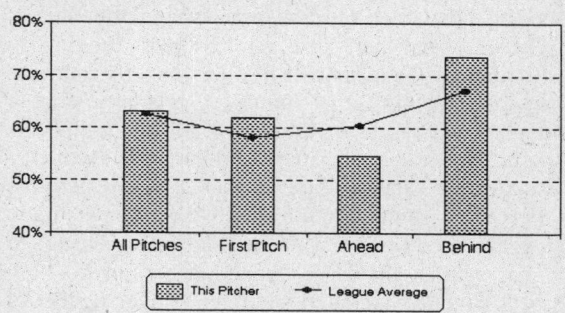

1996 Situational Stats

	W	L	ERA	Sv	IP		AB	H	HR	RBI	Avg
Home	1	2	1.39	1	32.1	LHB	86	22	1	10	.256
Road	1	1	2.88	0	40.2	RHB	185	43	2	18	.232
First Half	1	0	1.13	0	39.2	Sc Pos	66	19	0	24	.288
Scnd Half	1	3	3.51	1	33.1	Clutch	131	34	2	18	.260

1996 Rankings (National League)

→ 1st in highest percentage of inherited runners scored (50.0%)
→ 4th in relief ERA (2.22)
→ Led the Dodgers in lowest batting average allowed in relief with runners on base (.241) and relief ERA (2.22)

Todd Hollandsworth

1996 Season

Recovering from an injury-plagued 1995 campaign, Todd Hollandsworth was immediately thrown for a loop when his friend and mentor Brett Butler was diagnosed with throat cancer. Bouncing around the outfield, he played exclusively against right-handed pitchers and eventually won a job as the Dodgers' starting left fielder. Down the stretch, Hollandsworth was arguably the club's most outstanding player, and he was rewarded after the season with the National League Rookie of the Year Award—the fifth straight for a Dodger player.

Hitting

Hollandsworth is just as aggressive at the plate as he is everywhere else on the field, looking to pound the first fastball he likes into the outfield gaps. However, the youngster gets into trouble when he chases bad breaking balls and high heaters. He is a good situational hitter and can lay down the sacrifice bunt as well. Hollandsworth's greatest improvement last season was made against southpaws: when he finally got a chance to bat against them, he proved he could be very effective. An alert and intelligent player, he should only continue to improve.

Baserunning & Defense

Hollandsworth is a fine baserunner with an excellent stolen base percentage. Though he is capable in center field, Hollandsworth saw most of his playing time in left during the second half of the year. He gets a good jump on balls, but has just an average arm and will occasionally throw to the wrong base.

1997 Outlook

Hollandsworth is a player who actually surpassed the annual Dodger Rookie-of-the-Year hype. He's a real throwback: if you don't like the way this kid plays, you don't like baseball. If he can control his wild abandon enough to stay in the lineup, Hollandsworth should soon emerge as a team leader.

Position: LF/CF
Bats: L **Throws:** L
Ht: 6' 2" **Wt:** 193

Opening Day Age: 23
Born: 4/20/73 in Dayton, OH
ML Seasons: 2

Overall Statistics

	G	AB	R	H	D	T	HR	RBI	SB	BB	SO	Avg	OBP	Slg
1996	149	478	64	139	26	4	12	59	21	41	93	.291	.348	.437
Career	190	581	80	163	28	4	17	72	23	51	122	.281	.340	.430

Where He Hits the Ball

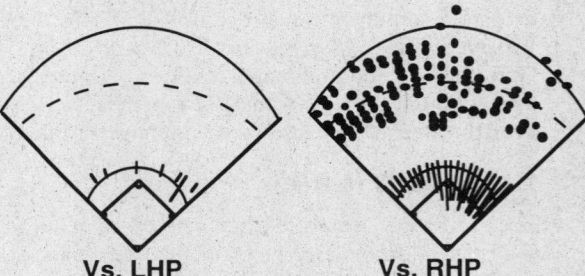

Vs. LHP **Vs. RHP**

1996 Situational Stats

	AB	H	HR	RBI	Avg		AB	H	HR	RBI	Avg
Home	218	62	2	19	.284	LHP	29	10	0	0	.345
Road	260	77	10	40	.296	RHP	449	129	12	59	.287
First Half	223	64	5	29	.287	Sc Pos	108	34	2	42	.315
Scnd Half	255	75	7	30	.294	Clutch	69	23	2	7	.333

1996 Rankings (National League)

→ 2nd in least GDPs per GDP situation (2.2%), lowest fielding percentage in left field (.973) and highest percentage of extra bases taken as a runner (72.1%)

→ 5th in errors in left field (5)

→ 9th in lowest batting average on a 3-1 count (.111)

→ Led the Dodgers in least GDPs per GDP situation (2.2%), batting average in the clutch (.333) and highest percentage of extra bases taken as a runner (72.1%)

Eric Karros

1996 Season

Eric Karros played very little last spring due to a pulled muscle in his side, and the injury hurt his early season performance. Hitting just .219 when June rolled around, the burly first baseman was struggling, but he just kept on swinging and re-bounded to put together another solid year. Karros was the main catalyst that ignited the Dodgers' playoff drive in August, churning out a team-high 27 RBI over the month.

Hitting

Karros is a pull hitter who has a short, powerful swing. He likes to hit pitches down and in, but has learned to drive the high fastballs to the opposite field. When Karros tries to pull those pitches, he runs into trouble—and usually adds to his league-leading double play total. While he is not the most patient hitter, Karros will take an occasional walk. However, he knows that his job is to drive in runs, so when the opportunity arises, he's not at all hesitant about swinging the bat.

Baserunning & Defense

Karros is big and slow, but surprised Dodger opponents by swiping eight bases without getting caught last season. He has good instincts and knows when to take the extra base. Over the years, Karros has developed a quality glove at first base. What he lacks in range, he makes up for in sure-handedness, and few balls, whether thrown or hit, get past him.

1997 Outlook

Karros is the leader of the Dodgers—and the main obstacle keeping ex-roommate Mike Piazza behind the plate. There is occasionally talk of giving Karros a shot across the diamond at third base, but he doesn't appear quick enough to handle the hot corner. Of course, the Dodgers might be willing to sacrifice some defense with 30 home run/100 RBI outputs coming from both sides of the diamond.

Position: 1B
Bats: R **Throws:** R
Ht: 6' 4" **Wt:** 222

Opening Day Age: 29
Born: 11/4/67 in Hackensack, NJ
ML Seasons: 6
Pronunciation: CARE-ose

Overall Statistics

	G	AB	R	H	D	T	HR	RBI	SB	BB	SO	Avg	OBP	Slg
1996	154	608	84	158	29	1	34	111	8	53	121	.260	.316	.479
Career	729	2743	355	724	137	8	123	431	16	215	480	.264	.317	.454

Where He Hits the Ball

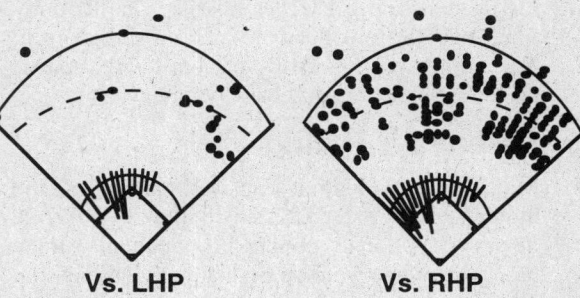

Vs. LHP   Vs. RHP

1996 Situational Stats

	AB	H	HR	RBI	Avg		AB	H	HR	RBI	Avg
Home	287	79	16	55	.275	LHP	101	33	6	24	.327
Road	321	79	18	56	.246	RHP	507	125	28	87	.247
First Half	314	80	20	53	.255	Sc Pos	170	47	8	74	.276
Scnd Half	294	78	14	58	.265	Clutch	96	18	2	11	.188

1996 Rankings (National League)

- → 1st in GDPs (27)
- → 2nd in errors at first base (15) and lowest fielding percentage at first base (.990)
- → 4th in lowest on-base percentage vs. right-handed pitchers (.295)
- → 5th in lowest percentage of extra bases taken as a runner (30.4%)
- → 7th in lowest batting average vs. right-handed pitchers (.247) and lowest cleanup slugging percentage (.479)
- → 8th in sacrifice flies (8), lowest on-base percentage and lowest batting average in the clutch (.188)
- → 9th in pitches seen (2,650)
- → Led the Dodgers in RBI and sacrifice flies (8)

Ramon Martinez

1996 Season

After missing time early last season with both a pulled groin muscle and a bad case of the flu, Ramon Martinez didn't get settled into the Dodger rotation until the middle of June. Once he was finally healthy, the staff ace put together a great second half and was unbeatable in the stretch drive, going 4-0 with a 2.45 ERA in September.

Pitching

Martinez attacks hitters with both two- and four-seam fastballs. While his four-seamer tails in on right-handed hitters, his two-seamer sinks devastatingly—to batters of all persuasions. Martinez' strikeout pitch is a change-up that looks just like his fastballs until it leaves his hand; he'll sometimes turn this pitch over to make it sink as well. To complement these weapons, he'll will also toss up a couple of flat curveballs per game.

Defense & Hitting

Martinez fields his position well, getting off the mound quickly and possessing a sure glove. While he pays attention to runners, his opponents' stolen base percentage went up dramatically last season. This was probably due to catcher Mike Piazza's throwing problems. At the plate, Martinez swings hard, but only occasionally makes contact.

1997 Outlook

Martinez is the ace of a strong Dodger rotation, turning in an excellent year despite missing a month-and-a-half. Since none of his injuries and ailments were arm-related, the club has every reason to expect more success from him next year. Martinez is truly the staff stopper: he went 9-1 with a 2.82 ERA in his 13 starts after an LA loss. With his home-park advantage and big-game experience, it would not be a reach to foresee a Cy Young award in his future, however, he'll need to work on cutting down his walks. Now if only Maddux, Smoltz and Glavine would leave the National League. . .

Position: SP
Bats: L **Throws:** R
Ht: 6' 4" **Wt:** 186

Opening Day Age: 29
Born: 3/22/68 in Santo Domingo, DR
ML Seasons: 9

Overall Statistics

	W	L	Pct.	ERA	G	GS	Sv	IP	H	BB	SO	HR	BR/IP
1996	15	6	.714	3.42	28	27	0	168.2	153	86	134	12	1.42
Career	106	69	.606	3.47	229	225	0	1496.1	1319	595	1104	126	1.28

How Often He Throws Strikes

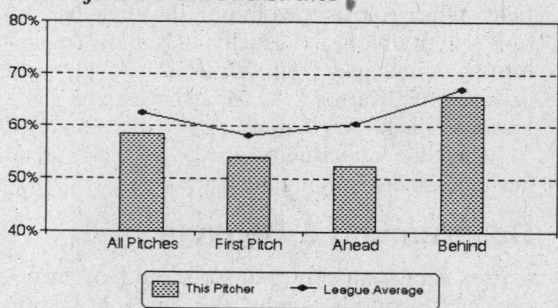

Legend: This Pitcher (bars) — League Average (line)

Y-axis: 40%, 50%, 60%, 70%, 80%
X-axis: All Pitches, First Pitch, Ahead, Behind

1996 Situational Stats

	W	L	ERA	Sv	IP		AB	H	HR	RBI	Avg
Home	8	3	3.09	0	84.1	LHB	267	66	6	24	.247
Road	7	3	3.74	0	84.1	RHB	358	87	6	34	.243
First Half	6	3	3.67	0	61.1	Sc Pos	147	32	3	45	.218
Scnd Half	9	3	3.27	0	107.1	Clutch	37	9	0	5	.243

1996 Rankings (National League)

- ➡ 2nd in shutouts (2) and winning percentage
- ➡ 3rd in most run support per 9 innings (6.0)
- ➡ 5th in stolen bases allowed (24), lowest slugging percentage allowed (.341) and least home runs allowed per 9 innings (.64)
- ➡ 6th in most pitches thrown per batter (3.87)
- ➡ 8th in walks allowed
- ➡ 9th in wins, lowest strikeout/walk ratio (1.6) and lowest batting average allowed with runners in scoring position (.218)
- ➡ 10th in highest stolen base percentage allowed (80.0%)
- ➡ Led the Dodgers in shutouts (2), walks allowed, winning percentage and lowest slugging percentage allowed (.341)

Raul Mondesi

1996 Season

At the end of July, Raul Mondesi was hitting .281 with 54 RBI, well on his way to a mediocre season. After catching fire for the last two months of year, Mondesi wound up with solid numbers. Only a player with Mondesi's talent could coast through two-thirds of a season and still put together dominating numbers like his. Should he ever stay focused for the whole six months, Dodger opponents will be in trouble.

Hitting

Any pitcher who throws Mondesi a first-pitch strike is asking for trouble. He's probably going to swing anyway, so why not put it a couple of inches outside? Not only is Mondesi impatient, but he simply does not have good strike zone judgment. In fact, he is just as likely to swing at a bad ball late in the count as on the first pitch. However, when he connects, he slams the ball very hard, resulting in tremendous home runs and ground balls that sometimes roll to the wall. Most of his longballs are to left, but Mondesi has power to all fields.

Baserunning & Defense

After a breakthrough year on the basepaths in 1995, Mondesi was more cautious in his approach last season. However, despite his incredible acceleration, his stolen base percentages plummeted. Defensively, Mondesi runs down fly balls with ease and has possibly the best throwing arm in the majors. Intimidating baserunners into stopping dead in their tracks, Mondesi's cannon is hardly tested anymore.

1997 Outlook

No one plays harder than Mondesi. Although he is a streaky hitter, he never takes his slumps out into the field. A true competitor, Mondesi plays hurt and runs hard on every ground ball. Bill Russell benched him late in the year for coming to the park late; it never happened again. Mondesi should patrol right field for the Dodgers for years to come.

Position: RF
Bats: R **Throws:** R
Ht: 5'11" **Wt:** 212

Opening Day Age: 26
Born: 3/12/71 in San Cristobal, DR
ML Seasons: 4
Pronunciation: MAHN-de-see

Overall Statistics

	G	AB	R	H	D	T	HR	RBI	SB	BB	SO	Avg	OBP	Slg
1996	157	634	98	188	40	7	24	88	14	32	122	.297	.334	.495
Career	450	1690	265	499	93	22	70	242	56	85	312	.295	.331	.501

Where He Hits the Ball

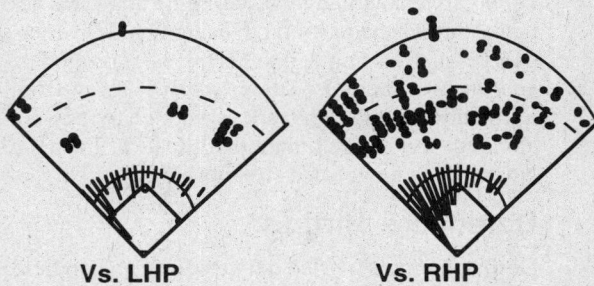

Vs. LHP **Vs. RHP**

1996 Situational Stats

	AB	H	HR	RBI	Avg		AB	H	HR	RBI	Avg
Home	298	92	11	40	.309	LHP	113	31	4	20	.274
Road	336	96	13	48	.286	RHP	521	157	20	68	.301
First Half	343	91	16	50	.265	Sc Pos	153	45	6	63	.294
Scnd Half	291	97	8	38	.333	Clutch	112	33	4	18	.295

1996 Rankings (National League)

- 1st in errors in right field (12)
- 3rd in lowest fielding percentage in right field (.967) and highest percentage of swings on the first pitch (45.7%)
- 5th in least GDPs per GDP situation (4.6%)
- 6th in at-bats and doubles
- 7th in lowest stolen base percentage (66.7%) and highest percentage of swings that missed (28.1%)
- 8th in triples
- 9th in lowest percentage of pitches taken (46.1%)
- 10th in hits and strikeouts
- Led the Dodgers in at-bats, runs scored, hits, doubles, total bases (314) and hit by pitch (5)

Los Angeles Dodgers

Hideo Nomo

1996 Season

It would have been too much to expect Hideo Nomo to repeat his stunning major league debut of 1995—and yet, despite the embarrassing midseason revelation of an extra-marital affair, he pitched just as well last season. His opponents hit just .218 against him, and in his last nine starts, Nomo went 5-2 with a 2.18 ERA, including an unbelievable no-hitter at Coors Field.

Pitching

Nomo usually starts hitters with a low-90s fastball high in the strike zone, and will occasionally showcase a rolling, offspeed curveball to complement his heater. When gunning for the strikeout, Nomo attacks with a devastating forkball. He actually throws the nasty pitch using two deliveries: a three-quarters angle, like his fastball, to righties, and an over-the-top motion to tail it away from left-handed hitters. Both are very tough to see—let alone hit. As a result, batters hit just .112 against Nomo when he got two strikes on them.

Defense & Hitting

Despite Nomo's twisted delivery, he's able to field his position well. Basestealers run at will with him on the mound; they stole 52 bases against him last season and were caught just 11 times. Although he struck out in more than half of his at-bats, he also slugged four doubles, three more than the rest of the Dodger pitching staff combined.

1997 Outlook

Nomo is a nice fit in the Dodgers' International House of Pitchers. How many other cities would embrace an Asian-American so easily and enthusiastically? His performance down the stretch cemented his position on the club and he should remain a member of the starting rotation as long as he stays healthy. Despite a history of shoulder problems, Nomo now has two solid seasons under his belt and has exhibited few dents in his armor.

Position: SP
Bats: R **Throws:** R
Ht: 6' 2" **Wt:** 210

Opening Day Age: 28
Born: 8/31/68 in Kobe, Japan
ML Seasons: 2
Pronunciation: hi-DAY-oh NO-mo

Overall Statistics

	W	L	Pct.	ERA	G	GS	Sv	IP	H	BB	SO	HR	BR/IP
1996	16	11	.593	3.19	33	33	0	228.1	180	85	234	23	1.16
Career	29	17	.630	2.90	61	61	0	419.2	304	163	470	37	1.11

How Often He Throws Strikes

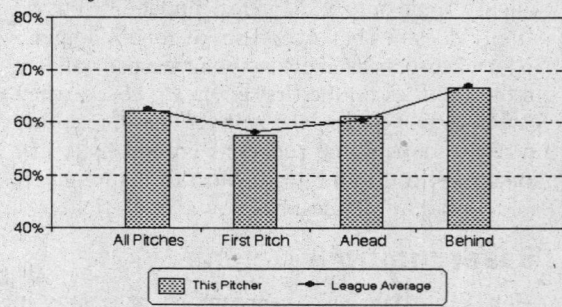

This Pitcher — League Average

1996 Situational Stats

	W	L	ERA	Sv	IP		AB	H	HR	RBI	Avg
Home	9	6	2.75	0	134.0	LHB	356	77	8	32	.216
Road	7	5	3.82	0	94.1	RHB	471	103	15	51	.219
First Half	9	7	3.51	0	120.2	Sc Pos	189	41	4	54	.217
Scnd Half	7	4	2.84	0	107.2	Clutch	68	12	2	7	.176

1996 Rankings (National League)

→ 1st in stolen bases allowed (52)
→ 2nd in shutouts (2), strikeouts, least GDPs induced per 9 innings (0.4) and most strikeouts per 9 innings (9.2)
→ 3rd in balks (3), lowest batting average allowed (.218) and lowest batting average allowed vs. left-handed batters (.216)
→ 5th in wins
→ 6th in lowest slugging percentage allowed (.343) and least baserunners allowed per 9 innings (10.5)
→ 7th in wild pitches (12), lowest on-base percentage allowed (.290), highest stolen base percentage allowed (82.5%) and ERA at home (2.75)

Antonio Osuna

Position: RP
Bats: R **Throws:** R
Ht: 5'11" **Wt:** 160

Opening Day Age: 23
Born: 4/12/73 in Sinaloa, Mexico
ML Seasons: 2
Pronunciation: oh-SOO-nuh

1996 Season

Antonio Osuna quickly settled into his role as a set-up man in 1996. He had a brilliant first half and entered the All-Star break with a 1.95 ERA. Though he wilted a bit in the latter part of the season, Osuna was regarded highly enough by the Dodgers' managerial staff to make 73 relief appearances, the fifth highest total in club history. It's no wonder—Osuna held opposing hitters to a .220 average and struck out more than one batter per inning.

Pitching

Osuna has a compact build and is a pure power reliever. In fact, managers voted his fastball as the third best in the National League, behind those of Mark Wohlers and Robb Nen. It's a four-seamer that he delivers high in the strike zone to generate a lot of fly balls. Because Osuna's fastball is so dominant, he really only needs to get his curves and change-ups over the plate to be effective. He possesses unusually good control for a pitcher with his velocity.

Defense & Hitting

Osuna's compact delivery keeps him in good fielding position and, like all the Dodgers' home-grown pitchers, he displays excellent fundamentals. He keeps runners close with an excellent pickoff move for a righthander. The reliever seldom gets a chance to swing the bat, reaching base once in three plate appearances last year.

1997 Outlook

In many bullpens, Osuna would have already been rushed into the closer role. However, with the resurgence of Todd Worrell and the arrival of Darren Dreifort, the Dodgers have the luxury of letting the hard thrower mature into the position. He will spend this season as the set-up man again, after which the club will evaluate their bullpen options. Osuna certainly has the ability to be the closer, but whether he has the makeup is still not certain.

Overall Statistics

	W	L	Pct.	ERA	G	GS	Sv	IP	H	BB	SO	HR	BR/IP
1996	9	6	.600	3.00	73	0	4	84.0	65	32	85	6	1.15
Career	11	10	.524	3.50	112	0	4	128.2	104	52	131	11	1.21

How Often He Throws Strikes

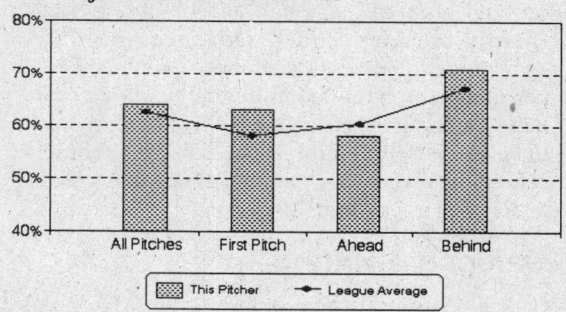

1996 Situational Stats

	W	L	ERA	Sv	IP		AB	H	HR	RBI	Avg
Home	3	4	3.32	3	40.2	LHB	109	26	3	13	.239
Road	6	2	2.70	1	43.1	RHB	187	39	3	19	.209
First Half	4	3	1.95	2	50.2	Sc Pos	82	16	4	26	.195
Scnd Half	5	3	4.59	2	33.1	Clutch	181	38	4	22	.210

1996 Rankings (National League)

→ 1st in relief wins (9)
→ 5th in relief losses (6)
→ 7th in holds (16)
→ 8th in games pitched
→ 9th in lowest percentage of inherited runners scored (28.9%) and relief innings (84.0)
→ 10th in least baserunners allowed per 9 innings in relief (10.6)
→ Led the Dodgers in games pitched, holds (16), lowest percentage of inherited runners scored (28.9%), relief wins (9), relief losses (6), relief innings (84.0), lowest batting average allowed in relief (.220) and least baserunners allowed per 9 innings in relief (10.6)

Los Angeles Dodgers

Chan Ho Park

1996 Season

Chan Ho Park made the Dodgers as the swing man out of the bullpen at the start of last season. Park entered the rotation when Ramon Martinez sat out for five weeks with a groin pull, going 2-2 with a 2.48 ERA through six starts. In 10 starts over the whole season, Park went 3-3 with a 3.26 ERA, but the young Korean pitched mostly in long relief, where he could work on his tools and poise.

Pitching

Park's stuff is, as one scout put it, "as good as you're ever going to see." The big righthander throws a mid-90s four-seam fastball that he moves all around the plate. To offset his heater, Park relies on both his tight curveball and his more erratic sharply-breaking slider. Opponents hit .209 against Park and he totalled more than a strikeout per inning, so dominating hitters is not his problem—rather, it is getting the ball consistently over the plate. Park's control is like a distant AM radio station; just when you think it's tuned in perfectly, everything goes static.

Defense & Hitting

Park is just an average fielder at best. He holds runners close with a decent pickoff move and by getting the ball to the plate so quickly. Park made just a handful of plate appearances last year and it seems that he's currently only capable of laying down bunts.

1997 Outlook

The Korean government has threatened to call Park back home for him to fulfill his mandatory year of military service, but they'll probably back off if the young fireballer is given a more prominent pitching role. Regardless of the blackmail, it is just a matter of time before Park joins the Dodger rotation. That time is probably now, and with his size, strength and mechanics, he could very well stay there for many years to come.

Position: RP/SP
Bats: R **Throws:** R
Ht: 6' 2" **Wt:** 195

Opening Day Age: 23
Born: 6/30/73 in Kong Ju City, Korea
ML Seasons: 3

Overall Statistics

	W	L	Pct.	ERA	G	GS	Sv	IP	H	BB	SO	HR	BR/IP
1996	5	5	.500	3.64	48	10	0	108.2	82	71	119	7	1.41
Career	5	5	.500	3.93	52	11	0	116.2	89	78	132	9	1.43

How Often He Throws Strikes

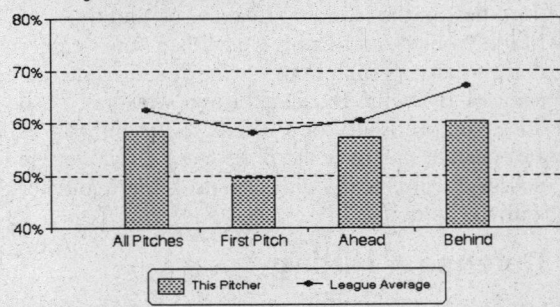

1996 Situational Stats

	W	L	ERA	Sv	IP		AB	H	HR	RBI	Avg
Home	2	3	2.10	0	55.2	LHB	160	42	3	20	.263
Road	3	2	5.26	0	53.0	RHB	233	40	4	21	.172
First Half	5	2	3.19	0	67.2	Scd Pos	114	28	1	35	.246
Scnd Half	0	3	4.39	0	41.0	Clutch	40	9	0	5	.225

1996 Rankings (National League)

→ 3rd in balks (3) and most strikeouts per 9 innings in relief (10.7)
→ Led the Dodgers in most strikeouts per 9 innings in relief (10.7)

Mike Piazza

1996 Season

Mike Piazza began last season with five multiple-hit games, but did not homer until his 66th at-bat, the longest dry spell of his career. He staggered out of the year after catching 148 games, but was nonetheless still perhaps the best hitter in the league. Piazza injured his right knee in late May, but refused to have surgery or even come out of the lineup. Though his ironman endurance may have hurt the club in the long run, the Dodgers offense was too weak to compete without him.

Hitting

Piazza gets on base and hits for power, a lethal combination. His lightning-quick bat enables him to see pitches an extra nanosecond before committing. As a result, Piazza can drive pitches to all fields. He can be beaten up and in and will occasionally wave at the down and away slider, but is excellent at adjusting from pitch to pitch. With improved strike zone judgment, Piazza more than doubled his walk total last year.

Baserunning & Defense

Piazza's bad legs slowed him considerably last season. He totalled only 16 doubles because he just couldn't leg out the gappers. Despite some midseason work with former Dodger Mike Scioscia, Piazza still has a slow release and his throws are often off-target. He's improved at blocking balls in the dirt, but still has not yet mastered the art of defending the plate from on-rushing baserunners.

1997 Outlook

How long the Dodgers allow their franchise player to get banged up behind the plate is a subject of great debate in Los Angeles. Were they in the American League, Piazza would no doubt DH 20-30 games per year, but they currently have nowhere else to put him. In the meantime, manager Bill Russell will have to consider resting his star slugger more often in the coming years or face dire consequences.

Position: C
Bats: R **Throws:** R
Ht: 6' 3" **Wt:** 215

Opening Day Age: 28
Born: 9/4/68 in Norristown, PA
ML Seasons: 5
Pronunciation: pee-AH-za

Overall Statistics

	G	AB	R	H	D	T	HR	RBI	SB	BB	SO	Avg	OBP	Slg
1996	148	547	87	184	16	0	36	105	0	81	93	.336	.422	.563
Career	537	2002	319	653	78	2	128	409	5	203	336	.326	.388	.559

Where He Hits the Ball

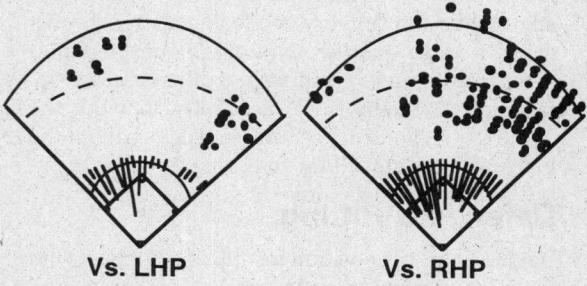

Vs. LHP   **Vs. RHP**

1996 Situational Stats

	AB	H	HR	RBI	Avg		AB	H	HR	RBI	Avg
Home	278	89	14	46	.320	LHP	93	38	6	19	.409
Road	269	95	22	59	.353	RHP	454	146	30	86	.322
First Half	300	109	24	63	.363	Sc Pos	140	49	8	65	.350
Scnd Half	247	75	12	42	.304	Clutch	89	24	9	19	.270

1996 Rankings (National League)

→ 1st in lowest percentage of extra bases taken as a runner (15.4%)
→ 2nd in intentional walks (21), batting average on the road (.353) and lowest percentage of runners caught stealing as a catcher (14.4%)
→ 3rd in GDPs (21) and batting average
→ 4th in on-base percentage
→ 5th in singles and on-base percentage vs. right-handed pitchers (.410)
→ 6th in batting average vs. right-handed pitchers (.322) and errors at catcher (9)
→ 7th in walks and times on base (266)
→ 8th in HR frequency (15.2 ABs per HR) and highest groundball/flyball ratio (1.9)
→ 9th in home runs and slugging percentage

Ismael Valdes

1996 Season

Ismael Valdes pitched very consistently in his first full season in the Dodgers rotation. The 23 year old reached the seventh inning in 25 of his 33 starts, giving his team a chance to win in almost every one of his outings. Valdes had a winning record in every month except August, and he ended the year with a four-game winning streak.

Pitching

Valdes throws four different pitches and has excellent command and control of all of them. He is not the hardest thrower on the staff, but his fastball sinks dramatically just before it reaches the hitter. The difference between his two curveballs is mainly where he releases them. One comes from an over-the-top delivery, while the other is thrown using a three-quarters motion. Valdes complements these pitches with an excellent change-up. His success stems from his ability to work the corners with amazing accuracy. Valdes can hit the black of the plate all day long.

Defense & Hitting

Valdes fields his position just like he pitches: with textbook accuracy and mistake-free precision. Holding runners, however, may be the one weakness in the young Mexican's game. His pickoff move is mediocre and his delivery is rather deliberate. Valdes handles the bat quite well and led the team in sacrifice bunts.

1997 Outlook

With his pinpoint control, Valdes reminds many people of Greg Maddux. While it may be a bit early to make that comparison, his numbers at this stage in his career match up fairly well with those of the four-time Cy Young Award winner. As long as he can stay healthy, this is a young hurler with a very bright future ahead of him.

Position: SP
Bats: R **Throws:** R
Ht: 6' 3" **Wt:** 207

Opening Day Age: 23
Born: 8/21/73 in Victoria, MX
ML Seasons: 3
Pronunciation: ISH-mail Val-DEZZ

Overall Statistics

	W	L	Pct.	ERA	G	GS	Sv	IP	H	BB	SO	HR	BR/IP
1996	15	7	.682	3.32	33	33	0	225.0	219	54	173	20	1.21
Career	31	19	.620	3.19	87	61	1	451.0	408	115	351	39	1.16

How Often He Throws Strikes

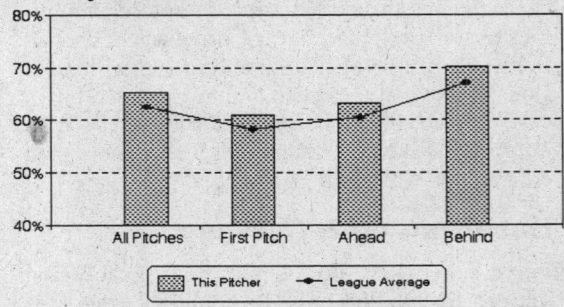

1996 Situational Stats

	W	L	ERA	Sv	IP		AB	H	HR	RBI	Avg
Home	7	2	2.60	0	114.1	LHB	381	93	7	30	.244
Road	8	5	4.07	0	110.2	RHB	493	126	13	54	.256
First Half	9	5	3.31	0	122.1	Sc Pos	190	43	5	60	.226
Scnd Half	6	2	3.33	0	102.2	Clutch	79	20	2	5	.253

1996 Rankings (National League)

- → 1st in balks (5)
- → 3rd in pickoff throws (208) and winning percentage
- → 4th in highest stolen base percentage allowed (85.2%)
- → 6th in ERA at home (2.60)
- → 8th in sacrifice bunts (13) and highest strike-out/walk ratio (3.2)
- → 9th in wins, hits allowed, stolen bases allowed (23) and lowest on-base percentage allowed (.294)

Todd Worrell

1996 Season

Todd Worrell has made a remarkable recovery from the arm injuries he suffered earlier in his career. After breaking the Dodger save record with 32 in 1995, he buried the pieces last season. The big righthander came out of the blocks blazing, not allowing a run in his first 11 appearances. Though he hit a "dead arm" period in May, Worrell remained amazingly consistent. He never once blew consecutive save chances all year long and converted 18 of his last 21 opportunities.

Pitching

Worrell is still a two-pitch reliever, though the particulars have changed a bit. He starts off batters with 90+ MPH fastballs, which especially stifle left-handed hitters by tailing in towards them. Since his elbow problems, Worrell has stopped throwing his slider, but has since developed a hard, knee-buckling curveball that he uses consistently for strikes. For a such a hard thrower, the veteran closer has great control. While he gives up his share of hits—more than one per inning last season—Worrell is always able to bear down and notch the strikeout when he needs it.

Defense & Hitting

Worrell is a big man and, consequently, he gets off the mound rather slowly. With an ineffective and seldom-used pickoff move, opponents run at will when he's on the mound. Over the last six years, enemy basestealers have been successful on 46 of 47 attempts against Worrell. He did not make a plate appearance last season and has not collected a hit since 1987.

1997 Outlook

Worrell was arguably the most dominant reliever in baseball last year. The Dodgers have already exercised their option for next season, so he will be closing out games in Los Angeles for at least one more year. However, with Antonio Osuna and Darren Dreifort both serving as apprentices in the bullpen, this could be the veteran's last tour in Los Angeles.

Position: RP
Bats: R **Throws:** R
Ht: 6' 5" **Wt:** 227

Opening Day Age: 37
Born: 9/28/59 in Arcadia, CA
ML Seasons: 10
Pronunciation: wor-RELL

Overall Statistics

	W	L	Pct.	ERA	G	GS	Sv	IP	H	BB	SO	HR	BR/IP
1996	4	6	.400	3.03	72	0	44	65.1	70	15	66	5	1.30
Career	48	46	.511	2.88	552	0	221	634.0	548	224	567	53	1.22

How Often He Throws Strikes

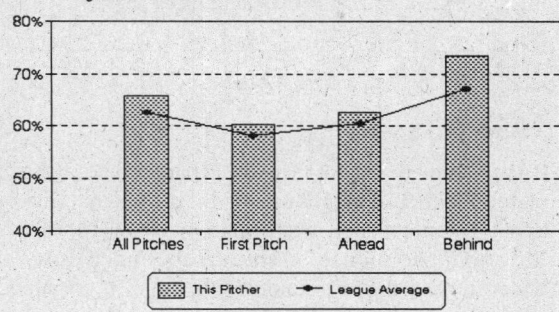

This Pitcher — League Average

1996 Situational Stats

	W	L	ERA	Sv	IP		AB	H	HR	RBI	Avg
Home	3	1	1.95	20	32.1	LHB	124	30	3	19	.242
Road	1	5	4.09	24	33.0	RHB	140	40	2	15	.286
First Half	3	4	2.97	23	36.1	Sc Pos	84	25	0	28	.298
Scnd Half	1	2	3.10	21	29.0	Clutch	208	53	4	29	.255

1996 Rankings (National League)

- → 1st in saves, games finished (67), save opportunities (53) and blown saves (9)
- → 4th in lowest save percentage (83.0%) and least GDPs induced per GDP situation (2.0%)
- → 5th in worst first batter efficiency (.333) and relief losses (6)
- → Led the Dodgers in saves, games finished (67), save opportunities (53), save percentage (83.0%), blown saves (9) and relief losses (6)

Billy Ashley

Position: LF
Bats: R **Throws:** R
Ht: 6' 7" **Wt:** 235

Opening Day Age: 26
Born: 7/11/70 in Taylor, MI
ML Seasons: 5

Overall Statistics

	G	AB	R	H	D	T	HR	RBI	SB	BB	SO	Avg	OBP	Slg
1996	71	110	18	22	2	1	9	25	0	21	44	.200	.331	.482
Career	197	463	41	105	13	1	19	58	0	53	179	.227	.308	.382

1996 Situational Stats

	AB	H	HR	RBI	Avg		AB	H	HR	RBI	Avg
Home	67	14	5	12	.209	LHP	79	19	8	23	.241
Road	43	8	4	13	.186	RHP	31	3	1	2	.097
First Half	72	11	4	10	.153	Sc Pos	37	9	3	18	.243
Scnd Half	38	11	5	15	.289	Clutch	19	5	4	8	.263

1996 Season

Billy Ashley began last season as part of a left field platoon with Todd Hollandsworth, but his inability to make contact soon sent him to manager Tommy Lasorda's doghouse. Ashley rebounded after Lasorda retired and pounded five pinch-hit home runs, one short of the major league record.

Hitting, Baserunning & Defense

When he makes contact, Ashley has considerable power to all fields. After striking out in an incredible 44 percent of his at-bats from May through July, he showed more patience and willingness to take the ball the other way. While he is vulnerable to high inside fastballs and breaking stuff thrown away from him, he's very dangerous when he makes pitchers throw strikes. Though he has a good arm, Ashley is quite slow and is out of place patrolling the outfield.

1997 Outlook

Ashley responded well to new Dodger skipper Bill Russell and was a potent weapon off the bench down the stretch. But LA has a lot of outfielders, and Ashley might not stick around. It would not be surprising to see Ashley traded to the American League—where he could DH—in the near future.

Brett Butler

Position: CF
Bats: L **Throws:** L
Ht: 5'10" **Wt:** 161

Opening Day Age: 39
Born: 6/15/57 in Los Angeles, CA
ML Seasons: 16

Overall Statistics

	G	AB	R	H	D	T	HR	RBI	SB	BB	SO	Avg	OBP	Slg
1996	34	131	22	35	1	1	0	8	8	9	22	.267	.313	.290
Career	2108	7837	1307	2278	269	128	54	560	543	1087	867	.291	.377	.378

1996 Situational Stats

	AB	H	HR	RBI	Avg		AB	H	HR	RBI	Avg
Home	72	18	0	6	.250	LHP	32	10	0	4	.313
Road	59	17	0	2	.288	RHP	99	25	0	4	.253
First Half	117	31	0	7	.265	Sc Pos	23	5	0	7	.217
Scnd Half	14	4	0	1	.286	Clutch	14	2	0	1	.143

1996 Season

After doctors found a cancerous tumor in his throat in May, Brett Butler was operated on and underwent six weeks of radiation treatments. In a courageous comeback, Butler made a miraculous return to the Los Angeles lineup in September. Unfortunately, he played just five more games before breaking his hand and ending his season.

Hitting, Baserunning & Defense

Butler looked uncharacteristically lethargic early last year, for what are now obvious reasons. Historically possessing excellent strike zone judgment, Butler is a spray hitter who remains one of the league's top bunters. Upon his return, he looked a few steps slower, especially on the basepaths. While he still gets a great jump on balls hit to the outfield and snares everything he can reach, Butler's arm has never been his strong suit.

1997 Outlook

The Dodgers re-signed Butler in early December, and the outfielder will try to prove that he can conquer cancer and return as an effective player. A thoughtful and intelligent leader, Butler would make a fine coach or manager—in fact, he saved several runs in September just by positioning outfielders from the dugout.

Roger Cedeno

Position: CF/LF
Bats: B **Throws:** R
Ht: 6' 1" **Wt:** 165

Opening Day Age: 22
Born: 8/16/74 in
Valencia Edo.
Carabobo, VZ
ML Seasons: 2
Pronunciation:
suh-DAYN-yo

Overall Statistics

	G	AB	R	H	D	T	HR	RBI	SB	BB	SO	Avg	OBP	Slg
1996	86	211	26	52	11	1	2	18	5	24	47	.246	.326	.336
Career	126	253	30	62	13	1	2	21	6	27	57	.245	.319	.328

1996 Situational Stats

	AB	H	HR	RBI	Avg		AB	H	HR	RBI	Avg
Home	93	22	0	4	.237	LHP	73	18	2	6	.247
Road	118	30	2	14	.254	RHP	138	34	0	12	.246
First Half	198	51	2	18	.258	Sc Pos	43	13	1	17	.302
Scnd Half	13	1	0	0	.077	Clutch	37	7	1	3	.189

1996 Season

When Brett Butler left the Dodgers, Roger Cedeno was given the first shot at the center field job. Clearly not ready for the majors, the 21 year old often looked overwhelmed and overmatched, and was promptly shipped back to the minors. He worked his way back to Los Angeles in September, but his duties were strictly limited to pinch running.

Hitting, Baserunning & Defense

Cedeno is a switch-hitter who sprays the ball to all fields from both sides of the plate. He has exhibited a good eye and the ability to make contact in his minor league career. Cedeno is deceptively quick, stealing 53 bases in his last two full years at Triple-A and going 5-for-6 for the Dodgers. Touted as a brilliant fielder, he was a disappointment, misplaying several balls during his brief time in the outfield.

1997 Outlook

Although everyone is waiting to hear what Brett Butler's plans are, Cedeno is clearly the Dodgers' center fielder of the future. He has hit over .300 in two straight years at Triple-A and, despite his initial defensive woes, should develop into a quality fielder.

Dave Clark

Position: LF/RF
Bats: L **Throws:** R
Ht: 6' 2" **Wt:** 209

Opening Day Age: 34
Born: 9/3/62 in Tupelo,
MS
ML Seasons: 11

Overall Statistics

	G	AB	R	H	D	T	HR	RBI	SB	BB	SO	Avg	OBP	Slg
1996	107	226	28	61	12	2	8	36	2	34	53	.270	.364	.447
Career	710	1690	217	448	66	8	57	248	17	189	372	.265	.337	.415

1996 Situational Stats

	AB	H	HR	RBI	Avg		AB	H	HR	RBI	Avg
Home	103	27	6	17	.262	LHP	29	6	1	4	.207
Road	123	34	2	19	.276	RHP	197	55	7	32	.279
First Half	110	32	3	21	.291	Sc Pos	68	19	3	27	.279
Scnd Half	116	29	5	15	.250	Clutch	60	16	1	5	.267

1996 Season

Dave Clark is a prime example of Pittsburgh ex-manager Jim Leyland's genius. A quintessential fourth outfielder, Clark has produced far better numbers with the Pirates than he has anywhere else in his travels. Acquired for the stretch run by the Dodgers on the last day of August, Clark made just one start and was a disappointment as a pinch hitter.

Hitting, Baserunning & Defense

Clark goes to the plate looking fastball, hitting almost .400 over the last six years when putting the first pitch into play. Though he has hit lefties pretty well in the past, he seldom gets the chance anymore. On defense, Clark can play either corner position, though his mediocre arm is more suited to left. He has average speed and makes smart decisions on the basepaths.

1997 Outlook

Clark was rented as bench insurance for the month of September. He did little to raise his stock with the Dodgers, so he will no doubt be signing up with yet another major league club next spring. It would not be surprising to see Clark reunited with Leyland in a Marlins uniform in 1997.

Chad Curtis

Position: CF/LF
Bats: R **Throws:** R
Ht: 5'10" **Wt:** 175

Opening Day Age: 28
Born: 11/6/68 in
Marion, IN
ML Seasons: 5

Overall Statistics

	G	AB	R	H	D	T	HR	RBI	SB	BB	SO	Avg	OBP	Slg
1996	147	504	85	127	25	1	12	46	18	70	88	.252	.341	.377
Career	696	2567	401	680	118	13	60	268	161	298	410	.265	.343	.391

1996 Situational Stats

	AB	H	HR	RBI	Avg		AB	H	HR	RBI	Avg
Home	218	46	3	18	.211	LHP	143	43	3	15	.301
Road	286	81	9	28	.283	RHP	361	84	9	31	.233
First Half	330	87	6	29	.264	Sc Pos	114	26	2	34	.228
Scnd Half	174	40	6	17	.230	Clutch	76	18	2	6	.237

1996 Season

Chad Curtis was acquired from Detroit right before the trading deadline as outfield insurance. The policy never really paid off. The longtime American Leaguer did not adjust particularly well to the Senior Circuit or to his platoon role with the Dodgers.

Hitting, Baserunning & Defense

Curtis is an aggressive hitter who nonetheless takes a lot of pitches. Though he has decent strike zone judgment, he has a weakness for high fastballs. Despite a power hitter's swing, Curtis never has the numbers to show for it, especially now that he's left Tiger Stadium. Curtis has a little speed, too, but is no longer the 40-plus stolen base man that he was earlier in his career. He is a good defensive outfielder and has a strong arm.

1997 Outlook

While Curtis has talent, he is a bit of a "tweener"; he is not quite a leadoff hitter, doesn't handle the bat well enough to hit second, and has too little power to be used in the middle of the order. The Dodgers don't want him back, and the way his career is going, it's possible that Curtis could start for one of the expansion teams in 1998.

Darren Dreifort

Position: RP
Bats: R **Throws:** R
Ht: 6' 2" **Wt:** 205

Opening Day Age: 24
Born: 5/18/72 in
Wichita, KS
ML Seasons: 2
Pronunciation:
DRY-fort

Overall Statistics

	W	L	Pct.	ERA	G	GS	Sv	IP	H	BB	SO	HR	BR/IP
1996	1	4	.200	4.94	19	0	0	23.2	23	12	24	2	1.48
Career	1	9	.100	5.64	46	0	6	52.2	68	27	46	2	1.80

1996 Situational Stats

	W	L	ERA	Sv	IP		AB	H	HR	RBI	Avg
Home	0	3	9.00	0	11.0	LHB	43	13	1	8	.302
Road	1	1	1.42	0	12.2	RHB	47	10	1	1	.213
First Half	0	0	-	0	0.0	Sc Pos	23	4	0	5	.174
Scnd Half	1	4	4.94	0	23.2	Clutch	52	16	0	6	.308

1996 Season

After sitting out the entire 1995 season due to elbow reconstructive surgery, Darren Dreifort recovered to such an extent that the Dodgers wanted him on their playoff roster. In order to get enough rehab innings, Dreifort began the season as a starter in Triple-A. He was called up in late July to serve in middle relief and in an occasional set-up role for Los Angeles the remainder of the year.

Pitching, Defense & Hitting

Dreifort throws one of the hardest fastballs in the league, complementing it with a nasty slider that arrives just a few ticks behind the heater. His incredible velocity in itself helps shut down enemy basestealers. Driefort's leg kick leaves him in poor fielding position, but he makes up for it with his athleticism. He seldom gets a chance to show it, but he was a designated hitter in college.

1997 Outlook

Dreifort has "future closer" written all over him. Since his arm problems probably stemmed from the abusive bullpen habits of the previous managerial administration, the current regime will no doubt exercise caution when using him. Dreifort will continue to develop as a middle reliever for at least another season.

Wayne Kirby

Position: CF
Bats: L **Throws:** R
Ht: 5'10" **Wt:** 190

Opening Day Age: 33
Born: 1/22/64 in Williamsburg, VA
ML Seasons: 6

Overall Statistics

	G	AB	R	H	D	T	HR	RBI	SB	BB	SO	Avg	OBP	Slg
1996	92	204	26	55	11	1	1	12	4	19	19	.270	.333	.348
Career	444	1102	172	285	49	8	14	115	43	87	147	.259	.314	.356

1996 Situational Stats

	AB	H	HR	RBI	Avg		AB	H	HR	RBI	Avg
Home	93	21	0	5	.226	LHP	15	3	0	1	.200
Road	111	34	1	7	.306	RHP	189	52	1	11	.275
First Half	26	4	0	1	.154	Sc Pos	47	12	0	10	.255
Scnd Half	178	51	1	11	.287	Clutch	37	12	0	3	.324

1996 Season

Last season, Wayne Kirby returned to the Dodgers organization, where he'd started his professional career 13 years ago. After Los Angeles grabbed him off the waiver wire for outfield insurance, Kirby did an excellent Brett Butler impersonation, filling in admirably at center field while hitting .283 in the leadoff spot.

Hitting, Baserunning & Defense

Reputed to be a hacker, Kirby took well to his spot at the top of the Dodger lineup, exhibiting good bat control and a solid knowledge of the strike zone. He has little power, and is likely to spray the ball in all directions. Though he swiped 51 bases in the minors as recently as 1992, Kirby is no longer much of a threat to steal. A versatile defender, he can play anywhere in the outfield. On most teams, he would have the strongest arm, but next to Mondesi. . .

1997 Outlook

Kirby was a nice addition to a stoic clubhouse. Though clearly not the everyday answer in center field, his wide variety of talents would be useful to almost any ballclub. The Dodgers have a particularly weak bench, and they re-signed Kirby to be a fourth outfielder again this year.

Scott Radinsky

Position: RP
Bats: L **Throws:** L
Ht: 6' 3" **Wt:** 204

Opening Day Age: 29
Born: 3/3/68 in Glendale, CA
ML Seasons: 6
Nickname: Rads

Overall Statistics

	W	L	Pct.	ERA	G	GS	Sv	IP	H	BB	SO	HR	BR/IP
1996	5	1	.833	2.41	58	0	1	52.1	52	17	48	2	1.32
Career	29	17	.630	3.43	374	0	33	328.0	313	146	249	20	1.40

1996 Situational Stats

	W	L	ERA	Sv	IP		AB	H	HR	RBI	Avg
Home	4	1	1.35	0	26.2	LHB	66	16	0	7	.242
Road	1	0	3.51	1	25.2	RHB	131	36	2	24	.275
First Half	0	1	2.42	1	26.0	Sc Pos	64	19	2	30	.297
Scnd Half	5	0	2.39	0	26.1	Clutch	82	22	1	16	.268

1996 Season

Scott Radinsky sat out the entire 1994 campaign while battling Hodgkin's disease, but he appears to have made a complete recovery. After starting last season on the disabled list, Radinsky came out firing, allowing just six hits and one earned run in his first 21-plus innings. While he couldn't keep up that pace, the big lefthander proved to be a very consistent short reliever throughout the year.

Pitching, Defense & Hitting

Radinsky throws just two pitches: a good moving fastball, and a wide-breaking slider. His main advantage, however, lies in his sidearm delivery, which strikes fear in the hearts of left-handed hitters. Radinsky does not get off the mound very well, though he is a solid fielder. Armed with a good pickoff move, he holds a tight reign on baserunners. Radinsky failed in his only plate appearance.

1997 Outlook

Radinsky did an excellent job for the Dodgers, especially because he was more effective against right-handed batters than some of their more recent left-handed specialists. As long as he continues to get hitters out, Radinsky will serve with Los Angeles in the same capacity next season.

Other Los Angeles Dodgers

Mike Busch (**Pos**: 3B, **Age**: 28, **Bats**: R)

	G	AB	R	H	D	T	HR	RBI	SB	BB	SO	Avg	OBP	Slg
1996	38	83	8	18	4	0	4	17	0	5	33	.217	.261	.410
Career	51	100	11	22	4	0	7	23	0	5	40	.220	.257	.470

Busch received regular playing time at third base in July when Mike Blowers went down with a knee injury. He was horrendous at the plate and suffered a season-ending elbow injury in August. 1997 Outlook: C

Juan Castro (**Pos**: SS/3B, **Age**: 24, **Bats**: R)

	G	AB	R	H	D	T	HR	RBI	SB	BB	SO	Avg	OBP	Slg
1996	70	132	16	26	5	3	0	5	1	10	27	.197	.254	.280
Career	81	136	16	27	5	3	0	5	1	11	28	.199	.259	.279

The club's utility man, Castro filled in at second, third, and shortstop during the season. That's about all he was good for, since his .197 average sure wasn't helping the team. He'll probably be back. 1997 Outlook: B

Chad Fonville (**Pos**: 2B/SS/LF/CF, **Age**: 26, **Bats**: B)

	G	AB	R	H	D	T	HR	RBI	SB	BB	SO	Avg	OBP	Slg
1996	103	201	34	41	4	1	0	13	7	17	31	.204	.266	.234
Career	205	521	77	130	10	2	0	29	27	40	73	.250	.304	.276

Fonville manned five different positions during his stay in Los Angeles. He struggled with the bat and spent August at Triple-A Albuquerque. He's young, so he'll probably be back in the same role this year. 1997 Outlook: B

Darren Hall (**Pos**: RHP, **Age**: 32)

	W	L	Pct.	ERA	G	GS	Sv	IP	H	BB	SO	HR	BR/IP
1996	0	2	.000	6.00	9	0	0	12.0	13	5	12	2	1.50
Career	2	7	.222	4.20	56	0	20	60.0	60	28	51	7	1.47

Hall started the year in the Dodger bullpen before recurring elbow problems sidelined him for the second straight year. Injury-plagued and 32 years old, Hall's career is just about through. 1997 Outlook: D

Dave Hansen (**Pos**: 3B, **Age**: 28, **Bats**: L)

	G	AB	R	H	D	T	HR	RBI	SB	BB	SO	Avg	OBP	Slg
1996	80	104	7	23	1	0	0	6	0	11	22	.221	.293	.231
Career	494	838	75	217	32	0	12	83	1	101	132	.259	.338	.340

Occasionally making infield starts in addition to his regular pinch-hitting duties, Hansen has a good eye at the plate but no power. The Dodgers released him, but someone will pick him up. 1997 Outlook: B

Carlos Hernandez (**Pos**: C, **Age**: 29, **Bats**: R)

	G	AB	R	H	D	T	HR	RBI	SB	BB	SO	Avg	OBP	Slg
1996	13	14	1	4	0	0	0	0	0	2	2	.286	.375	.286
Career	234	478	30	109	14	0	9	40	1	23	80	.228	.271	.314

Hernandez started the year as L.A.'s backup catcher before developing serious back problems. He spent the rest of the year at Triple-A Albuquerque and did not play well. 1997 Outlook: C

Oreste Marrero (**Pos**: 1B, **Age**: 27, **Bats**: L)

	G	AB	R	H	D	T	HR	RBI	SB	BB	SO	Avg	OBP	Slg
1996	10	8	2	3	1	0	0	1	0	1	3	.375	.444	.500
Career	42	89	12	20	6	1	1	5	1	15	19	.225	.337	.348

Marrero had very brief pinch hitting stints in June and September, and was not offered a contract from Los Angeles at the end of the season. It's unlikely that he'll see action this year. 1997 Outlook: D

Rick Parker (**Pos**: CF, **Age**: 34, **Bats**: R)

	G	AB	R	H	D	T	HR	RBI	SB	BB	SO	Avg	OBP	Slg
1996	16	14	2	4	1	0	0	1	1	0	2	.286	.333	.357
Career	163	225	36	55	9	0	2	24	9	16	36	.244	.300	.311

Now 34, Parker has yet to get more than 54 at-bats in a major league season. Despite good Triple-A numbers, he saw only minimal action with Los Angeles last summer. 1997 Outlook: C

Tom Prince (**Pos**: C, **Age**: 32, **Bats**: R)

	G	AB	R	H	D	T	HR	RBI	SB	BB	SO	Avg	OBP	Slg
1996	40	64	6	19	6	0	1	11	0	6	15	.297	.365	.438
Career	238	512	36	100	34	1	6	60	3	48	109	.195	.273	.301

Prince took over the backup catching responsibilities from Carlos Hernandez, finding his way into 40 games last season. He did so well with the bat that he was offered the chance to return. 1997 Outlook: A

Tim Wallach (**Pos**: 3B, **Age**: 39, **Bats**: R)

	G	AB	R	H	D	T	HR	RBI	SB	BB	SO	Avg	OBP	Slg
1996	102	352	37	82	10	1	12	42	1	30	79	.233	.297	.369
Career	2212	8099	908	2085	432	36	260	1125	51	649	1307	.257	.316	.416

Wallach manned third base down the stretch for the Dodgers after being waived by California. He was completely ineffective with the bat and announced his retirement at the end of the season. 1997 Outlook: D

Los Angeles Dodgers Minor League Prospects

Organization Overview:

Another Dodger captured the Rookie of the Year Award last year—this time it was Todd Hollandsworth. The scariest part is that they still have a ton of prospects lined up, waiting for the chance to extend the Dodgers' monopoly on the award. The best bet is second baseman Wilton Guerrero, although Paul Konerko could be a viable candidate if they can find a spot for him. With their massive international presence and deep pockets, the Dodgers are the trailblazers in developing and exploiting new sources of talent. Korean pitcher Chan Ho Park was another rookie find last year, and second-year Mexican native Antonio Osuna played a huge role as a set-up man. The talent in the system remains as impressive as ever, both on the mound and in the field, and the Dodgers figure to keep cranking out prospects for years to come.

Adrian Beltre

Position: 3B
Bats: R **Throws:** R
Ht: 5' 11" **Wt:** 165
Opening Day Age: 18
Born: 4/7/78 in Santo Domingo, DR

Recent Statistics

	G	AB	R	H	D	T	HR	RBI	SB	BB	SO	AVG
96 A Savannah	68	244	48	75	14	3	16	59	4	35	46	.307
96 A San Bernrdo	63	238	40	62	13	1	10	40	3	19	44	.261

At the age of 18, Adrian Beltre posted excellent power numbers at two levels of Class-A last year. The Dodgers know he's a long way off, but to hit with such authority is extremely rare for a teenager, not to mention one who was spending his first year in the United States. He showed the potential to become a good all-around offensive player, and in time, maturity may smooth out his glovework at third base. He won't be wearing Dodger blue next year, but you may hear his name mentioned before long.

Nate Bland

Position: P
Bats: L **Throws:** L
Ht: 6' 5" **Wt:** 195
Opening Day Age: 22
Born: 12/27/74 in Birmingham, AL

Recent Statistics

	W	L	ERA	G	GS	Sv	IP	H	R	BB	SO	HR
93 A Yakima	4	6	2.84	16	13	0	63.1	53	34	29	43	2
94 R Great Falls	0	0	0.96	2	1	0	9.1	6	2	3	12	0
94 A Bakersfield	2	6	5.36	12	9	0	50.1	58	31	27	19	10
95 A Bakersfield	4	9	5.22	27	23	0	122.1	155	89	55	46	13
96 A Savannah	1	0	1.63	5	5	0	27.2	24	8	10	24	0
96 A Vero Beach	10	4	3.09	17	17	0	96.0	99	42	35	69	3

Lefthander Nate Bland turned his career completely around last year. With newfound confidence and maturity, he added velocity and began to get his curve over consistently. The result was that he went from a non-entity to a prospect overnight. The Dodgers liked what they saw, and are eager to see what he can do as he continues to fill out and mature. He's only 22, and the Dodgers will give him every chance to establish himself at Double-A before pushing him up another rung.

Karim Garcia

Position: OF
Bats: L **Throws:** L
Ht: 6' 0" **Wt:** 172
Opening Day Age: 21
Born: 10/29/75 in Cd. Obregon, Sonora, Mexico

Recent Statistics

	G	AB	R	H	D	T	HR	RBI	SB	BB	SO	AVG
96 AA San Antonio	35	129	21	32	6	1	5	22	1	9	38	.248
96 AAA Alb'q'erq'e	84	327	54	97	17	10	13	58	6	29	67	.297
96 NL Los Angeles	1	1	0	0	0	0	0	0	0	0	1	.000
96 MLE	119	426	52	99	16	4	11	56	4	24	110	.232

All the superprospect hype may have gone to Karim Garcia's head a bit last year; after skipping Double-A the year before, he was demoted from Triple-A in midseason for disciplinary reasons. At the plate, he made no progress last season. He seemed to be getting a better grasp of the strike zone early in the year, but that trend reversed itself as the year wore on. He's still a little rough in right field, but his arm remains one of the best. He's got outstanding power potential, and few prospects have hit so well at so young an age. If his head is screwed on straight, he could be another exalted Dodger rookie one of these years.

Wilton Guerrero

Position: 2B
Bats: R **Throws:** R
Ht: 5' 11" **Wt:** 145
Opening Day Age: 22
Born: 10/24/74 in Nizao, Bani, Dr

Recent Statistics

	G	AB	R	H	D	T	HR	RBI	SB	BB	SO	AVG
96 AAA Alb'q'erq'e	98	425	79	146	17	12	2	38	26	26	48	.344
96 NL Los Angeles	5	2	1	0	0	0	0	0	0	0	2	.000
96 MLE	98	389	53	110	12	5	1	25	18	17	50	.283

He isn't half the prospect his brother Vlad is, but Wilton may give his little brother a run for his money in the Rookie of the Year race this season. A converted shortstop, Wilton has all the tools to play a fine second base, and he's capable of hitting for a good average. He has to learn how to wait for his pitch and use his speed more effectively, and he'll never hit with much power, but he's ready to play.

Paul Konerko

Position: 1B
Bats: R **Throws:** R
Ht: 6' 2" **Wt:** 205
Opening Day Age: 21
Born: 3/5/76 in Providence, RI

Recent Statistics

	G	AB	R	H	D	T	HR	RBI	SB	BB	SO	AVG
94 A Yakima	67	257	25	74	15	2	6	58	1	36	52	.288
95 A San Bernrdo	118	448	77	124	21	1	19	77	3	59	88	.277
96 AA San Antonio	133	470	78	141	23	2	29	86	1	72	85	.300
96 AAA Alb'q'erq'e	4	14	2	6	0	0	1	2	0	1	2	.429
96 MLE	137	455	62	118	17	0	21	68	0	47	93	.259

Former catcher Paul Konerko moved to first base last year, and just kept on hitting. Despite the fact that he was one of the youngest players in Double-A, he put up excellent power numbers in a park that strongly favors pitchers. His batting eye is fairly advanced, and he may hit for a good average by the time he's fully developed. Overall, he may be one of the best young power hitters in the high minors. He can help the Dodgers right now, but they may give him another year.

Jesus Martinez

Position: P
Bats: L **Throws:** L
Ht: 6' 2" **Wt:** 145
Opening Day Age: 23
Born: 3/13/74 in Santo Domingo, DR

Recent Statistics

	W	L	ERA	G	GS	Sv	IP	H	R	BB	SO	HR
93 A Bakersfield	4	13	4.14	30	21	0	145.2	144	95	75	108	12
94 AA San Antonio	0	1	4.50	1	1	0	4.0	3	2	2	3	0
94 A Vero Beach	7	9	6.26	18	18	0	87.2	91	65	43	69	7
95 AAA Alb'q'erq'e	1	1	4.50	2	0	0	4.0	4	2	4	5	0
95 AA San Antonio	6	9	3.54	24	24	0	139.2	129	64	71	83	6
96 AA San Antonio	10	13	4.40	27	27	0	161.2	157	90	92	124	7

Yes, the Dodgers have *another* Martinez brother in the system. This one's a lefty, although he doesn't have the pure stuff that his two older brothers do. Jesus' fastball cracks 90, and his biting curve is an effective pitch, but he struggles to throw strikes consistently. Last year, in his second season of Double-A, he showed that he has the tools to succeed, but still needs more time at that level. Unless he makes a sudden breakthrough with his control, he's probably at least two years away.

Gary Rath

Position: P
Bats: L **Throws:** L
Ht: 6' 2" **Wt:** 185
Opening Day Age: 24
Born: 1/10/73 in Gulfport, MS

Recent Statistics

	W	L	ERA	G	GS	Sv	IP	H	R	BB	SO	HR
94 A Vero Beach	5	6	2.73	13	11	0	62.2	55	26	23	50	3
95 AAA Alb'q'erq'e	3	5	5.08	8	8	0	39.0	46	31	20	23	4
95 AA San Antonio	13	3	2.77	18	18	0	117.0	96	42	48	81	4
96 AAA Alb'q'erq'e	10	11	4.19	30	30	0	180.1	177	97	89	125	13

In 1995, lefthander Gary Rath had a hard time making the transition from Double-A to Triple-A, but last year, he made the jump with no problems at all. Once he learned to keep the ball down and rely on his stuff, he was no longer spooked by the more hitter-friendly confines at Albuquerque. He doesn't throw hard, but his positive experience last year taught him a lot about pitching and proved a lot to the Dodgers.

Adam Riggs

Position: 2B
Bats: R **Throws:** R
Ht: 6' 0" **Wt:** 190
Opening Day Age: 24
Born: 10/4/72 in Steubenville, OH

Recent Statistics

	G	AB	R	H	D	T	HR	RBI	SB	BB	SO	AVG
94 R Great Falls	62	234	55	73	20	3	5	44	19	31	38	.312
94 A Yakima	4	7	1	2	1	0	0	0	0	0	1	.286
95 A San Bernrdo	134	542	111	196	39	5	24	106	31	59	93	.362
96 AA San Antonio	134	506	68	143	31	6	14	66	16	37	82	.283
96 MLE	134	478	53	115	24	2	10	51	11	24	87	.241

Adam Riggs' season couldn't possibly measure up to his '95 numbers, when he was voted MVP of the California League. Still, it was hardly a disappointing year for the hard-hitting second baseman. He proved that he could still juice the ball against more advanced competition, and his glovework was not the abomination that it had been made out to be. He makes more than his share of errors, but his range is decent, and he may be able to survive at the position. He's got an above-average bat for an infielder, and a year at Triple-A may be all the seasoning he needs.

Others to Watch

Ryan Luzinski's development has been a disappointment ever since the Dodgers took the big catcher with their first pick in the '92 draft. Luzinski fought injuries once again last year, but finally showed the maturity to make the jump to Double-A. At age 23, he still has a future. . . Catcher **Kyle Cooney** knows that there isn't much demand for a catcher in Los Angeles right now, but his solid season in the California League has him moving in that direction anyway. . . Australian southpaw **Kym Ashworth** seems like he's been around forever, but he'll be only 20 years old this year. The Dodgers have been babying his arm, but he still might become one the youngest players in Double-A next year. . . Lefthander **Dennis Reyes** fanned 176 batters in the California League last year at the age of 19. He's got great promise if his arm can stand up to the innings he's thrown. . . A good showing in the Arizona Fall League landed starter **Eric Weaver** on the Dodgers' 40-man roster last year, and he followed up with a strong season at Double-A. The big righthander reportedly hits 92 MPH on the radar gun, but he needs to prove he can survive the jump to Triple-A.

Felipe Alou

1996 Season

No manager in baseball is more highly respected than Felipe Alou. He is a superb handler of young players who exhibits both patience and no-nonsense authority. Veterans also appreciate his open approach to delineating roles on the club. There is never any question where you stand on a team managed by Alou, and most players appreciate that and play to their capabilities as a result. His Expos have almost always overachieved.

Offense

Alou is always trying to force the action and rarely sits on his hands hoping for big innings. He will try to run virtually anyone in his lineup if he feels the situation is in his favor. He sacrifices at any point in the game, often flying in the face of conventional wisdom. Alou is also adept at getting playing time for his entire bench through platoons, brief benchings of slumping regulars, or liberal use of pinch hitters.

Pitching & Defense

Alou has always had a quick hook with his starters, and he is not afraid to try relievers in a number of different roles. If his closer is struggling, Alou is quick to yank him in situations where many managers live or die with the same pitcher. He might call on his closer for two innings of work instead of using a set-up man who might be overworked. And he just as often might sit out his closer for extra rest and try to close a game with the committee approach.

1997 Outlook

No matter what the Expos look like in the spring, you can count on them to be better than expected. That's a tribute to Alou, who annually puts up with losing some of his top veterans when they start making too much money. He is likely to have the Expos in the playoff race again this year.

Born: 5/12/35 in Haina, Dominican Republic

Playing Experience: 1958-1974, SF, Mil, Atl, Oak, NYA, Mon, Mil

Managerial Experience: 5 seasons

Manager Statistics

Year Team, Lg	W	L	Pct	GB	Finish
1996 Montreal, NL	88	74	.543	8.0	2nd East
5 Seasons	392	315	.554	—	—

1996 Starting Pitchers by Days Rest

	≤3	4	5	6+
Expos Starts	1	86	56	10
Expos ERA	6.00	3.46	4.45	3.66
NL Avg Starts	4	86	41	21
NL ERA	4.06	4.28	4.23	4.58

1996 Situational Stats

	Felipe Alou	NL Average
Hit & Run Success %	35.0	39.0
Stolen Base Success %	76.1	71.6
Platoon Pct.	52.7	51.9
Defensive Subs	30	20
High-Pitch Outings	13	13
Quick/Slow Hooks	32/2	19/12
Sacrifice Attempts	97	92

1996 Rankings (National League)

→ 1st in stolen base percentage (76.1%), steals of home plate (3), least caught steals of second base (29), quick hooks (32) and saves with over 1 inning pitched (18)

→ 2nd in squeeze plays (10), defensive substitutions (30) and mid-inning pitching changes (178)

→ 3rd in least caught steals of third base (3) and relief appearances (433)

Moises Alou

1996 Season

Moises Alou was able to make a strong comeback in a season interrupted by a suspension and a stint on the disabled list. Alou had 12 home runs prior to the All-Star break, but was batting .262. He turned it on in the second half, batting .319 after July 25. His final tally of 21 home runs was one short of his career high, while his 96 RBI were a career best. Alou finished his season on a historical note by being the final regular-season hitter in Atlanta-Fulton County Stadium.

Hitting

Scouts have been whispering for over a year that Alou's bat speed has begun to slow down. But he regained much of his extra-base pop late last year, particularly to right-center. He is an outstanding fastball hitter but will slump when he starts chasing offspeed stuff. He also struggles through streaks of strikeouts when he starts pressing and fishing for breaking balls out of the strike zone. Alou should know better because he has quick hands which allow him to wait on pitches.

Baserunning & Defense

Alou has lost a couple of steps since his serious ankle injuries of three years ago. However, he picks his spots well and can still steal around 10 bases a year. He registered games at all three outfield positions but spent the large majority of time in right. He has good range and a strong arm wherever he plays.

1997 Outlook

One of the hostages of baseball's bungled labor deal, Alou became a free agent when the deal, with its service-time provisions, was finally ratified. He is now at a point where his salary is too expensive for the Expos' meager means. Wherever he winds up, Alou is one of the more complete outfielders in baseball.

Position: RF/LF
Bats: R **Throws:** R
Ht: 6' 3" **Wt:** 195

Opening Day Age: 30
Born: 7/3/66 in Atlanta, GA
ML Seasons: 6
Pronunciation: MOY-sezz ah-LOO

Overall Statistics

	G	AB	R	H	D	T	HR	RBI	SB	BB	SO	Avg	OBP	Slg
1996	143	540	87	152	28	2	21	96	9	49	83	.281	.339	.457
Career	610	2149	343	627	138	16	84	373	53	183	304	.292	.348	.488

Where He Hits the Ball

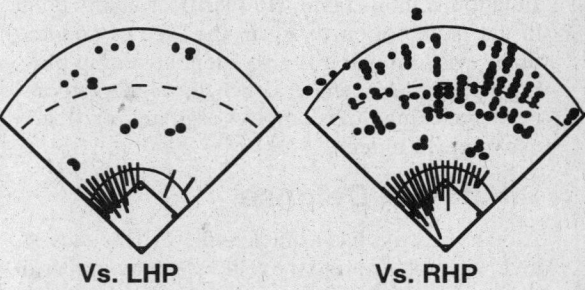

Vs. LHP   **Vs. RHP**

1996 Situational Stats

	AB	H	HR	RBI	Avg		AB	H	HR	RBI	Avg
Home	272	87	14	65	.320	LHP	114	38	4	19	.333
Road	268	65	7	31	.243	RHP	426	114	17	77	.268
First Half	324	85	12	54	.262	Sc Pos	162	52	8	76	.321
Scnd Half	216	67	9	42	.310	Clutch	93	25	3	20	.269

1996 Rankings (National League)

→ 1st in fielding percentage in right field (.995)
→ 4th in lowest cleanup slugging percentage (.452)
→ 9th in highest percentage of swings on the first pitch (42.3%)
→ 10th in batting average vs. left-handed pitchers (.333) and lowest percentage of extra bases taken as a runner (39.5%)
→ Led the Expos in sacrifice flies (7), batting average vs. left-handed pitchers (.333), cleanup slugging percentage (.452), slugging percentage vs. left-handed pitchers (.553) and on-base percentage vs. left-handed pitchers (.384)

Shane Andrews

1996 Season

In his first full season in the majors, Shane Andrews did a fine job as the Expos' primary third baseman. Andrews missed several weeks with a wrist injury but still managed to hit 19 homers, the third-best total on the club. His 64 RBI were also the third-best total on the club, despite being limited to only 375 at-bats.

Hitting

Andrews has a big swing that results in long home runs and a lot of strikeouts. He can go longball in any part of the ballpark, but he needs to learn to lay off the high pitches he can't handle. He also can be tied in knots by offspeed stuff. Andrews has worked on shortening his stroke, but quickly returns to a big swing when he struggles. That said, no pitcher in the league likes to leave a fastball over the plate to Andrews, because he can deposit it into the seats in a hurry.

Baserunning & Defense

Though hardly a fast runner, Andrews is much better conditioned than he was earlier in his career and can occasionally steal a base. By getting in better shape, Andrews has also improved his defense. His range has become markedly better over the last year. He always has had decent hands and an accurate arm, a combination that in time should make him one of the better third basemen in the league.

1997 Outlook

In an organization which routinely develops excellent talent, Andrews could be one of the next to emerge. He has only begun to scratch the surface of his considerable power potential. As he matures as a hitter and cuts down his strikes, Andrews should get his average up into the .260s and his home runs should approach the 25-to-30 range.

Position: 3B
Bats: R **Throws:** R
Ht: 6' 1"   **Wt:** 215

Opening Day Age: 25
Born: 8/28/71 in Dallas, TX
ML Seasons: 2

Overall Statistics

	G	AB	R	H	D	T	HR	RBI	SB	BB	SO	Avg	OBP	Slg
1996	127	375	43	85	15	2	19	64	3	35	119	.227	.295	.429
Career	211	595	70	132	25	3	27	95	4	52	187	.222	.286	.410

Where He Hits the Ball

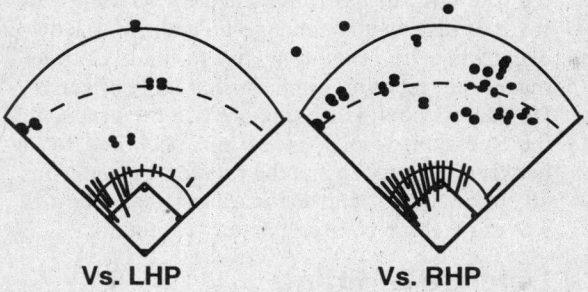

Vs. LHP   **Vs. RHP**

1996 Situational Stats

	AB	H	HR	RBI	Avg		AB	H	HR	RBI	Avg
Home	169	35	8	34	.207	LHP	90	19	1	11	.211
Road	206	50	11	30	.243	RHP	285	66	18	53	.232
First Half	209	55	11	39	.263	Sc Pos	115	29	6	49	.252
Scnd Half	166	30	8	25	.181	Clutch	66	10	1	6	.152

1996 Rankings (National League)

→ 1st in lowest batting average with two strikes (.115)
→ 2nd in lowest batting average in the clutch (.152)
→ 3rd in least GDPs per GDP situation (2.9%), highest percentage of swings that missed (30.7%) and lowest percentage of swings put into play (32.9%)
→ 5th in fielding percentage at third base (.955)
→ 7th in errors at third base (15)
→ Led the Expos in intentional walks (8) and least GDPs per GDP situation (2.9%)

Rheal Cormier

1996 Season

An integral part of the Expos' rotation from the beginning of the season, Rheal Cormier made 27 starts and could have had a much better record with better support. He was only 7-10, but the Expos averaged less than four runs in games he started. Along the way, he pitched the first complete-game shutout of his career before landing on the disabled list in late August with a sprained elbow ligament.

Pitching

Cormier was urged by manager Felipe Alou and then-Expos pitching coach Joe Kerrigan to place more trust in his fastball. He throws his heater in the low 90s but has often shied away from it in favor of his excellent change-up and slider. However, when he is spotting his fastball, Cormier makes the rest of his pitches much more effective. He had his confidence damaged in his year with the Red Sox, who bounced him back and forth between the bullpen and the rotation. A starter for all but a handful of appearances last year, Cormier was much more comfortable on the mound.

Defense & Hitting

An agile athlete whose compact delivery keeps him in good position, Cormier is an excellent fielding pitcher. He also does a good job of controlling the running game. A sneaky pickoff move and a slide-step allowed basestealers just a 50 percent success rate last year (11-for-22). Cormier handles the bat well, punching out eight hits last year including a triple, four RBI and 11 sacrifices.

1997 Outlook

On a staff of hard throwers, Cormier's ability to mix his pitches makes him a good change of pace in the Montreal rotation. He is a solid pitcher who would not surprise the Expos if he wins anywhere between 12 and 15 games this year.

Position: SP/RP
Bats: L **Throws:** L
Ht: 5'10" **Wt:** 187

Opening Day Age: 29
Born: 4/23/67 in Moncton, New Brunswick, Canada
ML Seasons: 6
Pronunciation: RAY-al KOR-mee-ay

Overall Statistics

	W	L	Pct.	ERA	G	GS	Sv	IP	H	BB	SO	HR	BR/IP
1996	7	10	.412	4.17	33	27	0	159.2	165	41	100	16	1.29
Career	38	38	.500	4.13	168	107	0	713.1	767	147	425	72	1.28

How Often He Throws Strikes

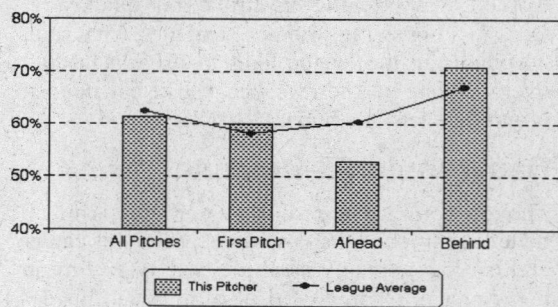

1996 Situational Stats

	W	L	ERA	Sv	IP		AB	H	HR	RBI	Avg
Home	6	6	3.82	0	96.2	LHB	108	29	2	12	.269
Road	1	4	4.71	0	63.0	RHB	504	136	14	54	.270
First Half	5	5	3.68	0	110.0	Sc Pos	134	32	2	47	.239
Scnd Half	2	5	5.26	0	49.2	Clutch	33	9	1	1	.273

1996 Rankings (National League)

- → 8th in runners caught stealing (11)
- → 9th in shutouts (1)
- → 10th in sacrifice bunts (11)
- → Led the Expos in shutouts (1), hit batsmen (9), wild pitches (8) and GDPs induced (14)

Omar Daal

1996 Season

For five months last year, Omar Daal was one of Montreal's only left-handed relievers, and he was a very busy fellow. The former Dodger made 58 relief appearances and allowed only 15 of 54 inherited runners to score. Then in late August, injuries to the starting rotation pressed Daal into service as a starter for the first time in his career. After winning his first outing—allowing one hit in five shutout innings—he managed a victory in only one of his five other starts.

Pitching

Prior to last season, Daal had a herky-jerky delivery which was deceptive but tended to take his arm out of its proper angle, hurting his control. His improvement as a pitcher last year was a direct result of lots of hard work to smooth out that delivery. It paid off in much better location with all his pitches. Daal's sinking fastball can hit 90 MPH, though his best strikeout pitch is a big-breaking curve that can dive several inches. When he has command of the hook, he can be tough. He will hang the occasional curve and surrender his share of home runs.

Defense & Hitting

Daal does a good job of handling the running game. He has an excellent pickoff move and there were only five steals attempted against him last year, just three of them successful. In the field, he committed only one error in his 87-plus innings of work. He got a chance to hit for the first time last year but was no factor at all, going hitless in seven at-bats.

1997 Outlook

Montreal thinks Daal has a chance to be a serviceable starter. However, with their bullpen lacking another seasoned lefthander, Daal will likely return to relief duty with the hope that his improved command will make him effective.

Position: RP/SP
Bats: L **Throws:** L
Ht: 6' 3" **Wt:** 185

Opening Day Age: 25
Born: 3/1/72 in Maracaibo, VZ
ML Seasons: 4
Pronunciation: DOLL

Overall Statistics

	W	L	Pct.	ERA	G	GS	Sv	IP	H	BB	SO	HR	BR/IP
1996	4	5	.444	4.02	64	6	0	87.1	74	37	82	10	1.27
Career	10	8	.556	4.61	163	6	0	156.1	151	78	121	17	1.46

How Often He Throws Strikes

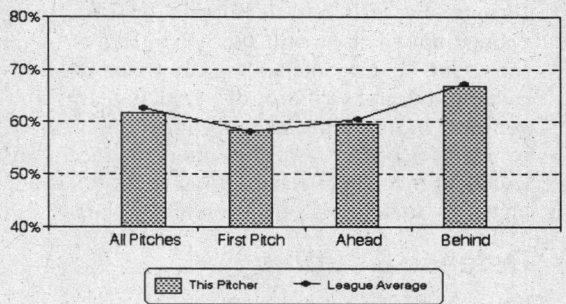

1996 Situational Stats

	W	L	ERA	Sv	IP		AB	H	HR	RBI	Avg
Home	2	2	2.76	0	49.0	LHB	97	24	1	15	.247
Road	2	3	5.63	0	38.1	RHB	227	50	9	33	.220
First Half	1	2	3.05	0	44.1	Sc Pos	92	24	2	37	.261
Scnd Half	3	3	5.02	0	43.0	Clutch	61	15	0	13	.246

1996 Rankings (National League)

→ 8th in lowest percentage of inherited runners scored (27.8%)

→ 9th in lowest batting average allowed in relief (.212)

→ Led the Expos in blown saves (4), first batter efficiency (.180) and lowest percentage of inherited runners scored (27.8%)

Jeff Fassero

1996 Season

With a strong performance from wire to wire, Jeff Fassero solidified his reputation as one of baseball's best lefthanders. Only Denny Neagle (16) and Al Leiter (16) had more wins among National League lefthanders. Fassero was also third in the N.L. with 222 strikeouts and third with five complete games.

Pitching

Fassero has one of the best sinkers in baseball, a heavy fastball that consistently reaches the plate in the low 90s. He also relies on a forkball and an excellent slider which he uses against right-handed hitters. In addition to those dangerous offerings, Fassero has developed an improving change-up which he will spot when he's ahead in the count. He has outstanding command of all his pitches and grabs control of most counts by specializing in first-pitch strikes, something he threw to nearly 70 percent of the hitters he faced. His excellent mechanics result in low walk totals and an ability to hold his stuff deep into games.

Defense & Hitting

Though he lacks a top-flight pickoff move, Fassero does a decent job of holding runners, using slide-steps and frequent throws to first in order to give his catchers a decent chance to throw out basestealers. Would-be thieves were thrown out 12 times in 25 attempts last year. He fields his position well and committed only one error in over 231 innings.

1997 Outlook

Fassero became too successful and too expensive to remain forever in Montreal. After being the constant subject of trade rumors over the last two years, he was dealt to Seattle where he could be the final piece of the puzzle in the Mariners' drive for their first World Series. With the support of Seattle's high-powered offense, Fassero should approach a 20-win season.

Position: SP
Bats: L **Throws:** L
Ht: 6' 1" **Wt:** 195

Opening Day Age: 34
Born: 1/5/63 in Springfield, IL
ML Seasons: 6
Pronunciation: fuh-SAIR-oh

Overall Statistics

	W	L	Pct.	ERA	G	GS	Sv	IP	H	BB	SO	HR	BR/IP
1996	15	11	.577	3.30	34	34	0	231.2	217	55	222	20	1.17
Career	58	48	.547	3.20	262	100	10	850.0	782	274	750	57	1.24

How Often He Throws Strikes

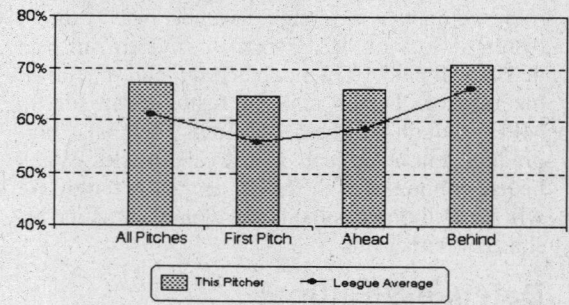

1996 Situational Stats

	W	L	ERA	Sv	IP		AB	H	HR	RBI	Avg
Home	8	5	2.77	0	117.0	LHB	111	26	0	7	.234
Road	7	6	3.85	0	114.2	RHB	777	191	20	77	.246
First Half	8	6	3.15	0	123.0	Sc Pos	195	49	5	65	.251
Scnd Half	7	5	3.48	0	108.2	Clutch	75	18	2	7	.240

1996 Rankings (National League)

→ 2nd in runners caught stealing (13) and bunts in play (25)
→ 3rd in complete games (5) and strikeouts
→ 5th in sacrifice bunts (14), highest strikeout/walk ratio (4.0) and least GDPs induced per 9 innings (0.5)
→ 6th in lowest on-base percentage allowed (.289), lowest stolen base percentage allowed (48.0%) and most strikeouts per 9 innings (8.6)
→ 7th in games started, innings pitched, batters faced (967), highest groundball/flyball ratio allowed (1.8), least pitches thrown per batter (3.53) and least baserunners allowed per 9 innings

Darrin Fletcher

1996 Season

Always rumored to be replaced, Darrin Fletcher again handled a majority of the catching duties for Montreal and had one of his best offensive seasons. He had a career-high 12 homers, just missed his career mark with 57 RBI and even hit a home run last year off a lefthander—a rare feat for Fletcher.

Hitting

Fletcher has worked on increasing his bat speed by starting his swing with his hands in hitting position and opening his stance to allow better plate coverage. This gives him a better chance to fight off pitches that crowd the inside corner. A low-ball hitter who struggles with pitches above the belt, he is still prone to uppercutting the ball too frequently. Though he rarely walks, Fletcher does put the ball into play most of the time. He is most dangerous when thrown a mistake breaking ball low on the inner half of the plate.

Baserunning & Defense

If you want proof of Fletcher's lack of speed, look no further than his grand total of zero stolen bases in his major league career. Once not entirely trusted by Felipe Alou and the Expos' coaches, Fletcher has improved significantly in his ability to call games and handle pitchers. He has also improved his ability to frame pitches behind the plate. However, he does not have a strong arm and his release is inconsistent, resulting in opponents succeeding on nearly 90 percent of their attempts against him last year.

1997 Outlook

Catcher is the one position at which the fertile Expos farm system has not been able to produce any prospects. As a result, Fletcher has remained the Montreal backstop longer than anyone would have believed a few years ago. He has made himself a solid receiver who can help many clubs if the Expos decide his price has become too steep.

Position: C
Bats: L **Throws:** R
Ht: 6' 1" **Wt:** 200

Opening Day Age: 30
Born: 10/3/66 in Elmhurst, IL
ML Seasons: 8

Overall Statistics

	G	AB	R	H	D	T	HR	RBI	SB	BB	SO	Avg	OBP	Slg
1996	127	394	41	105	22	0	12	57	0	27	42	.266	.321	.414
Career	609	1814	166	472	100	5	46	260	0	139	177	.260	.316	.397

Where He Hits the Ball

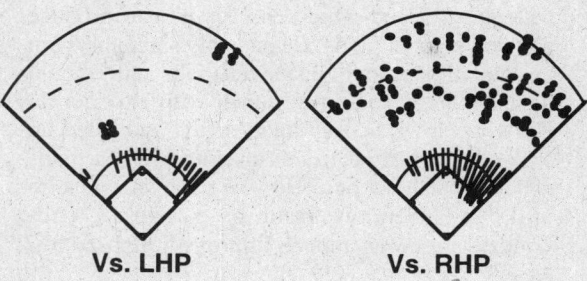

Vs. LHP　　　　**Vs. RHP**

1996 Situational Stats

	AB	H	HR	RBI	Avg		AB	H	HR	RBI	Avg
Home	199	55	7	29	.276	LHP	61	18	1	12	.295
Road	195	50	5	28	.256	RHP	333	87	11	45	.261
First Half	226	60	8	42	.265	Sc Pos	107	27	4	43	.252
Scnd Half	168	45	4	15	.268	Clutch	62	15	0	8	.242

1996 Rankings (National League)

- ➡ 1st in lowest percentage of runners caught stealing as a catcher (10.7%)
- ➡ 9th in lowest percentage of swings that missed (10.6%)
- ➡ Led the Expos in lowest percentage of swings that missed (10.6%) and highest percentage of swings put into play (50.9%)

Mark Grudzielanek

1996 Season

Montreal crossed its fingers last spring and handed the key jobs of shortstop and leadoff hitter to largely unproven Mark Grudzielanek. The results were remarkable. Grudzielanek started more games at short than any National League player. He also became the second Expos player ever with over 200 hits. Grudzielanek had a blistering April in which he had 45 hits and hit .328 in the first half to earn an All-Star berth. He hit 48 points lower in the second half but finished the year with a .322 September.

Hitting

Grudzielanek is a Paul Molitor-type hitter. He has an upright, slightly open stance and generates excellent bat speed which enables him to produce gap power to all fields. He had only six homers but he can turn around inside fastballs and should develop more home run punch with experience. He wore down in July and August and piled up strikeouts when he began chasing high fastballs and offspeed pitches. However, he is quick to make adjustments and by season's end, Grudzielanek was a much improved offspeed hitter.

Baserunning & Defense

There are dozens of players with better speed. But Grudzielanek has used the teachings of Expos coach Tommy Harper to become an excellent basestealer. He has worked hard to learn pitchers' moves and consistently gets good jumps. Though he's played second and third, Grudzielanek won't be moving away from shortstop. He has surprising range and a strong arm. His 27 errors were the second-most in the league, but he handled more chances than all but four N.L. shortstops.

1997 Outlook

In an era of great young shortstops, Grudzielanek is among the best. He has a great work ethic and a drive to improve. Shortstops like Alex Rodriguez, Derek Jeter and others may get more attention, but Grudzielanek should be a star for many years to come.

Position: SS
Bats: R **Throws:** R
Ht: 6' 1" **Wt:** 185

Opening Day Age: 26
Born: 6/30/70 in Milwaukee, WI
ML Seasons: 2
Pronunciation: gruzz-ELL-en-neck

Overall Statistics

	G	AB	R	H	D	T	HR	RBI	SB	BB	SO	Avg	OBP	Slg
1996	153	657	99	201	34	4	6	49	33	26	83	.306	.340	.397
Career	231	926	126	267	46	6	7	69	41	40	130	.288	.328	.374

Where He Hits the Ball

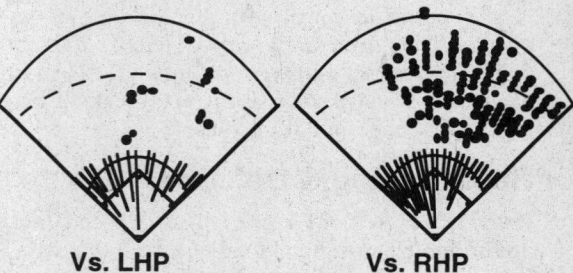

Vs. LHP   **Vs. RHP**

1996 Situational Stats

	AB	H	HR	RBI	Avg		AB	H	HR	RBI	Avg
Home	304	99	5	26	.326	LHP	133	41	1	5	.308
Road	353	102	1	23	.289	RHP	524	160	5	44	.305
First Half	357	117	5	30	.328	Sc Pos	139	39	0	40	.281
Scnd Half	300	84	1	19	.280	Clutch	98	33	1	4	.337

1996 Rankings (National League)

- 2nd in singles, lowest batting average with the bases loaded (.083) and errors at shortstop (27)
- 3rd in at-bats and lowest fielding percentage at shortstop (.959)
- 4th in hits
- 5th in lowest HR frequency (109.5 ABs per HR)
- 7th in stolen base percentage (82.5%) and lowest on-base percentage for a leadoff hitter (.329)
- 8th in plate appearances (696) and least pitches seen per plate appearance (3.39)
- 10th in highest groundball/flyball ratio (1.8)
- Led the Expos in at-bats, runs scored and hits

Mike Lansing

1996 Season

If there was a club leader for Montreal last year, it was second baseman Mike Lansing. Despite wrist, back and knee ailments, Lansing started all but three games for the Expos. He set career highs in virtually all offensive categories and finished among the league leaders with 40 doubles. The grind took its toll, however. After hitting .308 in the first half, Lansing tailed off down the stretch, hitting .259 in the second half and only .237 in August and September.

Hitting

Lansing is much stronger physically than he was when he first came to the majors, and he has continued to improve every year. He has made himself a better breaking-ball hitter by shortening his swing. When he gets tired, he will start lifting too many pitches, and he'll pile up strikeouts when he begins chasing breaking balls. Overall, though, Lansing is a tough hitter against all kinds of pitching. His gap power makes him very dangerous, especially when he works the count in his favor and puts himself in position to get a fastball, which he can crush.

Baserunning & Defense

An aggressive baserunner with good quickness, Lansing was 23-for-31 in stolen base attempts last year. He is always looking to press the action and take the extra base. He is also one of the best second basemen in the National League. His range is not exceptional, but he makes up for it with good hands and an accurate arm. Lansing turns the double play as well as anyone and was charged with only 11 errors last year in 749 chances.

1997 Outlook

On a ballclub that has loads of question marks because of its management's fiscal policies, there are no questions about the middle of the infield. Lansing has quietly developed into a top second baseman and a key part of the Expos' foundation. He has always improved from year to year, so expect more of the same in 1997.

Position: 2B
Bats: R **Throws:** R
Ht: 6' 0" **Wt:** 180

Opening Day Age: 28
Born: 4/3/68 in Rawlins, WY
ML Seasons: 4

Overall Statistics

	G	AB	R	H	D	T	HR	RBI	SB	BB	SO	Avg	OBP	Slg
1996	159	641	99	183	40	2	11	53	23	44	85	.285	.341	.406
Career	533	1993	254	548	120	7	29	195	85	148	243	.275	.331	.386

Where He Hits the Ball

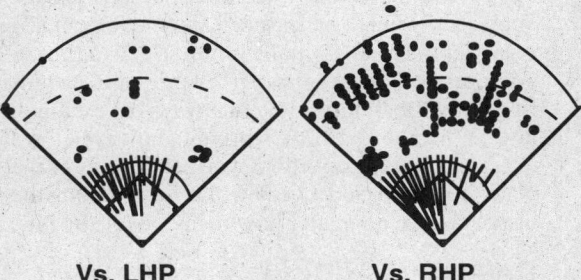

Vs. LHP   **Vs. RHP**

1996 Situational Stats

	AB	H	HR	RBI	Avg		AB	H	HR	RBI	Avg
Home	310	80	3	24	.258	LHP	135	40	1	4	.296
Road	331	103	8	29	.311	RHP	506	143	10	49	.283
First Half	344	106	5	29	.308	Sc Pos	131	39	4	43	.298
Scnd Half	297	77	6	24	.259	Clutch	90	25	2	13	.278

1996 Rankings (National League)

→ 5th in at-bats and fielding percentage at second base (.985)
→ 6th in doubles, batting average on the road (.311) and errors at second base (11)
→ 7th in plate appearances (705) and games played (159)
→ 8th in singles
→ 9th in hit by pitch (10)
→ 10th in GDPs (19)
→ Led the Expos in runs scored, caught stealing (8), times on base (237), GDPs (19), pitches seen (2,469), plate appearances (705), games played (159), on-base percentage, batting average on the road (.311) and highest percentage of extra bases taken as a runner (48.1%)

Mark Leiter

1996 Season

Acquired from San Francisco on July 30, Mark Leiter provided a boost to the Expos' starting rotation with a solid two months. The Expos lost Leiter's first start, but they would go on to win the next nine times he took the mound, with Leiter posting four victories. He didn't cool off until the end of the year, when he lost his final two starts.

Pitching

Leiter annually ranks among the league leaders in two dubious categories—home runs allowed and hit batsmen—and last season was no different. One reason for the lofty home run totals is Leiter's desire to throw his sinking fastball more often than he probably should. It often does not sink consistently, and when it lacks speed and movement it is a very enticing and hittable pitch. He also throws a big-breaking curve that often hangs and a split-fingered fastball that does not always have enough bite. When they're all working, however, he's tough. He has the ability to work both sides of the plate with good control and will keep pounding the inside corner, no matter how many people he hits.

Defense & Hitting

Leiter is a poor defensive player who is often out of position when fielding. He has a good right-handed pickoff move, but he was also hit with four balks last year. He is slow coming to the plate, which is one of the big reasons basestealers were successful on 23 of 31 attempts last year. Leiter makes infrequent contact with the bat but occasionally helps himself with an RBI or sacrifice.

1997 Outlook

In an Expos' rotation that has already lost Jeff Fassero, there are few set jobs. The veteran Leiter could stay in Montreal and at least give the Expos some serviceable work, producing 10 or so victories along the way.

Position: SP
Bats: R **Throws:** R
Ht: 6' 3" **Wt:** 210

Opening Day Age: 33
Born: 4/13/63 in Joliet, IL
ML Seasons: 7
Pronunciation: LITE-er

Overall Statistics

	W	L	Pct.	ERA	G	GS	Sv	IP	H	BB	SO	HR	BR/IP
1996	8	12	.400	4.92	35	34	0	205.0	219	69	164	37	1.40
Career	46	50	.479	4.48	213	115	3	875.2	888	305	633	116	1.36

How Often He Throws Strikes

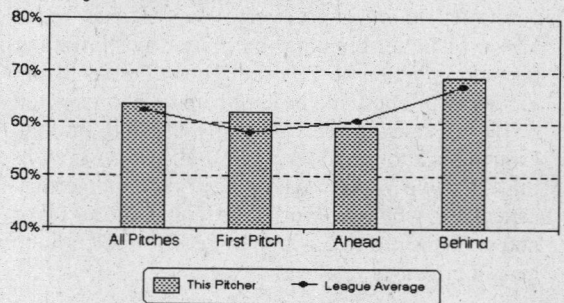

This Pitcher / League Average

1996 Situational Stats

	W	L	ERA	Sv	IP		AB	H	HR	RBI	Avg
Home	4	5	5.55	0	110.1	LHB	330	98	17	49	.297
Road	4	7	4.18	0	94.2	RHB	471	121	20	67	.257
First Half	4	7	4.71	0	116.2	Sc Pos	203	61	8	84	.300
Scnd Half	4	5	5.20	0	88.1	Clutch	27	6	0	0	.222

1996 Rankings (National League)

- → 1st in home runs allowed (37), hit batsmen (16) and most home runs allowed per 9 innings (1.62)
- → 2nd in balks (4), pickoff throws (231) and lowest groundball/flyball ratio allowed (0.9)
- → 3rd in highest slugging percentage allowed (.476) and highest ERA at home (5.55)
- → 6th in least GDPs induced per 9 innings (0.5)
- → 7th in games started (34) and most run support per 9 innings (5.7)
- → 8th in highest ERA (4.92)
- → 9th in losses (12), hits allowed (219) and stolen bases allowed (23)
- → 10th in highest batting average allowed vs. left-handed batters (.297)

Barry Manuel

Position: RP
Bats: R **Throws:** R
Ht: 5'11" **Wt:** 185

Opening Day Age: 31
Born: 8/12/65 in
Mamou, LA
ML Seasons: 3

1996 Season

Barry Manuel arrived at the Expos' spring training camp last year as a non-roster pitcher coming off a 5-12, 4.59 season at Triple-A Ottawa. Surprisingly, he earned a job and produced a solid season in middle relief. He was among the league leaders with 86 relief innings, and 23 of his 53 appearances lasted two innings or more. Manuel didn't just eat up innings, either. He held opponents to a .220 batting average.

Pitching

Manuel always had a live arm, but command had been his Achilles' heel. He made his delivery more compact last year and added velocity, to the point where he was throwing in the 92-MPH range. His fastball is somewhat straight, however, and his best pitch continues to be a big-breaking slider that is very tough on right-handed hitters. At times, he overthrows the slider and gets hurt by hangers; he allowed 10 home runs in 86 innings last season. Manuel is usually around the plate and had a very solid strikeout-to-walk ratio.

Defense & Hitting

A seasoned veteran of several minor-league seasons, Manuel does not panic in the field and is more than adequate with the glove. However, controlling the running game is one of his major weaknesses. He does almost nothing to hold runners. Combine that fact with his ponderous delivery, and you have the makings of a basestealers' dream pitcher. Baserunners torched him last year, stealing an amazing 19 bases in 20 attempts. Manuel is not a factor as a hitter and went without a base hit in seven at-bats.

1997 Outlook

Manuel was a pleasant surprise for the Expos, and he has the kind of resilient arm that is invaluable in this day and age where every team is desperate for strong arms out of the pen. For the first time in his career, the 31-year-old Manuel has a job waiting for him in spring training.

Overall Statistics

	W	L	Pct.	ERA	G	GS	Sv	IP	H	BB	SO	HR	BR/IP
1996	4	1	.800	3.24	53	0	0	86.0	70	26	62	10	1.12
Career	6	1	.857	3.01	64	0	0	107.2	83	33	76	12	1.08

How Often He Throws Strikes

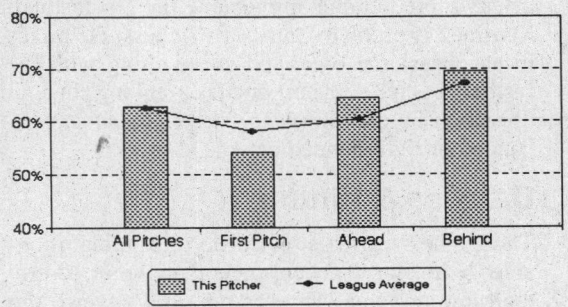

1996 Situational Stats

	W	L	ERA	Sv	IP		AB	H	HR	RBI	Avg
Home	2	0	2.87	0	37.2	LHB	107	25	1	6	.234
Road	2	1	3.54	0	48.1	RHB	211	45	9	35	.213
First Half	2	0	3.73	0	50.2	Sc Pos	102	19	3	31	.186
Scnd Half	2	1	2.55	0	35.1	Clutch	40	10	2	5	.250

1996 Rankings (National League)

➡ 8th in relief innings (86.0)
➡ Led the Expos in relief innings (86.0)

Pedro Martinez

1996 Season

At the age of 25, Pedro Martinez has firmly established himself as one of the National League's toughest righthanders. He was among the league leaders last year with four complete games and 222 strikeouts—a career high—and won in double-figures for the fourth season in a row.

Pitching

Martinez is not a comfortable at-bat for any hitter. His best weapon is a fastball that explodes near the plate and runs in on right-handed hitters. Since he throws in the mid-90s and has a well-earned reputation for pitching inside, he can be as intimidating as any hurler in the majors. But because of the often unpredictable movement on his fastball, Martinez is prone to bouts of wildness. He mixes in an occasional overhand curve along with the fastball, but his next best pitch is a sinking change-up which he can throw for strikes to either left-handed or right-handed batters.

Defense & Hitting

Though he's a good athlete, Martinez remains unable to develop a decent pickoff move or control the running game. Thieves ran wild against him last year, stealing 29 bases in 32 attempts. Only two other pitchers in the league allowed more stolen bases. He does help himself defensively with his ability to get in good fielding position. Martinez strikes out at least a third of the time he steps to the plate but also helps himself with the bat, rapping out six hits and a league-leading 16 sacrifice bunts in 1996.

1997 Outlook

Martinez has just begun to scratch the surface of his potential. He is a highly competitive pitcher with a good work ethic. If he can develop more maturity, he should break through as a 20-game winner in the very near future.

Position: SP
Bats: R **Throws:** R
Ht: 5'11" **Wt:** 170

Opening Day Age: 25
Born: 10/25/71 in Manoguyabo, DR
ML Seasons: 5

Overall Statistics

	W	L	Pct.	ERA	G	GS	Sv	IP	H	BB	SO	HR	BR/IP
1996	13	10	.565	3.70	33	33	0	216.2	189	70	222	19	1.20
Career	48	31	.608	3.39	154	89	3	671.0	544	239	665	56	1.17

How Often He Throws Strikes

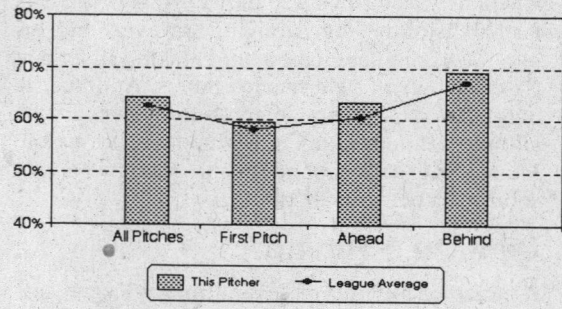

1996 Situational Stats

	W	L	ERA	Sv	IP		AB	H	HR	RBI	Avg
Home	8	3	3.06	0	97.0	LHB	395	100	6	40	.253
Road	5	7	4.21	0	119.2	RHB	418	89	13	45	.213
First Half	7	3	3.65	0	120.2	Sc Pos	186	41	5	63	.220
Scnd Half	6	7	3.75	0	96.0	Clutch	55	10	1	4	.182

1996 Rankings (National League)

→ 1st in sacrifice bunts (16) and highest stolen base percentage allowed (90.6%)
→ 3rd in strikeouts, stolen bases allowed (29) and most strikeouts per 9 innings (9.2)
→ 4th in lowest fielding percentage at pitcher (.903)
→ 5th in lowest batting average allowed vs. right-handed batters (.213)
→ 6th in errors at pitcher (3)
→ 7th in complete games (4), lowest batting average allowed (.232) and lowest ground-ball/flyball ratio allowed (1.0)
→ 8th in lowest slugging percentage allowed (.357) and lowest on-base percentage allowed (.294)

Henry Rodriguez

1996 Season

For the first two months of last season, there were few bigger stories in baseball than Henry Rodriguez. He set a National League record with 20 home runs by May 31 and became a big favorite with Montreal fans, who tossed "Oh Henry!" bars onto the field when he homered. Rodriguez' power tailed off sharply as the season progressed, though he did set a club record with 36 homers.

Hitting

Rodriguez is a dead fastball hitter who looks to jerk the first strike he sees out of the park, especially if it's down in the strike zone. He has the strength to hit the ball out to the opposite field, but he hit the skids in July and August when opposing hurlers fed him a steady diet of offspeed pitches. He could not stay back and wait on change-ups and slow curves and got so frustrated that the Expos coaches believed he was developing a mental block. Rodriguez began over-compensating for the change-up by guessing that offspeed pitches were coming. As a result, his ability to pull the trigger on fastballs was neutralized. He ended up leading the majors with 160 strikeouts.

Baserunning & Defense

Rodriguez' best position is probably first base, where he flashes average range and very sure hands. With the Expos, he spends the majority of his time in left field, where he does only a fair job of judging fly balls. His arm is below average. With his mediocre speed, he only occasionally attempts to steal a base.

1997 Outlook

Rodriguez has something to prove because many National League people think his big numbers were an aberration and that his true ability was shown in his sluggish second half. The truth is likely somewhere in between, which should mean around 25 homers and 80 RBI.

Position: LF/1B
Bats: L **Throws:** L
Ht: 6' 1" **Wt:** 205

Opening Day Age: 29
Born: 11/8/67 in Santo Domingo, DR
ML Seasons: 5

Overall Statistics

	G	AB	R	H	D	T	HR	RBI	SB	BB	SO	Avg	OBP	Slg
1996	145	532	81	147	42	1	36	103	2	37	160	.276	.325	.562
Career	423	1298	158	333	77	4	57	204	3	84	315	.257	.302	.454

Where He Hits the Ball

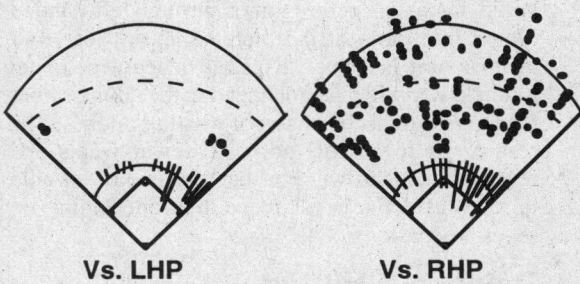

Vs. LHP   **Vs. RHP**

1996 Situational Stats

	AB	H	HR	RBI	Avg		AB	H	HR	RBI	Avg
Home	262	71	20	56	.271	LHP	110	24	7	24	.218
Road	270	76	16	47	.281	RHP	422	123	29	79	.291
First Half	319	89	25	70	.279	Sc Pos	154	43	12	67	.279
Scnd Half	213	58	11	33	.272	Clutch	85	28	7	15	.329

1996 Rankings (National League)

→ 1st in strikeouts and lowest percentage of swings put into play (31.7%)
→ 2nd in lowest groundball/flyball ratio (0.8), errors in left field (6) and highest percentage of swings that missed (33.3%)
→ 5th in doubles
→ 7th in HR frequency (14.8 ABs per HR)
→ 8th in slugging percentage vs. right-handed pitchers (.581)
→ 9th in home runs
→ Led the Expos in home runs, doubles, total bases (299), RBI, strikeouts, slugging percentage, HR frequency (14.8 ABs per HR), most pitches seen per plate appearance (3.92)

Mel Rojas

Signed By
CUBS

Position: RP
Bats: R **Throws:** R
Ht: 5'11" **Wt:** 195

Opening Day Age: 30
Born: 12/10/66 in Haina, DR
ML Seasons: 7
Pronunciation: ROH-hahss

1996 Season

Over the last three months of last season, there was no better closer in baseball than Mel Rojas. From July 19 to the end of the season, Rojas was perfect, registering 23 saves in 23 opportunities. He set a personal high with 36 saves while holding opposing hitters to a microscopic .193 average.

Pitching

The Expos always questioned Rojas' aggressiveness. . . until last season. He finally listened to manager Felipe Alou and went after every hitter with his best stuff. That "stuff" includes a fastball in the mid-90s with both heavy sinking and cutting action. He also throws one of the meanest split-fingered fastballs in the game, turning left-handed hitters into putty at the plate—they hit just .147 against him last year. Rojas also learned to put hitters away when he got ahead in the count, rather than give into his bad habit of wasting pitches. The result was fewer hits allowed, fewer walks and fewer pitches thrown. For that reason, he was able to pitch effectively for more than one inning on several occasions.

Defense & Hitting

Like many other closers, Rojas brings few defensive skills to the mound. His delivery sends him stumbling toward the first-base line, so he is never in good fielding position. He pays little attention to baserunners, who stole successfully on all seven of their attempts last season and are 28-for-29 over the last three years. He actually had three hits last year.

1997 Outlook

Rojas is another of those players whose status was affected by the botched labor deal. He gained his free agency when the new deal was ratified, and his breakthrough season put his price out of reach for the Expos. The Cubs quickly grabbed him, and if he stays aggressive, he will once again be one of the premier closers in the National League.

Overall Statistics

	W	L	Pct.	ERA	G	GS	Sv	IP	H	BB	SO	HR	BR/IP
1996	7	4	.636	3.22	74	0	36	81.0	56	28	92	5	1.04
Career	29	23	.558	3.04	385	0	109	509.2	423	179	418	35	1.18

How Often He Throws Strikes

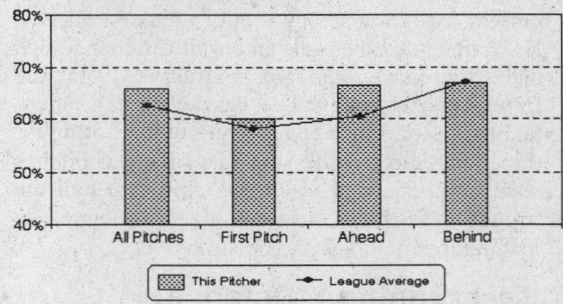

1996 Situational Stats

	W	L	ERA	Sv	IP		AB	H	HR	RBI	Avg
Home	4	2	4.15	19	43.1	LHB	129	19	2	14	.147
Road	3	2	2.15	17	37.2	RHB	161	37	3	21	.230
First Half	5	3	5.19	12	43.1	Sc Pos	71	18	1	29	.254
Scnd Half	2	1	0.96	24	37.2	Clutch	194	31	3	19	.160

1996 Rankings (National League)

→ 1st in save percentage (90.0%)
→ 3rd in games finished (64), lowest batting average allowed in relief (.193) and least baserunners allowed per 9 innings in relief (9.6)
→ 5th in saves, relief wins (7) and most strikeouts per 9 innings in relief (10.2)
→ 7th in games pitched and save opportunities (40)
→ Led the Expos in games pitched, saves, games finished (64), save opportunities (40), save percentage (90.0%), blown saves (4), relief ERA (3.22), relief wins (7) and lowest batting average allowed in relief (.193)

F.P. Santangelo

1996 Season

There was no more valuable Expo player last year than rookie F.P. Santangelo, Montreal's insurance policy at six different positions. He played his most games in center field during Rondell White's absence and gave the Expos solid offense and fine defensive play.

Hitting

A switch-hitter, Santangelo holds his own from both sides of the plate, but he has a little more power as a left-handed hitter. He is a good fastball hitter from either side. He tends to pull more as a left-handed hitter and is more easily jammed by righthanders. Santangelo usually sprays the ball when batting right-handed. He needs to improve against breaking stuff, but for a relatively inexperienced player he does a good job of handling offspeed stuff. He has some extra-base pop from either side of the plate.

Baserunning & Defense

Not blessed with great speed, Santangelo is nonetheless an aggressive baserunner who will force the action by trying to take an extra base when the opportunity presents itself. He is not a great basestealer but picks his spots well, and with regular playing time could steal 10 or so bases per year. Defensively, Santangelo is one of the most versatile players in baseball. As a center fielder, he has outstanding range and leaping ability. His arm might be a little short to play right field, but he won't hurt the Expos at any of the outfield spots. Santangelo also fills in ably at second, short and third and Montreal even had him catch batting practice during spring training for possible use as an emergency receiver.

1997 Outlook

Because of versatility and his low price, Santangelo is as untouchable as any Montreal player. He will be a very valuable jack-of-all-trades for the Expos again this season.

Position: CF/3B/LF/RF
Bats: B **Throws:** R
Ht: 5'10" **Wt:** 168

Opening Day Age: 29
Born: 10/24/67 in El Dorado Hills, CA
ML Seasons: 2
Pronunciation: san-TAN-jel-oh

Overall Statistics

	G	AB	R	H	D	T	HR	RBI	SB	BB	SO	Avg	OBP	Slg
1996	152	393	54	109	20	5	7	56	5	49	61	.277	.369	.407
Career	187	491	65	138	25	6	8	65	6	61	70	.281	.372	.405

Where He Hits the Ball

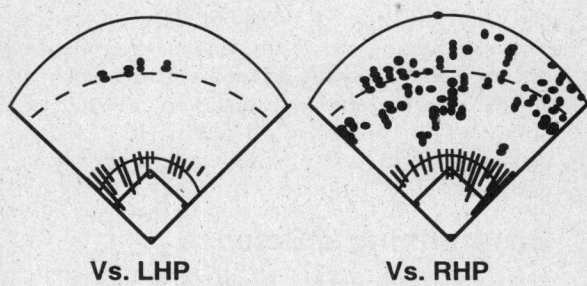

Vs. LHP   Vs. RHP

1996 Situational Stats

	AB	H	HR	RBI	Avg		AB	H	HR	RBI	Avg
Home	188	61	5	35	.324	LHP	75	23	1	13	.307
Road	205	48	2	21	.234	RHP	318	86	6	43	.270
First Half	196	53	3	32	.270	Sc Pos	98	31	2	47	.316
Scnd Half	197	56	4	24	.284	Clutch	72	17	2	16	.236

1996 Rankings (National League)

- ➡ 6th in errors in center field (4)
- ➡ 8th in hit by pitch (11) and batting average with the bases loaded (.533)
- ➡ Led the Expos in triples, hit by pitch (11) and highest percentage of pitches taken (55.8%)

David Segui

1996 Season

Well on his way to establishing his credentials as a top first baseman, David Segui went on the shelf for six weeks when his thumb was broken by a blistering pickoff throw from teammate Ugueth Urbina. Segui came back from the injury to post solid numbers, falling one home run short of matching his career high despite playing in only 115 games.

Hitting

Segui is a rare switch-hitter who is equally effective from both sides of the plate. He has the same short stroke and preference for low fastballs whether batting righty or lefty. He remained gun-shy about his thumb upon his return from the DL, and often got jammed. But by the last few weeks of the season, he was again hanging in on inside pitches. Segui keeps his strikeouts down thanks to a good eye, the ability to make contact and an ability to hit the ball to all fields. He has also become a very good offspeed hitter who is not easily fooled.

Baserunning & Defense

Segui may lack speed, but he will often take chances on the bases. It's not always the best policy. He attempted eight steals last year and was successful only four times. A very good first baseman, Segui has average range, his hands are excellent and his footwork around the bag is solid. He is also skillful at digging out low throws from the dirt. He is capable of fill-in duty in left or right, but his outfield days are likely behind him for good.

1997 Outlook

Segui won't evoke any comparisons to the classic Mo Vaughn/Mark McGwire types at first base. But he is a .300 hitter who should approach 15 to 20 home runs and 80 or so RBI if he stays healthy all year. The Expos could do a lot worse than having him in their lineup.

Position: 1B
Bats: B **Throws:** L
Ht: 6' 1" **Wt:** 202

Opening Day Age: 30
Born: 7/19/66 in Kansas City, KS
ML Seasons: 7
Pronunciation: suh-GHEE

Overall Statistics

	G	AB	R	H	D	T	HR	RBI	SB	BB	SO	Avg	OBP	Slg
1996	115	416	69	119	30	1	11	58	4	60	54	.286	.375	.442
Career	724	2182	287	597	122	6	48	283	10	234	254	.274	.343	.401

Where He Hits the Ball

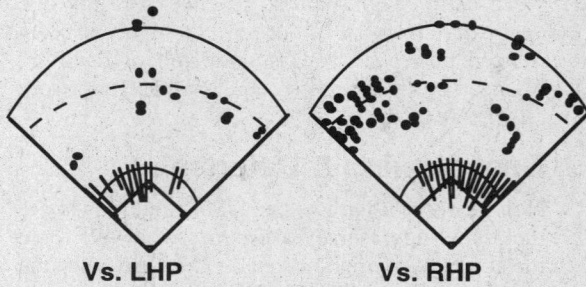

Vs. LHP   **Vs. RHP**

1996 Situational Stats

	AB	H	HR	RBI	Avg		AB	H	HR	RBI	Avg
Home	212	66	6	29	.311	LHP	110	33	4	25	.300
Road	204	53	5	29	.260	RHP	306	86	7	33	.281
First Half	268	75	5	34	.280	Sc Pos	98	32	3	43	.327
Scnd Half	148	44	6	24	.297	Clutch	64	21	1	8	.328

1996 Rankings (National League)

→ 1st in lowest batting average on an 0-2 count (.000)
→ 3rd in batting average with the bases loaded (.600)
→ 5th in lowest fielding percentage at first base (.993)
→ 9th in errors at first base (7)
→ Led the Expos in walks, batting average with runners in scoring position (.327) and batting average with the bases loaded (.600)

Rondell White

Position: CF
Bats: R **Throws:** R
Ht: 6' 1" **Wt:** 205

Opening Day Age: 25
Born: 2/23/72 in
Milledgeville, GA
ML Seasons: 4

Montreal
Expos

1996 Season

This was supposed be a coming-out year for talented outfielder Rondell White, but his season was dealt a serious blow when he suffered a bruised spleen while trying to make a diving catch on April 28. White was sidelined for over two months, and once he returned it took him a while to get back into the flow. He still managed to produce 41 RBI and 29 extra-base hits in what amounted to half a season.

Hitting

White has an exceptionally quick bat which generates power to all fields. An excellent fastball hitter who can catch up with most heaters, he also improved his ability to handle breaking balls and offspeed pitches. ... though he likely will always have his share of strikeouts. He remains noticeably more comfortable against left-handed pitching, but he's improved his ability to hang in against righthanders, and should become more comfortable against all pitching as he gains more experience. His home run power should also blossom thanks to his enormously strong wrists. He can go deep with a relatively short swing.

Baserunning & Defense

Nobody on the Expos has better speed than White. As he learns pitchers' moves and the art of getting a quicker jump, Montreal believes he can steal between 40 and 50 bases. He has all the tools to emerge as one of baseball's best center fielders. Because of his enormous range and closing ability, he plays shallow and gets rid of the ball quickly, making him a dangerous thrower from the outfield.

1997 Outlook

Last year was only a brief detour for White, who has a date with stardom. He is capable of becoming a big-time player with the potential to hit 20-plus home runs, bat .300 and steal 30 or so bases. It would not surprise the Expos if he reached those goals this year.

Overall Statistics

	G	AB	R	H	D	T	HR	RBI	SB	BB	SO	Avg	OBP	Slg
1996	88	334	35	98	19	4	6	41	14	22	53	.293	.340	.428
Career	281	978	147	284	65	10	23	126	41	79	174	.290	.348	.448

Where He Hits the Ball

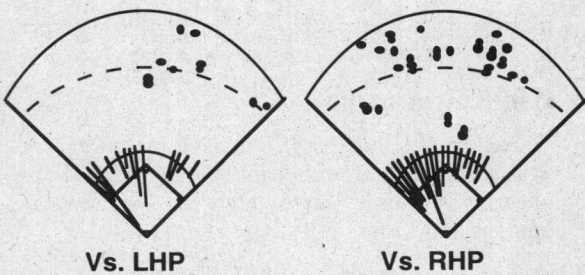

Vs. LHP   **Vs. RHP**

1996 Situational Stats

	AB	H	HR	RBI	Avg		AB	H	HR	RBI	Avg
Home	152	46	2	16	.303	LHP	95	36	0	13	.379
Road	182	52	4	25	.286	RHP	239	62	6	28	.259
First Half	100	30	3	19	.300	Sc Pos	101	28	2	36	.277
Scnd Half	234	68	3	22	.291	Clutch	52	12	0	6	.231

1996 Rankings (National League)

➡ 2nd in batting average on an 0-2 count (.367)
➡ Led the Expos in batting average on an 0-2 count (.367) and batting average with two strikes (.247)

Mike Dyer

Position: RP
Bats: R **Throws:** R
Ht: 6' 3" **Wt:** 200

Opening Day Age: 30
Born: 9/8/66 in Upland, CA
ML Seasons: 4

Overall Statistics

	W	L	Pct.	ERA	G	GS	Sv	IP	H	BB	SO	HR	BR/IP
1996	5	5	.500	4.40	70	1	2	75.2	79	34	51	7	1.49
Career	14	18	.438	4.60	155	13	6	236.2	249	113	154	19	1.53

1996 Situational Stats

	W	L	ERA	Sv	IP		AB	H	HR	RBI	Avg
Home	3	3	3.13	1	37.1	LHB	105	24	1	10	.229
Road	2	2	5.63	1	38.1	RHB	180	55	6	35	.306
First Half	4	2	4.01	2	42.2	Sc Pos	93	24	1	36	.258
Scnd Half	1	3	4.91	0	33.0	Clutch	84	23	3	17	.274

1996 Season

Picked up after Pittsburgh waived him, Mike Dyer was a durable and serviceable middle reliever for the Expos. He set career highs in appearances, innings and wins.

Pitching, Defense & Hitting

Dyer's best pitch is a good sinking fastball that occasionally will hit 90 MPH. However, it is not a dominating pitch, and at times he will labor with his location. He mixes in a slider, an occasional overhand curve and a forkball which he often tries to use as a strikeout pitch. He can't be trusted in save situations, blowing four of the six opportunities he had last year. Dyer is somewhat clumsy in his delivery, which doesn't help his fielding. He also does a poor job of holding runners. Basestealers were successful in 16 of 18 attempts when he was on the hill last year. He is also a non-factor as a hitter.

1997 Outlook

A classic journeyman, Dyer is capable of eating up innings in the key middle-relief role. Such utility arms have never been more valuable than they are today in the major leagues.

Cliff Floyd

Position: LF/CF
Bats: L **Throws:** R
Ht: 6' 4" **Wt:** 235

Opening Day Age: 24
Born: 12/5/72 in Chicago, IL
ML Seasons: 4

Overall Statistics

	G	AB	R	H	D	T	HR	RBI	SB	BB	SO	Avg	OBP	Slg
1996	117	227	29	55	15	4	6	26	7	30	52	.242	.340	.423
Career	256	661	81	165	35	8	12	77	20	60	146	.250	.318	.381

1996 Situational Stats

	AB	H	HR	RBI	Avg		AB	H	HR	RBI	Avg
Home	121	32	3	16	.264	LHP	34	8	0	4	.235
Road	106	23	3	10	.217	RHP	193	47	6	22	.244
First Half	77	22	2	11	.286	Sc Pos	51	10	2	18	.196
Scnd Half	150	33	4	15	.220	Clutch	53	16	2	6	.302

1996 Season

Cliff Floyd spent much of the year getting his strength back from his serious 1995 wrist injury. He was also fighting some weight problems. But over the last several weeks, Floyd showed flashes of his considerable talent.

Hitting, Baserunning & Defense

Floyd has begun showing aggressiveness at the plate, something the Expos had been hoping to see for a while. He has a big swing and big-time power. He still swings through too many pitches and will chase breaking balls out of the strike zone. However, he has started to wait better on pitches and no longer tries to pull everything. Floyd runs very well for a big man and is a smart baserunner who last year stole seven bases in eight attempts. Moved from the outfield to first base when he arrived in Montreal, he handles infield work adequately, but his future may be in the outfield. He has decent range and an average arm, but needs work on judging fly balls.

1997 Outlook

Floyd is a wild-card talent who could suddenly blossom. He should start the season healthy and, depending on where he fits in the lineup, he could deliver double-figure home runs and steals.

Jeff Juden

Position: RP
Bats: B **Throws:** R
Ht: 6' 8" **Wt:** 265

Opening Day Age: 26
Born: 1/19/71 in Salem, MA
ML Seasons: 5

Overall Statistics

	W	L	Pct.	ERA	G	GS	Sv	IP	H	BB	SO	HR	BR/IP
1996	5	0	1.000	3.27	58	0	0	74.1	61	34	61	8	1.28
Career	8	11	.421	4.27	83	18	0	187.2	166	88	148	22	1.35

1996 Situational Stats

	W	L	ERA	Sv	IP		AB	H	HR	RBI	Avg
Home	3	0	3.99	0	38.1	LHB	106	21	4	9	.198
Road	2	0	2.50	0	36.0	RHB	167	40	4	24	.240
First Half	4	0	4.10	0	41.2	Sc Pos	80	13	3	26	.163
Scnd Half	1	0	2.20	0	32.2	Clutch	73	16	0	4	.219

1996 Season

Jeff Juden's tour of National League franchises last year took him to Montreal, where he may have finally found a home. He appeared in a career-high 58 games and won all five of his decisions in his first full season in long- and middle-relief roles.

Pitching, Defense & Hitting

With his fourth organization in as many years, Juden remains an enigma. However, he still throws in the low 90s and finally found a fairly good release point last year, enabling him to throw a consistent sinking fastball and cutter as well as a slider. He has difficulty finishing his motion in decent fielding position and is often a defensive liability. He also is below average at holding runners and went 0-for-3 at the plate last year.

1997 Outlook

Previously viewed as a starting prospect, Juden seemed to adapt well to relief situations. He is still young and enormously talented, and if the Expos can continue to refine his abilities and his suspect attitude, they could have an imposing set-up man in their bullpen.

Sherman Obando

Position: RF
Bats: R **Throws:** R
Ht: 6' 4" **Wt:** 215

Opening Day Age: 27
Born: 1/23/70 in Bocas Del Toro, Panama
ML Seasons: 3

Overall Statistics

	G	AB	R	H	D	T	HR	RBI	SB	BB	SO	Avg	OBP	Slg
1996	89	178	30	44	9	0	8	22	2	22	48	.247	.332	.433
Career	136	308	38	79	12	0	11	40	3	28	86	.256	.321	.403

1996 Situational Stats

	AB	H	HR	RBI	Avg		AB	H	HR	RBI	Avg
Home	92	26	6	16	.283	LHP	69	13	2	9	.188
Road	86	18	2	6	.209	RHP	109	31	6	13	.284
First Half	135	33	5	16	.244	Sc Pos	52	9	0	11	.173
Scnd Half	43	11	3	6	.256	Clutch	47	9	2	3	.191

1996 Season

Acquired during spring training from Baltimore, Sherman Obando was a part-time outfielder and Montreal's busiest pinch hitter, with 48 plate appearances off the bench. He also made 36 starts and hit eight homers, but he struggled in clutch situations.

Hitting, Baserunning & Defense

A big swinger who is prone to strikeouts, Obando has had problems against left-handed pitching—despite the fact that he's a right-handed swinger. He managed a paltry .188 average against lefties last year with only two of his home runs. He has not shown the ability to hit anything except fastballs, so he usually sees a steady diet of breaking balls and change-ups. Obando has below-average speed but picks his spots and steals an occasional base. He is not a good outfielder, lacking range and often misplaying balls. He *does* have an above-average arm.

1997 Outlook

With all the youth and athleticism among the Expos' outfielders, Obando has little chance for significant playing time. However, he can be of some value as a pinch hitter with some power and occasional fill-in in the field.

Dave Silvestri

Position: 3B
Bats: R **Throws:** R
Ht: 6' 0" **Wt:** 196

Opening Day Age: 29
Born: 9/29/67 in St. Louis, MO
ML Seasons: 5

Overall Statistics

	G	AB	R	H	D	T	HR	RBI	SB	BB	SO	Avg	OBP	Slg
1996	86	162	16	33	4	0	1	17	2	34	41	.204	.340	.247
Career	168	307	42	66	11	3	6	35	4	56	92	.215	.334	.329

1996 Situational Stats

	AB	H	HR	RBI	Avg		AB	H	HR	RBI	Avg
Home	87	20	0	8	.230	LHP	29	5	0	4	.172
Road	75	13	1	9	.173	RHP	133	28	1	13	.211
First Half	112	25	0	11	.223	Sc Pos	48	11	0	15	.229
Scnd Half	50	8	1	6	.160	Clutch	29	7	0	2	.241

1996 Season

Ex-Yankee farmhand Dave Silvestri got playing time at third base for Shane Andrews when Andrews was injured early last year. He struck out in a quarter of his at-bats and managed only five extra-base hits. His main contribution was reaching base frequently via the walk.

Hitting, Baserunning & Defense

Silvestri once was a power-hitting infield prospect in the Yankees' farm system, but he has not converted that potential to the majors. He can be overpowered with just average hard stuff, and when he tries to make adjustments, he gets over-anxious against breaking balls. He has only average speed. In the field, Silvestri is very shaky at third. His range is average and his arm is unsure and erratic. However, he's versatile and capable of playing any of the four infield positions. Last year he even saw brief duty in the outfield.

1997 Outlook

Silvestri might stick as a utility man because of his ability to draw walks and fill a number of different roles in the field. If he does not show a little more with the bat, however, his spot will likely be taken by a younger player.

Ugueth Urbina

Position: SP/RP
Bats: R **Throws:** R
Ht: 6' 2" **Wt:** 185

Opening Day Age: 23
Born: 2/15/74 in Caracas, VZ
ML Seasons: 2
Pronunciation: ooo-GET ur-BEE-nuh

Overall Statistics

	W	L	Pct.	ERA	G	GS	Sv	IP	H	BB	SO	HR	BR/IP
1996	10	5	.667	3.71	33	17	0	114.0	102	44	108	18	1.28
Career	12	7	.632	4.13	40	21	0	137.1	128	58	123	24	1.35

1996 Situational Stats

	W	L	ERA	Sv	IP		AB	H	HR	RBI	Avg
Home	5	1	3.12	0	69.1	LHB	219	69	10	31	.315
Road	5	4	4.63	0	44.2	RHB	216	33	8	18	.153
First Half	4	2	4.53	0	49.2	Sc Pos	83	21	4	33	.253
Scnd Half	6	3	3.08	0	64.1	Clutch	54	9	2	2	.167

1996 Season

After making 17 starts as a member of the Expos' rotation, rookie righthander Ugueth Urbina was switched to the bullpen and showed huge potential. He ended the season with a 1.99 ERA in 16 relief outings while averaging more than a strikeout per inning out of the bullpen.

Pitching, Defense & Hitting

Urbina routinely hits the mid to upper 90s with his riding fastball and his three-quarter delivery makes him fearsome against right-handed hitters. Righty batters hit only .153 against Urbina. However, he still does not have consistency with his slider, and left-handed hitters get too good a look at his fastball. He has a somewhat wild delivery which does not contribute to good fielding. He pays little attention to opposing baserunners, who stole 18 bases in 22 attempts with Urbina pitching. He only occasionally makes contact as a hitter.

1997 Outlook

The Expos were projecting Urbina as their closer of the future, but with the departure of Mel Rojas to the Cubs, that future is probably now. He has the stuff and the makeup to be a success in the late-inning role.

Dave Veres

Position: RP
Bats: R **Throws:** R
Ht: 6' 2" **Wt:** 195

Opening Day Age: 30
Born: 10/19/66 in Montgomery, AL
ML Seasons: 3

Overall Statistics

	W	L	Pct.	ERA	G	GS	Sv	IP	H	BB	SO	HR	BR/IP
1996	6	3	.667	4.17	68	0	4	77.2	85	32	81	10	1.51
Career	14	7	.667	2.96	172	0	6	222.0	213	69	203	19	1.27

1996 Situational Stats

	W	L	ERA	Sv	IP		AB	H	HR	RBI	Avg
Home	4	0	4.45	2	32.1	LHB	123	38	3	14	.309
Road	2	3	3.97	2	45.1	RHB	184	47	7	25	.255
First Half	4	2	5.44	4	46.1	Sc Pos	102	21	2	29	.206
Scnd Half	2	1	2.30	0	31.1	Clutch	117	35	4	13	.299

1996 Season

After coming to the Expos in an offseason deal with the Astros, righty reliever Dave Veres had a miserable first half in which he had a 5.44 ERA and allowed eight home runs. But Veres got it together after the All-Star break. His ERA over the season's second half was 2.30, and he went on to set career highs in victories and saves.

Pitching, Defense & Hitting

Veres is consistently around the plate with an assortment of pitches including a fairly straight fastball, a splitter and a slider. His velocity is not exceptional, but he gets a high number of strikeouts because of his ability to work in and out and hit spots—particularly with the splitter and slider. His early-season home run problems were a product of overthrowing the splitter, which caused it to sit over the strike zone. Veres usually gets himself into good fielding position, but has some problems holding runners. He rarely gets a chance to hit.

1997 Outlook

There are few more consistent set-up men around than Veres. He should again be a busy and effective member of the Expos' bullpen this year.

Lenny Webster

Position: C
Bats: R **Throws:** R
Ht: 5' 9" **Wt:** 195

Opening Day Age: 32
Born: 2/10/65 in New Orleans, LA
ML Seasons: 8

Overall Statistics

	G	AB	R	H	D	T	HR	RBI	SB	BB	SO	Avg	OBP	Slg
1996	78	174	18	40	10	0	2	17	0	25	21	.230	.332	.322
Career	320	751	84	191	45	1	16	84	1	87	104	.254	.337	.381

1996 Situational Stats

	AB	H	HR	RBI	Avg		AB	H	HR	RBI	Avg
Home	90	20	1	7	.222	LHP	59	14	1	4	.237
Road	84	20	1	10	.238	RHP	115	26	1	13	.226
First Half	91	21	0	10	.231	Sc Pos	46	9	0	15	.196
Scnd Half	83	19	2	7	.229	Clutch	29	5	0	2	.172

1996 Season

The classic backup catcher, Lenny Webster shared time with Darrin Fletcher last year and contributed 17 RBI in 174 at-bats. He also saw a number of at-bats as a pinch hitter because the Expos carried three catchers during much of the season.

Hitting, Baserunning & Defense

Webster can hit fastballs and will occasionally surprise with his power if he gets a pitch up and over the plate. He has trouble with offspeed pitches but has good patience for a hitter who gets limited playing time. He is an adequate receiver and a good handler of pitchers, and though he doesn't have a strong arm, he has shown some improvement in his throwing mechanics, gunning down 38 percent of opposing basestealers last season. Webster is a below-average runner who is not a threat to do much on the bases.

1997 Outlook

Webster faces an annual battle to earn another year in the majors. Besides being a good role player and a positive influence in the clubhouse, he does a solid job catching for short periods of time. He should still be of value to some club.

Other Montreal Expos

Tavo Alvarez (Pos: RHP, Age: 25)

	W	L	Pct.	ERA	G	GS	Sv	IP	H	BB	SO	HR	BR/IP
1996	2	1	.667	3.00	11	5	0	21.0	19	12	9	0	1.48
Career	3	6	.333	5.40	19	13	0	58.1	65	26	26	2	1.56

Alvarez started and finished the season with the Expos, spending most of the year in the minors. Effective as a middle reliever, his strikeout/walk ratio is worrisome. 1997 Outlook: B

Derek Aucoin (Pos: RHP, Age: 27)

	W	L	Pct.	ERA	G	GS	Sv	IP	H	BB	SO	HR	BR/IP
1996	0	1	.000	3.38	2	0	0	2.2	3	1	1	0	1.50
Career	0	1	.000	3.38	2	0	0	2.2	3	1	1	0	1.50

Aucoin appeared in two games in May before spending the rest of the season at Triple-A Ottawa. His control was horrible, as he walked 53 batters in only 75 innings in the minors. 1997 Outlook: C

Tony Barron (Pos: 3B, Age: 30, Bats: R)

	G	AB	R	H	D	T	HR	RBI	SB	BB	SO	Avg	OBP	Slg
1996	1	1	0	0	0	0	0	0	0	0	1	.000	.000	.000
Career	1	1	0	0	0	0	0	0	0	0	1	.000	.000	.000

Despite posting excellent numbers throughout his career in the minors, Barron has never gotten significant playing time with any big-league club. He was signed by Philadelphia in November. 1997 Outlook: C

Raul Chavez (Pos: C, Age: 24, Bats: R)

	G	AB	R	H	D	T	HR	RBI	SB	BB	SO	Avg	OBP	Slg
1996	3	5	1	1	0	0	0	0	1	1	1	.200	.333	.200
Career	3	5	1	1	0	0	0	0	1	1	1	.200	.333	.200

Chavez spent September with the Expos, receiving very limited action as a backup catcher. He has struggled with the bat in the minors, but at 24, still has a shot to develop. 1997 Outlook: C

John Habyan (Pos: RHP, Age: 33)

	W	L	Pct.	ERA	G	GS	Sv	IP	H	BB	SO	HR	BR/IP
1996	1	1	.500	7.13	19	0	0	24.0	34	14	25	4	2.00
Career	26	24	.520	3.85	348	18	12	532.1	537	186	372	47	1.36

Habyan was signed to a minor league contract with the Expos' organization after becoming another pitching victim of Colorado's Coors Field. At 33, his days in the majors are probably finished. 1997 Outlook: D

Dave Leiper (Pos: LHP, Age: 34)

	W	L	Pct.	ERA	G	GS	Sv	IP	H	BB	SO	HR	BR/IP
1996	2	1	.667	7.20	33	0	0	25.0	40	9	13	4	1.96
Career	12	8	.600	3.98	264	0	7	278.0	282	114	150	25	1.42

Leiper was picked up by Montreal after being waived by the Phillies in June. He was shelled in September and was not offered another contract. His career is in trouble. 1997 Outlook: D

Rob Lukachyk (Pos: C, Age: 28, Bats: L)

	G	AB	R	H	D	T	HR	RBI	SB	BB	SO	Avg	OBP	Slg
1996	2	2	0	0	0	0	0	0	0	0	1	.000	.000	.000
Career	2	2	0	0	0	0	0	0	0	0	1	.000	.000	.000

Lukachyk spent most of last season at Triple-A Ottawa, receiving two pinch hit at-bats in July with the Expos. His age and lack of plate discipline will prevent him from having a big-league career. 1997 Outlook: C

Alex Pacheco (Pos: RHP, Age: 23)

	W	L	Pct.	ERA	G	GS	Sv	IP	H	BB	SO	HR	BR/IP
1996	0	0	-	11.12	5	0	0	5.2	8	1	7	2	1.59
Career	0	0	-	11.12	5	0	0	5.2	8	1	7	2	1.59

Montreal gave Pacheco three looks last season, none of which lasted longer than five days. He was hammered all year long, but he's young and strikes people out, so development is possible. 1997 Outlook: C

Rick Schu (Pos: 3B, Age: 35, Bats: R)

	G	AB	R	H	D	T	HR	RBI	SB	BB	SO	Avg	OBP	Slg
1996	1	4	0	0	0	0	0	0	0	0	0	.000	.000	.000
Career	580	1568	189	386	67	13	41	134	17	139	282	.246	.310	.384

A 35-year-old minor leaguer, Schu saw his first action in the majors in five years when he made an August appearance last season. He's not likely to last too much longer. 1997 Outlook: D

Tim Spehr (Pos: C, Age: 30, Bats: R)

	G	AB	R	H	D	T	HR	RBI	SB	BB	SO	Avg	OBP	Slg
1996	63	44	4	4	1	0	1	3	1	3	15	.091	.167	.182
Career	246	276	37	56	20	1	7	35	6	28	71	.203	.281	.359

After battling cancer in '95 and breaking his wrist in spring training, Spehr spent last season as the Expos' emergency catcher. He was horrendous at the plate, and his career is in jeopardy. 1997 Outlook: C

Andy Stankiewicz (Pos: 2B/SS, Age: 32, Bats: R)

	G	AB	R	H	D	T	HR	RBI	SB	BB	SO	Avg	OBP	Slg
1996	64	77	12	22	5	1	0	9	1	6	12	.286	.356	.377
Career	276	592	85	149	31	3	3	46	15	69	86	.252	.338	.329

Montreal's utility infielder last season, Stankiewicz had a good year with the bat in a limited role. His versatility and solid hitting performance should secure a job for him this year. 1997 Outlook: A

Montreal Expos Minor League Prospects

Organization Overview:

The game's economics have trapped the Montreal Expos in a perpetual rebuilding cycle, but their relentlessly productive farm system keeps bailing them out. In recent years, there have been concerns that the minor league talent was wearing thin, but the system redeemed itself once again last year. Rookies F.P. Santangelo and Ugueth Urbina graduated to the majors with flying colors, and down on the farm, Vladimir Guerrero emerged as perhaps the best prospect in the game. The Expos still have quality prospects at every position, at every level. In addition, the Expos have an excellent development record. Whether it's limiting their pitchers to reasonable workloads, allowing their players to advance through the system at their own pace, or providing quality instruction, the Expos seem to get more out of what they have than just about any other organization.

Yamil Benitez

Position: OF   **Opening Day Age:** 24
Bats: R **Throws:** R   **Born:** 10/5/72 in San
Ht: 6' 2" **Wt:** 180   Juan, PR

Recent Statistics

	G	AB	R	H	D	T	HR	RBI	SB	BB	SO	AVG
96 AAA Ottawa	114	439	56	122	20	2	23	81	11	28	120	.278
96 NL Montreal	11	12	0	2	0	0	0	2	0	0	4	.167
96 MLE	114	421	43	104	18	1	16	63	8	22	125	.247

Yamil Benitez has decent power and speed, but that may not be enough to enable him to break into the Expos' outfield. He's getting up in years, and his second season at Triple-A didn't bring the improvement that had been expected. Benitez still swings at too many bad pitches, and as a corner outfielder, his middling power and unimpressive average don't quite make up for his inability to draw walks. He's got fairly good speed, plays decent defense, and has a very strong arm, but the Expos may be losing interest in him.

Vladimir Guerrero

Position: OF   **Opening Day Age:** 21
Bats: R **Throws:** R   **Born:** 2/9/76 in Nizao
Ht: 6' 2" **Wt:** 158   Bani, DR

Recent Statistics

	G	AB	R	H	D	T	HR	RBI	SB	BB	SO	AVG
96 A W. Palm Bch	20	80	16	29	8	0	5	18	2	3	10	.363
96 AA Harrisburg	118	417	84	150	32	8	19	78	17	51	42	.360
96 NL Montreal	9	27	2	5	0	0	1	1	0	0	3	.185
96 MLE	118	398	67	131	30	5	13	62	12	35	44	.329

Yes, he really *is* that good. At the age of 20, Vlad Guerrero found that even Double-A baseball was unable to offer him a sufficient challenge. Let's quickly run through the five "tools." Hitting: he batted .360, the highest average in all of Double-A and Triple-A, and

was named the Eastern League's top hitting prospect. Power: for the season, he had 72 extra-base hits and only 52 strikeouts. He was named the top power prospect in the league. Speed: he stole 19 bases, hit eight triples, and scored 100 runs. Defense: he was named the best defensive outfielder in the league—and he played *right field*. Think about that. Throwing arm: you have to ask? Best in the league. If he plays regularly in the majors next year, he's an excellent bet to hit over .300, and he'll probably reach the 20-homer level sometime in the next couple of years. Next to Andruw Jones, he's the best.

Jose Paniagua

Position: P   **Opening Day Age:** 23
Bats: R **Throws:** R   **Born:** 8/20/73 in San
Ht: 6' 1" **Wt:** 160   Jose De Ocoa, DR

Recent Statistics

	W	L	ERA	G	GS	Sv	IP	H	R	BB	SO	HR
96 AA Harrisburg	3	0	0.00	3	3	0	18.0	12	1	2	16	0
96 AAA Ottawa	9	5	3.18	15	14	0	85.0	72	39	23	61	7
96 NL Montreal	2	4	3.53	13	11	0	51.0	55	24	23	27	7

Hard-throwing righthander Jose Paniagua was so impressive last spring that he began the year in the Expos rotation. That didn't last, but back in the minors, he showed much-improved command, and pitched well in seven late-season starts after Montreal called him back up. If he really has found the strike zone, his low-90s fastball and hard-biting slider could make him one of the better young pitchers in the league. Under Felipe Alou's careful watch, he should continue to progress.

Jon Saffer

Position: OF   **Opening Day Age:** 23
Bats: L **Throws:** R   **Born:** 7/6/73 in
Ht: 6' 2" **Wt:** 200   Ingelwood, CA

Recent Statistics

	G	AB	R	H	D	T	HR	RBI	SB	BB	SO	AVG
93 A W. Palm Bch	7	24	3	5	0	0	0	2	1	2	5	.208
93 A Jamestown	61	225	31	58	17	5	0	18	11	31	46	.258
94 A Vermont	70	263	44	83	18	5	3	43	14	33	47	.316
95 A W. Palm Bch	92	324	60	103	10	6	4	35	18	53	49	.318
95 AA Harrisburg	20	76	9	18	4	0	0	4	2	6	14	.237
96 AA Harrisburg	134	487	96	146	26	4	10	52	8	78	77	.300
96 MLE	134	472	77	131	24	2	7	41	5	55	82	.278

Jon Saffer has a future in the majors, because he's a left-handed hitter who makes great contact and gets on base. His speed, power, and defense in left field are not strengths, so it's highly unlikely that he'll ever be a regular. Still, he'd be an excellent pinch hitter, or maybe even a platoon player, given the right situation. He's ready to hit major league pitching, and at age 23, he may get even better. Felipe Alou likes his bench players to be able to play defense, however, so Saffer may have to go elsewhere to make it.

Everett Stull

Position: P **Opening Day Age:** 25
Bats: R **Throws:** R **Born:** 8/24/71 in Fort
Ht: 6' 3" **Wt:** 195 Riley, GA

Recent Statistics

	W	L	ERA	G	GS	Sv	IP	H	R	BB	SO	HR
93 A Burlington	4	9	3.83	15	15	0	82.1	68	44	59	85	8
94 A W. Palm Bch	10	10	3.31	27	26	0	147.0	116	60	78	165	3
95 AA Harrisburg	3	12	5.54	24	24	0	126.2	114	88	79	132	12
96 AA Harrisburg	6	3	3.15	14	14	0	80.0	64	31	52	81	8
96 AAA Ottawa	2	6	6.33	13	13	0	69.2	87	57	39	69	7

Everett Stull has a mid-90s fastball, a great curve, and, unfortunately, no command. At times, he seems to be on the verge of making a major breakthrough, but at other times, he works from behind and gets pounded mercilessly. The Expos know they will have to be patient with him, but they're willing to do that because of his tremendous upside. He had much more success in his second try at Double-A last year, but fell apart at Triple-A. Perhaps all he needs is a second tour around that league, too.

Jose Vidro

Position: 3B **Opening Day Age:** 22
Bats: B **Throws:** R **Born:** 8/27/74 in
Ht: 5' 11" **Wt:** 175 Mayaguez, PR

Recent Statistics

	G	AB	R	H	D	T	HR	RBI	SB	BB	SO	AVG
93 A Burlington	76	287	39	69	19	0	2	34	3	28	54	.240
94 A W. Palm Bch	125	465	57	124	30	2	4	49	8	51	56	.267
95 AA Harrisburg	64	246	33	64	16	2	4	38	3	20	37	.260
95 A W. Palm Bch	44	163	20	53	15	2	3	24	0	8	21	.325
96 AA Harrisburg	126	452	57	117	25	3	18	82	3	29	71	.259
96 MLE	126	438	45	103	25	2	13	66	2	20	76	.235

Jose Vidro has good tools, but in a very unusual sense—he's got *quantity*, rather than quality. He's a fairly good defender at both second and third base, he can hit for a fairly decent average, and he's developed some extra-base power. He doesn't have much foot speed or patience at the plate, but with a little improvement in a few areas, he can make it on what he's got.

Matt Wagner

Position: P **Opening Day Age:** 24
Bats: R **Throws:** R **Born:** 4/4/72 in Cedar
Ht: 6' 5" **Wt:** 215 Falls, IA

Recent Statistics

	W	L	ERA	G	GS	Sv	IP	H	R	BB	SO	HR
96 AAA Tacoma	9	2	2.41	15	15	0	93.1	89	30	30	82	8
96 AL Seattle	3	5	6.86	15	14	0	80.0	91	62	38	41	15

Righthander Matt Wagner also came over from the Mariners in the Fassero deal. He had been the M's top pitching prospect, but he experienced a rocky introduction to the majors in 14 starts last year. He pitched brilliantly at Triple-A, but seemed much more tentative in the majors. Wagner throws a low-90s fastball that was said to be the best in the Seattle system. He's had trouble finding a solid number-two pitch to go with it, but the Expos have an excellent track record working with struggling pitchers. Wagner may find moderate success in the Expos' rotation this year.

Chris Widger

Position: C **Opening Day Age:** 25
Bats: R **Throws:** R **Born:** 5/21/71 in
Ht: 6' 3" **Wt:** 195 Wilmington, DE

Recent Statistics

	G	AB	R	H	D	T	HR	RBI	SB	BB	SO	AVG
96 AAA Tacoma	97	352	42	107	20	2	13	48	7	27	62	.304
96 AL Seattle	8	11	1	2	0	0	0	0	0	0	5	.182
96 MLE	97	347	39	102	20	1	12	44	5	25	67	.294

The Expos knew that Chris Widger was the best catcher in baseball without a major league job, so they got him from Seattle as part of a package for Jeff Fassero. He'll see significant playing time in Montreal this year, and his production may be a pleasant surprise even to the Expos' brass. In addition to being a respected pitch-caller and strong thrower, Widger is also capable of hitting for both power and average. The expectations of a future 20-homer season are not unrealistic. He may be one of the better catchers in the league this year.

Others to Watch

Former second-round pick **Brad Fullmer** played his second full season after undergoing major surgery on his throwing shoulder. Now a first baseman, the left-handed hitter batted over .300 at Class A, rarely struck out, and wasn't fazed by a late-season promotion to Double-A. Scouts expect him to start turning some of his doubles into homers soon. . . After he batted .333 at Double-A in '95, the Expos snagged first baseman **Ryan McGuire** in the Wil Cordero deal. McGuire, however, suffered through a difficult season at Triple-A. He seemed to be trying to hit more home runs. While he did go deep slightly more often, his strikeouts shot up and his average plummeted 76 points. . . **Tom Phelps** is one of those lefties who doesn't do anything special except win. He went 12-4 between two levels and will open the season at Double-A. . . Lefthander **Neil Weber** throws a lot harder, and he finally found the plate in his second season at the Double-A level. He'll need to prove he's healthy after missing the second half with shoulder tendinitis. . . Former first-round pick **Hiram Bocachica** was limited to DH duties by a sore elbow. After a tremendous first half, he was forced to undergo surgery. He will remain one of their top prospects, even if the injury ends his days as a shortstop. . . The Expos took high school shortstop **Michael Barrett** in the first round of the '95 draft. Last year, they made the courageous decision to convert him into a catcher. It's too early to tell if he'll be able to master the subtleties of the position, but his power potential is still evident.

Bobby Valentine

1996 Season

Bobby Valentine is a player's manager. He brings a playful enthusiasm, appreciates youngsters, and likes defined roles with players knowing where they stand. "I can make a move that surprises writers, but I cannot surprise my players." With only a few weeks to evaluate talent in 1996, Valentine was highly experimental, giving chances to newcomers like Jason Hardtke, Matt Franco and Alberto Castillo, and testing various relievers. Winning was not his main objective, but he showed a low tolerance for anyone not giving 100 percent.

Offense

Valentine diminished the running game when he arrived, not wanting to give away any outs. He will run to stay out of the double play. Valentine isn't enamored with platooning, but his overlapping personnel often required it. He made many substitutions while experimenting in 1996. The flurry of in-game moves will not be so frequent in the future.

Pitching & Defense

With an injury-riddled and tired starting rotation, Valentine was quick to use his bullpen—even though his relievers were struggling, too. Valentine believes that in the National League, with lower scores, the real "save" may come in an eighth-inning situation. He will use John Franco early for that reason, and may let another pitcher work the ninth and get the statistical save. Valentine often had players out of their natural positions, but that was for testing purposes, not to de-emphasize defense.

1997 Outlook

Valentine managed most of the Mets' young players at Triple-A Norfolk. There will be a pronounced youth movement in New York in 1997, featuring players like outfielders Alex Ochoa and Jay Payton, infielder Edgardo Alfonzo and reliever Derek Wallace. The experimenting will come to an end at Port St. Lucie in March, however, as Valentine will be expected to field a winning team on Opening Day.

Born: 5/13/50 in Stamford, CT

Playing Experience: 1969-1979, LA, Cal, SD, NYN, Sea

Managerial Experience: 9 seasons

Manager Statistics

Year	Team, Lg	W	L	Pct	GB	Finish
1996	New York, NL	12	19	.387	25.0	4th East
9 Seasons		593	624	.487	—	—

1996 Starting Pitchers by Days Rest

	≤3	4	5	6+
Mets Starts	0	12	13	6
Mets ERA	0.00	2.67	3.15	3.27
NL Avg Starts	4	86	41	21
NL ERA	4.06	4.28	4.23	4.58

1996 Situational Stats

	Bobby Valentine*	NL Average
Hit & Run Success %	36.0	39.0
Stolen Base Success %	40.0	71.6
Platoon Pct.	63.4	51.9
Defensive Subs	3	20
High-Pitch Outings	0	13
Quick/Slow Hooks	6/0	19/12
Sacrifice Attempts	25	92

* Valentine managed the Mets for 31 games

1996 Rankings (National League)
➡ Did not rank near the top in any category

Edgardo Alfonzo

1996 Season

In early 1995 the Mets had a plan to use Edgardo Alfonzo as a utility infielder for one year, and then play him at second base alongside Rey Ordonez in 1996. That career path took a detour when Jose Vizcaino hit so well in 1995 that management decided to keep him in a full-time role. Vizcaino, not Alfonzo, played second base when Ordonez began his major league career. The trade of Vizcaino to Cleveland on July 29th finally opened the door for Alfonzo, who became a regular in August. He hit .352 in September.

Hitting

Alfonzo is a rare talent, of whom much is expected. He is young to be a major league regular, but extensive experience in winter ball has matured him. Alfonzo is an aggressive swinger who can pull a pitch or go the other way. He uses all fields and is developing home run power against righties and lefties alike. One aspect requiring improvement is patience; although he usually makes contact, Alfonzo needs to take more pitches and draw more walks.

Baserunning & Defense

Alfonzo once got 26 steals in a minor league season. He is alert when running and is always a threat to take an extra base. A shortstop in the minors before Ordonez emerged, Alfonzo has the ability to play all three infield skill positions. He already has above-average range at second base, and is improving his positioning as he learns the league's hitters better. His arm is clearly superior for second base, his most likely position.

1997 Outlook

When he played Double-A ball at age 20, Alfonzo drew comparisons to Ryne Sandberg, for steady defense and a combination of power and speed on offense. After a quiet year in 1996, Alfonzo is poised for one of the big breakout performances of 1997.

Position: 2B/3B/SS
Bats: R **Throws:** R
Ht: 5'11" **Wt:** 187

Opening Day Age: 23
Born: 11/8/73 in St. Teresa, VZ
ML Seasons: 2

Overall Statistics

	G	AB	R	H	D	T	HR	RBI	SB	BB	SO	Avg	OBP	Slg
1996	123	368	36	96	15	2	4	40	2	25	56	.261	.304	.345
Career	224	703	62	189	28	7	8	81	3	37	93	.269	.303	.363

Where He Hits the Ball

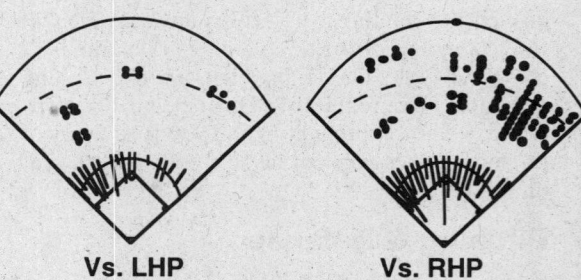

Vs. LHP   **Vs. RHP**

1996 Situational Stats

	AB	H	HR	RBI	Avg		AB	H	HR	RBI	Avg
Home	182	47	2	18	.258	LHP	89	23	1	13	.258
Road	186	49	2	22	.263	RHP	279	73	3	27	.262
First Half	132	34	0	8	.258	Sc Pos	99	24	1	36	.242
Scnd Half	236	62	4	32	.263	Clutch	73	16	0	8	.219

1996 Rankings (National League)

➡ 10th in errors at second base (8)
➡ Led the Mets in batting average with the bases loaded (.333)

Carlos Baerga

1996 Season

When the Mets acquired former All-Star second baseman Carlos Baerga in trade on July 29th, the deal looked like a coup for New York. Baerga never got it going with the Mets, however. A pulled abdominal muscle left him unable to play the field or run the bases. After slumping to a .182 batting average in August, Baerga got only seven at-bats in September. Management disappointment was no secret.

Hitting

When healthy, Baerga is an offensive terror, especially for a second baseman. Before coming to New York he had hit over .300 four years in a row, and topped 20 homers and 100 RBI two of those four years. Baerga hits well from both sides of the plate, with pull-hitter power against southpaws and straightaway home run power against righties. He does swing at too many pitches, especially high fastballs, but he is capable of getting more walks than strikeouts, as he did in 1995.

Baserunning & Defense

When healthy Baerga has good speed. He reached double-digit steals three of the four years 1992-1995. He is always a threat to take an extra base. Poor defense was a major reason why the Indians unloaded Baerga, but he didn't play badly for the Mets. His range is about average, and his throwing arm is superior for second base. He can play the other infield positions in a pinch.

1997 Outlook

At an age when he should be having his prime seasons, Baerga has been affected by nagging injuries from his hands to his feet (and some parts in between). Weight control and conditioning have been points of contention with management at times, even before he left Cleveland. There is massive talent inside Baerga, however, ready to come out when he's right. Another All-Star appearance might be a stretch for 1997, but he can be an offensive force in the middle infield.

Position: 2B/1B
Bats: B **Throws:** R
Ht: 5'11" **Wt:** 200

Opening Day Age: 28
Born: 11/4/68 in San Juan, PR
ML Seasons: 7
Pronunciation: by-AIR-ga

New York Mets

Overall Statistics

	G	AB	R	H	D	T	HR	RBI	SB	BB	SO	Avg	OBP	Slg
1996	126	507	59	129	28	0	12	66	1	21	27	.254	.293	.381
Career	945	3692	550	1100	193	15	105	571	48	199	378	.298	.338	.444

Where He Hits the Ball

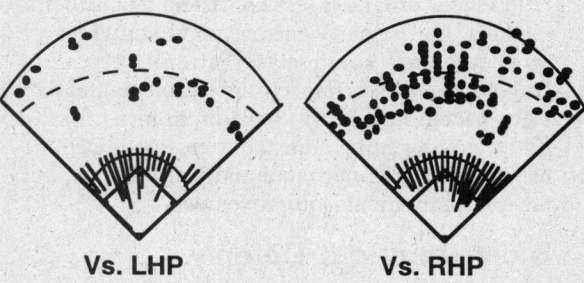

Vs. LHP   **Vs. RHP**

1996 Situational Stats

	AB	H	HR	RBI	Avg		AB	H	HR	RBI	Avg
Home	233	64	5	37	.275	LHP	123	27	0	12	.220
Road	274	65	7	29	.237	RHP	384	102	12	54	.266
First Half	365	94	9	50	.258	Sc Pos	155	35	0	49	.226
Scnd Half	142	35	3	16	.246	Clutch	73	15	1	5	.205

1996 Rankings (National League)

➡ Did not rank near the top or bottom in any category

Rico Brogna

1996 Season

Rico Brogna's season ended with shoulder surgery on June 21st. He was on a pace for a 20-homer, 90-RBI season building on his rookie and sophomore campaigns of 1994-1995. The Mets lost a first baseman, and Brogna lost a year to injury.

Hitting

After leaving the Tigers and joining the Mets three years ago, Brogna became a whole new player at the plate. He stopped trying to pull everything and showed that he can hit righty pitching with authority by using the whole field. He can go with an outside pitch or pull inside offerings over the right field fence. Brogna is less consistent against lefty pitchers, but he can generate good straightaway power against southpaws. Patient by nature, Brogna has pushed himself to be more aggressive since becoming a heart-of-the-order hitter for the Mets. While getting adjusted to this approach, he has been striking out more and walking less, but the long-term trend is improvement.

Baserunning & Defense

A slow runner, Brogna has only one stolen base in his career with New York. He isn't much of a threat to take an extra base, either. He does, however, shine on defense, with soft, sure hands that keep errors to a minimum—both Brogna's and those of the infielders he helps with his catches and scoops. He moves quickly around the bag and turns double plays well.

1997 Outlook

The Mets were reasonably happy with Brogna's work, but they had a surplus of players who were capable of playing first base. As a result, they traded Brogna to the Phillies after the season. The Phils envision him as their full-time first baseman, but he'll need to show he can handle lefties. . . and he'll need to stay healthy.

Position: 1B
Bats: L **Throws:** L
Ht: 6' 2" **Wt:** 205

Opening Day Age: 26
Born: 4/18/70 in Turner Falls, MA
ML Seasons: 4
Pronunciation: BRONE-yuh

Overall Statistics

	G	AB	R	H	D	T	HR	RBI	SB	BB	SO	Avg	OBP	Slg
1996	55	188	18	48	10	1	7	30	0	19	50	.255	.318	.431
Career	237	840	109	242	49	5	37	129	1	67	195	.288	.340	.490

Where He Hits the Ball

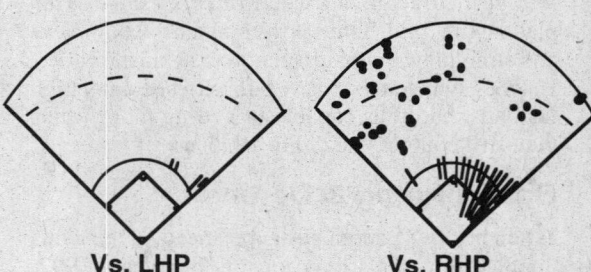

Vs. LHP   **Vs. RHP**

1996 Situational Stats

	AB	H	HR	RBI	Avg		AB	H	HR	RBI	Avg
Home	81	24	5	14	.296	LHP	32	4	0	3	.125
Road	107	24	2	16	.224	RHP	156	44	7	27	.282
First Half	188	48	7	30	.255	Sc Pos	44	12	0	20	.273
Scnd Half	0	0	0	0	-	Clutch	37	8	1	6	.216

1996 Rankings (National League)

➡ Did not rank near the top or bottom in any category

Mark Clark

1996 Season

Former Indian righthander Mark Clark joined the Mets at the end of spring training, and was expected to provide depth for their starting rotation. Clark did not figure as a prominent starter, and he would have found himself in the bullpen if Bobby Jones, Jason Isringhausen, Pete Harnisch, Paul Wilson and Bill Pulsipher had ever been healthy and productive at the same time; but that day never came. Clark not only stayed in the rotation, he emerged as the staff ace as the season unfolded.

Pitching

Clark has a good major league fastball with mid- to high-80s velocity and natural sink, but he does not blow hitters away. He succeeds by spotting the sinker and mixing in his slider, splitter and straight change. It is important for him to keep the ball down and stay ahead in the count. On a good day he gets many groundball outs. In tough situations, Clark can reach back for something extra and throw a four-seam fastball to get a strikeout or pop-up, but that's not his usual approach.

Defense & Hitting

A defensive asset, Clark helps himself by helping his infielders. He picks up grounders adeptly and gets over to first quickly. He has not made an error in over three years. Paying close attention to runners, Clark keeps them honest. He cut his number of steals allowed from 19 in 1995 to 12 in 1996. He is a weak hitter who strikes out 40 percent of the time.

1997 Outlook

After his strong performance anchoring an injury-riddled staff, Clark will go to spring training with a much bigger role than the swing man or fifth starter he was just a year ago. Clark has survived two trades, a broken wrist and a trip to the minors on his way to becoming a solid starter, but he has made it.

Position: SP
Bats: R **Throws:** R
Ht: 6' 5" **Wt:** 225

Opening Day Age: 28
Born: 5/12/68 in Bath, IL
ML Seasons: 6

New York Mets

Overall Statistics

	W	L	Pct.	ERA	G	GS	Sv	IP	H	BB	SO	HR	BR/IP
1996	14	11	.560	3.43	32	32	0	212.1	217	48	142	20	1.25
Career	45	37	.549	4.14	127	110	0	709.1	746	202	384	80	1.34

How Often He Throws Strikes

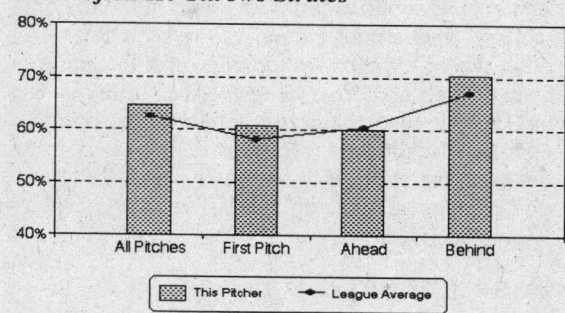

1996 Situational Stats

	W	L	ERA	Sv	IP		AB	H	HR	RBI	Avg
Home	6	6	3.19	0	104.1	LHB	368	102	10	43	.277
Road	8	5	3.67	0	108.0	RHB	452	115	10	36	.254
First Half	8	6	3.04	0	118.1	Sc Pos	160	38	2	53	.238
Scnd Half	6	5	3.93	0	94.0	Clutch	43	14	3	6	.326

1996 Rankings (National League)

→ 1st in fielding percentage at pitcher (1.000)
→ 3rd in GDPs induced (24) and highest stolen base percentage allowed (85.7%)
→ 5th in least pitches thrown per batter (3.47)
→ 6th in most GDPs induced per 9 innings (1.0) and most GDPs induced per GDP situation (18.3%)
→ 10th in most run support per 9 innings (5.4)
→ Led the Mets in sacrifice bunts (10), ERA, wins, games started, innings pitched, batters faced (883), strikeouts, pitches thrown (3,062), GDPs induced (24), highest strikeout/walk ratio (3.0), lowest on-base percentage allowed (.306) and least pitches thrown per batter (3.47)

Alvaro Espinoza

1996 Season

Veteran utility infielder Alvaro Espinoza came to New York from the Indians with Carlos Baerga on July 29th. At the time of the deal he looked like a throw-in, but when Baerga became sidelined, Espinoza emerged as the Mets' regular third baseman. He did well at the plate, too, having fun with pitchers who threw him too many fastballs down the middle. Overall it was a big boost for Espinoza to move from Cleveland to New York.

Hitting

It helped Espinoza to be reunited, even briefly, with coach Frank Howard in New York. Howard had taught Espinoza how to hit when he got his first shot at significant playing time in the majors in 1989. The key for Espinoza is to go with every pitch where it's thrown, looking for a fastball he can see well and drive. He generates little power but can hit line drives to all fields. The correct approach for pitchers is to show Espinoza nothing but breaking stuff away and fastballs in. The National Leaguers apparently didn't know that when Espinoza arrived.

Baserunning & Defense

A shortstop when he was in the minors, Espinoza can play all three infield skill positions, but his range is deficient at all three, and his arm is just average. Espinoza's major strength is his versatility. He is not a good enough defender to hold any job full-time. On the bases, he is quite slow for a middle infielder, but he is unusually alert and will take advantage of any lackadaisical fielding.

1997 Outlook

It is unlikely that Espinoza will ever again play as frequently as he did for the Mets in late 1996. He is, however, a useful utility player and pinch hitter and a good person for a clubhouse. He could hang around the majors for a few more years in these supporting roles. A free agent, he re-signed with the Mets after the season.

Position: 3B/1B/SS
Bats: R **Throws:** R
Ht: 6' 0" **Wt:** 190

Opening Day Age: 35
Born: 2/19/62 in Valencia, VZ
ML Seasons: 11

Overall Statistics

	G	AB	R	H	D	T	HR	RBI	SB	BB	SO	Avg	OBP	Slg
1996	107	246	31	66	11	4	8	27	1	10	37	.268	.303	.443
Career	909	2406	249	617	104	9	22	194	12	74	312	.256	.281	.335

Where He Hits the Ball

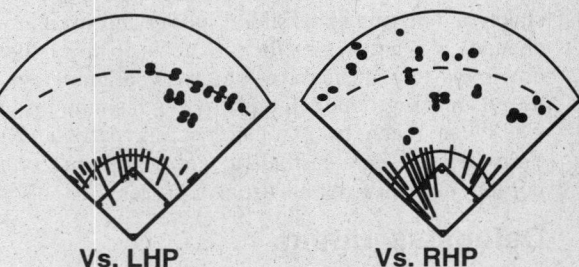

Vs. LHP   **Vs. RHP**

1996 Situational Stats

	AB	H	HR	RBI	Avg		AB	H	HR	RBI	Avg
Home	95	28	3	12	.295	LHP	82	22	4	12	.268
Road	151	38	5	15	.252	RHP	164	44	4	15	.268
First Half	75	18	2	6	.240	Sc Pos	59	13	1	17	.220
Scnd Half	171	48	6	21	.281	Clutch	48	12	2	6	.250

1996 Rankings (National League)

➡ Did not rank near the top or bottom in any category

Carl Everett

1996 Season

Carl Everett went to spring training last year as the Mets' starting right fielder. But he had a rough time in the Grapefruit League, looking helpless against lefty change-up artists like Steve Avery and Jimmy Key. While Everett was tying himself in knots at the plate, Butch Huskey was busy working on his "Roy Hobbs" impersonation in spring training. By Opening Day, Huskey was the right fielder. Later when Huskey moved to first base and Alex Ochoa came up, Everett sat and watched some more.

Hitting

Everett is a good hitter who just never quite found himself in 1996. He has patience, both in terms of drawing walks and working the count. Everett generates power from both sides of the plate. When he does catch a southpaw's fastball, it is likely to fly over the left field fence. Everett showed his potential in July, when he hit .500 coming off the bench.

Baserunning & Defense

Everett has fine speed and baserunning ability. He was six-for-six in steal attempts last year, and has twice exceeded 20 steals in the minors. In right field, Everett has a cannon arm. One of the mysteries of 1996 was how the Mets could keep one of the league's best right fielders out of their lineup. Everett did appear frequently as a defensive replacement.

1997 Outlook

When the Yankees lost their 1990 first-round pick in the expansion draft, spectators gasped and GM Gene Michael blushed. Everett never matured with the Marlins, and now he is taking his time with the Mets. For raw talent there hasn't been a better right field prospect in recent years; for opportunity, Everett has been as limited as anyone. One good sign was that new manager Bobby Valentine took a long look in September, to form his own opinion.

Position: RF/CF
Bats: B **Throws:** R
Ht: 6' 0" **Wt:** 190

Opening Day Age: 25
Born: 6/3/71 in Tampa, FL
ML Seasons: 4

Overall Statistics

	G	AB	R	H	D	T	HR	RBI	SB	BB	SO	Avg	OBP	Slg
1996	101	192	29	46	8	1	1	16	6	21	53	.240	.326	.307
Career	207	551	84	134	22	2	15	76	13	64	144	.243	.328	.372

Where He Hits the Ball

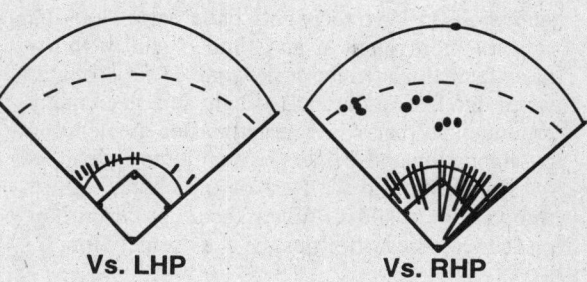

Vs. LHP   **Vs. RHP**

1996 Situational Stats

	AB	H	HR	RBI	Avg		AB	H	HR	RBI	Avg
Home	84	25	1	6	.298	LHP	36	9	0	5	.250
Road	108	21	0	10	.194	RHP	156	37	1	11	.237
First Half	76	14	0	5	.184	Sc Pos	53	10	0	15	.189
Scnd Half	116	32	1	11	.276	Clutch	62	15	0	8	.242

1996 Rankings (National League)

→ 1st in batting average on a 3-1 count (1.000)
→ 7th in batting average on a 3-2 count (.389)
→ 8th in errors in right field (5)
→ 9th in lowest batting average on an 0-2 count (.043)
→ 10th in lowest batting average with two strikes (.132)
→ Led the Mets in hit by pitch (4), batting average on a 3-1 count (1.000) and batting average on a 3-2 count (.389)

John Franco

1996 Season

For any pitcher except all-time lefty saves leader John Franco, 1996 would have been a great season. Franco was satisfied but not delighted. The casual observer sees 28 saves and an ERA under 2.00, but behind those numbers there were eight save opportunities missed, a hit per inning yielded for the first time since an elbow injury ruined his 1993 season, and one of the highest ratio of walks per inning in any year since Franco joined the Mets in 1990.

Pitching

Franco has been tough on righty and lefty batters alike, using a fadeaway change-up which flutters so much that right-handed batters have called it a screwball. In 1996 the righty batters tried looking at a lot more pitches, and Franco had to throw more fastballs up in the strike zone. He is strongest when he keeps the ball down and gets many grounders. Franco is a grandmaster at blending pitch location and fielder positioning to get batters out. In addition to the fastball and change-up, he throws a lot of sliders. When the umps call strikes on Franco's low offerings, he is extremely tough.

Defense & Hitting

Always adept, Franco has actually improved as a fielder in recent years. He covers his ground flawlessly and gets over to first quickly. He hasn't made an error since 1991. Franco holds runners very close. He has an excellent pickoff move. Franco almost never comes to bat (just once in 1996) and is an easy out when he does.

1997 Outlook

With 323 career saves, Franco says he would like to continue as an ace reliever until he has 400. The Mets helped him along the path to that career mark by re-signing him on October 18th. Franco may share an occasional save with a righty such as Derek Wallace in 1997, but Franco is still The Man.

Position: RP
Bats: L **Throws:** L
Ht: 5'10" **Wt:** 185

Opening Day Age: 36
Born: 9/17/60 in Brooklyn, NY
ML Seasons: 13

Overall Statistics

	W	L	Pct.	ERA	G	GS	Sv	IP	H	BB	SO	HR	BR/IP
1996	4	3	.571	1.83	51	0	28	54.0	54	21	48	2	1.39
Career	72	57	.558	2.57	712	0	323	876.0	806	336	648	48	1.30

How Often He Throws Strikes

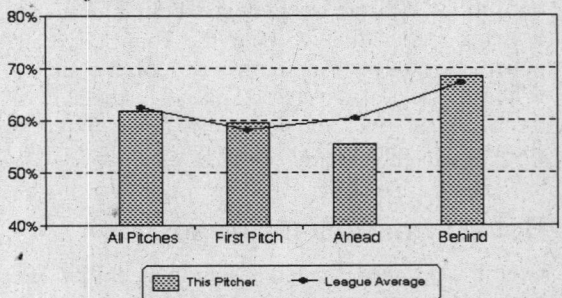

1996 Situational Stats

	W	L	ERA	Sv	IP		AB	H	HR	RBI	Avg
Home	4	1	2.31	16	35.0	LHB	47	7	0	3	.149
Road	0	2	0.95	12	19.0	RHB	161	47	2	20	.292
First Half	2	2	1.88	19	28.2	Sc Pos	68	19	0	21	.279
Scnd Half	2	1	1.78	9	25.1	Clutch	153	41	2	21	.268

1996 Rankings (National League)

- ➡ 2nd in lowest save percentage (77.8%), blown saves (8) and relief ERA (1.83)
- ➡ 6th in worst first batter efficiency (.304)
- ➡ 9th in save opportunities (36)
- ➡ 10th in saves
- ➡ Led the Mets in saves, games finished (44), save opportunities (36), save percentage (77.8%), blown saves (8), relief ERA (1.83), lowest batting average allowed in relief (.260) and least baserunners allowed per 9 innings in relief (12.5)

Bernard Gilkey

1996 Season

Never quite a full-time player with the Cardinals, Bernard Gilkey blossomed when the Mets obtained him and installed him as their number-three hitter last year. He reached career highs in just about every offensive category. Soaring far above his previous peaks in both home runs and walks, he delivered a total offensive package in 1996. Gilkey said he likes hitting in the same place in the batting order every day, and he likes batting third because of the opportunity to contribute RBI.

Hitting

With a more relaxed stance, improved patience, and a more compact swing, Gilkey has matured beautifully into the all-around hitter, both for average and power. He can pull any pitch over the left field wall, or go to right-center with long line-drive power. With good concentration, Gilkey has always been tough in the clutch. He was a good RBI producer even when batting first or second in past years.

Baserunning & Defense

Gilkey has above-average speed, and he is aggressive in all aspects of baserunning. He picks his spots for stolen bases, but he is constantly ready to get a big jump and take an extra base, and he breaks up double plays with enthusiasm. Always above average in the field, Gilkey improved notably in 1996, as he added more range to his left field play, and threw out 18 over-optimistic baserunners.

1997 Outlook

The Mets showed their appreciation for Gilkey's big season by re-signing him in October. By reaching the .300, 30-homer, 100-RBI triple milestone for the first time, Gilkey has made a bid to become one of the top dozen or so offensive players in the National League. A strong second half and a strong September offered signs that the long high peak will continue into 1997.

Position: LF
Bats: R **Throws:** R
Ht: 6' 0" **Wt:** 200

Opening Day Age: 30
Born: 9/24/66 in St. Louis, MO
ML Seasons: 7

Overall Statistics

	G	AB	R	H	D	T	HR	RBI	SB	BB	SO	Avg	OBP	Slg
1996	153	571	108	181	44	3	30	117	17	73	125	.317	.393	.562
Career	746	2704	427	783	170	21	82	367	97	296	416	.290	.362	.459

Where He Hits the Ball

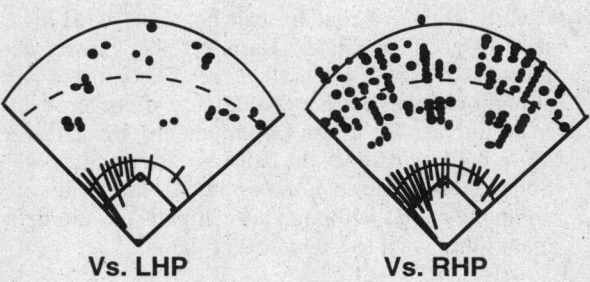

Vs. LHP   **Vs. RHP**

1996 Situational Stats

	AB	H	HR	RBI	Avg		AB	H	HR	RBI	Avg
Home	279	92	14	44	.330	LHP	134	46	7	18	.343
Road	292	89	16	73	.305	RHP	437	135	23	99	.309
First Half	318	96	16	62	.302	Sc Pos	155	63	9	90	.406
Scnd Half	253	85	14	55	.336	Clutch	90	28	6	22	.311

1996 Rankings (National League)

→ 1st in highest percentage of extra bases taken as a runner (74.5%)
→ 2nd in errors in left field (6)
→ 3rd in batting average with runners in scoring position (.406) and fielding percentage in left field (.982)
→ 4th in doubles
→ 5th in lowest stolen base percentage (65.4%)
→ 7th in strikeouts
→ 8th in RBI, sacrifice flies (8), batting average vs. left-handed pitchers (.343), slugging percentage vs. left-handed pitchers (.604) and batting average

Pete Harnisch

1996 Season

Pete Harnisch began last season on the disabled list, recovering from August 1995 shoulder surgery. It was his third trip to the DL in three years for shoulder problems. Harnisch was used cautiously, making only four starts in May and leaving most games before reaching 100 pitches. The careful usage paid off, as he peaked with a complete-game, four-hit shutout of the Pirates on July 29th. Harnisch pitched his steadiest in the final two months of the season, with a 3.86 ERA in August and a 3.13 ERA in September.

Pitching

A direct worker who doesn't nibble, Harnisch still throws his fastball over 90 MPH. His command is usually good, so that he can hit spots with his fastball and hard slider. Harnisch also throws a mid-80s forkball, a curve, a cut fastball and a straight change, but his fastball and slider are his main pitches. He doesn't mind leaving hard stuff up in the strike zone; fly balls are usually outs at Shea Stadium. He seldom has the stamina to pitch complete games, although his competitive attitude makes him want to stay in every game.

Defense & Hitting

Always a solid fielder, Harnisch had more batted balls coming his way in 1996, and ended the year with three errors, a career high, but he also made more assists than he had since 1991. At bat, Harnisch is not an automatic out. He collected five hits in 1996 including one double. He does strike out excessively.

1997 Outlook

With one year left on Harnisch's three-year contract, the Mets hope that he can regain some of the form he showed when he was 16-9 with a 2.98 ERA in 1993. Failing that, they hope he can at least stay healthy all year and fill the role of their number-three starter.

Position: SP
Bats: R **Throws:** R
Ht: 6' 0" **Wt:** 207

Opening Day Age: 30
Born: 9/23/66 in Commack, NY
ML Seasons: 9

Overall Statistics

	W	L	Pct.	ERA	G	GS	Sv	IP	H	BB	SO	HR	BR/IP
1996	8	12	.400	4.21	31	31	0	194.2	195	61	114	30	1.32
Career	71	75	.486	3.79	217	216	0	1345.2	1227	509	981	136	1.29

How Often He Throws Strikes

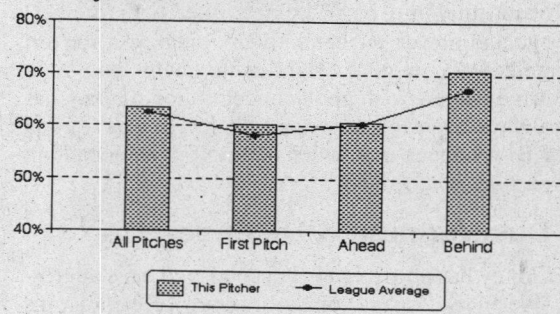

1996 Situational Stats

	W	L	ERA	Sv	IP		AB	H	HR	RBI	Avg
Home	5	6	3.83	0	112.2	LHB	353	97	11	44	.275
Road	3	6	4.72	0	82.0	RHB	396	98	19	51	.247
First Half	4	6	4.72	0	95.1	Sc Pos	167	37	8	64	.222
Scnd Half	4	6	3.71	0	99.1	Clutch	50	13	2	6	.260

1996 Rankings (National League)

- ➡ 1st in lowest groundball/flyball ratio allowed (0.8)
- ➡ 2nd in home runs allowed
- ➡ 3rd in balks (3)
- ➡ 4th in most home runs allowed per 9 innings (1.39) and least GDPs induced per 9 innings (0.5)
- ➡ 6th in highest stolen base percentage allowed (83.3%) and errors at pitcher (3)
- ➡ 8th in least strikeouts per 9 innings (5.3) and highest ERA on the road (4.72)
- ➡ 9th in losses and shutouts (1)
- ➡ Led the Mets in sacrifice bunts (10), shutouts (1), home runs allowed, balks (3) and lowest batting average allowed (.260)

Todd Hundley

Position: C
Bats: B **Throws:** R
Ht: 5'11" **Wt:** 185

Opening Day Age: 27
Born: 5/27/69 in Martinesville, VA
ML Seasons: 7

1996 Season

One of those special athletes who gets to the major leagues at a very young age because of defensive prowess, even without hitting, Todd Hundley has been learning to hit while in the majors. His progress reached a new high level in 1996 as Hundley broke Roy Campanella's all-time record for home runs by a catcher in one season. Hundley would have had an even bigger year, but a sore wrist limited him to three home runs and a .207 batting average during September.

Hitting

Although he has graduated from platooner to regular starter, Hundley still has room for improvement against lefty pitching. There is no visible hole in his swing from either side of the plate, but Hundley generates much less power batting from the right side, enabling lefty pitchers to get away with more mistakes. Overall improvement in batting average and on-base percentage can be expected with increased knowledge of the strike zone.

Baserunning & Defense

An aggressive and intelligent baserunner, Hundley lacks the raw speed to use his knowledge fully. Behind the plate, Hundley handles pitchers well and calls a good game. He has a strong and accurate throwing arm that forces the opposition to pick their spots for stolen bases. Hundley moves well on all plays around the plate. He had career highs in 1996 for putouts and assists, by wide margins.

1997 Outlook

Hundley is one of the key players around whom the Mets are building their team of the future. In 1997 he may share a little of his time with Alberto Castillo, who handled many of the Mets' young pitchers in the minors, and Hundley will take his days of rest when the opposing pitcher is a southpaw. Still, he has achieved status as a regular and now stands alongside Mike Piazza for hitting ability among National League catchers.

Overall Statistics

	G	AB	R	H	D	T	HR	RBI	SB	BB	SO	Avg	OBP	Slg
1996	153	540	85	140	32	1	41	112	1	79	146	.259	.356	.550
Career	644	2008	254	478	93	5	91	299	8	200	453	.238	.311	.425

Where He Hits the Ball

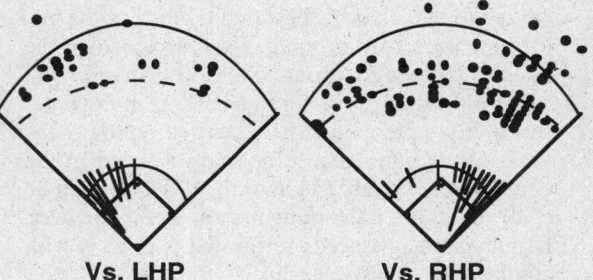

Vs. LHP   **Vs. RHP**

1996 Situational Stats

	AB	H	HR	RBI	Avg		AB	H	HR	RBI	Avg
Home	254	54	20	50	.213	LHP	153	30	6	21	.196
Road	286	86	21	62	.301	RHP	387	110	35	91	.284
First Half	290	75	23	66	.259	Sc Pos	166	42	15	77	.253
Scnd Half	250	65	18	46	.260	Clutch	102	23	6	15	.225

1996 Rankings (National League)

→ 1st in lowest batting average vs. left-handed pitchers (.196) and lowest batting average at home (.213)

→ 3rd in strikeouts, slugging percentage vs. right-handed pitchers (.620) and highest percentage of extra bases taken as a runner (70.5%)

→ 4th in home runs and HR frequency (13.2 ABs per HR)

→ 5th in most pitches seen per plate appearance (4.06), fielding percentage at catcher (.992) and lowest percentage of swings on the first pitch (19.2%)

→ 6th in intentional walks (15)

Jason Isringhausen

1996 Season

Much was expected from Jason Isringhausen in 1996, who shot through the minors and achieved major success as a rookie in 1995. Isringhausen began the '96 season with two quality starts, but he was undone by Mets errors on April 16th and got chased after four innings on April 26th. He then lost five consecutive starts in May. Isringhausen had one shutout, a six-hitter against Florida on June 9th, but overall it was a long and difficult season, especially in comparison to his rookie year. He missed the second half of August with a pulled ribcage muscle.

Pitching

Hitters have learned to look for Isringhausen's curveball, which is his best pitch. Many of the hits off him were hard grounders and shots down the lines as batters got around well on his curve and mid-80s fastball. Isringhausen became more tentative in his approach in 1996, not getting to use his good change-up because he wasn't ahead in the count often enough. Much of the difficulty can be chalked up as a learning experience, however. Isringhausen just needs to throw his pitches with confidence to be successful.

Defense & Hitting

Isringhausen needs a lot of work on fielding and holding runners. He is error-prone, and the opposition took 19 steals in 22 attempts in 1996. Isringhausen helps himself at the plate. He hit .255 with two home runs and nine RBI last year.

1997 Outlook

In retrospect it can be seen that in 1995, Isringhausen had fun with hitters who had never seen him before. Like many curveball specialists (Cal Eldred, for example), he had rookie success that didn't carry over. His place in the starting rotation remains solid, however, and Isringhausen just needs to go back to work in 1997 and make a few adjustments of his own.

Position: SP
Bats: R **Throws:** R
Ht: 6' 3" **Wt:** 196

Opening Day Age: 24
Born: 9/7/72 in Brighton, IL
ML Seasons: 2
Nickname: Izzy

Overall Statistics

	W	L	Pct.	ERA	G	GS	Sv	IP	H	BB	SO	HR	BR/IP
1996	6	14	.300	4.77	27	27	0	171.2	190	73	114	13	1.53
Career	15	16	.484	4.08	41	41	0	264.2	278	104	169	19	1.44

How Often He Throws Strikes

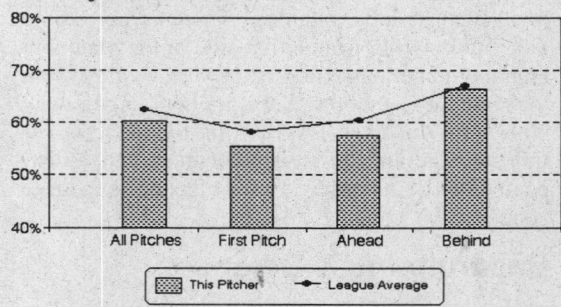

1996 Situational Stats

	W	L	ERA	Sv	IP		AB	H	HR	RBI	Avg
Home	5	6	3.11	0	101.1	LHB	276	87	3	39	.315
Road	1	8	7.17	0	70.1	RHB	393	103	10	45	.262
First Half	4	10	4.78	0	113.0	Sc Pos	173	52	1	64	.301
Scnd Half	2	4	4.76	0	58.2	Clutch	60	15	1	5	.250

1996 Rankings (National League)

- → 1st in errors at pitcher (5)
- → 2nd in wild pitches (14), highest stolen base percentage allowed (86.4%) and least run support per 9 innings (3.5)
- → 3rd in losses, lowest winning percentage and lowest fielding percentage at pitcher (.891)
- → 4th in most GDPs induced per 9 innings (1.0) and highest batting average allowed vs. left-handed batters (.315)
- → 5th in most baserunners allowed per 9 innings (14.2)
- → 6th in highest on-base percentage allowed (.357)
- → 9th in shutouts (1) and highest batting average allowed (.284)

Lance Johnson

1996 Season

The Mets got everything they hoped for, and more, after signing Lance Johnson prior to the 1996 season. He led the major leagues in hits, ran the bases with exciting speed that generated stolen bases and triples while delighting fans and helping the team. Johnson stole 15 bases just in the month of July and was an offensive spark all year. He was also a productive run-producer in RBI situations.

Hitting

Johnson is too impatient to be a truly great leadoff hitter, but he helps compensate for that with his other assets. His aggressiveness helps the team most when he comes up with men on base. Johnson drove in the same number of runners, other than himself (60), as Oriole leadoff man Brady Anderson, who had a 110-RBI season. Johnson likes all fastballs. He uses the whole ballpark against right-handed pitching and will generally try to go the other way against southpaws, though he is always looking for an inside mistake he can pull.

Baserunning & Defense

One of the game's best baserunners, Johnson has become a high-percentage basestealer in recent years. He's capable of running against any pitcher and any catcher. He is flat out fast and old-fashioned smart. His good range in center field makes him an asset in the spacious grass of Shea Stadium. Although his arm is not the strongest, Johnson gets respect from baserunners for his throwing accuracy.

1997 Outlook

Manager Bobby Valentine took pleasure in Johnson's success, talking up his center fielder's accomplishments. Johnson is a star in the field, on the bases and in the batting order, and he is a steady, quiet presence in the clubhouse. With a new contract as a reward for his great season, Johnson enters 1997 firmly established as the everyday center fielder and leadoff batter.

Position: CF
Bats: L **Throws:** L
Ht: 5'11" **Wt:** 160

Opening Day Age: 33
Born: 7/6/63 in Cincinnati, OH
ML Seasons: 10

Overall Statistics

	G	AB	R	H	D	T	HR	RBI	SB	BB	SO	Avg	OBP	Slg
1996	160	682	117	227	31	21	9	69	50	33	40	.333	.362	.479
Career	1139	4300	604	1258	139	99	26	403	282	247	304	.293	.330	.389

Where He Hits the Ball

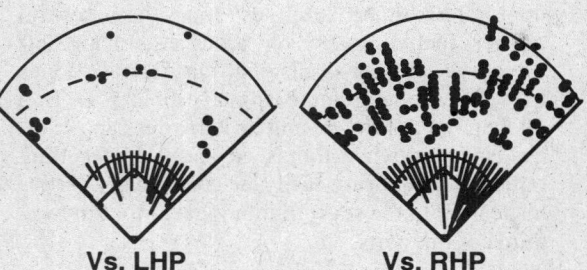

Vs. LHP   **Vs. RHP**

1996 Situational Stats

	AB	H	HR	RBI	Avg		AB	H	HR	RBI	Avg
Home	335	99	1	30	.296	LHP	182	60	0	20	.330
Road	347	128	8	39	.369	RHP	500	167	9	49	.334
First Half	376	121	5	40	.322	Sc Pos	127	41	3	59	.323
Scnd Half	306	106	4	29	.346	Clutch	114	42	2	17	.368

1996 Rankings (National League)

- → 1st in at-bats, hits, singles, triples, plate appearances (724), least pitches seen per plate appearance (2.98), batting average on the road (.369) and errors in center field (12)
- → 2nd in stolen bases, batting average with two strikes (.301), lowest fielding percentage in center field (.971), highest percentage of swings put into play (58.9%) and steals of third (10)
- → 3rd in highest groundball/flyball ratio (2.0), batting average in the clutch (.368) and batting average vs. right-handed pitchers (.334)
- → 4th in caught stealing and batting average
- → 5th in games played (160) and lowest percentage of swings that missed (9.3%)

Bobby Jones

1996 Season

Before spring training ended, Bobby Jones admitted that his command was not what he wanted it to be. He took his lumps in his first two regular season starts, not getting through the fourth inning of either. Eventually he settled down, however, crafting a 3.02 ERA for the month of May, and winning five consecutive decisions from April 28th to May 26th. After some ups and downs, Jones' best game was a four-hit shutout at Houston on September 24th.

Pitching

Jones needs good command to be effective. His biggest strength is not giving in to hitters with his mid-80s fastball. When he can't throw his change-up for strikes, he struggles. Jones uses several pitches, including a sinker, a curve, a change off the curve, and an occasional cut fastball. Jones uses finesse without being a nibbler; he is a pitcher, not a thrower, and he is fearless and cool-headed even when things go badly. Not getting rattled and not tiring easily, he consistently carries his team into the seventh inning or farther in two-thirds of his starts.

Defense & Hitting

A good fielder already, Jones is still improving. He moves well around the mound and gets over to first quickly. Jones watches runners attentively. He is a good bunter, and not quite an automatic out when he bats, with 22 hits in his career. He does strike out in more than a third of his plate appearances.

1997 Outlook

The Mets need Jones on their staff, gobbling up innings and producing double-digit wins as he has done three years in a row. Jones is assured of a spot in the starting rotation, though how high depends on who else is available. He is a steady if unspectacular presence on the field and in the clubhouse.

Position: SP
Bats: R **Throws:** R
Ht: 6' 4" **Wt:** 225

Opening Day Age: 27
Born: 2/10/70 in Fresno, California
ML Seasons: 4

Overall Statistics

	W	L	Pct.	ERA	G	GS	Sv	IP	H	BB	SO	HR	BR/IP
1996	12	8	.600	4.42	31	31	0	195.2	219	46	116	26	1.35
Career	36	29	.554	3.93	94	94	0	613.0	646	177	358	62	1.34

How Often He Throws Strikes

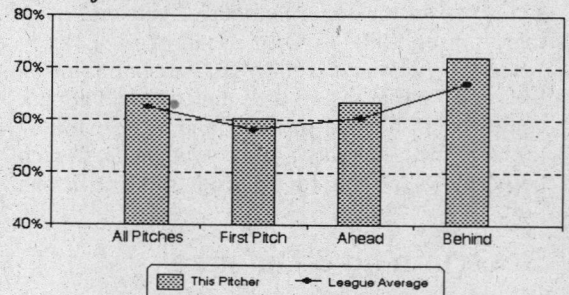

1996 Situational Stats

	W	L	ERA	Sv	IP		AB	H	HR	RBI	Avg
Home	5	4	3.91	0	94.1	LHB	343	99	10	42	.289
Road	7	4	4.88	0	101.1	RHB	417	120	16	47	.288
First Half	8	5	4.53	0	107.1	Sc Pos	144	37	5	56	.257
Scnd Half	4	3	4.28	0	88.1	Clutch	34	8	0	1	.235

1996 Rankings (National League)

→ 5th in highest batting average allowed (.288)
→ 6th in highest ERA on the road (4.88)
→ 9th in shutouts (1), hits allowed, GDPs induced (21), highest slugging percentage allowed (.446), least pitches thrown per batter (3.55), most GDPs induced per 9 innings (1.0) and least strikeouts per 9 innings (5.3)
→ Led the Mets in complete games (3), shutouts (1), hits allowed, runners caught stealing (8), winning percentage and lowest stolen base percentage allowed (57.9%)

Alex Ochoa

Position: RF
Bats: R **Throws:** R
Ht: 6' 0" **Wt:** 185

Opening Day Age: 25
Born: 3/29/72 in Miami
Lakes, FL
ML Seasons: 2
Pronunciation:
oh-CHO-uh

New York
Mets

1996 Season

The key player in the trade of Bobby Bonilla to the Orioles in July 1995, Alex Ochoa began the '96 season in the minors. He hit .339 with eight home runs in 223 at-bats for Triple-A Norfolk, while playing outstanding right field. He joined the Mets on June 21st and hit .357 in his first 28 at-bats. Carl Everett had already lost the right field job to Butch Huskey, and then Huskey was needed at first base when Rico Brogna got hurt. Ochoa became the regular right fielder, with Everett getting occasional starts against righty pitchers.

Hitting

Ochoa is a line-drive hitter with developing power. He came on strong in 1996 with increased patience and pitch selection. Ochoa should improve further as he gets to know the league's pitchers and gets a finer knowledge of the strike zone. He has no exploitable weaknesses in his swing and is already a dangerous hitter.

Baserunning & Defense

Blessed with good speed, Ochoa has stolen as many as 34 bases in a minor league season. He needs to pick his spots in the majors, however, and will probably not have a green light to run on his own in 1997. In the field he is a real gem with one of the best right field arms in all of baseball. His eight assists in just 76 major league games show that runners have not yet learned to fear him. They will.

1997 Outlook

The Mets ended 1996 with two excellent candidates for right field, Ochoa and Everett. Ochoa hits well against righties and lefties, but he is definitely better against the southpaws, the same pitchers who give Everett trouble. Manager Bobby Valentine would never say "platoon" concerning these players, and Ochoa will surely get more than half the starts, but with Everett around, right field is crowded.

Overall Statistics

	G	AB	R	H	D	T	HR	RBI	SB	BB	SO	Avg	OBP	Slg
1996	82	282	37	83	19	3	4	33	4	17	30	.294	.336	.426
Career	93	319	44	94	20	3	4	33	5	19	40	.295	.335	.414

Where He Hits the Ball

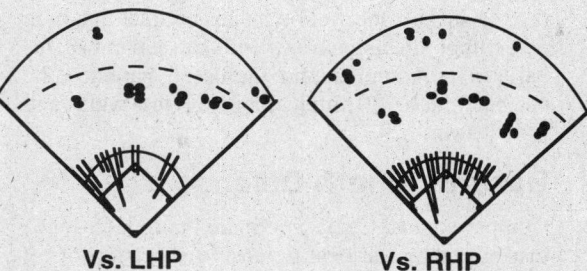

Vs. LHP   **Vs. RHP**

1996 Situational Stats

	AB	H	HR	RBI	Avg		AB	H	HR	RBI	Avg
Home	145	40	1	14	.276	LHP	91	30	2	12	.330
Road	137	43	3	19	.314	RHP	191	53	2	21	.277
First Half	58	19	3	15	.328	Sc Pos	70	22	1	29	.314
Scnd Half	224	64	1	18	.286	Clutch	55	13	2	6	.236

1996 Rankings (National League)

→ 4th in least GDPs per GDP situation (3.2%)
→ 8th in errors in right field (5)
→ Led the Mets in least GDPs per GDP situation (3.2%)

581

Rey Ordonez

1996 Season

If there was any question about Rey Ordonez being the Mets' Opening Day shortstop for 1996, the cheers of fans seeing him for the first time in spring training put an end to any doubt. Ordonez showed his ability with a from-the-knees throw from left field to home plate on Opening Day, and he just kept amazing fans and players alike as the season went on. He started well at the plate (.354 average for April) but struggled later, when pitchers approached him more cautiously.

Hitting

It would be a mistake to write off Ordonez as a no-hit defensive specialist. He came within one hit of winning the Puerto Rican winter batting title a year ago. He is an aggressive swinger, still learning the strike zone, yet he makes contact in a high percentage of his at-bats. With refinement of his ball/strike judgment and increased patience, he can become a .280 hitter, albeit with few walks and little power.

Baserunning & Defense

Comparisons to Ozzie Smith are natural. Ordonez just might be the best defensive shortstop of all time. Smith and Ordonez work different kinds of magic, however. The Ordonez specialties include a can't-believe-it play where he falls toward the third base line yet somehow fires a side-arm strike to first base without even attempting to plant his feet. Great range and the rifle arm will entertain fans and please his pitchers for many years. On the bases, Ordonez has good speed but hasn't yet learned how to use it well.

1997 Outlook

The only question about Ordonez' future is when he will move up from the number-eight spot in the batting order. He will be the starting shortstop for at least five more years, and longer if the Mets want to keep their fans.

Position: SS
Bats: R **Throws:** R
Ht: 5' 9" **Wt:** 159

Opening Day Age: 24
Born: 11/11/72 in Havana, Cuba
ML Seasons: 1
Pronunciation: Ray or-DOAN-yez

Overall Statistics

	G	AB	R	H	D	T	HR	RBI	SB	BB	SO	Avg	OBP	Slg
1996	151	502	51	129	12	4	1	30	1	22	53	.257	.289	.303
Career	151	502	51	129	12	4	1	30	1	22	53	.257	.289	.303

Where He Hits the Ball

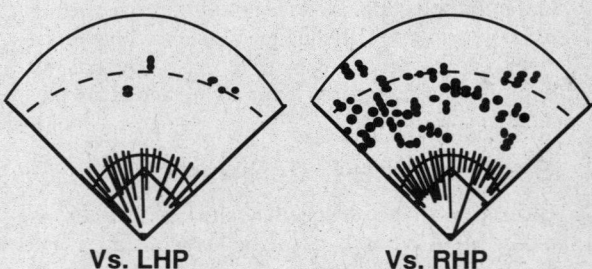

Vs. LHP   Vs. RHP

1996 Situational Stats

	AB	H	HR	RBI	Avg		AB	H	HR	RBI	Avg
Home	246	56	0	11	.228	LHP	120	31	0	10	.258
Road	256	73	1	19	.285	RHP	382	98	1	20	.257
First Half	272	71	0	13	.261	Sc Pos	115	28	0	27	.243
Scnd Half	230	58	1	17	.252	Clutch	83	22	0	8	.265

1996 Rankings (National League)

→ 1st in lowest HR frequency (502.0 ABs per HR) and highest groundball/flyball ratio (2.9)

→ 2nd in least pitches seen per plate appearance (3.01), lowest slugging percentage vs. right-handed pitchers (.306) and errors at shortstop (27)

→ 3rd in lowest slugging percentage, lowest on-base percentage and lowest on-base percentage vs. right-handed pitchers (.293)

→ 4th in lowest batting average at home (.228) and lowest fielding percentage at shortstop (.962)

→ 8th in intentional walks (12)

Paul Wilson

1996 Season

Before the 1996 season began, one opposing manager (off the record) said of Paul Wilson, "He will be a big winner some day, but I don't know about this year. It can take time." Translating great stuff into game results was indeed a challenge for Wilson throughout 1996. He was brilliant at times, as in an eight-inning, three-hit, no-walk appearance against the Giants on May 30th, but on other occasions he got knocked around. Wilson was also bothered by tendinitis and spent over five weeks on the DL from early June to mid July. He finished strongly, not giving up more than two earned runs in a game after August 24th, and crafting a 1.76 ERA in September.

Pitching

Wilson has the whole package of pitching talent: a mid-90s fastball, a deceptive change-up, a hard slider and a curve. He had fine control before 1996, although he became tentative at times in the majors. How can such a talent have trouble? Simple: mistakes. In between making some of the best major league hitters look foolish, Wilson will throw the wrong pitch at the wrong time too frequently. The good news is that this tendency can be easily remedied with experience.

Defense & Hitting

Wilson is a good athlete who covers first quickly, especially for a hard thrower. He is slightly prone to youthful mistakes, however. He needs to work on holding runners, too. Last year 24 of 28 steal attempts against him succeeded. At the plate, Wilson is a very weak hitter likely to strike out, although he did hit a home run in 1996.

1997 Outlook

The strong finish in 1996 suggests Wilson is ready for a breakthrough year in 1997. Like many young Mets, he is ready to move from on-the-job training to productive performance. Wilson is poised to be the staff ace for this young team.

Position: SP
Bats: R **Throws:** R
Ht: 6' 5" **Wt:** 235

Opening Day Age: 24
Born: 3/28/73 in Orlando, FL
ML Seasons: 1

Overall Statistics

	W	L	Pct.	ERA	G	GS	Sv	IP	H	BB	SO	HR	BR/IP
1996	5	12	.294	5.38	26	26	0	149.0	157	71	109	15	1.53
Career	5	12	.294	5.38	26	26	0	149.0	157	71	109	15	1.53

How Often He Throws Strikes

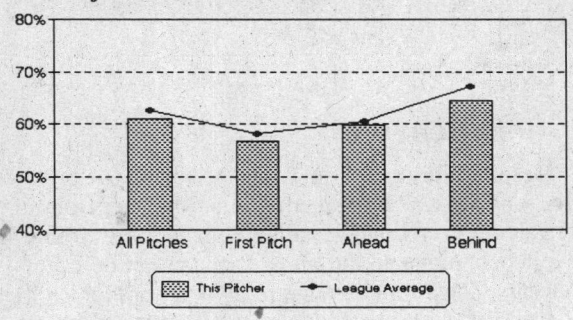

Legend: This Pitcher / League Average

Categories: All Pitches, First Pitch, Ahead, Behind (axis 40% to 80%)

1996 Situational Stats

	W	L	ERA	Sv	IP		AB	H	HR	RBI	Avg
Home	3	4	2.93	0	73.2	LHB	265	78	6	44	.294
Road	2	8	7.77	0	75.1	RHB	321	79	9	47	.246
First Half	3	5	6.06	0	68.1	Sc Pos	172	52	4	75	.302
Scnd Half	2	7	4.80	0	80.2	Clutch	27	2	1	4	.074

1996 Rankings (National League)

- ➡ 1st in lowest winning percentage
- ➡ 3rd in balks (3)
- ➡ 4th in pickoff throws (203)
- ➡ 5th in stolen bases allowed (24)
- ➡ 8th in hit batsmen (10) and highest batting average allowed with runners in scoring position (.302)
- ➡ 9th in losses
- ➡ Led the Mets in hit batsmen (10), balks (3), pickoff throws (203), stolen bases allowed (24) and lowest batting average allowed vs. right-handed batters (.246)

Alberto Castillo

Position: C
Bats: R **Throws:** R
Ht: 6' 0" **Wt:** 184

Opening Day Age: 27
Born: 2/10/70 in San Juan de la Maguana, DR
ML Seasons: 2

Overall Statistics

	G	AB	R	H	D	T	HR	RBI	SB	BB	SO	Avg	OBP	Slg
1996	6	11	1	4	0	0	0	0	0	0	4	.364	.364	.364
Career	19	40	3	7	0	0	0	0	1	3	13	.175	.250	.175

1996 Situational Stats

	AB	H	HR	RBI	Avg		AB	H	HR	RBI	Avg
Home	5	3	0	0	.600	LHP	5	1	0	0	.200
Road	6	1	0	0	.167	RHP	6	3	0	0	.500
First Half	0	0	0	0	-	Sc Pos	1	1	0	0	1.000
Scnd Half	11	4	0	0	.364	Clutch	1	0	0	0	.000

1996 Season

Despite hitting .208 at Triple-A Norfolk, Alberto Castillo got a September call-up. Manager Bobby Valentine credited Castillo with helping young pitchers move up the Mets' farm system in recent years. The promotion was partly a reward for a job well done, and partly to help the young pitchers called up with Castillo.

Hitting, Baserunning & Defense

Castillo has some pop in his bat, evidenced by his 11 homers at Norfolk in 1996. He is too free a swinger, however, an exploitable weakness in the majors. Castillo will steal a base once a year to keep the defense awake, but he really lacks speed. His strength is defense. Castillo is a mature, cool-headed pitcher-handler, and he will cut down over-optimistic baserunners attempting to steal. He has maintained a 35 to 40 percent throw-out average in his pro career.

1997 Outlook

Castillo has a chance to stay with the Mets after Opening Day. His manager likes him, and the pitchers like him. But the work will be strictly as a defensive backup.

Jerry DiPoto

Traded To ROCKIES

Position: RP
Bats: R **Throws:** R
Ht: 6' 2" **Wt:** 200

Opening Day Age: 28
Born: 5/24/68 in Jersey City, NJ
ML Seasons: 4
Pronunciation: da-POE-toe

Overall Statistics

	W	L	Pct.	ERA	G	GS	Sv	IP	H	BB	SO	HR	BR/IP
1996	7	2	.778	4.19	57	0	0	77.1	91	45	52	5	1.76
Career	15	12	.556	3.87	168	0	13	228.0	251	114	151	8	1.60

1996 Situational Stats

	W	L	ERA	Sv	IP		AB	H	HR	RBI	Avg
Home	5	1	4.40	0	43.0	LHB	129	40	2	20	.310
Road	2	1	3.93	0	34.1	RHB	176	51	3	32	.290
First Half	3	1	4.66	0	36.2	Sc Pos	128	33	0	41	.258
Scnd Half	4	1	3.76	0	40.2	Clutch	86	30	3	16	.349

1996 Season

Former Indians righthander Jerry DiPoto had a generally disappointing season as a set-up man and middle reliever for the Mets. He had many good games but was plagued by inconsistency. He did not build on his successful 1995 comeback season, and by year's end the Mets were looking at other right-handed relievers. DiPoto finished the year on a sour note, giving up two runs in each of his last two outings.

Pitching, Defense & Hitting

DiPoto throws a hard sinker, a slider and a split-fingered change-up. He converted to relief work in 1992 because he couldn't develop any other pitches, and his one offspeed pitch, the splitter, wasn't under control. DiPoto does have a resilient arm and likes to work frequently. He watches runners and is quick to the plate. In the field he is adequate, and he got through 1996 without an error. He rarely comes to bat (just once in '96).

1997 Outlook

The Mets had many options for right-handed relief in 1997, and they dealt DiPoto to the Rockies after the season. Pitching in Coors Field will be a whole new challenge for him.

Doug Henry

Position: RP
Bats: R **Throws:** R
Ht: 6' 4" **Wt:** 205

Opening Day Age: 33
Born: 12/10/63 in
Sacramento, CA
ML Seasons: 6

Overall Statistics

	W	L	Pct.	ERA	G	GS	Sv	IP	H	BB	SO	HR	BR/IP
1996	2	8	.200	4.68	58	0	9	75.0	82	36	58	7	1.57
Career	14	26	.350	3.94	288	0	74	329.1	309	147	258	35	1.38

1996 Situational Stats

	W	L	ERA	Sv	IP		AB	H	HR	RBI	Avg
Home	2	2	4.38	3	37.0	LHB	139	33	3	14	.237
Road	0	6	4.97	6	38.0	RHB	161	49	4	28	.304
First Half	2	2	3.60	6	45.0	Sc Pos	92	25	2	36	.272
Scnd Half	0	6	6.30	3	30.0	Clutch	141	41	4	27	.291

1996 Season

Doug Henry began the year as the Mets' top right-handed reliever. In addition to set-up work, he filled in as closer when John Franco was tired. Henry saved Bobby Valentine's first victory as New York's manager, but overall his performance under Valentine was disappointing. Henry gave up 10 earned runs while working only four-plus September innings.

Pitching, Defense & Hitting

Formerly a fastball-only reliever, Henry added offspeed and breaking stuff which resurrected his career. When he's going well, he can throw a slider, forkball or change-up for a strike. When his breaking stuff isn't over the plate, however, Henry's fastball becomes hittable. On defense he makes a good effort but is somewhat unsteady. Holding runners has been a problem. He is a weak hitter who went 0-for-5 in 1996.

1997 Outlook

Henry entered the winter with a cloud over his future. Bobby Valentine showed a preference for Derek Wallace. Nonetheless, Henry showed enough in 1995 and in his better outings of 1996 to get a look from another organization, if the Mets don't want him back.

Butch Huskey

Position: 1B/RF
Bats: R **Throws:** R
Ht: 6' 3" **Wt:** 244

Opening Day Age: 25
Born: 11/10/71 in
Anadarko, OK
ML Seasons: 3

Overall Statistics

	G	AB	R	H	D	T	HR	RBI	SB	BB	SO	Avg	OBP	Slg
1996	118	414	43	115	16	2	15	60	1	27	77	.278	.319	.435
Career	159	545	53	138	18	2	18	74	2	38	107	.253	.298	.393

1996 Situational Stats

	AB	H	HR	RBI	Avg		AB	H	HR	RBI	Avg
Home	243	70	9	33	.288	LHP	111	31	6	13	.279
Road	171	45	6	27	.263	RHP	303	84	9	47	.277
First Half	244	62	6	32	.254	Sc Pos	106	28	2	42	.264
Scnd Half	170	53	9	28	.312	Clutch	68	22	2	7	.324

1996 Season

Last spring, Butch Huskey broke Dave Kingman's all-time Mets record for spring training home runs. The offensive surge lifted Huskey into the Mets' starting right field job. Later when Alex Ochoa came up, Huskey played first base in place of the injured Rico Brogna. Huskey also appeared at third base, his original position. His first full season in the majors was an all-around success.

Hitting, Baserunning & Defense

Huskey's fine power was most visible in July, when he hit .337 with seven home runs. His wide stance helps generate power and also helps him remain patient by not committing too early. Huskey has good speed for a large guy; he once stole 22 bases in a minor league season. His biggest defensive asset is versatility. He is error-prone but gets the job done wherever he plays, first, third, or outfield.

1997 Outlook

Huskey will do well in 1997 just to play as much as he did in 1996. With Brogna returning to first and numerous other outfield and corner infield candidates, Huskey's role looks like utility and backup.

Brent Mayne

Position: C
Bats: L **Throws:** R
Ht: 6' 1" **Wt:** 190

Opening Day Age: 28
Born: 4/19/68 in Loma Linda, CA
ML Seasons: 7

Overall Statistics

	G	AB	R	H	D	T	HR	RBI	SB	BB	SO	Avg	OBP	Slg
1996	70	99	9	26	6	0	1	6	0	12	22	.263	.342	.354
Career	469	1212	113	301	56	3	9	125	6	106	192	.248	.309	.322

1996 Situational Stats

	AB	H	HR	RBI	Avg		AB	H	HR	RBI	Avg
Home	55	13	0	3	.236	LHP	10	3	0	1	.300
Road	44	13	1	3	.295	RHP	89	23	1	5	.258
First Half	54	14	1	4	.259	Sc Pos	21	5	0	4	.238
Scnd Half	45	12	0	2	.267	Clutch	33	7	1	3	.212

1996 Season

A first-round pick by the Royals in 1989, Brent Mayne came to the Mets in trade before the 1996 season. He is too good to be a backup catcher, but got adjusted to that role while in Kansas City. Playing behind Todd Hundley, Mayne produced a solid year on both offense and defense. He was hottest during August when he hit .333. In September, Mayne was used sparingly while new manager Bobby Valentine gave time to call-up Alberto Castillo.

Hitting, Baserunning & Defense

Mayne is a line-drive hitter with power to the gaps. For someone who doesn't hit home runs, he swings and misses a lot. Mayne is careful on the bases but has little speed. He is a good pitcher-handler and game-caller, and he moves well around the plate. He played all of 1996 without making an error.

1997 Outlook

Any team could use Mayne's lefty bat and solid defense. In another city, he might be a starting catcher, but in New York he is behind Todd Hundley. A free agent, he will likely end up elsewhere this year.

Dave Mlicki

Position: RP
Bats: R **Throws:** R
Ht: 6' 4" **Wt:** 205

Opening Day Age: 28
Born: 6/8/68 in Cleveland, OH
ML Seasons: 4

Overall Statistics

	W	L	Pct.	ERA	G	GS	Sv	IP	H	BB	SO	HR	BR/IP
1996	6	7	.462	3.30	51	2	1	90.0	95	33	83	9	1.42
Career	15	16	.484	3.97	87	34	1	285.2	289	109	229	37	1.39

1996 Situational Stats

	W	L	ERA	Sv	IP		AB	H	HR	RBI	Avg
Home	3	4	3.32	1	43.1	LHB	154	44	6	26	.286
Road	3	3	3.28	0	46.2	RHB	189	51	3	20	.270
First Half	4	3	3.16	1	51.1	Sc Pos	96	22	3	38	.229
Scnd Half	2	4	3.49	0	38.2	Clutch	132	42	2	19	.318

1996 Season

After working as a starter in 1995, his first season with the Mets, Dave Mlicki worked primarily out of the bullpen last season. He made two starts in early April when the Mets were plagued with pitching injuries, but he spent the rest of the year as a middle reliever and set-up man. He had a fine season and was at his best in September, when he had a 2.45 ERA.

Pitching, Defense & Hitting

Mlicki has a good fastball, but he needs other pitches to complement it. Those other pitches are a curve, knuckle curve, slider and change-up. He can also sink his fastball. Mlicki is a direct worker who doesn't nibble, but he uses all his pitches while moving the ball around and pitching to spots. He is below average on defense, but he has improved at holding runners. At bat he usually puts the ball in play, but he doesn't come to the plate very often.

1997 Outlook

Mlicki entered the winter with a bigger role than he had going into 1996. He has proven himself as a steady worker with a resilient arm, and the Mets were expected to re-sign him.

Robert Person

Position: RP/SP
Bats: R **Throws:** R
Ht: 6' 0" **Wt:** 185

Opening Day Age: 27
Born: 10/6/69 in St. Louis, MO
ML Seasons: 2

Overall Statistics

	W	L	Pct.	ERA	G	GS	Sv	IP	H	BB	SO	HR	BR/IP
1996	4	5	.444	4.52	27	13	0	89.2	86	35	76	16	1.35
Career	5	5	.500	4.07	30	14	0	101.2	91	37	86	17	1.26

1996 Situational Stats

	W	L	ERA	Sv	IP		AB	H	HR	RBI	Avg
Home	2	2	3.60	0	40.0	LHB	174	39	7	20	.224
Road	2	3	5.26	0	49.2	RHB	174	47	9	23	.270
First Half	2	3	3.93	0	34.1	Sc Pos	74	12	3	24	.162
Scnd Half	2	2	4.88	0	55.1	Clutch	25	5	2	3	.200

1996 Season

Robert Person went to the Arizona Fall League in 1994 to become a short reliever. A year later he went back as a starter. In 1996 he filled both roles with the Mets, making some April relief appearances. Then, back at Triple-A Norfolk, he was 5-0 as a starter. The Mets recalled him June 12th. Although he made a few more relief appearances, Person worked mainly as a starter until year's end.

Pitching, Defense and Hitting

A former outfielder, Person's strong arm got him into the pitching profession. He throws a 90 MPH fastball and mixes it with a hard slider and a straight change-up. As a starter he lacks stamina. Although he made four errors last year, Person is regarded as a good fielder. He hit just .087 as a minor league outfielder, but he handles a bat well for a pitcher.

1997 Outlook

Person has shown a positive attitude to do whatever it takes to help a major league pitching staff. On paper he isn't in the Mets rotation for 1997, but as 1996 showed, plans can change.

Derek Wallace

Position: RP
Bats: R **Throws:** R
Ht: 6' 3" **Wt:** 185

Opening Day Age: 25
Born: 9/1/71 in Van Nuys, CA
ML Seasons: 1

Overall Statistics

	W	L	Pct.	ERA	G	GS	Sv	IP	H	BB	SO	HR	BR/IP
1996	2	3	.400	4.01	19	0	3	24.2	29	14	15	2	1.74
Career	2	3	.400	4.01	19	0	3	24.2	29	14	15	2	1.74

1996 Situational Stats

	W	L	ERA	Sv	IP		AB	H	HR	RBI	Avg
Home	2	1	1.20	3	15.0	LHB	45	15	0	4	.333
Road	0	2	8.38	0	9.2	RHB	55	14	2	9	.255
First Half	0	0	-	0	0.0	Sc Pos	26	8	1	11	.308
Scnd Half	2	3	4.01	3	24.2	Clutch	63	17	1	7	.270

1996 Season

After collecting 26 saves with a 1.72 ERA as the ace reliever at Triple-A Norfolk, Derek Wallace joined the Mets on August 13th and made his first appearance that same day. He already had the confidence of manager Bobby Valentine, who had been at Norfolk with him. Although he struggled with his control at times, Wallace was prominent in Valentine's bullpen.

Pitching, Defense & Hitting

Wallace is a direct worker with a 90+ MPH fastball and a hard slider. He will mix in a straight change occasionally. His walks in 1996 were the result of intermittent control problems, not from nibbling. Wallace is a good fielder who covers his territory and gets to first quickly. He has only an average pickoff move but watches runners closely. Wallace did not come to bat in 1996.

1997 Outlook

Wallace is a better pitcher than his 1996 stats reflect—and that's a good thing, because Valentine plans to use him extensively in 1997. Wallace has a chance to take over the top righty relief role, succeeding Doug Henry.

Other New York Mets

Tim Bogar (Pos: 1B/3B/SS, Age: 30, Bats: R)

	G	AB	R	H	D	T	HR	RBI	SB	BB	SO	Avg	OBP	Slg
1996	91	89	17	19	4	0	0	6	1	8	20	.213	.287	.258
Career	297	491	58	119	24	0	6	57	3	35	85	.242	.297	.328

Bogar filled in at four infield positions last year, making occasional starts and providing late-inning defensive expertise. He didn't shine at the plate, but offense has never been his forte. 1997 Outlook: B

Paul Byrd (Pos: RHP, Age: 26)

	W	L	Pct.	ERA	G	GS	Sv	IP	H	BB	SO	HR	BR/IP
1996	1	2	.333	4.24	38	0	0	46.2	48	21	31	7	1.48
Career	3	2	.600	3.54	55	0	0	68.2	66	28	57	8	1.37

Returning to the majors in June after being sidelined with a bulging disk in his back, Byrd was mediocre in long relief throughout the remainder of the year. He was dealt to the Braves after the season, and should be in their bullpen this year. If he can regain full health, he'll be effective. 1997 Outlook: A

Matt Franco (Pos: 3B, Age: 27, Bats: L)

	G	AB	R	H	D	T	HR	RBI	SB	BB	SO	Avg	OBP	Slg
1996	14	31	3	6	1	0	1	2	0	1	5	.194	.235	.323
Career	30	48	6	11	2	0	1	3	0	1	9	.229	.255	.333

Franco saw some playing time at first and third base in September last year. He had a great season at Triple-A Norfolk, but he's now 27 and has to produce in the big leagues immediately. It didn't happen in '96. 1997 Outlook: C

Mike Fyhrie (Pos: RHP, Age: 27)

	W	L	Pct.	ERA	G	GS	Sv	IP	H	BB	SO	HR	BR/IP
1996	0	1	.000	15.43	2	0	0	2.1	4	3	0	0	3.00
Career	0	1	.000	15.43	2	0	0	2.1	4	3	0	0	3.00

After nearly six seasons in the minors, Fyhrie finally made it to the big leagues last season. However, he was shelled in both of his appearances with the Mets and might not receive a second chance soon. 1997 Outlook: D

Charlie Greene (Pos: C, Age: 26, Bats: R)

	G	AB	R	H	D	T	HR	RBI	SB	BB	SO	Avg	OBP	Slg
1996	2	1	0	0	0	0	0	0	0	0	0	.000	.000	.000
Career	2	1	0	0	0	0	0	0	0	0	0	.000	.000	.000

Greene has been mired in Double-A ball for the last three years, but he spent a few days in New York last September and picked up a lone at-bat. Not a major league prospect. 1997 Outlook: D

Jason Hardtke (Pos: 2B, Age: 25, Bats: B)

	G	AB	R	H	D	T	HR	RBI	SB	BB	SO	Avg	OBP	Slg
1996	19	57	3	11	5	0	0	6	0	2	12	.193	.233	.281
Career	19	57	3	11	5	0	0	6	0	2	12	.193	.233	.281

After his September call-up to the majors, Hardtke took over as the Mets' regular second baseman. Although outstanding defensively, he struggled at the plate. His minor league stats show that he can hit. 1997 Outlook: B

Chris Jones (Pos: RF/LF, Age: 31, Bats: R)

	G	AB	R	H	D	T	HR	RBI	SB	BB	SO	Avg	OBP	Slg
1996	89	149	22	36	7	0	4	18	1	12	42	.242	.307	.369
Career	381	732	111	194	29	10	21	92	17	46	201	.265	.309	.418

Jones was used extensively as a rotating outfield glove and a stopgap in right field whenever Carl Everett and Butch Huskey were unavailable. He hit decently considering his erratic playing time. 1997 Outlook: A

Bob MacDonald (Pos: LHP, Age: 31)

	W	L	Pct.	ERA	G	GS	Sv	IP	H	BB	SO	HR	BR/IP
1996	0	2	.000	4.26	20	0	0	19.0	16	9	12	2	1.32
Career	8	9	.471	4.34	197	0	3	234.1	234	107	142	26	1.46

MacDonald started the year in the Mets' bullpen as a middle reliever, but quickly grew out of favor with management after a series of poor outings in May and June. He pitched well at Triple-A, but he's not young. 1997 Outlook: C

Kevin Roberson (Pos: RF, Age: 29, Bats: B)

	G	AB	R	H	D	T	HR	RBI	SB	BB	SO	Avg	OBP	Slg
1996	27	36	8	8	1	0	3	9	0	7	17	.222	.348	.500
Career	165	309	44	61	10	1	20	51	0	27	93	.197	.275	.430

Roberson began the season as the Mets' fifth outfielder, but his free-swinging ways quickly earned him a trip to the minors. He drew walks, but also struck out in almost half of his major league at-bats. 1997 Outlook: C

Andy Tomberlin (Pos: LF, Age: 30, Bats: L)

	G	AB	R	H	D	T	HR	RBI	SB	BB	SO	Avg	OBP	Slg
1996	63	66	12	17	4	0	3	10	0	9	27	.258	.355	.455
Career	153	229	32	54	4	2	9	26	5	22	75	.236	.308	.389

Obtained in a May trade with Oakland, Tomberlin joined the Mets in June and served chiefly as a pinch hitter. He didn't exactly rekindle memories of Rusty Staub, but he was adequate. Age is now a factor. 1997 Outlook: C

Ricky Trlicek (Pos: RHP, Age: 27)

	W	L	Pct.	ERA	G	GS	Sv	IP	H	BB	SO	HR	BR/IP
1996	0	1	.000	3.38	5	0	0	5.1	3	3	3	0	1.13
Career	2	4	.333	5.11	60	1	1	93.1	96	42	52	8	1.48

After an outstanding season at Triple-A, Trlicek appeared in five September games after getting called up to the majors. He may have finally turned the corner on his career. 1997 Outlook: B

New York Mets Minor League Prospects

Organization Overview:

What happened? One year, the New York Mets' farm system is heralded as Baseball America's Organization of the Year, and their stock of young pitchers are the talk of baseball. The next year, a tidal wave of injuries sweeps through their system leveling nearly every prospect in sight, from the majors on down to Rookie ball. The injuries to Bill Pulsipher, Jason Isringhausen and Paul Wilson were just the tip of the iceberg. Top prospects like Jay Payton and Juan Acevedo suffered major injuries, and further down in the system, many long-range prospects went down for large parts of the season. Although Alex Ochoa, Rey Ordonez and Butch Huskey each made encouraging debuts, the overall level of talent has been decimated. For the next year or two, the focus will shift from development to rehabilitation. It's no exaggeration to say the future of the Mets organization lies largely in the hands of its medical staff.

Juan Acevedo

Position: P   **Opening Day Age:** 26
Bats: R **Throws:** R   **Born:** 5/5/70 in Juarez,
Ht: 6' 2" **Wt:** 195   Mexico

Recent Statistics

	W	L	ERA	G	GS	Sv	IP	H	R	BB	SO	HR
93 A Central Val	9	8	4.40	27	20	0	118.2	119	68	58	107	8
94 AA New Haven	17	6	2.37	26	26	0	174.2	142	56	38	161	16
95 AAA Norfolk	0	0	0.00	2	2	0	3.0	0	0	1	2	0
95 AAA Col. Sprng	1	1	6.14	3	3	0	14.2	18	11	7	7	0
96 AAA Norfolk	4	8	5.96	19	19	0	102.2	116	70	53	83	15

Juan Acevedo began the '96 season as one of the Mets' top prospects, just a step or two behind their other celebrated young starters. Like the others, Acevedo's season was wiped out by serious injuries. The Mets fooled with his delivery in the spring, he came down with a sore arm, lost his confidence, got sent to the minors, and suffered a season-ending stress fracture in his leg after the All-Star break. When he's healthy, he throws a vast assortment of pitches with excellent command, but it remains to be seen whether he can get back to where he was three years ago. At age 27, it's time for him to put it together.

Joe Crawford

Position: P   **Opening Day Age:** 26
Bats: L **Throws:** L   **Born:** 5/2/70 in
Ht: 6' 3" **Wt:** 225   Gainesville, FL

Recent Statistics

	W	L	ERA	G	GS	Sv	IP	H	R	BB	SO	HR
93 A St. Lucie	3	3	3.65	34	0	5	37.0	38	15	14	24	0
94 A St. Lucie	1	1	1.48	33	0	5	42.2	22	8	9	31	1
94 AA Binghamton	1	0	5.52	13	0	0	14.2	20	10	8	9	2
95 AAA Norfolk	1	1	1.93	8	0	0	18.2	9	5	4	13	0
95 AA Binghamton	7	2	2.23	42	1	0	60.2	48	17	17	43	4
96 AA Binghamton	5	1	1.45	7	7	0	49.2	34	10	9	34	4
96 AAA Norfolk	6	5	3.44	20	16	0	96.2	98	45	20	68	10

In late 1995, Joe Crawford was a left-handed middle reliever who'd been toiling in the Mets' system for years, with little hope. But the Red Sox were impressed with his solid '95 season at Double-A, and they took him in the Rule V draft. Unfortunately, they chose to return him to the Mets at the close of spring training, but then Crawford caught another break: the Mets sent him back to Double-A and put him in the rotation. The results were amazing—he blew through Double-A, and continued to pitch well in Triple-A. Crawford has great command of a sinking fastball, and could help the Mets as either a starter or a reliever.

Brian Daubach

Position: 1B   **Opening Day Age:** 25
Bats: L **Throws:** R   **Born:** 2/11/72 in
Ht: 6' 1" **Wt:** 201   Belleville, IL

Recent Statistics

	G	AB	R	H	D	T	HR	RBI	SB	BB	SO	AVG
93 A Capital Cty	102	379	50	106	19	3	7	72	6	52	84	.280
94 A St. Lucie	129	450	52	123	30	2	6	74	14	58	120	.273
95 AA Binghamton	135	469	61	115	25	2	10	72	6	51	104	.245
95 AAA Norfolk	2	7	0	0	0	0	0	0	0	2	0	.000
96 AAA Norfolk	17	54	7	11	2	0	0	6	1	6	14	.204
96 AA Binghamton	122	436	80	129	24	1	22	76	7	74	103	.296
96 MLE	139	474	72	124	21	0	18	67	4	55	124	.262

Another Double-A repeater, left-handed hitting first baseman Brian Daubach did much better the second time around. He raised his average 51 points, and more than doubled his home run output, raising the hope that he may someday approach the 20-homer level in the majors. It will be an uphill battle, though, as power is his only real skill. Now going on age 25, he'll need to catch a break soon in order to avoid becoming a career minor-leaguer.

Nelson Figueroa

Position: P   **Opening Day Age:** 22
Bats: B **Throws:** R   **Born:** 5/18/74 in
Ht: 6' 1" **Wt:** 165   Brooklyn, NY

Recent Statistics

	W	L	ERA	G	GS	Sv	IP	H	R	BB	SO	HR
95 R Kingsport	7	3	3.07	12	12	0	76.1	57	31	22	79	3
96 A Columbia	14	7	2.04	26	25	0	185.1	119	55	58	200	10

If you were to ask, "Who was the only minor league pitcher to register 200 strikeouts last season?", few would be knowledgeable enough to answer, "Nelson Figueroa." Down in the South Atlantic League, the former 30th-round pick went 14-7 and notched 200 Ks on the nose. And get this—his fastball doesn't even hit 90 MPH. Figueroa, who fashions himself after Greg Maddux, throws five pitches with superb control, and shows a great innate feel for the art of pitching. He's at least a couple of years away, but he's certainly one of the most unique prospects around.

Arnie Gooch

Position: P
Opening Day Age: 20
Bats: R **Throws:** R
Born: 11/12/76 in
Ht: 6' 2" **Wt:** 195
Levittown, PA

Recent Statistics

	W	L	ERA	G	GS	Sv	IP	H	R	BB	SO	HR
94 R Rockies	2	4	2.64	15	9	0	58.0	45	28	16	66	2
95 A Columbia	2	3	4.46	6	6	0	38.1	39	25	15	34	3
95 A Asheville	5	8	2.94	21	21	0	128.2	111	51	57	117	8
96 A St. Lucie	12	12	2.58	26	26	0	167.2	131	74	51	141	7

When the Mets obtained Arnold Gooch and Juan Acevedo from the Rockies in exchange for Bret Saberhagen, Gooch seemed like a mere throw-in. Last year, however, Gooch proved to be, by far, the more impressive of the two. As a teenager in the Florida State League, he pitched with a style that belied his age. His high-80s fastball has tremendous movement, and Gooch was able to keep it within the strike zone, with devastating results. He also throws a good curveball, and scouts believe he may get his velocity up into the 90s as he matures. He needs time, but he looks good so far.

Jay Payton

Position: DH
Opening Day Age: 24
Bats: R **Throws:** R
Born: 11/22/72 in
Ht: 5' 10" **Wt:** 190
Zanesville, OH

Recent Statistics

	G	AB	R	H	D	T	HR	RBI	SB	BB	SO	AVG
94 A Pittsfield	58	219	47	80	16	2	3	37	10	23	18	.365
94 AA Binghamton	8	25	3	7	1	0	0	1	1	2	3	.280
95 AA Binghamton	85	357	59	123	20	3	14	54	16	29	32	.345
95 AAA Norfolk	50	196	33	47	11	4	4	30	11	11	22	.240
96 R Mets	3	13	3	5	1	0	1	2	1	0	1	.385
96 AA Binghamton	4	10	0	2	0	0	0	2	0	2	2	.200
96 A St. Lucie	9	26	4	8	2	0	0	1	2	4	5	.308
96 AAA Norfolk	55	153	30	47	6	3	6	26	10	11	25	.307

Great promise in '95; severe injury in '96—Jay Payton sure fits right in with the Mets. Two years ago, he had a tremendous first half at Double-A, hitting for a great average, with power and very few strikeouts. When he got promoted to Triple-A later in the season, his elbow began to bother him, and after the season, he was forced to undergo the Tommy John surgery on his throwing arm. The rehab was slow, and another surgery to remove bone chips from the same elbow set him back last May. When he finally was able to play, his batting stroke returned, but his sore wing limited him mostly to DH duties. In winter ball, he still was unable to play the field full-time, and his status is still up in the air. If he can play, he can hit.

Roberto Petagine

Position: 1B
Opening Day Age: 25
Bats: L **Throws:** L
Born: 6/7/71 in Nueva
Ht: 6' 1" **Wt:** 172
Esparita, Venez

Recent Statistics

	G	AB	R	H	D	T	HR	RBI	SB	BB	SO	AVG
96 AAA Norfolk	95	314	49	100	24	3	12	65	4	51	75	.318
96 NL New York	50	99	10	23	3	0	4	17	0	9	27	.232
96 MLE	95	306	44	92	21	2	11	59	3	45	78	.301

Roberto Petagine just may be the best hitter in baseball without a major league job. He's been shuffled from Houston to San Diego to New York, missing opportunities at every turn. He can't run or field, but his smooth left-handed stroke is a thing of beauty. Petagine's got a great combination of line-drive power and plate discipline, and if he were to play regularly, he'd likely hit close to .300 with doubles power and a good number of walks. Sooner or later, a team is going to realize that he can contribute.

Chris Saunders

Position: 3B
Opening Day Age: 26
Bats: R **Throws:** R
Born: 7/19/70 in
Ht: 6' 2" **Wt:** 200
Harbor City, CA

Recent Statistics

	G	AB	R	H	D	T	HR	RBI	SB	BB	SO	AVG
93 A St. Lucie	123	456	45	115	14	4	4	64	6	40	89	.252
94 AA Binghamton	132	499	68	134	29	0	10	70	6	43	96	.269
95 AAA Norfolk	16	56	9	13	3	1	3	7	1	9	15	.232
95 AA Binghamton	122	441	58	114	22	5	8	66	3	45	98	.259
96 AA Binghamton	141	510	82	152	27	3	17	105	5	73	88	.298
96 MLE	141	490	67	132	23	2	13	86	3	50	94	.269

Third baseman Chris Sanders showed vast improvement at the plate in his third year at Double-A. His skills aren't amazing, but he's improved to the point where he may be considered for a spot on a major league bench. Saunders is a quality defender with good range afield, and his bat is decent, if unremarkable. He hits for an acceptable average, has a fair amount of power, and draws a few walks. At age 26, it's not likely that he'll go much further, but after last year, he's got an outside shot.

Others to Watch

Lefthander **Jesus Sanchez** made a stunning recovery from Tommy John surgery, posting a 9-3 record and 1.96 ERA in 16 starts at Class A. Sanchez isn't overpowering, but throws four pitches for strikes. . . One of the better bats in the system belongs to third baseman **Jose Lopez**. The 21 year old batted .291 in A-ball. He has excellent bat speed, but throwing problems may force a move from third base. . . Righthander **Mike Welch** notched 29 saves in the top two levels of the system. His stuff is unimpressive, but he's young and he throws strikes.

Terry Francona

1996 Season

Due to Philadelphia's recent struggles and front office bickering, owner Bill Giles felt it was time to replace frustrated skipper Jim Fregosi. Terry Francona, who at 37 will be the youngest manager in the majors, will try to restore the Phillies to respectability after the team's embarrassing 67-95 campaign last season. Francona coached in the Chicago White Sox farm system from 1992-95, and was named *Baseball America's* minor league manager of the year in 1993.

Offense

Francona was never a great hitter during his 10-year major-league career, but he knew how to handle the bat, and he appears to have the club headed in the right direction after naming the highly-respected Hal McRae (himself a candidate for the Phils' managerial job) as the Phillies' new hitting coach. Francona must emphasize that the only way to rebuild Philly's shell of a ballclub is to stock the roster with youth, speed, and power—if he can find it.

Pitching & Defense

Francona has repeatedly talked about how patient he will be with the team, but this year's Phillies could wear down even their most ardent supporters. The Phils are beset with major injuries throughout their pitching staff, and have only Curt Schilling to anchor down their starting rotation. Francona and GM Lee Thomas will have to work together and see if they can't repeat Thomas' winning strategy of the past: finding quality arms that other organizations have given up on.

1997 Outlook

After the disintegration of their '93 pennant-winning ballclub, the Phillies find themselves with a team lacking championship-quality talent at almost every position. Philadelphia will need at least three seasons before they'll be able to contend again, and how Francona handles the club during its time as the division doormat will decide whether he will be around by the time they return to prominence.

Born: 4/22/59 in Aberdeen, SD

Playing Experience: 1981-1990, Mon, ChN, Cin, Cle, Mil

Managerial Experience: No major league managerial experience

Manager Statistics

Year	Team, Lg	W	L	Pct	GB	Finish
—	—	—	—	—	—	—
—	—	—	—	—	—	—

1996 Starting Pitchers by Days Rest

	≤3	4	5	6+
Phillies Starts	—	—	—	—
Phillies ERA	—	—	—	—
NL Avg Starts	4	86	41	21
NL ERA	4.06	4.28	4.23	4.58

1996 Situational Stats

	Terry Francona	NL Average
Hit & Run Success %	—	39.0
Stolen Base Success %	—	71.6
Platoon Pct.	—	51.9
Defensive Subs	—	20
High-Pitch Outings	—	13
Quick/Slow Hooks	—	19/12
Sacrifice Attempts	—	92

1996 Rankings (National League)

➡ Did not manage in the majors last year

Toby Borland

Traded To
METS

1996 Season

In reprising his 1995 role, Toby Borland was one of the Phillies' primary set-up men, sharing the relieving duties with Ken Ryan. Like most of his teammates in the bullpen, Borland was streaky, struggling with his control and ineffective for long stretches at a time. Despite doing a poor job of keeping his inherited runners from crossing the plate, his teammates nevertheless contributed offensively when he *did* pitch well, resulting in his excellent 7-3 record.

Pitching

Borland is a sidearm-style pitcher who likes to employ both sinking and split-fingered fastballs against enemy hitters. Since Borland doesn't usually break the 90 MPH barrier, he's only successful when generating ground balls—running into trouble as soon as his pitches begin to rise. While Borland is always tough on right-handed batters, he frequently has trouble finding the plate against them, preferring to nibble around the strike zone rather than challenge the hitters. One of the team's most durable pitchers, he led the club in both appearances and relief innings.

Defense & Hitting

Both Borland's slow delivery and lack of a quality pickoff move hurt his ability to control enemy basestealers: they were successful in six of eight attempts last season. A solid glove on the mound, Borland was hitless in four appearances at the plate in 1996.

1997 Outlook

Borland's inconsistency bothered the Phillies, and they traded him to the Mets after the season. While he has has some shortcomings, his ability to throw 70-plus innings a year out of the bullpen makes him a useful guy to have around. He is an inexpensive stopgap for the Mets' pitching needs and will undoubtedly continue in a set-up role this season.

Position: RP
Bats: R   **Throws:** R
Ht: 6' 6"   **Wt:** 193

Opening Day Age: 27
Born: 5/29/69 in Quitman, LA
ML Seasons: 3
Pronunciation: buh-TAL-ih-coe

Overall Statistics

	W	L	Pct.	ERA	G	GS	Sv	IP	H	BB	SO	HR	BR/IP
1996	7	3	.700	4.07	69	0	0	90.2	83	43	76	9	1.39
Career	9	6	.600	3.66	143	0	7	199.0	195	94	161	13	1.45

How Often He Throws Strikes

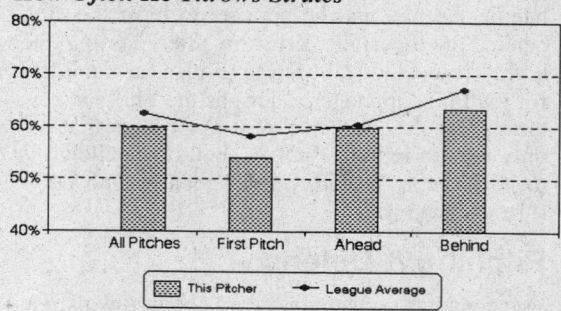

1996 Situational Stats

	W	L	ERA	Sv	IP		AB	H	HR	RBI	Avg
Home	6	1	3.14	0	51.2	LHB	134	38	3	17	.284
Road	1	2	5.31	0	39.0	RHB	214	45	6	32	.210
First Half	5	2	4.11	0	46.0	Sc Pos	105	25	1	36	.238
Scnd Half	2	1	4.03	0	44.2	Clutch	86	23	2	12	.267

1996 Rankings (National League)

→ 3rd in relief innings (90.2)
→ 5th in highest percentage of inherited runners scored (42.9%) and relief wins (7)
→ 8th in wild pitches (10)
→ 10th in first batter efficiency (.172)
→ Led the Phillies in games pitched, lowest batting average allowed in relief with runners in scoring position (.238), lowest percentage of inherited runners scored (42.9%), relief wins (7) and relief innings (90.2)

Ricky Bottalico

1996 Season

One of the few quality players to come up through the Phillies minor league system, Ricky Bottalico started the 1996 season as the team's new closer, replacing the departed Heathcliff Slocumb. Bottalico pitched well early on, compiling 14 saves and a 2.39 ERA through the end of May, and was named as the Phillies' lone representative to the All-Star Game. Following a midseason slump, during which some of his closing duties were shared with teammate Ken Ryan, Bottalico rebounded to close out the year strongly, racking up 34 saves for a losing cause.

Pitching

Bottalico mainly works with his powerful high-90s fastball and his sharp breaking ball. Since he likes to challenge the hitters, he can occasionally get burned with a longball, but usually he's able to keep his pitches low around the strike zone, forcing opponents to swing away. For a closer, Bottalico possesses mediocre control. He prefers to throw the ball as hard as possible and strike his way out of trouble if necessary.

Defense & Hitting

Like most relievers, Bottalico has struggled in the past to control his opponents' baserunning, but has now developed a decent pickoff move. Average on defense and a non-factor with the bat, Bottalico's main responsibility is to lock up those Philadelphia wins.

1997 Outlook

Being young and talented, Bottalico is definitely one of the most prized Phillies' assets. As such, he will no doubt continue to serve in the closer role in the bullpen next season—but he could have some competition in the near future. Recent first round pick Wayne Gomes is also being groomed as a closer, which could create some competition for Bottalico if Gomes reaches the majors in the next year or two.

Position: RP
Bats: L **Throws:** R
Ht: 6' 1" **Wt:** 208

Opening Day Age: 27
Born: 8/26/69 in New Britain, CT
ML Seasons: 3
Pronunciation: buh-TAL-ih-co

Philadelphia Phillies

Overall Statistics

	W	L	Pct.	ERA	G	GS	Sv	IP	H	BB	SO	HR	BR/IP
1996	4	5	.444	3.19	61	0	34	67.2	47	23	74	6	1.03
Career	9	8	.529	2.73	126	0	35	158.1	100	66	164	13	1.05

How Often He Throws Strikes

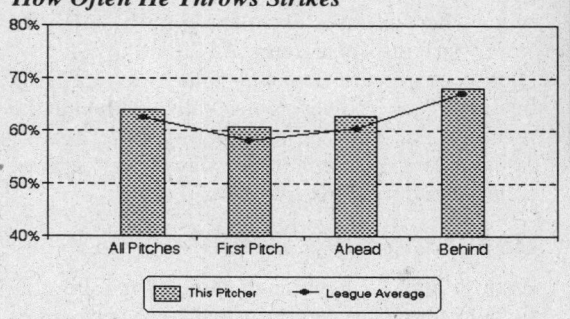

1996 Situational Stats

	W	L	ERA	Sv	IP		AB	H	HR	RBI	Avg
Home	3	3	4.04	15	35.2	LHB	92	20	3	12	.217
Road	1	2	2.25	19	32.0	RHB	146	27	3	15	.185
First Half	2	4	3.61	20	42.1	Sc Pos	58	14	2	22	.241
Scnd Half	2	1	2.49	14	25.1	Clutch	167	33	6	21	.198

1996 Rankings (National League)

- → 1st in first batter efficiency (.123)
- → 3rd in save percentage (89.5%)
- → 4th in least baserunners allowed per 9 innings in relief (9.6)
- → 5th in lowest batting average allowed in relief (.197)
- → 8th in saves, games finished (56), save opportunities (38) and most strikeouts per 9 innings in relief (9.8)
- → Led the Phillies in saves, games finished (56), save opportunities (38), save percentage (89.5%), first batter efficiency (.123), lowest batting average allowed in relief with runners on base (.207) and lowest batting average allowed in relief (.197)

Jim Eisenreich

1996 Season

One of Philadelphia's best-loved players, Jim Eisenreich turned in another outstanding year in 1996. Despite being hampered by Tourette's Syndrome, which limits his playing time, Eisenreich led the team in hitting and could have contended for the batting crown had not a broken foot cut short his season. Still an above-average fielder and baserunner, the veteran was usually platooned in left and right field with an assortment of rotating journeymen.

Hitting

Though he doesn't appear to be blessed with a great deal of bat speed, Eisenreich is a line-drive hitter who possesses excellent extra-base power. Rarely striking out, Eisenreich will often patiently choose to use the opposite field to avoid being beaten by overpowering fastballs. Although he receives the bulk of his playing time against righthanders, Eisenreich has played well against southpaws during his 14-year career.

Baserunning & Defense

Even at age 37, Eisenreich remains a solid outfielder in both left and right, and he has been used extensively as a defensive replacement during his stint in Philadelphia. While his throwing arm is only average, he gets a good jump on balls hit his way. Though he's never been a prolific basestealer, Eisenreich has had excellent success in his attempts, swiping 11 of 12 last year and 32 of 35 in four years with the Phillies.

1997 Outlook

Despite his fine 1996 performance, Eisenreich is at the career stage where a steep decline due to age is increasingly probable. His season-ending injury and ongoing illness problems only serve to hurt his chances. The Philadelphia front office would have loved to re-sign Eisenreich since they felt he would have been a great influence on the rookies who are sure to be populating the Philly clubhouse this year. However, he agreed to a two-year contract with the Marlins.

Position: RF/LF
Bats: L **Throws:** L
Ht: 5'11" **Wt:** 195

Opening Day Age: 37
Born: 4/18/59 in St. Cloud, MN
ML Seasons: 13
Pronunciation: EYE-zen-rike

Overall Statistics

	G	AB	R	H	D	T	HR	RBI	SB	BB	SO	Avg	OBP	Slg
1996	113	338	45	122	24	3	3	41	11	31	32	.361	.413	.476
Career	1197	3511	435	1037	199	36	49	430	99	278	371	.295	.345	.414

Where He Hits the Ball

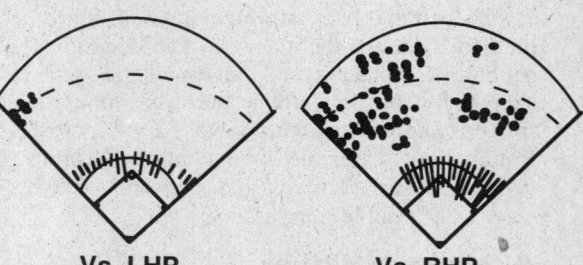

Vs. LHP   Vs. RHP

1996 Situational Stats

	AB	H	HR	RBI	Avg		AB	H	HR	RBI	Avg
Home	163	58	1	14	.356	LHP	40	15	0	7	.375
Road	175	64	2	27	.366	RHP	298	107	3	34	.359
First Half	200	68	2	22	.340	Sc Pos	83	32	0	33	.386
Scnd Half	138	54	1	19	.391	Clutch	75	23	0	7	.307

1996 Rankings (National League)

→ 1st in batting average with two strikes (.309)
→ 5th in batting average with runners in scoring position (.386)
→ Led the Phillies in doubles, intentional walks (9), batting average with runners in scoring position (.386) and batting average with two strikes (.309)

Sid Fernandez

Signed By
ASTROS

1996 Season

Beginning the season as the Phillies' number-one starter, Sid Fernandez proved why he's one of the most gifted—and maddening— pitchers in the National League. Unable to stay healthy, Fernandez finally saw his year come to a halt in June when he developed serious elbow ligament problems. This is nothing new for the portly southpaw: he's missed significant time in the past few years with shoulder strains, biceps tendinitis, knee cartilage tears, and rib cage problems.

Pitching

When he's healthy, Fernandez is still one of the more effective starters in the National League. Though he doesn't have much velocity on his pitches, Fernandez is a master at changing speeds and fooling hitters with his offspeed deliveries, and his unorthodox motion makes the ball extremely difficult to pick up. While he has struggled for stretches at a time, Fernandez has always maintained an excellent strikeout rate, lending credence to the belief that he will continue to be effective whenever unhampered by injury problems.

Defense & Hitting

Fernandez has never been known to pay attention to a baserunner. When combined with his slow delivery, opposing teams run on him at will. Injuries, along with his increasing weight, have sapped some of his mobility over the years, cutting down on his fielding range. Fernandez is a good hitting pitcher, with a career .182 average and 34 RBI to his credit.

1997 Outlook

A free agent when the '96 season ended, Fernandez signed a one-year deal with the Astros. It's a risky signing, since "El Sid" has become more fragile than the Middle East peace talks. He hasn't been healthy in over four years, and at the age of 34, one shouldn't look for him to begin now.

Position: SP
Bats: L **Throws:** L
Ht: 6' 1" **Wt:** 230

Opening Day Age: 34
Born: 10/12/62 in Honolulu, HI
ML Seasons: 14
Nickname: El Sid

Overall Statistics

	W	L	Pct.	ERA	G	GS	Sv	IP	H	BB	SO	HR	BR/IP
1996	3	6	.333	3.43	11	11	0	63.0	50	26	77	5	1.21
Career	113	96	.541	3.36	306	299	1	1861.2	1417	713	1740	190	1.14

How Often He Throws Strikes

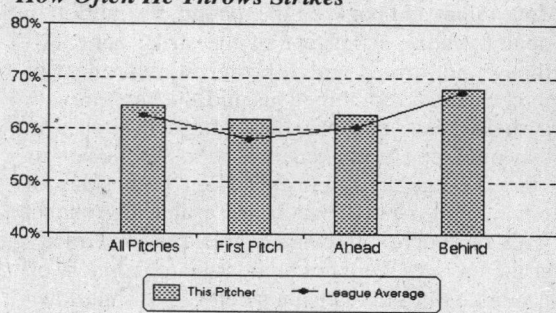

1996 Situational Stats

	W	L	ERA	Sv	IP		AB	H	HR	RBI	Avg
Home	1	3	1.95	0	37.0	LHB	32	10	1	5	.313
Road	2	3	5.54	0	26.0	RHB	201	40	4	16	.199
First Half	3	6	3.43	0	63.0	Sc Pos	45	9	1	15	.200
Scnd Half	0	0	-	0	0.0	Clutch	12	1	1	1	.083

1996 Rankings (National League)

➡ Did not rank near the top or bottom in any category

Mike Grace

1996 Season

Phillies pitcher Mike Grace surprised every-body—especially his doctors—when he burst out of the gate last year, going 7-2 in his first 12 starts in fighting back from several years of elbow and shoulder problems. Unfortunately, right about the time the media was starting to project him as a possible All-Star, the Philadelphia injury plague claimed another victim. Grace went down in early June with a strained right shoulder and was never to return, putting a heavy damper on what was shaping up to be a fine rookie season.

Pitching

Throughout his 12 starts, Grace exhibited tremen-dous talent and poise on the mound, in addition to demonstrating a mastery of the strike zone. Al-though not armed with a powerful assortment of pitches, Grace combined his mid-80s fastball with a sharp curve and excellent offspeed pitches to stay one step ahead of enemy hitters. While he was effective against opponents from both sides of plate, right-handed batters were able to connect with his curve for considerable power. Grace's strikeout rates were not high, as he relied more on ground balls and his team's defense to shut down offensive attacks.

Defense & Hitting

Grace is a good athlete who fields his position well, but has trouble keeping basestealers at bay due to his slow delivery and less-than-overpower-ing pitch velocity. While not a standout at the plate, Grace produced four hits in his limited hit-ting opportunities last season.

1997 Outlook

Due to the extent of Grace's layoff, it is not clear whether he'll be ready in time for the start of the 1997 season. Because he doesn't rely on an ex-tremely hard fastball, he should have less trouble regaining his arm strength than most other pitch-ers. However, his extensive history of elbow and shoulder problems weighs heavily against his chances of returning to the Philadelphia rotation anytime soon.

Position: SP
Bats: R **Throws:** R
Ht: 6' 4" **Wt:** 220

Opening Day Age: 26
Born: 6/20/70 in Joliet, IL
ML Seasons: 2

Overall Statistics

	W	L	Pct.	ERA	G	GS	Sv	IP	H	BB	SO	HR	BR/IP
1996	7	2	.778	3.49	12	12	0	80.0	72	16	49	9	1.10
Career	8	3	.727	3.45	14	14	0	91.1	82	20	56	9	1.12

How Often He Throws Strikes

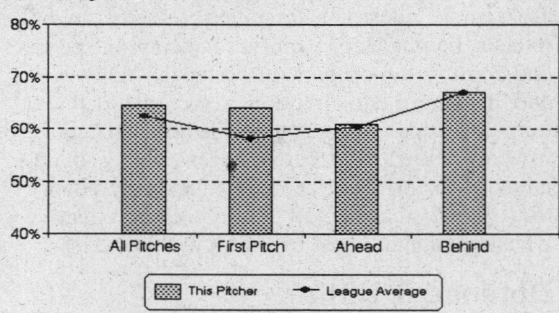

1996 Situational Stats

	W	L	ERA	Sv	IP		AB	H	HR	RBI	Avg
Home	4	0	2.98	0	42.1	LHB	137	35	1	11	.255
Road	3	2	4.06	0	37.2	RHB	165	37	8	21	.224
First Half	7	2	3.49	0	80.0	Sc Pos	54	12	2	21	.222
Scnd Half	0	0	-	0	0.0	Clutch	25	6	0	1	.240

1996 Rankings (National League)

➡ 9th in shutouts (1)

Gregg Jefferies

1996 Season

In the second year of his expensive multi-year contract, Gregg Jefferies' season started off on the wrong foot when he tore his left thumb ligament several days into the 1996 season. When he returned to the lineup in June, the Phillies began a swan dive that continued until the end of the year. Although his numbers looked decent, Jefferies failed to provide the production most teams expect from a first baseman or left fielder.

Hitting

Jefferies is a line-drive switch-hitter who always makes contact and sprays pitches to all fields. He doesn't have a problem handling any particular pitches, being able to both wait on the curve and get around quickly on the hard fastball. What hampers Jefferies is his plate discipline: though he is one of the hardest players to fan, he frequently chases pitches outside of the strike zone, resulting in low on-base percentages for such a high-average hitter.

Baserunning & Defense

Jefferies has lost some speed over the last few years, but he stole more bases last year than in any season since 1993. His desire to play first at the beginning of the season forced the horrendous Darren Daulton/outfield experiment, but by the end of the year he was content to man the outfield in order to provide playing time for some of Philly's rookie first basemen. Out in left, Jefferies is a stopgap at best, being blessed with neither quick feet nor an outstanding throwing arm. He did put up good defensive numbers last season in left field, however.

1997 Outlook

Since the Phillies aren't planning to contend for at least several years, it's probably safe to say that the investment in Jefferies has been a mistake. Nevertheless, Jefferies should provide decent offensive numbers this season—but he probably won't do all that much to help the team win. In fact, his large salary has be considered a drain on Philly's resources.

Position: 1B/LF
Bats: B **Throws:** R
Ht: 5'10" **Wt:** 184

Opening Day Age: 29
Born: 8/1/67 in Burlingame, CA
ML Seasons: 10
Nickname: Puggsly

Overall Statistics

	G	AB	R	H	D	T	HR	RBI	SB	BB	SO	Avg	OBP	Slg
1996	104	404	59	118	17	3	7	51	20	36	21	.292	.348	.401
Career	1080	4142	581	1224	231	21	98	525	169	361	268	.296	.351	.432

Where He Hits the Ball

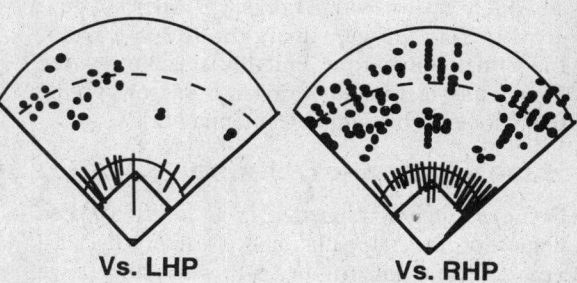

Vs. LHP   **Vs. RHP**

1996 Situational Stats

	AB	H	HR	RBI	Avg		AB	H	HR	RBI	Avg
Home	217	65	4	33	.300	LHP	87	25	1	12	.287
Road	187	53	3	18	.283	RHP	317	93	6	39	.293
First Half	124	29	2	15	.234	Sc Pos	92	32	1	44	.348
Scnd Half	280	89	5	36	.318	Clutch	55	11	1	7	.200

1996 Rankings (National League)

→ 1st in batting average on an 0-2 count (.375)
→ 2nd in batting average on a 3-2 count (.433)
→ 3rd in lowest percentage of swings that missed (8.4%)
→ 4th in batting average with two strikes (.286)
→ 5th in highest percentage of swings put into play (57.3%)
→ Led the Phillies in sacrifice flies (5), batting average on an 0-2 count (.375), batting average on a 3-2 count (.433) and highest percentage of swings put into play (57.3%)

Mike Lieberthal

Position: C
Bats: R **Throws:** R
Ht: 6' 0" **Wt:** 178

Opening Day Age: 25
Born: 1/18/72 in
Glendale, CA
ML Seasons: 3
Pronunciation:
LEE-ber-thal

1996 Season

A first-round draft pick by the Phillies back in 1990, Mike Lieberthal has long been heralded as the heir apparent to All-Star Darren Daulton at catcher. While he hasn't been brilliant, he's shown flashes of major league ability, playing sparingly behind both Daulton in '95 and Benito Santiago last year before suffering a season-ending knee injury in mid-August.

Hitting

As a hitter, Lieberthal visually resembles a right-handed version of teammate Lenny Dykstra with his compact stance and his crowding of the plate. The comparisons end there, though, as Lieberthal simply cannot command the strike zone, chasing any pitch thrown within his reach. After not generating any power throughout his career, Lieberthal stunned the Phils by smacking seven home runs in limited action last season, giving them hope for his future development.

Baserunning & Defense

Being a catcher, Lieberthal was never a speed demon on the basepaths, and it's likely that last year's serious knee injury will slow him down even further. Behind the plate, Lieberthal possesses a good throwing arm, catching 36 percent of baserunners attempting to steal against him last year. While the staff ERA was much higher with Lieberthal than without him, part of the difference probably stems from the fact that ace hurler Curt Schilling always insisted on working with Santiago, skewing the statistics.

1997 Outlook

Lieberthal's future in Philadelphia may have gotten a whole lot brighter with Benito Santiago's move to Toronto. Based on his past record, the Phils can't be overly eager to hand Lieberthal the starting job next season, but the door could be open for another opportunity to prove he's an everyday player.

Overall Statistics

	G	AB	R	H	D	T	HR	RBI	SB	BB	SO	Avg	OBP	Slg
1996	50	166	21	42	8	0	7	23	0	10	30	.253	.297	.428
Career	90	292	28	75	13	1	8	32	0	18	40	.257	.303	.390

Where He Hits the Ball

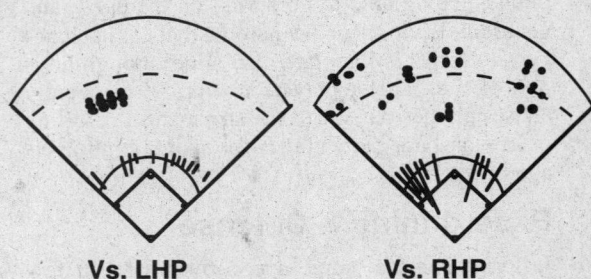

Vs. LHP   **Vs. RHP**

1996 Situational Stats

	AB	H	HR	RBI	Avg		AB	H	HR	RBI	Avg
Home	82	20	4	13	.244	LHP	29	7	1	4	.241
Road	84	22	3	10	.262	RHP	137	35	6	19	.255
First Half	121	35	7	18	.289	Sc Pos	49	9	1	15	.184
Scnd Half	45	7	0	5	.156	Clutch	28	4	1	3	.143

1996 Rankings (National League)

→ 1st in lowest batting average with the bases loaded (.000)

Michael Mimbs

Position: SP
Bats: L **Throws:** L
Ht: 6' 2" **Wt:** 190

Opening Day Age: 28
Born: 2/13/69 in Macon, GA
ML Seasons: 2

1996 Season

Coming off a semi-encouraging rookie season (9-7, 4.15), Michael Mimbs struggled mightily last year while shuttling back and forth between Triple-A Scranton and the majors. Philadelphia's lack of quality arms provided Mimbs with several opportunities to join their rotation, but he rebuffed them each time, never throwing more than four quality outings in a row and encountering a host of problems.

Pitching

A finesse pitcher, Mimbs is a poor man's—make that a pauper's—Sid Fernandez, changing speeds frequently to make a mediocre mid-80s fastball seem faster. Occasionally mixing in some curves with his offspeed pitches, Mimbs often finds himself behind in the count, which has led to walks, high pitch counts, and general ineffectiveness. Although his control was somewhat better last season than it has been in the past, Mimbs still frequently found himself pounded by opposing hitters, especially lefthanders. The alarming number of extra-base hits Mimbs surrendered, when combined with his poor strikeout/walk ratio, leaves serious doubts that he will ever be a consistent major league pitcher.

Defense & Hitting

Mimbs is a solid fielder who, despite his lack of velocity, does an excellent job in controlling the opposition running game. He is not a good hitting pitcher, with just four hits in 35 plate appearances last year.

1997 Outlook

Like many of his teammates, Mimbs has gotten his breaks from a situation that has forced management to dip repeatedly into its minor league pool of talent and fish him out, time and time again, despite his difficulties with big league hitters. With the departure of manager Jim Fregosi, the Phillies organization might soon decide to make a clean break with Mimbs and throw their support behind more promising arms.

Overall Statistics

	W	L	Pct.	ERA	G	GS	Sv	IP	H	BB	SO	HR	BR/IP
1996	3	9	.250	5.53	21	17	0	99.1	116	41	56	13	1.58
Career	12	16	.429	4.73	56	36	1	236.0	243	116	149	23	1.52

How Often He Throws Strikes

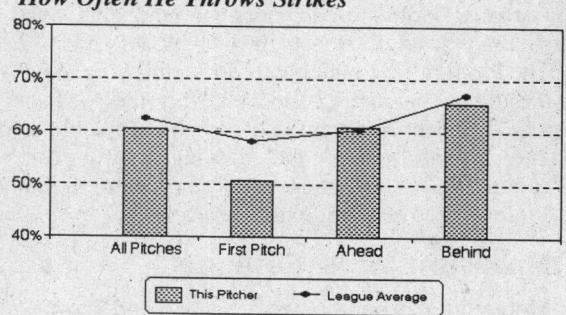

1996 Situational Stats

	W	L	ERA	Sv	IP		AB	H	HR	RBI	Avg
Home	1	6	5.70	0	53.2	LHB	80	29	1	10	.363
Road	2	3	5.32	0	45.2	RHB	314	87	12	45	.277
First Half	0	4	5.72	0	45.2	Sc Pos	93	26	5	42	.280
Scnd Half	3	5	5.37	0	53.2	Clutch	11	2	0	1	.182

1996 Rankings (National League)

→ Did not rank near the top or bottom in any category

Mickey Morandini

1996 Season

Dropping off substantially from his 1995 All-Star form, Mickey Morandini struggled with the bat for much of last season. Although never a power hitter, Morandini had trouble consistently driving the ball and, with his low on-base percentage, was a liability at the top of the Phillie lineup. He visited the disabled list with shoulder problems in June, so it's possible that the nagging injury affected his swing during the year.

Hitting

A spray hitter, Morandini possesses an uppercut stroke that hurts his ability to make contact with the ball. While he can be overpowered with hard fastballs, Morandini is more vulnerable to low sliders, especially those thrown by lefthanders. The Phillies have platooned Morandini off and on throughout his career, especially when they've had a quality backup from the other side of the plate. They might resurrect that idea again this year, depending on the success of teammate Kevin Jordan's recovery from knee surgery.

Baserunning & Defense

Morandini has good range at second and is especially adept at turning the double play. At this stage in his career, Morandini is not particularly fast, but he is an excellent baserunner. He had the best basestealing year of his career in '96 with 26 steals in 31 attempts.

1997 Outlook

Morandini will turn 31 a few weeks into next season and is not the type of player who'll last much beyond this age. With limited power and only an adequate control of the strike zone, Morandini will find it difficult to stay in the majors when he no longer has the speed to play his position. While there's a good chance he'll contribute a solid season in 1997, there's also a good chance he'll be platooned much more than he was in '96.

Position: 2B
Bats: L **Throws:** R
Ht: 5'11" **Wt:** 176

Opening Day Age: 30
Born: 4/22/66 in Leechburg, PA
ML Seasons: 7
Pronunciation: mor-an-DEE-nee

Overall Statistics

	G	AB	R	H	D	T	HR	RBI	SB	BB	SO	Avg	OBP	Slg
1996	140	539	64	135	24	6	3	32	26	49	87	.250	.321	.334
Career	724	2558	320	672	116	39	19	193	82	219	401	.263	.327	.361

Where He Hits the Ball

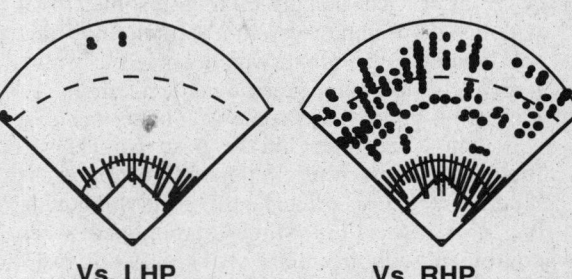

Vs. LHP   **Vs. RHP**

1996 Situational Stats

	AB	H	HR	RBI	Avg		AB	H	HR	RBI	Avg
Home	262	63	2	17	.240	LHP	104	25	0	8	.240
Road	277	72	1	15	.260	RHP	435	110	3	24	.253
First Half	285	77	2	16	.270	Sc Pos	106	31	0	25	.292
Scnd Half	254	58	1	16	.228	Clutch	79	20	0	8	.253

1996 Rankings (National League)

➡ 3rd in lowest HR frequency (179.7 ABs per HR)
➡ 4th in errors at second base (12) and lowest fielding percentage at second base (.982)
➡ 5th in stolen base percentage (83.9%)
➡ 6th in lowest slugging percentage and lowest percentage of extra bases taken as a runner (36.4%)
➡ 7th in lowest batting average at home (.240)
➡ 8th in lowest slugging percentage vs. right-handed pitchers (.340) and lowest batting average
➡ 9th in lowest on-base percentage
➡ Led the Phillies in at-bats, hits, singles, doubles, stolen bases and hit by pitch (9)

Ricky Otero

Position: CF
Bats: B **Throws:** R
Ht: 5' 5" **Wt:** 150

Opening Day Age: 24
Born: 4/15/72 in Vega Baja, PR
ML Seasons: 2

1996 Season

Acquired in a minor trade from the New York Mets last winter, Ricky Otero began the 1996 season at Triple-A Scranton Wilkes-Barre. After serious back injuries sidelined All-Star center fielder Lenny Dykstra for the remainder of the year, Otero was promoted to the majors to stabilize the club defensively and to inject much-needed speed into the Philadelphia attack. Although he was out of place in the team's leadoff slot, Otero nevertheless was solid with both the bat and the glove in his first season with the Phillies.

Hitting

Otero is a pesky hitter who loves to crowd the plate and rarely meets a pitch he doesn't like. While not showing much plate discipline, Otero is a contact hitter, slapping away grounders and pop flies out of curves and sliders thrown outside the strike zone. Despite his lack of power, Otero is able to turn on the inside fastball, but he has trouble catching up to anything thrown above his belt.

Baserunning & Defense

Although he was third on the Phils in steals last season, Otero certainly didn't choose his spots well, as evidenced by his poor 62 percent success rate. It was surprising to see manager Jim Fregosi give free reign to Otero over his basestealing, given the fact that he usually is very judicious with regards to sending runners. Defensively, Otero resembles his predecessor Dykstra, with his above-average speed helping to offset his lack of a quality throwing arm.

1997 Outlook

Since Otero is young (24)—and since he really doesn't have too much competition for his position anyway—he will most probably open the 1997 season as the Phillies' starting center fielder. The Philadelphia front office, having few other options, is eager to see if Otero might develop into a quality player.

Overall Statistics

	G	AB	R	H	D	T	HR	RBI	SB	BB	SO	Avg	OBP	Slg
1996	104	411	54	112	11	7	2	32	16	34	30	.273	.330	.348
Career	139	462	59	119	13	7	2	33	18	37	40	.258	.314	.329

Where He Hits the Ball

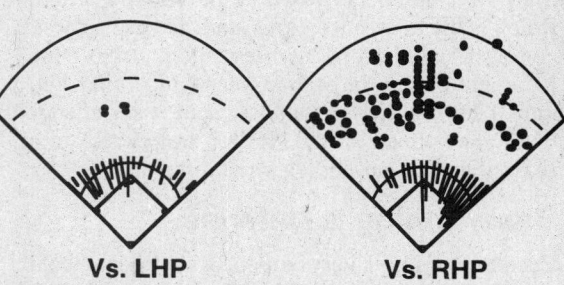

Vs. LHP   **Vs. RHP**

1996 Situational Stats

	AB	H	HR	RBI	Avg		AB	H	HR	RBI	Avg
Home	228	62	0	13	.272	LHP	75	17	0	3	.227
Road	183	50	2	19	.273	RHP	336	95	2	29	.283
First Half	156	41	2	15	.263	Sc Pos	80	23	0	26	.288
Scnd Half	255	71	0	17	.278	Clutch	59	14	1	4	.237

1996 Rankings (National League)

- ➡ 2nd in lowest stolen base percentage (61.5%) and lowest percentage of swings that missed (6.9%)
- ➡ 4th in lowest fielding percentage in center field (.985)
- ➡ 6th in errors in center field (4) and highest percentage of swings put into play (56.3%)
- ➡ 8th in triples
- ➡ 9th in lowest on-base percentage for a leadoff hitter (.331) and bunts in play (19)
- ➡ 10th in caught stealing (10)
- ➡ Led the Phillies in triples, caught stealing, bunts in play (19) and lowest percentage of swings that missed (6.9%)

Scott Rolen

1996 Season

Drafted by the Phillies in 1993, Scott Rolen has enjoyed a meteoric rise up the professional ranks, reaching the majors last July at the age of 21. By the time he arrived in Philly, Rolen had attracted a great deal of attention, both because he was so young—and also because Phillies fans had little else to look forward to. With the spotlight on, Rolen showed flashes, both offensively and defensively, of the ability that Philly hopes to harness at third base over the next decade.

Hitting

Most experts project Rolen as a high-average, line-drive hitter capable of 35-double, 15-home run power numbers. Based on his limited action, Rolen is off to an auspicious start. He has a short, compact swing along with excellent strike zone judgment. While he started very well, Rolen fell into a hitting slump that wrecked his statistics before he hopped off the Phillies' train wreck of a season with a year-ending wrist injury.

Baserunning & Defense

Because he's still very young, Rolen has decent speed and can run the field well, though he's not a basestealer by any stretch. While at times he's proved erratic with the glove, Rolen has shown great quickness and arm strength at third base, routinely barehanding bunt attempts like his predecessor Mike Schmidt.

1997 Outlook

Assuming he's healthy, it's clear that Rolen will be Philly's starting third baseman this year. If both the team and the fans will allow him to mature, Rolen could develop into a quality major league player. Because of his age, his potential for long-term success is probably much higher than most people would estimate. However, Philadelphia fans and media don't exactly have a patient reputation, and Rolen will have to show he can handle the pressure of being his club's top prospect.

Position: 3B
Bats: R **Throws:** R
Ht: 6' 4" **Wt:** 195

Opening Day Age: 21
Born: 4/4/75 in Evansville, IN
ML Seasons: 1

Overall Statistics

	G	AB	R	H	D	T	HR	RBI	SB	BB	SO	Avg	OBP	Slg
1996	37	130	10	33	7	0	4	18	0	13	27	.254	.322	.400
Career	37	130	10	33	7	0	4	18	0	13	27	.254	.322	.400

Where He Hits the Ball

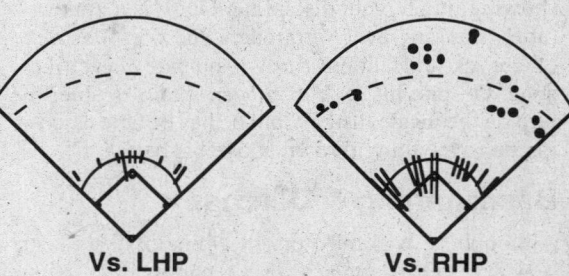

Vs. LHP **Vs. RHP**

1996 Situational Stats

	AB	H	HR	RBI	Avg		AB	H	HR	RBI	Avg
Home	87	22	2	12	.253	LHP	24	8	0	2	.333
Road	43	11	2	6	.256	RHP	106	25	4	16	.236
First Half	0	0	0	0	-	Sc Pos	36	9	2	14	.250
Scnd Half	130	33	4	18	.254	Clutch	20	3	0	3	.150

1996 Rankings (National League)

➡ Did not rank near the top or bottom in any category

Ken Ryan

1996 Season

Acquired from Boston last season in the Heathcliff Slocumb deal, reliever Ken Ryan proved to be a quality addition to the Philadelphia pitching staff. The hard-throwing righthander was effective both as a set-up man and a substitute for closer Ricky Bottalico. Like most of the Philly bullpen, Ryan had control problems and tended to be streaky, giving up the bulk of his runs in clusters of appearances. Nonetheless it rivaled his 1994 season as the best season of his five-year career.

Pitching

Ryan has both a low 90s heater and an effective curve, using them both to set up his hard slider when gunning for the strikeout—especially on right-handed hitters, whom he dominates. Ryan's problems lie in his wildness against lefties, as he seems to be hesitant to challenge them with fastballs over the plate. In addition, Ryan struggles to get comfortable on the mound, which hurts his consistency both in his delivery and his effectiveness. Unlike most of his teammates, he has been very stingy in giving up the longball.

Defense & Hitting

Like most relievers, Ryan hasn't developed much glove work or a pickoff move, and as such doesn't hold baserunners very well. After playing his entire career in the American League, Ryan finally got a chance to swing the bat last year, notching one hit in seven attempts.

1997 Outlook

Since Ryan was both effective and healthy throughout the entire 1996 year—a rare Philadelphia combo—he almost certainly will start next season holding the same role in the Phillies bullpen. Although his walk totals have been cause for concern, Ryan has always posted high strikeout rates throughout his career and should again serve to be a solid member of the Philly pitching staff.

Position: RP
Bats: R **Throws:** R
Ht: 6' 3" **Wt:** 230

Opening Day Age: 28
Born: 10/24/68 in Pawtucket, RI
ML Seasons: 5

Overall Statistics

	W	L	Pct.	ERA	G	GS	Sv	IP	H	BB	SO	HR	BR/IP
1996	3	5	.375	2.43	62	0	8	89.0	71	45	71	4	1.30
Career	12	14	.462	3.18	186	0	30	226.2	198	120	191	13	1.40

How Often He Throws Strikes

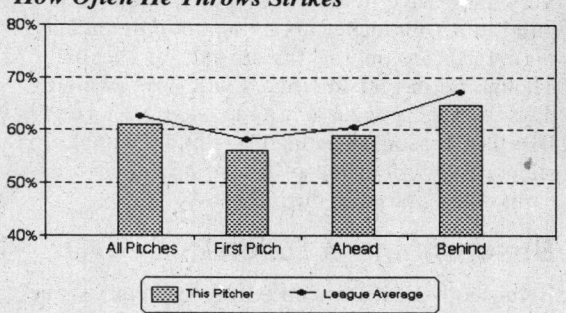

1996 Situational Stats

	W	L	ERA	Sv	IP		AB	H	HR	RBI	Avg
Home	2	3	2.68	6	50.1	LHB	133	32	0	16	.241
Road	1	2	2.09	2	38.2	RHB	186	39	4	12	.210
First Half	2	3	2.98	4	48.1	Sc Pos	78	20	0	23	.256
Scnd Half	1	2	1.77	4	40.2	Clutch	192	45	4	22	.234

1996 Rankings (National League)

➡ 3rd in balks (3)
➡ 4th in relief innings (89.0)
➡ 7th in relief ERA (2.43)
➡ 8th in holds (15)
➡ Led the Phillies in balks (3), holds (15), blown saves (5) and relief ERA (2.43)

Benito Santiago

Signed By
BLUE JAYS

1996 Season

Brought in as a free agent to replace the ailing Darren Daulton at catcher, Benito Santiago exploded offensively in 1996, posting career high marks in homers and runs scored. By September, when most of his teammates were packing it in for the year, Santiago maintained his intensity and finished the season very strongly—though of course, he had a bit of extra incentive to do so. Santiago is now again a free agent, and is likely to command $8-$10 million for the three-year contract he is currently seeking.

Hitting

Very aggressive in the batter's box, Santiago is a pull hitter who makes his living jumping on belt-high fastballs on the inside part of the plate. Though he has left his *really* wild free-swinging days behind him (reaching a career-high total of 49 BBs last season), Santiago is still vulnerable to sliders thrown outside of the strike zone—especially those placed in the dirt.

Baserunning & Defense

Being both a catcher and a 10-year veteran, one can't expect Santiago to possess a whole lot of speed. While he still is a hard runner, he's far from his days as a basestealing threat with San Diego. Behind the plate, Santiago has received praise from his teammates for his ability to handle pitchers. However, his once-excellent throwing ability has been permanently hampered by elbow troubles, as he threw out a mediocre 29 percent of basestealers last season.

1997 Outlook

Santiago figures to handle the bulk of the catching duties in Toronto, and the Blue Jays can only hope his 1996 numbers weren't an aberration. Despite his breakout season and the wishes of many of his teammates, the Phils were surprisingly lukewarm toward bringing him back. The Blue Jays signed him to a two-year deal in early December, and the 11-year vet will see his first tour of duty in the American League.

Position: C/1B
Bats: R **Throws:** R
Ht: 6' 1" **Wt:** 185

Opening Day Age: 32
Born: 3/9/65 in Ponce, PR
ML Seasons: 11
Pronunciation: sahn-tee-AH-go

Overall Statistics

	G	AB	R	H	D	T	HR	RBI	SB	BB	SO	Avg	OBP	Slg
1996	136	481	71	127	21	2	30	85	2	49	104	.264	.332	.503
Career	1246	4425	507	1161	198	25	150	595	77	274	813	.262	.306	.420

Where He Hits the Ball

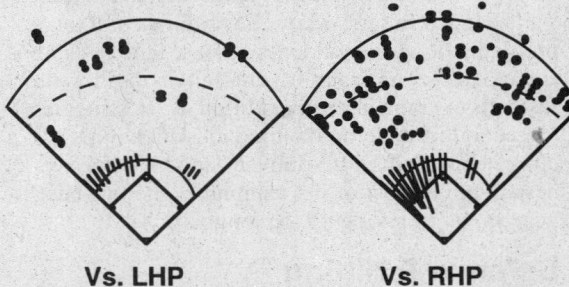

Vs. LHP   **Vs. RHP**

1996 Situational Stats

	AB	H	HR	RBI	Avg		AB	H	HR	RBI	Avg
Home	240	62	8	28	.258	LHP	72	24	6	14	.333
Road	241	65	22	57	.270	RHP	409	103	24	71	.252
First Half	263	64	13	43	.243	Sc Pos	133	33	13	58	.248
Scnd Half	218	63	17	42	.289	Clutch	95	17	4	14	.179

1996 Rankings (National League)

- ➡ 3rd in batting average on a 3-1 count (.778)
- ➡ 4th in lowest fielding percentage at catcher (.987)
- ➡ 5th in errors at catcher (10)
- ➡ 6th in lowest groundball/flyball ratio (0.9) and lowest batting average in the clutch (.179)
- ➡ 9th in lowest batting average vs. right-handed pitchers (.252)
- ➡ Led the Phillies in home runs, runs scored, total bases (242), RBI, strikeouts, slugging percentage, HR frequency (16.0 ABs per HR), least GDPs per GDP situation (7.1%), slugging percentage vs. right-handed pitchers (.482) and batting average on the road (.270)

Curt Schilling

1996 Season

When Curt Schilling missed the last half of the 1995 season with rotator cuff and bone spur problems—the second straight year he'd had serious injury problems—the Phillies became more than a little nervous about Schilling's future. The Philadelphia ace quickly dispelled those fears, however, as he entered the rotation in May in All-Star form, providing the hometown fans an occasional respite from their dreary season. The only constant in a staff racked with injuries, Schilling made a definitive return to the National League's top echelon of starting pitchers. The only question is: can he *stay* healthy?

Pitching

Armed with a mid-90's fastball and a sharp slider, Schilling keeps the ball low but always around the strike zone, preferring to challenge hitters rather than pitch around them. With two strikes on a batter, Schilling will often go to his sinker in an attempt to notch the strikeout. Not tailing away until the last five or 10 feet from the plate, the pitch has proven hard to resist—and lethal—for opposing hitters. For a pitcher with a history of several major injuries, Schilling is surprisingly durable, maintaining his effectiveness deep into a ballgame.

Defense & Hitting

Schilling has a good pickoff move and gets his pitches to the plate in a hurry, which helps choke off the opposition's running game. While just an average fielder, Schilling takes pride in his hitting.

1997 Outlook

Now that manager Jim Fregosi has been replaced by Terry Francona, one can't help but feel more positive about Schilling's future. Despite Schilling's injury record, Fregosi would commonly leave his ace in to rack up big pitch counts even at the end of the season, when the games were meaningless. There's no doubt that, as long as he isn't abused, Schilling will continue to pitch at an All-Star caliber level.

Position: SP
Bats: R **Throws:** R
Ht: 6' 4" **Wt:** 226

Opening Day Age: 30
Born: 11/14/66 in Anchorage, AK
ML Seasons: 9
Pronunciation: SHILL-ing

Overall Statistics

	W	L	Pct.	ERA	G	GS	Sv	IP	H	BB	SO	HR	BR/IP
1996	9	10	.474	3.19	26	26	0	183.1	149	50	182	16	1.09
Career	52	52	.500	3.49	232	121	13	988.1	880	291	800	80	1.18

How Often He Throws Strikes

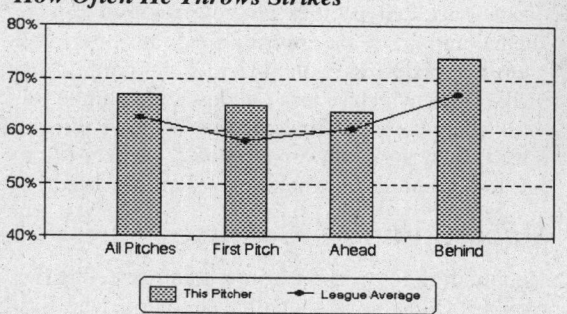

1996 Situational Stats

	W	L	ERA	Sv	IP		AB	H	HR	RBI	Avg
Home	4	5	3.05	0	79.2	LHB	297	64	7	30	.215
Road	5	5	3.30	0	103.2	RHB	372	85	9	33	.228
First Half	2	3	3.44	0	68.0	Sc Pos	133	33	2	43	.248
Scnd Half	7	7	3.04	0	115.1	Clutch	48	9	0	2	.188

1996 Rankings (National League)

→ 1st in complete games (8)
→ 2nd in shutouts (2), lowest stolen base percentage allowed (33.3%) and lowest batting average allowed vs. left-handed batters (.215)
→ 4th in lowest on-base percentage allowed (.278), most pitches thrown per batter (3.88) and least baserunners allowed per 9 innings (9.9)
→ 5th in lowest batting average allowed (.223), least run support per 9 innings (3.9) and most strikeouts per 9 innings (8.9)
→ 6th in highest strikeout/walk ratio (3.6), lowest groundball/flyball ratio allowed (1.0) and ERA on the road (3.30)
→ 7th in ERA

Kevin Stocker

1996 Season

Ever since his magical 1993 rookie season, Phillies infielder Kevin Stocker has struggled to recapture the offensive success that heralded him as one of the game's best up-and-coming young shortstops. Hitting rock bottom midway through the 1996 season, Stocker was jolted into action when the Phillies acquired Seattle prospect Desi Relaford to challenge him for the position. Ending the season on a torrid hitting streak, Stocker mightily strengthened his job security and will probably hold the starting job when spring training opens next year.

Hitting

Stocker is a switch-hitter who loves to choke up on the bat and hit to the opposite field. His problems stem from chasing fastballs and sliders out of the strike zone, which in turn cut down the number of walks he generates. Since he doesn't have the bat speed to sit and wait on a fastball, Stocker often has to commit early when facing hard throwers.

Baserunning & Defense

Rebounding last season from his earlier defensive troubles, Stocker is a quality shortstop who has excellent range, a solid throwing arm, and a strong ability to turn the double play. Although he has fairly decent speed and is a good baserunner, Stocker has stolen very few bases in his major league career. However, like most of his teammates, he is a good percentage stealer who picks his spots well.

1997 Outlook

The Phillies are encouraged by Stocker's second-half turnaround, and hope that he will stabilize in the future as a .250-.260 hitter. With his defense, they'll be more than happy with his current level of offensive production. After last year's season of mass casualties, the Phillies are relieved to have the durable Stocker holding down the fort respectably at such a critical position.

Position: SS
Bats: B **Throws:** R
Ht: 6' 1" **Wt:** 175

Opening Day Age: 27
Born: 2/13/70 in Spokane, WA
ML Seasons: 4

Overall Statistics

	G	AB	R	H	D	T	HR	RBI	SB	BB	SO	Avg	OBP	Slg
1996	119	394	46	100	22	6	5	41	6	43	89	.254	.336	.378
Career	396	1336	172	348	59	14	10	132	19	160	248	.260	.351	.348

Where He Hits the Ball

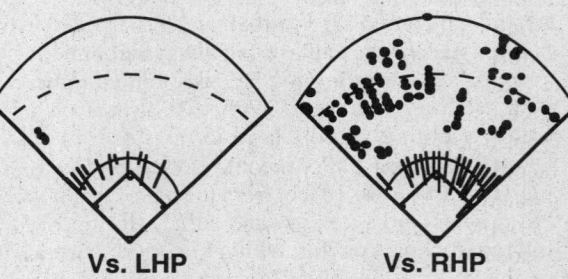

Vs. LHP   Vs. RHP

1996 Situational Stats

	AB	H	HR	RBI	Avg		AB	H	HR	RBI	Avg
Home	204	53	0	20	.260	LHP	60	17	0	4	.283
Road	190	47	5	21	.247	RHP	334	83	5	37	.249
First Half	165	33	3	19	.200	Sc Pos	94	22	1	32	.234
Scnd Half	229	67	2	22	.293	Clutch	71	22	0	8	.310

1996 Rankings (National League)

→ 3rd in fielding percentage at shortstop (.975)
→ 8th in lowest batting average vs. right-handed pitchers (.249) and lowest percentage of swings put into play (36.5%)
→ Led the Phillies in intentional walks (9) and batting average in the clutch (.310)

David West

1996 Season

Like many other Phillies hurlers, pitcher David West has been plagued with serious injuries over the past two seasons. West spent most of last year recovering from rotator cuff surgery that he underwent during the 1995 season, and was ineffective when he finally *did* return to action in August. After several unproductive starts, West was sent to the disabled list with groin problems, ending his comeback attempt.

Pitching

West is a big lefthander with a good mid-90s fastball and a sharp slider. In recent years, however, his arm problems have sapped a considerable amount of velocity out of his pitches. Without the strong fastball to threaten hitters, West runs into serious trouble, since he has difficulty throwing his sliders for strikes consistently. Even when he's pitching well, West has serious control problems, laboring often and accumulating high pitch counts in order to dig himself out of walks and other mistakes. Despite his recent setbacks, West has still proven he can do two things: dominate left-handed hitters and maintain fairly good strikeout rates.

Defense & Hitting

Possessing only a cursory pickoff move as well as a loping delivery, West is definitely not a detriment to the opposition running game. In addition, his size and lack of physical conditioning render him immobile on the mound defensively. He is a decent hitter who has knocked a few extra-base hits in his last couple of years.

1997 Outlook

West was not offered a contract by the Phillies after the season and became a free agent. He hasn't had an injury-free season since 1994, and he'll probably have to settle for an incentive-laden contract. If he's healthy he can be a useful pitcher, but that's a very big if.

Position: SP
Bats: L **Throws:** L
Ht: 6' 6" **Wt:** 247

Opening Day Age: 32
Born: 9/1/64 in Memphis, TN
ML Seasons: 9

Overall Statistics

	W	L	Pct.	ERA	G	GS	Sv	IP	H	BB	SO	HR	BR/IP
1996	2	2	.500	4.76	7	6	0	28.1	31	11	22	0	1.48
Career	31	38	.449	4.58	198	78	3	567.1	518	304	433	64	1.45

How Often He Throws Strikes

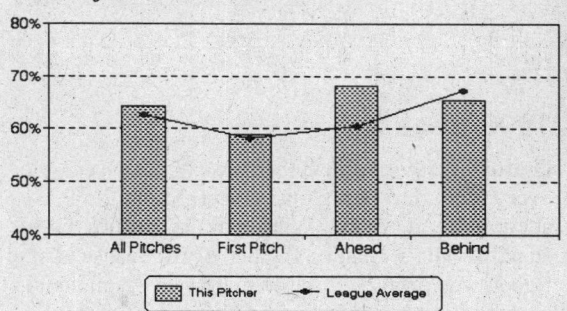

1996 Situational Stats

	W	L	ERA	Sv	IP		AB	H	HR	RBI	Avg
Home	2	1	4.22	0	21.1	LHB	15	3	0	1	.200
Road	0	1	6.43	0	7.0	RHB	99	28	0	11	.283
First Half	0	0	-	0	0.0	Sc Pos	32	11	0	10	.344
Scnd Half	2	2	4.76	0	28.1	Clutch	2	2	0	0	1.000

1996 Rankings (National League)

➡ Did not rank near the top or bottom in any category

Matt Beech

Position: SP
Bats: L **Throws:** L
Ht: 6' 2" **Wt:** 190

Opening Day Age: 25
Born: 1/20/72 in
Oakland, CA
ML Seasons: 1

Overall Statistics

	W	L	Pct.	ERA	G	GS	Sv	IP	H	BB	SO	HR	BR/IP
1996	1	4	.200	6.97	8	8	0	41.1	49	11	33	8	1.45
Career	1	4	.200	6.97	8	8	0	41.1	49	11	33	8	1.45

1996 Situational Stats

	W	L	ERA	Sv	IP		AB	H	HR	RBI	Avg
Home	0	3	7.57	0	27.1	LHB	28	7	1	2	.250
Road	1	1	5.79	0	14.0	RHB	132	42	7	28	.318
First Half	0	0	-	0	0.0	Sc Pos	38	10	2	21	.263
Scnd Half	1	4	6.97	0	41.1	Clutch	14	3	1	3	.214

1996 Season

Drafted in 1994, Matt Beech has shown success at every level during his march up through the Philadelphia farm system. Winner of the Phillies' Outstanding Minor League Pitcher Award last season, Beech was promoted to the majors in August and won his first big-league start against Atlanta legend Greg Maddux. His season then went downhill in a hurry, as he failed to win another game.

Pitching, Defense & Hitting

Despite excellent career strikeout rates, Beech doesn't throw exceptionally hard. Instead he combines a high 80s fastball with decent sliders and offspeed pitches. Beech's two main problems are that he very rarely challenges hitters inside and that he has problems keeping the ball down in the strike zone, encouraging enemy hitters to lean in on his hanging curveballs. He is average defensively, both with the glove and the pickoff move. Beech had only one hit last season.

1997 Outlook

Even when Beech was struggling, he was still striking people out, so there is a good chance that he will be successful in the future. He will get another chance this year, and should pitch better if the ballclub improves.

Ron Blazier

Position: RP
Bats: R **Throws:** R
Ht: 6' 5" **Wt:** 205

Opening Day Age: 25
Born: 7/30/71 in
Altoona, PA
ML Seasons: 1
Pronunciation:
BLAY-zure

Overall Statistics

	W	L	Pct.	ERA	G	GS	Sv	IP	H	BB	SO	HR	BR/IP
1996	3	1	.750	5.87	27	0	0	38.1	49	10	25	6	1.54
Career	3	1	.750	5.87	27	0	0	38.1	49	10	25	6	1.54

1996 Situational Stats

	W	L	ERA	Sv	IP		AB	H	HR	RBI	Avg
Home	2	1	6.43	0	21.0	LHB	54	13	2	7	.241
Road	1	0	5.19	0	17.1	RHB	104	36	4	17	.346
First Half	2	0	1.99	0	22.2	Sc Pos	43	13	3	17	.302
Scnd Half	1	1	11.49	0	15.2	Clutch	40	14	1	3	.350

1996 Season

A free-agent signing who finally made it to the big leagues last season, Ron Blazier was mostly used in middle relief to soak up innings during the frequent occasions when Philly's starters were knocked out early. After starting the year strongly, Blazier lost effectiveness in July and August and was subsequently benched.

Pitching, Defense & Hitting

Blazier is a big righthander with a fair fastball and slider whose pitches began to drift higher as the season progressed—traveling into prime striking range for opposing hitters. While he always maintained his control, Blazier was victimized by the longball. And though he's right-handed, he had a lot of problems with right-handed hitters. Defensively, Blazier is a decent glove on the mound but possesses a substandard pickoff move. At the plate, Blazier singled in his only appearance of the year.

1997 Outlook

Blazier didn't show much last season, but he's only 25, and his minor league record is excellent. With the Phillies hurting for pitching, he figures to get another chance this year.

Lenny Dykstra

Position: CF
Bats: L **Throws:** L
Ht: 5'10" **Wt:** 188

Opening Day Age: 34
Born: 2/10/63 in Santa Ana, CA
ML Seasons: 12
Pronunciation: DIKE-struh
Nickname: Nails

Overall Statistics

	G	AB	R	H	D	T	HR	RBI	SB	BB	SO	Avg	OBP	Slg
1996	40	134	21	35	6	3	3	13	3	26	25	.261	.387	.418
Career	1278	4559	802	1298	281	43	81	404	285	640	503	.285	.375	.419

1996 Situational Stats

	AB	H	HR	RBI	Avg		AB	H	HR	RBI	Avg
Home	63	15	1	5	.238	LHP	38	16	2	5	.421
Road	71	20	2	8	.282	RHP	96	19	1	8	.198
First Half	134	35	3	13	.261	Sc Pos	27	7	0	10	.259
Scnd Half	0	0	0	0	-	Clutch	22	6	1	3	.273

1996 Season

After encountering serious injury problems in both 1994 and 1995, Phillies outfielder Lenny Dykstra came roaring out of the gate last year, intent on proving that he was still one of the National League's best leadoff hitters. However, the injury jinx struck again. Dykstra's serious recurring back problems forced him out for the season in mid-May and threaten to end his career.

Hitting, Baserunning, & Defense

Though past injuries had sapped some of his bat speed, Dykstra was still able to get around against left-handed fastballs last season. While his strike zone judgment remains impeccable, his baserunning and fielding range are not what they once were, and when combined with his below-average throwing arm, a permanent shift to left is likely should Dykstra be able to return to the majors.

1997 Outlook

When last seen, Dykstra was walking around like a man twice his age, hobbling about with serious knee and back ailments—such has been the price of his wild and reckless playing style. Although he's eager to return, the chances are that his days as a regular are finished.

Rich Hunter

Position: SP
Bats: R **Throws:** R
Ht: 6' 1" **Wt:** 185

Opening Day Age: 22
Born: 9/25/74 in Pasadena, CA
ML Seasons: 1

Overall Statistics

	W	L	Pct.	ERA	G	GS	Sv	IP	H	BB	SO	HR	BR/IP
1996	3	7	.300	6.49	14	14	0	69.1	84	33	32	10	1.69
Career	3	7	.300	6.49	14	14	0	69.1	84	33	32	10	1.69

1996 Situational Stats

	W	L	ERA	Sv	IP		AB	H	HR	RBI	Avg
Home	1	6	6.75	0	40.0	LHB	136	46	3	22	.338
Road	2	1	6.14	0	29.1	RHB	140	38	7	22	.271
First Half	1	2	6.35	0	28.1	Sc Pos	69	21	1	33	.304
Scnd Half	2	5	6.59	0	41.0	Clutch	8	3	0	0	.375

1996 Season

Drafted out of high school by the Phillies in 1993, Rich Hunter made steady progress through the Phils system over the next two and a half seasons. Phils manager Jim Fregosi surprised many by taking the rookie righthander with the club as they left Florida last spring. Put in the rotation, Hunter got hammered and was eventually sent back down to Triple-A Scranton. Although he was recalled later in the season, he continued to struggle.

Pitching, Defense & Hitting

Although he had terrific control into the minors, Hunter completely fell apart in the major league ranks, serving up homers and walks in tremendous numbers on his previously unhittable fastballs and sliders. Hunter has a good pickoff move, severely hampering the opposition's running game. Average with the glove, Hunter knows how to help himself with the bat.

1997 Outlook

Hunter's struggles last year weren't too surprising, given that he'd only started three games above the Class-A level prior to the start of the season. Only 22, he'll have more opportunities to show what he can do, but there's a good chance he'll spend most of this year in Triple-A.

Ricardo Jordan  Traded To METS

Position: RP
Bats: L **Throws:** L
Ht: 6' 0" **Wt:** 180

Opening Day Age: 26
Born: 6/27/70 in Boynton Beach, FL
ML Seasons: 2

Overall Statistics

	W	L	Pct.	ERA	G	GS	Sv	IP	H	BB	SO	HR	BR/IP
1996	2	2	.500	1.80	26	0	0	25.0	18	12	17	0	1.20
Career	3	2	.600	3.60	41	0	1	40.0	36	25	27	3	1.53

1996 Situational Stats

	W	L	ERA	Sv	IP		AB	H	HR	RBI	Avg
Home	0	1	1.29	0	14.0	LHB	31	4	0	5	.129
Road	2	1	2.45	0	11.0	RHB	58	14	0	5	.241
First Half	0	1	3.68	0	7.1	Sc Pos	20	7	0	10	.350
Scnd Half	2	1	1.02	0	17.2	Clutch	21	5	0	5	.238

1996 Season

Acquired from Toronto after the '95 season, lefty Ricardo Jordan began last season in Triple-A. Jordan was promoted to Philadelphia in June and pitched very well, taking over the middle relief role from fellow rookie Ron Blazier in July.

Pitching, Defense & Hitting

When used primarily against lefthanders, Jordan was stifling, completely shutting down enemy attacks. Even against righthanders, Jordan pitched well, but he tended to have control problems in trying to keep his fastballs on the outside part of the plate. Defensively, Jordan didn't receive too many chances on the mound, and his quick move to the plate didn't encourage many basestealing attempts. Obviously unexperienced with the bat, Jordan failed in his only plate appearance last year.

1997 Outlook

Jordan was traded to the Mets, along with Toby Borland, for first baseman Rico Brogna after the season. Based on his 1996 success, Jordan figures to help the Mets this season as a middle reliever or set-up man. He'll need to show he's for real, but if he can continue to handle lefty swingers the way he did last year, he could fashion a career as a left-handed situational specialist.

Wendell Magee

Position: CF/RF
Bats: R **Throws:** R
Ht: 6' 0" **Wt:** 220

Opening Day Age: 24
Born: 8/3/72 in Hattiesburg, MS
ML Seasons: 1

Overall Statistics

	G	AB	R	H	D	T	HR	RBI	SB	BB	SO	Avg	OBP	Slg
1996	38	142	9	29	7	0	2	14	0	9	33	.204	.252	.296
Career	38	142	9	29	7	0	2	14	0	9	33	.204	.252	.296

1996 Situational Stats

	AB	H	HR	RBI	Avg		AB	H	HR	RBI	Avg
Home	76	21	2	9	.276	LHP	10	2	0	1	.200
Road	66	8	0	5	.121	RHP	132	27	2	13	.205
First Half	0	0	0	0	-	Sc Pos	44	11	0	12	.250
Scnd Half	142	29	2	14	.204	Clutch	26	4	1	2	.154

1996 Season

Advancing rapidly through the Phillies farm system, Wendell Magee received his first taste of the major leagues when he was called up in August to join their slipshod outfield corps. Starting in both center and right field, the free-swinging Magee shined defensively but struggled with the bat.

Hitting, Baserunning & Fielding

Armed with a huge swing, Magee proved to be a decent fastball hitter and showed that he has some power in his bat. However, he was very undisciplined and needs to learn how to layoff the unhittable sliders and curves that opposing pitchers started feeding him. Young and fast, Magee possesses good speed on the basepaths and is a quality fielder. His throwing arm has been mediocre but is improving.

1997 Outlook

Given the Phillies' chaotic 1997 spring training situation, it's a lock that Magee will be given a chance to earn a roster spot this season. While he may win a job with the team, his long-term success will be predicated on his ability to manage the strike zone.

Larry Mitchell

Position: RP
Bats: R **Throws:** R
Ht: 6' 1" **Wt:** 219

Opening Day Age: 25
Born: 10/16/71 in Flint, MI
ML Seasons: 1

Overall Statistics

	W	L	Pct.	ERA	G	GS	Sv	IP	H	BB	SO	HR	BR/IP
1996	0	0	-	4.50	7	0	0	12.0	14	5	7	1	1.58
Career	0	0	-	4.50	7	0	0	12.0	14	5	7	1	1.58

1996 Situational Stats

	W	L	ERA	Sv	IP		AB	H	HR	RBI	Avg
Home	0	0	4.50	0	6.0	LHB	19	5	0	2	.263
Road	0	0	4.50	0	6.0	RHB	26	9	1	7	.346
First Half	0	0	-	0	0.0	Sc Pos	22	6	0	7	.273
Scnd Half	0	0	4.50	0	12.0	Clutch	-	0	0	0	-

1996 Season

A starting pitcher for most of his minor league career, Larry Mitchell was shifted to the bullpen last year. After some quality outings at Triple-A Scranton-Wilkes Barre, he was recalled by the Phillies in midsummer. Mitchell got into seven games and did a so-so job.

Pitching, Defense & Hitting

A heavyset righthander, Mitchell throws a sinking fastball that can produce a lot of groundball outs when he's on his game. However, he has had tremendous control problems throughout his professional career. In his limited amount of appearances, he did not have much chance to show off his glove work, but he had problems holding baserunners. Mitchell was 0-for-2 with a strikeout at the plate last year.

1997 Outlook

Given Mitchell's lack of consistent minor-league success and his inability to master the strike zone, it's seems unlikely that he'll make the Phillies' roster this spring. He'll probably have to go back to the minors to work on his control, but with the Phils hurting for pitching, he could earn a quick recall if he improves.

Mike Williams

Position: SP
Bats: R **Throws:** R
Ht: 6' 3" **Wt:** 195

Opening Day Age: 28
Born: 7/29/68 in Radford, VA
ML Seasons: 5

Overall Statistics

	W	L	Pct.	ERA	G	GS	Sv	IP	H	BB	SO	HR	BR/IP
1996	6	14	.300	5.44	32	29	0	167.0	188	67	103	25	1.53
Career	13	25	.342	4.87	99	54	0	384.2	406	145	227	50	1.43

1996 Situational Stats

	W	L	ERA	Sv	IP		AB	H	HR	RBI	Avg
Home	4	4	4.97	0	87.0	LHB	258	73	9	34	.283
Road	2	10	5.96	0	80.0	RHB	390	115	16	63	.295
First Half	3	6	5.06	0	94.1	Sc Pos	169	51	7	71	.302
Scnd Half	3	8	5.94	0	72.2	Clutch	39	12	2	11	.308

1996 Season

Shuttling back and forth between Triple-A Scranton-Wilkes Barre and Philadelphia over the past few years, Mike Williams has proven to be one of the Phils' most erratic pitchers. For the first time in his career, he got significant playing time last season—and was dreadful.

Pitching, Defense & Hitting

Williams is a finesse hurler who serves up a variety of junk-ball offerings—many of which ended up in the bleachers last season. Possessing neither good control nor a "go-to" strikeout pitch, he's been hammered hard and often by enemy hitters. Williams has a good pickoff move, but his slow delivery to the plate encourages opponents to steal aggressively. Average with the glove and with the bat, Williams just doesn't last long enough in his starts to accumulate many plate appearances.

1997 Outlook

The Phils sure weren't counting on Williams getting 160-plus innings last year, so it's doubtful that his lack of ability will prevent him from getting playing time next season if their pitching woes persist. Philadelphia simply has too many question marks throughout their staff to write off Williams completely in 1997.

Other Philadelphia Phillies

Ruben Amaro (**Pos**: RF, **Age**: 32, **Bats**: B)

	G	AB	R	H	D	T	HR	RBI	SB	BB	SO	Avg	OBP	Slg
1996	61	117	14	37	10	0	2	15	0	9	18	.316	.380	.453
Career	276	645	74	157	32	8	13	69	14	61	89	.243	.321	.378

In his second stint with the Phillies, Amaro helped out in the outfield when most of the team's regulars went AWOL for the summer. He played well, but at 32, doesn't appear to have a place on this year's team. 1997 Outlook: C

Howard Battle (**Pos**: 3B, **Age**: 25, **Bats**: R)

	G	AB	R	H	D	T	HR	RBI	SB	BB	SO	Avg	OBP	Slg
1996	5	5	0	0	0	0	0	0	0	0	2	.000	.000	.000
Career	14	20	3	3	0	0	0	0	1	4	10	.150	.292	.150

Acquired from Toronto, this third baseman saw limited action at the end of last season. Shines defensively, but there is the matter of Scott Rolen... 1997 Outlook: C

Mike Benjamin (**Pos**: SS, **Age**: 31, **Bats**: R)

	G	AB	R	H	D	T	HR	RBI	SB	BB	SO	Avg	OBP	Slg
1996	35	103	13	23	5	1	4	13	3	12	21	.223	.316	.408
Career	334	740	92	148	31	4	17	64	24	48	163	.200	.259	.322

Benjamin was supposed to challenge Kevin Stocker for the starting shortstop position, but suffered a series of wrist and neck injuries and was sidelined for much of the season. 1997 Outlook: B

Gary Bennett (**Pos**: C, **Age**: 24, **Bats**: R)

	G	AB	R	H	D	T	HR	RBI	SB	BB	SO	Avg	OBP	Slg
1996	6	16	0	4	0	0	0	1	0	2	6	.250	.333	.250
Career	7	17	0	4	0	0	0	1	0	2	7	.235	.316	.235

Bennett saw some action at catcher in the waning moments of last season, but will be behind Mike Lieberthal and Bobby Estalella next year. 1997 Outlook: C

Carlos Crawford (**Pos**: RHP, **Age**: 25)

	W	L	Pct.	ERA	G	GS	Sv	IP	H	BB	SO	HR	BR/IP
1996	0	1	.000	4.91	1	1	0	3.2	7	2	4	1	2.45
Career	0	1	.000	4.91	1	1	0	3.2	7	2	4	1	2.45

Crawford got hammered in his only major league appearance of the year. However, he could surface again next season if the Phils' pitching woes persist. 1997 Outlook: C

Darren Daulton (**Pos**: LF, **Age**: 35, **Bats**: L)

	G	AB	R	H	D	T	HR	RBI	SB	BB	SO	Avg	OBP	Slg
1996	5	12	3	2	0	0	0	0	0	7	5	.167	.500	.167
Career	1025	3235	443	787	176	17	123	525	44	553	652	.243	.355	.422

It looks like the end of the line for this former All-Star. Although he says he's coming back, Daulton has suffered one too many knee injuries. 1997 Outlook: D

Glenn Dishman (**Pos**: LHP, **Age**: 26)

	W	L	Pct.	ERA	G	GS	Sv	IP	H	BB	SO	HR	BR/IP
1996	0	0	-	7.71	7	1	0	9.1	12	3	3	2	1.61
Career	4	8	.333	5.25	26	17	0	106.1	116	37	46	13	1.44

A marginal prospect whom the Phillies acquired off waivers in September, Dishman has since been picked up by Detroit and probably will get a shot next season. 1997 Outlook: C

David Doster (**Pos**: 2B, **Age**: 26, **Bats**: R)

	G	AB	R	H	D	T	HR	RBI	SB	BB	SO	Avg	OBP	Slg
1996	39	105	14	28	8	0	1	8	0	7	21	.267	.313	.371
Career	39	105	14	28	8	0	1	8	0	7	21	.267	.313	.371

A product of the Phillies farm system, Doster filled in adequately at second base when Mickey Morandini visited the DL in June. He should get a shot to compete for a utility infielder position in the spring. 1997 Outlook: B

Steve Frey (**Pos**: LHP, **Age**: 33)

	W	L	Pct.	ERA	G	GS	Sv	IP	H	BB	SO	HR	BR/IP
1996	0	1	.000	4.72	31	0	0	34.1	38	18	12	4	1.63
Career	18	15	.545	3.76	314	0	28	304.0	297	154	157	30	1.48

Frey is a journeyman who worked some middle relief innings for the Phils at the beginning of the year. With his horrendous control and 30ish age, Frey will be lucky to see the majors again next year. 1997 Outlook: D

Bronson Heflin (**Pos**: RHP, **Age**: 25)

	W	L	Pct.	ERA	G	GS	Sv	IP	H	BB	SO	HR	BR/IP
1996	0	0	-	6.75	3	0	0	6.2	11	3	4	1	2.10
Career	0	0	-	6.75	3	0	0	6.2	11	3	4	1	2.10

Heflin is a prospect who got shelled in his three appearances in the majors. He probably won't see too much action in 1997. 1997 Outlook: C

Kevin Jordan (**Pos**: 1B, **Age**: 27, **Bats**: R)

	G	AB	R	H	D	T	HR	RBI	SB	BB	SO	Avg	OBP	Slg
1996	43	131	15	37	10	0	3	12	2	5	20	.282	.309	.427
Career	67	185	21	47	11	0	5	18	2	7	29	.254	.286	.395

Jordan was off to a stellar season filling in at first and second base before tearing his knee up in June. Assuming his rehabilitation is successful, Jordan should contribute mightily next year. 1997 Outlook: A

Manny Martinez (**Pos**: RF, **Age**: 26, **Bats**: R)

	G	AB	R	H	D	T	HR	RBI	SB	BB	SO	Avg	OBP	Slg
1996	22	53	5	12	2	3	0	3	4	4	16	.226	.293	.377
Career	22	53	5	12	2	3	0	3	4	4	16	.226	.293	.377

A wild swinger who didn't seem to know how to hit or track a fly ball, Martinez was quickly expelled from the big leagues after his 13-game trial with the Phillies. 1997 Outlook: C

Bobby Munoz (**Pos**: RHP, **Age**: 29)

	W	L	Pct.	ERA	G	GS	Sv	IP	H	BB	SO	HR	BR/IP
1996	0	3	.000	7.82	6	6	0	25.1	42	7	8	5	1.93
Career	10	13	.435	4.24	68	23	1	191.0	206	77	106	16	1.48

Munoz has still not recovered from his 1995 elbow surgery, and time may be running out on this once-promising righthander. 1997 Outlook: C

Glenn Murray (**Pos**: RF, **Age**: 26, **Bats**: R)

	G	AB	R	H	D	T	HR	RBI	SB	BB	SO	Avg	OBP	Slg
1996	38	97	8	19	3	0	2	6	1	7	36	.196	.250	.289
Career	38	97	8	19	3	0	2	6	1	7	36	.196	.250	.289

Murray platooned in right field for part of the summer before a torn wrist ligament ended his season. At 26, he hasn't proven he can hit big league pitching. 1997 Outlook: B

Jeff Parrett (**Pos**: RHP, **Age**: 35)

	W	L	Pct.	ERA	G	GS	Sv	IP	H	BB	SO	HR	BR/IP
1996	3	3	.500	3.39	51	0	0	66.1	64	31	64	2	1.43
Career	56	43	.566	3.80	491	11	22	724.2	672	345	616	61	1.40

Parrett is a veteran journeyman reliever who pitched surprisingly well upon joining Philadelphia in August. He'll definitely get a crack at a job in spring training. 1997 Outlook: B

J.R. Phillips (**Pos**: 1B/RF, **Age**: 26, **Bats**: L)

	G	AB	R	H	D	T	HR	RBI	SB	BB	SO	Avg	OBP	Slg
1996	50	104	12	17	5	0	7	15	0	11	51	.163	.250	.413
Career	168	389	41	72	15	1	18	50	2	31	138	.185	.246	.368

A nightmare at the plate and in the field, Phillips struck out in almost half of his at-bats and made teammate Pete Incaviglia look like Kenny Lofton in the outfield. 1997 Outlook: D

Rafael Quirico (**Pos**: LHP, **Age**: 27)

	W	L	Pct.	ERA	G	GS	Sv	IP	H	BB	SO	HR	BR/IP
1996	0	1	.000	37.80	1	1	0	1.2	4	5	1	1	5.40
Career	0	1	.000	37.80	1	1	0	1.2	4	5	1	1	5.40

A career minor league pitcher, Quirico was shelled in his one and only appearance with the Phillies. He finished the season struggling at Double-A. 1997 Outlook: D

Desi Relaford (**Pos**: SS, **Age**: 23, **Bats**: B)

	G	AB	R	H	D	T	HR	RBI	SB	BB	SO	Avg	OBP	Slg
1996	15	40	2	7	2	0	0	1	1	3	9	.175	.233	.225
Career	15	40	2	7	2	0	0	1	1	3	9	.175	.233	.225

Brought in from Seattle to battle Kevin Stocker for the shortstop job, Relaford struggled with the bat while Stocker immediately began to hit. Competition at spring training will make it tough for him to snare a job. 1997 Outlook: C

Kevin Sefcik (**Pos**: SS/3B, **Age**: 26, **Bats**: R)

	G	AB	R	H	D	T	HR	RBI	SB	BB	SO	Avg	OBP	Slg
1996	44	116	10	33	5	3	0	9	3	9	16	.284	.341	.379
Career	49	120	11	33	5	3	0	9	3	9	18	.275	.331	.367

Filling in at third base following the exit of Scott Rolen, Sefcik is a solid utility infielder who should get some playing time next year. 1997 Outlook: B

Russ Springer (**Pos**: RHP, **Age**: 28)

	W	L	Pct.	ERA	G	GS	Sv	IP	H	BB	SO	HR	BR/IP
1996	3	10	.231	4.66	51	0	0	96.2	106	38	94	12	1.49
Career	7	20	.259	5.55	130	27	3	296.2	332	129	235	48	1.55

A set-up man/middle reliever, Springer has good strikeout/walk data but was hit fairly hard last season. He should contribute in '97. 1997 Outlook: A

Garrett Stephenson (**Pos**: RHP, **Age**: 25)

	W	L	Pct.	ERA	G	GS	Sv	IP	H	BB	SO	HR	BR/IP
1996	0	1	.000	12.79	3	0	0	6.1	13	3	3	1	2.53
Career	0	1	.000	12.79	3	0	0	6.1	13	3	3	1	2.53

Stephenson is a 25-year-old reliever who was shelled in three outings with Baltimore before being traded to Philly in September. He has had no signs of consistent minor league success. 1997 Outlook: D

Jon Zuber (**Pos**: 1B, **Age**: 27, **Bats**: L)

	G	AB	R	H	D	T	HR	RBI	SB	BB	SO	Avg	OBP	Slg
1996	30	91	7	23	4	0	1	10	1	6	11	.253	.296	.330
Career	30	91	7	23	4	0	1	10	1	6	11	.253	.296	.330

Zuber shared the first base duties with Gene Schall once Pete Incaviglia and Todd Zeile were traded. He's hit well in the minors, but was ineffective in 30 games last year. 1997 Outlook: B

Philadelphia Phillies Minor League Prospects

Organization Overview:

Well, it finally happened, and Juan Samuel lived to see it. The Phillies' long-inert farm system finally produced a Grade-A prospect—their first since Samuel debuted back in 1983. Yes, if Scott Rolen can manage to carry the hopes and dreams of Phillies fans on his shoulders, he should turn out to be quite a third baseman. With the arrival of pitchers like Mike Grace and Matt Beech, things may be turning around. The team has drafted much more effectively since Scouting Director Mike Arbuckle took over, but it will be at least a year or two before the new draftees make much of an impact at the major league level, and the upper levels of the system are still a wasteland. Arbuckle has focused on drafting young, raw, high-risk, high-payoff players, and the hope is that the strategy will yield a few more blue-chippers down the line. So far, few have stepped to the fore, but the lower end of the system contains more raw talent than it has in many years.

Bobby Estalella

Position: C   **Opening Day Age:** 22
Bats: R **Throws:** R   **Born:** 8/23/74 in
Ht: 6' 1" **Wt:** 200   Hialeah, FL

Recent Statistics

	G	AB	R	H	D	T	HR	RBI	SB	BB	SO	AVG
96 AA Reading	111	365	48	89	14	2	23	72	2	67	104	.244
96 AAA Scr't'n-WB	11	36	7	9	3	0	3	8	0	5	10	.250
96 NL Philadelphia	7	17	5	6	0	0	2	4	1	1	6	.353
96 MLE	122	385	41	82	14	1	18	60	1	45	123	.213

If the Phillies' catching position remains wide-open, Bobby Estalella may just grab it. Coming off another season where he showed surprising power, it's becoming clear that he's developing enough pop to survive as a slow, low-average hitter. His receiving skills are adequate, and he's got a fairly strong arm. Right now, he projects to approach the 20-homer mark in a full major league season, and in time, he may far surpass that level. If the Phillies don't hand him the job right now, he should inherit it in another year or so.

Wayne Gomes

Position: P   **Opening Day Age:** 24
Bats: R **Throws:** R   **Born:** 1/15/73 in
Ht: 6' 0" **Wt:** 215   Hampton, VA

Recent Statistics

	W	L	ERA	G	GS	Sv	IP	H	R	BB	SO	HR
93 A Batavia	1	0	1.23	5	0	0	7.1	1	1	8	11	0
93 A Clearwater	0	0	1.17	9	0	4	7.2	4	1	9	13	0
94 A Clearwater	6	8	4.74	23	21	0	104.1	85	63	82	102	5
95 AA Reading	7	4	3.96	22	22	0	104.2	89	54	70	102	8
96 AA Reading	0	4	4.48	67	0	24	64.1	53	35	48	79	7

The Phillies sure do have an interesting approach to developing prospects. They used the fourth-overall pick in the '93 draft on reliever Wayne Gomes, and decided that the best way to prepare him for a major league relief role was to make a starter out of him. Last year, they finally returned him to the pen, where he was sometimes effective, and sometimes hopelessly wild. There's hope for him because he throws a low-90s fastball and a terrific curve, but he still needs a guide dog to find the plate. The Phils will keep waiting him out.

Dan Held

Position: 1B   **Opening Day Age:** 26
Bats: R **Throws:** R   **Born:** 10/7/70 in
Ht: 6' 0" **Wt:** 200   Hartford, WI

Recent Statistics

	G	AB	R	H	D	T	HR	RBI	SB	BB	SO	AVG
93 A Batavia	45	151	18	31	8	1	3	16	2	16	40	.205
94 A Spartanburg	130	484	69	123	32	1	18	69	2	52	119	.254
95 A Clearwater	134	489	82	133	35	1	21	82	2	56	127	.272
95 AA Reading	2	4	2	2	1	0	1	3	1	2	1	.500
96 AA Reading	136	497	77	121	17	5	26	92	3	60	141	.243
96 AAA Scr't'n-WB	4	14	1	0	0	0	0	0	0	1	6	.000
96 MLE	140	492	57	102	15	3	19	69	2	38	160	.207

Dan Held is Dave Kingman, with less power. He can't hit for average, field his position, or outrun a retired catcher, but he occasionally reaches the fences, and that keeps allowing him to move up. It doesn't help that he's right-handed, either, but the upper levels of the Phillies' system are so bare that they may have to turn to him at some point out of sheer desperation.

Carlton Loewer

Position: P   **Opening Day Age:** 23
Bats: B **Throws:** R   **Born:** 9/24/73 in
Ht: 6' 6" **Wt:** 220   Lafayette, LA

Recent Statistics

	W	L	ERA	G	GS	Sv	IP	H	R	BB	SO	HR
95 AA Reading	4	1	2.16	8	8	0	50.0	42	17	31	35	3
95 A Clearwater	7	5	3.30	20	20	0	114.2	124	59	36	83	6
96 AA Reading	7	10	5.26	27	27	0	171.0	191	115	57	119	24

The Phillies have a 20-year string of wasted first-round draft picks, and they hope that Carlton Loewer won't end up as another poor choice. They took him in the first round of the '94 draft, and he pitched well in his professional debut in '95, finishing the year with eight solid starts at Double-A. Last year, he seemed to be making more of an effort to throw strikes, but the batters ended up feasting on his pitches. He doesn't throw nearly hard enough to blow people away, and he often misses the plate with his hard curve. He may need to add another pitch.

Calvin Maduro

Position: P   **Opening Day Age:** 22
Bats: R **Throws:** R   **Born:** 9/5/74 in
Ht: 6' 0" **Wt:** 175   Oranjestad, Aruba

Recent Statistics

	W	L	ERA	G	GS	Sv	IP	H	R	BB	SO	HR
96 AA Bowie	9	7	3.26	19	19	0	124.1	116	50	36	87	8
96 AAA Rochester	3	5	4.74	8	8	0	43.2	49	25	18	40	8
96 NL Phil'delphia	0	1	3.52	4	2	0	15.1	13	6	3	11	1

Calvin Maduro was the principal player acquired by the Phillies when they traded Todd Zeile to Baltimore. Maduro has always had superb command, and he's become a top prospect as he's filled out and added velocity. His fastball now reaches the 90s, and his curveball and change-up are plus pitches. Philadelphia brought him directly to the majors at age 21, and he was impressive in four games in September. He may need only a minimal adjustment period in order to pitch effectively in the majors.

Ryan Nye

Position: P   **Opening Day Age:** 23
Bats: R **Throws:** R   **Born:** 6/24/73 in Biloxi,
Ht: 6' 2" **Wt:** 195   MS

Recent Statistics

	W	L	ERA	G	GS	Sv	IP	H	R	BB	SO	HR
94 A Batavia	7	2	2.64	13	12	0	71.2	64	27	15	71	3
95 A Clearwater	12	7	3.40	27	27	0	167.0	164	71	33	116	8
96 AA Reading	8	2	3.84	14	14	0	86.2	76	41	30	90	9
96 AAA Scr't'n-WB	5	2	5.02	14	14	0	80.2	97	52	30	51	10

Ryan Nye is the most advanced starting pitcher in the Phillies' system. His fastball isn't overpowering, but he keeps the ball down and knows how to use his good change-up. He wasn't as successful in Triple-A as he had been in Double-A, but he's got good enough control to succeed there and move up to the majors in a year or two. His best asset has been his durability—a virtue that's always in short supply in Philadelphia.

Gene Schall

Position: 1B   **Opening Day Age:** 26
Bats: R **Throws:** R   **Born:** 6/5/70 in
Ht: 6' 3" **Wt:** 190   Abington, PA

Recent Statistics

	G	AB	R	H	D	T	HR	RBI	SB	BB	SO	AVG
96 AAA Scr't'n-WB	104	371	66	107	16	5	17	67	1	48	92	.288
96 NL Philadelphia	28	66	7	18	5	1	2	10	0	12	15	.273
96 MLE	104	356	51	92	15	3	13	52	0	37	98	.258

A right-handed first baseman without quite enough power to make it, Gene Schall was instructed to try to produce more longballs this year. He did, although it sapped his average, nearly doubled his strikeouts, and, on balance, left him just as mediocre as before. He's at the same point that Ricky Jordan was for most of his career—he's a good hitter, but not good enough to hold a job at first base. He may hang on as a pinch hitter for a time, but his long-term future is as someone who has to pay to get into the ballpark.

Keith Troutman

Position: P   **Opening Day Age:** 23
Bats: R **Throws:** R   **Born:** 5/29/73 in
Ht: 6' 1" **Wt:** 200   Asheville, NC

Recent Statistics

	W	L	ERA	G	GS	Sv	IP	H	R	BB	SO	HR
93 R Great Falls	1	1	1.71	27	0	16	42.0	26	12	12	48	2
94 A Vero Beach	3	2	3.91	43	0	0	78.1	69	39	35	66	6
95 AA San Antonio	1	2	3.15	38	0	2	65.2	64	24	18	50	3
96 AAA Scr't'n-WB	1	1	5.14	8	0	0	14.0	19	9	5	9	1
96 AA Reading	6	3	3.31	52	1	1	73.1	62	36	40	73	7

There's nothing special about Keith Troutman, except for the fact that he consistently gets outs. The word "prospect" never has been attached to his name, and his stuff isn't impressive. He was taken by the Dodgers in the 17th round of the '92 draft, and the Phils drafted him out of the Dodgers' system last year. He did decently in middle relief, and even made it up to Triple-A by season's end. If he keeps chugging along like this, he may surprise everyone and make the majors one of these years.

Others to Watch

Second baseman **Marlon Anderson** batted .273 and stole 43 bases between A-ball and Double-A last year. He's got great range and a quick pivot, but needs to cut down on his errors. He's a left-handed hitter, and only 23 years old. . . Righthander **Rob Burger** missed most of '95 with an eye problem, but returned to fan 171 batters in A-ball last year. . . **Jason Moler** never made it as a catcher, but he's developed a little power and can play several spots in the infield. At age 27, he's no longer a top prospect. . . **Aaron Royster** has a little bit more power than his father Jerry did, but it may not be enough for Aaron to make it as a left fielder. . . In his first full season of pro ball, righthander **Randy Knoll** fanned 153 batters and walked only 33, posting an 11-7 record at two stops at the A level. He's only 21 years old this year.

Gene Lamont

1996 Season

The Pirates hired third base coach Gene Lamont to replace Jim Leyland four days after the end of the 1996 season. Lamont, who had worked under Leyland for a number of years, was 258-210 as manager of the Chicago White Sox from 1992 to 1995, before they fired him. He was American League Manager of the Year in 1993 when he led the Sox to a division title.

Offense

Lamont inherits a rebuilding team which lacks both power and speed. Thus he will have to be creative offensively. He likes to run and put people in motion, and while the Pirates don't have great team speed and won't be among the league leaders in steals, look for Lamont to call for plenty of hit and runs and bunts. The Pirates will have to do the little things to manufacture runs.

Pitching & Defense

Lamont will try to build a pitching staff in Pittsburgh from a stable of good young arms. While his pitchers usually had set roles during his tenure with the White Sox, things are different with the Pirates. The team finished last season with a grand total of 41 saves and without a true closer in the bullpen. Lamont will have no choice but to experiment with his pitchers in different roles while he learns exactly who can do what.

1997 Outlook

Lamont signed a three-year contract to lead the Pirates' massive rebuilding project, and he's under no pressure to produce right away. Anything better than a 100-loss season will be considered a success. That will be quite a change from the stress he endured with the White Sox. The possible drawback is that Lamont is an extremely quiet man, someone a young team may feel uncomfortable with—and certainly not a guy who is going to turn on the fans of Pittsburgh after four straight losing seasons.

Born: 12/25/46 in Rockford, IL

Playing Experience: 1970-1975, Det

Managerial Experience: 4 seasons

Manager Statistics

Year Team, Lg	W	L	Pct	GB	Finish
— —	—	—	—	—	—
4 Seasons	258	210	.551	—	—

1996 Starting Pitchers by Days Rest

	≤3	4	5	6+
Pirates Starts	—	—	—	—
Pirates ERA	—	—	—	—
NL Avg Starts	4	86	41	21
NL ERA	4.06	4.28	4.23	4.58

1996 Situational Stats

	Gene Lamont	NL Average
Hit & Run Success %	—	39.0
Stolen Base Success %	—	71.6
Platoon Pct.	—	51.9
Defensive Subs	—	20
High-Pitch Outings	—	13
Quick/Slow Hooks	—	19/12
Sacrifice Attempts	—	92

1996 Rankings (National League)

➡ Did not manage in the majors last year

Jermaine Allensworth

1996 Season

Rookie outfield prospect Jermaine Allensworth made his long-awaited debut in center field with the Pirates last July 23, two weeks after starting for Calgary in the Triple-A All-Star Game. Allensworth started 55 games in center for the Pirates, and finished strongly after some initial struggles. Taking over the leadoff spot, he batted .347 in his last 19 games.

Hitting

Allensworth hit only .275 with six homers in three seasons in the minors before breaking through last year. Primarily a contact hitter, he has increased his strength and is capable of driving balls into the gaps and occasionally over the fence. Allensworth is a good fastball hitter who remains susceptible to good breaking stuff and offspeed pitches. He has particular trouble with breaking balls away from righthanders. He rarely tries to pull the ball and knows how to take advantage of his speed, getting numerous infield hits.

Baserunning & Defense

Allensworth is capable of stealing a lot of bases. However, he is still learning the nuances of thievery and must learn to read pitchers' moves. He has outstanding range in center field and soft hands which enable him to catch everything he gets his glove on. His arm is also above average. It is certainly not out of the question to think Allensworth will eventually blossom into a Gold Glove candidate.

1997 Outlook

Allensworth is a key part of the Pirates' rebuilding plan, and they feel he can be their center fielder and leadoff man for many years to come. He is intelligent and plays the game the right way. Some in the Pirates' organization questioned whether he would ever hit enough to be a major league regular. Allensworth answered those questions last season, and his future is bright.

Position: CF
Bats: R **Throws:** R
Ht: 6' 0" **Wt:** 190

Opening Day Age: 25
Born: 1/11/72 in Anderson, IN
ML Seasons: 1

Overall Statistics

	G	AB	R	H	D	T	HR	RBI	SB	BB	SO	Avg	OBP	Slg
1996	61	229	32	60	9	3	4	31	11	23	50	.262	.337	.380
Career	61	229	32	60	9	3	4	31	11	23	50	.262	.337	.380

Where He Hits the Ball

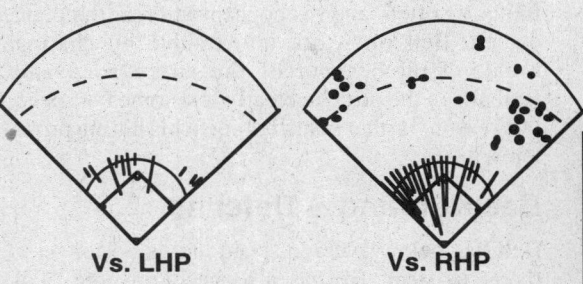

Vs. LHP　　　　**Vs. RHP**

1996 Situational Stats

	AB	H	HR	RBI	Avg		AB	H	HR	RBI	Avg
Home	105	26	4	19	.248	LHP	46	12	2	5	.261
Road	124	34	0	12	.274	RHP	183	48	2	26	.262
First Half	0	0	0	0	-	Sc Pos	58	16	1	28	.276
Scnd Half	229	60	4	31	.262	Clutch	30	7	1	7	.233

1996 Rankings (National League)

→ 3rd in batting average on an 0-2 count (.364)
→ 9th in errors in center field (3)
→ 10th in lowest on-base percentage for a leadoff hitter (.340)
→ Led the Pirates in batting average on an 0-2 count (.364).

Jay Bell

1996 Season

After spending the previous seven seasons as the Pirates' number-two hitter, Jay Bell was dropped to seventh in the order in an attempt to add some power to the bottom of the lineup. He *did* establish a career high with 71 RBI, but only a strong late-season push kept his season from being a disaster. He batted .338 in his last 43 games, raising his average from .216 to .250.

Hitting

Bell has always been a contradiction at the plate. He strikes out frequently, yet is one of the best hitters in the game when it comes to moving runners along with the bunt or the hit-and-run. Hitting lower in the order, he wasn't asked to do the little things as often, and his concentration at the plate waned. Bell often got into trouble by chasing breaking pitches out of the strike zone and fastballs in the dirt. He clearly lost some bat speed last season, further contributing to his hitting problems.

Baserunning & Defense

Bell has below-average speed and is no longer a threat to steal. He has also become more of a station-to-station baserunner. At shortstop he has always had average range at best, relying more on his good sense of defensive positioning. Bell still gets to balls up the middle, but struggles on those hit to the hole. He possesses a strong and accurate arm, which could help him make an eventual transition to third base.

1997 Outlook

The Pirates are rebuilding and would love to dump Bell's $4.8 million salary in this, the final year of his four-year contract. He showed signs of life late last season, but looks like a player whose skills are starting to erode at a relatively young age. He also admitted his desire to play was starting to wane after four straight losing seasons in Pittsburgh.

Position: SS
Bats: R **Throws:** R
Ht: 6' 0" **Wt:** 182

Opening Day Age: 31
Born: 12/11/65 in Eglin AFB, FL
ML Seasons: 11

Overall Statistics

	G	AB	R	H	D	T	HR	RBI	SB	BB	SO	Avg	OBP	Slg
1996	151	527	65	132	29	3	13	71	6	54	108	.250	.323	.391
Career	1222	4529	663	1202	249	46	83	461	64	457	867	.265	.335	.396

Where He Hits the Ball

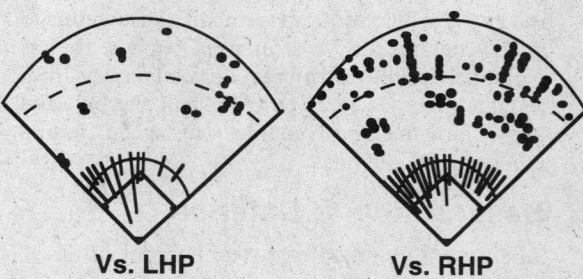

Vs. LHP   **Vs. RHP**

1996 Situational Stats

	AB	H	HR	RBI	Avg		AB	H	HR	RBI	Avg
Home	256	66	7	42	.258	LHP	103	24	3	15	.233
Road	271	66	6	29	.244	RHP	424	108	10	56	.255
First Half	297	67	6	38	.226	Sc Pos	135	32	4	53	.237
Scnd Half	230	65	7	33	.283	Clutch	84	22	0	6	.262

1996 Rankings (National League)
- ➙ 1st in fielding percentage at shortstop (.986)
- ➙ 8th in most pitches seen per plate appearance (4.00)
- ➙ 9th in lowest batting average
- ➙ Led the Pirates in most pitches seen per plate appearance (4.00)

Francisco Cordova

1996 Season

After spending the previous four years in the Mexican League, including a 13-0 season in 1995, Francisco Cordova came out of nowhere to make the Pirate club in spring training. He was soon closing games and established a Pirates' rookie record with 12 saves. He went 2-7 with a 4.21 ERA in 53 relief appearances before joining the starting rotation in September.

Pitching

Despite his slight build, Cordova is a power pitcher. He can bring a 90-MPH fastball which looks even faster because of its outstanding movement and a hard slider with a late break. That was enough to get him by during the first five months of last season when he worked as a short reliever. He began to add more pitches during the final month after moving to the rotation. He developed a curveball that seemed to get sharper with each outing and added a decent change-up. The big question about Cordova as a starter is his durability. He isn't very big and seemed to tire around the sixth or seventh inning.

Defense & Hitting

Like many young pitchers, particularly those on the Pirates' staff, Cordova doesn't hold runners particularly well and needs to improve his pickoff move. Cordova is quick off the mound and can handle those balls hit back through the box. His biggest problems defensively come when he gets rattled by bunts, often rushing his throws. Cordova was just 2-for-16 at the plate last year but showed promise as a bunter.

1997 Outlook

Cordova figures to start the season in the Pirates' rotation after his strong finish in 1996. The organization figures it can't lose with Cordova, especially with the ability he has demonstrated to perform well in either a starting or relief role. He has a bright future ahead of him regardless of which role he assumes.

Position: RP/SP
Bats: R **Throws:** R
Ht: 5'11" **Wt:** 163

Opening Day Age: 24
Born: 4/26/72 in Veracruz, MX
ML Seasons: 1

Overall Statistics

	W	L	Pct.	ERA	G	GS	Sv	IP	H	BB	SO	HR	BR/IP
1996	4	7	.364	4.09	59	6	12	99.0	103	20	95	11	1.24
Career	4	7	.364	4.09	59	6	12	99.0	103	20	95	11	1.24

How Often He Throws Strikes

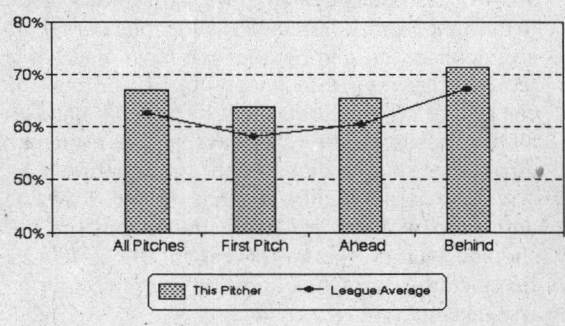

1996 Situational Stats

	W	L	ERA	Sv	IP		AB	H	HR	RBI	Avg
Home	2	5	4.56	5	51.1	LHB	149	54	4	27	.362
Road	2	2	3.59	7	47.2	RHB	242	49	7	23	.202
First Half	2	5	3.94	10	45.2	Sc Pos	102	31	4	38	.304
Scnd Half	2	2	4.22	2	53.1	Clutch	131	39	8	26	.298

1996 Rankings (National League)

→ 3rd in relief losses (7)
→ 8th in blown saves (6)
→ 9th in highest batting average allowed in relief with runners on base (.314)
→ Led the Pirates in saves, games finished (41), save opportunities (18), blown saves (6), first batter efficiency (.173), relief losses (7) and least baserunners allowed per 9 innings in relief (11.4)

John Ericks

1996 Season

John Ericks began the 1996 season in the Pirates' rotation and looked so bad in four starts that he was shipped back for an extended spring training in an effort to straighten out his mechanics. He eventually landed at Triple-A Calgary and was moved to the bullpen. He returned to Pittsburgh at the end of July and wound up converting eight of 10 save chances.

Pitching

Moving Ericks to the bullpen last season seems like a good move. He is a hard thrower and extremely aggressive. . . the type of pitcher suited to relief work. His fastball is consistently in the 90s—occasionally reaching 95 MPH—and rides in on right-handed hitters. His slider and curveball are inconsistent, and he does not have much of a feel for throwing the change-up. Ericks' control can also be erratic. Some days, he has command of all his pitches, but on other days, he can't seem to throw a strike. The biggest concern with Ericks as a reliever is his ability to pitch on back-to-back days, especially considering the reconstructive shoulder surgery he underwent in 1992. He is a fierce competitor who claims he can pitch four or five days in a row if needed.

Defense & Hitting

Ericks has an average move to first and occasionally tends to forget about runners. He is a lumbering fielder, though he gets to most bunts and has good reactions to balls hit up the middle. He isn't much of a hitter.

1997 Outlook

Ericks figures to come to spring training with first crack at the closer's job. His velocity and mentality make him an intriguing possibility, though his durability and his bouts with wildness raise questions. Ericks really enjoys the idea of short relief, and he has enough talent to be a big surprise.

Position: RP/SP
Bats: R **Throws:** R
Ht: 6' 7" **Wt:** 251

Opening Day Age: 29
Born: 9/16/67 in Oak Lawn, IL
ML Seasons: 2

Overall Statistics

	W	L	Pct.	ERA	G	GS	Sv	IP	H	BB	SO	HR	BR/IP
1996	4	5	.444	5.79	28	4	8	46.2	56	19	46	11	1.61
Career	7	14	.333	4.95	47	22	8	152.2	164	69	126	18	1.53

How Often He Throws Strikes

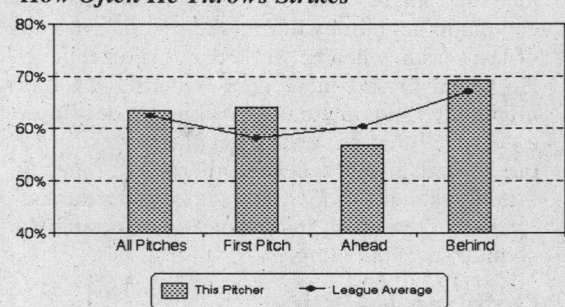

1996 Situational Stats

	W	L	ERA	Sv	IP		AB	H	HR	RBI	Avg
Home	3	1	2.95	4	21.1	LHB	77	21	2	7	.273
Road	1	4	8.17	4	25.1	RHB	115	35	9	27	.304
First Half	0	3	10.20	0	15.0	Sc Pos	61	22	4	26	.361
Scnd Half	4	2	3.69	8	31.2	Clutch	83	19	2	10	.229

1996 Rankings (National League)

→ Did not rank near the top or bottom in any category

Carlos Garcia

1996 Season

Carlos Garcia had a turbulent 1996 season which included time on the disabled list and a late-season position change. A strained right hamstring shelved him for parts of May, July and August. He then was moved from second base to third in September, starting 12 games at the hot corner after appearing there only twice in his previous six seasons in the big leagues.

Hitting

If he could stay healthy, Garcia looks like he could emerge as a decent hitter. He has decent pop in his bat, he hits to all fields and handles all types of pitches well. He does, however, go through spells where his swing tends to get long, slowing down his bat. Garcia is also a free swinger, and his aversion to drawing walks has prevented him from becoming the classic leadoff man.

Baserunning & Defense

Hamstring and knee injuries have ended Garcia's days as a 30-steal guy. He is still aggressive on the bases, though he should probably tone it down a notch due to his loss of speed. Garcia was a shortstop coming up through the Pirates' farm system and that's still his best position. However, the presence of Jay Bell has forced him to play second. There, Garcia is very good at flagging down balls up the middle, but struggles with balls in the hole and has yet to look comfortable turning the double play.

1997 Outlook

The Pirates were looking to deal Garcia in an effort to advance their youth movement, and it was no surprise when he was sent to the Blue Jays in a big nine-player deal following the season. He has a lot of skills and could again be poised for a big season if he stays healthy. However, staying healthy has been no small task for Garcia.

Position: 2B/3B/SS
Bats: R **Throws:** R
Ht: 6' 1" **Wt:** 205

Opening Day Age: 29
Born: 10/15/67 in Tachira, VZ
ML Seasons: 7

Overall Statistics

	G	AB	R	H	D	T	HR	RBI	SB	BB	SO	Avg	OBP	Slg
1996	101	390	66	111	18	4	6	44	16	23	58	.285	.329	.397
Career	482	1782	240	496	83	15	30	174	60	96	266	.278	.320	.392

Where He Hits the Ball

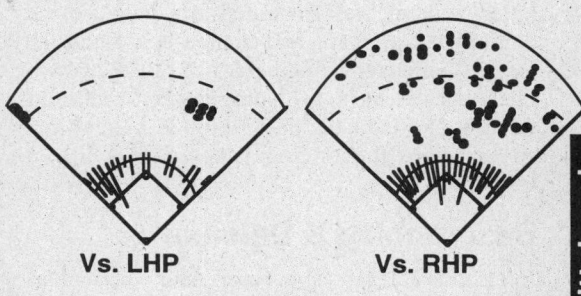

Vs. LHP   **Vs. RHP**

1996 Situational Stats

	AB	H	HR	RBI	Avg		AB	H	HR	RBI	Avg
Home	193	57	3	23	.295	LHP	72	21	1	7	.292
Road	197	54	3	21	.274	RHP	318	90	5	37	.283
First Half	241	70	3	28	.290	Sc Pos	86	25	3	39	.291
Scnd Half	149	41	3	16	.275	Clutch	51	13	1	9	.255

1996 Rankings (National League)

→ 7th in least GDPs per GDP situation (5.4%)
→ 10th in on-base percentage for a leadoff hitter (.344)
→ Led the Pirates in least GDPs per GDP situation (5.4%) and on-base percentage for a leadoff hitter (.344)

Pittsburgh Pirates

Mark Johnson

1996 Season

Mark Johnson got off to a great start in his role as a part-time first baseman and pinch hitter, smacking 12 homers in his first 197 at bats. The Pirates, starved for power and going nowhere in the standings, then decided to expand his role, making him a starter at first. He proceeded to hit just one homer in his last 45 games.

Hitting

Johnson was the ultimate all-or-nothing hitter when he came to the major leagues in 1995. He took some steps to improve last year, cutting down the exaggerated leg kick which started his swing. But his weaknesses were really exposed once he began to see regular duty. He is a dead fastball hitter, and pitchers frustrated him with a steady diet of breaking balls and change-ups. He usually lost his patience, swinging at bad pitches early in the count. He has outstanding power to all fields, though, and is at his best in tough pinch-hitting spots where the pitcher has to come in with fastballs.

Baserunning & Defense

Johnson is an aggressive baserunner who will take the extra base or pull off an occasional steal if the defense is napping. He has decent range at first base, but his footwork is shaky and his arm is poor, which is surprising considering that he was a quarterback at Dartmouth. Pittsburgh tried Johnson in left field for one game last season, but it was such a disaster—four runs scored on a routine fly ball—that he never left first base again.

1997 Outlook

The Pirates should have learned in the final months of last season that Johnson isn't an everyday player. The team desperately needs power, but was mistaken in thinking Johnson could turn into a 30-homer player. That isn't to say he doesn't have value as a pinch hitter and spot starter at first against right-handed pitching.

Position: 1B
Bats: L **Throws:** L
Ht: 6' 4" **Wt:** 230

Opening Day Age: 29
Born: 10/17/67 in Worcester, MA
ML Seasons: 2

Overall Statistics

	G	AB	R	H	D	T	HR	RBI	SB	BB	SO	Avg	OBP	Slg
1996	127	343	55	94	24	0	13	47	6	44	64	.274	.361	.458
Career	206	564	87	140	30	1	26	75	11	81	130	.248	.347	.443

Where He Hits the Ball

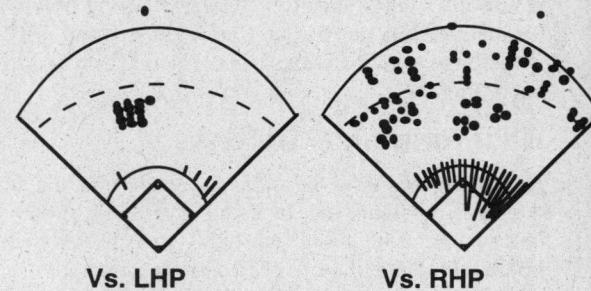

Vs. LHP   Vs. RHP

1996 Situational Stats

	AB	H	HR	RBI	Avg		AB	H	HR	RBI	Avg
Home	157	46	10	24	.293	LHP	30	7	2	4	.233
Road	186	48	3	23	.258	RHP	313	87	11	43	.278
First Half	127	39	7	21	.307	Sc Pos	92	24	2	27	.261
Scnd Half	216	55	6	26	.255	Clutch	62	18	3	11	.290

1996 Rankings (National League)

➝ 4th in fielding percentage at first base (.994)

Jason Kendall

Position: C
Bats: R **Throws:** R
Ht: 6' 0" **Wt:** 181

Opening Day Age: 22
Born: 6/26/74 in San Diego, CA
ML Seasons: 1

1996 Season

Jason Kendall made the jump to the majors after being named MVP of the Double-A Southern League in 1995. He quickly excelled, becoming the only rookie to appear in the All-Star Game in 1996 and the first in Pirates' history to play in the midsummer classic. *The Sporting News* named him N.L. Rookie Player of the Year.

Hitting

Kendall makes outstanding contact for a young hitter, rarely striking out and almost never getting fooled by a pitch. While he makes consistent contact, he doesn't always hit the ball hard. He lacks power, even to the gaps, at this stage of his career and is almost strictly a singles hitter. However, his big hands and strong forearms offer hope that he will add pop as he matures.

Baserunning & Defense

Kendall runs very well for a catcher. He always looks to take the extra base and has enough speed to steal on occasion. His defense—his calling card when the Pirates took him in the first round of the 1992 draft—was poor last season, however. He threw out just 23 percent of would-be basestealers and committed 18 errors. His arm strength is average, and his accuracy is a problem. However, Kendall is impressive in his ability to handle a pitching staff. He is reminiscent of his father Fred, a major league catcher from 1969-80.

1997 Outlook

Kendall is so adept at making contact that he could very well wind up hitting second in the Pirates' batting order, a rarity for a catcher. He proved he could hit .300 at the major league level and should gradually add some power to his game. He must improve his throwing mechanics if he is to have a long career behind the plate. The Pirates have another fine young catcher in Angelo Encarnacion, and that may push Kendall to second base (a la Craig Biggio in Houston).

Overall Statistics

	G	AB	R	H	D	T	HR	RBI	SB	BB	SO	Avg	OBP	Slg
1996	130	414	54	124	23	5	3	42	5	35	30	.300	.372	.401
Career	130	414	54	124	23	5	3	42	5	35	30	.300	.372	.401

Where He Hits the Ball

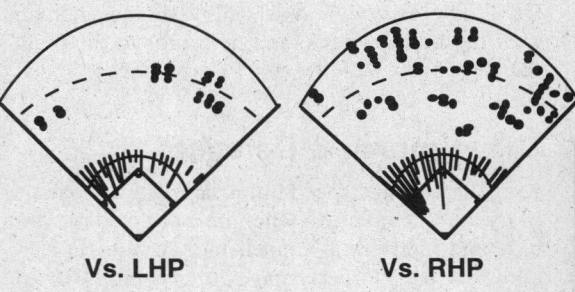

Vs. LHP   **Vs. RHP**

1996 Situational Stats

	AB	H	HR	RBI	Avg		AB	H	HR	RBI	Avg
Home	216	66	2	26	.306	LHP	78	23	0	5	.295
Road	198	58	1	16	.293	RHP	336	101	3	37	.301
First Half	228	67	1	26	.294	Sc Pos	100	30	0	35	.300
Scnd Half	186	57	2	16	.306	Clutch	67	23	2	14	.343

1996 Rankings (National League)
- → 1st in errors at catcher (18) and lowest fielding percentage at catcher (.980)
- → 4th in hit by pitch (15)
- → 7th in batting average in the clutch (.343) and lowest percentage of swings that missed (10.1%)
- → Led the Pirates in triples, intentional walks (11), hit by pitch (15), batting average in the clutch (.343), batting average on a 3-1 count (.429), on-base percentage vs. right-handed pitchers (.372), batting average with two strikes (.255), lowest percentage of swings that missed (10.1%) and highest percentage of swings put into play (50.8%)

Jeff King

Position: 1B/2B/3B
Bats: R **Throws:** R
Ht: 6' 1" **Wt:** 184

Opening Day Age: 32
Born: 12/26/64 in Marion, IN
ML Seasons: 8

1996 Season

In 1996 Jeff King had the kind of year the Pirates anticipated when they made him their first pick in the 1986 amateur draft. Establishing career highs in home runs and RBI, he became just the ninth player in Pirates' history to record a 30-homer season. King accomplished this while splitting time between first base (76 starts) and second base (63) after playing most of his career at third.

Hitting

King made an effort to add extra power to his game last season, and though it resulted in more strikeouts and less walks, it paid off in his overall stat line. He has good plate coverage with his erect stance and concentrates on hitting the ball hard up the middle. His quick wrists allow him to catch up with the best fastballs, and he brings to the plate the necessary patience to wait on the offspeed stuff.

Baserunning & Defense

King has average speed but is an extremely smart baserunner. He knows when he can take an extra base and rarely runs himself into an out. He also knows when the percentages are in his favor to steal and produced an outstanding 94-percent (15-of-16) success rate last season. King was an above-average third baseman, but chronic shoulder problems necessitated a move to the right side of the infield. He has good range and hands at first base, and was a revelation at second base last season. . . particularly in the way he smoothly turned the double play.

1997 Outlook

The Pirates made an effort to unload some of their high-salaried players over the winter, and King's services were very much in demand. It might be a bit much to expect another 30-homer season from King, but he is a proven run producer capable of driving in 100-plus RBI again. In addition, he can play first, second and third—and thus could fill holes for a number of teams.

Overall Statistics

	G	AB	R	H	D	T	HR	RBI	SB	BB	SO	Avg	OBP	Slg
1996	155	591	91	160	36	4	30	111	15	70	95	.271	.346	.497
Career	894	3161	419	817	173	16	99	493	47	296	405	.258	.320	.417

Where He Hits the Ball

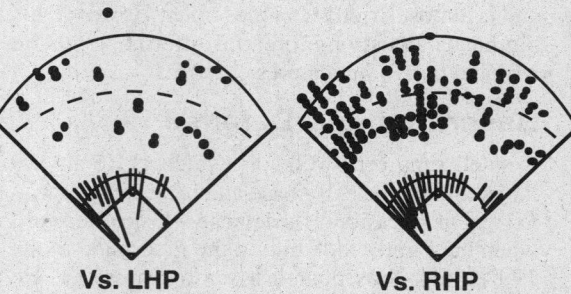

Vs. LHP   Vs. RHP

1996 Situational Stats

	AB	H	HR	RBI	Avg		AB	H	HR	RBI	Avg
Home	298	79	14	52	.265	LHP	137	39	7	21	.285
Road	293	81	16	59	.276	RHP	454	121	23	90	.267
First Half	336	94	21	64	.280	Sc Pos	159	47	6	75	.296
Scnd Half	255	66	9	47	.259	Clutch	88	18	2	18	.205

1996 Rankings (National League)

→ 7th in pitches seen (2,675) and lowest ground-ball/flyball ratio (0.9)

→ 8th in sacrifice flies (8)

→ 9th in batting average with the bases loaded (.500)

→ Led the Pirates in home runs, total bases (294), RBI, sacrifice flies (8), walks, GDPs (17), pitches seen (2,675), games played (155), slugging percentage, HR frequency (19.7 ABs per HR), batting average vs. left-handed pitchers (.285), slugging percentage vs. left-handed pitchers (.555), on-base percentage vs. left-handed pitchers (.387) and highest percentage of pitches taken (58.4%)

Mike Kingery

Position: CF/RF
Bats: L **Throws:** L
Ht: 6' 0" **Wt:** 185

Opening Day Age: 36
Born: 3/29/61 in St. James, MN
ML Seasons: 10

1996 Season

The Pirates had high hopes for Mike Kingery after signing him to a two-year, $1.5-million contract. Pittsburgh felt Kingery could become their starting first baseman and leadoff hitter in 1996. However, Kingery fell into a platoon with Jacob Brumfield by the time spring training ended, and he received few starts after his batting average skidded to .186 on May 18. He hit .274 in 83 games thereafter, but had his season cut short when he broke a bone in his left forearm.

Hitting

Kingery came to the Pirates with a reputation of being a solid contact hitter who drew a decent number of walks. He showed little of either ability last season, however. Kingery became pull-happy early in the season, perhaps trying to justify the first multi-year contract of his career, and his slowing bat couldn't get around on good fastballs. He also got in the habit of chasing bad pitches early in the count. Kingery's greatest success came when he hit the ball up the middle and to the opposite field, and his average improved when he returned to that approach.

Baserunning & Defense

Kingery seemed a step slower last season, but that perception is probably best attributed to age because he is still in outstanding shape. Kingery's defense was a disappointment. He had an awful time reading balls off the bat and continually got poor jumps. He still has enough arm to play right field in a reserve role.

1997 Outlook

Though he is signed with the Pirates through 1997, Kingery was contemplating retirement at the end of last season. *If* he decides to play one more season, it will certainly be in Pittsburgh. . . the Pirates won't find any takers for him on the trade market. One of the classiest people in baseball, Kingery is sadly nearing the end of the line.

Overall Statistics

	G	AB	R	H	D	T	HR	RBI	SB	BB	SO	Avg	OBP	Slg
1996	117	276	32	68	12	2	3	27	2	23	29	.246	.304	.337
Career	819	2034	292	546	108	26	30	219	45	191	248	.268	.330	.391

Where He Hits the Ball

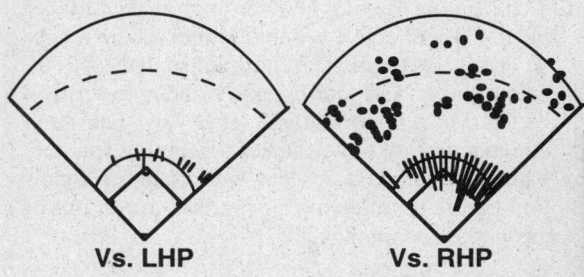

Vs. LHP   **Vs. RHP**

1996 Situational Stats

	AB	H	HR	RBI	Avg		AB	H	HR	RBI	Avg
Home	133	35	2	14	.263	LHP	22	8	0	0	.364
Road	143	33	1	13	.231	RHP	254	60	3	27	.236
First Half	176	43	0	13	.244	Sc Pos	65	14	1	23	.215
Scnd Half	100	25	3	14	.250	Clutch	45	9	0	4	.200

1996 Rankings (National League)

→ Did not rank near the top or bottom in any category

Jon Lieber

1996 Season

Jon Lieber began 1996 in the bullpen, pitching primarily in middle relief. The Pirates then moved him back to the more familiar role of starter after releasing Zane Smith halfway through the season. Lieber proceeded to go 7-2 with a 3.91 ERA in 15 starts. He reeled off two straight victories after losing his first start and finished the season with a three-game winning streak.

Pitching

After a disastrous 1995 campaign which saw him go from the Pirates' Opening Night starter to Triple-A Calgary, Lieber was a far better pitcher last season. He once again flashed the confidence he exhibited during a fine 1994 season, and he added a change-up. Having another pitch makes Lieber much more effective because hitters can no longer sit on his hard stuff. The change also makes his 90 MPH sinker and late-breaking slider look even better. Most importantly, Lieber now has good command of all three pitches, keeping walks to a bare minimum. Heavy legs and a lack of conditioning are a problem, causing him to run out of gas in the late innings.

Defense & Hitting

Lieber has a below-average pickoff move and needs to pay closer attention to runners. He isn't a very adept fielder, is tentative on bunts and slow to cover first base. He worked hard on his hitting last season, and though he still isn't dangerous with a bat, he's no longer an automatic out.

1997 Outlook

Lieber re-established himself with the Pirates last year and now appears to be one of the anchors of an extremely young starting rotation. Former Pirates manager Jim Leyland once said Lieber reminded him of Tom Seaver. That is probably a big stretch, but if he continues to progress, there's no reason he can't become a double-digit winner.

Position: RP/SP
Bats: L **Throws:** R
Ht: 6' 3" **Wt:** 220

Opening Day Age: 26
Born: 4/2/70 in Council Bluffs, IA
ML Seasons: 3
Pronunciation: LEE-burr

Overall Statistics

	W	L	Pct.	ERA	G	GS	Sv	IP	H	BB	SO	HR	BR/IP
1996	9	5	.643	3.99	51	15	1	142.0	156	28	94	19	1.30
Career	19	19	.500	4.43	89	44	1	323.1	375	67	210	38	1.37

How Often He Throws Strikes

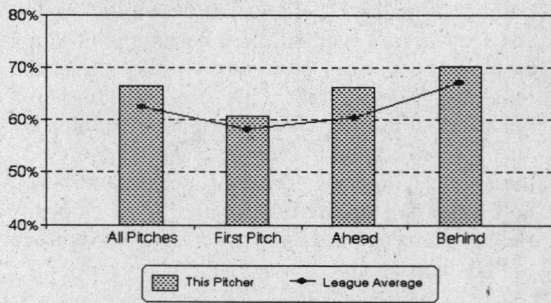

1996 Situational Stats

	W	L	ERA	Sv	IP		AB	H	HR	RBI	Avg
Home	6	1	4.15	0	80.1	LHB	259	73	5	33	.282
Road	3	4	3.79	1	61.2	RHB	300	83	14	34	.277
First Half	2	2	4.21	1	47.0	Sc Pos	126	36	4	47	.286
Scnd Half	7	3	3.88	0	95.0	Clutch	68	21	5	12	.309

1996 Rankings (National League)

➡ 1st in fielding percentage at pitcher (1.000)
➡ Led the Pirates in stolen bases allowed (19) and lowest batting average allowed vs. left-handed batters (.282)

Al Martin

1996 Season

Al Martin emerged as a star player in 1996, though few people noticed. He set single-season highs in almost every offensive category, and his 38 stolen bases were good for fifth in the National League. Martin got stronger as the season wore on, hitting .328 in his last 77 games.

Hitting

Martin became a complete hitter last season. Finally given a chance to play regularly against lefthanders, he proved he could handle the challenge and shed the platoon label. He is an aggressive hitter, sometimes overly aggressive as his high strikeout totals would indicate. Martin murders low-inside fastballs and is getting better at hitting offspeed stuff. He also has learned to use the whole field rather than trying to pull everything. His line-drive stroke, combined with his natural strength, could add to his home run total if he put a little lift in his swing.

Baserunning & Defense

Martin has tremendous speed and shows outstanding hustle on the bases. He runs hard at all times and can go from first to third and second to home on most hits. He is also a smart runner, particularly in basestealing situations. Where he once stole bases on pure speed, Martin now is more adept at reading pitchers' moves. Despite the fact that he displays good range, his fielding is below average. Poor eyesight causes him to have trouble following the flight of the ball, and his arm is rather weak.

1997 Outlook

Martin is one of the guys the Pirates want to rebuild around, and they extended his contract through 1999. All this for a player who never played baseball until his senior year of high school. He had a promising season last year and is capable of an even better one in 1997. The Pirates would be wise to drop Martin from second in the batting order to an RBI spot.

Position: LF/CF
Bats: L **Throws:** L
Ht: 6' 2" **Wt:** 210

Opening Day Age: 29
Born: 11/24/67 in West Covina, CA
ML Seasons: 5

Overall Statistics

	G	AB	R	H	D	T	HR	RBI	SB	BB	SO	Avg	OBP	Slg
1996	155	630	101	189	40	1	18	72	38	54	116	.300	.354	.452
Career	516	1837	305	529	103	17	58	212	89	174	391	.288	.350	.457

Where He Hits the Ball

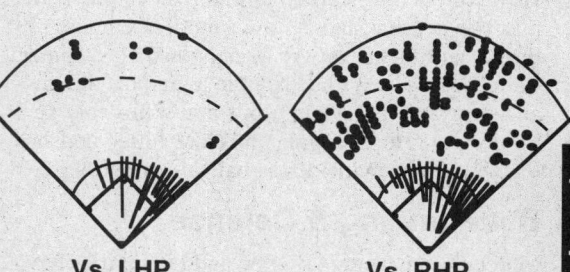

Vs. LHP   **Vs. RHP**

1996 Situational Stats

	AB	H	HR	RBI	Avg		AB	H	HR	RBI	Avg
Home	315	94	8	36	.298	LHP	135	27	4	19	.200
Road	315	95	10	36	.302	RHP	495	162	14	53	.327
First Half	353	103	11	40	.292	Sc Pos	141	35	4	50	.248
Scnd Half	277	86	7	32	.310	Clutch	89	22	2	7	.247

1996 Rankings (National League)

→ 1st in errors in left field (7) and lowest fielding percentage in left field (.964)
→ 2nd in lowest batting average vs. left-handed pitchers (.200)
→ 4th in caught stealing and batting average vs. right-handed pitchers (.327)
→ 5th in stolen bases
→ 6th in doubles and lowest on-base percentage vs. left-handed pitchers (.290)
→ 7th in lowest slugging percentage vs. left-handed pitchers (.326)
→ 8th in at-bats and singles
→ 9th in hits, plate appearances (694) and steals of third (6)

Orlando Merced

1996 Season

When he wasn't hurt, Orlando Merced had a solid, if unspectacular, 1996 season. He was on the disabled list three times, first with a strained right hamstring in May and then twice with a strained right calf in August. Like teammate Jay Bell, Merced got off to a slow start, hitting .230 through May 24 before batting .306 in his last 89 games. However, Merced didn't homer after July 28, not good for someone who spent the majority of the year as the team's cleanup hitter.

Hitting

Merced has been spraying line drives to all fields ever since he came to the major leagues in 1990. However, he has learned to pull inside pitches the past two seasons and is now a moderate home run threat, with better power to right and right-center. Merced has always had trouble laying off the low-and-away breaking pitch but that's his only real weak spot. He is a great mistake hitter and has learned to punch inside fastballs the other way.

Baserunning & Defense

Merced is an average runner, and leg injuries have cost him some speed. He has above-average instincts on the basepaths and has a knack of knowing when to take the extra base, particularly in clutch situations. Merced has never become comfortable in right field, and he rarely makes a fly ball routine. He has a below-average arm, but he compensates with outstanding accuracy. Runners who have tried to take advantage of his arm on shallow flies have paid the price.

1997 Outlook

One of the high-salaried vets who was part of the Pirates' fall and winter "fire sale," Merced went to the Blue Jays along with Carlos Garcia and Dan Plesac in exchange for a bunch of prospects. There's no reason to think he won't turn out another Merced-type season for the Blue Jays, meaning a batting average in the .280 range with decent home run and RBI totals.

Position: RF
Bats: L **Throws:** R
Ht: 5'11" **Wt:** 183

Opening Day Age: 30
Born: 11/2/66 in San Juan, PR
ML Seasons: 7
Pronunciation: mer-SED

Overall Statistics

	G	AB	R	H	D	T	HR	RBI	SB	BB	SO	Avg	OBP	Slg
1996	120	453	69	130	24	1	17	80	8	51	74	.287	.357	.457
Career	776	2613	396	739	146	19	65	394	35	339	423	.283	.364	.428

Where He Hits the Ball

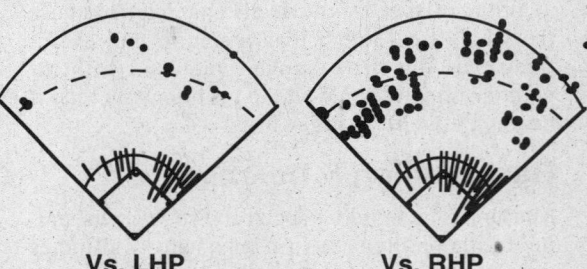

Vs. LHP   **Vs. RHP**

1996 Situational Stats

	AB	H	HR	RBI	Avg		AB	H	HR	RBI	Avg
Home	205	66	9	38	.322	LHP	114	30	2	16	.263
Road	248	64	8	42	.258	RHP	339	100	15	64	.295
First Half	268	77	12	36	.287	Sc Pos	124	40	5	64	.323
Scnd Half	185	53	5	44	.286	Clutch	73	21	2	12	.288

1996 Rankings (National League)

- ➡ 4th in fielding percentage in right field (.988)
- ➡ 5th in batting average with the bases loaded (.571)
- ➡ 8th in lowest cleanup slugging percentage (.494)
- ➡ Led the Pirates in on-base percentage, batting average with runners in scoring position (.323), batting average with the bases loaded (.571), cleanup slugging percentage (.494) and lowest percentage of swings on the first pitch (22.6%)

Dan Miceli

1996 Season

After saving a team-high 21 games for the Pirates in 1995—his first full season in the majors—1996 was a potpourri for Dan Miceli. He got off to an awful start and was dispatched to Double-A Carolina on May 6. He returned a few weeks later and moved into the rotation just before the All-Star break despite the fact that he hadn't started a game since high school. He went 1-5 with a 6.86 ERA in his nine starts before finishing the season back in the bullpen.

Pitching

Miceli is a power pitcher whose fastball routinely reaches 94 MPH and has been clocked as high as 98 MPH. The Pirates moved him into a starting role so he could work on his other pitches. His slider got a little sharper and he also learned how to throw a change, though it is still in the rudimentary stages. The key to Miceli's success is a good sinking motion on his fastball: he has had problems with home runs throughout his career because he often leaves the heater belt high and over the middle of the plate. His control also tends to be erratic, especially to the first batter.

Defense & Hitting

Players run at will against Miceli, who doesn't pay attention to runners and has a below-average pick-off move. He isn't much of a fielder, either, and is slow off the mound to scoop bunts and cover first. As a hitter, he gives advocates of the designated hitter fuel for their fire.

1997 Outlook

Miceli was traded to the Tigers for pitcher Clint Sodowsky shortly after the end of the '96 season. He has the physical ability to be an outstanding closer, and the Tigers are counting on him to fill that role. He'll need to improve on the mental parts of his game if he's going to succeed in Detroit.

Position: RP/SP
Bats: R **Throws:** R
Ht: 6' 0" **Wt:** 216

Opening Day Age: 26
Born: 9/9/70 in Newark, NJ
ML Seasons: 4
Pronunciation: mah-SELL-ee

Overall Statistics

	W	L	Pct.	ERA	G	GS	Sv	IP	H	BB	SO	HR	BR/IP
1996	2	10	.167	5.78	44	9	1	85.2	99	45	66	15	1.68
Career	8	15	.348	5.41	139	9	24	176.1	194	87	153	27	1.59

How Often He Throws Strikes

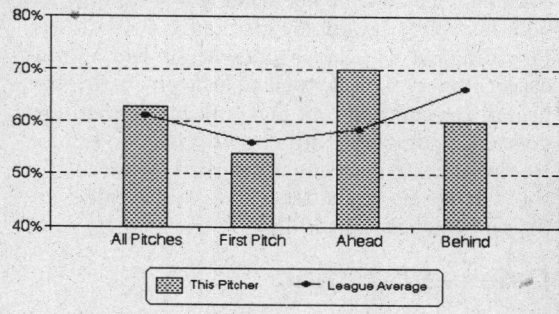

1996 Situational Stats

	W	L	ERA	Sv	IP		AB	H	HR	RBI	Avg
Home	2	5	5.63	0	40.0	LHB	132	39	5	24	.295
Road	0	5	5.91	1	45.2	RHB	208	60	10	40	.288
First Half	1	4	4.61	1	41.0	Sc Pos	95	29	3	45	.305
Scnd Half	1	6	6.85	0	44.2	Clutch	62	14	2	15	.226

1996 Rankings (National League)

➡ 6th in errors at pitcher (3)
➡ Led the Pirates in losses, walks allowed and wild pitches (9)

Pittsburgh Pirates

Dan Plesac

Position: RP
Bats: L **Throws:** L
Ht: 6' 5" **Wt:** 215

Opening Day Age: 35
Born: 2/4/62 in Gary, IN
ML Seasons: 11
Pronunciation:
PLEE-sac

1996 Season

For the first time since he starred in Milwaukee in the late 1980s, Dan Plesac showed he could still close out games. He also showed his durability, becoming just the third Pirates' lefthander in history to appear in 70 games. A horrible five-game stretch in late July and early August saw him go 0-4 with two blown saves, which inflated his final numbers.

Pitching

Plesac looked better in 1996 than he had in years. Since making three straight All-Star appearances from 1987-89, he had been dogged by shoulder tendinitis. However, his shoulder was healthy last season, and he went back to being a power pitcher, with his fastball routinely clocked at 92-94 MPH. Plesac had always been a power pitcher, and his career went downhill when he lost some zip off his heater. He can both cut and sink his fastball and gets a fair number of strikeouts off his good slider. He mixes in an occasional palmball, primarily for show. He is also a battler who took the ball every time he was asked in 1996.

Defense & Hitting

Plesac has a quick step-off move to first base which keeps baserunners honest, though all 10 stolen base attempts against him in 1996 were successful. He is an adequate fielder, but can be somewhat slow getting off the mound to field bunts. Plesac rarely hits and looks quite lost when he steps into the batter's box. He has one career hit.

1997 Outlook

Plesac signed a one-year contract extension last July that was to take him through the end of 1997. But then the Pirates decided to cut the payroll and go with a youth movement; as a result, Plesac was dealt to the Blue Jays after the season. He should be a good addition to the Toronto bullpen: a hard-throwing lefty who can perform as a set-up reliever as well as close an occasional game.

Overall Statistics

	W	L	Pct.	ERA	G	GS	Sv	IP	H	BB	SO	HR	BR/IP
1996	6	5	.545	4.09	73	0	11	70.1	67	24	76	4	1.29
Career	43	50	.462	3.54	607	14	148	772.1	715	271	681	69	1.28

How Often He Throws Strikes

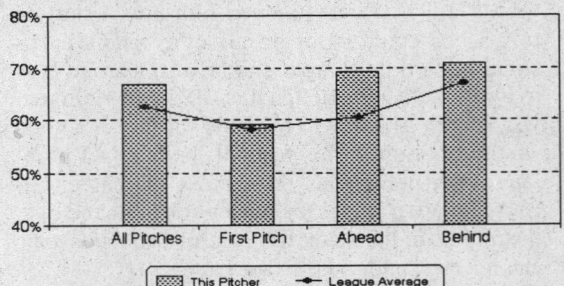

1996 Situational Stats

	W	L	ERA	Sv	IP		AB	H	HR	RBI	Avg
Home	2	2	3.50	8	36.0	LHB	80	20	1	13	.250
Road	4	3	4.72	3	34.1	RHB	191	47	3	23	.246
First Half	3	1	4.20	5	40.2	Sc Pos	69	19	0	28	.275
Scnd Half	3	4	3.94	6	29.2	Clutch	164	47	2	25	.287

1996 Rankings (National League)

- 8th in games pitched and blown saves (6)
- 9th in worst first batter efficiency (.299) and most strikeouts per 9 innings in relief (9.7)
- 10th in lowest percentage of inherited runners scored (28.9%) and relief wins (6)
- Led the Pirates in games pitched, holds (11), blown saves (6), lowest batting average allowed in relief with runners on base (.271), lowest percentage of inherited runners scored (28.9%), relief ERA (4.09), relief wins (6), relief innings (70.1), lowest batting average allowed in relief (.247) and most strikeouts per 9 innings in relief (9.7)

Jason Schmidt

1996 Season

Jason Schmidt began the year as the much-hyped rookie fifth starter in Atlanta's famed rotation. However, he went 3-4 with a 6.75 ERA in 13 games with the Braves and endured both a trip back to Triple-A Richmond and a stint on the disabled list with a stress fracture of one of his left ribs. On August 30, Schmidt was traded to the Pirates along with two minor leaguers for Denny Neagle. Immediately inserted into the rotation, Schmidt went 2-2 with a 4.06 ERA in six starts for the Pirates.

Pitching

At 6-foot-5 and 210 pounds, Schmidt looks like a power pitcher and plays the part well. His arsenal starts with a legitimate 94-MPH fastball, but it goes deeper than that. His slider tops out at 86 MPH, giving him a tough one-two combination. While his hard stuff is good enough to overpower many hitters, he still needs to develop his change-up—a pitch he tends to hang. He also dusted off a curveball which Atlanta had asked him to junk, and it showed the makings of a decent fourth pitch. Because of his size, Schmidt's mechanics tend to get out of whack at times and his control suffers as a result. He is extremely durable.

Defense & Hitting

Schmidt is slow to the plate and doesn't have a very good move to first. Runners therefore take liberties when he's on the mound. He is rather lumbering in the field and has trouble with bunts. Schmidt has a near disdain for swinging the bat, looking uncomfortable and overmatched at the plate.

1997 Outlook

The Pirates will enter the season with a good-looking young rotation of hard throwers. . . and Schmidt may be the best of them all. Few young pitchers in baseball have a better arm. He has the look of a big winner and figures to anchor the Pirates' staff for years to come.

Position: SP
Bats: R **Throws:** R
Ht: 6' 5" **Wt:** 185

Opening Day Age: 24
Born: 1/29/73 in Kelso, WA
ML Seasons: 2

Overall Statistics

	W	L	Pct.	ERA	G	GS	Sv	IP	H	BB	SO	HR	BR/IP
1996	5	6	.455	5.70	19	17	0	96.1	108	53	74	10	1.67
Career	7	8	.467	5.71	28	19	0	121.1	135	71	93	12	1.70

How Often He Throws Strikes

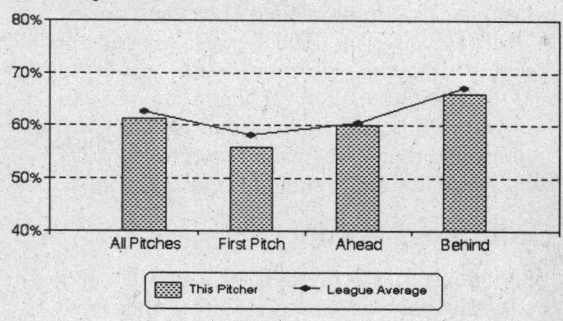

1996 Situational Stats

	W	L	ERA	Sv	IP		AB	H	HR	RBI	Avg
Home	3	4	6.32	0	57.0	LHB	152	51	4	28	.336
Road	2	2	4.81	0	39.1	RHB	225	57	6	30	.253
First Half	3	4	6.00	0	54.0	Sc Pos	97	29	5	51	.299
Scnd Half	2	2	5.31	0	42.1	Clutch	8	1	0	2	.125

1996 Rankings (National League)

➡ Led the Pirates in complete games (1)

Marc Wilkins

1996 Season

Marc Wilkins wasn't on the Pirates' 40-man roster last year and wasn't even a non-roster invitee to spring training. However, he became one of the Pirates' pleasant surprises after his contract was purchased from Double-A Carolina in May. All in all, his numbers in the majors were better than the 2-3 record and 4.01 ERA he posted at Carolina.

Pitching

When you size up his short and stocky build, Wilkins doesn't look much like a power pitcher. Looks are deceiving in his case, however, as he can run his fastball up in the low 90s with regularity. He also has a big-breaking curveball that is a weapon against right-handed hitters and can throw a decent change-up. The biggest question with Wilkins is stamina. He is not in the best of shape and tired late last season. In the minors the rap on him was that he often tired after just three or four innings and opponents would start to tee off. Obviously, conditioning should become a priority.

Defense & Hitting

Wilkins is surprisingly agile in spite of his physique. He handles choppers and bunts well, is quick to cover first base and fields just about everything hit back through the box. He also has a decent pickoff move which should only get better with experience. Wilkins hangs in the box well as a hitter and appears to have a little pop in his bat. He is a decent bunter, too.

1997 Outlook

Wilkins figures to be a key part of the Pirates' young pitching staff. His curveball makes him an effective right-handed set-up reliever and he looks like he might have enough ability to close if given an opportunity. He needs to get in better shape if he plans on having a long career.

Position: RP
Bats: R **Throws:** R
Ht: 5'11" **Wt:** 200

Opening Day Age: 26
Born: 10/21/70 in Mansfield, OH
ML Seasons: 1

Overall Statistics

	W	L	Pct.	ERA	G	GS	Sv	IP	H	BB	SO	HR	BR/IP
1996	4	3	.571	3.84	47	2	1	75.0	75	36	62	6	1.48
Career	4	3	.571	3.84	47	2	1	75.0	75	36	62	6	1.48

How Often He Throws Strikes

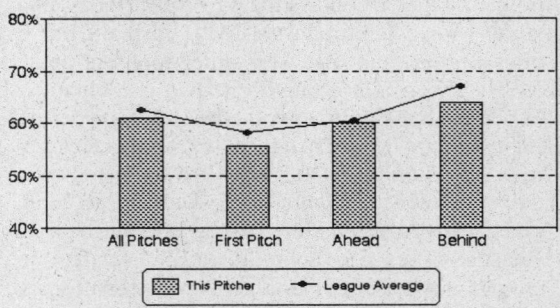

This Pitcher — League Average

1996 Situational Stats

	W	L	ERA	Sv	IP		AB	H	HR	RBI	Avg
Home	0	0	5.23	1	32.2	LHB	100	16	2	14	.160
Road	4	3	2.76	0	42.1	RHB	182	59	4	23	.324
First Half	1	0	3.44	0	36.2	Sc Pos	77	25	1	32	.325
Scnd Half	3	3	4.23	1	38.1	Clutch	83	22	3	18	.265

1996 Rankings (National League)

- ➡ 8th in most baserunners allowed per 9 innings in relief (14.1)
- ➡ 10th in highest batting average allowed in relief (.272)
- ➡ Led the Pirates in hit batsmen (6)

Jason Christiansen

Position: RP
Bats: R **Throws:** L
Ht: 6' 5" **Wt:** 230

Opening Day Age: 27
Born: 9/21/69 in
Omaha, NE
ML Seasons: 2

Overall Statistics

	W	L	Pct.	ERA	G	GS	Sv	IP	H	BB	SO	HR	BR/IP
1996	3	3	.500	6.70	33	0	0	44.1	56	19	38	7	1.69
Career	4	6	.400	5.27	96	0	0	100.2	105	53	91	12	1.57

1996 Situational Stats

	W	L	ERA	Sv	IP		AB	H	HR	RBI	Avg
Home	2	1	7.11	0	19.0	LHB	53	14	3	11	.264
Road	1	2	6.39	0	25.1	RHB	127	42	4	24	.331
First Half	3	3	6.96	0	42.2	Sc Pos	58	20	2	26	.345
Scnd Half	0	0	0.00	0	1.2	Clutch	20	6	1	3	.300

1996 Season

In his second season in the majors, Jason Christiansen was hit hard before being sent to Triple-A Calgary in mid-July to become a starter. The conversion to the rotation lasted only two starts before he underwent season-ending elbow surgery.

Pitching, Defense & Hitting

Christiansen is a big lefthander who throws hard, but the key to his success is his ability to control his breaking pitches. He commands a big, sweeping curveball and a sharp slider with a late break. If he has control of them, he is a very effective pitcher. However, he hasn't been able to throw them with any consistency since the first half of his rookie season in 1995. Christiansen does a good job of holding runners and is adequate defensively but he's not much of a hitter.

1997 Outlook

Christiansen's elbow operation clouds his future. The Pirates think he can be converted into a quality starting pitcher, but his arm problems may relegate him to the bullpen. He hasn't pitched well in over a year, and it's going to be an uphill climb.

Nelson Liriano

Position: 2B
Bats: B **Throws:** R
Ht: 5'10" **Wt:** 181

Opening Day Age: 32
Born: 6/3/64 in Puerto
Plata, DR
ML Seasons: 9

Overall Statistics

	G	AB	R	H	D	T	HR	RBI	SB	BB	SO	Avg	OBP	Slg
1996	112	217	23	58	14	2	3	30	2	14	22	.267	.308	.392
Career	735	2111	286	556	99	27	24	229	59	206	281	.263	.328	.370

1996 Situational Stats

	AB	H	HR	RBI	Avg		AB	H	HR	RBI	Avg
Home	104	25	0	10	.240	LHP	37	10	0	7	.270
Road	113	33	3	20	.292	RHP	180	48	3	23	.267
First Half	115	27	1	7	.235	Sc Pos	59	14	0	27	.237
Scnd Half	102	31	2	23	.304	Clutch	52	12	0	7	.231

1996 Season

Nelson Liriano had an outstanding year off the bench. His 17 pinch hits were two short of the Pirates' record set by Jose Pagan in 1969. Liriano also showed his usual versatility in the infield by starting 24 games at second base, seven at third base and three at shortstop.

Hitting, Baserunning & Defense

Liriano is a much more effective hitter from the left side of the plate, and he briefly abandoned switch-hitting early last season. He has also developed decent power from the left side. Liriano has slowed down over the years and rarely attempts a steal anymore. However, he is still capable of taking the extra base. Though he is a utility infielder, second base is by far his best position; his range has diminished at shortstop, and his arm isn't strong enough to play third base.

1997 Outlook

Liriano failed to become Toronto's second baseman a decade ago, but he has wound up fashioning a decent career as a bench player. He is a reliable pinch hitter and a decent defensive infielder. Put on waivers by the Pirates when the '96 season ended, he was quickly snapped up by the Dodgers.

Pittsburgh
Pirates

Esteban Loaiza

Position: SP
Bats: R **Throws:** R
Ht: 6' 4" **Wt:** 190

Opening Day Age: 25
Born: 12/31/71 in Tijuana, MX
ML Seasons: 2
Pronunciation: low-EYE-zuh

Overall Statistics

	W	L	Pct.	ERA	G	GS	Sv	IP	H	BB	SO	HR	BR/IP
1996	2	3	.400	4.96	10	10	0	52.2	65	19	32	11	1.59
Career	10	12	.455	5.11	42	41	0	225.1	270	74	117	32	1.53

1996 Situational Stats

	W	L	ERA	Sv	IP		AB	H	HR	RBI	Avg
Home	0	3	9.95	0	19.0	LHB	95	27	3	12	.284
Road	2	0	2.14	0	33.2	RHB	116	38	8	17	.328
First Half	0	0	11.57	0	7.0	Sc Pos	57	14	2	18	.246
Scnd Half	2	3	3.94	0	45.2	Clutch	6	3	2	2	.500

1996 Season

After tying for the N.L. lead with 31 starts as a rookie in 1995, Esteban Loaiza began the '96 season at Triple-A Calgary. Recalled after 11 starts, he was rocked for a horrid 11.57 ERA in two starts, which caused the Pirates to banish him to the Mexican League. He returned on August 22 and posted respectable numbers in his last eight starts.

Pitching, Defense & Hitting

Loaiza has all the makings of a fine major league pitcher. He has a 90 MPH fastball which sinks, an outstanding tight-breaking slider, a decent curveball and an improving change-up. He needs to develop the mental aspect of his game, however. He suddenly loses concentration and grooves pitches. Loaiza is a good athlete who handles the bat and knows how to field his position, though he needs to pay closer attention to runners.

1997 Outlook

Loaiza figures to begin the season in the Pirate rotation, but who knows where he'll be by year's end. He's that hard to figure. If he ever decides to get serious about his craft, he could be a consistent 15-game winner. Whether he'll ever get serious is anyone's guess.

Keith Osik

Position: C
Bats: R **Throws:** R
Ht: 6' 0" **Wt:** 185

Opening Day Age: 28
Born: 10/22/68 in Port Jefferson, NY
ML Seasons: 1

Overall Statistics

	G	AB	R	H	D	T	HR	RBI	SB	BB	SO	Avg	OBP	Slg
1996	48	140	18	41	14	1	1	14	1	14	22	.293	.361	.429
Career	48	140	18	41	14	1	1	14	1	14	22	.293	.361	.429

1996 Situational Stats

	AB	H	HR	RBI	Avg		AB	H	HR	RBI	Avg
Home	59	17	0	6	.288	LHP	23	6	0	4	.261
Road	81	24	1	8	.296	RHP	117	35	1	10	.299
First Half	83	26	0	7	.313	Sc Pos	34	10	1	10	.294
Scnd Half	57	15	1	7	.263	Clutch	20	6	0	1	.300

1996 Season

A year after reluctantly becoming a replacement player in an effort to jump-start his career, longtime minor leaguer Keith Osik made the Pirates last spring and spent the season as their backup catcher. He had a fine season in his bench role, though his progress was delayed by a broken right hand which sidelined him from mid-July to mid-August.

Hitting, Baserunning & Defense

Osik is a line-drive fastball hitter with little power. He showed some susceptibility to breaking pitches, but also displayed some patience at the plate. He has below-average speed and is not much of a defensive catcher. His receiving skills are shaky and his arm is inaccurate. However, he can play competently at both corners of the infield and in the outfield.

1997 Outlook

Osik is likely to make the club this season, but his chance of starting for the Pirates is slim to none with Jason Kendall in front of him. His hold on the backup job is also shaky with Angelo Encarnacion waiting in the wings. Osik can hit and play numerous positions, however, and could carve out a career as a utility player.

Chris Peters

Position: SP/RP
Bats: L **Throws:** L
Ht: 6' 1" **Wt:** 162

Opening Day Age: 25
Born: 1/28/72 in Ft. Thomas, KY
ML Seasons: 1

Overall Statistics

	W	L	Pct.	ERA	G	GS	Sv	IP	H	BB	SO	HR	BR/IP
1996	2	4	.333	5.63	16	10	0	64.0	72	25	28	9	1.52
Career	2	4	.333	5.63	16	10	0	64.0	72	25	28	9	1.52

1996 Situational Stats

	W	L	ERA	Sv	IP		AB	H	HR	RBI	Avg
Home	2	2	5.65	0	28.2	LHB	40	11	1	10	.275
Road	0	2	5.60	0	35.1	RHB	211	61	8	31	.289
First Half	0	0	-	0	0.0	Sc Pos	75	21	3	32	.280
Scnd Half	2	4	5.63	0	64.0	Clutch	25	10	1	5	.400

1996 Season

Lefthander Chris Peters shot through the Pirates' farm system last year, making 14 starts at Double-A Carolina and four more at Triple-A Calgary before landing in Pittsburgh on July 17. Peters went 1-4 in 10 starts with the Pirates, however, and was taken out of the starting rotation in September.

Pitching, Defense & Hitting

A lithe lefthander, Peters gets by on finesse. His primary pitch is a knuckle curve, which he struggled to control at the major league level. He also has a good change-up, which helps a below-average fastball that rarely comes in above 85 MPH. Peters gets off the mound quickly and adeptly handles shots up the middle. He also has the makings of a good pickoff move and pays close attention to runners. He hangs in extremely well at the plate and is capable of driving bad pitches.

1997 Outlook

The Pirates are leaning towards using Peters as a middle reliever, though he has had more professional success as a starter. He doesn't have great stuff, but with his moxie and his offspeed stuff, he could end up having a decent major league career.

Matt Ruebel

Position: RP/SP
Bats: L **Throws:** L
Ht: 6' 2" **Wt:** 180

Opening Day Age: 27
Born: 10/16/69 in Cincinnati, OH
ML Seasons: 1

Overall Statistics

	W	L	Pct.	ERA	G	GS	Sv	IP	H	BB	SO	HR	BR/IP
1996	1	1	.500	4.60	26	7	1	58.2	64	25	22	7	1.52
Career	1	1	.500	4.60	26	7	1	58.2	64	25	22	7	1.52

1996 Situational Stats

	W	L	ERA	Sv	IP		AB	H	HR	RBI	Avg
Home	1	0	3.12	1	34.2	LHB	45	7	2	6	.156
Road	0	1	6.75	1	24.0	RHB	186	57	5	23	.306
First Half	1	0	5.46	0	29.2	Sc Pos	59	13	1	19	.220
Scnd Half	0	1	3.72	1	29.0	Clutch	27	3	1	3	.111

1996 Season

Lefthander Matt Ruebel was called up from Triple-A Calgary on May 20 and went back a month later after going 1-0 with a 5.46 ERA. He returned to the majors for good on July 30 and had a 3.72 ERA in 20 appearances, 19 in relief, to finish the season.

Pitching, Defense & Hitting

Having mysteriously lost five MPH off his fastball after starting the Southern League All-Star game in 1995, Ruebel had to rely on finesse during his first stint in the majors. He was not a hard thrower to begin with, and his fastball rarely was clocked above 83 MPH last season. Ruebel has a good curveball which makes him tough on lefthanders and his change-up is fairly reliable. He's a good-fielding pitcher and has worked hard to improve what was once a weak pickoff move. He isn't much of a threat at the plate.

1997 Outlook

The Pirates believe Ruebel's niche is as a left-handed specialist out of the bullpen. His curveball freezes left-handed hitters, making him tailor-made for that role. His loss of velocity was alarming enough to put a bit of a cloud over his future.

Paul Wagner

Position: SP
Bats: R **Throws:** R
Ht: 6' 1" **Wt:** 209

Opening Day Age: 29
Born: 11/14/67 in Milwaukee, WI
ML Seasons: 5

Overall Statistics

	W	L	Pct.	ERA	G	GS	Sv	IP	H	BB	SO	HR	BR/IP
1996	4	8	.333	5.40	16	15	0	81.2	86	39	81	10	1.53
Career	26	40	.394	4.60	128	75	3	520.2	548	208	406	50	1.45

1996 Situational Stats

	W	L	ERA	Sv	IP		AB	H	HR	RBI	Avg
Home	2	5	4.93	0	49.1	LHB	140	36	1	17	.257
Road	2	3	6.12	0	32.1	RHB	173	50	9	25	.289
First Half	4	6	4.70	0	74.2	Sc Pos	87	26	2	33	.299
Scnd Half	0	2	12.86	0	7.0	Clutch	7	3	0	1	.429

1996 Season

Paul Wagner seemed ready to finally fulfill his vast potential in 1996. He started the season by building a 3-0 record with an 0.77 ERA in his first four games. Arm problems soon kicked in, however. He went 0-6 in his last nine starts and underwent reconstructive elbow surgery on August 7.

Pitching, Defense & Hitting

Before the injury, Wagner had some of the nastiest stuff in baseball with a 94 MPH fastball, a tough 87 MPH slider and a decent curveball. His potential never fully translated into results, however, for a couple of reasons: he often leaves his fastball up in the strike zone and lacks an effective offspeed pitch. He experimented with a straight change, palmball and forkball without much success. Wagner is a good fielder but horrible at holding runners. He has an idea at the plate and usually can get a bunt down.

1997 Outlook

Wagner's future depends on how well he recovers from his major arm surgery. He was a power pitcher before the operation, and no one knows how his arm will respond. The Pirates took a chance and re-signed him, hoping he can build on the early-season form he displayed in 1996.

John Wehner

Position: 3B/2B/CF
Bats: R **Throws:** R
Ht: 6' 3" **Wt:** 206

Opening Day Age: 29
Born: 6/29/67 in Pittsburgh, PA
ML Seasons: 6

Overall Statistics

	G	AB	R	H	D	T	HR	RBI	SB	BB	SO	Avg	OBP	Slg
1996	86	139	19	36	9	1	2	13	1	8	22	.259	.299	.381
Career	261	514	62	133	23	4	2	32	10	43	89	.259	.315	.331

1996 Situational Stats

	AB	H	HR	RBI	Avg		AB	H	HR	RBI	Avg
Home	76	24	1	7	.316	LHP	85	24	2	12	.282
Road	63	12	1	6	.190	RHP	54	12	0	1	.222
First Half	66	14	1	4	.212	Sc Pos	31	6	0	10	.194
Scnd Half	73	22	1	9	.301	Clutch	19	5	0	3	.263

1996 Season

John Wehner was his usual versatile self last year, making eight starts at third base, seven in center field, seven at second, four in left, three in right and also making his second career appearance at catcher. He has also hit his first two major league home runs (in his six seasons).

Hitting, Baserunning & Defense

Wehner has a slow bat and punches balls the opposite way from a wide-open stance. He flashed a little power last season but is primarily a singles hitter who is used as a pinch hitter when the bases are empty. A big guy, Wehner runs well and always hustles. He is capable of stealing a base and goes from second to home on most singles. He is solid at every position he plays, but is best at third base and center field. He has an adequate arm and decent range.

1997 Outlook

Wehner was claimed on waivers by Los Angeles at the end of the season. Wehner will fill a utility role in Los Angeles. His value lies more in his versatility than his statistics; he is a good 25th man to have on the roster.

Other Pittsburgh Pirates

Rich Aude (Pos: 1B, Age: 25, Bats: R)

	G	AB	R	H	D	T	HR	RBI	SB	BB	SO	Avg	OBP	Slg
1996	7	16	0	4	0	0	0	1	0	0	8	.250	.250	.250
Career	62	151	11	34	9	0	2	24	1	7	35	.225	.259	.325

Aude filled in at first for a few games in May when Jeff King switched over to second. He wasn't terribly impressive in his brief stint in the majors, but he'll probably surface again next season. 1997 Outlook: C

Joe Boever (Pos: RHP, Age: 36)

	W	L	Pct.	ERA	G	GS	Sv	IP	H	BB	SO	HR	BR/IP
1996	0	2	.000	5.40	13	0	2	15.0	17	6	6	2	1.53
Career	34	45	.430	3.93	516	0	49	754.1	751	343	541	75	1.45

Boever is a 36-year-old journeyman who spent time in the Pirates' bullpen during May and September. He appeared to have lost all effectiveness, but pitched very well in September and might return. 1997 Outlook: C

Steve Cooke (Pos: LHP, Age: 27)

	W	L	Pct.	ERA	G	GS	Sv	IP	H	BB	SO	HR	BR/IP
1996	0	0	-	7.56	3	0	0	8.1	11	5	7	1	1.92
Career	16	21	.432	4.35	71	55	1	376.1	397	114	223	46	1.36

After spending most of the season recovering from shoulder surgery, Cooke returned in June and made it clear that he still had a lot of rehab to finish. It remains to be seen if he'll be healthy this year. 1997 Outlook: C

Midre Cummings (Pos: CF, Age: 25, Bats: L)

	G	AB	R	H	D	T	HR	RBI	SB	BB	SO	Avg	OBP	Slg
1996	24	85	11	19	3	1	3	7	0	0	16	.224	.221	.388
Career	120	359	40	81	15	2	6	37	1	21	73	.226	.268	.329

Cummings allieviated some of Pittsburgh's early-season outfield problems by manning both right and center field in May and June. He has a bit of power, but his strikeout/walk ratios are horrendous. 1997 Outlook: C

Elmer Dessens (Pos: RHP, Age: 25)

	W	L	Pct.	ERA	G	GS	Sv	IP	H	BB	SO	HR	BR/IP
1996	0	2	.000	8.28	15	3	0	25.0	40	4	13	2	1.76
Career	0	2	.000	8.28	15	3	0	25.0	40	4	13	2	1.76

Called up from Calgary in June, Dessens was hammered so hard in his first three starts that he was relegated to the bullpen. He was more effective in relief, but not by much. 1997 Outlook: D

Lee Hancock (Pos: LHP, Age: 29)

	W	L	Pct.	ERA	G	GS	Sv	IP	H	BB	SO	HR	BR/IP
1996	0	0	-	6.38	13	0	0	18.1	21	10	13	5	1.69
Career	0	0	-	4.45	24	0	0	32.1	31	12	19	5	1.33

Hancock pitched so well at the end of '95 that he made the team in spring training. However, he started last season very poorly and never regained his stellar form. He was sent down to Triple-A in May. 1997 Outlook: C

John Hope (Pos: RHP, Age: 26)

	W	L	Pct.	ERA	G	GS	Sv	IP	H	BB	SO	HR	BR/IP
1996	1	3	.250	6.98	5	4	0	19.1	17	11	13	5	1.45
Career	1	5	.167	5.99	24	11	0	73.2	90	27	29	8	1.59

Hope was shelled during his four-week stint in the Pirates' rotation last spring, surrendering 11 walks and five home runs in just 19-plus innings. He has yet to show consistent success in the majors. 1997 Outlook: D

Rich Loiselle (Pos: RHP, Age: 25)

	W	L	Pct.	ERA	G	GS	Sv	IP	H	BB	SO	HR	BR/IP
1996	1	0	1.000	3.05	5	3	0	20.2	22	8	9	3	1.45
Career	1	0	1.000	3.05	5	3	0	20.2	22	8	9	3	1.45

Joining the big league club in September, Loiselle pitched well in his series of starts with the Pirates. He'll get a chance to prove his ability this spring. 1997 Outlook: B

Ramon Morel (Pos: RHP, Age: 22)

	W	L	Pct.	ERA	G	GS	Sv	IP	H	BB	SO	HR	BR/IP
1996	2	1	.667	5.36	29	0	0	42.0	57	19	22	4	1.81
Career	2	2	.500	5.03	34	0	0	48.1	63	21	25	4	1.74

Morel joined the Pittsburgh bullpen in June and was less than overwhelming, posting a 5.36 ERA in 29 appearances. Since he's still very young, he should appear again this season. 1997 Outlook: C

Steve Parris (Pos: RHP, Age: 29)

	W	L	Pct.	ERA	G	GS	Sv	IP	H	BB	SO	HR	BR/IP
1996	0	3	.000	7.18	8	4	0	26.1	35	11	27	4	1.75
Career	6	9	.400	5.82	23	19	0	108.1	124	44	88	16	1.55

Parris is a long-time minor leaguer who spent much of the season on the disabled list recovering from shoulder surgery. He's been hit hard in his big league starts and he may not recover from this setback. 1997 Outlook: D

Zane Smith (Pos: LHP, Age: 36)

	W	L	Pct.	ERA	G	GS	Sv	IP	H	BB	SO	HR	BR/IP
1996	4	6	.400	5.08	16	16	0	83.1	104	21	47	7	1.50
Career	100	115	.465	3.74	360	291	3	1919.1	1980	583	1011	122	1.34

Smith was ineffective throughout his 16 starts, surrendering 104 hits in just 83-plus innings, and was released in July. With his extensive injury history and age (36), he's a long shot to return. 1997 Outlook: D

Dale Sveum (Pos: 3B, Age: 33, Bats: B)

	G	AB	R	H	D	T	HR	RBI	SB	BB	SO	Avg	OBP	Slg
1996	12	34	9	12	5	0	1	5	0	6	6	.353	.450	.588
Career	657	2091	262	493	100	11	54	277	10	189	531	.236	.298	.372

After a half-decade of futility, Sveum hit surprisingly well in 12 September games last season. Although his chances of big league success are slim, he might receive a look in the majors this year. 1997 Outlook: C

Pittsburgh Pirates

David Wainhouse (Pos: RHP, Age: 29)

	W	L	Pct.	ERA	G	GS	Sv	IP	H	BB	SO	HR	BR/IP
1996	1	0	1.000	5.70	17	0	0	23.2	22	10	16	3	1.35
Career	1	1	.500	7.53	22	0	0	28.2	31	19	19	4	1.74

Wainhouse spent August and September in the Pirates' bullpen in his longest major league stint to date. He was hammered in middle relief (5.70 ERA) but was re-signed to a minor league deal at the end of the year. 1997 Outlook: C

Tony Womack (Pos: CF, Age: 27, Bats: L)

	G	AB	R	H	D	T	HR	RBI	SB	BB	SO	Avg	OBP	Slg
1996	17	30	11	10	3	1	0	7	2	6	1	.333	.459	.500
Career	37	66	20	16	3	1	0	8	4	11	7	.242	.359	.318

Womack played well following his September call-up, but his future in the majors is questionable. His minor league numbers show him as a player who can neither get on base nor hit for power. 1997 Outlook: C

Pittsburgh Pirates Minor League Prospects

Organization Overview:

With each salary-dumping trade, the Pittsburgh Pirates add another prospect or two to their well-stocked farm system. In the past year, they've added promising youngsters like Ron Wright, Rich Loiselle, Jose Pett, Jose Silva and Chris Corn, and the first pick in the '96 draft brought them Kris Benson, who may be only a year away. They had good position players on the farm to start with, and the recent moves have addressed their need for young pitching. It's obvious that the major league team will need an immediate infusion of talent, but there are good players on hand in the upper levels of the system to fill the void. Last year, Jason Kendall and Jermaine Allensworth gave them two players to build around, and next year's crop may be even more impressive. Lou Collier, Ron Wright and T.J. Staton are ready to step in, and several young arms figure to come forward in the next year or two. If everything goes according to plan, it may be only a few years before they'll need to start dumping payroll again.

Jimmy Anderson

Position: P
Bats: L **Throws:** L
Ht: 6' 1" **Wt:** 180
Opening Day Age: 21
Born: 1/22/76 in Portsmouth, VA

Recent Statistics

	W	L	ERA	G	GS	Sv	IP	H	R	BB	SO	HR
94 R Pirates	5	1	1.60	10	10	0	56.1	35	21	27	66	1
95 A Lynchburg	1	5	4.13	10	9	0	52.1	56	29	21	32	1
95 A Augusta	4	2	1.53	14	14	0	76.2	51	15	31	75	1
96 A Lynchburg	5	3	1.93	11	11	0	65.1	51	25	21	56	2
96 AA Carolina	8	3	3.34	17	16	0	97.0	92	40	44	79	3

Lefthander Jimmy Anderson solidified his position as one of the best pitching prospects in the minors last year. He rocketed through A-ball, and became the youngest pitcher in the Southern League when he arrived at Double-A in midseason. His stuff is fantastic—a sinking fastball in the low 90s, and a hard slider. He's got all the confidence in the world, and fully expects to succeed. The only concern is that his young arm may not be able to handle the innings he's been getting. Aside from that, there's no reason why he shouldn't arrive in Pittsburgh sometime in the next year or two.

Trey Beamon

Position: OF
Bats: L **Throws:** R
Ht: 6' 3" **Wt:** 195
Opening Day Age: 23
Born: 2/11/74 in Dallas, TX

Recent Statistics

	G	AB	R	H	D	T	HR	RBI	SB	BB	SO	AVG
96 AAA Calgary	111	378	62	109	15	3	5	52	16	55	63	.288
96 NL Pittsburgh	24	51	7	11	2	0	0	6	1	4	6	.216
96 MLE	111	362	46	93	13	1	3	39	11	41	66	.257

Young left fielder Trey Beamon took a big step backward last year. He's generated hype ever since he won the Southern League batting title at age 20 in '94. He was the youngest batting champ the league had ever had, and his future seemed bright. However, as it's become apparent that his defense will limit him to left field, the Pirates have asked him to try to hit for more power. His efforts to do so last year only served to mess up his swing, and he remains a singles-hitter at a power position. He's still very young, but to make it, it seems like he'll need to become an exceptional singles-and-doubles hitter. That will be difficult.

Lou Collier

Position: SS
Bats: R **Throws:** R
Ht: 5' 10" **Wt:** 170
Opening Day Age: 23
Born: 8/21/73 in Chicago, IL

Recent Statistics

	G	AB	R	H	D	T	HR	RBI	SB	BB	SO	AVG
93 A Welland	50	201	35	61	6	2	1	19	8	12	31	.303
94 A Augusta	85	318	48	89	17	4	7	40	32	25	53	.280
94 A Salem	43	158	25	42	4	1	6	16	5	15	29	.266
95 A Lynchburg	114	399	68	110	19	3	4	38	31	51	60	.276
96 AA Carolina	119	443	76	124	20	3	3	49	29	48	73	.280
96 MLE	119	433	66	114	19	2	2	42	21	35	78	.263

After a fine season at Double-A, young shortstop Lou Collier may have put himself in a position to be the Pirates' opening-day shortstop this year. He's not a well-developed hitter, but he'll keep his average high enough to remain in a major league lineup. It doesn't look like he'll develop any power, but he's got good speed and can steal a base. In the field, his tools are similar to those of Jay Bell—a powerful arm, but unremarkable range. But unlike Bell, Collier makes more than his share of errors. Still, if Bell is dealt, Collier is the most likely one to replace him.

Angelo Encarnacion

Position: C
Bats: R **Throws:** R
Ht: 5' 8" **Wt:** 180
Opening Day Age: 23
Born: 4/18/73 in Santo Domingo, DR

Recent Statistics

	G	AB	R	H	D	T	HR	RBI	SB	BB	SO	AVG
96 AAA Calgary	75	263	38	84	18	0	4	31	6	10	19	.319
96 NL Pittsburgh	7	22	3	7	2	0	0	1	0	0	5	.318
96 MLE	75	251	28	72	16	0	2	23	4	7	19	.287

Although there probably won't be a need for his services in Pittsburgh for a while, young catcher Angelo Encarnacion can play. A wildly impatient hitter, he still makes great contact and keeps his average up. On defense, he's got a fantastic arm, and isn't afraid to throw to any base at any time. Last year, his caught-stealing rate at Triple-A was 44.9 percent, an exceptional figure. If the Pirates really do convince themselves that Jason

Kendall ought to be converted to another position, Encarnacion could assume his duties capably.

Charles Peterson

Position: OF
Bats: R **Throws:** R
Ht: 6' 3" **Wt:** 200
Opening Day Age: 22
Born: 5/8/74 in Laurens, SC

Recent Statistics

	G	AB	R	H	D	T	HR	RBI	SB	BB	SO	AVG
93 R Pirates	49	188	28	57	11	3	1	23	8	22	22	.303
94 A Augusta	108	415	55	106	14	6	4	40	27	35	78	.255
95 A Lynchburg	107	391	61	107	9	4	7	51	31	43	73	.274
95 AA Carolina	20	70	13	23	3	1	0	7	2	9	15	.329
96 AA Carolina	125	462	71	127	24	2	7	63	33	50	104	.275
96 MLE	125	452	61	117	23	1	6	54	25	37	111	.259

Charles Peterson is a tremendous athlete, and he's still learning how to put his tools to work on the baseball field. He can use his good speed to steal bases and cover right field, and his strong throwing arm is an asset out there. What he really needs to do is to use his strength to hit for more power. He's kept his average up, but his run production has come up short. He's only 23, so the Pirates will continue to bring him along slowly.

Reed Secrist

Position: 3B
Bats: L **Throws:** R
Ht: 6' 1" **Wt:** 205
Opening Day Age: 26
Born: 5/7/70 in Bountiful, UT

Recent Statistics

	G	AB	R	H	D	T	HR	RBI	SB	BB	SO	AVG
93 A Augusta	90	266	38	71	16	3	6	47	4	27	43	.267
94 A Salem	80	221	29	54	12	0	10	35	2	22	58	.244
95 A Lynchburg	112	380	60	107	18	3	19	75	3	54	88	.282
96 AA Calgary	128	420	68	129	30	0	17	66	1	39	110	.307
96 MLE	128	401	51	110	27	0	12	49	1	39	110	.274

Reed Secrist is a marginal prospect who's likely past his time, but he can do two things: provide good production from the left side of the plate, and play third base—sort of. He's passable at the hot corner, and his bat may land him a platoon role if the Pirates get really desperate. His Triple-A stats are inflated because of the league and the ballpark he played in, but they remain impressive even after those factors are taken into account. He has no long-range potential, but he might play this year, and he might hit.

T.J. Staton

Position: OF
Bats: L **Throws:** L
Ht: 6' 3" **Wt:** 200
Opening Day Age: 22
Born: 2/17/75 in Norfolk, VA

Recent Statistics

	G	AB	R	H	D	T	HR	RBI	SB	BB	SO	AVG
93 R Pirates	32	115	23	41	9	2	1	18	10	8	14	.357
94 A Welland	12	45	4	8	3	0	0	4	5	0	7	.178
94 R Pirates	11	39	3	10	3	0	1	5	0	1	8	.256
94 A Augusta	37	125	9	27	6	1	0	5	6	10	38	.216
95 A Augusta	112	391	43	114	21	5	5	53	27	27	97	.292

	G	AB	R	H	D	T	HR	RBI	SB	BB	SO	AVG
96 AA Carolina	112	386	72	119	24	3	15	57	17	58	99	.308
96 MLE	112	376	62	109	23	2	12	49	12	42	106	.290

Another youngster who has a chance to break through for Pittsburgh this year is left fielder T.J. Staton. He's a speedy left-handed hitter who hits for a good average, and this year, he showed signs of becoming a power hitter. His production was exceptional for a 21 year old in Double-A, and he'll be ready to make the jump to the majors very soon. He may not be an RBI man right off the bat, but he could contribute as a number-two hitter until his power develops.

Ron Wright

Position: 1B
Bats: R **Throws:** R
Ht: 6' 0" **Wt:** 215
Opening Day Age: 21
Born: 1/21/76 in Delta, UT

Recent Statistics

	G	AB	R	H	D	T	HR	RBI	SB	BB	SO	AVG
94 R Braves	45	169	10	29	9	0	1	16	1	10	21	.172
95 A Macon	135	527	93	143	23	1	32	104	2	62	118	.271
96 A Durham	66	240	47	66	15	2	20	62	1	37	71	.275
96 AA Greenville	63	232	39	59	11	1	16	52	1	38	73	.254
96 AA Carolina	4	14	1	2	0	0	0	0	0	2	7	.143
96 MLE	67	237	30	52	10	0	12	40	0	26	85	.219

Ron Wright's half-season at Double-A convinced the Pirates that he wasn't far off from the majors, and they quickly snagged him in the Denny Neagle deal. At age 20, he showed that his power was not just the product of facing weaker competition at Class A. By the end of the season, many were convinced that his power potential was among the best in the minors. He's got a short stroke that enables him to hit with power to all fields, and he may be able to help the Pirates sometime next year.

Others to Watch

Center fielder **Adrian Brown** batted over .300 and stole 45 bases between A-ball and Double-A. Now only 23 years old, Brown has top-of-the-order potential. . . **Jose Pett** was one of the main acquisitions in the deal that sent Carlos Garcia and Orlando Merced to Toronto. Pett throws hard, but he's never been able to figure out how to use his low-90s fastball to get strikeouts. He's still very young, and has a lot more maturation coming. . . The Pirates had a pair of jewels at Class-A Lynchburg last year. Shortstop **Chad Hermansen**, the Pirates' top pick in the '95 draft, is a potential five-tool player. Meanwhile, right fielder **Jose Guillen** showed one of the most powerful throwing arms in baseball, and was named the league's MVP after hitting .322 with 21 homers. . . Shortstop **Brandon Cromer** came over from the Toronto system in the Carlos Garcia deal. Unlike his brother Tripp, he may not have the range to make it at shortstop, but he may develop into a good third base prospect. He's a patient left-handed hitter, and may need only one more year.

Tony La Russa

1996 Season

Tony La Russa's record is perhaps the most impressive among active managers, but leading the 1996 Cardinals to the National League Central crown and a berth in the NLCS may be his most glorious achievement. He is a pioneer of sorts, unafraid of attempting any strategy that he believes can succeed. Young players have thrived under La Russa's tutelage, but so have veterans such as Dennis Eckersley, Gary Gaetti, Ozzie Smith and Rick Honeycutt.

Offense

La Russa's Oakland teams relied to a great extent on the longball, but he has proven adept at manufacturing runs from unlikely sources, often getting contributions from players not expected to be as valuable. There's hasn't been a strategy invented that La Russa won't call on when the situation dictates. He'll bunt a power hitter one minute, then let a light-hitting middle infielder swing on 3-and-0 the next.

Pitching & Defense

La Russa has had Dave Duncan, one of the game's top pitching coaches, at his side for more than a decade, and he relies on him heavily. La Russa makes the pitching changes, though, and he's flexible in his approach. In his later years with Oakland, he spread the work around, but during the A's prime years, he'd look for a pitcher like Dave Stewart to carry much of the load. La Russa favors reliability on defense over athleticism. He'll accept the brilliant play turned less frequently, as long as the routine plays are executed consistently.

1997 Outlook

La Russa's success with the Cardinals is even more impressive considering it is his first managerial stint in the National League. After a few early mistakes—which he owned up to—he was able to run a smooth show. The Cardinals should continue to contend as long as they have at least a modest amount of talent. . . and as long as La Russa is the skipper.

Born: 10/04/44 in Tampa, FL

Playing Experience: 1963-1973, KCA, Oak, Atl, ChN

Managerial Experience: 18 seasons

Manager Statistics

Year	Team, Lg	W	L	Pct	GB	Finish
1996	St. Louis, NL	88	74	.543	—	1st Central
18 Seasons		1,408	1,257	.528	—	—

1996 Starting Pitchers by Days Rest

	≤3	4	5	6+
Cardinals Starts	3	88	42	18
Cardinals ERA	4.08	4.32	3.65	4.11
NL Avg Starts	4	86	41	21
NL ERA	4.06	4.28	4.23	4.58

1996 Situational Stats

	Tony La Russa	NL Average
Hit & Run Success %	38.5	39.0
Stolen Base Success %	72.0	71.6
Platoon Pct.	52.7	51.9
Defensive Subs	13	20
High-Pitch Outings	24	13
Quick/Slow Hooks	17/16	19/12
Sacrifice Attempts	117	92

1996 Rankings (National League)

→ 1st in sacrifice bunt attempts (117), hit-and-run attempts (143), starts with over 120 pitches (24), starts with over 140 pitches (1) and one-batter pitcher appearances (47)

→ 2nd in double steals (8), sacrifice bunt percentage (87.2%) and first batter platoon percentage (63.2%)

→ 3rd in starting lineups used (120), slow hooks (16) and 2+ pitching changes in low scoring games (25)

St. Louis Cardinals

641

Luis Alicea

1996 Season

Returning to the Cardinals after a year in Boston, Luis Alicea developed into the everyday second baseman in the absence of Mike Gallego. Alicea had some problems in the field, but he functioned as an effective number-eight hitter. He finished the year on a high note, batting .345 in September under pennant-race pressure.

Hitting

Alicea is a switch-hitter, but he generally hits for a better average right-handed. Although he has modest power at best, he can surprise you with a big hit from time to time. Alicea is a patient hitter, and adjusts relatively well to breaking stuff. He seems to have trouble catching up to high heat, but can drive the lower stuff into the gaps from either side of the plate.

Baserunning & Defense

Though he's a pretty good basestealer, Alicea doesn't run as effectively or as often as he should with his decent speed. He can take the extra base at any time. Alicea occasionally makes the spectacular plays at second, but his 24 errors—most of any major league second baseman—didn't meet with La Russa's approval. He has a tendency to come up on grounders too quickly, causing them to glance off his glove. He also seems to have difficulty going to his right and making the throw across his body, and he's not comfortable retreating on flares over his head.

1997 Outlook

Alicea's contract was up at the end of the year, and the signing of Delino DeShields virtually guarantees he won't return to St. Louis. He'll be looking for work over the winter, but he won't be on anybody's list of prime free agents. Alicea's best chance would be to hook on with someone looking for reserve infield help.

Position: 2B
Bats: B **Throws:** R
Ht: 5' 9" **Wt:** 177

Opening Day Age: 31
Born: 7/29/65 in Santurce, PR
ML Seasons: 7
Pronunciation: ah-la-SAY-ya

Overall Statistics

	G	AB	R	H	D	T	HR	RBI	SB	BB	SO	Avg	OBP	Slg
1996	129	380	54	98	26	3	5	42	11	52	78	.258	.350	.382
Career	698	1996	251	510	99	29	22	217	42	252	322	.256	.342	.367

Where He Hits the Ball

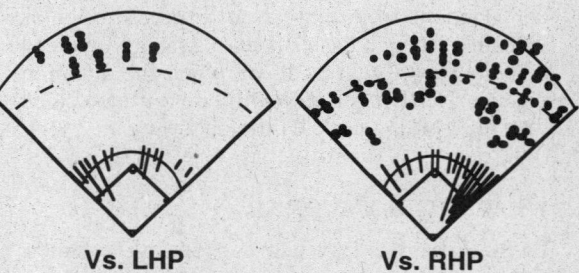

Vs. LHP   Vs. RHP

1996 Situational Stats

	AB	H	HR	RBI	Avg		AB	H	HR	RBI	Avg
Home	180	45	4	24	.250	LHP	64	17	1	5	.266
Road	200	53	1	18	.265	RHP	316	81	4	37	.256
First Half	260	62	4	29	.238	Sc Pos	89	21	3	37	.236
Scnd Half	120	36	1	13	.300	Clutch	78	25	3	15	.321

1996 Rankings (National League)

- ➡ 1st in errors at second base (24), lowest fielding percentage at second base (.957) and lowest batting average on an 0-2 count (.000)
- ➡ 6th in least GDPs per GDP situation (4.7%)
- ➡ Led the Cardinals in least GDPs per GDP situation (4.7%), lowest percentage of swings that missed (16.5%) and highest percentage of swings put into play (47.2%)

Alan Benes

1996 Season

Although other rookie pitchers got more preseason headlines, Alan Benes was probably the best of the lot. Benes made 32 starts, tops in the majors among rookie hurlers. He struggled with consistency from start to start, but he was downright brilliant on occasion while winning 13 games. His most impressive accomplishment may have been the fact that he largely lived up to everyone's expectations.

Pitching

Like his brother Andy, Benes is big and strong and throws hard. He throws a fastball and a cutter, and also offers a nice, tight-breaking curve. When he hits his spots, he's tough, but the problem is that he isn't able to do that consistently yet. He can overpower right-handed hitters, working up and in with the fastball and down and away with the curve, but he struggles against lefties. Benes' main attribute is poise—he's virtually unflappable, especially for a player so early in his overall development.

Defense & Hitting

Benes is a good athlete, but not especially adept around the mound. He is, however, excellent at holding runners. With runners on base, Benes will reduce his kick—although not to the point where he's using a true slide-step—and he'll stay primarily with the hard stuff. As a result, only eight of 21 would-be basestealers were successful against him. Benes had a friendly challenge with his brother for batting honors, and little brother lost by .003. He is an average hitter for a pitcher.

1997 Outlook

Insiders believe the younger Benes can eventually be every bit as good as his brother, and they hope he won't take as long to develop. He goes into the new season entrenched as the number-four starter, and is expected to continue to benefit from the presence of his brother as well as pitching coach Dave Duncan.

Position: SP
Bats: R **Throws:** R
Ht: 6' 5" **Wt:** 215

Opening Day Age: 25
Born: 1/21/72 in Evansville, IN
ML Seasons: 2
Pronunciation: BENN-ess

Overall Statistics

	W	L	Pct.	ERA	G	GS	Sv	IP	H	BB	SO	HR	BR/IP
1996	13	10	.565	4.90	34	32	0	191.0	192	87	131	27	1.46
Career	14	12	.538	5.17	37	35	0	207.0	216	91	151	29	1.48

How Often He Throws Strikes

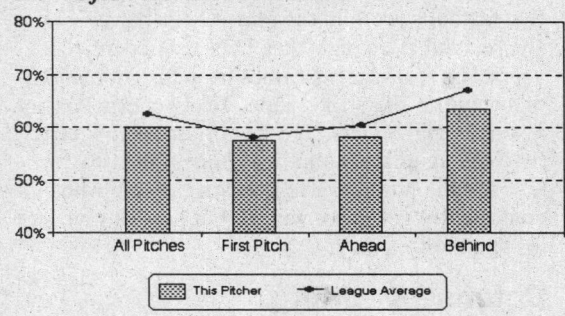

This Pitcher — League Average

1996 Situational Stats

	W	L	ERA	Sv	IP		AB	H	HR	RBI	Avg
Home	7	4	3.77	0	86.0	LHB	313	99	12	54	.316
Road	6	6	5.83	0	105.0	RHB	409	93	15	56	.227
First Half	8	5	5.09	0	106.0	Sc Pos	168	49	4	79	.292
Scnd Half	5	5	4.66	0	85.0	Clutch	49	18	5	13	.367

1996 Rankings (National League)

→ 1st in highest ERA on the road (5.83)
→ 2nd in runners caught stealing (13) and highest batting average allowed vs. left-handed batters (.316)
→ 3rd in lowest stolen base percentage allowed (38.1%)
→ 5th in lowest groundball/flyball ratio allowed (1.0)
→ 6th in lowest strikeout/walk ratio (1.5) and errors at pitcher (3)
→ 7th in walks allowed
→ 9th in highest ERA, shutouts (1), home runs allowed, most run support per 9 innings (5.4) and lowest batting average allowed vs. right-handed batters (.227)

St. Louis Cardinals

Andy Benes

1996 Season

Andy Benes went from the outhouse to the penthouse in a hurry in '96. He lost seven of his first eight decisions before capturing 17 of his last 20. It was often said that Benes lacked the intangibles necessary to be a big winner, but his extended hot streak went a long way toward putting those beliefs to rest. Benes ranked second in the league in wins and cracked the top 10 in several other categories, which garnered him some Cy Young consideration.

Pitching

To intimidate hitters, Benes relies on his size and strength, as well as his repertoire, which includes two fastballs (both in the mid-90s), a hard slider, a slurve, and a change that he's refined in recent years. His real success comes from his good movement within the strike zone. He is overpowering against righthanders, and has improved his effectiveness against southpaws. Benes likes to work letter-high on hitters. He's one of the few who can consistently get away with it, but he still gives up his share of taters.

Defense & Hitting

Benes soundly defends his territory. He fields bunts and liners alike with good effort, and easily makes it to first on plays to the right side. After making great strides in limiting the effectiveness of baserunners in 1995, he regressed in '96, as an eye-popping 21 of 25 basestealers were successful against him. Benes edged his brother Alan in overall batting, .151-.148, but in reality, he is a fair hitter at best who fans roughly half the time.

1997 Outlook

Benes is the ace of the Cardinals staff, period. He has flourished under Duncan and La Russa, and he's grateful for their faith and instruction. His stuff has never been questioned, but Benes has finally established himself as a reliable winner who can come out on top in the tough 2-1 games.

Position: SP
Bats: R **Throws:** R
Ht: 6' 6" **Wt:** 245

Opening Day Age: 29
Born: 8/20/67 in Evansville, IN
ML Seasons: 8
Pronunciation: BENN-ess
Nickname: Big Train, Rain Man

Overall Statistics

	W	L	Pct.	ERA	G	GS	Sv	IP	H	BB	SO	HR	BR/IP
1996	18	10	.643	3.83	36	34	1	230.1	215	77	160	28	1.27
Career	94	87	.519	3.70	235	232	1	1528.1	1415	512	1241	151	1.26

How Often He Throws Strikes

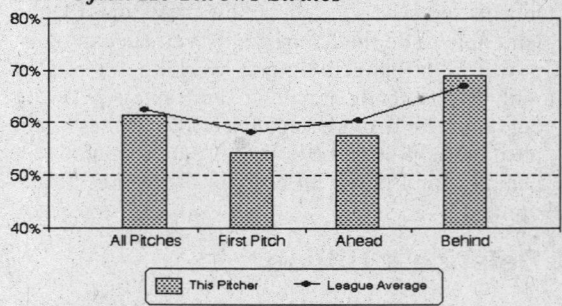

1996 Situational Stats

	W	L	ERA	Sv	IP		AB	H	HR	RBI	Avg
Home	8	4	3.93	1	112.1	LHB	368	99	11	45	.269
Road	10	6	3.74	0	118.0	RHB	504	116	17	53	.230
First Half	6	8	4.34	1	118.1	Sc Pos	171	45	4	62	.263
Scnd Half	12	2	3.29	0	112.0	Clutch	54	7	2	4	.130

1996 Rankings (National League)

→ 2nd in wins
→ 5th in home runs allowed, pitches thrown (3,654), winning percentage and highest stolen base percentage allowed (84.0%)
→ 7th in games started
→ 8th in innings pitched
→ 9th in shutouts (1), batters faced (963) and GDPs induced (21)
→ Led the Cardinals in wins, games started, innings pitched, hits allowed, batters faced (963), pitches thrown (3,654), pickoff throws (118), GDPs induced (21), winning percentage, highest groundball/flyball ratio allowed (1.2) and most GDPs induced per 9 innings (0.8)

Royce Clayton

1996 Season

Royce Clayton deserves a lot of credit for the way he handled the Ozzie Smith controversy. Clayton never disdained or disrespected Smith as he slowly displaced the living legend, and in the process, he put in a very respectable season to boot. When asked to sit down for a game or two, he didn't complain. When Smith offered pointers, he listened intently. The results were evident. Clayton wasn't brilliant in any aspect, but he was solid in virtually every facet of the game.

Hitting

Clayton still strikes out more than he should, but he's taken significant steps to improve his contact, developing a shorter, more disciplined swing. The approach produced line drives to all fields and improved offensive numbers. He is still a tad tardy on good heat, and he fishes for breaking balls now and then. Clayton doesn't utilize his excellent bunting skills enough, but he can go deep when he gets his pitch, and he gets down the line as quickly as anyone on the club.

Baserunning & Defense

Clayton ranked second on the team in stolen bases. His strength is getting a quick jump, using the crossover step popularized by Rickey Henderson. Clayton is a constant threat on the bases, often advancing 90 feet farther than the average runner. Last season, he improved more with the glove than in any other area, as he benefited greatly from Smith's tutelage. He has outstanding range and a throwing arm that is better than most shortstops. His errors come from occasional lapses in concentration.

1997 Outlook

Although Smith seems to be contemplating another "final" season, that shouldn't matter to Clayton, who has finally proven he deserves to be the Cardinals' everyday shortstop. What Clayton needs to work on next are the finer points of batting leadoff, a role he covets. In '97, he'll get every opportunity to establish himself in that spot, too.

Position: SS
Bats: R **Throws:** R
Ht: 6' 0" **Wt:** 183

Opening Day Age: 27
Born: 1/2/70 in Burbank, CA
ML Seasons: 6

Overall Statistics

	G	AB	R	H	D	T	HR	RBI	SB	BB	SO	Avg	OBP	Slg
1996	129	491	64	136	20	4	6	35	33	33	89	.277	.321	.371
Career	635	2281	243	581	92	22	24	219	99	166	432	.255	.306	.346

Where He Hits the Ball

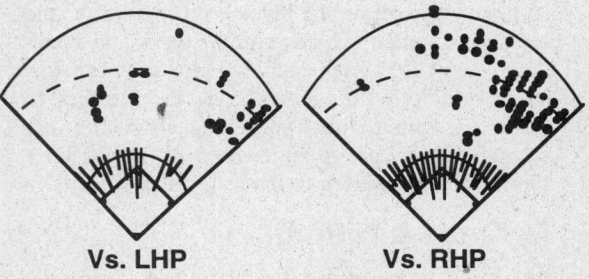

Vs. LHP **Vs. RHP**

1996 Situational Stats

	AB	H	HR	RBI	Avg		AB	H	HR	RBI	Avg
Home	237	60	6	20	.253	LHP	135	38	1	10	.281
Road	254	76	0	15	.299	RHP	356	98	5	25	.275
First Half	277	77	3	19	.278	Sc Pos	108	28	2	29	.259
Scnd Half	214	59	3	16	.276	Clutch	76	21	0	8	.276

1996 Rankings (National League)

- ➡ 2nd in caught stealing (15)
- ➡ 4th in highest groundball/flyball ratio (2.0)
- ➡ 5th in lowest on-base percentage for a leadoff hitter (.314), fielding percentage at shortstop (.972) and steals of third (8)
- ➡ 6th in most GDPs per GDP situation (18.3%) and lowest batting average with the bases loaded (.111)
- ➡ 7th in bunts in play (21)
- ➡ 8th in lowest stolen base percentage (68.8%)
- ➡ 9th in lowest HR frequency (81.8 ABs per HR) and errors at shortstop (15)
- ➡ 10th in lowest on-base percentage and lowest slugging percentage vs. left-handed pitchers (.356)

Dennis Eckersley

1996 Season

Dennis Eckersley is the Energizer Bunny of relievers. . . he just keeps going and going. At the age of 41, Eckersley came over to the Cardinals and enjoyed his best season since 1993. Back in Oakland, it looked like the end of a great career was near. It still may be, but it didn't appear to be any closer than it had been in '94 and '95. Eckersley endured some struggles in May and a DL stint in June, but righted the ship in time to be an effective closer in the stretch run and postseason. In six postseason games, he was 4-for-4 in save opportunities while posting a perfect 0.00 ERA.

Pitching

Eckersley still possesses pinpoint control. He spots his fastball on the black with regularity, and his slider, which crowds righthanders and backdoors lefties, is impeccable. Eckersley has lost some velocity with age, so he has been forced to throw first-pitch sliders more and go deeper into counts. Hitters get to him when he serves up a too-hittable first pitch or hangs his slider.

Defense & Hitting

Eckersley is awful at holding runners, primarily because he won't alter his patented delivery. As a fielder, Eckersley is outstanding, possessing a reaction time more like hurlers 10 years his junior. He is ultra-aggressive fielding sacrifices, going after the lead runner at every opportunity. After not swinging a bat much for the past 10 years, Eckersley was retired in his only plate appearance.

1997 Outlook

The Cardinals are grooming T.J. Mathews to eventually take the closer's role, but Eckersley—who re-signed with the Redbirds after the season—is still the man for now. At his age the end could come any time, but it's dangerous to predict he won't continue to be effective.

Position: RP
Bats: R **Throws:** R
Ht: 6' 2" **Wt:** 195

Opening Day Age: 42
Born: 10/3/54 in Oakland, CA
ML Seasons: 22
Nickname: The Eck

Overall Statistics

	W	L	Pct.	ERA	G	GS	Sv	IP	H	BB	SO	HR	BR/IP
1996	0	6	.000	3.30	63	0	30	60.0	65	6	49	8	1.18
Career	192	165	.538	3.48	964	361	353	3193.0	2981	722	2334	332	1.16

How Often He Throws Strikes

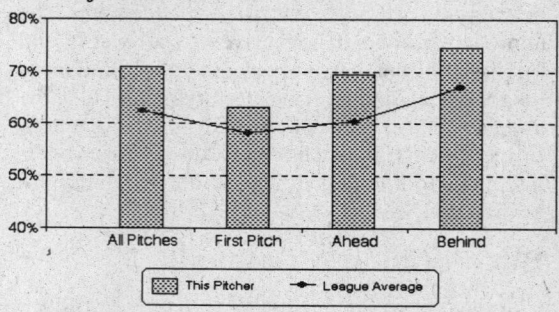

1996 Situational Stats

	W	L	ERA	Sv	IP		AB	H	HR	RBI	Avg
Home	0	1	2.70	14	33.1	LHB	100	29	4	10	.290
Road	0	5	4.05	16	26.2	RHB	137	36	4	20	.263
First Half	0	5	3.68	12	29.1	Sc Pos	57	16	2	21	.281
Scnd Half	0	1	2.93	18	30.2	Clutch	164	45	5	23	.274

1996 Rankings (National League)

→ 5th in save percentage (88.2%), relief losses (6) and highest batting average allowed in relief (.274)
→ 9th in saves
→ 10th in games finished (53) and save opportunities (34)
→ Led the Cardinals in saves, games finished (53), save opportunities (34), save percentage (88.2%) and relief losses (6)

Gary Gaetti

1996 Season

Lately, each year figures to be the last of Gary Gaetti's career, but somehow, each year he seems to play like a 28 year old. After nearly fading away, Gaetti has rebounded to put together back-to-back standout seasons with Kansas City and the Cardinals. Gaetti got the job done in '96 in every way, hitting for power and a respectable average and playing steady defense at third.

Hitting

Gaetti's approach to hitting has always been relatively simple: look for a pitch in your zone, preferably a fastball, and pull it as hard as you can. Gaetti rarely goes to right field, unless he's fooled by soft breaking stuff. Despite his age, he can still get around on decent heat with his uppercut swing, and he still has home run power. He takes his cuts, and is not afraid to strike out. He realizes as long as his power numbers are decent, he won't be expected to hit for a great average.

Baserunning & Defense

Gaetti is understandably limited on the bases, but he won't run you out of an inning. At third, he still has quick, soft hands and great natural instincts for the position. His arm isn't the strongest, but it's accurate and his release is quick. As efficient as Gaetti is at third, he's out of his element at first.

1997 Outlook

Gaetti, who re-signed with the Cardinals after the season, will enter '97 as the Cardinals' third baseman, and there are no hot prospects to displace him. It would be unfair to predict that he will do anything other than give the Redbirds another full season of solid play. As long as he can hit at least .240 with 20 homers, he'll be a major league third sacker. A veteran of one World Series, Gaetti is in St. Louis as much for his presence as for his production.

Position: 3B/1B
Bats: R **Throws:** R
Ht: 6' 0" **Wt:** 200

Opening Day Age: 38
Born: 8/19/58 in Centralia, IL
ML Seasons: 16
Pronunciation: guy-ETT-ee

Overall Statistics

	G	AB	R	H	D	T	HR	RBI	SB	BB	SO	Avg	OBP	Slg
1996	141	522	71	143	27	4	23	80	2	35	97	.274	.326	.473
Career	2113	7725	985	1975	376	36	315	1155	88	534	1398	.256	.307	.436

Where He Hits the Ball

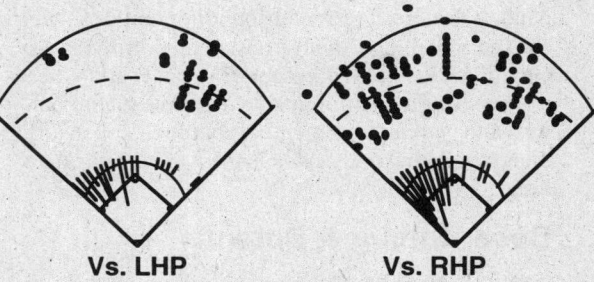

Vs. LHP   **Vs. RHP**

1996 Situational Stats

	AB	H	HR	RBI	Avg		AB	H	HR	RBI	Avg
Home	244	74	13	45	.303	LHP	105	26	3	13	.248
Road	278	69	10	35	.248	RHP	417	117	20	67	.281
First Half	255	64	8	35	.251	Sc Pos	143	38	5	55	.266
Scnd Half	267	79	15	45	.296	Clutch	83	28	6	14	.337

1996 Rankings (National League)

- ➡ 2nd in fielding percentage at third base (.969)
- ➡ 4th in highest percentage of swings on the first pitch (44.7%)
- ➡ 5th in lowest percentage of pitches taken (45.2%)
- ➡ 7th in least pitches seen per plate appearance (3.37)
- ➡ 10th in lowest batting average on a 3-1 count (.111)
- ➡ Led the Cardinals in hit by pitch (8), HR frequency (22.7 ABs per HR) and batting average with two strikes (.216)

St. Louis Cardinals

Ron Gant

1996 Season

Ron Gant didn't enjoy a "bang-up" season in the sense that the Cardinals hoped he would. Gant was the one who ended up getting banged-up, but he made his presence felt. He was slowed early in the season by a hamstring strain, and a torn rotator cuff hampered him late in the year. Still, he was an ever-threatening presence in the lineup down the stretch, and his 30 home runs provided suitable protection for Ray Lankford batting ahead of him in the Redbirds' order.

Hitting

Gant's primary goal these days is to hit the ball out of the park, which he's capable of doing against just about any pitcher. His struggles against left-handers last year were confounding, but not typical; he's pounded them consistently in the past. Gant likes the ball up in the strike zone, and when pitchers challenge him inside, he turns on the ball well and generates tremendous bat speed. A steady diet of breaking balls away is the way to neutralize him.

Baserunning & Defense

Gant is a good baserunner and routinely racks up steals in double figures, but doesn't run quite as often since breaking his leg in 1994. His outfield defense is good, but not great. His arm is average at best, possibly because he's too muscle-bound to get the flexibility needed for strong, accurate throws. He is adept at tracking down drives in the gap, however, and not afraid to crash into walls to make plays.

1997 Outlook

If Gant can stay healthy for an entire season, he can put up lofty numbers, even in Busch Stadium. The Cardinals' lineup is short on power without him, so his continued presence is critical to their success. Gant will be eligible for free agency after the '97 season, but if the Cardinals' success continues, he may be a part of their lineup for quite a while.

Position: LF
Bats: R **Throws:** R
Ht: 6' 0" **Wt:** 200

Opening Day Age: 32
Born: 3/2/65 in Victoria, TX
ML Seasons: 9

Overall Statistics

	G	AB	R	H	D	T	HR	RBI	SB	BB	SO	Avg	OBP	Slg
1996	122	419	74	103	14	2	30	82	13	73	98	.246	.359	.504
Career	1099	4021	668	1052	191	33	206	650	193	447	806	.262	.336	.479

Where He Hits the Ball

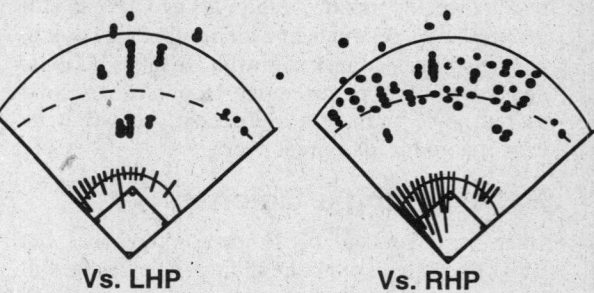

Vs. LHP   **Vs. RHP**

1996 Situational Stats

	AB	H	HR	RBI	Avg		AB	H	HR	RBI	Avg
Home	221	50	17	42	.226	LHP	94	19	5	10	.202
Road	198	53	13	40	.268	RHP	325	84	25	72	.258
First Half	174	41	12	41	.236	Sc Pos	110	29	7	51	.264
Scnd Half	245	62	18	41	.253	Clutch	67	18	3	8	.269

1996 Rankings (National League)

- ➡ 3rd in lowest batting average at home (.226)
- ➡ 5th in batting average on an 0-2 count (.310) and errors in left field (5)
- ➡ 6th in fielding percentage in left field (.978)
- ➡ 9th in highest percentage of swings that missed (27.8%)
- ➡ 10th in highest percentage of pitches taken (59.8%)
- ➡ Led the Cardinals in home runs, batting average on an 0-2 count (.310), slugging percentage vs. right-handed pitchers (.538) and highest percentage of pitches taken (59.8%)

Danny Jackson

1996 Season

Danny Jackson's career has been marred by frequent injuries, and 1996 was no different. Expected to lend left-handed depth and experience to the Cardinals' staff, Jackson was sidelined until August after undergoing ankle surgery. He ended up as an infrequently-used long reliever, making only four starts and winning only one game all year.

Pitching

Jackson has never quite recovered his strength after his cancer scare of '95, and he's been forced to try to evolve into a stereotypical "crafty left-hander." When he's at full strength, Jackson can bring heat in the low 90s along with a wicked slider that embarrasses left-handed hitters. He also mixes in an effective slurve in certain situations. Once a standout control pitcher, Jackson has been plagued by wildness in recent years—even when healthy—presumably because of rusty mechanics due to all his recent shelf time.

Defense & Hitting

Jackson struggles to field his position, and rarely gets rattled in tight spots. He's a decent athlete, and as a lefty, he makes some impressive plays on bunts to the third base side. Jackson laced a single and two doubles in nine at-bats last year, but he's basically a typical pitcher at the plate.

1997 Outlook

Halfway through his 30s and still fighting injuries, Jackson doesn't appear to have a clear role in the Cardinals' scheme. An excellent, pain-free spring could land him a spot as a lefty middle man and spot starter, but there are other qualified candidates around. Though his high salary is a barrier, Jackson might wind up somewhere else, perhaps with a team desperate for a left-handed set-up man or fifth starter.

Position: RP/SP
Bats: R **Throws:** L
Ht: 6' 0" **Wt:** 220

Opening Day Age: 35
Born: 1/5/62 in San Antonio, TX
ML Seasons: 14

Overall Statistics

	W	L	Pct.	ERA	G	GS	Sv	IP	H	BB	SO	HR	BR/IP
1996	1	1	.500	4.46	13	4	0	36.1	33	16	27	3	1.35
Career	110	122	.474	3.89	336	311	1	2005.0	2012	788	1193	122	1.40

How Often He Throws Strikes

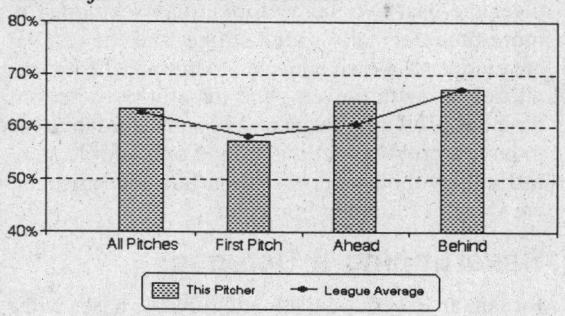

1996 Situational Stats

	W	L	ERA	Sv	IP		AB	H	HR	RBI	Avg
Home	1	0	3.10	0	20.1	LHB	33	12	1	8	.364
Road	0	1	6.19	0	16.0	RHB	103	21	2	10	.204
First Half	0	0	-	0	0.0	Sc Pos	27	9	1	13	.333
Scnd Half	1	1	4.46	0	36.1	Clutch	0	0	0	0	-

1996 Rankings (National League)

➡ Did not rank near the top or bottom in any category

Brian Jordan

1996 Season

Brian Jordan came on strong in 1996, putting to rest any thoughts that he was better off remaining in the NFL. Jordan led the St. Louis regulars in batting average and RBI, and stepped to the fore when Ron Gant went down with an injury early in the year. Jordan's numbers improved greatly upon Gant's return, however. His season was highlighted by numerous tape-measure home runs, some coming in game-breaking situations. Jordan also had many spectacular moments, both with the bat and glove, in the Cardinals' first postseason in nine years.

Hitting

Over the past two years, Jordan has developed a more fundamentally sound stroke, and the results are evident. His strikeouts have dropped, he hits to all fields—with power—and his ability to get on base has grown by leaps and bounds. Jordan used to have a problem getting around on major league fastballs without overswinging, but now pitchers are wary of throwing him heat.

Baserunning & Defense

Jordan, an exceptional athlete, runs the bases with a combination of pure speed and fury that is constantly on the minds of opposing players. He has the potential to steal even more bases when he gets a better idea of who to run against and when. His athletic ability is on display in the outfield, where he has developed into one of the premier right fielders in the game. His throwing arm is incredibly strong and usually on-line, and he covers as much territory as a center fielder. He really came through in key situations for the Cards last year, leading the majors with a remarkable .422 average with runners in scoring position.

1997 Outlook

Jordan has the potential to become the Cardinals' next superstar. The team's management shudders to think that, even now, his understanding of the game is still in its infancy. When his mental approach and perspective reach the level of his physical skills, he'll be truly awesome. This may be Jordan's first superstar campaign.

Position: RF/CF
Bats: R **Throws:** R
Ht: 6' 1" **Wt:** 215

Opening Day Age: 30
Born: 3/29/67 in Baltimore, MD
ML Seasons: 5

Overall Statistics

	G	AB	R	H	D	T	HR	RBI	SB	BB	SO	Avg	OBP	Slg
1996	140	513	82	159	36	1	17	104	22	29	84	.310	.349	.483
Career	446	1597	229	459	83	17	59	266	63	89	286	.287	.331	.472

Where He Hits the Ball

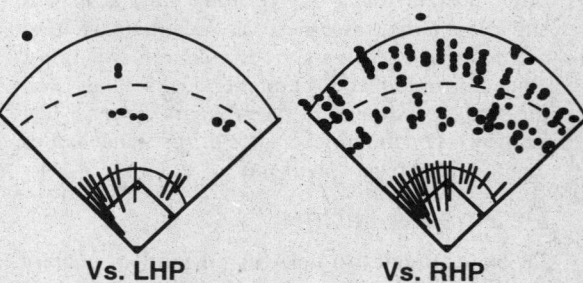

Vs. LHP   Vs. RHP

1996 Situational Stats

	AB	H	HR	RBI	Avg		AB	H	HR	RBI	Avg
Home	267	91	3	43	.341	LHP	108	37	3	17	.343
Road	246	68	14	61	.276	RHP	405	122	14	87	.301
First Half	264	79	9	50	.299	Sc Pos	147	62	10	93	.422
Scnd Half	249	80	8	54	.321	Clutch	75	25	2	11	.333

1996 Rankings (National League)

- ➡ 1st in batting average with runners in scoring position (.422)
- ➡ 2nd in batting average with the bases loaded (.684) and fielding percentage in right field (.993)
- ➡ 4th in sacrifice flies (9)
- ➡ 5th in highest percentage of extra bases taken as a runner (65.9%)
- ➡ 7th in cleanup slugging percentage (.524)
- ➡ 8th in stolen base percentage (81.5%) and batting average at home (.341)
- ➡ 10th in least pitches seen per plate appearance (3.42)
- ➡ Led the Cardinals in doubles, RBI and sacrifice flies (9)

Ray Lankford

1996 Season

Last year, Ray Lankford put together a very good year—perhaps his best overall in the major leagues. While he still whiffed more than his share, he provided the Cardinals with solid production, superlative defense in center field, and leadership for a team full of unfamiliar faces. The only sour note was a rotator-cuff injury that limited his effectiveness in the postseason.

Hitting

Lankford's problem at the plate has always been a lack of patience and a penchant for swinging at pitches well out of the strike zone. To an extent, he has learned to compensate by making his contact count, as he possesses excellent bat speed. He's worked diligently to get a better understanding of the hitting zone, and he's no longer intimidated by left-handed pitching (as seemed to be the case his first few seasons in the league). He does lack power against southpaws as evidenced by hitting no homers against them last year. Lankford still suffers from a habit of overswinging, but he's finally establishing himself as an all-around performer on offense.

Baserunning & Defense

Lankford is an ultra-aggressive baserunner who's always a threat to steal. He still has some things to learn about reading pitchers' moves and getting good jumps, but he's made good progress in that area. He led the team in steals, and was caught only seven times. Lankford is a burner in the outfield and he has a better-than-average throwing arm, but his defense is not without its flaws. He still has difficulty reacting to deep flies, especially when playing on the road.

1997 Outlook

As a five-tool player, Lankford has the potential to be among the very best in the league, but it has taken him a while to learn how to use his considerable talent. The Cardinals would love to see him break through with a monster season, but they're more than satisfied with his current level of production.

Position: CF
Bats: L **Throws:** L
Ht: 5'11" **Wt:** 200

Opening Day Age: 29
Born: 6/5/67 in Los Angeles, CA
ML Seasons: 7

Overall Statistics

	G	AB	R	H	D	T	HR	RBI	SB	BB	SO	Avg	OBP	Slg
1996	149	545	100	150	36	8	21	86	35	79	133	.275	.366	.486
Career	860	3141	516	845	186	40	104	437	178	407	755	.269	.353	.453

Where He Hits the Ball

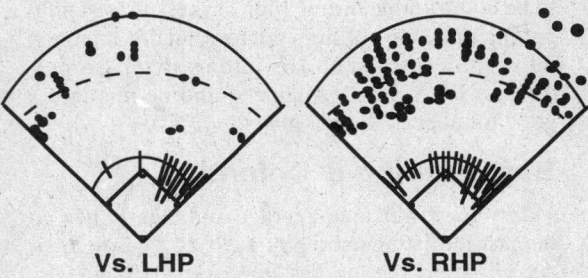

Vs. LHP   **Vs. RHP**

1996 Situational Stats

	AB	H	HR	RBI	Avg		AB	H	HR	RBI	Avg
Home	257	78	8	47	.304	LHP	122	30	0	22	.246
Road	288	72	13	39	.250	RHP	423	120	21	64	.284
First Half	301	84	14	49	.279	Sc Pos	135	42	3	58	.311
Scnd Half	244	66	7	37	.270	Clutch	101	24	3	21	.238

1996 Rankings (National League)

- → 1st in fielding percentage in center field (.997)
- → 3rd in lowest on-base percentage vs. left-handed pitchers (.278)
- → 4th in most pitches seen per plate appearance (4.08)
- → 5th in triples and strikeouts
- → 6th in stolen base percentage (83.3%)
- → 7th in lowest percentage of swings put into play (36.0%)
- → 9th in stolen bases, walks and lowest percentage of swings on the first pitch (22.4%)
- → 10th in lowest batting average vs. left-handed pitchers (.246)
- → Led the Cardinals in at-bats, runs scored, doubles, triples, total bases (265) and walks

John Mabry

1996 Season

John Mabry is the National League equivalent of Toronto's John Olerud, a left-handed-hitting first baseman with the capability to someday win a batting title. Mabry enjoyed a fine 1996 season, hitting close to .300 and playing a solid first base. At first, his conversion to first base seemed to be a stopgap solution, but by the end of the year, he had established himself as the regular there. Mabry also demonstrated some power after being labeled a contact hitter throughout his minor league career.

Hitting

Mabry is fundamentally sound, especially for a younger player, and he hits lefthanders surprisingly well. He is one of the few lefties who appears to be comfortable hitting high strikes, consistently getting on the top of high pitches and driving them into right-center field. His hitting style also produces a lot of hard grounders, and he hits into a good number of double plays.

Baserunning & Defense

Mabry is slower than average and clearly has no interest in distinguishing himself as a basestealer. As a first sacker, he has improved dramatically. His former weakness, throwing, is no longer a consistent problem. He is efficient at covering the required ground at first and has improved at digging low throws and stretching on close plays. He can play an average right field, giving the roster a bit more flexibility.

1997 Outlook

Mabry is still getting comfortable with his role as a big-league regular. Insiders like his stroke, and envision him as a consistent .300 hitter. While he lacks the home run power most clubs desire in a first baseman, he should be able to hold onto his job as long as he continues to be productive.

Position: 1B/RF
Bats: L **Throws:** R
Ht: 6' 4" **Wt:** 205

Opening Day Age: 26
Born: 10/17/70 in Wilmington, DE
ML Seasons: 3
Pronunciation: MAY-bree

Overall Statistics

	G	AB	R	H	D	T	HR	RBI	SB	BB	SO	Avg	OBP	Slg
1996	151	543	63	161	30	2	13	74	3	37	84	.297	.342	.431
Career	286	954	100	287	54	3	18	118	3	63	133	.301	.344	.420

Where He Hits the Ball

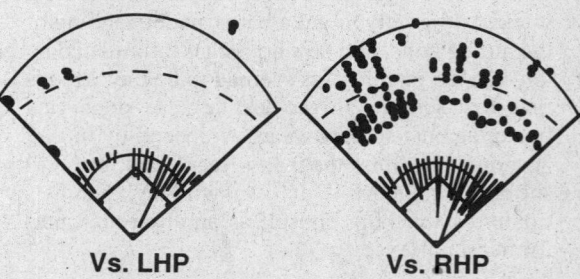

Vs. LHP   **Vs. RHP**

1996 Situational Stats

	AB	H	HR	RBI	Avg		AB	H	HR	RBI	Avg
Home	265	69	3	32	.260	LHP	97	34	3	19	.351
Road	278	92	10	42	.331	RHP	446	127	10	55	.285
First Half	299	99	7	42	.331	Sc Pos	139	42	1	56	.302
Scnd Half	244	62	6	32	.254	Clutch	87	22	1	8	.253

1996 Rankings (National League)

- → 2nd in highest percentage of swings on the first pitch (48.3%)
- → 3rd in GDPs (21), batting average on the road (.331) and lowest percentage of pitches taken (44.1%)
- → 4th in least pitches seen per plate appearance (3.21)
- → 5th in fielding percentage at first base (.994)
- → 6th in errors at first base (8)
- → 7th in most GDPs per GDP situation (17.6%)
- → 9th in highest groundball/flyball ratio (1.8)
- → Led the Cardinals in hits, singles, intentional walks (11), GDPs (21), games played (151) and batting average on the road (.331)

T.J. Mathews

1996 Season

Righthander T.J. Mathews underwent some on-the-job training in the St. Louis pen last year, learning from two of the better relievers in the game, Rick Honeycutt and Dennis Eckersley. He functioned primarily as a set-up man for Eckersley on a regular basis, but his true value lay in his versatility. In a bullpen full of specialists, Mathews was the jack-of-all-trades, performing capably in a variety of situations and leading the bullpen in innings. He continued his impressive pitching in the Cardinals' postseason.

Pitching

Mathews has the mentality of a workhorse: he wants the ball every day. Big and strong, he mixes a low-90s fastball and hard slider, and changes speeds to great effect. He was tough to hit and stranded most of the runners he inherited, which would suggest that he has the stuff and approach to be a major league closer eventually. Mathews is an intense competitor on the mound, with his emotions visibly riding on each pitch.

Defense & Hitting

In the field, Mathews is athletic and unafraid—if slightly error-prone. He's an active fielder, backing up when obligated and even when he's not. He's also sound at baffling baserunners, who were successful only once in four steal attempts. His pickoff move is deceiving, and he keeps the location of his pitches where his catcher can easily handle them during steal attempts. He can't hit.

1997 Outlook

Mathews' role depends on what happens to Dennis Eckersley, who could stick around a while longer as the Cardinals' closer. If that's the case, Mathews will continue to function as the primary right-handed set-up man. With his stuff, he could even be tested as a starter if the need arises. In any event, he has star potential, and figures to get plenty of important assignments this year.

Position: RP
Bats: R **Throws:** R
Ht: 6' 2" **Wt:** 200

Opening Day Age: 27
Born: 1/19/70 in Belleville, IL
ML Seasons: 2

Overall Statistics

	W	L	Pct.	ERA	G	GS	Sv	IP	H	BB	SO	HR	BR/IP
1996	2	6	.250	3.01	67	0	6	83.2	62	32	80	8	1.12
Career	3	7	.300	2.62	90	0	8	113.1	83	43	108	9	1.11

How Often He Throws Strikes

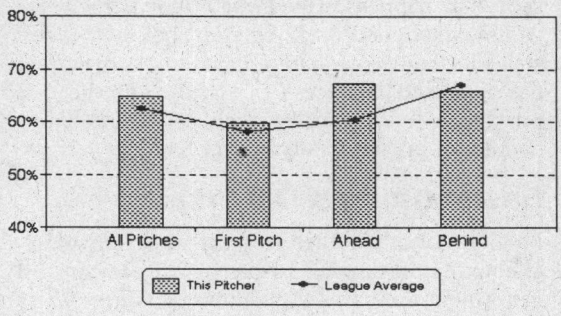

Legend: This Pitcher ▨ / League Average ●

1996 Situational Stats

	W	L	ERA	Sv	IP		AB	H	HR	RBI	Avg
Home	2	2	2.34	3	42.1	LHB	99	22	3	14	.222
Road	0	4	3.70	3	41.1	RHB	207	40	5	17	.193
First Half	1	2	2.27	3	47.2	Sc Pos	76	15	2	21	.197
Scnd Half	1	4	4.00	3	36.0	Clutch	144	30	3	15	.208

1996 Rankings (National League)

- ➡ 1st in lowest percentage of inherited runners scored (16.7%)
- ➡ 2nd in least GDPs induced per GDP situation (1.6%)
- ➡ 4th in first batter efficiency (.150)
- ➡ 5th in relief losses (6)
- ➡ 7th in lowest batting average allowed in relief (.203) and least baserunners allowed per 9 innings in relief (10.3)
- ➡ 10th in relief innings (83.2)
- ➡ Led the Cardinals in games pitched, blown saves (5), first batter efficiency (.150), lowest percentage of inherited runners scored (16.7%), relief losses (6) and relief innings (83.2)

Willie McGee

1996 Season

Reunited with the organization for which he won two batting titles and an MVP, Willie McGee revived his career in 1996. Gaining more playing time than he expected, McGee batted .307, playing all three outfield spots and serving as the team's top pinch hitter. He seemed a new man after returning to the place where he spent his glory years.

Hitting

McGee is a balanced switch-hitter, adept from either side of the plate. His unique knock-kneed stance allows him to execute that rare fundamental: hit down on the ball. McGee's theory has always been to put the ball in play, run hard, and see what happens. He doesn't fare particularly well against good breaking stuff, but he can still slap a fastball to any part of the field. As his career has advanced, McGee has looked to hit the first pitch more and more. He rarely sees more than a handful of pitches in a typical at-bat.

Baserunning & Defense

McGee doesn't bother to steal much anymore, attempting only seven swipes in '96. He can still get around the bases efficiently, taking the extra base when required, but he's not an instigator like he once was. He is still used as a pinch runner on occasion, more for his savvy than for his no-longer blazing speed. McGee used to be a Gold Glove-caliber outfielder, but he doesn't cover the territory he once did. His throwing arm isn't especially strong, but it is accurate and reliable.

1997 Outlook

McGee began to go stale in his last year in San Francisco, but his career has been resurrected back "home" in St. Louis. The Cards were happy enough to have him back—they signed the 38-year old to a one-year deal in December. Expect him to finish his playing career there in the next year or two, and possibly remain within the organization as a coach.

Position: RF/LF/CF
Bats: B **Throws:** R
Ht: 6' 1" **Wt:** 185

Opening Day Age: 38
Born: 11/2/58 in San Francisco, CA
ML Seasons: 15

Overall Statistics

	G	AB	R	H	D	T	HR	RBI	SB	BB	SO	Avg	OBP	Slg
1996	123	309	52	95	15	2	5	41	5	18	60	.307	.348	.417
Career	1827	6809	929	2028	314	89	73	764	330	395	1070	.298	.336	.402

Where He Hits the Ball

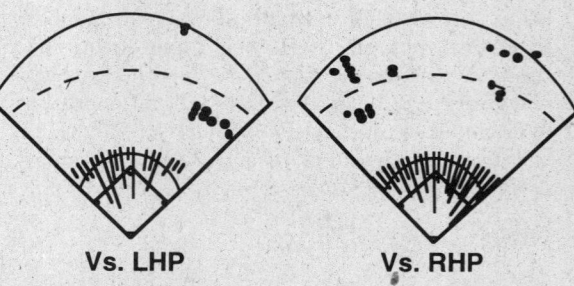

Vs. LHP   **Vs. RHP**

1996 Situational Stats

	AB	H	HR	RBI	Avg			AB	H	HR	RBI	Avg
Home	151	54	2	21	.358		LHP	88	26	3	13	.295
Road	158	41	3	20	.259		RHP	221	69	2	28	.312
First Half	188	59	3	29	.314		Sc Pos	79	25	2	36	.316
Scnd Half	121	36	2	12	.298		Clutch	71	24	0	13	.338

1996 Rankings (National League)

➡ 1st in lowest batting average on a 3-1 count (.000)
➡ 10th in batting average in the clutch (.338)
➡ Led the Cardinals in batting average in the clutch (.338)

Donovan Osborne

1996 Season

In 1993, many of the game's keenest observers saw a bright future for Donovan Osborne, but an assortment of injuries prevented him from strutting his stuff. . . until last season. Finally healthy for an entire season, Osborne developed into the steady, smart lefty the Cardinals had been lacking. He had the lowest ERA on the starting staff, and suddenly became one of the better lefthanders in the league.

Pitching

Osborne blends intelligence and poise with the southpaw's classic repertoire. Location is the key for him, as he mixes in an effective slider and change with a tailing fastball. The primary reason for his improved performance has been his ability to come inside and challenge righthanders. He rarely hurts himself with ill-advised pitches, and makes opposing hitters work for everything, eventually wearing them down.

Defense & Hitting

Osborne's pickoff move is among the better ones around. Its presence tends to keep runners close and resulted in 10 of 14 would-be basestealers being thrown out last year (although some of the credit goes to Tom Pagnozzi). Osborne plays good defense around the mound, and generally gets everywhere he's supposed to be. He's a solid, disciplined hitter. Last year he batted .220 and was the only St. Louis pitcher to go deep.

1997 Outlook

Osborne's year ended on a down note when he was blown out early in Game 7 of the NLCS, but that shouldn't do any permanent damage. The re-emergence of Osborne has given the Cardinals a formidable starting rotation. Good enough to be the number-two starter with most other teams, he actually could be considered a number-five starter on the Cardinals' deep staff. But Osborne certainly won't quibble over details like that, as long as his health allows him to continue to toe the rubber every fifth day.

Position: SP
Bats: L **Throws:** L
Ht: 6' 2" **Wt:** 195

Opening Day Age: 27
Born: 6/21/69 in Roseville, CA
ML Seasons: 4

Overall Statistics

	W	L	Pct.	ERA	G	GS	Sv	IP	H	BB	SO	HR	BR/IP
1996	13	9	.591	3.53	30	30	0	198.2	191	57	134	22	1.25
Career	38	31	.551	3.70	109	104	0	646.2	649	176	403	71	1.28

How Often He Throws Strikes

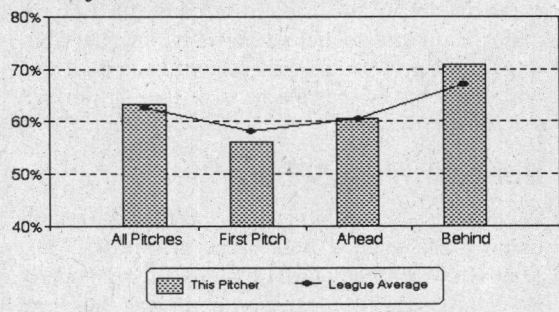

This Pitcher   League Average

1996 Situational Stats

	W	L	ERA	Sv	IP		AB	H	HR	RBI	Avg
Home	8	3	3.39	0	109.0	LHB	110	24	4	8	.218
Road	5	6	3.71	0	89.2	RHB	643	167	18	68	.260
First Half	8	4	3.13	0	103.2	Sc Pos	135	45	2	47	.333
Scnd Half	5	5	3.98	0	95.0	Clutch	57	18	3	11	.316

1996 Rankings (National League)

- ➤ 1st in lowest stolen base percentage allowed (28.6%)
- ➤ 3rd in highest batting average allowed with runners in scoring position (.333)
- ➤ 8th in least run support per 9 innings (4.2) and least GDPs induced per 9 innings (0.5)
- ➤ 9th in shutouts (1)
- ➤ Led the Cardinals in sacrifice bunts (10), ERA, highest strikeout/walk ratio (2.4), lowest on-base percentage allowed (.306), lowest stolen base percentage allowed (28.6%), least baserunners allowed per 9 innings (11.3), least home runs allowed per 9 innings (1.00) and ERA at home (3.39)

St. Louis Cardinals

Tom Pagnozzi

1996 Season

Tom Pagnozzi is one of those quiet, steady performers who does nothing except get the job done. In 1996, he enjoyed his best season ever offensively, carrying a .300-plus average into mid-July before slumping down the stretch. But Pagnozzi was at his best behind the plate. One of the game's best defensive catchers, he was invaluable to the Cardinals' pitching staff.

Hitting

Pagnozzi pulls most everything and sports occasional power. His improvement last year resulted from scaling back his propensity to dive after breaking pitches out of the strike zone. His bat speed is simply insufficient to catch up to most major league fastballs, so he relies on guess-hitting, cheating for that split-second head start that will allow him to get the head of the bat through the zone in time.

Baserunning & Defense

Pagnozzi is slow afoot, but he runs the bases intelligently and swiped four bases in five tries last year. His work behind the plate is simply superb. He calls as good of a game as anyone and his arm, although not the strongest in the league, is far and away the most accurate in the league. Pagnozzi's motion is flawless, and his other fundamentals are excellent as well. He is also an astute follower of the game and an on-field leader, and is especially valuable to the team's younger pitchers.

1997 Outlook

Pagnozzi was a free agent this winter, and the Cards found themselves in a bidding war as they tried to retain his services, which they did, inking him to a two-year deal in December. A veteran winding down his career, he seems to be a natural to move into a bullpen coaching role, or perhaps serve as a pitching coach. But for now, he should continue to be the Cards' number-one backstop.

Position: C
Bats: R **Throws:** R
Ht: 6' 1" **Wt:** 195

Opening Day Age: 34
Born: 7/30/62 in Tucson, AZ
ML Seasons: 10

Overall Statistics

	G	AB	R	H	D	T	HR	RBI	SB	BB	SO	Avg	OBP	Slg
1996	119	407	48	110	23	0	13	55	4	24	78	.270	.311	.423
Career	851	2686	236	687	141	11	42	302	18	174	406	.256	.301	.363

Where He Hits the Ball

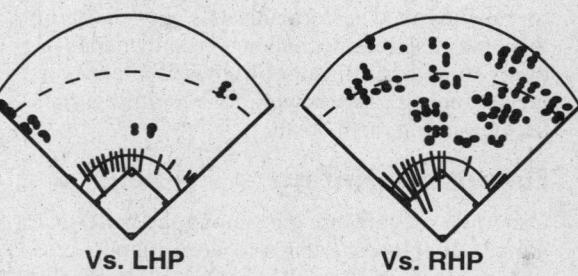

Vs. LHP   **Vs. RHP**

1996 Situational Stats

	AB	H	HR	RBI	Avg		AB	H	HR	RBI	Avg
Home	203	63	9	31	.310	LHP	76	23	3	11	.303
Road	204	47	4	24	.230	RHP	331	87	10	44	.263
First Half	193	58	6	30	.301	Sc Pos	102	26	1	37	.255
Scnd Half	214	52	7	25	.243	Clutch	79	21	4	9	.266

1996 Rankings (National League)

- → 3rd in highest percentage of runners caught stealing as a catcher (32.3%)
- → 8th in errors at catcher (8)
- → Led the Cardinals in batting average on a 3-1 count (.556)

Todd Stottlemyre

1996 Season

Long regarded as a disappointment, Todd Stottlemyre has become a completely different pitcher since hooking up with coach Dave Duncan in Oakland in 1995. In his first National League season, Stottlemyre became a bulwark of the St. Louis rotation, leading the team in strikeouts and complete games while working over 220 innings. He had been erratic and inconsistent in his earlier days with Toronto, but over the last two years, he has been among baseball's steadiest starters.

Pitching

Stottlemyre's mechanics have been overhauled by Duncan, and as a result, he now maintains his good stuff from start to start and goes deep into games with it. He throws a low-90s riding fastball to go with a slider, curve and change—all above-average pitches. He also throws a split-fingered fastball, which has boosted his strikeout totals the last two years. He does have occasional bouts of wildness, both in and out of the strike zone, and left-handed hitters give him trouble.

Defense & Hitting

Stottlemyre has gone back to his normal delivery after giving up trying to learn the slide-step. He was run on more than any other St. Louis pitcher, with opponents stealing successfully on 30 of 39 steal attempts. Stottlemyre helps himself with good defense, and his delivery leaves him in good fielding position. He was surprisingly effective in his first season as a hitter, batting .227 with seven walks, eight runs and two RBI.

1997 Outlook

After having won 14 games in each of the past two seasons, it's time for Stottlemyre to take the next step and approach the 18-20 victory plateau. Under the continuing tutelage of Duncan and La Russa, there's no reason why he can't continue to progress toward that level. He'll go into spring training as the team's number-two starter.

Position: SP
Bats: L **Throws:** R
Ht: 6' 3" **Wt:** 200

Opening Day Age: 31
Born: 5/20/65 in Yakima, WA
ML Seasons: 9
Pronunciation: STAH-till-my-er

Overall Statistics

	W	L	Pct.	ERA	G	GS	Sv	IP	H	BB	SO	HR	BR/IP
1996	14	11	.560	3.87	34	33	0	223.1	191	93	194	30	1.27
Career	97	88	.524	4.33	271	239	1	1572.0	1601	587	1061	171	1.39

How Often He Throws Strikes

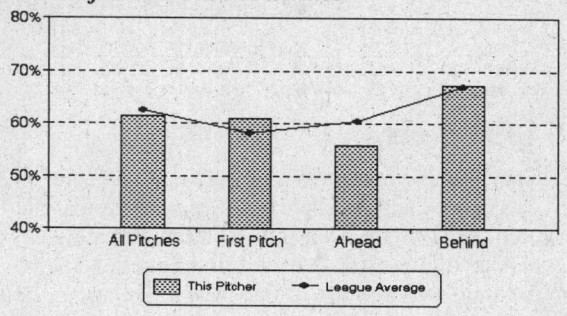

1996 Situational Stats

	W	L	ERA	Sv	IP		AB	H	HR	RBI	Avg
Home	6	7	4.01	0	128.0	LHB	371	101	15	41	.272
Road	8	4	3.68	0	95.1	RHB	455	90	15	51	.198
First Half	8	6	4.04	0	120.1	Sc Pos	196	40	11	64	.204
Scnd Half	6	5	3.67	0	103.0	Clutch	100	26	2	13	.260

1996 Rankings (National League)

→ 2nd in shutouts (2), home runs allowed, stolen bases allowed (30) and lowest batting average allowed vs. right-handed batters (.198)
→ 3rd in complete games (5) and lowest ground-ball/flyball ratio allowed (1.0)
→ 5th in walks allowed
→ 6th in lowest batting average allowed (.231) and lowest batting average allowed with runners in scoring position (.204)
→ 8th in strikeouts
→ 9th in pitches thrown (3,490), most strikeouts per 9 innings (7.8) and highest ERA at home (4.01)
→ Led the Cardinals in losses, complete games (5), shutouts (2) and home runs allowed

Cory Bailey

Position: RP
Bats: R **Throws:** R
Ht: 6' 1" **Wt:** 202

Opening Day Age: 26
Born: 1/24/71 in Herrin, IL
ML Seasons: 4

Overall Statistics

	W	L	Pct.	ERA	G	GS	Sv	IP	H	BB	SO	HR	BR/IP
1996	5	2	.714	3.00	51	0	0	57.0	57	30	38	1	1.53
Career	5	4	.556	3.79	70	0	0	80.2	81	47	58	3	1.59

1996 Situational Stats

	W	L	ERA	Sv	IP		AB	H	HR	RBI	Avg
Home	2	1	2.63	0	24.0	LHB	76	17	1	5	.224
Road	3	1	3.27	0	33.0	RHB	141	40	0	14	.284
First Half	3	1	4.71	0	28.2	Sc Pos	64	17	0	18	.266
Scnd Half	2	1	1.27	0	28.1	Clutch	98	28	0	7	.286

1996 Season

Cory Bailey got off to a rocky start in 1996, and he was sent to and recalled from Triple-A Louisville on three separate occasions. But he ultimately established himself as a useful middle reliever over the final two months of the season. He struggled with his control at times, but he was accomplished at avoiding the big inning.

Pitching, Defense & Hitting

Bailey doesn't have overpowering stuff, so he needs to hit his spots to be effective—which he managed to do just enough to stick around last year. Depending mostly on a sinking fastball, he allowed just one home run last year. Oddly enough, he had more trouble with righties. Bailey's defense is adequate and he's effective holding runners close. Only two of five would-be basestealers were successful. He was 0-for-1, but drew two walks at the plate last year.

1997 Outlook

Bailey was fortunate to spend so much time with the big club last year, but the fact that he was left off the postseason roster illustrates his precarious position on the Cardinals. If his control doesn't do him in, he may stick around a while longer as a middle man.

David Bell

Position: 3B/2B
Bats: R **Throws:** R
Ht: 5'10" **Wt:** 170

Opening Day Age: 24
Born: 9/14/72 in Cincinnati, OH
ML Seasons: 2

Overall Statistics

	G	AB	R	H	D	T	HR	RBI	SB	BB	SO	Avg	OBP	Slg
1996	62	145	12	31	6	0	1	9	1	10	22	.214	.268	.276
Career	103	291	25	67	13	2	3	28	2	14	47	.230	.271	.320

1996 Situational Stats

	AB	H	HR	RBI	Avg		AB	H	HR	RBI	Avg
Home	72	18	1	6	.250	LHP	64	16	0	4	.250
Road	73	13	0	3	.178	RHP	81	15	1	5	.185
First Half	136	29	1	8	.213	Sc Pos	35	5	0	8	.143
Scnd Half	9	2	0	1	.222	Clutch	30	9	0	0	.300

1996 Season

David Bell failed to impress in limited trials with the Cardinals early last year, and wound up back at Triple-A Louisville for most of the second half. Bell never found his batting stroke at the major league level, but he showed he's a bona fide utility player capable of playing second, third, or even shortstop if necessary.

Hitting, Baserunning & Defense

Bell, a third generation major leaguer and son of Detroit Tigers manager Buddy Bell, was too aggressive at the plate last year and tended to overswing, and it showed in his dismal average. He did show some power potential, but most of his hardest-hit balls go to the opposite field. Bell does not run particularly well, but he's a steady glove at third as well as a promising prospect at second base.

1997 Outlook

With Gary Gaetti refusing to yield to age, Bell's best shot may be to play his way into the second base competition. Tony La Russa, however, seemed to lose interest in him after his slow first half. He'll need to improve his approach at the plate to earn a better shot.

Tony Fossas

Position: RP
Bats: L **Throws:** L
Ht: 6' 0" **Wt:** 198

Opening Day Age: 39
Born: 9/23/57 in
Havana, Cuba
ML Seasons: 9

Overall Statistics

	W	L	Pct.	ERA	G	GS	Sv	IP	H	BB	SO	HR	BR/IP
1996	0	4	.000	2.68	65	0	2	47.0	43	21	36	7	1.36
Career	14	14	.500	3.68	450	0	7	340.1	336	137	260	30	1.39

1996 Situational Stats

	W	L	ERA	Sv	IP		AB	H	HR	RBI	Avg
Home	0	2	2.19	1	24.2	LHB	91	21	4	16	.231
Road	0	2	3.22	1	22.1	RHB	95	22	3	9	.232
First Half	0	4	3.33	2	27.0	Sc Pos	56	8	2	17	.143
Scnd Half	0	0	1.80	0	20.0	Clutch	65	19	3	17	.292

1996 Season

Tony Fossas' sole purpose in his baseball life is to retire the opposing team's left-handed hitters in pressure situations. Fossas did his job very well last year, holding lefties to a .231 average and finishing with the lowest ERA in the Cardinals' bullpen. He even pitched effectively against righties, against whom he's had problems through most of his career.

Pitching, Defense & Hitting

Fossas dominates left-handed hitters because he comes at them seemingly via first base. His slow, deep-breaking sliders are difficult for lefties to stay in on and his mediocre fastball runs in on their hands. He's also developed a cut fastball in case he has to face a righty. His age precludes him from being especially swift defensively, but he's effective at preventing teams from running wild on the bases. Fossas bunted into a double play in his only career plate appearance last year.

1997 Outlook

St. Louis re-signed the free agent, so there's no reason to believe Fossas will be any less effective in his limited role in '97. Despite his age and unathletic build, he is still one of the best at neutralizing left-handed hitters.

Mike Gallego

Position: 2B
Bats: R **Throws:** R
Ht: 5' 8" **Wt:** 175

Opening Day Age: 36
Born: 10/31/60 in
Whittier, CA
ML Seasons: 12
Pronunciation:
guy-YAY-go

Overall Statistics

	G	AB	R	H	D	T	HR	RBI	SB	BB	SO	Avg	OBP	Slg
1996	51	143	12	30	2	0	0	4	0	12	31	.210	.276	.224
Career	1084	2888	368	693	109	12	42	281	24	325	459	.240	.322	.330

1996 Situational Stats

	AB	H	HR	RBI	Avg		AB	H	HR	RBI	Avg
Home	78	16	0	3	.205	LHP	36	8	0	1	.222
Road	65	14	0	1	.215	RHP	107	22	0	3	.206
First Half	0	0	0	0	-	Sc Pos	30	6	0	4	.200
Scnd Half	143	30	0	4	.210	Clutch	21	5	0	0	.238

1996 Season

Mike Gallego missed the first half of 1996 with a badly strained hamstring, and when he finally returned, he didn't hit at all. But in the field, Gallego showed why Tony La Russa has always stuck by him. He played his usual brilliant defense, which was good enough in itself to earn him half of the second base job.

Hitting, Baserunning & Defense

Gallego has little value at the plate, although he can do a little damage to lefties from time to time. He no longer runs well, and hasn't stolen a base in years. His greatest asset is defense. He plays a flawless second base, with great footwork and soft hands, and can fill in acceptably at third base or shortstop.

1997 Outlook

The Cardinals signed free-agent second baseman Delino DeShields over the winter, and it's possible Gallego—a free agent himself—might not be back. If healthy, he still has plenty of value as a utility player and defensive sub. Since Tony La Russa thinks highly of him, a return to St. Louis is quite possible for Gallego.

St. Louis
Cardinals

Rick Honeycutt

Position: RP
Bats: L **Throws:** L
Ht: 6' 1" **Wt:** 195

Opening Day Age: 42
Born: 6/29/54 in
Chattanooga, TN
ML Seasons: 20

Overall Statistics

	W	L	Pct.	ERA	G	GS	Sv	IP	H	BB	SO	HR	BR/IP
1996	2	1	.667	2.85	61	0	4	47.1	42	7	30	3	1.04
Career	109	143	.433	3.71	795	268	38	2157.2	2178	656	1036	185	1.31

1996 Situational Stats

	W	L	ERA	Sv	IP		AB	H	HR	RBI	Avg
Home	2	1	2.00	2	27.0	LHB	67	16	3	9	.239
Road	0	0	3.98	2	20.1	RHB	108	26	0	15	.241
First Half	2	0	3.00	2	27.0	Sc Pos	48	17	1	22	.354
Scnd Half	0	1	2.66	2	20.1	Clutch	88	20	1	11	.227

1996 Season

Another Tony La Russa favorite, Rick Honeycutt was picked up by the Cardinals to be one of their two left-handed specialists out of the bullpen. Despite being the oldest player in the majors, Honeycutt posted a sub-3.00 ERA and appeared in more games than he had in five years.

Pitching, Defense & Hitting

Honeycutt's out pitch is a patented sinker which appears to sink twice, once upon its release and again as it reaches the plate. He complements it with a cut fastball that doesn't have much velocity, but remains enough to get lefties out. He keeps the ball down, induces ground balls, and has excellent control—he issued only four unintentional walks all year. The aged Honeycutt's fielding is below average, but his pickoff move freezes runners. Honeycutt was once a decent hitter, and walked twice in three plate appearances last year.

1997 Outlook

The club renewed its option on Honeycutt for '97, and the ancient lefty will be back for his 21st season. As long as he keeps getting hitters out, it won't matter *how* old Honeycutt is.

Mark Petkovsek

Position: RP/SP
Bats: R **Throws:** R
Ht: 6' 0" **Wt:** 195

Opening Day Age: 31
Born: 11/18/65 in
Beaumont, TX
ML Seasons: 4
Pronunciation:
pet-KY-zik

Overall Statistics

	W	L	Pct.	ERA	G	GS	Sv	IP	H	BB	SO	HR	BR/IP
1996	11	2	.846	3.55	48	6	0	88.2	83	35	45	9	1.33
Career	20	9	.690	4.57	104	28	0	267.2	283	83	136	31	1.37

1996 Situational Stats

	W	L	ERA	Sv	IP		AB	H	HR	RBI	Avg
Home	9	2	3.31	0	49.0	LHB	142	36	4	15	.254
Road	2	0	3.86	0	39.2	RHB	189	47	5	23	.249
First Half	5	0	4.53	0	43.2	Sc Pos	94	19	1	26	.202
Scnd Half	6	2	2.60	0	45.0	Clutch	77	19	1	9	.247

1996 Season

Mark Petkovsek was a part-time starter entering 1996, but ended up as the Cardinals' leading winner out of the pen. He started six games, winning three of those. His statistics were not flashy—except, of course, for his win-loss record. He finished the year with a shaky performance in the postseason.

Pitching, Defense & Hitting

Petkovsek's repertoire isn't overly impressive—medium-speed fastball, sinker, slider, changeup—but he throws them all for strikes and lives for getting ahead in the count. At his best, he gets hitters to swing at balls off their shoetops, inducing numerous double plays. At his worst, he walks people and then gives up one key hit. He's a decent fielder and can help himself with the bat, but he's had some problems holding runners.

1997 Outlook

Petkovsek wants to get back into the rotation, but the best he's likely to get with St. Louis are occasional spot starts. His fine work out of the pen may make the Cardinals reluctant to move him out of his swing role, where he should continue to pitch effectively.

Danny Sheaffer

Position: C/3B
Bats: R **Throws:** R
Ht: 6' 0" **Wt:** 195

Opening Day Age: 35
Born: 8/2/61 in Jacksonville, FL
ML Seasons: 6

Overall Statistics

	G	AB	R	H	D	T	HR	RBI	SB	BB	SO	Avg	OBP	Slg
1996	79	198	10	45	9	3	2	20	3	9	25	.227	.271	.333
Career	313	814	77	186	33	5	13	99	5	52	105	.229	.276	.329

1996 Situational Stats

	AB	H	HR	RBI	Avg		AB	H	HR	RBI	Avg
Home	92	16	1	11	.174	LHP	60	13	1	11	.217
Road	106	29	1	9	.274	RHP	138	32	1	9	.232
First Half	122	33	1	15	.270	Sc Pos	53	10	0	14	.189
Scnd Half	76	12	1	5	.158	Clutch	36	5	0	3	.139

1996 Season

As a backup catcher who's getting up there in years, Danny Sheaffer's opportunities are limited. Fortunately Sheaffer can play other positions and hit just well enough to make himself useful. He made some contributions to the Cardinal cause last year, playing pretty well behind the plate, filling in at other positions and often serving as Todd Stottlemyre's personal receiver.

Hitting, Baserunning & Defense

Sheaffer's hitting approach is aggressive—he doesn't take many pitches and rarely walks. If a pitcher makes a mistake, Sheaffer can make him pay, but that's really the extent of his power. He runs pretty well by catchers' standards, but he's no basestealer. As a receiver, he's not a star but he's fundamentally sound and throws pretty well. He's adequate at third, with a better-than-average arm, and he's also filled in at first base and in left field.

1997 Outlook

Sheaffer is the ideal backup catcher. He's versatile enough to play other positions, but not good enough to create confusion about who the first-stringer is. The Cardinals will be satisfied to get more of the same from him next year.

Mark Sweeney

Position: LF/1B
Bats: L **Throws:** L
Ht: 6' 1" **Wt:** 195

Opening Day Age: 27
Born: 10/26/69 in Framingham, ME
ML Seasons: 2

Overall Statistics

	G	AB	R	H	D	T	HR	RBI	SB	BB	SO	Avg	OBP	Slg
1996	98	170	32	45	9	0	3	22	3	33	29	.265	.387	.371
Career	135	247	37	66	11	0	5	35	4	43	44	.267	.375	.372

1996 Situational Stats

	AB	H	HR	RBI	Avg		AB	H	HR	RBI	Avg
Home	69	18	0	9	.261	LHP	16	6	0	3	.375
Road	101	27	3	13	.267	RHP	154	39	3	19	.253
First Half	120	32	3	17	.267	Sc Pos	36	16	0	19	.444
Scnd Half	50	13	0	5	.260	Clutch	34	10	0	6	.294

1996 Season

In his first full season in the majors, Mark Sweeney performed well offensively while showing off his versatility and competitiveness. He performed decently as one of the Cardinals' top pinch hitters and filled in capably at first base, left field and right field.

Hitting, Baserunning & Defense

Sweeney has a sweet stroke, hits to all fields, and is extremely disciplined. The Cardinals would like him to hit for more power, but he's proven to be valuable as a singles-and-doubles man. He's untested against lefthanders, but has done well in limited trials against them. Sweeney has average speed but knows how to pick his spots to run. His primary position is first base, and he's better than average there, but he's capable of playing either left or right field.

1997 Outlook

First base is currently occupied by John Mabry, a player with similar skills but more talent, so Sweeney seems destined to play a supporting role. Tony La Russa has indicated he'd be comfortable relying on Sweeney in the event of an injury, but unless that happens, his role is as a bench player.

Other St. Louis Cardinals

Brian Barber (Pos: RHP, Age: 24)

	W	L	Pct.	ERA	G	GS	Sv	IP	H	BB	SO	HR	BR/IP
1996	0	0	-	15.00	1	1	0	3.0	4	6	1	0	3.33
Career	2	1	.667	6.12	10	5	0	32.1	35	22	28	4	1.76

Barber was brought into St. Louis in April—and then promptly shipped down to the minors after walking six batters in three innings. His youth and good strikeout rates bode well for his future. 1997 Outlook: C

Richard Batchelor (Pos: RHP, Age: 29)

	W	L	Pct.	ERA	G	GS	Sv	IP	H	BB	SO	HR	BR/IP
1996	2	0	1.000	1.20	11	0	0	15.0	9	1	11	0	0.67
Career	2	0	1.000	3.96	20	0	0	25.0	23	4	15	1	1.08

In his three short stints in the Cardinal bullpen, Batchelor proved to be very effective (1.50 ERA). He's not young, but he boasts excellent control and could get a shot at the set-up role in spring training. 1997 Outlook: B

Terry Bradshaw (Pos: LF, Age: 28, Bats: L)

	G	AB	R	H	D	T	HR	RBI	SB	BB	SO	Avg	OBP	Slg
1996	15	21	4	7	1	0	0	3	0	3	2	.333	.417	.381
Career	34	65	10	17	2	1	0	5	2	5	12	.262	.314	.323

Bradshaw had an excellent season at Triple-A Louisville and saw limited September action in the majors last year. He played well, but the Cardinals' abundance of quality outfielders won't help him. 1997 Outlook: C

Mike Busby (Pos: RHP, Age: 24)

	W	L	Pct.	ERA	G	GS	Sv	IP	H	BB	SO	HR	BR/IP
1996	0	1	.000	18.00	1	1	0	4.0	9	4	4	4	3.25
Career	0	1	.000	18.00	1	1	0	4.0	9	4	4	4	3.25

Busby faced 28 batters in his only start in the majors last year, surrendering nine hits and four walks. That seemed to set the tone for his entire year, as he was horrendous at Triple-A Louisville. 1997 Outlook: C

Mike Difelice (Pos: C, Age: 27, Bats: R)

	G	AB	R	H	D	T	HR	RBI	SB	BB	SO	Avg	OBP	Slg
1996	4	7	0	2	1	0	0	2	0	0	1	.286	.286	.429
Career	4	7	0	2	1	0	0	2	0	0	1	.286	.286	.429

Difelice had a decent season at Triple-A Louisville (.285-9-33 in 79 games) and saw limited major league action behind the plate in September. With St. Louis solid at catcher, his potential is limited. 1997 Outlook: C

Brian Maxcy (Pos: RHP, Age: 25)

	W	L	Pct.	ERA	G	GS	Sv	IP	H	BB	SO	HR	BR/IP
1996	0	0	-	13.50	2	0	0	3.1	8	2	1	2	3.00
Career	4	5	.444	7.28	43	0	0	55.2	69	33	21	8	1.83

After struggling with Detroit (13.50 ERA in two appearances), Maxcy was traded to St. Louis in June and spent the remainder of the year in the minors. Major control problems. 1997 Outlook: C

Ozzie Smith (Pos: SS, Age: 42, Bats: B)

	G	AB	R	H	D	T	HR	RBI	SB	BB	SO	Avg	OBP	Slg
1996	82	227	36	64	10	2	2	18	7	25	9	.282	.358	.370
Career	2573	9396	1257	2460	402	69	28	793	580	1072	589	.262	.337	.328

"The Wizard" surprised everybody last season when he rebounded from injury problems at age 42 to post excellent numbers in a part-time role. He was planning to retire, but. . . 1997 Outlook: A (if he returns)

Ben VanRyn (Pos: LHP, Age: 25)

	W	L	Pct.	ERA	G	GS	Sv	IP	H	BB	SO	HR	BR/IP
1996	0	0	-	0.00	1	0	0	1.0	1	1	0	0	2.00
Career	0	0	-	0.00	1	0	0	1.0	1	1	0	0	2.00

Acquired from California in June, VanRyn spent the second half of the '96 season in the Triple-A Louisville bullpen. He struggled in middle relief (4.88 ERA) and probably won't reach the majors this year. 1997 Outlook: C

St. Louis Cardinals Minor League Prospects

Organization Overview:

The Cardinals' farm system keeps chugging along, producing a solid player or two every year or so. Last season, Alan Benes and T.J. Mathews were important newcomers, but the team's new ownership has relied heavily on the free agent market as of late. The team gives fair auditions to deserving rookies, but the youngsters are expected to do little more than flesh out the core of veteran talent. It is truly a team that has "built from without" over the last two years. That approach doesn't figure to change, based on the talent on hand in the minors. They have some top-flight position players ready to come up, and a few pitchers may become ready in the next year or so, but the talent is hardly overwhelming. The Cardinals will have little reason to change their systematic, one-at-a-time integration of young players into the lineup. Right now, Dmitri Young and Eli Marrero seem to be next in line. Recent drafts have stocked the lower levels of the system with hitters, but the effects won't be felt for a while.

Kris Detmers

Position: P **Opening Day Age:** 22
Bats: B **Throws:** L **Born:** 6/22/74 in
Ht: 6' 5" **Wt:** 215 Decatur, IL

Recent Statistics

	W	L	ERA	G	GS	Sv	IP	H	R	BB	SO	HR
94 A Madison	5	7	3.39	16	16	0	90.1	88	45	31	74	4
95 A St. Pete	10	9	3.25	25	25	0	146.2	120	64	57	150	12
96 AA Arkansas	12	8	3.35	27	27	0	163.2	154	72	70	97	15

At Double-A, lefty Kris Detmers continued to show how far you can go with an average fastball and an excellent curveball. He simply spots his pitches and moves the ball around, but he gets the job done. His strikeouts dropped dramatically last year, indicating that its may get tougher for him the higher he climbs. He probably needs at least another year or two before he'll be ready to make an impact at the major league level.

Micah Franklin

Position: OF **Opening Day Age:** 24
Bats: B **Throws:** R **Born:** 4/25/72 in San
Ht: 6' 0" **Wt:** 195 Francisco, CA

Recent Statistics

	G	AB	R	H	D	T	HR	RBI	SB	BB	SO	AVG
93 A Winston-Sal	20	69	10	16	1	1	3	6	0	10	19	.232
93 A Charlstn-WV	102	343	56	90	14	4	17	68	6	47	109	.262
94 A Winston-Sal	42	150	44	45	7	0	21	44	7	27	48	.300
94 AA Chattanooga	79	279	46	77	17	0	10	40	2	33	79	.276
95 AA Calgary	110	358	64	105	28	0	21	71	3	47	95	.293
96 AAA Toledo	53	179	32	44	10	1	7	21	3	27	60	.246
96 AAA Louisville	86	289	43	67	18	3	15	53	2	40	71	.232
96 MLE	139	454	58	97	26	1	16	58	3	51	136	.214

Micah Franklin is a young switch-hitter with power, but the Cardinals are the fourth organization he's played for in the last three years. What's the story? Catch-all euphemisms like "attitude" and "behavior" are all that's offered, so perhaps we'll never know the real story. From an objective standpoint, the most annoying thing he does is swing at too many bad pitches. His defense in right field is nothing special, but you might live with it to get his bat in the lineup. Maybe someone will give him a try someday.

Eric Ludwick

Position: P **Opening Day Age:** 25
Bats: R **Throws:** R **Born:** 12/14/71 in
Ht: 6' 5" **Wt:** 210 Whiteman AFB, MO

Recent Statistics

	W	L	ERA	G	GS	Sv	IP	H	R	BB	SO	HR
96 AAA Louisville	3	4	2.83	11	11	0	60.1	55	24	24	73	4
96 NL St. Louis	0	1	9.00	6	1	0	10.0	11	11	3	12	1

Eric Ludwick came over from the Mets' organization in the Bernard Gilkey trade. True to his heritage as a Met pitching prospect, Ludwick soon came down with an arm injury—a strained ligament in his elbow that knocked out for the first half of the season. When he returned, he quickly regained his low-90s fastball and sharp slider, and refined his command of his curveball. He pitched very well in 11 starts at Triple-A, and found even greater success over the winter as a closer in the Arizona Fall League. The Cardinals may use him as a set-up man next year, and he may be one of their biggest surprises.

Elieser Marrero

Position: C **Opening Day Age:** 23
Bats: R **Throws:** R **Born:** 11/17/73 in Cuba
Ht: 6' 1" **Wt:** 180

Recent Statistics

	G	AB	R	H	D	T	HR	RBI	SB	BB	SO	AVG
93 R Johnson Cty	18	61	10	22	8	0	2	14	1	12	9	.361
94 A Savannah	116	421	71	110	16	3	21	79	5	39	92	.261
95 A St. Pete	107	383	43	81	16	1	10	55	9	23	55	.211
96 AA Arkansas	116	374	65	101	17	3	19	65	9	32	55	.270
96 MLE	116	362	52	89	15	2	15	52	6	21	58	.246

After a disappointing '95 season, Eli Marrero rebounded with a terrific year in '96. He boosted his power and batting average, and emerged as a two-way prospect at catcher. His defensive prowess was unequaled in the Texas League: he nailed 42.9 percent of opposing basestealers, and made only three errors all year. His glove is already major-league caliber, and he already hits with enough power to hold a job. At age 23, he's only going to get better. The Cardinals may try to give him another year, but he may force their hand before long.

Miguel Mejia

Position: OF   **Opening Day Age:** 22
Bats: R **Throws:** R   **Born:** 3/25/75 in San
Ht: 6' 1" **Wt:** 155   Pedro De Macoris, DR

Recent Statistics

	G	AB	R	H	D	T	HR	RBI	SB	BB	SO	AVG
96 A St. Pete	8	26	2	3	0	0	0	0	2	1	12	.115
96 NL St. Louis	45	23	10	2	0	0	0	0	6	0	10	.087

After selecting him from the Baltimore organization in last year's Rule V draft, the Cardinals were forced to keep Miguel Mejia on the roster for the entire season. With no previous experience above A-ball, Mejia's only use was as a defensive replacement and occasional pinch runner. Now, he'll get to go back to the minors and work on his hitting. He's already a good center fielder and excellent basestealer. He won't hit for power, but the Cardinals hope to teach him to get on base. Switch-hitting may be in his future, and he's probably at least two years away from returning.

Matt Morris

Position: P   **Opening Day Age:** 22
Bats: R **Throws:** R   **Born:** 8/9/74 in
Ht: 6' 5" **Wt:** 210   Middletown, NY

Recent Statistics

	W	L	ERA	G	GS	Sv	IP	H	R	BB	SO	HR
95 A New Jersey	2	0	1.64	2	2	0	11.0	12	3	3	13	1
95 A St. Pete	5	2	2.20	8	8	0	45.0	34	19	14	44	2
96 AA Arkansas	12	12	3.88	27	27	0	167.0	178	79	48	120	14
96 AAA Louisville	0	1	3.38	1	1	0	8.0	8	3	1	9	0

Matt Morris was considered perhaps the finest pitching prospect in the '95 draft, and the Cardinals took him with the 12th-overall pick. His low-90s fastball and power curve were considered major league-ready, but his polish was questioned. He dispelled such concerns last year, displaying good enough command at Double-A to be named the Texas League's best pitching prospect. Even though he's only 22 this year, he may be able to jump directly to the majors and hold his own.

Brady Raggio

Position: P   **Opening Day Age:** 24
Bats: R **Throws:** R   **Born:** 9/17/72 in Los
Ht: 6' 4" **Wt:** 210   Angeles, CA

Recent Statistics

	W	L	ERA	G	GS	Sv	IP	H	R	BB	SO	HR
94 A New Jersey	3	0	1.67	4	4	0	27.0	28	7	4	20	0
94 A Madison	4	3	3.21	11	11	0	67.1	63	31	14	66	8
95 A Peoria	3	0	1.85	8	8	0	48.2	42	13	2	34	1
95 A St. Pete	2	3	3.80	20	30	0	47.1	43	24	13	35	2
96 AA Arkansas	9	10	3.22	26	24	0	162.1	160	68	40	123	17

Brady Raggio is a survivor. In 1992, he accidentally plunged off a 75-foot cliff and landed on a rock. The impact didn't kill him, but it left him with severe injuries

and a variety of hardware in his knee, elbow and upper leg. The doctors said he'd never play again. He took a year off, and then slowly came back. Last year was another big step for him, as he further refined his excellent control, and got by at Double-A with a very mediocre fastball. It's hard to have faith in his stuff, but you never can count this guy out.

Dmitri Young

Position: 1B   **Opening Day Age:** 23
Bats: B **Throws:** R   **Born:** 10/11/73 in
Ht: 6' 2" **Wt:** 215   Vicksburg, MS

Recent Statistics

	G	AB	R	H	D	T	HR	RBI	SB	BB	SO	AVG
96 AAA Louisville	122	459	90	153	31	8	15	64	16	34	67	.333
96 NL St. Louis	16	29	3	7	0	0	0	2	0	4	5	.241
96 MLE	122	441	73	135	29	5	11	51	11	27	70	.306

It's been a long, slow learning process for Dmitri Young, but last year signaled a huge step forward in his maturation. He took his conditioning more seriously, and finally found a home at first base. He had an excellent year at the plate, and showed signs of developing the power that everyone's always seen in him. He's ready for the majors, and the Cardinals are looking for a way to make room for the young switch-hitter. He's a strong Rookie of the Year candidate, and may develop into one of the game's top hitters down the line.

Others to Watch

The Cardinals' Minor League Pitcher of the Year was righthander **Britt Reames**, who went 15-7 with a 1.90 ERA at Class A. With a tremendous breaking pitch and excellent control, he had almost twice as many strikeouts (167) as hits allowed (98), and was named the Midwest League's best pitching prospect. At age 23, though, it's time for him to move up to a more challenging level. . . **Manny Aybar** is a young right-handed starter with sharp control. He posted good results at Double-A and Triple-A last year, and may not need much more seasoning. The Cardinals believe he'll add more zip to his above-average fastball as he fills out. . . Second baseman **Jeff Berblinger** is an above-average hitter for a middle infielder, and he'll have a chance to compete for the Dodgers' second-base position this year. He was selected by the Tigers in the Rule 5 draft and immediately traded to Los Angeles. . . There's still time left for second baseman **Aaron Holbert**, but recurring injuries have stalled his development. He doesn't look nearly as promising as he did two years ago. . . With a sharp slider and good command, righthander **Blake Stein** led the Florida State League in both wins and ERA last year. He doesn't throw all that hard, so we'll see if he can get by at Double-A this year.

Bruce Bochy

1996 Season

Bruce Bochy managed the Padres to the second National League West Division championship in franchise history last year, and finished in a tie in Manager of the Year voting with the Cardinals' Tony La Russa. Bochy achieved this success primarily by defining his team's roles and sticking with his philosophies throughout the season. Bochy was second-guessed on some of his strategic calls during the playoffs, but the general consensus was that he had done a great job.

Offense

The Padres weren't blessed with much team speed, so Bochy didn't have his team do a whole lot of running. However, they did use hit-and-run tactics regularly. Bochy probably relied on his best hitters too much down the stretch, but they delivered more often than not. He can be unconventional at times, basing his choices on hunches and instinct.

Pitching & Defense

Bochy likes young, hard-throwing hurlers, and so he featured them in prominent roles last season. Yet, he also respects veteran savvy, which is why soft-tossers Fernando Valenzuela and Bob Tewksbury played such vital roles on the Padre staff. Bochy placed his starters on strict pitch counts, putting major responsibility on his young bullpen. He also put a high priority on defense, opting to bench Greg Vaughn in certain spots, for example, despite the high price the team paid for his late-season acquisition. Bochy pitches out frequently and he's not afraid to walk or pitch around dangerous hitters.

1997 Outlook

The only real criticism of Bochy was that he seemed to become more conservative in the playoffs, managing not to lose rather than to win. This point will be brought up next season if the Padres contend again in the West. Still, Bochy has emerged as one of the game's top young managers.

Born: 4/16/55 in Landes de Bussac, France

Playing Experience: 1978-1987, Hou, NYN, SD

Managerial Experience: 2 seasons

Manager Statistics

Year	Team, Lg	W	L	Pct	GB	Finish
1996	San Diego, NL	91	71	.562	—	1st West
2 Seasons		161	145	.526	—	—

1996 Starting Pitchers by Days Rest

	≤3	4	5	6+
Padres Starts	7	81	51	16
Padres ERA	2.90	3.76	4.51	4.40
NL Avg Starts	4	86	41	21
NL ERA	4.06	4.28	4.23	4.58

1996 Situational Stats

	Bruce Bochy	NL Average
Hit & Run Success %	37.2	39.0
Stolen Base Success %	66.5	71.6
Platoon Pct.	54.3	51.9
Defensive Subs	15	20
High-Pitch Outings	10	13
Quick/Slow Hooks	23/8	19/12
Sacrifice Attempts	73	92

1996 Rankings (National League)

→ 1st in 2+ pitching changes in low scoring games (32)

→ 2nd in least caught steals of home plate (1) and pitchouts with a runner moving (18)

→ 3rd in pitchouts (65), starts on three days rest (7) and saves with over 1 inning pitched (12)

Andy Ashby

1996 Season

After a 12-win 1995 campaign that established him as one of the National League's better right-handed starters, Andy Ashby suffered through an injury-plagued 1996 season. Ashby made three visits to the disabled list because of shoulder problems, and he won only one game after the All-Star break. But when he was able to take the mound, he continued to be one of San Diego's most consistent starters.

Pitching

Ashby's best pitch is a cut fastball which is very effective against right-handed hitters. He also throws another fastball with a little more sink, along with a slider, curve and change-up. He has excellent control and consistently keeps his pitches down in the strike zone, resulting in lots of groundball outs. He likes to go right after the hitter and is reluctant to pitch around anyone, although his elbow problems have made him a little bit more cautious.

Defense & Hitting

Ashby has begun using a slide-step delivery with men on base, and as a result he has greatly improved his ability to hold baserunners. Always a fine bunter, he greatly improved his hitting last year; he batted .244 for the year, and five of his 11 hits went for extra bases. He's a solid fielder.

1997 Outlook

Ashby was back in the Padre rotation last September, but he wasn't at full strength, and he won only one of his six starts. Many experts believe that he could contend for a Cy Young Award if he can regain full health, but for now he remains a bit of a question mark. He'll enter spring training as the team's number-two starter behind Joey Hamilton, with a chance to move up if he shows his arm is sound.

Position: SP
Bats: R **Throws:** R
Ht: 6' 5" **Wt:** 190

Opening Day Age: 29
Born: 7/11/67 in Kansas City, MO
ML Seasons: 6

Overall Statistics

	W	L	Pct.	ERA	G	GS	Sv	IP	H	BB	SO	HR	BR/IP
1996	9	5	.643	3.23	24	24	0	150.2	147	34	85	17	1.20
Career	32	44	.421	4.20	129	116	1	709.2	723	235	483	80	1.35

How Often He Throws Strikes

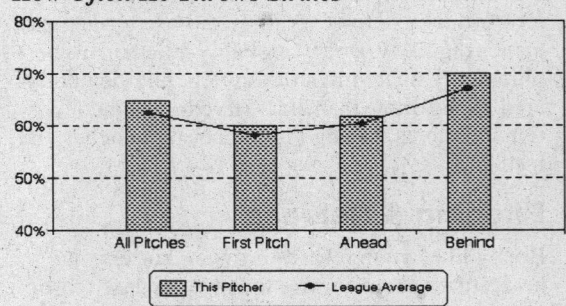

1996 Situational Stats

	W	L	ERA	Sv	IP		AB	H	HR	RBI	Avg
Home	3	3	3.36	0	64.1	LHB	252	70	6	20	.278
Road	6	2	3.13	0	86.1	RHB	315	77	11	33	.244
First Half	8	2	2.93	0	101.1	Sc Pos	107	27	1	30	.252
Scnd Half	1	3	3.83	0	49.1	Clutch	26	8	1	4	.308

1996 Rankings (National League)

- ➡ 5th in ERA on the road (3.13)
- ➡ 10th in most GDPs induced per GDP situation (18.0%)
- ➡ Led the Padres in runners caught stealing (10), most GDPs induced per GDP situation (18.0%) and ERA on the road (3.13)

Ken Caminiti

Position: 3B
Bats: B **Throws:** R
Ht: 6' 0" **Wt:** 200

Opening Day Age: 33
Born: 4/21/63 in
Hanford, CA
ML Seasons: 10
Pronunciation:
kam-un-NET-ee

1996 Season

A unanimous choice as the N.L.'s Most Valuable Player, Ken Caminiti not only had a huge offensive year, but he also set a single-season record by knocking home runs from both sides of the plate in the same game *six* times. Caminiti excelled in virtually every conceivable situation and seemed to get stronger as the season progressed, batting .360 with 28 home runs after the All-Star break.

Hitting

When Caminiti joined the Padres, San Diego believed it was getting a steady switch-hitter who had occasional power. What it got was arguably the N.L.'s most complete offensive player, a powerhouse from both sides of the plate. Caminiti likes to pull the ball, but doesn't insist on it. And he's not just a basher, shortening his stroke when he's behind in the count.

Baserunning & Defense

Caminiti is not exceptionally fast, but he'll steal a base when given the opportunity, and he circles the bases quickly when he gets a head of steam. Defensively, Caminiti has developed into the best third baseman in the game. With a cannon arm and soft, quick hands, Caminiti is extremely adept at scooping up slow rollers and gunning to first. He will commit errors, but he has exceptional range and covers both the hole and the line with equal dexterity.

1997 Outlook

It will be interesting to see if Caminiti can follow up his MVP campaign with another outstanding performance. Many doubt that he can, labeling last season's offensive show a "career year" for him. Others, though, believe it was the coming-out party of a somewhat tardy superstar. He'll be trying to duplicate his success this year. . . as well as hoping to lead the Padres back into the playoffs.

Overall Statistics

	G	AB	R	H	D	T	HR	RBI	SB	BB	SO	Avg	OBP	Slg
1996	146	546	109	178	37	2	40	130	11	78	99	.326	.408	.621
Career	1237	4513	592	1233	250	15	141	669	62	445	757	.273	.338	.429

Where He Hits the Ball

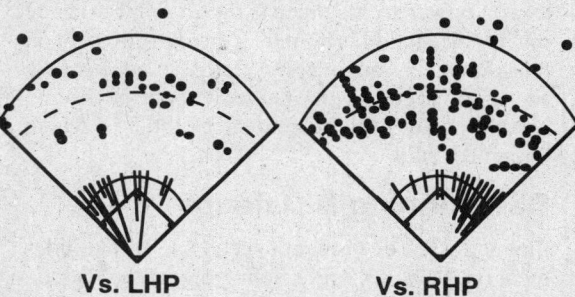

Vs. LHP   **Vs. RHP**

1996 Situational Stats

	AB	H	HR	RBI	Avg		AB	H	HR	RBI	Avg
Home	260	88	20	65	.338	LHP	165	59	15	46	.358
Road	286	90	20	65	.315	RHP	381	119	25	84	.312
First Half	279	82	12	49	.294	Sc Pos	155	60	15	100	.387
Scnd Half	267	96	28	81	.360	Clutch	95	24	9	25	.253

1996 Rankings (National League)

→ 1st in sacrifice flies (10)
→ 2nd in slugging percentage vs. left-handed pitchers (.721)
→ 3rd in RBI, slugging percentage and errors at third base (20)
→ 4th in batting average with runners in scoring position (.387), batting average vs. left-handed pitchers (.358), cleanup slugging percentage (.627) and lowest fielding percentage at third base (.954)
→ 5th in home runs, total bases (339), intentional walks (16) and batting average on the road (.315)
→ 6th in HR frequency (13.6 ABs per HR) and batting average

Steve Finley

Gold Glover

1996 Season

Somewhat lost in Ken Caminiti's MVP campaign was Steve Finley's best season in the majors. Never a power hitter during his years with Baltimore and Houston, Finley set career highs in home runs, RBI, and extra-base hits last year. In center field, Finley was again a pillar of stability, solidifying a defense that was suspect in both left and right field for much of the stretch drive.

Hitting

Finley attributes his success last season to two factors: becoming more aggressive at the plate, and not having to play 81 games per year in the Astrodome. Previously a slap-hitter, Finley strived to add power to his arsenal by turning on inside pitches. Many of his homers were golf shots hit on mistake pitches out over the plate. Finley was very successful at adding that power without sacrificing his average or on-base percentage, both of which remained solid.

Baserunning & Defense

Finley possesses excellent speed and sound judgment on the bases, representing one of the Padres' two primary basestealing threats along with Rickey Henderson. He stretches numerous singles into doubles, and legs typical two-baggers into triples. Finley is a take-charge center fielder whose coverage is first-rate, and who especially excels at snaring long fly balls. His arm is above average.

1997 Outlook

At 32, Finley is at an age where players don't normally show major improvement. Last season's performance could be viewed as an aberration, but there's no indication he won't continue to be productive. It's not likely that he'll hit 30 homers again, since he doesn't really sport a longball swing, but he's a good bet to churn out a .300-20-80 season without breaking a sweat. With his fielding and baserunning skills, that would more than satisfy the Padres.

Position: CF
Bats: L **Throws:** L
Ht: 6' 2" **Wt:** 180

Opening Day Age: 32
Born: 3/12/65 in Union City, TN
ML Seasons: 8

Overall Statistics

	G	AB	R	H	D	T	HR	RBI	SB	BB	SO	Avg	OBP	Slg
1996	161	655	126	195	45	9	30	95	22	56	88	.298	.354	.531
Career	1080	4019	612	1130	177	64	77	387	207	318	478	.281	.335	.415

Where He Hits the Ball

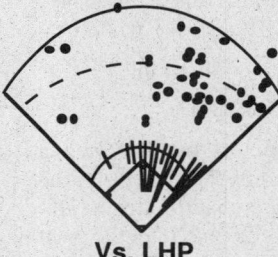

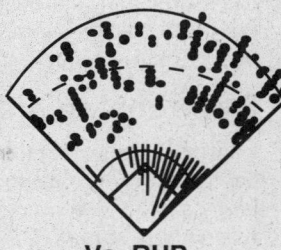

Vs. LHP　　　　**Vs. RHP**

1996 Situational Stats

	AB	H	HR	RBI	Avg		AB	H	HR	RBI	Avg
Home	312	104	15	46	.333	LHP	180	48	4	19	.267
Road	343	91	15	49	.265	RHP	475	147	26	76	.309
First Half	366	106	17	54	.290	Sc Pos	151	41	8	63	.272
Scnd Half	289	89	13	41	.308	Clutch	112	35	8	23	.313

1996 Rankings (National League)

- ➡ 2nd in runs scored and doubles
- ➡ 3rd in total bases (348), games played (161), errors in center field (7) and lowest fielding percentage in center field (.982)
- ➡ 4th in at-bats, triples and plate appearances (721)
- ➡ 5th in GDPs (20)
- ➡ 6th in hits
- ➡ 8th in pitches seen (2,654)
- ➡ Led the Padres in at-bats, runs scored, hits, doubles, triples, total bases (348), GDPs (20), plate appearances (721), games played (161), stolen base percentage (73.3%) and highest percentage of extra bases taken as a runner (61.8%)

John Flaherty

1996 Season

Not long after arriving in San Diego from the Detroit Tigers in a midseason trade, John Flaherty amassed a 27-game hitting streak. . . impressive for any player, but particularly a catcher who had been considered a light hitter. Flaherty's bat continued to be a pleasant surprise, especially since he had been acquired for his defense. He was a stabilizing force for the Padres down the stretch before suffering an assortment of injuries that sidelined him for the final week of the regular season as well as the playoffs.

Hitting

Flaherty joined the relatively small group of players who have enjoyed immediate success upon switching leagues. Adjusting his batting philosophy to deal with N.L. pitching, Flaherty now rarely swings at bad pitches and isn't afraid to go deep in the count, though he still rarely takes a base on balls. Enemy hurlers tend to nibble at the outside corner against him, firing the occasional high and inside fastball to bust his hands. Flaherty has shied away from trying to pull everything and now shows an increased propensity for hitting to the opposite field.

Baserunning & Defense

Flaherty is slow afoot, but he runs decently for a catcher. While he doesn't steal bases, he's not a baserunning liability either. Defensively, Flaherty helps his pitchers by framing their pitches effectively and by calling an efficient game. His throwing arm is strong, but he tends to hurry his tosses, leading to a majority of his errors.

1997 Outlook

While Flaherty was injured Brian Johnson took over as the Padres' catcher for the final two weeks of the season and the playoffs. Johnson and Flaherty may share the role this year, but don't count on it. If Flaherty can continue to produce offensively, he should supplant Johnson and snare 80 percent of the playing time. Flaherty signed a new two-year contract with the Padres in the offseason.

Position: C
Bats: R **Throws:** R
Ht: 6' 1" **Wt:** 200

Opening Day Age: 29
Born: 10/21/67 in New York, NY
ML Seasons: 5

Overall Statistics

	G	AB	R	H	D	T	HR	RBI	SB	BB	SO	Avg	OBP	Slg
1996	119	416	40	118	24	0	13	64	3	17	61	.284	.314	.435
Career	313	901	87	226	51	1	24	112	3	41	132	.251	.286	.390

Where He Hits the Ball

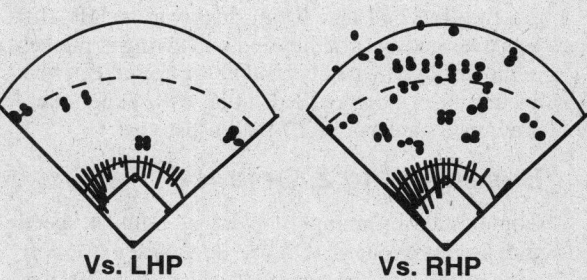

Vs. LHP   **Vs. RHP**

1996 Situational Stats

	AB	H	HR	RBI	Avg		AB	H	HR	RBI	Avg
Home	189	56	8	37	.296	LHP	93	29	1	17	.312
Road	227	62	5	27	.273	RHP	323	89	12	47	.276
First Half	215	58	8	35	.270	Sc Pos	111	32	3	53	.288
Scnd Half	201	60	5	29	.299	Clutch	57	15	2	7	.263

1996 Rankings (National League)

- → 5th in lowest percentage of runners caught stealing as a catcher (23.6%)
- → Led the Padres in batting average on an 0-2 count (.240)

Chris Gomez

1996 Season

When Chris Gomez came to the Padres in a mid-season trade with the Tigers, San Diego's expectations were modest: they were hoping he would provide steady defense while making a few contributions at the plate. They got pretty much what they expected, and Gomez' solid play was a key to the Padres' drive to the N.L. West title.

Hitting

Gomez will never be mistaken for Alex Rodriguez, but he's a good situational hitter who makes contact and can advance runners when needed. With above-average power for a shortstop, he's capable of reaching double figures in homers, but last year he concentrated mostly on meeting the ball and lifting his average. He still gets overanxious at times and will swing at pitches in the dirt even when behind in the count. But he's becoming a more patient hitter with experience, drawing a career-high 57 walks last year.

Baserunning & Defense

Gomez's baserunning is average, both in speed and aggressiveness. Oddly, he takes extremely wide turns around first and third, a habit that should long ago have been extinguished by an alert coach. He's not much of a threat to steal. While Gomez has improved his fielding considerably over the last few years, his throwing arm is still erratic. Because of his lack of arm strength, some people think Gomez would be better off at second base.

1997 Outlook

Gomez is the Padres' shortstop of the present and possibly the future. San Diego's front office was pleased with the results of the trade that brought him and John Flaherty to the club, and re-signed Gomez in early November. At 25, he is still just a young player, so utilizing the word "potential" when discussing him is still legitimate.

Position: SS
Bats: R **Throws:** R
Ht: 6' 1" **Wt:** 188

Opening Day Age: 25
Born: 6/16/71 in Los Angeles, CA
ML Seasons: 4

Overall Statistics

	G	AB	R	H	D	T	HR	RBI	SB	BB	SO	Avg	OBP	Slg
1996	137	456	53	117	21	1	4	45	3	57	84	.257	.347	.333
Career	390	1311	145	321	67	4	23	159	14	140	261	.245	.323	.355

Where He Hits the Ball

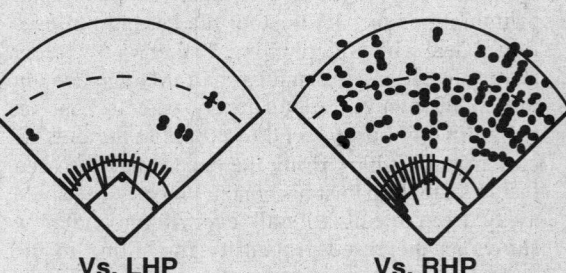

Vs. LHP   **Vs. RHP**

1996 Situational Stats

	AB	H	HR	RBI	Avg		AB	H	HR	RBI	Avg
Home	198	45	2	23	.227	LHP	82	19	0	3	.232
Road	258	72	2	22	.279	RHP	374	98	4	42	.262
First Half	187	49	2	23	.262	Sc Pos	99	30	0	37	.303
Scnd Half	269	68	2	22	.253	Clutch	74	15	1	4	.203

1996 Rankings (National League)

➝ Led the Padres in batting average on a 3-1 count (.467)

Tony Gwynn

1996 Season

Despite enduring one of the more injury-plagued seasons of his remarkable career, Tony Gwynn seized his seventh NL batting title last year. Gwynn fell a few plate appearances shy of the 502 needed to qualify, but his lead over Ellis Burks was big enough to give him the crown. Except for his injuries, last season was a typical Gwynn performance: he fanned only 17 times and continually cranked out hits to the opposite field.

Hitting

Gwynn is without question the best pure hitter in the game today—perhaps the best of the last 20 years. With phenomenal hand-eye coordination, Gwynn is capable of adjusting to any pitch and any delivery in an instant. He's never hit for much power, but his swing is one of the most efficient in baseball, producing no wasted motion with the exception of a little waggle of the bat as he awaits a pitch. Gwynn hits both righties and lefties successfully because he never bails out of the batter's box.

Baserunning & Defense

Plagued by a series of foot ailments, Gwynn has lost some speed and doesn't steal as often as he once did. But he's a smart baserunner and remains a high-percentage basestealer when he chooses to take off. In the outfield, he's no longer a Gold Glover, since he doesn't have the range he once had nor is he likely to make any spectacular catches. His arm is average at best for a right fielder, but it's as accurate as anyone's.

1997 Outlook

Injuries plague Gwynn from time to time, but nothing ever seems to affect his batting stroke. In 1997 he'll be looking for his fourth straight batting crown and hoping to match Honus Wagner's record of eight N.L. batting championships. Don't bet against him.

Position: RF
Bats: L **Throws:** L
Ht: 5'11" **Wt:** 220

Opening Day Age: 36
Born: 5/9/60 in Los Angeles, CA
ML Seasons: 15

Overall Statistics

	G	AB	R	H	D	T	HR	RBI	SB	BB	SO	Avg	OBP	Slg
1996	116	451	67	159	27	2	3	50	11	39	17	.353	.400	.441
Career	1946	7595	1140	2560	411	82	90	854	296	664	361	.337	.389	.448

Where He Hits the Ball

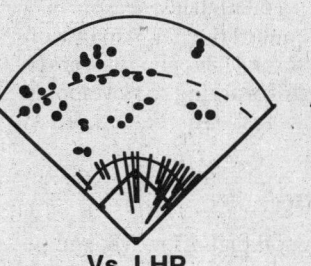
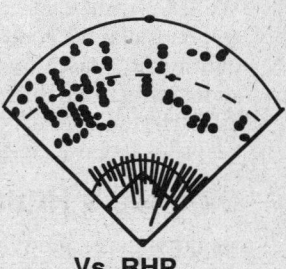

Vs. LHP   **Vs. RHP**

1996 Situational Stats

	AB	H	HR	RBI	Avg		AB	H	HR	RBI	Avg
Home	245	86	2	22	.351	LHP	136	48	1	20	.353
Road	206	73	1	28	.354	RHP	315	111	2	30	.352
First Half	269	91	3	34	.338	Sc Pos	84	32	1	44	.381
Scnd Half	182	68	0	16	.374	Clutch	85	40	1	10	.471

1996 Rankings (National League)

→ 1st in batting average in the clutch (.471), lowest percentage of swings that missed (6.7%), highest percentage of swings put into play (60.4%) and batting average

→ 3rd in batting average with two strikes (.296), fielding percentage in right field (.989) and lowest percentage of extra bases taken as a runner (27.7%)

→ 4th in batting average on a 3-2 count (.417)

→ 5th in batting average vs. left-handed pitchers (.353) and batting average at home (.351)

→ 6th in batting average with runners in scoring position (.381)

→ 8th in intentional walks (12)

→ 9th in most GDPs per GDP situation (17.3%)

Joey Hamilton

1996 Season

Joey Hamilton continues to confirm his ranking as one of the game's top young pitchers. Hamilton finished last season as the Padres' team leader in wins, innings, strikeouts, and complete games. His ERA crept up more than a run over his 1995 mark of 3.08, but that was due primarily to a poor six-week stretch in June and July. By season's end Hamilton had emerged the ace of the staff, usually going seven strong innings and almost always keeping his team in the ballgame.

Pitching

Hamilton throws hard and can record strikeouts, but the key to his effectiveness is a nasty sinking fastball which induces numerous groundball outs. While his walk total was a bit high last season, he's still considered a good control pitcher. Along with the sinker, Hamilton throws an above-average slider and curve. He's still working to develop an effective change-up. A fast worker, Hamilton keeps his defense alert.

Defense & Hitting

Hamilton has a pretty good pickoff move, and he does a decent job of holding runners, especially for a righthander. He is not a good glove man, however; among other things, he's downright clumsy when it comes to fielding bunt attempts. When Hamilton broke into the big leagues, he was a horrible hitter, going 0 for his first 57 at-bats. Although he's improved at the plate, he still strikes out nearly half the time—but he did lead the Padres with 11 sacrifice hits.

1997 Outlook

In light of his excellent performance last year, Hamilton will enter this season as the Padres' top starting pitcher and probable Opening Day starter. He has 20-win potential and only needs to improve his consistency to join the ranks of the N.L.'s elite.

Position: SP
Bats: R **Throws:** R
Ht: 6' 4" **Wt:** 230

Opening Day Age: 26
Born: 9/9/70 in Statesboro, GA
ML Seasons: 3

Overall Statistics

	W	L	Pct.	ERA	G	GS	Sv	IP	H	BB	SO	HR	BR/IP
1996	15	9	.625	4.17	34	33	0	211.2	206	83	184	19	1.37
Career	30	24	.556	3.50	81	79	0	524.2	493	168	368	43	1.26

How Often He Throws Strikes

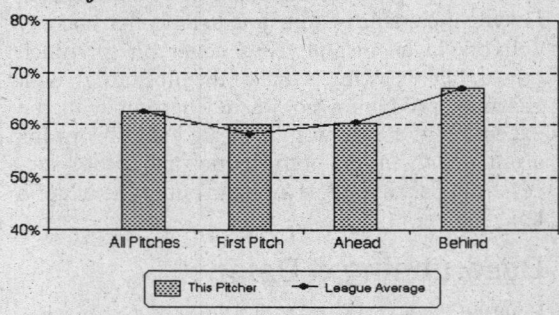

1996 Situational Stats

	W	L	ERA	Sv	IP		AB	H	HR	RBI	Avg
Home	12	2	3.03	0	113.0	LHB	383	109	9	45	.285
Road	3	7	5.47	0	98.2	RHB	422	97	10	45	.230
First Half	10	4	4.72	0	116.1	Sc Pos	199	55	3	66	.276
Scnd Half	5	5	3.49	0	95.1	Clutch	79	17	1	6	.215

1996 Rankings (National League)

→ 2nd in wild pitches (14)
→ 3rd in GDPs induced (24) and highest ground-ball/flyball ratio allowed (2.4)
→ 4th in highest ERA on the road (5.47)
→ 5th in most GDPs induced per 9 innings (1.0)
→ 8th in winning percentage and most strikeouts per 9 innings (7.8)
→ 9th in wins, shutouts (1) and strikeouts
→ 10th in sacrifice bunts (11)
→ Led the Padres in sacrifice bunts (11), wins, games started, complete games (3), shutouts (1), innings pitched, batters faced (908), home runs allowed, walks allowed, hit batsmen (9), strikeouts, wild pitches (14), pitches thrown (3,457) and GDPs induced (24)

Rickey Henderson

1996 Season

Rickey Henderson signed with the Padres as a free agent prior to last season and provided a veteran spark from the leadoff spot. Despite struggling to bat even .230 for much of the year, Henderson maintained an on-base percentage over .400 and came on strong down the stretch while sharing left field with newly-acquired slugger Greg Vaughn. In addition, the often moody Henderson fit in well with the Padre clubhouse.

Hitting

Although Henderson is now in the twilight of his fabulous career, he still creates many problems for opposing hurlers. He offers a very small strike zone, is very selective at the plate, and can instantly hurt you with his home run power. At his best, Henderson is a master at getting on base. Even when he doesn't reach, he wears out pitchers by working deep counts. Henderson's bat has slowed somewhat in recent years, and he strikes out against fastballs more than he ever has in his career.

Baserunning & Defense

He's no longer a threat to swipe 100, but Henderson is still one of the league's top basestealers. When you combine his quickness with his low-to-the ground running style and aggressive head-first sliding, Henderson becomes a constant migraine for opposing pitchers and catchers alike. In the outfield, Henderson has good range and is a decent glove, but does not possess a first-rate arm.

1997 Outlook

Henderson has indicated that he wishes to remain in San Diego, but that will probably be determined by the status of Vaughn, his "platoon" partner. The Padres would prefer to have Henderson at the top of the batting order instead of Tony Gwynn, who is better suited to hit second or third. However, they would also like to have Vaughn's power protecting Ken Caminiti. Something has to give, and it's possible Henderson will move on.

Position: LF/RF
Bats: R **Throws:** L
Ht: 5'10" **Wt:** 190

Opening Day Age: 38
Born: 12/25/58 in Chicago, IL
ML Seasons: 18

Overall Statistics

	G	AB	R	H	D	T	HR	RBI	SB	BB	SO	Avg	OBP	Slg
1996	148	465	110	112	17	2	9	29	37	125	90	.241	.410	.344
Career	2340	8528	1829	2450	412	59	244	887	1186	1675	1191	.287	.406	.435

Where He Hits the Ball

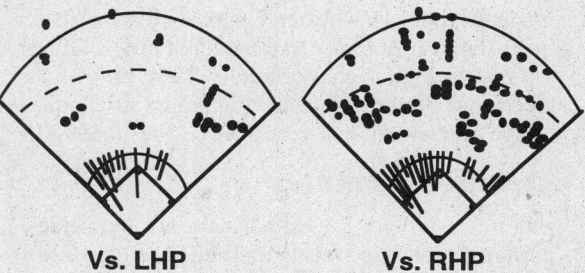

Vs. LHP   **Vs. RHP**

1996 Situational Stats

	AB	H	HR	RBI	Avg		AB	H	HR	RBI	Avg
Home	233	64	6	15	.275	LHP	114	30	4	12	.263
Road	232	48	3	14	.207	RHP	351	82	5	17	.234
First Half	264	62	7	21	.235	Sc Pos	77	14	2	20	.182
Scnd Half	201	50	2	8	.249	Clutch	80	17	0	0	.213

1996 Rankings (National League)

→ 1st in most pitches seen per plate appearance (4.48), on-base percentage for a leadoff hitter (.409) and highest percentage of pitches taken (69.4%)

→ 2nd in caught stealing (15), lowest batting average on the road (.207) , fielding percentage in left field (.985) and lowest percentage of swings on the first pitch (9.1%)

→ 3rd in lowest batting average with runners in scoring position (.182) and lowest batting average vs. right-handed pitchers (.234)

→ 4th in walks, pitches seen (2,696) and lowest batting average

→ 5th in on-base percentage and lowest slugging percentage vs. right-handed pitchers (.325)

San Diego Padres

Trevor Hoffman

1996 Season

Last season, Trevor Hoffman entrenched himself as one of the two or three top closers in the N.L.— and one of the top five in the game. His 42 saves and nine wins allowed him to finish second to Jeff Brantley of Cincinnati in the Rolaid's Relief Man N.L. sweepstakes. Hoffman's ratio of hits to innings pitched was the best in baseball. The fireballing righty averaged 11.4 strikeouts per nine innings pitched, an overpowering ratio.

Pitching

Hoffman comes right at hitters, as most hard-throwing closers do, with a sharply moving high-90s fastball. He also throws a hard slider and a slow curve to give hitters different looks, but his main weapon is his heater. Opposing hitters batted just .161 against him, and it mattered little whether he was facing a righty or a lefty. He'll give up an occasional longball, but he was far less susceptible to the gopher ball last year than he was in 1995.

Defense & Hitting

A former infielder, Hoffman is a steady fielder, although he has occasional mental lapses on throws to first base after spearing a comebacker. He gets off the mound quickly on sacrifices, but he usually opts to take the sure out. Despite a high leg kick, he does an effective job of controlling enemy running games. For an ex-shortstop, he's not much of a hitting threat.

1997 Outlook

Hoffman will enter the season looking for even bigger results from his awesome right arm. The Padres tend to play more than the usual number of close games, so Hoffman figures to get more save opportunities with San Diego than with most other teams. At 29, he's entering the prime of his career in excellent health. A 50-save season is not out of the question.

Position: RP
Bats: R **Throws:** R
Ht: 6' 0" **Wt:** 205

Opening Day Age: 29
Born: 10/13/67 in Bellflower, CA
ML Seasons: 4

Overall Statistics

	W	L	Pct.	ERA	G	GS	Sv	IP	H	BB	SO	HR	BR/IP
1996	9	5	.643	2.25	70	0	42	88.0	50	31	111	6	0.92
Career	24	19	.558	3.13	239	0	98	287.1	217	104	310	30	1.12

How Often He Throws Strikes

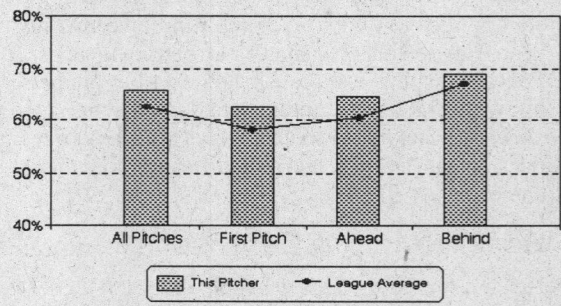

1996 Situational Stats

	W	L	ERA	Sv	IP		AB	H	HR	RBI	Avg
Home	5	1	1.35	19	40.0	LHB	135	21	2	8	.156
Road	4	4	3.00	23	48.0	RHB	176	29	4	19	.165
First Half	5	2	1.41	18	44.2	Sc Pos	72	10	2	20	.139
Scnd Half	4	3	3.12	24	43.1	Clutch	263	41	5	24	.156

1996 Rankings (National League)

→ 1st in relief wins (9)

→ 2nd in save opportunities (49), lowest batting average allowed in relief (.161), least baserunners allowed per 9 innings in relief (8.5) and most strikeouts per 9 innings in relief (11.4)

→ 3rd in saves, blown saves (7) and lowest percentage of inherited runners scored (17.1%)

→ 5th in games finished (62), lowest batting average allowed in relief with runners in scoring position (.139), relief ERA (2.25) and relief innings (88.0)

→ 6th in save percentage (85.7%)

→ 8th in first batter efficiency (.172)

Wally Joyner

1996 Season

After spending the first 10 years of his career in the American League, Wally Joyner made a successful transition to the Senior Circuit last season—at least until he suffered a broken thumb in early June. Joyner was among the league leaders in hitting before he took a six-week leave of absence, but when he returned, he was much less effective at the plate.

Hitting

Joyner is one of the game's most disciplined hitters. He rarely swings at bad pitches and concentrates on going the other way whenever possible. Joyner still offers up limited power and will occasionally turn on mistake pitches over the inner half of the plate, but he's primarily a contact hitter. Joyner struggled against lefties more last season than in 1995, forcing the Padres to sit him against southpaws on occasion. As has been the case for most of his career, Joyner was a strong hitter in the clutch, batting .306 with runners in scoring position, 29 points above his overall mark.

Baserunning & Defense

Joyner is very conservative on the basepaths, but usually is capable of taking extra bases when there are two outs. He'll steal a base now and then if a pitcher doesn't pay attention to him. An outstanding first sacker, Joyner has cat-like quickness around the bag along with a reliable throwing arm. He is exceptionally quick with the tag on pickoff attempts.

1997 Outlook

Despite his weak finish, the former American League Rookie of the Year runner-up is a good candidate to finish his career in San Diego. His presence lends stability to the lineup and the offense. Joyner's batting style is actually better suited to National League pitching because he is an effective low-ball hitter. Even if he leaves San Diego when his contract expires after this season, he'll likely opt to remain in the N.L.

Position: 1B
Bats: L **Throws:** L
Ht: 6' 2" **Wt:** 200

Opening Day Age: 34
Born: 6/16/62 in Atlanta, GA
ML Seasons: 11

Overall Statistics

	G	AB	R	H	D	T	HR	RBI	SB	BB	SO	Avg	OBP	Slg
1996	121	433	59	120	29	1	8	65	5	69	71	.277	.377	.404
Career	1485	5538	784	1601	319	20	166	854	55	629	627	.289	.361	.444

Where He Hits the Ball

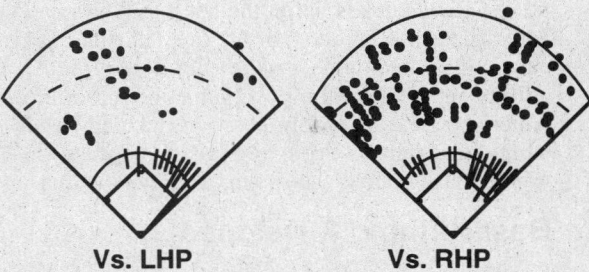

Vs. LHP   **Vs. RHP**

1996 Situational Stats

	AB	H	HR	RBI	Avg		AB	H	HR	RBI	Avg
Home	194	47	5	28	.242	LHP	117	25	2	21	.214
Road	239	73	3	37	.305	RHP	316	95	6	44	.301
First Half	184	59	5	33	.321	Sc Pos	121	37	3	57	.306
Scnd Half	249	61	3	32	.245	Clutch	76	22	2	12	.289

1996 Rankings (National League)

- ➡ 1st in fielding percentage at first base (.997)
- ➡ 3rd in lowest slugging percentage vs. left-handed pitchers (.316)
- ➡ 4th in lowest groundball/flyball ratio (0.8)
- ➡ 5th in lowest batting average vs. left-handed pitchers (.214) and lowest on-base percentage vs. left-handed pitchers (.290)
- ➡ 7th in on-base percentage vs. right-handed pitchers (.407) and lowest percentage of extra bases taken as a runner (37.2%)
- ➡ 9th in least GDPs per GDP situation (5.8%) and batting average on the road (.305)
- ➡ Led the Padres in least GDPs per GDP situation (5.8%) and on-base percentage vs. right-handed pitchers (.407)

San Diego Padres

Jody Reed

1996 Season

To some baseball insiders, Jody Reed is known mostly for his outrageous contract demands back in 1994 (he turned down an offer for $1.2 million from the Dodgers, then signed weeks later with the Brewers for $300,000). However, the sturdy veteran second baseman stabilized the Padres' infield last season and provided outstanding defense as well as the occasional timely hit.

Hitting

In his days with Boston, Reed used to love hitting shots off the Green Monster in left field—he once paced the American League in doubles. Today, he is effective as an opposite-field singles hitter who posts decent RBI numbers despite his lack of power. Reed chokes up on the bat these days and emphasizes putting the ball in play. He still can't catch up to the raw heat as he once could, but he adjusts better to breaking balls than he did in the American League. Oddly, the right-handed Reed struggled against lefties, reportedly because he tried to pull too many slow curves down the line.

Baserunning & Defense

Reed is an average runner who—though he doesn't steal much anymore—can still take the extra base when the situation demands it. Among the game's premier second basemen defensively, he's finished in the league's top two in fielding percentage twice. Reed doesn't make the amazing play very often, but he's automatic on the routine grounder and turns the double play flawlessly.

1997 Outlook

Though Reed performed capably for the Padres, San Diego made a deal for a young second baseman, Quilvio Veras, after the season. While Reed has experience at three other infield positions, it's doubtful that he would be content to fill a utility role. Reed would probably be shopped or released so that he can try and find a starting job elsewhere.

Position: 2B
Bats: R **Throws:** R
Ht: 5' 9" **Wt:** 165

Opening Day Age: 34
Born: 7/26/62 in Tampa, FL
ML Seasons: 10

Overall Statistics

	G	AB	R	H	D	T	HR	RBI	SB	BB	SO	Avg	OBP	Slg
1996	146	495	45	121	20	0	2	49	2	59	53	.244	.325	.297
Career	1232	4442	560	1209	261	10	27	384	37	532	392	.272	.351	.354

Where He Hits the Ball

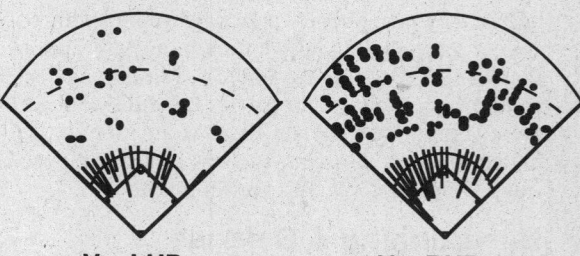

Vs. LHP   **Vs. RHP**

1996 Situational Stats

	AB	H	HR	RBI	Avg		AB	H	HR	RBI	Avg
Home	222	53	1	20	.239	LHP	118	25	0	9	.212
Road	273	68	1	29	.249	RHP	377	96	2	40	.255
First Half	304	72	1	29	.237	Sc Pos	118	31	0	45	.263
Scnd Half	191	49	1	20	.257	Clutch	90	20	0	5	.222

1996 Rankings (National League)

- → 1st in lowest slugging percentage and lowest slugging percentage vs. left-handed pitchers (.237)
- → 2nd in lowest HR frequency (247.5 ABs per HR)
- → 3rd in lowest slugging percentage vs. right-handed pitchers (.316)
- → 4th in lowest batting average vs. left-handed pitchers (.212), fielding percentage at second base (.987) and lowest percentage of swings that missed (8.9%)
- → 5th in lowest batting average at home (.239)
- → 6th in lowest percentage of swings on the first pitch (19.3%) and lowest batting average

Scott Sanders

1996 Season

For the third time in as many years, Scott Sanders was plagued by arm problems. He was shelved for more than half of last season. Still, Sanders was effective when he finally could start, going 8-3 after the All-Star break. He has averaged nearly a strikeout per inning in his brief career and showed signs of his ability to dominate down the stretch.

Pitching

By necessity, Sanders is working hard to alleviate his recent elbow troubles. Since his injuries have been attributed to mechanics that have maximized the strain on the arm, he's tried to incorporate his legs more into his motion. Elbow ailments not withstanding, Sanders is an excellent pitcher. He throws mid-90s fastballs, a good slider, and an improving change-up. He generally likes to work low in the zone, and he's fond of throwing his slider in the dirt, which yields plenty of strikeouts—and a few wild pitches. Sanders' control has improved each season, and he has maintained an excellent strikeout-to-walk ratio.

Defense & Hitting

Sanders is an outstanding athlete. He's adept around the mound, holds runners effectively, and boasts a sneaky pickoff move. Sanders has also established himself as a hitter to be respected: his .194 average was second among Padres pitchers and he fanned in less than a third of his at-bats.

1997 Outlook

The only real question about Sanders is his health. If he could stay around long enough to make 30 starts, he could be a 15-game winner. The Mariners are banking on that hope, and traded Sterling Hitchcock to acquire him. Still young and strong, Sanders is expected to overcome his elbow problems through a strict regimen of throwing and conditioning this past winter. He could turn out to be quite a complement to Randy Johnson.

Position: RP/SP
Bats: R **Throws:** R
Ht: 6' 4" **Wt:** 220

Opening Day Age: 28
Born: 3/25/69 in
Hannibal, MO
ML Seasons: 4

Overall Statistics

	W	L	Pct.	ERA	G	GS	Sv	IP	H	BB	SO	HR	BR/IP
1996	9	5	.643	3.38	46	16	0	144.0	117	48	157	10	1.15
Career	21	21	.500	4.08	95	60	1	397.1	353	150	391	38	1.27

How Often He Throws Strikes

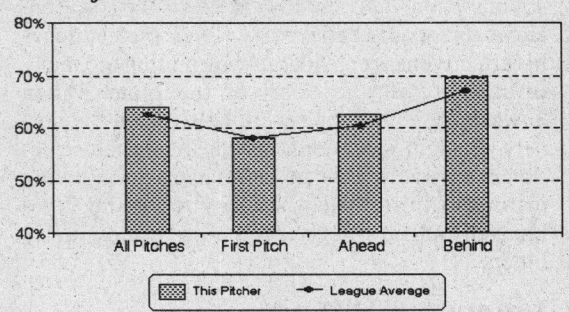

1996 Situational Stats

	W	L	ERA	Sv	IP		AB	H	HR	RBI	Avg
Home	4	3	3.00	0	66.0	LHB	249	57	4	20	.229
Road	5	2	3.69	0	78.0	RHB	281	60	6	23	.214
First Half	1	2	3.17	0	48.1	Sc Pos	112	21	2	31	.188
Scnd Half	8	3	3.48	0	95.2	Clutch	46	12	0	3	.261

1996 Rankings (National League)

→ 6th in lowest batting average allowed vs. right-handed batters (.214)
→ 7th in lowest batting average allowed vs. left-handed batters (.229)
→ Led the Padres in lowest batting average allowed vs. left-handed batters (.229) and lowest batting average allowed vs. right-handed batters (.214)

San Diego Padres

677

Bob Tewksbury

1996 Season

Bob Tewksbury came to the Padres with a reputation for consistency, but he didn't display much of it last year. After going through hot and cold streaks throughout the summer, Tewksbury pitched well in a losing effort in the N.L. playoffs against St. Louis, his former team. The Padres were baffled by his erratic performance throughout the year, but kept him in the rotation for all but a couple of starts.

Pitching

Tewksbury is the epitome of a "control pitcher." His walks-per-nine-innings career mark is the lowest among active pitchers, and he only allowed 43 bases on balls in his 33 starts last season. However, scouts believe that Tewksbury reduces his effectiveness considerably by putting too many offerings over the heart of the plate. When Tewksbury is throwing well, he lives on the corners, changing locations, speeds, and pitch selection extensively. He can fool batters by throwing his mediocre fastball when they're looking for a breaker, but he's never been able to blow away hitters.

Defense & Hitting

Tewksbury is perennially plagued by the stolen base, since his pickoff move is only average and he never delivers the ball to the plate in much of a hurry. His mechanics place him in good fielding position, but he's not quick and has trouble playing bunts. Tewksbury is a wretched hitter and finished last season as the worst in the N.L. after reaching safely only five times in 68 plate appearances.

1997 Outlook

The Padres held an option on Tewksbury's contract for 1997, but decided not to renew it. While 1996 wasn't one of his better years, Tewksbury shouldn't have much trouble finding another employer. Whoever signs him will hope he's a more consistent pitcher than he was in 1996.

Position: SP
Bats: R **Throws:** R
Ht: 6' 4" **Wt:** 205

Opening Day Age: 36
Born: 11/30/60 in Concord, NH
ML Seasons: 11

Overall Statistics

	W	L	Pct.	ERA	G	GS	Sv	IP	H	BB	SO	HR	BR/IP
1996	10	10	.500	4.31	36	33	0	206.2	224	43	126	17	1.29
Career	95	76	.556	3.80	250	226	1	1490.0	1669	241	660	111	1.28

How Often He Throws Strikes

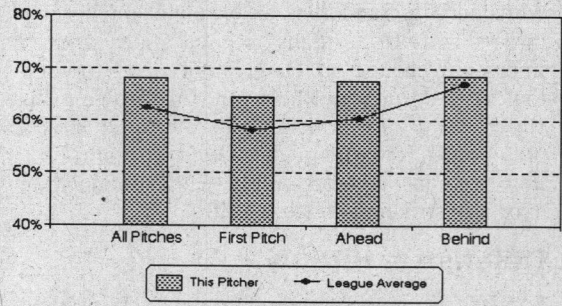

1996 Situational Stats

	W	L	ERA	Sv	IP		AB	H	HR	RBI	Avg
Home	5	4	3.64	0	94.0	LHB	320	85	4	44	.266
Road	5	6	4.87	0	112.2	RHB	494	139	13	52	.281
First Half	7	5	4.22	0	117.1	Sc Pos	180	54	5	77	.300
Scnd Half	3	5	4.43	0	89.1	Clutch	49	14	1	3	.286

1996 Rankings (National League)

- ➡ 1st in fielding percentage at pitcher (1.000)
- ➡ 2nd in least pitches thrown per batter (3.26)
- ➡ 3rd in balks (3)
- ➡ 4th in highest groundball/flyball ratio allowed (2.0)
- ➡ 7th in hits allowed and highest ERA on the road (4.87)
- ➡ 8th in pickoff throws (166)
- ➡ 10th in least home runs allowed per 9 innings (.74) and least strikeouts per 9 innings (5.5)
- ➡ Led the Padres in losses, games started, hits allowed, balks (3), pickoff throws (166), stolen bases allowed (22), highest strikeout/walk ratio (2.9) and lowest on-base percentage allowed (.310)

Fernando Valenzuela

1996 Season

It was an amazing resurrection for the 36-year-old Fernando Valenzuela, who struggled with four different teams between 1991 and 1995 before settling in as a reliable starter for the Padres last season. Valenzuela redefined the baseball term "crafty lefthander" by pitching well down the stretch at a time when San Diego's injury-plagued rotation was struggling.

Pitching

The Valenzuela of the early 1980s relied heavily on his screwball, and the pitch seems to be revitalized after being all but lost for the last five years. Valenzuela now curls his wrist back much more than he used to in an attempt to get more spring into his release. Combined with his cut fastball, which has become as important as his screwball, he keeps hitters perpetually off balance. Relying almost exclusively on outsmarting batters with his extensive pitching arsenal, Valenzuela no longer uses his trademark offering 80 percent of the time as he once did.

Defense & Hitting

Valenzuela is effective defensively despite his lack of conditioning. His pickoff move is still formidable, although he doesn't reveal it as often as he used to. At the plate, Valenzuela is one of the best hitting pitchers of the modern era. Ranking among the leaders among hurlers with 10 career home runs, his prowess with the bat has encouraged manager Bruce Bochy to utilize him as an occasional pinch hitter.

1997 Outlook

Valenzuela was signed two years ago as a attendance booster, but he's since pitched his way back into San Diego's plans. While he will eventually yield his spot to someone younger and stronger, Valenzuela works cheap by today's standards and is for now a legitimate member of the Padres' rotation.

Position: SP
Bats: L **Throws:** L
Ht: 5'11" **Wt:** 200

Opening Day Age: 36
Born: 11/1/60 in Navajoa, Sonora, MX
ML Seasons: 16

Overall Statistics

	W	L	Pct.	ERA	G	GS	Sv	IP	H	BB	SO	HR	BR/IP
1996	13	8	.619	3.62	33	31	0	171.2	177	67	95	17	1.42
Career	171	141	.548	3.50	435	406	2	2841.0	2612	1105	2013	214	1.31

How Often He Throws Strikes

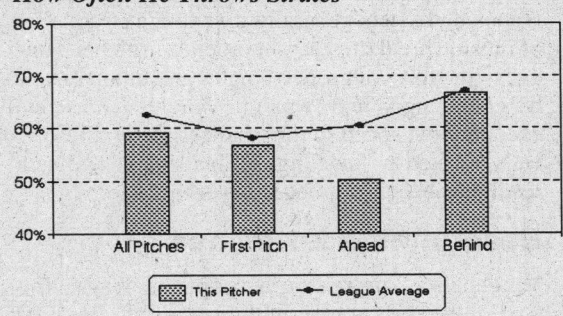

1996 Situational Stats

	W	L	ERA	Sv	IP		AB	H	HR	RBI	Avg
Home	8	5	3.61	0	102.1	LHB	92	24	1	6	.261
Road	5	3	3.63	0	69.1	RHB	567	153	16	65	.270
First Half	5	6	3.80	0	94.2	Sc Pos	167	38	2	48	.228
Scnd Half	8	2	3.39	0	77.0	Clutch	14	5	1	3	.357

1996 Rankings (National League)

- → 2nd in most pitches thrown per batter (3.94)
- → 5th in lowest strikeout/walk ratio (1.4) and least strikeouts per 9 innings (5.0)
- → 8th in most run support per 9 innings (5.7)
- → 10th in winning percentage
- → Led the Padres in ERA, lowest stolen base percentage allowed (68.0%), most run support per 9 innings (5.7) and lowest batting average allowed with runners in scoring position (.228)

San Diego Padres

Greg Vaughn

1996 Season

Greg Vaughn came to the Padres in an 11th-hour deadline deal with Milwaukee in which San Diego was forced to part with three promising prospects. The veteran slugger's plate appearances were either feast or famine, as he batted just .206 for the Padres but hit a home run every 14 at-bats. Vaughn finished the season sharing left field with Rickey Henderson and started only one of the Padres' three playoff games.

Hitting

Vaughn is a dead pull hitter who crushes mistake pitches. A free swinger, Vaughn can slam any pitch out of any park if he guesses correctly at the plate. Opposing hurlers generally give him a steady diet of outside breaking balls in order to limit his damage to the form of ground singles and bloop hits. If he's challenged high, though, Vaughn can use his excellent bat speed to turn on nearly any offering. He's worked on leveling out his swing, and as a result has become a more consistent hitter.

Baserunning & Defense

Vaughn is a surprise in a couple of ways. You wouldn't expect a man with his build to run well or swipe bases, but he has excellent speed and a steal success rate of better than 70 percent over the last two years. He's viewed as a liability in the outfield because he doesn't possess good instincts or a strong throwing arm, but he can cover ground quickly when he gets a head of steam.

1997 Outlook

The Padres have four legitimate everyday outfielders and just three open slots. That means that either Vaughn or Rickey Henderson won't be back. It's a tough choice for the Padres, who value both Vaughn's power and Henderson's ability to reach base. Wherever Vaughn ends up this year, he should continue to be a dangerous slugger.

Position: LF
Bats: R **Throws:** R
Ht: 6' 0" **Wt:** 202

Opening Day Age: 31
Born: 7/3/65 in Sacramento, CA
ML Seasons: 8

Overall Statistics

	G	AB	R	H	D	T	HR	RBI	SB	BB	SO	Avg	OBP	Slg
1996	145	516	98	134	19	1	41	117	9	82	130	.260	.365	.539
Career	946	3385	548	828	161	14	179	588	66	445	792	.245	.333	.459

Where He Hits the Ball

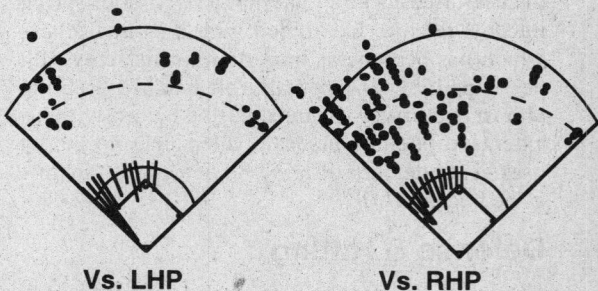

Vs. LHP   Vs. RHP

1996 Situational Stats

	AB	H	HR	RBI	Avg		AB	H	HR	RBI	Avg
Home	243	65	22	62	.267	LHP	139	32	10	26	.230
Road	273	69	19	55	.253	RHP	377	102	31	91	.271
First Half	305	87	24	75	.285	Sc Pos	174	39	10	79	.224
Scnd Half	211	47	17	42	.223	Clutch	68	14	2	8	.206

1996 Rankings (National League)

→ 7th in lowest batting average on a 3-2 count (.067)

Tim Worrell

1996 Season

Known primarily for being Todd Worrell's kid brother, Tim Worrell is quietly establishing himself as a bona fide major league pitcher. Although Worrell was bothered in the early part of the season by a variety of ailments, he settled in as one of the team's top set-up men as well as a spot starter. San Diego was counting on him to join the rotation before Fernando Valenzuela began his comeback-player-of-the-year bid. Returned to the pen, Worrell posted an outstanding 1.54 ERA in 39 relief appearances.

Pitching

Worrell has not allowed the reconstructive elbow surgery he underwent in 1994 to curtail his aggressiveness. He's still a hard thrower, mixing a moving fastball and darting slider with equal effectiveness. Although Worrell relies on location more than his brother, he has the ability to notch the key strikeouts. He's not afraid to work inside, either.

Defense & Hitting

Worrell is a former infielder, so he appears very comfortable both at making plays around the mound and covering first base. He keeps a close eye on baserunners and shuts down potential stealing threats. Worrell came to the plate only 20 times last season but helped himself at bat, particularly with his ability to lay down bunts.

1997 Outlook

Worrell makes no bones about his desire to start, but he insists that as long as San Diego is successful, he'll be content to toil from the bullpen. With Bob Tewksbury not returning and Fernando Valenzuela up there in years, a solid spring training by Worrell could catapult him into the Padres rotation. If not, he'll be entrenched as a right-handed set-up man and occasional long reliever until a job becomes available.

Position: RP/SP
Bats: R **Throws:** R
Ht: 6' 4" **Wt:** 220

Opening Day Age: 29
Born: 7/5/67 in Pasadena, CA
ML Seasons: 4
Pronunciation: wor-RELL

Overall Statistics

	W	L	Pct.	ERA	G	GS	Sv	IP	H	BB	SO	HR	BR/IP
1996	9	7	.563	3.05	50	11	1	121.0	109	39	99	9	1.22
Career	12	15	.444	3.93	83	30	1	249.2	238	93	178	22	1.33

How Often He Throws Strikes

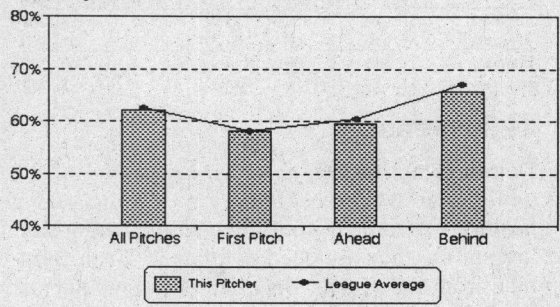

1996 Situational Stats

	W	L	ERA	Sv	IP		AB	H	HR	RBI	Avg
Home	4	7	4.48	0	70.1	LHB	206	53	0	16	.257
Road	5	0	1.07	1	50.2	RHB	255	56	9	30	.220
First Half	6	4	2.94	0	67.1	Sc Pos	119	28	1	34	.235
Scnd Half	3	3	3.19	1	53.2	Clutch	100	12	2	7	.120

1996 Rankings (National League)

→ 1st in relief ERA (1.54), lowest batting average allowed in relief (.137) and least baserunners allowed per 9 innings in relief (8.0)

→ 10th in relief wins (6)

→ Led the Padres in relief ERA (1.54), lowest batting average allowed in relief (.137) and least baserunners allowed per 9 innings in relief (8.0)

Sean Bergman

Position: RP/SP
Bats: R **Throws:** R
Ht: 6' 4" **Wt:** 230

Opening Day Age: 26
Born: 4/11/70 in Joliet, IL
ML Seasons: 4

Overall Statistics

	W	L	Pct.	ERA	G	GS	Sv	IP	H	BB	SO	HR	BR/IP
1996	6	8	.429	4.37	41	14	0	113.1	119	33	85	14	1.34
Career	16	23	.410	4.94	81	51	0	306.0	357	130	202	41	1.59

1996 Situational Stats

	W	L	ERA	Sv	IP		AB	H	HR	RBI	Avg
Home	1	5	4.66	0	56.0	LHB	180	52	5	24	.289
Road	5	3	4.08	0	57.1	RHB	255	67	9	35	.263
First Half	4	7	4.81	0	88.0	Sc Pos	107	34	3	46	.318
Scnd Half	2	1	2.84	0	25.1	Clutch	42	13	0	3	.310

1996 Season

Detroit is not exactly the pitching capital of the world, but when the Padres needed to add a healthy arm to their injury-depleted pitching staff last spring, they obtained righthander Sean Bergman from the Tigers. Bergman was a member of the Padre rotation for most of the first half of the season, with so-so results. He fared much better after a shift to the bullpen, posting a 2.75 ERA in 27 relief assignments.

Pitching, Defense & Hitting

Bergman is a sinker/slider pitcher with a fine groundball ratio and impressive strikeout rates. As a starter he had problems maintaining consistent location, but his control was much better after the Padres shifted him to the bullpen. Bergman is extremely easy to run on, and his defensive work isn't very good, either. He showed promise as a hitter and even belted a home run.

1997 Outlook

Bergman did well in relief last year, though the Padres didn't trust him with many important assignments. Since he's young and has a good arm, they'll probably keep him around in the same middle reliever/spot starter role he handled last year.

Willie Blair

Position: RP
Bats: R **Throws:** R
Ht: 6' 1" **Wt:** 185

Opening Day Age: 31
Born: 12/18/65 in Paintsville, KY
ML Seasons: 7

Overall Statistics

	W	L	Pct.	ERA	G	GS	Sv	IP	H	BB	SO	HR	BR/IP
1996	2	6	.250	4.60	60	0	1	88.0	80	29	67	13	1.24
Career	25	41	.379	4.73	260	50	4	609.0	672	218	406	69	1.46

1996 Situational Stats

	W	L	ERA	Sv	IP		AB	H	HR	RBI	Avg
Home	0	3	3.89	1	44.0	LHB	130	30	6	24	.231
Road	2	3	5.32	0	44.0	RHB	204	50	7	28	.245
First Half	1	5	4.22	0	53.1	Sc Pos	78	25	5	41	.321
Scnd Half	1	1	5.19	1	34.2	Clutch	80	26	6	24	.325

1996 Season

Veteran righty Willie Blair was expected to be one of the Padres' primary right-handed set-up men last year, but his performance was one of the staff's few disappointments. Although his control was solid and he didn't allow many hits, Blair had a knack for giving up key hits—particularly home runs—at bad times.

Pitching, Defense & Hitting

Blair's best pitch is referred to as a "12-to-6" slider, because it breaks virtually straight down. He also throws a moving fastball in the high 80s, an average curve, and a change-up that closely resembles his slider. Blair's major weakness is that he throws just the slider and fastball when he gets into trouble, and hitters have usually been able to sit on the heater. An average fielder, Blair has mastered the slide-step and holds baserunners well. He was hitless in three plate appearances last season.

1997 Outlook

Blair was a disappointment last year, and his future in San Diego is anything but secure. The Padres will look for major improvements from Blair if they choose to bring him back; if he doesn't produce, he probably won't stick around.

Doug Bochtler

Position: RP
Bats: R **Throws:** R
Ht: 6' 3" **Wt:** 200

Opening Day Age: 26
Born: 7/5/70 in West Palm Beach, FL
ML Seasons: 2
Pronunciaiton: BOCK-ler

Overall Statistics

	W	L	Pct.	ERA	G	GS	Sv	IP	H	BB	SO	HR	BR/IP
1996	2	4	.333	3.02	63	0	3	65.2	45	39	68	6	1.28
Career	6	8	.429	3.24	97	0	4	111.0	83	58	113	11	1.27

1996 Situational Stats

	W	L	ERA	Sv	IP		AB	H	HR	RBI	Avg
Home	1	2	4.58	1	37.1	LHB	111	21	1	10	.189
Road	1	2	0.95	2	28.1	RHB	120	24	5	18	.200
First Half	0	2	3.89	3	34.2	Sc Pos	67	13	1	21	.194
Scnd Half	2	2	2.03	0	31.0	Clutch	162	34	4	20	.210

1996 Season

Second-year man Doug Bochtler grabbed an important role in the Padres' bullpen last year and quickly developed into one of the best set-up relievers in the league. Bochtler walked 39 in just 65.2 innings, but his tremendous strikeout rate helped strand most of those runners. He took over the closer role when bullpen ace Trevor Hoffman needed a day off, saving three games in seven tries.

Pitching, Defense & Hitting

Bochtler suffered some shoulder woes during his minor league career, but he appears to have regained the full strength of his mid-90s fastball. His main weapon is his unusual delivery, which makes it very difficult for hitters to pick up the rotation of his breaking balls. Bochtler looks like he'd be easy to steal against, but he has three career pickoffs in just two short seasons. An average fielder, he did not bat last season.

1997 Outlook

A starter for most of his minor league career, Bochtler has made great strides since being shifted to the bullpen in 1995. He enters this season as the Padres' main set-up men, and he would be the Padres' first choice to close games if anything happened to Hoffman.

Archi Cianfrocco

Position: 1B/3B
Bats: R **Throws:** R
Ht: 6' 5" **Wt:** 215

Opening Day Age: 30
Born: 10/6/66 in Rome, NY
ML Seasons: 5
Pronunciation: sin-FROCK-oh

Overall Statistics

	G	AB	R	H	D	T	HR	RBI	SB	BB	SO	Avg	OBP	Slg
1996	79	192	21	54	13	3	2	32	1	8	56	.281	.315	.411
Career	371	984	107	245	44	7	29	154	8	50	258	.249	.290	.396

1996 Situational Stats

	AB	H	HR	RBI	Avg		AB	H	HR	RBI	Avg
Home	104	33	0	13	.317	LHP	67	24	0	8	.358
Road	88	21	2	19	.239	RHP	125	30	2	24	.240
First Half	142	40	1	23	.282	Sc Pos	63	18	0	27	.286
Scnd Half	50	14	1	9	.280	Clutch	48	7	0	5	.146

1996 Season

Archi Cianfrocco was slowed by injuries for much of the season, but he again showed his versatility as the Padres' power-hitting utility man. Cianfrocco played at least one game at every position except pitcher and center field. Even with part-time status, he managed more than 200 plate appearances and started at first base in Game 3 of the N.L. Divisional Series.

Hitting, Baserunning & Defense

Cianfrocco is a dead fastball hitter who likes to hack at the first pitch. Breaking balls outside of the plate have proven to be the downfall of the impatient Cianfrocco, but he hits for considerable power despite his lack of consistent playing time. With just average speed on the bases, he occasionally commits baserunning blunders. His defense isn't first-rate anywhere, but you have to admire a player who is so adaptable.

1997 Outlook

Although he's like everyone else in preferring to play regularly, Cianfrocco has come to grips with his utility role. He is an important member of the Padres' bench, and one of the best in the business at his role.

Brian Johnson

Position: C
Bats: R **Throws:** R
Ht: 6' 2" **Wt:** 210

Opening Day Age: 29
Born: 1/8/68 in
Oakland, CA
ML Seasons: 3

Overall Statistics

	G	AB	R	H	D	T	HR	RBI	SB	BB	SO	Avg	OBP	Slg
1996	82	.243	18	66	13	1	8	35	0	4	36	.272	.290	.432
Career	186	543	45	141	26	2	14	80	0	20	96	.260	.288	.392

1996 Situational Stats

	AB	H	HR	RBI	Avg		AB	H	HR	RBI	Avg
Home	117	35	3	15	.299	LHP	67	22	1	10	.328
Road	126	31	5	20	.246	RHP	176	44	7	25	.250
First Half	147	45	6	29	.306	Sc Pos	72	17	2	29	.236
Scnd Half	96	21	2	6	.219	Clutch	42	8	1	5	.190

1996 Season

Brian Johnson emerged over the second half of last season as a formidable offensive threat—and a defensive liability. Johnson played well after taking over at catcher for injured starter John Flaherty, and he was the club's main receiver as the Padres drove to the N.L. West crown. Although his defense was suspect, his handling of the Padres' pitching staff was adequate.

Hitting, Baserunning & Defense

Johnson became a more disciplined hitter last season and stopped swinging from the heels at every pitch. He shortened up when he got behind on the count and became a much better hitter with two strikes. While Johnson runs fairly well for a catcher, he's still sluggish on the basepaths. His biggest weakness is his erratic defense. With a strong but wild throwing arm, Johnson could use some instruction in the art of accurate throwing.

1997 Outlook

The Padres prefer the more well-rounded game of Flaherty, but Johnson would rank among the top backup catchers in baseball. As he continues to learn more about playing behind the plate and handling pitchers, he should become a valuable commodity.

Scott Livingstone

Position: 1B/3B
Bats: L **Throws:** R
Ht: 6' 0" **Wt:** 190

Opening Day Age: 31
Born: 7/15/65 in
Dallas, TX
ML Seasons: 6

Overall Statistics

	G	AB	R	H	D	T	HR	RBI	SB	BB	SO	Avg	OBP	Slg
1996	102	172	20	51	4	1	2	20	0	9	22	.297	.331	.366
Career	532	1356	158	397	68	4	17	159	8	81	163	.293	.329	.386

1996 Situational Stats

	AB	H	HR	RBI	Avg		AB	H	HR	RBI	Avg
Home	85	22	0	5	.259	LHP	13	1	0	1	.077
Road	87	29	2	15	.333	RHP	159	50	2	19	.314
First Half	130	35	1	12	.269	Sc Pos	51	18	1	19	.353
Scnd Half	42	16	1	8	.381	Clutch	46	13	1	9	.283

1996 Season

In his second full season with the Padres, Scott Livingstone continued to shine in his role as a pinch hitter and fill-in first/third baseman. Livingstone led the National League with 19 pinch hits and performed capably when asked to substitute at first or third—though, as usual, he didn't hit for much power.

Hitting, Baserunning & Defense

Livingstone is a singles hitter who is adept at putting the ball in play. The Padres used him almost exclusively against righthanders last year, but he's shown he can handle southpaws in the past. A below-average runner, Livingstone never steals and is a plodder on the bases. He is a solid defender at third base, his primary position, but merely adequate at first. He has trouble digging out low throws and executing long stretches.

1997 Outlook

There is a role on every team for a player who can pinch hit and slam line drives, so Livingstone should continue to be a deadly Padres weapon off the bench. His lack of power prevents him from getting a more substantial role than that, but he remains a very handy guy to have around.

Luis Lopez

Position: SS/2B
Bats: B **Throws:** R
Ht: 5'11" **Wt:** 175

Opening Day Age: 26
Born: 9/4/70 in Cidra, PR
ML Seasons: 3

Overall Statistics

	G	AB	R	H	D	T	HR	RBI	SB	BB	SO	Avg	OBP	Slg
1996	63	139	10	25	3	0	2	11	0	9	35	.180	.233	.245
Career	157	417	40	95	20	1	4	32	3	24	82	.228	.274	.309

1996 Situational Stats

	AB	H	HR	RBI	Avg		AB	H	HR	RBI	Avg
Home	73	13	1	7	.178	LHP	8	0	0	0	.000
Road	66	12	1	4	.182	RHP	131	25	2	11	.191
First Half	117	20	2	11	.171	Sc Pos	35	4	0	7	.114
Scnd Half	22	5	0	0	.227	Clutch	37	11	2	6	.297

1996 Season

Luis Lopez was a serious candidate for regular infield playing time with the Padres before injuring his shoulder last spring. It was the second year in a row he was hurt in training camp with a chance to be a starter. When Lopez returned, he was at less than full strength and didn't contribute much.

Hitting, Baserunning & Defense

Lopez is a switch-hitter who hits much better left-handed. He puts the ball in play and possesses above-average speed, and when healthy he's displayed decent power to the gaps for a middle infielder. He's not much of a basestealing threat. Defensively, Lopez is a slick-fielding infielder who's more comfortable at second than at shortstop, where he was slated to begin the 1994 season before getting hurt.

1997 Outlook

The Padres are still high on Lopez, but he hasn't stayed healthy enough over the last two years to truly display his skills. If he is at full speed this spring, he's capable of challenging Quilvio Veras for the second base job. However, Lopez is more likely to begin the season as San Diego's middle-infield utility man.

Craig Shipley

Position: 2B
Bats: R **Throws:** R
Ht: 6' 1" **Wt:** 190

Opening Day Age: 34
Born: 1/7/63 in Sydney, Australia
ML Seasons: 9

Overall Statistics

	G	AB	R	H	D	T	HR	RBI	SB	BB	SO	Avg	OBP	Slg
1996	33	92	13	29	5	0	1	7	7	2	15	.315	.337	.402
Career	442	1059	115	288	47	5	13	102	32	35	149	.272	.301	.363

1996 Situational Stats

	AB	H	HR	RBI	Avg		AB	H	HR	RBI	Avg
Home	40	9	0	2	.225	LHP	24	6	0	1	.250
Road	52	20	1	5	.385	RHP	68	23	1	6	.338
First Half	31	14	1	3	.452	Sc Pos	18	5	0	5	.278
Scnd Half	61	15	0	4	.246	Clutch	16	6	0	0	.375

1996 Season

Craig Shipley, the only native Australian in the National League, was a solid pinch hitter and defensive contributor—when he was able to play—after returning to the organization from Houston. He got into just 33 games last season, sitting out much of the summer due to a hamstring injury and finishing the year on the disabled list.

Hitting, Baserunning & Defense

Shipley is a gap hitter with a little bit of power. He occasionally knocks out home runs, but his power does not threaten enemy pitchers. Despite average speed, Shipley runs the bases intelligently and well. Defensively, his reactions at third are good, but his arm is suspect, and he often one-hops throws to first. At shortstop, he simply doesn't have the required range to be a regular.

1997 Outlook

The Padres will probably weed out one of their current crop of utility players and, on paper at least, that decision figures to end Shipley's stay with the team. If there is an infield injury in the spring, however, the team might keep its "mate from down under" a while longer.

Other San Diego Padres

Andres Berumen (Pos: RHP, Age: 25)

	W	L	Pct.	ERA	G	GS	Sv	IP	H	BB	SO	HR	BR/IP
1996	0	0	-	5.40	3	0	0	3.1	3	2	4	1	1.50
Career	2	3	.400	5.66	40	0	1	47.2	40	38	46	4	1.64

Berumen squeezed in three relief appearances with the Padres during his year at Triple-A Las Vegas. There, he achieved the incredible feat of walking 59 batters in 70-plus innings. 1997 Outlook: D

Doug Dascenzo (Pos: RF, Age: 32, Bats: B)

	G	AB	R	H	D	T	HR	RBI	SB	BB	SO	Avg	OBP	Slg
1996	21	9	3	1	0	0	0	0	0	1	2	.111	.200	.111
Career	540	1225	156	287	42	10	5	90	49	103	117	.234	.293	.297

Dascenzo provided pinch hitting and outfield insurance for the Padres during the latter half of the summer. At 33, his chances of returning to a significant major league role are nil. 1997 Outlook: D

Rob Deer (Pos: RF, Age: 36, Bats: R)

	G	AB	R	H	D	T	HR	RBI	SB	BB	SO	Avg	OBP	Slg
1996	25	50	9	9	3	0	4	9	0	14	30	.180	.359	.480
Career	1155	3881	578	853	148	13	230	600	43	575	1409	.220	.324	.442

Deer returned to the majors last season after a three-year exile. He quickly showed the Padres the error of their ways, striking out in 30 of his 50 at-bats and batting .180. Career might be through. 1997 Outlook: D

Chris Gwynn (Pos: RF, Age: 32, Bats: L)

	G	AB	R	H	D	T	HR	RBI	SB	BB	SO	Avg	OBP	Slg
1996	81	90	8	16	4	0	1	10	0	10	28	.178	.260	.256
Career	599	1007	119	263	36	11	17	118	2	71	171	.261	.308	.369

Contuining what is probably the diametric opposite of his brother's career, Gwynn was plagued with injuries and struggled horrifically at the plate (.176 BA). Tony's name can only carry him so long. 1997 Outlook: D

Dustin Hermanson (Pos: RHP, Age: 24)

	W	L	Pct.	ERA	G	GS	Sv	IP	H	BB	SO	HR	BR/IP
1996	1	0	1.000	8.56	8	0	0	13.2	18	4	11	3	1.61
Career	4	1	.800	7.35	34	0	0	45.1	53	26	30	11	1.74

A hard-throwing short reliever, Hermanson's fastball was voted the best in the Pacific Coast League last year. For the second straight year, he failed to catch on with the Padres, and they dealt him to Florida. 1997 Outlook: B

Sean Mulligan (Pos: 1B, Age: 26, Bats: R)

	G	AB	R	H	D	T	HR	RBI	SB	BB	SO	Avg	OBP	Slg
1996	2	1	0	0	0	0	0	0	0	0	0	.000	.000	.000
Career	2	1	0	0	0	0	0	0	0	0	0	.000	.000	.000

Mulligan received just two pinch-hit at-bats upon getting called up to the Padres in September. He's posted solid numbers at Triple-A, so he could get a shot at a job in spring training. 1997 Outlook: C

Mike Oquist (Pos: RHP, Age: 28)

	W	L	Pct.	ERA	G	GS	Sv	IP	H	BB	SO	HR	BR/IP
1996	0	0	-	2.35	8	0	0	7.2	6	4	4	0	1.30
Career	5	4	.556	4.92	55	9	0	131.2	144	79	78	13	1.69

Oquist, despite posting outstanding results at Triple-A Las Vegas in the minors, got only a brief look with San Diego last fall. He was recently signed to a minor league contract with Oakland. 1997 Outlook: B

Al Osuna (Pos: LHP, Age: 31)

	W	L	Pct.	ERA	G	GS	Sv	IP	H	BB	SO	HR	BR/IP
1996	0	0	-	2.25	10	0	0	4.0	5	2	4	0	1.75
Career	18	10	.643	3.83	218	0	14	192.2	156	109	143	17	1.38

Osuna pitched well for the Padres during his September stint in the bullpen, but was released at the end of the season. At 31, he's not young, but still should be able to latch on to another team. 1997 Outlook: C

Todd Steverson (Pos: SS, Age: 25, Bats: R)

	G	AB	R	H	D	T	HR	RBI	SB	BB	SO	Avg	OBP	Slg
1996	1	1	0	0	0	0	0	0	0	0	1	.000	.000	.000
Career	31	43	11	11	0	0	2	6	2	6	11	.256	.333	.395

Steverson spent most of the year in the minors after getting traded from Detroit a few weeks before the start of the season. He struggled at Triple-A (.239 BA) and got just one at-bat in the majors. 1997 Outlook: C

Jimmy Tatum (Pos: 3B, Age: 29, Bats: R)

	G	AB	R	H	D	T	HR	RBI	SB	BB	SO	Avg	OBP	Slg
1996	7	11	1	1	0	0	0	0	0	0	3	.091	.091	.091
Career	138	151	12	30	6	1	1	16	0	7	39	.199	.236	.272

Sold to San Diego by Boston in June, Tatum saw limited action at third base base in September. He had phenomenal minor league numbers (.343-12-56 in 233 AB's), but with MVP Ken Caminiti at third. . . 1997 Outlook: C

Pete Walker (Pos: RHP, Age: 27)

	W	L	Pct.	ERA	G	GS	Sv	IP	H	BB	SO	HR	BR/IP
1996	0	0	-	0.00	1	0	0	0.2	0	3	1	0	4.50
Career	1	0	1.000	4.42	14	0	0	18.1	24	8	6	3	1.75

Acquired from the Mets in March, Walker turned in a very poor year at Triple-A Las Vegas (6.83 ERA in 26 appearances) but managed to get to the majors in September, anyway. Probably not a prospect. 1997 Outlook: C

San Diego Padres Minor League Prospects

Organization Overview:

The San Diego Padres have unquestionably unseated the Atlanta Braves as the best producers of young pitching talent in baseball. Years of forward-looking trades and strong drafts have stocked the system with arms from top to bottom. This enables the Padres to pick and choose their favorites, while trading the rest at a premium to pitching-starved clubs. There are a few blue-chip position players on the horizon, but the system contains very few noteworthy bats right now. No one's worried, though, because such players can be easily acquired in exchange for the surplus pitching. The trade of Dustin Hermanson for Quilvio Veras may be the first of several moves along those lines. The major league staff already contains several home-grown products, and the coming years will bring many more. The management realizes what it has, and seems committed to developing its staff the way the Braves did several years ago. The Padres will spend a little money on position players to field a competitive major league team, while the young hurlers battle amongst themselves to grab the available pitching spots.

Gabe Alvarez

Position: 3B
Bats: R **Throws:** R
Ht: 6' 1" **Wt:** 185
Opening Day Age: 23
Born: 3/6/74 in Novojoa, Sonora, Mexico

Recent Statistics

	G	AB	R	H	D	T	HR	RBI	SB	BB	SO	AVG
95 A Rancho Cuca	59	212	41	73	17	2	6	36	1	29	30	.344
95 AA Memphis	2	9	0	5	1	0	0	4	0	1	1	.556
96 AA Memphis	104	368	58	91	23	1	8	40	2	64	87	.247
96 MLE	104	356	45	79	19	0	7	31	1	42	92	.222

It was a rough comedown for Gabe Alvarez, who starred in the California League in '95 after the Padres selected him in the second round of the draft. A move from shortstop to third base didn't remedy his erratic defense, and his hitting dropped off considerably. The Padres hope that a stress fracture in his foot was part of the problem. He remains a good offensive prospect, with a well-developed knowledge of the strike zone and enough power potential to make it at third base.

Homer Bush

Position: 2B
Bats: R **Throws:** R
Ht: 5' 11" **Wt:** 180
Opening Day Age: 24
Born: 11/12/72 in East St. Louis, IL

Recent Statistics

	G	AB	R	H	D	T	HR	RBI	SB	BB	SO	AVG
93 A Waterloo	130	472	63	152	19	3	5	51	19	19	87	.322
94 A Rancho Cuca	39	161	37	54	10	3	0	16	9	9	29	.335
94 AA Wichita	59	245	35	73	11	4	3	14	20	10	39	.298
95 AA Memphis	108	432	53	121	12	5	5	37	34	15	83	.280
96 AAA Las Vegas	32	116	24	42	11	1	2	3	3	3	33	.362

Homer Bush advanced through the Padres organization rather quickly by hitting for a good average wherever they sent him. Last year, he was off to a blazing start before a broken leg put him out for the season. He's a decent second baseman with good speed but absolutely zero power and no plate discipline. He doesn't have the talent to be a major league regular, but his flashy batting averages will continue to get him noticed. One of these years, he may sneak in and grab a bench role.

Brad Kaufman

Position: P
Bats: R **Throws:** R
Ht: 6' 2" **Wt:** 210
Opening Day Age: 24
Born: 4/26/72 in Marshalltown, PA

Recent Statistics

	W	L	ERA	G	GS	Sv	IP	H	R	BB	SO	HR
93 A Spokane	5	4	6.88	25	8	4	53.2	56	56	41	48	8
94 A Springfield	10	9	3.34	31	20	0	145.1	124	62	63	122	9
95 AA Memphis	11	10	5.76	27	27	0	148.1	142	112	90	119	17
96 AA Memphis	12	10	3.63	29	29	0	178.1	161	84	83	163	18

Never before considered a prospect, righthander Brad Kaufman suddenly became one in his second season at Double-A. Never overpowering, Kaufman made great strides in learning to mix his pitches and keep the ball down. The Padres got inquiries from other teams about him, but in the end, they preferred to keep Kaufman over some of their more advanced prospects. The Pacific Coast League will be his next big challenge.

Marc Kroon

Position: P
Bats: B **Throws:** R
Ht: 6' 2" **Wt:** 175
Opening Day Age: 23
Born: 4/2/73 in Bronx, NY

Recent Statistics

	W	L	ERA	G	GS	Sv	IP	H	R	BB	SO	HR
93 A Capital Cty	2	11	3.47	29	19	2	124.1	123	65	70	122	6
94 A Rancho Cuca	11	6	4.83	26	26	0	143.1	143	86	81	153	14
95 AA Memphis	7	5	3.51	22	19	2	115.1	90	49	61	123	12
96 AA Memphis	2	4	2.89	44	0	22	46.2	33	19	28	56	4

In one year, Marc Kroon went from being a hard-throwing starter with spotty control and no stamina to being the best short reliever in the Southern League. For the second straight year, his 95 MPH heater was voted the best fastball in the league, and his numbers would have been even better if a thumb injury hadn't ended his season in July. He's still got work to do on adding a breaking ball or an offspeed pitch, but his arm is one of the most coveted ones in the system. He could break in as a middle man as early as this year.

Derrek Lee

Position: 1B
Bats: R **Throws:** R
Ht: 6' 5" **Wt:** 220

Opening Day Age: 21
Born: 9/6/75 in
Sacramento, CA

Recent Statistics

	G	AB	R	H	D	T	HR	RBI	SB	BB	SO	AVG
93 R Padres	15	52	11	17	1	1	2	5	4	6	7	.327
93 A Rancho Cuca	20	73	13	20	5	1	1	10	0	10	20	.274
94 A Rancho Cuca	126	442	66	118	19	2	8	53	18	42	95	.267
95 A Rancho Cuca	128	502	82	151	25	2	23	95	11	49	130	.301
95 AA Memphis	2	9	0	1	0	0	0	1	0	0	2	.111
96 AA Memphis	134	500	98	140	39	2	34	104	13	65	170	.280
96 MLE	134	483	77	123	32	1	30	81	8	43	180	.255

Not only was Derrek Lee the youngest player in the
Southern League last year, he was also the league's
MVP. After topping the 30-homer mark last year at age
20, it's scary to think what the 6-foot, five-inch first
baseman might accomplish once he *really* matures. The
only thing he has to conquer is a serious—but understandable—tendency to strike out. The Padres may give
him another year to sort that out, but otherwise, he's
ready for prime time. A promotion to the hitter-friendly
Pacific Coast League may boost his numbers further and
accelerate his arrival in San Diego.

Heath Murray

Position: P
Bats: L **Throws:** L
Ht: 6' 4" **Wt:** 205

Opening Day Age: 23
Born: 4/19/73 in Troy,
OH

Recent Statistics

	W	L	ERA	G	GS	Sv	IP	H	R	BB	SO	HR
94 A Spokane	5	6	2.90	15	15	0	99.1	101	46	18	78	6
95 A Rancho Cuca	9	4	3.12	14	14	0	92.1	80	37	38	81	5
95 AA Memphis	5	4	3.38	14	14	0	77.1	83	36	42	71	1
96 AA Memphis	13	9	3.21	27	27	0	174.0	154	83	60	156	13

Heath Murray is a lefty with an average fastball and
great control. There had been concern that he didn't
have the stuff to get the big strikeout when he needed it,
but last year, he proved that his ability to paint the
corners was just as effective as sheer heat. He fanned
almost a batter per inning at Double-A, and will now test
his mettle against Triple-A hitters. His first run through
the Pacific Coast League may be a trial by fire, but if he
can survive there, he certainly should be able to hold his
own in the National League.

Jason Thompson

Position: 1B
Bats: L **Throws:** L
Ht: 6' 4" **Wt:** 200

Opening Day Age: 25
Born: 6/13/71 in
Orlando, FL

Recent Statistics

	G	AB	R	H	D	T	HR	RBI	SB	BB	SO	AVG
96 AAA Las Vegas	111	387	80	116	27	0	21	57	7	51	93	.300
96 NL San Diego	13	49	4	11	4	0	2	6	0	1	14	.224
96 MLE	111	367	60	96	22	0	16	43	4	38	96	.262

Jason Thompson always has been a bit old for the
leagues he's been playing in, and the Padres' handling

of him last year revealed that they'd never really taken
him seriously as a prospect. When an injury to Wally
Joyner created the need for a first baseman, the Padres
only gave Thompson a brief look before shipping him
back out. Down at Triple-A, he continued to prove that
he has acceptable power for a first baseman, but his age
left little hope that he'd develop much further. Concerns
about his ability to hit lefthanders remain, and the development of Derrek Lee leaves him in limbo within the
organization.

Dario Veras

Position: P
Bats: R **Throws:** R
Ht: 6' 2" **Wt:** 165

Opening Day Age: 24
Born: 3/13/73 in
Santiago, DR

Recent Statistics

	W	L	ERA	G	GS	Sv	IP	H	R	BB	SO	HR
96 AA Memphis	3	1	2.32	29	0	1	42.2	38	14	9	47	4
96 AAA Las Vegas	6	2	2.90	19	1	1	40.1	41	17	6	30	1
96 NL San Diego	3	1	2.79	23	0	0	29.0	24	10	10	23	3

Dario Veras was drafted out of the Dodgers' system in
1993 and has proven to be a real find. The skinny
Dominican righthander throws hard and has excellent
control. He pitched at three levels last year—Double-A,
Triple-A, and the majors—throwing 112 innings, and
issuing only 17 unintentional walks. The Padres called
him up in late July to replace the departed Ron Villone,
and Veras' work virtually assured him a spot in the
bullpen for next season.

Others to Watch

Young shortstop **Juan Melo** had a great year in the Class
A California League, batting .304 and showing good
power potential. He was also voted the league's best
defensive shortstop. . . One of last year's biggest surprises was lefty **Shane Dennis**. After a promotion to
Double-A, he was nearly unhittable, going 9-1 and fanning well over a batter per inning. He may be considered
as a set-up man this year. . . **Ben Davis**, the number-two
pick in the country in '95, struggled badly last year after
jumping from Rookie ball to advanced Class A. Calcium
deposits in his throwing elbow sidelined him for two
months, and often limited him to DH after he was
activated. The Padres still see a bright future for the
switch-hitting receiver. . . At age 21, **Jorge Velandia**
was extremely young for someone who spent his second
season in the high minors. His numbers weren't impressive on the surface, but his solid glove and his youth
provide hope that he'll develop into a decent enough
hitter to make it as a middle infielder. . . In his seventh
year of pro ball, righthander **Fernando Hernandez** had
a breakthrough of sorts, fanning 161 hitters at Double-
A. Now 26 years old, he doesn't have much hope of
elbowing his way past all the other young arms in the
system.

Dusty Baker

1996 Season

Well-regarded by his players and peers, Dusty Baker entered his fifth season at the helm of the Giants hoping to give direction to a struggling franchise. Though the results were disappointing, Baker earned respect for the way he handled an undermanned club. He remained patient with his players, especially youngsters, and handled his veterans adeptly as well. But while he continued to command the respect of both players and management, some are beginning to feel that Baker tends to stay too long with players who decline after enjoying career years.

Offense

Although his teams generally don't lack for power, Baker likes to use the running game and the hit and run. He tends to play for one run earlier in the game more than most managers do, and employs the sacrifice as often as anyone. He played the bulk of his career in the National League, and it shows.

Pitching & Defense

Baker shows confidence in his pitchers, always giving them a chance to work through slumps. He uses a lot of relievers, often for only a few batters at a time, in an effort to get favorable lefty-righty match-ups. He likes to pitch out, and he's had a fair amount of success with it. Baker is more willing than most managers to try a player at an unfamiliar position.

1997 Outlook

"Endurance" is the word that best describes Baker's tenure with the Giants. During 1996 he was given a two-year contract extension, and with new general manager Brian Sabean, the rebuilding process is set to begin. Aside from the question of Barry Bonds, the goal of 1997 should be to assemble a solid starting eight and push for .500. Baker's patience bodes well for a team trying to work several young players into the lineup.

Born: 6/15/49 in Riverside, CA

Playing Experience: 1968-1986, Atl, LA, SF, Oak

Managerial Experience: 4 seasons

Manager Statistics

Year	Team, Lg	W	L	Pct	GB	Finish
1996	San Francisco, NL	68	94	.420	23.0	4th West
4 Seasons		293	290	.503	—	—

1996 Starting Pitchers by Days Rest

	≤3	4	5	6+
Giants Starts	3	75	51	24
Giants ERA	9.22	4.64	4.40	5.05
NL Avg Starts	4	86	41	21
NL ERA	4.06	4.28	4.23	4.58

1996 Situational Stats

	Dusty Baker	NL Average
Hit & Run Success %	36.2	39.0
Stolen Base Success %	68.1	71.6
Platoon Pct.	51.0	51.9
Defensive Subs	15	20
High-Pitch Outings	15	13
Quick/Slow Hooks	12/16	19/12
Sacrifice Attempts	103	92

1996 Rankings (National League)

→ 1st in pitchouts (97), mid-inning pitching changes (193) and first batter platoon percentage (63.5%)

→ 2nd in least caught steals of home plate (1), starting lineups used (129) and one-batter pitcher appearances (35)

→ 3rd in sacrifice bunt attempts (103), pitchouts with a runner moving (16), intentional walks (45), slow hooks (16) and starts with over 120 pitches (15)

Rich Aurilia

1996 Season

Rich Aurilia backed up the middle infield for the Giants in the first half, and took over at shortstop after Shawon Dunston went down with an injury in August. The 24-year-old rookie failed to hit with much authority, but his defense was a pleasant surprise. All in all, his showing may end up convincing the Giants to give him a shot at a regular job.

Hitting

A line-drive hitter with a reputation for having decent power for a middle infielder, Aurilia looked overmatched last year, especially on high fastballs. He protected the plate with two strikes, but he didn't look for a pitch to drive when the count was in his favor as much as he probably should have. He was a fairly successful hitter in the minors, so he may improve with experience. He is a good bunter and has the ability to advance baserunners.

Baserunning & Defense

Aurilia has average speed, but he runs the bases well. He can steal a base when necessary and he pays attention when rounding them. He has an excellent glove, with good range and a strong arm. He can turn the double play, and could improve further with a consistent partner. Though he is a shortstop, he is comfortable at second base as well, and played errorless ball in 11 games there last year.

1997 Outlook

The Giants did not re-sign Shawon Dunston, so the regular shortstop job might be open for Aurilia to claim this spring. He has the tools to be a solid player, and another season of major league experience may bring some improvement at the plate for him. He is a smart player who knows his abilities, pays attention and learns. He'll likely develop if he's given the opportunity.

Position: SS/2B
Bats: R **Throws:** R
Ht: 6' 1" **Wt:** 170

Opening Day Age: 25
Born: 9/2/71 in Brooklyn, NY
ML Seasons: 2
Pronunciation: aw-REE-lee-uh

Overall Statistics

	G	AB	R	H	D	T	HR	RBI	SB	BB	SO	Avg	OBP	Slg
1996	105	318	27	76	7	1	3	26	4	25	52	.239	.295	.296
Career	114	337	31	85	10	1	5	30	5	26	54	.252	.305	.332

Where He Hits the Ball

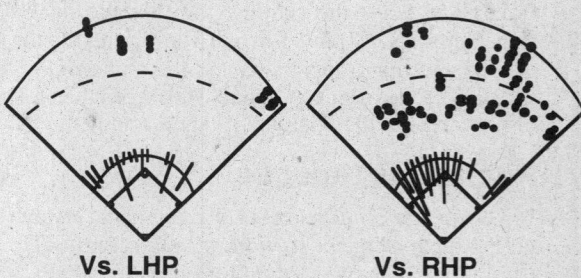

Vs. LHP   **Vs. RHP**

1996 Situational Stats

	AB	H	HR	RBI	Avg		AB	H	HR	RBI	Avg
Home	180	47	1	13	.261	LHP	67	15	1	5	.224
Road	138	29	2	13	.210	RHP	251	61	2	21	.243
First Half	108	24	3	10	.222	Sc Pos	79	18	0	20	.228
Scnd Half	210	52	0	16	.248	Clutch	56	12	0	3	.214

1996 Rankings (National League)

➡ 1st in least GDPs per GDP situation (1.7%)
➡ Led the Giants in least GDPs per GDP situation (1.7%) and batting average on an 0-2 count (.259)

Rod Beck

Position: RP
Bats: R **Throws:** R
Ht: 6' 1" **Wt:** 236

Opening Day Age: 28
Born: 8/3/68 in
Burbank, CA
ML Seasons: 6

1996 Season

The "Dr. Jekyll/Mr. Hyde" season of Rod Beck began with enough promise, as Beck didn't surrender a run over his first 15 appearances, notching nine saves in the process. Although he went on to save 26 more games from that point on, he also went 0-9 with an ERA well over 4.00. What began as a brilliant year for him ended up as an average one, and his poor finish mirrored the Giants' second-half collapse.

Pitching

On the mound, Beck has the size, looks and intimidating presence of a classic closer. The problem is that he no longer has the overpowering fastball to go with it. His curve and spilt-fingered fastball aren't good enough to fool anyone, so he must rely on pinpoint location to be effective. His girth and hard delivery cause his back to stiffen, making him useful for only an inning at a time, and limiting his ability to pitch on consecutive days.

Defense & Hitting

With his physical handicaps, Beck doesn't get off the mound too quickly, either, although he hasn't made an error in three years. He doesn't have any kind of a move to first; he's a closer, and baserunners are not his concern. He's done fairly well at the plate, but no one expects that to continue.

1997 Outlook

Beck is still plenty good enough to be the Giants' closer, but his contract may be a burden for the cost-cutting Giants. They reportedly shopped him around during his early hot streak last year, and the chances are that he'll be moved as soon as they can find a taker. Such a move might help Beck significantly; he could end up on a better team with many more leads to protect.

Overall Statistics

	W	L	Pct.	ERA	G	GS	Sv	IP	H	BB	SO	HR	BR/IP
1996	0	9	.000	3.34	63	0	35	62.0	56	10	48	9	1.06
Career	14	24	.368	2.89	343	0	162	393.0	337	85	340	45	1.07

How Often He Throws Strikes

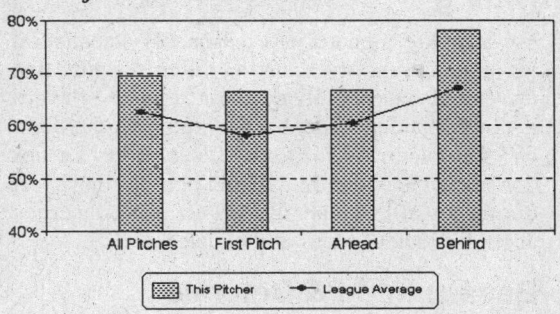

1996 Situational Stats

	W	L	ERA	Sv	IP		AB	H	HR	RBI	Avg
Home	0	4	3.31	20	35.1	LHB	105	23	4	16	.219
Road	0	5	3.38	15	26.2	RHB	130	33	5	16	.254
First Half	0	5	2.62	17	34.1	Sc Pos	54	13	4	24	.241
Scnd Half	0	4	4.23	18	27.2	Clutch	160	46	8	29	.288

1996 Rankings (National League)

- ➡ 1st in relief losses (9)
- ➡ 3rd in blown saves (7)
- ➡ 5th in save opportunities (42), lowest save percentage (83.3%) and first batter efficiency (.150)
- ➡ 6th in saves and least baserunners allowed per 9 innings in relief (9.7)
- ➡ 7th in games finished (58)
- ➡ Led the Giants in saves, games finished (58), save opportunities (42), save percentage (83.3%), blown saves (7), first batter efficiency (.150), lowest percentage of inherited runners scored (30.3%), relief losses (9) and lowest batting average allowed in relief (.238)

Marvin Benard

1996 Season

Rookie outfielder Marvin Benard was the Giants' full-time injury replacement last season. When Stan Javier went down in April with a strained hamstring, Benard took over in center field. Javier returned in May, but a broken wrist to right fielder Glenallen Hill allowed Benard to remain in the lineup. Two months later, Hill returned, but by then, Javier was gone for the season, and so Benard kept his tenuous hold on a regular job. He was an adequate center fielder and leadoff man, but he was also subject to mental lapses which concerned management, mostly because he didn't seem to be aware of them.

Hitting

For a rookie, Benard was reasonably selective at the plate. Primarily a singles hitter, he hits line drives and occasionally reaches the fences. Benard is not particularly adept at laying down the bunt, and must learn to hit to all fields more. Lefties don't seem to bother him. He sometimes looks lost during an at-bat, and the Giants are concerned about his lack of focus at the plate.

Baserunning & Defense

A real burner, Benard has tremendous speed. He is an adept basestealer and runs the bases with moxie. In the outfield, his speed doesn't make up for his poor jumps, so his range remains below average. He committed five errors last year, which is actually pretty good in light of his erratic play in the minors. Benard has an acceptable arm and gets his share of outfield assists.

1997 Outlook

The Giants would have loved to have seen Benard establish himself as the center fielder, but he proved to be little more than a fourth outfielder. With Javier presumably available again, Benard may end up coming off the bench as often as he starts. His modest talents should be better suited to that role.

Position: CF/RF
Bats: L **Throws:** L
Ht: 5' 9" **Wt:** 180

Opening Day Age: 27
Born: 1/20/70 in Bluefields, Nicaragua
ML Seasons: 2

Overall Statistics

	G	AB	R	H	D	T	HR	RBI	SB	BB	SO	Avg	OBP	Slg
1996	135	488	89	121	17	4	5	27	25	59	84	.248	.333	.330
Career	148	522	94	134	19	4	6	31	26	60	91	.257	.337	.343

Where He Hits the Ball

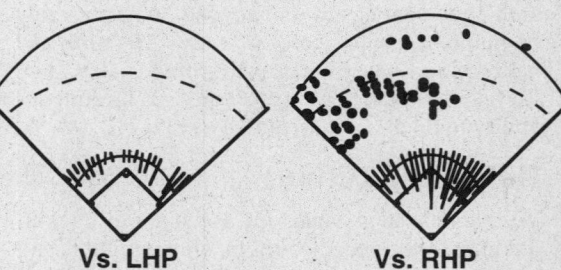

Vs. LHP   **Vs. RHP**

1996 Situational Stats

	AB	H	HR	RBI	Avg		AB	H	HR	RBI	Avg
Home	257	64	2	8	.249	LHP	69	18	0	4	.261
Road	231	57	3	19	.247	RHP	419	103	5	23	.246
First Half	232	60	0	11	.259	Sc Pos	79	16	1	21	.203
Scnd Half	256	61	5	16	.238	Clutch	71	21	3	11	.296

1996 Rankings (National League)

→ 3rd in fielding percentage in center field (.989)

→ 5th in lowest slugging percentage and bunts in play (22)

→ 6th in highest groundball/flyball ratio (2.0) and lowest batting average vs. right-handed pitchers (.246)

→ 7th in caught stealing, lowest slugging percentage vs. right-handed pitchers (.339) and lowest batting average

→ 8th in lowest HR frequency (97.6 ABs per HR) and lowest on-base percentage for a leadoff hitter (.330)

→ 9th in errors in center field (3)

→ 10th in lowest batting average at home (.249)

Barry Bonds

1996 Season

If ever there were a player you either hate to love or love to hate, Barry Bonds would have to be the man. Infuriating, misguided and egotistical, Bonds is nonetheless possibly the best all-around player in the game. In 1996, he hit his 300th home run and became the second player in history to attain 40 homers and 40 steals in the same season. Unfortunately, Bonds alienated just about everyone around him in the process, announcing at one point that his teammates weren't doing enough to help him reach that goal.

Hitting

Bonds is a powerful, disciplined hitter who has no appreciable weaknesses. Using hip torque and his strong wrists, Bonds can pull any pitcher's fastball. He always makes the pitcher come in to him—after Matt Williams went down last year, he refused to give in, even though no one would pitch to him in a tight spot. He set a National League record for most walks in a season last year (151). As is his custom, he stepped up his game ever further last year when there were ducks on the pond.

Baserunning & Defense

Late in the season, everyone knew Bonds was running to get the 40/40 mark, but they still couldn't stop him. He's both speedy and knowledgeable, and was caught only seven times all year. He also runs the bases very well. When he's focused, his defense in left field is stellar—arguably the best in the National League, if not the majors. He's got a good arm as well.

1997 Outlook

Bonds continues to excel at every aspect of the game, save humility. Still, his attitude—which probably helps to make him the player he is—alienates fans, management and media alike. When his father was fired as third base coach, he talked about wanting to leave San Francisco, and the Giants may finally oblige him. In the eyes of any potential employer, his terrific productivity will likely outweigh his personality and his contract.

Position: LF
Bats: L **Throws:** L
Ht: 6' 1" **Wt:** 190

Opening Day Age: 32
Born: 7/24/64 in Riverside, CA
ML Seasons: 11

Overall Statistics

	G	AB	R	H	D	T	HR	RBI	SB	BB	SO	Avg	OBP	Slg
1996	158	517	122	159	27	3	42	129	40	151	76	.308	.461	.615
Career	1583	5537	1121	1595	333	51	334	993	380	1082	871	.288	.404	.548

Where He Hits the Ball

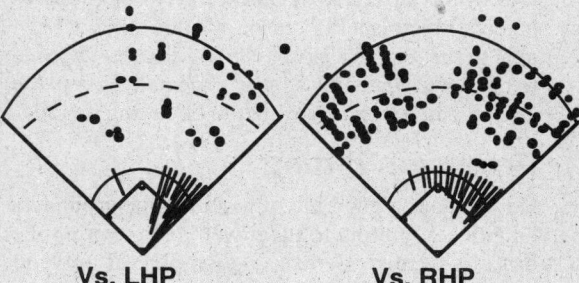

Vs. LHP   **Vs. RHP**

1996 Situational Stats

	AB	H	HR	RBI	Avg		AB	H	HR	RBI	Avg
Home	242	79	23	64	.326	LHP	150	46	12	39	.307
Road	275	80	19	65	.291	RHP	367	113	30	90	.308
First Half	319	96	23	68	.301	Sc Pos	115	43	9	80	.374
Scnd Half	198	63	19	61	.318	Clutch	70	14	6	18	.200

1996 Rankings (National League)

→ 1st in walks, intentional walks (30), HR frequency (12.3 ABs per HR), lowest ground-ball/flyball ratio (0.7), cleanup slugging percentage (.669), slugging percentage vs. right-handed pitchers (.624) and on-base percentage vs. right-handed pitchers (.483)

→ 2nd in home runs, on-base percentage and errors in left field (6)

→ 3rd in runs scored, times on base (311) and stolen base percentage (85.1%)

→ 4th in RBI, stolen bases, slugging percentage and fielding percentage in left field (.980)

→ 5th in highest percentage of pitches taken (62.6%)

Mark Dewey

1996 Season

Mark Dewey emerged as a critical component of the Giants bullpen last year, tying for third in the N.L. with a career-high 78 appearances. Unfortunately, all that work resulted in a rough stretch late in the year, but apart from that, he did good work as a set-up man and middle reliever.

Pitching

Relying primarily on a killer 88-MPH sinker and a very effective curve, Dewey also throws a slider and change-up. He uses his low-three-quarters motion to deceive and destroy right-handed hitters. Lefties, however, have no trouble picking him up, and batted .379 against him last year. Dewey has struggled against lefties throughout his career, which is a big reason why he's never been able to succeed as a closer. He was also susceptible to the home run ball last year, especially late in the season when fatigue seemed to be taking its toll.

Defense & Hitting

Dewey does a good job of handling the grounders he induces, getting to them well and covering the bases as needed. He uses a good pickoff move to keep runners close, and opposing basestealers have always fared poorly with him on the mound. At the plate, he doesn't do much except to draw an occasional walk.

1997 Season

Dewey did all that was asked of him last year, although he remained mostly anonymous until his reluctance to take part in an AIDS-awareness day created a public outcry in San Francisco. However, the Giants are paying him for his pitching, not his observations on social issues. He's become a valuable set-up man and should continue in that role in 1997. He probably should spend much of the spring working on a pitch that can help him better neutralize left-handed hitters.

Position: RP
Bats: R **Throws:** R
Ht: 6' 0" **Wt:** 216

Opening Day Age: 32
Born: 1/3/65 in Grand Rapids, MI
ML Seasons: 6

Overall Statistics

	W	L	Pct.	ERA	G	GS	Sv	IP	H	BB	SO	HR	BR/IP
1996	6	3	.667	4.21	78	0	0	83.1	79	41	57	9	1.44
Career	12	7	.632	3.65	205	0	8	249.0	243	102	168	18	1.39

How Often He Throws Strikes

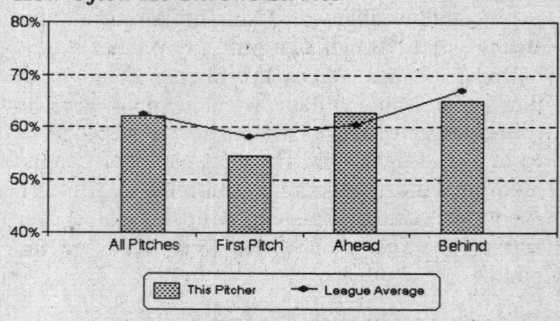

1996 Situational Stats

	W	L	ERA	Sv	IP		AB	H	HR	RBI	Avg
Home	5	1	3.48	0	41.1	LHB	95	36	3	18	.379
Road	1	2	4.93	0	42.0	RHB	212	43	6	36	.203
First Half	3	2	3.40	0	45.0	Sc Pos	89	24	4	46	.270
Scnd Half	3	1	5.17	0	38.1	Clutch	72	24	5	23	.333

1996 Rankings (National League)

➜ 3rd in games pitched

➜ 4th in highest percentage of inherited runners scored (44.6%)

➜ 10th in relief wins (6) and least strikeouts per 9 innings in relief (6.2)

➜ Led the Giants in games pitched, relief wins (6) and relief innings (83.1)

Shawon Dunston

1996 Season

In his first year in a Giants uniform, Shawon Dunston was enjoying a fairly solid season when he was kneed in the face while sliding into second base on August 4. The resulting fractures to his eye socket required surgery and sidelined him for the remainder of the season. Although his defense wasn't what it used to be, and his production was less impressive than it would appear at first glance, the Giants were pleased with his play and presence in the clubhouse.

Hitting

Dunston is a notorious hacker who just can't let four balls pass without taking a cut. He makes good contact, protects the plate with two strikes, and can pull the ball with some authority. He has good power for a shortstop, but his batting average is a bit misleading. The hits look good on paper, but he can't reach base any other way, which means that he can't be used effectively at the top of the order.

Baserunning & Defense

Still possessing very good speed, Dunston swiped eight bases without being caught last year. He's considered one of the better baserunners in the game. Dunston's back problems have affected his range, which is now no better than average. His throwing arm is still one of the strongest around, but a good number of his 15 errors came on wild throws.

1997 Outlook

A free agent again when the season ended, Dunston went back to the Cubs, signing a one-year contract. The Cubs are saying he'll be their shortstop in 1997, but it's possible they might try to shift Dunston to third base. If healthy, he figures to be a valuable member of the team.

Position: SS
Bats: R **Throws:** R
Ht: 6' 1" **Wt:** 180

Opening Day Age: 34
Born: 3/21/63 in Brooklyn, NY
ML Seasons: 12

Overall Statistics

	G	AB	R	H	D	T	HR	RBI	SB	BB	SO	Avg	OBP	Slg
1996	82	287	27	86	12	2	5	25	8	13	40	.300	.331	.408
Career	1222	4438	533	1186	220	46	103	473	154	176	746	.267	.296	.407

Where He Hits the Ball

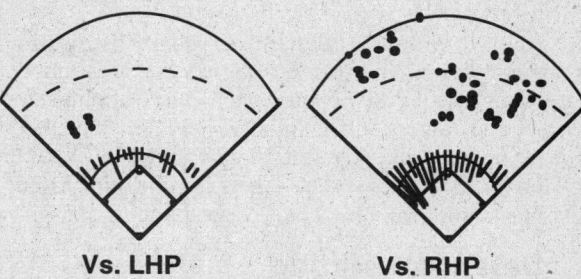

Vs. LHP   **Vs. RHP**

1996 Situational Stats

	AB	H	HR	RBI	Avg		AB	H	HR	RBI	Avg
Home	131	47	3	15	.359	LHP	55	14	0	3	.255
Road	156	39	2	10	.250	RHP	232	72	5	22	.310
First Half	212	66	5	22	.311	Sc Pos	80	22	1	17	.275
Scnd Half	75	20	0	3	.267	Clutch	45	10	1	3	.222

1996 Rankings (National League)

→ 5th in batting average on a 3-2 count (.412) and batting average with two strikes (.276)
→ 9th in errors at shortstop (15)
→ Led the Giants in batting average on a 3-2 count (.412) and batting average with two strikes (.276)

Shawn Estes

Position: SP
Bats: R **Throws:** L
Ht: 6' 2" **Wt:** 185

Opening Day Age: 24
Born: 2/18/73 in San Bernardino, CA
ML Seasons: 2

1996 Season

A youthful veteran of the Seattle organization who'd been held back by arm problems, lefthander Shawn Estes came to the Giants in the Salomon Torres deal early in 1995. He spent most of '95 and the first half of 1996 at Triple-A Phoenix before joining the big club last July. Estes threw seven shutout innings in his first start for San Francisco, allowing three hits and striking out 11. It proved to be no fluke, and he pitched very well before the Giants shut him down in September. He struck out nearly a batter per inning and was truly tough to hit. Although he struggled with his control at times, he showed one of the most impressive power arms of any young lefthander in the league.

Pitching

Blessed with a great hard curveball, Estes also possesses a mid-90s fastball and a very good change-up. In the Seattle organization, arm miseries and a questionable mindset held him back, but he matured quickly last year. Though he is still prone to fits of wildness, he's got the stuff to be outstanding and the time to learn how.

Defense & Hitting

Estes holds runners well, and didn't allow a single stolen base in 11 games. Although his delivery is rather long, it's difficult to read. He covers his position well and makes all the plays. Estes is not a bad hitter—he can make contact occasionally, and is good at bunting.

1997 Outlook

Estes is slated to remain in the starting rotation for this season and hopefully for many more. He's got a lot going for him, and his health and his command are the only things that could keep him from realizing his considerable potential. If his arm remains sound and he throws enough strikes to keep the hitters honest, the Giants may have themselves a rising star.

Overall Statistics

	W	L	Pct.	ERA	G	GS	Sv	IP	H	BB	SO	HR	BR/IP
1996	3	5	.375	3.60	11	11	0	70.0	63	39	60	3	1.46
Career	3	8	.273	4.23	14	14	0	87.1	79	44	74	5	1.41

How Often He Throws Strikes

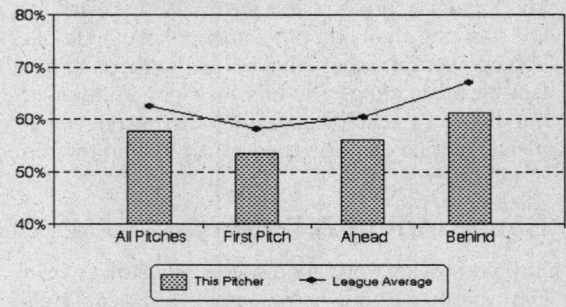

1996 Situational Stats

	W	L	ERA	Sv	IP		AB	H	HR	RBI	Avg
Home	1	2	4.02	0	31.1	LHB	31	8	0	3	.258
Road	2	3	3.26	0	38.2	RHB	228	55	3	19	.241
First Half	0	0	-	0	0.0	Sc Pos	77	14	0	16	.182
Scnd Half	3	5	3.60	0	70.0	Clutch	10	2	0	2	.200

1996 Rankings (National League)

→ Did not rank near the top or bottom in any category

Osvaldo Fernandez

1996 Season

Much like his cross-bay counterpart Ariel Prieto, Cuban emigre Osvaldo Fernandez had a lot of adjustments to make during his first major league season. In addition to overcoming culture shock, Fernandez had to adjust to throwing to big-league hitters. Had he been on a more prolific team, his struggle might have been lessened, but the run support he was afforded throughout the season was terrible. Fernandez pitched much better towards the end of the season when his family was allowed to emigrate from Cuba.

Pitching

During the second half of 1996, Fernandez settled down and started to throw strikes more consistently. He began coming inside with his high-80s fastball, junking his nibbling approach that he'd used in international play. Fernandez also throws a curve and a slider and is learning a change-up. His arm doesn't respond well to heavy use, and he sometimes needed extra rest after high-pitch outings last year.

Defense & Hitting

Fernandez covers his position very well and fielded far more balls than anyone else on the staff. He holds runners adequately, though he is improving. He has a very good pickoff move, one that was acceptable for international competition, but sometimes comes too close to being a balk in the majors. He can't do much at the plate except to lay down an occasional bunt.

1997 Outlook

Overcoming the tribulations of a new culture, Fernandez pitched with a lot more authority as the 1996 season progressed. With a year's worth of growth and adjustments behind him, Fernandez will be expected to apply what he's learned in '97. The Giants are counting on him to be a dependable member of their rotation.

Position: SP
Bats: R **Throws:** R
Ht: 6' 2" **Wt:** 190

Opening Day Age: 28
Born: 11/4/68 in Holguin, Cuba
ML Seasons: 1

Overall Statistics

	W	L	Pct.	ERA	G	GS	Sv	IP	H	BB	SO	HR	BR/IP
1996	7	13	.350	4.61	30	28	0	171.2	193	57	106	20	1.46
Career	7	13	.350	4.61	30	28	0	171.2	193	57	106	20	1.46

How Often He Throws Strikes

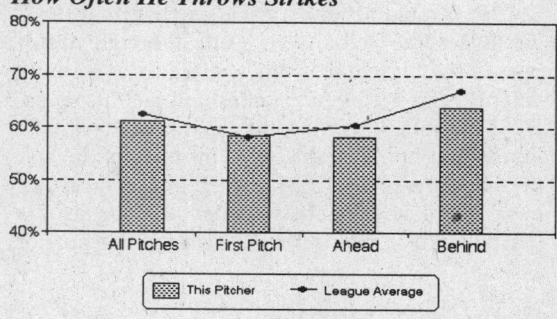

This Pitcher — League Average

1996 Situational Stats

	W	L	ERA	Sv	IP		AB	H	HR	RBI	Avg
Home	2	6	3.94	0	93.2	LHB	284	83	11	44	.292
Road	5	7	5.42	0	78.0	RHB	392	110	9	41	.281
First Half	4	9	5.61	0	101.0	Sc Pos	182	53	9	71	.291
Scnd Half	3	4	3.18	0	70.2	Clutch	53	16	1	6	.302

1996 Rankings (National League)

➡ 3rd in least run support per 9 innings (3.6)
➡ 6th in pickoff throws (187), lowest winning percentage and least pitches thrown per batter (3.48)
➡ 7th in losses and highest batting average allowed (.285)
➡ 8th in hit batsmen (10)
➡ 9th in highest on-base percentage allowed (.348), lowest groundball/flyball ratio allowed (1.1) and most baserunners allowed per 9 innings
➡ 10th in highest slugging percentage allowed (.439) and highest ERA at home (3.94)
➡ Led the Giants in hit batsmen (10), pickoff throws (187) and ERA at home (3.94)

Mark Gardner

1996 Season

Arriving as a free agent signing on the eve of the season opener, Mark Gardner provided veteran experience to San Francisco. He remained in the rotation all year and became their only pitcher to win in double digits. Gardner was particularly effective during the first half, but he was slowed by an appendectomy which limited him to three starts in July. He rebounded in September after working back up to full strength. He worked through his characteristic hot and cold streaks, but on balance, it was one of his best years.

Pitching

Garner's curveball isn't quite as sharp as it used to be, but it remains an excellent pitch. His fastball has lost some velocity as well, although it still pushes the high 80s at times. Gardner is a savvy veteran who mixes his pitches and hits his spots. He is hittable, though, so he must keep from falling behind in the count. As is his custom, he had trouble remaining effective deep into games, and even when healthy, he's tended to fade as the season wore on. His durability and stamina are not assets.

Defense & Hitting

Gardner's only above-average skill at the plate is his ability to bunt. He has a slow move to first, so he will step off the rubber repeatedly to keep runners close. That works pretty well for him. Gardner possesses a good enough glove to get by, and makes few mistakes in the field.

1997 Outlook

The Giants were very happy with Gardner's contribution to the team in 1996 and rewarded him with a contract extension. At age 35, he'll do well to put up numbers similar to last year's. The key for him, as always, will be to stay healthy and remain strong over the course of an entire season.

Position: SP
Bats: R **Throws:** R
Ht: 6' 1" **Wt:** 205

Opening Day Age: 35
Born: 3/1/62 in Los Angeles, CA
ML Seasons: 8

Overall Statistics

	W	L	Pct.	ERA	G	GS	Sv	IP	H	BB	SO	HR	BR/IP
1996	12	7	.632	4.42	30	28	0	179.1	200	57	145	28	1.43
Career	53	55	.491	4.39	200	156	1	992.2	971	373	738	120	1.35

How Often He Throws Strikes

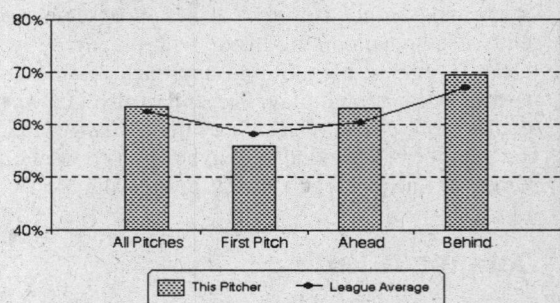

1996 Situational Stats

	W	L	ERA	Sv	IP		AB	H	HR	RBI	Avg
Home	7	2	4.13	0	104.2	LHB	332	92	12	37	.277
Road	5	5	4.82	0	74.2	RHB	374	108	16	59	.289
First Half	8	3	3.73	0	99.0	Sc Pos	168	46	7	66	.274
Scnd Half	4	4	5.27	0	80.1	Clutch	29	10	0	1	.345

1996 Rankings (National League)

➡ 2nd in most run support per 9 innings (6.8)
➡ 3rd in most home runs allowed per 9 innings (1.41)
➡ 5th in home runs allowed and most pitches thrown per batter (3.87)
➡ 7th in complete games (4), winning percentage and highest slugging percentage allowed (.456)
➡ 8th in lowest groundball/flyball ratio allowed (1.1), lowest stolen base percentage allowed (50.0%) and highest ERA at home (4.13)
➡ 9th in shutouts (1)
➡ 10th in highest batting average allowed (.283)
➡ Led the Giants in sacrifice bunts (8), ERA, wins, complete games (4) and shutouts (1)

Glenallen Hill

1996 Season

Yet another victim of the wave of injuries that hit the Giants, Glenallen Hill was in the midst of a solid second season as the Giants' right fielder when he was felled by a broken wrist on May 26. The injury—which looked worthy of an NFL highlight film in it's stomach-turning ugliness—kept Hill out of action until August. Despite the missed time, Hill maintained his 1995 level of production and solidified his status as a major league regular.

Hitting

Hill improved his presence at the plate in 1995, and he continued the improvement last year. A plate crowder, he crushes the inside fastball, particularly when there's a lefty on the mound. Although he's impatient at the plate, he's murder on knee-high pitches and his shots reach the depths of left field with regularity.

Baserunning & Defense

Hill has good speed and continues to work on his baserunning skills. He ran with caution after returning from the injury, so his basestealing numbers declined, but he's capable of duplicating his 25 steals of 1995 if he's healthy this year. Hill uses his speed to cover right field effectively. Though he committed seven errors during the '96 campaign, his arm remains terrific.

1997 Outlook

Hill's always had the talent—if not the focus—to be a successful major leaguer. Now, he finally appears to have proven himself. He is not only a good player, but he is still learning how to better exploit his talents. San Francisco has some question marks in the outfield, but Hill isn't one of them. If he can get 140 games under his belt, he's a good bet to establish some more career highs.

Position: RF
Bats: R **Throws:** R
Ht: 6' 2" **Wt:** 220

Opening Day Age: 32
Born: 3/22/65 in Santa Cruz, CA
ML Seasons: 8

Overall Statistics

	G	AB	R	H	D	T	HR	RBI	SB	BB	SO	Avg	OBP	Slg
1996	98	379	56	106	26	0	19	67	6	33	95	.280	.344	.499
Career	693	2308	326	607	116	13	107	351	83	182	522	.263	.318	.464

Where He Hits the Ball

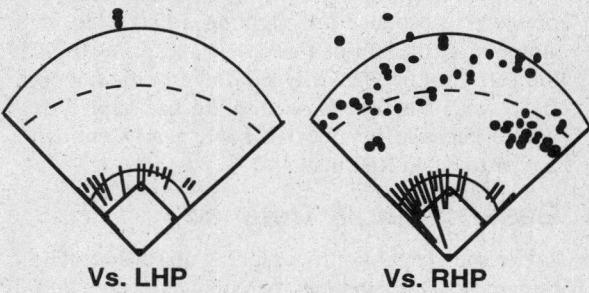

Vs. LHP   **Vs. RHP**

1996 Situational Stats

	AB	H	HR	RBI	Avg		AB	H	HR	RBI	Avg
Home	193	55	9	36	.285	LHP	71	26	7	15	.366
Road	186	51	10	31	.274	RHP	308	80	12	52	.260
First Half	170	46	10	31	.271	Sc Pos	108	36	2	42	.333
Scnd Half	209	60	9	36	.287	Clutch	56	10	0	6	.179

1996 Rankings (National League)

→ 5th in lowest batting average in the clutch (.179) and errors in right field (7)
→ Led the Giants in hit by pitch (6) and strike-outs

Stan Javier

1996 Season

Stan Javier was signed over the winter to bat lead-off and play center field, but he got hurt early on and never really got going. A strained hamstring put him on the disabled list in April and bothered him for most of the first half. The injury finally shelved him for good shortly after the All-Star break. When he was able to play, Javier posted what one would expect—nothing flashy, but decent workmanlike numbers.

Hitting

The switch-hitting Javier normally makes good contact and hits line drives from both sides of the plate, but doesn't draw quite enough walks to be a premier leadoff hitter. Last year, playing under pressure to produce and fighting a balky leg, he slumped at the top of the order, and didn't right himself until he was dropped down in the lineup. If he can't bat first or second, he has very little value, because he doesn't have nearly enough power to be an RBI man.

Baserunning & Defense

Javier's leg kept him from racking up steals, but he remained one of the best percentage basestealers around, swiping 14 bags in 16 attempts. He is a smart baserunner, utilizing his speed and smarts to score runs. Javier is a good defender with good range in center field. He hardly ever makes an error, but his arm is a bit weak.

1997 Outlook

Javier has a year left on his contract, so the Giants must find a way to use him. He seems to have fallen out of favor in center field, and his role may be reduced to that of a fourth outfielder. Still, with questions surrounding their other options in center, Javier could easily end up getting his regular job back.

Position: CF/RF
Bats: B **Throws:** R
Ht: 6' 0" **Wt:** 185

Opening Day Age: 33
Born: 1/9/64 in San Francisco de Macoris, DR
ML Seasons: 12
Pronunciation: HAHV-ee-air

Overall Statistics

	G	AB	R	H	D	T	HR	RBI	SB	BB	SO	Avg	OBP	Slg
1996	71	274	44	74	25	0	2	22	14	25	51	.270	.336	.383
Career	1160	3170	483	822	145	23	33	297	169	341	532	.259	.332	.351

Where He Hits the Ball

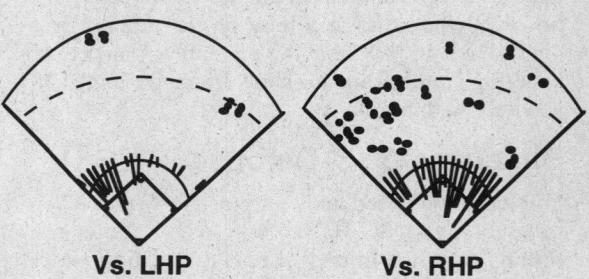

Vs. LHP   **Vs. RHP**

1996 Situational Stats

	AB	H	HR	RBI	Avg		AB	H	HR	RBI	Avg
Home	115	30	1	10	.261	LHP	78	22	1	5	.282
Road	159	44	1	12	.277	RHP	196	52	1	17	.265
First Half	251	67	2	18	.267	Sc Pos	71	14	0	18	.197
Scnd Half	23	7	0	4	.304	Clutch	33	8	0	7	.242

1996 Rankings (National League)

➡ 5th in batting average on a 3-1 count (.750)
➡ Led the Giants in batting average on a 3-1 count (.750)

Bill Mueller

1996 Season

Talk about a timely arrival. The promotion of Bill Mueller couldn't have been more fortuitous: it came a day after Matt Williams went on the disabled list. For the rest of the year, Mueller covered third base quite nicely, batting .330 and playing the field with confidence. By the end of the year it was clear that the Giants would need to find a spot for him, and after the season they stunned San Franciscans by trading Williams to the Indians, opening a position for Mueller. The only question is which position it will be, as Mueller can play both third and second.

Hitting

The switch-hitting Mueller doesn't pack the pop you'd expect from a third baseman. He makes up for it by spraying hits to all fields. Although his .330 average was a pleasant surprise, he's never hit lower than .297 as a professional. With good patience, a good eye and a great ability to make contact, Mueller makes an ideal number-two hitter.

Baserunning & Defense

Although he gets on base a lot, once he gets there, it's obvious that Mueller doesn't have much speed. He won't steal bases, but he is a good, smart baserunner. Mueller possesses sure hands and a strong arm at third, but his future seems to be at second base. He played eight games there last year, and looked fine.

1997 Outlook

The Giants obtained infielders Jeff Kent and Jose Vizcaino in the Williams deal, leaving them with several possible combinations for 1997. Vizcaino will probably succeed free agent Shawon Dunston as the shortstop, and Kent could wind up at either second or third, with Mueller taking the open position. Most likely Mueller will be the second sacker, and the Giants have confidence he'll do well.

Position: 3B
Bats: B **Throws:** R
Ht: 5'11" **Wt:** 175

Opening Day Age: 26
Born: 3/17/71 in Maryland Heights, MO
ML Seasons: 1
Pronunciation: MILL-err

Overall Statistics

	G	AB	R	H	D	T	HR	RBI	SB	BB	SO	Avg	OBP	Slg
1996	55	200	31	66	15	1	0	19	0	24	26	.330	.401	.415
Career	55	200	31	66	15	1	0	19	0	24	26	.330	.401	.415

Where He Hits the Ball

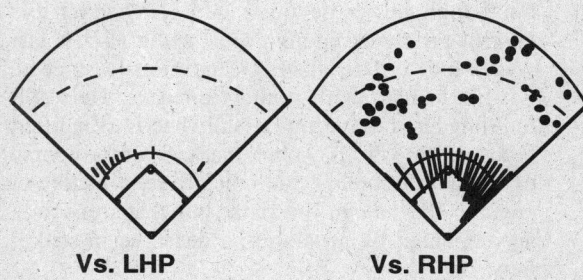

Vs. LHP   **Vs. RHP**

1996 Situational Stats

	AB	H	HR	RBI	Avg		AB	H	HR	RBI	Avg
Home	107	33	0	8	.308	LHP	28	9	0	3	.321
Road	93	33	0	11	.355	RHP	172	57	0	16	.331
First Half	2	1	0	0	.500	Sc Pos	40	15	0	19	.375
Scnd Half	198	65	0	19	.328	Clutch	30	9	0	5	.300

1996 Rankings (National League)

➡ Did not rank near the top or bottom in any category

William VanLandingham

1996 Season

After a terrible start, William VanLandingham rebounded to pitch decently over the last four months of the year. His year was a huge disappointment in light of his successful partial seasons in 1994 and '95, but he remained in the rotation and worked on his problems, and ended up leading the team with 32 games started. By the end of the year, he was showing occasional glimpses of his former effectiveness.

Pitching

VanLandingham's 90 MPH fastball has good movement—often too good. He's got a good sinker and slider, but when he can't control the fastball enough to get it over, he's lost. When he's on, though, he can be tough to hit. He had terrible control problems pitching out of the stretch last year, which inflated his ERA enormously, since he got hit so hard with runners on base. He's still building his stamina, and usually needs to be lifted before hitting the 100-pitch mark. Over the course of the season, he became much more effective at keeping the ball in the park, but that trend was accompanied by an alarming decrease in strikeouts.

Defense & Hitting

At the plate, VanLandingham fans half of the time and rarely does anything productive. He plays the field pretty well, but he has no move to first. Baserunners run on him until they run out of breath, and usually end up touching home plate before they return to the dugout.

1997 Outlook

VanLandingham's second-half recovery probably ensures that he'll begin 1997 in the starting rotation. Whether he remains there will depend on whether he conquers his control problems. If he's able to harness his talent, he has great upside, so Dusty Baker's characteristic patience may be VanLandingham's saving grace.

Position: SP
Bats: R **Throws:** R
Ht: 6' 2" **Wt:** 210

Opening Day Age: 26
Born: 7/16/70 in
Columbia, TN
ML Seasons: 3

Overall Statistics

	W	L	Pct.	ERA	G	GS	Sv	IP	H	BB	SO	HR	BR/IP
1996	9	14	.391	5.40	32	32	0	181.2	196	78	97	17	1.51
Career	23	19	.548	4.45	66	64	0	388.1	390	161	248	35	1.42

How Often He Throws Strikes

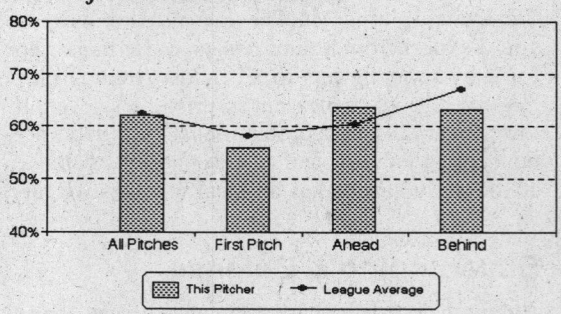

1996 Situational Stats

	W	L	ERA	Sv	IP		AB	H	HR	RBI	Avg
Home	4	9	5.80	0	99.1	LHB	301	87	9	43	.289
Road	5	5	4.92	0	82.1	RHB	410	109	8	58	.266
First Half	4	9	6.22	0	101.1	Sc Pos	179	60	3	81	.335
Scnd Half	5	5	4.37	0	80.1	Clutch	29	7	0	1	.241

1996 Rankings (National League)

➡ 1st in runners caught stealing (14)
➡ 2nd in highest ERA, highest ERA at home (5.80) and highest batting average allowed with runners in scoring position (.335)
➡ 3rd in losses and lowest strikeout/walk ratio (1.2)
➡ 4th in least strikeouts per 9 innings (4.8)
➡ 5th in stolen bases allowed (24) and highest ERA on the road (4.92)
➡ 8th in highest on-base percentage allowed (.352), most baserunners allowed per 9 innings (14.1) and lowest fielding percentage at pitcher (.935)
➡ 10th in lowest winning percentage
➡ Led the Giants in losses and games started

Allen Watson

Position: SP
Bats: L **Throws:** L
Ht: 6' 3" **Wt:** 195

Opening Day Age: 26
Born: 11/18/70 in
Jamaica, NY
ML Seasons: 4

1996 Season

A fresh start can be just the ticket for a player who hasn't realized his potential. Former first-round pick Allen Watson, who had never become the pitcher the Cardinals had hoped for, was sent to San Francisco as part of a package for Royce Clayton. Watson got off to a good start for the Giants before a tender elbow slowed him in the second half. Although he pitched in tough luck and got little run support, he was, all things considered, the closest thing the beleaguered staff had to an ace.

Pitching

Though not as hard a thrower as when he was drafted, Watson's fastball still hits the low 90s. He has a good curve which he disguises by dropping down. Watson also throws a change. He's aggressive at times, stubborn at others. Over the course of the season, he learned to come inside more with his fastball. He was throwing strikes more consistently last year, which boosted his strikeout-to-walk ratio to nearly two-to-one, but resulted in 28 longballs.

Defense & Hitting

Watson is a good fielder, but his pickoff move is adequate, at best. He has a high leg kick and runners will take off him, but his delivery is still reasonably quick, so a decent number are thrown out. An excellent athlete, Watson can hit by anyone's standards, not just a pitcher's. He batted .231 over 65 at bats, with three doubles and seven RBI. Dusty Baker even used him as a pinch hitter on three occasions, so it's possible he'll get to swing the bat even though he's been traded to an American League team.

1997 Season

Watson will get another fresh start in 1997; he's been dealt to the Angels for first baseman J.T. Snow. He pitched fairly well for the Giants last year considering the weak supporting cast behind him, and the Angels think he can win 10 or more games for them. If his elbow is sound, that's a very reachable goal.

Overall Statistics

	W	L	Pct.	ERA	G	GS	Sv	IP	H	BB	SO	HR	BR/IP
1996	8	12	.400	4.61	29	29	0	185.2	189	69	128	28	1.39
Career	27	33	.450	4.90	88	85	0	501.2	535	191	300	71	1.45

How Often He Throws Strikes

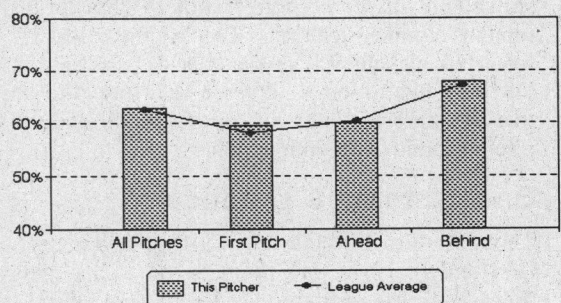

This Pitcher   League Average

1996 Situational Stats

	W	L	ERA	Sv	IP		AB	H	HR	RBI	Avg
Home	3	4	4.60	0	76.1	LHB	101	20	3	13	.198
Road	5	8	4.61	0	109.1	RHB	591	169	25	84	.286
First Half	6	8	4.11	0	116.0	Sc Pos	158	49	8	67	.310
Scnd Half	2	4	5.43	0	69.2	Clutch	48	16	3	12	.333

1996 Rankings (National League)

➡ 4th in lowest groundball/flyball ratio allowed (1.0) and highest batting average allowed with runners in scoring position (.310)
➡ 5th in home runs allowed
➡ 6th in highest slugging percentage allowed (.460) and most home runs allowed per 9 innings (1.36)
➡ 8th in runners caught stealing (11) and most GDPs induced per 9 innings (1.0)
➡ 9th in losses
➡ 10th in highest ERA on the road (4.61)
➡ Led the Giants in innings pitched, home runs allowed, wild pitches (9), GDPs induced (20), lowest batting average allowed (.273) and lowest on-base percentage allowed (.339)

S. F. Giants

Rick Wilkins

1996 Season

Ever since his monster 30-homer season with the Cubs in 1993, Rick Wilkins has been bothered by injuries and never has come close to that sort of production. In frustration, the Cubs dealt him to the Astros in '95, and last year, Houston sent him along to the Giants in a midseason deal. To everyone's surprise, he immediately recaptured the old magic, and for the final two months of the season, he played like it was 1993 all over again.

Hitting

Wilkins is a good fastball hitter, but has trouble adjusting to offspeed stuff. He's patient and generates good power to right field with his compact stroke, but his career-long problem with lefties remains a major weakness. Keeping the ball away from him negates his power, but he's learned to line base hits to left field when he's forced to do that. He almost always gets the ball in the air, and rarely grounds into double plays.

Baserunning & Defense

Though not a Gold Glove backstop, Wilkins is a first-rate receiver. He pounces on bunts, gets down-and-dirty on pitches in the dirt, and throws very well. The Giants used him a handful of times at first base, where he performed capably. On the basepaths, he's a slug, but always gives good effort and rarely overreaches himself.

1997 Outlook

The Giants were happy with Wilkins, and re-signed him to a one-year deal in December. He certainly will be the frontrunner to handle the starting catching duties. Wilkins may also be able to play first base part-time to keep his bat in the lineup while he rests his legs. If Wilkins has truly gotten over his ailments, he could put up surprisingly good numbers this year. Given his injury history, however, that may be a long shot.

Position: C
Bats: L **Throws:** R
Ht: 6' 2" **Wt:** 215

Opening Day Age: 29
Born: 6/4/67 in Jacksonville, FL
ML Seasons: 6

Overall Statistics

	G	AB	R	H	D	T	HR	RBI	SB	BB	SO	Avg	OBP	Slg
1996	136	411	53	100	18	2	14	59	0	67	121	.243	.344	.399
Career	606	1819	246	458	87	6	72	234	9	250	476	.252	.344	.425

Where He Hits the Ball

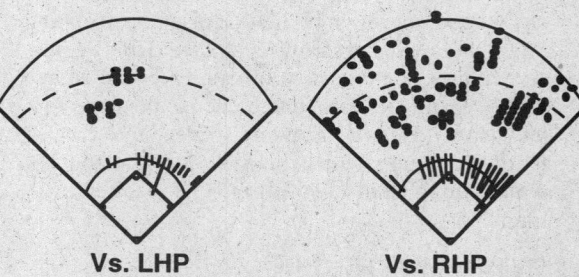

Vs. LHP   **Vs. RHP**

1996 Situational Stats

	AB	H	HR	RBI	Avg		AB	H	HR	RBI	Avg
Home	192	37	6	22	.193	LHP	64	11	3	9	.172
Road	219	63	8	37	.288	RHP	347	89	11	50	.256
First Half	221	50	6	21	.226	Sc Pos	114	25	4	44	.219
Scnd Half	190	50	8	38	.263	Clutch	63	16	1	14	.254

1996 Rankings (National League)

- ➡ 1st in sacrifice flies (10)
- ➡ 4th in lowest percentage of swings put into play (33.9%) and highest percentage of runners caught stealing as a catcher (29.0%)
- ➡ 6th in highest percentage of swings that missed (28.2%)
- ➡ 7th in intentional walks (13) and lowest batting average with runners in scoring position (.219)
- ➡ 8th in errors at catcher (8) and lowest percentage of extra bases taken as a runner (38.1%)

Matt Williams

Traded To
INDIANS

1996 Season

Matt Williams was on a Maris-like home run pace when the strike hit in 1994. Then he lost half of '95 to a broken foot. Last season he hoped to have a full campaign at last, but a bad throwing shoulder caused him to move to first base in July, and brought his season to a premature end soon thereafter. Although he managed to keep his average over .300, his power stroke wasn't as devastating as it had been when he was healthy. When the season ended the Giants traded him to the Cleveland Indians.

Hitting

An excellent fastball hitter, Williams has developed the patience to keep him from swinging at the curves which used to give him so much trouble. The other critical factor is his development as a hitter has been the way he's learned to hit the ball to all fields. This makes him particularly tough to pitch to because his opposite-field power is so deadly. He can go "up the ladder" and get to anything up in the strike zone.

Baserunning & Defense

When he's healthy, Williams is one of the best third basemen in the game. He's the total package, with a strong arm, soft hands and quick feet. He's an aggressive fielder, charging slowly-hit balls without hesitation. His complete lack of speed means that on the bases, all he tries to do is keep from running into outs.

1997 Outlook

Williams should be rehabbed and ready to go by Opening Day, which is good news for the Indians. The main question is whether his bad shoulder will allow him to play third base. If he can't, the Tribe will put him at first or DH and hope he stays healthy. If he does, he should be good for 40 or more homers.

Position: 3B/1B
Bats: R **Throws:** R
Ht: 6' 2" **Wt:** 216

Opening Day Age: 31
Born: 11/28/65 in Bishop, CA
ML Seasons: 10

Overall Statistics

	G	AB	R	H	D	T	HR	RBI	SB	BB	SO	Avg	OBP	Slg
1996	105	404	69	122	16	1	22	85	1	39	91	.302	.367	.510
Career	1120	4139	594	1092	179	25	247	732	29	272	872	.264	.312	.498

Where He Hits the Ball

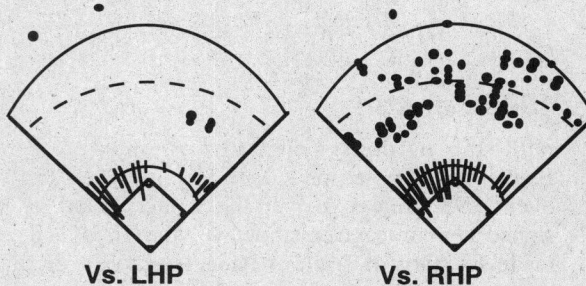

Vs. LHP   **Vs. RHP**

1996 Situational Stats

	AB	H	HR	RBI	Avg		AB	H	HR	RBI	Avg
Home	201	63	13	43	.313	LHP	90	21	7	21	.233
Road	203	59	9	42	.291	RHP	314	101	15	64	.322
First Half	321	96	17	68	.299	Sc Pos	126	40	8	64	.317
Scnd Half	83	26	5	17	.313	Clutch	54	14	2	8	.259

1996 Rankings (National League)

→ 5th in lowest percentage of swings put into play (35.5%)

→ 6th in lowest percentage of pitches taken (45.5%)

→ 9th in cleanup slugging percentage (.502) and errors at third base (13)

→ Led the Giants in sacrifice flies (6) and hit by pitch (6)

Jose Bautista

Position: RP
Bats: R **Throws:** R
Ht: 6' 2" **Wt:** 205

Opening Day Age: 32
Born: 7/26/64 in Bani, DR
ML Seasons: 8
Pronunciation: baugh-TEE-stah

Overall Statistics

	W	L	Pct.	ERA	G	GS	Sv	IP	H	BB	SO	HR	BR/IP
1996	3	4	.429	3.36	37	1	0	69.2	66	15	28	10	1.16
Career	30	40	.429	4.45	280	49	3	633.0	662	157	305	98	1.29

1996 Situational Stats

	W	L	ERA	Sv	IP		AB	H	HR	RBI	Avg
Home	3	2	3.61	0	42.1	LHB	115	33	6	21	.287
Road	0	2	2.96	0	27.1	RHB	150	33	4	19	.220
First Half	1	1	3.30	0	30.0	Sc Pos	67	20	4	31	.299
Scnd Half	2	3	3.40	0	39.2	Clutch	49	12	2	2	.245

1996 Season

Although hardly a celebrated triumph, Jose Bautista's 1996 season was a big improvement over 1995. Released over the winter, Bautista signed a minor league contract with the Giants and made six starts at Triple-A Phoenix before being called up in May. He was used infrequently, but pitched decently in a limited role.

Pitching, Defense & Hitting

Sporting a good slider and fastball in the high 80s, Bautista has good command but lacks the stuff to throw it past hitters. When he gets the ball up, it's easy to take him deep. He has a slide-step which holds runners well enough, and is a decent fielder. Bautista isn't any kind of hitter, but fortunately for the Giants, he didn't get too many chances.

1997 Outlook

Capable of long relief and spot starting, Bautista will be peddling his services now that the Giants have released him again. He pitched pretty well in 1996, and there are a lot of teams that need pitching. He should be able to hook on with somebody if his salary demands are reasonable.

Rich DeLucia

Position: RP
Bats: R **Throws:** R
Ht: 6' 0" **Wt:** 185

Opening Day Age: 32
Born: 10/7/64 in Wyomissing, PA
ML Seasons: 7
Pronunciation: de-LOOSH-uh

Overall Statistics

	W	L	Pct.	ERA	G	GS	Sv	IP	H	BB	SO	HR	BR/IP
1996	3	6	.333	5.84	56	0	0	61.2	62	31	55	8	1.51
Career	30	40	.429	4.69	217	49	1	499.0	486	217	378	72	1.41

1996 Situational Stats

	W	L	ERA	Sv	IP		AB	H	HR	RBI	Avg
Home	2	4	5.77	0	34.1	LHB	86	27	4	19	.314
Road	1	2	5.93	0	27.1	RHB	153	35	4	19	.229
First Half	3	2	5.45	0	33.0	Sc Pos	72	17	3	31	.236
Scnd Half	0	4	6.28	0	28.2	Clutch	128	34	2	17	.266

1996 Season

Bothered on-and-off all season by a pulled muscle in his rib cage, Rich DeLucia never really got untracked in 1996. The injury put him on the disabled list once and a shoulder injury put him there again. The injuries hampered him when he was able to pitch—especially when he tried to work on consecutive days.

Pitching, Defense & Hitting

DeLucia has a good fastball in the high 80s, along with a hard slider. His velocity is good but his pitches lack movement, and lefties give him tremendous trouble. He is good at holding runners and has a pretty good move to first. DeLucia also fields his position quite well and has been surprisingly successful in his infrequent at-bats.

1997 Outlook

DeLucia is signed through next season, so he'll probably be around to pitch middle relief. He's effective against right-handed hitters, which should be enough to give him a role in the Giants' bullpen. If he's healthy, he's capable of putting up much better numbers that he did last year.

Trent Hubbard

Position: CF/LF
Bats: R **Throws:** R
Ht: 5' 8" **Wt:** 180

Opening Day Age: 30
Born: 5/11/66 in
Chicago, IL
ML Seasons: 3

Overall Statistics

	G	AB	R	H	D	T	HR	RBI	SB	BB	SO	Avg	OBP	Slg
1996	55	89	15	19	5	2	2	14	2	11	27	.213	.307	.382
Career	97	172	31	44	10	3	6	26	4	22	37	.256	.344	.453

1996 Situational Stats

	AB	H	HR	RBI	Avg		AB	H	HR	RBI	Avg
Home	55	10	2	11	.182	LHP	30	6	1	5	.200
Road	34	9	0	3	.265	RHP	59	13	1	9	.220
First Half	58	13	1	12	.224	Sc Pos	29	8	0	9	.276
Scnd Half	31	6	1	2	.194	Clutch	20	3	0	1	.150

1996 Season

Still one more midseason pickup by the Giants, outfielder Trent Hubbard was claimed on waivers from the Rockies in August. He didn't get much of a chance to make an impression with his new club, but Hubbard has had four good years in a row at the Triple-A level, and the Giants hope to give him a longer look this spring.

Hitting, Baserunning & Defense

Hubbard never got a chance to play in Colorado, but his minor league record suggests that he's capable of hitting for a pretty good average and stealing some bases, albeit without much power or many walks. As a right-handed hitter, he's not an ideal bench player. He is a decent center fielder with good speed and a fair arm. After 49 major league games in the outfield, he still hasn't made an error.

1997 Outlook

At age 30, Hubbard can't be regarded as a hot prospect. However, he's a capable hitter, and if things break right for him in the Giants' muddled center field situation, he could end up getting his first real opportunity to play in the majors.

Tom Lampkin

Position: C
Bats: L **Throws:** R
Ht: 5'11" **Wt:** 185

Opening Day Age: 33
Born: 3/4/64 in
Cincinnati, OH
ML Seasons: 7

Overall Statistics

	G	AB	R	H	D	T	HR	RBI	SB	BB	SO	Avg	OBP	Slg
1996	66	177	26	41	8	0	6	29	1	20	22	.232	.324	.379
Career	281	557	67	123	21	2	12	70	12	63	75	.221	.305	.330

1996 Situational Stats

	AB	H	HR	RBI	Avg		AB	H	HR	RBI	Avg
Home	98	22	5	22	.224	LHP	24	5	1	5	.208
Road	79	19	1	7	.241	RHP	153	36	5	24	.235
First Half	99	25	3	13	.253	Sc Pos	52	13	3	25	.250
Scnd Half	78	16	3	16	.205	Clutch	36	10	1	9	.278

1996 Season

For a backup catcher, Tom Lampkin did a surprisingly good job last year. His offense was adequate, and his defense was a revelation. He had great success at throwing out basestealers, and worked particularly well with Mark Gardner and Allen Watson.

Hitting, Baserunning & Defense

As a hitter, Lampkin has no real strengths but very few weaknesses. He can draw a walk, and he hits with occasional power. He bats lefty, which helps, and southpaws don't seem to bother him very much. Although he has virtually no speed, he's a smart baserunner. His arm proved to be surprisingly strong last year, as he threw out over one-half of the runners who tried to steal on him.

1997 Outlook

An adequate backup, Lampkin will probably have to go elsewhere to see major league action next year. He is 33 years old, and the Giants have some younger receivers to break in, but he should be able to help some one else off the bench.

Jim Poole

Position: RP
Bats: L **Throws:** L
Ht: 6' 2" **Wt:** 203

Opening Day Age: 30
Born: 4/28/66 in
Rochester, NY
ML Seasons: 7

Overall Statistics

	W	L	Pct.	ERA	G	GS	Sv	IP	H	BB	SO	HR	BR/IP
1996	6	1	.857	2.86	67	0	0	50.1	44	27	38	5	1.41
Career	15	7	.682	3.17	253	0	3	227.1	185	97	173	22	1.24

1996 Situational Stats

	W	L	ERA	Sv	IP		AB	H	HR	RBI	Avg
Home	2	1	2.86	0	28.1	LHB	88	19	2	10	.216
Road	4	0	2.86	0	22.0	RHB	98	25	3	15	.255
First Half	4	0	3.04	0	26.2	Sc Pos	72	12	1	21	.167
Scnd Half	2	1	2.66	0	23.2	Clutch	82	15	2	8	.183

1996 Season

Acquired from Cleveland in a midseason trade, lefty reliever Jim Poole changed uniforms and kept right on rolling. Deadly against left-handed hitters, Poole pitched brilliantly for the Giants before tailing off in September. Giants' skipper Dusty Baker called for him often, and his 67 appearances marked a career high.

Pitching, Defense & Hitting

Poole's high-80s fastball and change are good enough to make him respectable against right-handed hitters, but his out pitch is a curveball that really dominates lefties. He can move it around both sides of the plate, tying hitters in knots. On the rare occasions when he can't get it over, he struggles. Poole holds runners decently and fields his position well. His first two career at-bats last year amounted to nothing.

1997 Outlook

It is no secret how valuable a lefty in the pen can be, so Poole will probably be back with the Giants for another 60-inning season. As a Madison Avenue genius might say, "Poole gets the job done, one lefty at a time."

Kirk Rueter

Position: SP
Bats: L **Throws:** L
Ht: 6' 3" **Wt:** 195

Opening Day Age: 26
Born: 12/1/70 in
Centralia, IL
ML Seasons: 4
Pronunciation:
REE-ter

Overall Statistics

	W	L	Pct.	ERA	G	GS	Sv	IP	H	BB	SO	HR	BR/IP
1996	6	8	.429	3.97	20	19	0	102.0	109	27	46	12	1.33
Career	26	14	.650	3.88	63	62	0	327.1	338	77	155	31	1.27

1996 Situational Stats

	W	L	ERA	Sv	IP		AB	H	HR	RBI	Avg
Home	3	6	4.65	0	62.0	LHB	74	24	2	8	.324
Road	3	2	2.93	0	40.0	RHB	322	85	10	31	.264
First Half	5	6	4.34	0	76.2	Sc Pos	80	20	3	24	.250
Scnd Half	1	2	2.84	0	25.1	Clutch	9	1	0	0	.111

1996 Season

Another midseason import, 26-year-old Kirk Rueter was acquired by San Francisco from the Expos at the trade deadline. Rueter had always given the Giants fits when he pitched for Montreal, and he turned in three very good starts after his September recall.

Pitching, Defense & Hitting

As a soft-tossing lefty, Rueter needs good control to be effective. He throws a fastball in the mid-80s, but relies on a great change and good curve to get batters out. During his time with the Giants, he was encouraged to throw his fastball inside more and the results were positive. Minor injuries and a lack of stamina have always been a problem. Rueter wields a good glove and has a very good pick-off move. He has a weak bat.

1997 Outlook

Ever since he ran off an 8-0 mark as a rookie in 1993, Rueter has been looking to recapture the magic. It may happen with the Giants, who like his style. They'll likely entrust him with a rotation spot and hope that he can withstand the physical toil for an entire season.

Steve Scarsone

Position: 2B/3B
Bats: R **Throws:** R
Ht: 6' 2" **Wt:** 195

Opening Day Age: 30
Born: 4/11/66 in Anaheim, CA
ML Seasons: 5
Pronunciation: scar-SONE-ee

Overall Statistics

	G	AB	R	H	D	T	HR	RBI	SB	BB	SO	Avg	OBP	Slg
1996	105	283	28	62	12	1	5	23	2	25	91	.219	.286	.322
Career	299	752	101	183	39	4	20	80	5	59	237	.243	.303	.386

1996 Situational Stats

	AB	H	HR	RBI	Avg		AB	H	HR	RBI	Avg
Home	142	36	4	16	.254	LHP	66	20	1	5	.303
Road	141	26	1	7	.184	RHP	217	42	4	18	.194
First Half	179	43	4	15	.240	Sc Pos	72	13	1	18	.181
Scnd Half	104	19	1	8	.183	Clutch	52	11	2	8	.212

1996 Season

Versatile Steve Scarsone had plenty of opportunities to play last year because of injuries to his teammates. No one expected him to keep producing the way he had in 1995, but his dropoff at the plate last year was still rather severe.

Hitting, Baserunning & Defense

Scarsone's a lowball hitter who can do some damage to a lefty. Righthanders have no problem with him, however. He has a little bit of power, but not much discipline at the plate, and he's struck out in nearly a third of his career at-bats. Scarsone can sub anywhere in the infield and do a pretty good job. His range isn't very good, but he has a good arm and good hands. He doesn't have a lot of speed, and doesn't try to run much, but he knows how to make the most of what he has when running the bases.

1997 Outlook

Although he was released by the Giants at season's end, Scarsone will probably show up somewhere on a major league bench next year. He can help a team in a variety of roles, and his bat will probably rebound a bit if he's given a chance.

Robby Thompson

Position: 2B
Bats: R **Throws:** R
Ht: 5'11" **Wt:** 173

Opening Day Age: 34
Born: 5/10/62 in West Palm Beach, FL
ML Seasons: 11

Overall Statistics

	G	AB	R	H	D	T	HR	RBI	SB	BB	SO	Avg	OBP	Slg
1996	63	227	35	48	11	1	5	21	2	24	69	.211	.301	.335
Career	1304	4612	671	1187	238	39	119	458	103	439	987	.257	.329	.403

1996 Situational Stats

	AB	H	HR	RBI	Avg		AB	H	HR	RBI	Avg
Home	112	21	2	10	.188	LHP	54	14	2	5	.259
Road	115	27	3	11	.235	RHP	173	34	3	16	.197
First Half	185	42	5	16	.227	Sc Pos	57	12	0	13	.211
Scnd Half	42	6	0	5	.143	Clutch	27	7	0	2	.259

1996 Season

It would be hard to find a player whose career has degenerated as quickly as Robby Thompson's has. Even since he signed a three-year contract after his career year in 1993, he's been plagued with injuries. Last year was more of the same: he missed time with assorted ailments, and didn't play well when he did manage to make it onto the field.

Hitting, Baserunning & Defense

Most of Thompson's skills are in the past tense. He used to be a good contact hitter, but injuries have forced him to make adjustments that have opened holes in his swing. Defense used to be his forte, but even with good positioning, his range is now below average. He's still good on the double play, but lacks his old flexibility. His speed is mostly gone, too, and he doesn't run much any more.

1997 Outlook

Thompson has always been well-liked, and it was difficult to see his career wind down this way. The Giants bought out the last year of his contract and released him just after season's end. He may get a tryout with another team, but don't bank on him sticking.

Other San Francisco Giants

Shawn Barton (Pos: LHP, Age: 33)

	W	L	Pct.	ERA	G	GS	Sv	IP	H	BB	SO	HR	BR/IP
1996	0	0	-	9.72	7	0	0	8.1	19	1	3	2	2.40
Career	4	2	.667	4.71	73	0	1	65.0	66	27	29	6	1.43

Barton was released by the Giants following the '96 season after surrendering 19 hits in only eight innings of relief work (9.72 ERA). At 34, he'll be hard-pressed to stay in the majors. 1997 Outlook: D

Kim Batiste (Pos: 3B, Age: 29, Bats: R)

	G	AB	R	H	D	T	HR	RBI	SB	BB	SO	Avg	OBP	Slg
1996	54	130	17	27	6	0	3	11	3	5	33	.208	.235	.323
Career	251	658	59	154	23	1	10	64	4	14	120	.234	.250	.318

After three stints with the Giants last season, Batiste was released in October. He's OK defensively at third and short, but his lack of plate discipline (14/120 lifetime BB/K ratio) has crippled his career. 1997 Outlook: C

Steve Bourgeois (Pos: RHP, Age: 22)

	W	L	Pct.	ERA	G	GS	Sv	IP	H	BB	SO	HR	BR/IP
1996	1	3	.250	6.30	15	5	0	40.0	60	21	17	4	2.03
Career	1	3	.250	6.30	15	5	0	40.0	60	21	17	4	2.03

Bourgeois has had a reasonable amount of success in the minors, but did not fare well in his 15 appearances with San Francisco. His poor control and low strikeout rates have hurt him, but he's still young. 1997 Outlook: C

Jay Canizaro (Pos: 2B, Age: 23, Bats: R)

	G	AB	R	H	D	T	HR	RBI	SB	BB	SO	Avg	OBP	Slg
1996	43	120	11	24	4	1	2	8	0	9	38	.200	.260	.300
Career	43	120	11	24	4	1	2	8	0	9	38	.200	.260	.300

Canizaro was useful as a utility infielder after the Giants called him up in the second half of the season, but he was a non-factor with the bat. That didn't faze San Francisco, so he should be back this year. 1997 Outlook: B

Dan Carlson (Pos: RHP, Age: 27)

	W	L	Pct.	ERA	G	GS	Sv	IP	H	BB	SO	HR	BR/IP
1996	1	0	1.000	2.70	5	0	0	10.0	13	2	4	2	1.50
Career	1	0	1.000	2.70	5	0	0	10.0	13	2	4	2	1.50

Carlson pitched well out of the bullpen last season in September after racking up impressive numbers at Triple-A Phoenix (13-6, 3.44 ERA, 124 K's in 146-plus innings). He should contribute this season. 1997 Outlook: B

Doug Creek (Pos: LHP, Age: 28)

	W	L	Pct.	ERA	G	GS	Sv	IP	H	BB	SO	HR	BR/IP
1996	0	2	.000	6.52	63	0	0	48.1	45	32	38	11	1.59
Career	0	2	.000	5.73	69	0	0	55.0	47	35	48	11	1.49

Creek is overpowering on the mound, but he needs a map to find the strike zone (32 BB's in 48-plus innings). The Giants would like to view him as insurance for struggling closer Rod Beck. 1997 Outlook: B

Wilson Delgado (Pos: SS, Age: 21, Bats: B)

	G	AB	R	H	D	T	HR	RBI	SB	BB	SO	Avg	OBP	Slg
1996	6	22	3	8	0	0	0	2	1	1	5	.364	.440	.364
Career	6	22	3	8	0	0	0	2	1	1	5	.364	.440	.364

In a meteoric rise through the minor league ranks, Delgado reached the majors in September (.364 BA in six starts). Depending upon what the Giants do with their myriad of infielders, Delgado could start next season. 1997 Outlook: B

Mel Hall (Pos: LF, Age: 36, Bats: L)

	G	AB	R	H	D	T	HR	RBI	SB	BB	SO	Avg	OBP	Slg
1996	25	25	3	3	0	0	0	5	0	1	4	.120	.148	.120
Career	1276	4237	568	1171	229	25	134	620	31	267	575	.276	.318	.437

Hall saw his first major league action in four years when he began last season as the Giants' primary left-handed pinch hitter. After he compiled a .120 average through May, he was quickly released. 1997 Outlook: D

Chris Hook (Pos: RHP, Age: 28)

	W	L	Pct.	ERA	G	GS	Sv	IP	H	BB	SO	HR	BR/IP
1996	0	1	.000	7.43	10	0	0	13.1	16	14	4	3	2.25
Career	5	2	.714	5.89	55	0	0	65.2	71	43	44	10	1.74

Hook was released at the end of last season after compiling a 5.89 ERA during his two years in the Giants' bullpen. He's still relatively young at 28, but he has never been able to find the strike zone. 1997 Outlook: D

Dax Jones (Pos: CF, Age: 26, Bats: R)

	G	AB	R	H	D	T	HR	RBI	SB	BB	SO	Avg	OBP	Slg
1996	34	58	7	10	0	2	1	7	2	8	12	.172	.269	.293
Career	34	58	7	10	0	2	1	7	2	8	12	.172	.269	.293

After a stellar year at Triple-A Phoenix, Jones spent August and September securing occasional playing time in the Giants' outfield. He struggled at the plate (.172 BA), but might return next season. 1997 Outlook: C

Dave McCarty (Pos: 1B/RF, Age: 27, Bats: R)

	G	AB	R	H	D	T	HR	RBI	SB	BB	SO	Avg	OBP	Slg
1996	91	175	16	38	3	0	6	24	2	18	43	.217	.294	.337
Career	270	731	84	164	30	5	9	63	7	50	177	.224	.281	.316

McCarty started extensively at first base in July and August following the trade of Mark Carreon, but did not swing the bat effectively, compiling a .217 average through 175 at-bats. His future is in doubt. 1997 Outlook: C

Dan Peltier (Pos: 1B, Age: 28, Bats: L)

	G	AB	R	H	D	T	HR	RBI	SB	BB	SO	Avg	OBP	Slg
1996	31	59	3	15	2	0	0	9	0	7	9	.254	.328	.288
Career	108	243	27	62	9	1	1	28	0	27	39	.255	.330	.313

Peltier garnered some playing time with the Giants at first base in June and July before returning to Triple-A Phoenix. He was unimpressive at the plate (.288 slugging), and at 29, is certainly no prospect. 1997 Outlook: C

Tim Scott (Pos: RHP, **Age:** 30)

	W	L	Pct.	ERA	G	GS	Sv	IP	H	BB	SO	HR	BR/IP
1996	5	7	.417	4.64	65	0	1	66.0	65	30	47	8	1.44
Career	23	12	.657	3.84	259	0	5	293.0	278	126	237	22	1.38

Cincinnati acquired him in October on waivers, Scott could be a valuable addition to the Reds' bullpen. Despite his recent problems, his strikeout rates are still high—a positive sign. 1997 Outlook: B

Steve Soderstrom (Pos: RHP, **Age:** 24)

	W	L	Pct.	ERA	G	GS	Sv	IP	H	BB	SO	HR	BR/IP
1996	2	0	1.000	5.27	3	3	0	13.2	16	6	9	1	1.61
Career	2	0	1.000	5.27	3	3	0	13.2	16	6	9	1	1.61

Soderstrom started three September games for the Giants, and won two of the decisions despite posting a 5.27 ERA. He might get a shot at the rotation this year, but his low strikeout rates are worrisome. 1997 Outlook: C

Keith Williams (Pos: RF, **Age:** 24, **Bats:** R)

	G	AB	R	H	D	T	HR	RBI	SB	BB	SO	Avg	OBP	Slg
1996	9	20	0	5	0	0	0	0	0	0	6	.250	.250	.250
Career	9	20	0	5	0	0	0	0	0	0	6	.250	.250	.250

Williams was one of the many substitutes that were used by the Giants to fill the shoes of injured outfielder Glenallen Hill last summer. He had a decent year in the minors and could surface again this year. 1997 Outlook: C

Desi Wilson (Pos: 1B, **Age:** 27, **Bats:** L)

	G	AB	R	H	D	T	HR	RBI	SB	BB	SO	Avg	OBP	Slg
1996	41	118	10	32	2	0	2	12	0	12	27	.271	.338	.339
Career	41	118	10	32	2	0	2	12	0	12	27	.271	.338	.339

As the regular first baseman for the last two months of the season, Wilson showed little power or ability to get on base. The Giants' lack of production at first base was a critical offensive weakness. 1997 Outlook: C

San Francisco Giants Minor League Prospects

Organization Overview:

Last season revealed a lot about the quality of the Giants' organization. At one time or another, just about every one of their starters went down with a serious injury. As a result, many of their minor leaguers were pressed into service at the major league level. Of the ones who got significant playing time, just about every single young player—with the notable exceptions of Bill Mueller and Shawn Estes—were huge disappointments. The Giants took another hit to their talent base when their first-round pick in the '96 draft, Matt White, was declared a free agent due to a procedural error on the part of the Giants. The blunder was only the latest embarassment during a series of fruitless drafts. The complete lack of young talent in the system has created even more problems for a cash-strapped operation that would like to try to build from within. The trade of Matt Williams was mostly dictated by financial considerations, but it also brought in something that had been in short supply: young pitching talent—namely, Julian Tavarez. Now there are even fewer veterans left to cash in, and the system is dangerously short of prospects. If the established players remain injury-prone, the lack of depth within the system may be further exposed.

Jacob Cruz

Position: OF **Opening Day Age:** 24
Bats: L **Throws:** L **Born:** 1/28/73 in
Ht: 6' 0" **Wt:** 175 Oxnard, CA

Recent Statistics

	G	AB	R	H	D	T	HR	RBI	SB	BB	SO	AVG
96 AAA Phoenix	121	435	60	124	26	4	7	75	5	62	77	.285
96 NL San Fran.	33	77	10	18	3	0	1	10	0	12	24	.234
96 MLE	121	417	49	106	22	2	5	61	3	51	81	.254

Jacob Cruz's stock sure took a tumble last year. The left-handed line-drive hitter needed to develop more power to make it in right field, but he did just the opposite. His power game regressed at Triple-A, and he failed to distinguish himself in a short trial with the Giants. He's a good right fielder, but the Giants expected more out of their supplemental first-round pick from '94. It's been a while since he was called "the best pure hitter in the system," and it's time to step it up now.

Keith Foulke

Position: P **Opening Day Age:** 24
Bats: R **Throws:** R **Born:** 10/19/72 in
Ht: 6' 1" **Wt:** 195 Ellsworth, SD

Recent Statistics

	W	L	ERA	G	GS	Sv	IP	H	R	BB	SO	HR
94 A Everett	2	0	0.93	4	4	0	19.1	17	4	3	22	0
95 A San Jose	13	6	3.50	28	26	0	177.1	166	85	32	168	16
96 AA Shreveport	12	7	2.76	27	27	0	182.2	149	61	35	129	16

Righthander Keith Foulke has good durability, remarkable control and a drop-dead change-up. The only problem is that his fastball is only good enough for batting practice. Obviously, he can get by with his limited arsenal; the point is that no one is going to give him the benefit of the doubt on his way to the majors. He was pitching in a great pitchers' park last year, but things will be different when he reaches the run-crazed Pacific Coast League this year. Now we'll see what he's really made of.

Marcus Jensen

Position: C **Opening Day Age:** 24
Bats: B **Throws:** R **Born:** 12/14/72 in
Ht: 6' 4" **Wt:** 195 Oakland, CA

Recent Statistics

	G	AB	R	H	D	T	HR	RBI	SB	BB	SO	AVG
96 AAA Phoenix	120	405	41	107	22	4	5	53	1	44	95	.264
96 NL San Fran.	9	19	4	4	1	0	0	4	0	8	7	.211
96 MLE	120	390	33	92	18	2	3	43	0	36	101	.236

For years, the Giants have been waiting patiently for Marcus Jensen to mature enough to be their full-time catcher. At last, the time may be at hand. The tall, lean, switch-hitting receiver put in a full year at Triple-A, refining his defensive technique and showing that he can hold his own at the plate. His arm and pitch-calling are well-respected, and his defense will be a major asset to the Giants. If they turn the catcher's job over to him this year, he'll probably hit enough to stay in the lineup. Down the line, he could add some power.

Doug Mirabelli

Position: C **Opening Day Age:** 26
Bats: R **Throws:** R **Born:** 10/18/70 in
Ht: 6' 1" **Wt:** 205 Kingman, AZ

Recent Statistics

	G	AB	R	H	D	T	HR	RBI	SB	BB	SO	AVG
96 AAA Phoenix	14	47	10	14	7	0	0	7	0	4	7	.298
96 AA Shreveport	115	380	60	112	23	0	21	70	0	76	49	.295
96 NL San Fran.	9	18	2	4	1	0	0	1	0	3	4	.222
96 MLE	129	412	59	111	26	0	18	64	0	58	60	.269

No one knew Doug Mirabelli was this good. He spent most of '94 and '95 backing up the Giants' other catching prospects, but last year he broke out with a season that moved him almost to the head of the class. He batted close to .300, hit for great power, showed remarkable strike-zone judgment, and threw out close to half of the runners who tried to steal on him. His season was so out of context with the rest of his career that the Giants still refuse to believe it. At best, they see him as a backup to their preferred catching prospect, Marcus Jensen. But if Jensen falters and Mirabelli sneaks into the lineup, he could continue to surprise.

Russ Ortiz

Position: P
Bats: R **Throws:** R
Ht: 6' 1" **Wt:** 190

Opening Day Age: 22
Born: 6/5/74 in Van Nuys, CA

Recent Statistics

	W	L	ERA	G	GS	Sv	IP	H	R	BB	SO	HR
95 A San Jose	0	1	1.50	5	0	0	6.0	4	1	2	7	0
95 A Bellingham	2	0	0.52	25	0	11	34.1	19	4	13	55	1
96 A San Jose	0	0	0.25	34	0	23	36.2	16	2	20	63	0
96 AA Shreveport	1	2	4.05	26	0	13	26.2	22	14	21	29	0

The next great closer for the Giants may be righthander Russ Ortiz. He throws in the mid-90s—harder than just about anyone in the system. In A-ball last year, he gave up one earned run in 34 games, and struck out almost *two* men per inning. That showing convinced the Giants that he was ready to move up to Double-A. He didn't fare nearly as well there, but he saved 13 more games to finish with 36 on the year. If the much-anticipated trade of Rod Beck finally happens, Ortiz may soon find himself in the San Francisco bullpen.

Dante Powell

Position: OF
Bats: R **Throws:** R
Ht: 6' 2" **Wt:** 185

Opening Day Age: 23
Born: 8/25/73 in Long Beach, CA

Recent Statistics

	G	AB	R	H	D	T	HR	RBI	SB	BB	SO	AVG
94 A Everett	41	165	31	51	15	1	5	25	27	19	47	.309
94 A San Jose	1	4	0	2	0	1	0	0	0	0	1	.500
95 A San Jose	135	505	74	125	23	8	10	70	43	46	131	.248
96 A Shreveport	135	508	92	142	27	2	21	78	43	72	92	.280
96 AAA Phoenix	2	8	0	2	0	1	0	0	0	2	3	.250
96 MLE	137	498	78	126	23	1	18	66	30	53	102	.253

With their first-round pick in the '92 draft, the Giants took a center fielder with exciting tools named Calvin Murray. Murray didn't work out, so in '94, they tried it again. They selected Dante Powell with their first-round pick, a raw center fielder in exactly the same mold. Powell, however, has developed into a multi-dimensional threat. He can draw a walk, steal a base, hit for power, cover center field with ease, and he was voted both the fastest and the most exciting player in the Texas League last year. Still only 23, he has a lot of growth left and possibly the highest ceiling of any prospect in the system.

Armando Rios

Position: OF
Bats: L **Throws:** L
Ht: 5' 9" **Wt:** 178

Opening Day Age: 25
Born: 9/13/71 in Santurce, PR

Recent Statistics

	G	AB	R	H	D	T	HR	RBI	SB	BB	SO	AVG
94 A Clinton	119	407	67	120	23	4	8	60	16	59	69	.295
95 A San Jose	128	488	76	143	34	3	8	75	51	74	75	.293
96 AA Shreveport	92	329	62	93	22	2	12	49	9	44	42	.283
96 MLE	92	316	52	80	19	1	9	41	6	32	45	.253

This kid just keeps surprising people. Everyone said he was too short to be a power hitter, but he started to really juice the ball last year. That, combined with his patience at the plate and ability to make good contact, has made him one of the best offensive prospects in the system. And he's hardly one-dimensional, either—he threw out 15 baserunners in only 85 games in right field, and his arm was voted the best in the Texas League. He's been a big basestealer in the past, although he didn't run much last year. That's some package. He's a little old at age 25, but he can play.

Benji Simonton

Position: 1B
Bats: R **Throws:** R
Ht: 6' 1" **Wt:** 225

Opening Day Age: 24
Born: 5/12/72 in Pittsburg, CA

Recent Statistics

	G	AB	R	H	D	T	HR	RBI	SB	BB	SO	AVG
93 A Clinton	100	310	52	79	18	4	12	49	8	40	112	.255
94 A Clinton	67	237	47	64	16	4	14	57	10	52	73	.270
94 A San Jose	68	259	41	77	20	0	14	51	0	32	86	.297
95 A San Jose	61	225	38	65	9	6	8	37	7	40	78	.289
95 AA Shreveport	38	108	18	33	9	3	4	30	3	11	32	.306
96 AA Shreveport	137	469	86	117	25	1	23	76	6	101	144	.249
96 AAA Phoenix	1	4	1	3	0	0	1	2	0	1	0	.750
96 MLE	138	458	73	105	22	0	19	65	4	73	155	.229

Big first baseman Benji Simonton gives you a lot of power and a lot of walks; the only question is whether he can make it on that alone. He's got no speed, strikes out too much, and plays indifferent defense, so he'll need to put on a real power show this spring to have any hope of grabbing the Giants' first base spot. Boston took a flyer on him in the '95 Rule V draft, but found his utility to be too limited, and returned him to the Giants shortly thereafter. Their estimation was probably accurate.

Others to Watch

The Giants' best long-term pitching prospect is righthander **Darin Blood**, who was named the California League Pitcher of the Year. Blood went 17-6 and led the league with 193 strikeouts. At age 22, he'll start the year at Double-A and go from there. . . Offseason knee surgery threatened to keep **Chris Singleton** out of the lineup well into the season, but the speedy outfielder returned for opening day and showed no ill effects. The left-handed hitter batted close to .300 at Double-A, and will advance to Triple-A to refine his plate discipline. . . The Giants took a risk by selecting high school pitcher **Joe Fontentot** with their first-round pick in the '95 draft, but so far, Fontentot has vindicated the selection. At age 19, he went 9-4 in the California League, holding his own in the advanced Class A league. With a good fastball and a hard slider, Fontenot has all the makings of a power pitcher. . . Switch-hitting first baseman **Jesse Ibarra** has a stellar glove, and hits for both power and average. The only problem is that he'll be making his first appearance above A-ball this year, at age 24.

About STATS, Inc.

STATS, Inc. is the nation's leading independent sports information and statistical analysis company, providing detailed sports services for a wide array of clients.

As one of the fastest-growing sports companies—in 1994, we ranked 144th on the "Inc. 500" list of fastest-growing privately held firms—STATS provides the most up-to-the-minute sports information to professional teams, print and broadcast media, software developers and interactive service providers around the country. Some of our major clients are ESPN, the Associated Press, *The Sporting News*, Electronic Arts, Motorola, SONY and Topps. Much of the information we provide is available to the public via STATS On-Line. With a computer and a modem, you can follow action in the four major professional sports, as well as NCAA football and basketball. . . as it happens!

STATS Publishing, a division of STATS, Inc., produces 11 annual books, including the *Major League Handbook*, *The Scouting Notebook*, the *Pro Football Handbook*, the *Pro Basketball Handbook* and the *Hockey Handbook*. These publications deliver STATS' expertise to fans, scouts, general managers and media around the country.

In addition, STATS offers the most innovative—and fun—fantasy sports games around, from *Bill James Fantasy Baseball* and *Bill James Classic Baseball* to *STATS Fantasy Football* and *STATS Fantasy Hoops*.

Information technology has grown by leaps and bounds in the last decade, and STATS will continue to be at the forefront as both a vendor and supplier of the most up-to-date, in-depth sports information available. For those of you on the information superhighway, you can always catch STATS at our site on America Online (Keyword: STATS).

For more information on our products, or on joining our reporter network, write us at:

STATS, Inc.
8131 Monticello Ave.
Skokie, IL 60076-3300

. . . or call us at 1-800-63-STATS (1-800-637-8287). Outside the U.S., dial 1-847-676-3383.

Index

Hartgraves, Dean	391	Hutton, Mark	476	Karl, Scott	204	Linton, Doug	192
Haselman, Bill	92	Hyers, Tim	169	Karros, Eric	527	Lira, Felipe	157
Hatteberg, Scott	95			Kaufman, Brad	687	Liriano, Nelson	633
Hawblitzel, Ryan	465			Keagle, Greg	169	Listach, Pat	205
Hawkins, LaTroy	243	**I**		Kelly, Mike	440	Little, Mark	344
Hayes, Charlie	264			Kelly, Pat	267	Livingstone, Scott	684
Haynes, Jimmy	67	Ibanez, Raul	319	Kelly, Roberto	227	Lloyd, Graeme	265
Heflin, Bronson	612	Incaviglia, Pete	67	Kelly, Tom	222	Loaiza, Esteban	634
Held, Dan	614	Isringhausen, Jason	578	Kendall, Jason	623	Lockhart, Keith	180
Helling, Rick	486			Kent, Jeff	142	Loewer, Carlton	614
Helms, Wesley	393			Key, Jimmy	254	Lofton, Kenny	129
Helton, Todd	467			Keyser, Brian	120	Loiselle, Rich	637
Henderson, Rickey	673			Kiefer, Mark	194	Lomon, Kevin	391
Henneman, Mike	328	**J**		Kieschnick, Brooks	417	Lopez, Albie	147
Henry, Doug	585			Kile, Darryl	504	Lopez, Javy	380
Hentgen, Pat	353	Jackson, Damian	146	King, Jeff	624	Lopez, Luis	685
Heredia, Felix	487	Jackson, Danny	649	Kingery, Mike	625	Lopez, Mendy	195
Heredia, Gil	339	Jackson, Mike	303	Kingsale, Gene	70	Loretta, Mark	215
Hermanson, Dustin	686	Jacome, Jason	191	Kirby, Wayne	539	Lovullo, Torey	292
Hernandez, Carlos	540	Jaha, John	203	Klassen, Danny	221	Ludwick, Eric	663
Hernandez, Jose	401	James, Dion	267	Klesko, Ryan	378	Lukachyk, Rob	564
Hernandez, Livan	492	James, Mike	35	Klingenbeck, Scott	243	Luke, Matt	267
Hernandez, Ramon	294	Janzen, Marty	363	Klink, Joe	317	Luuloa, Keith	47
Hernandez, Roberto	106	Jarvis, Kevin	436	Knackert, Brent	96	Lyons, Curt	443
Hernandez, Xavier	513	Javier, Stan	700	Knight, Ray	419		
Herrera, Jose	278	Jefferies, Gregg	597	Knoblauch, Chuck	228		
Hershiser, Orel	128	Jefferson, Reggie	82	Knorr, Randy	515	**M**	
Hiatt, Phil	169	Jenkins, Geoff	221	Konerko, Paul	542		
Hidalgo, Richard	517	Jennings, Robin	417	Koslofski, Kevin	218	Mabry, John	652
Higginson, Bobby	153	Jensen, Marcus	712	Kreuter, Chad	117	MacDonald, Bob	588
Hill, Glenallen	699	Jeter, Derek	253	Krivda, Rick	68	Macfarlane, Mike	181
Hill, Ken	329	Johns, Doug	279	Kroon, Marc	687	Machado, Robert	120
Hitchcock, Sterling	301	Johnson, Brian	684			Maddux, Greg	381
Hocking, Denny	243	Johnson, Charles	477			Maddux, Mike	93
Hoffman, Trevor	674	Johnson, Dane	366	**L**		Maduro, Calvin	615
Hoiles, Chris	56	Johnson, Davey	49			Magadan, Dave	414
Hollandsworth, Todd	526	Johnson, J.J.	244	Lacy, Kerry	96	Magee, Wendell	610
Hollins, Dave	302	Johnson, Jonathan	343	Lamont, Gene	616	Magnante, Mike	192
Holmes, Darren	449	Johnson, Lance	579	Lampkin, Tom	707	Magrane, Joe	120
Holt, Chris	518	Johnson, Mark	622	Langston, Mark	36	Mahomes, Pat	96
Holtz, Mike	42	Johnson, Randy	304	Lankford, Ray	651	Malave, Jose	93
Holzemer, Mark	45	Johnson, Russ	518	Lansing, Mike	551	Maloney, Sean	221
Honeycutt, Rick	660	Johnstone, John	515	Larkin, Andy	490	Mantei, Matt	490
Hook, Chris	710	Jones, Andruw	388	Larkin, Barry	428	Manto, Jeff	96
Hope, John	637	Jones, Bobby	580	LaRussa, Tony	641	Manuel, Barry	553
Hosey, Dwayne	96	Jones, Chipper	376	Lawton, Matt	240	Manwaring, Kirt	505
Houston, Tyler	414	Jones, Chris	588	Ledee, Ricky	269	Marrero, Elieser	663
Howard, David	179	Jones, Dax	710	Lee, Derrek	688	Marrero, Oreste	540
Howard, Matt	267	Jones, Doug	214	Leftwich, Phil	45	Martin, Al	627
Howard, Thomas	427	Jones, Ryan	368	Leiper, Dave	564	Martin, Norberto	118
Howe, Art	271	Jones, Stacy	120	Leiter, Al	478	Martinez, Dave	109
Howe, Steve	267	Jones, Terry	465	Leiter, Mark	552	Martinez, Dennis	130
Howell, Jack	43	Jones, Todd	503	Leius, Scott	145	Martinez, Edgar	305
Hubbard, Mike	416	Jordan, Brian	650	Lemke, Mark	379	Martinez, Jesus	542
Hubbard, Trent	707	Jordan, Kevin	612	Lennon, Patrick	292	Martinez, Manny	612
Hudek, John	513	Jordan, Ricardo	610	Lesher, Brian	292	Martinez, Pablo	391
Hudler, Rex	43	Jordan, Ricky	317	Leskanic, Curtis	450	Martinez, Pedro	554
Hudson, Joe	96	Joyner, Wally	675	Levine, Al	120	Martinez, Pedro A.	440
Huisman, Rick	194	Juden, Jeff	561	Levis, Jesse	215	Martinez, Ramon	528
Hundley, Todd	577	Justice, David	377	Lewis, Darren	108	Martinez, Sandy	354
Hunter, Brian	315			Lewis, Mark	154	Martinez, Tino	255
Hunter, Brian L.	502			Lewis, Richie	155	Marzano, John	317
Hunter, Rich	609			Leyland, Jim	469	Mashore, Damon	292
Hunter, Torii	244	**K**		Leyritz, Jim	264	Matheny, Mike	206
Hurst, Bill	490			Lieber, Jon	626	Mathews, T.J.	653
Hurst, Jimmy	123			Lieberthal, Mike	598	Mathews, Terry	70
Hurtado, Edwin	317	Kamieniecki, Scott	267	Lilliquist, Derek	440	Maxcy, Brian	662
Huskey, Butch	585	Karchner, Matt	117	Lima, Jose	156	May, Darrell	45
Huson, Jeff	70	Karkovice, Ron	107				

May, Derrick	506	Morandini, Mickey	600	Offerman, Jose	183	Petagine, Roberto	590
Mayne, Brent	586	Mordecai, Mike	388	Ogea, Chad	134	Peters, Chris	635
McCarthy, Greg	317	Morel, Ramon	637	Olerud, John	357	Peterson, Charles	640
McCarty, Dave	710	Morgan, Mike	440	Olivares, Omar	161	Petkovsek, Mark	660
McCaskill, Kirk	120	Morman, Alvin	514	Oliver, Darren	331	Pettitte, Andy	257
McClain, Scott	73	Morman, Russ	490	Oliver, Joe	437	Phillips, J.R.	613
McCracken, Quinton	451	Morris, Hal	430	Olson, Gregg	515	Phillips, Tony	111
McCurry, Jeff	169	Morris, Matt	664	Oquist, Mike	686	Piazza, Mike	533
McDonald, Ben	207	Mosquera, Julio	366	Ordonez, Magglio	123	Pichardo, Hipolito	193
McDowell, Jack	131	Moss, Damian	393	Ordonez, Rey	582	Piniella, Lou	296
McDowell, Roger	68	Mottola, Chad	440	Orie, Kevin	418	Pirkl, Greg	96
McElroy, Chuck	44	Mouton, James	514	Orosco, Jesse	60	Pittsley, Jim	196
McGee, Willie	654	Mouton, Lyle	110	Orsulak, Joe	489	Plantier, Phil	293
McGriff, Fred	382	Moyer, Jamie	306	Ortiz, Russ	713	Plesac, Dan	630
McGwire, Mark	280	Mueller, Bill	701	Osborne, Donovan	655	Plunk, Eric	144
McIntosh, Tim	267	Mulholland, Terry	307	Osik, Keith	634	Polley, Dale	268
McKeel, Walt	97	Mulligan, Sean	686	Osuna, Al	686	Polonia, Luis	391
McLemore, Mark	330	Munoz, Bobby	612	Osuna, Antonio	531	Poole, Jim	708
McMichael, Greg	383	Munoz, Jose	120	Otanez, Willis	73	Portugal, Mark	431
McMillon, Billy	493	Munoz, Mike	462	Otero, Ricky	601	Posada, Jorge	269
McRae, Brian	402	Munoz, Pedro	293	Owens, Eric	440	Potts, Mike	218
Meacham, Rusty	317	Murray, Eddie	57	Owens, Jayhawk	462	Powell, Dante	713
Meares, Pat	229	Murray, Glenn	613			Powell, Jay	481
Mecir, Jim	267	Murray, Heath	688			Pozo, Arquimedez	96
Medina, Rafael	269	Mussina, Mike	58			Pride, Curtis	162
Medrano, Tony	195	Myers, Greg	231	**P**		Prieto, Ariel	282
Mejia, Miguel	664	Myers, Jimmy	70			Prince, Tom	540
Mejia, Roberto	97	Myers, Mike	158			Pritchett, Chris	46
Meluskey, Mitch	518	Myers, Randy	59	Pacheco, Alex	320	Pugh, Tim	441
Mendoza, Ramiro	269	Myers, Rod	194	Pagnozzi, Tom	656	Pulliam, Harvey	466
Menhart, Paul	318	Myers, Rodney	415	Painter, Lance	463		
Merced, Orlando	628			Pall, Donn	490		
Mercedes, Henry	194			Palmeiro, Orlando	48		
Mercedes, Jose	218			Palmeiro, Rafael	61		
Mercker, Kent	143	**N**		Palmer, Dean	332	**Q**	
Mesa, Jose	132			Paniagua, Jose	565		
Miceli, Dan	629			Paquette, Craig	184	Quantrill, Paul	363
Mieske, Matt	216	Naehring, Tim	83	Parent, Mark	70	Quirico, Rafael	613
Milacki, Bob	318	Nagy, Charles	133	Park, Chan Ho	532		
Milchin, Mike	70	Natal, Bob	488	Parker, Rick	540		
Millar, Kevin	493	Naulty, Dan	232	Parra, Jose	241		
Miller, Kurt	487	Navarro, Jaime	403	Parrett, Jeff	613	**R**	
Miller, Orlando	507	Neagle, Denny	384	Parris, Steve	637		
Miller, Travis	243	Nelson, Jeff	265	Patterson, Bob	404	Raabe, Brian	244
Miller, Trever	171	Nen, Robb	479	Patterson, Danny	344	Radinsky, Scott	539
Milliard, Ralph	488	Nevin, Phil	159	Patzke, Jeff	368	Radke, Brad	233
Million, Doug	468	Newfield, Marc	208	Pavano, Carl	98	Radmanovich, Ryan	245
Mills, Alan	69	Newson, Warren	340	Pavlas, Dave	268	Raggio, Brady	664
Mimbs, Michael	599	Nied, Dave	465	Pavlik, Roger	333	Rain, Steve	418
Minchey, Nate	96	Nieves, Melvin	160	Payton, Jay	590	Raines, Tim	266
Minor, Blas	318	Nilsson, Dave	209	Peltier, Dan	710	Ramirez, Alex	147
Mirabelli, Doug	712	Nitkowski, C.J.	167	Pemberton, Rudy	98	Ramirez, Manny	135
Miranda, Angel	216	Nixon, Otis	355	Pena, Alejandro	490	Ramos, Edgar	518
Mitchell, Keith	440	Nixon, Trot	97	Pena, Geronimo	145	Randa, Joe	185
Mitchell, Kevin	429	Nomo, Hideo	530	Pena, Tony	143	Rapp, Pat	482
Mitchell, Larry	611	Norman, Les	194	Pendleton, Terry	389	Rath, Gary	542
Mlicki, Dave	586	Norton, Greg	123	Penn, Shannon	169	Reboulet, Jeff	241
Moehler, Brian	172	Nunnally, Jon	196	Pennington, Brad	46	Redman, Mark	245
Mohler, Mike	281	Nye, Ryan	615	Percival, Troy	37	Reed, Jeff	463
Molina, Izzy	292			Perez, Danny	218	Reed, Jody	676
Molitor, Paul	230			Perez, Eddie	389	Reed, Steve	452
Mondesi, Raul	529			Perez, Eduardo	440	Reese, Pokey	443
Monds, Wonder	393	**O**		Perez, Mike	416	Rekar, Bryan	466
Monteleone, Rich	45			Perez, Neifi	468	Relaford, Desi	613
Montgomery, Jeff	182			Perez, Robert	358	Remlinger, Mike	441
Montgomery, Ray	515	O'Brien, Charlie	356	Perez, Tomas	359	Renteria, Edgar	483
Montgomery, Steve	292	O'Leary, Troy	84	Perez, Yorkis	480	Reyes, Al	218
Moore, Kerwin	292	O'Neill, Paul	256	Perisho, Matt	48	Reyes, Carlos	283
Moore, Marcus	440	Oates, Johnny	321	Perry, Herbert	145	Reynolds, Shane	508
Morales, Willie	294	Obando, Sherman	561	Person, Robert	587	Reynoso, Armando	453
		Ochoa, Alex	581				

Wallace, Derek	587	Whiteman, Greg	172	Wilson, Desi	711
Wallach, Tim	540	Whiten, Mark	311	Wilson, Enrique	147
Walton, Jerome	392	Whiteside, Matt	342	Wilson, Nigel	145
Ward, Turner	219	Wickander, Kevin	219	Wilson, Paul	583
Ware, Jeff	366	Wickman, Bob	212	Witasick, Jay	295
Wasdin, John	291	Widger, Chris	566	Witt, Bobby	337
Washburn, Jarrod	48	Wilkins, Marc	632	Wohlers, Mark	386
Waszgis, B.J.	73	Wilkins, Rick	704	Wojciechowski, Steve	293
Watson, Allen	703	Williams, Bernie	262	Wolcott, Bob	316
Weathers, Dave	268	Williams, Brian	168	Wolff, Mike	48
Webster, Lenny	563	Williams, Eddie	170	Womack, Tony	638
Wehner, John	636	Williams, George	291	Woodall, Brad	394
Weiss, Walt	458	Williams, Gerald	213	Worrell, Tim	681
Wells, Bob	310	Williams, Jimy	74	Worrell, Todd	535
Wells, David	64	Williams, Juan	394	Worthington, Craig	342
Wendell, Turk	411	Williams, Keith	711	Wright, Jamey	459
Wengert, Don	286	Williams, Matt	705	Wright, Ron	640
West, David	607	Williams, Mike	611
Wetteland, John	261	Williams, Shad	46
White, Devon	485	Williams, Woody	365
White, Rondell	559	Williamson, Antone	221
Whitehurst, Wally	268	Wilson, Dan	312

Y

Yan, Esteban	71
Young, Anthony	516
Young, Dmitri	664
Young, Eric	460
Young, Ernie	287
Young, Kevin	194

Z

Zaun, Greg	491
Zeile, Todd	65
Zuber, Jon	613

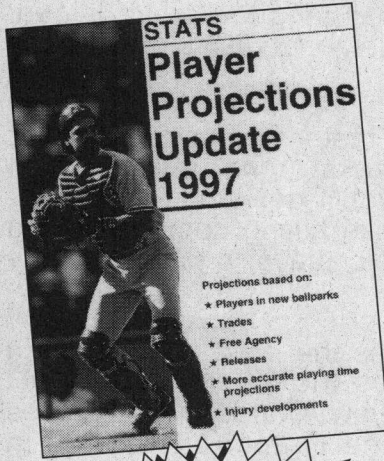 

Bill James Classic Baseball

Joe Jackson, Walter Johnson, and Roberto Clemente are back on the field of your dreams!

If you're not ready to give up baseball in the fall, or if you're looking to relive its glorious past, then Bill James Classic Baseball is the game for you! The Classic Game features players from all eras of Major League Baseball at all performance levels—not just the stars. You could see Honus Wagner, Josh Gibson, Carl Yastrzemski, Bob Uecker, Billy Grabarkewitz, and Masanori Murakami...on the SAME team!

As owner, GM and manager all in one, you'll be able to...

- "Buy" your team of up to 25 players from our catalog of over 2,000 historical players (You'll receive $1 million to buy your favorite players)
- Choose the park your team will call home—current or historical, 63 in all!
- Rotate batting lineups for a right- or left-handed starting pitcher
- Change your pitching rotation for each series. Determine your set-up man, closer, and long reliever
- Alter in-game strategies, including stealing frequency, holding runners on base, hit-and-run, and much more!
- Select your best pinch hitter and late-inning defensive replacements (For example, Curt Flood will get to more balls than Hack Wilson!)

How to Play The Classic Game:

1. Sign up to be a team owner TODAY! Leagues forming year-round
2. STATS, Inc. will supply you with a catalog of eligible players and a rule book
3. You'll receive $1 million to buy your favorite major leaguers
4. Take part in a player and ballpark draft with 11 other owners
5. Set your pitching rotation, batting lineup, and managerial strategies
6. STATS runs the game simulation...a 154-game schedule, 14 weeks!
7. You'll receive customized in-depth weekly reports, featuring game summaries, stats, and boxscores

Order from  Today!

Use Order Form in This Book, or Call 1-800-63-STATS or 847-676-3383 or e-mail: info@stats.com

STATS Fantasy Hoops

Soar into the 1996-97 season with STATS Fantasy Hoops! SFH puts YOU in charge. Don't just sit back and watch Grant Hill, Shawn Kemp, and Michael Jordan—get in the game and coach your team to the top!

How to Play SFH:
1. Sign up to coach a team.
2. You'll receive a full set of rules and a draft form with SFH point values for all eligible players - anyone who played in the NBA in 1995-96, plus all 1996 NBA draft picks.
3. Complete the draft form and return it to STATS.
4. You will take part in the draft with nine other owners, and we will send you league rosters.
5. You make unlimited weekly transactions including trades, free agent signings, activations, and benchings.
6. Six of the 10 teams in your league advance to postseason play, with two teams ultimately advancing to the Finals.

SFH point values are tested against actual NBA results, mirroring the real thing. Weekly reports will tell you everything you need to know to lead your team to the SFH Championship!

STATS Fantasy Football

STATS Fantasy Football puts YOU in charge! You draft, trade, cut, bench, activate players and even sign free agents each week. SFF pits you head-to-head against 11 other owners.

STATS' scoring system applies realistic values, tested against actual NFL results. Each week, you'll receive a superb in-depth report telling you all about both team and league performances.

How to Play SFF:
1. Sign up today!
2. STATS sends you a draft form listing all eligible NFL players.
3. Fill out the draft form and return it to STATS, and you will take part in the draft along with 11 other team owners.
4. Go head-to-head against the other owners in your league. You'll make week-by-week roster moves and transactions through STATS' Fantasy Football experts, via phone, fax, or on-line!

Order from  Today!

Use Order Form in This Book, or Call 1-800-63-STATS or 847-676-3383 or e-mail: info@stats.com

Bill James Presents:

STATS 1997 Batter Versus Pitcher Match-Ups!

- Complete stats for pitchers vs. batters (5+ career AB against them)
- Leader boards and stats for all 1996 major league players
- **Item #BP97, $14.95, Available Mid January, 1997!**

STATS Baseball Scoreboard 1997

- Lively analysis of all the hottest topics facing baseball today!
- Easy-to-understand charts answer the questions fans always ask
- Specific coverage for each major league team
- **Item #SB97, $18.95, Available March 1, 1997!**

STATS Pro Basketball Handbook 1996-97

- Career stats for every player who logged minutes during 1995-96
- Team game logs with points, rebounds, assists and much more
- Leader boards from points per game to triple doubles
- **Item #BH97, $17.95, Available NOW!**

STATS Pro Football Handbook 1997

- A complete season-by-season register for every active 1995 player
- Numerous statistical breakdowns for hundreds of NFL players
- Leader boards in a number of innovative and traditional categories
- **Item #FH97, $19.95, Available Early February 1997!**

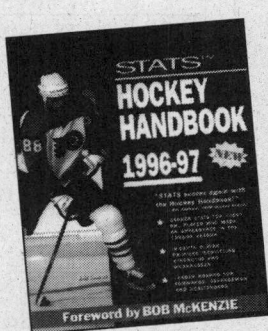

Pro Football Revealed:
The 100-Yard War (1997 Edition)

- Profiles each team, complete with essays, charts and play diagrams
- Detailed statistical breakdowns on players, teams and coaches
- Essays about NFL trends and happenings by leading experts
- **Price: $18.95, Item #PF97 , Available July 1997!**

STATS Hockey Handbook 1996-97

- A complete season-by-season register for every active 1996 player
- Numerous statistical breakdowns for hundreds of NHL players
- Leader boards in numerous innovative and traditional categories
- **Item #HH97, $17.95, Available NOW!**

STATS, Inc. Order Form

Name_____

Address_____

City_____ State_____ Zip_____

Phone_____ Fax_____ Internet Address_____

Method of Payment (U.S. Funds Only):
❏ Check　　❏ Money Order　　❏ Visa　　❏ MasterCard

Credit Card Information:
Cardholder Name_____

Credit Card Number_____ Exp. Date_____

Signature_____

BOOKS (STATS publications now include free first class shipping)

Qty.	Product Name	Item Number	Price	Total
	STATS Major League Handbook 1997	HB97	$19.95	
	STATS Major League Handbook 1997 (Comb-bound)	HC97	$21.95	
	STATS Projections Update 1997	PJUP	$9.95	
	The Scouting Notebook: 1997	SN97	$18.95	
	The Scouting Notebook: 1997 (Comb-bound)	SC97	$20.95	
	STATS Minor League Scouting Notebook 1997	MN97	$18.95	
	STATS Minor League Handbook 1997	MH97	$19.95	
	STATS Minor League Handbook 1997 (Comb-bound)	MC97	$21.95	
	STATS Player Profiles 1997	PP97	$19.95	
	STATS Player Profiles 1997 (Comb-bound)	PC97	$21.95	
	STATS 1997 BVSP Match-Ups!	BP97	$14.95	
	STATS Baseball Scoreboard 1997	SB97	$18.95	
	Pro Football Revealed: The 100 Yard War (1996 Edition)	PF97	$18.95	
	STATS Pro Football Handbook 1997	FH97	$19.95	
	STATS Basketball Handbook 1996-97	BH97	$17.95	
	STATS Hockey Handbook 1996-97	HH97	$17.95	
Prior Editions	(Please circle appropriate year)			
	STATS Major League Handbook '90 '91 '92 '93 '94 '95 '96		$9.95	
	The Scouting Report/Notebook '94 '95 '96		$9.95	
	STATS Player Profiles '93 '94 '95 '96		$9.95	
	STATS Minor League Handbook '92 '93 '94 '95 '96		$9.95	
	STATS BVSP Match-Ups! '94 '95 '96		$9.95	
	STATS Baseball Scoreboard '92 '93 '94 '95 '96		$9.95	
	STATS Basketball Scoreboard/Handbook '93-'94 '94-'95 '95-'96		$9.95	
	Pro Football Revealed: The 100 Yard War '94 '95 '96		$9.95	
	STATS Pro Football Handbook '95 '96		$9.95	
	STATS Minor League Scouting Notebook '95 '96		$9.95	

MULTIMEDIA PRODUCTS (Prices include shipping & handling charges)

Qty.	Product Name	Item Number	Price	Total
	Bill James Encyclopedia CD-Rom	BJCD	$49.95	
	Macmillan's Baseball Encyclopedia CD-Rom	MACD	$44.95	
	Motorola SportsTrax for Baseball	BBTX	$199.00	
	STATS On-Line	STON	$30.00	

SEASON FINAL & YEAR-END REPORTS (Prices include shipping & handling charges)

Qty.	Product Name	Circle Format				Price	Total
	Season Final Report	Paper	3 1/2" disk	5" disk	Mac	$12.95	
	Lefty/Righty Report	Paper	3 1/2" disk	5" disk	Mac	$19.95	
	Stolen Base Report	Paper	3 1/2" disk	5" disk	Mac	$34.95	
	Defensive Games by Position	Paper	3 1/2" disk	5" disk	Mac	$9.95	
	Catcher Report	Paper	3 1/2" disk	5" disk	Mac	$49.95	
	Relief Pitching Report	Paper	3 1/2" disk	5" disk	Mac	$49.95	
	Zone Ratings/Outfield Arms Report	Paper	3 1/2" disk	5" disk	Mac	$99.95	
	End of Season STATpak	Paper	3 1/2" disk	5" disk		$9.95	
	Team(s):						
	STATpak Subscription	Paper	3 1/2" disk	5" disk		$29.95	
	Team(s):						

FANTASY GAMES & STATSfax (STATSfax prices reflect the monthly charge for service)

Qty.	Product Name	Item Number	Price	Total
	Bill James Classic Baseball	BJCB	$129.00	
	How to Win the Classic Game	CGBK	$16.95	
	Classic Game STATSfax	CFX5	$20.00	
	STATS Fantasy Hoops	SFH	$85.00	
	STATS Fantasy Hoops STATSfax—5-Day	SFH5	$20.00	
	STATS Fantasy Hoops STATSfax—7-Day	SFH7	$25.00	
	STATS Fantasy Football	SFF	$69.00	
	STATS Fantasy Football STATSfax—3-Day	SFF3	$15.00	
	Bill James Fantasy Baseball	BJFB	$89.00	
	Fantasy Baseball STATSfax—5-Day	SFX5	$20.00	
	Fantasy Baseball STATSfax—7-Day	SFX7	$25.00	

1st Fantasy Team Name (ex. Colt 45's):_____ _____

What Fantasy Game is this team for?_____

2nd Fantasy Team Name (ex. Colt 45's):_____ _____

What Fantasy Game is this team for?_____

NOTE: $1.00/player is charged for all roster moves and transactions.

For Bill James Fantasy Baseball:

Would you like to play in a league drafted by Bill James? ❑ Yes ❑ No

---

For faster service, call:

1-800-63-STATS

or 847-676-3383,

or fax this form to STATS:

847-676-0821

TOTALS

	Price	Total
Product Total (excl. Fantasy Games)		
Canada—all orders—add:	$2.50/book	
Order 2 or more books—subtract:	$1.00/book	
(NOT to be combined with other specials)		
IL residents add 8.5% sales tax		
Subtotal		
Fantasy Games Total		
GRAND TOTAL		

All books now include free 1st class shipping!
Thanks for ordering from STATS, Inc.